I CHING

周易

I CHING

■

*The Classic Chinese
Oracle of Change*

■

*A Complete
Translation With
Concordance*

STEPHEN KARCHER

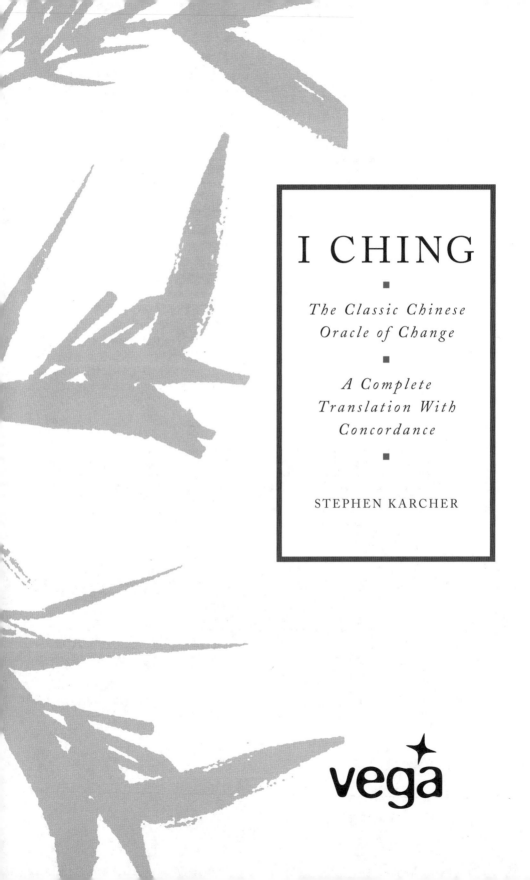

vega

ISBN 1-84333-003-2

A catalogue record for this book is available
from the British Library.

First published in 2002 by
Vega
64 Brewery Road
London, N7 9NT

A member of **Chrysalis** Books plc

Visit our website at www.chrysalisbooks.co.uk

Printed and bound in China
by Dai Nippon

The people who have contributed to the evolution of this book are many. I would first like to thank the pub-
lishers at Chrysalis/Vega Books for giving me the opportunity to revise it and make it available once again to
those who might benefit from its use. I would also like to thank the participants in the original seminars, conferences and consultations at *Eranos*, who gave of their insight, experience and spirit, and those many whom
I have taught and learned from in the years that followed. Thanks, too, to the *Eranos* Foundation itself: to the
memory of its founder, Olga-Fröbe-Kapteyn, and to Rudolf Ritsema, my co-Director during the years of the
I Ching Project. The appearance of the original version also owes much to Ian Fenton, a kind and long-suf-
fering editor. And, finally, many thanks to Dr. Michele O'Brian, without whose combination of editorial skill,
deep knowledge of the I Ching and psychological insight this new edition would have been impossible.

Through *Change*,
a Realizing Person knows the subtle and the obvious,
the strong and the supple.
So act with *Change* and be a model for the myriad people.

Stephen Karcher

CONTENTS

PART ONE

周易

INTRODUCTION

WHAT IS THE *I CHING*?

The *I Ching* offers a way to see into difficult situations, particularly those emotionally charged ones where rational knowledge fails us yet we are called upon to decide and act. It gives voice to a spirit concerned with how we can best live as individuals in contact with both inner and outer worlds.

The *I Ching* is able to do this because it is what the ancient world called an oracle. It is a particular kind of imaginative space set off for a dialogue with the gods or spirits, the creative basis of experience now called the unconscious. An oracle translates a problem or question brought to it into an image language like that of dreams. It changes the way you experience the situation in order to connect you with the inner forces that are shaping it. The oracle's images dissolve what is blocking the connection, making the spirits available.

This procedure is made for situations when you feel gripped by something behind the ordinary events of life. The *I Ching* portrays various sorts of crossroads. Its symbols make up a dictionary of the forces that move and change us. Working with these images dissolves your view of your situation and reforms your awareness in terms of these forces. The goal of this process is an intuitive clarity traditionally called *shen ming* or the *light of the gods*. It is a bright spirit that is creative, clear-seeing and connected.

Consulting an oracle and seeing yourself in terms of the symbols or magic spells it presents is a way of contacting what has been repressed in the creation of the modern world. It puts you back into what the ancients called the sea of soul by giving advice on attitudes and actions that lead to the experience of imaginative meaning. Oracular consultation insists on the importance of imagination. It is the heart of magic through which the living world speaks to you. The modern interest in alternative cultures and the old ways is a reflection of our need to recover this heart of magic, for it is the way our inner being speaks, thinks and acts.

The *I Ching* or *I* (pronounced "yee") was the fundamental text of traditional Chinese culture. It is a divinatory system with 3,000-year-old roots in the traditions of magic, shamanism and spiritual transformation. Nearly all that was significant in traditional China – philosophy, science, politics and popular culture – was founded on interpretations and adaptations of the I. The core of the book is the oldest and most complex divinatory system to survive into modern times.

This divinatory core is a set of 64 six-line figures or *kua*, usually called hexagrams, and a way to consult them. The figures represent all the possible combinations of six *opened* or supple — — and *whole* or strong —— lines. Each figure has a name and a group of short phrases associated with it. These combinations of texts and figures act like mirrors for the unconscious forces shaping any given moment, problem or situation. In traditional terms, the book provides symbols which comprehend the light of the gods, the unconscious forces that are creating what you experience. In itself still and unmoving, when stimulated by consultation the book produces an echo which can reach the depths, grasp the seeds, and penetrate the wills of all the beings under heaven.

The act of consultation is based upon chance, traditionally the random division of a set of 50 yarrow stalks or throwing and counting three coins six times. This chance event empowers a spirit beyond conscious control. It gives the forces behind your situation the chance to speak by singling out one or more of the book's symbols. Through this procedure, what you see as a problem to be mastered becomes a *sign* or *symbolic occurrence* that links you with another world. Like a shaman's drum and dance, these symbols can speak to you on many levels, beginning a creative process which, in traditional terms, completes the ceaseless activity of heaven. This is religion at its fundamental level. It reflects a sense of spirit that unites the great and the small, a spirit that moves in each individual.

These oracular texts only come to life in the context of a particular situation. They refer to unique events that evade scientific laws and rules. Your question, your life, your problem provide the necessary catalyst that creates meaning. The magic occurs when, in a particular situation and through your particular experience, you ask the spirit for an image to guide you.

The Name of the Book

The central concern of the *I Ching* is expressed by the key term in its name, *I*. Traditionally the book is simply called *I*. The second term, *Ching*, denotes a classic or fundamental text. It means a standard, a channel through which something passes, a loom. The *I Ching* is the classic, channel or loom of *I*. Though often translated as change or changes, the central term *I* is not simply orderly change – the change of the seasons, for example – or the change of one thing into another, like water changing to ice or a caterpillar to a butterfly. Unpredictable and, as the tradition says, unfathomable, *I* originates in and is a way of dealing with "trouble". It

articulates possible responses to fate, necessity or calamity – that which "crosses" your path.

The term *I* emphasizes imagination, openness and fluidity. It suggests the ability to change direction quickly and the use of a variety of imaginative stances to mirror the variety of being. It further suggests that this imaginative ability is the true root of a sense of security and spiritual well-being. The most adequate English translation of this might be *versatility*, the ability to remain available to and be moved by the unforeseen demands of time, fate and psyche. This term interweaves the *I* of the cosmos, the *I* of the book, and your own *I*, if you use it.

I in the human world is understood in terms of three other themes, *tao*, *te*, and *chün tzu*. *Tao*, literally "way", is the flow or stream of creative energy that makes life possible, the way *in which* everything happens and the way *on which* it occurs. *Te*, often translated as power or virtue, refers to the power to realize *tao* in action, to become what you are meant to be. A *chün tzu* is someone who seeks to acquire *te* through divination, to live connected with *tao*. The *I Ching*'s statements are invitations to a dialogue with the way, its power and its virtue. What the *chün tzu* finds through this dialogue is significance, the experience of spirit, meaning and connection.

The oldest name of this oracle was *Chou I*, for it was first developed as the *I* or versatility-book of the *Chou* kings (1100–400 BCE). Intrinsically, however, the term *chou* means universal, encompassing everything, moving in a circle. When stimulated by consultation, the *Chou I* describes the circle of events that connects the spirit world and the human heart. Using this book of magic spells is a way to encompass the ever-changing movement of *tao*. It is *Chou I, Encompassing Versatility*.

• What is Divination?

Antique civilization, both East and West, used divination and oracles to keep in contact with unseen powers. Sacrifices offered to the spirits and gods were not just bribes or pleas. They opened communication between humans and spirits so a dialogue could take place.

The idea that words, things and events can become omens that open communication with a spirit-world is based on an insight into the way the psyche works – that in every symptom, conflict or problem we experience there is a spirit trying to communicate with us. Each encounter with "trouble" is an opening to this spirit, usually opposed by an ego that wants to enforce its will on the world. Divination gives a voice to what this ego has rejected. It brings up the hidden complement or shadow of the situation in order to link you with the myths and spirits behind it. This changes the way you see yourself, your situation and the world around you.

Studies of divinatory systems in tribal cultures show that this process was and is consistently used to give information about individual questions, problems and choices for which rational knowledge or common social rules are not enough. It is the dark mirror that gives true answers, the place where the spirit of an individual can speak with all the other spirits in the world. These systems are often sponsored by an animal magician whose mysterious symbols offer an alternative to public laws and regulations. A procedure using chance provides a gap through which this spirit expresses itself by picking out one of the available symbols. A final diagnosis and plan of action come out of the creative interaction between the symbol, the inquirer and the diviner, over which the spirit presides. This interaction breaks down the old stories you are telling yourself in order to make up more effective ones. It produces advice on how to act in harmony with the "spirit of the time."

Thus divination is not an ideology or a belief but a creative way of contacting the spirit. It is imagination perceiving forces and inventing ways to deal with them. This involves a combination of analysis and intuition that normal thinking usually keeps apart. This process values imagination and creativity. It shifts the way you make decisions.

Opening this space, where identity becomes fluid and the spirits involve themselves in your life, is the purpose of divination. Using a divinatory system is an exploration of the unconscious side of a situation. The symbols evoked adjust the balance between you and the unknown forces behind it.

The language is the key to the contact. The words are, as the Chinese say, "fish-traps" for spirit or *tao*.

Origin, History and Development of the Classic of I

The *I Ching* is the oldest and most complex divinatory system to survive the disenchantment of the ancient world. It represents a way of knowing common to both magical or pre-technological cultures and to the world we contact each night in dreams. Central to both is the idea that life requires a proper relation to the spirit-world.

The traditional story of the origin of the *I Ching* reflects this concern.

In this account, the *I Ching* was created by three sage-kings who founded Chinese culture: Fu Hsi, King Wen and the Duke of Chou, his son.

Fu Hsi was the legendary First Emperor, a shaman, diviner, and magician. His rule represents the first Golden Age, when humans and spirits communicated freely. Fu Hsi contemplated the shapes of heaven, the patterns of the earth, bird and animal markings and the movements of his body and soul. Then he spontaneously brought forth the basic figures of the *I Ching*. They were a way to organize the world and communicate with its spirits. Through this magical communication a constant influx of spirit kept the human world in order.

The second part of this story occurs in a declining era full of troubles, anxiety and sorrow. It centers on the conflict between Chou the Tyrant, the last king of the Shang Dynasty (1520–1030 BCE), and King Wen, a spiritual reformer and founder of the Chou Dynasty (1100–480 BCE). King Wen, literally King Writing or King Pattern, spent several years in Shang prisons. As a prisoner, he meditated on the distance between the Golden Age of Fu Hsi and the complicated world which had developed since. He sought to understand how the Golden Age might be recovered.

King Wen first re-arranged the eight trigram figures to reflect the complexity of the human world. He then combined them to create 64 hexagrams and added writing to the figures, giving each hexagram a name and a divinatory message. This was the new magic. His son, the Duke of Chou, added a commentary to the lines. The new hexagrams and texts became the *Chou I*, the Oracle Book of the Kings of Chou. The Chou nobles used this magic in their struggle to restore the Golden Age of Fu Hsi, and, once in power, to stay in contact with the spirits and the Way of Heaven.

This story, popularized in the Han Dynasty (200 BCE–220 CE), reflects the importance of the *I Ching*'s power to connect humans and spiritual forces, making "spirit power" and knowledge available. As such, it is mythically true. But modern scholarship has shown that the factual origins of the book are the reverse of this account. The oldest part of the book is words, not diagrams and systems. It is made up of omens, images and magic spells from an oral shamanistic tradition. These phrases were assembled between 1000 and 750 BCE, probably first written down in connection with a simple system of whole or strong and opened or supple lines. At some point in this process the next level of symbolization emerged. This was the formation of the hexagrams, the six-line figures that display and organize the divinatory texts. Wu Hsien, literally the "Conjoining Shaman," discovered a numerical system of organizing the texts and the yarrow-stalk method of consultation. The development of the trigrams as a means of correlating systems of thought developed in the later Han Period.

So we might best think of the *I Ching* not simply as a book but as a Way, a living stream of images from the mythic past flowing into and through the present, connecting us with the future as it is evolving. One of the meanings of the term *I* relates to this practice. Among other things, *I* means "easy". The Yarrow-stalk Oracle with its texts and figures was much easier to use than Ancient China's other oracle system, consulting the cracks a heated bronze rod produced in specially prepared tortoise shells or ox bones. It was this easy quality that led to the most important development in the history of the *I Ching*: its imaginative use by individuals outside the ruling family.

A gap of five to seven hundred years occurs between the oldest parts of the *I Ching* and the next layer of the text. During this time the personal use of the Oracle developed. The Warring States Period (500–200 BCE) was a golden age of imaginative thought, the most creative period in Chinese culture. The creative thinking sprang up, however, against a background of political fragmentation and violence.

The personal use of the Yarrow-stalk Oracle grew out of this period, when being in accord with the time and the spirits was often a matter of life and death. So, too, did the sense that the use of the book opened a way or path through the chaos of a crumbling social order. Most probably, a group of diviners and magicians, the "technicians of the sacred," assembled the texts and developed the hexagrams to make this more powerful spirit available. It created a faith in the individual connection to the images of the psyche and a hope that this connection could "heal the time".

The political chaos finally ended with the emergence of the Han Dynasty (206 BCE–220 CE), which was the real beginning of Imperial China. During the Han, culture was consolidated and re-defined. This process included the codification of writing and the establishment of the *Ching* or Classics of antiquity. The *Chou I* became the *I Ching* or *Classic of I*.

Cosmologists of the Han discovered the perfect symbolism for the numerical structure of both the cosmos and the human mind in the trigrams and hexagrams of the *I Ching*. Confucian thinkers, developing an imperial philosophy, created a moral and social hierarchy for the lines and fixed interpretations of the texts based on this system. The system of the trigrams was expanded in this period to explain the hexagram structure and to link it with other image systems in the natural sciences and medicine.

However, in codifying the *Classic of I* the Han editors were in a strange position. They felt that the texts contained the magic of a Golden Age

when people were nearer to the gods and that such a time might be repeated through using them. The oldest texts, however, were not immediately understandable, for the divinatory tradition that explained their use had been lost. So the Han editors gathered and transcribed various oral traditions dealing with the use of the Yarrow-stalk Oracle that originated in the Warring States Period and added them to the older texts.

These treatises, called the *Ten Wings*, contain both oracular texts and interpretive strategies. One in particular, the *Hsi tz'u chuan* (*Commentary on the Attached Evidences*) or *Ta chuan* (*The Great Commentary*) defines an imaginative stance to be taken toward the book which preserves the core of the old shamanic tradition as it was developed for personal use.

According to this tradition, the function of the *I* is to provide symbols (*hsiang*). The text came into existence through a mysterious mode of imaginative induction, also called *hsiang*, which endows things with symbolic significance. Acted upon simultaneously by figures in heaven, patterns on earth and events in the psyche, the old shamans and magicians spontaneously *hsiang*-ed or symbolized to form the texts and figures as links to important spirits and energies.

The *chün tzu*, the ideal user of the book, can take advantage of this fundamental spirit power. He or she observes the figure obtained through divination and takes joy in its words, turning and rolling them in the heart. These words translate or symbolize (*hsiang*) the situation, connecting it with a level of reality from which the symbols flow. Through this action, the *chün tzu* becomes *hsiang* or symbolizing, linking the divinatory tools and the spirits connected with *I* directly to the ruling power of the personality. To do this is called *shen*, which refers to whatever is numinous, spiritually potent.

Like the shamans and sages of old, this tradition maintains, the person who uses these symbols to connect with *I* will have access to the numinous world and acquire a helping-spirit, a *shen*. The *I Ching* is more than a spirit; it channels or connects you to spirit. It puts its users in a position to create and experience their own spirit as a point of connection with the forces that govern the world. It is this imaginative power that was elaborated, re-interpreted and defined throughout later Chinese history as the basis of philosophy, morals and ethics. It is a way to connect with the creative imagination that underlies all systems and creeds. And it is the basis of what was called the "great enterprise," a spiritual practice that, through individual transformation, can reform or renew the time in which we live.

■

USING THE *I*

● *This Translation*

The *I Ching* is a diviner's manual or active sourcebook for what C. G. Jung called the archetypal forces. It organizes the play of these forces into images so that an individual reading becomes possible. Using it begins with a problem and a question. But there is a general question behind each specific demand: "How can I act in creative relation with the spirits or forces shaping this moment of time?" These forces represent the flow of life and the experience of meaning, its way or *tao*.

The *I Ching*'s response to a question comes through the texts of one of the hexagrams. These texts present clusters of images and ideas that mirror structures of the psyche, a quality they share with dreams and spontaneous fantasies. They act as corrections or interventions from an implicit order, the *tao*. Each opens a field of potential meaning that will support a specific series of stories while eliminating others. Spirit or energy moves through individual, creative interaction with the images. To use the *I Ching* as an oracle, we have to use this creative potential.

This book is an attempt to present the oracular core of the *I Ching* as a psychological tool. The purpose is to recover oracular language and the use of divination as a connection between the individual and the unseen – the world of images described by myth, dream, shamanic journey or mystery cult. Researched for over 40 years, the final form of the translation grew out of several years of seminars, conferences, individual and group consultations that included artists, thinkers and scholars from all over the world.

The fundamental concern of this book is to give people the means to live and choose in a meaningful way by making them aware of imaginative value. For the *I Ching* fills an important gap in the modern approach to the psyche. Its oracular texts connect the study of what C. G. Jung called the archetypes, and what the ancient world called the gods, directly to individual experience. The present translation is an attempt to revive the divinatory core, the psychological root of the book as a living practice.

We go to ancient China to find this way of seeing things because Old Chinese permitted the development of a special oracular language. It is made up of symbols with no rigid subject-verb, noun-adjective, pronoun or person distinctions. They combine and interact the way dream-images do. The *I Ching* is both an epitome of this language and of the divinatory view, that sees the world as "alive".

The basic text used for the translation is the *Chou-i-chê-chung*, the *Kang Hsi* or Palace Edition of 1715. It is the last of the classic versions of the text, and is used today throughout the East when someone consults the Oracle. This text served as the basis for Richard Wilhelm's translation and for the modern standard text, the *Harvard Yenching Edition.*

The Palace Edition is inclusive and represents the end of a long textual tradition. It systematically reproduces all the layers of the text and, in addition, a great number of commentaries that seek to explain the images. We have left most of these commentaries, based on Confucian moral philosophy and imperial political thought, aside. We have assembled and translated all the parts of the book that contain oracular texts. This is the core of the book, the images from which interpretations are made.

The translation of these images is an attempt to make their imaginative power available to the modern user. The possible meanings are gathered together with no presumption that they must conform to one single interpretation. The terms are seen as the centers of force-fields in the imagination that have gathered meanings over time. They are translated as functions, all of which can exist in any individual. They do not literally apply to any particular gender or social position. Bringing out this multivalence makes the individual quality of the encounter with the Oracle available for the first time in a western language. It presents the imaginative field from which interpretations are made.

There are four basic principles used in this approach. All of them represent a different way of using words than in ordinary language.

–Each Chinese character is translated throughout by the same English core-word or phrase. This one-to-one translation emphasizes a nuclear meaning of the term and makes possible the first Concordance in a western language.

–Each of these terms is provided with a group of possible meanings that resonate in the original. They provide an imaginative network that relates the terms to individual situations. These meanings are not limited to a single period or level of culture but are drawn from the history of the language. They include recent archeological findings as well as the traditional analysis of the ideogram.

–The word-order of the original statements is preserved wherever possible. Except for articles (a, an, the) and prepositions or connectives implied by the terms themselves, each word in the translation represents one and only one Chinese character in the order of the original. Contexts for the divinatory phrases, developed from both ancient and modern sources, provide an entrance into their range of meanings.

–The structural elements of the hexagrams are connected to the system of magic images from which traditional eastern science developed. Words that have acquired special meanings in the *I Ching* itself are also explored.

This way of looking at the *I Ching* is both very old and radically new, is based on a psychological re-creation of ancient divinatory practices. The focus is on the development of the divinatory tradition as it passed out of the hands of professionals associated with the Chinese Court and into the hands of private individuals, before it was made to serve a particular moral philosophy. This development began in a time of social breakdown and creative activity that offers many parallels to our own, a time when people needed to connect with the spirits outside of normal social structures. It feeds the development of the individual personality.

The circles of reference for the words and images revolve around you, the user. They are meant to eliminate the *a priori* moral or hierarchical interpretation a translation usually imposes, allowing you to position yourself within the dynamic field – the spirit – each term implies. Turning and rolling the words in your heart, the tradition suggests, is the key to contacting the numinous world opened by the Oracle. Like the sudden insight in a dream interpretation, intuitive meaning and a connection to the spirits is the result.

● *Questioning the Oracle*

The *I Ching* is a guide to decision making in situations when the flow of life is troubled. It helps you see what forces are at work, how they may develop, and how you can relate to them, an opportunity for spiritual growth It takes the way you are looking at things apart and opens up new insights.

The urge to consult the Oracle arises when you feel entangled with something that evades the usual methods of problem solving. Resistance, reluctance, anxiety, strong desire, the sense of something hidden or confusing, the sense of an important opportunity, the need to develop inner life and a connection to the spirit, all indicate a need to see behind or see through the situation. The Oracle can open this deeper perspective; the responsibility and decision remain yours.

The first step is making the question. The question is important, because it is the point of contact that will focus the divinatory images and connect them to your personal situation. It clarifies a moment of time and draws it out of the flux of experience to act as a link to fundamental energies.

Making a question has two parts. The first part is soul-searching. Search out the feelings, images and experiences that lie behind your immediate situation – what you feel, remember, are afraid of, what you think the effects of the problem might be, what it symbolizes for you, what relations and issues it involves, what is at stake, why you are uncertain or anxious about making a decision. This establishes the subjective field. The answer will focus on these concerns. Talking to someone about the situation can often help you bring these things out and clarify them.

This leads to the second step – a clear formulation of the question based on what you want to do in the situation. Be precise. Examine what you want to do with as much honesty and awareness as you can. And, if possible, come to a conclusion, presenting it as a question: "What about doing this?" "What will happen if I...?" "What should my attitude be toward ...?" The Oracle will connect you with an archetypal image through this question. This clarifies the dynamic forces at work in your psyche, the seeds of future events.

This process allows you to break through the wall that separates you from the spirit world, your own deeper intelligence, that usually lies beyond your immediate control. The response will not be a simple yes-or-no answer, though it will usually include specific advice. Be open to a surprise. What you are really asking for is an understanding in depth upon which you can base your decisions and actions. The question is the precise point of contact with the unknown, and it enables you to open and focus the divinatory space. It is part of a process of expansion and contraction that leads from an unconscious relation with a disturbing force to specific advice on how to handle the situation.

- ## *Getting an Answer*

The *I Ching* is organized through a set of 64 six-line figures or hexagrams. These hexagrams are the link between your question and the divinatory texts that answer it. Traditionally, you select a hexagram through one of two different methods. Both methods generate six numbers, each number being either 6, 7, 8, or 9. These numbers indicate the types of lines that make up your *Primary Hexagram.* This hexagram then keys the texts that answer your question.

Each hexagram is made up of six *opened* — — and/or *whole* —— lines. The lines have specific qualities, called *supple* and *strong*, which link them with the two primary agents in Eastern thought, yin and yang. Each hexagram can be thought of as a set of six empty places through which energy moves and changes. Energy comes into the hexagram from below and leaves at the top. The places are numbered accordingly; the lowest is the first and the highest the sixth. These six-line figures or hexagrams represent possible modes of change in the world, the dynamic qualities of time.

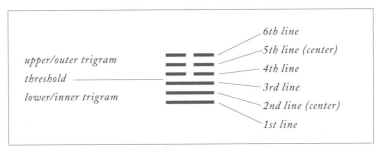

Each hexagram is also thought of as being composed of two *trigrams* or three-line figures. They represent basic elements or processes – wind and wood, fire and light, earth, heaven, mountain, marsh, running water, thunder – and have a wide range of associations. From this perspective each hexagram portrays the dynamic relation between a lower or *inner* element and an upper or *outer* element. This makes the division between the third and fourth lines particularly important as an interface between the inner and outer worlds. It also assigns a special value to the 2nd and 5th lines as centers of the inner and outer realms.

Each place in a hexagram, moving from below to above, can be occupied by one of four kinds of lines. These lines correspond to the four possible numbers that come from the traditional consultation procedure: 6, 7, 8 or 9. The yin, opened or *supple* lines correspond to the even numbers 6 and 8, the yang, *strong* or whole lines to the odd numbers 7 and 9.

The central numbers (7 and 8) constellate a *young* or *growing* line:

⑧ — — *young yin (does not change)*

⑦ —— *young yang (does not change)*

The extreme numbers (6 and 9) constellate an *old* line which is *transforming* (PIEN) into its opposite:

9 ——⊖—— old yang changes into — — young yin

6 —X— old yin changes into ——— young yang

These *Transforming Lines* have special significance. They represent precise points of change in the psyche and emphasize particular hexagram texts.

You get the numbers which produce these lines in two ways. The simplest is by tossing three coins six times. Heads are yang and have the value 3; tails are yin and have the value 2. Traditionally you would use copper *cash*, Chinese coins with a square hole in the center which are inscribed on one side (value 3) and empty (or with Manchu characters) on the other (value 2). Adding the results of each toss produces 6, 7, 8 or 9:

tails (2)+tails(2)+tails(2)= 6 = —X— *old or changing yin*

tails(2)+tails(2)+heads(3)= 7 = ——— *young yang*

tails(2)+heads(3)+heads(3)= 8 = — — *young yin*

heads(3)+heads(3)+heads(3)= 9 = —⊖— *old or changing yang*

Throwing the coins six times gives you six numbers. Arranged from the bottom up, and translated into lines, this produces the *Primary Hexagram.* When any of these lines are *Transforming Lines,* indicated by a 6 or a 9, they will change into their opposite. When they do this they generate a second hexagram, the *Relating Hexagram.* This figure indicates how you are related to the situation described in the Primary Hexagram. It describes the context or feeling that surrounds the answer given by the Primary Figure. It can show how the situation may develop, give the feeling tone of the encounter, describe a goal or desire, or an important experience that is shaping your perception. Which of the possibilities fits a given situation is determined through consideration of the question and its background: How does the Relating Figure actually "relate" you to the Primary Figure? Use the table on page 804 to find out which hexagram you have obtained. First identify the two trigrams, then look up the hexagram number. If there are *Transforming Lines,* indicated by a 6 or 9 in the consultation procedure, generate the new *Related Hexagram* which is produced when they change. Find that number in the same way.

The coin-oracle was popularized in the Southern Sung period (1127–1279) and has been used for several hundred years. It yields quick results. However it has a particular bias, for the mathematical odds involved are symmetrical. The probability that a yin line will transform is equal to that of a yang line, as is the proportion of stable yin and stable yang. This reflects binary choice and does not penetrate as deeply into the situation as the other, older and more complicated way of consulting the Oracle. This method, the yarrow-stalk method, uses a set of 50 thin sticks or batons about 12–18 inches long, traditionally yarrow-stalks (*achillea millefolium*) taken from the tips of the plant.

Using the yarrow-stalks reflects the nature of yin and yang as they were perceived in traditional Chinese science and allows time for reflection during the consultation process. The mathematical odds using yarrow-stalks are asymmetrical. These asymmetrical ratios reflect a *qualitative* difference, the intrinsic tendency of yin towards stability and of yang towards transformation.

The basic unit of this process of consultation is dividing and counting out the bunch of yarrow-stalks three times. Each time this is done a number, and thus a line of the Primary Hexagram, is produced.

Clear an open space on a table and quiet your mind. While thinking of your question and your plan of action, open yourself to whatever may come. You should note whatever emotions, images or memories come up, or whatever occurs around you during the process.

- Put the bunch of yarrow-stalks on the table in front of you. Make sure that you have 50. Take one stalk from the bunch and put it aside. This is the observer or witness, also called the center of the world. It will remain unused throughout the entire procedure of forming a hexagram.

- Divide the remaining bunch of 49 stalks into two random portions.

- Take one stalk from the pile on the left and put it between the 4th and 5th fingers of your left hand.

- Pick up the pile on the right and count it out in groups of 4, laying the groups out on the table in front of you, until you have a remainder of 1, 2, 3, or 4 stalks. Put this remainder between the 3rd and 4th fingers of your left hand.

- Take up the remaining pile and count it out in groups of 4, laying them out

in front of you, until you have a remainder of 1, 2, 3, or 4 stalks. Put this remainder between the 2nd and 3rd fingers of your left hand.

- Take all the stalks between fingers of your left hand and put them aside. They are out for this line.

- Make one bunch of the remaining groups of stalks. Repeat the entire procedure, again putting the stalks between your fingers aside.

- Repeat the procedure a third time. This time count the number of groups of 4 on the table in front of you. You will have either 6, 7, 8, or 9 groups. The number of groups gives you the first or bottom line of your hexagram.

- Go through this procedure 5 more times to form the complete hexagram, making the lines from the bottom up. At the end of the process gather the stalks together and return them to their wrapping or container. As in the coin method look up the numbers and names of the hexagrams you have formed.

The 16 Token Method

The coins and the yarrow stalks are the most frequently used traditional practices, but recently a new method was invented that combines the best features of the two. It is as simple and direct as the coins, and preserves the specific mathematical ratios between the different kinds of lines of the yarrow stalks. It is called the 16 Token Method.

To use this method, you need a small bowl and a total of 16 tokens (marbles are effective) of four different colors: one of the first color, three of the second color, five of the third color and seven of the fourth color. In this method, each color represents a different kind of line.

To use the 16 token oracle, put all sixteen tokens into a small bowl. The one token of the first color represents a yin line transforming into a yang line. The three marbles of the second color represent yang lines transforming into yin lines. The five marbles of the third color represent stable yang lines. The seven marbles of the fourth color represent stable yin lines. These ratios represent the innate tendency of yin to stay at rest and yang to move and change.

Now shake and mix the tokens. Without looking, pick one from the bowl. Note down the kind of line the color represents. This is the first line of your hexagram. Return the token to the bowl and pick again. Note the kind of line it represents. This is the second line of your hexagram. Repeat the procedure, each time returning the token to the bowl, until you have six lines, counting from the bottom up. This is your Primary Hexagram. If there are transforming lines, change them and create the Relating hexagram. Then use the Key to the Hexagrams to determine their names and numbers.

You are now ready to read the answer to your question.

● *Reading the Response*

The Oracle's response to the question you have asked comes through the texts of one of the 64 hexagrams. Turn to the hexagram texts indicated by your consultation. Read *all the basic texts in the Primary Hexagram* plus the texts of the *specific Transforming Lines* that are indicated by your consultation. Read *only the Image of the Related Hexagram.*

These texts describe energy fields and can generate many meanings. You will usually feel both an immediate intuitive connection and a sense of confusion as you begin to work with or "match" the symbols to your situation. This confusion is a necessary part of the process. Through it your sense of yourself and the situation becomes fluid, opened to new ways of seeing things.

This initial confusion triggers a sort of landslide of potential meaning. Being imaginatively open or versatile is the key to the interaction. The texts speak directly to your unconscious. When they touch a meaningful complex, *shen* or awareness of spirit is excited. Like key images in the remembering of a dream, certain definitions will emerge from the field. For the tradition insists that these words do not conform to a rule. Rather, as you walk around them, allowing them to act on your imagination, spontaneously the rules arrive. This is a living process. The images interact with, re-form and clarify the situation in your psyche.

Each reading begins with the Image of the *Primary Hexagram.* This is the basic context in which the Oracle sees both your question and its answer.

● *The* Image of the Situation *and the texts related to it describe an archetypal situation. It is each hexagram's central oracular statement, the ground in which all other parts of the hexagram are embedded. The name of the hexagram, usually the first word of the* Image, *generates both a description of your situation and advice as to the most effective way to deal with it. This places it in the dynamic of time, indicating key qualities and actions associated with it.*

The *Image* is the fundamental divinatory text. The first word of this text

forms the name or title of your hexagram. Together they are the hexagram's central oracular statement. The *Image* comes from the T'UAN, the oldest section of the text. The ideogram T'UAN consists of the graphs for swine and for a hog or boar's head. In China, pigs were a symbol of riches and intelligence, an essential sign of good fortune, and the boar's head was offered on sacrificial occasions. The *Image* suggests that knowing the image of the time, and basing your action upon it, is a key to realizing the riches and intelligence inherent in the situation.

All of the terms in the *Image*, and in the other sections that follow, are presented with their *Associated Contexts* and divinatory perspectives. These are possible meanings of the terms, usually including the traditional analysis of the ideogram. These *Associated Contexts* are given the first time a term appears in a hexagram; if the term is repeated you should refer back to the first occurrence. Punctuation marks give you a sense of the implicit pauses or emphases in the original text. Divinatory formulas such as **auspicious, pitfall, adversity, without fault, Advantageous Trial/Harvesting, Growing, nothing not advantageous** or **repenting extinguished**, give specific advice on whether the action you are contemplating leads toward or away from the experience of spirit and meaning.

As you read through the texts, certain terms will offer themselves as keys to your situation. Examine the meanings and let them suggest ways of understanding your situation. Use these meanings, even if they are contradictory, as you read through the other sections of your hexagram. The ultimate interpretation accumulates as the possible meanings interact.

The next section comments on the dynamic relation between the inner and the outer aspects of your situation. It describes the tension between your inner process and the outer world you are confronting.

• Outer and Inner Aspects *analyses the matter under consideration in terms of the dynamic relation of its outer and inner elements. This is described through the relation between the outer and inner trigrams and their nets of associated qualities.*

This section acts as a shorthand reference to the supplementary material on the Universal Compass dealing with traditional systems of correlative thinking. It gathers material from the 8th Wing and a Han Dynasty text central to the system of correlative thinking, *The Comprehensive Discussions in the White Tiger Hall.*

Hidden Possibility describes another figure at the core of the hexagram. It lets you see the potential of the situation, the possibility of resolving a core issue.

This section stems from the traditional view that the four inner lines of each hexagram form two overlapping Nuclear Trigrams, which thus form a Nuclear Hexagram. It focuses your understanding of the central Image by showing the possibility moving in its core or center.

The texts entitled *Contrasted Definitions, Sequence, Attached Evidences* (in certain hexagrams), *Symbol Tradition* and *Image Tradition* were composed later than the *Image*. They are interpretive strategies which come from the Ten Wings, each commenting on or amplifying the Image from a particular perspective.

The *Sequence* explains what led up to your present situation, thus suggesting why you are asking your question.

●   *The* Sequence *puts the* Image *in a series with the hexagram that precedes it in terms of a completed action which calls up a following action. It suggests that activating the energy of this hexagram depends upon understanding it as a part of a necessary succession of events.*

The *Sequence*, from the 9th Wing, represents a transitional area. It always contains the statement: "Accepting this lets you use use ..." This indicates that activating your hexagram's energies depends upon understanding and accepting as valid the succession of events the *Sequence* describes. The action of the preceding hexagram is conceived of as the point of departure for your present situation.

The *Contrasted Definitions* accent a particular quality of your hexagram as a clue to understanding how it works.

●   *The* Contrasted Definitions *offer a key to your situation by picking out a central feature and contrasting it with a central feature of an adjoining hexagram.*

The pairs of *Contrasted Definitions* are taken from the 10th Wing and are given with the hexagrams they describe.

In certain hexagrams there is a section called *Attached Evidences*. This indicates that the actions and attitudes described in the hexagram were felt to be particularly important in developing and deepening individual character, the ability to be independent and in touch with *tao*.

- *The* Attached Evidences *indicate the action of this hexagram is particularly relevant to actualizing-tao and describe how it can aid the process of realizing tao in action.*

These texts occur in only ten of the hexagrams and are drawn from the Eighth Wing.

The section called *Symbol Tradition* uses the Symbols of the trigrams to derive a particular attitude. They are linked with the *chün tzu*, the ideal user of the *I Ching*, or the *Earlier Kings*, who suggest a model from the Golden Age. This implies that part of being a *chün tzu* is being able to see things as symbols. It connects you with the way the *tao* is moving.

- *The* Symbol Tradition *describes the Image in terms of the relation between the Symbols of its two trigrams. It derives a specific action from this relation which gives access to the ideal of the chün tzu in this situation: a person who uses divination to order their life according to tao rather than personal desires.*

The trigrams and their attributes are described in the Reference Material. What is particularly relevant is that the *Symbol Tradition* derives a specific action from the relation of the trigrams. This action is said to typify the behavior of the *chün tzu* in conforming to and furthering the moment described.

The last interpretive section is called the *Image Tradition*. It repeats specific phrases from the Image and comments on them. It is probably the latest section, and has a distinct analytical quality.

- *The* Image Tradition *amplifies key terms and qualities of the* Image. *It also analyses the* Image *in terms of: the correspondence of pairs of lines; the actions and relations of supple and strong, assigned to the opened and whole lines; and the appropriateness of the lines to their places, particularly the center lines of the trigrams.*

The *Image Tradition* paraphrases the *Image* and analyses the actions described by the trigram symbols. It offers analogies to the central image and examines:

the resonance or correspondence of pairs of lines: 1 and 4, 2 and 5, 3 and 6;

the dynamic relation of supple and strong, qualities assigned to the opened and whole lines, and how they move in the situation;

the appropriateness of the lines to their places in the hierarchical structure of the hexagram, particularly in relation to the center lines of the trigrams:

opened lines are considered appropriate to even-numbered spaces, and whole lines appropriate to odd-numbered spaces.

The nature of this commentary is suggested by its characteristic term: Indeed/is/means, YEH. It is an intensifier and connective, which means: in truth, in actual fact, as a matter of fact, often translated as the verb "to be." This section of the Ten Wings sponsored an extensive commentary tradition called *i-li* or moral-principle analysis, which developed a view of the social value and function of the various line-positions.

The texts of the *Transforming Lines* are qualitatively different from the texts which surround and amplify the Image of your *Primary Hexagram.* These texts reflect the precise points of connection with the psychic forces involved in your question, "hot spots" where they cross and mix. They reveal the potential significance of individual action within the situation described by the Primary Hexagram as a whole, suggesting what your plan might lead to and how it might get there.

The Transforming Lines *represent precise points of connection with the psychic forces involved in your question, activated by a 6 or a 9 in the consultation procedure. They give you advice on the direction of specific actions and the potential consequences. As the activated lines change into their opposites they generate a second hexagram, the Relating Hexagram, which indicates how you are related to the basic situation.*

The texts of the Transforming Lines come from the T'UAN and from the commentaries on the lines in the 3rd and 4th Wings. These texts are constellated when a specific line is *transforming* (PIEN) into its contrary and thus *transforms* the hexagram in question, the *Primary Hexagram,* into the *Relating Hexagram.* You should read only those *Transforming Lines* constellated in the response to your question. The a) text is the oldest text, while the b) text is a clarifying comment on it. Like the Image Tradition, the b) text is characterized by the intensifier indeed, YEH, which means: in truth, in actual fact.

The Image of the *Relating Hexagram* generated when the Transforming Lines change into their opposites gives an indication of how you are related to the problem. This can be a goal, an image of desire, reassurance or warning. It is not an immutable future, but an indication of the potential contained in your present situation. Changing the way you act or perceive things can change this potential.

Keywords: Traps for Tao

Certain terms have a special significance in the *I Ching*, in addition to their ordinary meanings. These keywords evolved as the I became a tool used by private individuals. They reflect a troubled time, like our own, when people could not necessarily count on social structures to support them, but had to find their own path. Together, these keywords give a picture of the world of the *I Ching* and how it seeks to help you.

The most fundamental term is:

> **Tao**: way or path; ongoing process of being and course it traces for each specific being or thing; keyword. The ideogram: go and head, leading and the path it creates.

The term **tao** has no equivalent in English. The literal meaning is way or path, and the term describes both the movement on this way and the way itself. **Tao** is the ongoing, self-renewing and purposive energy of life, continually creating as it moves. It traces a way or path which is, potentially, reflected in each individual being. To be "in" **tao** or connected to tao is to experience meaning and move with the energy of life. This is fundamental value. It is experienced as meaning, joy, freedom, connection, compassion, creativity, insight.

Tao is not limited by any system or morality, and it continually undermines rational definitions. It is not predictable, but versatile.

> **Versatility**, I: sudden and unpredictable change; mental mobility and openness; easy and light, not difficult and heavy.

Versatility describes the way tao moves, a sudden substitution of one thing or image for another. This often appears as trouble or difficulty, for it challenges the fixity of things. Versatility also indicates the imaginative fluidity necessary to adapt to the movement of tao. It connects the way, the Book of I and the imagination, the continual flow of images in what the tradition calls the heart-mind, the heart of magic.

This connection occurs through symbols and symbolizing.

> **Symbol**, HSIANG: image invested with intrinsic power to connect visible and invisible; magic spell; figure, form, shape, likeness; pattern, model; create an image, imitate; act, play; writing.

The *I* – the "way" of the *I Ching* – provides **symbols**, direct analogies to the movement of energy in the invisible world. The **symbols** are **versatile**. They act like weirs or fishtraps in the flow of **tao**, accumulating the quality of mind it represents. You connect with the energy by imagining yourself through the **symbols**, a process which indicates what is and what is not in harmony with time and tao. The term **symbol** is connected with two other terms:

- **Trial**, CHEN: inquiry by divination and its result; righteous, firm; separating wheat from chaff; the kernel, the proven core; put your ideas to the trials; fourth stage of the Time Cycle. The ideogram: pearl and divination.

- **Vessel/holding**, TING: bronze cauldron with three feet and two ears, sacred vessel used to cook food for sacrifice to gods and ancestors; founding symbol of family or dynasty; melting pot, receptacle; hold, contain, transform; establish, secure; precious, respectable.

The **symbols** produced by the I through divination try or test an action by submitting it to the spirits and revealing its hidden roots. When you use these **symbols** in a **versatile** way, as imaginative models, they act like a sacred **vessel**, enacting a process of containment, sacrifice and transformation.

By doing this you acquire **te**, the virtue and power that comes through reflecting **tao** in the events of your life.

- **Actualize-tao**, TE: realize tao in action; power, virtue; ability to follow the course traced by the ongoing process of the cosmos; keyword. The ideogram: to go, straight, and heart. Linked with te, acquire: acquiring that which makes a being become what it is meant to be.

The movement of **tao** constantly offers **symbols** which the heart may respond to. Using these **symbols** to adapt to the movement of **tao** clarifies and deepens the heart, opening it to the spirit-power called *shen ming* or the *light of the gods*. **Actualizing-tao** suggests that the continual process of straightening, clarifying and deepening the heart enables you to become what you are meant to be, correcting and straightening movement on the path or way of life. Someone who seeks to acquire this virtue, and thus to live their life as a manifestation of **tao**, is a **chün tzu**.

- **Chün tzu**: ideal of a person who uses divination to order his/her life in accordance with tao rather than wilful intention.

The term **chün tzu**, literally son of the chief, has no real equivalent in English. It first described a lower order of nobility. As these orders fell apart, it evolved into the ideal of a person who uses *I* divination and its **versatile**

symbols to live life in connection with **tao,** acquiring the power and virtue of the spirits. You are a **chün tzu** when you use the oracle to understand what is in harmony with tao in any given situation in your life, to help and protect yourself through **tao** rather than seeking control by imposing your will. **Versatility** is the tool, an imaginative way of understanding and acting that opens the **tao** or way. The oracle is meant for those who strive for the ideal of **chün tzu.** It only makes sense from this perspective.

The **chün tzu** lives in **Heaven and Earth,** a world of continual change, of mixtures and movement, energies and spirits.

- **Heaven and Earth,** T'IEN TI: dynamic relation between the primal powers and the world it produces; cosmos, natural or human world; keyword.

This world is nowhere absolute. It results from the interaction of the two primal powers as they mix or **intertwine** to form a variegated cosmos. **Heaven and Earth** is the world of the myriad beings, humans, animals and spirits, where nothing is fixed. The I reflects this world; it is effective there. Through it, the **chün tzu** seeks to lead a meaningful and enjoyable human life, connected to the spirits, the **tao** and the living world. Part of this is a continual recognition of imperfection and change, and a careful reflection of the primal powers.

- **Heaven,** T'IEN: highest; sky, firmament, heavens; power above the human as opposed to earth, ti, below; the Symbol of the trigram Force, ch'ien. The ideogram: great and the one above.

- **Earth,** TI: ground on which the human world rests; basis of all things, nourishes all things; the Symbol of the trigram Field, K'UN.

Seeking neither purity nor immortality, the **chün tzu** lives in the stream of time that flows through **Heaven and Earth** as an image of the way. Two basic terms describe this flow.

- **Come,** LAI, and **Go,** WANG, describe the stream of time as it flows from the future through the present into the past; come, LAI, indicates what is approaching; move toward, arrive at; go, WANG, indicates what is departing; proceed, move on.

This time flows from and returns to a source. **Coming** events have an objective reality, and they cast images which may be seen through divination. **Come** and **go** also refer to the hexagrams as images of time. Lines enter a hexagram from below and within, **coming,** and leave above and outside, **going**, just as the stream of time, and the way or **tao**, originates within and flows through each individual. Thus **coming** and **going** contrasts with the sense of personal history in which life moves from the past into the future. It means that letting **go** of the places where you are bound to the past and paying attention to what is **coming** on the stream of time is part of being **versatile**. Through it you acquire **te**.

There are two basic orientations of the will used as the **chün tzu** seeks to adapt to the events that **come** on the stream of time. Between them, they implement imaginative **versatility**.

- **Great**, TA: big, noble, important, very; orient the will toward a self-imposed goal, impose direction; ability to lead or guide your life; contrasts to small, hsiao, flexible adaptation to what crosses your path.

- **Great People**, TA JEN: important, noble, influential; those who impose a ruling principle on their lives; effect of the great within an individual.

- **Small**, HSIAO: little, common, unimportant; adapting to what crosses your path; ability to move in harmony with the vicissitudes of life; contrasts with great, TA, self-imposed theme or goal.

- **Small People**, HSIAO JEN: lowly, common, humble; those who adjust to circumstances with the flexibility of the small; effect of the small within an individual.

Though these terms include the ordinary meanings of noble and humble, exceptional and common, powerful and weak, their significance lies in the direction they give to the will. The **chün tzu** seeks the freedom to move between these attitudes, picking them up and putting them down as the time demands. **Great** and **Great People**, the effect of the **great** on an individual, means imposing an idea on things, independent of what that idea might be. Only when it is connected to **actualizing-tao** is it valued in itself. **Small** and **Small People**, the effect of the small in an individual, is not simply the shadow of the **great**, but points at the ability to let go of self-importance, quickly and humbly adapting to what crosses your path. The **chün tzu** is not a **Great Person** or a **Small Person**, but seeks the capacity to act quickly and fluidly as both.

Divination with the *I* helps and supports connection with **tao** and the acquisition of **te**, the experience of meaning and the pleasure and benefit that comes with the connection. The basic divinatory terms of the *I* reflect this. Events are valued according to whether they lead towards or away from this experience.

- **Auspicious**, CHI: leads to the experience of meaning; favorable, propitious, advantageous, appropriate. The ideogram: scholar and mouth, wise words of a sage.

- **Pitfall**, HSIUNG: leads away from the experience of meaning; stuck and exposed to danger, unable to take in the situation; flow of life and spirit is blocked; unfortunate, baleful.

These terms emphasize that within the constant movement of things it is possible to choose. You may take advantage of the insight given by the *I* and its **symbols** to move with this flow. Implicit in this is the idea that through these **symbols** you not only acquire meaning and benefit, but that you can help the world around you by being in accord with **tao**.

- ## *Encounters with the Oracle*

The *I Ching* is meant to be used when you are troubled and you seek a meaning in the disturbance. It offers insight into the question you pose and practical advice on how to deal with it. Its images act as a guide to personal transformation, leading to a deeper knowledge of yourself and your actions. It is a way of thinking and imagining that gives you the tools to make changes.

The *I Ching*'s words and images have been called "magic spells" because of their uncanny ability to connect you with unseen forces. This opens a liminal space in which you can contact what is moving the soul. Inside this circle, your sense of yourself and your situation dissolves and re-forms. You receive information about what is possible and effective in a given situation. It shows your way or *tao* at work.

Because they are open symbols, the divinatory terms do not force you into the mold of a specific morality. All of the terms can refer to any person, regardless of age, gender or social position. They foster an imaginative process that both protects you and helps your spirit emerge. Your dialogue with them weaves a new story or context for your experience of yourself and your situation.

Using the *I* in this way is like working with dreams. The images do not offer standard predictions of an unalterable future. They describe the way energy is moving to create possible futures. This presents you with an opportunity to interact with the energy clusters or complexes of the psyche. Changing your relation to these forces can change what will happen to you.

You learn this "way" by doing it, by continually moving between the images and their connection to the events of your life. By involving yourself in these clusters of meaning, by trying out the stories they suggest, you open yourself to *I* and its function: to make conscious the imaginative background and the goal of the situation in which you find yourself, giving you the information necessary to make choices.

In a traditional culture, where myth is alive, people take a step back into the imagination before they start on any significant action. They encounter an image there and move into the action through the image that they have found. This oracular image carries them, keeping them connected with the imaginative ground. It acts as a sign and a talisman, gathering energy, warning, offering hope and direction. Similarly, these images answer the basic question that appears today in a moving or disturbing experience – What is going on? What will happen to me? What should I do? – in order to connect you with the creative ground beneath it.

The following series of Encounters with the Oracle gives you a sense of the ways the *I Ching* can be used and the sorts of situations in which people turn to it. Look at the hexagrams involved as you read through the consultations.

Perhaps the most fundamental quality of the Oracle is to recognize and act as a witness to your situation. This grounds you in an image that is larger than your personal awareness. Such recognition is the basic connection to the symbolic world.

● EXAMPLE 1

● *A Voice in the Wilderness*

He first encountered the I Ching *more than 30 years ago. Like other people at the time, he was searching for a better way to live his life. He had made a moral and political decision that put him into exile, and felt lost in a forest of conflicting emotions, thoughts, philosophies and possibilities, with no real sense of how to look at them. It was a dangerous time, full of sudden change and violence, and his life was in flux. Wandering in the wilderness of the time, he encountered the* I Ching *and asked this question.*

Question: Who are you? How should I use you?

Answer: Hexagram 50, no *Transforming Lines*

The answer was Hexagram 50, **The Vessel**, with no *Transforming Lines*.

Here, the book described itself and his relation to it:

The Vessel describes your situation in terms of imagination and the transformative capacity of a sacred vessel. Its symbol is the cast bronze cauldron, the sacrificial meal and the founding of a noble house. The way to deal with it is to contain and transform your problem through an image. Make an offering and you will succeed. You need to see deeply into what your problem means. Security and a new beginning will come from this awareness. It is a time for reflection, for slowly turning and examining things. This is the origin of great good fortune and meaningful events. It releases transformative energy. It is pleasing to the spirits. Through it they will give you success, effective power and the capacity to bring the situation to maturity.

 Vessel/holding, TING: bronze cauldron with three feet and two ears, sacred vessel used to cook food for sacrifice to gods and ancestors; founding symbol of family or dynasty; melting pot, receptacle; hold, contain, transform; establish, secure; precious, respectable.

The book presented itself as a process of imaginative transformation that could contain the fragmented pieces of his life. He should put what he needed to "cook" into the **Vessel** through posing it as a question, and it would respond. His problem would be held, contained, transformed, centered in another imaginative dimension. Through this process he could establish and secure himself.

He was amazed at the feeling of being talked to directly. The voice cut into his dislocation and loneliness, offering a way to understand and evaluate the things he was going through. Particularly, the *Contrasted Definitions* told him that he should understand the painful events leading to his present situation as **skinning,** a time of revolution.

 Skin, KO: take off the covering, skin or hide; change, renew, molt; remove, peel off; revolt, overthrow, degrade from office; leather armor, protection.

 This linked his personal feeling of being without protection to a kind of molting, an *objective* change. **Skinning** connects political revolt and personal vulnerability. It could open him to the imaginative practice of the **Vessel,** through which he could **grasp renewal:**

 Grasp, CH'Ü: lay hold of, take and use, seize, appropriate; grasp the meaning, understand. The ideogram: ear and hand, hear and grasp.

What was past, the bitter quarrels, old sorrows, previous causes, grievances and broken relationships that brought him to this situation, could simply depart.

Past, KU: come before as cause; formerly, ancient; reason, purpose, intention; grievance, quarrel, dissatisfaction, sorrow, mourning resulting from previous causes and intentions; situation leading to a divination.

Depart, CH'O: leave, quit, remove; repudiate, reject, dismiss.

Inner and Outer Aspects told him that this imaginative process could establish an inner **Ground**. It could bring disconnected things together to feed a spreading **Radiance**, a warm clarity of spirit. The *Hidden Possibility* told him that holding and containing things in the **Vessel** could lead to decisive action and **parting** from past sorrows. He should put all the disparate pieces of his life into the **Vessel** to be **cooked**. In this way, the *Symbol Tradition* told him, he could correct his situation.

Correct, CHENG rectify deviation or one-sidedness; proper, straight, exact, regular; constant, rule, model. The ideogram: stop and one, hold to one thing.

He could become aware of and live out his own destiny, giving a form to **fate**:

Fate, MING: individual destiny; birth and death as limits of life; issue orders with authority; consult the gods. The ideogram: mouth and order, words with heavenly authority.

For, in the words of the *Image Tradition*, the **Vessel** was a **symbol indeed**:

Symbol, HSIANG: image invested with intrinsic power to connect visible and invisible; magic spell; figure, form, shape, likeness; pattern; model; create an image, imitate; act, play; writing.

The *I Ching* offered itself to him personally as an imaginative process. This was like putting on a new fate, entering an imaginal world. The goal of the advice it gave was **auspiciousness**, the personal experience of meaning. Now, 35 years later, he realized that this is true in a much broader way. The feeling of being in touch with the hidden spirit of the time that the book offers is a counter to the alienation and fragmentation spreading throughout our world – the purpose for which the *I Ching* was originally assembled. It has been a guiding force in his life and work ever since.

EXAMPLE 2

The Invisible Woman

She asked the question because she felt cornered, frightened and desperate. The one thing she had to hang on to was her writing. She had staked almost everything on it. She had abandoned a professional training program, given up her house and friends. She was working at a menial job and took care of a sick old man in exchange for room and board. She was cut off from the man she was in love with. She wanted to write a book. She had thought she could do it quickly and well and the book would open a new life. Now she couldn't write. She blamed her impossible situation. She could see no way out. Panicked, shaky and heading for a breakdown, she decided to consult the I Ching.

Question: What can I do about my living and working situation?

Answer: Hexagram 47, no *Transforming Lines*

The answer was Hexagram 47, **Confining**, with no *Transforming Lines*.

The *Image* of this hexagram took hold of her desperation and loneliness and re-defined it:

> Confined and Oppressed describes your situation in terms of being cut off, oppressed and exhausted. Its symbol is the tree of life confined in a narrow enclosure. The way to deal with it is to collect the energy to break out of the enclosure and re-establish communication. Make an offering and you will succeed. This is pleasing to the spirits. Through it they will give you success, effective power and the capacity to bring the situation to maturity. Be great and master the situation from within. Find what is truly important to you. Seek those who can help and advise you. This generates meaning and good fortune by releasing transformative energy. The situation is not your fault. Words are not to be trusted. There is a breakdown of communication and you are being isolated by it. You are not believed when you speak. Don't believe what others are telling you to do.
>
> **Confine**, K'UN: enclose, restrict, limit; oppressed; impoverish, distress; afflicted, exhausted, disheartened, weary. The ideogram: an enclosed tree.

The emotional connection was immediate. She was **confined**, and the *Image* validated her feelings of being disheartened and weary, at the end of her rope. The image of the tree imprisoned in this distress – the Tree of Life, for her – was particularly vivid. It was the fundamental quality of this moment of her life.

At the same time, the Image advised her to go deeper into the situation, to accept and *internalize* it as part of her **fate**. The affirmation that **confining** had an objective quality brought a great sense of relief. She was not obliged to fight against it. The situation was, in the words of the *Image*, **without fault**, without personal error that leads to harm.

Outer and Inner Aspects gave her an image for the conflict she felt between her desires and her experience, a conflict that was pulling her apart. She was seeing the *Outer Aspect* through the **Open** and **stimulating** words: meeting with others, cheering and inspiring speech, widening acquaintance, working for mutual profit. She felt this *should* be happening. Her real situation was an empty caricature of what she wanted.

The *Inner Aspect* explained this emptiness. It showed the stream of psychic energy falling into danger and toiling through a dark passage, the **Gorge**. This was dissolving the inner forms she normally used to think about herself and her world. The possibility of contact in the outer world was being undermined and drawn in. The map was changing; it no longer fit the territory.

Confining had cut the links to family, friends and the cooperation of the workplace. It was drawing energy *in* and *down*. She felt this as oppression, affliction and isolation. The *Hidden Possibility* assured her that accepting and working through this could eventually lead to the security of people living and working together in a dwelling.

The "why" of this experience – and it was very important to find a purpose – emerged through the *Attached Evidences*. These texts relate the action of certain hexagrams to **actualizing-tao**, the struggle to acquire the power and the virtue to become an individual. **Confining** is characterized as **actualizing-tao's marking-off**.

> **Mark-off**, PIEN: distinguish by dividing; mark off a plot of land; frame which divides a bed from its stand; discuss and dispute. The ideogram: knife and acrid, biting division.

Her isolation, however it had been produced, had the deeper goal of clearly distinguishing her from others. Its acrid quality surrounded her, setting her off from teachers, friends, family, and lover.

Terms from the *Attached Evidences* and the *Contrasted Definitions* suggested that this bitter **confining** was also a time of **exhausting** the old.

Exhaust, CH'IUNG: bring to an end; limit, extremity; destitute; investigate exhaustively; end without a new beginning. The ideogram: cave and naked person, bent with disease or old age.

This connected to the inner dissolving and toil associated with **Gorge**, the night-sea journey. She was surrounded by the dying forms of things. **Confining** was challenging her to dis-identify with them, to become her own new person.

The *Image*, the central divinatory statement, linked **confining** and **success** or **Growing**.

Grow, HENG: success through a sacrifice; pervade, persevere; bring to full growth; enjoy; vigorous, effective; second stage of the Time Cycle.

Confining was a sacrifice offered to her spirit. The key to **growing** was accepting the inwardness of being confined, allowing it to stimulate *inner* growth and independence. Such acceptance was **without fault**.

Two things in the *Image* were of central importance. First was **Great People**:

Great People, TA JEN: important, noble, influential; those who impose a ruling principle on their lives; effect of the great within an individual; keyword.

Great People are not simply the important or influential people from whom she wanted approval. They are those who are able to impose a direction on their lives from within. The inner meaning of this term was very important. She was invited to develop the capacity to be **great** rather than continually searching for recognition and approval in other people's eyes. The inner **growth** of **confining** could produce the insight and courage to do so.

This was particularly important because at this crossroads of her life **possessing words** was not **trustworthy**.

Possess, YU: in possession of, have, own; opposite of lack, WU.

Trustworthy, HSIN: truthful, faithful, consistent over time; integrity; confide in, follow; credentials; contrasts with conforming, FU, connection in a specific moment. The ideogram: person and word, true speech.

Normally she was very facile with words, even glib. She never **lacked** them, but always had them in her **possession**. She had begun to write with this attitude, **trusting** her ability to impress people with **words**. But here, her **words** were not to be **trusted**. They would not endure. They were unconnected. They lacked integrity. This was the moment of truth, no way to escape. Her writer's block was part of **confining**.

The *Image Tradition* moved the deadlock. Here **confining** was described as a situation in which the **strong** − what is firm, strong and purposive, a focus she desperately needed − is **enshrouded**, shadowed and hidden from view.

> **Enshroud**, YEN: screen, shade from view, hide, cover. The ideogram: hand and cover.

As we looked at this image, the hand suddenly turned over. Her whole presence changed, relaxed and deepened. She admitted that she had begun to paint. The painting was a secret. No one knew about it. It expressed a separate, secret world, infusing images from her daily life with an intense feeling tone she could not explain with her usual facility. It was where the underground stream was moving, disconnected from ambition and approval. Staying in the situation, staying with her concerns and feelings, and abandoning the glib and **untrustworthy** relation to **words**, allowed the deepening process to work.

This process **reaches to her very chün tzu**, the possibility of becoming an individual rather than a random assemblage of collective desires. **Honoring the mouth** and its glib facility was being **exhausted**. Inner **stimulating** was **opening** new possibilities for living and, eventually, writing, that were not directly connected to **honoring the mouth**.

The reading ended with the *Symbol Tradition* and the **chün tzu** who **uses involving fate to release purpose**. At present she was completely **involved** in her problems.

> **Involve**, CHIH: include, entangle, implicate; induce, cause. The ideogram: person walking, induced to follow.

But by seeing and accepting this entanglement as **fate** and letting it induce inner movement, a **purpose** could be released that would, in turn, **release** her.

> **Purpose**, CHIH: focus of mind and heart; will, inclination, resolve. The ideogram: heart and scholar, high inner resolve, or heart and go, inner determination.

> **Release**, SUI: loose, let go, free; unhindered, in accord; follow, spread out, progress; penetrate, invade. The ideogram: go and follow your wishes, unimpeded movement.

Involving fate implied that the events of her life that were confusing her were given by creative forces beyond her direct control. This is how **fate** speaks. Confronting **fate's involvement** imaginatively puts you on the way to the **chün tzu**. Conscious **purpose** is released from **confinement** in unconscious drives, a transformation of ambition that connects it to the heart and to the **great**. This sense of **purpose** could **release** her. It was the reality of this moment of her life. As she let herself flow into this image, her panic dissolved. She was ready to discover the **purpose** in the dark moment where she was presently **confined**.

This reading shifted what seemed a practical concern into the area of inner development which shadowed it. **Confining** was offered as a talisman, a guiding image through a dark passage, and over time it did lead to a new kind of work and the establishment of a **dwelling** shared with others.

- EXAMPLE 3

- *The King and I*

This question was posed by a teacher, writer, psychologist and musician who had become involved with the fate of the Australian koala, considered by Aboriginal tribes as the secret knower and trickster. As he became acquainted with these remarkable animals, he found out that they were dying as a species. From a population of over 10 million in 1930, they had been reduced to fewer than 30,000. They seldom mated and most matings were non-productive. At the time of this reading, drought and severe bush fires were destroying the habitat of the remaining koalas. With no government support, he helped to build what was the only hospital and study center in the world devoted to koalas. Volunteer crews with mechanical "cherry-pickers" were dispatched to rescue the koalas from burning trees where they were trapped and dying. He developed a burn treatment protocol for use in the intensive care unit which proved highly successful. Treatment, however, was very expensive.

Surprisingly, the koalas, who had never seen a human being before and are quite capable of inflicting serious bites, knew they were being helped and cooperated with the sometimes painful treatment. An intense bonding resulted for both humans and animals.

When the time came for him to leave the hospital and return home, he became deeply upset. He was completely enervated and disoriented at the prospect of leaving before the results of the treatment on Terry Glen, an animal he had rescued, were known. He knew that his own depression and concern could very quickly prove contagious, affecting the animals and undermining the morale of the team of volunteers. He knew he must do something. So he posed the question to the I Ching.

Question: What is going on? How should I relate to the people who are working here with me?

Answer: Hexagram 55, no Transforming Lines

The answer was Hexagram 55, **Abounding**, with no *Transforming Lines*.

The *Image* of this hexagram described his situation:

Abounding describes your situation in terms of abundance and fertile profusion. Its symbol is the change in the mandate of heaven given to King Wu that bought a renewal of the time. The way to deal with it is to be exuberant and expansive. Overflow with good feeling, support and generosity. Give with both hands. This is pleasing to the spirits. Through it they will give you success, effective power and the capacity to bring the situation to maturity. Imagine yourself as the king whose power bestows wealth and happiness on all. Rid yourself of sorrow, melancholy and care. Be like the sun at midday. Shed light on all and eliminate the shadows.

Abound, FENG: abundant, plentiful, copious; grow wealthy; at the point of overflowing; exuberant, fertile, prolific; rich in talents, property, friends; fullness, culmination; ripe, sumptuous, fat.

The situation was described as something full to the brim, culminating, spilling over and thus moving to an end. The emotional tone, however, was exuberant, prolific, sumptuous, fertile, joyful, a hidden renewal of the time.

The *Image* brought an immediate connection, focusing his emotions. His experience as a counselor had taught him that when an **abundance** of powerful psychic material overflows into the personal it can cause panic and dysfunction. His contact with the koalas had activated deep feelings. Their overflow signalled that his consciousness was drawn too thin to handle it. It was spilling over into a whole range of symptoms, from panic to enervation. This had to be grounded by an image, a guideline for personal action.

The fundamental divinatory instruction was:

Abounding, Growing.
The king imagines it.

No grief. Properly the sun is at center.

Immersed in this very powerful emotional field, he was told he must not grieve over the fact it was culminating. The term described not only his confusion and anxious melancholy, but the hidden careworn quality that was enervating him.

> **Grieve(-over), YU:** sorrow, melancholy; mourn; anxious, careworn; hidden sorrow. The ideogram: heart, head, and limp, heart-sick and anxious.

He should not hide away. He must be like the sun as it reaches zenith, the **center** of the heavens, shedding its brightest rays as it begins to set. The *Outer and Inner Aspects* amplified the image of **the sun at the center**. He was to convert his inner sadness into positive **Radiance**, and let this **radiance** permeate and fertilize the outer world, **stirring up** action, germinating and inspiring. He was to increase the **Radiance** of everything, **abounding** but not entangled in grief or anxiety.

The *Sequence* suggested that he had been profoundly changed, **converted**, by coming to this **place**. The behavior of the koalas, who are among the oldest animals still living on earth, showed that something from the distant past, his totemic spirit, had found him. Working with the koalas, he had acquired something **great**, something that organized his life.

> **Convert, KUEI:** change to another form, persuade; return to yourself or the place where you belong; restore, revert, become loyal; turn into; give a young girl in marriage. The ideogram: arrive and wife, become mistress of a household.

> **Great, TA:** big, noble, important, very; orient the will toward a self-imposed goal, impose direction; ability to lead or guide your life; contrasts with small, HSIAO, flexible adaptation to what crosses your path; keyword.

The *Hidden Possibility* told him that this abounding generosity for all would lead him to traversing the great and difficult transition he confronted by giving him access to the creative energy hidden at its core.

> **Traverse/exceed, KU:** go beyond, pass over, make the passage; excessive, dominant, transgress.

The *Contrasted Definitions* showed the present situation contrasted with **sojourning**, an important image throughout his life:

Sojourn, LÜ: travel, stay in places other than your home; itinerant troops, temporary residents; visitor, guest, lodger. The ideogram: banner and people around it, loyal to a symbol rather than their temporary residence.

The **numerous past**, the many people who, each for his or her own reason, had come together here, was modulating once again into **connecting the few**, seeking out others in the world who could also be connected to what was happening here. He could **sojourn** under this banner. He has since published a significant book on these animals and the myths around them, *Koala: Australia's Ancient Ones*, (New York: MacMillan, 1994).

The *Symbol Tradition* reinforced the sense that everything in the situation was **culminating**.

Culminate, CHIH: bring to the highest degree; arrive at the end or summit; superlative.

It also connected to the other thing that was holding him. He was scheduled to be an expert witness for the defense in an upcoming trial. Here **severing litigating** spoke about cutting the connection to the litigation, allowing the **punishment** to occur.

Sever, CHE: break off, separate, sunder, cut in two; discriminate, judge the true and false.

It later proved that his testimony would have been useless, and that he would have become embroiled in an endless series of legal complications.

Finally the *Image* spoke to his deepest concern in the situation: how he could relate to the people and the extremely sensitive animals in the situation who could easily be infected by **grieving**. The way to deal with it was to **imagine it** as if he were a king. This was the sacrifice to the spirit that would ensure **growing**.

King(hood), WANG: effective ruler, by authority of the Emperor, from whom others derive their power.

Imagine, CHIA: create in the mind; fantasize, suppose, pretend, imitate; fiction; illusory, unreal; costume. The ideogram: person and borrow.

He was invited to **imagine** himself as the **king**, the one from whom blessings flow and others derive their **power**. The king's function was not to focus on a specific goal, but to stay in contact with **tao** or the way and pass the power on through a generosity that rivals the **sun** at midday. He was

invited to put on the **king**'s costume, to **radiate** its **abounding** and generous power with neither care nor sadness. This image would carry him through.

The last days in the hospital went well. Dressing himself in the costume of the **king**, he was able to encourage people at their work and remain **abundant** and joyful. Playing this role on the last day, he saw Terry Glen, the koala he had personally saved. These animals, whom the tribes consider to be clever and tricky as well as knowing, do not usually bond to humans. But this one had established a deep bond. When he approached, the koala put the soft, vulnerable part of his hand on his cheek, patted him knowingly and affectionately, then deliberately pushed him away. **No grieving**. It was time to go.

The hexagrams can give you images that carry you through dangerous situations. They can also reflect on your basic drives and attitudes, particularly when they are changing or they bring you into conflict with the world. Such reflection can save you from compulsive action and being trapped in a conflict that no one can win.

- EXAMPLE 4

- *Growing Pains*

He was a young doctor completing training in psychiatry. His drive was bringing him into a real conflict with some of his supervisors. He engaged in dangerous sports and held amateur records. He was interested in several spiritual disciplines and alternative approaches to medicine. He was convinced that he could only really help people by giving them a sense of spiritual meaning. Because of his passionate convictions, and the force with which they were expressed, his training was troubled. He was indignant about its narrow approach to problems of personal meaning. His supervisors told him, however, that his views on spirituality were a personal matter, that it was dangerous to all concerned to introduce his views in a psychoanalytical setting, and that he was being "unscientific." This conflict was threatening to explode, and he sought reflection on his drive through posing the question to the I Ching.

Question: What about my *drive* to bring spiritual practices into psychoanalytic therapy?

Answer: Hexagram 4, 6/6, Hexagram 7

The answer was Hexagram 4, **Enveloping/Ignorance**, with a *Transforming Line* at the top, leading to Hexagram 7, **Legions/Leading**.

The *Image* of the *Primary Hexagram* shifted his sense of championing a cause like a Zen master shocking a disciple. It saw him and his drive:

> Enveloping describes your situation in terms of staying under cover. It symbols are a fetus in the womb or the wordless seed of a new time. You are immature and your awareness of the problem is dull and clouded. The way to deal with it is to accept being hidden in order to nurture growing awareness. Pull the covers over. Put the lid on. There is much concealed from you. You don't really know what you are doing. But the beginnings are definitely there, even if you can't yet see them. You didn't ask for this problem. It asked for you and it belongs with you. The first time you consult the oracle about this, it will advise and inform you. If you keep on asking, you muddy the waters. Your awareness must grow and change. Put your ideas to the trial. That brings profit and insight. Keep working on your problem. It will educate you.
>
> **Envelop**, MENG: cover, pull over, hide, conceal; lid or cover; clouded awareness, dull; ignorance, immaturity; unseen beginnings. The ideogram: plant and covered, hidden growth.

The *Image* has two aspects: concealment and immaturity, unseen beginnings and ignorance. The first shock was: your desire is immature and your awareness confused. Because the terms extend to all the components in the situation, it also implies: the situation is immature, your idea "ahead of its time." So the second shock was: revealing your idea too soon will destroy its hidden growth. He was told: Keep it to yourself until you are ready. You are not ready yet.

The *Outer and Inner Aspects* revealed that the firm limit he was encountering in the outer world was there to *protect* his development. The defining top line of the outer trigram, **Bound**, was transforming. This would eventually transform his overabundant yang energy – his drive toward confrontation – into the primal receptive and structuring power of **Field**.

The inner world was characterized by **Gorge**, the night sea journey through toil and danger that dissolves the old forms of experience. This deep psychic process was what the outer limit was protecting. He had to do what was for him the most difficult thing possible: accept the limitation and wait, enveloped, trusting the inner breakdown and change.

The *Hidden Possibility* told him that enveloping's preparation for the future depends on returning to the source, and that this is what could lead to a re-birth. The message was trust in an unconscious process, not trying again and again.

The *Image* and *Image Tradition* brought out several things about the drive. This was a favorable divination – **Advantageous Trial/Harvesting** – and bringing the situation to full **growth** involved a sacrifice to the spirit. The question was what sacrifice was involved. The use of the pronoun **I/me/my** in these texts is unusual. It put the focus on his subjective experience, what he thought and felt, not what was being done to him. Other terms in the *Image* elicited the fact that he had asked this question before in many different ways, in fact he was constantly asking it. This going back again and again was **obscuring** the real problem.

> **Obscure**, TU: confuse, muddy, agitate; muddled, cloudy, turbid; agitated water; annoy through repetition.

But the *Image Tradition* indicated that this compulsive repetition could be focused on correcting the situation.

> **Correct**, CHENG: rectify deviation or one-sidedness; proper, straight, exact, regular; constant, rule, model. The ideogram: stop and one, hold to one thing.

By seeing the hostile response to his compulsive striving as a compensation of one-sidedness within himself, he could **achieve** a real degree of intuitive **wisdom**.

> **Achieve**, KUNG: work done, results; real accomplishment, praise, worth, merit. The ideogram: workman's square and forearm, combining craft and strength.

Understanding this one-sidedness was the center of the reading, the key to his desire. It gave access to the **all-wise**, the spiritual gift he sought to give to others.

> **All-wise**, SHENG: intuitive universal wisdom; mythical sages; holy, sacred; mark of highest distinction. The ideogram: ear and inform, one who knows all from a single sound.

Here several terms emerged. From the *Sequence* came **immaturity**.

> **Immature**, CHIH: small, tender, young, delicate; undeveloped; conceited, haughty; late grain.

Accepting that the drive was real but **immature** cautioned him against arrogance and protected the vulnerability of his idealism.

From the *Contrasted Definitions* came a conscious and public acceptance of a *lack* of clarity. He was to be **variegated and conspicuous**, emphasizing the display of his vulnerability and incompletion rather than fixed purpose.

The *Symbol Tradition* reinforced the move toward images of organic growth rather than spiritual drive, **using fruiting movement to nurture actualizing-tao.**

> **Fruit,** KUO: plants' annual produce; tree fruits; come to fruition, fruits of actions; produce, results, effects; reliable; conclude, surpass. The ideogram: tree topped by a round fruit.

> **Nurture,** YÜ: bring up, support, rear, raise; increase.

This is the long term process of **nurturing** and bearing **fruit**. It acts indirectly over time, not directly and immediately.

All these things formed a context for the *Transforming Line*. This line defined his "drive" – not the purpose behind it – as an attempt to **smite** what was **enveloping** him.

> **Smite,** CHI: hit, beat, attack; hurl against, rush a position; rouse to action. The ideogram: hand and hit, fist punching.

Such an attack, hurling himself against what was actually *protecting* his **immaturity**, transformed the quality of the **enveloping**. It became **smiting** in its turn, attacking him. In this adversarial situation one or the other party ends by having been seen as an **outlaw**.

> **Outlawry,** K'OU: break the laws; violent people, outcasts, bandits.

The only way to take advantage of this situation was to **resist** this **outlawry**.

> **Resist,** YÜ: withstand, oppose; bring to an end; prevent. The ideogram: rule and worship, imposing ethical or religious limits.

This implies ceasing to **smite** what was **enveloping**, ceasing to impose his will, break rules, or antagonize his superiors. The **enveloping** was not their fault. The only possibility of **achieving** something comes not through **smiting**, but through **yielding**.

> **Yield(-to),** SHUN: give way and bear produce; comply, agree, follow, obey; unresisting, docile, flexible; nourish, provide; the Action of the

trigram Field, K'UN. The ideogram: head and current, water flowing from the head of a river, yielding to the banks.

This was the only action that could connect **above** and **below**. He had a choice. He could accept this and **yield** or continue to **smite** the **envelopment** and be turned into an **outlaw**. This was the key to his inner process.

The right choice could result in a new way of acting. The *Image* of the *Relating Hexagram* described the beginning of this new focus:

> Legions/Leading describes your situation in terms of organizing a confused heap of things into functional units so you can take effective action. Its symbol is the great King Wu gathering the armies to overthrow the tyrant of Shang. The way to deal with it is to organize yourself and put yourself in order. Develop the capacity to lead. Look at the people you respect, and use them as models. Find who and what you need. This generates meaning and good fortune by releasing transformative energy. The ideal of this army is not just to fight. It brings order, and protects people who cannot protect themselves. It founds cities and defends what is necessary for people to live their lives. It is not a mistake to use force in this way.
>
> **Legions/leading,** SHIH: troops; an organized unit, a metropolis; leader, general, model, master; organize, make functional; take as a model, imitate. The ideogram: heap and whole, organize confusion into functional units.

The ideal of the **legions** represents a different way to organize drive and energy. They exist to **yield** and **serve**. They are seen not as an instrument of offensive war, **smiting** what opposes them, but as an instrument of culture. The **leader,** master or teacher — what he wished to become — provides a model, a pattern to be imitated. By **yielding** and **serving**, the potential **outlaws** can become the **legions**. The **leader,** at the moment **enveloped** in confusion and **immaturity,** is potentially the **all-wise,** a model or pattern of intuitive wisdom.

The final answer to his real and sincere drive to bring spirit into people's lives was first to bring order out of his own confusion. The **enveloping** was a gift; it was there to help him. Through **yielding** to it comes inner organization and the possibility to serve rather than impose his will. He could himself become a model, with an indirect yet deep effect on his surroundings. Then who he was rather than what he wanted would lead others to the spirit.

Each answer the Oracle gives is an attempt to provide you with the information you need in order to make a choice at a difficult moment in your life. It can also be used to explore the options open to you at these crossroads, helping you to see farther into the choices to be made.

EXAMPLE 5

The Dark Forest

She was about to take responsibility – financial, administrative and artistic – for a large training program. She wanted the responsibility and scope and felt a drive to succeed. But as the time to begin grew near, fears, anxieties and uncertainties which she couldn't understand would periodically overwhelm her. She felt something strange behind them, something dark in the ambition itself. So to find out what was lurking there, she posed a question to the I Ching.

First Question: What about wholeheartedly taking responsibility for this Program?

First Answer: Hexagram 26, no Transforming Lines

The answer was Hexagram 26, **Great Accumulating**, with no *Transforming Lines*.

The *Image* of this hexagram described her situation:

Great Accumulating describes your situation in terms of having a central idea that defines what is valuable. Its symbol is gathering the energy of heaven through an image of ancient virtue. The way to deal with it is to focus on a single idea and use that to impose a direction on your life. Concentrate everything on this goal. Gather all the different parts of yourself and all your many encounters. Take the long view. Think of yourself as raising animals, growing crops or bringing up children. Tolerate and nourish things. Develop an atmosphere in which things can grow. Putting your ideas to the trial brings profit and insight. It can culminate in great abundance. Don't stay at home. Be active. Take in what is coming. This generates meaning and good fortune by releasing transformative energy. This is the right time to enter the stream of life with a purpose or to embark on a significant enterprise.

Great, TA: big, noble, important, very; orient the will toward a self-

imposed goal, impose direction; ability to lead or guide your life; contrasts to small, HSIAO, flexible adaptation to what crosses your path; keyword.

Accumulate, CH'U: hoard, gather, retain, herd together; control, restrain; domesticate, tame, train; raise, feed, sustain, bring up. The ideogram: field and black, fertile black soil good for pastures, accumulated through retaining silt.

This seemed a very fortunate answer. It spoke of the necessity to subordinate everything to the one **great** concern, **accumulating** the people, things, ideas, contacts, experience to make it manifest. The time was right to **Step into the Great River,** to enter the stream of life with a goal or embark on a significant enterprise.

The fact that there were no *Transforming Lines* indicated the process of **accumulating** could take a long time and would permeate every part of her life. With this her fears suddenly appeared.

What came out was that she was very much afraid of losing herself in this **great** enterprise. She had been consumed by her work up till now, and deeply identified with her employer and teacher. Her personal life had been reduced to virtually nothing. So the reading suddenly focused on the opposite of **accumulating**, on what was being *lost*.

It was **not dwelling**.

Dwell, CHI: home, house, household, family; domestic, within doors; live in. The ideogram: roof and pig or dog, the most valued domestic animals.

The *Hidden Possibility* showed that this great accumulating put her into the position of the converting or marrying maiden, a young woman moved by forces beyond her control into a new life and station. What would be lost was **dwelling** – home, household, family – and her status as an adult. It suggested something fundamentally feminine would remain untouched.

The answer said it was possible to go ahead with the program if she was willing to submit everything to the rule of the **great**. She had already been put in this position for several years and suffered from the loss of a personal life. Lurking in her family history was a major business failure through badly timed ambition, the shadow of **great accumulating**. Her fears intensified rather than diminished with this favorable answer. So she asked for an image of the other fork in the road.

Second Question: What about *not* assuming responsibility for this Program?

Second Answer: Hexagram 41, 9/2, 6/3, 6/4, Hexagram 30

The answer to the second question, about not taking responsibility for the program, was Hexagram 41, **Diminishing**, with *Transforming Lines* in the second, third and fourth places, leading to Hexagram 30, **Radiance**.

The *Image* of the *Primary Hexagram* indicated that giving up the direction of the program would be a sacrifice. She would feel it as a real loss and would be made smaller by it.

> Diminishing describes your situation in terms of loss, sacrifice and the need for concentration. Its symbol is the empowering sacrifice to the spirit above. The way to deal with it is to decrease your involvements and free yourself from emotional entanglement. This makes energy available for new developments. Act this way with confidence, for you are connected to the spirits and they will carry you through. This is the origin of great good fortune and meaningful events. It is not a mistake. This is an enabling divination. Put your ideas to the trial. Have a place to go. Impose a direction on things. That brings profit and insight. Inquire into motivations; ask yourself why you are doing things. Use two ceremonial vessels to present your results to the spirits. Diminish the strong and augment the supple.
>
> **Diminish**, SUN: lessen, make smaller; take away from; lose, damage, spoil, wound; bad luck; blame, criticize; offer up, give away. The ideogram: hand and ceremonial vessel, offering sacrifice.

Unlike the fear that emerged from the first reading, this image of loss and sacrifice attracted her, drew her on to know more.

The *Image* revealed that **diminishing** could connect her to the spirits and bring her inner and outer life into accord.

> **There is a connection to the spirit,** YU FU: inner and outer are in accord; confidence of the spirits has been captured; sincere, truthful; proper to take action.

It was **without fault**, without error or harm, and could be a source or spring of auspiciousness, significance and growth. In this situation, it was advantageous to **have a direction**, a goal or purpose. Finding out what this purpose was involved **asking why**.

> **Ask why,** HO: interjection, why? how?; question, inquire into motives; interrupt, demand attention. The ideogram: speak and beg, demanding an answer.

This involves questioning your concerns, demanding answers, cutting into things, breaking into patterns of behavior, the things one does unquestioningly.

The *Contrasted Definitions* show that **diminishing** and **augmenting**, the following hexagram, form a pair. **Diminishing** is the hidden **beginning** of **increase** and **augmenting**. If you want to **augment** something, you must first **decrease** it.

> **Decrease,** SHUAI: grow or make smaller; fade, decline, decay, diminish, cut off; grow old; adversity, misfortune.

Decreasing makes energy available for the **beginning** of a new cycle. It is *not* going back to start over. The *Hidden Possibility* showed that this diminishing could lead to a return of spirit, a re-birth. **Diminishing** begins something new. Its **inner stimulation begins** a new formative process, and **diminishing** involvement makes this energy available. But you must have a sacrificial utensil, a method or tool here described as **two platters**, to **avail of** this power and apply it to your own situation.

The *Image Tradition* explains that these **two platters**, the sacrificial method or utensil, are **diminishing** the **strong** and **augmenting** the **supple**.

> **Strong,** KANG: quality of the whole lines; firm, strong, unyielding, persisting.

> **Supple,** JOU: quality of the opened lines; flexible, pliant, tender, adaptable.

You use **asking why** to **diminish** what was formerly **strong**, firm, purposeful, solid. This emptying out of former purposes enables you to **associate with** the spiritual quality of the time.

> **Associate(-with),** YÜ: consort with, combine; companions; group, band, company; agree with, comply, help. The ideogram: pair of hands reaching downward meets a pair of hands reaching upward, helpful association.

The *Attached Evidences* indicated that the action she was asking about – **diminishing** her commitment – was connected with **actualizing-tao**, acquiring the virtue and power to become an individual. **Diminishing** is **actualizing-tao's adjusting**.

> **Adjust,** HSIU: regulate, repair, clean up, renovate.

This is at first **heavy** and hard to bear. She would suffer from it, feeling the loss, the decrease, growing personally smaller, held down and unable to fly.

> **Heavy**, NAN: arduous, grievous, difficult; hardship, distress; harass; contrasts with versatile, I, deal lightly with. The ideogram: domestic bird with clipped tail and drying sticky earth.

But what comes out of this heavy work is **change** or **versatility**, imaginative mobility and the capacity to adjust to the movement of **tao**.

Because **tao** is **moving** in what is **above** in this situation, the **chün tzu curbs anger** in order to **block appetites**.

> **Curb**, CH'ENG: reprimand, reprove, repress; warn, caution; corrective punishment. The ideogram: heart and action, the heart acting on itself.

> **Curbing anger**, forcing **anger** to act on itself, **blocks** or obstructs the unconscious drive of the **appetites** in order to make you aware of them.

> **Appetites**, YÜ: drives, instinctive craving; wishes, passions, desires, aspirations; long for, seek ardently; covet.

Through **diminishing** you are made aware that what you are seeking in others is actually part of yourself. **Asking why, diminishing** the **strong** and **blocking** the **appetites** frees you from the stuck quality of unconscious involvements. This makes energy available to what was excluded or repressed in the former situation.

With this, she found herself in the center of a net of compulsions fighting their way to the surface through her fears. Even if the time was propitious for launching her program, what was at stake in **diminishing** it was her own life and her ability to live it, her **actualizing-tao**.

The *Transforming Lines* gave each of her fears a face. They indicated that each could be resolved through the **diminishing** implied by her question, giving up direction of this new program. The **transforming** lines suggested the possibility of **transformation**.

> **Transform**, PIEN: abrupt, radical, fundamental mutation from one state of being to another; transformation of lines in hexagrams; contrasts with change, HUA, gradual metamorphosis.

The *Transforming Line* at the second place indicated that what she had asked about was an **Advantageous Trial** that leads to **Harvesting**. It would **nowhere diminish** her but **augment** her. Its **purpose** was **activated** from her own **center**. In this situation, the act of **chastising** was a **trap or pitfall**.

Chastise, CHENG: punish, subjugate, discipline; reduce to order; punishing expedition. The ideogram: step and correct, a rectifying move.

This line separated her from a particular role she had created for herself, a combination of bearing responsibility, enforcing order and isolation that she called "the Policewoman." The late childhood fears were lurking here. Because she was afraid that this program was her only chance for financial security, she found herself constantly **chastising** others in order to make her place secure.

The *Transforming Line* in the third place addressed a deep fear of isolation and loneliness. It affirmed that where there were **three people moving** they would be **diminished** by **one**. **The-one** person, herself, was separating from a group. But she should not fear. Through the **diminishing** of walking alone, this **one person** would join hands with a **friend**.

Friend, YU: companion, associate; of the same mind; attached, fraternal, in pairs. The ideogram: two hands joined.

The *Transforming Line* in the fourth place showed her **affliction diminished** by this action.

Afflict, CHI: sickness, disorder, defect, calamity; injurious; pressure and consequent anger, hate or dislike. The ideogram: sickness and dart, a sudden affliction.

This described the panic, fear and disorientation that would suddenly grip her, as well as the explosive anger of **chastising** and the continual pressure to succeed. **Diminishing** what created this, and doing it swiftly, would permit **rejoicing**, returning joy to **afflicted** parts of her life.

Rejoice, HSI: feel and give joy; delight, exult; cheerful, merry. The ideogram: joy (music) and mouth, expressing joy.

The result of this **diminishing**, and the quality best suited to deal with the situation shown by the *Relating Hexagram*, was Hexagram 30, **Radiance** and its action, **congregating**.

The *Image* of this hexagram described the evolution of her situation:

Radiance describes your situation in terms of awareness and coherence. It is the bright presence expressed in the omens that shows the spirit is near. The way to deal with it is to articulate and spread light and warmth. Illuminate, articulate, discriminate, make things conscious. Bring together what belongs together. This is a time of intelligent effort and accumulating awareness. It includes unexpected and meaningful encounters, separations from the old and experiences outside the ordinary. Put your ideas to the trial. That brings profit and insight. It is pleasing to the spirits. Through it they will give you effective power, enjoyment, and the capacity to bring things to maturity. Nurturing the receptive strength that can carry burdens generates meaning and good fortune by releasing transformative energy.

Radiance, LI: glowing light, spreading in all directions; light-giving, discriminating, articulating; divide and arrange in order; the power of consciousness. The ideogram: bird and weird, the magical fire-bird with brilliant plumage.

Congregate, LI: cling together; depend on, attached to, rely on; couple, pair, herd. The ideogram: deer flocking together.

Here the dark forest was illuminated, and the way was clear. Behind **diminishing** and growing smaller was not isolation, loneliness and affliction but the potential for awareness. It pointed at another, warmer and more conscious connection, **congregating** with **people**. Both forks in this road were possible, the decision was hers. But this reading indicated that one of them was the way of **transformation**. **Heavy** at first with a sense of loss and sacrifice, it led to **joy** and companionship. It would free her from the dark forest, the **afflicting** drives and fears of compulsion.

THE GLOBAL SYSTEM *THE UNIVERSAL COMPASS*

- ### *Divination and Traditional Science*

Much of traditional Chinese science began in the *I Ching*. The system behind it, first codified in the Han dynasty, grew out of imagistic, correlative or magical thinking. It connects to terms and figures used in the *I Ching*, and can extend and amplify the oracular images. This system describes the way psychic energy moves in the world and in the individual in a precise yet imaginative way. It formed the basic categories of traditional Chinese thought and perception, providing a way to navigate the world by pointing out what would develop from a particular moment or experience.

This system is organic and complicated. You should not expect to remember or master it all in one reading. Use it as reference material. The section of the Hexagrams called *Outer and Inner Aspects* gives you a concentrated version of these systems as they relate to individual hexagrams. From there you can refer back to the full system. Let it gradually penetrate the way you think about things as you use it.

This system uses three categories – the Time Cycle, Yin-Yang Dynamics, and the Correspondence of Qualities – to describe the quality and direction of moving energy. It is expressed in a fundamental chart called the *Universal Compass* that portrays a constantly moving world made up of organically interdependent forces.

The *Universal Compass* consists of a set of concentric circles that represent interlocking cycles:

- *1* The Time Cycle

- *2* The Yin and Yang Hemicycles

- *3* The Eight Phases of Yin-Yang Dynamics

- *4* The Five Transformative Moments

These cycles connect with:

- *5* The Cycle of the Eight Trigrams

The cycle of trigrams connects in turn with the hexagrams of the *I Ching*. Thus the hexagrams are linked to the interaction of all these qualities in a dynamic and systematic way.

The basic premise of the *Universal Compass* is that it describes energetic processes of the world-organism or world-soul. Through this system your question and your situation are linked with an organic, constantly moving world.

- *The Time Cycle*

The basic connection between *I Ching* divination and the system of the *Universal Compass* is the quality of time. This connection is expressed in the four fundamental terms of the Time Cycle: **Spring**, YÜAN; **Growing, Growth**, HENG; **Harvest, Harvesting**, LI; and **Trial**, CHEN. These terms have divinatory meanings that come from the oldest layers of the *I Ching's* texts: **Source of Success: Advantageous Trial.** They developed into the model of a dynamic process used to describe all units or spans of time.

- **Spring**, YÜAN, as a divinatory term, refers to the power to originate something. It is an adjective meaning great, excellent, very much, very potent and indicates that you are connected to the source or origin of things. As the first phase of the Time Cycle it refers to: the vernal season, the East, sunrise; issue forth, begin to appear, arise; rising or issuing from the ground, thus source or origin; the first sign of day, the beginning, the first cause or generating power of the cosmos; the eldest, the head, original, primary; the head of a river, the source of thoughts in the individual, the source of authority in the social field. It is the primal originating power itself and the place in space or time where it appears.

- **Grow, Growing**, HENG, as a divinatory term, indicates that something can be successful, vigorous and effective if a sacrifice is offered to the proper spirits at the proper time. As the second phase of the Time Cycle it refers to: summer, the South, midday; any manifestation of vigorous life; all pervading; increase gradually, become by degrees, pervade, spread; influence throughout as heaven influences, penetrates and increases all things; prosperous, successful, effectual, carried to completion. It is the

power that gives full-grown form to what is initiated or sprouted in **Spring**, YÜAN. The ideogram suggests success through offering a gift to a superior.

- **Harvest, Harvesting**, LI, as a divinatory term, indicates what is advantageous, profitable, of great benefit and full of insight. As the third phase of the Time Cycle it refers to: autumn, the West, sunset; the season's yield of natural produce; the product of an action or effort, gains, profit, interest on money; reaping and gathering in; benefit, nourish; the edge or point of a knife; sharp, acute. It stands for both the sharpness of the blade that reaps and for the profit gathered. The ideogram suggests a knife and ripe grain standing in the field.

- **Trial**, CHEN, refers to the act of divination itself, trying or proving something by submitting it to the judgement of the spirits. As the fourth and final phase of the Time Cycle it refers to: winter, the North, midnight; test, ordeal, proof; separating wheat from chaff, the valuable from the useless; the test-withstanding, resistant part of something, the kernel; undefiled, uncorrupted and incorruptible, pure, virtuous, righteous, firm. It stands for testing by ordeal and the lasting solid core that emerges from it. The ideogram suggests a pearl and divination.

The core that emerges from Trial or Winter is the seed of Spring, beginning the cycle anew.

- *Yin and Yang: Struction and Action*

Yin and *yang* are the fundamental categories of this system, but translating these terms is difficult. We can call *yang* Action, but then are left with words like passive or static for *yin*. Struction, derived from Latin *struere*, to erect or construct, suggests that each of these powers exists in its own right.

The categories *yin* and *yang* grew from a wide range of shifting qualities:

YIN	*YANG*
Yin / **struction** applies to:	*Yang* / **action** applies to:
the shady, cool southern ▮ *bank of a river*	▮ *the bright, warm northern* *bank of a river*
the shady, cool northern ▮ *slope of a mountain*	▮ *the bright, warm southern* *slope of a mountain*
Water ▮	▮ *Fire*
Moon ▮	▮ *Sun*
Lower ▮	▮ *Upper*
Interior ▮	▮ *Exterior*
Dark ▮	▮ *Bright*
Moist ▮	▮ *Dry*
Soft ▮	▮ *Hard*
Obscure ▮	▮ *Manifest*
Contracting ▮	▮ *Expanding*
Reaction ▮	▮ *Stimulus*
Incoming ▮	▮ *Outgoing*
Completing ▮	▮ *Beginning*
Response ▮	▮ *Move*
Receptive ▮	▮ *Initiating*
To be ▮	▮ *To do*
The ideogram *yin* suggests hillshadows and clouds	The ideogram *yang* suggests sunrise and a sunlit flag.

The terms evolved into dynamic categories through which all phenomena could be analysed:

- Yang, **action**, is the light, active aspect of all phenomena. It refers to: movement, dynamic development, thrust, stimulus, drive; focusing on a goal, giving direction to something. By creating the future, yang destroys the present, negating anything that exists in a positive or consolidated sense. The yang aspect of phenomena is their dynamic mode of becoming: arousal, transformation and dissolution. It is united, continuous, uni-directional, a closed system where all things are categorically equal.

Yin, **struction**, is the shadowy, structive aspect of phenomena. It refers to: build, make concrete, establish; limited, bound, given specific being; consolidating, conserving, structuring something. By consolidating the present, yin stops forward motion, drive or purpose. The yin aspect of phenomena is the result of contraction and concentration; it is their positive (from *ponere*, to place, to put) mode of existence. It is diverse, adaptable extension in space, an open system where all things are categorically discontinuous.

However, with one exception, the actual terms *yin* and *yang* do not occur in the oldest layers of the *I Ching*. What does occur is the pair of **opened** or **supple** — — and **whole** or **strong** —— lines. These lines and the qualities associated with them are the divinatory basis underlying the categories *yin* and *yang*.

Opened or supple, P'I, refers to: open up, disclose, burst forth; develop through germinating each thing. The ideogram suggests a double door, toil, and the body: the literal womb and the separateness of each physical being. The corresponding quality in a person or a situation is **supple**, JOU: flexible, pliant, tender, adaptable. This term advises adapting to what is given, developing each thing in its turn through yielding to it.

Whole, HO, refers to: all, unite all; together. The ideogram suggests a double door and a cover, an image of uniting everything for one purpose. The corresponding quality in a person or a situation is **strong**, KANG: firm, strong, unyielding, persisting. This term advises taking the initiative, acting in a spirited, focused way to impose an idea on things.

The *Universal Compass* is divided into two basic hemicyles which reflect these primary categories. All things in the world, inner or outer, female or male, human or non-human are made up of a mixture of these two powers. In a divinatory sense they represent two fundamental ways of acting or being in the world, stances each person can take at different times to connect with the flow of *tao* or energy.

• *Yin and Yang: Choice and Change*

The oldest form of the *I* oracle was a series of phrases connected to single lines which indicated the choice made by a spirit. These lines may have been related to cracks that appeared in the bones used in ritual pyromancy. There were four kinds of lines associated with the oracle, even in its oldest form. Two of these indicate relatively stable conditions; the other two indicate changing conditions that are open to surprise and intervention. These lines and numbers are still used to build a hexagram.

8 = an unvarying opened or supple line ——   ——

6 = a transforming opened or supple line — X —

7 = an unvarying whole or strong line ————

9 = a transforming whole or strong line ——⊖——

The extreme quality of the transforming lines indicated gaps or openings in the fabric of the world. As the hexagrams were assembled, this transformative quality evolved into the process through which one hexagram could change into another, showing the direction the original situation may evolve through the intervention of a spirit.

The transformation of lines was also used to show the way *yin* and *yang* interact. It evolved into a description of how each of these primal spirits enters a situation, comes to predominate, and leaves, calling up its contrary or complement. This kind of thinking was joined to the Time Cycle by identifying each kind of line with a season.

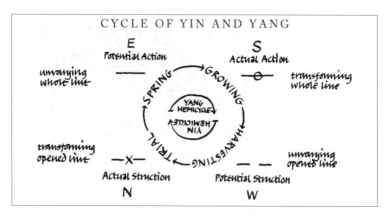

CYCLE OF YIN AND YANG

The yin and yang hemicycles were then elaborated around a central axis or
Pivot of Equalization by articulating each of them into three analogous
phases:

- The *Pivoting Phase* is the first move out of the center. The qualities emerge
  as hidden germs, interior or *in potentia*.
  Pivot, SHU, refers to: hinge, axis, center; starting point, fundamental.
  The *Pivoting Phase* produces *youngest yin* and *youngest yang, Potential
  Struction* or *Potential Action*.

- The *Phase of Wholeness* is a threshold. The qualities are full grown but still
  contained or **whole**.
  Whole, HO, refers to: all, unite all; uniting everything within.
  The *Phase of Wholeness* produces *contracted yin*, the opaque, concentrated
  inwardness of Struction, and *bright yang*, the clear outward essence of
  Action.

- The *Disclosing Phase* breaks the boundaries. The qualities expand and
  exhaust themselves. This leads back to the neutral center from which the
  opposite hemicycle begins.

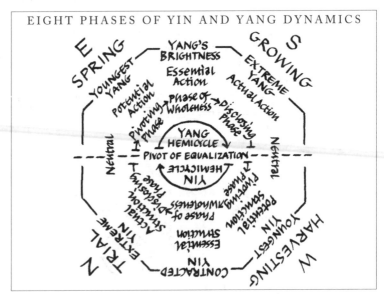

EIGHT PHASES OF YIN AND YANG DYNAMICS

Disclose, K'AI, refers to: open, reveal, unfold; enact rites, clear land. The
ideogram suggests a house bursting open through rising inner pressure.

The *Disclosing Phase* produces *extreme yin* and *extreme yang*, *Actual Struction* and *Actual Action, flooding below* and *flaming above.*

The central Pivot of Equalization is a gate through which the two primary agencies pass. It is common to both hemicycles and acts as the transition between them. The agencies either cancel each other out at the end of a complete cycle or come into an active balance at its midpoint.

• *The Five Transformative Moments*

In the middle Han Dynasty, a large convention of scholars was gathered by Imperial Edict to standardize and systematize the *Ching* or Classics. The official report of this convention, PO HU T'UNG, *The Comprehensive Discussions in the White Tiger Hall,* combined the other systems of correspondence which had evolved with a cycle of five processes or *Transformative Moments,* the WU HSING.

These five processes are not substances, but stages of transformation. They are translated as adjectives: **Woody, Fiery, Earthy, Metallic, Streaming.** The term *Moment* expresses their function as both points of time and qualities of transformation. These *Transformative Moments* evoke each other in a particular order. They form a cycle which was combined

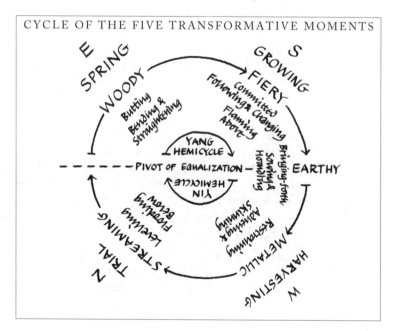

CYCLE OF THE FIVE TRANSFORMATIVE MOMENTS

with the Time Cycle and the Cycle of Yin-Yang Interaction and linked to the trigrams of the *I Ching*. To make the systems interlock, the Earthy Moment was made into an axis corresponding to the *Pivot of Equalization*. This allowed the Seasons and the Moments to coincide.

- **Woody,** MU, describes organic growth or development. It refers to: origins, beginnings; break open, burst forth; Spring, East, daybreak. It is associated with youngest yang and Potential Action, which arise after the Yin Hemicycle is exhausted. Its Action is **butt,** CHU: to push against something with the horns. It manifests as the *bending* and *straightening* of sprouting plants pushing their way through the surface of the earth. This germinating thrust inaugurates the Yang Hemicycle of the *Universal Compass*.

- **Fiery,** HUO, describes combustion, heat, and light. It refers to: fire, flame; flame up, blaze, glow; burning and consuming; upward motion; Summer, South, midday. It is associated with extreme yang and Actual Action flaring up, blazing out and spreading. Its Actions are **committed following,** WEI SUI, and **changing,** HUA. They manifest as *flaming above*. The Fiery Moment consumes Wood and changes it to ashes or Earth. It brings the Yang Hemicycle of the *Universal Compass* to a close.

- **Earthy,** T'U, describes soil, ground, dust, clay, ashes. It is the point around which the seasons, the cardinal points, and the alternation of day and night revolve. It represents the *Pivot of Equalization* where yin and yang, Action and Struction, are in balance, neutralizing each other or creatively interacting. Its Action is **bringing forth,** T'U. It manifests as *sowing* and *hoarding* a crop. The Earthy Moment connects the hemicycles. It is the moment of balance and transition.

- **Metallic,** CHIN, describes metals, and particularly gold as their quintessence. It refers to: ore; smelting, crystalization, concentration, coagulation; the hard forms of cast metal resulting from those processes; Autumn, West, sunset. It is associated with youngest yin and Potential Struction. Its Action is **restraining,** CHIN, holding something in a specific form. It manifests as *adhering*, casting molten metal in molds, and skinning, stripping the molds away. The Metallic Moment casts Earth into fixed forms. It begins the Yin Hemicycle of the *Universal Compass*.

- **Streaming,** SHUI, describes fluids and flowing. It refers to: floods, tides; dissolving, liquefying; flowing water, streams, rivers; downward motion; Winter, North, midnight. It is associated with extreme yin and Actual Struction overflowing and spreading out. Its Action is **leveling,** CHUN, equalizing and evening out differences. It manifests as *flooding below*, which disappears into the neutral Pivot of Equalization. The Streaming Moment dissolves the fixed forms of Metal. It brings the Yin Hemicycle of the *Universal Compass* to a close.

- ## The Trigram Cycle

The most important connection between *I* divination and the Universal Compass is the Cyclic Order of the Eight Trigrams. The arrangement of these trigrams and their attributes in a cyclic order enabled scholars, magicians and diviners to correlate hundreds of different systems of magical correspondence with the divinatory practice of the *I Ching*. All of these systems could then be entered simultaneously by manipulating the yarrow-stalks, the mysterious pointers of *yin* and *yang*.

- ## The Eight Trigrams and Their Attributes

The eight trigrams represent all the possible combinations of three opened or supple and whole or strong lines. Each of the hexagrams in the *I Ching* is seen as the dynamic relation between two of these trigrams. The bottom trigram with all its associated qualities represents the inner aspect of the situation, the upper trigram with its net of associations represents the outer aspect. The hexagram itself is thus a dynamic relation between the inner and the outer, the individual and the cosmos. The integration of the trigrams into the *Universal Compass* means that the other systems of association can be used to describe the way energy is moving in a particular divinatory situation.

The trigrams and their attributes are arranged in three different systems or orders: a conceptual order, a family order and, most significant, the cyclic order.

EIGHT TRIGRAMS AND THEIR ATTRIBUTES			
TRIGRAM	*IMAGE*	*ACTION*	*SYMBOL*
☰	FORCE CH'IEN	PERSISTING	HEAVEN
☷	FIELD K'UN	YIELDING	EARTH
☳	SHAKE CHEN	STIRRING-UP	THUNDER
☵	GORGE K'AN	VENTURING FALLING	STREAM
☶	BOUND KEN	STOPPING	MOUNTAIN
☴	GROUND SUN	ENTERING	WOOD WIND
☲	RADIANCE LI	CONGREGATING	FIRE BRIGHTNESS
☱	OPEN TUI	STIMULATING	MARSH

● *Trigrams in Pairs: the Conceptual Order*

In the simplest order the trigrams form pairs, which polarizes their qualities. These pairs of opposites are called the arrangement according to Fu Hsi.

THE CONCEPTUAL ORDER ACCORDING TO FU HSI			
FORCE/FIELD	SHAKE/GROUND	GORGE/RADIANCE	BOUND/OPEN
☰ ☷	☳ ☴	☵ ☲	☶ ☱

● *The Trigrams as a Family*

In this arrangement the trigrams articulate an ideal family, which was thought to reflect the organization of the cosmos. The trigrams are grouped as parents, sons and daughters.

THE TRIGRAMS AS A FAMILY

FATHER	MOTHER
☰	☷
FORCE	FIELD

SONS

ELDEST	MIDDLE	YOUNGEST
☳	☵	☶
SHAKE	GORGE	BOUND

DAUGHTERS

ELDEST	MIDDLE	YOUNGEST
☴	☲	☱
GROUND	RADIANCE	OPEN

Father and Mother, Force, CH'IEN, and Field, K'UN, represent pure cosmic principles. They intermingle to produce the six variegated trigrams through **twining**, SO, twisting together. The variegated trigrams signify the different ages of womanhood, NÜ, and manhood, NAN: the long lived or senior, CHANG; the central or middle, CHUNG; and the junior or youngest, SHAO.

The Cycle of Trigrams

In the cyclic order the trigrams are seen as phases of a continuing process. Their meaning in the 64 hexagrams of the *I Ching* refers mainly to their place in this order of evocation. This order is called the arrangement according to King Wen. In it each trigram has an *Image*, an *Action* and a *Symbol*, as well as a location within the *Family* of trigrams. Other specific actions are thought to connect one trigram with the next.

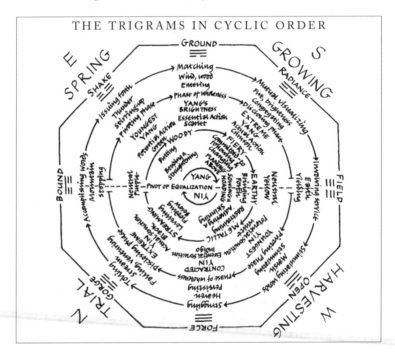

THE TRIGRAMS IN CYCLIC ORDER

• **Shake,** CHEN

Shake, CHEN, begins the cyclic order. A stirring whole or strong line emerges below two watery opened lines, causing things to *issue forth from the concealing Earth.*

Shake, CHEN: arouse, excite, inspire; thunder rising from below; awe, alarm, trembling; fertilizing intrusion. The ideogram: excite and rain.

Symbol: **Thunder,** LEI: rising, arousing power.

Actions: **Stir up,** TUNG: excite, influence, move, affect; work, take action; come out of the egg or the bud. The ideogram: strength and heavy, able to move weighty things.

Family: the first or eldest son, **long lived manhood,** CHANG NAN, energetic and inspiring.

In the *Universal Compass*, **Shake,** CHEN, is related to the beginning of the Woody Moment and belongs to the East, where seeds break open and development originates. Its color is green, the color of spring, nature and beginnings.

- **Ground,** SUN ☴

After the issuing-forth of **Shake,** CHEN, things *match* and *couple*, giving birth to new generations. **Ground,** SUN, brings *matching* and *coupling*. An opened line, supple yin, subtly penetrates from below.

Ground, SUN: base on which things rest; support, foundation; mild, subtly penetrating; nourishing. The ideogram: stand and things arranged on it, the subtle influence of the ground.

Symbols: **Wood/tree,** MU: all things woody or wooden, alive or constructed from wood; associated with the Woody Moment. The ideogram: a tree with roots and branches.

Wind, FENG: moving air, breeze, gust; weather and its influence on mood and humor; fashion, usage.

Action: **Enter,** JU: penetrate, go into, enter on, progress; put into, encroach on; contrary of issue forth, CH'U.

Family: eldest or first daughter, **long lived womanhood,** CHANG NÜ, influencing and nourishing.

In the *Universal Compass*, **Ground,** SUN, is related to the culmination of the Woody Moment. Its color is scarlet, a vivid red connoting luck, honor, marriage and riches.

- **Radiance,** LI ☲

Through the *matching* and *coupling* of **Ground,** SUN, things give birth to new generations. Together they *mutually see* new possibilities. **Radiance,** LI, brings *mutual seeing*, envisioning common goals. It is represented by the

single opened or supple line which holds two whole or strong lines together.

Radiance, LI: glowing light, spreading in all directions; light-giving, discriminating, articulating; divide and arrange in order; the power of consciousness. The ideogram: bird and weird, the magical fire-bird with brilliant plumage.

Symbols: **Brightness,** MING: light-giving aspect of burning, heavenly bodies and consciousness. The ideogram: sun and moon.

Fire, HUO: warming and consuming aspect of burning.

Action: **Congregate,** LI: cling together; depend on, attached to, rely on; couple, pair, herd. The ideogram: deer flocking together.

Family: middle or second daughter, **central womanhood,** CHUNG NÜ, mature and supportive.

In the *Universal Compass* **Radiance,** LI, relates to the Fiery Moment and belongs to the South, the realm of change through combustion. Its color is crimson, which connotes fire, burning, stripping and denuding.

- **Field,** K'UN ☷

After the *mutual seeing* of **Radiance,** LI, comes the common labor of serving, sowing and hoarding the produce of the Earth. **Field,** K'UN, brings involving service, difficult labor undertaken together.

Field, K'UN, surface of the world; concrete extension; basis of all existence, where Force or heaven exerts its power; all-involving service; earth; moon, wife, mother; courtiers, servants. The ideogram: terrestrial globe and stretch out, stability and extension.

Symbol: **Earth,** TI: ground on which the human world rests; basis of all things, nourishes all things form.

Action: **Yield(-to),** SHUN: give way and bear produce; comply, agree, follow, obey; unresisting, docile, flexible; nourish, provide. The ideogram: head and current, water flowing from the head of a river, yielding to the banks.

Family: mother as the essence of yin, origin of the opened lines in the six variegated trigrams.

In the *Universal Compass,* **Field,** K'UN, is related to the Earthy Moment and belongs to the South-West, where things are reduced to dust and fertile soil. Its color is yellow, the color of the middle, the soil of central China and the Emperor.

- Open, TUI ☱

After the common labor of **Field**, K'UN, the joy of Harvest breaks forth in *stimulating words*. **Open**, TUI, brings stimulating words that cheer and inspire. It is represented by the single opened or supple line leading two whole lines.

   Open, TUI: an open surface, promoting interaction and interpenetration; responsive, free, unhindered, pleasing; opening, passage; the mouth; exchange, barter; straight, direct; meet, gather; place where water accumulates. The ideogram: person, mouth and vapor, speaking with others.

   Symbol: **Marsh**, TSE: open surface of a flat body of water and the vapors rising from it; fertilize, enrich; kindness, favor.

   Action: **Stimulate**, SHUO: rouse to action and good feeling; stir up, urge on; persuade; set out in words; free from constraint, cheer, delight. The ideogram: words and exchange.

   Family: youngest or third daughter, **junior womanhood**, SHAO NÜ, light-hearted, whimsical and magical.

In the *Universal Compass*, **Open**, TUI, relates to the beginning of the Metallic Moment and belongs to the West, the realm of restraining to essential form. Its color is white, the color of mourning, which connotes clear, pure, immaculate, plain.

- Force, CH'IEN ☰

After the *stimulation* of **Open**, TUI, comes a *struggle* for survival, giving form to each being and feeling. **Force**, CH'IEN, brings *struggling*, lonely single grappling with primary forces.

   Force, CH'IEN: spirit power, creative and destructive; unceasing forward motion; dynamic, enduring, untiring; firm, stable; heaven, sovereign, father; also: dry up, parched, exhausted, cleared away. The ideogram: sprouts or vapors rising from the ground and sunlight, both fecundating moisture and scorching drought.

   Symbol: **Heaven**, T'IEN: highest; sky, firmament, heavens; power above the human as opposed to earth, TI, below. The ideogram: great and the one above.

   Action: **Persist**, CHIEN: strong, robust, dynamic, tenacious; continuous; unwearied heavenly bodies in their orbits.

   Family: father as the essence of yang, ancestor of the whole or strong lines in the six variegated trigrams.

In the *Universal Compass*, **Force**, CH'IEN, relates to the culmination of the Metallic Moment. Its color is indigo, the color of the sky's depths, the venerability of gods and spiritual agencies.

● **Gorge**, K'AN ☵

With the *struggle* of **Force**, CH'IEN, comes heavy labor and isolation. **Gorge**, K'AN, brings toiling, difficult but worthy labor. It is represented by the whole or strong line venturing on between two opened or supple lines.

    Gorge, K'AN: dangerous place; hole, cavity, hollow; pit, snare, trap, grave, precipice; critical time, test; risky. The ideogram: earth and pit.

    Symbol: **Stream**, SHUI: flowing water; fluid, dissolving; river, tide, flood. The ideogram: rippling water.

    Action: **Venture falling**, HSIEN HSIEN: risk falling until a bottom is reached, filling and overcoming the danger of the Gorge.

    Fall, HSIEN: fall down or into, sink, drop, descend; falling water; be captured.

    Venture, HSIEN: risk without reserve; key point, point of danger; difficulty, obstruction that must be confronted; water falling and filling the holes on its way. The ideogram: mound and all or whole, everything engaged at one point.

    Family: middle or second son, **central manhood**, CHUNG NAN, courageous and venturesome.

In the *Universal Compass*, **Gorge**, K'AN, relates to the Streaming Moment and belongs to the North where direction and shape are dissolved. Its color is black, suggesting dark obscure toiling.

● **Bound**, KEN ☶

Venturing, falling and filling all obstacles, the toiling of **Gorge**, K'AN, streams out and encounters the limits. **Bound**, KEN, brings accomplishing words that articulate the end of a cycle. It is represented by the whole or strong line capping two opened or supple lines.

    Bound, KEN: limit, boundary; encounter an obstacle, stop; still, quiet, motionless; confine, enclose, mark off; turn around to look behind; hard, adamant, obstinate; perverse. The ideogram: eye and person turning round to compare and group what is behind.

    Symbol: **Mountain**, SHAN: limit, boundary. The ideogram: three peaks, a mountain range.

Action: **Stop,** CHIH: bring or come to a standstill. The ideogram: a foot stops walking.

Family: youngest or third son, **junior manhood,** SHAO NAN, the limit or bound.

In the *Universal Compass,* **Bound,** KEN, relates to the neutral end point between Yin and Yang Hemicycles, where the primary agencies cancel each other out. Its color is purple, suggesting a dark weather-beaten face and the Heavenly Palace of the Immortals. The immobility of the Mountain prepares the *issuing-forth* of a new cycle.

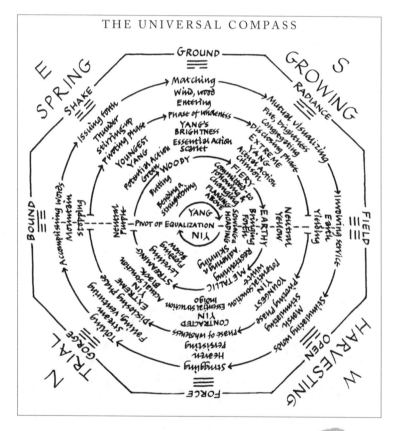

THE UNIVERSAL COMPASS

Using the Universal Compass

The previous diagram connects the Time Cycle, the phases of Yin and Yang, the Five Transformative Moments and the Cyclic Order of the Trigrams. Through these interconnections, the trigrams of a given hexagram are related to a web of qualities that give you insight into how psychic energy is moving and transforming the dynamics of your situation.

The *Universal Compass* represents a fluid, changing world whose ground is imaginative energy. It can be applied to any kind of situation. It particularly helps to place you in the image of your situation by describing the relation between its inner and outer aspects and the direction of their probable development. Use it along with the *Image of the Situation* to open the imaginative background to a question you pose to the *I Ching*.

PART TWO

周
易

HEXAGRAMS

A QUICK GUIDE TO THE ORACLE

This procedure for asking a question and reading the response summarizes the information in Using the I.

- *1* Find your question. Establish the background, your hopes and fears, desires and anxieties, memories and dreams. Clarify the alternatives – What do you really want to know? What information do you need? Use your desire, what you want to do, to help focus your question: "What about doing ... X?" See pages 18-19 for more information.

- *2* Decide which method you want to use and assemble the equipment – coins, yarrow stalks or 16 tokens and a bowl. Each method will let you generate the six lines of your *Primary Hexagram*, starting from the bottom up. If there are any *transforming lines* in your reading, change them to generate the *Relating Hexagram*. See pages 18-23 for the procedures.

- *3* Find the number of your *Primary Hexagram*, and of the *Related Hexagram* if there are *Transforming Lines*, in the Key on page 804. Locate the lower trigram (the lower three lines) on the left side of the chart and the upper trigram (the upper three lines) on the top.

- *4* Turn to the Hexagram Texts indicated by these numbers (pages 86–677). You can use all the basic texts of the *Primary Hexagram*, the *Transforming Lines* indicated in your reading, and the *Image* of the *Relating Hexagram*, the one generated when your *Transforming Lines* change. These sections are described briefly on the next page.

- *5* Read the *Image of the Situation* at the beginning of the *Primary Hexagram*. This is the *I Ching*'s basic advice. Then read through the other sections. Don't worry if you are confused at first; it is part of the process. See which terms and definitions connect with your problem, your feelings and your state of mind. Then focus on the *Transforming Lines*, if there are any, and the *Image* of the *Relating Hexagram*.

● *6* The *Primary Hexagram* gives you a picture of what is happening now, the *Transforming Line* shows how the situation is likely to change if you go ahead with the action you asked about, and the *Relating Hexagram* establishes how you are connected to that situation. Guidance in your situation comes from the interaction of the divinatory terms in your imagination. Take the time to let the terms that have struck you make stories about the way you should act. This is a real, living process and there is a spirit behind it. The section *Encounters with the Oracle*, which starts on page 32, gives examples of questions, answers and the process of interpretation.

● *Hexagram Texts and their Functions*

The Image of the Situation *and the texts connected with it describe an archetypal situation. They are each hexagram's central oracular statement, the ground in which all other parts of the hexagram are embedded. The name of the hexagram, the first word of the* Image, *provides both a description of your situation and advice as to the most effective way to deal with it. The texts place it in the dynamic of time, indicating key qualities and actions associated with it.*

● Outer and Inner Aspects *analyses the matter under consideration in terms of your dynamic relation to its outer and inner elements. This is described through the relation between the outer and inner trigrams and their nets of associated qualities. This section acts as a shorthand reference to the supplementary material on the* Universal Compass *dealing with traditional systems of correlative thinking.*

● Hidden Possibility *describes another figure at the core of the hexagram. It lets you see the potential of the situation, the possibility of resolving a core issue.*

● *The* Sequence *puts the* Image *in a series with the hexagram that precedes it in terms of a completed action which calls up a following action. It suggests that activating the energy of this hexagram depends upon understanding it as a part of a necessary succession of events.*

● *The* Contrasted Definitions *offer a key to your situation by picking out a central feature and contrasting it with a central feature of an adjoining hexagram.*

- *The* Attached Evidences *see the action of this hexagram as particularly relevant to* actualizing-tao *and describe how it can aid the process of realizing tao in action.*

- *The* Symbol Tradition *describes the* Image *in terms of the relation between the Symbols of its two trigrams. It derives a specific action from this relation which gives access to the ideal of the* chün tzu *in this situation: a person who uses divination to order their life according to tao rather than personal desires.*

- *The* Image Tradition *amplifies key terms and qualities of the* Image. *It also analyses the* Image *in terms of: the correspondence of pairs of lines; the actions and relations of supple and strong, assigned to the opened and whole lines; and the appropriateness of the lines to their places, particularly the center lines of the trigrams.*

- *The* Transforming Lines *represent precise points of connection with the psychic forces involved in your question. They are activated by a 6 or a 9 in the consultation procedure. They give you advice on the direction of specific actions and the potential consequences. As the activated lines change into their opposites they produce a new hexagram, the* Relating Hexagram, *which is an image of overall future potential.*

- *The* Image *of the* Relating Hexagram *produced when the* Transforming Lines *change into their opposites shows your relation to the basic situation as potential outcome, goal, desire, predominant feeling or hidden motivation, reassurance or warning. Changing the way you act or perceive things can change this potential.*

• *Orthography and Punctuation*

Punctuation, orthographic signs and the use of **bold**, *italic* and SMALL CAPITALS are consistent throughout the translation and have specific meanings:

Bold in the Hexagram texts always indicates a **core word** or **phrase**, the particular English word used to translate a Chinese ideogram, for example: **Force**.

SMALL CAPITALS, usually following a **bold core word** or **phrase**, indicate the transliteration of the Chinese word (according to the Wade-Giles system), for example: **Force**, CH'IEN.

Italics indicates the title of a major section of a Hexagram, such as *Image of the Situation, Sequence,* or *Transforming Lines,* or the *Associated Contexts,* the circles of definitions given with each Chinese term. Remember that the *Associated Contexts* for a term are only given *the first time a term appears in a hexagram* or *when it only appears in a* Transforming Line.

A full stop (.) indicates the end of a line or internal punctuation in the Chinese text. Such punctuation is rare. We have used the *colon* (:) and *comma* (,) to indicate implicit pauses and emphases in the lines that show the relation between terms. The *colon* should be read as an equal sign, the *comma* as indicating a series of connected things.

Indentation of a line in the *Associated Contexts* corresponds to the beginning of a line in the Chinese text. Definitions for the first term in a line *that has not already appeared* are given there. A space between sections in the *Associated Contexts* corresponds to the beginning of a new sub-section of the text. In the section *Image Tradition,* the longest section in each hexagram, these subsections are indicated by Roman Numerals (I, II, III, IV, V). *Transforming Lines a)* and *b)* indicate different kinds of texts: the oldest is the Line text *a),* the commentary is Line text *b).*

	HEXAGRAM		HEXAGRAM
1	FORCE CH'IEN *page 86*	17	FOLLOWING SUI *page 238*
2	FIELD K'UN *page 95*	18	CORRUPTION/RENOVATION KUI *page 247*
3	SPROUTING CHUN *page 106*	19	NEARING LIN *page 256*
4	ENVELOPING/IGNORANCE MENG *page 116*	20	VIEWING KUAN *page 265*
5	ATTENDING HSÜ *page 125*	21	GNAWING BITE SHIH HO *page 273*
6	ARGUING SUNG *page 135*	22	ADORNING PI *page 281*
7	LEGIONS/LEADING SHIH *page 144*	23	STRIPPING PO *page 290*
8	GROUPING PI *page 154*	24	RETURNING FU *page 298*
9	SMALL ACCUMULATING HSIAO CH'U *page 163*	25	DISENTANGLING WU WANG *page 308*
10	TREADING LÜ *page 172*	26	GREAT ACCUMULATING TA CH'U *page 316*
11	PERVADING T'AI *page 181*	27	JAWS/SWALLOWING YI *page 324*
12	OBSTRUCTION PI *page 192*	28	GREAT TRAVERSES TA KUO *page 333*
13	CONCORDING PEOPLE T'UNG JEN *page 201*	29	GORGE K'AN *page 342*
14	GREAT POSSESSING TA YU *page 210*	30	RADIANCE LI *page 351*
15	HUMBLING CH'IEN *page 219*	31	CONJOINING HSIEN *page 360*
16	PROVIDING FOR YÜ *page 228*	32	PERSEVERING HENG *page 370*

•*A list*
of the
Hexagrams

HEXAGRAM	HEXAGRAM
33 RETIRING TUN *page 380*	**49** SKINNING/REVOLUTION KO *page 531*
34 GREAT INVIGORATING TA CHUANG *page 388*	**50** THE VESSEL TING *page 541*
35 PROSPERING CHIN *page 396*	**51** SHAKE CHEN *page 551*
36 BRIGHTNESS HIDING MING YI *page 405*	**52** BOUND KEN *page 560*
37 DWELLING PEOPLE CHIA JEN *page 414*	**53** GRADUAL ADVANCE CHIEN *page 568*
38 DIVERGING K'UEI *page 423*	**54** MARRYING THE MAIDEN KUEI MEI *page 578*
39 DIFFICULTIES/LIMPING CHIEN *page 434*	**55** ABOUNDING FENG *page 587*
40 LOOSENING/DELIVERANCE HSIEH *page 443*	**56** SOJOURNING LÜ *page 597*
41 DIMINISHING SUN *page 453*	**57** GROUND SUN *page 607*
42 AUGMENTING YI *page 463*	**58** OPEN TUI *page 616*
43 DECIDING/PARTING KUAI *page 474*	**59** DISPERSING HUAN *page 624*
44 COUPLING KOU *page 484*	**60** ARTICULATING CHIEH *page 633*
45 CLUSTERING TS'UI *page 493*	**61** CENTERING/CONNECTING CHUNG FU *page 641*
46 ASCENDING SHENG *page 503*	**62** SMALL TRAVERSES HSIAO KUO *page 650*
47 CONFINING K'UN *page 511*	**63** ALREADY FORDING CHI CHI *page 660*
48 THE WELL CHING *page 522*	**64** NOT YET FORDING WEI CHI *page 669*

● The
Sections
of the
Hexagrams

*The following table
compares the names
and the locations of
the various texts
that make up a
hexagram in the
present translation
with the Chinese
original and the
Wilhem/Baynes
translation.*

*Chinese terms are
romanized accord-
ing to the Wade-
Giles system, used in
most references to
classical Chinese lit-
erature in the last
hundred years.
Other publications
using the Pin yin
method will include
conversion tables
between the two
systems.*

THIS TRANSLATION	K'ANG HSI EDITION	WILHELM/BAYNES
● *Image of the Situation*	1st & 2nd Wings, T'UAN CHUAN	The Name The Judgement
● *Outer and Inner Aspects*	From 8th Wing, SHUO KUA; amplified by PO HU T'UNG, The Comprehensive Discussions in the White Tiger Hall	Discussion of the Trigrams
● *Hidden Possibility*	HO KUA or Nuclear Trigrams	HO KUA or Nuclear Trigrams
● *Contrasted Definitions*	10th Wing, TSA KUA	Miscellaneous Notes
● *Attached Evidences*	Extracts from 8th Wing, HSI TZ'U CHUAN	Appended Judgements
● *Sequence*	9th Wing, HSÜ KUA	The Sequence
● *Symbol Tradition*	3rd & 4th Wing, HSIANG CHUAN	The Image
● *Image Tradition*	1st & 2nd Wings, T'UAN CHUAN	Commentary on the Decision
● *Transforming Lines a)*	1st & 2nd Wing, T'UAN CHUAN	The Lines a)
● *Transforming Lines b)*	3rd & 4th Wing, HSIANG CHUAN	The Lines b)

FORCE/DRAGON ■ *CH'IEN*

Creative energy; persist, create, endure; power to guide and inspire, dynamic and enduring.

Force describes your situation in terms of the primal power of spirit to create and destroy. Its symbols are the inspiring power of heaven, the light of the sun that causes everything to grow, the fertilizing rain and the creative energy of the dragon that breaks through boundaries. You are confronted with many obstacles. The way to deal with them is to persist, for you are in contact with fundamental creative energy. Take action. Be dynamic, strong, untiring, tenacious and enduring. Continue on your path and don't be dismayed. Ride the power of the dragon, the mythical shape-changer with inspiring power, and bring the fertilizing rain. Your situation contains great creative potential. It can open up a whole new cycle of time.

● *Image of the Situation*

Force. Source of Success: Advantageous Trial.

Associated Contexts **Force**, CH'IEN: spirit power, creative and destructive; unceasing forward motion; dynamic, enduring, untiring; firm, stable; heaven, sovereign, father; also: dry up, parched, exhausted, cleared away. The ideogram: sprouts or vapors rising from the ground and sunlight, both fecundating moisture and scorching drought. **Force** is the Heaven trigram doubled and includes that trigram's attributes: *Symbol*: **Heaven**, T'IEN: highest; sky, firmament, heavens; power above the human as opposed to earth, TI, below. The ideogram: great and the one above. *Action*: **Persist**, CHIEN: strong, robust, dynamic, tenacious; continuous; unwearied heavenly bodies in their orbits. **Source of Success: Advantageous Trial**, Lit: Spring Growing Harvesting Trial: **Spring**, YÜAN; **Grow**, HENG; **Harvest**, LI; and **Trial**, CHEN, are the four stages of the Time Cycle, the model for all dynamic processes. They indicate that your question is connected to the cycle as a whole rather than a part of it, and that the origin (Spring) of a favorable result (Harvesting Trial) is an offering to the spirits (Growing).

- ## Outer and Inner Aspects

☰ **Force**: The force of heaven struggles on, persistent and unwearied; heavenly bodies persist in their orbits. **Force** is born at the center of the yin hemicycle, completing the formative process.

Connection to both inner and outer: struggling forces are bound together in dynamic tension, the Metallic Moment culminating. Force brings elements to grips, creating enduring relations.

- ## Contrasted Definitions

> Force: strong.
> Field: supple.

Associated Contexts **Strong**, KANG: quality of the whole lines; firm, strong, unyielding, persisting.

Field, K'UN: surface of the world; concrete extension; basis of all existence, where Force or heaven exerts its power; all-involving service; earth; moon, wife, mother; courtiers, servants. The ideogram: terrestrial globe and stretch out, stability and extension. Image of Hexagram 2. **Supple**, JOU: quality of the opened lines; flexible, pliant, tender, adaptable.

- ## Symbol Tradition

> **Heaven moves persistingly.**
> **A chün tzu uses originating strength not to pause.**

Associated Contexts **Move**, HSING: move or move something; motivate, emotionally moving; walk, act, do. The ideogram: stepping left then right.

Chün tzu: ideal of a person who uses divination to order his/her life in accordance with tao rather than wilful intention; keyword. **Use(of)**, YI: make use of, by means of, owing to; employ, make functional. **Origin**, TZU: source, beginning, ground; cause, reason, motive; line of descent; path to the origin; yourself, intrinsic. **Strengthen**, CH'IANG: invigorate, test; compel, rely on force; determined, sturdy; overcome a desire. **Pause**, HSI: stop and rest, repose; breathe, a breathing spell; suspended.

● *Image Tradition*

The great Force, Spring in fact. [I]
The myriad beings's own beginning.

Thereupon primary heaven. [II]
Clouds moving, rain spreading out.
The kinds: being diffusing into forms.

Great brightening completes the beginning. [III]
The six situations: the seasons accomplishing.
The season riding six dragons used going to meet heaven.

Force: tao transforming changes. [IV]
Each one correcting innate fate.
Protecting and uniting the great harmony.

Thereupon Advantageous Trial. [V]
Heads issue forth from the multitudinous beings,
the Myriad cities conjoined and soothed.

Associated Contexts [I] **Great**, TA: big, noble, important, very; orient the will toward a self-imposed goal, impose direction; ability to lead or guide your life; contrasts with small, hsiao, flexible adaptation to what crosses your path; keyword. Image of Hexagrams 14, 26, 28, 34. **Spring**, YÜAN: source, origin, head; great, excellent; arise, begin, generating power; first stage of the Time Cycle. **In fact**, TSAI: in actual fact, currently.

Myriad, WAN: countless; many, everyone; lit.: ten thousand. The ideogram: swarm of insects. **Being(s)**, WU: creature, thing, any single being; matter, substance, essence; nature of things. **'s/have(it)/it/them**, CHIH: expresses possession, directly or as an object pronoun. **Own**, TZU: possession and the things possessed; avail of, depend on; property, riches. **Begin**, SHIH: commence, start, open; earliest, first; beginning of a time-span, ended by completion, chung. The ideogram: woman and eminent, beginning new life.

[II] **Thereupon**, NAI: on that ground, because of. **Primary**, T'UNG: origin, beginning; first of a class; clue, hint; whole, general.

Clouds, YÜN: fog, mist, water vapor; connects to the Streaming Moment and Stream, the Symbol of the trigram Gorge, K'AN. **Rain,** YÜ: all precipitation; sudden showers, fast and furious; associated with the trigram Gorge, K'AN and the Streaming Moment. **Spread out,** SHIH: expand, diffuse, distribute, arrange, exhibit; add to, aid. The ideogram: flag and indeed, claiming new country.

Kinds, P'IN: species and their essential qualities; sorts, classes; classify, select. **Diffuse,** LIU: flow out, spread, permeate. **Form,** HSING: shape; body, bodily; material appearance.

[III] **Brightness,** MING: light-giving aspect of burning, heavenly bodies and consciousness; with fire, the Symbol of the trigram Radiance, LI. **Complete,** CHUNG: end of a cycle that begins the next; last, whole, all; contrasts with exhaust, CH'IUNG, final end. The ideogram: silk cocoons, follow and ice, winter linking one year with the next.

Six, LU: transforming opened line; six lines or places of a hexagram; sixth. **Situation,** WEI: place or seat according to rank; post, position, command; right, proper; established, arranged. The ideogram: person and stand, servants in their places. **Season,** SHIH: quality of the time; the right time, opportune, in harmony; planning in accord with the time; seasons of the year. The ideogram: sun and temple, time as sacred. **Accomplish,** CH'ENG: complete, finish, bring about; perfect, full, whole; play your part, do your duty; mature. The ideogram: weapon and man, able to bear arms, thus fully developed.

Ride, CH'ENG: ride an animal or a chariot; have the upper hand, seize the right time; control strong power; overcome the nature of the other; supple opened line above a solid whole line. **Dragon,** LUNG: powerful spirit-energy emerging from waters below; mythical shape-changer with supreme power; connected with heaven, T'IEN, and the trigram Force, CH'IEN. **Go to meet,** YA: advance to encounter and receive; invoke; anticipate, face, provide for; govern; drive or tame a horse; extending everywhere, as the imperial power.

[IV] **Tao:** way or path; ongoing process of being and the course it traces for each specific person or thing; keyword. The ideogram: go and head, leading and the path it creates. **Transform,** PIEN: abrupt, radical, fundamental mutation from one state of being to another; transformation of lines in hexagrams; contrasts with change, HUA, gradual metamorphosis. **Change,** HUA: gradual, continuous metamorphosis; influence someone; contrasts with transform, PIEN, sudden mutation. The ideogram: person alive and dead, the life-process.

Each one, KO: every, all, wherever; each separate thing. **Correct,** CHENG: rectify deviation or one-sidedness; proper, straight, exact, regular; constant, rule, model. The ideogram: stop and one, hold to one thing. **Innate,** HSING: inborn character; spirit, quality, ability; naturally, without constraint. The ideogram: heart and produce, spontaneous feeling. **Fate,** MING: individual destiny; birth and death as limits of life; issue orders with authority; consult the gods. The ideogram: mouth and order, words with heavenly authority.

Protect, PAO: guard, defend, keep safe; secure. **Unite,** HO: join, match, correspond, agree, collect, reply; unison, harmony; also: close, shut the mouth. The ideogram: mouth and assemble. **Harmony,** HO: concord, union; conciliate; at peace, mild; fit, tune, adjust.

[V] **Advantageous Trial,** LI CHIEN: advantageous divination; putting the action in question to the test is beneficial, harvesting.

Head, SHOU: literal head; leader, foremost; subject headings; beginning, model; superior, upper, front. **Issue forth(from),** CH'U: emerge from, come out of, proceed from, spring from; the Action of the trigram Shake, CHEN; contrary of enter, JU. The ideogram: stem with branches and leaves emerging. **Multitude,** SHU: the people; mass, herd; all, the whole.

City, KUO: area of only human constructions; political unit, polis. First of the territorial zones: city, suburbs, countryside, forests. **Conjoin,** HSIEN: come into contact with, influence; reach, join together; put together as parts of a previously separated whole; come into conjunction, as the celestial bodies; totally, completely; lit.: broken piece of pottery, the halves of which join to identify partners. Image of Hexagram 31. **Soothe,** NING: calm, pacify; create peace of mind; tranquil, quiet. The ideogram: shelter above heart, dish and breath, physical and spiritual comfort.

● *Transforming Lines*

Initial nine

a) **Immersed dragon, do not avail of it.**

b) **Immersed dragon, do not avail of it.**
   Yang located below indeed.

The situation feels confused and uncertain, for you lack a clear goal. You would like to take hold and set things right. Don't do yet. The creative energy is still under water. Have no fear, it will soon emerge.

Associated Contexts a) **Immerse**, CH'IEN: submerge, hide in water; make away with; secret, reserved; carefully. **No**, WU: simple negative; un-, dis-. **Avail of**, YUNG: take advantage of; benefit from, profit by; use for a specific purpose; apply to advantage. The ideogram: to divine and center, applying divination to central concerns.

b) **Yang**: Action; dynamic and light aspect of phenomena: arouses, transforms, dissolves existing structures; linear thrust; stimulus, drive, focus; direct or orient something. **Locate (in)**, TSAI: live in, dwell, reside; belong to, involved with, depend on; within. The ideogram: earth and persevere, place on the earth. **Below**, HSIA: anything below, in all senses; lower, inner; lower trigram; opposite of above, SHANG. **Indeed**, YEH: intensifier; indicates comment on previous statement.

> **Nine at second**

> *a)* **See the dragon located in the fields.**
>   **Advantageous to see the Great People.**

> *b)* **See the dragon located in the fields.**
>   **Actualizing tao is spreading throughout indeed.**

You have the ability to realize things now. Take the advice of people you know and trust and seek what is great in yourself.

Associated Contexts a) **See**, CH'IEN: seeing in all its aspects: vision, being visible, forming mental images; visit, call on, consult. The ideogram: eye above person, active and receptive sight. **Locate (in)**, TSAI: live in, dwell, reside; belong to, involved with, depend on; within. The ideogram: earth and persevere, place on the earth. **Fields**, T'IEN: cultivated land, plantation; also: hunting, game in the fields cannot escape the hunt. The ideogram: square divided into four sections, delineating fields.

Advantageous Harvest, LI: advantageous, profitable; acute, insightful; benefit, nourish; third stage of the Time Cycle. **Great People**, TA JEN: important, noble, influential; those who impose a ruling principle on their lives; effect of the great within an individual; keyword.

b) **Actualize tao**, TE: realize tao in action; power, virtue; ability to follow the course traced by the ongoing process of the cosmos; keyword. The ideogram: to go, straight, and heart. Linked with acquire, TE: acquiring that which makes a being become what it is meant to be. **Throughout**, P'U: universal, all; great, pervading light. The ideogram: sun and equal, equal to the sun. **Indeed/is/means**, YEH: intensifier connective; indicates comment on previous statement.

Nine at third

a) A chün tzu completing the day: Force, Force.
At nightfall, alarms, like adversity.
Without fault.

b) Completing the day: Force, Force.
This means reversing and returning to tao.

A transitional time of incessant activity, plagued by practical and emotional problems. Don't worry. This is a very important change and creative energy is available to help you. Turn your back on the past. This marks the return of the Way in your life.

Associated Contexts a) **Day/sun,** JIH: actual sun and the time of a sun-cycle, a day. **Force,** CH'IEN: the doubled character intensifies this quality.

Nightfall, HSI: day's end, dusk; late; last day of month or year. **Alarms,** T'I: alarmed and cautious; respect, regard, fear; stand in awe of. The ideogram: heart and versatile, the heart aware of sudden change. **-Like,** JO: same as; just as, similar to. **Adversity,** LI: danger; threatening, malevolent demon. This has two aspects: grind, sharpen, improve, perfect, stimulate; and: poisonous, sinister, cruel, contrary. It indicates a spirit or ghost that seeks revenge by inflicting suffering upon the living. Pacifying or exorcizing such a spirit can have a healing effect. The ideogram: sheltering cliff and stinging insect.

Without fault, WU CHIU: no error or harm in the situation.

b) **Reverse,** FAN: turn and move in the opposite direction; turn around or upside down (180 degrees); change to the opposite position; contrary. **Return,** FU: go back, turn back to the starting point; recur, reappear, come again; restore, recover, retrace; an earlier time or place. The ideogram: step and retrace a path. Image of Hexagram 24. **Indeed/is/means:** intensifier, connective; indicates comment on previous statement.

Nine at fourth

a) "Someone" capering located in the abyss.
Without fault.

b) "Someone" capering located in the abyss.
Advancing without fault indeed.

Even in dealing with big issues, don't lose the playful spirit. Joy is the key to creation in this situation. Don't get frozen into a single stance. Advancing now is a mistake.

Associated Contexts a) **Maybe/someone,** HUO: possible, perhaps; term indicating spirit is active. **Caper,** YO: play, frolic, dance and leap for joy, frisk, gambol. The ideogram: foot and feather, light-footed. **Locate(in),** TSAI: live in, dwell, reside; belong to, involved with, depend on; within. The ideogram: earth and persevere, place on the earth. **Abyss,** YÜAN: deep hole or gulf, where backwaters eddy and accumulate; whirlpool; deep water.

Without fault, WU CHIN: no error or harm in the situation.

b) **Advance,** CHIN: exert yourself, make progress, climb; be promoted; further the development of, augment; adopt a religion or conviction; offer, introduce. **Indeed/is/means,** YEH: intensifier, connective; indicates comment on previous statement.

Nine at fifth

a) Flying dragon located in heaven.
   Advantageous to see the Great People.

b) Flying dragon located in heaven.
   Great People creating indeed.

Spread your wings. Let your creative power emerge. Now is the time to build something enduring. Listen to people you know and trust. Seek out what is great in yourself.

Associated Contexts a) **Fly,** FEI: spread your wings, fly away; let free; swift. **Locate(in),** TSAI: live in, dwell, reside; belong to, involved with, depend on; within. The ideogram: earth and persevere, place on the earth.

Advantageous, LI: advantageous, profitable; acute, insightful; benefit, nourish; third stage of the Time Cycle. **See,** CH'IEN: seeing in all its aspects: vision, being visible, forming mental images; visit, call on, consult. The ideogram: eye above person, active and receptive sight. **Great People,** TA JEN: important, noble, influential; those who impose a ruling principle on their lives; effect of the great within an individual; keyword.

b) **Create,** TSAO: make, construct, build, form, establish. **Indeed/is/means,** YEH: intensifier, connective ; indicates comment on previous statement.

Nine above

a) Overbearing dragon possesses repenting.

b) Overbearing dragon possesses repenting.
   Overfilling does not permit lasting indeed.

Associated Contexts a) **Overbearing**, K'ANG: excessive, overpowering authority; disparage; rigid, unbending; excessive display of force. **Possess**, YU: in possession of, have, own; opposite of lack, WU. **Repent**, HUI: dissatisfaction with past conduct causing a change of heart; proceeds from **abashment**, LIN, shame and confusion at having lost the right way.

b) **Overfill**, YING: at the point of overflowing; more than wanted, stretch beyond; replenished, full; arrogant. The ideogram: vessel and too much. **Not permitting**, PU K'O: not possible; contradicts an inherent principle. The ideogram: mouth and breath, silent consent. **Last**, CHIU: long, protracted; enduring. **Indeed/is/means**, YEH: intensifier connective; indicates comment on previous statement.

> Availing of the Nines (all lines are transforming)

> *a)* See the flocking dragons without a head.
>   Auspicious.

> *b)* Availing of the nines.
>   Heavenly actualizing tao does not permit
>   activating the heads indeed.

Associated Contexts a) **See**, CH'IEN: seeing in all its aspects: vision, being visible, forming mental images; visit, call on, consult. The ideogram: eye above person, active and receptive sight. **Flock**, CH'ÜN: herd, group; people of same kind, friends, equals; all, entire; move in unison, flock together. The ideogram: chief and sheep, flock around a leader. **Without**, WU: devoid of; -less as suffix.

Auspicious, CHI: leads to the experience of meaning; favorable, propitious, advantageous, appropriate; keyword. The ideogram: scholar and mouth, wise words of a sage.

b) **Avail of**, YUNG: take advantage of; benefit from, profit by; use for a specific purpose; apply to advantage. The ideogram: to divine and center, applying divination to central concerns. **Nine**, CHIU: number of a transforming whole line; superlative: best, perfect; ninth.

Actualize tao, TE: realize tao in action; power, virtue; ability to follow the course traced by the ongoing process of the cosmos; keyword. The ideogram: to go, straight, and heart. Linked with acquire, TE: acquiring that which makes a being become what it is meant to be. **Not permitting**, PU K'O: not possible; contradicts an inherent principle. The ideogram: mouth and breath, silent consent. **Activate**, WEI: act or cause to act; do, make, manage; make active; attend to, help; because of. **Indeed/is/means**, YEH: intensifier, connective; indicates comment on previous statement.

2

FIELD ▮ *K'UN*

Yield, nourish, provide for; gentle, receptive, welcoming; give all things form.

Field describes your situation in terms of the primal power to nourish and give things form. Its symbols are the earth, the moon, the mother, the devoted servant, and the mare. You are confronted with many conflicting forces. The way to deal with them is to yield to each thing, nourishing it and providing what it needs to exist. You are in contact with the fundamental power to give things form. This will yield results. It will open up a whole new cycle of time. At first you will be confused by the profusion of things. Keep your sense of purpose. Do whatever presents itself to be done without judging it. This brings profit and insight. You can acquire what you desire and achieve mastery. Join with others in concrete projects, and look to the future, the southwest. Let go of the past, the northeast, and go on alone when necessary. Put your ideas to the trial. You are safe and secure. This generates meaning and good fortune by releasing transformative energy.

● *Image of the Situation*

> **Field. Source of Success: Advantageous Trial for the female horse.**
> **A chün tzu has a direction to go.**
> **Beforehand delusion, afterwards acquiring a lord. Harvesting.**
>
> **Western South: acquiring partners.**
> **Eastern North: losing partnering.**
> **Security Trial auspicious.**

Associated Contexts **Field**, K'UN: surface of the world; concrete extension; basis of all existence, where Force or heaven exerts its power; all-involving service; earth; moon, wife, mother; courtiers, servants. The ideogram: terrestrial globe and stretch out, stability and extension. **Field**, K'UN, is the **Earth** trigram doubled and includes that trigram's attributes: *Symbol*: **Earth**, TI: ground on which the human world rests; basis of all things, nourishes all things **form**. *Action*: **Yield (to)**, SHUN: give way and bear produce; comply, agree, follow, obey; unresisting, docile, flexible;

95

nourish, provide. The ideogram: head and current, water flowing from the head of a river, yielding to the banks. **Source … Trial** Lit: Spring Growing Harvesting Trial: **Spring**, YÜAN: **Grow**, HENG; **Harvest**, LI; and **Trial**, CHEN, are the four stages of the Time Cycle, the model for all dynamic processes. They indicate that your question is connected to the cycle as a whole rather than a part of it, and that the origin (Spring) of a favorable result (Harvesting Trial) is an offering to the spirits (Growing). **Female**, P'IN: female sexual organs, particularly of farm animals; concave, hollow. The ideogram: cattle and ladle, a hollow, reproductive organ. **Horse**, MA: symbol of spirited strength in the natural world, counterpart of dragon, LUNG; associated with the trigram Force, CH'IEN, heaven, T'IEN, and high noon. **For/have (it)/it/them**, CHIH: expresses possession, directly or as an object pronoun.

Chün tzu: ideal of a person who uses divination to order his/her life in accordance with tao rather than wilful intention; keyword. **Have a direction to go**, YU YU WANG: imposing a direction on the flow of time from present to past; have a specific goal or purpose.

Before(hand)/earlier, HSIEN: come before in time; first, at first; formerly, past, previous; begin, go ahead of. **Delude**, MI: confused, stupefied, infatuated; blinded by vice; bewitch, fascinate, deceive. **After(wards)/later**, HOU: come after in time, subsequent; put oneself after; the second; attendant, heirs, successors, posterity. **Acquire**, TE: obtain the desired object; wish for, desire covetously; gains, possessions. The ideogram: go and obstacle, going through obstacles to the goal. **Lord**, CHU: ruler, master, chief; authority. The ideogram: lamp and flame, giving light.

Harvest, LI: advantageous, profitable; acute, insightful; benefit, nourish; third stage of the Time Cycle.

Western South: the neutral Earthy Moment between the yang and yin hemicycles; bring forth concrete results, ripe fruits of late summer. **Partner**, P'ENG: associate for mutual benefit; two equal or similar things; companions, friends, peers; join in; commercial ventures. The ideogram: linked strings of cowries or coins.

Eastern North: border, limit, completion; boundary between cycles: Mountain; accomplishing words, summing up before new germination; dark, cold, lonely winter night. **Lose**, SANG: fail to obtain, cease, become obscure; forgotten, destroyed; lament, mourn; funeral. The ideogram: weep and the dead.

Secure, AN: safe; peaceful, still, settled; calm, tranquilize. The ideogram: woman under a roof, a tranquil home. **Trial,** CHEN: inquiry by divination and its result; righteous, firm; separating wheat from chaff; the kernel, the proven core; fourth stage of the Time Cycle. The ideogram: pearl and divination. **Auspicious,** CHI: leads to the experience of meaning; favorable, propitious, advantageous, appropriate; keyword. The ideogram: scholar and mouth, wise words of a sage.

- *Outer and Inner Aspects*

⚏ **Field:** The field of earth yields and sustains, serving in order to produce. **Field** is the equalizing point between yin and yang where things labor and serve.

Connection to both inner and outer: the common labor of sowing and hoarding, the Earthy Moment. **Field** produces concrete results through serving.

- *Contrasted Definitions*

Force: strong.
Field: supple.

Associated Contexts **Force,** CH'IEN: spirit power, creative and destructive; unceasing forward motion; dynamic, enduring, untiring; firm, stable; heaven, sovereign, father; also: dry up, parched, exhausted, cleared away. The ideogram: sprouts or vapors rising from the ground and sunlight, both fecundating moisture and scorching drought. Image of Hexagram 1. **Strong,** KANG: quality of the whole lines; firm, strong, unyielding, persisting.

Supple, JOU: quality of the opened lines; flexible, pliant, tender, adaptable.

- *Symbol Tradition*

    Earth potency: Field.
    A chün tzu uses munificent actualizing tao to carry the beings.

    Associated Contexts **Potency**, SHIH: power, influence, strength; authority, dignity; virility. The ideogram: strength and skill.

    Use (of), YI: make use of, by means of, owing to; employ, make functional. **Munificence**, HOU: liberal, kind, generous; create abundance; thick, large. The ideogram: gift of a superior to an inferior. **Actualize tao**, TE: realize tao in action; power, virtue; ability to follow the course traced by the ongoing process of the cosmos; keyword. The ideogram: to go, straight, and heart. Linked with acquire, TE: acquiring that which makes a being become what it is meant to be. **Carry**, TSAI: bear, carry with you; contain, sustain; load a ship or cart, cargo; fill in, complete. **Being(s)**, WU: creature, thing, any single being; matter, substance, essence; nature of things.

- *Image Tradition*

    Culminating Field, Spring in fact. [I]
    The myriad beings' own birth.
    Thereupon yielding receives heaven.
    Field: munificence carrying the beings.

    Actualizing tao unites without delimiting. [II]
    Containing generosity, the shining great.
    The kinds: beings conjoin and Grow.
    The female horse: earth sorting.
    Moving over the earth without delimiting.

    Supple yielding, Advantageous Trial. [III]
    A chün tzu's direction moving.
    Beforehand delusion letting go tao.
    Afterwards yielding acquires the rules.

Western South: acquiring partners. [IV]
Thereupon associating sorts the movement.
Eastern North: losing partners.
Thereupon completing possesses reward.

Security Trial is auspicious, [V]
Corresponding to the earth without delimiting.

Associated Contexts **[I] Culminate,** CHIH: bring to the highest degree; arrive at the end or summit; superlative. **Spring,** YÜAN: source, origin, head; great, excellent; arise, begin, generating power; first stage of the Time Cycle. **In fact,** TSAI: in actual fact, currently.

Myriad, WAN: countless; many, everyone; lit.: ten thousand. The ideogram: swarm of insects. **Own,** TZU: possession and the things possessed; avail of, depend on; property, riches. **Birth/give birth to,** SHENG: produce, beget, grow, bear, arise; life, vitality. The ideogram: earth and sprout.

Thereupon, NAI: on that ground, because of. **Receive,** CH'ENG: receive gifts or commands from superiors or customers; take in hand; catch falling water. The ideogram: accepting a seal of office. **Heaven,** T'IEN: highest; sky, firmament, heavens; power above the human as opposed to earth, TI, below; the Symbol of the trigram Force, CH'IEN. The ideogram: great and the one above.

[II] Unite, HO: join, match, correspond, agree, collect, reply; unison, harmony; also: close, shut the mouth. The ideogram: mouth and assemble. **Without,** WU: devoid of; -less as suffix. **Delimit,** CHIANG: define frontiers, draw limits; boundary, border.

Contain, HAN: retain, embody, cherish; withhold, tolerate; lit.: contain in the mouth, put a coin in a corpse's mouth. **Generous,** HUNG: liberal, large; vast, expanded; give or share willingly, munificent; develop fully. **Shine,** KUANG: illuminate; give off brilliant, bright light; honor, glory, éclat; result of action, contrasts with brightness, MING, light of heavenly bodies. The ideogram: fire above person, lifting the light. **Great,** TA: big, noble, important, very; orient the will toward a self-imposed goal, impose direction; ability to lead or guide your life; contrasts with small, HSIAO, flexible adaptation to what crosses your path; keyword. Image of Hexagrams 14, 26, 28, 34.

Kinds, P'IN: species and their essential qualities; sorts, classes; classify, select. **Conjoin,** HSIEN: come into contact with, influence; reach, join together; put together as parts of a previously separated whole; come into

conjunction, as the celestial bodies; totally, completely; lit.: broken piece of pottery, the halves of which join to identify partners. Image of Hexagram 31. **Grow**, HENG: success through a sacrifice; pervade, persevere; bring to full growth; enjoy; vigorous, effective; second stage of the Time Cycle.

Sort, LEI: group according to kind, class with; like nature or purpose; species, class, genus.

Move, HSING: move or move something; motivate, emotionally moving; walk, act, do. The ideogram: stepping left then right.

[III] Advantageous Trial, LI CHEN: advantageous divination; putting the action in question to the test is beneficial; harvesting.

Let go, SHIH: lose, omit, miss, fail, let slip; out of control. The ideogram: drop from the hand. **Tao**: way or path; ongoing process of being and the course it traces for each specific person or thing; keyword. The ideogram: go and head, leading and the path it creates.

Rules, CH'ANG: unchanging principles; regular, constant, habitual; maintain laws and customs.

[IV] Associate(with), YÜ: consort with, combine; companions; group, band, company; agree with, comply, help. The ideogram: pair of hands reaching downward meets a pair of hands reaching upward, helpful association.

Complete, CHUNG: end of a cycle that begins the next; last, whole, all; contrasts with exhaust, CH'IUNG, final end. The ideogram: silk cocoons, follow and ice, winter linking one year with the next. **Reward**, CH'ING: gift given from gratitude or benevolence; favor from heaven; congratulate with gifts. The ideogram: heart, follow and deer (wealth), the heart expressed through gifts.

[V] Correspond, YING: be in agreement or harmony; resonate together, invoke and fulfil each other; answer to, suitable; relation between the lines (1:4, 2:5, 3:6) when they form the pair opened and whole, supple and strong. The ideogram: heart and obey.

- *Transforming Lines*

  Initial six

  a) Treading frost, hardening ice, culminating.

  b) Treading frost hardens the ice:
  Yin begins solidifying indeed.

> Docilely involving one's tao:
> Culminating in hardening the ice indeed.

Things solidify and take form out of the watery mass. Act slowly, carefully and persistently to build a base. Yield to this impulse.

Associated Contexts a) **Tread**, LÜ: step, path, track; footsteps; walk a path or way; course of the stars; act, practice; conduct; salary, means of subsistence. The ideogram: body and repeating steps, following a trail. Image of Hexagram 10. **Frost**, SHUANG: frozen dew, hoar-frost, rime; crystallized; severe, frigid. **Harden**, CHIEN: make or become hard; establish, strengthen; durable, resolute. **Ice**, PING: frozen water; icy, freezing; clear, pure.

b) **Yin**: Struction: consolidating, shadowy aspect of phenomena: conserves, substantializes, creates structures; spacial extension; limited, bound, given specific being; build, make something concrete. **Begin**, SHIH: commence, start, open; earliest, first; beginning of a time-span, ended by completion, CHUNG. The ideogram: woman and eminent, beginning new life. **Solidify**, NING: congeal, freeze, curdle, stiffen; coagulate, make strong or firm. **Indeed**, YEH: intensifier; indicates comment on previous statement.

    Docile, HSÜN: amiable, mild, yielding; tame; gradually attained. **Involve**, CHIH: include, entangle, implicate; induce, cause. The ideogram: person walking, induced to follow. **One's/one**, CH'I: third person pronoun; also: it/its, he/his, she/hers, they/theirs.

> Six at second

> *a)* Straight on all sides and great.
>   Not repeating: nothing not advantageous.

> *b)* Six at second's stirring up.
>   Straightening used on all sides indeed.
>   Not repeating: nothing not advantageous.
>   Earthly tao shining indeed.

The time is ripe. Commit yourself fully. Go right to the point. You don't have to plan or rehearse anything. Everything is there. This will benefit everything in your life.

Associated Contexts a) **Straighten**, CHIH: correct the crooked, reform, repay injustice; proceed directly; sincere, upright, just; blunt, outspoken. **Sides(on all sides)**, FANG: limits, boundaries; square, surface of

the earth extending to the four cardinal points; everywhere.

Repeat, HSI: series of similar acts; practice, rehearse; familiar with, skilled. The ideogram: two wings and a cap, thought carried by repeated movements. **Nothing not advantageous**, WU PU LI: nothing for which this will not be beneficial; advantageous potential, borderline where the balance is swinging from not Harvesting to actually Harvesting.

b) **Stir up**, TUNG: excite, influence, move, affect; work, take action; come out of the egg or the bud; the Action of the trigram Shake, CHEN. The ideogram: strength and heavy, move weighty things.

Indeed/is/means, YEH: intensifier, connective; indicates comment on previous statement.

Six at third

a) Containing composition permitting Trial.
Maybe adhering to a king's affairs:
Without accomplishment there is completion.

b) Containing composition permitting Trial.
Using the season to shoot forth indeed.
Maybe adhering to a king's affairs:
Knowing the shining great indeed.

Act through a design that contains and conceals. This is the place of hidden excellence, an enabling divination. You can bring all your plans to a beautiful completion. This is a far-reaching time with far-reaching effects.

Associated Contexts a) **Composition**, CHANG: a well-composed whole and its structure; beautiful creations; elegant, clear, brilliant; contrasts with pattern, WEN, beauty of intrinsic design. **Permit**, K'O: possible because in harmony with an inherent principle. The ideogram: mouth and breath, silent consent.

Maybe/someone, HUO: possible, perhaps; term indicating spirit is active. **Adhere(to)**, TS'UNG: follow a way, hold to a doctrine, school, or person; hear and comply with, agree to; forced to follow, follower. The ideogram: two men walking, one following the other. **King(hood)**, WANG: effective ruler, by authority of the Emperor, from whom others derive their power. **Affairs**, SHIH: all kinds of personal activity; matters at hand; business, occupation; manage a business, case in court.

Without, WU: devoid of; -less as suffix. **Accomplish**, CH'ENG: complete, finish, bring about; perfect, full, whole; play your part, do your duty; mature. The ideogram: weapon and man, able to bear arms, thus fully developed.

b) **Season**, SHIH: quality of the time; the right time, opportune, in harmony; planning in accord with the time; seasons of the year. The ideogram: sun and temple, time as sacred. **Shoot forth**, FA: expand, send out; shoot an arrow; ferment, rise; be displayed. The ideogram: stance, bow and arrow, shooting from a strong base. **Indeed/is/means**, YEH: intensifier; connective; indicates comment on previous statement.

Know, CHIH: understand, perceive, remember; informed, aware, wise. The ideogram: arrow and mouth, words focused and swift.

Six at fourth

a) **Bundled in the bag.**
   Without fault, without praise.

b) **Bundled in the bag, without fault.**
   Consideration not harmful indeed.

The situation is pregnant with possibilities. There is nothing to blame or praise, for what you want is already there. Think things over carefully.

Associated Contexts a) **Bundle in**, KUA: enclose, envelop, tie up; embrace, include. **Bag**, NANG: sack, purse; put in a bag; property, salary.

Without fault, WU CHIU: no error or harm in the situation. **Praise**, YÜ: admire and approve; magnify, eulogize; flatter. The ideogram: words and give, offering words.

b) **Consider**, SHEN: act carefully, seriously; cautious, attentive, circumspect; still, quiet, sincere. The ideogram: heart and true. **Harm**, HAI: damage, injure, offend; suffer; hurtful, hindrance; fearful, anxious. **Indeed/is/means**, YEH: intensifier, connective; indicates comment on previous statement.

Six at fifth

a) **A yellow apron. Spring, auspicious.**

b) **A yellow apron, Spring auspicious.**
   Pattern located in the center indeed.

There are processes at work that open the way to enduring connections. Accept them. What is happening now will affect you deeply and positively.

Associated Contexts a) **Yellow**, HUANG: color of the productive

middle; associated with the Earthy Moment between yang and yin hemicycles; color of soil in central China; emblematic and imperial color of China since the Yellow Emperor (2500 BCE). **Apron**, SHANG: ceremonial garment; skirt, clothes; curtains of a carriage; ritual at the earth altar. The ideogram: garment and manifest, clothing as display.

b) **Pattern**, WEN: intrinsic or natural design and its beauty; stylish, elegant; noble; contrasts with composition, CHANG, a conscious creation. **Locate (in)**, TSAI: live in, dwell, reside; belong to, involved with, depend on; within. The ideogram: earth and persevere, place on the earth. **Center**, CHUNG: inner, central; put in the center; middle, stable point enabling you to face inner and outer changes; middle line of trigram. The ideogram: field divided in two equal parts. Image of Hexagram 61. **Indeed**, YEH: intensifier; connective; indicates comment on previous statement.

> Six above
>
> *a)* Dragons struggling in the countryside.
>   Their blood: indigo, yellow.
>
> *b)* Dragons struggling in the countryside.
>   Their tao exhausted indeed.

The rains flow down. The new time is coming. Yield, give way, restore the peace. Do not try to dominate the situation.

Associated Contexts a) **Dragon**, LUNG: powerful spirit-energy emerging from waters below; mythical shape-changer with supreme power; connected with heaven, T'IEN and the trigram Force, CH'IEN. **Struggle**, CHAN: fight with, combat; make war, join battle; hostilities; alarmed, terrified. **Countryside**, YEH: cultivated fields and grassland, where nature and human construction interact; third of the territorial zones: city, suburbs, countryside, forests.

    Their/they, CH'I: third person pronoun; also: one/one's, it/its, he/his, she/hers. **Blood**, HSÜEH: yin fluid that maintains life; rain; money, property. **Indigo**, HSÜAN: color associated with the Metallic Moment; deep blue-black, color of the sky's depths; profound, subtle, deep; veneration of the gods and spirits. **Yellow**, HUANG: color of the productive middle; associated with the Earthy Moment between yang and yin hemicycles; color of soil in central China; emblematic and imperial color of China since the Yellow Emperor (2500 BCE).

b) **Exhaust**, CH'IUNG: bring to an end; limit, extremity; destitute;

investigate exhaustively; end without a new beginning. The ideogram: cave and naked person, bent with disease or old age. **Indeed/is/means**, YEH: intensifier, connective; indicates comment on previous statement.

Availing of Sixes (all lines are transforming)

a) **Trial: perpetual Harvesting.**

b) **Availing of the sixes, perpetual Trial.**
Using the great completion indeed.

A great project from which great benefit will flow, an enduring source of creative energy. Use all your efforts to bring this to completion.

Associated Contexts a) **Perpetual**, YUNG: continuing; everlasting, ever-flowing. The ideogram: flowing water.

b) **Avail of**, YUNG: take advantage of; benefit from, profit by; use for a specific purpose; apply to advantage. The ideogram: to divine and center, applying divination to central concerns. **Six**, LU: transforming opened line; six lines or places of a hexagram; sixth.

Indeed/is/means, YEH: intensifier, connective; indicates comment on previous statement.

3

SPROUTING ▌ *CHUN*

Begin, establish, found; gather your strength, surmount difficulties.

Sprouting describes your situation in terms of beginning growth. Its symbol is the world tree, horsemen going to fetch the bride, soldiers massing at the borders. The way to deal with it is to assemble things and accumulate energy for a difficult yet exciting task. Like young plants breaking through the covering earth, this will open an entire new cycle of time. It is the tenderness of the sprout, the inexorable power of the yielding path that reaches out towards Heaven. Don't try to impose your ideas or direct things. There are many new possibilities emerging. Take advantage of them by installing helpers and delegating responsibilities. Stake out your territory, establish bases of operation, assemble the troops, and collect your possessions. That brings profit and insight.

- *Image of the Situation*

> Sprouting.
> Source of Success: Advantageous Trial.
> Do not avail of having a direction to go.
> Advantageous to install feudatories. Harvesting.

Associated Contexts **Sprout**, CHUN: begin or cause to grow; assemble, accumulate, bring under control; hoard possessions; establish a military camp; difficult, arduous. The ideogram: sprout piercing hard soil.

Source of ... Trial Lit: Spring Growing Harvesting Trial: **Spring**, YAN; **Grow**, HENG; **Harvest**, LI; and **Trial**, CHEN, are the four stages of the Time Cycle, the model for all dynamic processes. They indicate that your question is connected to the cycle as a whole rather than a part of it, and that the origin (Spring) of a favorable result (Harvesting Trial) is an offering to the spirits (Growing).

Avail of, YUNG: take advantage of; benefit from, profit by; use for a specific purpose; apply to advantage. The ideogram: to divine and center, applying divination to central concerns. **Have a direction to go**, YU YU WANG: imposing a direction on the flow of time from present to past; have a specific goal or purpose.

Advantageous/Harvesting, LI: advantageous, profitable; acute, insightful; benefit, nourish; third stage of the Time Cycle. **Install**, CHIEN: set up, establish; confirm a position or law. **Feudatory**, HOU: nobles entrusted with governing the provinces; active in daily life rather than governing from the center; contrasts with prince, KUNG, executives at the court.

- *Outer and Inner Aspects*

☵ **Gorge**: Stream ventures and falls into the gorge, flowing on through toil and danger. **Gorge** ends the yin hemicycle by leveling and dissolving forms.

Connection to the outer: flooding and leveling dissolve direction and shape, the Streaming Moment. **Gorge** ventures, falls, toils and flows on.

☳ **Shake**: Thunder rises from below, shaking and stirring things up. **Shake** begins the yang hemicycle by germinating new action.

Connection to the inner: sprouting energies thrusting from below, the Woody Moment beginning. **Shake** stirs things up to issue forth.

The outer trigram completes a cycle, the inner begins a new one. Inner stirring up is **sprouting**, pushing through the leveling stream.

- *Hidden Possibility*

Nuclear trigrams **Bound**, KEN, and **Field**, K'UN, result in Nuclear Hexagram 23, **Stripping**, PO. Sprouting's abundant new energy depends on **stripping** things and reducing them to the essential.

- *Sequence*

> There is Heaven and Earth.
> Therefore afterwards the myriad beings give birth in truth.
> Overfilling Heaven and Earth's interspace
> > implies verily the myriad beings.
> Accepting this lets you use Sprouting.
> Sprouting implies overfilling indeed.
> Sprouting implies beings's beginning is giving birth indeed.

Associated Contexts **Possess**, YU: in possession of, have, own; opposite of lack, WU. **Heaven[and]Earth**, T'IEN TI: dynamic relation between the primal powers and the world it produces; cosmos, natural or human world; keyword.

Therefore afterwards, JAN HOU: logical consequence of, necessarily follows in time. **Myriad**, WAN: countless; many, everyone; lit.: ten thousand. The ideogram: swarm of insects. **Being(s)**, WU: creature, thing, any single being; matter, substance, essence; nature of things. **Birth/give birth to**, SHENG: produce, beget, grow, bear, arise; life, vitality. The ideogram: earth and sprout. **In truth**, YEN: statement is complete and correct.

Overfill, YING: at the point of overflowing; more than wanted, stretch beyond; replenished, full; arrogant. The ideogram: vessel and too much. **'s/have(it)/it/them**, CHIH: expresses possession, directly or as an object pronoun. **Interspace**, HSIEN: space between, interval, crevice; vacant, empty. **Imply**, CHE: further signify; additional meaning. **Verily**, WEI: the epitome of; in truth, the only; very important. **Indeed/is/means**, YEH: intensifier, connective; indicates comment on previous statement.

Accepting ... use: activating this hexagram depends on understanding and accepting the previous statement.

Begin, SHIH: commence, start, open; earliest, first; beginning of a time-span, ended by completion, CHUNG. The ideogram: woman and eminent, beginning new life.

● *Contrasted Definitions*

Enveloping: variegated and conspicuous.
Sprouting: being seen and not letting go one's residence.

Associated Contexts **Envelop**, MENG: cover, pull over, hide, conceal; lid or cover; clouded awareness, dull; ignorance, immaturity; unseen beginnings. The ideogram: plant and covered, hidden growth. Image of Hexagram 4. **Motley**, TSA: mingled, variegated, mixed; disorder. **Conspicuous**, CHU: manifest, obvious, clear.

See, CHIEN: seeing in all its aspects: vision, being visible, forming mental images; visit, call on, consult. The ideogram: eye above person, active and receptive sight. **Let go**, SHIH: lose, omit, miss, fail, let slip; out of control. The ideogram: drop from the hand. **One's/one**, CH'I third person pronoun; also: it/its, he/his, she/hers, they/theirs. **Reside(in)**, CHÜ: dwell, live in, stay; sit down, fill an office; settled parts of a country. The ideogram: body and seat.

- *Symbol Tradition*

Clouds, Thunder, Sprouting.
A chün tzu uses the canons to coordinate.

Associated Contexts **Clouds,** YÜN: fog, mist, water vapor; connects to the Streaming Moment and Stream, the Symbol of the trigram **Gorge,** K'AN: **Thunder,** LEI: rising, arousing power; the Symbol of the trigram **Shake,** CHEN.

Chün tzu: ideal of a person who uses divination to order his/her life in accordance with tao rather than wilful intention; keyword. **Use(of),** YI: make use of, by means of, owing to; employ, make functional. **Canons,** CHING: standards, laws; regular, regulate; the Five Classics. The ideogram: warp-threads in a loom. **Coordinate,** LUN: classify, bind, adjust; weave together; lit.: unravel and twist silk together into threads.

- *Image Tradition*

Sprouting. [I]
Strong and Supple begin to mingle and heaviness gives birth indeed.

Stirring up reaches the venturing center. [II]
Great Growing: Trial.
Thunder and Rain's stirring up, overfilling, fullness.
Heaven creating grass and duskiness.
Proper to install feudatories and not to soothe them.

Associated Contexts **[I] Strong and Supple,** KANG JOU: field of creative tension between the whole and opened lines and their qualities; field of psychic movement. **Mingle,** CHIAO: blend with, communicate, join, exchange; trade, business; copulation; friendship. **Heavy,** NAN: arduous, grievous, difficult; hardship, distress; harass; contrasts with versatile, I, deal lightly with. The ideogram: domestic bird with clipped tail and drying sticky earth.

[II] Stir up, TUNG: excite, influence, move, affect; work, take action; come out of the egg or the bud; the Action of the trigram Shake, CHEN. The ideogram: strength and heavy, move weighty things. **Reach(to),** HU: arrive at a goal; reach towards and achieve; connect; contrasts with tend-towards, YU. **Venture,** HSIEN: risk without reserve; key point, point of danger; difficulty, obstruction that must be confronted; water falling and filling the holes on its way; the Action of the trigram Gorge, K'AN. The ideogram:

109

mound and all or whole, everything engaged at one point. **Center**, CHUNG: inner, central; put in the center; middle, stable point enabling you to face inner and outer changes; middle line of trigram. The ideogram: field divided in two equal parts. Image of Hexagram 61.

Great, TA: big, noble, important, very; orient the will toward a self-imposed goal, impose direction; ability to lead or guide your life; contrasts with small, HSIAO, flexible adaptation to what crosses your path; keyword. Image of Hexagrams 14, 26, 28, 34. **Grow**, HENG: success through a sacrifice; pervade, persevere; bring to full growth; enjoy; vigorous, effective; second stage of the Time Cycle. **Trial**, CHEN: inquiry by divination and its result; righteous, firm; separating wheat from chaff; the kernel, the proven core; fourth stage of the Time Cycle. The ideogram: pearl and divination.

Thunder[and]Rain, LEI YÜ: fertilizing shock of storms; associated with the trigrams Shake, CHEN, and Gorge, K'AN. **Full**, MAN: as much as possible; replete, bulging, stuffed, abounding; complete; proud.

Heaven, T'IEN: highest; sky, firmament, heavens; power above the human as opposed to earth, TI, below; the Symbol of the trigram Force, CH'IEN. The ideogram: great and the one above. **Create**, TSAO: make, construct, build, form, establish. **Grass**, TS'AO: all grassy plants and herbs; young, tender plants; rough draft; hastily. **Duskiness**, MAI: obscure, indistinct; insufficient light; times of day when it is not fully light. The ideogram: day and not-yet.

Proper, YI: reasonable of itself; fit and right, harmonious; ought, should. **Soothe**, NING: calm, pacify; create peace of mind; tranquil, quiet. The ideogram: shelter above heart, dish and breath, physical and spiritual comfort.

● *Transforming Lines*

Initial nine

a) **A stone pillar.**
Advantageous residence Trial: Harvesting.
Advantageous to install feudatories.

b) **Although a stone pillar, the purpose is moving correctly indeed.**
Use valuing the mean below.
This means the great acquires the commoners.

Establish your foundation. Connect this experience to your own deep roots. Involve other people. Don't be secretive about your plans.

Associated Contexts a) **Stone**, P'AN: large conspicuous rock, found-ation stone; stable, immovable. **Pillar**, HUAN: post or tablet marking a grave.

b) **Although**, SUI: even though, supposing that, if, even if. **Purpose**, CHIH: focus of mind and heart; will, inclination, resolve. The ideogram: heart and scholar, high inner resolve, or heart and go, inner determination. **Move**, HSING: move or move something; motivate, emotionally moving; walk, act, do. The ideogram: stepping left then right. **Correct**, CHENG: rectify deviation or one-sidedness; proper, straight, exact, regular; constant, rule, model. The ideogram: stop and one, hold to one thing.

Value, KUEI: regard as valuable, give worth and dignity to; precious, high priced; honorable, exalted, illustrious. The ideogram: cowries (coins) and basket. **Mean**, CHIEN: low, poor, cheap; depreciate, undervalue; opposite of **value**, KUEI. **Below**, HSIA: anything below, in all senses; lower, inner; lower trigram; opposite of **above**, SHANG.

Acquire, TE: obtain the desired object; wish for, desire covetously; gains, possessions. The ideogram: go and obstacle, going through obstacles to the goal. **Commoners**, MIN: class of workers the state draws on to sustain the social hierarchy; undeveloped potential outside the organized personality.

Six at second

a) **Sprouting thus, quitting thus.**
  Riding a horse, arrayed thus.
  In no way outlaws, seek matrimonial allying.
  Woman and Son, Trial: not nursing.
  Ten years revolve, thereupon nursing.

b) **Six at second's heaviness.**
  Riding a strong indeed.
  Ten years revolve, thereupon nursing.
  Reversing the rules indeed.

You reach out, then turn away from them. You are prepared for an encounter then see the others as outlaws. Drop the hostility. Seek a permanent connection. It will be a while before this bears fruit, but in the end all will come right.

Associated Contexts a) **Thus ... thus**, JU ... JU: when there is one thing, then there must be the second thing. **Quit**, CHAN: stop, change because unsuccessful; unable to advance.

Ride, CH'ENG: ride an animal or a chariot; have the upper hand, seize

the right time; control strong power; overcome the nature of the other; supple opened line above a strong whole line. **Horse**, MA: symbol of spirited strength in the natural world, counterpart of dragon, LUNG; associated with the trigram Force, CH'IEN, heaven, T'IEN, and high noon. **Array**, PAN: classify and display; arrange according to rank; assign to a group, as soldiers to their units. The ideogram: knife between two gems, separating values.

In no way, FEI: strong negative; not so. The ideogram: a box filled with opposition. **Outlawry**, K'OU: break the laws; violent people, outcasts, bandits. **Matrimonial allying**, HUN KOU: legal institution of marriage; make alliances through marriage rather than force.

Woman[and]Son, NÜ TZU: particular relation between a woman and her child. **Nurse**, TZU: love, care for and shelter; act as a mother. The ideogram: child and shelter.

Ten, SHIH: goal and end of reckoning; whole, complete, all; entire, perfected, the full amount; reach everywhere, receive everything. The ideogram: East–West line crosses North–South line, a grid that contains all. **Years revolved**, NIEN: number of years elapsed; a person's age; contrasts with year's-time, SUI, length of time in a year. **Thereupon**, NAI: on that ground, because of.

b) **Strong**, KANG: quality of the whole lines; firm, strong, unyielding, persisting.

Reverse, FAN: turn and move in the opposite direction; turn around or upside down (180 degrees); change to the opposite position; contrary. **Rules**, CH'ANG: unchanging principles; regular, constant, habitual; maintain laws and customs.

Six at third

a) Approaching stag, lacking precaution.
Namely, entering into the forest center.
A chün tzu almost does not stow it away.
Going, distress.

b) Approaching stag, without precaution.
Using adhering to the wildfowl indeed.
A chün tzu stowing it away:
This means going distress is exhausted.

You are losing yourself in the difficulties, following impulses without a second thought. You are on the edge of disaster. Stop now before you lose sight of what is really worthwhile. Recognize this and you will not be ashamed.

Associated Contexts a) **Approach**, CHI: come near to, advance toward; about to do; soon. **Stag**, LU: mature male deer with horns. **Lacking**, WU: strong negative; does not possess. **Precaution**, YÜ: provide against, preventive measures; anxious, vigilant, ready; preoccupied with, think about, expect; mishap, accident.

Namely, WEI: precisely, only that. **Enter**, JU: penetrate, go into, enter on, progress; put into, encroach on; Action of the trigram Ground, SUN, contrary of issue-forth, CH'U. **Forest**, LIN: area with no mark of human construction; woods, wild luxuriance; wilderness; last of the territorial zones: city, suburbs, countryside, forests.

Almost, CHI: nearly, about to; subtle, almost imperceptible; the first sign. **Thus**, JU: as, in this way. **Stow (away)**, SHE: set aside, put away, store; halt, rest in; temporary lodgings, breathing-spell.

Go, WANG, and come, LAI, describe the stream of time as it flows from future through present to past; go, WANG, indicates what is departing from present to past; proceed, move on; keyword. **Distress**, LIN: shame, regret, humiliation; aware of having lost the right track; leads to repenting, HUI, correcting the direction of mind and life.

b) **Adhere(to)**, TS'UNG: follow a way, hold to a doctrine, school, or person; hear and comply with, agree to; forced to follow, follower. The ideogram: two men walking, one following the other. **Wildfowl**, CH'IN: all wild and game birds; untamed.

It/them/have(it)/'s, CHIH: expresses possession, directly or as an object pronoun.

Exhaust, CH'IUNG: bring to an end; limit, extremity; destitute; investigate exhaustively; end without a new beginning. The ideogram: cave and naked person, bent with disease or old age.

Six at fourth

a) **Riding a horse, arrayed thus.**
Seek matrimonial allying.
Going auspicious.
Nothing not advantageous.

b) **Seeking and going:**
Brightness indeed.

The time is right. The difficulties are over. Make the connection. Pledge yourself in front of the community. This will be of great benefit to everyone concerned.

Associated Contexts a) **Ride**, CH'ENG: ride an animal or a chariot; have the upper hand, seize the right time; control strong power; overcome the nature of the other; supple opened line above a strong whole line. **Horse**, MA: symbol of spirited strength in the natural world, counterpart of dragon, LUNG; associated with the trigram Force, CH'IEN, heaven, T'IEN, and high noon. **Array**, PAN: classify and display; arrange according to rank; assign to a group, as soldiers to their units. The ideogram: knife between two gems, separating values. **Thus**, JU: as, in this way.

Seek, CH'IU: search for, aim at, wish for, desire; implore, supplicate; covetous. **Matrimonial allying**, HUN KOU: legal institution of marriage; make alliances through marriage rather than force.

Go, WANG, and come, LAI, describe the stream of time as it flows from future through present to past; go, WANG, indicates what is departing from present to past; proceed, move on; keyword. **Auspicious**, CHI: leads to the experience of meaning; favorable, propitious, advantageous, appropriate; keyword. The ideogram: scholar and mouth, wise words of a sage.

Nothing not advantageous, WU PU LI: nothing for which this will not be beneficial; advantageous potential, borderline where the balance is swinging from not Harvesting to actually Harvesting.

b) **Brightness**, MING: light-giving aspect of burning, heavenly bodies and consciousness; with fire, the Symbol of the trigram Radiance, LI.

Nine at fifth

a) Sprouting: its juice.
   The small, Trial: auspicious.
   The great, Trial: pitfall.

b) Sprouting: its juice.
   Spreading out is not yet shining indeed.

You have found this source of vital growth. Make no great moves now. Adapt to what happens. Make sure everything gets what it needs. Don't impose your will. Your purpose is expanding but not shining yet.

Associated Contexts a) **Juice**, KAO: active principle, essence; oil, grease, ointment; fertilizing, rich; genius.

Small, HSIAO: little, common, unimportant; adapting to what crosses your path; ability to move in harmony with the vicissitudes of life; contrasts with great, TA, self-imposed theme or goal; keyword. Image of Hexagrams 9 and 62. **Auspicious**, CHI: leads to the experience of meaning; favorable, propitious, advantageous, appropriate; keyword. The ideogram: scholar and mouth, wise words of a sage.

Pitfall, HSIUNG: leads away from the experience of meaning; stuck and exposed to danger, unable to take in the situation; flow of life and spirit is blocked; unfortunate, baleful; keyword.

b) **Spread out**, SHIH: expand, diffuse, distribute, arrange, exhibit; add to, aid. The ideogram: flag and indeed, claiming new country. **Not yet**, WEI: temporal negative; something will but has not yet occurred; contrary of already, CHI. Image of Hexagram 64. **Shine**, KUANG: illuminate; give off brilliant, bright light; honor, glory, éclat; result of action, contrasts with brightness, MING, light of heavenly bodies. The ideogram: fire above person, lifting the light.

Six above

a) Riding a horse, arrayed thus.
    Weeping blood, coursing thus.

b) Weeping blood, coursing thus.
    Why permit long living indeed?

A disastrous way to proceed, bleeding you in literal and emotional ways. Don't think you can simply fix it. Let go of it now before it gets worse.

Associated Contexts a) **Ride**, CH'ENG: ride an animal or a chariot; have the upper hand, seize the right time; control strong power; overcome the nature of the other; supple opened line above a strong whole line. **Horse**, MA: symbol of spirited strength in the natural world, counterpart of dragon, LUNG; associated with the trigram Force, CH'IEN, heaven, T'IEN, and high noon. **Array**, PAN: classify and display; arrange according to rank; assign to a group, as soldiers to their units. The ideogram: knife between two gems, separating values. **Thus**, JU: as, in this way.

Weep, CH'I: lament wordlessly; grieved, heart-broken. **Blood**, HSÜEH: yin fluid that maintains life; money, property. **Course**, LIEN: move, flow like ripples spreading on water; unceasing.

b) **Why**, HO: interrogative: why? for what reason? what is? and affirmation: therefore, for that reason. **Permit**, K'O: possible because in harmony with an inherent principle. The ideogram: mouth and breath, silent consent. **Long-living**, CHANG: enduring, constant; senior, superior, greater; increase, prosper; respect, elevate.

ENVELOPING/
IGNORANCE ▌ *MENG*

Immature, unaware, foolish; hidden, concealed; nurture hidden growth.

Enveloping describes your situation in terms of staying under cover. Its symbols are a fetus in the womb or the wordless seed of a new time. You are immature and your awareness of the problem is dull and clouded. The way to deal with it is to accept being hidden in order to nurture growing awareness. Pull the covers over. Put the lid on. There is much concealed from you. You don't really know what you are doing. But the beginnings are definitely there, even if you can't yet see them. You didn't ask for this problem. It asked for you and it belongs with you. The first time you consult the oracle about this, it will advise and inform you. If you keep on asking, you muddy the waters. Your awareness must grow and change. Put your ideas to the trial. That brings profit and insight. Keep working on your problem. It will educate you.

● *Image of the Situation*

> **Enveloping, Growing.**
> **In no way me seeking the young and ignorant.**
> **The young and ignorant seek me.**
> **The initial oracle consultation notifies you.**
> **Twice, three times obscures it.**
> **Obscuring, by consequence not notifying.**
> **Advantageous Trial, Harvesting.**

Associated Contexts **Envelop**, MENG: cover, pull over, hide, conceal; lid or cover; clouded awareness, dull; ignorance, immaturity; unseen beginnings. The ideogram: plant and covered, hidden growth. **Grow**, HENG: success through a sacrifice; pervade, persevere; bring to full growth; enjoy; vigorous, effective; second stage of the Time Cycle.

In no way, FEI: strong negative; not so. The ideogram: a box filled with opposition. **Me/I/my**, WO: first person pronoun; indicates an unusually strong emphasis on your own subjective experience. **Seek**, CH'IU: search for, aim at, wish for, desire; implore, supplicate; covetous. **Youthful**, T'UNG: young person between eight and fifteen; young animals and plants.

Initial, CH'U: first step or part; beginning, incipient; bottom line of hexagram. The ideogram: knife and garment, cutting out the pattern. **Oracle consulting**, SHIH: yarrow stalk divination; find your allotted destiny. **Notify**, KAO: proclaim, order, decree; advise, inform, tell. The ideogram: mouth and ox head, imposing speech.

Twice, three times, TSAI SAN: serial repetition. **Obscure**, TU: confuse, muddy, agitate; muddled, cloudy, turbid; agitated water; annoy through repetition.

By consequence(of), TSE: very strong connection; reason, cause, result; rule, law, pattern, standard; therefore.

Advantageous Trial, LI CHEN: advantageous divination; putting the action in question to the test is beneficial, harvesting.

● *Outer and Inner Aspects*

☶ **Bound**: Mountains bound, limit and set a place off, stopping forward movement. **Bound** completes a full yin-yang cycle.

Connection to the outer: accomplishing words, which express things fully. **Bound** articulates what is complete and suggests what is beginning.

☵ **Gorge**: Stream ventures and falls into the gorge, flowing on through toil and danger. **Gorge** ends the yin hemicycle by leveling and dissolving forms.

Connection to the inner: flooding and leveling dissolve direction and shape, the Streaming Moment. **Gorge** ventures, falls, toils and flows on.

An outer limit hides and shields inner venturing; inner growth is **enveloped** and awareness of new growth is clouded.

● *Hidden Possibility*

Nuclear trigrams **Field**, K'UN, and **Shake**, CHEN, result in Nuclear Hexagram 24, **Returning**, FU. **Enveloping**'s preparation for moving on depends on **returning** to the source.

● *Sequence*

Beings giving birth are necessarily Enveloped.
Accepting this lets you use Enveloping.
Enveloping implies envelopment
And beings's immaturity indeed.

Associated Contexts **Being(s)**, WU: creature, thing, any single being; matter, substance, essence; nature of things. **Birth/give birth to**, SHENG: produce, beget, grow, bear, arise; life, vitality. The ideogram: earth and sprout. **Necessarily**, PI: unavoidably, indispensably, certainly.

Accepting … use: activating this hexagram depends on understanding and accepting the previous statement.

Imply, CHE: further signify; additional meaning. **'s/have(it)/it/them**, CHIH: expresses possession, directly or as an object pronoun. **Indeed/is/means**, YEH: intensifier, connective; indicates comment on previous statement.

Immature, CHIH: small, tender, young, delicate; undeveloped; conceited, haughty; late grain.

- *Contrasted Definitions*

> Sprouting: being seen and not letting go one's residence.
> Enveloping: variegated and conspicuous.

Associated Contexts **Sprout**, CHUN: begin or cause to grow; assemble, accumulate, bring under control; hoard possessions; gather soldiers in a military camp; difficult, arduous. The ideogram: sprout piercing hard soil. Image of Hexagram 3. **See**, CHIEN: seeing in all its aspects: vision, being visible, forming mental images; visit, call on, consult. The ideogram: eye above person, active and receptive sight. **Let go**, SHIH: lose, omit, miss, fail, let slip; out of control. The ideogram: drop from the hand. **One's/one**, CH'I: third person pronoun; also: it/its, he/his, she/hers, they/theirs. **Reside(in)**, CHÜ: dwell, live in, stay; sit down, fill an office; settled parts of a country. The ideogram: body and seat.

Variegated, TSA: mingled, various, mixed; disordered. **Conspicuous**, CHU: manifest, obvious, clear.

- *Symbol Tradition*

> Below mountain issuing forth springwater. Enveloping.
> A chün tzu uses fruiting movement to nurture actualizing tao.

Associated Contexts **Below**, HSIA: anything below, in all senses; lower, inner; lower trigram; opposite of above, SHANG. **Mountain**, SHAN: limit, boundary; the Symbol of the trigram Bound, KEN. The ideogram: three peaks, a mountain range. **Issue forth(from)**, CH'U: emerge from, come out of, proceed from, spring from; the Action of the trigram Shake, CHEN; contrary of enter, JU. The ideogram: stem with branches and leaves emerging. **Springwater,** CH'ÜAN: headwaters of a river; pure water. The ideogram: water and white, pure water at the source.

Chün tzu: ideal of a person who uses divination to order his/her life in accordance with tao rather than willful intention; keyword. **Use(of),** YI: make use of, by means of, owing to; employ, make functional. **Fruit,** KUO: plant's annual produce; tree fruits; come to fruition, fruits of actions; produce, results, effects; reliable; conclude, surpass. The ideogram: tree topped by a round fruit. **Move,** HSING: move or move something; motivate, emotionally moving; walk, act, do. The ideogram: stepping left then right. **Nurture,** YÜ: bring up, support, rear, raise; increase. **Actualize tao,** TE: realize tao in action; power, virtue; ability to follow the course traced by the ongoing process of the cosmos; keyword. The ideogram: to go, straight, and heart. Linked with acquire, TE: acquiring that which makes a being become what it is meant to be.

● *Image Tradition*

> Enveloping. Below mountain possesses venturing. [I]
> Venturing and stopping. Enveloping.
>
> Enveloping, Growing. [II]
> Using Growing movement.
> The Season centered indeed.
>
> In no way me seeking the young and ignorant. [III]
> The young and ignorant seeking me.
> Purposes corresponding indeed.
>
> The initial oracle consulting notifying. [IV]
> Using the strong center indeed.
> Twice, three times: obscuring.
> Obscuring, by consequence not notifying.
> Obscuring Enveloping indeed.
> Of Enveloping is used to nourish correcting:
> The all wise is achieved indeed.

Associated Contexts [I] **Possess,** YU: in possession of, have, own; opposite of lack, WU. **Venture,** HSIEN: risk without reserve; key point, point of danger; difficulty, obstruction that must be confronted; water falling and filling the holes on its way; the Action of the trigram Gorge, K'AN. The ideogram: mound and all or whole, everything engaged at one point.

Stop, CHIH: bring or come to a standstill; the Action of the trigram

Bound, KEN. The ideogram: a foot stops walking.

[II] **Season**, SHIH: quality of the time; the right time, opportune, in harmony; planning in accord with the time; seasons of the year. The ideogram: sun and temple, time as sacred. **Center**, CHUNG: inner, central; put in the center; middle, stable point enabling you to face inner and outer changes; middle line of trigram. The ideogram: field divided in two equal parts. Image of Hexagram 61.

[III] **Purpose**, CHIH: focus of mind and heart; will, inclination, resolve. The ideogram: heart and scholar, high inner resolve, or heart and go, inner determination. **Correspond**, YING: be in agreement or harmony; resonate together, invoke and fulfil each other; answer to, suitable; relation between the lines (1:4, 2:5, 3:6) when they form the pair opened and whole, supple and strong. The ideogram: heart and obey.

[IV] **Strong**, KANG: quality of the whole lines; firm, strong, unyielding, persisting.

Nourish, YANG: feed, sustain, support; provide, care for; bring up, improve, grow, develop. **Correct**, CHENG: rectify deviation or one sidedness; proper, straight, exact, regular; constant, rule, model. The ideogram: stop and one, hold to one thing.

All wise, SHENG: intuitive universal wisdom; mythical sages; holy, sacred; mark of highest distinction. The ideogram: ear and inform, one who knows all from a single sound. **Achieve**, KUNG: work done, results; real accomplishment, praise, worth, merit. The ideogram: workman's square and forearm, combining craft and strength.

● *Transforming Lines*

Initial six

a) Shooting forth Enveloping.
  Advantageous to avail of punishing people.
  Avail of loosening the fettering shackles.
  Using going: distress.

b) Harvesting: availing of punishing people.
  Use correcting the laws indeed.

You have to correct a far-reaching error. Be discriminating with the people around you. Free the youthful energy that you are now confining. Simply going on will cover you with confusion.

Associated Contexts a) **Shoot forth**, FA: expand, send out; shoot an arrow; ferment, rise; be displayed. The ideogram: stance, bow and arrow, shooting from a strong base.

Advantageous Harvest, LI: advantageous, profitable; acute, insightful; benefit, nourish; third stage of the Time Cycle. **Avail of**, YUNG: take advantage of; benefit from, profit by; use for a specific purpose; apply to advantage. The ideogram: to divine and center, applying divination to central concerns. **Punish**, HSING: legal punishment; physical penalties for severe criminal offenses; whip, torture, behead. **People, person**, JEN: humans individually and collectively; an individual; humankind. Image of Hexagrams 13 and 37.

Loosen/Stimulate, SHUO: rouse to action and good feeling; free from constraint, stir up, urge on; persuade, cheer, delight; set out in words; the Action of the trigram Open, TUI. The ideogram: words and exchange. **Fetter**, CHIH: tie, manacle; restrain and hinder movement, clog wheels; impede. **Shackles**, KU: chains used to secure prisoners; restrain freedom of action; self-restraint, good principles.

Go, WANG, and come, LAI, describe the stream of time as it flows from future through present to past; go, WANG, indicates what is departing from present to past; proceed, move on; keyword. **Distress**, LIN: distress, shame, regret, humiliation; aware of having lost the right track; leads to repenting, HUI, correcting the direction of mind and life.

b) **Laws**, FA: rules, statutes, model, method.

Nine at second

a) **Enwrapped and Enveloped, Auspicious.**
Letting in the wife. Auspicious.
The son controls the dwelling.

b) **The son controls the dwelling.**
Strong and Supple articulated indeed.

Being enveloped turns into caring for and protecting someone. The time is right to take a wife and establish a dwelling. You have the ability to control this change.

Associated Contexts a) **Enwrap**, PAO: envelop, hold, contain; patient; take on responsibility, engaged. The ideogram: enfold and self, a fetus in the womb. **Auspicious**, CHI: leads to the experience of meaning; favorable, propitious, advantageous, appropriate; keyword. The ideogram: scholar and mouth, wise words of a sage.

Let in, NA: allow to enter; take in, grow smaller; insert; collect. The

ideogram: silk and enter, shrinking silk threads. **Wife**, FU: responsible position of married woman within the household; contrasts with consort, CH'I, her legal position and concubine, CH'IEH, secondary wives. The ideogram: woman, hand and broom, household duties.

Son(hood), TZU: living up to ideal of ancestors as highest human development; act with concern and reverence; male child; offspring, posterity; seed, kernel, egg; sage, teacher; nadir, deepest point, midnight, mid-winter. **Control**, K'O: command; check, impede, prevail, obstruct, repress; adequate, able. The ideogram: roof beams support a house, controlling the structure. **Dwell**, CHI: home, house, household, family; domestic, within doors; live in. The ideogram: roof and pig or dog, the most valued domestic animals. Image of Hexagram 37.

b) **Strong and Supple**, KANG JOU: field of creative tension between the whole and opened lines and their qualities; field of psychic movement. **Articulate**, CHIEH: separate and distinguish, as well as join, different things; express thought through speech; joint, section, chapter, interval, unit of time; zodiacal sign; moderate, regulate; lit.: nodes on bamboo stalks. Image of Hexagram 60.

Six at third

a) Do not avail of grasping the woman.
See the metal husband,
Do not possess the body.
No advantageous direction.

b) No availing of grasping the woman.
Movement not yielding indeed.

You are flirting with something beyond you. If you become involved you lose your independence and your capacity to express yourself. There is nothing of value here for you. Let it go. Don't grasp this possibility.

Associated Contexts a) **Avail of**, YUNG: take advantage of; benefit from, profit by; use for a specific purpose; apply to advantage. The ideogram: to divine and center, applying divination to central concerns. **Grasp**, CH'Ü: lay hold of, take and use, seize, appropriate; grasp the meaning, understand. The ideogram: ear and hand, hear and grasp. **Woman(hood)**, NÜ: a woman; what is inherently female.

Metallic, CHIN: smelting and casting; all things pertaining to metal, particularly gold; autumn, West, sunset; one of the Five Moments. **Husband**, FU: household manager; administer with thrift and prudence;

responsible for; sustain with your earnings; old enough to assume responsibility; married man.

Body, KUNG: physical being, power and self expression; contrasts with individuality, SHEN, the total personality.

No advantageous direction, WU YU LI: no plan or direction is advantageous; in order to take advantage of the situation, do not impose a direction on events.

b) **Yield(to)**, SHUN: give way and bear produce; comply, agree, follow, obey; unresisting, docile, flexible; nourish, provide; the Action of the trigram Field, K'UN. The ideogram: head and current, water flowing from the head of a river, yielding to the banks.

Six at fourth

a) Confining Enveloping. Distress.

b) Confining Enveloping's distress.
Solitariness distances substance indeed.

You are locking yourself in a prison. You don't have to confine yourself like this. You are cutting yourself off from what is real.

Associated Contexts a) **Confine**, K'UN: enclose, restrict, limit; oppressed; impoverish, distress; afflicted, exhausted, disheartened, weary. The ideogram: an enclosed tree. Image of Hexagram 47. **Distress**, LIN: shame, regret, humiliation; aware of having lost the right track; leads to repenting, HUI, correcting the direction of mind and life.

b) **Solitary**, TI: alone, single; isolated, abandoned. **Distance**, YÜAN: far off, remote; keep at a distance; alienated. The ideogram: go and a long way. **Substance**, SHIH: real, solid, full; results, fruits, possessions; essence; honest, sincere. The ideogram: string of coins under a roof, riches in the house.

Six at fifth

a) Youthful Enveloping. Auspicious.

b) Youth Enveloping it. Auspicious.
Yielding uses Ground indeed.

You have accepted your immaturity and the fact that there is something hidden in the situation. The way opens and leads to real connection and understanding. Be patient and have faith.

Associated Contexts a) **Auspicious**, CHI: leads to the experience of meaning; favorable, propitious, advantageous, appropriate; keyword. The ideogram: scholar and mouth, wise words of a sage.

b) **Yield(to)**, SHUN: give way and bear produce; comply, agree, follow, obey; unresisting, docile, flexible; nourish, provide; the Action of the trigram Field, K'UN. The ideogram: head and current, water flowing from the head of a river, yielding to the banks. **Ground**, SUN: base on which things rest; support, foundation; mild, subtly penetrating; nourishing. The ideogram: stand and things arranged on it, the subtle influence of the ground. Image of Hexagram 57.

> **Nine above**

> *a)* **Smiting the Enveloping.**
>   **Not Advantageous: activating outlawry.**
>   **Advantageous: resisting outlawry.**

> *b)* **Harvesting: availing of resisting outlawry.**
>   **Above and Below yielding indeed.**

You are fighting against the very processes that, in the long run, will give you what you need. Resist the temptation to act impulsively. Then the fruit will literally fall into your hand.

Associated Contexts a) **Smite**, CHI: hit, beat, attack; hurl against, rush a position; rouse to action. The ideogram: hand and hit, fist punching.

Advantageous Harvest, LI: advantageous, profitable; acute, insightful; benefit, nourish; third stage of the Time Cycle. **Activate**, WEI: act or cause to act; do, make, manage; make active; attend to, help; because of. **Outlawry**, K'OU: break the laws; violent people, outcasts, bandits.

Resist, YÜ: withstand, oppose; bring to an end; prevent. The ideogram: rule and worship, imposing ethical or religious limits.

b) **Avail-of**, YUNG: take advantage of; benefit from, profit by; use for a specific purpose; apply to advantage. The ideogram: to divine and center, applying divination to central concerns.

Above[and]Below, SHANG HSIA: realm of dynamic interaction between the upper and the lower; the vertical dimension. **Yield(-to)**, SHUN: give way and bear produce; comply, agree, follow, obey; unresisting, docile, flexible; nourish, provide; the Action of the trigram Field, K'UN. The ideogram: head and current, water flowing from the head of a river, yielding to the banks.

ATTENDING ∎ *HSÜ*

Wait for, wait on, attend to what is needed; wait for the right moment.

Attending describes your situation in terms of waiting for and serving something. Its symbol is the attendant at a sacrifice through which ancestral blessing will flow like the rain. The way to deal with it is to find out what is needed and carefully wait for the right moment to act. You aren't in control of things, but in time you can provide what is needed. Act this way with confidence. You are connected to the spirits and they will carry you through. One day you will bring the rain. Look after things. Think about what is necessary. Illuminate the situation through repeated efforts. This is pleasing to the spirits. Through it they will give you success, effective power and the capacity to bring the situation to maturity. Put your ideas to the trial. That generates meaning and good fortune by releasing transformative energy. This is the right time to enter the stream of life with a goal or embark on a significant enterprise. That brings profit and insight.

● *Image of the Situation*

> **Attending, there is a connection to the spirits.**
> **Shining Growing, Trial: auspicious.**
> **Advantageous to step into the Great Stream.**

Associated Contexts **Attend**, HSÜ: take care of, look out for, serve; turn your mind to what is necessary; wait, await, wait on; hesitate, doubt; obstinate, fixed. The ideogram: rain and stop, compelled to wait, or rain and origin, providing what is needed. **There is a connection to the spirits**, YU FU: inner and outer are in accord; confidence of the spirits has been captured; sincere, truthful; proper to take action.

Shine, KUANG: illuminate; give off brilliant, bright light; honor, glory, éclat; result of action, contrasts with brightness, MING, light of heavenly bodies. The ideogram: fire above person, lifting the light. **Grow**, HENG: success through a sacrifice; pervade, persevere; bring to full growth; enjoy; vigorous, effective; second stage of the Time Cycle. **Trial**, CHEN: inquiry by divination and its result; righteous, firm; separating wheat from chaff; the kernel, the proven core; fourth stage of the Time Cycle. The ideogram:

pearl and divination. **Auspicious,** CHI: leads to the experience of meaning; favorable, propitious, advantageous, appropriate; keyword. The ideogram: scholar and mouth, wise words of a sage.

Advantageous/Harvest, LI: advantageous, profitable; acute, insightful; benefit, nourish; third stage of the Time Cycle. **Step into the Great River,** SHE TA CH'UAN: consciously move into the flow of time; enter the stream of life with a goal or purpose; embark on a significant enterprise.

- *Outer and Inner Aspects*

☵ **Gorge:** Stream ventures and falls into the gorge, flowing on through toil and danger. **Gorge** ends the yin hemicycle by leveling and dissolving forms.

Connection to the outer: flooding and leveling dissolve direction and shape, the Streaming Moment. **Gorge** ventures, falls, toils and flows on.

☰ **Force:** The force of heaven struggles on, persistent and unwearied; heavenly bodies persist in their orbits. **Force** is the center of the yin hemicycle, completing the formative process.

Connection to the inner: struggling forces are bound together in dynamic tension, the Metallic Moment culminating. **Force** brings elements to grips, creating enduring relations.

Persistent inner concentration confronts outer danger by careful **attending** on events.

- *Hidden Possibility*

Nuclear trigrams **Radiance,** LI, and **Open,** TUI, result in Nuclear Hexagram 38, **Diverging,** K'UEI. **Attending** to the needs at hand depends on **diverging** from the norm.

- *Sequence*

> **Being immature does not permit not nourishing indeed.**
> **Accepting this lets you use Attending.**
> **Attending implies drinking and eating's tao indeed.**

Associated Contexts **Being(s),** WU: creature, thing, any single being; matter, substance, essence; nature of things. **Immature,** CHIH: small, tender, young, delicate; undeveloped; conceited, haughty; late grain. **Not permitting,** PU K'O: not possible; contradicts an inherent principle. The ideogram: mouth and breath, silent consent. **Nourish,** YANG: feed, sustain,

126

support; provide, care for; bring up, improve, grow, develop. **Indeed/is/means**, YEH: intensifier, connective; indicates comment on previous statement.

Anterior ... use: activating this hexagram depends on understanding and accepting the previous statement.

Imply, CHE: further signify; additional meaning. **Drinking and eating**, YIN SHIH: comprehensive term for eating, drinking and breathing; a meal, eating together. **'s/have(it)/it/them**, CHIH: expresses possession, directly or as an object pronoun. **Tao**: way or path; ongoing process of being and the course it traces for each specific person or thing; keyword. The ideogram: go and head, leading and the path it creates.

- *Contrasted Definitions*

> **Attending means not advancing.**
> **Arguing means not connecting.**

Associated Contexts **Advance**, CHIN: exert yourself, make progress, climb; be promoted; further the development of, augment; adopt a religion or conviction; offer, introduce.

Argue, SUNG: dispute, plead in court, contend before a ruler, demand justice; wrangles, quarrels, litigation. The ideogram: words and public, public disputation. Image of Hexagram 6. **Connect**, CH'IN: attach to, approach, come near; cherish, help, favor; intimate; relatives, kin.

- *Symbol Tradition*

> **Above clouds with respect to heaven. Attending.**
> **A chün tzu uses drinking and eating to repose delighting.**

Associated Contexts **Above**, SHANG: anything above, in all senses; higher, upper, outer; upper trigram; opposite of below, HSIA. **Clouds**, YÜN: fog, mist, water vapor; connects to the Streaming Moment and Stream, the Symbol of the trigram Gorge, K'AN. **With respect to**, YÜ: relates to, refers to; hold a position in. **Heaven**, T'IEN: highest; sky, firmament, heavens; power above the human as opposed to earth, TI, below; the Symbol of the trigram Force, CH'IEN. The ideogram: great and the one above.

Chün tzu: ideal of a person who uses divination to order his/her life in accordance with tao rather than wilful intention; keyword. **Use(of)**, YI: make use of, by means of, owing to; employ, make functional. **Repose**, YEN: rest, leisure, peace of mind; banquet, feast. The ideogram: shelter and rest,

a wayside inn. **Delight**, LO: take joy or pleasure in; pleasant, relaxed; also: music as harmony, elegance and pleasure.

- *Image Tradition*

> Attending means patience. [I]
> Venturing located in precedence indeed.
> Strong persists and does not fall.
> Actually one's righteousness, not confining exhaustion.
>
> Attending, there is a connection to the spirits. [II]
> Shining Growing, Trial: auspicious.
> The situation reaches to the heavenly situation.
> Use correcting and centering indeed.
>
> Advantageous: to step into the Great River. [III]
> Going possesses achievement indeed.

Associated Contexts [I] **Patience**, HSÜ: patience symbolized as waiting for hair to grow; hold back, wait for; slow; necessary.

Venture, HSIEN: risk without reserve; key point, point of danger; difficulty, obstruction that must be confronted; water falling and filling the holes on its way; the Action of the trigram Gorge, K'AN. The ideogram: mound and all or whole, everything engaged at one point. **Locate(in)**, TSAI: live in, dwell, reside; belong to, involved with, depend on; within. The ideogram: earth and persevere, place on the earth. **Precede**, CH'IEN: come before in time and thus in value; anterior, former, ancient; lead forward.

Strong, KANG: quality of the whole lines; firm, strong, unyielding, persisting. **Persist**, CHIEN: strong, robust, dynamic, tenacious; continuous; unwearied heavenly bodies in their orbits; the Action of the trigram Force, CH'IEN. **Fall**, HSIEN: fall down or into, sink, drop, descend; falling water; the Action of the trigram Gorge, K'AN.

Actually, YI: truly, really, at present. The ideogram: a dart and done, strong intention fully expressed. **One's/one**, CH'I: third person pronoun; also: it/its, he/his, she/hers, they/theirs. **Righteous**, YI: proper and just, meets the standards; things in their proper place; the heart that rules itself; upright, moral rule; contrasts with Harvest, LI, advantage or profit. **Confine**, K'UN: enclose, restrict, limit; oppressed; impoverish, distress; afflicted, exhausted, disheartened, weary. The ideogram: an enclosed tree. Image of Hexagram 47. **Exhaust**, CH'IUNG: bring to an end; limit, extremity; destitute; investigate exhaustively; end without a new beginning. The ideogram: cave and naked person, bent with disease or old age.

[II] Situation, WEI: place or seat according to rank; post, position, command; right, proper; established, arranged. The ideogram: person and stand, servants in their places. **Reach(to)**, HU: arrive at a goal; reach towards and achieve; connect; contrasts with tend-toward, YU.

Correct, CHENG: rectify deviation or one-sidedness; proper, straight, exact, regular; constant, rule, model. The ideogram: stop and one, hold to one thing. **Center**, CHUNG: inner, central; put in the center; middle, stable point enabling you to face inner and outer changes; middle line of trigram. The ideogram: field divided in two equal parts. Image of Hexagram 61.

[III] Go, WANG, and come, LAI, describe the stream of time as it flows from future through present to past; go, WANG, indicates what is departing from present to past; proceed, move on; keyword. **Possess**, YU: in possession of, have, own; opposite of lack, WU. **Achieve**, KUNG: work done, results; real accomplishment, praise, worth, merit. The ideogram: workman's square and forearm, combining craft and strength.

● *Transforming Lines*

Initial nine

a) Attending in the outskirts.
Advantageous to avail of persevering.
Without fault.

b) Attending in the suburbs.
Not opposing heavy moving indeed.
Harvesting: availing of persevering, without fault.
Not yet letting go the rules indeed.

It feels like the spirit is far away. But underneath, the connection is there. Persevere! Don't lose patience. You are not making a mistake.

Associated Contexts a) **Outskirts**, CHIAO: area adjoining a city where human constructions and nature interpenetrate; second of the territorial zones: city, suburbs, countryside, forests.

Avail of, YUNG: take advantage of; benefit from, profit by; use for a specific purpose; apply to advantage. The ideogram: to divine and center, applying divination to central concerns. **Persevere**, HENG: continue in the same way or spirit; constant, perpetual, regular; self-renewing; extend everywhere. Image of Hexagram 32.

Without fault, WU CHIU: no error or harm in the situation.

b) **Oppose,** FAN: resist; violate, offend, attack; possessed by an evil spirit; criminal. The ideogram: violate and dog, brutal offense. **Heavy,** NAN: arduous, grievous, difficult; hardship, distress; harass; contrasts with versatile, I, deal lightly with. The ideogram: domestic bird with clipped tail and drying sticky earth. **Move,** HSING: move or move something; motivate, emotionally moving; walk, act, do. The ideogram: stepping left then right.

Not yet, WEI: temporal negative; something will but has not yet occurred; contrary of **already,** CHI. Image of Hexagram 64. **Let go,** SHIH: lose, omit, miss, fail, let slip; out of control. The ideogram: drop from the hand. **Rules,** CH'ANG: unchanging principles; regular, constant, habitual; maintain laws and customs.

Nine at second

a) Attending on the sands.
   The small possesses words.
   Completing auspicious.

b) Attending on the sands.
   Overflowing and located in the center indeed.
   Although the small possesses words,
   use completing to be auspicious.

You are a bit closer but the situation keeps shifting. All around you voices are chattering. Don't worry. Keep your eye on what is important and go through this. The way to the center opens from here.

Associated Contexts a) **Sands,** SHA: beach, sandbanks, shingle; gravel, pebbles; granulated. The ideogram: water and few, areas laid bare by receding water.

Small, HSIAO: little, common, unimportant; adapting to what crosses your path; ability to move in harmony with the vicissitudes of life; contrasts with great, TA, self-imposed theme or goal; keyword. Image of Hexagrams 9 and 62. **Word,** YEN: speech, spoken words, sayings; talk, discuss, address. The ideogram: mouth and rising vapor, words as speech.

Complete, CHUNG: end of a cycle that begins the next; last, whole, all; contrasts with exhaust, CH'IUNG, final end. The ideogram: silk cocoons, follow and ice, winter linking one year with the next.

b) **Overflow,** YEN: flow over the top; inundate, spread out; abundant, rich.
Although, SUI: even though, supposing that, if, even if.

Nine at third

a) Attending in the bogs.
Involving outlaws at the culmination.

b) Attending in the bogs.
Calamity located outside indeed.
Originating from my involvement with outlawry.
Respectful consideration will not destroy you indeed.

You have lost the sense of attending on something precious. This leaves you vulnerable to attack and loss of what you care for. There is still time, so think it over.

Associated Contexts a) **Bog,** NI: wet spongy soil; mire, slush, quicksand; unable to move.

Involve, CHIH: include, entangle, implicate; induce, cause. The ideogram: person walking, induced to follow. **Outlawry,** K'OU: break the laws; violent people, outcasts, bandits. **Culminate,** CHIH: bring to the highest degree; arrive at the end or summit; superlative.

b) **Calamity,** TSAI: disaster from outside; flood, plague, drought, blight, ruin; contrasts with blunder, SHENG, indicating personal fault. The ideogram: water and fire, elemental powers. **Outside,** WAI: outer, exterior, external; people working in places other than their home; unfamiliar, foreign; the upper trigram, as opposed to inside, NEI, the lower.

Origin, TZU: source, beginning, ground; cause, reason, motive; line of descent; path to the origin; yourself, intrinsic. **My/me/I,** WO: first person pronoun; indicates an unusually strong emphasis on your own subjective experience.

Respect(ful), CHING: reverent, attentive; stand in awe of, honor; inner respect; contrasts with courtesy, KUNG, good manners. The ideogram: teacher's rod taming speech and attitude. **Consider,** SHEN: act carefully, seriously; cautious, attentive, circumspect; still, quiet, sincere. The ideogram: heart and true. **Destroy,** PAI: ruin, defeat, violate, subvert, break.

Six at fourth

a) Attending in blood.
　Issue forth from the origin in the cave.

b) Attending in blood.
　Yield and use hearkening indeed.

You are in immediate danger. Whatever you are doing, stop! Get out of the place where you are trapped. You can save things now if you will only listen.

Associated Contexts a) **Blood**, HSÜEH: yin fluid that maintains life; rain; money, property.
　　Issue forth(from), CH'U: emerge from, come out of, proceed from, spring from; the Action of the trigram Shake, CHEN; contrary of enter, JU. The ideogram: stem with branches and leaves emerging. **Origin**, TZU: source, beginning, ground; cause, reason, motive; line of descent; path to the origin; your self, intrinsic. **Cave**, HSÜEH: hole used for dwelling; cavern, den, pit; open grave.

b) **Yield(to)**, SHUN: give way and bear produce; comply, agree, follow, obey; unresisting, docile, flexible; nourish, provide; the Action of the trigram Field, K'UN. The ideogram: head and current, water flowing from the head of a river, yielding to the banks. **Hearken**, T'ING: listen to, obey, accept, acknowledge; examine, judge, decide. The ideogram: ear and actualizing-tao, hear and obey.

Nine at fifth

a) Attending on liquor and eating.
　Trial: auspicious.

b) Liquor and eating, Trial: auspicious.
　Use centering and correcting indeed.

This is the meal shared with the spirits, the ancestors and noble people. Let pleasure, harmony, peace and joy open the way. Gather with others. This cheer brings you out of your isolation.

Associated Contexts a) **Liquor**, CHIU: alcoholic beverages, distilled spirits; spirit which perfects the good and evil in human nature. The ideogram: liquid above fermenting must, separating the spirits. **Eat**, SHIH: eat, ingest, swallow, devour; incorporate.

b) **Centering correcting,** CHUNG CHENG: central and correct; make rectifying one-sidedness and error your central concern; reaching a stable center in yourself can correct the situation.

Six above

a) **Entering into the cave.**
   Possessing, not urging, visitors.
   Three people are coming.
   Respect them: completing is auspicious.

b) **Not urging's visitors coming.**
   Respect them: completing is auspicious.
   Although not an appropriate situation, this means
                                 not yet letting go the great.

Associated Contexts a) **Enter,** JU: penetrate, go into, enter on, progress; put into, encroach on; the Action of the trigram Ground, SUN, contrary of issue-forth, CH'U. **Cave,** HSÜEH: hole used for dwelling; cavern, den, pit; open grave.

Urge, SU: strong specific desire; quick, hurried; call, invite. **Visitor,** K'O: guest; stranger, foreign, from afar; squatter.

Three, SAN: number three, third time or place; active phases of a cycle; superlative; beginning of repetition. **People,** person, JEN: humans individually and collectively; an individual; humankind. Image of Hexagrams 13 and 37. **Come,** LAI, and go, WANG, describe the stream of time as it flows from future through present to past; come, LAI, indicates what is approaching; move toward, arrive at; keyword.

Respect(ful), CHING: reverent, attentive; stand in awe of, honor; inner respect; contrasts with courtesy, KUNG, good manners. The ideogram: teacher's rod taming speech and attitude. **Them/it, have(it)/'s,** CHIH: expresses possession, directly or as an object pronoun. **Complete,** CHUNG: end of a cycle that begins the next; last, whole, all; contrasts with exhaust, CH'IUNG, final end. The ideogram: silk cocoons, follow and ice, winter linking one year with the next.

b) **Although,** SUI: even though, supposing that, if, even if. **Appropriate,** TANG: suitable; opportune, convenient; adequate, competent; equal to; whole lines in uneven places and opened lines in even places. **Not-yet,** WEI: temporal negative; something will but has not yet occurred; contrary of already, CHI. Image of Hexagram 64. **Great,** TA: big, noble, important, very; orient the will toward a self-imposed goal, impose direction; ability to lead or guide your life; contrasts with small, HSIAO, flexible adaptation to what crosses your path; keyword. Image of Hexagrams 14, 26, 28, 34. **Let-go**, SHIH: lose, omit, miss, fail, let slip; out of control. The ideogram: drop from the hand.

6

ARGUING ▮ *SUNG*

Conflict, quarrels, arguments; express what you feel; resolve or retreat from conflict.

Arguing describes your situation in terms of a dispute. Its symbols are a council of war, pleading a case before the Prince or a lover's complaint. The way to deal with it is to clarify and actively express your viewpoint without trying to escalate the conflict. Act this way with confidence. You are linked to the spirits and they will carry you through. Dispute things. Present your case. Ask for justice. Don't be afraid or intimidated. Restrain your fear of authority. Don't give in, but don't exaggerate or get involved in petty wrangles. Staying in the center will generate meaning and good fortune by releasing transformative energy. It is advantageous to see great people. Visit those who are important and can give you advice. Try to become aware of the real purpose behind your desire. This will bring profit and insight. Don't try to bring your plans to completion. You would be cut off from the spirits and left open to danger. It is not the right time to embark on a significant enterprise or enter the stream of life with a purpose.

● *Image of the Situation*

> Arguing, there is a connection to the spirits. Blocking alarm.
> Centering auspicious. Completing: pitfall.
> Advantageous: to see the Great People.
> Not Advantageous: step into the Great River.

Associated Contexts **Argue**, SUNG: dispute, plead in court, contend before a ruler, demand justice; wrangles, quarrels, litigation. The ideogram: words and public, public disputation. **Connection to the spirits**, YU FU: inner and outer are in accord; confidence of the spirits has been captured; sincere, truthful; proper to take action. **Block**, CHIH: obstruct, stop up, close, restrain, fill up. **Alarm**, T'I: alarmed and cautious; respect, regard, fear; stand in awe of. The ideogram: heart and versatile, the heart aware of sudden change.

Center, CHUNG: inner, central; put in the center; middle, stable point enabling you to face inner and outer changes; middle line of trigram. The

ideogram: field divided in two equal parts. Image of Hexagram 61. **Auspicious**, CHI: leads to the experience of meaning; favorable, propitious, advantageous, appropriate; keyword. The ideogram: scholar and mouth, wise words of a sage. **Complete**, CHUNG: end of a cycle that begins the next; last, whole, all; contrasts with exhaust, CH'IUNG, final end. The ideogram: silk cocoons, follow and ice, winter linking one year with the next. **Pitfall**, HSIUNG: leads away from the experience of meaning; stuck and exposed to danger, unable to take in the situation; flow of life and spirit is blocked; unfortunate, baleful; keyword.

Advantageous/Harvest, LI: advantageous, profitable; acute, insightful; benefit, nourish; third stage of the Time Cycle. **See**, CHIEN: seeing in all its aspects: vision, being visible, forming mental images; visit, call on, consult. The ideogram: eye above person, active and receptive sight. **Great People**, TA JEN: important, noble, influential; those who impose a ruling principle on their lives; effect of the great within an individual; keyword.

Step into the Great River, SHE TA CH'UAN: consciously moving into the flow of time; enter the stream of life with a goal or purpose; embark on a significant enterprise.

- *Outer and Inner Aspects*

☰**Force**: The force of heaven struggles on, persistent and unwearied; heavenly bodies persist in their orbits. **Force** is the center of the yin hemicycle, completing the formative process.

Connection to the outer: struggling forces are bound together in dynamic tension, the Metallic Moment culminating. **Force** brings elements to grips, creating enduring relations.

☵**Gorge**: Stream ventures and falls into the gorge, flowing on through toil and danger. Gorge ends the yin hemicycle by leveling and dissolving forms.

Connection to the inner: flooding and leveling dissolve direction and shape, the Streaming Moment. **Gorge** ventures, falls, toils and flows on.

Without a strong inner base for action, outer struggle must expresses itself as verbal **arguing**.

- *Hidden Possibilities*

Nuclear trigrams **Ground**, SUN, and **Radiance**, LI, result in Nuclear Hexagram 37, **Dwelling People**, CHIA JEN. The opposition and contradiction in **arguing** can be resolved by the fellow feeling of people **dwelling** and living together.

- *Sequence*

> Drinking and eating necessarily possesses Arguing.
> Accepting this lets you use Arguing.

Associated Contexts **Drinking and eating,** YIN SHIH: comprehensive term for eating, drinking and breathing; a meal, eating together. **Necessarily,** PI: unavoidably, indispensably, certainly. **Possess,** YU: in possession of, have, own; opposite of lack, WU.

Accepting ... use: activating this hexagram depends on understanding and accepting the previous statement.

- *Contrasted Definitions*

> Attending means not advancing.
> Arguing means not connecting.

Associated Contexts **Attend,** HSÜ: take care of, look out for, care or service of; turn your mind to; needs; obstinate, fixed on; wait, await, wait on; hesitate, doubt. The ideogram: rain and stopped, compelled to wait, or rain and origin, providing what is needed. Image of Hexagram 5. **Advance,** CHIN: exert yourself, make progress, climb; be promoted; further the development of, augment; adopt a religion or conviction; offer, introduce. **Indeed/is/means,** YEH: intensifier, connective; indicates comment on previous statement.

Connect, CH'IN: attach to, approach, come near; cherish, help, favor; intimate; relatives, kin.

- *Symbol Tradition*

> Heaven associating with stream,
> contradicting movements. Arguing.
> A chün tzu uses arousing affairs to plan beginnings.

Associated Contexts **Heaven,** T'IEN: highest; sky, firmament, heavens; power above the human as opposed to earth, TI, below; the Symbol of the trigram Force, CH'IEN. The ideogram: great and the one above. **Associate(with),** YÜ: consort with, combine; companions; group, band, company; agree with, comply, help. The ideogram: pair of hands reaching downward meets a pair of hands reaching upward, helpful association. **Stream,** SHUI: flowing water; fluid, dissolving; river, tide, flood; the Symbol of the trigram Gorge, K'AN. The ideogram: rippling water. **Contradict,**

WEI: oppose, disregard, disobey; seditious, perverse. **Move**, HSING: move or move something; motivate, emotionally moving; walk, act, do. The ideogram: stepping left then right.

Chün tzu: ideal of a person who uses divination to order his/her life in accordance with tao rather than wilful intention; keyword. **Use(of)**, YI: make use of, by means of, owing to; employ, make functional. **Arouse**, TSO: stir up, stimulate, rouse from inactivity; generate; appear, arise. The ideogram: person and beginning. **Affairs**, SHIH: all kinds of personal activity; matters at hand; business, occupation; manage a business, case in court. **Plan**, MOU: plot, ponder, deliberate; project, device, stratagem. **Begin**, SHIH: commence, start, open; earliest, first; beginning of a time-span, ended by completion, CHUNG. The ideogram: woman and eminent, beginning new life.

● *Image Tradition*

> Arguing. The Strong above, venturing below. [I]
> Venturing and persisting. Arguing.

> Arguing, there is a connection to the spirits. [II]
> Blocking alarm, centering is auspicious.
> Strong coming and acquiring the center indeed.

> Completing: pitfall. [III]
> Arguing does not permit accomplishment indeed.

> Advantageous: to see the Great People. [IV]
> Honor centering and correcting indeed.

> Not Harvesting: to step into the Great River. [V]
> This means entering into the abyss.

Associated Contexts **[I] Strong**, KANG: quality of the whole lines; firm, strong, unyielding, persisting. **Above**, SHANG: anything above, in all senses; higher, upper, outer; upper trigram; opposite of below, HSIA. **Venture**, HSIEN: risk without reserve; key point, point of danger; difficulty, obstruction that must be confronted; water falling and filling the holes on its way; the Action of the trigram Gorge, K'AN. The ideogram: mound and all or whole, everything engaged at one point. **Below**, HSIA: anything below, in all senses; lower, inner; lower trigram; opposite of above, SHANG.

Persist, CHIEN: strong, robust, dynamic, tenacious; continuous; unwearied heavenly bodies in their orbits; the Action of the trigram Force, CH'IEN.

[II] Come, LAI, and **go,** WANG, describe the stream of time as it flows from future through present to past; come, LAI, indicates what is approaching; move toward, arrive at; keyword. **Acquire,** TE: obtain the desired object; wish for, desire covetously; gains, possessions. The ideogram: go and obstacle, going through obstacles to the goal.

[III] Not permitting, PU K'O: not possible; contradicts an inherent principle. The ideogram: mouth and breath, silent consent. **Accomplish,** CH'ENG: complete, finish, bring about; perfect, full, whole; play your part, do your duty; mature. The ideogram: weapon and man, able to bear arms, thus fully developed.

[IV] Honor, SHANG: esteem, give high rank to; eminent; put one thing on top of another. **Centering correcting,** CHUNG CHENG: central and correct; make rectifying one-sidedness and error your central concern; reaching a stable center in yourself can correct the situation.

[V] Enter, JU: penetrate, go into, enter on, progress; put into, encroach on; the Action of the trigram Ground, SUN, contrary of issue-forth, CH'U. **Abyss,** YÜAN: deep hole or gulf, where backwaters eddy and accumulate; whirlpool; deep water.

● *Transforming Lines*

Initial six

a) Not a perpetual place, affairs.
The small possesses words, completing auspicious.

b) Not a perpetual place, affairs.
Arguing not permitting long living indeed.
Although the small possesses words,
one's differentiation brightening indeed.

This is not the place for you to be of service. You are discussing trivial affairs. Be done with it. End it and leave. The way is open to you. Brighten your awareness and you will see things clearly.

Associated Contexts a) **Perpetual,** YUNG: continuing; everlasting, ever-flowing. The ideogram: flowing water. **Place,** SO: where something belongs or comes from; residence, dwelling; habitual focus or object.
   Small, HSIAO: little, common, unimportant; adapting to what crosses your path; ability to move in harmony with the vicissitudes of life; contrasts

with great, TA, self-imposed theme or goal; keyword. Image of Hexagrams 9 and 62. **Word**, YEN: speech, spoken words, sayings; talk, discuss, address. The ideogram: mouth and rising vapor, words as speech.

b) **Long living**, CHANG: enduring, constant; senior, superior, greater; increase, prosper; respect, elevate.

Although, SUI: even though, supposing that, if, even if. **One's/one**, CH'I: third person pronoun; also: it/its, he/his, she/hers, they/theirs. **Differentiate**, PIEN: argue, dispute, criticize; sophisticated, artful. The ideogram: words and sharp or pungent. **Brightness**, MING: light-giving aspect of burning, heavenly bodies and consciousness; with fire, the Symbol of the trigram Radiance, LI.

Nine at second

a) Not controlling through Arguing.
Convert and escape to your capital,
To your people, three hundred doors.
Without blunder.

b) Not controlling through Arguing.
Converting and escaping, skulking indeed.
Below an origin, above Arguing.
The distress culminating means reaping.

You cannot win this fight, so change your plans. Go back to your own people, where the doors are open. Use any means necessary to effect your escape. This is not a mistake. When the distress comes to an end, you can emerge from hiding. Your return will be welcomed.

Associated Contexts a) **Control**, K'O: command; check, impede, prevail, obstruct, repress; adequate, able. The ideogram: roof beams support a house, controlling the structure.

Convert, KUEI: change to another form, persuade; return to yourself or the place where you belong; restore, revert, become loyal; turn into; give a young girl in marriage. The ideogram: arrive and wife, become mistress of a household. Image of Hexagram 54. **Escape**, P'U: flee, run away, turn tail; deserter, fugitive. The ideogram: go and first, precipitous flight. **One's/one**, CH'I: third person pronoun; a,lso: it/its, he/his, she/hers, they/theirs. **Capital**, YI: populous fortified city, center and symbol of the domain it rules. The ideogram: enclosure and official seal.

People, person, JEN: humans individually and collectively; an individual; humankind. Image of Hexagrams 13 and 37. **Three,** SAN: number three, third time or place; active phases of a cycle; superlative; beginning of repetition. **Hundred,** PO: numerous, many, all; a whole class or type. **Door,** HU: inner door, chamber door; a household; contrasts with gate, MEN, the outer door.

Without, WU: devoid of; -less as suffix. **Blunder,** SHENG: mistake due to ignorance or fault; contrasts with calamity, TSAI, disaster from without. The ideogram: eye and grow, a film clouding sight.

b) **Skulk,** TS'UAN: sneak away and hide; furtive, stealthy; seduce into evil. The ideogram: cave and rat, rat lurking in its hole.

Origin, TZU: source, beginning, ground; cause, reason, motive; line of descent; path to the origin; yourself, intrinsic.

Distress, HUAN: tribulation, grief, affliction. The ideogram: heart and clamour, the heart distressed. **Culminate,** CHIH: bring to the highest degree; arrive at the end or summit; superlative. **Reap,** TO: harvest, collect, gather up, pick; arrange. The ideogram: hand and join, taking in both hands.

Six at third

a) **Take in the ancient actualizing tao. Trial.**
   Adversity, completing is auspicious.
   Maybe adhering to a king's affairs:
   Without accomplishment.

b) **Taking in ancient actualizing tao.**
   Adhering to the above is auspicious indeed.

To deal with this you need the power and the insight of the ancient sages. You are facing a hoard of things from the past that come back to haunt you. Take heart and fight your way through, even though your social duties may suffer.

Associated Contexts a) **Eat,** SHIH: eat, ingest, swallow, devour; incorporate, take in. **Ancient,** CHIU: of old, long before; worn out, spoiled; defunct. **Actualize tao,** TE: realize tao in action; power, virtue; ability to follow the course traced by the ongoing process of the cosmos; keyword. The ideogram: to go, straight, and heart. Linked with acquire, TE: acquiring that which makes a being become what it is meant to be. **Trial,** CHEN: inquiry by divination and its result; righteous, firm; separating wheat from chaff; the kernel, the proven core; fourth stage of the Time Cycle. The ideogram: pearl and divination.

Adversity, LI: danger; threatening, malevolent demon. This has two

aspects: grind, sharpen, improve, perfect, stimulate; and: poisonous, sinister, cruel, contrary. It indicates a spirit or ghost that seeks revenge by inflicting suffering upon the living. Pacifying or exorcizing such a spirit can have a healing effect. The ideogram: sheltering cliff and stinging insect.

Maybe/"someone", HUO: possible but not certain, perhaps. **Adhere(to)**, TS'UNG: follow a way, hold to a doctrine, school, or person; hear and comply with, agree to; forced to follow, follower. The ideogram: two men walking, one following the other. **King(hood)**, WANG: effective ruler, by authority of the Emperor, from whom others derive their power.

Without, WU: devoid of; -less as suffix.

Nine at fourth

a) **Not controlling through Arguing.**
Returning, approaching fate.
Deny it Security Trial: auspicious.

b) **Returning, approaching fate.**
Denying quiet Trial.
Not letting go indeed.

You cannot win, so change your plans. Return to yourself. A change of fate is approaching. Have no fear. You are safe. Stay quiet, accepting and peaceful. This is a crucial moment.

Associated Contexts a) **Control**, K'O: command; check, impede, prevail, obstruct, repress; adequate, able. The ideogram: roof beams support a house, controlling the structure.

Return, FU: go back, turn back to the starting point; recur, reappear, come again; restore, recover, retrace; an earlier time or place. The ideogram: step and retrace a path. Image of Hexagram 24. **Approach**, CHI: come near to, advance toward; about to do; soon. **Fate**, mandate, MING: individual destiny; birth and death as limits of life; issue orders with authority; consult the gods. The ideogram: mouth and order, words with heavenly authority.

Deny, YÜ: retract, repudiate; deterioration, regress. **Secure**, AN: peaceful, still, settled; calm, tranquilize. The ideogram: woman under a roof, a tranquil home. **Trial**, CHEN: test by ordeal; inquiry by divination and its result; righteous, firm; separating wheat from chaff; the kernel, the proven core; fourth stage of the Time Cycle. The ideogram: pearl and divination.

b) **Let go**, SHIH: lose, omit, miss, fail, let slip; out of control. The ideogram: drop from the hand.

Nine at fifth

a) Arguing. Spring, auspicious.

b) Arguing, Spring auspicious.
Use centering and correcting indeed.

Now is the time to convince people. State your case with confidence and expect positive results. This resolves the situation and opens the way. The bonds created lead to great things.

Associated Contexts a) **Spring,** YUAN: source, origin, head; great, excellent; arise, begin, generating power; first stage of the Time Cycle.

Nine above

a) Maybe bestowing this pouched belt.
Completing dawn three times strips it away.

b) Using Arguing to accept submitting.
Truly not standing respectfully indeed.

You are contesting for mastery. If you think you can win this way, then think again. Anything you gain will soon vanish. This really is not worthy of you. It will bring you no respect at all.

Associated Contexts a) **Maybe/"someone",** HUO: possible but not certain, perhaps. **Bestow,** HSI: grant, confer upon; reward, gift. The ideogram: metal used in coins and insignia. **'s/have(it)/it/them,** CHIH: expresses possession, directly or as an object pronoun. **Pouched belt,** P'AN TAI: sash that serves as a purse; money-belt.

Dawn, CHAO: early morning, before daybreak; opposite of nightfall, HSI. **Three-times,** SAN: serial repetition. **Strip away:** CH'IH: strip (of rank), take away; undress; put an end to. **It/them/have(-it)/'s,** CHIH: expresses possession, directly or as an object pronoun.

b) **Accept,** SHOU: accept, make peace with, agree to; at rest, satisfied; patient. **Submit,** FU: yield to, serve; undergo.

Truly, YI: statement is true and precise. **Stand,** TSU: base, foot, leg; rest on, support; stance. The ideogram: foot and calf resting. **Respect(ful),** CHING: reverent, attentive; stand in awe of, honor; inner respect; contrasts with courtesy, KUNG: good manners. The ideogram: teacher's rod taming speech and attitude.

LEGIONS/LEADING ▪ *SHIH*

Organize, mobilize, lead; armies and soldiers; a master craftsman, martial arts master; discipline, power.

Legions/Leading describes your situation in terms of organizing a confused heap of things into functional units so you can take effective action. Its symbol is the great King Wu gathering the armies to overthrow the tyrant of Shang. The way to deal with it is to organize yourself and put yourself in order. Develop the capacity to lead. Look at the people you respect, and use them as models. Find who and what you need. This generates meaning and good fortune by releasing transformative energy. The ideal of this army is not just to fight. It brings order, and protects people who cannot protect themselves. It founds cities and defends what is necessary for people to live their lives. It is not a mistake to use force in this way.

- *Image of the Situation*

> **Legions: Trial.**
> **Experienced people auspicious.**
> **Without fault.**

Associated Contexts **Legions/leading,** SHIH: troops; an organized unit, a metropolis; leader, general, model, master; organize, make functional; take as a model, imitate. The ideogram: heap and whole, organize confusion into functional units. **Trial,** CHEN: inquiry by divination and its result; righteous, firm; separating wheat from chaff; the kernel, the proven core; fourth stage of the Time Cycle. The ideogram: pearl and divination.

Experienced, CHANG: worthy of respect; standard by which others are measured. **People, person,** JEN: humans individually and collectively; an individual; humankind. Image of Hexagrams 13 and 37. **Auspicious,** CHI: leads to the experience of meaning; favorable, propitious, advantageous, appropriate; keyword. The ideogram: scholar and mouth, wise words of a sage.

Without fault, WU CHIU: no error or harm in the situation.

● *Outer and Inner Aspects*

☷ **Field**: The field of earth yields and sustains, serving in order to produce. **Field** is the equalizing point between yin and yang where things labor and serve.

Connection to the outer: the common labor of sowing and hoarding, the Earthy Moment. **Field** produces concrete results through serving.

☵ **Gorge**: Stream ventures and falls into the gorge, flowing on through toil and danger. **Gorge** ends the yin hemicycle by leveling and dissolving forms.

Connection to the inner: flooding and leveling dissolve direction and shape, the Streaming Moment. **Gorge** ventures, falls, toils and flows on.

An inner willingness for work and danger sustains the **legions** and their **leaders** involving service.

● *Hidden Possibility*

Nuclear trigrams **Field**, K'UN, and **Shake**, CHEN, result in Nuclear Hexagram 24, **Returning**, FU. **Legions** constant forward thrust depends on continually **returning** to the starting point to begin again.

● *Sequence*

> **Arguing necessarily possesses crowds rising up.**
> **Accepting this lets you use Legions.**
> **Legions imply crowds indeed.**

Associated Contexts **Argue**, SUNG: dispute, plead in court, contend before a ruler, demand justice; wrangles, quarrels, litigation. The ideogram: words and public, public disputation. Image of Hexagram 6. **Necessarily**, PI: unavoidably, indispensably, certainly. **Possess**, YU: in possession of, have, own; opposite of lack, WU. **Crowds**, CHUNG: many people, large group; majority; in common. **Rise up**, CH'I: stand up, lift; undertake, begin, originate.

Accepting ... use: activating this hexagram depends on understanding and accepting the previous statement.

Imply, CHE: further signify; additional meaning. **Indeed/is/means**, YEH: intensifier, connective; indicates comment on previous statement.

- *Contrasted Definitions*

  Grouping: delighting.
  Legions: grieving.

  Associated Contexts **Group**, PI: compare and select, order things and put them in classes; find what you belong with; sort, examine correspondences; choose and harmonize; unite. The ideogram: person who stops walking, looking around to examine and compare. Image of Hexagram 8. **Delight**, LO: take joy or pleasure in; pleasant, relaxed; also: music as harmony, elegance and pleasure.

  Grieve(over), YU: sorrow, melancholy; mourn; anxious, careworn; hidden sorrow. The ideogram: heart, head, and limp, heart-sick and anxious.

- *Symbol Tradition*

  Earth center possessing stream. Legions.
  A chün tzu uses tolerating the commoners to accumulate crowds.

  Associated Contexts **Earth**, TI: ground on which the human world rests; basis of all things, nourishes all things; the Symbol of the trigram Field, K'UN: **Center**, CHUNG: inner, central; put in the center; middle, stable point enabling you to face inner and outer changes; middle line of trigram. The ideogram: field divided in two equal parts. Image of Hexagram 61. **Stream**, SHUI: flowing water; fluid, dissolving; river, tide, flood; the Symbol of the trigram Gorge, K'AN. The ideogram: rippling water.

  Chün tzu: ideal of a person who uses divination to order his/her life in accordance with tao rather than wilful intention; keyword. **Use(of)**, YI: make use of, by means of, owing to; employ, make functional. **Tolerate**, JUNG: allow, contain, endure, bear with; accept graciously. The ideogram: full stream bed, tolerating and containing. **Commoners**, MIN: class of workers the state draws on to sustain the social hierarchy; undeveloped potential outside the organized personality. **Accumulate**: CH'U: retain, hoard, gather, herd together; control, restrain; domesticate, tame, train; raise, feed, sustain, bring up. The ideogram: field and black, fertile black soil good for pastures, accumulated through retaining silt. Image of Hexagrams 9 and 26.

● *Image Tradition*

> Legions: crowds indeed. [I]
> Trial: correcting indeed.
> The ability to use the crowds correctly
>
> Actually permits using kinghood. [II]
> Strong centered and corresponding.
>
> Movement venturing and yielding. [III]
> Using the latter poisons Below Heaven and
> the commoners adhere to it.
> Actually auspicious, furthermore wherefore faulty?

Associated Contexts [I] **Correct**, CHENG: rectify deviation or one-sidedness; proper, straight, exact, regular; constant, rule, model. The ideogram: stop and one, hold to one thing.

Able, NENG: enable; ability, power, skill, art; competent, talented; duty, function, capacity. The ideogram: an animal with strong hooves and bones, able to carry and defend.

[II] **Actually**, YI: truly, really, at present. The ideogram: a dart and done, strong intention fully expressed. **Permit**, K'O: possible because in harmony with an inherent principle. The ideogram: mouth and breath, silent consent. **King(hood)**, WANG: effective ruler, by authority of the Emperor, from whom others derive their power.

Strong, KANG: quality of the whole lines; firm, strong, unyielding, persisting. **Correspond**, YING: be in agreement or harmony; resonate together, invoke and fulfil each other; answer to, suitable; relation between the lines (1:4, 2:5, 3:6) when they form the pair opened and whole, supple and strong. The ideogram: heart and obey.

[III] **Move**, HSING: move or move something; motivate, emotionally moving; walk, act, do. The ideogram: stepping left then right. **Venture**, HSIEN: risk without reserve; key point, point of danger; difficulty, obstruction that must be confronted; water falling and filling the holes on its way; the Action of the trigram Gorge, K'AN. The ideogram: mound and all or whole, everything engaged at one point. **Yield(to)**, SHUN: give way and bear produce; comply, agree, follow, obey; unresisting, docile, flexible; nourish, provide; the Action of the trigram Field, K'UN. The ideogram: head and current, water flowing from the head of a river, yielding to the banks.

Latter, TZ'U: what was last spoken of. **Poison**, TU: noxious, malignant, hurtful, destructive; despise. **Below Heaven**, T'IEN HSIA: the human world,

between heaven and earth. **Adhere(to)**, TS'UNG: follow a way, hold to a doctrine, school, or person; hear and comply with, agree to; forced to follow, follower. The ideogram: two men walking, one following the other. **It/them/have(it)/'s**, CHIH: expresses possession, directly or as an object pronoun.

Furthermore, YU: in addition to; higher degree of. **Wherefore**, HO: interrogative: why? for what reason? what is? and affirmation: therefore, for that reason. **Fault**, CHIU: unworthy conduct that leads to harm, illness, misfortune. The ideogram: person and differ, differ from what you should be.

- *Transforming Lines*

    Initial six

    a) Legions issue forth using ordinance.
       Obstructing virtue: pitfall.

    b) Legions issuing forth using ordinance.
       Letting go ordinance: pitfall indeed.

Everything needs rules and regulations. Without them, energy and enthusiasm disintegrate. But be sure the rules you set are not obstructing your real power.

Associated Contexts a) **Issue forth(from)**, CH'U: emerge from, come out of, proceed from, spring from; the Action of the trigram Shake, CHEN; contrary of enter, JU. The ideogram: stem with branches and leaves emerging. **Ordinance**, LÜ: law, fixed regulation; regulate by law, divide into right and wrong. The ideogram: writing and move, codes that govern action.

    Obstruct, P'I: closed, stopped; bar the way; obstacle; unfortunate, wicked; refuse, disapprove, deny. The ideogram: mouth and not, blocked communication. Image of Hexagram 12. **Virtue**, TSANG: essential force or quality; generous, good, dexterous. **Pitfall**, HSIUNG: leads away from the experience of meaning; stuck and exposed to danger, unable to take in the situation; flow of life and spirit is blocked; unfortunate, baleful; keyword.

b) **Let go**, SHIH: lose, omit, miss, fail, let slip; out of control. The ideogram: drop from the hand.

Nine at second

a) Located in the Legions' center, auspicious.
Without fault.
The king three times bestows a mandate.

b) Located in the Legions' center, auspicious.
Receiving heavenly favor indeed.
The king three times bestows a mandate.
Cherishing the myriad fiefdoms indeed.

You are in the leader's position, at the center of a well-organized force. You receive a mandate to act. Make no mistake. This is an honor. Carrying this through will change your life.

Associated Contexts a) **Locate(in)**, TSAI: live in, dwell, reside; belong to, involved with, depend on; within. The ideogram: earth and persevere, place on the earth.

Three times, SAN: serial repetition. **Bestow**, HSI: grant, confer upon; reward, gift. The ideogram: metal used in coins and insignia. **Fate/ mandate**, MING: individual destiny; birth and death as limits of life; issue orders with authority; consult the gods. The ideogram: mouth and order, words with heavenly authority.

b) **Receive**, CH'ENG: receive gifts or commands from superiors or customers; take in hand; catch falling water. The ideogram: accepting a seal of office. **Heaven**, T'IEN: highest; sky, firmament, heavens; power above the human as opposed to earth, TI, below; the Symbol of the trigram Force, CH'IEN. The ideogram: great and the one above. **Favor**, CH'UNG: receive or confer gifts, obtain grace, win favor; dote on a woman; gifted for.

Cherish, HUAI: dwell on, think of; carry in the heart or womb; cling to. The ideogram: heart and hide, cherish in the heart. **Myriad**, WAN: countless; many, everyone; lit.: ten thousand. The ideogram: swarm of insects. **Fiefdom**, PANG: region governed by a feudatory, an order of nobility.

Six at third

a) Legions maybe carting corpses.
Pitfall.

b) Legions maybe carting corpses.
The great will be without achievement indeed.

Dead bodies, old memories, useless ideas and false images – mourning the past will defeat you. Get rid of it. Carry your inspiration with you and trust in the spirit. You must do it now. If you go on mourning the past you will lose your real sense of purpose.

Associated Contexts a) **Maybe, "someone"**, HUO: possible, perhaps; term indicating that spirit is active. **Cart**, YÜ: carrying capacity of a vehicle; contain, hold, sustain. **Corpse**, SHIH: dead human body; effigy, statue; inefficient, useless; impersonate.

    Pitfall, HSIUNG: leads away from the experience of meaning; stuck and exposed to danger, unable to take in the situation; flow of life and spirit is blocked; unfortunate, baleful; keyword.

b) **Great**, TA: big, noble, important, very; orient the will toward a self-imposed goal, impose direction; ability to lead or guide your life; contrasts with small, HSIAO, flexible adaptation to what crosses your path; keyword. Image of Hexagrams 14, 26, 28, 34. **Achieve**, KUNG: work done, results; real accomplishment, praise, worth, merit. The ideogram: workman's square and forearm, combining craft and strength.

    Six at fourth

    a) Legions on the left, resting.
       Without fault.

    b) The left resting, without fault.
       Not yet letting go the rules indeed.

A tactical retreat or a move towards peace. In any case, value this time of rest. It is not a mistake.

Associated Contexts a) **Left**, TSO: left side, left hand; secondary; peace, retreat; deputy, assistant; inferior. **Rest(ing place)**, TZ'U: camp, inn, shed; halting-place, breathing-spell; put in consecutive order. The ideogram: two and breath, pausing to breath.

b) **Not yet**, WEI: temporal negative; something will but has not yet occurred; contrary of already, CHI. Image of Hexagram 64. **Let go**, SHIH: lose, omit, miss, fail, let slip; out of control. The ideogram: drop from the hand. **Rules**, CH'ANG: unchanging principles; regular, constant, habitual; maintain laws and customs.

Six at fifth

a) In the fields there are wildfowl.
　Advantageous: holding on to words.
　Without fault.
　The long living son conducts the Legions.
　The junior son carting corpses.
　"Stay in mourning?"; Trial, pitfall.

b) The long living son conducts the Legions.
　Using the center to move indeed.
　The junior son carts the corpses.
　Commissioning not appropriate indeed.

Conflict has broken out and you must engage whether you like it or not. Keep hold of your tongue and you will avoid mistakes. Seize the enemy. Be aggressive. Do not leave the dirty work to others. Get rid of old ideas, irrelevant images and bad memories. Do not stay in mourning. Carry your inspiration with you and trust in the spirit.

Associated Contexts a) **Fields**, T'IEN: cultivated land, plantation; also: hunting, game in the fields cannot escape the hunt. The ideogram: square divided into four sections, delineating fields. **Wildfowl**, CH'IN: all wild and game birds; game animals untamed; military leaders.

Advantageous/Harvest, LI: advantageous, profitable; acute, insightful; benefit, nourish; third stage of the Time Cycle. **Hold on(to)**, CHIH: lay hold of, seize, take in hand; keep, maintain, look after. The ideogram: criminal and seize. **Word**, YEN: speech, spoken words, sayings; talk, discuss, address. The ideogram: mouth and rising vapor, words as speech.

Long living, CHANG: enduring, constant; senior, superior, greater; increase, prosper; respect, elevate. **Son(hood)**, TZU: living up to ideal of ancestors as highest human development; act with concern and reverence; male child; offspring, posterity; seed, kernel, egg; sage, teacher; nadir, deepest point, midnight, mid-winter. **Conduct**, SHUAI: lead; leader, chief, commander; follow, follower.

Junior, TI: younger relatives who owe respect to their elders. **Cart**, YÜ: carrying capacity of a vehicle; contain, hold, sustain. **Corpse**, SHIH: dead human body; effigy, statue; inefficient, useless; impersonate.

Pitfall, HSIUNG: leads away from the experience of meaning; stuck and exposed to danger, unable to take in the situation; flow of life and spirit is blocked; unfortunate, baleful; keyword.

b) **Commission,** SHIH: employ for a task; command, order; messenger, agent. The ideogram: person and office. **Appropriate,** TANG: suitable; opportune, convenient; adequate, competent; equal to; whole lines in uneven places and opened lines in even places.

Six above

a) The Great Chief possesses a mandate.
Disclosing the city, receiving the dwellers.
Small People not availed of.

b) The Great Chief possesses a mandate.
Use correcting to achieve it indeed.
Small People not availed of.
Necessarily disarraying the fiefdoms indeed.

You have received a mandate to found a new city. Use all your powers to create a beautiful place. Don't simply adapt. Though you must disturb things, have no fear. Simply do what you have to do.

Associated Contexts a) **Great,** TA: big, noble, important, very; orient the will toward a self-imposed goal, impose direction; ability to lead or guide your life; contrasts with small, HSIAO, flexible adaptation to what crosses your path; keyword. Image of Hexagrams 14, 26, 28, 34. **Chief,** CHÜN: effective ruler; preside over, take the lead; influence others; term of respect. The ideogram: mouth and director, giving orders. **Fate/mandate:** MING: individual destiny; birth and death as limits of life; issue orders with authority; consult the gods. The ideogram: mouth and order, words with heavenly authority.

Disclose, K'AI: open, reveal, unfold, display; enact rites, clear land; final phase of hemicycles in Universal Compass. The ideogram: house doors bursting open. **City,** KUO: area of only human constructions; political unit, polis. First of the territorial zones: city, suburbs, countryside, forests. **Receive,** CH'ENG: receive gifts or commands from superiors or customers; take in hand; catch falling water. The ideogram: accepting a seal of office. **Dwell,** CHI: home, house, household, family; domestic, within doors; live in. The ideogram: roof and pig or dog, the most valued domestic animals. Image of Hexagram 37.

Small People, HSIAO JEN: lowly, common, humble; those who adjust to circumstances with the flexibility of the small; effect of the small within an individual; keyword. **Avail of**, YUNG: take advantage of; benefit from, profit by; use for a specific purpose; apply to advantage. The ideogram: to divine and center, applying divination to central concerns.

b) **Achieve**, KUNG: work done, results; real accomplishment, praise, worth, merit. The ideogram: workman's square and forearm, combining craft and strength.

Disarray, LUAN: throw into disorder, mislay, confuse; out of place; discord, insurrection, anarchy. **Fiefdom**, PANG: region governed by a feudatory, an order of nobility.

GROUPING ▮ *PI*

Mutual support, spiritual kin; change how you think about things and who you are grouped with.

Grouping describes your situation in terms of the people and things with which your spirit connects you. Its symbol is the gathering of the spiritual husbandmen after the great hero Yü saved humanity by channeling off the waters of the flood. The way to deal with it is to look at who you group yourself with, and how you use ideas to categorize things. The way you put things and people together is changing. Stop and take a look around. Try to perceive essential qualities in order to get to the heart of the matter. Compare things and sort them out. Find what you belong with. You can ask your question in many different ways. The oracle will help you. This is not a mistake. It generates meaning and good fortune by releasing transformative energy. This is not a soothing time. Things are coming at you from all sides, demanding that you consider them. Do it now. Do not be late. If you put it off and try to manage it later, you will be cut off from the spirits and left open to danger.

● *Image of the Situation*

> Grouping, auspicious.
> Retracing the oracle consulting, Trial: a perpetual spring
> Without fault.
> Not soothing, on all sides coming.
> The late husbandman: pitfall.

Associated Contexts **Group,** PI: order things and put them in classes, compare and select; find what you belong with; compare, sort, examine correspondences; select and harmonize; unite. The ideogram: person who stops walking, looking around to examine and compare. **Auspicious,** CHI: leads to the experience of meaning; favorable, propitious, advantageous, appropriate; keyword. The ideogram: scholar and mouth, wise words of a sage.

Retrace, YÜAN: repeat, another; trace to the source. The ideogram: pure water at its source. **Oracle consulting,** SHIH: yarrow stalk divination; find your allotted destiny. **Spring,** YÜAN: source, origin, head; great, excellent;

arise, begin, generating power; first stage of the Time Cycle. **Perpetual**, YUNG: continuing; everlasting, ever-flowing. The ideogram: flowing water. **Trial**, CHEN: inquiry by divination and its result; righteous, firm; separating wheat from chaff; the kernel, the proven core; fourth stage of the Time Cycle. The ideogram: pearl and divination.

Without fault, WU CHIU: no error or harm in the situation.

Soothe, NING: calm, pacify; create peace of mind; tranquil, quiet. The ideogram: shelter above heart, dish and breath, physical and spiritual comfort. **Sides (on all sides)**, FANG: limits, boundaries; square, surface of the earth extending to the four cardinal points; everywhere. **Come**, LAI, and **go**, WANG, describe the stream of time as it flows from future through present to past; come, LAI, indicates what is approaching; move toward, arrive at; keyword.

After(wards)/later, HOU: come after in time, subsequent; put oneself after; the second; attendants, heirs, successors, posterity. **Husband**, FU: household manager; administer with thrift and prudence; responsible for; sustain with your earnings; old enough to assume responsibility; married man. **Pitfall**, HSIUNG: leads away from the experience of meaning; stuck and exposed to danger, unable to take in the situation; flow of life and spirit is blocked; unfortunate, baleful; keyword.

- *Outer and Inner Aspects*

☵ Gorge: Stream ventures and falls into the gorge, flowing on through toil and danger. **Gorge** ends the yin hemicycle by leveling and dissolving forms.

Connection to the outer: flooding and leveling dissolve direction and shape, the Streaming Moment. **Gorge** ventures, falls, toils and flows on.

☷ Field: The field of earth yields and sustains, serving in order to produce. **Field** is the equalizing point between yin and yang where things labor and serve.

Connection to the inner: the common labor of sowing and hoarding, the Earthy Moment. **Field** produces concrete results through serving.

The relation to the outer world dissolves and changes. New ways to **group** people and things appear on the inner field.

- *Hidden Possibility*

Nuclear trigrams **Bound**, KEN, and **Field**, KUN, result in Nuclear Hexagram 23, **Stripping**, PO. Finding new ways to **group** people and things depends on **stripping** away old ideas.

- *Sequence*

> Crowds necessarily possess a place to Group.
> Accepting this lets you use Grouping.
> Grouping implies Groups.

Associated Contexts **Crowds,** CHUNG: many people, large group; majority; in common. **Necessarily,** PI: unavoidably, indispensably, certainly. **Possess,** YU: in possession of, have, own; opposite of lack, WU. **Place,** SO: where something belongs or comes from; residence, dwelling; habitual focus or object.

    Accepting ... use: activating this hexagram depends on understanding and accepting the previous statement.

    Imply, CHE: further signify; additional meaning.

- *Contrasted Definitions*

> Grouping: delighting.
> Legions: grieving.

Associated Contexts **Delight,** LO: take joy or pleasure in; pleasant, relaxed; also: music as harmony, elegance and pleasure.

    Legions/leading, SHIH: troops; an organized unit, a metropolis; leader, general, model, master; organize, make functional; take as a model, imitate. The ideogram: heap and whole, organize confusion into functional units. Image of Hexagram 7. **Grieve,** YU: sorrow, melancholy; mourn; anxious, careworn; hidden sorrow. The ideogram: heart, head, and limp, heart-sick and anxious.

- *Symbol Tradition*

> Above earth possessing stream. Grouping.
> The Early Kings used installing myriad cities
> to connect the connoted feudatories.

Associated Contexts **Above,** SHANG: anything above, in all senses; higher, upper, outer; upper trigram; opposite of below, HSIA. **Earth,** TI: ground on which the human world rests; basis of all things, nourishes all things; the Symbol of the trigram Field, K'UN. **Stream,** SHUI: flowing water; fluid, dissolving; river, tide, flood; the Symbol of the trigram Gorge, K'AN. The ideogram: rippling water.

    Early Kings, HSIEN WANG: ideal rulers of old; the golden age, primal time, power in harmony with nature; model for the chün tzu. **Use(of)**, YI: make use of, by means of, owing to; employ, make functional. **Install,** CHIEN: set up, establish; confirm a position or law. **Myriad,** WAN: countless; many, everyone; lit.: ten thousand. The ideogram: swarm of insects. **City,** KUO: area of only human constructions; political unit, polis. First of the territorial zones: city, suburbs, countryside, forests. **Connect,** CH'IN: attach to, approach, come near; cherish, help, favor; intimate; relatives, kin. **Connote,** CHU: imply the meaning; signify. The ideogram: words and imply. **Feudatory,** HOU: nobles entrusted with governing the provinces; active in daily life rather than governing from the center; contrasts with prince, KUNG, executives at the court.

- *Image Tradition*

Grouping auspicious indeed. [I]
Grouping bracing indeed.
Yielding adhering to the below indeed.

Retrace the oracle consulting, Trial: perpetual Spring [II]
Without fault.
Using the strong center indeed.

Not soothing, on all sides coming. [III]
Above and Below corresponding indeed.
The late husbandman: pitfall.
His tao exhausted indeed.

Associated Contexts **[I] Indeed/is/means:** YEH: intensifier, connective; indicates comment on previous statement.

Brace/jawbones, FU: support, consolidate, reinforce, strengthen, stiffen, prop up, fix; steady, firm, rigid; help, rescue; support the speaking mouth. The ideogram: cart and great.

Yield(to), SHUN: give way and bear produce; comply, agree, follow, obey; unresisting, docile, flexible; nourish, provide; the Action of the trigram Field, K'UN. The ideogram: head and current, water flowing from the head of a river, yielding to the banks. **Adhere(to),** TS'UNG: follow a way, hold to a doctrine, school, or person; hear and comply with, agree to; forced to follow, follower. The ideogram: two men walking, one following the other. **Below,** HSIA: anything below, in all senses; lower, inner; lower trigram; opposite of above, SHANG.

[II] Strong, KANG: quality of the whole lines; firm, strong, unyielding,

persisting. **Center,** CHUNG: inner, central; put in the center; middle, stable point enabling you to face inner and outer changes; middle line of trigram. The ideogram: field divided in two equal parts. Image of Hexagram 61.

[III] **Above and Below,** SHANG HSIA: realm of dynamic interaction between the upper and the lower; the vertical dimension. **Correspond,** YING: be in agreement or harmony; resonate together, invoke and fulfil each other; answer to, suitable; relation between the lines (1:4, 2:5, 3:6) when they form the pair opened and whole, supple and strong. The ideogram: heart and obey.

One's/one, CH'I: third person pronoun; also: it/its, he/his, she/hers, they/theirs. **Tao:** way or path; ongoing process of being and the course it traces for each specific person or thing; keyword. The ideogram: go and head, leading and the path it creates. **Exhaust,** CH'IUNG: bring to an end; limit, extremity; destitute; investigate exhaustively; end without a new beginning. The ideogram: cave and naked person, bent with disease or old age.

- *Transforming Lines*

    Initial six

    a) There is a connection to the spirits, Grouping them.
    Without fault.
    There is a connection to the spirits, overfilling the jar.
    Completing coming possesses more auspiciousness.

    b) Grouping's initial six.
    Possessing more auspiciousness indeed.

Becoming part of this group will connect you with the flow of the spirit. This connection is certain. There is no mistake here. This group overflows with love and care. You will find there is more on the way.

Associated Contexts a) **There is ... spirits,** YU FU: inner and outer are in accord; confidence of the spirits has been captured; sincere, truthful; proper to take action. **It/them/have(it)/'s,** CHIH: expresses possession, directly or as an object pronoun.

Overfill, YING: at the point of overflowing; more than wanted, stretch beyond; replenished, full; arrogant. The ideogram: vessel and too much. **Jar,** FOU: earthenware vessels; wine-jars and drums. The ideogram: jar containing liquor.

Complete, CHUNG: end of a cycle that begins the next; last, whole, all; contrasts with exhaust, CH'IUNG, final end. The ideogram: silk cocoons, follow and ice, winter linking one year with the next. **More,** T'O: another; add to.

b) **s/have(it)/it/them,** CHIH: expresses possession, directly or as an object pronoun.

Six at second

a) Grouping them, the origin inside.
    Trial: auspicious.

b) Grouping them, the origin inside.
    Not originating from letting go indeed.

Your connection puts you at the center of this group, a part of its origin. The way is open to you. Gather people around this. Don't let the connection slip through your fingers.

Associated Contexts a) 's/have(it)/it/them, CHIH: expresses possession, directly or as an object pronoun. **Origin,** TZU: source, beginning, ground; cause, reason, motive; line of descent; path to the origin; yourself, intrinsic. **Inside,** NEI: within, inner, interior; inside of the house and those who work there, particularly women; the lower trigram, as opposed to outside, WAI, the upper. The ideogram: border and enter, cross a border.

b) **Let go,** SHIH: lose, omit, miss, fail, let slip; out of control. The ideogram: drop from the hand.

Six at third

a) Grouping them: in no way people.

b) Grouping them: in no way people.
    Reaching, not truly injuring.

The people you are involved with will do you no good. These are the wrong people for you. Leave now before they do you harm. Reach out and you can escape injury.

Associated Contexts a) s/have(it)/it/them, CHIH: expresses possession, directly or as an object pronoun. **In no way people,** FEI JEN: there are no people, no people are involved; also: worthless people; barbarians, rebels, foreign slaves, captives.

b) **Reach(to)**, HU: arrive at a goal; reach toward and achieve; connect. **Truly**, YI: statement is true and precise. **Injure**, SHANG: hurt, wound, grieve, distress; mourn, sad at heart, humiliated.

Six at fourth

a) Outside Grouping them.
   Trial: auspicious.

b) Outside Grouping with respect to eminence.
   Use adhering to the above indeed.

You are outside this group, but don't let it bother you. You are in this position because of your moral and intellectual worth. Stick to your work and your values and you will influence them.

Associated Contexts a) **Outside**, WAI: outer, exterior, external; people working in places other than their home; unfamiliar, foreign; the upper trigram, as opposed to inside, NEI, the lower. **It/them/have(it)/'s**, CHIH: expresses possession, directly or as an object pronoun.

b) **With respect to**, YÜ: relates to, refers to; hold a position in. **Eminent**, HSIEN: moral and intellectual power; worthy, excellent, virtuous; sage second to the all-wise, SHENG.

Nine at fifth

a) Manifest Grouping.
   The king avails of three beaters,
   Lets go the preceding wildfowl.
   Capital people not admonished. Auspicious.

b) Manifest Grouping's auspicious.
   Situation correctly centered indeed.
   Stow away countering, grasp yielding.
   Letting go the preceding wildfowl indeed.
   This means capital people not admonished.
   This means commissioning the center above.

You are looking for connections and a social identity. Don't try to coerce or impress people. Don't admonish the people in the group. Let your virtue shine. This creates a true and willing bond. Deep affinities have a chance to work. Acting like this opens the way to real connections.

Associated Contexts a) **Manifest**, HSIEN: apparent, conspicuous; illustrious; make clear.

King(hood), WANG: effective ruler, by authority of the Emperor, from whom others derive their power. **Avail of,** YUNG: take advantage of; benefit from, profit by; use for a specific purpose; apply to advantage. The ideogram: to divine and center, applying divination to central concerns. **Three**, SAN: number three, third time or place; active phases of a cycle; superlative; beginning of repetition. **Beater**, CH'U: servants who drive animals toward hunters; order people to their places; drive on, whip up, animate, exhort.

Let go, SHIH: lose, omit, miss, fail, let slip; out of control. The ideogram: drop from the hand. **Precede**, CH'IEN: come before in time and thus in value; anterior, former, ancient; lead forward. **Wildfowl**, CH'IN: all wild and game birds; untamed game animals; military leaders.

Capital, YI: populous fortified city, center and symbol of the domain it rules. The ideogram: enclosure and official seal. **People, person,** JEN: humans individually and collectively; an individual; humankind. Image of Hexagrams 13 and 37. **Admonish**, CHIEH: make someone obey; rule of conduct, precept, warning. The ideogram: words and warning.

b) **'s/have(it)/it/them**, CHIH: expresses possession, directly or as an object pronoun.

Situation, WEI: place or seat according to rank; post, position, command; right, proper; established, arranged. The ideogram: person and stand, servants in their places. **Correct**, CHENG: rectify deviation or one-sidedness; proper, straight, exact, regular; constant, rule, model. The ideogram: stop and one, hold to one thing.

Stow(away), SHE: set aside, put away, store; halt, rest in; temporary lodgings, breathing-spell. **Counter**, NI: oppose, resist, seek out; contrary, rebellious, refractory. The ideogram: go and rise against, active revolt. **Grasp**, CH'Ü: lay hold of, take and use, seize, appropriate; grasp the meaning, understand. The ideogram: ear and hand, hear and grasp.

Commission, SHIH: employ for a task; command, order; messenger, agent. The ideogram: person and office.

Six above

a) **Without a head, Grouping them.**
　Pitfall.

b) **Without a head, Grouping them.**
　Without a place to complete indeed.

This is not the group for you. It has no goal and no purpose. Leave now or face disaster.

Associated Contexts a) **Head,** SHOU: literal head; leader, foremost; subject headings; beginning, model; superior, upper, front. **It/them/have(-it)/'s,** CHIH: expresses possession, directly or as an object pronoun.

b) **Complete,** CHUNG: end of a cycle that begins the next; last, whole, all; contrasts with exhaust, CH'IUNG, final end. The ideogram: silk cocoons, follow and ice, winter linking one year with the next.

9

SMALL ACCUMULATING
AND NURTURING ▪
HSIAO CH'U

Accumulate the small to do the great; helping one another; nurture, raise, support; develop through the small; dealings with the ghost world.

Small Accumulating describes your situation in terms of confronting a great variety of things that don't seem to be related. Its symbol is a procession that calls, gathers and feeds the ghosts and the seeds of new beings. The way to deal with it is to adapt to each thing that crosses your path in order to accumulate something great. Make an offering and you will succeed. Take the long view. Gather, herd together, retain and hoard all the little things that might seem unimportant. Think of yourself as raising animals, growing crops or bringing up children. Be flexible and adaptable. Tolerate and nourish things. The rain hasn't come yet, but the dense clouds that bring it are rolling in from the western frontier. The successful completion of your efforts is not far away.

- *Image of the Situation*

> Small Accumulating, Growing.
> Shrouding clouds, not raining.
> Originate from my Western outskirts.

Associated Contexts **Small,** HSIAO: little, common, unimportant; adapting to what crosses your path; ability to move in harmonious relation to the vicissitudes of life; contrasts with great, TA, self-imposed theme or goal; keyword. **Accumulate,** CH'U: hoard, gather, retain, herd together; control, restrain; domesticate, tame, train; raise, feed, sustain, bring up. The ideogram: field and black, fertile black soil good for pastures, accumulated through retaining silt. **Grow,** HENG: success through a sacrifice; pervade, persevere; bring to full growth; enjoy; vigorous, effective; second stage of the Time Cycle.

Shroud, MI: dense, close together, thick, tight; hidden, secret; retired, intimate. **Clouds,** YÜN: fog, mist, water vapor; connects to the Streaming Moment and Stream, the Symbol of the trigram Gorge,

K'AN. **Rain**, YÜ: all precipitation; sudden showers, fast and furious; associated with the trigram Gorge, K'AN, and the Streaming Moment.

Origin, TZU: source, beginning, ground; cause, reason, motive; line of descent; path to the origin; yourself, intrinsic. **My/me/I**, WO: first person pronoun; indicates an unusually strong emphasis on your own subjective experience. **West**, HSI: corresponds to autumn, Harvest and the Streaming Moment; begins yin hemicycle of Universal Compass. **Outskirts**, CHIAO: area adjoining a city where human constructions and nature interpenetrate; second of the territorial zones: city, suburbs, countryside, forests.

- ### Outer and Inner Aspects

☴**Ground**: Wind and wood subtly enter from the ground, penetrating and pervading. **Ground** is the center of the yang hemicycle, spreading pervasive action.

Connection to the outer: penetrating and bringing together, the Woody Moment culminating. **Ground** pervades, matches and couples, seeding a new generation.

☰**Force**: The force of heaven struggles on, persistent and unwearied; heavenly bodies persist in their orbits. **Force** is the center of the yin hemicycle, completing the formative process.

Connection to the inner: struggling forces bound together in dynamic tension, the Metallic Moment culminating. **Force** brings elements to grips, creating enduring relations.

An enduring force **accumulates** and is nurtured within through penetrating and matching the **small**.

- ### Hidden Possibility

Nuclear trigrams **Radiance**, LI, and **Open**, TUI, result in Nuclear Hexagram 38, **Diverging**, K'UEI: **Accumulating small** things through flexible adaptation depends on **diverging** from the norms.

- ### Sequence

Grouping necessarily possesses a place to Accumulate.
Accepting this lets you use Small Accumulating.

Associated Contexts **Group**, PI: compare and select, order things and put them in classes; find what you belong with; sort, examine correspondences; choose and harmonize; unite. The ideogram: person who stops walking, looking around to examine and compare. **Necessarily**, PI: unavoidably, indispensably, certainly. **Possess**, YU: in possession of, have, own; opposite of lack, WU. **Place**, SO: where something belongs or comes from; residence, dwelling; habitual focus or object.

Accepting ... use: activating this hexagram depends on understanding and accepting the previous statement.

● *Contrasted Definitions*

> Small Accumulating: few indeed.
> Treading: not abiding indeed.

Associated Contexts **Few**, KUA: small number; seldom, rarely; unusual, solitary. **Indeed, is/means**, YEH: intensifier, connective; indicates comment on previous statement.

Tread, LÜ: step, path, track; footsteps; walk a path or way; course of the stars; act, practice; conduct; salary, means of subsistence. The ideogram: body and repeating steps, following a trail. Image of Hexagram 10. **Abide**, CH'U: rest in, dwell; stop yourself; arrive at a place or condition; distinguish, decide; do what is proper. The ideogram: tiger, stop and seat, powerful movement coming to rest.

● *Symbol Tradition*

> Wind moving above heaven. Small Accumulating.
> A chün tzu uses highlighting the pattern to actualize tao.

Associated Contexts **Wind**, FENG: moving air, breeze, gust; weather and its influence on mood and humor; fashion, usage; wind and wood are the Symbols of the trigram Ground, SUN. **Move**, HSING: move or move something; motivate, emotionally moving; walk, act, do. The ideogram: stepping left then right. **Above**, SHANG: anything above, in all senses; higher, upper, outer; upper trigram; opposite of below, HSIA. **Heaven**, T'IEN: highest; sky, firmament, heavens; power above the human as opposed to earth, TI, below; the Symbol of the trigram Force, CH'IEN. The ideogram: great and the one above.

Chün tzu: ideal of a person who uses divination to order his/her life in accordance with tao rather than wilful intention; keyword. **Use(of)**, YI make

use of, by means of, owing to; employ, make functional. **Highlight**, YI: emphasize what is inherently good; concentrate, focus on; virtuous, worthy; an accomplished, graceful woman. **Pattern**, WEN: intrinsic or natural design and its beauty; stylish, elegant; noble; contrasts with composition, CHANG, a conscious creation. **Actualize tao**, TE: realize tao in action; power, virtue; ability to follow the course traced by the ongoing process of the cosmos; keyword. The ideogram: to go, straight, and heart. Linked with acquire, TE: acquiring that which makes a being become what it is meant to be.

- *Image Tradition*

> Small Accumulating. [I]
> Supple acquires the situation and also
> Above and Below correspond to it.
> Spoken thus: Small Accumulating.
>
> Persisting and Grounding. [II]
> Strong centering and purpose moving.
> Thereupon Growing.
>
> Shrouding clouds, not raining: [III]
> Honoring going indeed.
> Originating from my Western suburbs:
> Spreading out, not yet moving indeed.

Associated Contexts [I] **Supple**, JOU: quality of the opened lines; flexible, pliant, tender, adaptable. **Acquire**, TE: obtain the desired object; wish for, desire covetously; gains, possessions. The ideogram: go and obstacle, going through obstacles to the goal. **Situation**, WEI: place or seat according to rank; post, position, command; right, proper; established, arranged. The ideogram: person and stand, servants in their places.

Above and Below, SHANG HSIA: realm of dynamic interaction between the upper and the lower; the vertical dimension. **Correspond(to)**, YING: be in agreement or harmony; resonate together, invoke and fulfil each other; answer to, suitable; relation between the lines (1:4, 2:5, 3:6) when they form the pair opened and whole, supple and strong. The ideogram: heart and obey. **It/them/have(it)/'s**, CHIH: expresses possession, directly or as an object pronoun.

Spoken thus, YÜEH: designated, termed, called. The ideogram: open mouth and tongue.

[II] **Persist**, CHIEN: strong, robust, dynamic, tenacious; continuous;

unwearied heavenly bodies in their orbits; the Action of the trigram Force, CH'IEN. **Ground,** SUN: base on which things rest; support, foundation; mild, subtly penetrating; nourishing. The ideogram: stand and things arranged on it, the subtle influence of the ground. Image of Hexagram 57.

Strong, KANG: quality of the whole lines; firm, strong, unyielding, persisting. **Center,** CHUNG: inner, central; put in the center; middle, stable point enabling you to face inner and outer changes; middle line of trigram. The ideogram: field divided in two equal parts. Image of Hexagram 61. **Purpose,** CHIH: focus of mind and heart; will, inclination, resolve. The ideogram: heart and scholar, high inner resolve, or heart and go, inner determination.

Thereupon, NAI: on that ground, because of.

[III] **Honor,** SHANG: esteem, give high rank to; eminent; put one thing on top of another. **Go,** WANG, and **come,** LAI, describe the stream of time as it flows from future through present to past; go, WANG, indicates what is departing from present to past; proceed, move on; keyword.

Spread out, SHIH: expand, diffuse, distribute, arrange, exhibit; add to; aid. The ideogram: flag and indeed, claiming new country. **Not yet,** WEI: temporal negative; something will but has not yet occurred; contrary of already, CHI. Image of Hexagram 64.

●   *Transforming Lines*

Initial Nine

a) Returning to the origins of tao.
Wherefore one's fault? Auspicious.

b) Returning to the origins of tao.
One's righteousness auspicious indeed.

You have been lost in a cloud of details, but now you see the way once more. Don't hesitate to return. How could this be a mistake?

Associated Contexts a) **Return,** FU: go back, turn back to the starting point; recur, reappear, come again; restore, recover, retrace; an earlier time or place. The ideogram: step and retrace a path. Image of Hexagram 24. **Tao:** way or path; ongoing process of being and the course it traces for each specific person or thing; keyword. The ideogram: go and head, leading and the path it creates.

Wherefore, HO: interrogative: why? for what reason? what is? and affirmation: therefore, for that reason. **One's/one,** CH'I: third person

pronoun; also: it/its, he/his, she/hers, they/theirs. **Fault**, CHIU: unworthy conduct that leads to harm, illness, misfortune. The ideogram: person and differ, differ from what you should be. **Auspicious**, CHI: leads to the experience of meaning; favorable, propitious, advantageous, appropriate; keyword. The ideogram: scholar and mouth, wise words of a sage.

b) **Righteous**, YI: proper and just, meets the standards; things in their proper place; the heart that rules itself; upright, moral rule; contrasts with Harvest, LI, advantage or profit.

Nine at second

a) Hauled along, returning. Auspicious.

b) Hauling along, returning, located in the center.
Truly not originating from letting go indeed.

Lost and confused, you are simply hauled back to the way like an animal dragged on a leash. How fortunate! The way is open to you.

Associated Contexts a) **Haul along**, CH'IEN: haul or pull, drag behind; pull an animal on a rope; pull toward. The ideogram: ox and halter. **Return**, FU: go back, turn back to the starting point; recur, reappear, come again; restore, recover, retrace; an earlier time or place. The ideogram: step and retrace a path. Image of Hexagram 24. **Auspicious**, CHI: leads to the experience of meaning; favorable, propitious, advantageous, appropriate; keyword. The ideogram: scholar and mouth, wise words of a sage.

b) **Locate(in)**, TSAI: live in, dwell, reside; belong to, involved with, depend on; within. The ideogram: earth and persevere, place on the earth.

Truly, YI: statement is true and precise. **Let go**, SHIH: lose, omit, miss, fail, let slip; out of control. The ideogram: drop from the hand.

Nine at third

a) Carting loosens the spokes.
Husband and consort, reversing eyes.

b) Husband and consort, reversing eyes.
Not able to correct the home indeed.

A real family quarrel. The cart breaks down. You and your friend are standing there rolling your eyes in indignation and nothing gets done. This is no way to put your house in order.

Associated Contexts a) **Cart**, YÜ: carrying capacity of a vehicle; contain, hold, sustain. **Stimulate**, loosen, SHUO: rouse to action and good feeling; free from constraint, stir up, urge on; persuade, cheer, delight; set out in words; the Action of the trigram Open, TUI. The ideogram: words and exchange. **Spokes**, FU: braces that connect hub and rim of wheel; tributaries.

Husband, FU: household manager; administer with thrift and prudence; responsible for; sustain with your earnings; old enough to assume responsibility; married man. **Consort**, CH'I: single official partner; legal status of married woman (first wife); contrasts with function of wife, FU, head of household, and concubine, CH'IEH, secondary wives. **Reverse**, FAN: turn and move in the opposite direction; turn around or upside down (180 degrees); change to the opposite position; contrary. **Eye**, MU: eye and its functions: look, see, glance, observe.

b) **Able**, NENG: enable; ability, power, skill, art; competent, talented; duty, function, capacity. The ideogram: an animal with strong hooves and bones, able to carry and defend. **Correct**, CHENG: rectify deviation or one-sidedness; proper, straight, exact, regular; constant, rule, model. The ideogram: stop and one, hold to one thing. **Home**, SHIH: place of rest, dwelling, family; the grave.

Nine at fourth

a) There is a connection to the spirits.
Blood departs, awe issues forth.
Without fault.

b) There is a connection to the spirits, awe issuing forth.
Uniting purposes above indeed.

You can act with confidence now. The spirits are with you. Forget about old quarrels and resentments. Announce yourself. This is not a mistake. Your purpose is united with those above.

Associated Contexts a) **There is ... spirits**, YU FU: inner and outer are in accord; confidence of the spirits has been captured; sincere, truthful; proper to take action.

Blood, HSÜEH: yin fluid that maintains life; rain; money, property. **Depart**, CH'Ü: leave, quit, remove; repudiate, reject, dismiss. **Awe**, T'I: alarmed and cautious; respect, regard, fear; stand in awe of. The ideogram: heart and versatile, the heart aware of sudden change. **Issue forth(from)**,

CH'U: emerge from, come out of, proceed from, spring from; the Action of the trigram Shake, CHEN; contrary of enter, JU. The ideogram: stem with branches and leaves emerging.

Without fault, WU CHIU: no error or harm in the situation.

b) **Unite**, HO: join, match, correspond, agree, collect, reply; unison, harmony; also: close, shut the mouth. The ideogram: mouth and assemble.

Six at fifth

a) There is a connection to the spirits, binding thus.
Affluence: use one's neighbor.

b) There is a connection to the spirits, binding thus.
Not solitary affluence indeed.

You are not alone. There is a spiritual connection that binds you to the people around you. Don't be afraid to make use of this connection. Take hold of things and use them for the good of all.

Associated Contexts a) **There is ... spirits**: YU FU: inner and outer are in accord; confidence of the spirits has been captured; sincere, truthful; proper to take action. **Bind**, LÜAN: tie, connect, take hold of; bent, contracted. The ideogram: hand and connect, binding things. **Thus**, JU: as, in this way.

Affluence, FU: rich, abundant; wealth; enrich, provide for; flow toward, accrue. **One's/one**, CH'I: third person pronoun; also: it/its, he/his, she/hers, they/theirs. **Neighbor**, LIN: person living nearby; extended family; assist, support.

b) **Solitary**, TI: alone, single; isolated, abandoned.

Nine above

a) Already rain, already abiding.
Honoring actualizing tao, carrying.
The wife, Trial: adversity.
The moon almost facing.
A chün tzu chastising: pitfall.

b) Already rain, already abiding.
Actualizing tao, amassing and carrying indeed.
A chün tzu chastising: pitfall.
There is a place to doubt indeed.

You have achieved your goal. The rain has fallen to bless you and you live in honor and virtue. Don't worry, carry on. If the wife divines now, she will face danger with its roots in the past. Don't try to put everything in order. Don't set out on an expedition. Accept things as they are and the happiness you know will endure.

Associated Contexts a) **Already,** CHI: completed, done, has occurred; past tense, contrary of not-yet, WEI. Image of Hexagram 63.

Carry, TSAI: bear, carry with you; contain, sustain; load a ship or cart, cargo; fill in, complete.

Wife, FU: responsible position of married woman within the household; contrasts with consort, CH'I, her legal position and concubine, CH'IEH, secondary wives. The ideogram: woman, hand and broom, household duties. **Trial,** CHEN: inquiry by divination and its result; righteous, firm; separating wheat from chaff; the kernel, the proven core; fourth stage of the Time Cycle. The ideogram: pearl and divination. **Adversity,** LI: danger; threatening, malevolent demon. This has two aspects: grind, sharpen, improve, perfect, stimulate; and: poisonous, sinister, cruel, contrary. It indicates a spirit or ghost that seeks revenge by inflicting suffering upon the living. Pacifying or exorcizing such a spirit can have a healing effect. The ideogram: sheltering cliff and stinging insect.

Moon, YÜEH: actual moon and moon-month; yin, the sun being yang. **Almost,** CHI: nearly, about to; subtle, almost imperceptible; the first sign. **Face,** WANG: full moon; moon directly facing the sun; 15th day of the moon-month; look at hopefully.

Chastise, CHENG: punish, subjugate, discipline; reduce to order; punishing expedition. The ideogram: step and correct, a rectifying move. **Pitfall,** HSIUNG: leads away from the experience of meaning; stuck and exposed to danger, unable to take in the situation; flow of life and spirit is blocked; unfortunate, baleful; keyword.

b) **Amass,** CHI: hoard, accumulate, pile up, store up, add up, increase.

Doubt, YI: suspect, distrust; dubious; surmise, conjecture.

10

T R E A D I N G ▮ *L Ü*

Make your way a step at a time; trust in the outcome; conduct, support, sustain; good cheer, good luck.

Treading describes your situation in terms of how you find and make your way. Its symbol is the time when the shamaness opens the fields and goes up to the Hidden Temple to acquire a new fate. The way to deal with it is to proceed step by step. Make an offering and you will succeed. The path is there. Practice. Think about the right way to act and how to gain your livelihood. You are walking in the tracks of a tiger, a powerful and dangerous being. If you are careful, this being will give you what you need to exist and frighten off what is trying to harm you. Speak with it and partake of its power and intelligence. Don't do anything to make it bite you and don't snap at people yourself. You can't afford to sneer and scold. This is pleasing to the spirits. Through it they will give you success, effective power and the capacity to bring the situation to maturity.

● *Image of the Situation*

> Treading a tiger tail.
> Not mauling people. Growing.

Associated Contexts **Tread**, LÜ: step, path, track; footsteps; walk a path or way; course of the stars; act, practice; conduct; salary, means of subsistence. The ideogram: body and repeating steps, following a trail. **Tiger**, HU: fierce king of animals; extreme yang; opposed to and protects against demoniacs on North–South axis of Universal Compass. **Tail**, WEI: animal's tail; last, extreme; remnants, unimportant.

Maul, TIEH: bite, seize with the teeth, maul; sneering laughter, rebuke. The ideogram: mouth and reach. **People, person**, JEN: humans individually and collectively; an individual; humankind. Image of Hexagrams 13 and 37. **Grow**, HENG: success through a sacrifice; pervade, persevere; bring to full growth; enjoy; vigorous, effective; second stage of the Time Cycle.

● *Outer and Inner Aspects*

☰**Force**: The force of heaven struggles on, persistent and unwearied; heavenly bodies persist in their orbits. **Force** is the center of the yin hemicycle, completing the formative process.

Connection to the outer: struggling forces are bound together in dynamic tension, the Metallic Moment culminating. **Force** brings elements to grips, creating enduring relations.

☱**Open**: vapor rising from the marsh's open surface stimulates and fertilizes; stimulating words cheer and inspire. **Open** begins the yin hemicycle by initiating the formative process.

Connection to the inner: liquifying, casting, skinning off the mold, the Metallic Moment beginning. **Open** stimulates, cheers and reveals innate form.

Inner stimulation alternates with outer struggle, **treading** a path step by step.

● *Hidden Possibility*

Nuclear trigrams **Ground**, SUN, and **Radiance**, LI, result in Nuclear Hexagram 37, **Dwelling People**, CHIA JEN. **Treading** and moving along a path leads to living with **people** and founding a **dwelling**.

● *Sequence*

Beings Accumulate, therefore afterwards they possess codes.
Accepting this lets you use Treading.

Associated Contexts **Being(s)**, WU: creature, thing, any single being; matter, substance, essence; nature of things. **Accumulate**, CH'U: retain, hoard, gather, herd together; control, restrain; domesticate, tame, train; raise, feed, sustain, bring up. The ideogram: field and black, fertile black soil good for pastures, accumulated through retaining silt. Image of Hexagrams 9 and 26. **Therefore afterwards**, JAN HOU: logical consequence of, necessarily follows in time. **Possess**, YU: in possession of, have, own; opposite of lack, WU. **Codes**, LI: rites, rules, ritual; usage, manners; worship, ceremony, observance. The ideogram: worship and sacrificial vase, handling a sacred vessel.

Accepting ... use: activating this hexagram depends on understanding and accepting the previous statement.

● *Contrasted Definitions*

> Small Accumulating: few indeed.
> Treading: not abiding indeed.

Associated Contexts **Small,** HSIAO: little, common, unimportant; adapting to what crosses your path; ability to move in harmony with the vicissitudes of life; contrasts with great, TA, self-imposed theme or goal; keyword. **Small Accumulating,** HSIAO CH'U, is the Image of Hexagram 9. **Few,** KUA: small number; seldom, rarely; unusual, solitary. **Indeed/is/means:** YEH: intensifier, connective; indicates comment on previous statement.

    Abide, CH'U: rest in, dwell; stop yourself; arrive at a place or condition; distinguish, decide; do what is proper. The ideogram: tiger, stop and seat, powerful movement coming to rest.

● *Attached Evidences*

> Treading: actualizing tao's foundation indeed.
> Treading: harmonizing and culminating.
> Treading: using harmonizing movement.

Associated Contexts **Actualize tao,** TE: realize tao in action; power, virtue; ability to follow the course traced by the ongoing process of the cosmos; keyword. The ideogram: to go, straight, and heart. Linked with acquire, TE: acquiring that which makes a being become what it is meant to be. **'s/have(it)/it/them,** CHIH: expresses possession, directly or as an object pronoun. **Foundation,** CHI: base of wall or building; basis, starting point; found, establish.

    Harmony, HO: concord, union; conciliate; at peace, mild; fit, tune, adjust. **Culminate,** CHIH: bring to the highest degree; arrive at the end or summit; superlative.

    Use(of), YI: make use of, by means of, owing to; employ, make functional. **Move,** HSING: move or move something; motivate, emotionally moving; walk, act, do. The ideogram: stepping left then right.

● *Symbol Tradition*

> Heaven above, marsh below. Treading.
> A chün tzu uses differentiating Above and Below.
> [A chün tzu uses] setting right the commoner's, purpose.

Associated Contexts **Heaven,** T'IEN: highest; sky, firmament, heavens; power above the human as opposed to earth, TI, below; the Symbol of the trigram Force, CH'IEN. The ideogram: great and the one above. **Above,** SHANG: anything above, in all senses; higher, upper, outer; upper trigram; opposite of below, HSIA. **Marsh,** TSE: open surface of a flat body of water and the vapors rising from it; fertilize, enrich; kindness, favor; the Symbol of the trigram Open, TUI. **Below,** HSIA: anything below, in all senses; lower, inner; lower trigram; opposite of above, SHANG.

Chün tzu: ideal of a person who uses divination to order his/her life in accordance with tao rather than wilful intention; keyword. **Differentiate,** PIEN: argue, dispute, criticize; sophisticated, artful. The ideogram: words and sharp or pungent. **Above and Below,** SHANG HSIA: realm of dynamic interaction between the upper and the lower; the vertical dimension.

Set right, TING: settle, fix, put in place; at rest, repose. **Commoners,** MIN: class of workers the state draws on to sustain the social hierarchy; undeveloped potential outside the organized personality. **Purpose,** CHIH: focus of mind and heart; will, inclination, resolve. The ideogram: heart and scholar, high inner resolve, or heart and go, inner determination.

● *Image Tradition*

> Treading. Supple Treading on strong indeed. [I]
> Stimulating and corresponding reaching to Force.
> That uses Treading a tiger tail.
>
> Not mauling people. Growing. [II]
> Strong centering correctly.
> Treading the supreme situation and not ailing.
> Shining brightness indeed.

Associated Contexts **[I] Supple,** JOU: quality of the opened lines; flexible, pliant, tender, adaptable. **Strong,** KANG: quality of the whole lines; firm, strong, unyielding, persisting.

Stimulate loosen, SHUO: rouse to action and good feeling; free from constraint, stir up, urge on; persuade, cheer, delight; set out in words; the Action of the trigram Open, TUI. The ideogram: words and exchange. **Correspond(to),** YING: be in agreement or harmony; resonate together, invoke and fulfil each other; answer to, suitable; relation between the lines (1:4, 2:5, 3:6) when they form the pair opened and whole, supple and strong. The ideogram: heart and obey. **Reach(to),** HU: arrive at a goal; reach toward and achieve; connect. **Force,** CH'IEN: spirit power, creative and

destructive; unceasing forward motion; dynamic, enduring, untiring; firm, stable; heaven, sovereign, father; also: dry up, parched, exhausted, cleared away. The ideogram: sprouts or vapors rising from the ground and sunlight, both fecundating moisture and scorching drought. Image of Hexagram 1. **That uses**, SHIH YI: involves and is involved by.

[II] Centering correcting, CHUNG CHENG: central and correct; make rectifying one-sidedness and error your central concern; reaching a stable center in yourself can correct the situation.

Supreme, TI: highest, above all on earth; sovereign lord, source of power; emperor. **Situation**, WEI: place or seat according to rank; post, position, command; right, proper; established, arranged. The ideogram: person and stand, servants in their places. **Ail**, CHIU: chronic disease; disheartened, distressed by.

Shine, KUANG: illuminate; give off brilliant, bright light; honor, glory, éclat; result of action, contrasts with brightness, MING, light of heavenly bodies. The ideogram: fire above person, lifting the light. **Brightness**, MING: light-giving aspect of burning, heavenly bodies and consciousness; with fire, the Symbol of the trigram Radiance, LI.

● *Transforming Lines*

Initial nine

a) Sheer Treading going.
   Without fault.

b) Sheer Treading's going.
   Solitarily moving desire indeed.

Go your own way. Be simple and pure about your efforts. Move with your real desire. How could this be a mistake?

Associated Contexts a) **Sheer**, SU: plain, unadorned; original color or state; clean, pure. The ideogram: white silk, symbol of mourning. **Go**, WANG, and **come**, LAI, describe the stream of time as it flows from future through present to past; go, WANG, indicates what is departing from present to past; proceed, move on; keyword.
   Without fault, WU CHIU: no error or harm in the situation.

b) **Solitary**, TI: alone, single; isolated, abandoned. **Desire**, YÜAN: wish, hope or long for; covet; desired object.

Nine at second

a) Treading tao, smoothing, smoothing.
Shade people, Trial: auspicious.

b) Shade people, Trial: auspicious.
Centering, not originating from disarray indeed.

You are treading the Way, so be calm about everything. This is not the time to come out of hiding. Stay in the shade for now, hidden away. The spirit is there. Your time will come.

Associated Contexts a) **Tao**: way or path; ongoing process of being and the course it traces for each specific person or thing; keyword. The ideogram: go and head, leading and the path it creates. **Smooth**, T'AN: plain, leveled; even, make smooth; tranquil, composed, at ease. The doubled character intensifies this quality.

Shade, YU: hidden from view; retired, solitary, secret; dark, obscure, occult, mysterious; ignorant. The ideogram: small within hill, a cave or grotto. **Trial**, CHEN: inquiry by divination and its result; righteous, firm; separating wheat from chaff; the kernel, the proven core; fourth stage of the Time Cycle. The ideogram: pearl and divination. **Auspicious**, CHI: leads to the experience of meaning; favorable, propitious, advantageous, appropriate; keyword. The ideogram: scholar and mouth, wise words of a sage.

b) **Center**, CHUNG: inner, central; put in the center; middle, stable point enabling you to face inner and outer changes; middle line of trigram. The ideogram: field divided in two equal parts. Image of Hexagram 61. **Origin**, TZU: source, beginning, ground; cause, reason, motive; line of descent; path to the origin; yourself, intrinsic. **Disarray**, LUAN: throw into disorder, mislay, confuse; out of place; discord, insurrection, anarchy.

Six at third

a) Squinting may enable you to observe.
Halting may enable you to Tread.
Treading a tiger tail.
Mauling people: pitfall.
A Martial Person acting as a Great Chief.

b) Squinting may enable you to observe.
Not the stand to use possessing brightness indeed.

> Halting may enable you to Tread.
> Not the stand to use associating with moving indeed.
> Mauling people's pitfall.
> Situation not appropriate indeed.
> A Martial Person acting as a Great Chief.
> Purpose strong indeed.

This is not the way to act. Give it up now. You are presuming on inadequate powers. Go on like this and the tiger will maul you. The only reason to act this way is if you had specific orders to sacrifice yourself.

Associated Contexts a) **Squint**, MIAO: look at with one eye, glance at; obstructed vision. **Able**, NENG: enable; ability, power, skill, art; competent, talented; duty, function, capacity. The ideogram: an animal with strong hooves and bones, able to carry and defend. **Observe**, SHIH: see and inspect carefully; gain knowledge of; compare and imitate. The ideogram: see and omen, taking account of what you see.

    Halt, P'O: limp; lame, crippled; indecorous.

    Pitfall, HSIUNG: leads away from the experience of meaning; stuck and exposed to danger, unable to take in the situation; flow of life and spirit is blocked; unfortunate, baleful; keyword.

    Martial, WU: military, warlike; strong, stern; power to make war. The ideogram: fight and stop, force deterring aggression. **Activate**, WEI: act or cause to act; do, make, manage; make active; attend to, help; because of. **Great**, TA: big, noble, important, very; orient the will toward a self-imposed goal, impose direction; ability to lead or guide your life; contrasts with small, HSIAO, flexible adaptation to what crosses your path; keyword. Image of Hexagrams 14, 26, 28, 34. **Chief**, CHÜN: effective ruler; preside over, take the lead; influence others; term of respect. The ideogram: mouth and director, giving orders.

b) **Stand**, TSU: base, foot, leg; rest on, support; stance. The ideogram: foot and calf resting.

    Associate(with), YÜ: consort with, combine; companions; group, band, company; agree with, comply, help. The ideogram: pair of hands reaching downward meets a pair of hands reaching upward, helpful association.

    Appropriate, TANG: suitable; opportune, convenient; adequate, competent; equal to; whole lines in uneven places and opened lines in even places.

Nine at fourth

a) Treading a tiger tail.
Pleading, pleading: completing auspicious.

b) Pleading, pleading: completing auspicious.
Purpose moving indeed.

You meet the great person, the source of power. Present your case clearly and persuasively. Don't be intimidated. Your purpose is moving.

Associated Contexts a) **Plead,** SU: defend or prosecute a case in court; enter a plea; statement of grievance. The doubled character intensifies this quality. **Complete,** CHUNG: end of a cycle that begins the next; last, whole, all; contrasts with exhaust, CH'IUNG: final end. The ideogram: silk cocoons, follow and ice, winter linking one year with the next. **Auspicious,** CHI: leads to the experience of meaning; favorable, propitious, advantageous, appropriate; keyword. The ideogram: scholar and mouth, wise words of a sage.

Nine at fifth

a) Parting Treading. Trial: adversity.

b) Parting Treading, Trial: adversity.
Situation correcting appropriate indeed.

This next step takes courage, because you must decisively separate yourselves from a dangerous past influence. Have no fear. Correcting the situation is definitely the right thing to do.

Associated Contexts a) **Part,** KUAI: separate, fork, cut off, decide; pull or flow in different directions; certain, settled; prompt, decisive, stern. Image of Hexagram 43. **Trial,** CHEN: inquiry by divination and its result; righteous, firm; separating wheat from chaff; the kernel, the proven core; fourth stage of the Time Cycle. The ideogram: pearl and divination. **Adversity,** LI: danger; threatening, malevolent demon. This has two aspects: grind, sharpen, improve, perfect, stimulate; and: poisonous, sinister, cruel, contrary. It indicates a spirit or ghost that seeks revenge by inflicting suffering upon the living. Pacifying or exorcizing such a spirit can have a healing effect. The ideogram: sheltering cliff and stinging insect.

b) **Correct,** CHENG: rectify deviation or one-sidedness; proper, straight, exact, regular; constant, rule, model. The ideogram: stop and one, hold to

one thing. **Appropriate**, TANG: suitable; opportune, convenient; adequate, competent; equal to; whole lines in uneven places and opened lines in even places.

> Nine above

> *a)* Observing Treading, the predecessors omens.
> Their recurring Spring: auspicious.

> *b)* Spring: auspicious and located above.
> The great possesses reward indeed.

If you look at the things you have been doing, you will see that they connect with something larger than personal desires. Keep to this path, for the ancestors bless you. It is their presence that opens the Way.

Associated Contexts a) **Observe**, SHIH: see and inspect carefully; gain knowledge of; compare and imitate. The ideogram: see and omen, taking account of what you see. **Predecessor**, K'AO: deceased ancestor, especially the grandfather; the ancients; aged, long-lived; consult, verify. The ideogram: old and ingenious, the old wise man. **Omen**, HSIANG: omen of good luck and prosperity; sign, auspices.

One's/one, CH'I: third person pronoun; also: it/its, he/his, she/hers, they/theirs. **Recur**, HSÜAN: return to the same point; orbit, revolve; spiral. **Spring**, YÜAN: source, origin, head; great, excellent; arise, begin, generating power; first stage of the Time Cycle. **Auspicious**, CHI: leads to the experience of meaning; favorable, propitious, advantageous, appropriate; keyword. The ideogram: scholar and mouth, wise words of a sage.

b) **Locate(in)**, TSAI: live in, dwell, reside; belong to, involved with, depend on; within. The ideogram: earth and persevere, place on the earth.

Great, TA: big, noble, important, very; orient the will toward a self-imposed goal, impose direction; ability to lead or guide your life; contrasts with small, HSIAO, flexible adaptation to what crosses your path; keyword. Image of Hexagrams 14, 26, 28, 34. **Reward**, CH'ING: gift given from gratitude or benevolence; favor from heaven; congratulate with gifts. The ideogram: heart, follow and deer (wealth), the heart expressed through gifts.

11

PERVADING ▮ *T'AI*

Expand, communicate; harmony, abundance, flowering, connection.

Pervading describes your situation in terms of an influx of spirit that brings flowering and prosperity. Its symbol is the great sacrifice on Mount T'ai that opened the flow of blessing for all. The way to deal with it is to spread the prosperity and good feeling by communicating it. Make an offering and you will succeed. You are connected to the flow of energy. Be great, abounding and fertile. What is unimportant is departing, along with the necessity to be small and adapt to whatever crosses your path. The time that is coming offers you the chance to develop your fundamental ideas. It generates meaning and good fortune by releasing transformative energy. This is pleasing to the spirits. Through it they will give you success, effective power and the capacity to bring the situation to maturity.

● *Image of the Situation*

> **Pervading.**
> **The small going, the great coming.**
> **Auspicious Growing.**

Associated Contexts **Pervade**, T'AI: spread and reach everywhere, permeate, diffuse; communicate; great, extensive, abundant, prosperous; smooth, slippery; extreme, extravagant, prodigal. Mount T'AI in eastern China was a sacred mountain connecting heaven and earth. The emperor made offerings there to establish harmony between humans and the great spirits. The ideogram: person in water, connected to the universal medium.

    Small, HSIAO: little, common, unimportant; adapting to what crosses your path; ability to move in harmony with the vicissitudes of life; contrasts with great, TA, self-imposed theme or goal; keyword. Image of Hexagrams 9 and 62. **Go**, WANG, and **Come**, LAI, describe the stream of time as it flows from future through present to past. Go, WANG, indicates: what is departing; proceed, move on; Come, LAI, indicates: what is approaching; move toward, arrive at; keywords. **Great**, TA: big, noble, important, very; orient the will toward a self-imposed goal, impose direction; ability to lead or guide your life; contrasts with small, HSIAO, flexible adaptation to what crosses your path; keyword. Image of Hexagrams 14, 26, 28, 34.

Auspicious, CHI: leads to the experience of meaning; favorable, propitious, advantageous, appropriate; keyword. The ideogram: scholar and mouth, wise words of a sage. **Grow**, HENG: success through a sacrifice; pervade, persevere; bring to full growth; enjoy; vigorous, effective; second stage of the Time Cycle.

● *Outer and Inner Aspects*

☷ **Field**: The field of earth yields and sustains, serving in order to produce. **Field** is the equalizing point between yin and yang where things labor and serve.

Connection to the outer: the common labor of sowing and hoarding, the Earthy Moment. **Field** produces concrete results through serving.

☰ **Force**: The force of heaven struggles on, persistent and unwearied; heavenly bodies persist in their orbits. **Force** is the center of the yin hemicycle, completing the formative process.

Connection to the inner: struggling forces are bound together in dynamic tension, the Metallic Moment culminating. **Force** brings elements to grips, creating enduring relations.

An enduring creative force spreads from within, **pervading** the earth which yields and brings-forth. This is a time of creative abundance.

● *Hidden Possibility*

Nuclear trigrams **Shake**, CHEN, and **Open**, TUI, result in Nuclear Hexagram 54, **Converting Maidenhood**, KUEI MEI. **Pervading** and spreading in all directions leads the **maiden** to the specific place where she belongs.

● *Sequence*

> Treading and Pervading.
> Therefore afterwards quieting.
> Accepting this lets you use Pervading.
> Pervading implies interpenetrating indeed.

Associated Contexts **Tread**, LÜ: step, path, track; footsteps; walk a path or way; course of the stars; act, practice; conduct; salary, means of subsistence. The ideogram: body and repeating steps, following a trail. Image of Hexagram 10.

Therefore afterwards, JAN HOU: logical consequence of, necessarily follows in time. **Quiet,** AN: peaceful, still, settled; calm, tranquilize. The ideogram: woman under a roof, a tranquil home.

Accepting ... use: activating this hexagram depends on understanding and accepting the previous statement.

Imply, CHE: further signify; additional meaning. **Interpenetrate,** T'UNG: mutually penetrate; permeate, flow through, reach everywhere; see clearly, communicate with. **Indeed** YEH: intensifier, connective; indicates comment on previous statement.

- *C o n t r a s t i n g   D e f i n i t i o n s*

Obstructing, Pervading: reversing one's sorting indeed.

Associated Contexts **Obstruct,** P'I: closed, stopped; bar the way; obstacle; unfortunate, wicked; refuse, disapprove, deny. The ideogram: mouth and not, blocked communication. Image of Hexagram 12. **Reverse,** FAN: turn and move in the opposite direction; turn around or upside down (180 degrees); change to the opposite position; contrary. **One's/one,** CH'I: third person pronoun; also: it/its, he/his, she/hers, they/theirs. **Sort,** LEI: group according to kind, class with; like nature or purpose; species, class, genus.

- *S y m b o l   T r a d i t i o n*

Heaven and Earth mingling. Pervading.
The crown prince uses property
                              to accomplish Heaven and Earth's tao.
[The crown prince uses] bracing
                              to mutualize Heaven and Earth's propriety
[The crown prince] uses the left to right the commoners.

Associated Contexts **Heaven and Earth,** T'IEN TI: dynamic relation between the primal powers and the world it produces; cosmos, natural or human world; keyword. **Mingle,** CHIAO: blend with, communicate, join, exchange; trade, business; copulation; friendship.

Crown prince, HOU: successor to the sovereign. The ideogram: one, mouth and shelter, one with the sovereign's orders. **Use(of),** YI: make use of, by means of, owing to; employ, make functional. **Property,** TS'AI: possessions, goods, substance, wealth. The ideogram: pearl and value.

Accomplish, CH'ENG: complete, finish, bring about; perfect, full, whole; play your part, do your duty; mature. The ideogram: weapon and man, able to bear arms, thus fully developed. **'s/have(it)/it/them,** CHIH: expresses possession, directly or as an object pronoun. **Tao:** way or path; ongoing process of being and the course it traces for each specific person or thing; keyword. The ideogram: go and head, leading and the path it creates.

Brace/jawbones, FU: support, consolidate, reinforce, strengthen, stiffen, prop up, fix; steady, firm, rigid; help, rescue; support the speaking mouth. The ideogram: cart and great. **Mutual,** HSIANG: reciprocal assistance, encourage, help; bring together, blend with; examine, inspect; by turns. **Proper,** YI: reasonable of itself; fit and right, harmonious; ought, should.

Left, TSO: left side, left hand; secondary; deputy, assistant; inferior. **Right,** YU: right side, right hand; noble, honorable; make things right. **Commoners,** MIN: class of workers the state draws on to sustain the social hierarchy; undeveloped potential outside the organized personality.

- *Image Tradition*

> The small going, the great coming: auspiciousness Growing. [I]
> By consequence of that Heaven and Earth mingle
> and the myriad beings interpenetrate indeed.
> Above and Below mingling and
> one's purpose concording indeed.
>
> Inside yang and outside yin. [II]
> Inside persisting and outside yielding.
> Inside chün tzu and outside Small People.
> A chün tzu: tao long living.
> Small People: tao dissolving indeed.

Associated Contexts [I] **By consequence(of),** TSE: very strong connection; reason, cause, result; rule, law, pattern, standard; therefore. **That,** SHIH: preceding statement; what has passed. **Myriad,** WAN: countless; many, everyone; lit.: ten thousand. The ideogram: swarm of insects. **Being(s),** WU: creature, thing, any single being; matter, substance, essence; nature of things.

Above and Below, SHANG HSIA: realm of dynamic interaction between the upper and the lower; the vertical dimension. **Purpose,** CHIH: focus of mind and heart; will, inclination, resolve. The ideogram: heart and scholar, high inner resolve, or heart and go, inner determination. **Concord,** T'UNG:

harmonize, unite, equalize, assemble; agree, share in; together, at once, same time and place. The ideogram: cover and mouth, silent understanding and perfect fit. Image of Hexagram 13.

[II] **Inside**, NEI: within, inner, interior; inside of the house and those who work there, particularly women; the lower trigram, as opposed to outside, WAI, the upper. The ideogram: border and enter, cross a border. **Yang:** Action; dynamic and light aspect of phenomena: arouses, transforms, dissolves existing structures; linear thrust; stimulus, drive, focus; direct or orient something. **Outside**, WAI: outer, exterior, external; people working in places other than their home; unfamiliar, foreign; the upper trigram, as opposed to **inside**, NEI, the lower. **Yin:** Struction; consolidating, shadowy aspect of phenomena: conserves, substantializes, creates structures; spacial extension; limited, bound, given specific being; build, make something concrete.

    Persist, CHIEN: strong, robust, dynamic, tenacious; continuous; unwearied heavenly bodies in their orbits; the Action of the trigram Force, CH'IEN. **Yield(to)**, SHUN: give way and bear produce; comply, agree, follow, obey; unresisting, docile, flexible; nourish, provide; the Action of the trigram Field, K'UN. The ideogram: head and current, water flowing from the head of a river, yielding to the banks.

    Chün tzu: ideal of a person who uses divination to order his/her life in accordance with tao rather than wilful intention; keyword. **Small People,** HSIAO JEN: lowly, common, humble; those who adjust to circumstances with the flexibility of the small; effect of the small within an individual; keyword.

    Long living, CHANG: enduring, constant; senior, superior, greater; increase, prosper; respect, elevate. **Dissolve**, HSIAO: liquify, melt, thaw; diminish, disperse; eliminate, exhaust. The ideogram: water dissolving differences.

● *Transforming Lines*

    Initial Nine

        a) **Eradicate thatch grass intertwisting.**
            Using one's classification.
            Chastising auspicious.

        b) **Eradicating thatch grass, chastising auspicious.**
            Purpose located outside indeed.

Take vigorous action to get out of this lowly place and find the people you really belong with. Be firm. Put things in order and set out. The way is open.

Associated Contexts a) **Eradicate**, PA: pull up, root out, extirpate; extricate from difficulties; elevate, promote. **Thatch grass**, MAO: thick grass used for the roofs of humble houses. **Intertwist,** JU: interlaced; entangled roots.

Classification, HUI: class, collection, series; same kind; put or group together. **Chastise**, CHENG: punish, subjugate, discipline; reduce to order; punishing expedition. The ideogram: step and correct, a rectifying move.

b) **Locate(in)**, TSAI: live in, dwell, reside; belong to, involved with, depend on; within. The ideogram: earth and persevere, place on the earth.

Nine at second

a) Enwrapping wasteland.
   Avail of crossing the channel.
   Do not put off abandoning.
   Partnering extinguished.
   Acquiring honor, moving towards center.

b) Enwrapping wasteland, acquiring honor,
   moving towards center.
   Using the shining great indeed.

You are surrounded by a wasteland. Get out of this situation. Cross the river. Move toward the vibrant center. The people you now identify with will disappear, but there is no other choice. Your integrity will be honored and your desire fulfiled.

Associated Contexts a) **Enwrap**, PAO: envelop, hold, contain; patient; take on responsibility, engaged. The ideogram: enfold and self, a fetus in the womb. **Wasteland**, HUANG: wild, barren, deserted, unproductive; jungle, moor, heath; reckless, neglectful.

Avail of, YUNG: take advantage of; benefit from, profit by; use for a specific purpose; apply to advantage. The ideogram: to divine and center, applying divination to central concerns. **Cross**, P'ING: cross a river without a boat; cross a dry or frozen river. The ideogram: horse and ice. **Channel**, HO: bed of river or stream; running water.

Put off, HSIA: delay; put at a distance; far away, remote in time. **Abandon**, YI: leave behind, forget; die; lose through unawareness. The ideogram: go and value, value is gone.

Partner, P'ENG: associate for mutual benefit; two equal or similar things; companions, friends, peers; join in; commercial ventures. The ideogram: linked strings of cowries or coins. **Extinguish**, WANG: ruin, destroy; gone, dead, lost without trace; extinct, forgotten, out of mind. The ideogram: person concealed by a wall, out of sight.

Acquire, TE: obtain the desired object; wish for, desire covetously; gains, possessions. The ideogram: go and obstacle, going through obstacles to the goal. **Honor**, SHANG: esteem, give high rank to; eminent; put one thing on top of another. **Center**, CHUNG: inner, central; put in the center; middle, stable point enabling you to face inner and outer changes; middle line of trigram. The ideogram: field divided in two equal parts. Image of Hexagram 61. **Move**, HSING: move or move something; motivate, emotionally moving; walk, act, do. The ideogram: stepping left then right.

b) **Shine**, KUANG: illuminate; give off brilliant, bright light; honor, glory, éclat; result of action, contrasts with brightness, MING, light of heavenly bodies. The ideogram: fire above person, lifting the light.

Nine at third

a) Without the even, no uneven.
Without going, no returning.
Drudgery, Trial: without fault.
No cares: you are connected to the spirits.
Tending towards eating possesses blessing.

b) Without going, not returning.
Heaven and Earth, the border indeed.

You are facing a difficult time. After a level road there is always a difficult climb. But if you don't let go of your joy, it will never come back to you. This difficulty is not a mistake. Don't worry, it has a real spiritual meaning. Going through the hardship draws the blessing down. Join with others in this loving spirit.

Associated Contexts a) **Without**, WU: devoid of; -less as suffix. **Even**, P'ING: level, make even or equal; uniform, peaceful, tranquil; restore quiet, harmonize. **Uneven**, PEI: any difference in level; inclined, falling down, tipped over, dilapidated; also: rising; bank, shore, dam, dikes.

Return, FU: go back, turn back to the starting point; recur, reappear, come again; restore, recover, retrace; an earlier time or place. The ideogram: step and retrace a path. Image of Hexagram 24.

Drudgery, CHIEN: difficult, hard, repetitive work; hard to cultivate; distressing, sorrowful. The ideogram: sticky earth and a person looking around, hard work in comparison to others. **Trial,** CHEN: test by ordeal; inquiry by divination and its result; righteous, firm; separating wheat from chaff; the kernel, the proven core; fourth stage of the Time Cycle. The ideogram: pearl and divination. **Without fault,** WU CHIU: no error or harm in the situation.

Care, HSÜ: fear, doubt, concern; heartfelt attachment; relieve, soothe, aid; sympathy, compassion, consolation. The ideogram: heart and blood, the heart's blood affected. **Connection,** FU: accord between inner and outer in a particular moment; sincere, truthful, verified, reliable, in accord with the spirits; capture; prisoners, spoils; contrasts with trustworthy, HSIN, consistent over time. The ideogram: bird's claw enclosing young animals, possessive grip. Image of Hexagram 61.

Tend towards, YÜ: move toward, reach, in the direction of. **Eat,** SHIH: eat, ingest, swallow, devour; take in, incorporate. **Possess,** YU: in possession of, have, own; opposite of lack, WU. **Bless,** FU: heavenly gifts; make happy; spiritual power and goodwill. The ideogram: spirit and plenty, heavenly gifts in abundance.

b) **Border,** CHI: limit, frontier, line which joins and divides. The ideogram: place and sacrifice, border between human and spirit.

Six at fourth

a) Fluttering, fluttering.
   Not affluent: use one's neighbor.
   Not warning: use the connection to the spirits.

b) Fluttering, fluttering: not affluence.
   Altogether letting go substance indeed.
   Not warning: using the connection to the spirits.
   Centering the heart desiring indeed.

You are afraid to leave the nest. Don't worry, come out and live in the great world. If you need help, then ask for it. It will be there. Use your basic connection to people who are your spiritual kin. Act on your heart's desire.

Associated Contexts a) **Flutter,** P'IEN: fly or run about; bustle, fussy. The ideogram: young bird leaving the nest. The doubled character intensifies this quality.

Affluence, FU: rich, abundant; wealth; enrich, provide for; flow towards, accrue. **Neighbor,** LIN: person living nearby; extended family; assist, support.

Warn, CHIEH: alert, alarm, put on guard; caution, inform; guard against, refrain from (as in a diet). The ideogram: spear held in both hands, warning enemies and alerting friends. **Connection,** FU: accord between inner and outer in a particular moment; sincere, truthful, verified, reliable, in accord with the spirits; capture; prisoners, spoils. The ideogram: bird's claw enclosing young animals, possessive grip. Image of Hexagram 61.

b) **Altogether,** CHIEH: all, the whole; the same sort, all alike; entirely. **Let go,** SHIH: lose, omit, miss, fail, let slip; out of control. The ideogram: drop from the hand. **Substance,** SHIH: real, solid, full; results, fruits, possessions; essence; honest, sincere. The ideogram: string of coins under a roof, riches in the house.

Center, CHUNG: inner, central; put in the center; middle, stable point enabling you to face inner and outer changes; middle line of trigram. The ideogram: field divided in two equal parts. Image of Hexagram 61. **Heart,** HSIN: heart as center of being; seat of mind's images and affections; moral nature; source of desires, intentions, will. **Desire,** YÜAN: wish, hope or long for; covet; desired object.

Six at fifth

a) The supreme burgeoning converts the maiden.
Using satisfaction, Spring auspicious.

b) Using satisfaction, Spring auspicious.
Center uses moving desire indeed.

This is a great union that will have repercussions through the generations. It is an omen of future happiness that, in time, will gratify your desires and realize all your aims. Take joy in this connection. The way to the source is open.

Associated Contexts a) **Supreme,** TI: highest, above all on earth; sovereign lord, source of power; emperor. **Burgeon,** YI: beginning of growth after seedburst, CHIA; early spring; associated with the Woody Moment. **Supreme Burgeoning,** TI YI, refers to the great Shang emperor (1191–1151 BCE) who took a wife from the family of King Wen's ancestors in order to assure an heir. This ennobled the line from which the Chou Dynasty would come. It is an omen of great happiness and good fortune in the future. **Convert,** KUEI: change to another form, persuade; return to yourself or the place where you belong; restore, revert, become loyal; turn into; give a young girl in marriage. The ideogram: arrive and wife, become mistress of a household. **Maiden(hood)**, MEI: girl not yet nubile, virgin; younger sister; daughter of a secondary wife. The ideogram: woman and not-yet. **Converting Maidenhood** is the Image of Hexagram 54.

Satisfaction, CHIH: fulfilment, gratification, happy in realizing your aim; take pleasure in, fulfil a need. **Spring**, YÜAN: source, origin, head; great, excellent; arise, begin, generating power; first stage of the Time Cycle.

b) **Center**, CHUNG: inner, central; put in the center; middle, stable point enabling you to face inner and outer changes; middle line of trigram. The ideogram: field divided in two equal parts. Image of Hexagram 61. **Move**, HSING: move or move something; motivate, emotionally moving; walk, act, do. The ideogram: stepping left then right. **Desire**, YÜAN: wish, hope or long for; covet; desired object.

Six above

a) The bulwark returned to the moat.
Do not avail of legions.
Originating from the capital, notifying fate.
Trial: distress.

b) The bulwark returned to the moat.
One's fate disarrayed indeed.

The structure of things is collapsing. Don't try to force a change by acting aggressively. This has fate behind it. You may be distressed, but you are in the right position to change your thinking. Collect the energy and insight to try anew.

Associated Contexts a) **Bulwark**, CH'ENG: city wall, citadel, place walled for defence. **Return**, FU: go back, turn back to the starting point; recur, reappear, come again; restore, recover, retrace; an earlier time or place. The ideogram: step and retrace a path. Image of Hexagram 24. **Moat**, HUANG: ditch around city or fort.

Avail of, YUNG: take advantage of; benefit from, profit by; use for a specific purpose; apply to advantage. The ideogram: to divine and center, applying divination to central concerns. **Legions/leading**, SHIH: troops; an organized unit, a metropolis; leader, general, model, master; organize, make functional; take as a model, imitate. The ideogram: heap and whole, organize confusion into functional units. Image of Hexagram 7.

Origin, TZU: source, beginning, ground; cause, reason, motive; line of descent; path to the origin; yourself, intrinsic. **Capital,** YI: populous fortified city, center and symbol of the domain it rules. The ideogram: enclosure and official seal. **Notify,** KAO: proclaim, order, decree; advise, inform, tell. The ideogram: mouth and ox head, imposing speech. **Fate, mandate,** MING: individual destiny; birth and death as limits of life; issue orders with authority; consult the gods. The ideogram: mouth and order, words with heavenly authority.

Trial, CHEN: inquiry by divination and its result; righteous, firm; separating wheat from chaff; the kernel, the proven core; fourth stage of the Time Cycle. The ideogram: pearl and divination. **Distress,** LIN: shame, regret, humiliation; aware of having lost the right track; leads to **repenting,** HUI, correcting the direction of mind and life.

b) **Disarray,** LUAN: throw into disorder, mislay, confuse; out of place; discord, insurrection, anarchy.

OBSTRUCTION ▌ *PI*

Stop!; obstacles, blocked communication; cut off, closed, failure; people of no use or worth to you.

Obstruction describes your situation in terms of being blocked or interfered with. Its symbol is the place of the victim in a sacrifice, the thing to be banished or cut off. The way to deal with it is to stop what you are doing and accept the obstruction. Communication is cut off. You are connected with the wrong people. If you try to act, you will encounter misfortune. Your proposals will be rejected. You will be personally disapproved of. There is no way for someone who wants to stay in touch with the Way to take advantage of this situation. What is important is departing, along with your ability to realize your plans. The time that is coming is small and mean. You will have to adapt to it. Don't seek to impose your ideas. Retreat and be patient.

● *Image of the Situation*

> **Obstructing it, in no way people.**
> **Chün tzu, Trial: not advantageous.**
> **The great going, the small coming.**

Associated Contexts **Obstruct**, P'I: closed, stopped; bar the way; obstacle; unfortunate, wicked; refuse, disapprove, deny. The ideogram: mouth and not, blocked communication. **It/them/have(it)/'s**, CHIH: expresses possession, directly or as an object pronoun. **In no way people**, FEI JEN: there are no people, no people are involved; also: worthless people; barbarians, rebels, foreign slaves, captives.

Advantageous/Harvest, LI: advantageous, profitable; acute, insightful; benefit, nourish; third stage of the Time Cycle. **Chün tzu**: ideal of a person who uses divination to order his/her life in accordance with tao rather than wilful intention; keyword. **Trial**, CHEN: inquiry by divination and its result; righteous, firm; separating wheat from chaff; the kernel, the proven core; fourth stage of the Time Cycle. The ideogram: pearl and divination.

Great, TA: big, noble, important, very; orient the will toward a self-imposed goal, impose direction; ability to lead or guide your life; contrasts with small, HSIAO, flexible adaptation to what crosses your path; keyword. Image of Hexagrams 14, 26, 28, 34. **Go,** WANG, and **Come,** LAI, describe the stream of time as it flows from future through present to past. **Go,** WANG, indicates: what is departing; proceed, move on; **Come,** LAI, indicates: what is approaching; move toward, arrive at; keywords. **Small,** HSIAO, little, common, unimportant; adapting to what crosses your path; ability to move in harmony with the vicissitudes of life; contrasts with great, TA, self-imposed theme or goal; keyword. Image of Hexagrams 9 and 62.

- *Outer and Inner Aspects*

☰**Force:** The force of heaven struggles on, persistent and unwearied; heavenly bodies persist in their orbits. **Force** is the center of the yin hemicycle, completing the formative process.

Connection to the outer: struggling forces are bound together in dynamic tension, the Metallic Moment culminating. **Force** brings elements to grips, creating enduring relations.

☷**Field:** The field of earth yields and sustains, serving in order to produce. **Field** is the equalizing point between yin and yang where things labor and serve.

Connection to the inner: the common labor of sowing and hoarding, the Earthy Moment. **Field** produces concrete results through serving.

An outer struggle blocks bringing-forth; the productivity of the field is **obstructed** and confined within.

- *Hidden Possibility*

Nuclear trigrams **Ground,** SUN, and **Bound,** KEN, result in Nuclear Hexagram 53, **Gradual Advance,** CHIEN. **Obstructed** communication is overcome by the subtle and continual penetration of **Gradual Advance.**

- *Sequence*

Beings not permitted to use complete interpenetrating.
Accepting this lets you use Obstruction.

Associated Contexts **Beings not permitted to use ...** : no one is allowed to make use of; nothing can exist by means of. **Complete,** CHUNG: end of a cycle that begins the next; last, whole, all; contrasts with exhaust, CH'IUNG, final end. The ideogram: silk cocoons, follow and ice, winter linking one

year with the next. **Interpenetrate**, T'UNG: mutually penetrate; permeate, flow through, reach everywhere; see clearly, communicate with.

Accepting ... use: activating this hexagram depends on understanding and accepting the previous statement.

- *Contrasted Definitions*

    Obstruction, Pervading: reversing one's sorting indeed.

    Associated Contexts **Pervade**, T'AI: spread and reach everywhere, permeate, diffuse; communicate; extensive, abundant, prosperous; smooth, slippery; extreme, extravagant, prodigal. The ideogram: person in water, connected to the universal medium. Image of Hexagram 11. **Reverse**, FAN: turn and move in the opposite direction; turn around or upside down (180 degrees); change to the opposite position; contrary. **One's/one**, CH'I: third person pronoun; also: it/its, he/his, she/hers, they/theirs. **Sort**, LEI: group according to kind, class with; like nature or purpose; species, class, genus. **Indeed/is/means**: YEH: intensifier, connective; indicates comment on previous statement.

- *Symbol Tradition*

    Heaven, earth, not mingling. Obstruction.
    A chün tzu uses parsimonious actualizing tao to cast out heaviness.
    [A chün tzu uses] not permitting splendor in using benefits.

    Associated Contexts **Heaven**, T'IEN: highest; sky, firmament, heavens; power above the human as opposed to earth, TI, below; the Symbol of the trigram Force, CH'IEN. The ideogram: great and the one above. **Earth**, TI: ground on which the human world rests; basis of all things, nourishes all things; the Symbol of the trigram Field, K'UN: **Mingle**, CHIAO: blend with, communicate, join, exchange; trade, business; copulation; friendship.

    Use(of), YI: make use of, by means of, owing to; employ, make functional. **Parsimonious**, CHIEN: thrifty; moderate, temperate; stingy, scanty. **Actualize tao**, TE: realize tao in action; power, virtue; ability to follow the course traced by the ongoing process of the cosmos; keyword. The ideogram: to go, straight, and heart. Linked with acquire, TE: acquiring that which makes a being become what it is meant to be. **Cast out**, P'I: expel, repress, exclude, punish; exclusionary laws and their enforcement. The ideogram: punish, authority and mouth, give orders to expel. **Heavy**, NAN: arduous, grievous, difficult; hardship, distress; harass; contrasts with versatile, I, deal lightly with. The ideogram: domestic bird with clipped tail and drying sticky earth.

Not permitting, PI K'O:: not possible; contradicts an inherent principle. The ideogram: mouth and breath, silent consent. **Splendor**, JUNG: glory, elegance, honor, beauty; flowering; elaborate carved corners of a temple roof. **Benefits**, LU: pay, salary, income; have the use of; goods received, revenues; official recognition.

● *Image Tradition*

> Obstructing it, in no way people. [I]
> Chün tzu, Trial: not advantageous
> The great going, the small coming.
> By consequence of that Heaven and Earth do not mingle
> and the myriad beings do not interpenetrate indeed.
> Above and Below not mingling and
> Below Heaven without fiefdoms indeed.
>
> Inside yin and outside yang. [II]
> Inside supple and outside strong.
> Inside Small People and outside chün tzu.
> Small People: tao long living.
> A chün tzu: tao dissolving indeed.

Associated Contexts [I] **By consequence(of)**, TSE: very strong connection; reason, cause, result; rule, law, pattern, standard; therefore. **That**, SHIH: preceding statement. **Myriad**, WAN: countless; many, everyone; lit.: ten thousand. The ideogram: swarm of insects. **Being(s)**, WU: creature, thing, any single being; matter, substance, essence; nature of things.

Above and Below, SHANG HSIA: realm of dynamic interaction between the upper and the lower; the vertical dimension. **Below Heaven**, T'IEN HSIA: the human world, between heaven and earth. **Fiefdom**, PANG: region governed by a feudatory, an order of nobility.

[II] **Inside**, NEI: within, inner, interior; inside of the house and those who work there, particularly women; the lower trigram, as opposed to outside, WAI, the upper. The ideogram: border and enter, cross a border. **Yin**: Struction; consolidating, shadowy aspect of phenomena: conserves, substantializes, creates structures; spacial extension; limited, bound, given

specific being; build, make something concrete. **Outside**, WAI: outer, exterior, external; people working in places other than their home; unfamiliar, foreign; the upper trigram, as opposed to inside, NEI, the lower. **Yang**: Action; dynamic and light aspect of phenomena: arouses, transforms, dissolves existing structures; linear thrust; stimulus, drive, focus; direct or orient something.

Supple, JOU: quality of the opened lines; flexible, pliant, tender, adaptable. **Strong**, KANG: quality of the whole lines; firm, strong, unyielding, persisting.

Small People, HSIAO JEN: lowly, common, humble; those who adjust to circumstances with the flexibility of the small; effect of the small within an individual; keyword.

Tao: way or path; ongoing process of being and the course it traces for each specific person or thing; keyword. The ideogram: go and head, leading and the path it creates. **Long living**, CHANG: enduring, constant; senior, superior, greater; increase, prosper; respect, elevate. **Dissolve**, HSIAO: liquify, melt, thaw; diminish, disperse; eliminate, exhaust. The ideogram: water dissolving differences.

- *Transforming Lines*

    Initial six

    a) **Eradicate thatch grass intertwisting.**
    Using one's classification.
    Trial: auspicious. Growing.

    b) **Eradicating thatch grass, Trial: auspicious.**
    Purpose located in a chief indeed.

It is time to pull back. Take vigorous action together with others to get out of this place and find the people you really belong with. Be firm. Put things in order and set out. Make an offering and you will succeed.

Associated Contexts a) **Eradicate**, PA: pull up, root out, extirpate; extricate from difficulties; elevate, promote. **Thatch grass**, MAO: thick grass used for the roofs of humble houses. **Intertwist**, JU: interlaced; entangled roots.

Classification, HUI: class, collection, series; same kind; put or group together.

Auspicious, CHI: leads to the experience of meaning; favorable, propitious, advantageous, appropriate; keyword. The ideogram: scholar and mouth, wise words of a sage. **Grow,** HENG: success through a sacrifice; pervade, persevere; bring to full growth; enjoy; vigorous, effective; second stage of the Time Cycle.

b) **Purpose,** CHIH: focus of mind and heart; will, inclination, resolve. The ideogram: heart and scholar, high inner resolve, or heart and go, inner determination. **Locate(in),** TSAI: live in, dwell, reside; belong to, involved with, depend on; within. The ideogram: earth and persevere, place on the earth. **Chief,** CHÜN: effective ruler; preside over, take the lead; influence others; term of respect. The ideogram: mouth and director, giving orders.

   Six at second

   a) **Enwrapped and receiving.**
   Small People auspicious.
   Great People Obstructed. Growing.

   b) **Great People Obstructed. Growing.**
   Not disarraying the flock indeed.

Accept isolation. Make a hidden offering. Don't disturb the flock. Those who adapt to what crosses their path may succeed, but your great idea is obstructed. Do not worry. Stay true to yourself and the way will open.

Associated Contexts a) **Enwrap,** PAO: envelop, hold, contain; patient; take on responsibility, engaged. The ideogram: enfold and self, a fetus in the womb. **Receive,** CH'ENG: receive gifts or commands from superiors or customers; take in hand; catch falling water. The ideogram: accepting a seal of office.

   Great People, TA JEN: important, noble, influential; those who impose a ruling principle on their lives; effect of the great within an individual; keyword. **Grow,** HENG: success through a sacrifice; pervade, persevere; bring to full growth; enjoy; vigorous, effective; second stage of the Time Cycle.

b) **Disarray,** LUAN: throw into disorder, mislay, confuse; out of place; discord, insurrection, anarchy. **Flock,** CH'ÜN: herd, group; people of same kind, friends, equals; all, entire; move in unison, flock together. The ideogram: chief and sheep, flock around a leader.

Six at third

a) Enwrapped and embarrassed.

b) Enwrapping embarrassing.
Situation not appropriate indeed.

Do nothing. Simply wait. Stop and examine yourself. Make inner preparations. The time is not right for action. Be like the fetus in the womb. Let your sense of shame correct you.

Associated Contexts a) **Enwrap**, PAO: envelop, hold, contain; patient; take on responsibility, engaged. The ideogram: enfold and self, a fetus in the womb. **Embarrassed**, HSIU: conscious of guilt or fault; unworthy; ashamed, confused; shy, blushing. The ideogram: sheep, sheepish feeling.

b) **Situation**, WEI: place or seat according to rank; post, position, command; right, proper; established, arranged. The ideogram: person and stand, servants in their places. **Appropriate**, TANG: suitable; opportune, convenient; adequate, competent; equal to; whole lines in uneven places and opened lines in even places.

Nine at fourth

a) Possessing a mandate, without fault.
Cultivating radiant satisfaction.

b) Possessing a mandate, without fault.
Purpose moving indeed.

In the middle of this terrible time, you experience a real connection. This is a lovely fate offered by heaven and it is your job to cultivate it. Whatever happens, it is not a mistake. Work at it. In the end it can bring joy and satisfaction, spreading light to all.

Associated Contexts a) **Possess**, YU: in possession of, have, own; opposite of lack, WU. **Fate/mandate**, MING: individual destiny; birth and death as limits of life; issue orders with authority; consult the gods. The ideogram: mouth and order, words with heavenly authority. **Without fault**, WU CHIU: no error or harm in the situation.

Cultivate, CHOU: till fields or gardens; continue successively, like annual plowing. The ideogram: fields and long life. **Radiance**, LI: glowing light, spreading in all directions; light-giving, discriminating, articulating; divide and arrange in order; the power of consciousness. The ideogram: bird and weird, the magical fire-bird with brilliant plumage. Image of Hexagram 30. **Satisfaction,** CHIH: fulfilment, gratification, happy in realizing your aim; take pleasure in, fulfil a need.

b) **Purpose,** CHIH: focus of mind and heart; will, inclination, resolve. The ideogram: heart and scholar, high inner resolve, or heart and go, inner determination. **Move,** HSING: move or move something; motivate, emotionally moving; walk, act, do. The ideogram: stepping left then right.

> **Nine at fifth**
>
> *a)* Relinquishing Obstruction.
>   Great People auspicious.
>   Its extinction, its extinction.
>   Attached to the bushy mulberry trees.
>
> *b)* Great People's auspiciousness.
>   Situation correcting appropriate indeed.

If you are fighting the obstruction, it is time to let go. The obstacles and troubles are disappearing. Imagine that you are in a quiet rural retreat, attached to the mulberry grove. That is the place for you. It will correct the whole situation.

Associated Contexts a) **Relinquish,** HSIU: let go of, stop temporarily, rest; resign, release; act gently, enjoy; relaxed. The ideogram: person leaning on a tree.
   Great People, TA JEN: important, noble, influential; those who impose a ruling principle on their lives; effect of the great within an individual; keyword. **Auspicious,** CHI: leads to the experience of meaning; favorable, propitious, advantageous, appropriate; keyword. The ideogram: scholar and mouth, wise words of a sage.
   Its/it, CH'I: third person pronoun; also: one/one's, he/his, she/hers, they/theirs. **Extinguish,** WANG: ruin, destroy; gone, dead, lost without trace; extinct, forgotten, out of mind. The ideogram: person concealed by a wall, out of sight. The doubled character intensifies this quality.
   Attach, HSI: fasten to, bind, tie; retain, continue; keep in mind, emotionally attached. **Bushy,** PAO: luxuriant growth, dense thicket; conceal; screen; sleeping-mats; wrap as a gift. The ideogram: wrap and bushes. **Mulberry tree,** SANG: literal tree and silk production; tranquility; retired, rural place.

b) **'s/have(it)/it/them,** CHIH: expresses possession, directly or as an object pronoun.

Situation, WEI: place or seat according to rank; post, position, command; right, proper; established, arranged. The ideogram: person and stand, servants in their places. **Correct**, CHENG: rectify deviation or one-sidedness; proper, straight, exact, regular; constant, rule, model. The ideogram: stop and one, hold to one thing. **Appropriate**, TANG: suitable; opportune, convenient; adequate, competent; equal to; whole lines in uneven places and opened lines in even places.

Nine above

a) Subverting Obstruction.
Beforehand Obstruction, afterwards rejoicing.

b) Obstruction completed, by consequence subverting.
Wherefore permitting long living indeed?

The very thing causing you pain is suddenly turned on its head. What used to be an obstruction becomes a cause to rejoice. Thank heavens the bad time is over! Let it all go. Move freely and firmly with the new time. Why regret what is past?

Associated Contexts a) **Subvert**, CHING: undermine, overturn, overthrow; falling; pour out, empty; waste, squander. The ideogram: man, head and ladle, emptying out old ideas.

Before(hand)/earlier, HSIEN: come before in time; first, at first; formerly, past, previous; begin, go ahead of. **After(wards)/later**, HOU: come after in time, subsequent; put oneself after; the second; attendants, heirs, successors, posterity. **Rejoice(in)**, HSI: feel and give joy; delight, exult; cheerful, merry. The ideogram: joy (music) and mouth, expressing joy.

b) **Wherefore**, HO: interrogative: why? for what reason? what is? and affirmation: therefore, for that reason. **Permit**, K'O: possible because in harmony with an inherent principle. The ideogram: mouth and breath, silent consent.

13

CONCORDING PEOPLE ▌
T'UNG JEN

Bring people together, harmonize; share an idea or goal; welcome others, co-operate.

Concording People describes your situation in terms of sharing something with others. Its symbol is people gathering at the Outskirts Altar for the great sacrifices and dances that unite them in love, war or the opening of the fields. The way to deal with it is to find ways to unite the people involved. Make an offering and you will succeed. This is the kind of task that can best be done together and brings mutual advantage in the end. Find places of agreement where goals can be shared. Develop group spirit and a bond of common understanding. This is pleasing to the spirits. Through it they will give you success, effective power and the ability to bring the situation to maturity. This is the right time to embark on a significant enterprise or enter the stream of life with a goal. Use the oracle and put your ideas to the trial.

●   *Image of the Situation*

> **Concording People move towards the countryside. Growing.**
> **Advantageous to step into the Great River.**
> **A chün tzu: Advantageous Trial, Harvesting.**

Associated Contexts **Concord,** T'UNG: harmonize, unite, equalize, assemble; agree, share in; together, at once, same time and place. The ideogram: cover and mouth, silent understanding and perfect fit. **People, person,** JEN: humans individually and collectively; an individual; humankind. **Move towards,** YÜ: move toward, in the direction of; arrive at, in. **Countryside,** YEH: cultivated fields and grassland, where nature and human construction interact; third of the territorial zones: city, suburbs, countryside, forests. **Grow,** HENG: success through a sacrifice; pervade, persevere; bring to full growth; enjoy; vigorous, effective; second stage of the Time Cycle.

   Advantageous/Harvest, LI: advantageous, profitable; acute, insightful; benefit, nourish; third stage of the Time Cycle. **Step into the Great River,**

SHE TA CH'UAN: consciously moving into the flow of time; enter the stream of life with a goal or purpose; embark on a significant enterprise.

Chün tzu: ideal of a person who uses divination to order his/her life in accordance with tao rather than wilful intention; keyword. **Trial**, CHEN: inquiry by divination and its result; righteous, firm; separating wheat from chaff; the kernel, the proven core; fourth stage of the Time Cycle. The ideogram: pearl and divination.

• *Outer and Inner Aspects*

☰**Force**: The force of heaven struggles on, persistent and unwearied; heavenly bodies persist in their orbits. **Force** is the center of the yin hemicycle, completing the formative process.

Connection to the outer: struggling forces are bound together in dynamic tension, the Metallic Moment culminating. **Force** brings elements to grips, creating enduring relations.

☲**Radiance**: Fire and brightness radiate light and warmth, attached to their support; congregating people see and become aware. **Radiance** ends the yang hemicycle, consuming action in awareness.

Connection to the inner: light, heat, consciousness bring about continual change, the Fiery Moment. **Radiance** spreads outward, congregating, becoming aware and changing.

Warmth and brightness radiate outward through **people's** enduring struggle to find ways to **concord**.

• *Hidden Possibility*

Nuclear trigrams **Force**, CH'IEN, and **Ground**, SUN, result in Nuclear Hexagram 44, **Coupling**, KOU. **Concording people's** conscious attempt to create enduring forms of union leads to spontaneous **coupling**.

• *Sequence*

Beings not permitted to use completing Obstruction.
Accepting this lets you use Concording People.

Associated Contexts **Beings not permitted to use ...** : no one is allowed to make use of; nothing can exist by means of. **Complete**, CHUNG: end of a cycle that begins the next; last, whole, all; contrasts with exhaust, CH'IUNG: final end. The ideogram: silk cocoons, follow and ice, winter linking one year with the next. **Obstruct**, P'I: closed, stopped; bar the way; obstacle; unfortunate, wicked; refuse, disapprove, deny. The ideogram: mouth and not, blocked communication. Image of Hexagram 12.

Accepting ... use: activating this hexagram depends on understanding and accepting the previous statement.

- ## Contrasted Definitions

> Great Possessing: crowds indeed.
> Concording People: connecting indeed.

Associated Contexts **Great**, TA: big, noble, important, very; orient the will toward a self-imposed goal, impose direction; ability to lead or guide your life; contrasts with small, HSIAO, flexible adaptation to what crosses your path; keyword. Image of Hexagrams 14, 26, 28, 34. **Possess**, YU: in possession of, have, own; opposite of lack, WU. **Great Possessing** is the Image of Hexagram 14. **Crowds**, CHUNG: many people, large group; majority; in common. **Indeed/is/means**: YEH: intensifier, connective; indicates comment on previous statement.

Connect, CH'IN: attach to, approach, come near; cherish, help, favor; intimate; relatives, kin.

- ## Symbol Tradition

> Heaven associating with fire. Concording People.
> A chün tzu uses sorting the clans to mark off the beings.

Associated Contexts **Heaven**, T'IEN: highest; sky, firmament, heavens; power above the human as opposed to earth, TI, below; the Symbol of the trigram Force, CH'IEN. The ideogram: great and the one above. **Associate(with)**, YÜ: consort with, combine; companions; group, band, company; agree with, comply, help. The ideogram: pair of hands reaching downward meets a pair of hands reaching upward, helpful association. **Fire**, HUO: warming and consuming aspect of burning; fire and brightness are the Symbols of Radiance, LI.

Use(of), YI: make use of, by means of, owing to; employ, make functional. **Sort**, LEI: group according to kind, class with; like nature or purpose; species, class, genus. **Clan**, TSU: extended family with same ancester and surname; kin, relatives; tribe, class, kind. The ideogram: flag and spear, a rallying point. **Mark off**, PIEN: distinguish by dividing; mark off a plot of land; frame which divides a bed from its stand; discuss and dispute. The

ideogram: knife and acrid, biting division. **Being(s)**, WU: creature, thing, any single being; matter, substance, essence; nature of things.

● *Image Tradition*

> Concording People. [I]
> Supple acquiring the situation.
> Acquiring the center and corresponding
> reaches to Force.
> Spoken thus: Concording People.

> Concording People: spoken thus. [II]
> Concording People moving toward the countryside. Growing.
> Advantageous to step into the Great River.
> Force moving indeed.

> Pattern brightening and using persisting. [III]
> Center correct and corresponding.
> A chün tzu correcting indeed.
> Verily a chün tzu activating enables
> interpenetrating Below Heaven's purpose.

Associated Contexts [I] **Supple**, JOU: quality of the opened lines; flexible, pliant, tender, adaptable. **Acquire**, TE: obtain the desired object; wish for, desire covetously; gains, possessions. The ideogram: go and obstacle, going through obstacles to the goal. **Situation**, WEI: place or seat according to rank; post, position, command; right, proper; established, arranged. The ideogram: person and stand, servants in their places.

Center, CHUNG: inner, central; put in the center; middle, stable point enabling you to face inner and outer changes; middle line of trigram. The ideogram: field divided in two equal parts. Image of Hexagram 61. **Correspond(to)**, YING: be in agreement or harmony; resonate together, invoke and fulfil each other; answer to, suitable; relation between the lines (1:4, 2:5, 3:6) when they form the pair opened and whole, supple and strong. The ideogram: heart and obey. **Reach(to)**, HU: arrive at a goal; reach towards and achieve; connect; contrasts with tend-towards, YU. **Force**, CH'IEN: spirit power, creative and destructive; unceasing forward motion; dynamic, enduring, untiring; firm, stable; heaven, sovereign, father; also: dry up, parched, exhausted, cleared away. The ideogram: sprouts or vapors rising from the ground and sunlight, both fecundating moisture and scorching drought. Image of Hexagram 1.

Spoken thus, YÜEH: designated, termed, called. The ideogram: open mouth and tongue.

[II] Move, HSING: move or move something; motivate, emotionally moving; walk, act, do. The ideogram: stepping left then right.

[III] Pattern, WEN: intrinsic or natural design and its beauty; stylish, elegant; noble; contrasts with composition, CHANG, a conscious creation. **Brightness**, MING: light-giving aspect of burning, heavenly bodies and consciousness; with fire, the Symbol of the trigram Radiance, LI. **Persist**, CHIEN: strong, robust, dynamic, tenacious; continuous; unwearied heavenly bodies in their orbits; the Action of the trigram Force, CH'IEN.

Centering correcting, CHUNG CHENG: central and correct; make rectifying one-sidedness and error your central concern; reach,ing a stable center in yourself can correct the situation.

Verily, WEI: the epitome of; in truth, the only; very important. **Activate**, WEI: act or cause to act; do, make, manage; make active; attend to, help; because of. **Able**, NENG: enable; ability, power, skill, art; competent, talented; duty, function, capacity. The ideogram: an animal with strong hooves and bones, able to carry and defend. **Interpenetrate**, T'UNG: mutually penetrate; permeate, flow through, reach everywhere; see clearly, communicate with. **Below Heaven**, T'IEN HSIA: the human world, between heaven and earth. **'s/have(it)/it/them**, CHIH: expresses possession, directly or as an object pronoun. **Purpose**, CHIH: focus of mind and heart; will, inclination, resolve. The ideogram: heart and scholar, high inner resolve, or heart and go, inner determination.

● *Transforming Lines*

Initial nine

a) **Concording People at the gate.**
Without fault.

b) **Issuing forth from the gate, Concording People.**
Furthermore whose fault indeed?

You are poised on the threshold. Join with others and take the first step. This is certainly not a mistake.

Associated Contexts a) **Gate**, MEN: outer door, between court-yard and street; a text or master as gate to a school of thought.

Without fault, WU CHIU: no error or harm in the situation.

b) **Issue forth(from),** CH'U: emerge from, come out of, proceed from, spring from; the Action of the trigram Shake, CHEN; contrary of enter, JU. The ideogram: stem with branches and leaves emerging.

Furthermore, YU: in addition to; higher degree of. **Whose,** SHUI: relative and interrogative pronoun; also: whose? **Fault,** CHIU: unworthy conduct that leads to harm, illness, misfortune. The ideogram: person and differ, differ from what you should be.

Six at second

a) Concording People at the ancestral temple.
Distress.

b) Concording People at the ancestral temple.
Distress: tao indeed.

Announcing the new, you stand before the ancestors and the ideals they represent. As you think about it you will see the right way to act. Let your distress be your guide.

Associated Contexts a) **Ancestry,** TSUNG: clan, kin, origin; those who bear the same surname; ancestral hall and tablets; honor, revere; a doctrine; contrasts with predecessor, K'AO: individual ancestors.
Distress, LIN: shame, regret, humiliation; aware of having lost the right track; leads to repenting, HUI, correcting the direction of mind and life.

b) **Tao:** way or path; ongoing process of being and the course it traces for each specific person or thing; keyword. The ideogram: go and head, leading and the path it creates.

Nine at third

a) Hiding away arms in the thickets.
Ascending one's high mound.
Three year's time not rising up.

b) Hiding away arms in the thickets.
Antagonistic strong indeed.
Three year's time not rising.
Secure movement indeed.

You have been treated badly and withdraw from contact. Be careful of the thickets of resentment. Are you sure you want to act like this? It may keep you isolated for quite a long time, though in the end you will succeed.

Associated Contexts a) **Hide away**, FU: conceal, place in ambush; secretly, silently; prostrate, fall on your face; humble. The ideogram: man and dog, man crouching. **Arms**, JUNG: weapons; armed people, soldiers; military, violent. The ideogram: spear and armor, offensive and defensive weapons. **Thicket**, MANG: underbrush, tangled vegetation, thick grass, jungle; rustic, rude, socially inept.

Ascend, SHENG: go up; climb step by step; rise in office; advance through effort; accumulate; bring out and fulfil; lit.: a measure for fermented liquor, ascension as distillation. Image of Hexagram 46. **One's/one**, CH'I: third person pronoun; also: it/its, he/his, she/hers, they/theirs. **High(ness)**, KAO: high, elevated, lofty, eminent; excellent, advanced. **Mound**, LING: grave-mound, barrow; small hill.

Three, SAN: number three, third time or place; active phases of a cycle; superlative; beginning of repetition. **Year's time**, SUI: actual length of time in a year; contrasts with years-revolved, NIEN, number of years elapsed. **Rise**, HSING: get up, grow, lift; begin, give rise to, construct; be promoted; flourishing, fashionable. The ideogram: lift, two hands and unite, lift with both hands.

b) **Antagonistic**, TI: opposed and equal; competitor, enemy; a contest between equals. **Strong**, KANG: quality of the whole lines; firm, strong, unyielding, persisting.

Secure, AN: safe, peaceful, still, settled; calm, tranquilize. The ideogram: woman under a roof, a tranquil home.

Nine at fourth

a) **Riding one's rampart.**
   Nothing controlling or attacking.
   Auspicious.

b) **Riding one's rampart.**
   Righteously nothing controlling (its auspiciousness) indeed.
   By consequence confining and reversing indeed.

Stand in your city and on your accomplishments. Have no doubts. Trust your purpose. This will reverse what feels like an oppressive situation.

Associated Contexts a) **Ride**, CH'ENG: ride an animal or a chariot; have the upper hand, seize the right time; control strong power; overcome the nature of the other; supple opened line above a strong whole line. **One's/one**, CH'I: third person pronoun; also: it/its, he/his, she/hers, they/theirs. **Rampart**, YUNG: defensive wall; bulwark, redoubt.

Nothing/nowhere, FU: strong negative; not a single thing/place. **Control**, K'O: command; check, impede, prevail, obstruct, repress; adequate, able. The ideogram: roof beams support a house, controlling the structure. **Attack**, KUNG: fight with; aggression; go to work, apply to; rouse by criticizing, put in order; stimulate vital power; urgent desire. The ideogram: toil and strike.

Auspicious, CHI: leads to the experience of meaning; favorable, propitious, advantageous, appropriate; keyword. The ideogram: scholar and mouth, wise words of a sage.

b) **Righteous**, YI: proper and just, meets the standards; things in their proper place; the heart that rules itself; upright, moral rule; contrasts with Harvest, LI, advantage or profit.

By consequence(of), TSE: very strong connection; reason, cause, result; rule, law, pattern, standard; therefore. **Confine**, K'UN: enclose, restrict, limit; oppressed; impoverish, distress; afflicted, exhausted, disheartened, weary. The ideogram: an enclosed tree. Image of Hexagram 47. **Reverse**, FAN: turn and move in the opposite direction; turn around or upside down (180 degrees); change to the opposite position; contrary.

Nine at fifth

a) Concording People beforehand crying and sobbing
and afterwards laughing.
Great leaders control mutual meeting.

b) Beforehand Concording People have it:
Using centering and straightening indeed.
Great leaders control mutual meeting.
Words mutualize controlling indeed.

The way to a real connection between people is not always easy. But when you work your way through the tears, the joy will soon be there. As long as your hearts are firm, everything you encounter will conspire to help you. This is the time when great leaders come together in friendship and pool their powers for the good of all.

Associated Contexts a) **Before(hand)/earlier,** HSIEN: come before in time; first, at first; formerly, past, previous; begin, go ahead of. **Cry out/outcry,** HAO: call out, proclaim; signal, order, command; mark, label, sign. **Sob,** T'AO: cry, weep aloud; wailing children. The ideogram: mouth and omen, ominous sounds. **After(wards)/later,** HOU: come after in time, subsequent; put oneself after; the second; attendant, heirs, successors, posterity. **Laugh,** HSIAO: manifest joy or mirth; giggle, laugh at, ridicule; pleased, merry; associated with the Fiery Moment.

Legions/leading, SHIH: troops; an organized unit, a metropolis; leader, general, model, master; organize, make functional; take as a model, imitate. The ideogram: heap and whole, organize confusion into functional units. Image of Hexagram 7. **Control,** K'O: command; check, impede, prevail, obstruct, repress; adequate, able. The ideogram: roof beams support a house, controlling the structure. **Mutual,** HSIANG: reciprocal assistance, encourage, help; bring together, blend with; examine, inspect; by turns. **Meet,** YÜ: come on unexpectedly, encounter; occur, happen; pleasant meeting, lucky coincidence; agree.

b) **Have(it)/it/them/'s,** CHIH: expresses possession, directly or as an object pronoun. **Straighten,** CHIH: correct the crooked, reform, repay injustice; proceed directly; sincere, upright, just; blunt, outspoken. **Word,** YEN: speech, spoken words, sayings; talk, discuss, address. The ideogram: mouth and rising vapor, words as speech.

Nine above

a) Concording People at the outskirts altar.
   Without repenting.

b) Concording People at the outskirts altar.
   Purpose acquired indeed.

Concording people gather to welcome the spirit and open the fields. Commit yourself to this. Enjoy it with others. You won't have any cause to regret it.

Associated Contexts a) **Outskirts,** CHIAO: area adjoining a city where human constructions and nature interpenetrate; second of the territorial zones: city, suburbs, countryside, forests. **Without repenting,** WU HUI: devoid of the sort of trouble that leads to sorrow, regret and the necessity to change your attitude.

14

GREAT POSSESSING ▮ *TA YU*

Great idea, great being; great power to realize; organization, concentration; wealth, abundance, possessions; share your wealth.

Great Possessing describes your situation in terms of acquiring great abundance and prosperity through the development of a central idea. Its symbol is the great person who spreads the blessing of heaven. The way to the source is open. Make an offering and you will succeed. The way to deal with it is to concentrate your energies in one place and share the fruits of your efforts. Focus on a single idea and impose a direction on things. Be noble and magnanimous with the results. This can be a continuing source of fertility and excellence. It is pleasing to the spirits. Through it they will give you success, effective power and the capacity to bring the situation to maturity. Make a great offering and share with others.

● *Image of the Situation*

Great Possessing, Spring Growing.

Associated Contexts **Great,** TA: big, noble, important, very; orient the will toward a self-imposed goal, impose direction; ability to lead or guide your life; contrasts to small, HSIAO: flexible adaptation to what crosses your path; keyword. **Possess,** YU: be in possession of, have, own; possessions; opposite of lack, WU. **Spring,** YÜAN: source, origin, head; great, excellent; arise, begin, generating power; first stage of the Time Cycle. **Grow,** HENG: success through a sacrifice; pervade, persevere; bring to full growth; enjoy; vigorous, effective; second stage of the Time Cycle.

● *Outer and Inner Aspects*

Radiance: Fire and brightness radiate light and warmth, attached to their support; congregating people see and become aware. **Radiance** ends the yang hemicycle, consuming action in awareness.

Connection to the outer: light, heat, consciousness bring continual change, the Fiery Moment. **Radiance** spreads outward, congregating, becoming aware and changing.

☰**Force**: The force of heaven struggles on, persistent and unwearied; heavenly bodies persist in their orbits. **Force** is the center of the yin hemicycle, completing the formative process.

Connection to the inner: struggling forces are bound together in dynamic tension, the Metallic Moment culminating. **Force** brings elements to grips, creating enduring relations.

Great force within **possesses** and spreads brightness and warmth, congregating with people and being seen. This is a time of abundance.

● *Hidden Possibilities*

Nuclear trigrams **Open**, TUI, and **Force**, CH'IEN, result in Nuclear Hexagram 43, **Deciding**, KUAI. Being **possessed** by a single **great** idea demands decisive words and **parting** with the past.

● *Sequence*

> Associating with People Concording implies
> beings necessarily converting in truth.
> Accepting this lets you use Great Possessing.

Associated Contexts **Associate(with)**, YÜ: consort with, combine; companions; group, band, company; agree with, comply, help. The ideogram: pair of hands reaching downward meets a pair of hands reaching upward, helpful association. **People, person,** JEN: humans individually and collectively; an individual; humankind. **Concord**, T'UNG: harmonize, unite, equalize, assemble; agree, share in; together, at once, same time and place. The ideogram: cover and mouth, silent understanding and perfect fit. **Concording People** is the Image of Hexagram 13. **Imply**, CHE: further signify; additional meaning. **Being(s)**, WU: creature, thing, any single being; matter, substance, essence; nature of things. **Necessarily**, PI: unavoidably, indispensably, certainly. **Convert**, KUEI: change to another form, persuade; return to yourself or the place where you belong; restore, revert, become loyal; turn into; give a young girl in marriage. The ideogram: arrive and wife, become mistress of a household. Image of Hexagram 54. **In truth**, YEN: statement is complete and correct.

Accepting ... use: activating this hexagram depends on understanding and accepting the previous statement.

Contrasted Definitions

Great Possessing: crowds indeed.
Concording People: connecting indeed.

Associated Contexts **Crowds**, CHUNG: many people, large group; majority; in common. **Indeed/is/means**, YEH: intensifier, connective; indicates comment on previous statement.

Connect, CH'IN: attach to, approach, come near; cherish, help, favor; intimate; relatives, kin.

Symbol Tradition

Fire located above heaven. Great Possessing.
A chün tzu uses terminating hate to display improvement.
[A chün tzu uses] yielding to heaven to relinquish fate.

Associated Contexts **Fire**, HUO: warming and consuming aspect of burning; fire and brightness are the Symbols of the trigram Radiance, LI. **Locate(in)**, TSAI: live in, dwell, reside; belong to, involved with, depend on; within. The ideogram: earth and persevere, place on the earth. **Above**, SHANG: anything above, in all senses; higher, upper, outer; upper trigram; opposite of below, HSIA. **Heaven**, T'IEN: highest; sky, firmament, heavens; power above the human as opposed to earth, TI, below; the Symbol of the trigram Force, CH'IEN. The ideogram: great and the one above.

Chün tzu: ideal of a person who uses divination to order his/her life in accordance with tao rather than wilful intention; keyword. **Use(of)**, YI: make use of, by means of, owing to; employ, make functional. **Terminate**, O: cut off, check, extinguish, bring to a standstill. The ideogram: go and why, no reason to move. **Hate**, WU: dislike, dread; averse to, ashamed of; repulsive, vicious, vile, ugly, wicked. The ideogram: twisted bowels and heart, heart entangled in emotion. **Display**, YANG: spread, extend, scatter, divulge; publish abroad, make famous. The ideogram: hand and expand, spreading a message. **Improve**, SHAN: make better, reform, perfect, repair; virtuous, wise; mild, docile; clever, skillful, handy. The ideogram: mouth and sheep, gentle speech.

Yield(to), SHUN: give way and bear produce; comply, agree, follow, obey; unresisting, docile, flexible; nourish, provide; the Action of the trigram Field, K'UN. The ideogram: head and current, water flowing from the head of a river, yielding to the banks. **Relinquish**, HSIU: let go of, stop temporarily, rest; resign, release; act gently, enjoy; relaxed. The ideogram:

person leaning on a tree. **Fate,** MING: individual destiny; birth and death as limits of life; issue orders with authority; consult the gods. The ideogram: mouth and order, words with heavenly authority.

● *Image Tradition*

> Great Possessing. [I]
> Supple acquires the dignifying situation, the great center,
> And Above and Below correspond to it.
> Spoken thus: Great Possessing.
>
> One's actualizing tao: strong persists and the pattern brightens [II].
> Corresponding reaching to heaven and the season moving.
> That uses Spring Growing.

Associated Contexts [I] **Supple,** JOU: quality of the opened lines; flexible, pliant, tender, adaptable. **Acquire,** TE: obtain the desired object; wish for, desire covetously; gains, possessions. The ideogram: go and obstacle, going through obstacles to the goal. **Dignify,** TSUN: honor, make eminent; noble, respected. The ideogram: presenting wine to a guest. **Situation,** WEI: place or seat according to rank; post, position, command; right, proper; established, arranged. The ideogram: person and stand, servants in their places. **Center,** CHUNG: inner, central; put in the center; middle, stable point enabling you to face inner and outer changes; middle line of trigram. The ideogram: field divided in two equal parts. Image of Hexagram 61.

Above and Below, SHANG HSIA: realm of dynamic interaction between the upper and the lower; the vertical dimension. **Correspond(to),** YING: be in agreement or harmony; resonate together, invoke and fulfil each other; answer to, suitable; relation between the lines (1:4, 2:5, 3:6) when they form the pair opened and whole, supple and strong. The ideogram: heart and obey. **It/them/have(it)/'s,** CHIH: expresses possession, directly or as an object pronoun.

Spoken thus, YÜEH: designated, termed, called. The ideogram: open mouth and tongue.

[II] **One's/one,** CH'I: third person pronoun; also: it/its, he/his, she/hers, they/theirs. **Actualize tao,** TE: realize tao in action; power, virtue; ability to follow the course traced by the ongoing process of the cosmos; keyword. The ideogram: to go, straight, and heart. Linked with acquire, TE: acquiring that which makes a being become what it is meant to be. **Strong,**

KANG: quality of the whole lines; firm, strong, unyielding, persisting. **Persist**, CHIEN: strong, robust, dynamic, tenacious; continuous; unwearied heavenly bodies in their orbits; the Action of the trigram Force, CH'IEN: **Pattern**, WEN: intrinsic or natural design and its beauty; stylish, elegant; noble; contrasts with composition, CHANG, a conscious creation. **Brightness**, MING: lightgiving aspect of burning, heavenly bodies and consciousness; with fire, the Symbol of the trigram Radiance, LI.

Reach(to), HU: arrive at a goal; reach toward and achieve; connect; contrasts with tend-towards, YU. **Season**, SHIH: quality of the time; the right time, opportune, in harmony; planning in accord with the time; seasons of the year. The ideogram: sun and temple, time as sacred. **Move**, HSING: move or move something; motivate, emotionally moving; walk, act, do. The ideogram: stepping left then right.

That uses, SHIH YI: involves and is involved by.

- *Transforming Lines*

   Initial nine

   a) **Without mingling harm.**
   In no way faulty.
   Drudgery by consequence without fault.

   b) **Great Possessing, the initial nine.**
   Without mingling harm indeed.

There is nothing harmful mingled in your aims and desires. You are not making a mistake in feeling the way you do. There is a lot of hard work involved. This isn't a mistake either. Success is assured.

Associated Contexts a) **Without**, WU: devoid of; -less as suffix. **Mingle**, CHIAO: blend with, communicate, join, exchange; trade, business; copulation; friendship. **Harm**, HAI: damage, injure, offend; suffer; hurtful, hindrance; fearful, anxious.

   In no way, FEI: strong negative; not so. The ideogram: a box filled with opposition. **Fault**, CHIU: unworthy conduct that leads to harm, illness, misfortune. The ideogram: person and differ, differ from what you should be.

   Drudgery, CHIEN: difficult, hard, repetitive work; hard to cultivate; distressing, sorrowful. The ideogram: sticky earth and a person looking around, hard work in comparison to others. **By consequence(of)**, TSE: very strong connection; reason, cause, result; rule, law, pattern, standard; therefore. **Without fault,** WU CHIU: no error or harm in the situation.

Nine at second

a) The great chariot used to carry.
  Having a direction to go. Without fault.

b) The great chariot used to carry.
  Amassing centering, not destroying indeed.

You have to have a vehicle, an inspiring idea that can carry your feelings and desires. Make a plan. Dedicate yourself. You will not be making a mistake.

Associated Contexts a) **Chariot,** CH'E: wheeled travelling vehicle; contrasts with cart, YÜ, which carries. **Carry,** TSAI: bear, carry with you; contain, sustain; load a ship or cart, cargo; fill in, complete.

  Have a direction to go, YU YU WANG: imposing a direction on the flow of time from present to past; have a specific goal or purpose. **Without fault,** WU CHIU: no error or harm in the situation.

b) **Amass,** CHI: hoard, accumulate, pile up, store up, add up, increase. **Destroy,** PAI: ruin, defeat, violate, subvert, break.

Nine at third

a) A prince avails of Growing,
  a sacrifice to the heavenly son.
  Small People nowhere controlling.

b) A prince availing of Growing,
  a sacrifice to the heavenly son.
  Small People harmful indeed.

Concentrate everything you have and feel now and offer it to the highest principle you know. Do not let others control your ideas. This can create a firm and lasting connection.

Associated Contexts a) **Prince,** KUNG: nobles acting as ministers of state in the capital; governing from the center rather than active in daily life; contrasts with feudatory, HOU, governors of the provinces. **Avail of,** YUNG: take advantage of; benefit from, profit by; use for a specific purpose; apply to advantage. The ideogram: to divine and center, applying divination to central concerns. **Son(hood),** TZU: living up to ideal of ancestors as highest

human development; act with concern and reverence; male child; offspring, posterity; seed, kernel, egg; sage, teacher; nadir, deepest point, midnight, mid-winter.

    Small People, HSIAO JEN: lowly, common, humble; those who adjust to circumstances with the flexibility of the small; effect of the small within an individual; keyword. **Nothing/nowhere**, FU: strong negative; not a single thing/place. **Control**, K'O: command; check, impede, prevail, obstruct, repress; adequate, able. The ideogram: roof beams support a house, controlling the structure.

b) **Harm**, HAI: damage, injure, offend; suffer; hurtful, hindrance; fearful, anxious.

    Nine at fourth

    a) **In no way one's preponderance.**
      Without fault.

    b) **In no way one's preponderance. Without fault.**
      Brightness differentiating clearly indeed.

Don't try to dominate or polarize the issues. This is not the time for aggression or insistence on your rights. Let others shine. Bring out their qualities. Be very clear about this. You will not be making a mistake.

Associated Contexts a) **In no way**, FEI: strong negative; not so. The ideogram: a box filled with opposition. **Preponderance**, P'ENG: forceful, dominant; overbearing, encroaching. The ideogram: drum beats, dominating sound.

    Without fault, WU CHIU: no error or harm in the situation.

b) **Differentiate**, PIEN: argue, dispute, criticize; sophisticated, artful. The ideogram: words and sharp or pungent. **Clearly**, CHE: make clear, illuminate; shine, emit light; starlight.

    Six at fifth

    a) **Your connection to the spirits: mingling thus, impressing thus.**
      Auspicious.

    b) **Your conforming, mingling thus.**
      Trustworthiness uses shooting forth with purpose indeed.
      Impressing thus, having auspiciousness.
      Versatility and without preparing indeed.

You have made a connection to the spirits and everyone will be legitimately impressed. Act with complete confidence. Stay true to your purpose and send out new shoots. With spirit like this you can deal with anything.

Associated Contexts a) **Your,** CHÜEH: intensifying personal pronoun, specifically you! your!; intensify, concentrate, tense, contract; lit.: muscle spasms. **Connection,** FU: accord between inner and outer in a particular moment; sincere, truthful, verified, reliable, in accord with the spirits; capture; prisoners, spoils; contrasts with trustworthy, HSIN, consistent over time. The ideogram: bird's claw enclosing young animals, possessive grip. Image of Hexagram 61. **Mingle,** CHIAO: blend with, communicate, join, exchange; trade, business; copulation; friendship. **Thus,** JU: as, in this way. **Impress,** WEI: impose on, intimidate; august, solemn; pomp, majesty. **Auspicious,** CHI: leads to the experience of meaning; favorable, propitious, advantageous, appropriate; keyword. The ideogram: scholar and mouth, wise words of a sage.

b) **Trustworthy,** HSIN: truthful, faithful, consistent over time; integrity; confide in, follow; credentials; contrasts with conforming, FU, connection in a specific moment. The ideogram: person and word, true speech. **Shoot forth,** FA: expand, send out; shoot an arrow; ferment, rise; be displayed. The ideogram: stance, bow and arrow, shooting from a strong base. **Purpose,** CHIH: focus of mind and heart; will, inclination, resolve. The ideogram: heart and scholar, high inner resolve, or heart and go, inner determination.

Versatility, I: sudden and unpredictable change; mental mobility and openness; easy and light, not difficult and heavy; occurs in name of the I CHING. **Without,** WU: devoid of; -less as suffix. **Prepare,** PEI: make ready, provide for; sufficient.

Nine above

a) Originating from heaven shielding it.
Auspicious. Nothing not advantageous.

b) Great Possessing the above: auspicious.
Originating from heaven shielding indeed.

Heaven protects you and the birth of your plans. The way is open to you. In the long run, this will benefit everyone you contact.

Associated Contexts a) **Origin,** TZU: source, beginning, ground; cause, reason, motive; line of descent; path to the origin; yourself, intrinsic. **Shield,** YU: protect; defended by spirits; heavenly kindness and protection.

The ideogram: numinous and right hand, spirit power.

Auspicious, CHI: leads to the experience of meaning; favorable, propitious, advantageous, appropriate; keyword. The ideogram: scholar and mouth, wise words of a sage. **Nothing not advantageous**, WU PU LI: nothing for which this will not be beneficial; advantageous potential, borderline where the balance is swinging from not Harvesting to actually Harvesting.

HUMBLING ▮ *CH'IEN*

Balance, adjust, cut through pride and complications; stay close to fundamentals; think of yourself and your desires in a modest way; unconscious creative processes are activated.

Humbling describes your situation in terms of cutting through pride and complication. Its symbol is an omen animal, the Grey Rat, which indicates unconscious creative powers have been activated. The way to deal with it is to keep your words and thoughts simple and connected to fundamental things. Make an offering and you will succeed. Think and speak of yourself in a modest way. Take the lower position. By yielding you acquire the power to realize the Way. This is pleasing to the spirits. Through it they will give you success, effective power and the capacity to bring the situation to maturity. If you use the oracle to keep in touch with the Way, you can complete what you want to do. Your acts will not bring things to an end, but will open new possibilities. Cutting through pride and the need to dominate brings a great power of realization. Be clear about this, then act directly.

● *Image of the Situation*

> **Humbling, Growing.**
> **A chün tzu possesses completing.**

Associated Contexts **Humble**, CH'IEN: think and speak of yourself in a modest way; respectful, unassuming, retiring, unobtrusive; yielding, compliant, reverent, lowly. The ideogram: words and unite, keeping words close to underlying facts. **Grow**, HENG: success through a sacrifice; pervade, persevere; bring to full growth; enjoy; vigorous, effective; second stage of the Time Cycle.

    Chün tzu: ideal of a person who uses divination to order his/her life in accordance with tao rather than wilful intention; keyword. **Possess**, YU: in possession of, have, own; opposite of lack, WU. **Complete**, CHUNG: end of a cycle that begins the next; last, whole, all; contrasts with exhaust, CH'IUNG, final end. The ideogram: silk cocoons, follow and ice, winter linking one year with the next.

- ## *Outer and Inner Aspects*

☷ **Field**: The field of earth yields and sustains, serving in order to produce. **Field** is the equalizing point between yin and yang where things labor and serve.

Connection to the outer: the common labor of sowing and hoarding, the Earthy Moment. **Field** produces concrete results through serving.

☶ **Bound**: Mountains bound, limit and set a place off, stopping forward movement. **Bound** completes a full yin-yang cycle.

Connection to the inner: accomplishing words, which express things. **Bound** articulates what is complete to suggest what is beginning.

Articulating inner limits sustains **humble** service on the wide field of earth. These trigrams form the Pivot of Equalization, where yin and yang come into creative balance.

- ## *Hidden Possibility*

Nuclear trigrams **Shake**, CHEN, and **Gorge**, K'AN, result in Nuclear Hexagram 40, **Loosening**, HSIEH. Keeping words and actions together through **humbling** leads to **loosening** and freeing bound energy.

- ## *Sequence*

> **Possessing the Great implies not permitting using overfilling.**
> **Accepting this lets you use Humbling.**

Associated Contexts **Great**, TA: big, noble, important, very; orient the will toward a self-imposed goal, impose direction; ability to lead or guide your life; contrasts with small, HSIAO, flexible adaptation to what crosses your path; keyword. **Great Possessing** is the Image of Hexagram 14. **Imply**, CHE: further signify; additional meaning. **Not permitting**, PU K'O: not possible; contradicts an inherent principle. The ideogram: mouth and breath, silent consent. **Use(of)**, YI: make use of, by means of, owing to; employ, make functional. **Overfill**, YING: at the point of overflowing; more than wanted, stretch beyond; replenished, full; arrogant. The ideogram: vessel and too much.

Accepting ... use: activating this hexagram depends on understanding and accepting the previous statement.

● *Contrasted Definitions*

Humbling: levity indeed.
Provision: indolence indeed.

Associated Contexts **Levity**, CH'ING: frivolous, think lightly of, unimportant; alert, agile; gentle. The ideogram: cart and stream, empty cart floating downstream. **Indeed/is/means**, YEH: intensifier, connective; indicates comment on previous statement.

Provide for/provision, YÜ: ready, prepared for; pre-arrange, take precaution, think beforehand; satisfied, contented, at ease. The ideogram: sonhood and elephant, careful, reverent and very strong. Image of Hexagram 16. **Indolence**, TAI: idle, inattentive, careless; self-indulgent; disdainful, contemptuous.

● *Attached Evidences*

Humbling: actualizing tao's handle indeed.
Humbling: dignifying and shining.
Humbling: using paring the codes.

Associated Contexts **Actualize tao**, TE: realize tao in action; power, virtue; ability to follow the course traced by the ongoing process of the cosmos; keyword. The ideogram: to go, straight, and heart. Linked with acquire, TE: acquiring that which makes a being become what it is meant to be. **'s/have(it)/it/them**, CHIH: expresses possession, directly or as an object pronoun. **Handle**, PING: haft; control of, power to.

Dignify, TSUN: honor, make eminent; noble, respected. The ideogram: presenting wine to a guest. **Shine**, KUANG: illuminate; give off brilliant, bright light; honor, glory, éclat; result of action, contrasts with brightness, MING, light of heavenly bodies. The ideogram: fire above person, lifting the light.

Pare, CHIH: cut away; form, tailor, carve; invent; limit, prevent. The ideogram: knife and incomplete. **Codes**, LI: rites, rules, ritual; usage, manners; worship, ceremony, observance. The ideogram: worship and sacrificial vase, handling a sacred vessel.

● *Symbol Tradition*

Earth center possessing mountain. Humbling.
A chün tzu uses reducing the numerous to augment the few.
[A chün tzu uses] evaluating beings to even spreading out.

Associated Contexts **Earth,** TI: ground on which the human world rests; basis of all things, nourishes all things; the Symbol of the trigram Field, K'UN. **Center,** CHUNG: inner, central; put in the center; middle, stable point enabling you to face inner and outer changes; middle line of trigram. The ideogram: field divided in two equal parts. Image of Hexagram 61. **Mountain,** SHAN: limit, boundary; the Symbol of the trigram Bound, KEN. The ideogram: three peaks, a mountain range.

Reduce, P'OU: diminish in number; collect in fewer, larger groups. **Numerous,** TO: great number, many; often. **Augment,** YI: increase, advance, promote, benefit, strengthen; pour in more; full, superabundant; restorative. The ideogram: water and vessel, pouring in more. Image of Hexagram 42. **Few,** KUA: small number; seldom, rarely; unusual, solitary.

Evaluate, CH'ENG: assess, appraise; weigh, estimate, reckon; designate, name. The ideogram: weigh and grain, attributing value. **Being(s),** WU: creature, thing, any single being; matter, substance, essence; nature of things. **Even,** P'ING: level, make even or equal; uniform, peaceful, tranquil; restore quiet, harmonize. **Spread out,** SHIH: expand, diffuse, distribute, arrange, exhibit; add to, aid. The ideogram: flag and indeed, claiming new country.

- *Image Tradition*

> Humbling, Growing. [I]
> Heavenly tao fording below and shining brightness.
> Earthly tao lowly and moving above.
> Heavenly tao lessening overfilling also augmenting Humbling. [II]

> Earthly tao transforming overfilling and diffusing Humbling.
> Souls[and]Spirits harming overfilling and blessing Humbling. [III]
> People tao hating overfilling and loving Humbling.

> Humbling dignifying and shining. [IV]
> Lowliness and not permitting passing beyond it.
> A chün tzu's completion indeed.

Associated Contexts **[I] Heaven,** T'IEN highest; sky, firmament, heavens; power above the human as opposed to earth, TI, below; the Symbol of the trigram Force, CH'IEN. The ideogram: great and the one above. **Tao:** way or path; ongoing process of being and the course it traces for each specific person or thing; keyword. The ideogram: go and head, leading and the path it creates. **Ford**, CHI: cross a river at a ford or shallow place; overcome an obstacle, embark on a course of action; help, relieve; cease. The ideogram: water and level, running smooth over a flat bottom. Image of Hexagrams 63 and 64. **Below**, HSIA: anything below, in all senses; lower, inner; lower trigram; opposite of above, SHANG. **Brightness**, MING: light-giving aspect of burning, heavenly bodies and consciousness; with fire, the Symbol of the trigram Radiance, LI.

Lowly, PEI: speak and think of yourself humbly; modest, yielding; base, mean, contemptible. **Move**, HSING: move or move something; motivate, emotionally moving; walk, act, do. The ideogram: stepping left then right. **Above**, SHANG: anything above, in all senses; higher, upper, outer; upper trigram; opposite of below, HSIA.

[II] Lessen, K'UEI: diminish, injure, wane; lack, defect, failure.

Transform, PIEN: abrupt, radical, fundamental mutation from one state of being to another; transformation of lines in hexagrams; contrasts with change, HUA, gradual metamorphosis. **Diffuse**, LIU: flow out, spread, permeate.

[III] Souls and Spirits, KUEI SHEN: the whole range of imaginal beings both inside and outside the individual; spiritual powers, gods, demons, ghosts, powers, faculties. **Harm**, HAI: damage, injure, offend; suffer; hurtful, hindrance; fearful, anxious. **Bless**, FU: heavenly gifts; make happy; spiritual power and goodwill. The ideogram: spirit and plenty, heavenly gifts in abundance.

People, person, JEN: humans individually and collectively; an individual; humankind. Image of Hexagrams 13 and 37. **Hate**, WU: dislike, dread; averse to, ashamed of; repulsive, vicious, vile, ugly, wicked. The ideogram: twisted bowels and heart, heart entangled in emotion. **Love**, HAO: affection; fond of, take pleasure in; fine, graceful.

[IV] Pass beyond, YÜ: go beyond set time or limits; get over a wall or obstacle; pass to the other side.

● *Transforming Lines*

Initial six

a) Humbling, Humbling: chün tzu.
Avail of stepping into the Great River. Auspicious.

b) Humbling, Humbling: chün tzu.
Lowliness uses originating in the herd indeed.

Work hard at this. Keep your pride out of the way. Think it through, then take the big step. The way is open to you. Unconscious creative powers are at work. You are starting from a humble position. Work hard and keep your pride out of the way.

Associated Contexts a) **Humbling**, CH'IEN, The doubled character intensifies this quality.

Avail of, YUNG: take advantage of; benefit from, profit by; use for a specific purpose; apply to advantage. The ideogram: to divine and center, applying divination to central concerns. **Step into the Great River**, SHE TA CH'UAN: consciously moving into the flow of time; enter the stream of life with a goal or purpose; embark on a significant enterprise. **Auspicious**, CHI: leads to the experience of meaning; favorable, propitious, advantageous, appropriate; keyword. The ideogram: scholar and mouth, wise words of a sage.

b) **Origin**, TZU: source, beginning, ground; cause, reason, motive; line of descent; path to the origin; yourself, intrinsic. **Herd**, MU: tend cattle; watch over, superintend; ruler, teacher.

Six at second

a) Calling Humbling. Trial: auspicious.

b) Calling Humbling, Trial: auspicious.
Centering the heart, acquiring indeed.

The inner work you are doing calls out to others. Unconscious creative powers are at work. Don't hesitate. The way is open. You acquire what you desire.

Associated Contexts a) **Call**, MING: bird and animal cries, through which they recognize each other; distinctive sound, song, statement. The ideogram: bird and mouth, a distinguishing call. **Trial**, CHEN: inquiry by divination and its result; righteous, firm; separating wheat from chaff; the kernel, the proven core; fourth stage of the Time Cycle. The ideogram: pearl and divination. **Auspicious**, CHI: leads to the experience of meaning; favorable, propitious, advantageous, appropriate; keyword. The ideogram: scholar and mouth, wise words of a sage.

b) **Heart,** HSIN: heart as center of being; seat of mind's images and affections; moral nature; source of desires, intentions, will. **Acquire,** TE: obtain the desired object; wish for, desire covetously; gains, possessions. The ideogram: go and obstacle, going through obstacles to the goal.

Nine at third

a) Toiling Humbling: chün tzu.
   Possessing completing, auspicious.

b) Toiling Humbling: chün tzu.
   The myriad commoners submitting indeed.

Humbly work at this idea, following its connection to the Way. Carry on. Unconscious creative powers are at work. You don't need to advertise. Work at rousing the undeveloped potential in yourself and the situation.

Associated Contexts a) **Toil,** LAO: labor, take pains, exert yourself; burdened, careworn; worthy actions. The ideogram: strength and fire, producing heat.
   Auspicious, CHI: leads to the experience of meaning; favorable, propitious, advantageous, appropriate; keyword. The ideogram: scholar and mouth, wise words of a sage.

b) **Myriad,** WAN: countless; many, everyone; lit.: ten thousand. The ideogram: swarm of insects. **Commoners,** MIN: class of workers the state draws on to sustain the social hierarchy; undeveloped potential outside the organized personality. **Submit,** FU: yield to, serve; undergo.

Six at fourth

a) Nothing not advantageous, demonstrating Humbling.

b) Nothing not advantageous, demonstrating Humbling.
   Not contradicting by consequence indeed.

Let your actions show what humbling really is. Cut through pride and complication. If you can do this, everything will benefit. Unconscious creative powers are at work. Don't be attached to your ideas and do not get involved in arguments. Everything will fall into your hands.

Associated Contexts a) **Nothing not advantageous,** WU PU LI: nothing for which this will not be beneficial; advantageous potential, borderline where the balance is swinging from not Harvesting to actually

Harvesting. **Demonstrate,** HUI: show, signal, point out. The ideogram: hand and act, giving signals.

b) **Contradict,** WEI: oppose, disregard, disobey; seditious, perverse. **By consequence(of),** TSE: very strong connection; reason, cause, result; rule, law, pattern, standard; therefore.

Six at fifth

a) **Not affluence: use your neighbor.**
  Advantageous to avail of encroaching subjugating. Harvesting.
  Nothing not advantageous.

b) **Advantageous to avail of encroaching and subjugating.**
  Chastising, not submitting indeed.

It is time to expand. You have a real purpose. Do not be timid. Attack your problems aggressively. Use what others have to offer. Everything will benefit from this behavior. Unconscious creative powers are at work.

Associated Contexts a) **Affluence,** FU: rich, abundant; wealth; enrich, provide for; flow toward, accrue. **One's/one,** CH'I: third person pronoun; also: it/its, he/his, she/hers, they/theirs. **Neighbor,** LIN: person living nearby; extended family; assist, support.
  Advantageous/Harvest, LI: advantageous, profitable; acute, insightful; benefit, nourish; third stage of the Time Cycle. **Avail of,** YUNG: take advantage of; benefit from, profit by; use for a specific purpose; apply to advantage. The ideogram: to divine and center, applying divination to central concerns. **Encroach,** CH'IN: invade, usurp, appropriate; advance stealthily, enter secretly; possessed by a spirit. **Subjugate,** FA: chastise rebels, make dependent; cut down, subject to rule. The ideogram: man and lance, armed soldiers.
  Nothing not advantageous, WU PU LI: nothing for which this will not be beneficial; advantageous potential, borderline where the balance is swinging from not Harvesting to actually Harvesting.

b) **Chastise,** CHENG: punish, subjugate, discipline; reduce to order; punishing expedition. The ideogram: step and correct, a rectifying move. **Submit,** FU: yield to, serve; undergo.

Six above

a) **Calling Humbling.**
  Advantageous to avail of moving legions. Harvesting.
  Chastising the capital city.

b) Calling Humbling.
  Purpose not yet acquired indeed.
  Permitting availing of moving legions:
  Chastising the capital city indeed.

The inner power of your purpose calls out to others. Focus your energies on a major plan, marshal your forces and attack. You can set right your place in the social world, eliminate negativity and help others.

Associated Contexts a) **Call,** MING: bird and animal cries, through which they recognize each other; distinctive sound, song, statement. The ideogram: bird and mouth, a distinguishing call.

  Advantageous/Harvest, LI: advantageous, profitable; acute, insightful; benefit, nourish; third stage of the Time Cycle. **Avail of,** YUNG: take advantage of; benefit from, profit by; use for a specific purpose; apply to advantage. The ideogram: to divine and center, applying divination to central concerns. **Legions/leading,** SHIH: troops; an organized unit, a metropolis; leader, general, model, master; organize, make functional; take as a model, imitate. The ideogram: heap and whole, organize confusion into functional units. Image of Hexagram 7.

  Chastise, CHENG: punish, subjugate, discipline; reduce to order; punishing expedition. The ideogram: step and correct, a rectifying move. **Capital,** YI: populous fortified city, center and symbol of the domain it rules. The ideogram: enclosure and official seal. **City,** KUO: area of only human constructions; political unit, polis. First of the territorial zones: city, suburbs, countryside, forests.

b) **Purpose,** CHIH: focus of mind and heart; will, inclination, resolve. The ideogram: heart and scholar, high inner resolve, or heart and go, inner determination. **Not yet,** WEI: temporal negative; something will but has not yet occurred; contrary of already, CHI. Image of Hexagram 64. **Acquire,** TE: obtain the desired object; wish for, desire covetously; gains, possessions. The ideogram: go and obstacle, going through obstacles to the goal.

  Permit, K'O: possible because in harmony with an inherent principle. The ideogram: mouth and breath, silent consent.

16

PROVIDING FOR/
PROVISION ▮ YÜ

Prepare, collect what you need to meet the future; spontaneous, direct response, enthusiastic; enjoy, take pleasure.

Providing for describes your situation in terms of gathering what is needed to meet and enjoy the future. Its symbols is a child riding an elephant. You can deal with it by accumulating strength and resources so you can respond spontaneously and fully when the time comes. Prepare things. Take precautions. Think things through so you can move smoothly with the flow of events. Get rid of negative attitudes. It is like riding an elephant that you have previously tamed, a creature of great grace and power. Establish and empower helpers, so your forces can be easily mobilized to respond to any situation. That brings profit and insight.

● *Image of the Situation*

> **Providing-for, advantageous to install feudatories to move legions.
> Harvesting.**

Associated Contexts **Provide(-for)/provision**, YÜ: ready, prepared for; prearrange, take precaution, think beforehand; satisfied, contented, at ease. The ideogram: son and elephant, careful, reverent and very strong. **Advantageous/Harvest**, LI: advantageous, profitable; acute, insightful; benefit, nourish; third stage of the Time Cycle. **Install**, CHIEN: set up, establish; confirm a position or law. **Feudatory**, HOU: nobles entrusted with governing the provinces; active in daily life rather than governing from the center; contrasts with prince, KUNG, executives at the court. **Move**, HSING: move or move something; motivate, emotionally moving; walk, act, do. The ideogram: stepping left then right. **Legions/leading**, SHIH: troops; an organized unit, a metropolis; leader, general, model, master; organize, make functional; take as a model, imitate. The ideogram: heap and whole, organize confusion into functional units. Image of Hexagram 7.

- *Outer and Inner Aspects*

☳ **Shake**: Thunder rises from below, shaking and stirring things up. **Shake** begins the yang hemicycle by germinating new action.

Connection to the outer: sprouting energies thrusting from below, the Woody Moment beginning. **Shake** stirs things up to issue-forth.

☷ **Field**: The field of earth yields and sustains, serving in order to produce. **Field** is the equalizing point between yin and yang where things labor and serve.

Connection to the inner: the common labor of sowing and hoarding, the Earthy Moment. **Field** produces concrete results through serving.

Inner sowing and hoarding **provides-for** a rousing summons to action that comes from outside.

- *Hidden Possibility*

Nuclear trigrams **Gorge**, K'AN, and **Bound**, KEN, result in Nuclear Hexagram 39, **Difficulties**, CHIEN. Building up reserves to **provide-for** the future lets you re-imagine a **difficult** situation.

- *Sequence*

> Possessing the Great and enabling Humbling
> necessarily Provides-for.
> Accepting this lets you use Providing-for.

Associated Contexts **Possess**, YU: in possession of, have, own; opposite of lack, WU. **Great**, TA: big, noble, important, very; orient the will toward a self-imposed goal, impose direction; ability to lead or guide your life; contrasts with small, HSIAO, flexible adaptation to what crosses your path; keyword. **Great Possessing** is the Image of Hexagram 14. **Able**, NENG: enable; ability, power, skill, art; competent, talented; duty, function, capacity. The ideogram: an animal with strong hooves and bones, able to carry and defend. **Humble**, CH'IEN: think and speak of yourself in a modest way; respectful, unassuming, retiring, unobtrusive; yielding, compliant, reverent, lowly. The ideogram: words and unite, keeping words close to underlying facts. Image of Hexagram 15. **Necessarily**, PI: unavoidably, indispensably, certainly.

Accepting ... use: activating this hexagram depends on understanding and accepting the previous statement.

- *Contrasted Definitions*

   Humbling: levity indeed.
   Provision: indolence indeed.

Associated Contexts **Levity,** CH'ING: frivolous, think lightly of, unimportant; alert, agile; gentle. The ideogram: cart and stream, empty cart floating downstream. **Indeed is/means,** YEH: intensifier, connective; indicates comment on previous statement.
   Indolence, TAI: idle, inattentive, careless; self-indulgent; disdainful, contemptuous.

- *Attached Evidences*

   Redoubling the gates, smiting the clappers.
   Used to await violent visitors.
   Surely, grasping connotes Providing for.

Associated Contexts **Redouble,** CH'UNG: repeat, reiterate, add to; build up by layers. **Gate,** MEN: outer door, between court-yard and street; a text or master as gate to a school of thought. **Smite,** CHI: hit, beat, attack; hurl against, rush a position; rouse to action. The ideogram: hand and hit, fist punching. **Clapper,** T'O: board used by watchmen to strike the hours.
   Use(-of), YI: make use of, by means of, owing to; employ, make functional. **Await,** TAI: expect, wait for, welcome (friendly or hostile), provide against. **Violent,** PAO: fierce, oppressive, cruel; strike hard. **Visitor,** K'O: guest; stranger, foreign, from afar; squatter.
   Surely, KAI: preceding statement is undoubtedly true. **Grasp,** CH'U: lay hold of, take and use, seize, appropriate; grasp the meaning, understand. The ideogram: ear and hand, hear and grasp. **Connote,** CHU: imply the meaning; signify. The ideogram: words and imply.

- *Symbol Tradition*

   Thunder issuing forth from earth impetuously. Providing for.
   The Earlier Kings used arousing delight to extol actualizing-tao,
   Exalting worship of the Supreme Above
   Used to equal the grandfathers and predecessors.

Associated Contexts **Thunder,** LEI: rising, arousing power; the Symbol of the trigram Shake, CHEN. **Issue forth(from),** CH'U: emerge from, come out of, proceed from, spring from; the Action of the trigram Shake, CHEN;

contrary of enter, JU. The ideogram: stem with branches and leaves emerging. **Earth**, TI: ground on which the human world rests; basis of all things, nourishes all things; the Symbol of the trigram Field, K'UN. **Impetuous**, FEN: sudden energy; lively, spirited, impulsive; excite, arouse; press on.

Earlier Kings, HSIEN WANG: ideal rulers of old; the golden age, primal time, power in harmony with nature; model for the chün tzu. **Arouse**, TSO: stir up, stimulate, rouse from inactivity; generate; appear, arise. The ideogram: person and beginning. **Delight**, LO: take joy or pleasure in; pleasant, relaxed; also: music as harmony, elegance and pleasure. **Extol**, CH'UNG: praise, honor, magnify, revere; eminent, lofty; worthy of worship. **Actualize tao**, TE: realize tao in action; power, virtue; ability to follow the course traced by the ongoing process of the cosmos; keyword. The ideogram: to go, straight, and heart. Linked with acquire, TE: acquiring that which makes a being become what it is meant to be.

Exalting worship, YIN CHIEN: superlative of worship; glorify; intensify feelings of praise and awe. **'s/have(-it)/it/them**, CHIH: expresses possession, directly or as an object pronoun. **Supreme Above**, SHANG TI: highest power in universe, lord of all.

Equal, P'EI: on the same level; pair, husband or wife; together. **Grandfather**, TSU: second ancestor generation; deceased grandfather, honored more than actual father. **Predecessor**, K'AO: deceased ancestor; the ancients; aged, long-lived; consult, verify. The ideogram: old and ingenious, the old wise man.

- *Image Tradition*

> Providing for. Strong corresponding and purpose moving. [I]
> Yielding uses stirring up. Providing-for.
>
> Providing for: yielding uses stirring up. [II]
> Anterior Heaven and Earth thus have it.
> And even more installing feudatories to move legions is reached.
>
> Heaven and Earth uses yielding and stirring up. [III]
> Anterior Sun and Moon not exceeding
> And the four seasons not straying.
>
> The all wise person uses yielding and stirring up. [IV]
> By consequence punishing and flogging purifies
> and the commoners submit.
> Actually Provision's season righteously great in fact.

Associated Contexts **[I] Strong**, KANG: quality of the whole lines; firm, strong, unyielding, persisting. **Correspond(-to)**, YING: be in agreement or harmony; resonate together, invoke and fulfil each other; answer to, suitable; relation between the lines (1:4, 2:5, 3:6) when they form the pair opened and whole, supple and strong. The ideogram: heart and obey. **Purpose**, CHIH: focus of mind and heart; will, inclination, resolve. The ideogram: heart and scholar, high inner resolve, or heart and go, inner determination.

Yield(to), SHUN: give way and bear produce; comply, agree, follow, obey; unresisting, docile, flexible; nourish, provide; the Action of the trigram Field, K'UN. The ideogram: head and current, water flowing from the head of a river, yielding to the banks. **Stir up**, TUNG: excite, influence, move, affect; work, take action; come out of the egg or the bud; the Action of the trigram Shake, CHEN. The ideogram: strength and heavy, move weighty things.

[II] Anterior, KU: come before as cause; formerly, ancient; reason, purpose, intention; grievance, quarrel, dissatisfaction, sorrow, mourning resulting from previous causes and intentions; situation leading to a divination. **Heaven and Earth**, T'IEN TI: dynamic relation between the primal powers and the world it produces; cosmos, natural or human world; keyword. **Thus**, JU: as, in this way.

Even more, K'UANG: even more so, all the more. **Reach(to)**, HU: arrive at a goal; reach towards and achieve; connect; contrasts with tend-towards, YU.

[III] Sun and Moon, JIH YŪEH: the two dimensions of calendar time that define any specific moment; time as interlocking cycles. **Not**, PU: simple negative. **Exceed**, KU: go beyond, pass by, pass over; excessive, transgress; error, fault. Image of Hexagrams 28 and 62.

Four seasons, SSU SHIH: the four dynamic qualities of time that make up the year and the Time Cycle; the right time, in accord with the time; time as sacred; all-encompassing. **Stray**, T'E: wander blindly; deviate, err, alter, doubt; excess.

[IV] All wise, SHENG: intuitive universal wisdom; mythical sages; holy, sacred; mark of highest distinction. The ideogram: ear and inform, one who knows all from a single sound. **People, person**, JEN: humans individually and collectively; an individual; humankind. Image of Hexagrams 13 and 37.

By consequence(of), TSE: very strong connection; reason, cause, result; rule, law, pattern, standard; therefore. **Punish**, HSING: legal punishment;

physical penalties for severe criminal offenses; whip, torture, behead. **Flog,** FA: punish with blows, beat, whip; used to find out the truth. **Purify,** CH'ING: clean a water course; limpid, unsullied; right principles. **Commoners,** MIN: class of workers the state draws on to sustain the social hierarchy; undeveloped potential outside the organized personality. **Submit,** FU: yield to, serve; undergo.

Actually ... in fact, YI TSAI: stresses the importance of a statement. The ideogram: a dart and done, strong intention fully expressed. **Righteous,** YI: proper and just, meets the standards; things in their proper place; the heart that rules itself; upright, moral rule; contrasts with Harvest, LI, advantage or profit.

● *Transforming Lines*

Initial six

a) **Calling for Provision.**
Pitfall.

b) **Initial six, calling for Provision.**
Purpose exhausted, pitfall indeed.

You are trying to get others to take care of you. It doesn't work like that. If you keep calling for help you will exhaust all your strength.

Associated Contexts a) **Call,** MING: bird and animal cries, through which they recognize each other; distinctive sound, song, statement. The ideogram: bird and mouth, a distinguishing call.

Pitfall, HSIUNG: leads away from the experience of meaning; stuck and exposed to danger, unable to take in the situation; flow of life and spirit is blocked; unfortunate, baleful; keyword.

b) **Exhaust,** CH'IUNG: bring to an end; limit, extremity; destitute; investigate exhaustively; end without a new beginning. The ideogram: cave and naked person, bent with disease or old age.

Six at second

a) **The limits are petrifying.**
Do not complete the day.
Trial: auspicious.

b) **Not completing the day, Trial: auspicious.**
Using centering and correcting indeed.

The limits imposed on you, or those you impose on yourself, have become so rigid they are turning to stone. Don't wait. Let go of them now. Correct yourself and release the bound energy.

Associated Contexts a) **Limits/chain mail**, CHIEH: chain-armor; tortoise or crab shell; protective covering; border, limit; protection, support. **Petrify**, SHIH: become stone or stony; rocks, stony land; objects made of stone; firm, decided; a barren womb.

Complete, CHUNG: end of a cycle that begins the next; last, whole, all; contrasts with exhaust, CH'IUNG: final end. The ideogram: silk cocoons, follow and ice, winter linking one year with the next. **Day/sun**, JIH: actual sun and the time of a sun-cycle, a day.

Trial, CHEN: inquiry by divination and its result; righteous, firm; separating wheat from chaff; the kernel, the proven core; fourth stage of the Time Cycle. The ideogram: pearl and divination. **Auspicious**, CHI: leads to the experience of meaning; favorable, propitious, advantageous, appropriate; keyword. The ideogram: scholar and mouth, wise words of a sage.

b) **Centering correcting**, CHUNG CHENG: central and correct; make rectifying one-sidedness and error your central concern; reaching a stable center in yourself can correct the situation.

Six at third

a) Skeptical Providing for, repenting.
   Procrastinating possesses repenting.

b) Skeptical Providing for possesses repenting.
   Situation not appropriate indeed.

Don't be skeptical about this and don't hold back. It will only bring you sorrow. Provide what is needed, simply and directly.

Associated Contexts a) **Skeptical**, YÜ: doubtful, cynical; wonder at, wide-eyed surprise. **Repent**, HUI: dissatisfaction with past conduct causing a change of heart; proceeds from abashment, LIN, shame and confusion at having lost the right way.

Procrastinate, CH'IH: delay, act at leisure, retard; slow, late.

b) **Situation**, WEI: place or seat according to rank; post, position, command; right, proper; established, arranged. The ideogram: person and stand, servants in their places. **Appropriate**, TANG: suitable; opportune, convenient; adequate, competent; equal to; whole lines in uneven places and opened lines in even places.

Nine at fourth

a) Antecedent Provision.
   The great possesses acquiring.
   No doubting.
   Partners join and clasp together.

b) Antecedent Provision, the great possesses acquiring.
   Purpose: the great moving indeed.

This is sent from heaven. It gives you everything you need. Have no doubts. Partners join together freely and spontaneously. Together your purpose can give you all you desire.

Associated Contexts a) **Antecedent**, YU: come before as origin and cause; through, by, from; depend on; permit, enter by way of.
   Acquire, TE: obtain the desired object; wish for, desire covetously; gains, possessions. The ideogram: go and obstacle, going through obstacles to the goal.
   Doubt, YI: suspect, distrust; dubious; surmise, conjecture.
   Partner, P'ENG: associate for mutual benefit; two equal or similar things; companions, friends, peers; join in; commercial ventures. The ideogram: linked strings of cowries or coins. **Join-together**, HO: unite for a purpose; assemble friends for a specific aim. **Clasp**, TSAN: quick, prompt, abrupt action; collect together. The ideogram: clasp used to gather the hair.

Six at fifth

a) Trial: affliction.
   Persevering, not dying.

b) Six at-fifth, Trial: affliction.
   Riding a strong indeed.
   Persevering, not dying.
   Center not yet extinguished indeed.

This is a hard time – sickness, hostility, isolation, disorder – but don't give up. You will certainly survive. Learn from it. Gather the wisdom it offers you.

Associated Contexts a) **Trial,** CHEN: inquiry by divination and its result; righteous, firm; separating wheat from chaff; the kernel, the proven core; fourth stage of the Time Cycle. The ideogram: pearl and divination. **Afflict,** CHI: sickness, disorder, defect, calamity; injurious; pressure and consequent anger, hate or dislike. The ideogram: sickness and dart, a sudden affliction.

Persevere, HENG: continue in the same way or spirit; constant, perpetual, regular; self-renewing; extend everywhere. Image of Hexagram 32. **Die,** SSU: sudden or untimely death; run out of energy; immobile, fixed.

b) **Ride,** CH'ENG: ride an animal or a chariot; have the upper hand, seize the right time; control strong power; overcome the nature of the other; supple opened line above a strong whole line. **Strong,** KANG: quality of the whole lines; firm, strong, unyielding, persisting.

Center, CHUNG: inner, central; put in the center; middle, stable point enabling you to face inner and outer changes; middle line of trigram. The ideogram: field divided in two equal parts. Image of Hexagram 61. **Not-yet,** WEI: temporal negative; something will but has not yet occurred; contrary of already, CHI. Image of Hexagram 64. **Extinguish,** WANG: ruin, destroy; gone, dead, lost without trace; extinct, forgotten, out of mind. The ideogram: person concealed by a wall, out of sight.

Six above

a) **Dim Providing for.**
   Accomplishment: possessing denial.
   Without fault.

b) **Dim Providing for located above.**
   Wherefore permitting long living indeed?

You are working in the dark to provide for the future. Put away your current status. This is not a mistake. You will find what you need and climb out of the cave. Everything will be better in the end.

Associated Contexts a) **Dim,** MING: dark, obscure; misinformed, immature, cavern, the underworld. The ideogram: 16th day of moon-month, when the moon begins to dim.

Accomplish, CHENG: complete, finish, bring about; perfect, full, whole; play your part, do your duty; mature. The ideogram: weapon and man, able to bear arms thus fully developed. **Deny,** YÜ: retract, repudiate; deterioration, regress.

Without fault, WU CHIU: no error or harm in the situation.

b) **Locate(in),** TSAOI: live in, dwell, reside; belong to, involved with, depend on; within. The ideogram: earth and persevere, place on the earth. **Above,** SHANG: anything above, in all senses; higher, upper, outer; upper trigram; opposite of below, HSIA.

Wherefore, HO: interrogative: why? for what reason? what is? and affirmation: therefore, for that reason. **Permit,** K'O: possible because in harmony with an inherent principle. The ideogram: mouth and breath, silent consent. **Long living,** CHANG: enduring, constant; senior, superior, greater; increase, prosper; respect, elevate.

17

FOLLOWING ▮ *SUI*

Move with the flow, strong, natural attraction; inevitable, natural, correct; influence, guidance.

Following describes your situation in terms of been drawn forward. The way to deal with it is to follow the inevitable course of events. Go with the flow. Yield to the path set out in front of you. Be guided by the way things are moving. You are involved in a series of events that are firmly connected. Don't fight it, move with it. It opens a whole new cycle of time. This is not a mistake. The situation cannot harm you. This is pleasing to the spirits. Through it they will give you success, effective power and the capacity to bring the situation to maturity.

● *Image of the Situation*

> Following.
> Source of Success: Advantageous Trial.
> Without fault.

Associated Contexts **Follow,** SUI: come or go after; pursue, impelled to move; come after in inevitable sequence; move in the same direction, comply with what is ahead; follow a way or religion; according to, next, subsequent. The ideogram: go and fall, unavoidable movement.

  Source ... Trial, lit: Spring Growing Harvesting Trial: **Spring,** YÜAN: **Grow,** HENG: **Harvest,** LI; and **Trial,** CHEN, are the four stages of the Time Cycle, the model for all dynamic processes. They indicate that your question is connected to the cycle as a whole rather than a part of it, and that the origin (Spring) of a favorable result (Harvesting Trial) is an offering to the spirits (Growing).

  Without fault, WU CHIU: no error or harm in the situation.

● *Outer and Inner Aspects*

  ☱ **Open:** vapor rising from the marsh's open surface stimulates and fertilizes; stimulating words cheer and inspire. **Open** begins the yin hemicycle by initiating the formative process.

Connection to the outer: liquifying, casting, skinning off the mold, the Metallic Moment beginning. **Open** stimulates, cheers and reveals innate form.

☵☰ **Shake**: Thunder rises from below, shaking and stirring things up. **Shake** begins the yang hemicycle by germinating new action.

Connection to the inner: sprouting energies thrusting from below, the Woody Moment beginning. **Shake** stirs things up to issue-forth.

Stimulating words in the outer world stir-up **following** within. These trigrams emphasize the Pivoting Phase, initiating new actions.

- *Hidden Possibility*

Nuclear trigrams **Ground**, SUN, and **Bound**, KEN, result in Nuclear Hexagram 53, **Gradual Advance**, CHIEN. Actively **following** a specific model lets you **gradually advance** to your goal.

- *Sequence*

Providing for necessarily possesses Following.
Accepting this lets you use Following.

Associated Contexts **Provide for/provision**, YÜ: ready, prepared for; pre-arrange, take precaution, think beforehand; satisfied, contented, at ease. The ideogram: son and elephant, careful, reverent and very strong. Image of Hexagram 16. **Necessarily**, PI: unavoidably, indispensably, certainly. **Possess**, YU: in possession of, have, own; opposite of lack, WU.

Accepting ... use: activating this hexagram depends on understanding and accepting the previous statement.

- *Contrasted Definitions*

Following: without the past indeed.
Corrupting: by consequence stability indeed.

Associated Contexts **Without**, WU: devoid of; -less as suffix. **Past** (cause), KU: come before as cause; formerly, ancient; reason, purpose, intention; grievance, quarrel, dissatisfaction, sorrow, mourning resulting from previous causes and intentions; situation leading to a divination. **Indeed/is/means**, YEH: intensifier, connective; indicates comment on previous statement.

Corrupt, KU: rotting, poisonous; intestinal worms, venomous insects; evil magic; disorder, error; pervert by seduction, flattery; unquiet ghost. The ideogram: dish and worms, putrefaction and poisonous decay. Image of Hexagram 18. **By consequence(of),** TSE: very strong connection; reason, cause, result; rule, law, pattern, standard; therefore. **Stability,** CH'IH: firm, prepared for; careful, respectful.

- *Symbol Tradition*

> Marsh center possessing thunder. Following.
> A chün tzu uses turning to darkening to enter a reposing pause.

Associated Contexts **Marsh,** TSE: open surface of a flat body of water and the vapors rising from it; fertilize, enrich; kindness, favor; the Symbol of the trigram Open, TUI. **Center,** CHUNG: inner, central; put in the center; middle, stable point enabling you to face inner and outer changes; middle line of trigram. The ideogram: field divided in two equal parts. Image of Hexagram 61. **Thunder,** LEI: rising, arousing power; the Symbol of the trigram Shake, CHEN.

Chün tzu: ideal of a person who uses divination to order his/her life in accordance with tao rather than wilful intention; keyword. **Use(of),** YI: make use of, by means of, owing to; employ, make functional. **Turn to,** HSIANG: direct your mind toward, seek. **Darken,** HUI: make or become dark; last day of the moon; obscure, night, mist. **Enter,** JU: penetrate, go into, enter on, progress; put into, encroach on; the Action of the trigram Ground, SUN, contrary of issue-forth, CH'U. **Repose,** YEN: rest, leisure, peace of mind; banquet, feast. The ideogram: shelter and rest, a wayside inn. **Pause,** HSI: stop and rest, repose; breathe, a breathing-spell; suspended.

- *Image Tradition*

> Following. Strong coming and supple below. [I]
> Stirring up and stimulating. Following.

> Great Growing, Trial: without fault. [II]
> And Below Heaven Following the season.
> Actually Following the season's righteous great in fact.

Associated Contexts [I] **Strong,** KANG: quality of the whole lines; firm, strong, unyielding, persisting. **Come,** LAI, and go, WANG, describe the stream of time as it flows from future through present to past; come,

LAI, indicates what is approaching; move toward, arrive at; keyword. **Supple,** JOU: quality of the opened lines; flexible, pliant, tender, adaptable. **Below,** HSIA: anything below, in all senses; lower, inner; lower trigram; opposite of above, SHANG.

Stir up, TUNG: excite, influence, move, affect; work, take action; come out of the egg or the bud; the Action of the trigram Shake, CHEN. The ideogram: strength and heavy, move weighty things. **Stimulate,** SHUO: rouse to action and good feeling; free from constraint, stir up, urge on; persuade, cheer, delight; set out in words; the Action of the trigram Open, TUI. The ideogram: words and exchange.

[II] Great, TA: big, noble, important, very; orient the will toward a self-imposed goal, impose direction; ability to lead or guide your life; contrasts with small, HSIAO, flexible adaptation to what crosses your path; keyword. Image of Hexagrams 14, 26, 28, 34. **Grow,** HENG: success through a sacrifice; pervade, persevere; bring to full growth; enjoy; vigorous, effective; second stage of the Time Cycle. **Trial,** CHEN inquiry by divination and its result; righteous, firm; separating wheat from chaff; the kernel, the proven core; fourth stage of the Time Cycle. The ideogram: pearl and divination.

Below Heaven, T'IEN HSIA: the human world, between heaven and earth. **Season,** SHIH: quality of the time; the right time, opportune, in harmony; planning in accord with the time; seasons of the year. The ideogram: sun and temple, time as sacred.

Actually ... in fact, YI TSAI: stresses the importance of a statement. The ideogram: a dart and done, strong intention fully expressed. **'s/have(it)/it/them,** CHIH: expresses possession, directly or as an object pronoun. **Righteous,** YI: proper and just, meets the standards; things in their proper place; the heart that rules itself; upright, moral rule; contrasts with Harvest, LI, advantage or profit.

● *Transforming Lines*

Initial nine

a) **An office: possessing denial. Trial: auspicious.**
Issue forth from the gate, mingling possesses achievement.

b) **An office: possessing denial.**
Adhering to correcting auspicious indeed.
Issuing forth from the gate, mingling possesses achievement.
Not letting go indeed.

Leave your old life behind. Following this influence will transform you. Walk out of your old thoughts and mix with new people. This will definitely produce achievements.

Associated Contexts a) **Office**, KUAN: government officials, magistrates, dignitaries. **Deny**, YÜ: retract, repudiate; deterioration, regress. **Auspicious**, CHI: leads to the experience of meaning; favorable, propitious, advantageous, appropriate; keyword. The ideogram: scholar and mouth, wise words of a sage.

Issue forth(from), CH'U: emerge from, come out of, proceed from, spring from; the Action of the trigram Shake, CHEN; contrary of enter, JU. The ideogram: stem with branches and leaves emerging. **Gate**, MEN: outer door, between court-yard and street; a text or master as gate to a school of thought. **Mingle**, CHIAO: blend with, communicate, join, exchange; trade, business; copulation; friendship. **Achieve**, KUNG: work done, results; real accomplishment, praise, worth, merit. The ideogram: workman's square and forearm, combining craft and strength.

b) **Adhere(to)**, TS'UNG: follow a way, hold to a doctrine, school, or person; hear and comply with, agree to; forced to follow, follower. The ideogram: two men walking, one following the other. **Correct**, CHENG: rectify deviation or one-sidedness; proper, straight, exact, regular; constant, rule, model. The ideogram: stop and one, hold to one thing.

Let go, SHIH: lose, omit, miss, fail, let slip; out of control. The ideogram: drop from the hand.

Six at second

a) Tied to the small son.
  Letting go the respectable husband.

b) Tied to the small son.
  Nowhere joining associates indeed.

You have picked the wrong impulse to follow. You will end up alone, without anyone to trust. All you can do then is adapt to whatever crosses your path.

Associated Contexts a) **Tie(to)**, HSI: connect, attach to, bind; devoted to; relatives. The ideogram: person and connect, ties between humans. **Small**, HSIAO: little, common, unimportant; adapting to what crosses your path; ability to move in harmony with the vicissitudes of life; contrasts with great, TA, self-imposed theme or goal; keyword. Image of Hexagrams 9 and

62. **Son(hood)**, TZU: living up to ideal of ancestors as highest human development; act with concern and reverence; male child; offspring, posterity; seed, kernel, egg; sage, teacher; nadir, deepest point, midnight, mid-winter.

Let go, SHIH: lose, omit, miss, fail, let slip; out of control. The ideogram: drop from the hand. **Respectable**, CHANG: worthy of respect; standard by which others are measured. **Husband**, FU: household manager; administer with thrift and prudence; responsible for; sustain with your earnings; old enough to assume responsibility; married man.

b) **Nothing/nowhere**, FU: strong negative; not a single thing/place. **Join**, CHIEN: add or bring together; unite, absorb; attend to many things. The ideogram: hand grasps two grain stalks, two things at once. **Associate(with)**, YÜ: consort with, combine; companions; group, band, company; agree with, comply, help. The ideogram: pair of hands reaching downward meets a pair of hands reaching upward, helpful association.

> **Six at third**
>
> *a)* Tied to the respectable husband.
>   Letting go the small son.
>   Following possesses seeking and acquiring.
>   Advantageous residence Trial. Harvesting.
>
> *b)* Tied to the respectable husband.
>   Below, purpose stowed away indeed.

You have made the right choice. You are following the right person. You will get everything you desire from this connection. Staying in this flow brings you profit and insight.

Associated Contexts a) **Tie(to)**, HSI: connect, attach to, bind; devoted to; relatives. The ideogram: person and connect, ties between humans. **Respectable**, CHANG: worthy of respect; standard by which others are measured. **Husband**, FU: household manager; administer with thrift and prudence; responsible for; sustain with your earnings; old enough to assume responsibility; married man.

Let go, SHIH: lose, omit, miss, fail, let slip; out of control. The ideogram: drop from the hand. **Small**, HSIAO: little, common, unimportant; adapting to what crosses your path; ability to move in harmony with the vicissitudes of life; contrasts with great, TA, self-imposed theme or goal; keyword. Image of Hexagrams 9 and 62. **Son(hood)**, TZU: living up to ideal of ancestors as highest human development; act with concern and reverence; male child; offspring, posterity; seed, kernel, egg; sage, teacher; nadir, deepest point, midnight, mid-winter.

Seek, CH'IU: search for, aim at, wish for, desire; implore, supplicate; covetous. **Acquire,** TE: obtain the desired object; wish for, desire covetously; gains, possessions. The ideogram: go and obstacle, going through obstacles to the goal.

Advantageous/Harvest, LI: advantageous, profitable; acute, insightful; benefit, nourish; third stage of the Time Cycle. **Reside(in),** CHÜ: dwell, live in, stay; sit down, fill an office; settled parts of a country. The ideogram: body and seat.

b) **Purpose,** CHIH: focus of mind and heart; will, inclination, resolve. The ideogram: heart and scholar, high inner resolve, or heart and go, inner determination. **Stow(away),** SHE: set aside, put away, store; halt, rest in; temporary lodgings, breathing-spell.

Nine at fourth

a) Following to possess catching. Trial: pitfall.
Connecting to the spirits, locating in tao to use brightening.
Wherefore faulty?

b) Following to possess catching.
One's righteousness: pitfall indeed.
Connecting to the spirits located in tao.
Brightening achieved indeed.

You have turned following into a kind of hunt. This will trap you and cut you off from the spirit. Connect with the flow of events rather than your ego, and put yourself in harmony with the Way. Use what you have been given by heaven. Then things will come of themselves because you have understood the situation correctly.

Associated Contexts a) **Catch,** HUO: take in hunt; catch a thief; obtain, seize; hit the mark, opportune moment; prisoner, spoils, prey; slave, servant. **Pitfall,** HSIUNG: leads away from the experience of meaning; stuck and exposed to danger, unable to take in the situation; flow of life and spirit is blocked; unfortunate, baleful; keyword.

Connection the spirits, YU FU: inner and outer are in accord; confidence of the spirits has been captured; sincere, truthful; proper to take action. **Locate(in),** TSAI: live in, dwell, reside; belong to, involved with, depend on;

within. The ideogram: earth and persevere, place on the earth. **Tao**: way or path; ongoing process of being and the course it traces for each specific person or thing; keyword. The ideogram: go and head, leading and the path it creates. **Brightness**, MING: light-giving aspect of burning, heavenly bodies and consciousness; with fire, the Symbol of the trigram Radiance, LI.

Wherefore, HO: interrogative: why? for what reason? what is? and affirmation: therefore, for that reason. **Fault**, CHIU: unworthy conduct that leads to harm, illness, misfortune. The ideogram: person and differ, differ from what you should be.

b) **One's/one**, CH'I: third person pronoun; also: it/its, he/his, she/hers, they/theirs. **Achieve**, KUNG: work done, results; real accomplishment, praise, worth, merit. The ideogram: workman's square and forearm, combining craft and strength.

Nine at fifth

a) **Connecting with excellence. Auspicious.**

b) **Connecting with excellence auspicious.**
Situation correctly centering indeed.

You have made the connection. It will lead you on to real achievements. Have no doubts. Follow it. The way is open to you.

Associated Contexts a) **Connection**, FU: accord between inner and outer in a particular moment; sincere, truthful, verified, reliable, in accord with the spirits; capture; prisoners, spoils; contrasts with trustworthy, HSIN, consistent over time. The ideogram: bird's claw enclosing young animals, possessive grip. **Excellence**, CHIA: superior quality; fine, delicious, glorious; happy, pleased; rejoice in, praise. The ideogram: increasing goodness, pleasure and happiness. **Auspicious**, CHI: leads to the experience of meaning; favorable, propitious, advantageous, appropriate; keyword. The ideogram: scholar and mouth, wise words of a sage.

b) **Situation**, WEI: place or seat according to rank; post, position, command; right, proper; established, arranged. The ideogram: person and stand, servants in their places. **Correct**, CHENG: rectify deviation or one-sidedness; proper, straight, exact, regular; constant, rule, model. The ideogram: stop and one, hold to one thing.

Six above

a) Grappled and tied to it.
Thereupon the adherents holding fast to it.
The king avails of Growing, a sacrifice on the Western mountain.

b) Grappled and tied to it.
Exhausting the above indeed.

You are firmly attached to the principles you follow. Others are held fast through your devotion. Offer up what you know. You will be enshrined in the hall of ancestors. You help in the flow of blessings. You can go no farther than this.

Associated Contexts a) **Grapple**, CHÜ: grasp and detain; restrain, attach to, hook. **Tie(to)**, HSI: connect, attach to, bind; devoted to; relatives. The ideogram: person and connect, ties between humans. **It/them/have(it)'s**, CHIH: expresses possession, directly or as an object pronoun.

Thereupon, NAI: on that ground, because of. **Adhere(to)**, TS'UNG: follow a way, hold to a doctrine, school, or person; hear and comply with, agree to; forced to follow, follower. The ideogram: two men walking, one following the other. **Hold fast(to)**, WEI: hold together; tie to, connect; reins, net.

King(hood), WANG: effective ruler, by authority of the Emperor, from whom others derive their power. **Avail of**, YUNG: take advantage of; benefit from, profit by; use for a specific purpose; apply to advantage. The ideogram: to divine and center, applying divination to central concerns. **West**, HSI: corresponds to autumn, Harvest and the Streaming Moment; begins yin hemicycle of Universal Compass. **Mountain**, SHAN: limit, boundary; the Symbol of the trigram Bound, KEN. The ideogram: three peaks, a mountain range.

b) **Exhaust**, CH'IUNG: bring to an end; limit, extremity; destitute; investigate exhaustively; end without a new beginning. The ideogram: cave and naked person, bent with disease or old age. **Above**, SHANG: anything above, in all senses; higher, upper, outer; upper trigram; opposite of below, HSIA.

18

CORRUPTION/ RENOVATION ∎ *KU*

Perversion, decay, negative effects of the past, of parents on children; black, sexual magic; renew, renovate, new beginning.

Corruption/Renovation describes your situation in terms of poison, putrefaction, black magic, and the evil deeds done by parents that are manifested in their children. Its symbol is a sacrificial vessel full of rotting meat. The way to deal with it is to help things rot away so that a new beginning can be found. Make an offering and you will succeed. You are facing something that has turned to poison. Search out the source so new growth can begin. This is pleasing to the spirits. Through it they will give you success, effective power and the capacity to bring the situation to maturity. This is the right time to enter the stream of life with a goal, or to embark on a significant enterprise. That brings profit and insight. Prepare the moment when the new time arrives and carefully watch over its first growth. It will take three days, a whole period of activity, before the seed of the new energy bursts open, and a similar period afterwards to stabilize it.

● *Image of the Situation*

> **Corruption, Spring Growing.**
> **Advantageous to step into the Great River. Harvesting.**
> **Before seedburst three days, after seedburst three days.**

Associated Contexts **Corrupt**, KU: rotting, poisonous; intestinal worms, venomous insects; evil magic; disorder, error; pervert by seduction, flattery; unquiet ghost. The ideogram: dish and worms, putrefaction and poisonous decay. **Spring**, YÜAN: source, origin, head; great, excellent; arise, begin, generating power; first stage of the Time Cycle. **Grow**, HENG: success through a sacrifice; pervade, persevere; bring to full growth; enjoy; vigorous, effective; second stage of the Time Cycle.

Advantageous/Harvest, LI: advantageous, profitable; acute, insightful; benefit, nourish; third stage of the Time Cycle. **Step into the Great River**, SHE TA CH'UAN: consciously moving into the flow of time; enter the stream of life with a goal or purpose; embark on a significant enterprise.

Before(hand)/earlier, HSIEN: come before in time; first, at first; formerly, past, previous; begin, go ahead of. **Seedburst,** CHIA: seeds bursting forth in spring; first of the Ten Heavenly Barriers in calendar system; begin, first, number one; associated with the Woody Moment. **Three,** SAN: number three, third time or place; active phases of a cycle; superlative; beginning of repetition. **Day/sun,** JIH: actual sun and the time of a sun-cycle, a day. **After(wards)/later,** HOU: come after in time, subsequent; put oneself after; the second; attendants, heirs, successors, posterity.

- *Outer and Inner Aspects*

⚏ **Bound**: Mountains bound, limit and set a place off, stopping forward movement. **Bound** completes a full yin-yang cycle.

Connection to the outer: accomplishing words, which express things fully. **Bound** articulates what is complete and suggests what is beginning.

⚎ **Ground**: Wind and wood subtly enter from the ground, penetrating and pervading. **Ground** is the center of the yang hemicycle, spreading pervasive action.

Connection to the inner: penetrating and bringing together, the Woody Moment culminating. **Ground** pervades, matches and couples, seeding a new generation.

The outer limit blocks penetration and matching, turning growth in on itself and **corrupting** it.

- *Hidden Possibility*

Nuclear trigrams **Shake**, CHEN, and **Open**, TUI, result in Nuclear Hexagram 54, **Converting Maidenhood**, KUEI MEI. Stagnation and rotting away through **corrupting** let you realize hidden potential through **converting maidenhood**.

- *Sequence*

> Using rejoicing and Following people
> implies necessarily possessing affairs.
> Accepting this lets you use Corrupting.
> Corrupting implies affairs indeed.

Associated Contexts **Use(of)**, YI: make use of, by means of, owing to; employ, make functional. **Rejoice(in)**, HSI: feel and give joy; delight, exult;

cheerful, merry. The ideogram: joy (music) and mouth, expressing joy. **Follow**, SUI: come or go after; pursue, impelled to move; come after in inevitable sequence; move in the same direction, comply with what is ahead; follow a way or religion; according to, next, subsequent. The ideogram: go and fall, unavoidable movement. Image of Hexagram 17. **People, person,** JEN: humans individually and collectively; an individual; humankind. Image of Hexagrams 13 and 37. **Imply**, CHE: further signify; additional meaning. **Necessarily**, PI: unavoidably, indispensably, certainly. **Possess**, YU: in possession of, have, own; opposite of lack, WU. **Affairs**, SHIH: all kinds of personal activity; matters at hand; business, occupation; manage a business, case in court.

Accepting ... use: activating this hexagram depends on understanding and accepting the previous statement. **Indeed/is/means**, YEH: intensifier, connective; indicates comment on previous statement.

- *Contrasted Definitions*

> Following: without the past indeed.
> Corruption: by consequence stability indeed.

Associated Contexts **Without**, WU: devoid of; -less as suffix. **Past (cause)**, KU: come before as cause; formerly, ancient; reason, purpose, intention; grievance, quarrel, dissatisfaction, sorrow, mourning resulting from previous causes and intentions; situation leading to a divination.

By consequence(of), TSE: very strong connection; reason, cause, result; rule, law, pattern, standard; therefore. **Stability**, CH'IH: firm, prepared for; careful, respectful.

- *Symbol Tradition*

> Below mountain possessing wind. Corruption.
> A chün tzu uses rousing the commoners to nurture actualizing tao.

Associated Contexts **Below**, HSIA: anything below, in all senses; lower, inner; lower trigram; opposite of above, SHANG. **Mountain**, SHAN: limit, boundary; the Symbol of the trigram Bound, KEN. The ideogram: three peaks, a mountain range. **Wind**, FENG: moving air, breeze, gust; weather and its influence on mood and humor; fashion, usage; wind and wood are the Symbols of the trigram **Ground**, SUN.

Chün tzu: ideal of a person who uses divination to order his/her life in accordance with tao rather than wilful intention; keyword. **Rouse**, CHEN: stir up, excite, stimulate; issue forth; put in order. The ideogram: hand and shake, shaking things up. **Commoners**, MIN: class of workers the state draws on to sustain the social hierarchy; undeveloped potential outside the organized personality. **Nurture**, YÜ: bring up, support, rear, raise; increase. **Actualize tao**, TE: realize tao in action; power, virtue; ability to follow the course traced by the ongoing process of the cosmos; keyword. The ideogram: to go, straight, and heart. Linked with acquire, TE: acquiring that which makes a being become what it is meant to be.

● *Image Tradition*

> Corruption. Above strong and below supple. [I]
> Ground and stopping. Corruption.

> Corruption, Spring Growing. [II]
> And Below Heaven regulated indeed.

> Advantageous to step into the Great River. Harvesting. [III]
> Going possesses affairs indeed.

> Before seedburst three days, after seedburst three days. [IV]
> Completing, by consequence possessing the beginning.
> Heaven moving indeed.

Associated Contexts [I] **Above**, SHANG: anything above, in all senses; higher, upper, outer; upper trigram; opposite of below, HSIA. **Strong**, KANG: quality of the whole lines; firm, strong, unyielding, persisting. **Supple**, JOU: quality of the opened lines; flexible, pliant, tender, adaptable.

Ground, SUN: base on which things rest; support, foundation; mild, subtly penetrating; nourishing. The ideogram: stand and things arranged on it, the subtle influence of the ground. Image of Hexagram 57. **Stop**, CHIH: bring or come to a standstill; the Action of the trigram Bound, KEN. The ideogram: a foot stops walking.

[II] **Below Heaven**, T'IEN HSIA: the human world, between heaven and earth. **Regulate**, CHIH: govern well, ensure prosperity; remedy disorder, heal; someone fit to govern land, house and heart.

[III] **Go**, WANG, and **come**, LAI, describe the stream of time as it flows from future through present to past; go, WANG, indicates what is departing from present to past; proceed, move on; keyword.

[IV] **Complete**, CHUNG: end of a cycle that begins the next; last, whole, all; contrasts with exhaust, CH'IUNG, final end. The ideogram: silk cocoons, follow and ice, winter linking one year with the next. **Begin**, SHIH: commence, start, open; earliest, first; beginning of a time-span, ended by completion, CHUNG. The ideogram: woman and eminent, beginning new life.

Heaven, T'IEN: highest; sky, firmament, heavens; power above the human as opposed to earth, TI, below; the Symbol of the trigram Force, CH'IEN. The ideogram: great and the one above. **Move**, HSING: move or move something; motivate, emotionally moving; walk, act, do. The ideogram: stepping left then right.

● *Transforming Lines*

Initial six

a) **Managing the father's Corruption.**
Possessing sonhood.
Predecessors without fault.
Adversity, completing auspicious.

b) **Managing the father's Corruption.**
Intention receiving the predecessors indeed.

You must deal with the corruption of authority. This means danger with roots in the past. If you can manage this, the way will open. Take on the responsibility like a son or daughter who redeems the ancestors and go through it to the end.

Associated Contexts a) **Manage**, KAN: cope with, deal with, able; undertake, attend to business; trunk, stem, spine, skeleton. **Father(hood)**, FU: ruler of the family; act as a father, paternal, patriarchal; authoritative rule. The ideogram: hand and rod, the chastising father. **'s/have(it)/it/them**, CHIH: expresses possession, directly or as an object pronoun.

Son(hood), TZU: living up to ideal of ancestors as highest human development; act with concern and reverence; male child; offspring, posterity; seed, kernel, egg; sage, teacher; nadir, deepest point, midnight, mid-winter.

Predecessor, K'AO: deceased ancestor, especially the grandfather; the ancients; aged, long-lived; consult, verify. The ideogram: old and ingenious, the old wise man. **Without fault,** WU CHIU: no error or harm in the situation.

Adversity, LI: danger; threatening, malevolent demon. This has two aspects: grind, sharpen, improve, perfect, stimulate; and: poisonous, sinister, cruel, contrary. It indicates a spirit or ghost that seeks revenge by inflicting suffering upon the living. Pacifying or exorcizing such a spirit can have a healing effect. The ideogram: sheltering cliff and stinging insect. **Auspicious,** CHI: leads to the experience of meaning; favorable, propitious, advantageous, appropriate; keyword. The ideogram: scholar and mouth, wise words of a sage. ,

b) **Intention,** YI: thought, meaning, idea, will, motive; what gives words their significance. The ideogram: heart and sound, heartfelt expression. **Receive,** CH'ENG: receive gifts or commands from superiors or customers; take in hand; catch falling water. The ideogram: accepting a seal of office.

Nine at second

a) Managing the mother's Corruption.
   Not permitting Trial.

b) Managing the mother's Corruption.
   Acquiring centering tao indeed.

You must deal with the corruption of nourishment and care. Do not let the source of trouble make the divination. Put yourself in the middle of the situation and try to find the Way. Then you can change things.

Associated Contexts a) **Manage,** KAN: cope with, deal with, able; undertake, attend to business; trunk, stem, spine, skeleton. **Mother(hood),** MU: child-bearing and nourishing. The ideogram: two breasts. **'s/have(it)/it/them,** CHIH: expresses possession, directly or as an object pronoun.

Not permitting, PU K'O: not possible; contradicts an inherent principle. The ideogram: mouth and breath, silent consent. **Trial,** CHEN: inquiry by divination and its result; righteous, firm; separating wheat from chaff; the kernel, the proven core; fourth stage of the Time Cycle. The ideogram: pearl and divination.

b) **Acquire,** TE: obtain the desired object; wish for, desire covetously; gains, possessions. The ideogram: go and obstacle, going through obstacles to the goal. **Center,** CHUNG: inner, central; put in the center; middle, stable point enabling you to face inner and outer changes; middle line of trigram. The ideogram: field divided in two equal parts. Image of Hexagram 61. **Tao:** way or path; ongoing process of being and the course it traces for each specific person or thing; keyword. The ideogram: go and head, leading and the path it creates.

Nine at third

a) Managing the father's Corruption.
The small possesses repenting.
Without the great: fault.

b) Managing the father's Corruption.
Completing without fault indeed.

You must deal with the corruption of authority. There will be regrets that you co-operated with it. You must have a strong central purpose to come through.

Associated Contexts a) **Manage,** KAN: cope with, deal with, able; undertake, attend to business; trunk, stem, spine, skeleton. **Father(hood),** FU: ruler of the family; act as a father, paternal, patriarchal; authoritative rule. The ideogram: hand and rod, the chastising father. **'s/have(it)/it/them,** CHIH: expresses possession, directly or as an object pronoun.

Small, HSIAO: little, common, unimportant; adapting to what crosses your path; ability to move in harmony with the vicissitudes of life; contrasts with great, TA, self-imposed theme or goal; keyword. Image of Hexagrams 9 and 62. **Repent,** HUI: dissatisfaction with past conduct causing a change of heart; proceeds from abashment, LIN, shame and confusion at having lost the right way.

Great, TA: big, noble, important, very; orient the will toward a self-imposed goal, impose direction; ability to lead or guide your life; contrasts with small, HSIAO, flexible adaptation to what crosses your path; keyword. Image of Hexagrams 14, 26, 28, 34. **Fault,** CHIU: unworthy conduct that leads to harm, illness, misfortune. The ideogram: person and differ, differ from what you should be.

b) **Without fault,** WU CHIU: no error or harm in the situation.

Six at fourth

a) Enriching the father's Corruption.
Going: seeing distress.

b) Enriching the father's Corruption.
   Going not yet acquiring indeed.

You are colluding with the corruption of authority. Don't simply follow the old ways. If you do you will end up both lonely and confused, cut off from the Way.

Associated Contexts a) **Enrich**, YÜ: make richer (excluding land); material, mental or spiritual wealth; bequeath; generous, abundant. The ideogram: garments, portable riches. **Father(hood)**, FU: ruler of the family; act as a father, paternal, patriarchal; authoritative rule. The ideogram: hand and rod, the chastising father. **'s/have(it)/it/them/'s**, CHIH: expresses possession, directly or as an object pronoun.

   See, CHIEN: seeing in all its aspects: vision, being visible, forming mental images; visit, call on, consult. The ideogram: eye above person, active and receptive sight. **Distress**, LIN: distress, shame, regret, humiliation; aware of having lost the right track; leads to repenting, HUI, correcting the direction of mind and life.

b) **Not yet**, WEI: temporal negative; something will but has not yet occurred; contrary of already, CHI. Image of Hexagram 64. **Acquire**, TE: obtain the desired object; wish for, desire covetously; gains, possessions. The ideogram: go and obstacle, going through obstacles to the goal.

   Six at fifth

a) Managing the father's Corruption.
   Avail of praise.

b) Managing the father, availing of praise.
   Receiving uses actualizing tao indeed.

You must deal with the corruption of authority. Don't attack it directly. Use praise to accomplish the task. You will disarm your opponent and reclaim your own power. In the process you will find the power to actualize your plans.

Associated Contexts a) **Manage**, KAN: cope with, deal with, able; undertake, attend to business; trunk, stem, spine, skeleton. **Father(hood)**, FU: ruler of the family; act as a father, paternal, patriarchal; authoritative rule. The ideogram: hand and rod, the chastising father. **'s/have(it)/it/them**, CHIH: expresses possession, directly or as an object pronoun.

Avail of, YUNG: take advantage of; benefit from, profit by; use for a specific purpose; apply to advantage. The ideogram: to divine and center, applying divination to central concerns. **Praise,** YÜ: admire and approve; magnify, eulogize; flatter. The ideogram: words and give, offering words.

b) **Receive,** CH'ENG: receive gifts or commands from superiors or customers; take in hand; catch falling water. The ideogram: accepting a seal of office.

Nine above

a) Not affairs, kings and feudatories.
Honoring highness: one's affair.

b) Not affairs, kings and feudatories.
Purpose permitted by consequence indeed.

You should keep clear of the current corruption of business and politics. You have another job, finding and honoring what is truly noble in the human spirit. You will be rewarded for this.

Associated Contexts a) **King(hood),** WANG: effective ruler, by authority of the Emperor, from whom others derive their power. **Feudatory,** HOU: nobles entrusted with governing the provinces; active in daily life rather than governing from the center; contrasts with prince, KUNG, executives at the court.

Honor, SHANG: esteem, give high rank to; eminent; put one thing on top of another. **High(ness),** KAO: high, elevated, lofty, eminent; excellent, advanced. **One's/one,** CH'I: third person pronoun; also: it/its, he/his, she/hers, they/theirs.

b) **Purpose,** CHIH: focus of mind and heart; will, inclination, resolve. The ideogram: heart and scholar, high inner resolve, or heart and go, inner determination. **Permit,** K'O: possible because in harmony with an inherent principle. The ideogram: mouth and breath, silent consent.

19

NEARING ▌ *LIN*

Arrival of the new; approach of something powerful and meaningful; welcome, draw nearer and closer; spirit and meaning emerge from sadness.

Nearing describes your situation in terms of something great approaching. Its symbol is the arrival of a powerful ancestor spirit. This is the first arrival and point of new contact. The way to deal with it is to move towards what is approaching without expecting to get what you want immediately. Look at things with care and sympathy. Welcome the approach of others. Keep your expectations modest. This contact opens a whole new cycle of time. It is particularly favorable for what is growing. So beware. Trying to rush to completion and an early harvest will cut you off from the spirits and leave you open to danger.

● *Image of the Situation*

> **Nearing, Source of Success: Advantageous Trial.**
> **Culminating in the eighth moon: possessing a pitfall.**

Associated Contexts **Near**, LIN: approach, behold with care, look down on sympathetically; condescend; bless or curse by coming nearer; a superior visiting an inferior. **Source ... Trial**, lit. Spring Growing Harvesting Trial: **Spring**, YÜAN: **Grow**, HENG; **Harvest**, LI; and **Trial**, CHEN, are the four stages of the Time Cycle, the model for all dynamic processes. They indicate that your question is connected to the cycle as a whole rather than a part of it, and that the origin (Spring) of a favorable result (Harvesting Trial) is an offering to the spirits (Growing).

 Culminate, CHIH: bring to the highest degree; arrive at the end or summit; superlative. **Reach(to)**, HU, actually arriving. **Eight**, PA: number of highly valued essentials: eight trigrams, eight immortals, eight compass points; eighth. **Moon**, YÜEH: actual moon and moon-month; yin, the sun being yang. **Possess**, YU: in possession of, have, own; opposite of lack, WU. **Pitfall**, HSIUNG: leads away from the experience of meaning; stuck and exposed to danger, unable to take in the situation; flow of life and spirit is blocked; unfortunate, baleful; keyword.

● *Outer and Inner Aspects*

☷ **Field**: The field of earth yields and sustains, serving in order to produce. **Field** is the equalizing point between yin and yang where things labor and serve.

Connection to the outer: the common labor of sowing and hoarding, the Earthy Moment. **Field** produces concrete results through serving.

☱ **Open**: vapor rising from the marsh's open surface stimulates and fertilizes; stimulating words cheer and inspire. **Open** begins the yin hemicycle by initiating the formative process.

Connection to the inner: liquifying, casting, skinning off the mold, the Metallic Moment beginning. **Open** stimulates, cheers and reveals innate form.

Inner stimulation combined with an outer willingness to serve invites **nearing**.

● *Hidden Possibility*

Nuclear trigrams **Field**, K'UN and **Shake**, CHEN, result in Nuclear Hexagram 24, **Returning**, FU. The spirit which is **nearing** lets you **return** to a starting point to begin again.

● *Sequence*

> **Possessing affairs and afterwards permitting the great.**
> **Accepting this lets you use Nearing.**
> **Nearing implies the great indeed.**

Associated Contexts **Affairs**, SHIH: all kinds of personal activity; matters at hand; business, occupation; manage a business, case in court. **Also**, ERH: joins and contrasts two terms. **After(wards)/later**, HOU: come after in time, subsequent; put oneself after; the second; attendants, heirs, successors, posterity. **Permit**, K'O: possible because in harmony with an inherent principle. The ideogram: mouth and breath, silent consent. **Great**, TA: big, noble, important, very; orient the will toward a self-imposed goal, impose direction; ability to lead or guide your life; contrasts with **small**, HSIAO, flexible adaptation to what crosses your path; keyword. Image of Hexagrams 14, 26, 28, 34.

Anterior ... the use of: activating this hexagram depends on understanding and accepting the previous statement.

Imply, CHE: further signify; additional meaning. **Indeed,** YEH: intensifier, connective; indicates comment on previous statement.

- *Contrasted Definitions*

    Nearing and Viewing's righteousness.
    "Someone" is associating with it, "someone" is seeking.

    Associated Contexts **View,** KUAN: contemplate, observe from a distance; look at carefully, gaze at; also: a monastery, an observatory; scry, divine through liquid in a cup. The ideogram: see and waterbird, observe through air or water. Image of Hexagram 20. **'s/have(it)/it/them,** CHIH: expresses possession, directly or as an object pronoun. **Righteous,** YI: proper and just, meets the standards; things in their proper place; the heart that rules itself; upright, moral rule; contrasts with Harvest, LI, advantage or profit.

    Maybe, "someone" HUO: possible but not certain, perhaps. **Associate(with),** YÜ: consort with, combine; companions; group, band, company; agree with, comply, help. The ideogram: pair of hands reaching downward meets a pair of hands reaching upward, helpful association. **Seek,** CH'IU: search for, aim at, wish for, desire; implore, supplicate; covetous.

- *Symbol Tradition*

    Above marsh possessing earth. Nearing.
    A chün tzu uses teaching to ponder without exhausting.
    [A chün tzu uses] tolerating
    to protect the commoners without delimiting.

    Associated Contexts **Above,** SHANG: anything above, in all senses; higher, upper, outer; upper trigram; opposite of below, HSIA. **Marsh,** TSE: open surface of a flat body of water and the vapors rising from it; fertilize, enrich; kindness, favor; the Symbol of the trigram Open, TUI. **Earth,** TI: ground on which the human world rests; basis of all things, nourishes all things; the Symbol of the trigram Field, K'UN.

    Chün tzu: ideal of a person who uses divination to order his/her life in accordance with tao rather than wilful intention; keyword. **Use(of),** YI: make use of, by means of, owing to; employ, make functional. **Teach,** CHIAO: instruct, show; precept, doctrine. **Ponder,** SSU: reflect, consider, remember; deep thought; desire, wish. The ideogram: heart and field, the heart's concerns. **Without,** WU: devoid of; -less as suffix. **Exhaust,** CH'IUNG: bring to an end; limit, extremity; destitute; investigate exhaustively; end without a new beginning. The ideogram: cave and naked person, bent with disease or old age.

Tolerate, JUNG: allow, contain, endure, bear with; accept graciously. The ideogram: full stream bed, tolerating and containing. **Protect**, PAO: guard, defend, keep safe; secure. **Commoners**, MIN: class of workers the state draws on to sustain the social hierarchy; undeveloped potential outside the organized personality. **Delimit**, CHIANG: define frontiers, draw limits; boundary, border.

● *Image Tradition*

> Nearing. [I]
> Strong drenched and long living.
> Stimulating and yielding.
> Strong centered and corresponding.
>
> Great Growing uses correcting. [II]
> Heavenly tao indeed.
> Culminating in the eighth moon: possessing a pitfall. [III]
> Dissolving, not lasting indeed.

Associated Contexts **Strong**, KANG: quality of the whole lines; firm, strong, unyielding, persisting. **Drench**, CH'IN: soak, penetrate, immerse, steep in; imbued with. **Long living**, CHANG: enduring, constant; senior, superior, greater; increase, prosper; respect, elevate.

Stimulate, SHUO: rouse to action and good feeling; free from constraint, stir up, urge on; persuade, cheer, delight; set out in words; the Action of the trigram Open, TUI. The ideogram: words and exchange. **Yield(to)**, SHUN: give way and bear produce; comply, agree, follow, obey; unresisting, docile, flexible; nourish, provide; the Action of the trigram Field, K'UN. The ideogram: head and current, water flowing from the head of a river, yielding to the banks.

Center, CHUNG: inner, central; put in the center; middle, stable point enabling you to face inner and outer changes; middle line of trigram. The ideogram: field divided in two equal parts. Image of Hexagram 61. **Correspond(to)**, YING: be in agreement or harmony; resonate together, invoke and fulfil each other; answer to, suitable; relation between the lines (1:4, 2:5, 3:6) when they form the pair opened and whole, supple and strong. The ideogram: heart and obey.

[II] **Grow**, HENG: success through a sacrifice; pervade, persevere; bring to full growth; enjoy; vigorous, effective; second stage of the Time Cycle. **Correct**, CHENG: rectify deviation or one-sidedness; proper, straight, exact, regular; constant, rule, model. The ideogram: stop and one, hold to one thing.

Heaven, T'IEN: highest; sky, firmament, heavens; power above the human as opposed to earth, TI, below; the Symbol of the trigram Force, CH'IEN. The ideogram: great and the one above. **Tao**: way or path; ongoing process of being and the course it traces for each specific person or thing; keyword. The ideogram: go and head, leading and the path it creates.

[III] **Dissolve**, HSIAO: liquify, melt, thaw; diminish, disperse; eliminate, exhaust. The ideogram: water dissolving differences. **Not**, PU: simple negative. **Last**, CHIU: long, protracted; enduring.

- *Transforming Lines*

  Initial nine

  a) **Conjunction Nearing, Trial: auspicious.**

  b) **Conjunction Nearing, Trial: auspicious.**
  Purpose moving, correcting indeed.

What is approaching belongs with you like parts of a previously separated whole. This is a marriage made in heaven. It will stimulate and inspire you. Have no doubts. The way is open.

Associated Contexts a) **Conjoin**, HSIEN: come into contact with, influence; reach, join together; put together as parts of a previously separated whole; come into conjunction, as the celestial bodies; totally, completely; lit.: broken piece of pottery, the halves of which join to identify partners. Image of Hexagram 31. **Trial**, CHEN: inquiry by divination and its result; righteous, firm; separating wheat from chaff; the kernel, the proven core; fourth stage of the Time Cycle. The ideogram: pearl and divination. **Auspicious**, CHI: leads to the experience of meaning; favorable, propitious, advantageous, appropriate; keyword. The ideogram: scholar and mouth, wise words of a sage.

b) **Purpose**, CHIH: focus of mind and heart; will, inclination, resolve. The ideogram: heart and scholar, high inner resolve, or heart and go, inner determination. **Move**, HSING: move or move something; motivate, emotionally moving; walk, act, do. The ideogram: stepping left then right.

Nine at second

a) Conjunction Nearing: auspicious.
Nothing not advantageous.

b) Conjunction Nearing: auspicious.
Nothing not advantageous.
Not yet yielding to fate indeed.

What is approaching belongs with you like parts of a previously separated whole. This is a marriage made in heaven. It will stimulate and inspire you. There is nothing that will not benefit from this connection. You are not the victim of fate.

Associated Contexts a) **Conjoin,** HSIEN: come into contact with, influence; reach, join together; put together as parts of a previously separated whole; come into conjunction, as the celestial bodies; totally, completely; lit.: broken piece of pottery, the halves of which join to identify partners. Image of Hexagram 31. **Auspicious,** CHI: leads to the experience of meaning; favorable, propitious, advantageous, appropriate; keyword. The ideogram: scholar and mouth, wise words of a sage.

Nothing not advantageous, WU PU LI: nothing for which this will not be beneficial; advantageous potential, borderline where the balance is swinging from not Harvesting to actually Harvesting.

b) **Not yet,** WEI: temporal negative; something will but has not yet occurred; contrary of already, CHI. Image of Hexagram 64. **Fate,** MING: individual destiny; birth and death as limits of life; issue orders with authority; consult the gods. The ideogram: mouth and order, words with heavenly authority.

Six at third

a) Sweetness Nearing.
Nothing not advantageous.
Already grieving over it:
Without fault.

b) Sweetness Nearing.
Situation not appropriate indeed.
Already grieving over it:
Fault not long living indeed.

What is approaching may look sweet but no good can come of it. This is simply not right for you. Painful though it may be, if you have already realized it you won't make mistakes.

Associated Contexts a) **Sweet**, KAN: taste corresponding to the Earthy Moment; agreeable, happy, delightful, refreshing; grateful.

Nothing not advantageous, WU YU LI: no plan or direction is advantageous; in order to take advantage of the situation, do not impose a direction on events.

Already, CHI: completed, done, has occurred; past tense, contrary of not-yet, WEI. Image of Hexagram 63. **Grieve(over)**, YU: sorrow, melancholy; mourn; anxious, careworn; hidden sorrow. The ideogram: heart, head, and limp, heart-sick and anxious. **It/them/have(it)/'s**, CHIH: expresses possession, directly or as an object pronoun.

Without fault, WU CHIU: no error or harm in the situation.

b) **Situation**, WEI: place or seat according to rank; post, position, command; right, proper; established, arranged. The ideogram: person and stand, servants in their places. **Appropriate**, TANG: suitable; opportune, convenient; adequate, competent; equal to; whole lines in uneven places and opened lines in even places.

Fault, CHIU: unworthy conduct that leads to harm, illness, misfortune. The ideogram: person and differ, differ from what you should be.

Six at fourth

a) **Culmination Nearing.**
Without fault.

b) **Culmination Nearing, without fault.**
Situation appropriate indeed.

This is the climax. Don't hold back. Give yourself fully. This is not a mistake.

Associated Contexts a) **Without fault**, WU CHIU: no error or harm in the situation.

b) **Situation**, WEI: place or seat according to rank; post, position, command; right, proper; established, arranged. The ideogram: person and stand, servants in their places. **Appropriate**, TANG: suitable; opportune, convenient; adequate, competent; equal to; whole lines in uneven places and opened lines in even places.

Six at fifth

a) **Knowledge Nearing.**
A Great Chief's propriety.
Auspicious.

b) **A Great Chief's propriety.**
Moving the center's designation indeed.

This connection has a special quality, the knowledge a great leader uses to help and change people. It is time to take action. Launch the armies. The spirit will be with you. This can change the way you see yourself and your life.

A s s o c i a t e d   C o n t e x t s   a) **Know,** CHIH: understand, perceive, remember; informed, aware, wise. The ideogram: arrow and mouth, words focused and swift.

Chief, CHÜN: effective ruler; preside over, take the lead; influence others; term of respect. The ideogram: mouth and director, giving orders.
Proper, YI: reasonable of itself; fit and right, harmonious; ought, should.
Auspicious, CHI: leads to the experience of meaning; favorable, propitious, advantageous, appropriate; keyword. The ideogram: scholar and mouth, wise words of a sage.

b) **Move,** HSING: move or move something; motivate, emotionally moving; walk, act, do. The ideogram: stepping left then right. **Designate,** WEI: represent in words, assign a name or meaning; report on, talk about. The ideogram: words and belly, describing the essential.

Six above

a) **Magnanimity Nearing.**
Auspicious. Without fault.

b) **Magnanimity Nearing's Auspicious.**
Purpose located inside indeed.

Generosity, wealth and the power of enjoyment enter your life through this connection. Be generous with what you acquire. Hold on to your sense of inner purpose. Your desires will be satisfied.

A s s o c i a t e d   C o n t e x t s   a) **Magnanimous,** TUN: generous; honest, substantial, important, wealthy; honor, increase; firm, strong. The ideogram: strike and accept, warrior magnanimous in attack and defense.

Auspicious, CHI: leads to the experience of meaning; favorable, propitious, advantageous, appropriate; keyword. The ideogram: scholar and mouth, wise words of a sage. **Without fault,** WU CHIU: no error or harm in the situation.

b) **Purpose,** CHIH: focus of mind and heart; will, inclination, resolve. The ideogram: heart and scholar, high inner resolve, or heart and go, inner determination. **Locate(in),** TSAI: live in, dwell, reside; belong to, involved with, depend on; within. The ideogram: earth and persevere, place on the earth. **Inside,** NEI: within, inner, interior; inside of the house and those who work there, particularly women; the lower trigram, as opposed to outside, WAI, the upper. The ideogram: border and enter, cross a border.

20

VIEWING ▮ KUAN

Let everything come into view, examine, contemplate, divine the meaning; spirit manifests through the omens.

Viewing describes your situation in terms of the need to look without acting in order to find the right perspective. Its symbol is a tower used to observe the signs in heaven and earth. The way to deal with it is to let everything emerge and divine the central meaning. Particularly, look at what you usually don't want to see or think about. This figure describes a particular moment in a religious ceremony, when the purification has been made and the libation is about to be poured out. Have confidence. Examining things will bring you the insight you need. When you have made the preparations, the spirit presence will arrive and carry you through.

- ## Image of the Situation

  Viewing: hand washing and also not worshipping.
  There is a connection to the spirits like a presence.

  Associated Contexts **View**, KUAN: contemplate, observe from a distance; look at carefully, gaze at; also: a monastery, an observatory; scry, divine through liquid in a cup. The ideogram: see and waterbird, observe through air or water. **Hand washing**, KUAN: wash the hands before a sacramental act; ablutions, a basin. **Worship**, CHIEN: honor the gods and ancestors; make sacrifice; recommend or introduce yourself. The ideogram: leading animals to green pastures.

  There is ... spirits, YU FU: inner and outer are in accord; confidence of the spirits has been captured; sincere, truthful; proper to take action. **Like**, JO: same as; just as, similar to. **Presence**, YUNG: noble bearing; prestige, dignity; imposing; lit.: a great head.

- ## Outer and Inner Aspects

  ☷ **Ground**: Wind and wood subtly enter from the ground, penetrating and pervading. **Ground** is the center of the yang hemicycle, spreading pervasive action.

Connection to the outer: penetrating and bringing together, the Woody Moment culminating. **Ground** pervades, matches and couples, seeding a new generation.

☷ **Field**: The field of earth yields and sustains, serving in order to produce. **Field** is the equalizing point between yin and yang where things labor and serve.

Connection to the inner: the common labor of sowing and hoarding, the Earthy Moment. **Field** produces concrete results through serving.

Entering and penetrating the inner field, images of distant actions come into **view**.

- *Hidden Possibility*

Nuclear trigrams **Bound**, KEN, and **Field**, K'UN, result in Nuclear Hexagram 23, **Stripping**, PO. **Viewing** the entire field of action lets you **strip** away old ideas.

- *Sequence*

> **Being great therefore afterwards permits Viewing.**
> **Accepting this lets you use Viewing.**

Associated Contexts **Being(s)**, WU: creature, thing, any single being; matter, substance, essence; nature of things. **Great**, TA: big, noble, important, very; orient the will toward a self-imposed goal, impose direction; ability to lead or guide your life; contrasts with small, HSIAO, flexible adaptation to what crosses your path; keyword. Image of Hexagrams 14, 26, 28, 34. **Therefore afterwards**, JAN HOU: logical consequence of, necessarily follows in time. **Permit**, K'O: possible because in harmony with an inherent principle. The ideogram: mouth and breath, silent consent.

Accepting ... use: activating this hexagram depends on understanding and accepting the previous statement.

- *Contrasted Definitions*

> **Nearing and Viewing's righteousness.**
> **"Someone" is associating with it, "someone" is seeking.**

Associated Contexts **Near**, LIN: approach or be approached: behold with care, look on sympathetically; condescend; bless or curse by coming nearer; a superior visits an inferior. Image of Hexagram 19. **'s/have(it)/it/them**, CHIH: expresses possession, directly or as an object pronoun. **Righteous**, YI: proper and just, meets the standards; things in their proper place; the heart that rules itself; upright, moral rule; contrasts with Harvest, LI, advantage or profit.

Maybe/"someone", HUO: possible but not certain, perhaps. **Associate(with)**, YÜ: consort with, combine; companions; group, band, company; agree with, comply, help. The ideogram: pair of hands reaching downward meets a pair of hands reaching upward, helpful association. **Seek**, CH'IU: search for, aim at, wish for, desire; implore, supplicate; covetous.

● *Symbol Tradition*

> **Wind moving above earth. Viewing.**
> **The Earlier Kings used inspecting on all sides,**
> **Viewing the commoners to set up teaching.**

Associated Contexts **Wind**, FENG: moving air, breeze, gust; weather and its influence on mood and humor; fashion, usage; wind and wood are the Symbols of the trigram Ground, SUN. **Move**, HSING: move or move something; motivate, emotionally moving; walk, act, do. The ideogram: stepping left then right. **Above**, SHANG: anything above, in all senses; higher, upper, outer; upper trigram; opposite of below, HSIA. **Earth**, TI: ground on which the human world rests; basis of all things, nourishes all things; the Symbol of the trigram Field, K'UN.

Earlier Kings, HSIEN WANG: ideal rulers of old; the golden age, primal time, power in harmony with nature; model for the chün tzu. **Use(of)**, YI: make use of, by means of, owing to; employ, make functional. **Inspect**, HSING: examine on all sides, careful inquiry; watchful. **Sides (on all sides)**, FANG: limits, boundaries; square, surface of the earth extending to the four cardinal points; everywhere. **Commoners**, MIN: class of workers the state draws on to sustain the social hierarchy; undeveloped potential outside the organized personality. **Set up**, SHE: establish, institute; arrange, set in order; spread a net. The ideogram: words and impel, establish with words. **Teach**, CHIAO: instruct, show; precept, doctrine.

● *Image Tradition*

The great: Viewing located above. [I]
Yielding to the Ground.
Centering and correcting uses Viewing Below Heaven.

Viewing: hand washing and also not worshipping. [II]
There is a connection to the spirits, like a presence.
Viewing below and changing indeed.

Viewing heaven's spirit tao, [III]
And the four seasons not straying.
The all wise person uses spirit tao to set up teaching.
And actually Below Heaven submits.

Associated Contexts **Locate(in)**, TSAI: live in, dwell, reside; belong to, involved with, depend on; within. The ideogram: earth and persevere, place on the earth.

Yield(to), SHUN: give way and bear produce; comply, agree, follow, obey; unresisting, docile, flexible; nourish, provide; the Action of the trigram Field, K'UN. The ideogram: head and current, water flowing from the head of a river, yielding to the banks. **Ground**, SUN: base on which things rest; support, foundation; mild, subtly penetrating; nourishing. The ideogram: stand and things arranged on it, the subtle influence of the ground. Image of Hexagram 57.

Centering correcting, CHUNG CHENG: central and correct; make rectifying one-sidedness and error your central concern; reaching a stable center in yourself can correct the situation. **Below Heaven**, T'IEN HSIA: the human world, between heaven and earth.

[II] **Below**, HSIA: anything below, in all senses; lower, inner; lower trigram; opposite of above, SHANG. **Change**, HUA: gradual, continuous metamorphosis; influence someone; contrasts with transform, PIEN, sudden mutation. The ideogram: person alive and dead, the life-process. **Indeed/is/means**, YEH: intensifier, connective; comment on previous statement.

[III] **Heaven**, T'IEN: highest; sky, firmament, heavens; power above the human as opposed to earth, TI, below; the Symbol of the trigram Force, CH'IEN. The ideogram: great and the one above. **Spirit(s)**, SHEN: independent spiritual powers that confer intensity on heart and mind by acting on the soul, KUEI; gods, daimons. **Tao**: way or path; ongoing process of being and the course it traces for each specific person or thing; keyword. The ideogram: go and head, leading and the path it creates.

Four seasons, SSU SHIH: the four dynamic qualities of time that make up the year and the Time Cycle; the right time, in accord with the time; time as sacred; all-encompassing. **Stray,** T'E: wander blindly; deviate, err, alter, doubt; excess.

All wise, SHENG: intuitive universal wisdom; mythical sages; holy, sacred; mark of highest distinction. The ideogram: ear and inform, one who knows all from a single sound. **People, person,** JEN: humans individually and collectively; an individual; humankind. Image of Hexagrams 13 and 37.

Actually, YI: truly, really, at present. The ideogram: a dart and done, strong intention fully expressed. **Submit,** FU: yield to, serve; undergo.

● *Transforming Lines*

Initial six

a) Youthful Viewing.
   Small People: without fault.
   Chün tzu: distress.

b) Initial six, youthful Viewing.
   Small People: tao indeed.

Watching the children play. These are beginnings of danger. Help the small people if you want to overcome the distress. Don't see things like a child yourself.

Associated Contexts a) **Youthful,** T'UNG: young person between eight and fifteen; young animals and plants.

Small People, HSIAO JEN: lowly, common, humble; those who adjust to circumstances with the flexibility of the small; effect of the small within an individual; keyword. **Without fault,** WU CHIU: no error or harm in the situation.

Chün tzu: ideal of a person who uses divination to order his/her life in accordance with tao rather than wilful intention; keyword. **Distress,** LIN: distress, shame, regret, humiliation; aware of having lost the right track; leads to repenting, HUI, correcting the direction of mind and life.

Six at second

a) Peeping through Viewing.
   Advantageous woman Trial. Harvesting.

b) Peeping through Viewing: woman Trial.
Truly permitting the demoniac indeed.

Rather than watching furtively, trying to steal secrets, empower those you are spying on to ask the questions and learn how the spirit is moving. Don't fall into negative emotions.

Associated Contexts a) **Peep through,** K'UEI: observe from hiding; stealthily, furtive.

Advantageous/Harvest, LI: advantageous, profitable; acute, insightful; benefit, nourish; third stage of the Time Cycle. **Woman(hood),** NÜ: a woman; what is inherently female. **Trial,** CHEN: inquiry by divination and its result; righteous, firm; separating wheat from chaff; the kernel, the proven core; fourth stage of the Time Cycle. The ideogram: pearl and divination.

b) **Truly,** YI: statement is true and precise. **Demon(iac),** CH'OU: possessed by a malignant genius; ugly, physically or morally deformed; vile, disgraceful, shameful; drunken. The ideogram: fermenting liquor and soul. Demoniac and tiger are opposed on the Universal Compass North–South axis; the tiger (Extreme Yang) scares away and protects against demoniacs (Extreme Yin).

Six at third

a) Viewing my birth, advancing, withdrawing.

b) Viewing my birth, advancing, withdrawing.
Not yet letting go tao indeed.

This is a transition. You have to decide whether to go on with this or to pull back. Look at the things you do, what you give birth to. Don't let go of your real purpose.

Associated Contexts a) **My/me/I,** WO: first person pronoun; indicates an unusually strong emphasis on your own subjective experience. **Birth/give birth to,** SHENG: produce, beget, grow, bear, arise; life, vitality. The ideogram: earth and sprout. **Advance,** CHIN: exert yourself, make progress, climb; be promoted; further the development of, augment; adopt a religion or conviction; offer, introduce. **Withdraw(from),** T'UI: draw back, retreat, recede; decline, refuse.

b) **Not yet,** WEI: temporal negative; something will but has not yet occurred; contrary of already, CHI. Image of Hexagram 64. **Let go,** SHIH: lose, omit, miss, fail, let slip; out of control. The ideogram: drop from the hand.

Six at fourth

a) Viewing the city's shining.
  Advantageous to be a guest of the king. Harvesting.

b) Viewing the city's shining.
  Honoring guesting indeed.

This connection can bring you power and wealth. The city is spread out before you. Remember, however, you are a guest. Be politic and polite. This is a long-term experience. Its true purpose is not clear yet.

Associated Contexts a) **City,** KUO: area of only human constructions; political unit, polis. First of the territorial zones: city, suburbs, countryside, forests. **Shine,** KUANG: illuminate; give off brilliant, bright light; honor, glory, éclat; result of action, contrasts with brightness, MING, light of heavenly bodies. The ideogram: fire above person, lifting the light.

  Advantageous/Harvest, LI: advantageous, profitable; acute, insightful; benefit, nourish; third stage of the Time Cycle. **Avail of,** YUNG: take advantage of; benefit from, profit by; use for a specific purpose; apply to advantage. The ideogram: to divine and center, applying divination to central concerns. **Guest,** PIN: entertain a guest; visit someone, enjoy hospitality; receive a stranger. **King(hood),** WANG: effective ruler, by authority of the Emperor, from whom others derive their power.

b) **Honor,** SHANG: esteem, give high rank to; eminent; put one thing on top of another.

Nine at fifth

a) Viewing my birth.
  A chün tzu: without fault.

b) Viewing my birth.
  Viewing the commoners indeed.

Look deeply at this connection and your relation to it. Look at the things you do, what you give birth to, then commit yourself. If you measure your desires against the ideal of the Noble Son, you won't make any mistakes.

Associated Contexts a) **My/me/I,** WO: first person pronoun; indicates an unusually strong emphasis on your own subjective experience. **Birth/give birth to,** SHENG: produce, beget, grow, bear, arise; life, vitality. The ideogram: earth and sprout.

Chün tzu: ideal of a person who uses divination to order his/her life in accordance with tao rather than wilful intention; keyword. **Without fault,** WU CHIU: no error or harm in the situation.

> **Nine above**
>
> *a)* **Viewing one's birth.**
>   **A chün tzu: without fault.**
>
> *b)* **Viewing one's birth.**
>   **Purpose not yet evened indeed.**

Look deeply at this connection. Look at where and how it started and the effect it has had on your life and the lives of others. Measure it against the ideal of Noble Son, then commit yourself. You won't be making a mistake.

Associated Contexts a) **One's/one,** CH'I: third person pronoun; also: it/its, he/his, she/hers, they/theirs. **Birth/give birth to,** SHENG: produce, beget, grow, bear, arise; life, vitality. The ideogram: earth and sprout.

Chün tzu: ideal of a person who uses divination to order his/her life in accordance with tao rather than wilful intention; keyword. **Without fault,** WU CHIU: no error or harm in the situation.

b) **Purpose,** CHIH: focus of mind and heart; will, inclination, resolve. The ideogram: heart and scholar, high inner resolve, or heart and go, inner determination. **Not yet,** WEI: temporal negative; something will but has not yet occurred; contrary of already, CHI. Image of Hexagram 64. **Even,** P'ING: level, make even or equal; uniform, peaceful, tranquil; restore quiet, harmonize.

21

GNAWING BITE ▌ *SHIH HO*

Confront the problem, bite through the obstacle, tenacious, determined, enduring.

Gnawing Bite describes your situation in terms of confronting a tenacious obstacle. Its symbol is "eating ancient virtue," the ancestral feats and the scribes eating through the books to find the core meanings. The way to deal with it is to gnaw away what is unnecessary and bite through the core of the problem. Make an offering and you will succeed. Something is keeping the jaws from coming together. Take decisive action. Gnaw away at the obstacles until you reach the hidden center, then bite through what is keeping things apart. This is pleasing to the spirits and they will help you. Take things to court. Plead for justice and make demands on authorities. That brings profit and insight. This is a time for legal action, punishment and a warning against criminal activity.

● *Image of the Situation*

> **Gnawing Bite, Growing.**
> **Advantageous to avail of litigating. Harvesting**

Associated Contexts **Gnaw,** SHIH: bite away, chew; bite persistently and remove; snap at, nibble; reach the essential by removing the unnecessary. The ideogram: mouth and divination, revealing the essential. **Bite,** HO: close the jaws, bite through, crush between the teeth. The ideogram: mouth and cover, jaws fit together as a lid fits a vessel. **Grow,** HENG: success through a sacrifice; pervade, persevere; bring to full growth; enjoy; vigorous, effective; second stage of the Time Cycle.

Advantageous/Harvest, LI: advantageous, profitable; acute, insightful; benefit, nourish; third stage of the Time Cycle. **Avail of,** YUNG: take advantage of; benefit from, profit by; use for a specific purpose; apply to advantage. The ideogram: to divine and center, applying divination to central concerns. **Litigate,** YÜ: legal proceedings; take a case to court. The ideogram: two dogs and words, barking arguments at each other.

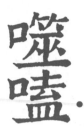

Outer and Inner Aspects

☲ **Radiance**: Fire and brightness radiate light and warmth, attached to their support; congregating people see and become aware. **Radiance** ends the yang hemicycle, consuming action in awareness.

Connection to the outer: light, heat, consciousness bring continual change, the Fiery Moment. **Radiance** spreads outward, congregating, becoming aware and changing.

☳ **Shake**: Thunder rises from below, shaking and stirring things up. **Shake** begins the yang hemicycle by germinating new action.

Connection to the inner: sprouting energies thrusting from below, the Woody Moment beginning. **Shake** stirs things up to issue-forth.

Inner stirring-up spreads outer awareness, **gnawing** through obstacles with thunder's incisive **bite**. These trigrams begin and end the yang hemicycle; they emphasize taking action.

Hidden Possibility

Nuclear trigrams **Gorge**, K'AN, and **Bound**, KEN, result in Nuclear Hexagram 39, **Difficulties**, CHIEN. The resolute action necessary to **gnaw** and **bite** through lets you re-imagine a **difficult** situation.

Sequence

Permitting Viewing and afterwards possessing a place to unite.
Accepting this lets you use Gnawing Bite.
Gnawing Bite implies uniting indeed.

Associated Contexts **Permit**, K'O: possible because in harmony with an inherent principle. The ideogram: mouth and breath, silent consent. **View**, KUAN: contemplate, observe from a distance; look at carefully, gaze at; also: a monastery, an observatory; scry, divine through liquid in a cup. The ideogram: see and waterbird, observe through air or water. Image of Hexagram 20. **After(wards)/later**, HOU: come after in time, subsequent; put oneself after; the second; attendant, heirs, successors, posterity. **Possess**, YU: in possession of, have, own; opposite of lack, WU. **Place**, SO: where something belongs or comes from; residence, dwelling; habitual focus or object. **Unite**, HO: join, match, correspond, agree, collect, reply; unison, harmony; also: close, shut the mouth. The ideogram: mouth and assemble.

Accepting ... use: activating this hexagram depends on understanding and accepting the previous statement.

Imply, CHE: further signify; additional meaning. **Indeed/is/means**, YEH: intensifier, connective; indicates comment on previous statement.

- ## Contrasted Definitions

Gnawing Bite: eating indeed.
Adorning: without complexion indeed.

Associated Contexts **Eat**, SHIH: eat, ingest, swallow, devour; incorporate, take in.

Adorn, PI: embellish, ornament, deck out, beautify; variegated (flowers); elegant, brilliant; also: energetic, passionate, eager, intrepid; capable of great effort; brave. The ideogram: cowrie shells (money) and flowers, linking ornaments and value. Image of Hexagram 22. **Without**, WU: devoid of; -less as suffix. **Complexion**, SE: appearance, expression; color, hue; air, manner, deportment; beautiful.

- ## Symbol Tradition

Thunder, lightning. Gnawing Bite.
The Earlier Kings used brightening through flogging to enforce the laws.

Associated Contexts **Thunder**, LEI: rising, arousing power; the Symbol of the trigram **Shake**, CHEN. **Lightning**, TIEN: lighting flash, electric discharge; sudden clarity; look attentively.

Earlier Kings, HSIEN WANG: ideal rulers of old; the golden age, primal time, power in harmony with nature; model for the chün tzu. **Use(of)**, YI: make use of, by means of, owing to; employ, make functional. **Brightness**, MING: light-giving aspect of burning, heavenly bodies and consciousness; with fire, the Symbol of the trigram Radiance, LI. **Flog**, FA: punish with blows, beat, whip; used to find out the truth. **Enforce**, LAI: compel obedience; have charge of; imposed by highest authority; arrest, deliver for punishment. **Laws**, FA: rules, statutes, model, method.

- ## Image Tradition

Jaws center possesses being. Spoken thus: Gnawing Bite. [I]
Gnawing Bite and Growing.
Strong and Supple apportioned.

Stirring up and brightening. [II]
Thunder and lightning, uniting and composing.

Supple acquiring the center and moving above. [III]
Although not an appropriate situation,
Advantageous to avail of litigating indeed.

Associated Contexts [I] **Jaws/swallow**, YI: mouth, jaws, cheeks, chin; take in, ingest; feed, nourish, sustain, rear; furnish what is necessary. The ideogram: open jaws. Image of Hexagram 27. **Center**, CHUNG: inner, central; put in the center; middle, stable point enabling you to face inner and outer changes; middle line of trigram. The ideogram: field divided in two equal parts. Image of Hexagram 61. **Being(s)**, WU: creature, thing, any single being; matter, substance, essence; nature of things. **Spoken thus**, YÜEH: designated, termed, called. The ideogram: open mouth and tongue.

Strong and Supple, KANG JOU: field of creative tension between the whole and opened lines and their qualities; field of psychic movement. **Apportion**, FEN: divide for distribution; sort out; allot to.

[II] **Stir up**, TUNG: excite, influence, move, affect; work, take action; come out of the egg or the bud; the Action of the trigram Shake, CHEN. The ideogram: strength and heavy, move weighty things.

Composition, CHANG: a well-composed whole and its structure; beautiful creations; elegant, clear, brilliant; contrasts with pattern, WEN, beauty of intrinsic design.

[III] **Supple**, JOU: quality of the opened lines; flexible, pliant, tender, adaptable. **Acquire**, TE: obtain the desired object; wish for, desire covetously; gains, possessions. The ideogram: go and obstacle, going through obstacles to the goal. **Move**, HSING: move or move something; motivate, emotionally moving; walk, act, do. The ideogram: stepping left then right. **Above**, SHANG: anything above, in all senses; higher, upper, outer; upper trigram; opposite of below, HSIA.

Although, SUI: even though, supposing that, if, even if. **Appropriate**, TANG: suitable; opportune, convenient; adequate, competent; equal to; whole lines in uneven places and opened lines in even places. **Situation**, WEI: place or seat according to rank; post, position, command; right, proper; established, arranged. The ideogram: person and stand, servants in their places.

● *Transforming Lines*

Initial nine

a) Shoes in the lock up, submerging the feet.
Without fault.

b) Shoes in the lock up, submerging the feet.
Not moving indeed.

You have been locked up and cannot move. Don't worry. This is for your own good. It is the right thing to do now. It will free you from impulsive reactions before you can act them out.

Associated Contexts a) **Shoes,** CHÜ: footwear, sandals. **Lock up,** CHIAO: imprison, lock up the feet; prison, pen. **Submerge,** MIEH: plunge under water, put out a fire; exterminate, finish, cut off. The ideogram: water and destroy. **Foot,** CHIH: literal foot; foundation, base.

Without fault, WU CHIU: no error or harm in the situation.

Six at second

a) Gnawing flesh, submerging the nose.
Without fault.

b) Gnawing flesh, submerging the nose.
Riding a strong indeed.

Enthusiastically biting through obstacles, you go a little overboard. Don't worry about your enthusiasm. Keep it up. This is not a mistake. You are on the right track.

Associated Contexts a) **Flesh,** FU: muscles, organs, skin, in contrast to bones. **Submerge,** MIEH: plunge under water, put out a fire; exterminate, finish, cut off. The ideogram: water and destroy. **Nose,** PI: literal nose; the first, original.

Without fault, WU CHIU: no error or harm in the situation.

b) **Ride,** CH'ENG: ride an animal or a chariot; have the upper hand, seize the right time; control strong power; overcome the nature of the other; supple opened line above a strong whole line. **Strong,** KANG: quality of the whole lines; firm, strong, unyielding, persisting.

Six at third

a) Gnawing seasoned meat. Meeting poison.
The small distressed.
Without fault.

b) Meeting poison.
Situation not appropriate indeed.

Biting through the obstacles, you encounter something old and dangerous. Take it on. Don't try to hide it. If you simply adapt, you will be ashamed and confused. Bring it out into the open. This is not a mistake.

Associated Contexts a) **Seasoned,** HSI: dried meat, prepared for a journey. **Meat,** JU: flesh of animals, pulp of fruit. **Meet,** YÜ: come on unexpectedly, encounter; occur, happen; pleasant meeting, lucky coincidence; agree. **Poison,** TU: noxious, malignant, hurtful, destructive; despise.

Small, HSIAO: little, common, unimportant; adapting to what crosses your path; ability to move in harmony with the vicissitudes of life; contrasts with great, TA, self-imposed theme or goal; keyword. Image of Hexagrams 9 and 62. **Abashment,** LIN: distress, shame, regret, humiliation; aware of having lost the right track; leads to repenting, HUI, correcting the direction of mind and life.

Without fault, WU CHIU: no error or harm in the situation.

Nine at fourth

a) Gnawing parched meat bones.
Acquiring a metal arrow.
Trial: drudgery advantageous.
Auspicious.

b) Drudgery advantageous, Trial auspicious.
Not yet shining indeed.

Getting through this confrontation is a long, arduous task, but you will find something of great value. The drudgery will definitely be worth it in the end. This will open the way for you and the generations to come.

Associated Contexts a) **Parch,** KAN: dry up; dried, exhausted, desiccated; cleaned away, gone. **Meat bones,** TZU: meat with bones; bones left after a meal.

Metallic, CHIN: smelting and casting; all things pertaining to metal, particularly gold; autumn, West, sunset; one of the Five Moments. **Arrow,** SHIH: arrow, javelin, dart; swift, direct as an arrow; marshal together.

Drudgery, CHIEN: difficult, hard, repetitive work; hard to cultivate; distressing, sorrowful. The ideogram: sticky earth and a person looking around, hard work in comparison to others. **Trial,** CHEN: inquiry by divination and its result; righteous, firm; separating wheat from chaff; the kernel, the proven core; fourth stage of the Time Cycle. The ideogram: pearl and divination.

Auspicious, CHI: leads to the experience of meaning; favorable, propitious, advantageous, appropriate; keyword. The ideogram: scholar and mouth, wise words of a sage.

b) **Not yet,** WEI: temporal negative; something will but has not yet occurred; contrary of already, CHI. Image of Hexagram 64. **Shine,** KUANG: illuminate; give off brilliant, bright light; honor, glory, éclat; result of action, contrasts with brightness, MING, light of heavenly bodies. The ideogram: fire above person, lifting the light.

Six at fifth

a) Gnawing parched meat. Acquiring yellow metal.
   Trial: adversity.
   Without fault.

b) Trial: adversity, without fault.
   Acquiring the appropriate indeed.

Getting through this confrontation is a long, arduous task. In the end you acquire something of very great value, wealth and the possibility it gives to establish a line of descent. You are going to have to confront your own ghosts and shadows in the process. Have no fear, this is not a mistake.

Associated Contexts a) **Parch,** KAN: dry up; dried, exhausted, desiccated; cleaned away, gone. **Meat,** JU: flesh of animals, pulp of fruit. **Yellow,** HUANG: color of the productive middle; associated with the Earthy Moment between yang and yin hemicycles; color of soil in central China; emblematic and imperial color of China since the Yellow Emperor (2500 BCE). **Metallic,** CHIN: smelting and casting; all things pertaining to metal, particularly gold; autumn, West, sunset; one of the Five Moments.

Trial, CHEN: inquiry by divination and its result; righteous, firm; separating wheat from chaff; the kernel, the proven core; fourth stage of the

Time Cycle. The ideogram: pearl and divination. **Adversity**, LI: danger; threatening, malevolent demon. This has two aspects: grind, sharpen, improve, perfect, stimulate; and: poisonous, sinister, cruel, contrary. It indicates a spirit or ghost that seeks revenge by inflicting suffering upon the living. Pacifying or exorcizing such a spirit can have a healing effect. The ideogram: sheltering cliff and stinging insect.

   Without fault, WU CHIU: no error or harm in the situation.

   Nine above

   a) Wherefore locking up submerging the ears?
      Pitfall.

   b) Wherefore locking up submerging the ears?
      Understanding not brightened indeed.

You are stuck in an old habit, an ineffective pattern. This time you have seriously cut yourself off. You may have lost relationships and goals. Why can't you hear this? You certainly won't understand anything this way!

Associated Contexts a) **Wherefore**, HO: interrogative: why? for what reason? what is? and affirmation: therefore, for that reason. **Lock up**, CHIAO: imprison, lock up the feet; prison, pen. **Submerge**, MIEH: plunge under water, put out a fire; exterminate, finish, cut off. The ideogram: water and destroy. **Ear**, ERH: organ of hearing; handle, sides.

   Pitfall, HSIUNG: leads away from the experience of meaning; stuck and exposed to danger, unable to take in the situation; flow of life and spirit is blocked; unfortunate, baleful; keyword.

b) **Understand**, TS'UNG: perceive quickly, astute, sharp; discriminate intelligently. The ideogram: ear and quick.

22

ADORNING ∎ *PI*

Beautify, embellish; display courage and beauty; elegance; make appearance reflect inner worth.

Adorning describes your situation in terms of its outward appearance. Its symbol is a festive marriage procession. You can deal with it by decorating, beautifying and embellishing the way things are presented. Make an offering and you will succeed. This builds up intrinsic value. Be elegant. Be brilliant. Display your valor. Think of this as a festive marriage procession. Let the way you present yourself signal the changes in your life. This is pleasing to the spirits. Through it they will give you success, effective power and the capacity to bring the situation to maturity. Be flexible and adapt to what presents itself to be done. Have a place to go. Impose a direction on things. That brings profit and insight.

● *Image of the Situation*

> **Adorning, Growing.**
> **The small, advantageous to have a direction to go. Harvesting**

Associated Contexts **Adorn**, PI: embellish, ornament, deck out, beautify; variegated (flowers); elegant, brilliant; also: energetic, passionate, eager, intrepid; capable of great effort; brave. The ideogram: cowrie shells (money) and flowers, linking ornaments and value. **Grow**, HENG: success through a sacrifice; pervade, persevere; bring to full growth; enjoy; vigorous, effective; second stage of the Time Cycle.

   Small, HSIAO: little, common, unimportant; adapting to what crosses your path; ability to move in harmony with the vicissitudes of life; contrasts with great, TA, self-imposed theme or goal; keyword. Image of Hexagrams 9 and 62. **Advantageous/Harvest**, LI: advantageous, profitable; acute, insightful; benefit, nourish; third stage of the Time Cycle. **Have a direction to go**, YU YU WANG: imposing a direction on the flow of time from present to past; have a specific goal or purpose.

● *Outer and Inner Aspects*

⚏ **Bound**: Mountains bound, limit and set a place off, stopping forward movement. **Bound** completes a full yin-yang cycle.

Connection to the outer: accomplishing words, which express things fully. **Bound** articulates what is complete and suggests what is beginning.

⚎ **Radiance**: Fire and brightness radiate light and warmth, attached to their support; congregating people see and become aware. **Radiance** ends the yang hemicycle, consuming action in awareness.

Connection to the inner: light, heat, consciousness bring about continual change, the Fiery Moment. **Radiance** spreads outward, congregating, becoming aware and changing.

The outer boundary limits spreading brightness to **adorning** what can be seen.

● *Hidden Possibility*

Nuclear trigrams **Shake**, CHEN, and **Gorge**, K'AN, result in Nuclear Hexagram 40, **Loosening**, HSIEH. **Adorning** the outward appearance lets you **loosen** and liberate bound energy.

● *Sequence*

> Beings not permitted to use unconsidered uniting and climaxing.
> Accepting this lets you use Adorning
> Adorning implies embellishing indeed.

Associated Contexts **Beings not permitted to use ...**: no one is allowed to make use of; nothing can exist by means of. **Unconsidered**, KOU: offhand, impromptu, improvised; careless, improper; illicit. **Unite**, HO: join, match, correspond, agree, collect, reply; unison, harmony; also: close, shut the mouth. The ideogram: mouth and assemble. **Climax**, YI: come to a high point and stop, bring to an end; use up, lay aside; decline, reject.

Accepting ... use: activating this hexagram depends on understanding and accepting the previous statement.

Imply, CHE: further signify; additional meaning. **Embellish**, SHIH: ornament, paint, brighten, patch up the appearance; apply cosmetics; pretend, make believe. **Indeed/is/means**, YEH: intensifier, connective; indicates comment on previous statement.

- *Contrasted Definitions*

> Gnawing Bite: taking in indeed.
> Adorning: without complexion indeed.

Associated Contexts **Gnaw**, SHIH: bite away, chew; bite persistently and remove; snap at, nibble; reach the essential by removing the unnecessary. The ideogram: mouth and divination, revealing the essential. **Bite**, HO: close the jaws, bite through, crush between the teeth. The ideogram: mouth and cover, jaws fit together as a lid fits a vessel. **Gnawing Bite** is the Image of Hexagram 21. **Take in/eat**, SHIH: eat, ingest, swallow, devour; incorporate.

Without, WU: devoid of; -less as suffix. **Complexion**, SE: appearance, expression; color, hue; air, manner, deportment; beautiful.

- *Symbol Tradition*

> Below mountain possessing fire. Adorning.
> A chün tzu uses brightening the multitudinous standards
> without daring to sever litigation.

Associated Contexts **Below**, HSIA: anything below, in all senses; lower, inner; lower trigram; opposite of above, SHANG. **Mountain**, SHAN: limit, boundary; the Symbol of the trigram **Bound**, KEN. The ideogram: three peaks, a mountain range. **Possess**, YU: in possession of, have, own; opposite of lack, WU. **Fire**, HUO: warming and consuming aspect of burning; fire and brightness are the Symbols of the trigram **Radiance**, LI.

Chün tzu: ideal of a person who uses divination to order his/her life in accordance with tao rather than wilful intention; keyword. **Use(of)**, YI: make use of, by means of, owing to; employ, make functional. **Brightness**, MING: light-giving aspect of burning, heavenly bodies and consciousness; with fire, the Symbol of the trigram **Radiance**, LI. **Multitude**, SHU: the people; mass, herd; all, the whole. **Standard**, CHENG: measure, test, limit, rule; musical interval; subjugate, regulate; capacity, endurance. **Dare**, KAN: have the courage to, try, permit yourself: bold, intrepid; rash, offensive. **Sever**, CHE: break off, separate, sunder, cut in two; discriminate, judge the true and false. **Litigate**, YÜ: legal proceedings; take a case to court. The ideogram: two dogs and words, barking arguments at each other.

● *Image Tradition*

Adorning, Growing. [I]
Supple coming and patterning the strong.
The past cause is growing.
Above apportions the strong and patterns the supple.

The anterior small, advantageous to have a direction to go. [II]
Heavenly pattern indeed.
Pattern brightening and stopping:
People's pattern indeed.

Viewing reaches to the heavenly pattern, [III]
Using scrutinizing the seasons transforming.
Viewing reaches to the people's pattern,
Using changes accomplishing Below Heaven.

Associated Contexts [I] **Supple**, JOU: quality of the opened lines; flexible, pliant, tender, adaptable. **Come**, LAI, and go, WANG: describe the stream of time as it flows from future through present to past; come, LAI, indicates what is approaching; move toward, arrive at; keyword. **Pattern**, WEN: intrinsic or natural design and its beauty; stylish, elegant; noble; contrasts with composition, CHANG, a conscious creation. **Strong**, KANG: quality of the whole lines; firm, strong, unyielding, persisting.

Past (cause), KU: come before as cause; formerly, ancient; reason, purpose, intention; grievance, quarrel, dissatisfaction, sorrow, mourning resulting from previous causes and intentions; situation leading to a divination.

Above, SHANG: anything above, in all senses; higher, upper, outer; upper trigram; opposite of below, HSIA. **Apportion**, FEN: divide for distribution; sort out; allot to.

[II] **Heaven**, T'IEN: highest; sky, firmament, heavens; power above the human as opposed to earth, TI, below; the Symbol of the trigram Force, CH'IEN. The ideogram: great and the one above.

Stop, CHIH: bring or come to a standstill; the Action of the trigram Bound, KEN. The ideogram: a foot stops walking.

People, person, JEN: humans individually and collectively; an individual; humankind. Image of Hexagrams 13 and 37.

[III] **View**, KUAN: contemplate, observe from a distance; look at carefully, gaze at; also: a monastery, an observatory; scry, divine through liquid in a cup. The ideogram: see and waterbird, observe through air or water. Image of Hexagram 20. **Reach(to)**, HU: arrive at a goal; reach towards and achieve; connect; contrasts with tend-towards, YU.

    Scrutinize, CH'A: investigate, observe carefully, learn the particulars, get at the truth. The ideogram: sacrifice as central to understanding. **Season**, SHIH: quality of the time; the right time, opportune, in harmony; planning in accord with the time; seasons of the year. The ideogram: sun and temple, time as sacred. **Transform**, PIEN: abrupt, radical, fundamental mutation from one state of being to another; transformation of lines in hexagrams; contrasts with change, HUA, gradual metamorphosis.

    Change, HUA: gradual, continuous metamorphosis; influence someone; contrasts with transform, PIEN, sudden mutation. The ideogram: person alive and dead, the life-process. **Accomplish**, CH'ENG: complete, finish, bring about; perfect, full, whole; play your part, do your duty; mature. The ideogram: weapon and man, able to bear arms, thus fully developed. **Below Heaven**, T'IEN HSIA: the human world, between heaven and earth.

●   *Transforming Lines*

    Initial nine

    a) **Adorning one's feet.**
       Stowing away the chariot and afoot.

    b) **Stowing away the chariot and afoot.**
       Righteously nothing to ride indeed.

Adorn yourself with courage and independence. Make your own way. Don't take the easy way out.

Associated Contexts a) **One's/one**, CH'I: third person pronoun; also: it/its, he/his, she/hers, they/theirs. **Foot**, CHIH: literal foot; foundation, base.

    Stow(away), SHE: set aside, put away, store; halt, rest in; temporary lodgings, breathing-spell. **Chariot**, CH'E: wheeled travelling vehicle; contrasts with cart, YÜ, which carries. **Afoot**, T'U: travel on foot; footman, foot-soldier; follower, disciple; ruffian, bond-servant.

b) **Righteous**, YI: proper and just, meets the standards; things in their proper place; the heart that rules itself; upright, moral rule; contrasts with Harvest, LI, advantage or profit. **Nothing/nowhere**, FU: strong negative; not a single thing/place. **Ride**, CH'ENG: ride an animal or a chariot; have the upper hand, seize the right time; control strong power; overcome the nature of the other; supple opened line above a strong whole line.

Six at second

a) Adorning one's patience.

b) Adorning: one's patience.
Associating with the above, rising indeed.

Be brave and patient. If you adorn yourself with elegance and patience, it will lift you into a better sphere.

Associated Contexts a) **One's/one**, CH'I: third person pronoun; also: it/its, he/his, she/hers, they/theirs. **Patience**, HSÜ: beard, hair; patience symbolized as waiting for hair to grow; hold back, wait for; slow; necessary.

b) **Associate(with)**, YÜ: consort with, combine; companions; group, band, company; agree with, comply, help. The ideogram: pair of hands reaching downward meets a pair of hands reaching upward, helpful association. **Rise**, HSING: get up, grow, lift; begin, give rise to, construct; be promoted; flourishing, fashionable. The ideogram: lift, two hands and unite, lift with both hands.

Nine at third

a) Adorning thus, soaking thus.
Trial perpetually auspicious.

b) Perpetual Trial's auspiciousness.
Complete absolutely nothing and you will have a mound indeed.

Let this connection impregnate you. Don't try to bring it to an end. This can open the way for you and all your descendants.

Associated Contexts a) **Thus ... thus**, JU ... JU: when there is one thing, then there must be the second thing. **Soak**, JU: immerse, steep; damp, wet; stain, pollute, blemish; urinate on.
Perpetual, YUNG: continuing; everlasting, ever-flowing. The ideogram: flowing water. **Trial**, CHEN: inquiry by divination and its result; righteous, firm; separating wheat from chaff; the kernel, the proven core; fourth stage of the Time Cycle. The ideogram: pearl and divination. **Auspicious**, CHI: leads to the experience of meaning; favorable, propitious, advantageous, appropriate; keyword. The ideogram: scholar and mouth, wise words of a sage.

b) **'s/have(it)/it/them**, CHIH: expresses possession, directly or as an object pronoun.

Complete, CHUNG: end of a cycle that begins the next; last, whole, all; contrasts with exhaust, CH'IUNG, final end. The ideogram: silk cocoons, follow and ice, winter linking one year with the next. **Absolutely no(thing)**, MO: complete elimination; not any, by no means. **Mound**, LING: grave-mound, barrow; small hill.

Six at fourth

a) Adorning thus, hoary thus.
   A white horse, soaring thus.
   In no way an outlaw, matrimonial allying.

b) Six at fourth. Appropriate situation to doubt indeed.
   In no way an outlaw, matrimonial allying.
   Completing without surpassing indeed.

Attribute great wisdom and worth to this connection. It can carry you like the sacred flying horse. These people are not trying to steal anything from you. This is a time for a marriage, not distrust. This can be an ever-flowing source of inspiration and pleasure.

Associated Contexts a) **Thus ... thus,** JU ... JU: when there is one thing, then there must be the second thing. **Hoary**, PO: silvery grey hair; old and venerable, aging.

   White, PO: associated with autumn, Harvest and the Metallic Moment; clear, immaculate; plain, pure, essential; explicit; color of death and mourning. **Horse**, MA: symbol of spirited strength in the natural world, counterpart of dragon, LUNG; associated with the trigram Force, CH'IEN, heaven, T'IEN, and high noon. **Soar**, HAN: fly high; rising sun, the firebird with red plumage; trunk or stem of a plant; vertical support. The ideogram: feathers and dawn. **Thus,** JU: as, in this way.

   In no way, FEI: strong negative; not so. The ideogram: a box filled with opposition. **Outlawry**, K'OU: break the laws; violent people, outcasts, bandits. **Matrimonial allying**, HUN KOU: legal institution of marriage; make alliances through marriage rather than force.

b) **Appropriate**, TANG: suitable; opportune, convenient; adequate, competent; equal to; whole lines in uneven places and opened lines in even places. **Situation**, WEI: place or seat according to rank; post, position, command; right, proper; established, arranged. The ideogram: person and stand, servants in their places. **Doubt**, YI: suspect, distrust; dubious; surmise, conjecture.

Complete, CHUNG: end of a cycle that begins the next; last, whole, all; contrasts with exhaust, CH'IUNG: final end. The ideogram: silk cocoons, follow and ice, winter linking one year with the next. **Surpass,** YU: exceed; beyond measure, excessive; extraordinary; transgress, blame.

Six at fifth

a) **Adorning in a hill top garden.**
Rolled plain silk: little, little.
Distress. Completing auspicious.

b) **Six at fifth's auspicious.**
Possessing rejoicing indeed.

You are asked to become a formal member of this group. You must offer something at the shrine, but you have very little to give. Go through with this, even if you are embarrassed, for it will open the way. Soon you will have great cause to rejoice.

Associated Contexts a) **Hill top,** CH'IU: hill with hollow top used for worship and as grave-site; knoll, hillock. **Garden,** YÜAN: enclosed garden; park, yard; imperial tombs.

Roll, SHU: gather into a bundle, bind together; restrain. **Plain silk,** PAI: unbleached, undyed silk. **Little,** CHIEN: small, narrow, insignificant, petty; diminish, contract. The doubled character intensifies this quality.

Distress, LIN: distress, shame, regret, humiliation; aware of having lost the right track; leads to repenting, HUI, correcting the direction of mind and life. **Complete,** CHUNG: end of a cycle that begins the next; last, whole, all; contrasts with exhaust, CH'IUNG, final end. The ideogram: silk cocoons, follow and ice, winter linking one year with the next. **Auspicious,** CHI: leads to the experience of meaning; favorable, propitious, advantageous, appropriate; keyword. The ideogram: scholar and mouth, wise words of a sage.

b) **'s/have(it)/it/them,** CHIH: expresses possession, directly or as an object pronoun.

Rejoice(in), HSI: feel and give joy; delight, exult; cheerful, merry. The ideogram: joy (music) and mouth, expressing joy.

Nine above

a) **White Adorning.**
Without fault.

b) **White Adorning, without fault.**
Acquiring purpose above indeed.

Bring out the essentials now. Adorn yourself with real virtue. It is necessary to know the truth here, no matter what it costs. This is not a mistake. You find a real purpose.

Associated Contexts a) **White,** PO: associated with autumn, Harvest and the Metallic Moment; clear, immaculate; plain, pure, essential; explicit; color of death, and mourning.

Without fault, WU CHIU: no error or harm in the situation.

b) **Acquire,** TE: obtain the desired object; wish for, desire covetously; gains, possessions. The ideogram: go and obstacle, going through obstacles to the goal. **Purpose,** CHIH: focus of mind and heart; will, inclination, resolve. The ideogram: heart and scholar, high inner resolve, or heart and go, inner determination.

23

STRIPPING ∎ *PO*

Strip away old ideas, eliminate what is outmoded or worn out.

Stripping describes your situation in terms of habits and ideas that are outmoded and worn out. Its symbol is the burial practice that strips away the flesh from the bones to release the spirit for rebirth. The way to deal with it is to strip away what has become unusable. This brings renewal. Remove and uncover things. Cut into the problem and strip away the unessential without thought of immediate gain. If you can do that, then you can impose a direction on things or have a place to go.

- ## *Image of the Situation*

   Stripping, not advantageous to have a direction to go.

   Associated Contexts **Strip**, PO: flay, peel, skin; remove, uncover, degrade; split, slice; reduce to essentials; slaughter an animal. The ideogram: knife and carve, trenchant action. **Advantageous/Harvest**, LI: advantageous, profitable; acute, insightful; benefit, nourish; third stage of the Time Cycle. **Have a direction to go**, YU YU WANG: imposing a direction on the flow of time from present to past; have a specific goal or purpose.

- ## *Outer and Inner Aspects*

   ☶ **Bound**: Mountains bound, limit and set a place off, stopping forward movement. **Bound** completes a full yin-yang cycle.
   Connection to the outer: accomplishing words, which express things fully. **Bound** articulates what is complete and suggests what is beginning.

   ☷ **Field**: The field of earth yields and sustains, serving in order to produce. **Field** is the equalizing point between yin and yang where things labor and serve.
   Connection to the inner: the common labor of sowing and hoarding, the Earthy Moment. **Field** produces concrete results through serving.

   Outer accomplishing **strips** away the previous cycle, while inner bringing-forth prepares the new. These trigrams form the Pivot of Equalization, where yin and yang come into creative balance.

● *Hidden Possibility*

The doubled nuclear trigram **Field**, K'UN, results in Nuclear Hexagram 2, **Field**, K'UN. The trenchant action in **stripping** opens a new **field of action**.

● *Sequence*

> Actually involving embellishing,
> therefore afterwards Growing by consequence used up.
> Accepting this lets you use Stripping.
> Stripping implies a Stripper indeed.

Associated Contexts **Actually,** YI: truly, really, at present. The ideogram: a dart and done, strong intention fully expressed. **Involve,** CHIH: include, entangle, implicate; induce, cause. The ideogram: person walking, induced to follow. **Embellish,** SHIH: ornament, paint, brighten, patch up the appearance; apply cosmetics; pretend, make believe. **Therefore afterwards,** JAN HOU: logical consequence of, necessarily follows in time. **Grow,** HENG: success through a sacrifice; pervade, persevere; bring to full growth; enjoy; vigorous, effective; second stage of the Time Cycle. **By consequence(of),** TSE: very strong connection; reason, cause, result; rule, law, pattern, standard; therefore. **Use up,** CHIN: exhaust, use all; ended, an empty vessel.

Accepting ... use: activating this hexagram depends on understanding and accepting the previous statement.

Imply, CHE: further signify; additional meaning. **Indeed/is/means,** YEH: intensifier, connective; indicates comment on previous statement.

● *Contrasted Definitions*

> Stripping: rotten indeed.
> Returning: reversing indeed.

Associated Contexts **Rotten,** LAN: corrupt, putrid, antiquated, worn out, dirty; a running sore; boil over. **Return,** FU: go back, turn back to the starting point; recur, reappear, come again; restore, recover, retrace; an earlier time or place. The ideogram: step and retrace a path. Image of Hexagram 24. **Reverse,** FAN: turn and move in the opposite direction; turn around or upside down (180 degrees); change to the opposite position; contrary.

- *Symbol Tradition*

> Mountain adjoining with respect to earth. Stripping.
> Using munificence above to quiet the position below.

Associated Contexts **Mountain**, SHAN: limit, boundary; the Symbol of the trigram Bound, KEN. The ideogram: three peaks, a mountain range. **Adjoin**, FU: next to, lean on; join; near, approaching. **With respect to**, YÜ: relates to, refers to; hold a position in. **Earth**, TI: ground on which the human world rests; basis of all things, nourishes all things; the Symbol of the trigram Field, K'UN.

Use(of), YI: make use of, by means of, owing to; employ, make functional. **Munificence**, HOU: liberal, kind, generous; create abundance; thick, large. The ideogram: gift of a superior to an inferior. **Above**, SHANG: anything above, in all senses; higher, upper, outer; upper trigram; opposite of below, HSIA. **Quiet/secure**, AN: peaceful, still, settled; calm, tranquilize. The ideogram: woman under a roof, a tranquil home. **Position**, CHAI: dwelling site, good situation in life; consolidate, reside, fill an office. **Below**, HSIA: anything below, in all senses; lower, inner; lower trigram; opposite of above, SHANG.

- *Image Tradition*

> Stripping. A Stripper indeed. [I]
> Supple transforming the strong indeed.

> Not Harvesting: having a direction to go. [II]
> Small People long living indeed.

> Yielding and stopping it. [III]
> Viewing the symbols indeed.

> A chün tzu honors the dissolving pause to overfill emptiness. [IV]
> Heaven moving indeed.

Associated Contexts **[I] Supple**, JOU: quality of the opened lines; flexible, pliant, tender, adaptable. **Transform**, PIEN: abrupt, radical, fundamental mutation from one state of being to another; transformation of lines in hexagrams; contrasts with change, HUA, gradual metamorphosis. **Strong**, KANG: quality of the whole lines; firm, strong, unyielding, persisting.

[II] Small People, HSIAO JEN: lowly, common, humble; those who adjust to circumstances with the flexibility of the small; effect of the small within an individual; keyword. **Long living,** CHANG: enduring, constant; senior, superior, greater; increase, prosper; respect, elevate.

[III] **Yield(to),** SHUN: give way and bear produce; comply, agree, follow, obey; unresisting, docile, flexible; nourish, provide; the Action of the trigram Field, K'UN. The ideogram: head and current, water flowing from the head of a river, yielding to the banks. **Stop,** CHIH: bring or come to a standstill; the Action of the trigram Bound, KEN. The ideogram: a foot stops walking. **It/them/have(it)/'s,** CHIH: expresses possession, directly or as an object pronoun.

View, KUAN: contemplate, observe from a distance; look at carefully, gaze at; also: a monastery, an observatory; scry, divine through liquid in a cup. The ideogram: see and waterbird, observe through air or water. Image of Hexagram 20. **Symbol,** HSIANG: image invested with intrinsic power to connect visible and invisible; magic spell; figure, form, shape, likeness; pattern, model; create an image, imitate; act, play; writing.

[IV] **Chün tzu:** ideal of a person who uses divination to order his/her life in accordance with tao rather than wilful intention; keyword. **Honor,** SHANG: esteem, give high rank to; eminent; put one thing on top of another. **Dissolving pause,** HSIAO HSI: yin or structure dissolves so that yang or action may emerge; transitional phase of Universal Compass. **Overfill,** YING: at the point of overflowing; more than wanted, stretch beyond; replenished, full; arrogant. The ideogram: vessel and too much. **Empty,** HSÜ: no images or concepts; vacant, unsubstantial; empty yet fertile space.

Heaven, T'IEN: highest; sky, firmament, heavens; power above the human as opposed to earth, TI, below; the Symbol of the trigram Force, CH'IEN. The ideogram: great and the one above. **Move,** HSING: move or move something; motivate, emotionally moving; walk, act, do. The ideogram: stepping left then right.

● *Transforming Lines*

Initial six

a) Stripping the bed, use the stand.
Discarding the Trial: pitfall.

b) Stripping the bed, using the stand.
Below using the submerged indeed.

You have to confront basic questions of support and intimacy, the place where you feel at home. Take a stand for change. This is important. If you simply ignore the message, the way will close.

Associated Contexts a) **Bed,** CH'UANG: sleeping place; couch, sofa, lounge; bench around a well. **Stand,** TSU: base, foot, leg; rest on, support; stance. The ideogram: foot and calf resting.

 Discard, MIEH: disregard, ignore; petty, worthless, insignificant; trash. **Trial,** CHEN: inquiry by divination and its result; righteous, firm; separating wheat from chaff; the kernel, the proven core; fourth stage of the Time Cycle. The ideogram: pearl and divination. **Pitfall,** HSIUNG: leads away from the experience of meaning; stuck and exposed to danger, unable to take in the situation; flow of life and spirit is blocked; unfortunate, baleful; keyword.

b) **Submerge,** MIEH: plunge under water, put out a fire; exterminate, finish, cut off. The ideogram: water and destroy.

> **Six at second**

> *a)* Stripping the bed, use marking off.
> Discarding the Trial: pitfall.

> *b)* Stripping the bed, using marking off.
> Not yet possessing associates indeed.

You have to confront basic questions of support and intimacy, the place where you feel at home. Mark things off. Differentiate yourself from others. This is important. If you simply ignore the message, the way will close.

Associated Contexts a) **Bed,** CH'UANG: sleeping place; couch, sofa, lounge; bench around a well. **Mark off,** PIEN: distinguish by dividing; mark off a plot of land; frame which divides a bed from its stand; discuss and dispute. The ideogram: knife and acrid, biting division.

 Discard, MIEH: disregard, ignore; petty, worthless, insignificant; trash. **Trial,** CHEN: inquiry by divination and its result; righteous, firm; separating wheat from chaff; the kernel, the proven core; fourth stage of the Time Cycle. The ideogram: pearl and divination. **Pitfall,** HSIUNG: leads away from the experience of meaning; stuck and exposed to danger, unable to take in the situation; flow of life and spirit is blocked; unfortunate, baleful; keyword.

b) **Not yet,** WEI: temporal negative; something will but has not yet occurred; contrary of already, CHI. Image of Hexagram 64. **Possess,** YU: in possession of, have, own; opposite of lack, WU. **Associate(with),** YU: consort with, combine; companions; group, band, company; agree with, comply, help. The ideogram: pair of hands reaching downward meets a pair of hands reaching upward, helpful association.

Six at third

a) Strip it, without fault.

b) Stripping it, without fault.
  Letting go Above and Below indeed.

The time is now. Do it! By taking decisive action you can renew yourself and your relations. This is not a mistake. Don't be side-tracked.

Associated Contexts a) **Without fault,** WU CHIU: no error or harm in the situation.

b) **Let go,** SHIH: lose, omit, miss, fail, let slip; out of control. The ideogram: drop from the hand. **Above and Below,** SHANG HSIA: realm of dynamic interaction between the upper and the lower; the vertical dimension.

Six at fourth

a) Stripping the bed, using the flesh.
  Pitfall.

b) Stripping the bed, using the flesh.
  Slicing close to calamity indeed.

You are getting carried away with the renovation of your life. You are about to do serious harm. This is not what the time is about. Pull back, let go for now, or you may see yourself all alone.

Associated Contexts a) **Bed,** CH'UANG: sleeping place; couch, sofa, lounge; bench around a well. **Flesh,** FU: muscles, organs, skin, in contrast to bones.

   Pitfall, HSIUNG: leads away from the experience of meaning; stuck and exposed to danger, unable to take in the situation; flow of life and spirit is blocked; unfortunate, baleful; keyword.

b) **Slice,** CH'IEH: cut, carve, mince; urge, press; a resumé. **Close to,** CHIN: near in time or place, next to; approach; recently, lately; familiar. **Calamity,** TSAI: disaster from outside; flood, plague, drought, blight, ruin; contrasts with blunder, SHENG, indicating personal fault. The ideogram: water and fire, elemental powers.

Six at fifth

a) Threading fish.
Using the "housing people's" favor.
Nothing not advantageous.

b) Using the housing people's favor.
Completing without surpassing indeed.

Pull things together now. There is profit and fertility hidden in the stream of events. The palace women confer their grace and favor. Use your connections and trust your imagination. Anything is possible. There is nothing that will not benefit from the connection you are making now.

Associated Contexts a) **Thread,** KUAN: string together; string of a thousand coins. **Fish,** YÜ: scaly, aquatic beings hidden in the water; symbol of abundance; connected with the Streaming Moment.

House, KUNG: palace residence, mansion; surround; fence, walls, roof. **People, person,** JEN: humans individually and collectively; an individual; humankind. Image of Hexagrams 13 and 37. **Housing People** refers to the women of the royal palace. **Favor,** CH'UNG: receive or confer gifts, obtain grace, win favor; dote on a woman; gifted for.

Nothing not advantageous, WU PU LI: nothing for which this will not be beneficial; advantageous potential, borderline where the balance is swinging from not Harvesting to actually Harvesting.

b) **Complete,** CHUNG: end of a cycle that begins the next; last, whole, all; contrasts with exhaust, CH'IUNG, final end. The ideogram: silk cocoons, follow and ice, winter linking one year with the next. **Without,** WU: devoid of; -less as suffix. **Surpass,** YU: exceed; beyond measure, excessive; extraordinary; transgress, blame.

Nine above

a) A ripe fruit not eaten.
A chün tzu acquires a cart.
Small People Strip the hut.

b) A chün tzu acquiring a cart.
Commoners place to carry indeed.
Small People Strip the hut.
Completing, not permitting availing of indeed.

You have stripped away the outmoded and found the new. Move on, carry it all away with you. Don't go back to your old ways. It would be like painting your house to avoid moving.

Associated Contexts a) **Ripe**, SHIH: mature, full-grown; great, eminent. **Fruit**, KUO: plants' annual produce; tree fruits; come to fruition, fruits of actions; produce, results, effects; reliable; conclude, surpass. The ideogram: tree topped by a round fruit. **Eat/take in**, SHIH: eat, ingest, swallow, devour; incorporate, take in.

Acquire, TE: obtain the desired object; wish for; desire covetously; gains, possessions. The ideogram: go and obstacle, going through obstacles to the goal. **Cart**, YŪ: carrying capacity of a vehicle; contain, hold, sustain.

Hut, LU: thatched hut, cottage, roadside lodge, hovel; house as personal shelter.

b) **Commoners**, MIN: class of workers the state draws on to sustain the social hierarchy; undeveloped potential outside the organized personality. **Place**, SO: where something belongs or comes from; residence, dwelling; habitual focus or object. **Carry**, TSAI: bear, carry with you; contain, sustain; load a ship or cart, cargo; fill in, complete.

Complete, CHUNG: end of a cycle that begins the next; last, whole, all; contrasts with exhaust, CH'IUNG, final end. The ideogram: silk cocoons, follow and ice, winter linking one year with the next. **Not permitting**, PU K'O: not possible; contradicts an inherent principle. The ideogram: mouth and breath, silent consent. **Avail of**, YUNG: take advantage of; benefit from, profit by; use for a specific purpose; apply to advantage. The ideogram: to divine and center, applying divination to central concerns.

24

RETURNING ▌ *FU*

Love and spirit return after a difficult time; renewal, rebirth, re-establish; go back to the beginning; new hope.

Returning describes your situation in terms of re-emergence and re-birth. The way to deal with it is to go back to meet the returning energy in order to begin anew. Make an offering and you will succeed. Retrace your path, return to the source, re-establish what is important, restore the way. Find the intensity of the earlier time and the purity of the original feeling. This is pleasing to the spirits. Through it they will give you success, effective power and the capacity to bring the situation to maturity. Let things emerge and come back without pressure or upset. People will suggest mutually profitable projects. It is not a mistake to join them. Turning and moving in the opposite direction from your former path will return you to the way on the seventh day. Have a place to go. Impose a direction on things. That brings profit and insight.

● *Image of the Situation*

> Returning, Growing.
> Issuing forth and entering without affliction.
> Partners come without fault.
> Reversing returns one's tao.
> The seventh day comes: Returning.
> Advantageous to have a direction to go.

Associated Contexts **Return,** FU: go back, turn back to the starting point; recur, reappear, come again; restore, recover, retrace; an earlier time or place. The ideogram: step and retrace a path. **Grow,** HENG: success through a sacrifice; pervade, persevere; bring to full growth; enjoy; vigorous, effective; second stage of the Time Cycle.

Issue forth(from), CH'U: emerge from, come out of, proceed from, spring from; the Action of the trigram Shake, CHEN; contrary of enter, JU. The ideogram: stem with branches and leaves emerging. **Enter,** JU: penetrate, go into, enter on, progress; put into, encroach on; the Action of the trigram Ground, SUN, contrary of issue forth, CH'U. **Without,** WU:

devoid of; -less as suffix. **Afflict,** CHI: sickness, disorder, defect, calamity; injurious; pressure and consequent anger, hate or dislike. The ideogram: sickness and dart, a sudden affliction.

Partner, P'ENG: associate for mutual benefit; two equal or similar things; companions, friends, peers; join in; commercial ventures. The ideogram: linked strings of cowries or coins. **Come,** LAI, and **go,** WANG, describe the stream of time as it flows from future through present to past; come, LAI, indicates what is approaching; move toward, arrive at; keyword. **Without fault,** WU CHIU: no error or harm in the situation.

Reverse, FAN: turn and move in the opposite direction; turn around or upside down (180 degrees); change to the opposite position; contrary. **One's/one,** CH'I: third person pronoun; also: it/its, he/his, she/hers, they/theirs. **Tao:** way or path; ongoing process of being and the course it traces for each specific person or thing; keyword. The ideogram: go and head, leading and the path it creates.

Seven, CH'I: number seven, seventh; seven planets; seventh day when moon changes from crescent to waxing; the Tangram game makes pictures of all phenomena from seven basic shapes. **Day/sun,** JIH: actual sun and the time of a sun-cycle, a day.

Advantageous/Harvest, LI: advantageous, profitable; acute, insightful; benefit, nourish; third stage of the Time Cycle. **Have a direction to go,** YU YU WANG: imposing a direction on the flow of time from present to past; have a specific goal or purpose.

- *Outer and Inner Aspects*

⚏ **Field:** The field of earth yields and sustains, serving in order to produce. **Field** is the equalizing point between yin and yang where things labor and serve.

Connection to the outer: the common labor of sowing and hoarding, the Earthy Moment. **Field** produces concrete results through serving.

⚎ **Shake:** Thunder rises from below, shaking and stirring things up. **Shake** begins the yang hemicycle by germinating new action.

Connection to the inner: sprouting energies thrusting from below, the Woody Moment beginning. **Shake** stirs things up to issue-forth.
Returning to the energy germinating within prepares and opens a new **field** of activity.

- ### *Hidden Possibility*

The doubled nuclear trigram **Field**, K'UN, results in Nuclear Hexagram 2, **Field**, K'UN. Actively **returning** to the starting point opens a new **field** of activity.

- ### *Sequence*

> Beings not permitted to use completely using it up.
> Above Stripping exhausted, below reversing.
> Accepting this lets you use Returning.

Associated Contexts **Beings not permitted to use ...**: no one is allowed to make use of; nothing can exist by means of. **Complete**, CHUNG: end of a cycle that begins the next; last, whole, all; contrasts with exhaust, CH'IUNG, final end. The ideogram: silk cocoons, follow and ice, winter linking one year with the next. **Use up**, CHIN: exhaust, use all; ended, an empty vessel.

Above, SHANG: anything above, in all senses; higher, upper, outer; upper trigram; opposite of below, HSIA. **Strip**, PO: flay, peel, skin; remove, uncover, degrade; split, slice; reduce to essentials; slaughter an animal. The ideogram: knife and carve, trenchant action. Image of Hexagram 23. **Exhaust**, CH'IUNG: bring to an end; limit, extremity; destitute; investigate exhaustively; end without a new beginning. The ideogram: cave and naked person, bent with disease or old age. **Below**, HSIA: anything below, in all senses; lower, inner; lower trigram; opposite of above, SHANG.

Accepting ... use: activating this hexagram depends on understanding and accepting the previous statement.

- ### *Contrasted Definitions*

> Stripping: rotten indeed.
> Returning: reversing indeed.

Associated Contexts **Rotten**, LAN: corrupt, putrid, antiquated, worn out, dirty; a running sore; boil over. **Indeed/is/means**, YEH: intensifier, connective; indicates comment on previous statement.

- ### *Attached Evidences*

> Returning: actualizing tao's root indeed.
> Returning: the small and marking off with respect to beings.
> Returning: using originating knowledge.

Associated Contexts **Actualize tao**, TE: realize tao in action; power, virtue; ability to follow the course traced by the ongoing process of the cosmos; keyword. The ideogram: to go, straight, and heart. Linked with acquire, TE: acquiring that which makes a being become what it is meant to be. **'s/have(it)/it/them**, CHIH: expresses possession, directly or as an object pronoun. **Root**, PEN: origin, cause, source of nourishment; essential. The ideogram: tree with roots in earth.

Small, HSIAO: little, common, unimportant; adapting to what crosses your path; ability to move in harmony with the vicissitudes of life; contrasts with great, TA, self-imposed theme or goal; keyword. Image of Hexagrams 9 and 62. **Also**, ERH: joins and contrasts two terms. **Mark off**, PIEN: distinguish by dividing; mark off a plot of land; frame which divides a bed from its stand; discuss and dispute. The ideogram: knife and acrid, biting division. **With respect to**, YÜ: relates to, refers to; hold a position in. **Being(s)**, WU: creature, thing, any single being; matter, substance, essence; nature of things.

Use(of), YI: make use of, by means of, owing to; employ, make functional. **Origin**, TZU: source, beginning, ground; cause, reason, motive; line of descent; path to the origin; yourself, intrinsic. **Know**, CHIH: understand, perceive, remember; informed, aware, wise. The ideogram: arrow and mouth, words focused and swift.

● *Symbol Tradition*

> Thunder located in earth center. Returning.
> The Earlier Kings used culminating sun to bar the passages.
> Bargaining sojourners [used culminating sun] not to move.
> The crown prince [used culminating sun] not to inspect on all sides.

Associated Contexts **Thunder**, LEI: rising, arousing power; the Symbol of the trigram Shake, CHEN. **Locate(in)**, TSAI: live in, dwell, reside; belong to, involved with, depend on; within. The ideogram: earth and persevere, place on the earth. **Earth**, TI: ground on which the human world rests; basis of all things, nourishes all things; the Symbol of the trigram Field, K'UN. **Center**, CHUNG: inner, central; put in the center; middle, stable point enabling you to face inner and outer changes; middle line of trigram. The ideogram: field divided in two equal parts. Image of Hexagram 61.

Earlier Kings, HSIEN WANG: ideal rulers of old; the golden age, primal time, power in harmony with nature; model for the chün tzu. **Culminating sun**, CHIH JIH: acme of any time period; midday, summer solstice; midpoint of life. **Bar**, PI: close a door, stop up a hole; obstruct, exclude, screen. The ideogram: door and hand, closing the door. **Passage**, KUAN: market gate, customs house, frontier post; limit, crisis, important point.

Bargain, SHANG: argue over prices; consult, deliberate, do business; dealers, travelling merchants; hour before sunrise and sunset. The ideogram: stutter and sentences, repetitive speaking. **Sojourn**, LÜ: travel, stay in places other than your home; itinerant troops, temporary residents; visitor, guest, lodger. The ideogram: banner and people around it, loyal to a symbol rather than their temporary residence. Image of Hexagram 56. **Move**, HSING: move or move something; motivate, emotionally moving; walk, act, do. The ideogram: stepping left then right.

Crown prince, HOU: successor to the sovereign. The ideogram: one, mouth and shelter, one with the sovereign's orders. Inspect, HSING: examine on all sides, careful inquiry; watchful. **Sides (on all sides)**, FANG: limits, boundaries; square, surface of the earth extending to the four cardinal points; everywhere.

● *Image Tradition*

Returning, Growing. The Strong reversing. [I]
Stirring up and using yielding to move.
That uses issuing forth and entering, without affliction.

Partners coming, without fault. [II]
Reversing, Returning to one's tao.
The seventh day coming: Returning.
Heaven moving indeed.

Advantageous to have a direction to go. [III]
The Strong long living indeed.
Reaching to Returning, you see Heaven and Earth's heart.

Associated Contexts [I] **Strong**, KANG: quality of the whole lines; firm, strong, unyielding, persisting.

Stir up, TUNG: excite, influence, move, affect; work, take action; come out of the egg or the bud; the Action of the trigram Shake, CHEN. The ideogram: strength and heavy, move weighty things. **Yield (to)**, SHUN: give way and bear produce; comply, agree, follow, obey; unresisting, docile, flexible; nourish, provide; the Action of the trigram Field, K'UN. The ideogram: head and current, water flowing from the head of a river, yielding to the banks.

That uses, SHIH YI: involves and is involved by.

[II] Heaven, T'IEN: highest; sky, firmament, heavens; power above the human as opposed to earth, TI, below; the Symbol of the trigram Force, CH'IEN. The ideogram: great and the one above.

[III] Long living, CHANG: enduring, constant; senior, superior, greater; increase, prosper; respect, elevate.

Reach(to), HU: arrive at a goal; reach toward and achieve; connect. **See,** CHIEN: seeing in all its aspects: vision, being visible, forming mental images; visit, call on, consult. The ideogram: eye above person, active and receptive sight. **Heaven and Earth,** T'IEN TI: dynamic relation between the primal powers and the world it produces; cosmos, natural or human world; keyword. **Heart,** HSIN: heart as center of being; seat of mind's images and affections; moral nature; source of desires, intentions, will.

● *Transforming Lines*

Initial nine

a) **Not distancing Returning.**
Without merely repenting.
Spring auspicious.

b) **Not distancing's Returning.**
Using adjusting the individuality indeed.

You have been keeping at a distance. Now is the time to let it go. Don't just think about. Do something. The way to the source is open.

Associated Contexts a) **Distance,** YÜAN: far off, remote; keep at a distance; alienated. The ideogram: go and a long way.

Merely, CHIH: nothing more than. **Repent,** HUI: dissatisfaction with past conduct causing a change of heart; proceeds from abashment, LIN, shame and confusion at having lost the right way.

Spring, YÜAN: source, origin, head; great, excellent; arise, begin, generating power; first stage of the Time Cycle. **Auspicious,** CHI: leads to the experience of meaning; favorable, propitious, advantageous, appropriate; keyword. The ideogram: scholar and mouth, wise words of a sage.

b) **Adjust,** HSIU: regulate, repair, clean up, renovate. **Individuality,** SHEN: total person: psyche, body and lifespan; character, virtue, duty; contrasts with body, KUNG, physical being.

Six at second

a) **Relinquishing Returning.**
 Auspicious.

b) **Relinquishing Returning's auspiciousness.**
 Using humanity below indeed.

Let things Relax your grip. Be unselfish and benevolent. The way is open to you.

Associated Contexts a) **Relinquish,** HSIU: let go of, stop temporarily, rest; resign, release; act gently, enjoy; relaxed. The ideogram: person leaning on a tree.
 Auspicious, CHI: leads to the experience of meaning; favorable, propitious, advantageous, appropriate; keyword. The ideogram: scholar and mouth, wise words of a sage.

b) **Humanity,** JEN: fellow-feeling, regard for others; benevolence, fulfil social duties; unselfish, kind, merciful.

Six at third

a) **Imminent Returning. Adversity.**
 Without fault.

b) **Imminent Returning's adversity.**
 Righteous, without fault indeed.

Pulling back from a crisis, you return to yourself. You confront danger with its roots in the past. Difficult though this may be, it is not a mistake.

Associated Contexts a) **Imminent,** P'IN: on the brink of; pressing, urgent. **Adversity,** LI: danger; threatening, malevolent demon. This has two aspects: grind, sharpen, improve, perfect, stimulate; and: poisonous, sinister, cruel, contrary. It indicates a spirit or ghost that seeks revenge by inflicting suffering upon the living. Pacifying or exorcizing such a spirit can have a healing effect. The ideogram: sheltering cliff and stinging insect.

b) **Righteous,** YI: proper and just, meets the standards; things in their proper place; the heart that rules itself; upright, moral rule; contrasts with Harvest, LI, advantage or profit.

Six at fourth

a) **Centering movement, solitary Returning.**

b) **Centering movement, solitary Returning.**
   Using adhering to tao indeed.

The center of life is shifting. Move with it even if it involves going on alone. This returns you to yourself. You are following the way.

Associated Contexts a) **Solitary,** TI: alone, single; isolated, abandoned.

b) **Adhere(to),** TS'UNG: follow a way, hold to a doctrine, school, or person; hear and comply with, agree to; forced to follow, follower. The ideogram: two men walking, one following the other.

Six at fifth

a) **Magnanimous Returning.**
   Without repenting.

b) **Magnanimous Returning, without repenting.**
   Center originating from the predecessor indeed.

Wealth and pleasure return. As the time renews itself, give with open arms. You will meet the same qualities in return. You will have no cause to regret what you do.

Associated Contexts a) **Magnanimous,** TUN: generous; honest, substantial, important, wealthy; honor, increase; firm, strong. The ideogram: strike and accept, warrior magnanimous in attack and defense.

   Without repenting, WU HUI: devoid of the sort of trouble that leads to sorrow, regret and the necessity to change your attitude.

b) **Predecessor,** K'AO: deceased ancestor, especially the grandfather; the ancients; aged, long-lived; consult, verify. The ideogram: old and ingenious, the old wise man.

Six above

a) **Delusion Returning. Pitfall.**
   Possessing Calamity and Blunder.

Availing of moving the legions:
Completing possesses great destruction.
Using one's city chief: pitfall.
The culmination is ten years revolved
of uncontrolled chastisement.

b) Delusion Returning's pitfall.
Reversing the chief: tao indeed.

This is an old delusion returning. You are blinded by self-deception and
infatuation. If you go on in this way, your hard won growth will be
destroyed. It will take at least ten years to deal with the repercussions of this
catastrophe. Think about where this desire comes from. Don't set the
armies marching. Don't act this out.

Associated Contexts a) **Delude**, MI: confused, stupefied, infatuated;
blinded by vice; bewitch, fascinate, deceive. **Pitfall**, HSIUNG: leads away
from the experience of meaning; stuck and exposed to danger, unable to
take in the situation; flow of life and spirit is blocked; unfortunate, baleful;
keyword.

    Possess, YU: in possession of, have, own; opposite of lack, WU. **Calamity
and Blunder**, TSAI SHENG: disaster from without and within; natural
disaster combined with misfortune due to ignorance or fault; ruin, defeat,
rout, collapse.

    Avail of, YUNG: take advantage of; benefit from, profit by; use for a
specific purpose; apply to advantage. The ideogram: to divine and center,
applying divination to central concerns. **Legions/leading**, SHIH: troops; an
organized unit, a metropolis; leader, general, model, master; organize, make
functional; take as a model, imitate. The ideogram: heap and whole,
organize confusion into functional units. Image of Hexagram 7.

    Great, TA: big, noble, important, very; orient the will toward a self-
imposed goal, impose direction; ability to lead or guide your life; contrasts
with small, HSIAO, flexible adaptation to what crosses your path; keyword.
Image of Hexagrams 14, 26, 28, 34. **Destroy**, PAI: ruin, defeat, violate,
subvert, break.

    City, KUO: area of only human constructions; political unit, polis. First
of the territorial zones: city, suburbs, countryside, forests. **Chief**, CHÜN:
effective ruler; preside over, take the lead; influence others; term of respect.
The ideogram: mouth and director, giving orders.

    Culminate, CHIH: bring to the highest degree; arrive at the end or
summit; superlative.

Ten, SHIH: goal and end of reckoning; whole, complete, all; entire, perfected, the full amount; reach everywhere, receive everything. The ideogram: East–West line crosses North–South line, a grid that contains all. **Years revolved,** NIEN: number of years elapsed; a person's age; contrasts with year's-time, SUI, length of time in a year. **Control,** K'O: command; check, impede, prevail, obstruct, repress; adequate, able. The ideogram: roof beams support a house, controlling the structure. **Chastise,** CHENG: punish, subjugate, discipline; reduce to order; punishing expedition. The ideogram: step and correct, a rectifying move.

25

DISENTANGLING ▌
WU WANG

Disentangle yourself; spontaneous, unplanned; free from confusion; clean, pure.

Disentangling describes your situation in terms of acquiring the capacity to act spontaneously and confidently. Its symbol is casting out a plague demon. The way to deal with it is to free yourself from disorder. Disentangle yourself from compulsive ideas, confusion, vanity, anger, lust, hatred and the desire for revenge. By freeing your awareness from these entanglements, you gain the capacity to act directly. This opens up a whole new cycle of time. If you do not correct yourself, you will consistently make mistakes through ignorance and faulty perception. Your sight will be clouded. Then imposing a direction on things or having a place to go will bring you no advantage.

● *Image of the Situation*

> **Disentangling.**
> **Source of Success: Advantageous Trial.**
> **One in no way correcting: possessing a blunder.**
> **Advantageous to have a direction to go.**

Associated Contexts **Without is,** WU: devoid of; -less as suffix. **Tangle,** WANG: caught up in, entangled, involved; disorder, incoherence; foolish, wild, reckless; false, brutish behaviour; vain, idle, futile.

   Source … Trial, lit: Spring Growing Harvesting Trial: **Spring,** YÜAN: **Grow,** HENG; **Harvest,** LI; and **Trial,** CHEN, are the four stages of the Time Cycle, the model for all dynamic processes. They indicate that your question is connected to the cycle as a whole rather than a part of it, and that the origin (Spring) of a favorable result (Harvesting Trial) is an offering to the spirits (Growing).

   One's/one, CH'I: third person pronoun; also: he/his, she/hers, they/theirs, it/its. **In no way,** FEI: strong negative; not so. The ideogram: a box filled with opposition. **Correct,** CHENG: rectify deviation or one-sidedness; proper, straight, exact, regular; constant, rule, model. The ideogram: stop and one, hold to one thing. **Possess,** YU: in possession of, have, own; opposite of lack, WU. **Blunder,** SHENG: mistake due to ignorance or fault; contrasts with calamity, TSAI, disaster from without. The ideogram: eye and grow, a film clouding sight.

Advantageous/Harvest, LI: advantageous, profitable; acute, insightful; benefit, nourish; third stage of the Time Cycle. **Have a direction to go,** YU YU WANG: imposing a direction on the flow of time from present to past; have a specific goal or purpose.

- *Outer and Inner Aspects*

☰ **Force:** The force of heaven struggles on, persistent and unwearied; heavenly bodies persist in their orbits. **Force** is the center of the yin hemicycle, completing the formative process.

Connection to the outer: struggling forces are bound together in dynamic tension, the Metallic Moment culminating. **Force** brings elements to grips, creating enduring relations.

☳ **Shake:** Thunder rises from below, shaking and stirring things up. Shake begins the yang hemicycle by germinating new action.

Connection to the inner: sprouting energies thrusting from below, the Woody Moment beginning. **Shake** stirs things up to issue-forth.

Germinating inner growth remains **without embroiling** through its connection to heaven's persistent struggle.

- *Hidden Possibility*

Nuclear trigrams **Ground,** SUN, and **Bound,** KEN, result in Nuclear Hexagram 53, **Gradual Advance,** CHIEN. **Disentangling** yourself from confusion lets you **gradually advance** to a real goal.

- *Sequence*

> **Actually Returning, by consequence Disentangling.**
> **Accepting this lets you use Disentangling.**

Associated Contexts **Actually,** YI: truly, really, at present. The ideogram: a dart and done, strong intention fully expressed. **Return,** FU: go back, turn back to the starting point; recur, reappear, come again; restore, recover, retrace; an earlier time or place. The ideogram: step and retrace a path. Image of Hexagram 24. **By consequence(of),** TSE: very strong

connection; reason, cause, result; rule, law, pattern, standard; therefore.

Accepting ... use: activating this hexagram depends on understanding and accepting the previous statement.

- *Contrasted Definitions*

> Great Accumulating: the season indeed.
> Disentangling from calamity indeed.

Associated Contexts **Great**, TA: big, noble, important, very; orient the will toward a self-imposed goal, impose direction; ability to lead or guide your life; contrasts with small, HSIAO, flexible adaptation to what crosses your path; keyword. **Accumulate**, CH'U: retain, hoard, gather, herd together; control, restrain; domesticate, tame, train; raise, feed, sustain, bring up. The ideogram: field and black, fertile black soil good for pastures, accumulated through retaining silt. **Great Accumulating** is the Image of Hexagram 26. **Season**, SHIH: quality of the time; the right time, opportune, in harmony; planning in accord with the time; seasons of the year. The ideogram: sun and temple, time as sacred. **Indeed/is/means**, YEH: intensifier, connective; indicates comment on previous statement.

Calamity, TSAI: disaster from outside; flood, plague, drought, blight, ruin; contrasts with blunder, SHENG, indicating personal fault. The ideogram: water and fire, elemental powers.

- *Symbol Tradition*

> Below heaven thunder moving.
> Beings associating and disentangling.
> The Earlier Kings used luxuriance suiting the season
> to nurture the myriad beings.

Associated Contexts **Below**, HSIA: anything below, in all senses; lower, inner; lower trigram; opposite of above, SHANG. **Heaven**, T'IEN: highest; sky, firmament, heavens; power above the human as opposed to earth, TI, below; the Symbol of the trigram Force, CH'IEN. The ideogram: great and the one above. **Thunder**, LEI: rising, arousing power; the Symbol of the trigram Shake, CHEN. **Move**, HSING: move or move something; motivate, emotionally moving; walk, act, do. The ideogram: stepping left then right. **Being(s)**, WU: creature, thing, any single being; matter, substance, essence; nature of things. **Associate(with)**, YÜ: consort with, combine; companions; group, band, company; agree with, comply, help.

The ideogram: pair of hands reaching downward meets a pair of hands reaching upward, helpful association.

Earlier Kings, HSIEN WANG: ideal rulers of old; the golden age, primal time, power in harmony with nature; model for the chün tzu. **Use(of)**, YI: make use of, by means of, owing to; employ, make functional. **Luxuriance**, MAO: thriving, flourishing, vigorous; highly developed, elegant. The ideogram: plants and flourish. **Suiting**, TUI: correspond to, agree with, consistent; pair; parallel sentences in poetic language. **Nurture**, YÜ: bring up, support, rear, raise; increase. **Myriad**, WAN: countless; many, everyone; lit.: ten thousand. The ideogram: swarm of insects.

- *Image Tradition*

> Disentangling. [I]
> Strong originating from the outside coming and
> activating a lord with respect to the inside.
> Stirring up and persisting.
>
> Strong centering and corresponding. [II]
> Great Growing using correcting.
> Heaven's fate indeed.
>
> One in no way correcting: possessing a blunder. [III]
> Not advantageous to have a direction to go.
> Disentangling's going.
> Actually wherefore having it?
> Heavenly fate not shielding it.
> Actually moving in fact.

Associated Contexts [I] **Strong**, KANG: quality of the whole lines; firm, strong, unyielding, persisting. **Origin**, TZU: source, beginning, ground; cause, reason, motive; line of descent; path to the origin; yourself, intrinsic. **Outside**, WAI: outer, exterior, external; people working in places other than their home; unfamiliar, foreign; the upper trigram, as opposed to inside, NEI, the lower. **Come**, LAI, and **go**, WANG, describe the stream of time as it flows from future through present to past. Come, LAI, indicates what is approaching; move toward, arrive at; Go, WANG, indicates what is departing; proceed, move on; keywords. **Activate**, WEI: act or cause to act; do, make, manage; make active; attend to, help; because of. **Lord**, CHU: ruler, master, chief; authority. The ideogram: lamp and flame, giving light. **With respect to**, YÜ: relates to, refers to; hold a position in. **Inside**, NEI:

within, inner, interior; inside of the house and those who work there, particularly women; the lower trigram, as opposed to outside, WAI, the upper. The ideogram: border and enter, cross a border.

Stir up, TUNG: excite, influence, move, affect; work, take action; come out of the egg or the bud; the Action of the trigram Shake, CHEN. The ideogram: strength and heavy, move weighty things. **Persist**, CHIEN: strong, robust, dynamic, tenacious; continuous; unwearied heavenly bodies in their orbits; the Action of the trigram Force, CH'IEN.

[II] Center, CHUNG: inner, central; put in the center; middle, stable point enabling you to face inner and outer changes; middle line of trigram. The ideogram: field divided in two equal parts. Image of Hexagram 61. **Correspond(to)**, YING: be in agreement or harmony; resonate together, invoke and fulfil each other; answer to, suitable; relation between the lines (1:4, 2:5, 3:6) when they form the pair opened and whole, supple and strong. The ideogram: heart and obey.

Grow, HENG: success through a sacrifice; pervade, persevere; bring to full growth; enjoy; vigorous, effective; second stage of the Time Cycle.

's/have(it)/it/them, CHIH: expresses possession, directly or as an object pronoun. **Fate/Mandate**, MING: individual destiny; birth and death as limits of life; issue orders with authority; consult the gods. The ideogram: mouth and order, words with heavenly authority.

[III] Actually, YI: truly, really, at present. The ideogram: a dart and done, strong intention fully expressed. **Wherefore**, HO: interrogative: why? for what reason? what is? and affirmation: therefore, for that reason. **Have(it)/it/them's**, CHIH: expresses possession, directly or as an object pronoun.

Shield, YU: protect; defended by spirits; heavenly kindness and protection. The ideogram: numinous and right hand, spirit power.

Actually ... in fact, YI TSAI: stresses the importance of a statement. The ideogram: a dart and done, strong intention fully expressed.

- *Transforming Lines*

    Initial nine

    a) Disentangling. Going auspicious.

    b) Disentangling's going.
        Acquiring the purpose indeed.

Disentangle yourself, then go forward. You can do what you wish to do now, counting on the fact that you will not get tied up in negative emotions.

Associated Contexts a) **Auspicious**, CHI: leads to the experience of meaning; favorable, propitious, advantageous, appropriate; keyword. The ideogram: scholar and mouth, wise words of a sage.

b) **Acquire**, TE: obtain the desired object; wish for, desire covetously; gains, possessions. The ideogram: go and obstacle, going through obstacles to the goal. **Purpose**, CHIH: focus of mind and heart; will, inclination, resolve. The ideogram: heart and scholar, high inner resolve, or heart and go, inner determination.

> **Six at second**
>
> *a)* Not tilling the crop. Not clearing the plowland.
>   By consequence, Advantageous to have a direction to go. Harvesting
>
> *b)* Not tilling the crop.
>   Not yet affluence indeed.

This is not the time or place to start something. Things will not respond to direct effort. If you realize what this means, your plans will bring you success. Move on. The possibility to realize your plans lies ahead of you.

Associated Contexts a) **Till**, KENG: plow; labor at, cultivate. **Crop**, HUO: grain gathered in autumn; reap, harvest. **Clear**, TZU: cultivate wild or overgrown land; reclaim. **Plowland**, YÜ: newly opened fields, after two or three years plowing.

b) **Not yet**, WEI: temporal negative; something will but has not yet occurred; contrary of already, CHI. Image of Hexagram 64. **Affluence**, FU: rich, abundant; wealth; enrich, provide for; flow towards, accrue.

> **Six at third**
>
> *a)* Disentangling's calamity.
>   Maybe attaching's cattle.
>   Moving people's acquiring them:
>   Capital people's calamity.
>
> *b)* Moving people acquiring cattle.
>   Capital people, calamity indeed.

Even though you are without blame, you have lost something you care

about. Understand that you can see your loss two ways. If you identify with the capital people, if you stay where you are, it is a disaster. If you identify with the moving people who are on their way to a new place, you actually acquire new strength. This may rid you of an old affliction.

Associated Contexts a) **Maybe/"someone"** HUO: possible but not certain, perhaps, indicates spirit is active. **Attach,** HSI: fasten to, bind, tie; retain, continue; keep in mind, emotionally attached. **Cattle,** NIU: ox, bull, cow, calf; kine; power and strength of work animals.

People, person, JEN: humans individually and collectively; an individual; humankind. Image of Hexagrams 13 and 37. **Acquire,** TE: obtain the desired object; wish for, desire covetously; gains, possessions. The ideogram: go and obstacle, going through obstacles to the goal.

Capital, YI: populous fortified city, center and symbol of the domain it rules. The ideogram: enclosure and official seal.

Nine at fourth

a) Permitting Trial.
  Without fault.

b) Permitting Trial, without fault.
  Firmly possessing it indeed.

Go through with your plan. This is an enabling divination. You are empowered and free of mistakes.

Associated Contexts a) **Permit,** K'O: possible because in harmony with an inherent principle. The ideogram: mouth and breath, silent consent. **Trial,** CHEN: inquiry by divination and its result; righteous, firm; separating wheat from chaff; the kernel, the proven core; fourth stage of the Time Cycle. The ideogram: pearl and divination. **Without fault,** WU CHIU: no error or harm in the situation.

b) **Firm,** KU: constant, fixed, steady; chronic, recurrent. The ideogram: old and enclosure, long preserved. **It/them/have(it)/'s,** CHIH: expresses possession, directly or as an object pronoun.

Nine at fifth

a) Disentangling's affliction.
  No medicinal herbs, possessing rejoicing.

b) Disentangling's medicinal herbs.

Not permitting testing indeed.

You are suffering from sickness, anger, or negative emotion. Though you may be in pain, don't treat it as a medical or a literal problem. See it imaginatively and spiritually. It will soon clear up and you will have cause to rejoice.

Associated Contexts a) **Afflict**, CHI: sickness, disorder, defect, calamity; injurious; pressure and consequent anger, hate or dislike. The ideogram: sickness and dart, a sudden affliction.

Medicinal herbs, YAO: plants used as remedies; medical as opposed to other ways of healing. **Rejoice(in)**, HSI: feel and give joy; delight, exult; cheerful, merry. The ideogram: joy (music) and mouth, expressing joy.

b) **Not permitting**, PU K'O: not possible; contradicts an inherent principle. The ideogram: mouth and breath, silent consent. **Test**, SHIH: compare, try, experiment; tempt.

Nine above

a) Disentangling. Moving possesses blundering.
No advantageous direction.

b) Disentangling's moving:
Exhaustion's calamity indeed.

Even though you are not caught up in negative emotions, there is nothing you can do for now. The time is wrong. No plan you could make will help you now.

Associated Contexts a) **No advantageous direction**, WU YU LI: no plan or direction is advantageous; in order to take advantage of the situation, do not impose a direction on events.

b) **Exhaust**, CH'IUNG: bring to an end; limit, extremity; destitute; investigate exhaustively; end without a new beginning. The ideogram: cave and naked person, bent with disease or old age.

26

GREAT ACCUMULATING ▮
TA CH'U

Concentrate, focus on one idea; accumulate energy, support, nourish; bring everything together; great effort and great achievement.

Great Accumulating describes your situation in terms of having a central idea that defines what is valuable. Its symbol is gathering the energy of heaven through an image of ancient virtue. The way to deal with it is to focus on a single idea and use that to impose a direction on your life. Concentrate everything on this goal. Gather all the different parts of yourself and all your many encounters. Take the long view. Think of yourself as raising animals, growing crops or bringing up children. Tolerate and nourish things. Develop an atmosphere in which things can grow. Putting your ideas to the trial brings profit and insight. It can culminate in great abundance. Don't stay at home. Be active. Take in what is coming. This generates meaning and good fortune by releasing transformative energy. This is the right time to enter the stream of life with a purpose or to embark on a significant enterprise.

● *Image of the Situation*

> Great Accumulating.
> Advantageous Trial: Harvesting.
> Not dwelling, taking in. Auspicious.
> Advantageous to step into the Great River.

Associated Contexts **Great,** TA: big, noble, important, very; orient the will toward a self-imposed goal, impose direction; ability to lead or guide your life; contrasts to small, HSIAO, flexible adaptation to what crosses your path; keyword. **Accumulate,** CH'U: hoard, gather, retain, herd together; control, restrain; domesticate, tame, train; raise, feed, sustain, bring up. The ideogram: field and black, fertile black soil good for pastures, accumulated through retaining silt.

 Advantageous Trial, LI CHEN: advantageous divination; putting the action in question to the test is beneficial.

 Dwell, CHI: home, house, household, family; domestic, within doors;

live in. The ideogram: roof and pig or dog, the most valued domestic animals. Image of Hexagram 37. **Take in/eat** SHIH: eat, ingest, swallow, devour; incorporate. **Auspicious,** CHI: leads to the experience of meaning; favorable, propitious, advantageous, appropriate; keyword. The ideogram: scholar and mouth, wise wordsof a sage.

Advantageous/Harvest, LI: advantageous, profitable; acute, insightful; benefit, nourish; third stage of the Time Cycle. **Step into the Great River,** SHE TA CH'UAN: consciously moving into the flow of time; enter the stream of life with a goal or purpose; embark on a significant enterprise.

● *Outer and Inner Aspects*

☷ **Bound**: Mountains bound, limit and set a place off, stopping forward movement. **Bound** completes a full yin-yang cycle.

Connection to the outer: accomplishing words, which express things fully. **Bound** articulates what is complete and suggests what is beginning.

☰ **Force**: The force of heaven struggles on, persistent and unwearied; heavenly bodies persist in their orbits. **Force** is the center of the yin hemicycle, completing the formative process.

Connection to the inner: struggling forces are bound together in dynamic tension, the Metallic Moment culminating. **Force** brings elements to grips, creating enduring relations.

The outer limit retains and **accumulates** heaven's **great** inner force, bringing it to expression. This is a time of abundance.

● *Hidden Possibility*

Nuclear trigrams **Shake,** CHEN, and **Open,** TUI, result in Nuclear Hexagram 54, **Converting Maidenhood,** KUEI MEI. The will and power that grows from **great accumulating** leads to realizing the hidden potential of the **converting maiden.**

● *Sequence*

Possessing Disentangling,
therefore afterwards permitting Accumulating.
Accepting this lets you use Great Accumulating.

Associated Contexts **Possess,** YU: in possession of, have, own; opposite of **lack,** WU. **Disentangling** is the Image of Hexagram 25.

Therefore afterwards, JAN HOU: logical consequence of, necessarily follows in time. **Permit,** K'O: possible because in harmony with an inherent principle. The ideogram: mouth and breath, silent consent.

Accepting ... use: activating this hexagram depends on understanding and accepting the previous statement.

- *Contrasted Definitions*

> Great Accumulating: the season indeed.
> Disentangling from calamity indeed.

Associated Contexts **Season,** SHIH: quality of the time; the right time, opportune, in harmony; planning in accord with the time; seasons of the year. The ideogram: sun and temple, time as sacred. **Indeed/is/means,** YEH: intensifier, connective; indicates comment on previous statement.

Calamity, TSAI: disaster from outside; flood, plague, drought, blight, ruin; contrasts with blunder, SHENG, indicating personal fault. The ideogram: water and fire, elemental powers.

- *Symbol Tradition*

> Heaven located in mountain center. Great Accumulating.
> A chün tzu uses
> the numerous records, precedents and words going to move.
> [A chün tzu] uses accumulating his actualizing tao.

Associated Contexts **Heaven,** T'IEN: highest; sky, firmament, heavens; power above the human as opposed to earth, TI. below; the Symbol of the trigram Force, CH'IEN. The ideogram: great and the one above. **Locate(in),** TSAI: live in, dwell, reside; belong to, involved with, depend on; within. The ideogram: earth and persevere, place on the earth. **Mountain,** SHAN: limit, boundary; the Symbol of the trigram Bound, KEN. The ideogram: three peaks, a mountain range. **Center,** CHUNG: inner, central; put in the center; middle, stable point enabling you to face inner and outer changes; middle line of trigram. The ideogram: field divided in two equal parts. Image of Hexagram 61.

Chün tzu: ideal of a person who uses divination to order his/her life in accordance with tao rather than wilful intention; keyword. **Use(of),** YI: make use of, by means of, owing to; employ, make functional. **Numerous,** TO: great number, many; often. **Record,** SHIH: write down, inscribe; memorize, learn; recognize; annals, monuments. **Precede,** CH'IEN: come before in time and thus in value; anterior, former, ancient; lead forward. **Word,** YEN: speech, spoken words, sayings; talk, discuss, address. The ideogram: mouth and rising vapor, words as speech. **Go,** WANG, and **come,** LAI, describe the stream of time as it flows from future through present to past; go, WANG, indicates what is departing from present to past; proceed, move on; keyword. **Move,** HSING: move or move something; motivate, emotionally moving; walk, act, do. The ideogram: stepping left then right.

One/one's, CH'I: third person pronoun; also: it/its, he/his, she/hers, they/theirs. **Actualize tao,** TE: realize tao in action; power, virtue; ability to follow the course traced by the ongoing process of the cosmos; keyword The ideogram: to go, straight, and heart. Linked with acquire, TE: acquiring that which makes a being become what it is meant to be.

● *Image Tradition*

> Great Accumulating. [I]
> Strong persisting: staunch substance, resplendent shining.
> A day renews one's actualizing tao.
> Above strong and honoring eminence.
>
> Ability to stop and persist. [II]
> The great correcting indeed.
>
> Not dwelling, taking in auspicious. [III]
> Nourishing eminence indeed.
> Advantageous to step into the Great River.
> Corresponding reaching to heaven indeed.

Associated Contexts **[I] Strong,** KANG: quality of the whole lines; firm, strong, unyielding, persisting. **Persist,** CHIEN: strong, robust, dynamic, tenacious; continuous; unwearied heavenly bodies in their orbits; the Action of the trigram Force, CH'IEN. **Staunch,** TU: firm, strong, reliable; pure; consolidate, establish; sincere, honest. **Substance,** SHIH: real, strong, full; results, fruits, possessions; essence; honest, sincere. The ideogram: string of coins under a roof, riches in the house. **Resplendent,** HUI: glorious, sun-like, refulgent; brighten. **Shine,** KUANG: illuminate; give off brilliant, bright light; honor, glory, éclat; result of action, contrasts with brightness, MING, light of heavenly bodies. The ideogram: fire above person, lifting the light.

Day/sun, JIH: actual sun and the time of a sun-cycle, a day. **Renew,** HSIN: restore, improve, make or get better; new, fresh; the best, the latest.

Above, SHANG: anything above, in all senses; higher, upper, outer; upper trigram; opposite of below, HSIA. **Honor,** SHANG: esteem, give high rank to; eminent; put one thing on top of another. **Eminent,** HSIEN: moral and intellectual power; worthy, excellent, virtuous; sage second to the all-wise, SHENG.

[II] Able, NENG: enable; ability, power, skill, art; competent, talented; duty, function, capacity. The ideogram: an animal with strong hooves and bones, able to carry and defend. **Stop,** CHIH: bring or come to a standstill; the Action of the trigram Bound, KEN. The ideogram: a foot stops walking.

Correct, CHENG: rectify deviation or one-sidedness; proper, straight, exact, regular; constant, rule, model. The ideogram: stop and one, hold to one thing.

[III] Nourish, YANG: feed, sustain, support; provide, care for; bring up, improve, grow, develop.

Correspond(to), YING: be in agreement or harmony; resonate together, invoke and fulfil each other; answer to, suitable; relation between the lines (1:4, 2:5, 3:6) when they form the pair opened and whole, supple and strong. The ideogram: heart and obey. **Reach(to),** HU: arrive at a goal; reach towards and achieve; connect; contrasts with tend-towards, YU.

●   *Transforming Lines*

   Initial nine

   a) **Possessing adversity.**
      Harvesting: climaxing.

   b) **Possessing adversity, Harvesting: climaxing.**
      Not opposing calamity indeed.

This is heading into danger. Stop. End the adversity now. If you brings things to a head and leave, you will reap the crop. Things will turn out to your advantage.

Associated Contexts a) **Adversity,** LI: danger; threatening, malevolent demon. This has two aspects: grind, sharpen, improve, perfect, stimulate; and: poisonous, sinister, cruel, contrary. It indicates a spirit or ghost that seeks revenge by inflicting suffering upon the living. Pacifying or exorcizing such a spirit can have a healing effect. The ideogram: sheltering cliff and stinging insect.

Climax, YI: come to a high point and stop, bring to an end; use up, lay aside; decline, reject.

b) **Oppose**, FAN: resist; violate, offend, attack; possessed by an evil spirit; criminal. The ideogram: violate and dog, brutal offense.

Nine at second

a) Carting, loosening the axle straps.

b) Carting, loosening the axle straps.
Centering without surpassing indeed.

Forward movement stopped, you cluster round. Draw up the wagons and make contact. Nurture things. You need a show of beauty and bravery to release the bound energy.

Associated Contexts a) **Cart**, YÜ: carrying capacity of a vehicle; contain, hold, sustain. **Loosen/stimulate**, SHUO: rouse to action and good feeling; free from constraint, stir up, urge on; persuade, cheer, delight; set out in words; the Action of the trigram Open, TUI. The ideogram: words and exchange. **Axle strap**, FU: fastens the body of a cart to axle and wheels.

b) **Surpass**, YU: exceed; beyond measure, excessive; extraordinary; transgress, blame.

Nine at third

a) A fine horse, pursuing.
Trial: drudgery advantageous. Harvesting.
Spoken thus: an enclosed cart, escorting.
Advantageous to have a direction to go.

b) Harvesting: have a direction to go.
Uniting purposes above indeed.

You are pursuing your ideal. Don't lose heart, the drudgery will bring you profit and insight in the end. Think of it this way: you are escorting a covered cart with your secret treasure inside. Stay focused and work together. Circle the wagons at night and be careful all the day. Having a plan will help you.

Associated Contexts a) **Fine**, LIANG: excellent, refined, valuable; gentle, considerate, kind; natural. **Horse**, MA: symbol of spirited strength in the natural world, counterpart of dragon, LUNG; associated with Force,

CH'IEN, heaven, T'IEN, and high noon. **Pursue,** CHU: chase, follow closely, press hard; expel, drive out. The ideogram: pig (wealth) and go, chasing fortune.

Drudgery, CHIEN: difficult, hard, repetitive work; hard to cultivate; distressing, sorrowful. The ideogram: sticky earth and a person looking around, hard work in comparison to others. **Trial,** CHEN: inquiry by divination and its result; righteous, firm; separating wheat from chaff; the kernel, the proven core; fourth stage of the Time Cycle. The ideogram: pearl and divination.

Spoken thus, YÜEH: designated, termed, called. The ideogram: open mouth and tongue. **Enclose,** HSIEN: put inside a fence or barrier; restrain, obstruct, forbid; pen, corral. **Cart,** YÜ: carrying capacity of a vehicle; contain, hold, sustain. **Escort,** WEI: accompany, protect, guard, defend, honor; restrain; military outpost.

Have a direction to go, YU YU WANG: imposing a direction on the flow of time from present to past; have a specific goal or purpose.

b) **Unite,** HO: join, match, correspond, agree, collect, reply; unison, harmony; also: close, shut the mouth. The ideogram: mouth and assemble. **Purpose,** CHIH: focus of mind and heart; will, inclination, resolve. The ideogram: heart and scholar, high inner resolve, or heart and go, inner determination.

Six at fourth

a) **Youthful cattle's stable.**
   Spring auspicious.

b) **Six at fourth, Spring auspicious.**
   Possessing rejoicing indeed.

Accumulate the strength to carry heavy loads and confront difficult situations. Don't give up now, the way to the source is open. In the end you will have cause to rejoice.

Associated Contexts a) **Youthful,** T'UNG: young person between eight and fifteen; young animals and plants. **Cattle,** NIU: ox, bull, cow, calf; kine; power and strength of work animals. **'s/have(it)/it/them,** CHIH: expresses possession, directly or as an object pronoun. **Stable,** KU: shed or pen for cattle and horses.

Spring, YÜAN: source, origin, head; great, excellent; arise, begin, generating power; first stage of the Time Cycle.

b) **Rejoice(in)**, HSI: feel and give joy; delight, exult; cheerful, merry. The ideogram: joy (music) and mouth, expressing joy.

Six at fifth

a) **A gelded pig's tusks.**
Auspicious.

b) **Six at fifth's auspiciousness.**
Possessing reward indeed.

You have managed to confront and disable what could have been a powerful enemy. The way is open. This will bring rewards in the end.

Associated Contexts a) **Geld**, FEN: castrate a pig; deprive, take out. **Pig,** SHIH: all swine; sign of wealth and good fortune; associated with Streaming Moment. **'s/have(it)/it/them,** CHIH: expresses possession, directly or as an object pronoun. **Tusk,** YA: teeth of animals; toothlike, jagged, gnaw; ivory; a tax collector.

b) **Reward,** CH'ING: gift given from gratitude or benevolence; favour from heaven; congratulate with gifts. The ideogram: heart, follow and deer (wealth), the heart expressed through gifts.

Nine above

a) **Wherefore heaven's highway? Growing.**

b) **Wherefore heaven's highway?**
Tao: the great moving indeed.

You are walking heaven's highway. Make an offering and you will succeed. There is no doubt about your success.

Associated Contexts a) **Wherefore,** HO: interrogative: why? for what reason? what is? and affirmation: therefore, for that reason. **'s/have(it)/it/them,** CHIH: expresses possession, directly or as an object pronoun. **Highway,** CH'Ü: main road, thoroughfare; where many ways meet.

Grow, HENG: success through a sacrifice; pervade, persevere; bring to full growth; enjoy; vigorous, effective; second stage of the Time Cycle.

b) **Tao:** way or path; ongoing process of being and the course it traces for each specific person or thing; keyword. The ideogram: go and head, leading and the path it creates.

27

JAWS/SWALLOWING ▮ *YI*

Nourishing and being nourished; take things in; the mouth, daily bread; speaking, words.

Jaws describes your situation in terms of the sources of nourishment. Its symbol is what goes in and out of an open mouth. The way to deal with it is to take things in to provide for yourself and others. Take in what has been said and done and let it nourish the new. Provide what is necessary to feed yourself and those connected with you. Putting your ideas to the trial generates meaning and good fortune by releasing transformative energy. Contemplate what nourishes people and what you are nourishing. Think about what you give and what you ask for. Seek out the source of what goes in and out of your mouth and the mouths of others. The answer to your question lies there.

● *Image of the Situation*

> **Jaws, Trial: auspicious.**
> **Viewing the Jaws.**
> **Originating from seeking mouth substance.**

Associated Contexts **Jaws/swallow,** YI: mouth, jaws, cheeks, chin; take in, ingest; feed, nourish, sustain, rear; furnish what is necessary. The ideogram: open jaws. **Trial,** CHEN: inquiry by divination and its result; righteous, firm; separating wheat from chaff; the kernel, the proven core; fourth stage of the Time Cycle. The ideogram: pearl and divination. **Auspicious,** CHI: leads to the experience of meaning; favorable, propitious, advantageous, appropriate; keyword. The ideogram: scholar and mouth, wise words of a sage.

View, KUAN: contemplate, observe from a distance; look at carefully, gaze at; also: a monastery, an observatory; descry, divine through liquid in a cup. The ideogram: see and waterbird, observe through air or water. Image of Hexagram 20.

Origin, TZU: source, beginning, ground; cause, reason, motive; line of descent; path to the origin; yourself, intrinsic. **Seek,** CH'IU: search for, aim at, wish for, desire; implore, supplicate; covetous. **Mouth,** K'OU: literal mouth, words going out and food coming in; entrance, hole. **Substance,** SHIH: real, strong, full; results, fruits, possessions; essence; honest, sincere. The ideogram: string of coins under a roof, riches in the house.

- ## *Outer and Inner Aspects*

☶ **Bound**: Mountains bound, limit and set a place off, stopping forward movement. **Bound** completes a full yin-yang cycle.

Connection to the outer: accomplishing words, which express things fully. **Bound** articulates what is complete and suggests what is beginning.

☳ **Shake**: Thunder rises from below, shaking and stirring things up. **Shake** begins the yang hemicycle by germinating new action.

Connection to the inner: sprouting energies thrusting from below, the Woody Moment beginning. **Shake** stirs things up to issue-forth.

Previous accomplishments are **swallowed** in order to nourish germinating new energies.

- ## *Hidden Possibility*

The doubled nuclear trigram **Field**, K'UN, results in Nuclear Hexagram 2, **Field**, K'UN. Actively **swallowing** and taking things in opens a new **field** of activity.

- ## *Sequence*

Beings accumulating therefore afterwards permitting nourishing.
Accepting this lets you use Jaws.
Jaws imply nourishing indeed.

Associated Contexts **Being(s)**, WU: creature, thing, any single being; matter, substance, essence; nature of things. **Accumulate**, CH'U: retain, hoard, gather, herd together; control, restrain; domesticate, tame, train; raise, feed, sustain, bring up. The ideogram: field and black, fertile black soil good for pastures, accumulated through retaining silt. Image of Hexagrams 9 and 26. **Therefore afterwards**, JAN HOU: logical consequence of, necessarily follows in time. **Permit**, K'O: possible because in harmony with an inherent principle. The ideogram: mouth and breath, silent consent. **Nourish**, YANG: feed, sustain, support; provide, care for; bring up, improve, grow, develop.

Accepting ... use: activating this hexagram depends on understanding and accepting the previous statement.

Imply, CHE: further signify; additional meaning. **Indeed/is/means**, YEH: intensifier, connective; indicates comment on previous statement.

- *Contrasted Definitions*

> Great Traverses: toppling indeed.
> Jaws: nourishing and correcting indeed.

Associated Contexts **Great**, TA: big, noble, important, very; orient the will toward a self-imposed goal, impose direction; ability to lead or guide your life; contrasts with small, HSIAO, flexible adaptation to what crosses your path; keyword. **Traverse/exceed**, KU: go beyond, pass by, pass over; excessive, transgress; error, fault. **Great Traverses** is the Image of Hexagram 28. **Topple**, TIEN: fall over because top-heavy; overthrow, subvert; top, summit.

Correct, CHENG: rectify deviation or one-sidedness; proper, straight, exact, regular; constant, rule, model. The ideogram: stop and one, hold to one thing.

- *Symbol Tradition*

> Below mountain possessing thunder. Jaws.
> A chün tzu uses considering words to inform.
> [A chün tzu uses] articulating to drink and eat.

Associated Contexts **Below**, HSIA: anything below, in all senses; lower, inner; lower trigram; opposite of above, SHANG. **Mountain**, SHAN: limit, boundary; the Symbol of the trigram Bound, KEN. The ideogram: three peaks, a mountain range. **Possess**, YU: in possession of, have, own; opposite of lack, WU. **Thunder**, LEI: rising, arousing power; the Symbol of the trigram Shake, CHEN.

Chün tzu: ideal of a person who uses divination to order his/her life in accordance with tao rather than wilful intention; keyword. **Use(of)**, YI: make use of, by means of, owing to; employ, make functional. **Consider**, SHEN: act carefully, seriously; cautious, attentive, circumspect; still, quiet, sincere. The ideogram: heart and true. **Word**, YEN: speech, spoken words, sayings; talk, discuss, address. The ideogram: mouth and rising vapor, words as speech. **Inform**, YÜ: tell, warn; talk with, converse, exchange ideas.

Articulate, CHIEH: separate and distinguish, as well as join, different things; express thought through speech; joint, section, chapter, interval, unit of time; zodiacal sign; moderate, regulate; lit.: nodes on bamboo stalks.

Image of Hexagram 60. **Drinking and eating,** YIN SHIH: comprehensive term for eating, drinking and breathing; a meal, eating together.

● *Image Tradition*

Jaws. Trial: auspicious. [I]
Nourishing correcting, by consequence auspicious indeed.

Viewing Jaws. [II]
Viewing one's place to nourish indeed.
Originating from seeking mouth substance.
Viewing the origin of nourishing indeed.

Heaven and Earth nourishes the myriad beings. [III]
The all wise person nourishes eminence
used to extend to the myriad commoners.
Actually Jaws's season great in fact.

Associated Contexts **[I] By consequence(of),** TSE: very strong connection; reason, cause, result; rule, law, pattern, standard; therefore.

[II] One's/one, CH'I: third person pronoun; also: it/its, he/his, she/hers, they/theirs. **Place,** SO: where something belongs or comes from; residence, dwelling; habitual focus or object.

[III] Heaven and Earth, T'IEN TI: dynamic relation between the primal powers and the world it produces; cosmos, natural or human world; keyword. **Myriad,** WAN: countless; many, everyone; lit.: ten thousand. The ideogram: swarm of insects.

All wise, SHENG: intuitive universal wisdom; mythical sages; holy, sacred; mark of highest distinction. The ideogram: ear and inform, one who knows all from a single sound. **People, person,** JEN: humans individually and collectively; an individual; humankind. Image of Hexagrams 13 and 37. **Eminent,** HSIEN: moral and intellectual power; worthy, excellent, virtuous; sage second to the all-wise, SHENG. **Extend(to),** CHI: reach to, draw out, prolong; continuous, enduring. **Commoners,** MIN: class of workers the state draws on to sustain the social hierarchy; undeveloped potential outside the organized personality.

Actually ... in fact, YI TSAI: stresses the importance of a statement. The ideogram: a dart and done, strong intention fully expressed. **'s/have(it)/it/them,** CHIH: expresses possession, directly or as an object pronoun. **Season,** SHIH: quality of the time; the right time, opportune, in harmony; planning in accord with the time; seasons of the year. The ideogram: sun and temple, time as sacred.

● *Transforming Lines*

Initial nine

a) Stowing away simply the psyche tortoise.
Viewing my pendent Jaws.
Pitfall.

b) Viewing my pendent Jaws.
Truly not the stand to value indeed.

When you confront the problems involved, you simply give up and fall into self-pity. You put aside your imagination, its magical power and the omens you have been given. So of course the way closes. This sort of attitude has no value at all.

Associated Contexts a) **Stow(away)**, SHE: set aside, put away, store; halt, rest in; temporary lodgings, breathing-spell. **Simply**, ERH: just so, only. **Psyche**, LING: life force, vital energy; spirit of a being; magical action or influence. **Tortoise**, KUEI: turtles; armored animals, shells and shields; long-living; oracle-consulting by tortoise shell; image of the macrocosm: heaven and earth, between them the soft flesh of humans.

My/me/I, WO: first person pronoun; indicates an unusually strong emphasis on your own subjective experience. **Pendent**, TO: hanging; flowering branch, date or grape clusters.

Pitfall, HSIUNG: leads away from the experience of meaning; stuck and exposed to danger, unable to take in the situation; flow of life and spirit is blocked; unfortunate, baleful; keyword.

b) **Truly**, YI: statement is true and precise. **Stand**, TSU: base, foot, leg; rest on, support; stance. The ideogram: foot and calf resting. **Value**, KUEI: regard as valuable, give worth and dignity to; precious, high priced; honorable, exalted, illustrious. The ideogram: cowries (coins) and basket.

Six at second

a) Toppling Jaws.
Rejecting the canons, move to the hilltop.
Jaws chastising: pitfall.

b) Six at second, chastising: pitfall.
   Movement letting go sorting indeed.

The source of nourishment is disturbed. This shakes things up and clears the channels through which spirit and energy flow. Don't follow the rules now. Move to the place where you feel secure and contact your ideals. Even though this is a difficult time, don't try to punish people or set out on expeditions.

Associated Contexts a) **Reject**, FU: push away, expel, brush off; oppose, contradict; perverse, proud. The ideogram: hand and do not, pushing something away. **Canons**, CHING: standards, laws; regular, regulate; the Five Classics. The ideogram: warp-threads in a loom. **Hilltop**, CH'IU: hill with hollow top used for worship and as grave-site; knoll, hillock.
   Chastise, CHENG: punish, subjugate, discipline; reduce to order; punishing expedition. The ideogram: step and correct, a rectifying move. **Pitfall**, HSIUNG: leads away from the experience of meaning; stuck and exposed to danger, unable to take in the situation; flow of life and spirit is blocked; unfortunate, baleful; keyword.

b) **Move**, HSING: move or move something; motivate, emotionally moving; walk, act, do. The ideogram: stepping left then right. **Let go**, SHIH: lose, omit, miss, fail, let slip; out of control. The ideogram: drop from the hand. **Sort**, LEI: group according to kind, class with; like nature or purpose; species, class, genus.

   Six at third

   a) Rejecting the Jaws. Trial: pitfall.
      Ten years revolved, no availing of.
      No advantageous direction.

   b) Ten years revolved, no availing of.
      Tao, the great rebelling indeed.

You reject the hand that feeds you. If you go on like this, you will be paralyzed for an entire cycle of time. There is nothing that you can do here. You idea goes against the Way.

Associated Contexts a) **Reject**, FU: push away, expel, brush off; oppose, contradict; perverse, proud. The ideogram: hand and do not, pushing something away. **Pitfall**, HSIUNG: leads away from the experience of meaning; stuck and exposed to danger, unable to take in the situation; flow of life and spirit is blocked; unfortunate, baleful; keyword.

Ten, SHIH: goal and end of reckoning; whole, complete, all; entire, perfected, the full amount; reach everywhere, receive everything. The ideogram: East–West line crosses North–South line, a grid that contains all. **Years revolved,** NIEN: number of years elapsed; a person's age; contrasts with year's-time, SUI, length of time in a year. **Avail of,** YUNG: take advantage of; benefit from, profit by; use for a specific purpose; apply to advantage. The ideogram: to divine and center, applying divination to central concerns.

No advantageous direction, WU YU LI: no plan or direction is advantageous; in order to take advantage of the situation, do not impose a direction on events.

b) **Tao:** way or path; ongoing process of being and the course it traces for each specific person or thing; keyword. The ideogram: go and head, leading and the path it creates. **Rebel,** PEI: go against nature or usage; insubordinate; perverse, unreasonable.

Six at fourth

> *a)* Toppling Jaws. Auspicious.
> Tiger observing: glaring, glaring.
> His appetites: pursuing, pursuing.
> Without fault.

> *b)* Toppling Jaws' auspiciousness.
> Spreading out and shining above indeed.

The source of nourishment is disturbed. This action will shake things up and free you. Search out the new with the ferocity and passion of a tiger. Be full of force and concentration. This energy is not a mistake. It brings light and clarity to the situation.

Associated Contexts a) **Tiger,** HU: fierce king of animals; extreme yang; opposed to and protects against demoniacs on North–South axis of Universal Compass. **Observe,** SHIH: see and inspect carefully; gain knowledge of; compare and imitate. The ideogram: see and omen, taking account of what you see. **Glare,** TAN: stare intensely; obstruct, prevent. The ideogram: look and hesitate, staring without acting. The doubled character intensifies this quality.

His/he, CH'I: third person pronoun; also: one/one's, it/its, she/hers, they/theirs. **Appetites**, YÜ: drives, instinctive craving; wishes, passions, desires, aspirations; long for, seek ardently; covet. **Pursue**, CHU: chase, follow closely, press hard; expel, drive out. The ideogram: pig (wealth) and go, chasing fortune. The doubled character intensifies this quality.

Without fault, WU CHIU: no error or harm in the situation.

b) **Spread out**, SHIH: expand, diffuse, distribute, arrange, exhibit; add to, aid. The ideogram: flag and indeed, claiming new country. **Shine**, KUANG: illuminate; give off brilliant, bright light; honor, glory, éclat; result of action, contrasts with brightness, MING, light of heavenly bodies. The ideogram: fire above person, lifting the light. **Above**, SHANG: anything above, in all senses; higher, upper, outer; upper trigram; opposite of below, HSIA.

Six at fifth

a) Rejecting the canons.
   Residence Trial auspicious.
   Not permitting stepping into the Great River.

b) Residing in Trial's auspiciousness.
   Yielding uses adhering to the above indeed.

Nourishment is disturbed. This clears the channels through which spirit and energy flow. You are rejecting the rules most people live by. The way is open if you stay where you are and don't start any big projects for now. What you feel in doing this is entirely correct. It will connect you with a higher ideal.

Associated Contexts a) **Reject**, FU: push away, expel, brush off; oppose, contradict; perverse, proud. The ideogram: hand and do not, pushing something away. **Canons**, CHING: standards, laws; regular, regulate; the Five Classics. The ideogram: warp-threads in a loom.

Reside(in), CHÜ: dwell, live in, stay; sit down, fill an office; settled parts of a country. The ideogram: body and seat.

Not permitting, PU K'O: not possible; contradicts an inherent principle. The ideogram: mouth and breath, silent consent. **Step into the Great River**, SHE TA CH'UAN: consciously moving into the flow of time; enter the stream of life with a goal or purpose; embark on a significant enterprise.

b) **Yield(to)**, SHUN: give way and bear produce; comply, agree, follow, obey; unresisting, docile, flexible; nourish, provide; the Action of the trigram Field, K'UN: The ideogram: head and current, water flowing from the head of a river, yielding to the banks. **Adhere(to)**, TS'UNG: follow a way, hold to a doctrine, school, or person; hear and comply with, agree to; forced to follow, follower. The ideogram: two men walking, one following the other. **Above**, SHANG: anything above, in all senses; higher, upper, outer; upper trigram; opposite of below, HSIA.

Nine above

a) Antecedent Jaws. Adversity auspicious.
   Advantageous to step into the Great River.

b) Antecedent Jaws, adversity auspicious.
   The great possessing reward indeed.

You are nourished by what came before you, a legacy of ancient virtue. Go back to the source and correct things. Have no fear, the way is open. The best way to deal with things now is launch into a brand new enterprise. Your ideas will be rewarded if you do.

Associated Contexts a) **Antecedent**, YU: come before as origin and cause; through, by, from; depend on; permit, enter by way of. **Adversity**, LI: danger; threatening, malevolent demon. This has two aspects: grind, sharpen, improve, perfect, stimulate; and: poisonous, sinister, cruel, contrary. It indicates a spirit or ghost that seeks revenge by inflicting suffering upon the living. Pacifying or exorcizing such a spirit can have a healing effect. The ideogram: sheltering cliff and stinging insect.

   Advantageous/Harvest, LI: advantageous, profitable; acute, insightful; benefit, nourish; third stage of the Time Cycle. **Step into the Great River**, SHE TA CH'UAN: consciously moving into the flow of time; entering the stream of life with a goal or purpose; keyword.

b) **Reward**, CH'ING: gift given from gratitude or benevolence; favor from heaven; congratulate with gifts. The ideogram: heart, follow and deer (wealth), the heart expressed through gifts.

28
GREAT TRAVERSES ▮
TA KUO

Transition, crisis; gather all your strength to make the passage; hold on to your ideals.

Great Traverses describes your situation in terms of how to act in a time of crisis. Its symbol is the ridgepole, the strong idea that all other things depend on. The way to deal with it is to push your principles beyond ordinary limits and accept the movement it brings. Have a noble purpose. Make an offering and you will succeed. Find what is truly important and organize yourself accordingly. The ridgepole of your house is warped and sagging. The structure of your life is in danger of collapse. But there is a creative force at work in this breakdown. So impose a direction on things. Have a place to go. This is pleasing to the spirits. Through it they will give you success, effective power and the capacity to bring things to maturity.

● *Image of the Situation*

> **Great Traverses, the ridgepole sagging.**
> **Advantageous to have a direction to go.**
> **Growing.**

Associated Contexts **Great**, TA: big, noble, important, very; orient the will toward a self-imposed goal, impose direction; ability to lead or guide your life; contrasts to small, HSIAO, flexible adaptation to what crosses your path; keyword. **Traverse/exceed**, KU: go beyond, make a passage, pass over; excessive, transgress; error, fault. **Ridgepole**, TUNG: highest and key beam in a house; summit, crest. **Sag**, NAO: yield, bend, distort, twist; disturbed, confused.
> **Advantageous/Harvest**, LI: advantageous, profitable; acute, insightful; benefit, nourish; third stage of the Time Cycle. **Have a direction to go**, YU YU WANG: imposing a direction on the flow of time from present to past; have a specific goal or purpose.
> **Grow**, HENG: success through a sacrifice; pervade, persevere; bring to full growth; enjoy; vigorous, effective; second stage of the Time Cycle.

Outer and Inner Aspects

⚌ **Open**: vapor rising from the marsh's open surface stimulates and fertilizes; stimulating words cheer and inspire. **Open** begins the yin hemicycle by initiating the formative process.

Connection to the outer: liquifying, casting, skinning off the mold, the Metallic Moment beginning. **Open** stimulates, cheers and reveals innate form.

⚏ **Ground**: Wind and wood subtly enter from the ground, penetrating and pervading. **Ground** is the center of the yang hemicycle, spreading pervasive action.

Connection to the inner: penetrating and bringing together, the Woody Moment culminating. **Ground** pervades, matches and couples, seeding a new generation.

Great inner penetration, stimulated in the outer world, **traverses** and **exceeds** all normal forms and relations.

Hidden Possibility

The doubled nuclear trigram **Force**, CH'IEN, results in Nuclear Hexagram 1, **Force**, CH'IEN. The creative drive of **great traverses** connects you with the creative energy of **force**.

Sequence

> Not nourishing, by consequence not permitting stirring up.
> Accepting this lets you use Great Traverses.

Associated Contexts **Nourish**, YANG: feed, sustain, support; provide, care for; bring up, improve, grow, develop. **By consequence(of)**, TSE: very strong connection; reason, cause, result; rule, law, pattern, standard; therefore. **Not permitting**, PU K'O: not possible; contradicts an inherent principle. The ideogram: mouth and breath, silent consent. **Stir up**, TUNG: excite, influence, move, affect; work, take action; come out of the egg or the bud; the Action of the trigram Shake, CHEN. The ideogram: strength and heavy, move weighty things.

Accepting ... use: activating this hexagram depends on understanding and accepting the previous statement.

- *Contrasted Definitions*

> Great Traverses: toppling indeed.
> Jaws: nourishing correcting indeed.

Associated Contexts **Topple**, TIEN: fall over because top-heavy; overthrow, subvert; top, summit. **Indeed/is/means**, YEH: intensifier, connective; indicates comment on previous statement.

Jaws/swallow, YI: mouth, jaws, cheeks, chin; take in, ingest; feed, nourish, sustain, rear; furnish what is necessary. The ideogram: open jaws. Image of Hexagram 27. **Correct**, CHENG: rectify deviation or one-sidedness; proper, straight, exact, regular; constant, rule, model. The ideogram: stop and one, hold to one thing.

- *Symbol Tradition*

> Marsh submerging wood. Great Traverses.
> A chün tzu uses solitary establishing not to fear.
> [A chün tzu uses] retiring from the age without melancholy.

Associated Contexts **Marsh**, TSE: open surface of a flat body of water and the vapors rising from it; fertilize, enrich; kindness, favor; the Symbol of the trigram **Open**, TUI. **Submerge**, MIEH: plunge under water, put out a fire; exterminate, finish, cut off. The ideogram: water and destroy. **Wood/tree**, MU: all things woody or wooden, alive or constructed from wood; associated with the Woody Moment; wood and wind are the Symbols of the trigram Ground, SUN. The ideogram: a tree with roots and branches.

Chün tzu: ideal of a person who uses divination to order his/her life in accordance with tao rather than wilful intention; keyword. **Use(of)**, YI: make use of, by means of, owing to; employ, make functional. **Solitary**, TI: alone, single; isolated, abandoned. **Establish**, LI: set up, institute, order, arrange; stand erect; settled principles. **Fear**, CHÜ: afraid, intimidated, apprehensive; stand in awe of.

Retire, TUN: withdraw; run away, flee; conceal yourself, become obscure, invisible; secluded, non-social. The ideogram: walk and swine (wealth and luck), satisfaction through walking away. Image of Hexagram 33. **Age**, SHIH: an age, an epoch, a generation; the world, mankind; the time, as "in the time of." **Without**, WU: devoid of; -less as suffix. **Melancholy**, MEN: sad, unhappy, chagrined, heavy-hearted. The ideogram: gate and heart, the heart confined.

Image Tradition

Great Traverses. [I]
Great implies Traversing indeed.
The ridgepole sagging.
Roots, tips, fading indeed.

Strong Exceeding and centering. [II]
Ground and stimulating movement.
Advantageous to have a direction to go.

Thereupon Growing. [III]
Actually Great Traverses' season great in fact.

Associated Contexts **[I] Imply**, CHE: further signify; additional meaning.

Root, PEN: origin, cause, source of nourishment; essential. The ideogram: tree with roots in earth. **Tips**, MO: growing ends, outermost twigs; last, most distant. **Fade**, JO: lose strength or freshness, wither, wane; fragile, feeble, weak; decayed, ruined; infirm purpose.

[II] Strong, KANG: quality of the whole lines; firm, strong, unyielding, persisting. **Center**, CHUNG: inner, central; put in the center; middle, stable point enabling you to face inner and outer changes; middle line of trigram. The ideogram: field divided in two equal parts. Image of Hexagram 61.

Ground, SUN: base on which things rest; support, foundation; mild, subtly penetrating; nourishing. The ideogram: stand and things arranged on it, the subtle influence of the ground. Image of Hexagram 57. **Stimulate/ loosen**, SHUO: rouse to action and good feeling; free from constraint, stir up, urge on; persuade, cheer, delight; set out in words; the Action of the trigram Open, TUI. The ideogram: words and exchange. **Move**, HSING: move or move something; motivate, emotionally moving; walk, act, do. The ideogram: stepping left then right.

[III] Thereupon, NAI: on that ground, because of.

Actually ... in fact, YI TSAI: stresses the importance of a statement. The ideogram: a dart and done, strong intention fully expressed. **'s/have(it)/it/them**, CHIH: expresses possession, directly or as an object pronoun. **Season**, SHIH: quality of the time; the right time, opportune, in harmony; planning in accord with the time; seasons of the year. The ideogram: sun and temple, time as sacred.

• *Transforming Lines*

Initial six

a) A sacrifice availing of white thatch grass.
  Without fault.

b) A sacrifice availing of white thatch grass.
  Supple located below indeed.

Prepare your move very carefully. Think about your motives. Be clear and pure. This is not a mistake. The beginning is humble, but the result will be great. Make a sacrifice.

Associated Contexts a) **Sacrifice**, CHIEH: make offerings to gods and the dead; depend on, call on, borrow; lit.: straw mat used to hold offerings. **Avail of**, YUNG: take advantage of; benefit from, profit by; use for a specific purpose; apply to advantage. The ideogram: to divine and center, applying divination to central concerns. **White**, PO: associated with autumn, Harvest and the Metallic Moment; clear, immaculate; plain, pure, essential; explicit; color of death and mourning. **Thatch grass**, MAO: thick grass used for the roofs of humble houses.
  Without fault, WU CHIU: no error or harm in the situation.

b) **Supple**, JOU: quality of the opened lines; flexible, pliant, tender, adaptable. **Locate(in)**, TSAI: live in, dwell, reside; belong to, involved with, depend on; within. The ideogram: earth and persevere, place on the earth. **Below**, HSIA: anything below, in all senses; lower, inner; lower trigram; opposite of above, SHANG.

Nine at second

a) A withered willow giving birth to a sprig.
  A venerable husband acquiring his woman consort.
  Nothing not advantageous.

b) A venerable husband, a woman consort.
  Exceeding uses mutual associating indeed.

In the midst of the crisis, something happens that gives it a whole new lease on life. A new branch emerges, a new start. This will benefit everything. Associate with others for mutual benefit.

Associated Contexts a) **Withered**, K'U: dry up; dry wood, dried up bogs; decayed, rotten. The ideogram: tree and old. **Willow**, YANG: all thriving, fast growing trees; willow, poplar, tamarisk, aspen. The ideogram: tree and expand. **Birth/give birth to**, SHENG: produce, beget, grow, bear, arise; life, vitality. The ideogram: earth and sprout. **Sprig**, T'I: tender new shoot of a tree, twig, new branch.

Venerable, LAO: term of respect due to old age. **Husband**, FU: household manager; administer with thrift and prudence; responsible for; sustain with your earnings; old enough to assume responsibility; married man. **Acquire**, TE: obtain the desired object; wish for, desire covetously; gains, possessions. The ideogram: go and obstacle, going through obstacles to the goal. **His/he**, CH'I: third person pronoun; also: one/one's, it/its, she/hers, they/theirs. **Woman(hood)**, NÜ: a woman; what is inherently female. **Consort**, CH'I: single official partner; legal status of married woman (first wife); contrasts with function of wife, FU, head of household, and concubine, CH'IEH, secondary wives.

Nothing not advantageous, WU PU LI: nothing for which this will not be beneficial; advantageous potential, borderline where the balance is swinging from not Harvesting to actually Harvesting.

b) **Mutual**, HSIANG: reciprocal assistance, encourage, help; bring together, blend with; examine, inspect; by turns. **Associate(with)**, YÜ: consort with, combine; companions; group, band, company; agree with, comply, help. The ideogram: pair of hands reaching downward meets a pair of hands reaching upward, helpful association.

Nine at third

a) The ridgepole buckling. Pitfall.

b) The ridgepole buckling's pitfall.
Not permitted to use possessing bracing indeed.

The structure of your life buckles and fails. There is nothing you can do to brace it up now.

Associated Contexts a) **Buckle**, JAO: distort, wrench out of shape, collapse, break; weak; flexible, lithe. **Pitfall**, HSIUNG: leads away from the experience of meaning; stuck and exposed to danger, unable to take in the situation; flow of life and spirit is blocked; unfortunate, baleful; keyword.

b) **Possess**, YU: in possession of, have, own; opposite of lack, WU. **Brace/jawbones**, FU: support, consolidate, reinforce, strengthen, stiffen, prop up, fix; steady, firm, rigid; help, rescue; support the speaking mouth. The ideogram: cart and great.

Nine at fourth

a) **The ridgepole crowned. Auspicious.**
  Possessing more: distress.

b) **The ridgepole crowning's auspiciousness.**
  Not sagging, reaching to the below indeed.

You have come through the crisis. The structure of your life is strengthened and crowned. The way is open. You have all you need. If you try for more, you will only see distress and confusion and lose what you have.

Associated Contexts a) **Crown**, LUNG: place above all others; peak; high, surpassing. **Auspicious**, CHI: leads to the experience of meaning; favorable, propitious, advantageous, appropriate; keyword. The ideogram: scholar and mouth, wise words of a sage.

  Possess, YU: in possession of, have, own; opposite of lack, WU. **More**, T'O: another; add to. **Distress**, LIN: distress, shame, regret, humiliation; aware of having lost the right track; leads to repenting, HUI, correcting the direction of mind and life.

b) **Reach(to)**, HU: arrive at a goal; reach toward and achieve; connect; contrasts with tend-towards, YU. **Below**, HSIA. anything below, in all senses; lower, inner; lower trigram; opposite of above, SHANG.

Nine at fifth

a) **A withered willow giving birth to flowers.**
  A venerable wife acquiring her notable husband.
  Without fault, without praise.

b) **A withered willow giving birth to flowers.**
  Wherefore permitting lasting indeed?
  A venerable wife, a notable husband.
  Truly permitting the demoniac indeed.

As the crisis passes, something happens to produce a burst of beauty. There is neither blame nor praise involved. Enjoy it, for it may soon be over. Allow even the demons to have a place.

Associated Contexts a) **Withered**, K'U: dry up; dry wood, dried up bogs; decayed, rotten. The ideogram: tree and old. **Willow**, YANG: all thriving, fast growing trees; willow, poplar, tamarisk, aspen. The ideogram: tree and expand. **Birth/give birth to**, SHENG: produce, beget, grow, bear, arise; life, vitality. The ideogram: earth and sprout. **Flower**, HUA: beauty, abundance; variegated, elegant, blooming, garden-like; symbol of culture and literature.

Venerable, LAO: term of respect due to old age. **Wife**, FU: responsible position of married woman within the household; contrasts with consort, CH'I, her legal position and concubine, CH'IEH, secondary wives. The ideogram: woman, hand and broom, household duties. **Acquire**, TE: obtain the desired object; wish for, desire covetously; gains, possessions. The ideogram: go and obstacle, going through obstacles to the goal. **Hers/she**, CH'I: third person pronoun; also: one/one's, it/its, he/his, they/their. **Notable**, SHIH: learned, upright, important man; scholar, gentleman. **Husband**, FU: household manager; administer with thrift and prudence; responsible for; sustain with your earnings; old enough to assume responsibility; married man.

Without fault, WU CHIU: no error or harm in the situation. **Praise**, YÜ: admire and approve; magnify, eulogize; flatter. The ideogram: words and give, offering words.

b) **Wherefore**, HO: interrogative: why? for what reason? what is? and affirmation: therefore, for that reason. **Permit**, K'O: possible because in harmony with an inherent principle. The ideogram: mouth and breath, silent consent. **Last**, CHIU: long, protracted; enduring.

Truly, YI: statement is true and precise. **Demon(iac)**, CH'OU: possessed by a malignant genius; ugly, physically or morally deformed; vile, disgraceful, shameful; drunken. The ideogram: fermenting liquor and soul. Demoniac and tiger are opposed on the Universal Compass North–South axis; the tiger (Extreme Yang) scares away and protects against demoniacs (Extreme Yin).

Six above

a) Traversing. Stepping in submerges the peak. Pitfall.
   Without fault.

b) Traversing and stepping in's pitfall.
   Not permitting fault indeed.

These are deep and troubled waters. Be clear about how much you can become involved. If you do more than get your feet wet, chances are you will be swept away. It is not a mistake to realize this. When you do, the potential cause of sorrow disappears.

Associated Contexts a) **Step into**, SHE: walk in or through the water; spend time on something; contrasts with ford, CHI, to cross. The ideogram: step and water. **Peak**, TING: top, summit, crown; carry on the head; superior. **Pitfall**, HSIUNG: leads away from the experience of meaning; stuck and exposed to danger, unable to take in the situation; flow of life and spirit is blocked; unfortunate, baleful; keyword.

   Without fault, WU CHIU: no error or harm in the situation.

b) **Fault**, CHIU: unworthy conduct that leads to harm, illness, misfortune. The ideogram: person and differ, differ from what you should be.

29

G O R G E ▮ *K ' A N*

Collect your forces, confront your fears, take the plunge; practice, repeat, rehearse; rise to the challenge.

Gorge describes your situation in terms of repeatedly confronting something dangerous and difficult. Its symbols are the earth pit and the ghost river, danger and the one who dances with ghosts. The way to deal with it is to take the risk without holding back. Make an offering and you will succeed. You cannot avoid this obstacle. Conquer your fear and faintheartedness. Jump in, like water that pours into a hole, fills it up and flows on. Practice, train, accustom yourself to danger. This is a critical point. It is a pit that could trap you and become a grave. But there is no way around it. Summon your energy and concentration. Repeatedly confront the challenge. You can act this way with confidence, for you are linked to the spirits and they will carry you forward. Hold fast to your heart and its growth. This is pleasing to the spirits. Through it they will give you success, effective power and the capacity to bring the situation to maturity. Moving, acting, motivating things will bring you honor, so give them first place.

● *Image of the Situation*

> **Repeating Gorge.**
> **There is a connection to the spirits.**
> **Hold fast the heart. Growing.**
> **Movement possesses honor.**

Associated Contexts **Repeat**, HSI: series of similar acts; practice, rehearse; familiar with, skilled. The ideogram: two wings and a cap, thought carried by repeated movements. **Gorge**, K'AN: dangerous place; hole, cavity, hollow; pit, snare, trap, grave, precipice; critical time, test; risky. The ideogram: earth and pit.

Gorge is the **Stream** trigram doubled and includes that trigram's attributes: *Symbol:* **Stream**, SHUI: flowing water; fluid, dissolving; river, tide, flood. The ideogram: rippling water. *Action:* **Venture falling**, HSIEN HSIEN: risk falling until a bottom is reached, filling and overcoming the danger of the Gorge. **Fall**, HSIEN: fall down or into, sink, drop, descend;

falling water; be captured. **Venture,** HSIEN: risk without reserve; key point, point of danger; difficulty, obstruction that must be confronted; water falling and filling the holes on its way. The ideogram: mound and all or whole, everything engaged at one point.

There is … spirits, YU FU: inner and outer are in accord; confidence of the spirits has been captured; sincere, truthful; proper to take action.

Hold fast, WEI: hold together; tie to, connect; reins, net. **Heart,** HSIN: heart as center of being; seat of mind's images and affections; moral nature; source of desires, intentions, will. **Grow,** HENG: success through a sacrifice; pervade, persevere; bring to full growth; enjoy; vigorous, effective; second stage of the Time Cycle.

Move, HSING: move or move something; motivate, emotionally moving; walk, act, do. The ideogram: stepping left then right. **Possess,** YU: in possession of, have, own; opposite of lack, WU. **Honor,** SHANG: esteem, give high rank to; eminent; put one thing on top of another.

- *Outer and Inner Aspects*

☵ Gorge: Stream ventures and falls into the gorge, flowing on through toil and danger. **Gorge** ends the yin hemicycle by leveling and dissolving forms.

Connection to both inner and outer: flooding and leveling dissolve direction and shape, the Streaming Moment. **Gorge** ventures, falls, toils and flows on.

- *Hidden Possibility*

Nuclear trigrams **Bound,** KEN, and **Shake,** CHEN, result in Nuclear Hexagram 27, **Jaws/Swallowing,** YI. Wholehearted outer venturing into the danger of the **gorge** lets you provide nourishment for yourself and others through **jaws.**

- *Sequence*

Beings not permitted to use completing Traversing.
Accepting this lets you use Gorge.
Gorge implies falling indeed.

Associated Contexts **Beings not permitted to use … :** no one is allowed to make use of; nothing can exist by means of. **Complete,** CHUNG: end of a cycle that begins the next; last, whole, all; contrasts with exhaust, CH'IUNG:

final end. The ideogram: silk cocoons, follow and ice, winter linking one year with the next. **Traverse/xceed**, KU: go beyond, pass by, pass over; excessive, transgress; error, fault. Image of Hexagrams 28 and 62.

Accepting ... use: activating this hexagram depends on understanding and accepting the previous statement.

Imply, CHE: further signify; additional meaning. **Indeed**, YEH: intensifier, connective; indicates comment on previous statement.

- ### Contrasted Definitions

    Above Radiance and below Gorge indeed.

    Associated Contexts **Above**, SHANG: anything above, in all senses; higher, upper, outer; upper trigram; opposite of below, HSIA. **Radiance**, LI: glowing light, spreading in all directions; light-giving, discriminating, articulating; divide and arrange in order; the power of consciousness. The ideogram: bird and weird, the magical fire-bird with brilliant plumage. Image of Hexagram 30. **Also**, ERH: joins and contrasts two terms. **Below**, HSIA: anything below, in all senses; lower, inner; lower trigram; opposite of above, SHANG.

- ### Symbol Tradition

    Streams reiterating culminating. Repeating Gorge.
    A chün tzu uses rules actualizing tao to move.
    [A chün tzu uses] repeating to teach affairs.

    Associated Contexts **Reiterate**, CHIEN: repeat, duplicate; successive. **Culminate**, CHIH: bring to the highest degree; arrive at the end or summit; superlative.

    Chün tzu: ideal of a person who uses divination to order his/her life in accordance with tao rather than wilful intention; keyword. **Use(of)**, YI: make use of, by means of, owing to; employ, make functional. **Rules**, CH'ANG: unchanging principles; regular, constant, habitual; maintain laws and customs. **Actualize tao**, TE: realize tao in action; power, virtue; ability to follow the course traced by the ongoing process of the cosmos; keyword. The ideogram: to go, straight, and heart. Linked with acquire, TE: acquiring that which makes a being become what it is meant to be.

    Teach, CHIAO: instruct, show; precept, doctrine. **Affairs**, SHIH: all kinds of personal activity; matters at hand; business, occupation; manage a business, case in court.

- *Image Tradition*

> Repeating Gorge. [I]
> Redoubling and venturing indeed.
> Stream diffusing and not overfilling.
> Movement venturing and not letting go one's trustworthiness.
>
> Hold fast the heart's Growing, [II]
> thereupon using the strong center indeed.
> Movement possesses honor. Going possesses achievement indeed.
> Heaven venturing, not permitting ascending indeed.
> Earth venturing, mountains, rivers, hill tops, mounds indeed.
>
> The kingly prince sets up venturing used to guard his city. [III]
> Actually venturing's season to avail of the great in fact.

Associated Contexts **[I]** **Redouble**, CH'UNG: repeat, reiterate, add to; build up by layers.

Diffuse, LIU: flow out, spread, permeate. **Overfill**, YING: at the point of overflowing; more than wanted, stretch beyond; replenished, full; arrogant. The ideogram: vessel and too much.

Let go, SHIH: lose, omit, miss, fail, let slip; out of control. The ideogram: drop from the hand. **One's/one, his/he**, CH'I: third person pronoun; also: it/its, she/hers, they/theirs. **Trustworthy**, HSIN: truthful, faithful, consistent over time; integrity; confide in, follow; credentials; contrasts with conforming, FU, connection in a specific moment. The ideogram: person and word, true speech.

[II] **'s/have(it)/it/them**, CHIH: expresses possession, directly or as an object pronoun. **Thereupon**, NAI: on that ground, because of. **Strong**, KANG: quality of the whole lines; firm, strong, unyielding, persisting. **Center**, CHUNG: inner, central; put in the center; middle, stable point enabling you to face inner and outer changes; middle line of trigram. The ideogram: field divided in two equal parts. Image of Hexagram 61.

Go, WANG, and **come**, LAI, describe the stream of time as it flows from future through present to past; go, WANG, indicates what is departing from present to past; proceed, move on; keyword. **Achieve**, KUNG: work done, results; real accomplishment, praise, worth, merit. The ideogram: workman's square and forearm, combining craft and strength.

Heaven, T'IEN: highest; sky, firmament, heavens; power above the human as opposed to earth, TI, below; the Symbol of the trigram Force,

CH'IEN. The ideogram: great and the one above. **Not permitting**, PU K'O: not possible; contradicts an inherent principle. The ideogram: mouth and breath, silent consent. **Ascend**, SHENG: go up; climb step by step; rise in office; advance through effort; accumulate; bring out and fulfil; lit.: a measure for fermented liquor, ascension as distillation. Image of Hexagram 46.

Earth, TI: ground on which the human world rests; basis of all things; nourishes all things; the Symbol of the trigram Field, K'UN. **Mountain**, SHAN: limit, boundary; the Symbol of the trigram Bound, KEN. The ideogram: three peaks, a mountain range. **River**, CH'UAN: water flowing between banks; current, channel; associated with the Streaming Moment and the trigram Gorge, K'AN. **Hilltop**, CH'IU: hill with hollow top used for worship and as grave-site; knoll, hillock. **Mound**, LING: grave-mound, barrow; small hill.

[III] **King(hood)**, WANG: effective ruler, by authority of the Emperor, from whom others derive their power. **Prince**, KUNG: nobles acting as ministers of state in the capital; governing from the center rather than active in daily life; contrasts with feudatory, HOU, governors of the provinces. **Set up**, SHE: establish, institute; arrange, set in order; spread a net. The ideogram: words and impel, establish with words. **Guard**, SHOU: keep in custody; protect, ward off harm, attend to, supervise. **City**, KUO: area of only human constructions; political unit, polis. First of the territorial zones: city, suburbs, countryside, forests.

Actually ... in fact, YI TSAI: stresses the importance of a statement. The ideogram: a dart and done, strong intention fully expressed. **Season**, SHIH: quality of the time; the right time, opportune, in harmony; planning in accord with the time; seasons of the year. The ideogram: sun and temple, time as sacred. **Avail of**, YUNG: take advantage of; benefit from, profit by; use for a specific purpose; apply to advantage. The ideogram: to divine and center, applying divination to central concerns. **Great**, TA: big, noble, important, very; orient the will toward a self-imposed goal, impose direction; ability to lead or guide your life; contrasts with small, HSIAO, flexible adaptation to what crosses your path; keyword. Image of Hexagrams 14, 26, 28, 34.

● *Transforming Lines*

Initial six

a) **Repeating Gorge.**
Entering into the Gorge, the recess.
Pitfall.

b) **Repeating Gorge, entering Gorge.**
Letting go tao: pitfall indeed.

By responding in the same way again and again, you get caught in a dead end. This is the pit of melancholy, a pit within the gorge. Don't get caught here.

Associated Contexts a) **Enter**, JU: penetrate, go into, enter on, progress; put into, encroach on; the Action of the trigram Ground, SUN, contrary of issue-forth, CH'U. **Recess**, TAN: pit within a large cave, entered from the side.

Pitfall, HSIUNG: leads away from the experience of meaning; stuck and exposed to danger, unable to take in the situation; flow of life and spirit is blocked; unfortunate, baleful; keyword.

b) **Tao**: way or path; ongoing process of being and the course it traces for each specific person or thing; keyword. The ideogram: go and head, leading and the path it creates.

Nine at second

a) **Gorge, possessing venturing.**
Seeking, the small acquiring.

b) **Seeking, the small acquiring.**
Not yet issuing forth from the center indeed.

As you venture into danger, you will get what you need by being flexible and adaptable. Have modest goals, don't impose your will and you will succeed.

Associated Contexts a) **Seek**, CH'IU: search for, aim at, wish for, desire; implore, supplicate; covetous. **Small**, HSIAO: little, common, unimportant; adapting to what crosses your path; ability to move in harmony with the vicissitudes of life; contrasts with **great**, TA, self-imposed theme or goal; keyword. Image of Hexagrams 9 and 62. **Acquire**, TE: obtain the desired object; wish for, desire covetously; gains, possessions. The ideogram: go and obstacle, going through obstacles to the goal.

b) **Not yet,** WEI: temporal negative; something will but has not yet occurred; contrary of already, CHI. Image of Hexagram 64. **Issue forth(from),** CH'U: emerge from, come out of, proceed from, spring from; the Action of the trigram Shake, CHEN; contrary of enter, JU. The ideogram: stem with branches and leaves emerging.

Six at third

a) It is coming: Gorge, the Gorge.
  Venturing moreover is reclining.
  Entering into the Gorge, the recess.
  No availing of.

b) It is coming: Gorge, the Gorge.
  Completing without achieving indeed.

Relax and pull back. What is coming is more than you can handle right now. If you push on, you will be trapped in a pit, a fatal diversion. Think about this desire.

Associated Contexts a) **Come,** LAI, and **go,** WANG, describe the stream of time as it flows from future through present to past; come, LAI, indicates what is approaching; move toward, arrive at; keyword.

  Moreover, CH'IEH: further, and also. **Recline,** CHEN: lean back or on; soften, relax; head rest, back support; stake to tie cattle.

  Enter, JU: penetrate, go into, enter on, progress; put into, encroach on; the Action of the trigram Ground, SUN, contrary of issue-forth, CH'U.

b) **Without,** WU: devoid of; -less as suffix. **Achieve,** KUNG: work done, results; real accomplishment, praise, worth, merit. The ideogram: workman's square and forearm, combining craft and strength.

Six at fourth

a) A cup, liquor, a platter added.
  Availing of a jar.
  Let in the bonds originating from the window.
  Completing, without fault.

b) A cup, liquor, a platter added.
  Strong and Supple, the border indeed.

If you are trapped or cut off, don't fight it. Lay out an offering, give of yourself. Open the window and let the spirit in. Your rescuers are coming.

You are right on the border, the liminal place where events emerge. Go through with your plans. This is not a mistake.

Associated Contexts a) **Cup,** TSUN: quantity a libation vessel contains; glass, decanter, bottle. **Liquor,** CHIU: alcoholic beverages, distilled spirits; spirit which perfects the good and evil in human nature. The ideogram: liquid above fermenting must, separating the spirits. **Platter,** KUEI: wood or bamboo plate; sacrificial utensil. **Add,** ERH: join to something previous; reiterate, repeat; second, double; assistant.

Jar, FOU: earthenware vessels; wine-jars and drums. The ideogram: jar containing liquor.

Let in, NA: allow to enter; take in, grow smaller; insert; collect. The ideogram: silk and enter, shrinking silk threads. **Bonds,** YO: cords, ropes; contracts, treaties, legal and moral obligations; moderate, restrain, restrict. **Origin,** TZU: source, beginning, ground; cause, reason, motive; line of descent; path to the origin; yourself, intrinsic. **Window,** YU: opening in wall or roof to let in light; open, instruct, enlighten.

Without fault, WU CHIU: no error or harm in the situation.

b) **Strong and Supple,** KANG JOU: field of creative tension between the whole and opened lines and their qualities; field of psychic movement. **Border,** CHI: limit, frontier, line which joins and divides. The ideogram: place and sacrifice, border between human and spirit.

Nine at fifth

a) **Gorge not overfilled.**
  Merely already evened.
  Without fault.

b) **Gorge not overfilled.**
  Centering, not yet great indeed.

The danger is over. The spirits are appeased. Go on with your life. Be happy with your release. Move to the center and your real purpose will come clear.

Associated Contexts a) **Merely,** CHIH: nothing more than. **Already,** CHI: completed, done, has occurred; past tense, contrary of **not yet,** WEI. Image of Hexagram 63. **Even,** P'ING: level, make even or equal; uniform, peaceful, tranquil; restore quiet, harmonize.

Without fault, WU CHIU: no error or harm in the situation.

b) **Not yet,** WEI: temporal negative; something will but has not yet occurred; contrary of already, CHI. Image of Hexagram 64.

Six above

a) Tying availing of stranded ropes.
  Dismissed to the dense jujube trees.
  Three year's time, no acquiring. Pitfall.

b) Six above, letting go tao.
  Pitfall: three year's time indeed.

If you go on like this, you will commit a serious transgression. You will be bound and judged and imprisoned. Change now or be trapped.

Associated Contexts a) **Tie(to),** HSI: connect, attach to, bind; devoted to; relatives. The ideogram: person and connect, ties between humans. **Stranded ropes,** HUI MO: three stranded ropes; royal garments; beautiful, honorable.

Dismiss, CHIH: put aside; judge and find wanting. **Dense,** TS'UNG: close-set, bushy, crowded; a grove. **Jujube tree,** CHI: thorny bush or tree; sign of a court of justice or site of official literary examinations.

Three, SAN: number three, third time or place; active phases of a cycle; superlative; beginning of repetition. **Year's time,** SUI: actual length of time in a year; contrasts with years-revolved, NIEN, number of years elapsed. **Acquire,** TE: obtain the desired object; wish for, desire covetously; gains, possessions. The ideogram: go and obstacle, going through obstacles to the goal. **Pitfall,** HSIUNG: leads away from the experience of meaning; stuck and exposed to danger, unable to take in the situation; flow of life and spirit is blocked; unfortunate, baleful; keyword.

b) **Tao:** way or path; ongoing process of being and the course it traces for each specific person or thing; keyword. The ideogram: go and head, leading and the path it creates.

RADIANCE ▮ *LI*

Light, warmth, awareness; join with, adhere to; articulate and spread the light, see clearly.

Radiance describes your situation in terms of awareness and coherence. It is the bright presence in expressed in the omens that shows the spirit is near. The way to deal with it is to articulate and spread light and warmth. Illuminate, articulate, discriminate, make things conscious. Bring together what belongs together. This is a time of intelligent effort and accumulating awareness. It includes unexpected and meaningful encounters, separations from the old and experiences outside the ordinary. Put your ideas to the trial. That brings profit and insight. It is pleasing to the spirits. Through it they will give you effective power, enjoyment, and the capacity to bring things to maturity. Nurturing the receptive strength that can carry burdens generates meaning and good fortune by releasing transformative energy.

● *Image of the Situation*

> **Radiance, Advantageous Trial. Harvesting.**
> **Growing.**
> **Accumulating female cattle. Auspicious.**

Associated Contexts **Radiance**, LI: glowing light, spreading in all directions; light-giving, discriminating, articulating; divide and arrange in order; the power of consciousness. The ideogram: bird and weird, the magical fire-bird with brilliant plumage. **Radiance** is the **Brightness** and **Fire** trigram doubled and includes that trigram's attributes: *Symbols:* **Brightness**, MING: light-giving aspect of burning, heavenly bodies and consciousness. The ideogram: sun and moon. **Fire**, HUO: warming and consuming aspect of burning. *Action:* **Congregate**, LI: cling together; depend on, attached to, rely on; couple, pair, herd. The ideogram: deer flocking together. **Advantageous Trial**, LI CHEN: advantageous divination; putting the action in question to the test is beneficial, harvesting.

    Grow, HENG: success through a sacrifice; pervade, persevere; bring to full growth; enjoy; vigorous, effective; second stage of the Time Cycle.

Accumulate, CH'U: retain, hoard, gather, herd together; control, restrain; domesticate, tame, train; raise, feed, sustain, bring up. The ideogram: field and black, fertile black soil good for pastures, accumulated through retaining silt. Image of Hexagrams 9 and 26. **Female**, P'IN: female sexual organs, particularly of farm animals; concave, hollow. The ideogram: cattle and ladle, a hollow, reproductive organ. **Cattle**, NIU: ox, bull, cow, calf; kine; power and strength of work animals. **Auspicious**, CHI: leads to the experience of meaning; favorable, propitious, advantageous, appropriate; keyword. The ideogram: scholar and mouth, wise words of a sage.

- *Outer and Inner Aspects*

☲ **Radiance**: Fire and brightness radiate light and warmth, attached to their support; congregating people see and become aware. **Radiance** ends the yang hemicycle, consuming action in awareness.

Connection to both inner and outer: light, heat, consciousness bring continual change, the Fiery Moment. **Radiance** spreads outward, congregating, becoming aware and changing.

- *Hidden Possibility*

Nuclear trigrams **Open**, TUI, and **Ground**, SUN, result in Nuclear Hexagram 28, **Great Traverses**, TA KUO. **Radiance** spreading in all directions lets you make the **great transition**.

- *Sequence*

Falling necessarily possesses a place to congregate.
Accepting this lets you use Radiance.
Radiance implies congregating indeed.

Associated Contexts **Fall**, HSIEN: fall down or into, sink, drop, descend; falling water; the Action of the trigram Gorge, K'AN: **Necessarily**, PI: unavoidably, indispensably, certainly. **Possess**, YU: in possession of, have, own; opposite of lack, WU: **Place**, SO: where something belongs or comes from; residence, dwelling; habitual focus or object.

Accepting ... use: activating this hexagram depends on understanding and accepting the previous statement.

Imply, CHE: further signify; additional meaning. **Indeed**, YEH: intensifier, connective; indicates comment on previous statement.

- *Contrasted Definitions*

    Above Radiance and below Gorge indeed.

Associated Contexts **Above,** SHANG: anything above, in all senses; higher, upper, outer; upper trigram; opposite of below, HSIA. **Below,** HSIA: anything below, in all senses; lower, inner; lower trigram; opposite of above, SHANG. **Gorge,** K'AN: dangerous place; hole, cavity, hollow; pit, snare, trap, grave, precipice; critical time, test; risky. The ideogram: earth and pit. Image of Hexagram 29.

- *Symbol Tradition*

    Brightness doubled arousing Radiance.
    Great People use consecutive brightening
    to illuminate the four sides.

Associated Contexts **Doubled,** LIANG: twice, both, again, dual, a pair. **Arouse,** TSO: stir up, stimulate, rouse from inactivity; generate; appear, arise. The ideogram: person and beginning.

    Great People, TA JEN: important, noble, influential; those who impose a ruling principle on their lives; effect of the great within an individual; keyword. **Use(of),** YI: make use of, by means of, owing to; employ, make functional. **Consecutive,** CHI: follow after, continue; take another's place; line of succession, adopt an heir. The ideogram: silk thread and continuous. **Illuminate,** CHAO: shine light on; enlighten, reflect: care for, supervise. The ideogram: fire and brightness. **Four sides,** SSU FANG: the cardinal points; the limits or boundaries of the earth; everywhere, all around.

- *Image Tradition*

    Radiance. Congregating indeed. [I]
    Sun and Moon congregating reach to heaven.
    The hundred grains, grasses, trees congregating reach to earth.
    Redoubling brightness uses congregating to reach to correcting.
    Thereupon changes accomplished Below Heaven.

    Supple congregating reaches to centering correcting. [II]
    The past causes Growing.
    That uses accumulating female cattle, auspicious indeed.

Associated Contexts **[I] Sun and Moon**, JIH YÜEH: the two dimensions of calendar time that define any specific moment; time as interlocking cycles. **Reach(to)**, HU: arrive at a goal; reach towards and achieve; connect; contrasts with tend-towards, YU. **Heaven**, T'IEN: highest; sky, firmament, heavens; power above the human as opposed to earth, TI, below; the Symbol of the trigram Force, CH'IEN: The ideogram: great and the one above.

Hundred, PO: numerous, many, all; a whole class or type. **Grains**, KU: cereal crops, corn; substantial, well-off; income; bless with plenty. **Grass**, TS'AO: all grassy plants and herbs; young, tender plants; rough draft; hastily. **Tree/wood**, MU: all things woody or wooden, alive or constructed from wood; associated with the Woody Moment; wood and wind are the Symbols of the trigram Ground, SUN. The ideogram: a tree striking its roots down and sending up branches. **Earth**, TI: ground on which the human world rests; basis of all things, nourishes all things; the Symbol of the trigram Field, K'UN.

Redouble, CH'UNG: repeat, reiterate, add to; build up by layers. **Correct**, CHENG: rectify deviation or one-sidedness; proper, straight, exact, regular; constant, rule, model. The ideogram: stop and one, hold to one thing.

Thereupon, NAI: on that ground, because of. **Change**, HUA: gradual, continuous metamorphosis; influence someone; contrasts with transform, PIEN, sudden mutation. The ideogram: person alive and dead, the life-process. **Accomplish**, CH'ENG: complete, finish, bring about; perfect, full, whole; play your part, do your duty; mature. The ideogram: weapon and man, able to bear arms, thus fully developed. **Below Heaven**, T'IEN HSIA: the human world, between heaven and earth.

[II] Supple, JOU: quality of the opened lines; flexible, pliant, tender, adaptable. **Centering correcting**, CHUNG CHENG: central and correct; make rectifying one-sidedness and error your central concern; reaching a stable center in yourself can correct the situation.

Past (cause), KU: come before as cause; formerly, ancient; reason, purpose, intention; grievance, quarrel, dissatisfaction, sorrow, mourning resulting from previous causes and intentions; situation leading to a divination.

That uses, SHIH YI: involves and is involved by.

● *Transforming Lines*

Initial nine

a) Treading, polishing therefore.
   Respecting it.
   Without fault.

b) Treading, polishing it respectfully.
   Using casting out fault indeed.

The crosswise pattern of things now is a good omen for the beginning. Be very careful with the first steps. Polish and clarify your motives and feelings. Treat this with real respect. You won't be making a mistake.

Associated Contexts a) **Tread**, LÜ: step, path, track; footsteps; walk a path or way; course of the stars; act, practice; conduct; salary, means of subsistence. The ideogram: body and repeating steps, following a trail. Image of Hexagram 10. **Polish**, TS'O: file away imperfections; wash or plate with gold; confused, in disorder, mixed. The ideogram: metal and old, clearing away accumulated disorder. **Therefore**, JAN: follows logically, thus.

   Respect(ful), CHING: reverent, attentive; stand in awe of, honor; inner respect; contrasts with courtesy, KUNG, good manners. The ideogram: teacher's rod taming speech and attitude. **It/them/have(it)/'s**, CHIH: expresses possession, directly or as an object pronoun.

   Without fault, WU CHIU: no error or harm in the situation.

b) **Cast out**, P'I: expel, repress, exclude, punish; exclusionary laws and their enforcement. The ideogram: punish, authority and mouth, give orders to expel. **Fault**, CHIU: unworthy conduct that leads to harm, illness, misfortune. The ideogram: person and differ, differ from what you should be.

Six at second

a) Yellow Radiance. Spring auspicious.

b) Yellow Radiance, Spring auspicious.
   Acquiring centering tao indeed.

You have found the connection here. Light and power surge up from below. The way to the source is open.

Associated Contexts a) **Yellow**, HUANG: color of the productive middle; associated with the Earthy Moment between yang and yin

hemicycles; color of soil in central China; emblematic and imperial color of China since the Yellow Emperor (2500 BCE). **Spring**, YÜAN: source, origin, head; great, excellent; arise, begin, generating power; first stage of the Time Cycle.

b) **Acquire**, TE: obtain the desired object; wish for, desire covetously; gains, possessions. The ideogram: go and obstacle, going through obstacles to the goal. **Center**, CHUNG: inner, central; put in the center; middle, stable point enabling you to face inner and outer changes; middle line of trigram. The ideogram: field divided in two equal parts. Image of Hexagram 61. **Tao**: way or path; ongoing process of being and the course it traces for each specific person or thing; keyword. The ideogram: go and head, leading and the path it creates.

> **Nine at third**
>
> *a)* Sun going down's Radiance.
>   Not drumbeating a jar and singing,
>   By consequence great old age's lament. Pitfall.
>
> *b)* Sun going down's Radiance.
>   Wherefore permit lasting indeed?

Instead of spreading light and warmth, you see everything in the light of the setting sun. You don't beat your drum or sing your songs. Instead, you lament all the terrible things that have happened in your life. Why go on like this?

Associated Contexts a) **Sun/day**, JIH: actual sun and the time of a suncycle, a day. **Go down**, TSE: sun setting, afternoon; waning moon; decline. **'s/have(it)/it/them**, CHIH: expresses possession, directly or as an object pronoun.

  Drumbeating, KU: skin or earthenware drums; play a drum; excite, arouse, encourage; joyous, happy. **Jar**, FOU: earthenware vessels; wine-jars and drums. The ideogram: jar containing liquor. **Sing**, KO: chant, sing elegies, sad or mournful songs; associated with the Earthy Moment, turning from yang to yin.

  By consequence(of), TSE: very strong connection; reason, cause, result; rule, law, pattern, standard; therefore. **Great**, TA: big, noble, important, very; orient the will toward a self-imposed goal, impose direction; ability to lead or guide your life; contrasts with **small**, HSIAO, flexible adaptation to what crosses your path; keyword. Image of Hexagrams 14, 26, 28, 34. **Old**

age, TIEH: seventy or older; aged, no longer active. **Lament**, CHÜEH: express intense regret or sorrow; mourn over; painful recollections. **Pitfall**, HSIUNG: leads away from the experience of meaning; stuck and exposed to danger, unable to take in the situation; flow of life and spirit is blocked; unfortunate, baleful; keyword.

b) **Wherefore**, HO: interrogative: why? for what reason? what is? and affirmation: therefore, for that reason. **Permit**, K'O: possible because in harmony with an inherent principle. The ideogram: mouth and breath, silent consent. **Last**, CHIU: long, protracted; enduring.

Nine at fourth

a) Assailing thus, its coming thus.
　Burning thus. Dying thus. Thrown out thus.

b) Assailing thus, its coming thus.
　Without a place to tolerate indeed.

This affair is a flash in the pan. It comes on strong, burns out and dies. Throw it away. It has no place in your life.

Associated Contexts a) **Assail**, T'U: rush against; abrupt attack; suddenly stricken; insolent, offensive. **Thus**, JU: as, in this way. **Its/it**, CH'I: third person pronoun; also: one/one's, he/his, she/hers, they/theirs. **Come**, LAI, and **go**, WANG, describe the stream of time as it flows from future through present to past; come, LAI, indicates what is approaching; move toward, arrive at; keyword.

　Burn, FEN: set fire to, destroy completely. **Die**, SSU: sudden or untimely death; run out of energy; immobile, fixed. **Throw out**, CH'I: reject, discard, abandon, push aside, break off: renounce, forget.

b) **Without**, WU: devoid of; -less as suffix. **Tolerate**, JUNG: allow, contain, endure, bear with; accept graciously. The ideogram: full stream bed, tolerating and containing.

Six at fifth

a) Issuing forth tears like gushing. Sadness like lamenting.
　Auspicious.

b) Six at fifth's auspiciousness.
　Radiance: the kingly prince indeed.

It feels as if you have lost a connection with someone important. Cry and mourn. Let your sadness be seen. This will open the way again and bring those above you to their senses.

Associated Contexts a) **Issue forth(from)**, CH'U: emerge from, come out of, proceed from, spring from; the Action of the trigram Shake, CHEN; contrary of enter, JU. The ideogram: stem with branches and leaves emerging. **Tears**, T'I: weep, cry; water from the eyes. **Like**, JO: same as; just as, similar to. **Gush**, T'O: water surging in streams; falling tears; heavy rain. **Sad**, CH'I: unhappy, low in spirits, distressed; mourn, sorrow over; commiserate with. **Lament**, CHÜEH: express intense regret or sorrow; mourn over; painful recollections.

b) **'s/have(it)/it/them**, CHIH: expresses possession, directly or as an object pronoun. **King(hood)**, WANG: effective ruler, by authority of the Emperor, from whom others derive their power. **Prince**, KUNG: nobles acting as ministers of state in the capital; governing from the center rather than active in daily life; contrasts with feudatory, HOU, governors of the provinces.

> **Nine above**
>
> *a)* The king avails of issuing forth to chastise.
>   Possessing excellence.
>   Severing the head. Catching in no way its demons.
>   Without fault.
>
> *b)* The king availing of issuing forth chastising.
>   Using correcting the fiefdoms indeed.

This is a time to take decisive measures. Be determined and aggressive. You will have excellent results. Get rid of the leaders. Seize what is truly important. This is not a mistake. Opposition will fall apart.

Associated Contexts a) **King(hood)**, WANG: effective ruler, by authority of the Emperor, from whom others derive their power. **Avail of**, YUNG: take advantage of; benefit from, profit by; use for a specific purpose; apply to advantage. The ideogram: to divine and center, applying divination to central concerns. **Issue forth(from)**, CH'U: emerge from, come out of, proceed from, spring from; the Action of the trigram Shake, CHEN; contrary of enter, JU. The ideogram: stem with branches and leaves emerging. **Chastise**, CHENG: punish, subjugate, discipline; reduce to order; punishing expedition. The ideogram: step and correct, a rectifying move.

  Excellence, CHIA: superior quality; fine, delicious, glorious; happy, pleased; rejoice in, praise. The ideogram: increasing goodness, pleasure and happiness.

Sever, CHE: break off, separate, sunder, cut in two; discriminate, judge the true and false. **Head**, SHOU: literal head; leader, foremost; subject headings; beginning, model; superior, upper, front. **Catch**, HUO: take in hunt; catch a thief; obtain, seize; hit the mark, opportune moment; prisoner, spoils, prey; slave, servant. **In no way**, FEI: strong negative; not so. The ideogram: a box filled with opposition. **Its/it**, CH'I: third person pronoun; also: one/one's, he/his, she/hers, they/theirs. **Demon(iac)**, CH'OU: possessed by a malignant genius; ugly, physically or morally deformed; vile, disgraceful, shameful; drunken. The ideogram: fermenting liquor and soul. Demoniac and tiger are opposed on the Universal Compass North–South axis; the tiger (Extreme Yang) scares away and protects against demoniacs (Extreme Yin).

Without fault, WU CHIU: no error or harm in the situation.

b) **Fiefdom**, PANG: region governed by a feudatory, an order of nobility.

31

CONJOINING ▌ *HSIEN*

Excite, stimulate, influence; strong attraction; bring together what belongs together; a sacred place.

Conjoining describes your situation in terms of an influence that excites, mobilizes or triggers you into action. Its symbol is the sacred place where humans and spirits conjoin. The way to deal with it is to find the best way to bring things together. Make an offering and you will succeed. This influence is working to unite the separated parts of something that belongs together. Reach out, join things, and allow yourself to be moved. This is pleasing to the spirits. Through it they will give you success, effective power, enjoyment, and the capacity to bring the situation to maturity. Put your ideas to the trial. That brings profit and insight. The woman and the yin are the keys to the situation. Understanding, accepting and acting through the woman generates meaning and good fortune by releasing transformative energies.

● *Image of the Situation*

> Conjoining, Growing.
> Advantageous Trial. Harvesting.
> Grasping the woman auspicious.

Associated Contexts **Conjoin,** HSIEN: come into contact with, influence; reach, join together; put together as parts of a previously separated whole; come into conjunction, as the celestial bodies; totally, completely; lit.: broken piece of pottery, the halves of which join to identify partners. **Grow,** HENG: success through a sacrifice; pervade, persevere; bring to full growth; enjoy; vigorous, effective; second stage of the Time Cycle.

> **Advantageous Trial,** LI CHEN: advantageous divination; putting the action in question to the test is beneficial, harvesting.

> **Grasp,** CH'Ü: lay hold of, take and use, seize, appropriate; grasp the meaning, understand. The ideogram: ear and hand, hear and grasp. **Woman(hood),** NÜ: a woman; what is inherently female. **Auspicious,** CHI: leads to the experience of meaning; favorable, propitious, advantageous, appropriate; keyword. The ideogram: scholar and mouth, wise words of a sage.

- *Outer and Inner Aspects*

☱ **Open**: vapor rising from the marsh's open surface stimulates and fertilizes; stimulating words cheer and inspire. **Open** begins the yin hemicycle by initiating the formative process.

Connection to the outer: liquifying, casting, skinning off the mold, the Metallic Moment beginning. **Open** stimulates, cheers and reveals innate form.

☶ **Bound**: Mountains bound, limit and set a place off, stopping forward movement. **Bound** completes a full yin-yang cycle.

Connection to the inner: accomplishing words, which express things. **Bound** articulates what is complete to suggest what is beginning.

Inner accomplishment provides the foundation for **conjoining** through outer stimulation and cheer.

- *Hidden Possibility*

Nuclear trigrams **Force**, CH'IEN, and **Ground**, SUN, result in Nuclear Hexagram 44, **Coupling**, KOU. **Conjoining's** active drive to restore an intrinsic whole leads to a **coupling** of the primal powers.

- *Sequence*

> Possessing Heaven and Earth:
> Therefore afterwards possessing the myriad beings.
> Possessing the myriad beings:
> Therefore afterwards possessing Man and Woman.
> Possessing Man and Woman:
> Therefore afterwards possessing Husband and Wife.
> Possessing Husband and Wife:
> Therefore afterwards possessing Father and Son.
> Possessing Father and Son:
> Therefore afterwards possessing Chief and Servant.
> Possessing Chief and Servant:
> Therefore afterwards possessing Above and Below.
> Possessing Above and Below:
> Therefore afterwards the code's righteousness
> possesses a place to be polished.

Associated Contexts **Possess**, YU: in possession of, have, own; opposite of lack, WU. **Heaven and Earth**, T'IEN TI: dynamic relation between the primal powers and the world it produces; cosmos, natural or human world; keyword.

Therefore afterwards, JAN HOU: logical consequence of, necessarily follows in time. **Myriad**, WAN: countless; many, everyone; lit.: ten thousand. The ideogram: swarm of insects. **Being(s)**, WU: creature, thing, any single being; matter, substance, essence; nature of things.

Man and Woman, NAN NÜ: creative relation between what is inherently male and what is inherently female.

Husband and Wife, FU FU: the cooperative effort of man and woman in establishing and maintaining a home.

Father and Son, FU TZU: proper relation between generations serving and living up to the ideal of the ancestors, carrying on a tradition.

Chief and Servant, CHÜN CH'EN: cooperative relation between those who give orders and those who carry them out.

Above and Below, SHANG HSIA: realm of dynamic interaction between the upper and the lower; the vertical dimension.

Codes, LI: rites, rules, ritual; usage, manners; worship, ceremony, observance. The ideogram: worship and sacrificial vase, handling a sacred vessel. **Righteous**, YI: proper and just, meets the standards; things in their proper place; the heart that rules itself; upright, moral rule; contrasts with Harvest, LI, advantage or profit. **Place**, SO: where something belongs or comes from; residence, dwelling; habitual focus or object. **Polish**, TS'O: file away imperfections; wash or plate with gold; confused, in disorder, mixed. The ideogram: metal and old, clearing away accumulated disorder.

● *Contrasted Definitions*

> Conjoining: urging indeed.
> Persevering: lasting indeed.

Associated Contexts **Urge**, SU: strong specific desire; quick, hurried; call, invite. **Indeed**, YEH: intensifier; indicates comment on previous statement.

Persevere, HENG: continue in the same way or spirit; constant, perpetual, regular; self-renewing; extend everywhere. Image of Hexagram 32. **Last**, CHIU: long, protracted; enduring.

● *Symbol Tradition*

> Above mountain possessing marsh. Conjoining.
> A chün tzu uses emptiness to accept people.

Associated Contexts **Above**, SHANG: anything above, in all senses; higher, upper, outer; upper trigram; opposite of below, HSIA. **Mountain**, SHAN: limit, boundary; the Symbol of the trigram Bound, KEN. The ideogram: three peaks, a mountain range. **Marsh**, TSE: open surface of a flat body of water and the vapors rising from it; fertilize, enrich; kindness, favor; the Symbol of the trigram Open, TUI.

Chün tzu: ideal of a person who uses divination to order his/her life in accordance with tao rather than wilful intention; keyword. **Use(of)**, YI: make use of, by means of, owing to; employ, make functional. **Empty**, HSÜ: no images or concepts; vacant, unsubstantial; empty yet fertile space. **Accept**, SHOU: accept, make peace with, agree to; at rest, satisfied; patient. **People, person**, JEN: humans individually and collectively; an individual; humankind. Image of Hexagrams 13 and 37.

● *Image Tradition*

> Conjoining. Influencing indeed. [I]
> Above supple and below strong.
> The two agency's influence corresponds and uses mutual associating.
>
> Stopping and stimulating. [II]
> Below manhood, womanhood.
> That uses Growing, Advantageous Trial,
> grasping the woman auspicious.
>
> Heaven and Earth influencing
> and the myriad beings changing give birth. [III]
> The all wise person influences the people at heart
> and Below Heaven harmoniously evens it.
>
> Viewing one's place to influence. [IV]
> And actually Heaven and Earth,
> and the myriad beings' motives permit seeing.

Associated Contexts [I] **Influence**, KAN: excite, act on, touch; affect someone's feelings, move the heart. The ideogram: heart and all, pervasive influence.

Supple, JOU: quality of the opened lines; flexible, pliant, tender, adaptable. **Below**, HSIA: anything below, in all senses; lower, inner; lower trigram; opposite of above, SHANG. **Strong**, KANG: quality of the whole lines; firm, strong, unyielding, persisting.

Two, ERH: pair, even numbers, binary, duplicate. **Agencies**, CH'I: fluid energy, configurative power, vital force; interacts with essence, CHING, to produce things and beings. The ideogram: vapor and rice, heat and moisture producing substance. **Correspond(to)**, YING: be in agreement or harmony; resonate together, invoke and fulfil each other; answer to, suitable; relation between the lines (1:4, 2:5, 3:6) when they form the pair opened and whole, supple and strong. The ideogram: heart and obey. **Mutual**, HSIANG: reciprocal assistance, encourage, help; bring together, blend with; examine, inspect; by turns. **Associate(with)**, YÜ: consort with, combine; companions; group, band, company; agree with, comply, help. The ideogram: pair of hands reaching downward meets a pair of hands reaching upward, helpful association.

[II] **Stop**, CHIH: bring or come to a standstill; the Action of the trigram Bound, KEN. The ideogram: a foot stops walking. **Stimulate**, SHUO: rouse to action and good feeling; free from constraint, stir up, urge on; persuade, cheer, delight; set out in words; the Action of the trigram Open, TUI. The ideogram: words and exchange.

Man(hood), NAN: a man; what is inherently male. The ideogram: fields and strength, hard labor in the fields.

That uses, SHIH YI: involves and is involved by.

[III] **Change**, HUA: gradual, continuous metamorphosis; influence someone; contrasts with transform, PIEN, sudden mutation. The ideogram: person alive and dead, the life process. **Birth/give birth to**, SHENG: produce, beget, grow, bear, arise; life, vitality. The ideogram: earth and sprout.

All wise, SHENG: intuitive universal wisdom; mythical sages; holy, sacred; mark of highest distinction. The ideogram: ear and inform, one who knows all from a single sound. **Heart**, HSIN: heart as center of being; seat of mind's images and affections; moral nature; source of desires, intentions, will. **Below Heaven**, T'IEN HSIA: the human world, between heaven and earth. **Harmony**, HO: concord, union; conciliate; at peace, mild; fit, tune, adjust. **Even**, P'ING: level, make even or equal; uniform, peaceful, tranquil; restore quiet, harmonize.

[IV] **View**, KUAN: contemplate, observe from a distance; look at carefully, gaze at; also: a monastery, an observatory; descry, divine through liquid in a cup. The ideogram: see and waterbird, observe through air or water. Image of Hexagram 20. **One's/one**, CH'I: third person pronoun; also: it/its, he/his, she/hers, they/theirs.

Actually, YI: truly, really, at present. The ideogram: a dart and done, strong intention fully expressed. **'s/have(it)/it/them**, CHIH: expresses possession, directly or as an object pronoun. **Motive**, CH'ING: true nature; feelings, desires, passions. The ideogram: heart and green, germinated in the heart. **Permit**, K'O: possible because in harmony with an inherent principle. The ideogram: mouth and breath, silent consent. **See**, CHIEN: seeing in all its aspects: vision, being visible, forming mental images; visit, call on, consult. The ideogram: eye above person, active and receptive sight.

● *Transforming Lines*

Initial six

a) **Conjoining one's big toes.**

b) **Conjoining one's big toes.**
   Purpose located outside indeed.

You feel the first stirrings of creative desire. The influence is just beginning. There is no telling what will happen. This impulse could change the way you see your life. Something is calling to you.

Associated Contexts a) **Big toe/thumb**, MU: in lower trigram: big-toe; in upper trigram: thumb; the big-toe enables the foot to walk, the thumb enables the hand to grasp.

b) **Purpose**, CHIH: focus of mind and heart; will, inclination, resolve. The ideogram: heart and scholar, high inner resolve, or heart and go, inner determination. **Locate(in)**, TSAI: live in, dwell, reside; belong to, involved with, depend on; within. The ideogram: earth and persevere, place on the earth. **Outside**, WAI: outer, exterior, external; people working in places other than their home; unfamiliar, foreign; the upper trigram, as opposed to inside, NEI, the lower.

Six at second

a) **Conjoining one's calves.**
   Pitfall. Residing auspicious.

b) **Although a pitfall, residing auspicious.**
    Yielding, not harming indeed.

Don't get swept off your feet. A hasty move will lead to nothing but trouble. Stay right where you are and you'll soon have what you want.

Associated Contexts a) **Calf,** FEI: muscle of lower leg; rely on; prop, rest.
    Pitfall, HSIUNG: leads away from the experience of meaning; stuck and exposed to danger, unable to take in the situation; flow of life and spirit is blocked; unfortunate, baleful; keyword. **Reside(in),** CHÜ: dwell, live in, stay; sit down, fill an office; settled parts of a country. The ideogram: body and seat.

b) **Although,** SUI: even though, supposing that, if, even if.
    Yield(to), SHUN: give way and bear produce; comply, agree, follow, obey; unresisting, docile, flexible; nourish, provide; the Action of the trigram Field, K'UN: The ideogram: head and current, water flowing from the head of a river, yielding to the banks. **Harm,** HAI: damage, injure, offend; suffer; hurtful, hindrance; fearful, anxious.

   Nine at third

   a) **Conjoining one's thighs.**
       Holding on to one's following.
       Going: distress.

   b) **Conjoining one's thighs.**
       Truly not abiding indeed.
       Purpose located in following people.
       A place to hold on to the below indeed.

You are in danger of becoming obsessive. This will do you no good. Hold on to yourself and what supports you. If you go on running after this, you will simply be covered in distress.

Associated Contexts a) **Thigh,** KU: upper leg that provides power for walking; strands of a rope. **Hold on(to),** CHIH: lay hold of, seize, take in hand; keep, maintain, look after. The ideogram: criminal and seize. **Follow,** SUI: come or go after; pursue, impelled to move; come after in inevitable sequence; move in the same direction, comply with what is ahead; follow a way or religion; according to, next, subsequent. The ideogram: go and fall, unavoidable movement. Image of Hexagram 17.

Go, WANG, and come, LAI, describe the stream of time as it flows from future through present to past; go, WANG, indicates what is departing from present to past; proceed, move on; keyword. **Distress**, LIN: shame, regret, humiliation; aware of having lost the right track; leads to repenting, HUI, correcting the direction of mind and life.

b) **Truly**, YI: statement is true and precise. **Abide**, CH'U: rest in, dwell; stop yourself; arrive at a place or condition; distinguish, decide; do what is proper. The ideogram: tiger, stop and seat, powerful movement coming to rest.

Purpose, CHIH: focus of mind and heart; will, inclination, resolve. The ideogram: heart and scholar, high inner resolve, or heart and go, inner determination. **Locate(in)**, TSAI: live in, dwell, reside; belong to, involved with, depend on; within. The ideogram: earth and persevere, place on the earth.

Nine at fourth

a) Trial: auspicious, repenting extinguished.
    Wavering, wavering: going, coming.
    Partners adhere to simply pondering.

b) Trial: auspicious, repenting extinguished.
    Not yet influencing harming indeed.
    Wavering, wavering: going, coming.
    Not yet the shining great indeed.

Express your aims and desires. This is a very favorable influence. Your sorrow over the past will simply disappear. The way is open. You go back and forth in your thoughts, trying to understand this new feeling. Have no fears. Your friends will be there for you.

Associated Contexts a) **Trial**, CHEN: inquiry by divination and its result; righteous, firm; separating wheat from chaff; the kernel, the proven core; fourth stage of the Time Cycle. The ideogram: pearl and divination. **Repenting extinguished**, HUI WANG: previous troubles and consequent remorse will disappear.

Waver, CH'UNG: irresolute, hesitating; unsettled, disturbed; fluctuate, sway to and fro. The doubled character intensifies this quality. **Come**, LAI, and **go**, WANG, describe the stream of time as it flows from future through present to past. Come, LAI, indicates: what is approaching; move toward, arrive at; go, WANG, indicates: what is departing; proceed, move on; keywords.

Partner, P'ENG: associate for mutual benefit; two equal or similar things; companions, friends, peers; join in; commercial ventures. The ideogram: linked strings of cowries or coins. **Adhere(to),** TS'UNG: follow a way, hold to a doctrine, school, or person; hear and comply with, agree to; forced to follow, follower. The ideogram: two men walking, one following the other. **Simply,** ERH: just so, only. **Ponder,** SSU: reflect, consider, remember; deep thought; desire, wish. The ideogram: heart and field, the heart's concerns.

b) **Not yet,** WEI: temporal negative; something will but has not yet occurred; contrary of already, CHI. Image of Hexagram 64. **Harm,** HAI: damage, injure, offend; suffer; hurtful, hindrance; fearful, anxious.

Shine, KUANG: illuminate; give off brilliant, bright light; honor, glory, éclat; result of action, contrasts with brightness, MING, light of heavenly bodies. The ideogram: fire above person, lifting the light. **Great,** TA: big, noble, important, very; orient the will toward a self-imposed goal, impose direction; ability to lead or guide your life; contrasts with small, HSIAO, flexible adaptation to what crosses your path; keyword. Image of Hexagrams 14, 26, 28, 34.

Nine at fifth

a) Conjoining one's neck.
　Without repenting.

b) Conjoining one's neck.
　Purpose, the tips indeed.

This is a very deep connection that will endure over time. You are feeling the beginnings. This will wipe away past sorrows.

Associated Contexts a) **Neck,** MEI: muscular base of neck, shoulders and arms; source of strength in arms and shoulders; persist.

Without repenting, WU HUI: devoid of the sort of trouble that leads to sorrow, regret and the necessity to change your attitude.

b) **Purpose,** CHIH: focus of mind and heart; will, inclination, resolve. The ideogram: heart and scholar, high inner resolve, or heart and go, inner determination. **Tips,** MO: growing ends, outermost twigs; last, most distant.

Six above

a) **Conjoining one's jawbones, cheeks, tongue.**

b) **Conjoining one's jawbones, cheeks, tongue.**
   The spouting mouth stimulating indeed.

This influence inspires you to burst forth in passionate speech. It may not last long, so be ready to retreat when words run out.

Associated Contexts a) **Jawbones/brace,** FU: support, consolidate, reinforce, strengthen, stiffen, prop up, fix; rigid, steady, firm; help, rescue; support the mouth that speaks. The ideogram: cart and great. **Cheeks,** CHIA: sides of the face; speak, articulate. **Tongue,** SHE: tongue in the mouth; clapper in a bell, valve in a pump, hook of a clasp; talkative, wordy.

b) **Spout,** T'ENG: spurt, burst forth; open mouth, loud talk. **Mouth,** K'OU: literal mouth, words going out and food coming in; entrance, hole.

P E R S E V E R I N G ▮ *H E N G*

Continue, endure; constant, consistent, durable; self-renewing; married couple; understand the signs and omens.

Persevering describes your situation in terms of what continues and endures. Its symbols are the married couple, the boat between two shores and the spirit-medium realizing the significance in an omen. The way to deal with it is to continue on the Way. Be constant, regular, and stable. Persist in your normal way of life and what you feel is right. Make an offering to the spirits. Through it they will give you success, effective power and the capacity to bring things to maturity. Proceeding in this way is not a mistake. Put your ideas and desires to the trial. Impose a direction. Have a place to go. This brings profit and insight.

● *Image of the Situation*

> Persevering, Growing.
> Without fault.
> Advantageous Trial. Harvesting.
> Advantageous to have a direction to go.

Associated Contexts **Persevere**, HENG: continue in the same way or spirit; constant, perpetual, regular; self-renewing; extend everywhere; the moon almost full. **Grow**, HENG: success through a sacrifice; pervade, persevere; bring to full growth; enjoy; vigorous, effective; second stage of the Time Cycle.

Without fault, WU CHIU: no error or harm in the situation.

Advantageous Trial, LI CHEN: advantageous divination; putting the action in question to the test is beneficial, harvesting.

Advantageous/Harvest, LI: advantageous, profitable; acute, insightful; benefit, nourish; third stage of the Time Cycle. **Have a direction to go**, YU YU WANG: imposing a direction on the flow of time from present to past; have a specific goal or purpose.

● *Outer and Inner Aspects*

☷ **Shake:** Thunder rises from below, shaking and stirring things up. **Shake** begins the yang hemicycle by germinating new action.

Connection to the outer: sprouting energies thrusting from below, the Woody Moment beginning. **Shake** stirs things up to issue-forth.

☴ **Ground:** Wind and wood subtly enter from the ground, penetrating and pervading. **Ground** is the center of the yang hemicycle, spreading pervasive action.

Connection to the inner: penetrating and bringing together, the Woody Moment culminating. **Ground** pervades, matches and couples, seeding a new generation.

Inner penetration and coupling provide the basis for dynamic **persevering** in the outer world.

● *Hidden Possibility*

Nuclear trigrams **Open**, TUI, and **Force**, CH'IEN, result in Nuclear Hexagram 43, **Deciding**, KUAI. Lasting cohesion through **persevering** leads to **decisive** action and words.

● *Sequence*

> **Husband and Wife's tao.**
> **Not permitting using not lasting indeed.**
> **Accepting this lets you use Persevering.**
> **Persevering implies lasting indeed.**

Associated Contexts **Husband and Wife**, FU FU: the cooperative effort of man and woman in establishing and maintaining a home. **'s/have(it)/it/them**, CHIH: expresses possession, directly or as an object pronoun. **Tao**: way or path; ongoing process of being and the course it traces for each specific person or thing; keyword. The ideogram: go and head, leading and the path it creates.

Not permitting, PU K'O: not possible; contradicts an inherent principle. The ideogram: mouth and breath, silent consent. **Use(of)**, YI: make use of, by means of, owing to; employ, make functional. **Last**, CHIU: long, protracted; enduring. **Indeed/is/means**, YEH: intensifier, connective; indicates comment on previous statement.

Accepting ... use: activating this hexagram depends on understanding and accepting the previous statement.

Imply, CHE: further signify; additional meaning.

- *Contrasted Definitions*

Conjoining: urging indeed.
Persevering: lasting indeed.

Associated Contexts **Conjoin,** HSIEN: come into contact with, influence; reach, join together; put together as parts of a previously separated whole; come into conjunction, as the celestial bodies; totally, completely; lit.: broken piece of pottery, the halves of which join to identify partners. Image of Hexagram 31. **Urge,** SU: strong specific desire; quick, hurried; call, invite.

- *Attached Evidences*

Persevering: actualizing tao's firmness indeed.
Persevering: variegated and not restricted.
Persevering: using the One to actualize tao.

Associated Contexts **Actualize tao,** TE: realize tao in action; power, virtue; ability to follow the course traced by the ongoing process of the cosmos; keyword. The ideogram: to go, straight, and heart. Linked with acquire, TE: acquiring that which makes a being become what it is meant to be. **Firm,** KU: constant, fixed, steady; chronic, recurrent. The ideogram: old and enclosure, long preserved.

Variegated, TSA: mingled, variegated, mixed; disorder. **Restrict,** YEN: keep in order, maintain discipline; subjugate, repress; narrow, obedient.

One, the one, YI: single unit; number one; undivided, simple, whole; any one of; first, the first.

- *Symbol Tradition*

Thunder, wind, Persevering.
A chün tzu uses establishing, not change on all sides.

Associated Contexts **Thunder,** LEI: rising, arousing power; the Symbol of the trigram Shake, CHEN. **Wind,** FENG: moving air, breeze, gust; weather and its influence on mood and humor; fashion, usage; wind and wood are the Symbols of the trigram Ground, SUN.

Chün tzu: ideal of a person who uses divination to order his/her life in accordance with tao rather than wilful intention; keyword. **Establish,** LI: set up, institute, order, arrange; stand erect; settled principles. **Versatility/change** I: sudden and unpredictable change; mental mobility and openness; easy and light, not difficult and heavy; occurs in name of the I CHING. **Sides (on all sides),** FANG: limits, boundaries; square, surface of the earth extending to the four cardinal points; everywhere.

● *Image Tradition*

Persevering. Lasting indeed. [I]
Above strong and below supple.
Thunder and wind, mutually associating.
Ground and stirring up.
Strong and Supple altogether corresponding. Persevering.

Persevering Growing, without fault. [II]
Advantageous Trial. Harvesting.
Lasting with respect to one's tao indeed.
Heaven and Earth's tao.
Persevering lasting and not climaxing indeed.
Advantageous to have a direction to go.
Completing by consequence possesses a beginning indeed.

Sun and Moon acquiring heaven
and enabling lasting illumination. [III]
The four seasons transform and change and
enable lasting accomplishment.
The all wise person lasting with respect to his tao
and Below Heaven the changes are accomplished.

Viewing one's place to Persevere. [IV]
Actually Heaven and Earth,
and the myriad beings's motives permit seeing.

Associated Contexts [I] **Above,** SHANG: anything above, in all senses; higher, upper, outer; upper trigram; opposite of below, HSIA. **Strong,** KANG: quality of the whole lines; firm, strong, unyielding, persisting. **Below,** HSIA: anything below, in all senses; lower, inner; lower trigram; opposite of above, SHANG. **Supple,** JOU: quality of the opened lines; flexible, pliant, tender, adaptable.

Mutual, HSIANG: reciprocal assistance, encourage, help; bring together, blend with; examine, inspect; by turns. **Associate(with)**, YÜ: consort with, combine; companions; group, band, company; agree with, comply, help. The ideogram: pair of hands reaching downward meets a pair of hands reaching upward, helpful association.

Ground, SUN: base on which things rest; support, foundation; mild, subtly penetrating; nourishing. The ideogram: stand and things arranged on it, the subtle influence of the ground. Image of Hexagram 57. **Stir up**, TUNG: excite, influence, move, affect; work, take action; come out of the egg or the bud; the Action of the trigram Shake, CHEN. The ideogram: strength and heavy, move weighty things.

Strong and Supple, KANG JOU: field of creative tension between the whole and opened lines and their qualities; field of psychic movement. **Altogether**, CHIEH: all, the whole; the same sort, all alike; entirely. **Correspond(to)**, YING: be in agreement or harmony; resonate together, invoke and fulfil each other; answer to, suitable; relation between the lines (1:4, 2:5, 3:6) when they form the pair opened and whole, supple and strong. The ideogram: heart and obey.

[II] With respect to, YÜ: relates to, refers to; hold a position in. **One's/one**, CH'I: third person pronoun; also: it/its, he/his, she/hers, they/theirs. **Heaven and Earth**, T'IEN TI: dynamic relation between the primal powers and the world it produces; cosmos, natural or human world; keyword. **Climax**, YI: come to a high point and stop, bring to an end; use up, lay aside; decline, reject.

Complete, CHUNG: end of a cycle that begins the next; last, whole, all; contrasts with exhaust, CH'IUNG: final end. The ideogram: silk cocoons, follow and ice, winter linking one year with the next. **By consequence(of)**, TSE: very strong connection; reason, cause, result; rule, law, pattern, standard; therefore. **Possess**, YU: in possession of, have, own; opposite of lack, WU. **Begin**, SHIH: commence, start, open; earliest, first; beginning of a time-span, ended by completion, CHUNG. The ideogram: woman and eminent, beginning new life.

[III] Sun and Moon, YIH YÜEH: the two dimensions of calendar time that define any specific moment; time as interlocking cycles. **Acquire**, TE: obtain the desired object; wish for, desire covetously; gains, possessions. The ideogram: go and obstacle, going through obstacles to the goal. **Heaven**, T'IEN: highest; sky, firmament, heavens; power above the human as opposed to earth, TI, below; the Symbol of the trigram Force, CH'IEN. The ideogram: great and the one above. **Able**, NENG: enable; ability, power, skill, art; competent, talented; duty, function, capacity. The ideogram: an animal with strong hooves and bones, able to carry and defend. **Illuminate,** CHAO: shine light on; enlighten, reflect: care for, supervise. The ideogram: fire and brightness.

Four seasons, SSU SHIH: the four dynamic qualities of time that make up the year and the Time Cycle; the right time, in accord with the time; time as sacred; all-encompassing. **Transform,** PIEN: abrupt, radical, fundamental mutation from one state of being to another; transformation of lines in hexagrams; contrasts with change, HUA, gradual metamorphosis. **Change,** HUA: gradual, continuous metamorphosis; influence someone; contrasts with transform, PIEN, sudden mutation. The ideogram: person alive and dead, the life-process. **Accomplish,** CH'ENG: complete, finish, bring about; perfect, full, whole; play your part, do your duty; mature. The ideogram: weapon and man, able to bear arms, thus fully developed.

All wise, SHENG: intuitive universal wisdom; mythical sages; holy, sacred; mark of highest distinction. The ideogram: ear and inform, one who knows all from a single sound. **People, person,** JEN: humans individually and collectively; an individual; humankind. Image of Hexagrams 13 and 37. **Below Heaven,** T'IEN HSIA: the human world, between heaven and earth.

[IV] **View,** KUAN: contemplate, observe from a distance; look at carefully, gaze at; also: a monastery, an observatory; descry, divine through liquid in a cup. The ideogram: see and waterbird, observe through air or water. Image of Hexagram 20. **Place,** SO: where something belongs or comes from; residence, dwelling; habitual focus or object.

Actually, YI: truly, really, at present. The ideogram: a dart and done, strong intention fully expressed. **Myriad,** WAN: countless; many, everyone; lit.: ten thousand. The ideogram: swarm of insects. **Being(s),** WU: creature, thing, any single being; matter, substance, essence; nature of things. **Motive,** CH'ING: true nature; feelings, desires, passions. The ideogram: heart and green, germinated in the heart. **Permit,** K'O: possible because in harmony with an inherent principle. The ideogram: mouth and breath, silent consent. **See,** CHIEN: seeing in all its aspects: vision, being visible, forming mental images; visit, call on, consult. The ideogram: eye above person, active and receptive sight.

● *Transforming Lines*

Initial six

a) **Deepening Persevering, Trial: pitfall.**
No advantageous direction.

b) Deepening Persevering's pitfall.
  Beginning seeking depth indeed.

You are going into this affair too deeply, too soon. This is the wrong way to go about it. The way is closed. No plan or direction can help you.

Associated Contexts a) **Deepen,** CHÜN: jump into deep water; deepen; serious, abstruse. **Trial,** CHEN: inquiry by divination and its result; righteous, firm; separating wheat from chaff; the kernel, the proven core; fourth stage of the Time Cycle. The ideogram: pearl and divination. **Pitfall,** HSIUNG: leads away from the experience of meaning; stuck and exposed to danger, unable to take in the situation; flow of life and spirit is blocked; unfortunate, baleful; keyword.

  No advantageous direction, WU YU LI: no plan or direction is advantageous; in order to take advantage of the situation, do not impose a direction on events.

b) **Seek,** CH'IU: search for, aim at, wish for, desire; implore, supplicate; covetous. **Depth,** SHEN: deep water; profound, abstruse; ardent, strong, intense, inner; sound the depths.

  Nine at second

  a) Repenting extinguished.

  b) Nine at second, repenting extinguished.
    Ability lasting, the center indeed.

If you persevere in what you have established, your cares and sorrows will disappear. Commit yourself. The ability to last and endure will center you.

Associated Contexts a) **Repenting extinguished,** HUI WANG: previous troubles and consequent remorse will disappear.

b) **Center,** CHUNG: inner, central; put in the center; middle, stable point enabling you to face inner and outer changes; middle line of trigram. The ideogram: field divided in two equal parts. Image of Hexagram 61.

  Nine at third

  a) Not Persevering in one's actualizing tao.
    Maybe receiving's embarrassing.
    Trial: distress.

b) Not Persevering in one's actualizing tao.
Without a place to tolerate this indeed.

You are betraying your own promise. Everything you receive will lead to
embarrassment, because you cannot keep your heart steady. Surely you can
do better. This simply should not be tolerated.

Associated Contexts a) **Maybe/"someone"**, HUO: possible but not
certain, perhaps. **Receive**, CH'ENG: receive gifts or commands from superiors
or customers; take in hand; catch falling water. The ideogram: accepting a seal
of office. **Embarrassed**, HSIU: conscious of guilt or fault; unworthy; ashamed,
confused; shy, blushing. The ideogram: sheep, sheepish feeling.

   Trial, CHEN: inquiry by divination and its result; righteous, firm;
separating wheat from chaff; the kernel, the proven core; fourth stage of the
Time Cycle. The ideogram: pearl and divination. **Distress**, LIN: shame,
regret, humiliation; aware of having lost the right track; leads to repenting,
HUI, correcting the direction of mind and life.

b) **Without**, WU: devoid of; -less as suffix. **Tolerate**, JUNG: allow, contain,
endure, bear with; accept graciously. The ideogram: full stream bed,
tolerating and containing.

   Nine at fourth

a) The fields without wildfowl.

b) No lasting whatever in one's situation.
Quietly acquiring the wildfowl indeed.

There is simply nothing in sight, no possibility of a real connection. The
best thing to do is to leave quietly. Then you may find what you need.

Associated Contexts a) **Fields**, T'IEN: cultivated land, plantation; also:
hunting, game in the fields cannot escape the hunt. The ideogram: square
divided into four sections, delineating fields. **Without**, WU: devoid of; -less
as suffix. **Wildfowl**, CH'IN: wild game, all wild and game birds; untamed;
military leaders.

b) **No ... whatever**, FEI: strongest negative; not at all! **Situation**, WEI: place or
seat according to rank; post, position, command; right, proper; established,
arranged. The ideogram: person and stand, servants in their places.

   Quiet/secure, AN: peaceful, still, settled; calm, tranquilize. The
ideogram: woman under a roof, a tranquil home.

Six at fifth

a) Persevering one's actualizing tao.
   Trial: Wife people auspicious.
   The husband, the son: pitfall.

b) Wife people, Trial auspicious.
   Adhering to the one and completing indeed.
   The husband, the son: paring righteously.
   Adhering to the wife: pitfall indeed.

Persevere in your virtue. This is a time of transition. You must choose how to act. If you choose the woman's way, the way is open. Adhere to this one thing. If you choose the man's way, the way closes. You must cut yourself off and leave.

Associated Contexts a) **Trial**, CHEN: inquiry by divination and its result; righteous, firm; separating wheat from chaff; the kernel, the proven core; fourth stage of the Time Cycle. The ideogram: pearl and divination.

   Wife, FU: responsible position of married woman within the household; contrasts with consort, CH'I, her legal position and concubine, CH'IEH, secondary wives. The ideogram: woman, hand and broom, household duties. **Auspicious**, CHI: leads to the experience of meaning; favorable, propitious, advantageous, appropriate; keyword. The ideogram: scholar and mouth, wise words of a sage.

   Husband, FU: household manager; administer with thrift and prudence; responsible for; sustain with your earnings; old enough to assume responsibility; married man. **Son(hood)**, TZU: living up to ideal of ancestors as highest human development; act with concern and reverence; male child; offspring, posterity; seed, kernel, egg; sage, teacher; nadir, deepest point, midnight, mid-winter. **Pitfall**, HSIUNG: leads away from the experience of meaning; stuck and exposed to danger, unable to take in the situation; flow of life and spirit is blocked; unfortunate, baleful; keyword.

b) **Adhere(to)**, TS'UNG: follow a way, hold to a doctrine, school, or person; hear and comply with, agree to; forced to follow, follower. The ideogram: two men walking, one following the other.

   Pare, CHIH: cut away; form, tailor, carve; invent; limit, prevent. The ideogram: knife and incomplete. **Righteous**, TI: proper and just, meets the standards; things in their proper place; the heart that rules itself; upright, moral rule; contrasts with Harvest, LI, advantage or profit.

Six above

a) Rousing Persevering: pitfall.

b) Rousing Persevering located in the above.
The great without achievement indeed.

You won't make anything happen like this. Too much excitement and agitation, trying to drum up support that is not there. You will not achieve great things like this.

Associated Contexts a) **Rouse**, CHEN: stir up, excite, stimulate; issue forth; put in order. The ideogram: hand and shake, shaking things up. **Pitfall**, HSIUNG: leads away from the experience of meaning; stuck and exposed to danger, unable to take in the situation; flow of life and spirit is blocked; unfortunate, baleful; keyword.

b) **Locate(in)**, TSAI: live in, dwell, reside; belong to, involved with, depend on; within. The ideogram: earth and persevere, place on the earth.

Great, TA: big, noble, important, very; orient the will toward a self-imposed goal, impose direction; ability to lead or guide your life; contrasts with small, HSIAO, flexible adaptation to what crosses your path; keyword. Image of Hexagrams 14, 26, 28, 34. **Without**, WU: devoid of; -less as suffix. **Achieve**, KUNG: work done, results; real accomplishment, praise, worth, merit. The ideogram: workman's square and forearm, combining craft and strength.

RETIRING ▌ *TUN*

Withdraw, conceal yourself, pull back; retreat in order to advance later.

Retiring describes your situation in terms of facing conflict and withdrawal. Its symbol is the mountain retreat or shrine. The way to deal with it is to pull back and seclude yourself in order to prepare for a better time. Make an offering and you will succeed. This is pleasing to the spirits. Through it they will give you success, power and the capacity to bring the situation to maturity. Putting your ideas to the trial brings profit and insight. Don't impose yourself on the world. Be small. Adapt to whatever crosses your path.

- *Image of the Situation*

   Retiring, Growing.
   The small: Advantageous Trial. Harvesting.

   Associated Contexts **Retire**, TUN: withdraw; run away, flee; conceal yourself, become obscure, invisible; secluded, non-social. The ideogram: walk and swine (wealth and luck), satisfaction through walking away. **Grow**, HENG: success through a sacrifice; pervade, persevere; bring to full growth; enjoy; vigorous, effective; second stage of the Time Cycle.
   Small, HSIAO: little, common, unimportant; adapting to what crosses your path; ability to move in harmony with the vicissitudes of life; contrasts with great, TA, self-imposed theme or goal; keyword. Image of Hexagrams 9 and 62. **Advantageous Trial**, LI CHEN: advantageous divination; putting the action in question to the test is beneficial; harvesting.

- *Outer and Inner Aspects*

   ☰ **Force**: The force of heaven struggles on, persistent and unwearied; heavenly bodies persist in their orbits. **Force** is the center of the yin hemicycle, completing the formative process.
   Connection to the outer: struggling forces are bound together in dynamic tension, the Metallic Moment culminating. **Force** brings elements to grips, creating enduring relations.

☶ **Bound**: Mountains bound, limit and set a place off, stopping forward movement. **Bound** completes a full yin-yang cycle.

Connection to the inner: accomplishing words, which express things. **Bound** articulates what is complete to suggest what is beginning.

Inner accomplishing draws heaven's creative force into **retiring** from the world.

- *Hidden Possibility*

Nuclear trigrams **Force**, CH'IEN, and **Ground**, SUN, result in Nuclear Hexagram 44, **Coupling**, KOU. **Retiring** from active involvements **couples** you with a creative force.

- *Sequence*

Beings not permitted to use lasting and residing in their place.
Accepting this lets you use Retiring.
Retiring implies withdrawing indeed.

Associated Contexts **Beings not permitted to use ...** : no one is allowed to make use of; nothing can exist by means of. **Last,** CHIU: long, protracted; enduring. **Reside(in),** CHÜ: dwell, live in, stay; sit down, fill an office; settled parts of a country. The ideogram: body and seat. **Their,** CH'I: third person pronoun; also: one/one's, he/his, she/hers, they/theirs, it/its. **Place,** SO: where something belongs or comes from; residence, dwelling; habitual focus or object.

Accepting ... use: activating this hexagram depends on understanding and accepting the previous statement.

Imply, CHE: further signify; additional meaning. **Withdraw(from),** T'UI: draw back, retreat, recede; decline, refuse. **Indeed/is/means,** YEH: intensifier, connective; indicates comment on previous statement.

- *Contrasted Definitions*

Great Invigorating: by consequence stopping.
Retiring: by consequence withdrawing indeed.

Associated Contexts **Great,** TA: big, noble, important, very; orient the will toward a self-imposed goal, impose direction; ability to lead or guide your life; contrasts with small, HSIAO, flexible adaptation to what crosses your path; keyword. **Invigorate,** CHUANG: inspirit, animate; strong, robust;

full grown, flourishing, abundant; attain manhood (at 30); damage through unrestrained strength. The ideogram: strength and scholar, intellectual impact. **Great Invigorating** is the Image of Hexagram 34. **By consequence(of)**, TSE: very strong connection; reason, cause, result; rule, law, pattern, standard; therefore. **Stop**, CHIH: bring or come to a standstill; the Action of the trigram Bound, KEN. The ideogram: a foot stops walking.

● *Symbol Tradition*

> Below heaven possessing mountain. Retiring.
> A chün tzu uses distancing Small People.
> [A chün tzu uses] not hating and intimidating.

Associated Contexts **Below**, HSIA: anything below, in all senses; lower, inner; lower trigram; opposite of above, SHANG. **Heaven**, T'IEN: highest; sky, firmament, heavens; power above the human as opposed to earth, TI, below; the Symbol of the trigram **Force**, CH'IEN. The ideogram: great and the one above. **Possess**, YU: in possession of, have, own; opposite of lack, WU. **Mountain**, SHAN: limit, boundary; the Symbol of the trigram Bound, KEN. The ideogram: three peaks, a mountain range.

 Chün tzu: ideal of a person who uses divination to order his/her life in accordance with tao rather than wilful intention; keyword. **Use(of)**, YI: make use of, by means of, owing to; employ, make functional. **Distance**, YÜAN: far off, remote; keep at a distance; alienated. The ideogram: go and a long way. **Small people**, HSIAO JEN: lowly, common, humble; those who adjust to circumstances with the flexibility of the small; effect of the small within an individual; keyword.

 Hate, WU: dislike, dread; averse to, ashamed of; repulsive, vicious, vile, ugly, wicked. The ideogram: twisted bowels and heart, heart entangled in emotion. **Intimidate**, YEN: inspire with fear or awe; severe, rigid, strict, austere, demanding; a severe father; tight, a closed door.

● *Image Tradition*

> Retiring, Growing. [I]
> Retiring and Growing indeed.
> Strong situation appropriate and corresponding.
> Associating with the season, moving indeed.

The small: Advantageous Trial. [II]
Drenched and long living indeed.
Actually Retiring's season is righteously great in fact.

Associated Contexts **[I] Strong**, KANG: quality of the whole lines; firm, strong, unyielding, persisting. **Appropriate**, TANG: suitable; opportune, convenient; adequate, competent; equal to; whole lines in uneven places and opened lines in even places. **Situation**, WEI: place or seat according to rank; post, position, command; right, proper; established, arranged. The ideogram: person and stand, servants in their places. **Correspond(to)**, YING: be in agreement or harmony; resonate together, invoke and fulfil each other; answer to, suitable; relation between the lines (1:4, 2:5, 3:6) when they form the pair opened and whole, supple and strong. The ideogram: heart and obey.

Associate(with), YÜ: consort with, combine; companions; group, band, company; agree with, comply, help. The ideogram: pair of hands reaching downward meets a pair of hands reaching upward, helpful association. **Season**, SHIH: quality of the time; the right time, opportune, in harmony; planning in accord with the time; seasons of the year. The ideogram: sun and temple, time as sacred. **Move**, HSING: move or move something; motivate, emotionally moving; walk, act, do. The ideogram: stepping left then right.

[II] Drench, CH'IN: soak, penetrate, immerse, steep in; imbued with. **Long living**, CHANG: enduring, constant; senior, superior, greater; increase, prosper; respect, elevate.

Actually ... in fact, YI TSAI: stresses the importance of a statement. The ideogram: a dart and done, strong intention fully expressed. **'s/have(it)/it/them**, CHIH: expresses possession, directly or as an object pronoun. **Righteous**, YI: proper and just, meets the standards; things in their proper place; the heart that rules itself; upright, moral rule; contrasts with Harvest, LI, advantage or profit.

● *Transforming Lines*

   Initial six

   a) Retiring tail, adversity.
      No availing of having a direction to go.

b) **Retiring tail's adversity.**
Not going, wherefore calamity indeed.

You get caught in old plans and old promises. You cannot cut through this yet. Be ready. Have a plan to use when you get a chance.

Associated Contexts a) **Tail**, WEI: animal's tail; last, extreme; remnants, unimportant. **Adversity**, LI: danger; threatening, malevolent demon. This has two aspects: grind, sharpen, improve, perfect, stimulate; and: poisonous, sinister, cruel, contrary. It indicates a spirit or ghost that seeks revenge by inflicting suffering upon the living. Pacifying or exorcizing such a spirit can have a healing effect. The ideogram: sheltering cliff and stinging insect.

Avail of, YUNG: take advantage of; benefit from, profit by; use for a specific purpose; apply to advantage. The ideogram: to divine and center, applying divination to central concerns. **Have a direction to go**, YU YU WANG: imposing a direction on the flow of time from present to past; have a specific goal or purpose.

b) **Go**, WANG, and **come**, LAI, describe the stream of time as it flows from future through present to past; go, WANG, indicates what is departing from present to past; proceed, move on; keyword. **Wherefore**, HO: interrogative: why? for what reason? what is? and affirmation: therefore, for that reason. **Calamity**, TSAI: disaster from outside; flood, plague, drought, blight, ruin; contrasts with blunder, SHENG, indicating personal fault. The ideogram: water and fire, elemental powers.

Six at second

a) **Holding avails of a yellow cow's skin.**
Absolutely nothing can master or loosen it.

b) **Holding avails of the yellow cow.**
Firm purpose indeed.

Held in the yellow cowskin, put on the shaman's mask. This is an inner retreat through which you see into things. Do not let go of what you have seen. It is your purpose and belongs with you. Work with these plans and these people.

Associated Contexts a) **Hold on(to)**, CHIH: lay hold of, seize, take in hand; keep, maintain, look after. The ideogram: criminal and seize. **Avail of**, YUNG: take advantage of; benefit from, profit by; use for a specific purpose; apply to advantage. The ideogram: to divine and center, applying divination to central concerns. **Yellow,** HUANG: color of the productive middle; associated with the Earthy Moment between yang and yin hemicycles; color of soil in central China; emblematic and imperial color of China since the Yellow Emperor (2500 BCE). **Cattle,** NIU: ox, bull, cow, calf; kine; power and strength of work animals. **Skin,** KO: take off the covering, skin or hide; change, renew, molt; remove, peel off; revolt, overthrow, degrade from office; leather armor, protection. Image of Hexagram 49.

Absolutely no(thing), MO: complete elimination; not any, by no means. **Master,** SHENG: have the upper hand, conquer; worthy of, able to; control, check, command. **Stimulate,** SHUO: rouse to action and good feeling; free from constraint, stir up, urge on; persuade, cheer, delight; set out in words; the Action of the trigram Open, TUI. The ideogram: words and exchange.

b) **Firm,** KU: constant, fixed, steady; chronic, recurrent. The ideogram: old and enclosure, long preserved. **Purpose,** CHIH: focus of mind and heart; will, inclination, resolve. The ideogram: heart and scholar, high inner resolve, or heart and go, inner determination.

Nine at third

a) Tied Retiring. Possessing affliction and adversity.
Accumulating servants and concubines, auspicious.

b) Tied Retiring's adversity.
Possessing afflicting weariness indeed.
Accumulating servants and concubines, auspicious.
Not permitting Great Affairs indeed.

Entangled in a web of difficulties, duties and connections, you can't get out of this alone. Let others help you: servants (who carry out orders) and concubines (who create a pleasant mood). Then you can begin to put it all at a distance.

Associated Contexts a) **Tie(to),** HSI: connect, attach to, bind; devoted to; relatives. The ideogram: person and connect, ties between humans. **Afflict,** CHI: sickness, disorder, defect, calamity; injurious; pressure and consequent anger, hate or dislike. The ideogram: sickness and dart, a sudden affliction. **Adversity,** LI: danger; threatening, malevolent demon. This has two aspects: grind, sharpen, improve, perfect, stimulate; and: poisonous, sinister, cruel, contrary. It indicates a spirit or ghost that seeks revenge by inflicting suffering upon the living. Pacifying or exorcizing such a spirit can have a healing effect. The ideogram: sheltering cliff and stinging insect.

Accumulate, CH'U: retain, hoard, gather, herd together; control, restrain; domesticate, tame, train; raise, feed, sustain, bring up. The ideogram: field and black, fertile black soil good for pastures, accumulated through retaining silt. Image of Hexagrams 9 and 26. **Servant**, CH'EN: attendant, minister, vassal; courtier who can speak to the sovereign; wait on, serve in office. The ideogram: person bowing low.

Concubine, CH'IEH: secondary wife taken without ceremony to ensure a male descendant; handmaid. **Auspicious**, CHI: leads to the experience of meaning; favorable, propitious, advantageous, appropriate; keyword. The ideogram: scholar and mouth, wise words of a sage.

b) **Weariness**, PAI: fatigue; debilitated, exhausted, distressed; weak.

Not permitting, PU K'O: not possible; contradicts an inherent principle. The ideogram: mouth and breath, silent consent. **Affairs**, SHIH: all kinds of personal activity; matters at hand; business, occupation; manage a business, case in court.

Nine at fourth

a) Loving Retiring.
   A chün tzu: auspicious.
   Small People: obstructed.

b) A chün tzu lovingly Retiring.
   Small People obstructed indeed.

Goodness and love come through retiring. Think about what you care for. It will open the way. Keep greedy people who are eager to serve you at a distance now.

Associated Contexts a) **Love**, HAO: affection; fond of, take pleasure in; fine, graceful.

Auspicious, CHI: leads to the experience of meaning; favorable, propitious, advantageous, appropriate; keyword. The ideogram: scholar and mouth, wise words of a sage.

Obstruct, P'I: closed, stopped; bar the way; obstacle; unfortunate, wicked; refuse, disapprove, deny. The ideogram: mouth and not, blocked communication. Image of Hexagram 12.

Nine at fifth

a) Excellence Retiring, Trial: auspicious.

b) Excellence Retiring, Trial: auspicious.
　Using correcting the purpose indeed.

Excellence comes through retiring. It will open the way and give you things to do. Have no regrets. The way is open.

Associated Contexts a) **Excellence**, CHIA: superior quality; fine, delicious, glorious; happy, pleased; rejoice in, praise. The ideogram: increasing goodness, pleasure and happiness. **Trial**, CHEN: inquiry by divination and its result; righteous, firm; separating wheat from chaff; the kernel, the proven core; fourth stage of the Time Cycle. The ideogram: pearl and divination. **Auspicious**, CHI: leads to the experience of meaning; favorable, propitious, advantageous, appropriate; keyword. The ideogram: scholar and mouth, wise words of a sage.

b) **Correct**, CHENG: rectify deviation or one-sidedness; proper, straight, exact, regular; constant, rule, model. The ideogram: stop and one, hold to one thing. **Purpose**, CHIH: focus of mind and heart; will, inclination, resolve. The ideogram: heart and scholar, high inner resolve, or heart and go, inner determination.

Nine above

a) Rich Retiring, nothing not advantageous. Harvesting.

b) Rich Retiring, nothing not advantageous.
　Without a place to doubt indeed.

By retiring, you bring wealth and fertility to everything around you. You are doing exactly what is needed and will be very successful at it.

Associated Contexts a) **Rich**, FEI: fertile, abundant, fat; manure, fertilizer. **Nothing not advantageous**, WU PU LI: advantageous nothing for which this will not be beneficial; advantageous potential, borderline where the balance is swinging from not Harvesting to actually Harvesting.

b) **Without**, WU: devoid of; -less as suffix. **Doubt**, YI: suspect, distrust; dubious; surmise, conjecture.

34

GREAT INVIGORATING ▮
TA CHUANG

Great strength and invigoration, a great idea; focus, drive, advance; injury, wound, harm.

Great Invigorating describes your situation in terms of strength and invigorating power. Its symbol is driving or herding animals. The way to deal with it is to focus your strength through a central creative idea. Putting your ideas to the trial will bring profit and insight. Beware of hurting others through excessive use of force.

● *Image of the Situation*

Great Invigorating, Advantageous Trial. Harvesting

Associated Contexts **Great,** TA: big, noble, important, very; orient the will toward a self-imposed goal; impose direction; ability to lead or guide your life; contrasts to small, HSIAO, flexible adaptation to what crosses your path; keyword. **Invigorate,** CHUANG: inspirit, animate; strong, robust; full grown, flourishing, abundant; attain manhood (at 30); damage through unrestrained strength. The ideogram: strength and scholar, intellectual impact. **Advantageous Trial,** LI CHEN: advantageous divination; putting the action in question to the test is beneficial, harvesting.

● *Outer and Inner Aspects*

☳ **Shake:** Thunder rises from below, shaking and stirring things up. **Shake** begins the yang hemicycle by germinating new action.

Connection to the outer: sprouting energies thrusting from below, the Woody Moment beginning. **Shake** stirs things up to issue-forth.

☰ **Force:** The force of heaven struggles on, persistent and unwearied; heavenly bodies persist in their orbits. **Force** is the center of the yin hemicycle, completing the formative process.

Connection to the inner: struggling forces are bound together in dynamic tension, the Metallic Moment culminating. **Force** brings elements to grips, creating enduring relations.

Great inner force is directly expressed through the outward thrust of **invigorating** action.

● *Hidden Possibility*

Nuclear trigrams **Open**, TUI, and **Force**, CH'IEN, result in Nuclear Hexagram 43, **Deciding/Parting**, KUAI. Concentrating effort through **invigorating** the **great** depends on **decisive** action.

● *Sequence*

> Beings not permitted to use completing Retiring.
> Accepting this lets you use Great Invigorating.

Associated Contexts **Beings not permitted to use ...** : no one is allowed to make use of; nothing can exist by means of. **Complete**, CHUNG: end of a cycle that begins the next; last, whole, all; contrasts with exhaust, CH'IUNG: final end. The ideogram: silk cocoons, follow and ice, winter linking one year with the next. **Retire**, TUN: withdraw; run away, flee; conceal yourself, become obscure, invisible; secluded, non-social. The ideogram: walk and swine (wealth and luck), satisfaction through walking away. Image of Hexagram 33.

> **Accepting ... use**: activating this hexagram depends on understanding and accepting the previous statement.

● *Contrasted Definitions*

> Great Invigorating: by consequence stopping.
> Retiring: by consequence withdrawing indeed.

Associated Contexts **By consequence(of)**, TSE: very strong connection; reason, cause, result; rule, law, pattern, standard; therefore. **Stop**, CHIH: bring or come to a standstill; the Action of the trigram Bound, KEN. The ideogram: a foot stops walking.

> **Withdraw(from)**, T'UI: draw back, retreat, recede; decline, refuse. **Indeed**, YEH: intensifier; indicates comment on previous statement.

● *Symbol Tradition*

> Thunder located above heaven. Great Invigorating.
> A chün tzu uses no codes whatever, nowhere treading.

Associated Contexts **Thunder,** LEI: rising, arousing power; the Symbol of the trigram Shake, CHEN. **Locate(in),** TSAI: live in, dwell, reside; belong to, involved with, depend on; within. The ideogram: earth and persevere, place on the earth. **Above,** SHANG: anything above, in all senses; higher, upper, outer; upper trigram; opposite of below, HSIA. **Heaven,** T'IEN: highest; sky, firmament, heavens; power above the human as opposed to earth, TI, below; the Symbol of the trigram Force, CH'IEN. The ideogram: great and the one above.

Chün tzu: ideal of a person who uses divination to order his/her life in accordance with tao rather than wilful intention; keyword. **Use(of),** YI: make use of, by means of, owing to; employ, make functional. **No ... whatever,** FEI: strongest negative; not at all! **Codes,** LI: rites, rules, ritual; usage, manners; worship, ceremony, observance. The ideogram: worship and sacrificial vase, handling a sacred vessel. **Nothing/nowhere,** FU: strong negative; not a single thing/place. **Tread,** LÜ: step, path, track; footsteps; walk a path or way; course of the stars; act, practice; conduct; salary, means of subsistence. The ideogram: body and repeating steps, following a trail. Image of Hexagram 10.

●   *Image Tradition*

> Great Invigorating. The Great implies Invigorating indeed. [I]
> Strong uses stirring up. Anterior Invigorating.

> Great Invigorating, Advantageous Trial. [II]
> The Great implies correcting indeed.
> Actually correcting the Great
> permits seeing Heaven and Earth's motives.

Associated Contexts **[I] Imply,** CHE: further signify; additional meaning.

Strong, KANG: quality of the whole lines; firm, strong, unyielding, persisting. **Stir up,** TUNG: excite, influence, move, affect; work, take action; come out of the egg or the bud; the Action of the trigram Shake, CHEN. The ideogram: strength and heavy, move weighty things. **Anterior,** KU: come before as cause; formerly, ancient; reason, purpose, intention; grievance, quarrel, dissatisfaction, sorrow, mourning resulting from previous causes and intentions; situation leading to a divination.

[II] Correct, CHENG: rectify deviation or one-sidedness; proper, straight, exact, regular; constant, rule, model. The ideogram: stop and one, hold to one thing.

Actually, YI: truly, really, at present. The ideogram: a dart and done, strong intention fully expressed. **Heaven and Earth**, T'IEN TI: dynamic relation between the primal powers and the world it produces; cosmos, natural or human world; keyword. **'s/have(it)/it/them**, CHIH: expresses possession, directly or as an object pronoun. **Motive**, CH'ING: true nature; feelings, desires, passions. The ideogram: heart and green, germinated in the heart. **Permit**, K'O: possible because in harmony with an inherent principle. The ideogram: mouth and breath, silent consent. **See**, CHIEN: seeing in all its aspects: vision, being visible, forming mental images; visit, call on, consult. The ideogram: eye above person, active and receptive sight.

● *Transforming Lines*

Initial nine

a) **Invigorating in the feet.**
Chastising: pitfall, there is a connection to the spirits.

b) **Invigorating in the feet.**
One's connection exhausted indeed.

You are out to conquer the world. Hold back just a moment. Don't try to tell other people what to do and don't set out on any adventurous expeditions. The spirits are with you, but start slowly.

Associated Contexts a) **Foot**, CHIH: literal foot; foundation, base.

Chastise, CHENG: punish, subjugate, discipline; reduce to order; punishing expedition. The ideogram: step and correct, a rectifying move. **Pitfall**, HSIUNG: leads away from the experience of meaning; stuck and exposed to danger, unable to take in the situation; flow of life and spirit is blocked; unfortunate, baleful; keyword. **There is ... spirits**, YU FU: inner and outer are in accord; confidence of the spirits has been captured; sincere, truthful; proper to take action.

b) **One's/one**, CH'I: third person pronoun; also: it/its, he/his, she/hers, they/theirs. **Exhaust**, CH'IUNG: bring to an end; limit, extremity; destitute; investigate exhaustively; end without a new beginning. The ideogram: cave and naked person, bent with disease or old age.

Nine at second

a) Trial: auspicious.

b) Nine at second, Trial: auspicious.
  Using centering indeed.

This is using the center. Whatever you want to do will be successful. This begins a flourishing time.

Associated Contexts a) **Trial,** CHEN: inquiry by divination and its result; righteous, firm; separating wheat from chaff; the kernel, the proven core; fourth stage of the Time Cycle. The ideogram: pearl and divination. **Auspicious,** CHI: leads to the experience of meaning; favorable, propitious, advantageous, appropriate; keyword. The ideogram: scholar and mouth, wise words of a sage.

b) **Center,** CHUNG: inner, central; put in the center; middle, stable point enabling you to face inner and outer changes; middle line of trigram. The ideogram: field divided in two equal parts. Image of Hexagram 61.

Nine at third

a) Small People avail of Invigorating.
  A chün tzu avails of a net.
  Trial: adversity.
  The he goat butts a hedge, ruining his horns.

b) Small People avail of Invigorating.
  A chün tzu: a net indeed.

You are trying to catch something. Don't force it. Use strategy and an open heart rather than aggression. You are confronting some troublesome past experiences. If you use force, like the aggressive ram you will only get yourself entangled.

Associated Contexts a) **Small People,** HSIAO JEN: lowly, common, humble; those who adjust to circumstances with the flexibility of the small; effect of the small within an individual; keyword. **Avail of,** YUNG: take advantage of; benefit from, profit by; use for a specific purpose; apply to advantage. The ideogram: to divine and center, applying divination to central concerns. **Net,** WANG: emptiness, vacancy; lit.: a net, open spaces between threads. The ideogram: net and lost, empty spaces divide what is kept from what is lost.

Trial, CHEN: inquiry by divination and its result; righteous, firm; separating wheat from chaff; the kernel, the proven core; fourth stage of the Time Cycle. The ideogram: pearl and divination. **Adversity**, LI: danger; threatening, malevolent demon. This has two aspects: grind, sharpen, improve, perfect, stimulate; and: poisonous, sinister, cruel, contrary. It indicates a spirit or ghost that seeks revenge by inflicting suffering upon the living. Pacifying or exorcizing such a spirit can have a healing effect. The ideogram: sheltering cliff and stinging insect.

He goat, TI YANG: ram or buck; three-year-old male at peak of strength. **Butt**, CHU: push or strike with the horns; attack, oppose, offend; stirred up, excited; obnoxious; associated with the Woody Moment. **Hedge**, FAN: row of bushes, fence, boundary; protect, fend off, enclose.

Ruin, LEI: destroy, break, overturn; debilitated, meager, emaciated; entangled. **His/he**, CH'I: third person pronoun; also: one/one's, it/its, she/hers, they/theirs. **Horns**, CHIO: strength and power; gore; dispute, test your strength; headland.

Nine at fourth

a) Trial: auspicious.
　Repenting extinguished.
　The hedge broken up, not ruined.
　Invigorating in the Great cart's axle straps.

b) The hedge broken up, not ruined.
　Honoring and going indeed.

The obstacle vanishes and together you can do what you want. The past simply disappears. There is nothing holding you back. Attack. Put your shoulders to the wheel and do the great things that are in you to do.

Associated Contexts a) **Trial**, CHEN: inquiry by divination and its result; righteous, firm; separating wheat from chaff; the kernel, the proven core; fourth stage of the Time Cycle. The ideogram: pearl and divination. **Auspicious**, CHI: leads to the experience of meaning; favorable, propitious, advantageous, appropriate; keyword. The ideogram: scholar and mouth, wise words of a sage.

Repenting extinguished, HUI WANG: previous troubles and consequent remorse will disappear.

Hedge, FAN: row of bushes, fence, boundary; protect, fend off, enclose. **Break up**, CHÜEH: streams diverging; break through an obstacle and scatter; separate, break into parts; cut or bite through; decide, pass sentence.

The ideogram: water and parting. **Ruin**, LEI: destroy, break, overturn; debilitated, meager, emaciated; entangled.

Cart, YÜ: carrying capacity of a vehicle; contain, hold, sustain. **Axle strap**, FU: fastens the body of a cart to axle and wheels.

b) **Honor**, SHANG: esteem, give high rank to; eminent; put one thing on top of another. **Go**, WANG, and **come**, LAI, describe the stream of time as it flows from future through present to past; go, WANG, indicates what is departing from present to past; proceed, move on; keyword.

Six at fifth

a) Losing the goat, through versatility.
   Without repenting.

b) Losing the goat through versatility.
   Situation not appropriate indeed.

Let go of forward drive. Change your considerable strength into imagination. Don't always charge into obstacles. There are more interesting ways to deal with things. If you realize this, your sorrows will simply disappear.

Associated Contexts a) **Lose**, SANG: fail to obtain, cease, become obscure; forgotten, destroyed; lament, mourn; funeral. The ideogram: weep and the dead. **Goat**, YANG: sheep and goats; direct thought and action. **Versatility/change**, I: sudden and unpredictable change; mental mobility and openness; easy and light, not difficult and heavy; occurs in name of the I CHING.

Without repenting, WU HUI: devoid of the sort of trouble that leads to sorrow, regret and the necessity to change your attitude.

b) **Situation**, WEI: place or seat according to rank; post, position, command; right, proper; established, arranged. The ideogram: person and stand, servants in their places. **Appropriate**, TANG: suitable; opportune, convenient; adequate, competent; equal to; whole lines in uneven places and opened lines in even places.

Six above

a) The he goat butts a hedge.
   Not enabling withdrawing, not enabling releasing.
   No advantageous direction.
   Drudgery by consequence auspicious.

b) Not enabling withdrawing, not enabling releasing.
Not ruminating indeed.
Drudgery by consequence auspicious.
Fault not long living indeed.

You are stuck and in for a bit of hard work. You can't force your way out of this one. Just sit there and go through the painful analysis of your mistakes. As you do this, the way will open of itself.

Associated Contexts a) **He goat,** TI YANG: ram or buck; three-year-old male at peak of strength. **Butt,** CHU: push or strike with the horns; attack, oppose, offend; stirred up, excited; obnoxious; associated with the Woody Moment. **Hedge,** FAN: row of bushes, fence, boundary; protect, fend off, enclose.

Able, NENG: enable; ability, power, skill, art; competent, talented; duty, function, capacity. The ideogram: an animal with strong hooves and bones, able to carry and defend. **Release,** SUI: loose, let go, free; unhindered, in accord; follow, spread out, progress; penetrate, invade. The ideogram: go and follow your wishes, unimpeded movement.

No advantageous direction, WU YU LI: no plan or direction is advantageous; in order to take advantage of the situation, do not impose a direction on events.

Drudgery, CHIEN: difficult, hard, repetitive work; hard to cultivate; distressing, sorrowful. The ideogram: sticky earth and a person looking around, hard work in comparison to others. **Auspicious,** CHI: leads to the experience of meaning; favorable, propitious, advantageous, appropriate; keyword. The ideogram: scholar and mouth, wise words of a sage.

b) **Ruminate,** HSIANG: ponder and discuss; examine minutely, learn fully, watch over, pay attention to. The ideogram: word and sheep, ruminating on words.

Fault, CHIU: unworthy conduct that leads to harm, illness, misfortune. The ideogram: person and differ, differ from what you should be. **Long living,** CHANG: enduring, constant; senior, superior, greater; increase, prosper; respect, elevate.

PROSPERING ▪ *CHIN*

Emerge into the light; advance, be noticed; give and receive gifts; dawn of a new day.

Prospering describes your situation in terms of emerging slowly and surely into the full light of day. Its symbols are the rising sun and the recognition of the able person. The way to deal with it is to give freely in order to help things emerge and flourish. Be calm in your strength and poise. Take delight in things. Give gifts of strength and spirit to enhance those connected with you. You will be received by the higher powers three times in a single day.

● *Image of the Situation*

> **Prospering, the calm feudatory**
> **avails of bestowing horses, multiplying in multitudes.**
> **A day's sun: three times an audience.**

Associated Contexts **Prosper,** CHIN: grow and flourish, as young plants in the sun; increase, progress, permeate, impregnate; attached to. The ideogram: sun and reach, the daylight world. **Calm,** K'ANG: confident strength and poise; stability, peace, ease; joy, delight. **Feudatory,** HOU: nobles entrusted with governing the provinces; active in daily life rather than governing from the center; contrasts with prince, KUNG, executives at the court. **Avail of,** YUNG: take advantage of; benefit from, profit by; use for a specific purpose; apply to advantage. The ideogram: to divine and center, applying divination to central concerns. **Bestow,** HSI: grant, confer upon; reward, gift. The ideogram: metal used in coins and insignia. **Horse,** MA: symbol of spirited strength in the natural world, counterpart of dragon, LUNG; associated with the trigram Force, CH'IEN, heaven, T'IEN, and high noon. **Multiply,** FAN: augment, enhance, increase; thriving, plentiful. **Multitude,** SHU: the people; mass, herd; all, the whole.

Day time, CHOU: daylight half of 24-hour cycle. **Sun/day,** JIH: actual sun and the time of a sun-cycle, a day. **Three times,** SAN: serial repetition. **Audience,** CHIEH: received by the higher powers; follow in office; inherit, as father and son; associate with. The ideogram: hand and concubine, received into the court.

● *Outer and Inner Aspects*

☲ **Radiance**: Fire and brightness radiate light and warmth, attached to their support; congregating people see and become aware. **Radiance** ends the yang hemicycle, consuming action in awareness.

Connection to the outer: light, heat, consciousness bring continual change, the Fiery Moment. **Radiance** spreads outward, congregating, becoming aware and changing.

☷ **Field**: The field of earth yields and sustains, serving in order to produce. **Field** is the equalizing point between yin and yang where things labor and serve.

Connection to the inner: the common labor of sowing and hoarding, the Earthy Moment. **Field** produces concrete results through serving.

Spreading outer light fertilizes the inner field, whose yielding service in turn spreads **prospering**.

● *Hidden Possibility*

Nuclear trigrams **Gorge**, K'AN, and **Bound**, KEN, result in Nuclear Hexagram 39, **Difficulties**, CHIEN. **Prospering's** flourishing brightness lets you re-imagine a **difficult** situation.

● *Sequence*

> **Beings not permitted to use completing Invigorating.**
> **Accepting this lets you use Prospering.**
> **Prospering implies advancing indeed.**

Associated Contexts **Beings not permitted to use ...** : no one is allowed to make use of; nothing can exist by means of. **Complete**, CHUNG: end of a cycle that begins the next; last, whole, all; contrasts with exhaust, CH'IUNG: final end. The ideogram: silk cocoons, follow and ice, winter linking one year with the next. **Invigorate**, CHUANG: inspirit, animate; strong, robust; full grown, flourishing, abundant; attain manhood (at 30); damage through unrestrained strength. The ideogram: strength and scholar, intellectual impact. Image of Hexagram 34.

Accepting ... use: activating this hexagram depends on understanding and accepting the previous statement.

Imply, CHE: further signify; additional meaning. **Advance**, CHIN: exert yourself, make progress, climb; be promoted; further the development of, augment; adopt a religion or conviction; offer, introduce. **Indeed/is/means**: YEH: intensifier, connector; indicates comment on previous statement.

- *Contrasted Definitions*

    Prospering: day time indeed.
    Brightness Hiding: proscribed indeed.

    Associated Contexts **Brightness**, MING: light-giving aspect of burning, heavenly bodies and consciousness; with fire, the Symbol of the trigram Radiance, LI. **Hide, YI**: keep out of sight; remote, distant from the center; equalize by lowering; squat, level, make ordinary; pacified, colorless; cut, wound, destroy, exterminate. **Brightness Hiding** is the Image of Hexagram 36. **Proscribe**, CHU: exclude, reject by proclamation; denounce, forbid; reprove, seek as a criminal; condemn to death; clear away.

- *Symbol Tradition*

    Brightness issuing forth above earth. Prospering.
    A chün tzu uses originating enlightening
    to brighten actualizing tao.

    Associated Contexts **Issue forth(from)**, CH'U: emerge from, come out of, proceed from, spring from; the Action of the trigram Shake, CHEN; contrary of enter, JU. The ideogram: stem with branches and leaves emerging. **Above**, SHANG: anything above, in all senses; higher, upper, outer; upper trigram; opposite of below, HSIA. **Earth**, TI: ground on which the human world rests; basis of all things, nourishes all things; the Symbol of the trigram Field, K'UN.

    Chün tzu: ideal of a person who uses divination to order his/her life in accordance with tao rather than wilful intention; keyword. **Use(of)**, YI: make use of, by means of, owing to; employ, make functional. **Origin**, TZU: source, beginning, ground; cause, reason, motive; line of descent; path to the origin; yourself, intrinsic. **Enlighten**, CHAO: cast light on, display, show; instruct, give knowledge; manifest, bright, splendid. The ideogram: sun and call, bring into the light. **Actualize tao**, TE: realize tao in action; power, virtue; ability to follow the course traced by the ongoing process of the cosmos; keyword. The ideogram: to go, straight, and heart. Linked with acquire, TE: acquiring that which makes a being become what it is meant to be.

• *Image Tradition*

> Prospering. Advancing indeed. [I]
> Brightness issuing forth above earth.
> Yielding and congregating reaches to great brightening.
>
> Supple advancing and moving above. [II]
> That uses the calm feudatory
> to avail of bestowing horses multiplying in multitudes.
> A day's sun three times an audience indeed.

Associated Contexts [I] **Yield(to)**, SHUN: give way and bear produce; comply, agree, follow, obey; unresisting, docile, flexible; nourish, provide; the Action of the trigram Field, K'UN. The ideogram: head and current, water flowing from the head of a river, yielding to the banks. **Congregate,** LI: cling together; depend on, attached to, rely on; couple, pair, herd; the Action of the trigram Radiance, LI. The ideogram: deer flocking together. **Reach(to)**, HU: arrive at a goal; reach towards and achieve; connect; contrasts with tend-towards, YU. **Great**, TA: big, noble, important, very; orient the will toward a self-imposed goal, impose direction; ability to lead or guide your life; contrasts with small, HSIAO, flexible adaptation to what crosses your path; keyword. Image of Hexagrams 14, 26, 28, 34.

[II] **Supple**, JOU: quality of the opened lines; flexible, pliant, tender, adaptable. **Move,** HSING: move or move something; motivate, emotionally moving; walk, act, do. The ideogram: stepping left then right.

That uses, SHIH YI: involves and is involved by.

• *Transforming Lines*

> Initial six
>
> *a)* Prospering thus, arresting thus.
>   Trial: auspicious. A net of connections.
>   Enriching, without fault.
>
> *b)* Prospering thus, arresting thus.
>   Solitary moving correcting indeed.
>   Enriching, without fault.
>   Not yet acquiescing in fate indeed.

Emerging, you are held back. Don't worry. You are connected through a net of spiritual relations. Advance vigorously. This situation will enrich you. It is definitely not a mistake.

Associated Contexts a) **Thus ... thus,** JU ... JU: when there is one thing, then there must be the second thing. **Arrest,** TS'UI: stop, drive back, repress; force obedience, overpower, impel; scorn; destroy, break.

Trial, CHEN: inquiry by divination and its result; righteous, firm; separating wheat from chaff; the kernel, the proven core; fourth stage of the Time Cycle. The ideogram: pearl and divination. **Auspicious,** CHI: leads to the experience of meaning; favorable, propitious, advantageous, appropriate; keyword. The ideogram: scholar and mouth, wise words of a sage.

Net, WANG: emptiness, vacancy; lit.: a net, open spaces between threads; used as a negative. The ideogram: net and lost, empty spaces divide what is kept from what is lost. **Connection,** FU: accord between inner and outer in a particular moment; sincere, truthful, verified, reliable, in accord with the spirits; capture; prisoners, spoils; contrasts with trustworthy, HSIN, consistent over time. The ideogram: bird's claw enclosing young animals, possessive grip. Image of Hexagram 61.

Enrich, YÜ: make richer (excluding land); material, mental or spiritual wealth; bequeath; generous, abundant. The ideogram: garments, portable riches. **Without fault,** WU CHIU: no error or harm in the situation.

b) **Solitary,** TI: alone, single; isolated, abandoned. **Correct,** CHENG: rectify deviation or one-sidedness; proper, straight, exact, regular; constant, rule, model. The ideogram: stop and one, hold to one thing.

Not yet, WEI: temporal negative; something will but has not yet occurred; contrary of already, CHI. Image of Hexagram 64. **Acquiesce(in),** SHOU: accept, make peace with, agree to; at rest, satisfied; patient. **Fate/Mandate,** MING: individual destiny; birth and death as limits of life; issue orders with authority; consult the gods. The ideogram: mouth and order, words with heavenly authority.

Six at second

a) Prospering thus, apprehensive thus.
  Trial: auspicious.
  Accept the closely woven chain mail
  and blessing of one's kingly mother.

b) Accepting the closely woven chain mail and blessing.
  Using centering and correcting indeed.

You set out, but feel anxious and sorrowful. Don't worry. The way is open. Take on this task and receive the Queen Mother's blessing.

Associated Contexts a) **Thus ... thus**, JU ... JU: when there is one thing, then there must be the second thing. **Apprehensive**, CH'OU: anticipating adversity, afraid of what approaches; chagrined, grieved. The ideogram: heart and autumn, dreading the coming winter.

Trial, CHEN: inquiry by divination and its result; righteous, firm; separating wheat from chaff; the kernel, the proven core; fourth stage of the Time Cycle. The ideogram: pearl and divination. **Auspicious**, CHI: leads to the experience of meaning; favorable, propitious, advantageous, appropriate; keyword. The ideogram: scholar and mouth, wise words of a sage.

Accept, SHOU: accept, make peace with, agree to; at rest, satisfied; patient. **Closely woven**, TZU: compact, close textured, dense, strong, impenetrable. The ideogram: herbs and silk, dense fabric or foliage. **Chain mail/limit**, CHIEH: chain-armor; tortoise or crab shell; protective covering; border, limit; protection, support. **Bless**, FU: heavenly gifts; make happy; spiritual power and goodwill. The ideogram: spirit and plenty, heavenly gifts in abundance.

One's/one, CH'I: third person pronoun; also: it/its, he/his, she/hers, they/theirs. **King(hood)**, WANG: effective ruler, by authority of the Emperor, from whom others derive their power. **Mother(hood)**, MU: child-bearing and nourishing. The ideogram: two breasts.

b) **Centering correcting**, CHUNG CHENG: central and correct; make rectifying one-sidedness and error your central concern; reaching a stable center in yourself can correct the situation.

Six at third

a) Crowds, sincerity, repenting extinguished.

b) Crowds: sincerity's purpose.
   Moving above indeed.

Everything is in order. People have confidence in you. Don't hold back. Give of yourself unstintingly. Your sorrows will vanish.

Associated Contexts a) **Crowds**, CHUNG: many people, large group; majority; in common. **Sincere**, YÜN: true, honest, loyal; according to the facts; have confidence in, permit, assent. The ideogram: vapor rising, words directed upwards. **Repenting extinguished**, HUI WANG: previous troubles and consequent remorse will disappear.

b) **'s/have(it)/it/them**, CHIH: expresses possession, directly or as an object pronoun. **Purpose**, CHIH: focus of mind and heart; will, inclination, resolve. The ideogram: heart and scholar, high inner resolve, or heart and go, inner determination.

Nine at fourth

a) **Prospering, thus bushy tailed rodents.**
  Trial: adversity.

b) **Bushy tailed rodents, Trial: adversity.**
  Situation not appropriate indeed.

You are being timid, furtive and scattered. Thus as you prosper, greedy people and bad memories may attack you. Make a bold move. Don't give up what you know is right.

Associated Contexts a) **Thus**, JU: as, in this way. **Bushy tailed rodent**, SHIH SHU: timid, fearful; mean, thieving people; skulking, mournful, brooding.

Trial, CHEN: inquiry by divination and its result; righteous, firm; separating wheat from chaff; the kernel, the proven core; fourth stage of the Time Cycle. The ideogram: pearl and divination. **Adversity**, LI: danger; threatening, malevolent demon. This has two aspects: grind, sharpen, improve, perfect, stimulate; and: poisonous, sinister, cruel, contrary. It indicates a spirit or ghost that seeks revenge by inflicting suffering upon the living. Pacifying or exorcizing such a spirit can have a healing effect. The ideogram: sheltering cliff and stinging insect.

b) **Situation**, WEI: place or seat according to rank; post, position, command; right, proper; established, arranged. The ideogram: person and stand, servants in their places. **Appropriate**, TANG: suitable; opportune, convenient; adequate, competent; equal to; whole lines in uneven places and opened lines in even places.

Six at fifth

a) **Repenting extinguished.**
  Letting go, acquiring, no cares.
  Going auspicious, nothing not advantageous.

b) **Letting go, acquiring, no cares.**
  Going possesses reward indeed.

All your sorrows will vanish. Don't worry about anything; simply give yourself to the work. The way is open and the time is right. Everything will benefit from this endeavor.

Associated Contexts a) **Repenting extinguished**, HUI WANG: previous troubles and consequent remorse will disappear.

Let go, SHIH: lose, omit, miss, fail, let slip; out of control. The ideogram: drop from the hand. **Acquire**, TE: obtain the desired object; wish for, desire covetously; gains, possessions. The ideogram: go and obstacle, going through obstacles to the goal. **Care**, HSÜ: fear, doubt, concern; heartfelt attachment; relieve, soothe, aid; sympathy, compassion, consolation. The ideogram: heart and blood, the heart's blood affected.

Go, WANG, and **come**, LAI, describe the stream of time as it flows from future through present to past; go, WANG, indicates what is departing from present to past; proceed, move on; keyword. **Auspicious**, CHI: leads to the experience of meaning; favorable, propitious, advantageous, appropriate; keyword. The ideogram: scholar and mouth, wise words of a sage. **Nothing not advantageous**, WU PU LI: nothing for which this will not be beneficial; advantageous potential, borderline where the balance is swinging from not Harvesting to actually Harvesting.

b) **Possess**, YU: in possession of, have, own; opposite of lack, WU. **Reward**, CH'ING: gift given from gratitude or benevolence; favour from heaven; congratulate with gifts. The ideogram: heart, follow and deer (wealth), the heart expressed through gifts.

Nine above

a) **Prospering with one's horns.**
   Hold fast to avail of subjugating the capital.
   Adversity auspicious, without fault.

b) **Holding fast to avail of subjugating the capital.**
   Tao not yet shining indeed.

You can control the situation through direct action. Hold fast and deal with your own troubles first. You have to confront the negative images you have of things. This is difficult, but it opens the way. Though you may feel distressed, this is not a mistake. Attack and take the capital city.

Associated Contexts a) **One's/one**, CH'I: third person pronoun; also: it/its, he/his, she/hers, they/theirs. **Horns**, CHIO: strength and power; gore; dispute, test your strength; headland.

Hold fast, WEI: hold together; tie to, connect; reins, net. **Subjugate,** FA: chastise rebels, make dependent; cut down, subject to rule. The ideogram: man and lance, armed soldiers. **Capital,** YI: populous fortified city, center and symbol of the domain it rules. The ideogram: enclosure and official seal.

Adversity, LI: danger; threatening, malevolent demon. This has two aspects: grind, sharpen, improve, perfect, stimulate; and: poisonous, sinister, cruel, contrary. It indicates a spirit or ghost that seeks revenge by inflicting suffering upon the living. Pacifying or exorcizing such a spirit can have a healing effect. The ideogram: sheltering cliff and stinging insect. **Auspicious,** CHI: leads to the experience of meaning; favorable, propitious, advantageous, appropriate; keyword. The ideogram: scholar and mouth, wise words of a sage. **Without fault,** WU CHIU: no error or harm in the situation.

b) **Tao**: way or path; ongoing process of being and the course it traces for each specific person or thing; keyword. The ideogram: go and head, leading and the path it creates. **Not yet,** WEI: temporal negative; something will but has not yet occurred; contrary of already, CHI. Image of Hexagram 64. **Shine,** KUANG: illuminate; give off brilliant, bright light; honor, glory, éclat; result of action, contrasts with brightness, MING, light of heavenly bodies. The ideogram: fire above person, lifting the light.

36

BRIGHTNESS HIDING ∎
MING YI

Hide your light; protect yourself; accept and begin a difficult task; hidden positive influences.

Brightness Hiding describes your situation in terms of entering the darkness to protect yourself, or to begin a difficult new endeavor. Its symbols are the setting sun and travelling through the demon's country. The way to deal with it is to hide your light. Conceal your intelligence by voluntarily entering what is beneath you, like the sun as it sets in the evening. There is a real possibility of injury in the situation. By dimming the light of your awareness and entering the darkness you can avoid being hurt. You have the chance to release yourself from your problems and inaugurate a new time. Putting your ideas to the trial by accepting drudgery and difficulty will bring you profit and insight.

- *Image of the Situation*

    Brightness Hiding, Harvesting. Trial: drudgery advantageous.

    Associated Contexts **Brightness**, MING: light-giving aspect of burning, heavenly bodies and consciousness; with fire, the Symbol of the trigram Radiance, LI. **Hide**, YI: keep out of sight; remote, distant from the center; equalize by lowering; squat, level, make ordinary; pacified, colorless; cut, wound, destroy, exterminate. **Advantageous/Harvest**, LI: advantageous, profitable; acute, insightful; benefit, nourish; third stage of the Time Cycle. **Drudgery**, CHIEN: difficult, hard, repetitive work; hard to cultivate; distressing, sorrowful. The ideogram: sticky earth and a person looking around, hard work in comparison to others. **Trial**, CHEN: inquiry by divination and its result; righteous, firm; separating wheat from chaff; the kernel, the proven core; fourth stage of the Time Cycle. The ideogram: pearl and divination.

- *Outer and Inner Aspects*

    ☷ **Field**: The field of earth yields and sustains, serving in order to

produce. **Field** is the equalizing point between yin and yang where things labor and serve.

Connection to the outer: the common labor of sowing and hoarding, the Earthy Moment. **Field** produces concrete results through serving.

☲ **Radiance**: Fire and brightness radiate light and warmth, attached to their support; congregating people see and become aware. **Radiance** ends the yang hemicycle, consuming action in awareness.

Connection to the inner: light, heat, consciousness bring about continual change, the Fiery Moment. **Radiance** spreads outward, congregating, becoming aware and changing.

Congregating with what is below the common earth **hides brightness** and awareness.

- *Hidden Possibility*

Nuclear trigrams **Shake**, CHEN, and **Gorge**, K'AN, result in Nuclear Hexagram 40, **Loosening**, HSIEH. Dimming the intelligence when **brightness hides** leads to **loosening** and liberating bound energy.

- *Sequence*

> Advancing there is necessarily a place to be injured.
> Accepting this lets you use Brightness Hiding.
> Hiding implies injury.

Associated Contexts **Advance**, CHIN: exert yourself, make progress, climb; be promoted; further the development of, augment; adopt a religion or conviction; offer, introduce. **Necessarily**, PI: unavoidably, indispensably, certainly. **Possess there is**, YU: in possession of, have, own; opposite of lack, WU. **Place**, SO: where something belongs or comes from; residence, dwelling; habitual focus or object. **Injure**, SHANG: hurt, wound, grieve, distress; mourn, sad at heart, humiliated.

Accepting ... use: activating this hexagram depends on understanding and accepting the previous statement.

Imply, CHE: further signify; additional meaning.

- *Contrasted Definitions*

> Prospering: day time indeed.
> Brightness Hiding: proscribed indeed.

Associated Contexts **Prospering,** CHIN: grow and flourish as young plants in the sun; increase, progress, permeate, impregnate; attached to. The ideogram: sun and reaching, the daylight world. Image of Hexagram 35. **Day time,** CHOU: daylight half of 24-hour cycle. **Indeed/is/means:** YEH: intensifier, connective; indicates comment on previous statement.

Proscribe, CHU: exclude, reject by proclamation; denounce, forbid; reprove, seek as a criminal; condemn to death; clear away.

● *Symbol Tradition*

> Brightness entering earth center. Brightness Hiding.
> A chün tzu uses supervising the crowds
> to avail of darkening and Brightening.

Associated Contexts **Enter,** JU: penetrate, go into, enter on, progress; put into, encroach on; the Action of the trigram Ground, SUN, contrary of issue-forth, CH'U. **Earth,** TI: ground on which the human world rests; basis of all things, nourishes all things; the Symbol of the trigram Field, K'UN. **Center,** CHUNG: inner, central; put in the center; middle, stable point enabling you to face inner and outer changes; middle line of trigram. The ideogram: field divided in two equal parts. Image of Hexagram 61.

Chün tzu: ideal of a person who uses divination to order his/her life in accordance with tao rather than wilful intention; keyword. **Use(of),** YI: make use of, by means of, owing to; employ, make functional. **Supervise,** LI: oversee, inspect, administer; visit subordinates; headquarters. **Crowds,** CHUNG: many people, large group; majority; in common. **Avail of,** YUNG: take advantage of; benefit from, profit by; use for a specific purpose; apply to advantage. The ideogram: to divine and center, applying divination to central concerns. **Darken,** HUI: make or become dark; last day of the moon; obscure, night, mist.

● *Image Tradition*

> Brightness entering earth center. Brightness Hiding. [I]
> Inside pattern Brightening and outside supple yielding.

> Using the enveloped great heaviness. [II]
> The pattern king used it.
> Harvesting Trial: drudgery advantageous.
> Darkening one's Brightness indeed.

Inside heaviness and the ability to correct one's purpose. [III]
The winnowing son used it.

Associated Contexts [I] **Inside**, NEI: within, inner, interior; inside of
the house and those who work there, particularly women; the lower trigram,
as opposed to outside, WAI, the upper. The ideogram: border and enter,
cross a border. **Pattern**, WEN: intrinsic or natural design and its beauty;
stylish, elegant; noble; contrasts with composition, CHANG, a conscious
creation. **Outside**, WAI: outer, exterior, external; people working in places
other than their home; unfamiliar, foreign; the upper trigram, as opposed to
inside, NEI, the lower. **Supple**, JOU: quality of the opened lines; flexible,
pliant, tender, adaptable. **Yield(to)**, SHUN: give way and bear produce;
comply, agree, follow, obey; unresisting, docile, flexible; nourish, provide;
the Action of the trigram Field, K'UN: The ideogram: head and current,
water flowing from the head of a river, yielding to the banks.

[II] **Envelop**, MENG: cover, pull over, hide, conceal; lid or cover; clouded
awareness, dull; ignorance, immaturity; unseen beginnings. The ideogram:
plant and covered, hidden growth. Image of Hexagram 4. **Great**, TA: big,
noble, important, very; orient the will toward a self-imposed goal, impose
direction; ability to lead or guide your life; contrasts with small, HSIAO,
flexible adaptation to what crosses your path; keyword. Image of
Hexagrams 14, 26, 28, 34. **Heavy**, NAN: arduous, grievous, difficult;
hardship, distress; harass; contrasts with versatile, I, deal lightly with. The
ideogram: domestic bird with clipped tail and drying sticky earth.

King(hood), WANG: effective ruler, by authority of the Emperor, from
whom others derive their power. **It/them/have(it)/'s**, CHIH: expresses
possession, directly or as an object pronoun.

One's/one, CH'I: third person pronoun; also: it/its, he/his, she/hers,
they/theirs.

[III] **Able**, NENG: enable; ability, power, skill, art; competent, talented;
duty, function, capacity. The ideogram: an animal with strong hooves and
bones, able to carry and defend. **Correct**, CHENG: rectify deviation or one-
sidedness; proper, straight, exact, regular; constant, rule, model. The
ideogram: stop and one, hold to one thing. **Purpose**, CHIH: focus of mind
and heart; will, inclination, resolve. The ideogram: heart and scholar, high
inner resolve, or heart and go, inner determination.

Winnow, CHI: separate grain from chaff by tossing it in the wind;
separate the valuable from the worthless, good from bad; sieve, winnowing-
basket; fan out. **Son(hood)**, TZU: living up to ideal of ancestors as highest

human development; act with concern and reverence; male child; offspring, posterity; seed, kernel, egg; sage, teacher; nadir, deepest point, midnight, mid-winter.

This text evokes the troubled time at the end of the Shang Dynasty (1100 BCE) when the figures who were to found the new Chou Dynasty were oppressed or held captive.

The Pattern King is King Wen, a pattern of justice and wisdom and a master diviner. He was the founding figure of the new Chou dynasty and was imprisoned by the last Shang tyrant for his outspoken rectitude.

The Winnowing Son is Prince Chi, a model of moral discrimination. As a diviner serving the last Shang tyrant, he shone like a light in the darkness. He refused to serve the new Dynasty, but passed on his wisdom and experience of ritual. He thus carefully discriminated between moral integrity and personal advantage.

Legend has it that Keng Wen and Prince Chi composed the fundamental texts of the I CHING.

● *Transforming Lines*

Initial nine

a) **Brightness Hiding in flight.**
   Drooping one's wings.
   A chün tzu moving:
   Three days, not eating.
   Have a direction to go.
   A lord: the people possess words.

b) **A chün tzu moving:**
   Righteously not eating indeed.

You are escaping from an impossible situation, embarked on a dangerous and important mission. Have courage and stamina. Have a plan. You can convince people of anything if you master your words.

Associated Contexts a) **Fly**, FEI: spread your wings, fly away; let free; swift.

   Droop, CH'UI: hang down, let fall; bow; condescend to inferiors; almost, near; suspended; hand down from past to future. **Wings**, YI: birds' wings; sails, flanks, side-rooms; brood over, shelter and defend.

   Move, HSING: move or move something; motivate, emotionally

moving; walk, act, do. The ideogram: stepping left then right.

Three, SAN: number three, third time or place; active phases of a cycle; superlative; beginning of repetition. **Day/sun**, JIH: actual sun and the time of a sun-cycle, a day. **Eat**, SHIH: eat, ingest, swallow, devour; incorporate, take in.

Have a direction to go, YU YU WANG: imposing a direction on the flow of time from present to past; have a specific goal or purpose.

Lord, CHU: ruler, master, chief; authority. The ideogram: lamp and flame, giving light. **People, person**, JEN: humans individually and collectively; an individual; humankind. Image of Hexagrams 13 and 37. **Word**, YEN: speech, spoken words, sayings; talk, discuss, address. The ideogram: mouth and rising vapor, words as speech.

b) **Righteous**, YI: proper and just, meets the standards; things in their proper place; the heart that rules itself; upright, moral rule; contrasts with Harvest, LI, advantage or profit.

Six at second

a) Brightness Hiding. Injured in the left thigh.
　Avail of a rescuing horse, invigorating auspicious.

b) Six at second's auspiciousness.
　Yielding used by consequence indeed.

This is a serious but not deadly wound. You can deal with it. Mobilize your spirit. Come to the rescue. If you can invigorate your imaginative power the way will open and you will free yourself and your loved ones.

Associated Contexts a) **Left**, TSO: left side, left hand; secondary; deputy, assistant; inferior. **Thigh**, KU: upper leg that provides power for walking; strands of a rope.

Rescue, CHENG: aid, deliver from trouble; pull out, raise up, lift. The ideogram: hand and aid, a helping hand. **Horse**, MA: symbol of spirited strength in the natural world, counterpart of dragon, LUNG; associated with the trigram Force, CH'IEN, heaven, T'IEN, and high noon. **Invigorate**, CHUANG: inspirit, animate; strong, robust; full grown, flourishing, abundant; attain manhood (at 30); damage through unrestrained strength. The ideogram: strength and scholar, intellectual impact. Image of Hexagram 34. **Auspicious**, CHI: leads to the experience of meaning; favorable, propitious, advantageous, appropriate; keyword. The ideogram: scholar and mouth, wise words of a sage.

b) 's/have(it)/it/them, CHIH: expresses possession, directly or as an object pronoun. **By consequence(of)**, TSE: very strong connection; reason, cause, result; rule, law, pattern, standard; therefore.

Nine at third

a) Brightness Hiding in the Southern hunt.
Acquiring its great, head.
Not permitting affliction: Trial.

b) The South: hounding's purpose.
Thereupon acquiring the great indeed.

In the midst of very considerable difficulties, you find the central illusion that is causing this chaos. Though it may act slowly, this will release you from the pain and sadness that afflict you. It lets you open your heart once more.

Associated Contexts a) **South**, NAN: corresponds to summer, Growing, and the Fiery Moment; end of the yang hemicycle; reference point of compass; rulers face South, thus true principles and correct decisions. **Hunt**, SHOU: hunt with dogs; annual winter hunt; military expedition, pursue closely, press hard; burn dry fields to drive game; inspect the frontiers.

Acquire, TE: obtain the desired object; wish for, desire covetously; gains, possessions. The ideogram: go and obstacle, going through obstacles to the goal. **Its/it**, CH'I: third person pronoun; also: one/one's, he/his, she/hers, they/theirs. **Head**, SHOU: literal head; leader, foremost; subject headings; beginning, model; superior, upper, front.

Not permitting, PU K'O: not possible; contradicts an inherent principle. The ideogram: mouth and breath, silent consent. **Afflict**, CHI: sickness, disorder, defect, calamity; injurious; pressure and consequent anger, hate or dislike. The ideogram: sickness and dart, a sudden affliction.

b) **Thereupon**, NAI: on that ground, because of.

Six at fourth

a) Entering into the left belly.
Catching Brightness Hiding's heart.
Issue forth from the gate chambers.

b) Entering into the left belly.
Catching the heart and intention indeed.

Get out of this terrible place. Take aggressive action. Go right to the heart of it and reclaim your lost intelligence. Leave this situation and don't come back.

Associated Contexts a) **Left belly**, TSO FU: the belly contains the internal organs; also: middle, thick, substantial; intimate, dear; left belly holds the heart and spleen, organs considered the seat of emotional drives.

Catch, HUO: take in hunt; catch a thief; obtain, seize; hit the mark, opportune moment; prisoner, spoils, prey; slave, servant. **Heart**, HSIN: heart as center of being; seat of mind's images and affections; moral nature; source of desires, intentions, will.

Issue forth(from), CH'U: emerge from, come out of, proceed from, spring from; the Action of the trigram Shake, CHEN; contrary of enter, JU. The ideogram: stem with branches and leaves emerging. **Gate**, MEN: outer door, between court-yard and street; text or master as gate to a school of thought. **Chambers**, T'ING: family room, courtyard, hall; domestic. The ideogram: shelter and hall, a secure place.

b) **Intention**, YI: thought, meaning, idea, will, motive; what gives words their significance. The ideogram: heart and sound, heartfelt expression.

Six at fifth

a) Winnowing Son's Brightness Hiding.
Advantageous Trial. Harvesting.

b) Winnowing Son's Trial.
Brightness not permitted to pause indeed.

You have to pretend to be a part of this situation. Disguise yourself. Don't lose your integrity. You will survive. This will bring you profit and insight in the end. Be clear about what is really happening.

Associated Contexts a) **'s/have(it)/it/them**, CHIH: expresses possession, directly or as an object pronoun.

Advantageous Trial LI CHEN: advantageous divination; fruit of an action is a test or trial, harvesting.

b) **Not permitting**, PU K'O: not possible; contradicts an inherent principle. The ideogram: mouth and breath, silent consent. **Pause**, HSI: stop and rest, repose; breathe, a breathing-spell; suspended.

Six above

a) Not Brightening, darkening.
Initially mounting to heaven.
Afterwards entering into earth.

b) Initially mounting to heaven.
Illuminating the four cities indeed.
Afterwards entering into earth.
Letting go by consequence indeed.

This cycle is over. The tyrant falls. The darkening ends and you are free. Life once more comes forth from hardship. Think about this set of events and how it started. Can you understand why? There is a lesson to be learned.

Associated Contexts a) **Initial**, CH'U: first step or part; beginning, incipient; bottom line of hexagram. The ideogram: knife and garment, cutting out the pattern. **Mount**, TENG: ascend, step up; ripen, complete. **Heaven**, T'IEN: highest; sky, firmament, heavens; power above the human as opposed to earth, TI, below; the Symbol of the trigram Force, CH'IEN. The ideogram: great and the one above.

After(wards)/later, HOU: come after in time, subsequent; put oneself after; the second; attendants, heirs, successors, posterity.

b) **Illuminate**, CHAO: shine light on; enlighten, reflect: care for, supervise. The ideogram: fire and brightness. **Four**, SSU: number four, fourth; everywhere, all around; the earth with four sides, FANG. **City**, KUO: area of only human constructions; political unit, polis. First of the territorial zones: city, suburbs, countryside, forests.

Let go, SHIH: lose, omit, miss, fail, let slip; out of control. The ideogram: drop from the hand. **By consequence(of)**, TSE: very strong connection; reason, cause, result; rule, law, pattern, standard; therefore.

37

DWELLING PEOPLE ▋
CHIA JEN

Hold together, family, clan, intimate group; support, nourish, stay in your group; people who live and work together.

Dwelling People describes your situation in terms of living and working with others. Its symbols are the hearth fire, the husband and wife who tend it and the extended family dwelling. The way to deal with it is to care for your relationship with the people who share your space and your activities. Take care of the dwelling and what is within it. Profit and insight come through the woman and through a flexible, nourishing attitude. Dwell in the yin.

● *Image of the Situation*

Dwelling People, Trial: the woman is advantageous. Harvesting.

Associated Contexts **Dwell**, CHI: home, house, household, family; domestic, within doors; live in. The ideogram: roof and pig or dog, the most valued domestic animals. **People, person**, JEN: humans individually and collectively; an individual; humankind. **Advantageous/Harvest**, LI: advantageous, profitable; acute, insightful; benefit, nourish; third stage of the Time Cycle. **Woman(hood)**, NÜ: a woman; what is inherently female. **Trial**, CHEN: inquiry by divination and its result; righteous, firm; separating wheat from chaff; the kernel, the proven core; fourth stage of the Time Cycle. The ideogram: pearl and divination.

● *Outer and Inner Aspects*

☴ **Ground**: Wind and wood subtly enter from the ground, penetrating and pervading. **Ground** is the center of the yang hemicycle, spreading pervasive action.

Connection to the outer: penetrating and bringing together, the Woody Moment culminating. **Ground** pervades, matches and couples, seeding a new generation.

☲ **Radiance**: Fire and brightness radiate light and warmth, attached to their support; congregating people see and become aware. **Radiance** ends the yang hemicycle, consuming action in awareness.

Connection to the inner: light, heat, consciousness bring about continual change, the Fiery Moment. **Radiance** spreads outward, congregating, becoming aware and changing.

Warm awareness inside the **dwelling** brings **people** together through gentle penetration.

- *Hidden   Possibility*

Nuclear trigrams **Radiance**, LI, and **Gorge**, K'AN, result in Nuclear Hexagram 64, **Not yet Fording**, WEI CHI. **People's** sense of being in the right place in their **dwelling** allows you to gather energy for an important new move.

- *Sequence*

> Injury with respect to the outside
> necessarily implies reversing with respect to the Dwelling.
> Accepting this lets you use Dwelling People.

Associated Contexts **Injure**, SHANG: hurt, wound, grieve, distress; mourn, sad at heart, humiliated. **With respect to,** YÜ: relates to, refers to; hold a position in. **Outside,** WAI: outer, exterior, external; people working in places other than their home; unfamiliar, foreign; the upper trigram, as opposed to inside, NEI, the lower. **Imply,** CHE: further signify; additional meaning. **Necessarily,** PI: unavoidably, indispensably, certainly. **Reverse,** FAN: turn and move in the opposite direction; turn around or upside down (180 degrees); change to the opposite position; contrary.

Accepting ... use: activating this hexagram depends on understanding and accepting the previous statement.

- *Contrasted   Definitions*

> Diverging: outside indeed.
> Dwelling People: inside indeed.

Associated Contexts **Diverge**, K'UEI: separate, oppose; contrary, mutually exclusive; distant from, absent, remote; animosity, anger; astronomical or polar opposition: the ends of an axis, 180 degrees apart. Image of Hexagram 38. **Indeed/is/means,** YEH: intensifier, connective;

indicates comment on previous statement.

Inside, NEI: within, inner, interior; inside of the house and those who work there, particularly women; the lower trigram, as opposed to outside, WAI, the upper. The ideogram: border and enter, cross a border.

● *Symbol Tradition*

> Wind originating from fire issues forth. Dwelling People.
> A chün tzu uses words to possess beings
> and movement to possess perseverance.

Associated Contexts **Wind**, FENG: moving air, breeze, gust; weather and its influence on mood and humor; fashion, usage; wind and wood are the Symbols of the trigram Ground, SUN. **Origin**, TZU: source, beginning, ground; cause, reason, motive; line of descent; path to the origin; yourself, intrinsic. **Fire**, HUO: warming and consuming aspect of burning; fire and brightness are the Symbols of the trigram Radiance, LI. **Issue forth(from)**, CH'U: emerge from, come out of, proceed from, spring from; the Action of the trigram Shake, CHEN; contrary of enter, JU. The ideogram: stem with branches and leaves emerging.

Chün tzu: ideal of a person who uses divination to order his/her life in accordance with tao rather than wilful intention; keyword. **Use(of)**, YI: make use of, by means of, owing to; employ, make functional. **Word**, YEN: speech, spoken words, sayings; talk, discuss, address. The ideogram: mouth and rising vapor, words as speech. **Possess**, YU: in possession of, have, own; opposite of lack, WU. **Being(s)**, WU: creature, thing, any single being; matter, substance, essence; nature of things. **Move**, HSING: move or move something; motivate, emotionally moving; walk, act, do. The ideogram: stepping left then right. **Persevere**, HENG: continue in the same way or spirit; constant, perpetual, regular; self-renewing; extend everywhere. Image of Hexagram 32.

● *Image Tradition*

> Dwelling People. [I]
> The woman correcting the situation reaching to the inside.
> The man correcting the situation reaching to the outside.
> Man and Woman correcting.
> Heaven and Earth's great righteousness indeed.

Dwelling People possess an intimidating chief in truth. [II]
This means Father and Mother's designating.
The father, a father. The son, a son.
The senior, a senior. The junior, a junior.
The husband, a husband. The wife, a wife.
And Dwelling tao is corrected.
Actually correct the Dwelling and Below Heaven is set right.

Associated Contexts [I] **Correct**, CHENG: rectify deviation or one-sidedness; proper, straight, exact, regular; constant, rule, model. The ideogram: stop and one, hold to one thing. **Situation**, WEI: place or seat according to rank; post, position, command; right, proper; established, arranged. The ideogram: person and stand, servants in their places. **Reach(to)**, HU: arrive at a goal; reach towards and achieve; connect.

Man(hood), NAN: a man; what is inherently male. The ideogram: fields and strength, hard labor in the fields.

Man and Woman, NAN NÜ: creative relation between what is inherently male and what is inherently female.

Heaven and Earth, T'IEN TI: dynamic relation between the primal powers and the world it produces; cosmos, natural or human world; keyword. **'s/have(it)/it/them**, CHIH: expresses possession, directly or as an object pronoun. **Great**, TA: big, noble, important, very; orient the will toward a self-imposed goal, impose direction; ability to lead or guide your life; contrasts with small, HSIAO, flexible adaptation to what crosses your path; keyword. Image of Hexagrams 14, 26, 28, 34. **Righteous**, YI: proper and just, meets the standards; things in their proper place; the heart that rules itself; upright, moral rule; contrasts with Harvest, LI, advantage or profit.

[II] **Intimidate**, YEN: inspire with fear or awe; severe, rigid, strict, austere, demanding; a severe father; tight, a closed door. **Chief**, CHÜN: effective ruler; preside over, take the lead; influence others; term of respect. The ideogram: mouth and director, giving orders. **In truth**, YEN: statement is complete and correct.

Father and Mother, FU MU: cooperative relation between man and woman in ruling and caring for a family. **Designate**, WEI: represent in words, assign a name or meaning; report on, talk about. The ideogram: words and belly, describing the essential.

Father, FU: ruler of the family; act as a father, paternal, patriarchal; authoritative rule. The ideogram: hand and rod, the chastising father. **Son(hood)**, TZU: living up to ideal of ancestors as highest human

development; act with concern and reverence; male child; offspring, posterity; seed, kernel, egg; sage, teacher; nadir, deepest point, midnight, mid-winter.

Senior, HSIUNG: elder; recognized as one to whom respect is due. **Junior**, TI: younger relatives who owe respect to their elders.

Husband, FU: household manager; administer with thrift and prudence; responsible for; sustain with your earnings; old enough to assume responsibility; married man. **Wife**, FU: responsible position of married woman within the household; contrasts with consort, CH'I, her legal position and concubine, CH'IEH, secondary wives. The ideogram: woman, hand and broom, household duties.

Tao: way or path; ongoing process of being and the course it traces for each specific person or thing; keyword. The ideogram: go and head, leading and the path it creates.

Actually, YI: truly, really, at present. The ideogram: a dart and done, strong intention fully expressed. **Below Heaven**, T'IEN HSIA: the human world, between heaven and earth. **Set right**, TING: settle, fix, put in place; at rest, repose.

● *Transforming Lines*

Initial nine

a) Enclosing: possessing a Dwelling.
Repenting extinguished.

b) Enclosing: possessing a Dwelling.
Purpose not yet transformed indeed.

Stay inside your group of friends and co-workers. Don't take chances now. Your sorrows will disappear. You are not ready to act yet. Through this enclosure you create the sense of the secure group.

Associated Contexts a) **Enclose**, HSIEN: put inside a fence or barrier; restrain, obstruct, forbid; pen, corral.

Repenting extinguished, HUI WANG: previous troubles and consequent remorse will disappear.

b) **Purpose**, CHIH: focus of mind and heart; will, inclination, resolve. The ideogram: heart and scholar, high inner resolve, or heart and go, inner determination. **Not yet**, WEI: temporal negative; something will but has not yet occurred; contrary of already, CHI. Image of Hexagram 64. **Transform,** PIEN: abrupt, radical, fundamental mutation from one state of being to another; transformation of lines in hexagrams; contrasts with change, HUA, gradual metamorphosis.

Six at second

a) **Without direction, releasing.**
Located in the center, feeding.
Trial: auspicious.

b) **Six at second's auspiciousness.**
Yielding uses Ground indeed.

You and your work are the center of this group. Give open-handedly. Don't impose yourself on anyone. Help and nourish the others in your group. This will open the way for all of you.

Associated Contexts a) **Without,** WU: devoid of; -less as suffix. **Direct,** YU: move toward a specific place or goal; have a focus. The ideogram: person moving through or over water, direction without visible landmarks. **Release,** SUI: loose, let go, free; unhindered, in accord; follow, spread out, progress; penetrate, invade. The ideogram: go and follow your wishes, unimpeded movement.

Locate(in), TSAI: live in, dwell, reside; belong to, involved with, depend on; within. The ideogram: earth and persevere, place on the earth. **Center,** CHUNG: inner, central; put in the center; middle, stable point enabling you to face inner and outer changes; middle line of trigram. The ideogram: field divided in two equal parts. Image of Hexagram 61. **Feed,** K'UEI: prepare and present food; provisions.

Auspicious, CHI: leads to the experience of meaning; favorable, propitious, advantageous, appropriate; keyword. The ideogram: scholar and mouth, wise words of a sage.

b) **Yield(to),** SHUN: give way and bear produce; comply, agree, follow, obey; unresisting, docile, flexible; nourish, provide; the Action of the trigram Field, K'UN. The ideogram: head and current, water flowing from the head of a river, yielding to the banks. **Ground,** SUN: base on which things rest; support, foundation; mild, subtly penetrating; nourishing. The ideogram: stand and things arranged on it, the subtle influence of the ground. Image of Hexagram 57.

Nine at third

a) Dwelling People, scolding, scolding:
Repenting adversity auspicious.
The wife, the son, giggling, giggling:
Completing: distress.

b) Dwelling People, scolding, scolding:
Not yet letting it go indeed.
The wife, the son, giggling, giggling:
Letting go articulating the Dwelling indeed.

Make sure your house is in order and that people know their places and roles. It may be time to move. Don't just let things slide by. The confrontation isn't easy, but facing old habits will open the way. This calls for honest repentance of past mistakes, cleaning house, opening the heart. If you simply let things go on, everything will be confused. Take charge! Articulate relations clearly.

Associated Contexts a) **Scold**, HO: rebuke, blame, demand and enforce obedience; severe, stern. The doubled character intensifies this quality.

Repent, HUI: dissatisfaction with past conduct causing a change of heart; proceeds from abashment, LIN, shame and confusion at having lost the right way. **Adversity**, LI: danger; threatening, malevolent demon. This has two aspects: grind, sharpen, improve, perfect, stimulate; and: poisonous, sinister, cruel, contrary. It indicates a spirit or ghost that seeks revenge by inflicting suffering upon the living. Pacifying or exorcizing such a spirit can have a healing effect. The ideogram: sheltering cliff and stinging insect. **Auspicious**, CHI: leads to the experience of meaning; favorable, propitious, advantageous, appropriate; keyword. The ideogram: scholar and mouth, wise words of a sage.

Giggle, HSI: laugh or titter uncontrollably; merriment, delight, surprise; foolish.

Complete, CHUNG: end of a cycle that begins the next; last, whole, all; contrasts with exhaust, CH'IUNG: final end. The ideogram: silk cocoons, follow and ice, winter linking one year with the next. **Distress**, LIN: distress, shame, regret, humiliation; aware of having lost the right track; leads to repenting, HUI, correcting the direction of mind and life.

b) **Not yet**, WEI: temporal negative; something will but has not yet occurred; contrary of already, CHI. Image of Hexagram 64. **Let go**, SHIH: lose, omit, miss, fail, let slip; out of control. The ideogram: drop from the hand.

Articulate, CHIEH: separate and distinguish, as well as join, different things; express thought through speech; joint, section, chapter, interval, unit of time; zodiacal sign; moderate, regulate; lit.: nodes on bamboo stalks. Image of Hexagram 60.

Six at fourth

a) **Affluence Dwelling, great auspiciousness.**

b) **Affluence Dwelling, great auspiciousness.
Yielding located in the situation indeed.**

Wealth and family connections. Goodness, riches and happiness will flow in this dwelling. The way is open. Make this abundance serve a real purpose.

Associated Contexts a) **Affluence**, FU: rich, abundant; wealth; enrich, provide for; flow toward, accrue. **Auspicious**, CHI: leads to the experience of meaning; favorable, propitious, advantageous, appropriate; keyword. The ideogram: scholar and mouth, wise words of a sage.

b) **Yield(to)**, SHUN: give way and bear produce; comply, agree, follow, obey; unresisting, docile, flexible; nourish, provide; the Action of the trigram Field, K'UN. The ideogram: head and current, water flowing from the head of a river, yielding to the banks. **Locate(in)**, TSAI: live in, dwell, reside; belong to, involved with, depend on; within. The ideogram: earth and persevere, place on the earth.

Nine at fifth

a) **The king imagines possessing a Dwelling.
Beings care auspicious.**

b) **The king imagines possessing a Dwelling.
Mingling mutual affection indeed.**

You can create a world around you like a temple or a house of the spirit. Act from your heart. Try to help others. Your care for other people will open the way.

Associated Contexts a) **King(hood)**, WANG: effective ruler, by authority of the Emperor, from whom others derive their power. **Imagine**, CHIA: create in the mind; fantasize, suppose, pretend, imitate; fiction;

illusory, unreal; costume. The ideogram: person and borrow.

Care, HSÜ: fear, doubt, concern; heartfelt attachment; relieve, soothe, aid; sympathy, compassion, consolation. The ideogram: heart and blood, the heart's blood affected. **Auspicious**, CHI: leads to the experience of meaning; favorable, propitious, advantageous, appropriate; keyword. The ideogram: scholar and mouth, wise words of a sage.

b) **Mingle**, CHIAO: blend with, communicate, join, exchange; trade, business; copulation; friendship. **Mutual**, HSIANG: reciprocal assistance, encourage, help; bring together, blend with; examine, inspect; by turns. **Affection**, AI: love, show affection; benevolent feelings; kindness, regard.

   Nine above

   a) There is a connection to the spirits, impressing thus.
      Completing auspicious.

   b) Impressing thus, having auspiciousness.
      Reversing individuality's designation indeed.

Whatever you want to do is possible. You have the intelligence to carry all before you. Act on your desires. Do what you need to do. The way is open. The spirits are with you.

Associated Contexts a) **There is … spirits**, YU FU: inner and outer are in accord; confidence of the spirits has been captured; sincere, truthful; proper to take action. **Impress**, WEI: impose on, intimidate; august, solemn; pomp, majesty. **Thus**, JU: as, in this way.

   Complete, CHUNG: end of a cycle that begins the next; last, whole, all; contrasts with exhaust, CH'IUNG, final end. The ideogram: silk cocoons, follow and ice, winter linking one year with the next. **Auspicious**, CHI: leads to the experience of meaning; favorable, propitious, advantageous, appropriate; keyword. The ideogram: scholar and mouth, wise words of a sage.

b) **Individuality**, SHEN: total person: psyche, body and lifespan; character, virtue, duty; contrasts with body, KUNG, physical being.

DIVERGING ▮ *K'UEI*

Opposition, discord, conflicting purposes; outside the norms, outcast; strange meetings with spirits and ghosts; change conflict to creative tension through awareness.

Diverging describes your situation in terms of opposition and discord. Its symbol is strife in the home and the outcast, alone and outside the norms. The way to deal with it is to change potential conflict into dynamic tension. Separate and clarify what is in conflict while acknowledging the essential connection. Small things are important now. Be flexible and adaptable in all your affairs. That generates meaning and good fortune by releasing transformative energy. Be open to strange occurrences, sudden visions and non-normal ways of seeing things.

● *Image of the Situation*

Diverging, Small Affairs auspicious.

Associated Contexts **Diverging**, K'UEI: separate, oppose; contrary, mutually exclusive; distant from, absent, remote; animosity, anger; astronomical or polar opposition: the ends of an axis, 180 degrees apart. **Small**, HSIAO: little, common, unimportant; adapting to what crosses your path; ability to move in harmony with the vicissitudes of life; contrasts with great, TA, self-imposed theme or goal; keyword. Image of Hexagrams 9 and 62. **Affairs**, SHIH: all kinds of personal activity; matters at hand; business, occupation; manage a business, case in court. **Auspicious**, CHI: leads to the experience of meaning; favorable, propitious, advantageous, appropriate; keyword. The ideogram: scholar and mouth, wise words of a sage.

● *Outer and Inner Aspects*

☲ **Radiance:** Fire and brightness radiate light and warmth, attached to their support; congregating people see and become aware. **Radiance** ends the yang hemicycle, consuming action in awareness.
  Connection to the outer: light, heat, consciousness bring continual

change, the Fiery Moment. **Radiance** spreads outward, congregating, becoming aware and changing.

☱ **Open**: vapor rising from the marsh's open surface stimulates and fertilizes; stimulating words cheer and inspire. **Open** begins the yin hemicycle by initiating the formative process.

Connection to the inner: liquifying, casting, skinning off the mold, the Metallic Moment beginning. **Open** stimulates, cheers and reveals innate form.

The conflict between inner form and outer radiance **polarizes** relationships.

- *Hidden Possibility*

Nuclear trigrams **Gorge**, K'AN, and **Radiance**, LI, result in Nuclear Hexagram 63, **Already Fording**, CHI CHI. The opposition in diverging **already** contains the possibility of resolution.

- *Sequence*

> Dwelling tao exhausted, you necessarily turn away.
> Accepting this lets you use Diverging.
> Diverging implies turning away indeed.

Associated Contexts **Dwell**, CHI: home, house, household, family; domestic, within doors; live in. The ideogram: roof and pig or dog, the most valued domestic animals. Image of Hexagram 37. **Tao**: way or path; ongoing process of being and the course it traces for each specific person or thing; keyword. The ideogram: go and head, leading and the path it creates. **Exhaust**, CH'IUNG: bring to an end; limit, extremity; destitute; investigate exhaustively; end without a new beginning. The ideogram: cave and naked person, bent with disease or old age. **Necessarily**, PI: unavoidably, indispensably, certainly. **Turn away**, KUAI: turn your back on something and focus on its opposite; contradict, cross purposes; cunning, crafty; perverse; contrasts with return, FU, going back to the start.

Accepting ... use: activating this hexagram depends on understanding and accepting the previous statement.

Imply, CHE: further signify; additional meaning. **Indeed/is/means**, YEH: intensifier, connective; indicates comment on previous statement.

● *Contrasted Definitions*

> Diverging: outside indeed.
> Dwelling People: inside indeed.

Associated Contexts **Outside,** WAI: outer, exterior, external; people working in places other than their home; unfamiliar, foreign; the upper trigram, as opposed to inside, NEI, the lower.

People, person, JEN: humans individually and collectively; an individual; humankind. **Dwelling People** is the Image of Hexagram 37. **Inside,** NEI: within, inner, interior; inside of the house and those who work there, particularly women; the lower trigram, as opposed to outside, WAI, the upper. The ideogram: border and enter, cross a border.

● *Symbol Tradition*

> Fire above, marsh below. Diverging.
> A chün tzu uses concording and dividing.

Associated Contexts **Fire,** HUO: warming and consuming aspect of burning; fire and brightness are the Symbols of the trigram Radiance, LI. **Above,** SHANG: anything above, in all senses; higher, upper, outer; upper trigram; opposite of below, HSIA. **Marsh,** TSE: open surface of a flat body of water and the vapors rising from it; fertilize, enrich; kindness, favor; the Symbol of the trigram Open, TUI. **Below,** HSIA: anything below, in all senses; lower, inner; lower trigram; opposite of above, SHANG.

Chün tzu: ideal of a person who uses divination to order his/her life in accordance with tao rather than wilful intention; keyword. **Use(of),** YI: make use of, by means of, owing to; employ, make functional. **Concord,** T'UNG: harmonize, unite, equalize, assemble; agree, share in; together, at once, same time and place. The ideogram: cover and mouth, silent understanding and perfect fit. Image of Hexagram 13. **Divide,** YI: separate, break apart, sever; oppose; different, foreign, strange, unusual, rare.

● *Image Tradition*

> Polarizing. [I]
> Fire stirring up and above.
> Marsh stirring up and below.

Two women concording in residing. [II]
Their purposes not concording: moving.
Stimulating and congregating reach to brightness.

Supple advancing and moving above. [III]
Acquiring the center and corresponding reach the strong.
That uses Small Affairs, auspicious.

Heaven and Earth, Diverging, their affairs concording indeed. [IV]
Man and Woman, Diverging, their purposes interpenetrate indeed.
The myriad beings Diverging and their affairs are sorted indeed.
Actually Diverging's season to avail of the great in fact.

Associated Contexts **[I] Stir up**, TUNG: excite, influence, move, affect; work, take action; come out of the egg or the bud; the Action of the trigram Shake, CHEN. The ideogram: strength and heavy, move weighty things.

[II] Two, ERH: pair, even numbers, binary, duplicate. **Woman(hood)**, NÜ: a woman; what is inherently female. **Reside(in)**, CHÜ: dwell, live in, stay; sit down, fill an office; settled parts of a country. The ideogram: body and seat.

Their/they, CH'I: third person pronoun; also: one/one's, it/its, he/his, she/hers. **Purpose**, CHIH: focus of mind and heart; will, inclination, resolve. The ideogram: heart and scholar, high inner resolve, or heart and go, inner determination. **Move**, HSING: move or move something; motivate, emotionally moving; walk, act, do. The ideogram: stepping left then right.

Stimulate/loosen, SHUO: rouse to action and good feeling; free from constraint, stir up, urge on; persuade, cheer, delight; set out in words; the Action of the trigram Open, TUI. The ideogram: words and exchange. **Congregate**, LI: cling together; depend on, attached to, rely on; couple, pair, herd; the Action of the trigram Radiance, LI. The ideogram: deer flocking together. **Reach(to)**, HU: arrive at a goal; reach toward and achieve; connect. **Brightness**, MING: light-giving aspect of burning, heavenly bodies and consciousness; with fire, the Symbol of the trigram Radiance, LI.

[III] Supple, JOU: quality of the opened lines; flexible, pliant, tender, adaptable. **Advance**, CHIN: exert yourself, make progress, climb; be promoted; further the development of, augment; adopt a religion or conviction; offer, introduce.

Acquire, TE: obtain the desired object; wish for, desire covetously; gains, possessions. The ideogram: go and obstacle, going through obstacles to the goal. **Center,** CHUNG: inner, central; put in the center; middle, stable point enabling you to face inner and outer changes; middle line of trigram. The ideogram: field divided in two equal parts. Image of Hexagram 61. **Correspond(to),** YING: be in agreement or harmony; resonate together, invoke and fulfil each other; answer to, suitable; relation between the lines (1:4, 2:5, 3:6) when they form the pair opened and whole, supple and strong. The ideogram: heart and obey. **Strong,** KANG: quality of the whole lines; firm, strong, unyielding, persisting.

That uses, SHIH YI: involves and is involved by.

[IV] Heaven, T'IEN: highest; sky, firmament, heavens; power above the human as opposed to earth, TI, below; the Symbol of the trigram Force, CH'IEN. The ideogram: great and the one above. **Earth,** TI: ground on which the human world rests; basis of all things, nourishes all things; the Symbol of the trigram Field, K'UN. **One's/one,** CH'I: third person pronoun; also: it/its, he/his, she/hers, they/theirs. **Man(hood),** NAN: a man; what is inherently male. The ideogram: fields and strength, hard labor in the fields. **Interpenetrate,** T'UNG: mutually penetrate; permeate, flow through, reach everywhere; see clearly, communicate with.

Myriad, WAN: countless; many, everyone; lit.: ten thousand. The ideogram: swarm of insects. **Being(s),** WU: creature, thing, any single being; matter, substance, essence; nature of things. **Sort,** LEI: group according to kind, class with; like nature or purpose; species, class, genus.

Actually ... in fact, YI TSAI: stresses the importance of a statement. The ideogram: a dart and done, strong intention fully expressed. **'s/have(it)/it/them,** CHIH: expresses possession, directly or as an object pronoun. **Season,** SHIH: quality of the time; the right time, opportune, in harmony; planning in accord with the time; seasons of the year. The ideogram: sun and temple, time as sacred. **Avail of,** YUNG: take advantage of; benefit from, profit by; use for a specific purpose; apply to advantage. The ideogram: to divine and center, applying divination to central concerns. **Great,** TA: big, noble, important, very; orient the will toward a self-imposed goal, impose direction; ability to lead or guide your life; contrasts with small, HSIAO, flexible adaptation to what crosses your path; keyword. Image of Hexagrams 14, 26, 28, 34.

● *Transforming Lines*

Initial nine

a) **Repenting extinguished.**
Losing the horse, no pursuit, returning to the origin.
See hateful people without fault.

b) **Seeing hateful people.**
Use casting out fault indeed.

Don't try to prove your point. Don't worry over what seems gone. Let it all go. Harmony, strength and love will return by themselves. The sorrow and disconnection you feel will vanish. It is vital that you don't let your own or other people's negativity poison your mind. Keep your thoughts warm and clear and you will make no mistakes.

Associated Contexts a) **Repenting extinguished,** HUI WANG: previous troubles and consequent remorse will disappear.

Lose, SANG: fail to obtain, cease, become obscure; forgotten, destroyed; lament, mourn; funeral. The ideogram: weep and the dead. **Horse,** MA: symbol of spirited strength in the natural world, counterpart of dragon, LUNG; associated with the trigram Force, CH'IEN, heaven, T'IEN, and high noon. **Pursue,** CHU: chase, follow closely, press hard; expel, drive out. The ideogram: pig (wealth) and go, chasing fortune. **Origin,** TZU: source, beginning, ground; cause, reason, motive; line of descent; path to the origin; yourself, intrinsic. **Return,** FU: go back, turn back to the starting point; recur, reappear, come again; restore, recover, retrace; an earlier time or place. The ideogram: step and retrace a path. Image of Hexagram 24.

See, CHIEN: seeing in all its aspects: vision, being visible, forming mental images; visit, call on, consult. The ideogram: eye above person, active and receptive sight. **Hate,** WU: dislike, dread; averse to, ashamed of; repulsive, vicious, vile, ugly, wicked. The ideogram: twisted bowels and heart, heart entangled in emotion.

Without fault, WU CHIU: no error or harm in the situation.

b) **Cast out,** P'I: expel, repress, exclude, punish; exclusionary laws and their enforcement. The ideogram: punish, authority and mouth, give orders to expel. **Fault,** CHIU: unworthy conduct that leads to harm, illness, misfortune. The ideogram: person and differ, differ from what you should be.

Nine at second

a) Meeting a lord in the street.
Without fault.

b) Meeting a lord in the street.
Not yet letting go tao indeed.

In an unexpected way, in an unexpected place, you meet something of great importance. This enters your heart and makes everything clear. Don't be afraid. This is not a mistake.

Associated Contexts a) **Meet,** YÜ: come on unexpectedly, encounter; occur, happen; pleasant meeting, lucky coincidence; agree. **Lord,** CHU: ruler, master, chief; authority. The ideogram: lamp and flame, giving light. **Street,** HSIANG: public space between dwellings, public square; side-street, alley, lane. The ideogram: place and public.

Without fault, WU CHIU: no error or harm in the situation.

b) **Not yet,** WEI: temporal negative; something will but has not yet occurred; contrary of already, CHI. Image of Hexagram 64. **Let go,** SHIH: lose, omit, miss, fail, let slip; out of control. The ideogram: drop from the hand.

Six at third

a) Seeing the cart pulled back, One's cattle hampered.
One's person stricken, moreover nose cut.
Without initiating possessing completion.

b) Seeing the cart pulled back.
Situation not appropriate indeed.
Without initiating possessing completion.
Meeting the strong indeed.

A serious setback, the end of your plans. You have tried to force your way through and have met unexpectedly strong opposition. Nothing can come to fruition now.

Associated Contexts a) **See,** CHIEN: seeing in all its aspects: vision, being visible, forming mental images; visit, call on, consult. The ideogram: eye above person, active and receptive sight. **Cart,** YÜ: carrying capacity of a vehicle; contain, hold, sustain. **Pull back,** YI: pull or drag something toward you; drag behind, take by the hand; leave traces.

One's/one, CH'I: third person pronoun; also: it/its, he/his, she/hers, they/theirs. **Cattle,** NIU: ox, bull, cow, calf; kine; power and strength of work animals. **Hamper,** CH'E: hinder, obstruct, hold or pull back; embarrass; select. The ideogram: hand and limit, grasp and control.

Stricken, YAO: afflicted by fate; untimely, premature death; tender, delicate, young; pleasing. The ideogram: great with a broken point, interrupted growth. **Moreover,** CH'IEH: further, and also. **Nose cutting,** YI: punish through loss of public face or honor; contrasts with **foot cutting,** YÜEH, crippling punishment for serious crime.

Without, WU: devoid of; -less as suffix. **Initial,** CH'U: first step or part; beginning, incipient; bottom line of hexagram. The ideogram: knife and garment, cutting out the pattern. **Possess,** YU: in possession of, have, own; opposite of lack, WU. **Complete,** CHUNG: end of a cycle that begins the next; last, whole, all; contrasts with exhaust, CH'IUNG, final end. The ideogram: silk cocoons, follow and ice, winter linking one year with the next.

b) **Situation,** WEI: place or seat according to rank; post, position, command; right, proper; established, arranged. The ideogram: person and stand, servants in their places. **Appropriate,** TANG: suitable; opportune, convenient; adequate, competent; equal to; whole lines in uneven places and opened lines in even places.

Meet, YÜ: come on unexpectedly, encounter; occur, happen; pleasant meeting, lucky coincidence; agree.

Nine at fourth

a) Diverging alone.
  Meeting the Spring Husband.
  Mingling and connecting.

b) Adversity, without fault.
  Mingling and connecting, without fault.
  Purpose moving indeed.

Alone and feeling isolated by your own thoughts, you encounter something or someone inspiring, a primal source. Though there may seem to be danger, don't be afraid. Joining with this force will put you in touch with the spirits. What you have in your heart will come to pass.

Associated Contexts a) **Alone,** KU: solitary; without a protector; fatherless, orphan-like; as a title: the only, unequalled.

Meet, YÜ: come on unexpectedly, encounter; occur, happen; pleasant meeting, lucky coincidence; agree. **Spring,** TÜAN: source, origin, head; great, excellent; arise, begin, generating power; first stage of the Time Cycle. **Husband,** FU: household manager; administer with thrift and prudence; responsible for; sustain with your earnings; old enough to assume responsibility; married man.

Mingle, CHIAO: blend with, communicate, join, exchange; trade, business; copulation; friendship. **Connection,** FU: accord between inner and outer in a particular moment; sincere, truthful, verified, reliable, in accord with the spirits; capture; prisoners, spoils; contrasts with trustworthy, HSIN, consistent over time. The ideogram: bird's claw enclosing young animals, possessive grip.

b) **Adversity,** LI: danger; threatening, malevolent demon. This has two aspects: grind, sharpen, improve, perfect, stimulate; and: poisonous, sinister, cruel, contrary. It indicates a spirit or ghost that seeks revenge by inflicting suffering upon the living. Pacifying or exorcizing such a spirit can have a healing effect. The ideogram: sheltering cliff and stinging insect. **Without fault,** WU CHIU: no error or harm in the situation.

Six at fifth

a) Repenting extinguished.
   Your ancestor gnaws through the flesh.
   Going wherefore faulty?

b) Your ancestor gnawing flesh.
   Going possesses reward indeed.

Lost in the wilderness, you find the ancient virtue and power. You are blessed by your ancestors. They bite their way through this ordinary life and confer their blessings. This is the meal shared with spirits and great ones. Your sorrows will soon vanish. There is no way in which this can be a mistake.

Associated Contexts a) **Repenting extinguished,** HUI WANG: previous troubles and consequent remorse will disappear.

Your, CHÜEH: intensifying personal pronoun, specifically you! your!; intensify, concentrate, tense, contract; lit.: muscle spasms. **Ancestry,** TSUNG: clan, kin, origin; those who bear the same surname; ancestral hall and tablets; honor, revere; a doctrine; contrasts with predecessor, K'AO, individual ancestors. **Gnaw,** SHIH: bite away, chew; bite persistently and

remove; snap at, nibble; reach the essential by removing the unnecessary. The ideogram: mouth and divination, revealing the essential. Image of Hexagram 21. **Flesh,** FU: muscles, organs, skin, in contrast to bones.

Go, WANG, and **come,** LAI, describe the stream of time as it flows from future through present to past; go, WANG, indicates what is departing from present to past; proceed, move on; keyword. **Wherefore,** HO: interrogative: why? for what reason? what is? and affirmation: therefore, for that reason. **Fault,** CHIU: unworthy conduct that leads to harm, illness, misfortune. The ideogram: person and differ, differ from what you should be.

b) **Possess,** YU: in possession of, have, own; opposite of lack, WU. **Reward,** CH'ING: gift given from gratitude or benevolence; favor from heaven; congratulate with gifts. The ideogram: heart, follow and deer (wealth), the heart expressed through gifts.

Nine above

a) Diverging alone.

Seeing pigs bearing mire.
　Carrying souls in the one chariot.
　Beforehand stretching the bow.
　Afterwards loosening the bow.
　In no way outlaws, seek matrimonial allying.
　Going and meeting rain, by consequence auspicious.

b) Meeting rain's auspiciousness.
　The flock's doubt extinguished indeed.

Alone and isolated, you see the people around you as dirty pigs or a carload of ghosts. At first you are hostile, but then you relax. Where does this hostility come from? These people are not trying to hurt you. Reach out and seek an alliance. As you begin, the falling rain will wash the past away and the way will open.

Associated Contexts a) **Alone,** KU: solitary; without a protector; fatherless, orphan-like; as a title: the only, unequalled.

See, CHIEN: seeing in all its aspects: vision, being visible, forming mental images; visit, call on, consult. The ideogram: eye above person, active and receptive sight. **Pig,** SHIH: all swine; sign of wealth and good fortune; associated with the Streaming Moment. **Bear,** FU: carry on your back; take on a responsibility; rely on, depend on; loaded down; burden, duty; math term for minus. **Mire,** T'U: mud, dirt, filth; besmear, blot out;

stupid, pig-headed. The ideogram: earth and water.

Carry, TSAI: bear, carry with you; contain, sustain; load a ship or cart, cargo; fill in, complete. **Soul**, KUEI: power that creates individual existence; union of volatile-soul, HUN, spiritual and intellectual power, and dense-soul, P'O, bodily strength and movement. The HUN rises after death, the P'O remains with the body and may communicate with the living. **One, the one**, YI: single unit; number one; undivided, simple, whole; any one of; first, the first. **Chariot**, CH'E: wheeled travelling vehicle; contrasts with cart, YÜ, which carries.

Before(hand)/earlier, HSIEN: come before in time; first, at first; formerly, past, previous; begin, go ahead of. **Stretch**, CHANG: draw a bow taut; open, extend, spread, display; make much of. **Bow**, HU: wooden bow; curved flag pole; curved, arched.

After(wards)/later, HOU: come after in time, subsequent; put oneself after; the second; attendant, heirs, successors, posterity.

In no way, FEI: strong negative; not so. The ideogram: a box filled with opposition. **Outlawry**, K'OU: break the laws; violent people, outcasts, bandits. **Matrimonial allying**, HUN KOU: legal institution of marriage; make alliances through marriage rather than force.

Go, WANG, and **come**, LAI, describe the stream of time as it flows from future through present to past; go, WANG, indicates what is departing from present to past; proceed, move on; keyword. **Meet**, YÜ: come on unexpectedly, encounter; occur, happen; pleasant meeting, lucky coincidence; agree. **Rain**, YÜ: all precipitation; sudden showers, fast and furious; associated with the trigram **Gorge**, K'AN, and the Streaming Moment. **By consequence(of)**, TSE: very strong connection; reason, cause, result; rule, law, pattern, standard; therefore.

b) **Flock**, CH'ÜN: herd, group; people of same kind, friends, equals; all, entire; move in unison, flock together. The ideogram: chief and sheep, flock around a leader. **Doubt**, YI: suspect, distrust; dubious; surmise, conjecture. **Extinguish**, WANG: ruin, destroy; gone, dead, lost without trace; extinct, forgotten, out of mind. The ideogram: person concealed by a wall, out of sight.

39

DIFFICULTIES/LIMPING ∎
CHIEN

Obstacles, afflictions, feeling hampered; overcome difficulties by re-imagining the situation.

Difficulties/Limping describes your situation in terms of confronting obstacles and feeling afflicted. Its symbol is the limping hero, Yu the Great, who through both yielding and advancing caused a new world to rise from the waters. The way to deal with it is to see through the situation in a new way and pull back to gather energy for a decisive new move. Don't magnify your problems. You are limping along and your circulation is impeded. Retreat and join with others in view of future gains. That brings profit and insight. Attack, lonely efforts and dwelling on the past won't help at all. See great people. Contact important people who can help you and think about what your central idea really is. Putting your ideas to the trial generates meaning and good fortune by releasing transformative energy.

● *Image of the Situation*

> **Difficulties. Limping. Western South advantageous. Harvesting.**
> **Not Advantageous: Eastern North.**
> **Advantageous to see Great People.**
> **Trial: auspicious.**

Associated Contexts **Difficulties/Limping,** CHIEN: walk lamely, proceed haltingly; weak-legged, afflicted, crooked; feeble, weak; unfortunate, difficult. The ideogram: foot and cold, impeded circulation in the feet. **Advantageous/Harvest,** LI: advantageous, profitable; acute, insightful; benefit, nourish; third stage of the Time Cycle. **Western South:** the neutral Earthy Moment between the yang and yin hemicycles; bring forth concrete results, ripe fruits of late summer.

Eastern North: border, limit, completion; boundary between cycles: Mountain; accomplishing words, summing up before new germination; dark, cold, lonely winter night.

See, CHIEN: seeing in all its aspects: vision, being visible, forming mental images; visit, call on, consult. The ideogram: eye above person, active and receptive sight. **Great People**, TA JEN: important, noble, influential; those who impose a ruling principle on their lives; effect of the great within an individual; keyword.

Trial, CHEN: inquiry by divination and its result; righteous, firm; separating wheat from chaff; the kernel, the proven core; fourth stage of the Time Cycle. The ideogram: pearl and divination. **Auspicious**, CHI: leads to the experience of meaning; favorable, propitious, advantageous, appropriate; keyword. The ideogram: scholar and mouth, wise words of a sage.

● *Outer and Inner Aspects*

☵ **Gorge**: Stream ventures and falls into the gorge, flowing on through toil and danger. **Gorge** ends the yin hemicycle by leveling and dissolving forms.

Connection to the outer: flooding and leveling dissolve direction and shape, the Streaming Moment. **Gorge** ventures, falls, toils and flows on.

☶ **Bound**: Mountains bound, limit and set a place off, stopping forward movement. **Bound** completes a full yin-yang cycle.

Connection to the inner: accomplishing words, which express things. **Bound** articulates what is complete to suggest what is beginning.

The inner limit intermittently blocks outer venturing, producing **limping**.

● *Hidden Possibility*

Nuclear trigrams **Radiance**, LI, and **Gorge**, K'AN, result in Nuclear Hexagram 64, **Not yet Fording**, WEI CHI. Re-imagining a difficult situation lets you gather resources to **ford** the stream of events.

● *Sequence*

Turning away necessarily possesses heaviness.
Accepting this lets you use Difficulties.
Difficulties imply heaviness indeed.

Associated Contexts **Turn away**, KUAI: turn your back on something and focus on its opposite; contradict, cross purposes; cunning, crafty; perverse; contrasts with return, FU, going back to the start. **Necessarily**, PI: unavoidably, indispensably, certainly. **Possess**, YU: in possession of, have, own; opposite of lack, WU. **Heavy**, NAN: arduous, grievous, difficult; hardship, distress; harass; contrasts with versatile, I, deal lightly with. The ideogram: domestic bird with clipped tail and drying sticky earth.

Accepting ... use: activating this hexagram depends on understanding and accepting the previous statement.

Imply, CHE: further signify; additional meaning. **Indeed/is/means**, YEH: intensifier, connective; indicates comment on previous statement.

● *Contrasted Definitions*

> Loosening: delay indeed.
> Difficulties: heaviness indeed.

Associated Contexts **Loosening**, HSIEH: loosen, disjoin, untie, sever, scatter; analyse, explain, understand; release, dispel sorrow; eliminate effects, solve problems; resolution, deliverance. The ideogram: horns and knife, cutting into forward thrust. Image of Hexagram 40. **Delay**, HUAN: retard, put off; let things take their course, tie loosely; gradually, leisurely; lax, tardy, negligent.

● *Symbol Tradition*

> Above mountain possessing stream. Difficulties.
> A chün tzu uses reversing individuality to renovate actualizing tao.

Associated Contexts **Above**, SHANG: anything above, in all senses; higher, upper, outer; upper trigram; opposite of below, HSIA. **Mountain**, SHAN: limit, boundary; the Symbol of the trigram Bound, KEN. The ideogram: three peaks, a mountain range. **Stream**, SHUI: flowing water; fluid, dissolving; river, tide, flood; the Symbol of the trigram Gorge, K'AN. The ideogram: rippling water.

Chün tzu: ideal of a person who uses divination to order his/her life in accordance with tao rather than wilful intention; keyword. **Use(of)**, YI: make use of, by means of, owing to; employ, make functional. **Reverse**, FAN: turn and move in the opposite direction; turn around or upside down (180 degrees); change to the opposite position; contrary. **Individuality**, SHEN: total person: psyche, body and lifespan; character, virtue, duty; contrasts with body, KUNG, physical being. **Renovate**, HSIU: repair, mend, clean, adorn; adjust, regulate; cultivate, practice, acquire skills. **Actualize tao**, TE: realize tao in action; power, virtue; ability to follow the course traced by the ongoing process of the cosmos; keyword. The ideogram: to go, straight, and heart. Linked with acquire, TE: acquiring that which makes a being become what it is meant to be.

- *Image Tradition*

> Difficulties. Heaviness indeed. [I]
> Venturing located in precedence indeed.
> Seeing danger and enabling stopping.
> Actually knowing in fact.

> Difficulties: Western South advantageous. [II]
> Going acquires the center indeed.
> Not advantageous: Eastern North.
> One's tao exhausted indeed.

> Advantageous to see Great People. [III]
> Going possesses achievement indeed.
> Appropriate situation, Trial: auspicious.
> Using correcting the fiefdoms indeed.
> Actually Difficulty's season to avail of the great in fact.

Associated Contexts [I] **Venture, Danger,** HSIEN: risk without reserve; key point, point of danger; difficulty, obstruction that must be confronted; water falling and filling the holes on its way; the Action of the trigram Gorge, K'AN. The ideogram: mound and all or whole, everything engaged at one point. **Locate(in),** TSAI: live in, dwell, reside; belong to, involved with, depend on; within. The ideogram: earth and persevere, place on the earth. **Precede,** CH'IEN: come before in time and thus in value; anterior, former, ancient; lead forward.

Able, NENG: enable; ability, power, skill, art; competent, talented; duty, function, capacity. The ideogram: an animal with strong hooves and bones, able to carry and defend. **Stop,** CHIH: bring or come to a standstill; the Action of the trigram Bound, KEN. The ideogram: a foot stops walking.

Actually ... in fact, YI TSAI: stresses the importance of a statement. The ideogram: a dart and done, strong intention fully expressed. **Know,** CHIH: understand, perceive, remember; informed, aware, wise. The ideogram: arrow and mouth, words focused and swift.

[II] **Go,** WANG, and **come,** LAI, describe the stream of time as it flows from future through present to past; go, WANG, indicates what is departing from present to past; proceed, move on; keyword. **Acquire,** TE: obtain the desired object; wish for, desire covetously; gains, possessions. The ideogram: go and obstacle, going through obstacles to the goal. **Center**, CHUNG: inner, central; put in the center; middle, stable point enabling you to face inner and outer changes; middle line of trigram. The ideogram: field divided in two equal parts. Image of Hexagram 61.

One's/one, CH'I: third person pronoun; also: it/its, he/his, she/hers, they/theirs. **Tao**: way or path; ongoing process of being and the course it traces for each specific person or thing; keyword. The ideogram: go and head, leading and the path it creates. **Exhaust**, CH'IUNG: bring to an end; limit, extremity; destitute; investigate exhaustively; end without a new beginning. The ideogram: cave and naked person, bent with disease or old age.

[III] **Achieve**, KUNG: work done, results; real accomplishment, praise, worth, merit. The ideogram: workman's square and forearm, combining craft and strength.

Appropriate, TANG: suitable; opportune, convenient; adequate, competent; equal to; whole lines in uneven places and opened lines in even places. **Situation**, WEI: place or seat according to rank; post, position, command; right, proper; established, arranged. The ideogram: person and stand, servants in their places.

Correct, CHENG: rectify deviation or one-sidedness; proper, straight, exact, regular; constant, rule, model. The ideogram: stop and one, hold to one thing. **Fiefdom**, PANG: region governed by a feudatory, an order of nobility.

's/have(it)/it/them, CHIH: expresses possession, directly or as an object pronoun. **Season**, SHIH: quality of the time; the right time, opportune, in harmony; planning in accord with the time; seasons of the year. The ideogram: sun and temple, time as sacred. **Avail of**, YUNG: take advantage of; benefit from, profit by; use for a specific purpose; apply to advantage. The ideogram: to divine and center, applying divination to central concerns. **Great**, TA: big, noble, important, very; orient the will toward a self-imposed goal, impose direction; ability to lead or guide your life; contrasts with small, HSIAO, flexible adaptation to what crosses your path; keyword. Image of Hexagrams 14, 26, 28, 34.

● *Transforming Lines*

Initial six

a) Limping. Going Difficulties, coming praise.

b) Limping. Going Difficulties, coming praise.
   Proper to await indeed.

You are cut off and feel frustrated. Resist the temptation to push your way through. If you wait and open yourself to new thoughts, all these frustrations will disappear. You will be praised for doing this.

Associated Contexts a) **Come**, LAI, and **go**, WANG, describe the stream of time as it flows from future through present to past. Come, LAI, indicates what is approaching; move toward, arrive at; go, WANG, indicates what is departing; proceed, move on; keywords. **Praise**, YÜ: admire and approve; magnify, eulogize; flatter. The ideogram: words and give, offering words.

b) **Proper**, YI: reasonable of itself; fit and right, harmonious; ought, should. **Await**, TAI: expect, wait for, welcome (friendly or hostile), provide against.

   Six at second

   a) A king, a servant: Limping, Limping.
      In no way his person is the cause.

   b) A king, a servant: Limping, Limping.
      Completing without surpassing indeed.

You are pushing on through a sea of troubles, and you don't really know why everything is so complicated. Be calm in your heart. The difficulties you are facing are not your fault. Though it doesn't make it any easier, you are truly called on to confront them. Much good will come of this.

Associated Contexts a) **King(hood)**, WANG: effective ruler, by authority of the Emperor, from whom others derive their power. **Servant**, CH'EN: attendant, minister, vassal; courtier who can speak to the sovereign; wait on, serve in office. The ideogram: person bowing low. **Limping**, CHIEN: the doubled character intensifies this quality.

   In no way, FEI: strong negative; not so. The ideogram: a box filled with opposition. **Body/person**, KUNG: physical being, power and self expression; contrasts with individuality, SHEN, the total personality. **Anterior cause**, KU: come before as cause; formerly, ancient; reason, purpose, intention; grievance, quarrel, dissatisfaction, sorrow, mourning resulting from previous causes and intentions; situation leading to a divination.

b) **Complete**, CHUNG: end of a cycle that begins the next; last, whole, all;

contrasts with exhaust, CH'IUNG, final end. The ideogram: silk cocoons, follow and ice, winter linking one year with the next. **Without**, WU: devoid of; -less as suffix. **Surpass**, YU: exceed; beyond measure, excessive; extraordinary; transgress, blame.

Nine at third

a) Limping. Going difficulties, coming reversing.

b) Limping. Going difficulties, coming reversing.
Inside rejoicing in it indeed.

Don't keep chasing what you want. Don't force it. If you just wait calmly, the whole situation will reverse itself. Then you will truly have cause to rejoice.

Associated Contexts a) **Come**, LAI, and **go**, WANG, describe the stream of time as it flows from future through present to past. Come, LAI, indicates what is approaching; move toward, arrive at; go, WANG, indicates what is departing; proceed, move on; keywords.

b) **Inside**, NEI: within, inner, interior; inside of the house and those who work there, particularly women; the lower trigram, as opposed to outside, WAI, the upper. The ideogram: border and enter, cross a border. **Rejoice(in)**, HSI: feel and give joy; delight, exult; cheerful, merry. The ideogram: joy (music) and mouth, expressing joy. **It/them/have(it)/'s**, CHIH: expresses possession, directly or as an object pronoun.

Six at fourth

a) Limping. Going difficulties, coming continuity.

b) Limping. Going difficulties, coming continuity.
Appropriate situation, substance indeed.

You feel lonely and think the world is against you. But you are beating your head against a brick wall. Relax. There are people looking for you right now who can see how valuable you are. Keep the faith.

Associated Contexts a) **Come**, LAI, and **go**, WANG, describe the stream of time as it flows from future through present to past. Come, LAI, indicates what is approaching; move toward, arrive at; go, WANG, indicates what is departing; proceed, move on; keywords. **Continuity**, LIEN: connected, continuous, attached, annexed, consistent; follow, reach, stick to, join; series.

b) **Substance**, SHIH: real, strong, full; results, fruits, possessions; essence; honest, sincere. The ideogram: string of coins under a roof, riches in the house.

Nine at fifth

a) Limping. Great difficulties, partners coming.

b) Limping. Great difficulties, partners coming.
  Using centering and articulating indeed.

You are in the middle of great difficulties, about to give up. New spirit and new partners will soon be there to help you. What you are doing is very important. Don't give up now.

Associated Contexts a) **Partner**, P'ENG: associate for mutual benefit; two equal or similar things; companions, friends, peers; join in; commercial ventures. The ideogram: linked strings of cowries or coins. **Come**, LAI, and **go**, WANG, describe the stream of time as it flows from future through present to past; come, LAI, indicates what is approaching; move toward, arrive at; keyword.

b) **Articulate**, CHIEH: separate and distinguish, as well as join, different things; express thought through speech; joint, section, chapter, interval, unit of time; zodiacal sign; moderate, regulate; lit.: nodes on bamboo stalks. Image of Hexagram 60.

Six above

a) Limping. Going difficulties, coming ripening.
  Auspicious.
  Advantageous to see Great People. Harvesting.

b) Limping. Going difficulties, coming ripening.
  Purpose located inside indeed.
  Advantageous to see Great People. Harvesting.
  Using adhering to valuing indeed.

If you try to impose your will on people, you will most certainly be unhappy. Let go and the situation will drop into your hand like a ripe plum. Things are full of promise, if you can only hear it. Talk to someone who can help you reflect on what is going on. See the spirit at the heart of the situation.

Associated Contexts a) **Come,** LAI, and **go,** WANG. describe the stream of time as it flows from future through present to past. Come, LAI, indicates what is approaching; move toward, arrive at; go, WANG, indicates what is departing; proceed, move on; keywords. **Ripe,** SHIH: mature, full-grown; great, eminent.

b) **Purpose,** CHIH: focus of mind and heart; will, inclination, resolve. The ideogram: heart and scholar, high inner resolve, or heart and go, inner determination. **Inside,** NEI: within, inner, interior; inside of the house and those who work there, particularly women; the lower trigram, as opposed to outside, WAI, the upper. The ideogram: border and enter, cross a border.

Adhere(to), TS'UNG: follow a way, hold to a doctrine, school, or person; hear and comply with, agree to; forced to follow, follower. The ideogram: two men walking, one following the other. **Value,** KUEI: regard as valuable, give worth and dignity to; precious, high priced; honorable, exalted, illustrious. The ideogram: cowries (coins) and basket.

40

LOOSENING/DELIVERANCE ▮
HSIEH

Solve problems, untie knots, release blocked energy; liberation, freed from suffering.

Loosening/Deliverance describes your situation in terms of a release from tension and the new energy that it makes available. Its symbol is untying knots and liberating energy. The way to deal with it is to dispel sorrows, solve problems and understand motivations. Forgive and forget, wipe the slate clean. Join with others to realize plans for future gain. That brings profit and insight. If you have no unfinished business to attend to, simply wait for the energy to return. It will generate meaning and good fortune. If you do have directions to impose or places to go, the first light of dawn generates meaning and good fortune by releasing transformative energy. Be up and doing and greet the new day.

- ● *Image of the Situation*

> Loosening. Western South advantageous. Harvesting.
> Without a place to go:
> Coming and returning auspicious.
> Having a direction to go:
> Daybreak auspicious.

Associated Contexts **Loosening/Deliverance**, HSIEH: loosen, disjoin, untie, sever, scatter; analyse, explain, understand; release, dispel sorrow; eliminate effects, solve problems; resolution, deliverance. The ideogram: horns and knife, cutting into forward thrust. **Harvest/Advantageous**, LI: advantageous, profitable; acute, insightful; benefit, nourish; third stage of the Time Cycle: reaping the crop. **Western South**: the neutral Earthy Moment between the yang and yin hemicycles; bring forth concrete results, ripe fruits of late summer.

    Without, WU: devoid of; -less as suffix. **Place**, SO: where something belongs or comes from; residence, dwelling; habitual focus or object. **Go**, WANG, and **come**, LAI, describe the stream of time as it flows from future through present to past. **Go**, WANG, indicates what is departing; proceed, move on; come, LAI, indicates: what is approaching; move toward, arrive at; keywords.

One's/one, CH'I: third person pronoun; also: it/its, he/his, she/hers, they/theirs. **Return**, FU: go back, turn back to the starting point; recur, reappear, come again; restore, recover, retrace; an earlier time or place. The ideogram: step and retrace a path. Image of Hexagram 24. **Auspicious**, CHI: leads to the experience of meaning; favorable, propitious, advantageous, appropriate; keyword. The ideogram: scholar and mouth, wise words of a sage.

Have a direction to go, YU YU WANG: imposing a direction on the flow of time from present to past; have a specific goal or purpose. **Daybreak**, SU: first light, after dawn; early morning; early, careful attention.

- *Inner and Outer Aspects*

☳ **Shake**: Thunder rises from below, shaking and stirring things up. **Shake** begins the yang hemicycle by germinating new action.

Connection to the outer: sprouting energies thrusting from below, the Woody Moment beginning. **Shake** stirs things up to issue-forth.

☵ **Gorge**: Stream ventures and falls into the gorge, flowing on through toil and danger. **Gorge** ends the yin hemicycle by leveling and dissolving forms.

Connection to the inner: flooding and leveling dissolve direction and shape, the Streaming Moment. Gorge ventures, falls, toils and flows on.

The outer trigram begins a new cycle while the inner completes the previous one. Leveling inside **takes** outer stimuli **apart** and releases blocked energy.

- *Hidden Possibility*

Nuclear trigrams **Gorge**, K'AN, and **Radiance**, LI, result in Nuclear Hexagram 63, **Already Fording**, CHI CHI. Loosening and deliverance are part of a process **already** underway.

- *Sequence*

> Beings not permitted to use completing heaviness.
> Accepting this lets you use Loosening.
> Loosening implies delay indeed.

Associated Contexts **Beings not permitted to use ...** : no one is allowed to make use of; nothing can exist by means of. **Complete,** CHUNG: end of a cycle that begins the next; last, whole, all; contrasts with exhaust, CH'IUNG: final end. The ideogram: silk cocoons, follow and ice, winter linking one year with the next. **Heavy,** NAN: arduous, grievous, difficult; hardship, distress; harass; contrasts with versatile, I, deal lightly with. The ideogram: domestic bird with clipped tail and drying sticky earth.

Accepting ... use: activating this hexagram depends on understanding and accepting the previous statement.

Imply, CHE: further signify; additional meaning. **Delay,** HUAN: retard, put off; let things take their course, tie loosely; gradually, leisurely; lax, tardy, negligent. **Indeed/is/means,** YEH: intensifier, connective; indicates comment on previous statement.

● *Contrasted Definitions*

> Loosening: delay indeed.
> Difficulties: heaviness indeed.

Associated Contexts **Difficulties,** CHIEN: walk lamely, proceed haltingly; weak-legged, afflicted, crooked; feeble, weak; unfortunate, difficult. The ideogram: foot and cold, impeded circulation in the feet. Image of Hexagram 39.

● *Symbol Tradition*

> Thunder, rain, arousing. Loosening and Deliverance.
> A chün tzu uses forgiving excess to pardon offenses.

Associated Contexts **Thunder,** LEI: rising, arousing power; the Symbol of the trigram Shake, CHEN. **Rain,** YÜ: all precipitation; sudden showers, fast and furious; associated with the trigram Gorge, K'AN, and the Streaming Moment. **Arouse,** TSO: stir up, stimulate, rouse from inactivity; generate; appear, arise. The ideogram: person and beginning.

Chün tzu: ideal of a person who uses divination to order his/her life in accordance with tao rather than wilful intention; keyword. **Use(of),** YI: make use of, by means of, owing to; employ, make functional. **Forgive,** SHE: excuse, pass over, set aside, reprieve. **Exceed/traverse,** KU: go beyond, pass by, pass over; excessive, transgress; error, fault. Image of Hexagrams 28 and 62. **Pardon,** YU: forgive, indulge, relax; lenient. **Offense,** TSUI: crime, sin, fault; violate laws or rules; incur blame, incriminated. The ideogram: net and wrong, entangled in guilt.

- *Image Tradition*

> Loosening. Venturing uses stirring up. [I]
> Stirring up and evading reach to venturing. Loosening.
>
> Loosening, Western South advantageous. [II]
> Going acquiring crowds indeed.
> Coming and returning auspicious.
> Thereupon acquiring the center indeed.
> Having a direction to go: daybreak auspicious.
> Going possesses achievement indeed.
>
> Heaven and Earth Loosening and
> Thunder and Rain arousing. [III]
> Thunder and Rain arousing and the hundred fruits,
> grasses, trees, altogether seedburst boundary.
> Actually Loosening's season great in fact.

Associated Contexts [I] **Venture**, HSIEN: risk without reserve; key point, point of danger; difficulty, obstruction that must be confronted; water falling and filling the holes on its way; the Action of the trigram Gorge, K'AN. The ideogram: mound and all or whole, everything engaged at one point. **Stir up**, TUNG: excite, influence, move, affect; work, take action; come out of the egg or the bud; the Action of the trigram Shake, CHEN. The ideogram: strength and heavy, move weighty things.

Evade, MIEN: avoid, escape from, get away; be free of, dispense with; remove from office. The ideogram: a hare, known for its evasive skill. **Reach(to)**, HU: arrive at a goal; reach towards and achieve; connect; contrasts with tend-towards, YU.

[II] **Acquire**, TE: obtain the desired object; wish for, desire covetously; gains, possessions. The ideogram: go and obstacle, going through obstacles to the goal. **Crowds**, CHUNG: many people, large group; majority; in common.

Thereupon, NAI: on that ground, because of. **Center**, CHUNG: inner, central; put in the center; middle, stable point enabling you to face inner and outer changes; middle line of trigram. The ideogram: field divided in two equal parts. Image of Hexagram 61.

Possess, YU: in possession of, have, own; opposite of lack, WU. **Achieve**, KUNG: work done, results; real accomplishment, praise, worth, merit. The ideogram: workman's square and forearm, combining craft and strength.

[III] Heaven and Earth, T'IEN TI: dynamic relation between the primal powers and the world it produces; cosmos, natural or human world; keyword. **Thunder and Rain**, LEI YÜ: fertilizing shock of storms; associated with the trigrams Shake, CHEN, and Gorge, K'AN.

Hundred, PO: numerous, many, all; a whole class or type. **Fruit**, KUO: plants' annual produce; tree fruits; come to fruition, fruits of actions; produce, results, effects; reliable; conclude, surpass. The ideogram: tree topped by a round fruit. **Grass**, TS'AO: all grassy plants and herbs; young, tender plants; rough draft; hastily. **Tree/wood**, MU: all things woody or wooden, alive or constructed from wood; associated with the Woody Moment; wood and wind are the Symbols of the trigram Ground, SUN. The ideogram: a tree striking its roots down and sending up branches. **Altogether**, CHIEH: all, the whole; the same sort, all alike; entirely. **Seedburst**, CHIA: seeds bursting forth in spring; first of the Ten Heavenly Barriers in calendar system; begin, first, number one; associated with the Woody Moment. **Boundary**, CHI: border, limit, frontier; confine.

Actually ... in fact, YI TSAI: stresses the importance of a statement. The ideogram: a dart and done, strong intention fully expressed. **'s/have(it)/it/them**, CHIH: expresses possession, directly or as an object pronoun. **Season**, SHIH: quality of the time; the right time, opportune, in harmony; planning in accord with the time; seasons of the year. The ideogram: sun and temple, time as sacred. **Great**, TA: big, noble, important, very; orient the will toward a self-imposed goal, impose direction; ability to lead or guide your life; contrasts with small, HSIAO, flexible adaptation to what crosses your path; keyword. Image of Hexagrams 14, 26, 28, 34.

● *Transforming Lines*

Initial six

a) **Without fault.**

b) **Strong and Supple's border.**
   Righteous, without fault indeed.

Act on your plans. Be vigorous. You are in exactly the right position. This is not a mistake.

Associated Contexts a) **Without fault,** WU CHIU: no error or harm in the situation.

b) **Strong and Supple,** KANG JOU: field of creative tension between the whole and opened lines and their qualities; field of psychic movement. **Border,** CHI: limit, frontier, line which joins and divides. The ideogram: place and sacrifice, border between human and spirit.

 Righteous, YI: proper and just, meets the standards; things in their proper place; the heart that rules itself; upright, moral rule; contrasts with Harvest, LI, advantage or profit.

Nine at second

a) The fields, catching three foxes.
   Acquiring a yellow arrow.
   Trial: auspicious.

b) Nine at second, Trial: auspicious.
   Acquiring and centering tao indeed.

Vigorously pursue your objectives. There are forces that seem to be threatening you, but you catch them in the act and acquire their power. You have the ability to realize your desires, which are in harmony with the Way.

Associated Contexts a) **Fields,** T'IEN: cultivated land, plantation; also: hunting, game in the fields cannot escape the hunt. The ideogram: square divided into four sections, delineating fields. **Catch,** HUO: take in hunt; catch a thief; obtain, seize; hit the mark, opportune moment; prisoner, spoils, prey; slave, servant. **Three,** SAN: number three, third time or place; active phases of a cycle; superlative; beginning of repetition. **Fox,** HU: crafty, shape-changing animal; used by spirits, often female; ambivalent night-spirit that can create havoc and bestow abundance.

 Yellow, HUANG: color of the productive middle; associated with the Earthy Moment between yang and yin hemicycles; color of soil in central China; emblematic and imperial color of China since the Yellow Emperor (2500 BCE). **Arrow,** SHIH: arrow, javelin, dart; swift, direct as an arrow; marshal together.

 Trial, CHEN: inquiry by divination and its result; righteous, firm; separating wheat from chaff; the kernel, the proven core; fourth stage of the Time Cycle. The ideogram: pearl and divination.

b) **Tao:** way or path; ongoing process of being and the course it traces for each specific person or thing; keyword. The ideogram: go and head, leading and the path it creates.

Six at third

a) **Bearing, moreover riding.**
Involving outlawry at the culmination.
Trial: distress.

b) **Bearing, moreover riding.**
Truly permitting the demoniac indeed.
Originating from my involving arms.
Furthermore whose fault indeed.

If you are truly committed to what you are doing, you will be freed from the constriction you feel. Hold fast to what you believe. It opens the way and connects you to the spirits. Ordinary people will feel this and help.

Associated Contexts a) **Bear,** FU: carry on your back; take on a responsibility; rely on, depend on; loaded down; burden, duty; math term for minus. **Moreover,** CH'IEH: further, and also. **Ride,** CH'ENG: ride an animal or a chariot; have the upper hand, seize the right time; control strong power; overcome the nature of the other; supple opened line above a strong whole line.

   Involve, CHIH: include, entangle, implicate; induce, cause. The ideogram: person walking, induced to follow. **Outlawry,** K'OU: break the laws; violent people, outcasts, bandits. **Culminate,** CHIH: bring to the highest degree; arrive at the end or summit; superlative.

   Trial, CHEN: inquiry by divination and its result; righteous, firm; separating wheat from chaff; the kernel, the proven core; fourth stage of the Time Cycle. The ideogram: pearl and divination. **Distress,** LIN: distress, shame, regret, humiliation; aware of having lost the right track; leads to repenting, HUI, correcting the direction of mind and life.

b) **Truly,** YI: statement is true and precise. **Permit,** K'O: possible because in harmony with an inherent principle. The ideogram: mouth and breath, silent consent. **Demon(iac),** CH'OU: possessed by a malignant genius; ugly, physically or morally deformed; vile, disgraceful, shameful; drunken. The ideogram: fermenting liquor and soul. Demoniac and tiger are opposed on the Universal Compass North–South axis; the tiger (Extreme Yang) scares away and protects against demoniacs (Extreme Yin).

Origin, TZU: source, beginning, ground; cause, reason, motive; line of descent; path to the origin; yourself, intrinsic. **My/me/I,** WO: first person pronoun; indicates an unusually strong emphasis on your own subjective experience. **Arms,** JUNG: weapons; armed people, soldiers; military, violent. The ideogram: spear and armor, offensive and defensive weapons.

Furthermore, YU: in addition to; higher degree of. **Whose,** SHUI: relative and interrogative pronoun; also: whose? **Fault,** CHIU: unworthy conduct that leads to harm, illness, misfortune. The ideogram: person and differ, differ from what you should be.

Nine at fourth

a) **Loosening and the thumbs.**
   Partnering culminating, splitting off connects you to the spirits.

b) **Loosening and the thumbs.**
   Not yet an appropriate situation indeed.

Associated Contexts a) **Thumb/big toe,** MU: in lower trigram: big-toe; in upper trigram: thumb; the big-toe enables the foot to walk, the thumb enables the hand to grasp.

Partner, P'ENG: associate for mutual benefit; two equal or similar things; companions, friends, peers; join in; commercial ventures. The ideogram: linked strings of cowries or coins. **Culminate,** CHIH: bring to the highest degree; arrive at the end or summit; superlative. **Split off,** SSU: lop off, split with an ax, rive; white (color eliminated). The ideogram: ax and possessive, splitting what belongs together. **Connection,** FU: accord between inner and outer in a particular moment; sincere, truthful, verified, reliable, in accord with the spirits; capture; prisoners, spoils; contrasts with trustworthy, HSIN, consistent over time. The ideogram: bird's claw enclosing young animals, possessive grip. Image of Hexagram 61.

b) **Not yet,** WEI: temporal negative; something will but has not yet occurred; contrary of already, CHI. Image of Hexagram 64. **Appropriate,** TANG: suitable; opportune, convenient; adequate, competent; equal to; whole lines in uneven places and opened lines in even places. **Situation,** WEI: place or seat according to rank; post, position, command; right, proper; established, arranged. The ideogram: person and stand, servants in their places.

Six at fifth

a) A chün tzu held fast possesses Loosening.
Auspicious.
There is a connection to the spirits, moving towards Small People.

b) A chün tzu possessing Loosening.
Small People withdrawing indeed.

Associated Contexts a) **Hold fast(to)**, WEI: hold together; tie to; connect; reins, net. **There is … spirits**, YU FU: inner and outer are in accord; confidence of the spirits has been captured; sincere, truthful; proper to take action. **Small People**, HSIAO JEN: lowly, common, humble; those who adjust to circumstances with the flexibility of the small; effect of the small within an individual; keyword.

b) **Withdraw(from)**, T'UI: draw back, retreat, recede; decline, refuse.

Six above

a) A prince avails of shooting a hawk,

on the high rampart above them.
Nothing not advantageous: catching it.

b) A prince avails of shooting a hawk.
Using Loosening the rebels indeed.

You capture the force opposing your plans and desires. Don't worry. Be brave. Attack now and you will most certainly win. This will begin a new cycle of time. Everything will benefit.

Associated Contexts a) **Prince**, KUNG: nobles acting as ministers of state in the capital; governing from the center rather than active in daily life; contrasts with feudatory, HOU, governors of the provinces. **Avail of**, YUNG: take advantage of; benefit from, profit by; use for a specific purpose; apply to advantage. The ideogram: to divine and center, applying divination to central concerns. **Shoot**, SHE: shoot with a bow, point at and hit; project from, spurt, issue forth; glance at; scheme for. The ideogram: arrow and body. **Hawk**, SHUN: bird of prey used in hunting; falcon, kestrel. **High(ness)**, KAO: high, elevated, lofty, eminent; excellent, advanced. **Rampart**, YUNG: defensive wall; bulwark, redoubt. **Above**, SHANG: anything above, in all senses; higher, upper, outer; upper trigram; opposite of below, HSIA.

Nothing not advantageous, WU PU LI: nothing for which this will not be beneficial; advantageous potential, borderline where the balance is swinging from not Harvesting to actually Harvesting. **Catch,** HUO: take in hunt; catch a thief; obtain, seize; hit the mark, opportune moment; prisoner, spoils, prey; slave, servant. **It/them/have(it)/'s,** CHIH: expresses possession, directly or as an object pronoun.

b) **Rebel,** PEI: go against nature or usage; insubordinate; perverse, unreasonable.

41

DIMINISHING ▌ SUN

Decrease, sacrifice, loss; concentrate, diminish your involvement, decrease your desire; aim at a higher goal.

Diminishing describes your situation in terms of loss, sacrifice and the need for concentration. Its symbol is the empowering sacrifice to the spirit above. The way to deal with it is to decrease your involvements and free yourself from emotional entanglements. This makes energy available for new developments. Act this way with confidence, for you are connected to the spirits and they will carry you through. This is the origin of great good fortune and meaningful events. It is not a mistake. This is an enabling divination. Put your ideas to the trial. Have a place to go. Impose a direction on things. That brings profit and insight. Inquire into motivations; ask yourself why you are doing things. Use two ceremonial vessels to present your results to the spirits. Diminish the strong and augment the supple.

- *Image of the Situation*

> Diminishing, there is a connection to the spirits.
> Spring auspicious.
> Without fault, permitting Trial.
> Advantageous to have a direction to go. Harvesting.
> Asking why avails of it.
> Two platters permit availing of presenting.

Associated Contexts **Diminish**, SUN: lessen, make smaller; take away from; lose, damage, spoil, wound; bad luck; blame, criticize; offer up, give away. The ideogram: hand and ceremonial vessel, offering sacrifice. **There is … spirits**, YU FU: inner and outer are in accord; confidence of the spirits has been captured; sincere, truthful; proper to take action.

    Spring, YÜAN: source, origin, head; great, excellent; arise, begin, generating power; first stage of the Time Cycle. **Auspicious**, CHI: leads to the experience of meaning; favorable, propitious, advantageous, appropriate; keyword. The ideogram: scholar and mouth, wise words of a sage.

    Without fault, WU CHIU: no error or harm in the situation. **Permit**, K'O:

possible because in harmony with an inherent principle. The ideogram: mouth and breath, silent consent. **Trial**, CHEN: inquiry by divination and its result; righteous, firm; separating wheat from chaff; the kernel, the proven core; fourth stage of the Time Cycle. The ideogram: pearl and divination.

Advantageous/Harvest, LI: advantageous, profitable; acute, insightful; benefit, nourish; third stage of the Time Cycle. **Have a direction to go**, YU YU WANG: imposing a direction on the flow of time from present to past; have a specific goal or purpose. **Ask why**, HO: why? how? why not?; question, inquire into motives. The ideogram: speak and beg, demanding an answer. **Have(it)/it/them/'s**, CHIH: expresses possession, directly or as an object pronoun. **Avail of**, YUNG: take advantage of; benefit from, profit by; use for a specific purpose; apply to advantage. The ideogram: to divine and center, applying divination to central concerns.

Two, ERH: pair, even numbers, binary, duplicate. **Platter**, KUEI: wood or bamboo plate; sacrificial utensil. **Present(to)**, HSIANG: present in sacrifice, offer with thanks, give to the gods or a superior; confer dignity on.

● *Outer and Inner Aspects*

⚏ **Bound**: Mountains bound, limit and set a place off, stopping forward movement. **Bound** completes a full yin-yang cycle.

Connection to the outer: accomplishing words, which express things fully. **Bound** articulates what is complete and suggests what is beginning.

⚌ **Open**: vapor rising from the marsh's open surface stimulates and fertilizes; stimulating words cheer and inspire. **Open** begins the yin hemicycle by initiating the formative process.

Connection to the inner: liquifying, casting, skinning off the mold, the Metallic Moment beginning. **Open** stimulates, cheers and reveals innate form.

The outer limit **diminishes** involvement, stimulating new inner development.

● *Hidden Possibility*

Nuclear trigrams **Field**, K'UN, and **Shake**, CHEN, result in Nuclear Hexagram 24, **Returning**, FU. **Diminishing** and decreasing outer involvement lets you **return** to the source to start over again.

- *Sequence*

> Delaying necessarily possesses a place to let go.
> Accepting this lets you use Diminishing.

Associated Contexts **Delay,** HUAN: retard, put off; let things take their course, tie loosely; gradually, leisurely; lax, tardy, negligent. **Necessarily,** PI: unavoidably, indispensably, certainly. **Possess,** YU: in possession of, have, own; opposite of lack, WU. **Place,** SO: where something belongs or comes from; residence, dwelling; habitual focus or object. **Let go,** SHIH: lose, omit, miss, fail, let slip; out of control. The ideogram: drop from the hand.

Accepting ... use: activating this hexagram depends on understanding and accepting the previous statement.

- *Contrasted Definitions*

> Diminishing, Augmenting.
> Increasing and decreasing's beginning indeed.

Associated Contexts **Augment,** YI: increase, advance, promote, benefit, strengthen; pour in more; full, superabundant; restorative. The ideogram: water and vessel, pouring in more. Image of Hexagram 42.

Increase, SHENG: grow or make larger; flourishing, exuberant, full, abundant; heaped up; excellent, fine. **Decrease,** SHUAI: grow or make smaller; fade, decline, decay, diminish, cut off; grow old; adversity, misfortune. **'s/have(it)/it/them,** CHIH: expresses possession, directly or as an object pronoun. **Begin,** SHIH: commence, start, open; earliest, first; beginning of a time-span, ended by completion, CHUNG. The ideogram: woman and eminent, beginning new life. **Indeed is/means,** YEH: intensifier, connective; indicates comment on previous statement.

- *Attached Evidences*

> Diminishing: actualizing tao's adjustment indeed.
> Diminishing: beforehand heaviness and afterwards versatility.
> Diminishing: use it to distance harm.

Associated Contexts **Actualize tao,** TE: realize tao in action; power, virtue; ability to follow the course traced by the ongoing process of the cosmos; keyword. The ideogram: to go, straight, and heart. Linked with acquire, TE: acquiring that which makes a being become what it is meant to be. **Adjust,** HSIU: regulate, repair, clean up, renovate.

Before(hand)/earlier, HSIEN: come before in time; first, at first; formerly, past, previous; begin, go ahead of. **Heavy**, NAN: arduous, grievous, difficult; hardship, distress; harass; contrasts with versatile, I, deal lightly with. The ideogram: domestic bird with clipped tail and drying sticky earth. **After(wards)/later**, HOU: come after in time, subsequent; put oneself after; the second; attendant, heirs, successors, posterity. **Versatility/change**, I: sudden and unpredictable change; mental mobility and openness; easy and light, not difficult and heavy; occurs in name of the I CHING.

Use(of), YI: make use of, by means of, owing to; employ, make functional. **Distance**, YÜAN: far off, remote; keep at a distance; alienated. The ideogram: go and a long way. **Harm**, HAI: damage, injure, offend; suffer; hurtful, hindrance; fearful, anxious.

- *Symbol Tradition*

> Below mountain possessing marsh. Diminishing.
> A chün tzu uses curbing anger to block the appetites.

Associated Contexts **Below**, HSIA: anything below, in all senses; lower, inner; lower trigram; opposite of above, SHANG. **Mountain**, SHAN: limit, boundary; the Symbol of the trigram Bound, KEN. The ideogram: three peaks, a mountain range. **Marsh**, TSE: open surface of a flat body of water and the vapors rising from it; fertilize, enrich; kindness, favor; the Symbol of the trigram Open, TUI.

Chün tzu: ideal of a person who uses divination to order his/her life in accordance with tao rather than wilful intention; keyword. **Curb**, CH'ENG: reprimand, reprove, repress; warn, caution; corrective punishment. The ideogram: heart and action, the heart acting on itself. **Anger**, FEN: resentment; cross, wrathful; irritated at, indignant. The ideogram: heart and divide, the heart dividing people. **Block**, CHIH: obstruct, stop up, close, restrain, fill up. **Appetites**, YÜ: drives, instinctive craving; wishes, passions, desires, aspirations; long for, seek ardently; covet.

- *Image Tradition*

> Diminishing. [I]
> Below Diminishing, above augmenting.
> One's tao moving above.
> Diminishing and possessing conformity.

Spring auspicious. [II]
Without fault, permitting Trial.
Advantageous to have a direction to go. Harvesting.
Asking why avails of it.
Two platters permit availing of presenting.

Two platters correspond and possess the season. [III]
Diminishing the strong, augmenting the supple, possessing the season.
Diminishing augments it, overfilling emptiness,
Associating with the season, and accompanying the movement.

Associated Contexts [I] **Above,** SHANG: anything above, in all senses; higher, upper, outer; upper trigram; opposite of below, HSIA.

One's/one, CH'I: third person pronoun; also: it/its, he/his, she/hers, they/theirs. **Tao:** way or path; ongoing process of being and the course it traces for each specific person or thing; keyword. The ideogram: go and head, leading and the path it creates. **Move,** HSING: move or move something; motivate, emotionally moving; walk, act, do. The ideogram: stepping left then right.

[III] **Correspond(to),** YING: be in agreement or harmony; resonate together, invoke and fulfil each other; answer to, suitable; relation between the lines (1:4, 2:5, 3:6) when they form the pair opened and whole, supple and strong. The ideogram: heart and obey. **Season,** SHIH: quality of the time; the right time, opportune, in harmony; planning in accord with the time; seasons of the year. The ideogram: sun and temple, time as sacred.

Strong, KANG: quality of the whole lines; firm, strong, unyielding, persisting. **Supple,** JOU: quality of the opened lines; flexible, pliant, tender, adaptable.

Overfill, YING: at the point of overflowing; more than wanted, stretch beyond; replenished, full; arrogant. The ideogram: vessel and too much. **Empty,** HSÜ: no images or concepts; vacant, unsubstantial; empty yet fertile space.

Associate(with), YÜ: consort with, combine; companions; group, band, company; agree with, comply, help. The ideogram: pair of hands reaching downward meets a pair of hands reaching upward, helpful association. **Accompany,** HSIEH: take or go along with; jointly, all at once.

● *Transforming Lines*

Initial nine

a) Climaxing affairs, swiftly going.
   Without fault.
   Discussing Diminishing it.

b) Climaxing affairs, swiftly going.
   Honoring uniting purposes indeed.

This involvement is a mistake. Leave now. Don't even discuss it. Don't let it diminish your resolve.

Associated Contexts a) **Climax**, YI: come to a high point and stop, bring to an end; use up, lay aside; decline, reject. **Affairs**, SHIH: all kinds of personal activity; matters at hand; business, occupation; manage a business, case in court. **Swiftly**, CH'UAN: quickly; hurry, hasten. **Go**, WANG, and **come**, LAI, describe the stream of time as it flows from future through present to past; go, WANG, indicates what is departing from present to past; proceed, move on; keyword.

Discuss, CHO: deliberate; hear opinions; reach and act on a decision. The ideogram: wine and ladle, pouring out wine to open discussion. **It/them/have(it)/'s**, CHIH: expresses possession, directly or as an object pronoun.

b) **Honor**, SHANG: esteem, give high rank to; eminent; put one thing on top of another. **Unite**, HO: join, match, correspond, agree, collect, reply; unison, harmony; also: close, shut the mouth. The ideogram: mouth and assemble. **Purpose**, CHIH: focus of mind and heart; will, inclination, resolve. The ideogram: heart and scholar, high inner resolve, or heart and go, inner determination.

Nine at second

a) Advantageous Trial. Harvesting.
   Chastising: pitfall.
   Nowhere Diminishing, augmenting it.

b) Nine at second, Advantageous Trial. Harvesting.
   Centering using activating purposes indeed.

This is a very advantageous connection. Everyone will benefit. But it won't help if you try to discipline people and set things in order. That will close the way. This connection won't diminish things, it will augment them.

Associated Contexts a) **Harvesting Trial,** LI CHEN: advantageous divination; putting the action in question to the test is beneficial.

Chastise, CHENG: punish, subjugate, discipline; reduce to order; punishing expedition. The ideogram: step and correct, a rectifying move. **Pitfall,** HSIUNG: leads away from the experience of meaning; stuck and exposed to danger, unable to take in the situation; flow of life and spirit is blocked; unfortunate, baleful; keyword.

Nothing/nowhere, FU: strong negative; not a single thing/place. **It/them/have(it)/'s,** CHIH: expresses possession, directly or as an object pronoun.

b) **Center,** CHUNG: inner, central; put in the center; middle, stable point enabling you to face inner and outer changes; middle line of trigram. The ideogram: field divided in two equal parts. Image of Hexagram 61. **Activate,** WEI: act or cause to act; do, make, manage; make active; attend to, help; because of. **Purpose,** CHIH: focus of mind and heart; will, inclination, resolve. The ideogram: heart and scholar, high inner resolve, or heart and go, inner determination.

Six at third

a) **Three people moving.**
   By consequence Diminishing by one person.
   The one person moving.
   By consequence acquiring one's friend.

b) **The one person moving.**
   Three by consequence doubting indeed.

If you are involved in a triangle, it will soon become a couple. If you are alone, you will soon have a friend.

Associated Contexts a) **Three,** SAN: number three, third time or place; active phases of a cycle; superlative; beginning of repetition. **People, person,** JEN: humans individually and collectively; an individual; humankind. Image of Hexagrams 13 and 37.

By consequence(of), TSE: very strong connection; reason, cause, result; rule, law, pattern, standard; therefore. **One, the one,** YI: single unit; number one; undivided, simple, whole; any one of; first, the first.

Acquire, TE: obtain the desired object; wish for, desire covetously; gains, possessions. The ideogram: go and obstacle, going through obstacles to the goal. **One's/one**, CH'I: third person pronoun; also: it/its, he/his, she/hers, they/theirs. **Friend**, YU: companion, associate; of the same mind; attached, in pairs. The ideogram: two hands joined.

b) **Doubt**, YI: suspect, distrust; dubious; surmise, conjecture.

Six at fourth

a) Diminishing one's affliction.
Commissioning swiftly possesses rejoicing.
Without fault.

b) Diminishing one's affliction.
Truly permitting rejoicing indeed.

This connection is seriously harming you. Diminish your involvement. Send someone quickly to give the message. Then you will have cause to rejoice. Have no doubts, this is not a mistake.

Associated Contexts a) **One's/one**, CH'I: third person pronoun; also: he/his, she/hers, they/theirs, it/its. **Afflict**, CHI: sickness, disorder, defect, calamity; injurious; pressure and consequent anger, hate or dislike. The ideogram: sickness and dart, a sudden affliction.

Commission, CHIH: employ for a task; command, order; messenger, agent. The ideogram: person and office. **Swiftly**, CH'UAN: quickly; hurry, hasten. **Rejoice(in)**, HSI: feel and give joy; delight, exult; cheerful, merry. The ideogram: joy (music) and mouth, expressing joy.

b) **Truly**, YI: statement is true and precise.

Six at fifth

a) "Someone" augments it: ten partnered tortoises.
Nowhere a controlling contradiction.
Spring auspicious.

b) Six at fifth, Spring auspicious.
Originating from shielding above indeed.

What a fortunate answer! A blessing and a mandate from Heaven. The way to the source is open. Nothing can get in the way of your plans and your desires. You will be showered with blessings. Enjoy it!

Associated Contexts a) **Maybe/"someone"**, HUO: possible perhaps; term indicating spirit is active. **Ten**, SHIH: goal and end of reckoning; whole, complete, all; entire, perfected, the full amount; reach everywhere, receive everything. The ideogram: East–West line crosses North–South line, a grid that contains all. **Partner,** P'ENG: associate for mutual benefit; two equal or similar things; companions, friends, peers; join in; commercial ventures. The ideogram: linked strings of cowries or coins. **Tortoise,** KUEI: turtles; armored animals, shells and shields; long-living; oracle-consulting by tortoise shell; image of the macrocosm: heaven and earth, between them the soft flesh of humans.

Nothing/nowhere, FU: strong negative; not a single thing/place. **Control,** K'O: command; check, impede, prevail, obstruct, repress; adequate, able. The ideogram: roof beams support a house, controlling the structure. **Contradict,** WEI: oppose, disregard, disobey; seditious, perverse.

b) **Origin,** TZU: source, beginning, ground; cause, reason, motive; line of descent; path to the origin; yourself, intrinsic. **Shield,** YU: protect; defended by spirits; heavenly kindness and protection. The ideogram: numinous and right hand, spirit power.

Nine above

a) **Nowhere Diminishing, augmenting it.**
  Without fault.
  Trial: auspicious.
  Advantageous to have a direction to go. Harvesting.
  Acquiring a servant, without a dwelling.

b) **Nowhere Diminishing, augmenting it.**
  The great acquiring purpose indeed.

Your involvement will not be diminished but augmented. It will bring good things everyone involved. The feelings you have now are not a mistake. They actually open the way. Draw up a plan. Be sure of yourself. You will get considerable help, but not a dwelling place.

Associated Contexts a) **Nothing/nowhere,** FU: strong negative; not a single thing/place. **It/them/have(it)/'s,** CHIH: expresses possession, directly or as an object pronoun.

Acquire, TE: obtain the desired object; wish for, desire covetously; gains, possessions. The ideogram: go and obstacle, going through obstacles to the goal. **Servant,** CH'EN: attendant, minister, vassal; courtier who can speak to the sovereign; wait on, serve in office. The ideogram: person bowing low. **Without,** WU: devoid of; -less as suffix. **Dwell,** CHI: home, house, household, family; domestic, within doors; live in. The ideogram: roof and pig or dog, the most valued domestic animals. Image of Hexagram 37.

b) **Great**, TA: big, noble, important, very; orient the will toward a self-imposed goal, impose direction; ability to lead or guide your life; contrasts with small, HSIAO, flexible adaptation to what crosses your path; keyword. Image of Hexagrams 14, 26, 28, 34. **Purpose**, CHIH: focus of mind and heart; will, inclination, resolve. The ideogram: heart and scholar, high inner resolve, or heart and go, inner determination.

42

AUGMENTING ▮ *YI*

Increase, expand, develop, pour in more; fertile and expansive.

Augmenting describes your situation in terms of increase, advance and development. It is the response of the spirit above to the sacrifice, an outpouring of blessings. The way to deal with it is to increase your involvements and pour in more energy. This is a time of gain, profit and expansion. Have a place to go. Impose a direction on things. Enter the stream of life with a purpose or embark on a significant enterprise. These things bring profit and insight.

- *Image of the Situation*

    Augmenting, advantageous to have a direction to go. Harvesting. Advantageous to step into the Great River.

    Associated Contexts **Augment**, YI: increase, advance, promote, benefit, strengthen; pour in more; full, superabundant; restorative. The ideogram: water and vessel, pouring in more. **Advantageous/Harvest**, LI: advantageous, profitable; acute, insightful; benefit, nourish; third stage of the Time Cycle. **Have a direction to go**, YU YU WANG: imposing a direction on the flow of time from present to past; have a specific goal or purpose.
    Step into the Great River, SHE TA CH'UAN: consciously moving into the flow of time; enter the stream of life with a goal or purpose; embark on a significant enterprise.

- *Outer and Inner Aspects*

    ☴ **Ground**: Wind and wood subtly enter from the ground, penetrating and pervading. **Ground** is the center of the yang hemicycle, spreading pervasive action.

    Connection to the outer: penetrating and bringing together, the Woody Moment culminating. **Ground** pervades, matches and couples, seeding a new generation.

    ☳ **Shake**: Thunder rises from below, shaking and stirring things up. **Shake** begins the yang hemicycle by germinating new action.

Connection to the outer: sprouting energies thrusting from below, the Woody Moment beginning. **Shake** stirs things up to issue-forth.

Germinating inner energy continually **augments** and expands outer pervading and growth.

● *Hidden Possibility*

Nuclear trigrams **Bound**, KEN, and **Field**, K'UN, result in Nuclear Hexagram 23, **Stripping**, PO. Increase and expansion through **augmenting** depends on **stripping** away old ideas.

● *Sequence*

> **Diminishing and not climaxing necessarily Augments.**
> **Accepting this lets you use Augmenting.**

Associated Contexts **Diminish**, SUN: lessen, make smaller; take away from; lose, damage, spoil, wound; bad luck; blame, criticize; offer up, give away. The ideogram: hand and ceremonial vessel, offering sacrifice. Image of Hexagram 41. **Climax**, YI: come to a high point and stop, bring to an end; use up, lay aside; decline, reject. **Necessarily**, PI: unavoidably, indispensably, certainly.

Accepting ... use: activating this hexagram depends on understanding and accepting the previous statement.

● *Contrasted Definitions*

> **Diminishing, Augmenting.**
> **Increasing and decreasing's beginning indeed.**

Associated Contexts **Increase**, SHENG: grow or make larger; flourishing, exuberant, full, abundant; heaped up; excellent, fine. **Decrease**, SHUAI: grow or make smaller; fade, decline, decay, diminish, cut off; grow old; adversity, misfortune. **'s/have(it)/it/them**, CHIH: expresses possession, directly or as an object pronoun. **Begin**, SHIH: commence, start, open; earliest, first; beginning of a time-span, ended by completion, CHUNG. The ideogram: woman and eminent, beginning new life. **Indeed**, YEH: intensifier, connective; indicates comment on previous statement.

● *Attached Evidences*

> Augmenting: actualizing tao's enriching indeed.
> Augmenting: long living enriching and not setting up.
> Augmenting: using the rising advantage. Harvesting.

Associated Contexts **Actualize tao**, TE: realize tao in action; power, virtue; ability to follow the course traced by the ongoing process of the cosmos; keyword. The ideogram: to go, straight, and heart. Linked with acquire, TE: acquiring that which makes a being become what it is meant to be. **Enrich**, YÜ: make richer (excluding land); material, mental or spiritual wealth; bequeath; generous, abundant. The ideogram: garments, portable riches.

Long living, CHANG: enduring, constant; senior, superior, greater; increase, prosper; respect, elevate. **Set up**, SHE: establish, institute; arrange, set in order; spread a net. The ideogram: words and impel, establish with words.

Use(of), YI: make use of, by means of, owing to; employ, make functional. **Rise**, HSING: get up, grow, lift; begin, give rise to, construct; be promoted; flourishing, fashionable. The ideogram: lift, two hands and unite, lift with both hands.

● *Symbol Tradition*

> Wind, thunder. Augmenting.
> A chün tzu uses seeing improvement, by consequence shifting.
> [A chün tzu uses] possessing and traversing, by consequence amending.

Associated Contexts **Wind**, FENG: moving air, breeze, gust; weather and its influence on mood and humor; fashion, usage; wind and wood are the Symbols of the trigram Ground, SUN. **Thunder**, LEI: rising, arousing power; the Symbol of the trigram Shake, CHEN.

Chün tzu: ideal of a person who uses divination to order his/her life in accordance with tao rather than wilful intention; keyword. **See**, CHIEN: seeing in all its aspects: vision, being visible, forming mental images; visit, call on, consult. The ideogram: eye above person, active and receptive sight. **Improve**, SHAN: make better, reform, perfect, repair; virtuous, wise; mild, docile; clever, skillful, handy. The ideogram: mouth and sheep, gentle speech. **By consequence(of)**, TSE: very strong connection; reason, cause, result; rule, law, pattern, standard; therefore. **Shift**, CH'IEN: move, change, transpose; improve, ascend, be promoted; deport, dismiss, remove.

Possess, YU: in possession of, have, own; opposite of lack, WU. **Traverse/exceed,** KU: go across, pass over; excessive, transgress. Image of Hexagrams 28 and 62. **Amend,** KAI: correct, reform, make new, alter, mend. The ideogram: self and strike, fighting your own errors.

● *Image Tradition*

> Above diminishing, below Augmenting. [I]
> The commoners stimulated without delimiting.
> Above origin, below the below.
> One's tao, the great shining.
>
> Advantageous to have a direction to go. Harvesting. [II]
> Centering and correcting possess reward.
> Advantageous to step into the Great River. Harvesting.
> Woody tao, thereupon moving.
>
> Augmenting stirring up and Grounding. [III]
> Sun advancing without delimiting.
> Heaven spreading out, earth giving birth.
> One's Augmenting without sides.
> Total Augmenting's tao:
> Associate with the season, accompany the movement.

Associated Contexts **[I] Above,** SHANG: anything above, in all senses; higher, upper, outer; upper trigram; opposite of below, HSIA. **Below,** HSIA: anything below, in all senses; lower, inner; lower trigram; opposite of above, SHANG.

Commoners, MIN: class of workers the state draws on to sustain the social hierarchy; undeveloped potential outside the organized personality. **Stimulate,** SHUO: rouse to action and good feeling; free from constraint, stir up, urge on; persuade, cheer, delight; set out in words; the Action of the trigram Open, TUI. The ideogram: words and exchange. **Without,** WU: devoid of; -less as suffix. **Delimit,** CHIANG: define frontiers, draw limits; boundary, border.

Origin, TZU: source, beginning, ground; cause, reason, motive; line of descent; path to the origin; yourself, intrinsic.

One's/one, CH'I: third person pronoun; also: it/its, he/his, she/hers, they/theirs. **Tao:** way or path; ongoing process of being and the course it traces for each specific person or thing; keyword. The ideogram: go and head, leading and the path it creates. **Great,** TA: big, noble, important, very;

orient the will toward a self-imposed goal, impose direction; ability to lead or guide your life; contrasts with small, HSIAO, flexible adaptation to what crosses your path; keyword. Image of Hexagrams 14, 26, 28, 34. **Shine**, KUANG: illuminate; give off brilliant, bright light; honor, glory, éclat; result of action, contrasts with brightness, MING, light of heavenly bodies. The ideogram: fire above person, lifting the light.

[II] **Centering correcting**, CHUNG CHENG: central and correct; make rectifying one-sidedness and error your central concern; reaching a stable center in yourself can correct the situation. **Reward**, CH'ING: gift given from gratitude or benevolence; favor from heaven; congratulate with gifts. The ideogram: heart, follow and deer (wealth), the heart expressed through gifts.

Wood/tree, MU: all things woody or wooden, alive or constructed from wood; associated with the Woody Moment; wood and wind are the Symbols of the trigram Ground, SUN. The ideogram: a tree with roots and branches. **Thereupon**, NAI: on that ground, because of. **Move**, HSING: move or move something; motivate, emotionally moving; walk, act, do. The ideogram: stepping left then right.

[III] **Stir up**, TUNG: excite, influence, move, affect; work, take action; come out of the egg or the bud; the Action of the trigram Shake, CHEN. The ideogram: strength and heavy, move weighty things. **Ground**, SUN: base on which things rest; support, foundation; mild, subtly penetrating; nourishing. The ideogram: stand and things arranged on it, the subtle influence of the ground. Image of Hexagram 57.

Sun/day, JIH: actual sun and the time of a sun-cycle, a day. **Advance**, CHIN: exert yourself, make progress, climb; be promoted; further the development of, augment; adopt a religion or conviction; offer, introduce.

Heaven, T'IEN: highest; sky, firmament, heavens; power above the human as opposed to earth, TI, below; the Symbol of the trigram Force, CH'IEN. The ideogram: great and the one above. **Spread out**, SHIH: expand, diffuse, distribute, arrange, exhibit; add to, aid. The ideogram: flag and indeed, claiming new country. **Earth**, TI: ground on which the human world rests; basis of all things, nourishes all things; the Symbol of the trigram Field, K'UN. **Birth/give birth to**, SHENG: produce, beget, grow, bear, arise; life, vitality. The ideogram: earth and sprout.

Sides (on all sides), FANG: limits, boundaries; square, surface of the earth extending to the four cardinal points; everywhere. **Total**, FAN: all, everything; world, humankind.

Associate(with), YÜ: consort with, combine; companions; group, band, company; agree with, comply, help. The ideogram: pair of hands reaching downward meets a pair of hands reaching upward, helpful association. **Season,** SHIH: quality of the time; the right time, opportune, in harmony; planning in accord with the time; seasons of the year. The ideogram: sun and temple, time as sacred. **Accompany,** HSIEH: take or go along with; jointly, all at once.

● *Transforming Lines*

Initial nine

a) Advantageous to avail of activating the great arousing.
   Spring auspicious, without fault.

b) Spring auspicious, without fault.
   The below, not munificent affairs indeed.

You need a purpose, a great idea around which you can organize yourself and your passion. Build the city, cast the vessel. The way to the source is open. It is the right time to act. Go forward. This is definitely not a mistake.

Associated Contexts a) **Avail of,** YUNG: take advantage of; benefit from, profit by; use for a specific purpose; apply to advantage. The ideogram: to divine and center, applying divination to central concerns. **Activate,** WEI: act or cause to act; do, make, manage; make active; attend to, help; because of. **Arouse,** TSO: stir up, stimulate, rouse from inactivity; generate; appear, arise. The ideogram: person and beginning.

 Spring, YÜAN: source, origin, head; great, excellent; arise, begin, generating power; first stage of the Time Cycle. **Auspicious,** CHI: leads to the experience of meaning; favorable, propitious, advantageous, appropriate; keyword. The ideogram: scholar and mouth, wise words of a sage. **Without fault,** WU CHIU: no error or harm in the situation.

b) **Munificence,** HOU: liberal, kind, generous; create abundance; thick, large. The ideogram: gift of a superior to an inferior. **Affairs,** SHIH: all kinds of personal activity; matters at hand; business, occupation; manage a business, case in court.

Six at second

a) "Someone" augments it: ten partnered tortoises.
   Nowhere a controlling contradiction.
   Perpetually advantageous Trial.
   The king availing of presenting to the supreme, auspicious.

b) "Someone" Augmenting it.
   Originating from outside, coming indeed.

What a fortunate answer! A blessing, a mandate from Heaven. Anything you wish to do will prosper. The way is open to your ideas, not just now, but in the future. Enjoy it! But remember the spirit in your happiness. Then the way will truly be open.

Associated Contexts a) **Maybe/"Someone"**, HUO: possible, perhaps; indicates spirit is active. **Ten**, SHIH: goal and end of reckoning; whole, complete, all; entire, perfected, the full amount; reach everywhere, receive everything. The ideogram: East–West line crosses North–South line, a grid that contains all. **Partner**, P'ENG: associate for mutual benefit; two equal or similar things; companions, friends, peers; join in; commercial ventures. The ideogram: linked strings of cowries or coins. **Tortoise**, KUEI: turtles; armored animals, shells and shields; long-living; oracle-consulting by tortoise shell; image of the macrocosm: heaven and earth, between them the soft flesh of humans.

Nothing/nowhere, FU: strong negative; not a single thing/place. **Control**, K'O: command; check, impede, prevail, obstruct, repress; adequate, able. The ideogram: roof beams support a house, controlling the structure. **Contradict**, WEI: oppose, disregard, disobey; seditious, perverse.

Perpetual, YUNG: continuing; everlasting, ever-flowing. The ideogram: flowing water. **Trial**, CHEN: inquiry by divination and its result; righteous, firm; separating wheat from chaff; the kernel, the proven core; fourth stage of the Time Cycle. The ideogram: pearl and divination. **Auspicious**, CHI: leads to the experience of meaning; favorable, propitious, advantageous, appropriate; keyword. The ideogram: scholar and mouth, wise words of a sage.

King(hood), WANG: effective ruler, by authority of the Emperor, from whom others derive their power. **Avail of**, YUNG: take advantage of; benefit from, profit by; use for a specific purpose; apply to advantage. The ideogram: to divine and center, applying divination to central concerns. **Present(to)**, HSIANG: present in sacrifice, offer with thanks, give to the gods or a superior; confer dignity on. **Supreme**, TI: highest, above all on earth; sovereign lord, source of power; emperor.

b) **It/them/have(it)/'s**, CHIH: expresses possession, directly or as an object pronoun.

Outside, WAI: outer, exterior, external; people working in places other than their home; unfamiliar, foreign; the upper trigram, as opposed to inside, NEI, the lower. **Come,** LAI, and **go,** WANG, describe the stream of time as it flows from future through present to past; come, LAI, indicates what is approaching; move toward, arrive at; keyword.

> **Six at third**
>
> *a)* Augmenting's availing of pitfall affairs.
>   Without fault.
>   There is a connection to the spirit, center moving.
>   Notify the prince, avail of the scepter.
>
> *b)* Augmenting availing of pitfall affairs.
>   Firmly possessing it indeed.

What seems like an unfortunate happening will turn out to your benefit. Act on your ideas. This is not a mistake. The capital city is being shifted and you are part of it. Tell your prince and your people what is happening. Insist on your right to speak. You are connected to the spirits and they will carry you through.

Associated Contexts a) **Avail of,** YUNG: take advantage of; benefit from, profit by; use for a specific purpose; apply to advantage. The ideogram: to divine and center, applying divination to central concerns. **Pitfall,** HSIUNG: leads away from the experience of meaning; stuck and exposed to danger, unable to take in the situation; flow of life and spirit is blocked; unfortunate, baleful; keyword. **Affairs,** SHIH: all kinds of personal activity; matters at hand; business, occupation; manage a business, case in court.

Without fault, WU CHIU: no error or harm in the situation.

There is … spirit, YU FU: inner and outer are in accord; confidence of the spirits has been captured; sincere, truthful; proper to take action. **Center,** CHUNG: inner, central; put in the center; middle, stable point enabling you to face inner and outer changes; middle line of trigram. The ideogram: field divided in two equal parts. Image of Hexagram 61.

Notify, KAO: proclaim, order, decree; advise, inform, tell. The ideogram: mouth and ox head, imposing speech. **Prince,** KUNG: nobles acting as ministers of state in the capital; governing from the center rather than active in daily life; contrasts with feudatory, HOU, governors of the provinces. **Scepter,** KUEI: sign of rank that gives you freedom to report to the prince.

b) **Firm,** KU: constant, fixed, steady; chronic, recurrent. The ideogram: old and enclosure, long preserved. **It/them/have(it)/'s,** CHIH: expresses possession, directly or as an object pronoun.

Six at fourth

a) Center moving.
   Notify the prince, adhere to him.
   Advantageous to avail of activating depending on shifting the city.
   Harvesting.

b) Notifying the prince, adhering.
   Using Augmenting purpose indeed.

This is a great change in the center of power. The center of life is shifting. Stay loyal to your friends. Act on your ideas. Depend on the fact that everything is changing. You are an important part of it.

Associated Contexts a) **Center**, CHUNG: inner, central; put in the center; middle, stable point enabling you to face inner and outer changes; middle line of trigram. The ideogram: field divided in two equal parts. Image of Hexagram 61.

   Notify, KAO: proclaim, order, decree; advise, inform, tell. The ideogram: mouth and ox head, imposing speech. **Prince**, KUNG: nobles acting as ministers of state in the capital; governing from the center rather than active in daily life; contrasts with feudatory, HOU, governors of the provinces. **Adhere(to)**, TS'UNG: follow a way, hold to a doctrine, school, or person; hear and comply with, agree to; forced to follow, follower. The ideogram: two men walking, one following the other.

   Avail of, YUNG: take advantage of; benefit from, profit by; use for a specific purpose; apply to advantage. The ideogram: to divine and center, applying divination to central concerns. **Activate**, WEI: act or cause to act; do, make, manage; make active; attend to, help; because of. **Depend on**, YI: rely on, trust; conform to; image, illustration. **City**, KUO: area of only human constructions; political unit, polis. First of the territorial zones: city, suburbs, countryside, forests.

b) **Purpose**, CHIH: focus of mind and heart; will, inclination, resolve. The ideogram: heart and scholar, high inner resolve, or heart and go, inner determination.

Nine at fifth

a) There is a connection to the spirit and a benevolent heart.
   No question, Spring auspicious.
   There is a connection to the spirit. "Benevolence is my actualizing tao."

b) There is a connection to the spirit, a benevolent heart.
  Actually no questioning it.
  "Benevolence is my actualizing tao."
  The great acquiring a purpose indeed.

Act through your virtue and kindness. You have a kind, generous heart and a noble spirit. Don't question this. Use it. The way is fundamentally open. Your benevolence connects you to the Way.

Associated Contexts a) **There is … spirit**, YU FU: inner and outer are in accord; confidence of the spirits has been captured; sincere, truthful; proper to take action. **Benevolence**, HUI: regard for others, humanity; fulfil social duties; unselfish, kind, merciful. **Heart**, HSIN: heart as center of being; seat of mind's images and affections; moral nature; source of desires, intentions, will.

Question, WEN: ask, inquire about, examine; clear up doubts; convict and sentence. **Spring**, YÜAN: source, origin, head; great, excellent; arise, begin, generating power; first stage of the Time Cycle. **Auspicious**, CHI: leads to the experience of meaning; favorable, propitious, advantageous, appropriate; keyword. The ideogram: scholar and mouth, wise words of a sage.

My/me/I, WO: first person pronoun; indicates an unusually strong emphasis on your own subjective experience.

b) **Actually**, YI: truly, really, at present. The ideogram: a dart and done, strong intention fully expressed. **It/them/have(it)/'s**, CHIH: expresses possession, directly or as an object pronoun.

Acquire, TE: obtain the desired object; wish for, desire covetously; gains, possessions. The ideogram: go and obstacle, going through obstacles to the goal. **Purpose**, CHIH: focus of mind and heart; will, inclination, resolve. The ideogram: heart and scholar, high inner resolve, or heart and go, inner determination.

Nine above

a) Absolutely not Augmenting it.
  Maybe smiting it.
  Establishing the heart, no persevering.
  Pitfall.

b) Absolutely not Augmenting it.
   One sided evidence indeed.
   Maybe smiting it.
   Originating from outside, coming indeed.

This means disaster comes from outside. You are being fickle, wayward, and perhaps deceitful. Nothing good can come of this. The way will close and you will be left open to danger. Fix and steady your emotions.

Associated   Contexts   a) **Absolutely no(thing)**, MO: complete elimination; not any, by no means. **It/them/have(it)/'s**, CHIH: expresses possession, directly or as an object pronoun.

   Maybe/"someone", HUO: possible but not certain, perhaps; indicates spirit is active. **Smite**, CHI: hit, beat, attack; hurl against, rush a position; rouse to action. The ideogram: hand and hit, fist punching.

   Establish, LI: set up, institute, order, arrange; stand erect; settled principles. **Heart**, HSIN: heart as center of being; seat of mind's images and affections; moral nature; source of desires, intentions, will. **Persevere**, HENG: continue in the same way or spirit; constant, perpetual, regular; self-renewing; extend everywhere. Image of Hexagram 32.

   Pitfall, HSIUNG: leads away from the experience of meaning; stuck and exposed to danger, unable to take in the situation; flow of life and spirit is blocked; unfortunate, baleful; keyword.

b) **One sided**, P'IEN: excessive, partial, selfish; long for, bent on; lit.: inclined to one side. **Evidence**, TZ'U: verbal proof; instructions, orders, arguments; apology.

   Outside, WAI: outer, exterior, external; people working in places other than their home; unfamiliar, foreign; the upper trigram, as opposed to inside, NEI, the lower. **Come**, LAI, and go, WANG, describe the stream of time as it flows from future through present to past; come, LAI, indicates what is approaching; move toward, arrive at; keyword.

DECIDING/PARTING ▮ *KUAI*

Resolution, act clearly, make a decision and announce it; breakthrough; part from the past, separate; clean it out and bring it to light.

Deciding/Parting describes your situation in terms of resolutely confronting difficulties. Its symbol is announcing the results of an oracle and the parting of two streams. The way to deal with it is to clarify what you must do and act on it, even if you must leave something behind. Move quickly. Display your decision resolutely at the center of effective power. Have confidence in proclaiming it, for you are connected to the spirits and they will carry you through. You will confront difficulties. There is an angry old ghost in the situation that has returned to take revenge for past mistreatment. Notify those who love, trust and depend on you. Don't resort to arms, attack or build up defenses. Have a place to go. Impose a direction on things. That brings profit and insight.

● *Image of the Situation*

> Parting, display it in the king's chambers.
> A connection to the spirits, cry out, possessing adversity.
> This notifying originates from the capital.
> Not advantageous: approaching with arms.
> Advantageous to have a direction to go. Harvesting.

Associated Contexts **Decide/Part**, KUAI: separate, fork, cut off, decide; pull or flow in different directions; certain, settled; prompt, decisive, stern. **Display**, YANG: spread, extend, scatter, divulge; publish abroad, make famous. The ideogram: hand and expand, spreading a message. **King(hood)**, WANG: effective ruler, by authority of the Emperor, from whom others derive their power. **Chambers**, T'ING: family room, courtyard, hall; domestic. The ideogram: shelter and hall, a secure place.

Connection, FU: accord between inner and outer in a particular moment; sincere, truthful, verified, reliable, in accord with the spirits; capture; prisoners, spoils; contrasts with trustworthy, HSIN, consistent over time. The ideogram: bird's claw enclosing young animals, possessive grip.

Image of Hexagram 61. **Cry out/outcry**, HAO: call out, proclaim; signal, order, command; mark, label, sign. **Possess**, YU: in possession of, have, own; opposite of lack, WU. **Adversity**, LI: danger; threatening, malevolent demon. This has two aspects: grind, sharpen, improve, perfect, stimulate; and: poisonous, sinister, cruel, contrary. It indicates a spirit or ghost that seeks revenge by inflicting suffering upon the living. Pacifying or exorcizing such a spirit can have a healing effect. The ideogram: sheltering cliff and stinging insect.

Notify, KAO: proclaim, order, decree; advise, inform, tell. The ideogram: mouth and ox head, imposing speech. **Origin**, TZU: source, beginning, ground; cause, reason, motive; line of descent; path to the origin; yourself, intrinsic. **Capital**, YI: populous fortified city, center and symbol of the domain it rules. The ideogram: enclosure and official seal.

Advantageous/Harvest, LI: advantageous, profitable; acute, insightful; benefit, nourish; third stage of the Time Cycle. **Approach**, CHI: come near to, advance toward; about to do; soon. **Arms**, JUNG: weapons; armed people, soldiers; military, violent. The ideogram: spear and armor, offensive and defensive weapons.

Have a direction to go, YU YU WANG: imposing a direction on the flow of time from present to past; have a specific goal or purpose.

● *Outer and Inner Aspects*

☱ **Open**: vapor rising from the marsh's open surface stimulates and fertilizes; stimulating words cheer and inspire. **Open** begins the yin hemicycle by initiating the formative process.

Connection to the outer: liquifying, casting, skinning off the mold, the Metallic Moment beginning. **Open** stimulates, cheers and reveals innate form.

☰ **Force**: The force of heaven struggles on, persistent and unwearied; heavenly bodies persist in their orbits. **Force** is the center of the yin hemicycle, completing the formative process.

Connection to the inner: struggling forces are bound together in dynamic tension, the Metallic Moment culminating. **Force** brings elements to grips, creating enduring relations.

Inner struggle is broken up by outer stimulation, **parting** the grappling powers.

● *Hidden Possibility*

The doubled Nuclear trigram **Force**, CH'IEN, results in Nuclear Hexagram 1, **Force**, CH'IEN. **Decisive** words and actions connect you with the creative drive of **force**.

● *Sequence*

> Augmenting and not climaxing necessarily breaks up.
> Accepting this lets you use Parting.
> Parting implies breaking up indeed.

Associated Contexts **Augment**, YI: increase, advance, promote, benefit, strengthen; pour in more; full, superabundant; restorative. The ideogram: water and vessel, pouring in more. Image of Hexagram 42. **Climax**, YI: come to a high point and stop, bring to an end; use up, lay aside; decline, reject. **Necessarily**, PI: unavoidably, indispensably, certainly. **Break up**, CHÜEH: streams diverging; break through an obstacle and scatter; separate, break into parts; cut or bite through; decide, pass sentence. The ideogram: water and parting.

Accepting ... use: activating this hexagram depends on understanding and accepting the previous statement.

Imply, CHE: further signify; additional meaning. **Indeed/is/means**, YEH: intensifier; indicates comment on previous statement.

● *Contrasted Definitions*

> Coupling: meeting indeed.
> Supple meeting strong indeed.
> Parting: breaking up indeed.
> Strong breaking up supple indeed.

Associated Contexts **Couple**, KOU: driven encounter, at once transitory and enduring, that is the reflection of primal yin and yang; meet, encounter, copulate; mating animals; magnetism, gravity; to be gripped by impersonal forces. Image of Hexagram 44. **Meet**, YÜ: come on unexpectedly, encounter; occur, happen; pleasant meeting, lucky coincidence; agree.

Supple, JOU: quality of the opened lines; flexible, pliant, tender, adaptable. **Strong**, KANG: quality of the whole lines; firm, strong, unyielding, persisting.

● *Symbol Tradition*

> Above marsh with respect to heaven. Parting.
> A chün tzu uses spreading out benefits to extend to the below.
> [A chün tzu uses] residing in actualizing tao,
> by consequence keeping aloof.

Associated Contexts **Above,** SHANG: anything above, in all senses; higher, upper, outer; upper trigram; opposite of below, HSIA. **Marsh,** TSE: open surface of a flat body of water and the vapors rising from it; fertilize, enrich; kindness, favor; the Symbol of the trigram Open, TUI. **With respect to,** YÜ: relates to, refers to; hold a position in. **Heaven,** T'IEN: highest; sky, firmament, heavens; power above the human as opposed to earth, TI, below; the Symbol of the trigram Force, CH'IEN. The ideogram: great and the one above.

Chün tzu: ideal of a person who uses divination to order his/her life in accordance with tao rather than wilful intention; keyword. **Use(of),** YI: make use of, by means of, owing to; employ, make functional. **Spread out,** SHIH: expand, diffuse, distribute, arrange, exhibit; add to, aid. The ideogram: flag and indeed, claiming new country. **Benefits,** LU: pay, salary, income; have the use of; goods received, revenues; official recognition. **Extend(to),** CHI: reach to, draw out, prolong; continuous, enduring. **Below,** HSIA: anything below, in all senses; lower, inner; lower trigram; opposite of above, SHANG.

Reside(in), CHÜ: dwell, live in, stay; sit down, fill an office; settled parts of a country. The ideogram: body and seat. **Actualize tao,** TE: realize tao in action; power, virtue; ability to follow the course traced by the ongoing process of the cosmos; keyword. The ideogram: to go, straight, and heart. Linked with acquire, TE: acquiring that which makes a being become what it is meant to be. **By consequence(of),** TSE: very strong connection; reason, cause, result; rule, law, pattern, standard; therefore. **Keep aloof,** CHI: keep at a distance; avoid, fear, shun; antipathy. The ideogram: heart and self, keeping to yourself.

● *Image Tradition*

> Parting. Breaking up indeed. [I]
> Strong breaking up supple indeed.
> Persisting and stimulating.
> Breaking up and harmonizing.

Display it in the king's chambers. [II]
Supple riding five strongs indeed.
Connection to the spirits, crying out, possessing adversity.
One's exposure thereupon shining indeed.

This notifying originates from the capital. [III]
Not advantageous: approaching with arms.
The place to honor is thereupon exhausted.
Advantageous to have a direction to go. Harvesting.
Strong long living, thereupon completing indeed.

Associated Contexts [I] **Persist,** CHIEN: strong, robust, dynamic, tenacious; continuous; unwearied heavenly bodies in their orbits; the Action of the trigram Force, CH'IEN. **Stimulate,** SHUO: rouse to action and good feeling; free from constraint, stir up, urge on; persuade, cheer, delight; set out in words; the Action of the trigram Open, TUI. The ideogram: words and exchange.

Harmony, HO: concord, union; conciliate; at peace, mild; fit, tune, adjust.

[II] **Ride,** CH'ENG: ride an animal or a chariot; have the upper hand, seize the right time; control strong power; overcome the nature of the other; supple opened line above a strong whole line. **Five,** WU: number for active groups: Five Moments, Directions, colors, smells, tastes, tones, feelings; fifth.

One's/one, CH'I: third person pronoun; also: it/its, he/his, she/hers, they/theirs. **Expose,** WEI: exposed to danger, precipitous, unsteady; too high, not upright; uneasy. The ideogram: overhanging rock, person and limit, exposure in an extreme position. **Thereupon,** NAI: on that ground, because of. **Shine,** KUANG: illuminate; give off brilliant, bright light; honor, glory, éclat; result of action, contrasts with brightness, MING, light of heavenly bodies. The ideogram: fire above person, lifting the light.

[III] **Place,** SO: where something belongs or comes from; residence, dwelling; habitual focus or object. **Honor,** SHANG: esteem, give high rank to; eminent; put one thing on top of another. **Exhaust,** CH'IUNG: bring to an end; limit, extremity; destitute; investigate exhaustively; end without a new beginning. The ideogram: cave and naked person, bent with disease or old age.

Long living, CHANG: enduring, constant; senior, superior, greater; increase, prosper; respect, elevate. **Complete,** CHUNG: end of a cycle that begins the next; last, whole, all; contrasts with exhaust, CH'IUNG, final end.

The ideogram: silk cocoons, follow and ice, winter linking one year with the next.

● *Transforming Lines*

Initial nine

a) Invigorating the preceding foot.
   Going and not mastering, activating faulty.

b) Not mastering and going.
   Fault indeed.

If you try to take the lead, you will most certainly fail. You simply aren't prepared for it yet. This is not the way to go about things.

Associated Contexts a) **Invigorate**, CHUANG: inspirit, animate; strong, robust; full grown, flourishing, abundant; attain manhood (at 30); damage through unrestrained strength. The ideogram: strength and scholar, intellectual impact. Image of Hexagram 34. **Precede**, CH'IEN: come before in time and thus in value; anterior, former, ancient; lead forward. **Foot**, CHIH: literal foot; foundation, base.

   Go, WANG, and **come**, LAI, describe the stream of time as it flows from future through present to past; go, WANG, indicates what is departing from present to past; proceed, move on; keyword. **Master**, SHENG: have the upper hand, conquer; worthy of, able to; control, check, command. **Activate**, WEI: act or cause to act; do, make, manage; make active; attend to, help; because of. **Fault**, CHIU: unworthy conduct that leads to harm, illness, misfortune. The ideogram: person and differ, differ from what you should be.

Nine at second

a) Alarms, outcries.
   Absolutely no night time, possessing arms.
   No cares.

b) Possessing arms, no cares.
   Acquiring centering tao indeed.

A tense and invigorating situation, with things coming from all sides. Don't worry. Bring out the hidden. Let past sorrows go. You will obtain what you want. This can renew your creative life.

Associated Contexts a) **Alarm**, T'I: alarmed and cautious; respect, regard, fear; stand in awe of. The ideogram: heart and versatile, the heart aware of sudden change.

Absolutely no(thing), MO: complete elimination; not any, by no means. **Night time**, YEH: dark half of 24 hour cycle.

Care, HSÜ: fear, doubt, concern; heartfelt attachment; relieve, soothe, aid; sympathy, compassion, consolation. The ideogram: heart and blood, the heart's blood affected.

b) **Acquire**, TE: obtain the desired object; wish for, desire covetously; gains, possessions. The ideogram: go and obstacle, going through obstacles to the goal. **Center**, CHUNG: inner, central; put in the center; middle, stable point enabling you to face inner and outer changes; middle line of trigram. The ideogram: field divided in two equal parts. Image of Hexagram 61. **Tao**: way or path; ongoing process of being and the course it traces for each specific person or thing; keyword. The ideogram: go and head, leading and the path it creates.

Nine at third

a) Invigorating in the cheek bones:
  Possessing a pitfall.
  A chün tzu: Parting, Parting.
  Solitary going, meeting rain.
  Like being soaked, possessing indignation.
  Without fault.

b) A chün tzu: Parting, Parting.
  Completing without fault indeed.

You are involved with cruel people intent on their mastery. This way is closed. See this clearly and leave now. You will be caught in a flood of insults and abuse. This is not a mistake. Be very clear and leave now.

Associated Contexts a) **Invigorate**, CHUANG: inspirit, animate; strong, robust; full grown, flourishing, abundant; attain manhood (at 30); damage through unrestrained strength. The ideogram: strength and scholar, intellectual impact. Image of Hexagram 34. **Cheek bones**, CH'ÜAN: facial feature denoting character; high cheek-bones indicate cruelty.

Pitfall, HSIUNG: leads away from the experience of meaning; stuck and exposed to danger, unable to take in the situation; flow of life and spirit is blocked; unfortunate, baleful; keyword.

Parting: The doubled character intensifies this quality. **Solitary,** TI: alone, single; isolated, abandoned. **Go,** WANG, and come, LAI, describe the stream of time as it flows from future through present to past; go, WANG, indicates what is departing from present to past; proceed, move on; keyword. **Rain,** YÜ: all precipitation; sudden showers, fast and furious; associated with the trigram Gorge, K'AN, and the Streaming Moment.

Like, JO: same as; just as, similar to. **Soak,** JU: immerse, steep; damp, wet; stain, pollute, blemish; urinate on. **Indignation,** WEN: irritated, wrathful; feeling of injustice, rage; hateful.

Without fault, WU CHIU: no error or harm in the situation.

Nine at fourth

a) The sacrum without flesh.
One moves the resting place moreover.
Haul along the goat, repenting extinguished.
Hearing words untrustworthy.

b) One moves the resting place moreover.
Situation not appropriate indeed.
Hearing words, untrustworthy.
Understanding not brightened indeed.

You have been punished or hurt and are isolated. You must move to a new location. Stay adaptable. See this as a gift from fate. Don't get caught up in negative emotions. Fear not. Your sorrows will soon disappear. Don't believe what people tell you right now, and keep your own speech guarded.

Associated Contexts a) **Sacrum,** T'UN: lower back where it joins legs; buttocks, seat, lower spine. **Without,** WU: devoid of; -less as suffix. **Flesh,** FU: muscles, organs, skin, in contrast to bones.

Move, HSING: move or move something; motivate, emotionally moving; walk, act, do. The ideogram: stepping left then right. **Rest(ing place),** TZ'U: camp, inn, shed; halting-place, breathing-spell; put in consecutive order. The ideogram: two and breath, pausing to breathe. **Moreover,** CH'IEH: further, and also.

Haul along, CH'IEN: haul or pull, drag behind; pull an animal on a rope; pull toward. The ideogram: ox and halter. **Goat,** YANG: sheep and goats; direct thought and action. **Repenting extinguished,** HUI WANG: previous troubles and consequent remorse will disappear.

Hear, WEN: perceive sound; learn by report; news, fame. The ideogram: ear and door. **Word,** YEN: speech, spoken words, sayings; talk, discuss, address. The ideogram: mouth and rising vapor, words as speech. **Trustworthy**, HSIN: truthful, faithful, consistent over time; integrity; confide in, follow; credentials; contrasts with conforming, FU, connection in a specific moment. The ideogram: person and word, true speech.

b) **Situation**, WEI: place or seat according to rank; post, position, command; right, proper; established, arranged. The ideogram: person and stand, servants in their places. **Appropriate**, TANG: suitable; opportune, convenient; adequate, competent; equal to; whole lines in uneven places and opened lines in even places.

Understand, TS'UNG: perceive quickly, astute, sharp; discriminate intelligently. The ideogram: ear and quick. **Brightness**, MING: light-giving aspect of burning, heavenly bodies and consciousness; with fire, the Symbol of the trigram Radiance, LI.

   Nine at fifth

   a) Reeds, highlands: Parting, Parting.
   Center moving, without fault.

   b) Center moving, without fault.
   Center not yet shining indeed.

You have to choose between two clear alternatives. Decide now. Don't be afraid of radical change. There is a creative force at work. It is time to move the center of your world. Do it now!

Associated Contexts a) **Reeds**, KUAN: marsh and swamp plants, rushes. **Highlands**, LU: high, dry land as distinct from swamps; plateau. **Parting**: the doubled character intensifies this quality.

   Center, CHUNG: inner, central; put in the center; middle, stable point enabling you to face inner and outer changes; middle line of trigram. The ideogram: field divided in two equal parts. Image of Hexagram 61. **Move**, HSING: move or move something; motivate, emotionally moving; walk, act, do. The ideogram: stepping left then right. **Without fault**, WU CHIU: no error or harm in the situation.

b) **Not yet**, WEI: temporal negative; something will but has not yet occurred; contrary of already, CHI. Image of Hexagram 64. **Shine**, KUANG: illuminate; give off brilliant, bright light; honor, glory, éclat; result of action, contrasts with brightness, MING, light of heavenly bodies. The ideogram: fire above person, lifting the light.

Six above

a) Without crying out.
   Completing: possessing a pitfall.

b) Without crying out's pitfall.
   Completing not permitting long living indeed.

If you don't communicate about what you are doing, you will be cut off and isolated. Call out. Tell us about it.

Associated Contexts a) **Without,** WU: devoid of; -less as suffix. **Pitfall,** HSIUNG: leads away from the experience of meaning; stuck and exposed to danger, unable to take in the situation; flow of life and spirit is blocked; unfortunate, baleful; keyword.

b) **'s/have(it)/it/them,** CHIH: expresses possession, directly or as an object pronoun.
   Not permitting, PU K'O: not possible; contradicts an inherent principle. The ideogram: mouth and breath, silent consent.

44

COUPLING ▮ KOU

Welcome, encounter, open yourself to; intense contact; all forms of sexual intercourse; don't grasp things, act through the yin.

Coupling describes your situation in terms of opening yourself to welcome what comes. Its symbol is the strong woman who carries a hidden fate. You can deal with it by realizing that the brief and intense moment of encounter reflects a connection of the primal powers. Don't try to grasp the woman. The connection is there, full of invigorating strength. Don't try to grasp and hold on to things. What seems a brief contact connects you with creative force.

● *Image of the Situation*

> **Coupling, womanhood invigorating.**
> **Do not avail of grasping the woman.**

Associated Contexts **Couple**, KOU: intense, driven encounter, at once transitory and enduring, that is the reflection of primal yin and yang; meet, encounter, copulate; mating animals; magnetism, gravity; to be gripped by impersonal forces. **Woman(hood)**, NÜ: a woman; what is inherently female. **Invigorate**, CHUANG: inspirit, animate; strong, robust; full grown, flourishing, abundant; attain manhood (at 30); damage through unrestrained strength. The ideogram: strength and scholar, intellectual impact. Image of Hexagram 34.

Avail of, YUNG: take advantage of; benefit from, profit by; use for a specific purpose; apply to advantage. The ideogram: to divine and center, applying divination to central concerns. **Grasp**, CH'Ü: lay hold of, take and use, seize, appropriate; grasp the meaning, understand. The ideogram: ear and hand, hear and grasp.

● *Outer and Inner Aspects*

☰ **Force**: The force of heaven struggles on, persistent and unwearied; heavenly bodies persist in their orbits. **Force** is the center of the yin hemicycle, completing the formative process.

Connection to the outer: struggling forces are bound together in dynamic tension, the Metallic Moment culminating. **Force** brings elements to grips, creating enduring relations.

☷ **Ground**: Wind and wood subtly enter from the ground, penetrating and pervading. **Ground** is the center of the yang hemicycle, spreading pervasive action.

Connection to the inner: penetrating and bringing together, the Woody Moment culminating. **Ground** pervades, matches and couples, seeding a new generation.

Primal forces **couple** in the inner world, seeding enduring new forms. These trigrams form the vertical axis of yin and yang.

● *Hidden Possibility*

The doubled Nuclear trigram **Force**, CH'IEN, results in Nuclear Hexagram 1, **Force**, CH'IEN. The intensity of **coupling** connects you with the creative energy of **force**.

● *Sequence*

> Breaking up necessarily possesses meeting.
> Accepting this lets you use Coupling.
> Coupling implies meeting indeed.

Associated Contexts **Break up**, CHÜEH: streams diverging; break through an obstacle and scatter; separate, break into parts; cut or bite through; decide, pass sentence. The ideogram: water and parting. **Necessarily**, PI: unavoidably, indispensably, certainly. **Possess**, YU: in possession of, have, own; opposite of lack, WU. **Meet**, YÜ: come on unexpectedly, encounter; occur, happen; pleasant meeting, lucky coincidence; agree.

Accepting ... use: activating this hexagram depends on understanding and accepting the previous statement.

Imply, CHE: further signify; additional meaning. **Indeed/is/means**, YEH: intensifier, connective; indicates comment on previous statement.

● *Contrasted Definitions*

> Coupling: meeting indeed.
> Supple meeting solid indeed.
> Parting: breaking up indeed.
> Strong breaking up supple indeed.

Associated Contexts **Supple,** JOU: quality of the opened lines; flexible, pliant, tender, adaptable. **Strong,** KANG: quality of the whole lines; firm, strong, unyielding, persisting. **Part,** KUAI: separate, fork, cut off, decide; pull or flow in different directions; certain, settled; prompt, decisive, stern. Image of Hexagram 43.

- ● *Symbol Tradition*

> Below heaven possessing wind. Coupling.
> The crown prince uses spreading out the mandate
> to command the four sides.

Associated Contexts **Below,** HSIA: anything below, in all senses; lower, inner; lower trigram; opposite of above, SHANG. **Heaven,** T'IEN: highest; sky, firmament, heavens; power above the human as opposed to earth, TI, below; the Symbol of the trigram Force, CH'IEN. The ideogram: great and the one above. **Wind,** FENG: moving air, breeze, gust; weather and its influence on mood and humor; fashion, usage; wind and wood are the Symbols of the trigram Ground, SUN.

Crown prince, HOU: successor to the sovereign. The ideogram: one, mouth and shelter, one with the sovereign's orders. **Use(of),** YI: make use of, by means of, owing to; employ, make functional. **Spread out,** SHIH: expand, diffuse, distribute, arrange, exhibit; add to, aid. The ideogram: flag and indeed, claiming new country. **Fate/mandate,** MING: individual destiny; birth and death as limits of life; issue orders with authority; consult the gods. The ideogram: mouth and order, words with heavenly authority. **Command,** KAO: give orders; insist on, express wishes; official seal. The ideogram: words and announce, verbal commands. **Four sides,** SSU FANG: the cardinal points; the limits or boundaries of the earth; everywhere, all around.

- ● *Image Tradition*

> Coupling. Meeting indeed. [I]
> Supple meeting strong indeed.
> Do not avail of grasping the woman.
> Not permitting associating with long living indeed.
>
> Heaven, Earth: mutually meeting. [II]
> The kinds: beings conjoining composition indeed.

Strong meeting, centered and correct. [III]
Below Heaven, the great moving indeed.
Actually Coupling's season righteously great in fact.

Associated Contexts [I] **Not permitting**, PU K'O: not possible; contradicts an inherent principle. The ideogram: mouth and breath, silent consent. **Associate(with)**, YÜ: consort with, combine; companions; group, band, company; agree with, comply, help. The ideogram: pair of hands reaching downward meets a pair of hands reaching upward, helpful association. **Long living**, CHANG: enduring, constant; senior, superior, greater; increase, prosper; respect, elevate.

[II] **Heaven**, T'IEN: highest; sky, firmament, heavens; power above the human as opposed to earth, TI, below; the Symbol of the trigram Force, CH'IEN. The ideogram: great and the one above. **Earth**, TI: ground on which the human world rests; basis of all things, nourishes all things; the Symbol of the trigram Field, K'UN. **Mutual**, HSIANG: reciprocal assistance, encourage, help; bring together, blend with; examine, inspect; by turns.

Kinds, P'IN: species and their essential qualities; sorts, classes; classify, select. **Being(s)**, WU: creature, thing, any single being; matter, substance, essence; nature of things. **Conjoin**, HSIEN: come into contact with, influence; reach, join together; put together as parts of a previously separated whole; come into conjunction, as the celestial bodies; totally, completely; lit.: broken piece of pottery, the halves of which join to identify partners. Image of Hexagram 31. **Composition**, CHANG: a well-composed whole and its structure; beautiful creations; elegant, clear, brilliant; contrasts with pattern, WEN, beauty of intrinsic design.

[III] **Centering correcting**, CHUNG CHENG: central and correct; make rectifying one-sidedness and error your central concern; reaching a stable center in yourself can correct the situation.

Below Heaven, T'IEN HSIA: the human world, between heaven and earth. **Great**, TA: big, noble, important, very; orient the will toward a self-imposed goal, impose direction; ability to lead or guide your life; contrasts with small, HSIAO, flexible adaptation to what crosses your path; keyword. Image of Hexagrams 14, 26, 28, 34. **Move**, HSIANG: move or move something; motivate, emotionally moving; walk, act, do. The ideogram: stepping left then right.

Actually ... in fact, YI TSAI: stresses the importance of a statement. The ideogram: a dart and done, strong intention fully expressed. **'s/have(it)/it/them**, CHIH: expresses possession, directly or as an object pronoun. **Season,** SHIH: quality of the time; the right time, opportune, in harmony; planning in accord with the time; seasons of the year. The ideogram: sun and temple, time as sacred. **Righteous,** YI: proper and just, meets the standards; things in their proper place; the heart that rules itself; upright, moral rule; contrasts with Harvest, LI, advantage or profit.

● *Transforming Lines*

> **Initial six**
>
> *a)* **Attaching to a metallic chock.**
> **Trial: auspicious.**
> **Having a direction to go.**
> **You will see a pitfall.**
> **Ruining the pig connection, hoof dragging.**
>
> *b)* **Attaching to a metallic chock.**
> **Supple tao hauling along indeed.**

Hold back. Don't act this impulse out. If you have a plan to act, the Way will close. Accept the sacrifice represented by the pig. Give up your immediate plans and sort this out. If you try to control things, you'll get all tangled up.

Associated Contexts a) **Attach,** HSI: fasten to, bind, tie; retain, continue; keep in mind, emotionally attached. **Metallic,** CHIN: smelting and casting; all things pertaining to metal, particularly gold; autumn, West, sunset; one of the Five Moments. **Chock,** NI: block used to stop a cart wheel; inquire, investigate.

Trial, CHEN: inquiry by divination and its result; righteous, firm; separating wheat from chaff; the kernel, the proven core; fourth stage of the Time Cycle. The ideogram: pearl and divination. **Auspicious,** CHI: leads to the experience of meaning; favorable, propitious, advantageous, appropriate; keyword. The ideogram: scholar and mouth, wise words of a sage.

Have a direction to go, YU YU WANG: imposing a direction on the flow of time from present to past; have a specific goal or purpose.

See, CHIEN: seeing in all its aspects: vision, being visible, forming mental images; visit, call on, consult. The ideogram: eye above person, active and receptive sight. **Pitfall,** HSIUNG: leads away from the experience of meaning; stuck and exposed to danger, unable to take in the situation; flow of life and spirit is blocked; unfortunate, baleful; keyword.

Ruin, LEI: destroy, break, overturn; debilitated, meager, emaciated; entangled. **Pig**, SHIH: all swine; sign of wealth and good fortune; associated with the Streaming Moment. **Connection**, FU: accord between inner and outer in a particular moment; sincere, truthful, verified, reliable, in accord with the spirits; capture; prisoners, spoils; contrasts with trustworthy, HSIN, consistent over time. The ideogram: bird's claw enclosing young animals, possessive grip. Image of Hexagram 61. **Hoof**, TI: pig's trotters and horse's hooves. **Drag**, CHU: pull along a hurt or malfunctioning foot; limping, lame. The ideogram: foot and worm, an infected foot.

b) **Tao**: way or path; ongoing process of being and the course it traces for each specific person or thing; keyword. The ideogram: go and head, leading and the path it creates. **Haul along**, CH'IEN: haul or pull, drag behind; pull an animal on a rope; pull toward. The ideogram: ox and halter.

Nine at second

a) **Enwrapping possessing fish.**
   Without fault.
   Not advantageous: guesting.

b) **Enwrapping possessing fish.**
   Righteously not extending to guesting indeed.

Stay quiet and withdrawn. Your ideas have born fruit and the womb is full. They need quiet and intimacy. It won't help you to be or receive a guest.

Associated Contexts a) **Enwrap**, PAO: envelop, hold, contain; patient; take on responsibility, engaged. The ideogram: enfold and self, a fetus in the womb. **Fish**, YÜ: scaly, aquatic beings hidden in the water; symbol of abundance; connected with the Streaming Moment.
   Without fault, WU CHIU: no error or harm in the situation.
   Advantageous/Harvest, LI: advantageous, profitable; acute, insightful; benefit, nourish; third stage of the Time Cycle. **Guest**, PIN: entertain a guest; visit someone, enjoy hospitality; receive a stranger.

b) **Extend(to)**, CHI: reach to, draw out, prolong; continuous, enduring.

Nine at third

a) **The sacrum without flesh.**
   One moves the resting place moreover.
   Adversity.
   Without the great: fault.

b) One moves the resting place moreover.
Moving, not yet hauling along indeed.

You are isolated and have been punished or hurt. Move to a new place. You will have to confront your past, but don't give in! Find and believe in your central idea, for will gather new friends.

Associated Contexts a) **Sacrum**, T'UN: lower back where it joins legs; buttocks, seat, lower spine. **Without**, WU: devoid of; -less as suffix. **Flesh**, FU: muscles, organs, skin, in contrast to bones.

One's/one, CH'I: third person pronoun; also: it/its, he/his, she/hers, they/theirs. **Rest(ing place)**, TZ'U: camp, inn, shed; halting-place, breathing-spell; put in consecutive order. The ideogram: two and breath, pausing to breath. **Moreover**, CH'IEH: further, and also.

Adversity, LI: danger; threatening, malevolent demon. This has two aspects: grind, sharpen, improve, perfect, stimulate; and: poisonous, sinister, cruel, contrary. It indicates a spirit or ghost that seeks revenge by inflicting suffering upon the living. Pacifying or exorcizing such a spirit can have a healing effect. The ideogram: sheltering cliff and stinging insect.

Fault, CHIU: unworthy conduct that leads to harm, illness, misfortune. The ideogram: person and differ, differ from what you should be.

b) **Not yet**, WEI: temporal negative; something will but has not yet occurred; contrary of already, CHI. Image of Hexagram 64. **Haul along**, CH'IEN: haul or pull, drag behind; pull an animal on a rope; pull toward. The ideogram: ox and halter.

Nine at fourth

a) Enwrapping without fish.
Rising up: pitfall.

b) Without fish's pitfall.
Distancing the commoners indeed.

There are no creative possibilities in this situation at the moment. Objecting or rebelling won't help. You are cut off from common experience.

Associated Contexts a) **Enwrap**, PAO: envelop, hold, contain; patient; take on responsibility, engaged. The ideogram: enfold and self, a fetus in the womb. **Without**, WU: devoid of; -less as suffix. **Fish**, YÜ: scaly, aquatic beings hidden in the water; symbol of abundance; connected with the Streaming Moment.

Rise up, CH'I: stand up, lift; undertake, begin, originate. **Pitfall**, HSIUNG: leads away from the experience of meaning; stuck and exposed to danger, unable to take in the situation; flow of life and spirit is blocked; unfortunate, baleful; keyword.

b) **Distance**, YÜAN: far off, remote; keep at a distance; alienated. The ideogram: go and a long way. **Commoners**, MIN: class of workers the state draws on to sustain the social hierarchy; undeveloped potential outside the organized personality.

Nine at fifth

a) Using osier, to enwrap the melons.
    A containing composition.
    Possessing tumbling from the origin in heaven.

b) Nine at fifth, a containing composition.
    Centering correctness indeed.
    Possessing tumbling from the origin in heaven.
    A purpose, not stowing away fate indeed.

This is a beautiful inspiration, literally made in heaven. What you do now will add elegance and beauty to your life. It inaugurates a wonderful new time.

Associated Contexts a) **Osier**, CH'I: willow branches used to make baskets. **Enwrap**, PAO: envelop, hold, contain; patient; take on responsibility, engaged. The ideogram: enfold and self, a fetus in the womb. **Melon**, KUA: general term for melon, gourd, squash, cucumber; symbol of Heaven and Earth, the cosmos.
    Contain, HAN: retain, embody, cherish; withhold, tolerate; lit.: contain in the mouth, put a coin in a corpse's mouth.
    Tumble, YÜN: fall with a crash, fall from the sky; roll down. **Origin**, TZU: source, beginning, ground; cause, reason, motive; line of descent; path to the origin; yourself, intrinsic. **Heaven**, T'IEN: highest; sky, firmament, heavens; power above the human as opposed to earth, TI, below; the Symbol of the trigram Force, CH'IEN. The ideogram: great and the one above.

b) **Purpose**, CHIH: focus of mind and heart; will, inclination, resolve. The ideogram: heart and scholar, high inner resolve, or heart and go, inner determination. **Stow(away)**, SHE: set aside, put away, store; halt, rest in; temporary lodgings, breathing-spell.

Nine above

a) Coupling: one's horns.
   Distress.
   Without fault.

b) Coupling: one's horns.
   Exhausting distress above indeed.

You are turning a joyous experience into a trial of strength and prowess. This is not a serious mistake, but it does leave you quite confused about what things are all about.

Associated Contexts a) **One's/one,** CH'I: third person pronoun; also: it/its, he/his, she/hers, they/theirs. **Horns,** CHIO: strength and power; gore; dispute, test your strength; headland.

   Distress, LIN: distress, shame, regret, humiliation; aware of having lost the right track; leads to repenting, HUI, correcting the direction of mind and life.

   Without fault, WU CHIU: no error or harm in the situation.

b) **Exhaust,** CH'IUNG: bring to an end; limit, extremity; destitute; investigate exhaustively; end without a new beginning. The ideogram: cave and naked person, bent with disease or old age. **Above,** SHANG: anything above, in all senses; higher, upper, outer; upper trigram; opposite of below, HSIA.

CLUSTERING ❚ *TS'UI*

Gather, assemble, bunch together, collect; crowds; a great effort brings a great reward.

Clustering describes your situation in terms of collecting and gathering. Its symbol is a great collective effort, like building dams, a great house or a great harvest. The way to deal with it is to unite people and things through a common feeling or goal. Concentrate the crowd and turn it into an organized whole. Make a great sacrifice and you will succeed. This is pleasing to the spirits. Through it they will give you success, effective power and the capacity to bring the situation to maturity. This is the time for great projects. Be like the king who imagines a temple full of images that unite people and connect them with greater forces. See great people. Visit those who can help and advise you. Look at your own central idea and how you organize your thoughts. Reach out and touch others. Making a great offering to the spirit of this time generates meaning and good fortune by releasing transformative energy. Put your ideas to the trial. Have a place to go. Impose a direction on things. This brings profit and insight.

● *Image of the Situation*

> Clustering, Growing.
> The king imagines possessing a temple.
> Advantageous for the Great People. Growing.
> Advantageous Trial. Availing of the great sacrificial victims auspicious.
> Advantageous to have a direction to go. Harvesting.

Associated Contexts **Cluster,** TS'UI: call or pack together; tight groups of people, animals, things; collect, gather, assemble, concentrate; bunch, crowd, collection; lit.: dense, tussocky grass. **Grow,** HENG: success through a sacrifice; pervade, persevere; bring to full growth; enjoy; vigorous, effective; second stage of the Time Cycle.

King(hood), WANG: effective ruler, by authority of the Emperor, from whom others derive their power. **Imagine,** CHIA: create in the mind; fantasize, suppose, pretend, imitate; fiction; illusory, unreal; costume. The ideogram: person and borrow. **Possess,** YU: in possession of, have, own;

opposite of lack, WU. **Temple**, MIAO: building used to honor gods and ancestors.

Advantageous/Harvest, LI: advantageous, profitable; acute, insightful; benefit, nourish; third stage of the Time Cycle. **See**, CHIEN: seeing in all its aspects: vision, being visible, forming mental images; visit, call on, consult. The ideogram: eye above person, active and receptive sight. **Great People**, TA JEN: important, noble, influential; those who impose a ruling principle on their lives; effect of the great within an individual; keyword.

Advantageous Trial, LI CHEN: advantageous divination; putting the action in question to the test is beneficial. **Avail of**, YUNG: take advantage of; benefit from, profit by; use for a specific purpose; apply to advantage. The ideogram: to divine and center, applying divination to central concerns. **Great**, TA: big, noble, important, very; orient the will toward a self-imposed goal, impose direction; ability to lead or guide your life; contrasts with small, HSIAO, flexible adaptation to what crosses your path; keyword. Image of Hexagrams 14, 26, 28, 34. **Sacrificial victims**, SHENG: the six sacrificial animals: horse, ox, lamb, cock, dog and pig. **Auspicious**, CHI: leads to the experience of meaning; favorable, propitious, advantageous, appropriate; keyword. The ideogram: scholar and mouth, wise words of a sage.

Have a direction to go, YU YU WANG: imposing a direction on the flow of time from present to past; have a specific goal or purpose.

● *Outer and Inner Aspects*

☱ **Open**: vapor rising from the marsh's open surface stimulates and fertilizes; stimulating words cheer and inspire. **Open** begins the yin hemicycle by initiating the formative process.

Connection to the outer: liquifying, casting, skinning off the mold, the Metallic Moment beginning. **Open** stimulates, cheers and reveals innate form.

☷ **Field**: The field of earth yields and sustains, serving in order to produce. **Field** is the equalizing point between yin and yang where things labor and serve.

Connection to the inner: the common labor of sowing and hoarding, the Earthy Moment. **Field** produces concrete results through serving.

Inner willingness to yield and serve **clusters** through stimulating, revealing the forms that bring people together.

- *Hidden Possibility*

Nuclear trigrams **Ground**, SUN, and **Bound**, KEN, result in Nuclear Hexagram 53, **Gradual Advance**, CHIEN. **Clustering** things results in an inexorable **gradual advance** to the goal.

- *Sequence*

> Beings mutually meeting and afterwards assembling.
> Accepting this lets you use Clustering.
> Clustering implies assembling indeed.

Associated Contexts **Being(s)**, WU: creature, thing, any single being; matter, substance, essence; nature of things. **Mutual**, HSIANG: reciprocal assistance, encourage, help; bring together, blend with; examine, inspect; by turns. **Meet**, YÜ: come on unexpectedly, encounter; occur, happen; pleasant meeting, lucky coincidence; agree. **After(wards)/later**, HOU: come after in time, subsequent; put oneself after; the second; attendants, heirs, successors, posterity. **Assemble**, CHÜ: gather, bring together, collect; call to assembly; dwell together, converge; meeting, reunion, collection; meeting place, dwelling place. The ideogram: three (= many) people.

    Accepting ... use: activating this hexagram depends on understanding and accepting the previous statement.

    Imply, CHE: further signify; additional meaning. **Indeed/is/means**, YEH: intensifier, connective; indicates comment on previous statement.

- *Contrasted Definitions*

> Clustering: assembling and
> Ascending: not coming indeed.

Associated Contexts **Ascend**, SHENG: go up; climb step by step; rise in office; advance through effort; accumulate; bring out and fulfil; lit.: a measure for fermented liquor, ascension as distillation. Image of Hexagram 46. **Come**, LAI, and go, WANG, describe the stream of time as it flows from future to present; come, LAI, indicates what is approaching; keyword.

- *Symbol Tradition*

> Above marsh with respect to earth. Clustering.
> A chün tzu uses eliminating arms to implement.
> [A chün tzu uses] warning, not precautions.

Associated Contexts **Above**, SHANG: anything above, in all senses; higher, upper, outer; upper trigram; opposite of below, HSIA. **Marsh**, TSE: open surface of a flat body of water and the vapors rising from it; fertilize, enrich; kindness, favor; the Symbol of the trigram Open, TUI. **With respect to**, YÜ: relates to, refers to; hold a position in. **Earth**, TI: ground on which the human world rests; basis of all things, nourishes all things; the Symbol of the trigram Field, K'UN.

Chün tzu: ideal of a person who uses divination to order his/her life in accordance with tao rather than wilful intention; keyword. **Use(of)**, YI: make use of, by means of, owing to; employ, make functional. **Eliminate**, CH'U: root out, remove, do away with, take off, keep out; vacate, exchange. **Arms**, JUNG: weapons; armed people, soldiers; military, violent. The ideogram: spear and armor, offensive and defensive weapons. **Implements**, CH'I: utensils, tools; molded or carved objects; use a person or thing suitably; capacity, talent, intelligence. **Warn**, CHIEH: alert, alarm, put on guard; caution, inform; guard against, refrain from (as in a diet). The ideogram: spear held in both hands, warning enemies and alerting friends. **Precaution**, YÜ: provide against, preventive measures; anxious, vigilant, ready; preoccupied with, think about, expect; mishap, accident.

●   *Image Tradition*

> Clustering, assembling indeed. [I]
> Yielding uses stimulating.
> Strong centering and corresponding.
> Anterior assembling indeed.
>
> The king imagines possessing a temple. [II]
> Involving reverence presenting it indeed.
> Advantageous to see it Growing.
> Assembling uses correcting indeed.
>
> Availing of the great sacrificial victims auspicious. [III]
> Advantageous to have a direction to go.
> Yielding to heavenly fate indeed.
> Actually viewing one's place to assemble,
> Actually permit seeing Heaven and Earth
> and the myriad beings's motives.

Associated Contexts [I] **Yield(to)**, SHUN: give way and bear produce; comply, agree, follow, obey; unresisting, docile, flexible; nourish, provide;

the Action of the trigram Field, K'UN. The ideogram: head and current, water flowing from the head of a river, yielding to the banks. **Stimulate**, SHOU: rouse to action and good feeling; free from constraint, stir up, urge on; persuade, cheer, delight; set out in words; the Action of the trigram Open, TUI. The ideogram: words and exchange.

Strong, KANG: quality of the whole lines; firm, strong, unyielding, persisting. **Center**, CHUNG: inner, central; put in the center; middle, stable point enabling you to face inner and outer changes; middle line of trigram. The ideogram: field divided in two equal parts. Image of Hexagram 61. **Correspond(to)**, YING: be in agreement or harmony; resonate together, invoke and fulfil each other; answer to, suitable; relation between the lines (1:4, 2:5, 3:6) when they form the pair opened and whole, supple and strong. The ideogram: heart and obey.

Anterior/past, KU: come before as cause; formerly, ancient; reason, purpose, intention; grievance, quarrel, dissatisfaction, sorrow, mourning resulting from previous causes and intentions; situation leading to a divination.

[II] Involve, CHIH: include, entangle, implicate; induce, cause. The ideogram: person walking, induced to follow. **Reverence**, HSIAO: filial duty, respect and obedience owed to elders; loyalty, dignity, confidence, self-respect; brave in battle; period of mourning for deceased parents. **Present(to)**, HSIANG: present in sacrifice, offer with thanks, give to the gods or a superior; confer dignity on.

Correct, CHENG: rectify deviation or one-sidedness; proper, straight, exact, regular; constant, rule, model. The ideogram: stop and one, hold to one thing.

[III] Heaven, T'IEN: highest; sky, firmament, heavens; power above the human as opposed to earth, TI, below; the Symbol of the trigram Force, CH'IEN. The ideogram: great and the one above. **Fate/mandate**, MING: individual destiny; birth and death as limits of life; issue orders with authority; consult the gods. The ideogram: mouth and order, words with heavenly authority.

Actually, YI: truly, really, at present. The ideogram: a dart and done, strong intention fully expressed. **View**, KUAN: contemplate, observe from a distance; look at carefully, gaze at; also: a monastery, an observatory; scry, divine through liquid in a cup. The ideogram: see and waterbird, observe through air or water. Image of Hexagram 20. **One's/one**, CH'I: third person pronoun; also: it/its, he/his, she/hers, they/theirs. **Place**, SO: where something belongs or comes from; residence, dwelling; habitual focus or object.

Heaven and Earth, T'IEN TI: dynamic relation between the primal powers and the world it produces; cosmos, natural or human world;

keyword. **Myriad**, WAN: countless; many, everyone; lit.: ten thousand. The ideogram: swarm of insects. **'s/have(it)/it/them**, CHIH: expresses possession, directly or as an object pronoun. **Motive**, CH'ING: true nature; feelings, desires, passions. The ideogram: heart and green, germinated in the heart. **Permit**, K'O: possible because in harmony with an inherent principle. The ideogram: mouth and breath, silent consent.

● *Transforming Lines*

Initial six

a) There is a connection to the spirits, not completion.
Thereupon disarraying, thereupon Clustering.
Like an outcry, the one hand clasp activates laughing.
No cares.
Going without fault.

b) Thereupon disarraying, thereupon Clustering.
One's purpose disarrayed indeed.

You are connected to a deep source of energy, but the link is unclear. That is why things are so uneven, one moment joyous, the next moment confused. Don't worry. Reach out and touch each other and the tension will dissolve into laughter and joy. This is certainly not a mistake. The connection is real.

Associated Contexts a) **There … spirits**, YU FU: inner and outer are in accord; confidence of the spirits has been captured; sincere, truthful; proper to take action. **Complete**, CHUNG: end of a cycle that begins the next; last, whole, all; contrasts with **exhaust**, CH'IUNG, final end. The ideogram: silk cocoons, follow and ice, winter linking one year with the next.

Thereupon, NAI: on that ground, because of. **Disarray**, LUAN: throw into disorder, mislay, confuse; out of place; discord, insurrection, anarchy. **Like**, JO: same as; just as, similar to.

Cry out/outcry, HAO: call out, proclaim; signal, order, command; mark, label, sign. **One, the one**, YI: single unit; number one; undivided, simple, whole; any one of; first, the first. **Hand clasp**, WU: as much as the hand can hold; a little; grasp, hold. **Activate**, WEI: act or cause to act; do, make, manage; make active; attend to, help; because of. **Laugh**, HSIAO: manifest joy or mirth; giggle, laugh at, ridicule; pleased, merry; associated with the Fiery Moment.

Care, HSÜ: fear, doubt, concern; heartfelt attachment; relieve, soothe, aid; sympathy, compassion, consolation. The ideogram: heart and blood, the heart's blood affected.

Go, WANG, and **come**, LAI, describe the stream of time as it flows from future through present to past; go, WANG, indicates what is departing from present to past; proceed, move on; keyword. **Without fault**, WU CHIU: no error or harm in the situation.

b) **Purpose**, CHIH: focus of mind and heart; will, inclination, resolve. The ideogram: heart and scholar, high inner resolve, or heart and go, inner determination.

   Six at second

   a) Protracted auspiciousness, without fault.
     A connection to the spirits,
     thereupon advantageous to avail ofdedicating. Harvesting.

   b) Protracted auspiciousness, without fault.
     Centering, not yet transforming indeed.

Extend the group and the activity, include more and draw the time out. Then you can make the sacrifice to the gathered group of ancestors that opens the way to achievement. This is a time for great things, a time of extended good fortune.

Associated Contexts a) **Protract**, YIN: draw out, prolong; carried on; lead on, to bring forward; lit.: drawing a bow. **Without fault**, WU CHIU: no error or harm in the situation.

   Connection, FU: accord between inner and outer in a particular moment; sincere, truthful, verified, reliable, in accord with the spirits; capture; prisoners, spoils; contrasts with trustworthy, HSIN, consistent over time. The ideogram: bird's claw enclosing young animals, possessive grip. Image of Hexagram 61. **Thereupon**, NAI: on that ground, because of. **Dedicate**, YO: offering at the spring equinox, when stores were low; offer a sacrifice with limited resources. The ideogram: spring and thin.

b) **Not yet**, WEI: temporal negative; something will but has not yet occurred; contrary of already, CHI. Image of Hexagram 64. **Transform**, PIEN: abrupt, radical, fundamental mutation from one state of being to another; transformation of lines in hexagrams; contrasts with **change**, HUA, gradual metamorphosis.

Six at third

a) Clustering thus, lamenting thus.
No advantageous direction.
Going without fault.
The Small distressed.

b) Going without fault.
Ground above indeed.

As soon as you begin, a flood of sorrow and painful memories swamps you. There is really nothing you can do here. Leave gently and quietly. It is not a mistake. If you simply try to adapt to the situation, you will be covered in distress and confusion.

Associated Contexts a) **Thus ... thus**, JU ... JU: when there is one thing, then there must be the second thing. **Lament**, CHÜEH: express intense regret or sorrow; mourn over; painful recollections.

No advantageous direction, WU YU LI: no plan or direction is advantageous; in order to take advantage of the situation, do not impose a direction on events.

Go, WANG, and **come**, LAI, describe the stream of time as it flows from future through present to past; go, WANG, indicates what is departing from present to past; proceed, move on; keyword. **Without fault**, WU CHIU: no error or harm in the situation.

Small, HSIAO: little, common, unimportant; adapting to what crosses your path; ability to move in harmony with the vicissitudes of life; contrasts with great, TA, self-imposed theme or goal; keyword. Image of Hexagrams 9 and 62. **Distress**, LIN: distress, shame, regret, humiliation; aware of having lost the right track; leads to repenting, HUI, correcting the direction of mind and life.

b) **Ground**, SUN: base on which things rest; support, foundation; mild, subtly penetrating; nourishing. The ideogram: stand and things arranged on it, the subtle influence of the ground. Image of Hexagram 57.

Nine at fourth

a) The great auspicious, without fault.

b) The great auspicious, without fault.
Situation not appropriate indeed.

You can do anything you want to do now if you act with a full and loving heart. The Great Way is open. Nothing you do would be a mistake. Move on. Take action.

Associated Contexts a) **Without fault,** WU CHIU: no error or harm in the situation.

b) **Situation,** WEI: place or seat according to rank; post, position, command; right, proper; established, arranged. The ideogram: person and stand, servants in their places. **Appropriate,** TANG: suitable; opportune, convenient; adequate, competent; equal to; whole lines in uneven places and opened lines in even places.

> **Nine at fifth**
>
> *a)* Clustering: possessing the situation.
>   In no way a fault: a connection to the spirits.
>   Perpetual Spring: Trial.
>   Repenting extinguished.
>
> *b)* Clustering: possessing the situation.
>   Purpose not yet shining indeed.

You have a position here. This can be a long-term source of energy and inspiration. You do not need to make a sacrifice. Keep exploring it by asking the oracle. As you do, doubt and sorrow will disappear and all will come clear.

Associated Contexts a) **Situation,** WEI: place or seat according to rank; post, position, command; right, proper; established, arranged. The ideogram: person and stand, servants in their places.

Without fault, WU CHIU: no error or harm in the situation. **In no way,** FEI: strong negative; not so. The ideogram: a box filled with opposition. **Connection to the spirits,** FU: accord between inner and outer in a particular moment; sincere, truthful, verified, reliable, in accord with the spirits; capture; prisoners, spoils; contrasts with trustworthy, HSIN, consistent over time. The ideogram: bird's claw enclosing young animals, possessive grip. Image of Hexagram 61.

Spring, YÜAN: source, origin, head; great, excellent; arise, begin, generating power; first stage of the Time Cycle. **Perpetual,** YUNG: continuing; everlasting, ever-flowing. The ideogram: flowing water. **Trial,** CHEN: inquiry by divination and its result; righteous, firm; separating wheat from chaff; the kernel, the proven core; fourth stage of the Time Cycle. The ideogram: pearl and divination.

Repenting extinguished, HUI WANG: previous troubles and consequent remorse will disappear.

b) **Purpose,** CHIH: focus of mind and heart; will, inclination, resolve. The ideogram: heart and scholar, high inner resolve, or heart and go, inner determination. **Not yet,** WEI: temporal negative; something will but has not yet occurred; contrary of already, CHI. Image of Hexagram 64. **Shine,** KUANG: illuminate; give off brilliant, bright light; honor, glory, éclat; result of action, contrasts with brightness, MING, light of heavenly bodies. The ideogram: fire above person, lifting the light.

Six above

a) **Paying tribute: sighs, tears, snot.**
Without fault.

b) **Paying tribute: sighs, tears, snot.**
The above not yet quiet indeed.

Like rites at a funeral, these tears will make a greater connection between people. Expressing emotion is not a mistake. It is entirely apropos. It opens blocked communication.

Associated Contexts a) **Pay tribute,** CHI: compulsory payments; present property to a superior. **Sigh,** TZU: lament, express grief, sorrow or yearning. **Tears,** T'I: weep, cry; water from the eyes. **Snot,** YI: mucus from the nose; snivel, whine.

Without fault, WU CHIU: no error or harm in the situation.

b) **Not yet,** WEI: temporal negative; something will but has not yet occurred; contrary of already, CHI. Image of Hexagram 64. **Quiet/secure,** AN: peaceful, still, settled; calm, tranquilize. The ideogram: woman under a roof, a tranquil home.

46

ASCENDING ▮ SHENG

Make the effort, don't worry; climb the mountain step by step; lift yourself, fulfil the potential; advance, rise.

Ascending describes your situation in terms of rising to a higher level and getting something done. Its symbol is a plant pushing through the earth and climbing the sacred mountain to the ancestral temple. The way to deal with it is set a goal and work towards it step by step. Make an offering and you will succeed. Root yourself and push towards the heights. Climb the mountain and connect with the spirits. Bring out and fulfil the hidden potential. This is a very favorable situation. It is pleasing to the spirits. It is the origin of growth, effective power and the capacity to bring things to maturity. See great people, those who can help and advise you. Look at the great in yourself and how you organize your ideas. Have no cares, fears or anxiety. Set out towards the south, the region of summer, growth, intensity and action. This generates meaning and good fortune by releasing transformative energy. Correct, discipline and put things in order.

● *Image of the Situation*

> **Ascending, Spring Growing.**
> **Avail of seeing the Great People.**
> **No cares.**
> **The South, chastising auspicious.**

Associated Contexts **Ascend,** SHENG: go up; climb step by step; rise in office; advance through effort; accumulate; bring out and fulfil; lit.: a measure for fermented liquor, ascension as distillation. **Spring,** YÜAN: source, origin, head; great, excellent; arise, begin, generating power; first stage of the Time Cycle. **Grow,** HENG: success through a sacrifice; pervade, persevere; bring to full growth; enjoy; vigorous, effective; second stage of the Time Cycle.

  Avail of, YUNG: take advantage of; benefit from, profit by; use for a specific purpose; apply to advantage. The ideogram: to divine and center, applying divination to central concerns. **See,** CHIEN: seeing in all its aspects: vision, being visible, forming mental images; visit, call on, consult. The ideogram: eye above person, active and receptive sight. **Great People,** TA

JEN: important, noble, influential; those who impose a ruling principle on their lives; effect of the great within an individual; keyword.

Care, HSÜ: fear, doubt, concern; heartfelt attachment; relieve, soothe, aid; sympathy, compassion, consolation. The ideogram: heart and blood, the heart's blood affected.

South, NAN: corresponds to summer, Growing, and the Fiery Moment; end of the yang hemicycle; reference point of compass; rulers face South, thus true principles and correct decisions. **Chastise**, CHENG: punish, subjugate, discipline; reduce to order; punishing expedition. The ideogram: step and correct, a rectifying move. **Auspicious**, CHI: leads to the experience of meaning; favorable, propitious, advantageous, appropriate; keyword. The ideogram: scholar and mouth, wise words of a sage.

- ## *Outer and Inner Aspects*

☷ **Field**: The field of earth yields and sustains, serving in order to produce. **Field** is the equalizing point between yin and yang where things labor and serve.

Connection to the outer: the common labor of sowing and hoarding, the Earthy Moment. **Field** produces concrete results through serving.

☴ **Ground**: Wind and wood subtly enter from the ground, penetrating and pervading. **Ground** is the center of the yang hemicycle, spreading pervasive action.

Connection to the inner: penetrating and bringing together, the Woody Moment culminating. **Ground** pervades, matches and couples, seeding a new generation.

Subtle penetration and coupling within slowly **ascends** to a higher field of activity.

- ## *Hidden Possibility*

Nuclear trigrams **Shake**, CHEN, and **Open**, TUI, result in Nuclear Hexagram 54, **Converting Maidenhood**, KUEI MEI. The effort needed to **ascend converts** the **maiden**, realizing her hidden potential.

- ## *Sequence*

Assembling and the above implies designating it as Ascending.
Accepting this lets you use Ascending.

Associated Contexts **Assemble**, CHÜ: gather, bring together, collect; call to assembly; dwell together, converge; meeting, reunion, collection; meeting place, dwelling place. The ideogram: three (= many) people. **Above**, SHANG: anything above, in all senses; higher, upper, outer; upper trigram; opposite of below, HSIA. **Imply**, CHE. further signify; additional meaning. **Designate**, WEI: represent in words, assign a name or meaning; report on, talk about. The ideogram: words and belly, describing the essential. **'s/have(it)/it/them**, CHIH: expresses possession, directly or as an object pronoun.

Accepting ... use: activating this hexagram depends on understanding and accepting the previous statement.

- *Contrasted Definitions*

> Clustering: assembling and
> Ascending: not coming indeed.

Associated Contexts **Cluster**, TS'UI: call or pack together; tight groups of people, animals, things; collect, gather, assemble, concentrate; bunch, crowd, collection; lit.: dense, tussocky grass. Image of Hexagram 45.

Come, LAI, and **go**, WANG, describe the stream of time as it flows from future through present to past; come, LAI, indicates what is approaching; move toward, arrive at; keyword. **Indeed**, YEH: intensifier, connective; indicates comment on previous statement.

- *Symbol Tradition*

> Earth center giving birth to wood. Ascending.
> A chün tzu uses yielding to actualize tao.
> [A chün tzu uses] amassing the small to use the high great.

Associated Contexts **Earth**, TI: ground on which the human world rests; basis of all things, nourishes all things; the Symbol of the trigram Field, K'UN. **Center**, CHUNG: inner, central; put in the center; middle, stable point enabling you to face inner and outer changes; middle line of trigram. The ideogram: field divided in two equal parts. Image of Hexagram 61. **Birth/give birth to**, SHENG: produce, beget, grow, bear, arise; life, vitality. The ideogram: earth and sprout. **Wood/tree**, MU: all things woody or wooden, alive or constructed from wood; associated with the Woody Moment; wood and wind are the Symbols of the trigram Ground, SUN. The ideogram: a tree with roots and branches.

Chün tzu: ideal of a person who uses divination to order his/her life in accordance with tao rather than wilful intention; keyword. **Use(of)**, YI: make use of, by means of, owing to; employ, make functional. **Yield(to)**, SHUN: give way and bear produce; comply, agree, follow, obey; unresisting, docile, flexible; nourish, provide; the Action of the trigram Field, K'UN. The ideogram: head and current, water flowing from the head of a river, yielding to the banks. **Actualize tao**, TE: realize tao in action; power, virtue; ability to follow the course traced by the ongoing process of the cosmos; keyword. The ideogram: to go, straight, and heart. Linked with acquire, TE: acquiring that which makes a being become what it is meant to be.

Amass, CHI: hoard, accumulate, pile up, store up, add up, increase. **Small**, HSIAO: little, common, unimportant; adapting to what crosses your path; ability to move in harmony with the vicissitudes of life; contrasts with great, TA, self-imposed theme or goal; keyword. Image of Hexagrams 9 and 62. **High(ness)**, KAO: high, elevated, lofty, eminent; excellent, advanced. **Great**, TA: big, noble, important, very; orient the will toward a self-imposed goal, impose direction; ability to lead or guide your life; contrasts with small, HSIAO, flexible adaptation to what crosses your path; keyword. Image of Hexagrams 14, 26, 28, 34.

● *Image Tradition*

> Supple using the season, Ascending. [I]
> Ground and yielding.
> Strong centering and corresponding.
> That uses great Growing to avail of seeing the Great People.
>
> No cares. [II]
> Possessing reward indeed.
> The South, chastising auspicious.
> Purpose moving indeed.

Associated Contexts [I] **Supple**, JOU: quality of the opened lines; flexible, pliant, tender, adaptable. **Season**, SHIH: quality of the time; the right time, opportune, in harmony; planning in accord with the time; seasons of the year. The ideogram: sun and temple, time as sacred.

Ground, SUN: base on which things rest; support, foundation; mild, subtly penetrating; nourishing. The ideogram: stand and things arranged on it, the subtle influence of the ground. Image of Hexagram 57.

Strong, KANG: quality of the whole lines; firm, strong, unyielding, persisting. **Correspond(to)**, YING: be in agreement or harmony; resonate together, invoke and fulfil each other; answer to, suitable; relation between the lines (1:4, 2:5, 3:6) when they form the pair opened and whole, supple and strong. The ideogram: heart and obey.

That uses, SHIH YI: involves and is involved by.

[II] Possess, YU: in possession of, have, own; opposite of lack, WU. **Reward**, CH'ING: gift given from gratitude or benevolence; favor from heaven; congratulate with gifts. The ideogram: heart, follow and deer (wealth), the heart expressed through gifts.

Purpose, CHIH: focus of mind and heart; will, inclination, resolve. The ideogram: heart and scholar, high inner resolve, or heart and go, inner determination. **Move**, HSING: move or move something; motivate, emotionally moving; walk, act, do. The ideogram: stepping left then right.

● *Transforming Lines*

Initial six

a) **Sincere Ascending, the great auspicious.**

b) **Sincere Ascending, the great auspicious.**
   Uniting purposes above indeed.

You have been recognized. The ancestors have become aware of your value. Now all the doors are open to you. Be sincere. Climb the mountain and find what you desire.

Associated Contexts a) **Sincere**, YÜN: true, honest, loyal; according to the facts; have confidence in, permit, assent. The ideogram: vapor rising, words directed upwards.

b) **Unite**, HO: join, match, correspond, agree, collect, reply; unison, harmony; also: close, shut the mouth. The ideogram: mouth and assemble.

Nine at second

a) **Connecting to the spirits, thereupon advantageous**
   to avail of dedicating. Harvesting.
   Without fault.

b) **Nine at second's connection.**
   Possessing rejoicing indeed.

The connection is established. Make the offering and climb the sacred mountain. Dedicate yourself to what you believe in and sacrifice to the gathered ancestors. It is all there if you want it to be.

Associated Contexts a) **Connection,** FU: accord between inner and outer in a particular moment; sincere, truthful, verified, reliable, in accord with the spirits; capture; prisoners, spoils; contrasts with trustworthy, HSIN, consistent over time. The ideogram: bird's claw enclosing young animals, possessive grip. Image of Hexagram 61. **Thereupon,** NAI: on that ground, because of. **Advantageous/Harvest,** LI: advantageous, profitable; acute, insightful; benefit, nourish; third stage of the Time Cycle. **Dedicate,**YO: offering at the spring equinox, when stores were low; offer a sacrifice with limited resources. The ideogram: spring and thin.

Without fault, WU CHIU: no error or harm in the situation.

b) **Rejoice(in),** HSI: feel and give joy; delight, exult; cheerful, merry. The ideogram: joy (music) and mouth, expressing joy.

Nine at third

a) Ascending into an empty capital.

b) Ascending into an empty capital.
Without a place to doubt indeed.

There is no resistance to your efforts. The gates are open. The ceremony is being performed. Don't stop, push on.

Associated Contexts a) **Empty,** HSÜ: no images or concepts; vacant, unsubstantial; empty yet fertile space. **Capital,** YI: populous fortified city, center and symbol of the domain it rules. The ideogram: enclosure and official seal.

b) **Without,** WU: devoid of; -less as suffix. **Place,** SO: where something belongs or comes from; residence, dwelling; habitual focus or object. **Doubt,** YI: suspect, distrust; dubious; surmise, conjecture.

Six at fourth

a) The king avails of Growing,
a sacrifice on the twin peaked mountain.
Auspicious.
Without fault.

b) The king avails of Growing,
   a sacrifice on the twin peaked mountain.
   Yielding affairs indeed.

You have found a powerful place in the symbolic life. Make an offering and you will succeed. You are part of the great sacrifices that connect us to the ancestors. Dedicate your efforts to the common good. The way is open. This is not a mistake.

Associated Contexts a) **King(hood)**, WANG: effective ruler, by authority of the Emperor, from whom others derive their power. **Twin peaked**, CH'I: mountain with two peaks; forked road; diverge, ambiguous. The ideogram: mountain and branched. **Mountain**, SHAN: limit, boundary; the Symbol of the trigram Bound, KEN. The ideogram: three peaks, a mountain range. **Twin peaked Mountain**, CH'I SHAN, was the ancestral shrine of the Chou Dynasty.

   Without fault, WU CHIU: no error or harm in the situation.

b) **Affairs**, SHIH: all kinds of personal activity; matters at hand; business, occupation; manage a business, case in court.

Six at fifth

a) Trial: auspicious, Ascending the steps.

b) Trial: auspicious, Ascending the steps.
   The great acquiring the purpose indeed.

There are no barriers to your progress. You are welcomed into the temple. Proceed step by step. The way is open to you.

Associated Contexts a) **Trial**, CHEN: inquiry by divination and its result; righteous, firm; separating wheat from chaff; the kernel, the proven core; fourth stage of the Time Cycle. The ideogram: pearl and divination. **Steps**, CHIEH: stairs leading to a gate or hall; grade, degree, rank; emulate, rise.

b) **Acquire**, TE: obtain the desired object; wish for, desire covetously; gains, possessions. The ideogram: go and obstacle, going through obstacles to the goal.

Six above

a) Dim Ascending.
   Advantageous Trial: do not pause.

b) Dim Ascending located above.
Dissolving, not affluence indeed.

You are climbing in the dark as things begin to wane. Don't stop now. Pushing on and emerging will bring both profit and insight in the end.

Associated Contexts a) **Dim**, MING: dark, obscure; misinformed, immature, cavern, the underworld. The ideogram: 16th day of moon-month, when the moon begins to dim.

Advantageous/Harvest, LI: advantageous, profitable; acute, insightful; benefit, nourish; third stage of the Time Cycle. **Pause**, HSI: stop and rest, repose; breathe, a breathing-spell; suspended. **Trial**, CHEN: inquiry by divination and its result; righteous, firm; separating wheat from chaff; the kernel, the proven core; fourth stage of the Time Cycle. The ideogram: pearl and divination.

b) **Locate(in)**, TSAI: live in, dwell, reside; belong to, involved with, depend on; within. The ideogram: earth and persevere, place on the earth.

Dissolve, HSIAO: liquify, melt, thaw; diminish, disperse; eliminate, exhaust. The ideogram: water dissolving differences. **Affluence**, FU: rich, abundant; wealth; enrich, provide for; flow toward, accrue.

CONFINING ▮ K'UN

Oppressed, restricted, exhausted, cut off; at the end of your resources; the moment of truth; search within to find the way out.

Confining describes your situation in terms of being cut off, oppressed and exhausted. Its symbol is the tree of life confined in a narrow enclosure. The way to deal with it is to collect the energy to break out of the enclosure and re-establish communication. Make an offering and you will succeed. This is pleasing to the spirits. Through it they will give you success, effective power and the capacity to bring the situation to maturity. Be great and master the situation from within. Find what is truly important to you. Seek those who can help and advise you. This generates meaning and good fortune by releasing transformative energy. The situation is not your fault. Words are not to be trusted. There is a breakdown of communication and you are being isolated by it. You are not believed when you speak. Don't believe what others are telling you to do.

● *Image of the Situation*

> **Confining, Growing.**
> **Trial: Great People auspicious. Without fault.**
> **Possessing words not trustworthy.**

Associated Contexts **Confine**, K'UN: enclose, restrict, limit; oppressed; impoverish, distress; afflicted, exhausted, disheartened, weary. The ideogram: an enclosed tree. **Grow**, HENG: success through a sacrifice; pervade, persevere; bring to full growth; enjoy; vigorous, effective; second stage of the Time Cycle.

   Trial, CHEN: inquiry by divination and its result; righteous, firm; separating wheat from chaff; the kernel, the proven core; fourth stage of the Time Cycle. The ideogram: pearl and divination. **Great People**, TA JEN: important, noble, influential; those who impose a ruling principle on their lives; effect of the great within an individual; keyword. **Auspicious**, CHI: leads to the experience of meaning; favorable, propitious, advantageous, appropriate; keyword. The ideogram: scholar and mouth, wise words of a sage.

Without fault, WU CHIU: no error or harm in the situation.

Possess, YU: in possession of, have, own; opposite of lack, WU. **Word**, YEN: speech, spoken words, sayings; talk, discuss, address. The ideogram: mouth and rising vapor, words as speech. **Trustworthy**, HSIN: truthful, faithful, consistent over time; integrity; confide in, follow; credentials; contrasts with conforming, FU, connection in a specific moment. The ideogram: person and word, true speech.

• *Outer and Inner Aspects*

☱ **Open**: vapor rising from the marsh's open surface stimulates and fertilizes; stimulating words cheer and inspire. **Open** begins the yin hemicycle by initiating the formative process.

Connection to the outer: liquifying, casting, skinning off the mold, the Metallic Moment beginning. **Open** stimulates, cheers and reveals innate form.

☵ **Gorge**: Stream ventures and falls into the gorge, flowing on through toil and danger. **Gorge** ends the yin hemicycle by leveling and dissolving forms.

Connection to the inner: flooding and leveling dissolve direction and shape, the Streaming Moment. **Gorge** ventures, falls, toils and flows on.

Drawn in by the falling stream, outer stimulation and cheer are **confined** to creating inner forms.

• *Hidden Possibility*

Nuclear trigrams **Ground**, SUN, and **Radiance**, LI, result in Nuclear Hexagram 37, **Dwelling People**, CHIA JEN. Accepting and working through confining leads to the security of **people** working together in their **dwelling**.

• *Sequence*

Ascending and not climaxing necessarily Confines.
Accepting this lets you use Confining.

Associated Contexts **Ascend**, SHENG: go up; climb step by step; rise in office; advance through effort; accumulate; bring out and fulfil; lit.: a measure for fermented liquor, ascension as distillation. Image of Hexagram 46. **Climax**, YI: come to a high point and stop, bring to an end;

use up, lay aside; decline, reject. **Necessarily**, PI: unavoidably, indispensably, certainly.

Accepting ... use: activating this hexagram depends on understanding and accepting the previous statement.

● *Contrasted Definitions*

> The Well: interpenetrating and
> Confining: mutual meeting indeed.

Associated Contexts **Well**, CHING: water well at the center of the fields; rise and flow of water in a well, rise and surge from an inner source; life-water, nucleus of life; found a capital city. The ideogram: two vertical lines crossing two horizontal ones, eight fields with a well at the center. Image of Hexagram 48. **Interpenetrate**, T'UNG: mutually penetrate; permeate, flow through, reach everywhere; see clearly, communicate with.

Mutual, HSIANG: reciprocal assistance, encourage, help; bring together, blend with; examine, inspect; by turns. **Meet**, YÜ: come on unexpectedly, encounter; occur, happen; pleasant meeting, lucky coincidence; agree. **Indeed/is/means**, YEH: intensifier, connective; indicates comment on previous statement.

● *Attached Evidences*

> Confining: actualizing-tao's marking off indeed.
> Confining: exhausting and interpenetrating.
> Confining: using few grudges.

Associated Contexts **Actualize tao** TE: realize tao in action; power, virtue; ability to follow the course traced by the ongoing process of the cosmos; keyword. The ideogram: to go, straight, and heart. Linked with acquire, TE: acquiring that which makes a being become what it is meant to be. **'s/have(it)/it/them**, CHIH: expresses possession, directly or as an object pronoun. **Mark off**, PIEN: distinguish by dividing; mark off a plot of land; frame which divides a bed from its stand; discuss and dispute. The ideogram: knife and acrid, biting division.

Exhaust, CH'IUNG: bring to an end; limit, extremity; destitute; investigate exhaustively; end without a new beginning. The ideogram: cave and naked person, bent with disease or old age.

Use(of), YI: make use of, by means of, owing to; employ, make functional. **Few**, KUA: small number; seldom, rarely; unusual, solitary.

Grudges, YÜAN: bitter feelings, ill-will; hate, abhor; murmur against. The ideogram: heart and overturn, upset emotion.

● *Symbol Tradition*

> Marsh without stream. Confining.
> A chün tzu uses involving fate to release purpose.

Associated Contexts **Marsh**, TSE: open surface of a flat body of water and the vapors rising from it; fertilize, enrich; kindness, favor; the Symbol of the trigram Open, TUI. **Without**, WU: devoid of; -less as suffix. **Stream**, SHUI: flowing water; fluid, dissolving; river, tide, flood; the Symbol of the trigram Gorge, K'AN. The ideogram: rippling water.

Chün tzu: ideal of a person who uses divination to order his/her life in accordance with tao rather than wilful intention; keyword. **Involve**, CHIH: include, entangle, implicate; induce, cause. The ideogram: person walking, induced to follow. **Fate/mandate**, MING: individual destiny; birth and death as limits of life; issue orders with authority; consult the gods. The ideogram: mouth and order, words with heavenly authority. **Release**, SUI: loose, let go, free; unhindered, in accord; follow, spread out, progress; penetrate, invade. The ideogram: go and follow your wishes, unimpeded movement. **Purpose**, CHIH: focus of mind and heart; will, inclination, resolve. The ideogram: heart and scholar, high inner resolve, or heart and go, inner determination.

● *Image Tradition*

> Confining. [I]
> Strong enshrouded indeed.
> Venturing uses stimulating.
> Confining and not letting go one's place: Growing.
>
> Reaching to one's very chün tzu. [II]
> Trial: Great People auspicious.
> Using strong centering indeed.
> Possessing words not trustworthy.
> Honoring the mouth, thereupon exhaustion indeed.

Associated Contexts [I] **Strong**, KANG: quality of the whole lines; firm, strong, unyielding, persisting. **Enshroud**, YEN: screen, shade from view, hide, cover. The ideogram: hand and cover.

Venture, HSIEN: risk without reserve; key point, point of danger;

difficulty, obstruction that must be confronted; water falling and filling the holes on its way; the Action of the trigram Gorge, K'AN. The ideogram: mound and all or whole, everything engaged at one point. **Stimulate**, SHUO: rouse to action and good feeling; free from constraint, stir up, urge on; persuade, cheer, delight; set out in words; the Action of the trigram Open, TUI. The ideogram: words and exchange.

Let go, SHIH: lose, omit, miss, fail, let slip; out of control. The ideogram: drop from the hand. **One's/one**, CH'I: third person pronoun; also: it/its, he/his, she/hers, they/theirs. **Place**, SO: where something belongs or comes from; residence, dwelling; habitual focus or object.

Reach(to), HU: arrive at a goal; reach toward and achieve; connect; contrasts with tend-towards, YU. **Verily, very**, WEI: the epitome of; in truth, the only; very important.

[II] **Center**, CHUNG: inner, central; put in the center; middle, stable point enabling you to face inner and outer changes; middle line of trigram. The ideogram: field divided in two equal parts. Image of Hexagram 61.

Honor, SHANG: esteem, give high rank to; eminent; put one thing on top of another. **Mouth**, K'OU: literal mouth, words going out and food coming in; entrance, hole. **Thereupon**, NAI: on that ground, because of.

● *Transforming Lines*

Initial six

a) **The sacrum Confined by a wooden post.**
Entering into a shady gully.
Three year's time, no encounters.

b) **Entering into a shady gully.**
Shady, not bright indeed.

You have been hurt or punished, but you are your own worst enemy now. Do not retreat into melancholy darkness and isolation. You will completely cut yourself off.

Associated Contexts a) **Sacrum**, T'UN: lower back where it joins legs; buttocks, seat, lower spine. **Post**, CHU: trunk, bole, stalk; wooden post; keep down, degrade. **Wood/tree**, MU: all things woody or wooden, alive or constructed from wood; associated with the Woody Moment; wood and wind are the Symbols of the trigram Ground, SUN. The ideogram: a tree with roots and branches.

Enter, JU: penetrate, go into, enter on, progress; put into, encroach on; the Action of the trigram Ground, SUN, contrary of issue-forth, CH'U. Shade, YU: hidden from view; retired, solitary, secret; dark, obscure, occult, mysterious; ignorant. The ideogram: small within hill, a cave or grotto. Gully, KU: valley, ravine, river bed, gap. The ideogram: divide and river, a river bed separating hills.

Three, SAN: number three, third time or place; active phases of a cycle; superlative; beginning of repetition. Year's time, SUI: actual length of time in a year; contrasts with years-revolved, NIEN, number of years elapsed. Encounter, TI: see face to face; admitted to an audience; visit, interview.

b) Brightness, MING: light-giving aspect of burning, heavenly bodies and consciousness; with fire, the Symbol of the trigram Radiance, LI.

Nine at second

a) Confined at drinking liquor and eating.
Scarlet sashes coming on all sides.
Advantageous to avail of presenting oblations. Harvesting.
Chastising: pitfall, without fault.

b) Confined at drinking liquor and eating.
Center possessing reward indeed.

You ostensibly have all you need. But you are not recognized. Don't worry, recognition is on its way. It will change the way you see yourself and your relationships with others. Offer a sacrifice to the things you believe in. Stay where you are and wait. Don't try to make others take the blame for your situation. This is not a mistake.

Associated Contexts a) Liquor, CHIU: alcoholic beverages, distilled spirits; spirit which perfects the good and evil in human nature. The ideogram: liquid above fermenting must, separating the spirits. Eat, SHIH: eat, ingest, swallow, devour; incorporate to be in.

Scarlet, CHU: vivid red signifying honor, luck, marriage, riches, literary accomplishment; culmination of the Woody Moment. Sash, FU: ceremonial belt of official which holds seal of office. Sides (on all sides), FANG: limits, boundaries; square, surface of the earth extending to the four cardinal points; everywhere. Come, LAI, and go, WANG, describe the stream of time as it flows from future through present to past; come, LAI, indicates what is approaching; move toward, arrive at; keyword.

Advantageous/Harvest, LI: advantageous, profitable; acute, insightful;

benefit, nourish; third stage of the Time Cycle. **Avail of,** YUNG: take advantage of; benefit from, profit by; use for a specific purpose; apply to advantage. The ideogram: to divine and center, applying divination to central concerns. **Present(to),** HSIANG: present in sacrifice, offer with thanks, give to the gods or a superior; confer dignity on. **Oblations,** SSU: sacrifices offered situation; flow of life and spirit is blocked; unfortunate, baleful; keyword.

Chastise, CHENG: punish, subjugate, discipline; reduce to order; punishing expedition. The ideogram: step and correct, a rectifying move. **Pitfall,** HSIUNG: leads away from the experience of meaning; stuck and exposed to danger, unable to take in the situation; flow of life and spirit is blocked; unfortunate, baleful; keyword.

b) **Reward,** CH'ING: gift given from gratitude or benevolence; favor from heaven; congratulate with gifts. The ideogram: heart, follow and deer (wealth), the heart expressed through gifts.

Six at third

a) **Confined by petrification.**
Seizing on star thistles.
Entering into one's house,
Not seeing one's consort.
Pitfall.

b) **Seizing on star thistles.**
Riding a strong indeed.
Entering into one's house,
Not seeing one's consort.
Not auspicious indeed.

You don't need anyone else to oppress you. You do it very well yourself at the moment. You beat yourself against impossible obstacles and grasp at things that hurt you. You can't even see your friend, who loves you and is eager to support you. This kind of behavior will get you absolutely nowhere.

Associated Contexts a) **Petrify,** SHIH: become stone or stony; rocks, stony land; objects made of stone; firm, decided; a barren womb.

Seize, CHÜ: grasp, lay hands on; lean on, rely on; maintain, become concrete; testimony, evidence. **Star thistles,** CHI LI: spiny weeds that entangle the feet; caltrops, metal snares.

Enter, JU: penetrate, go into, enter on, progress; put into, encroach on;

the Action of the trigram Ground, SUN, contrary of issue-forth, CH'U. **House,** KUNG: residence, mansion; surround; fence, walls, roof. **See,** CHIEN: seeing in all its aspects: vision, being visible, forming mental images; visit, call on, consult. The ideogram: eye above person, active and receptive sight. **Consort,** CH'I: single official partner; legal status of married woman (first wife); contrasts with function of wife, FU, head of household, and concubine, CH'IEH, secondary wives.

    Pitfall, HSIUNG: leads away from the experience of meaning; stuck and exposed to danger, unable to take in the situation; flow of life and spirit is blocked; unfortunate, baleful; keyword.

b) **Ride,** CH'ENG: ride an animal or a chariot; have the upper hand, seize the right time; control strong power; overcome the nature of the other; supple opened line above a strong whole line. **Auspicious,** HSIANG: omen of good luck and prosperity; sign, auspices.

> **Nine at fourth**
>
> *a)* **Coming, ambling, ambling.**
>   **Confined in a metal chariot.**
>   **Distress.**
>   **Possessing completion.**
>
> *b)* **Coming, ambling, ambling.**
>   **Purpose located below indeed.**
>   **Although not an appropriate situation,**
>   **possessing associates indeed.**

The solution to your problems will arrive very slowly. This is partially because you are bound up in a metal chariot of old duties and thoughts. This distresses you. It will take a change of heart to recognize the truth, but all will turn out well in the end.

Associated Contexts a) **Come,** LAI, and **go,** WANG, describe the stream of time as it flows from future through present to past; come, LAI, indicates what is approaching; move toward, arrive at; keyword. **Amble,** HSÜ: walk quietly and carefully; leisurely, tardy, slow; composed, dignified. The doubled character intensifies this quality.

    Metallic, CHIN: smelting and casting; all things pertaining to metal, particularly gold; autumn, West, sunset; one of the Five Moments. **Chariot,** CH'E: wheeled travelling vehicle; contrasts with cart, YÜ, which carries.

    Distress, LIN: distress, shame, regret, humiliation; aware of having lost the right track; leads to repenting, HUI, correcting the direction of mind and life.

Complete, CHUNG: end of a cycle that begins the next; last, whole, all; contrasts with exhaust, CH'IUNG, final end. The ideogram: silk cocoons, follow and ice, winter linking one year with the next.

b) **Locate(in)**, TSAI: live in, dwell, reside; belong to, involved with, depend on; within. The ideogram: earth and persevere, place on the earth. **Below**, HSIA: anything below, in all senses; lower, inner; lower trigram; opposite of above, SHANG.

Although, SUI: even though, supposing that, if, even if. **Appropriate**, TANG: suitable; opportune, convenient; adequate, competent; equal to; whole lines in uneven places and opened lines in even places. **Situation**, WEI: place or seat according to rank; post, position, command; right, proper; established, arranged. The ideogram: person and stand, servants in their places. **Associate(with)**, YÜ: consort with, combine; companions; group, band, company; agree with, comply, help. The ideogram: pair of hands reaching downward meets a pair of hands reaching upward, helpful association.

Nine at fifth

a) **Nose cutting, foot cutting.**
   Confined by the crimson sashes.
   Thereupon ambling possesses loosening.
   Advantageous to avail of offering oblations. Harvesting.

b) **Nose cutting, foot cutting.**
   Purpose not yet acquired indeed.
   Thereupon ambling possesses loosening.
   Using centering and straightening indeed.
   Advantageous to avail of offering oblations. Harvesting.
   Acquiescing in blessing indeed.

You are punished and oppressed by authority. This is serious, but the bitter feelings will slowly loosen and you will be set free. Until this day comes, make offerings to your ideals. What your heart feels deeply will help you through. The spirits will help you.

Associated Contexts a) **Nose cutting**, YI: punish through loss of public face or honor. **Foot cutting**, YÜEH: crippling punishment for serious crimes.
   Crimson, CH'IH: color associated with the Fiery Moment, South and

Actualized Yang; fire, burning; dark complexion; color of new-born child; drunk, angry; polished metal; strip, naked, barren; also: sign of official rank. **Sash,** FU: ceremonial belt of official which holds seal of office.

Amble, HSÜ: walk quietly and carefully; leisurely, tardy, slow; composed, dignified.

Advantageous/Harvest, LI: advantageous, profitable; acute, insightful; benefit, nourish; third stage of the Time Cycle. **Avail of,** YUNG: take advantage of; benefit from, profit by; use for a specific purpose; apply to advantage. The ideogram: to divine and center, applying divination to central concerns. **Offer,** CHI: gifts to gods and spirits. The ideogram: hand, meat and worship. **Oblations,** SSU: sacrifices offered to the gods and the dead.

b) **Not yet,** WEI: temporal negative; something will but has not yet occurred; contrary of already, CHI. Image of Hexagram 64. **Acquire,** TE: obtain the desired object; wish for, desire covetously; gains, possessions. The ideogram: go and obstacle, going through obstacles to the goal.

Straighten, CHIH: correct the crooked, reform, repay injustice; proceed directly; sincere, upright, just; blunt, outspoken.

Acquiesce(in), SHOU: accept, make peace with, agree to; at rest, satisfied; patient. **Bless,** FU: heavenly gifts; make happy; spiritual power and goodwill. The ideogram: spirit and plenty, heavenly gifts in abundance.

Six above

a) **Confined by trailing creepers,**
  by the unsteady and unsettled.
  Spoken thus: stirring up repenting possesses repenting.
  Chastising auspicious.

b) **Confined by trailing creepers.**
  Not yet appropriate indeed.
  Stirring up repenting possesses repenting.
  Auspicious to move indeed.

Stop indulging yourself! This shouldn't even bother you. If you sit around and groan all the time, all you will hear is lamentation. Take yourself in hand. Get yourself in order. That will open the way. Don't just sit around trying to make everyone feel guilty.

Associated Contexts a) **Trailing creeper,** KO LEI: lush, fast-growing hanging plants; spread rapidly and widely; numerous progeny.

Unsteady and unsettled, NIEH WU: badly based; unquiet, hazardous; uneasy, anxious; dizzy, giddy as on a high place.

Spoken thus, YÜEH: designated, termed, called. The ideogram: open mouth and tongue. **Stir up,** TUNG: excite, influence, move, affect; work, take action; come out of the egg or the bud; the Action of the trigram Shake, CHEN. The ideogram: strength and heavy, move weighty things. **Repent,** HUI: dissatisfaction with past conduct causing a change of heart; proceeds from abashment, LIN, shame and confusion at having lost the right way.

Chastise, CHENG: punish, subjugate, discipline; reduce to order; punishing expedition. The ideogram: step and correct, a rectifying move.

b) **Not yet,** WEI: temporal negative; something will but has not yet occurred; contrary of already, CHI. Image of Hexagram 64. **Appropriate,** TANG: suitable; opportune, convenient; adequate, competent; equal to; whole lines in uneven places and opened lines in even places.

Move, HSING: move or move something; motivate, emotionally moving; walk, act, do. The ideogram: stepping left then right.

THE WELL ▮ CHING

Communicate, interact; the underlying structure, the network; source of life-water needed by all.

The Well describes your situation in terms of an underlying social structure and the natural force that flows through it. Its symbol is the well in the middle of the fields and the social order that gives access to the life water. The way to deal with it is to clarify and renew your connection to the source. The water is there for all to draw on. The well that gives you access to it must be cleaned and maintained. You can change where you live and who you associate with, but you can't change the well and the needs it represents. Losing and acquiring, coming and going, all are part of the well and its water. If all you find is mud in the well, you haven't gone deep enough. Your rope is too short. If you ruin the pitcher used to draw the water, you will be cut off from the spirits and left open to danger.

● *Image of the Situation*

> The Well: amending the capital, not amending the Well.
> Without losing, without acquiring,
> Going and coming, the Well is the Well.
> A muddy culmination, truly not yet a well rope in the Well,
> Ruining one's pitcher:
> Pitfall.

Associated Contexts **Well**, CHING: water well at the center of the fields; rise and flow of water in a well, rise and surge from an inner source; life-water, nucleus of life; found a capital city. The ideogram: two vertical lines crossing two horizontal ones, eight fields with a well at the center. **Amend**, KAI: correct, reform, make new, alter, mend. The ideogram: self and strike, fighting your own errors. **Capital**, YI: populous fortified city, center and symbol of the domain it rules. The ideogram: enclosure and official seal.

Without, WU: devoid of; -less as suffix. **Lose**, SANG: fail to obtain, cease, become obscure; forgotten, destroyed; lament, mourn; funeral. The ideogram: weep and the dead. **Acquire**, TE: obtain the desired object; wish for, desire covetously; gains, possessions. The ideogram: go and obstacle, going through obstacles to the goal.

Come, LAI, and **go**, WANG, describe the stream of time as it flows from future through present to past. Come, LAI, indicates what is approaching; move toward, arrive at; go, WANG, indicates what is departing; proceed, move on; keywords.

Mud, HSI: ground left wet by water, muddy shores; danger; shed tears; nearly. **Culminate**, CHIH: bring to the highest degree; arrive at the end or summit; superlative. **Truly**, YI: statement is true and precise. **Not yet**, WEI: temporal negative; something will but has not yet occurred; contrary of already, CHI, Image of Hexagram 64. **Well rope**, YÜ: rope used to draw water.

Ruin, LEI: destroy, break, overturn; debilitated, meager, emaciated; entangled. **One's/one**, CH'I: third person pronoun; also: it/its, he/his, she/hers, they/theirs. **Pitcher**, P'ING: clay jug or vase.

Pitfall, HSIUNG: leads away from the experience of meaning; stuck and exposed to danger, unable to take in the situation; flow of life and spirit is blocked; unfortunate, baleful; keyword.

- ## *Outer and Inner Aspects*

☵ **Gorge**: Stream ventures and falls into the gorge, flowing on through toil and danger. **Gorge** ends the yin hemicycle by leveling and dissolving forms.

Connection to the outer: flooding and leveling dissolve direction and shape, the Streaming Moment. **Gorge** ventures, falls, toils and flows on.

☴ **Ground**: Wind and wood subtly enter from the ground, penetrating and pervading. **Ground** is the center of the yang hemicycle, spreading pervasive action.

Connection to the inner: penetrating and bringing together, the Woody Moment culminating. **Ground** pervades, matches and couples, seeding a new generation.

Outer venturing and falling reach an inner ground where nourishment **wells** up from the depths.

- ## *Hidden Possibility*

Nuclear trigrams **Radiance**, LI, and **Open**, TUI, result in Nuclear Hexagram 38, **Diverging**, K'UEI. The **well**'s inner center which is open to all lets you resolve discord and diverging.

- *Sequence*

> Confining reaching to the above
> implies necessarily reversing the below.
> Accepting this lets you use The Well.

Associated Contexts **Confine**, K'UN: enclose, restrict, limit; oppressed; impoverish, distress; afflicted, exhausted, disheartened, weary. The ideogram: an enclosed tree. Image of Hexagram 47. **Reach(to)**, HU: arrive at a goal; reach towards and achieve; connect. **Above**, SHANG: anything above, in all senses; higher, upper, outer; upper trigram; opposite of below, HSIA. **Imply**, CHE: further signify; additional meaning. **Necessarily**, PI: unavoidably, indispensably, certainly. **Reverse**, FAN: turn and move in the opposite direction; turn around or upside down (180 degrees); change to the opposite position; contrary. **Below**, HSIA: anything below, in all senses; lower, inner; lower trigram; opposite of above, SHANG.

Accepting ... use: activating this hexagram depends on understanding and accepting the previous statement.

- *Contrasted Definitions*

> The Well: interpenetrating and
> Confining: mutual meeting indeed.

Associated Contexts **Interpenetrate**, T'UNG: mutually penetrate; permeate, flow through, reach everywhere; see clearly, communicate with.

Mutual, HSIANG: reciprocal assistance, encourage, help; bring together, blend with; examine, inspect; by turns. **Meet**, YÜ: come on unexpectedly, encounter; occur, happen; pleasant meeting, lucky coincidence; agree. **Indeed/is/means**, YEH: intensifier, connective; indicates comment on previous statement.

- *Attached Evidences*

> The Well: actualizing tao's earth indeed.
> The Well: residing in one's place and shifting.
> The Well uses differentiating righteousness.

Associated Contexts **Actualize tao**, TE: realize tao in action; power, virtue; ability to follow the course traced by the ongoing process of the cosmos; keyword. The ideogram: to go, straight, and heart. Linked with acquire, TE: acquiring that which makes a being become what it is meant to be. 's/have(it)/it/them, CHIH: expresses possession, directly or as an object pronoun. **Earth**, TI: ground on which the human world rests; basis of all things, nourishes all things; the Symbol of the trigram Field, K'UN.

Reside(in), CHU: dwell, live in, stay; sit down, fill an office; settled parts of a country. The ideogram: body and seat. **Place**, SO: where something belongs or comes from; residence, dwelling; habitual focus or object. **Shift**, CH'IEN: move, change, transpose; improve, ascend, be promoted; deport, dismiss, remove.

Use(of), YI: make use of, by means of, owing to; employ, make functional. **Differentiate**, PIEN: argue, dispute, criticize; sophisticated, artful. The ideogram: words and sharp or pungent. **Righteous**, YI: proper and just, meets the standards; things in their proper place; the heart that rules itself; upright, moral rule; contrasts with Harvest, LI, advantage or profit.

- *Symbol Tradition*

> **Above wood possessing stream. The Well.**
> **A chün tzu uses toiling with the commoners to encourage mutualizing.**

Associated Contexts **Wood/tree**, MU: all things woody or wooden, alive or constructed from wood; associated with Woody Moment ; wood and wind are the Symbols of the trigram Ground, SUN. The ideogram: a tree with roots and branches. **Possess**, YU: in possession of, have, own; opposite of lack, WU. **Stream**, SHUI: flowing water; fluid, dissolving; river, tide, flood; the Symbol of the trigram Gorge, K'AN. The ideogram: rippling water.

Chün tzu: ideal of a person who uses divination to order his/her life in accordance with tao rather than wilful intention; keyword. **Toil**, LAO: labor, take pains, exert yourself; burdened, careworn; worthy actions. The ideogram: strength and fire, producing heat. **Commoners**, MIN: class of workers the state draws on to sustain the social hierarchy; undeveloped potential outside the organized personality. **Encourage**, CH'ÜAN: exhort, stimulate, influence; admonish.

- *Image Tradition*

> **Ground reaching to stream and the stream above. The Well. [I]**
> **The Well nourishes and is not exhausted.**

Amending the capital, not amending the Well. [II]
Thereupon using strong centering indeed.

Muddy culmination, truly not yet a well rope in the Well. [III]
Not yet possessing achievement indeed.
Ruining one's pitcher.
That uses a pitfall indeed.

Associated Contexts **[I] Ground**, SUN: base on which things rest;
support, foundation; mild, subtly penetrating; nourishing. The ideogram:
stand and things arranged on it, the subtle influence of the ground. Image
of Hexagram 57.

Nourish, YANG: feed, sustain, support; provide, care for; bring up,
improve, grow, develop. **Exhaust**, CH'IUNG: bring to an end; limit,
extremity; destitute; investigate exhaustively; end without a new beginning.
The ideogram: cave and naked person, bent with disease or old age.

[II] Thereupon, NAI: on that ground, because of. **Strong**, KANG: quality of
the whole lines; firm, strong, unyielding, persisting. **Center**, CHUNG: inner,
central; put in the center; middle, stable point enabling you to face inner
and outer changes; middle line of trigram. The ideogram: field divided in
two equal parts. Image of Hexagram 61.

[III] Achieve, KUNG: work done, results; real accomplishment, praise,
worth, merit. The ideogram: workman's square and forearm, combining
craft and strength.

That uses, SHIH YI: involves and is involved by.

• *Transforming Lines*

Initial six

a) The Well: a bog, not taking it in.
The ancient Well without wildfowl.

b) The Well: a bog, not taking it in.
The below indeed.
The ancient Well without wildfowl.
The season stowed away indeed.

The sources of life and order are muddy and bogged down. Nothing good
will come of doing things this way. It is time to change.

Associated Contexts a) **Bog**, NI: wet spongy soil; mire, slush, quicksand; unable to move. **Take in/eat**, SHIH: eat, ingest, swallow, devour; incorporate.

Ancient, CHIU: of old, long before; worn out, spoiled; defunct. **Wildfowl**, CH'IN: all wild and game birds; untamed.

b) **Season**, SHIH: quality of the time; the right time, opportune, in harmony; planning in accord with the time; seasons of the year. The ideogram: sun and temple, time as sacred. **Stow(away)**, SHE: set aside, put away, store; halt, rest in; temporary lodgings, breathing-spell.

Nine at second

> *a)* The Well: a gully, shooting bass.
>   The jug cracked and leaking.

> *b)* The Well: a gully, shooting bass.
>   Without associates indeed.

The sources of life and order are not taken care of. Each seeks his own gain. There is no container. Time to change.

Associated Contexts a) **Gully**, KU: valley, ravine, river bed, gap. The ideogram: divide and river, a river bed separating hills. **Shoot**, SHE: shoot with a bow, point at and hit; project from, spurt, issue forth; glance at; scheme for. The ideogram: arrow and body. **Bass**, FU: freshwater fish, said to go in pairs and be faithful.

Jug, WENG: earthen jar; jug used to draw water. **Cracked**, PI: broken, ruined, tattered; unfit, unworthy. The ideogram: strike and break. **Leak**, LOU: seep, drip, ooze out; reveal; forget, let slip.

b) **Associate(with)**, YÜ: consort with, combine; companions; group, band, company; agree with, comply, help. The ideogram: pair of hands reaching downward meets a pair of hands reaching upward, helpful association.

Nine at third

> a) The Well: oozing, not taking it in.
>   Activating my heart aching.
>   Permitting availing of drawing the water:
>   Kingly brightness.
>   Together we could accept the blessing.

b) **The Well: oozing, not taking it in.**
Moving: aching indeed.
Seeking kingly brightness:
Acquiescing in blessing indeed.

This is the sorrow of someone who has much to give, but no one to give it to. There is nothing you can do, except think of the common good. Be prepared to move on. In the end you will be recognized and blessings will flow.

Associated Contexts a) **Ooze,** TIEH: exude moisture; mud, slime; turbid, tainted. **Take in/eat,** SHIH: ingest, swallow, devour; incorporate.

Activate, WEI: act or cause to act; do, make, manage; make active; attend to, help; because of. **My/me/I,** WO: first person pronoun; indicates an unusually strong emphasis on your own subjective experience. **Heart,** HSIN: heart as center of being; seat of mind's images and affections; moral nature; source of desires, intentions, will. **Ache,** TS'E: acute pain or grief; pity, sympathy, sorrow, grief.

Permit, K'O: possible because in harmony with an inherent principle. The ideogram: mouth and breath, silent consent. **Avail of,** YUNG: take advantage of; benefit from, profit by; use for a specific purpose; apply to advantage. The ideogram: to divine and center, applying divination to central concerns. **Draw water,** CHI: draw water from a well; draw forth, lead; take in a doctrine or example. The ideogram: water and reach to.

King(hood), WANG: effective ruler, by authority of the Emperor, from whom others derive their power. **Brightness,** MING: light-giving aspect of burning, heavenly bodies and consciousness; with fire, the Symbol of the trigram Radiance, LI.

Together with, PING: also, both, at the same time. The ideogram: two people standing together. **Accept,** SHOU: accept, make peace with, agree to; at rest, satisfied; patient. **Bless,** FU: heavenly gifts; make happy; spiritual power and goodwill. The ideogram: spirit and plenty, heavenly gifts in abundance.

b) **Move,** HSING: move or move something; motivate, emotionally moving; walk, act, do. The ideogram: stepping left then right.

Seek, CH'IU: search for, aim at, wish for, desire; implore, supplicate; covetous.

Six at fourth

a) The Well being lined, without fault.

b) The Well being lined, without fault.
Adjusting the Well indeed.

A time of inner work and improvement. You may feel cut off from those around you, but have no fears. This is inner work is not a mistake.

Associated Contexts a) **Lining**, TS'OU: line or repair a well. **Without fault**, WU CHIU: no error or harm in the situation.

b) **Adjust**, HSIU: regulate, repair, clean up, renovate.

Nine at fifth

a) The Well: limpid, cold springwater taken in.

b) Cold springwater's taking in.
Centering and correcting indeed.

This connection is a clear, pure source of life water for everyone to draw on. Use it and give thanks.

Associated Contexts a) **Limpid**, LIEH: pure, clear, clean liquid; wash clean. **Cold**, HAN: chilled, wintry; destitute, poor; shiver; fear; associated with the Streaming Moment. The ideogram: person huddled in straw under a roof. **Springwater**, CH'ÜAN: headwaters of a river; pure water. The ideogram: water and white, pure water at the source. **Take in/eat**, SHIH: ingest, swallow, devour; incorporate.

b) **Centering correcting**, CHUNG CHENG: central and correct; make rectifying one-sidedness and error your central concern; reaching a stable center in yourself can correct the situation.

Six above

a) The Well: collecting, no cover.
There is a connection to the spirits, Spring auspicious.

b) Spring auspicious located in the above.
The great accomplishing indeed.

Receive and give things freely. This is a source of spiritual nourishment for everyone. Don't hide it away. The way to the source is open. You can accomplish great things.

Associated Contexts a) **Collect**, SHOU: gather, harvest; receive what is

due; involve, snare, bind, restrain. **Cover,** MU: canvas covering; tent, booth, screen, tarpaulin.

There is ... **spirits,** YU FU: inner and outer are in accord; confidence of the spirits has been captured; sincere, truthful; proper to take action. **Spring,** YÜAN: source, origin, head; great, excellent; arise, begin, generating power; first stage of the Time Cycle. **Auspicious,** CHI: leads to the experience of meaning; favorable, propitious, advantageous, appropriate; keyword. The ideogram: scholar and mouth, wise words of a sage.

b) **Locate(in),** TSAI: live in, dwell, reside; belong to, involved with, depend on; within. The ideogram: earth and persevere, place on the earth.

Great, TA: big, noble, important, very; orient the will toward a self-imposed goal, impose direction; ability to lead or guide your life; contrasts with small, HSIAO, flexible adaptation to what crosses your path; keyword. Image of Hexagrams 14, 26, 28, 34. **Accomplish,** CH'ENG: complete, finish, bring about; perfect, full, whole; play your part, do your duty; mature. The ideogram: weapon and man, able to bear arms thus, fully developed.

SKINNING/REVOLUTION ▌ *KO*

Strip away the old; let the new life emerge; revolt and renew; molting.

Skinning/Revolution describes your situation in terms of stripping away the protective cover. Its symbols are animal transformations, melting bronze and casting the sacred vessels, and changing the mandate of heaven. The way to deal with it is to change and renew radically the way things are presented. Make an offering and you will succeed. Eliminate what has grown old and useless so that the new can be seen. You must wait for the right moment to act, when the snake is ready to shed its skin and the sun is approaching the zenith. When the right moment arrives, act with confidence. You will be linked to the spirits and they will carry you through. This begins a whole new cycle of time. All your doubts and sorrows will be extinguished.

● *Image of the Situation*

> **Skinning: your own day, thereupon a connection to the spirits.**
> **Source of Success: Advantageous Divination.**
> **Repenting extinguished.**

Associated Contexts **Skin**, KO: take off the covering, skin or hide; change, renew, molt; remove, peel off; revolt, overthrow, degrade from office; leather armor, protection. **Your own day**, SSU JIH; lit: before-zenith sun, the moment when the serpent sheds its skin; the double hour from 9-11 am, June; on the point of, the right time, the moment of transformation. **Thereupon**, NAI: on that ground, because of. **Connection to the spirits**, FU: accord between inner and outer in a particular moment; sincere, truthful, verified, reliable, in accord with the spirits; capture; prisoners, spoils. The ideogram: bird's claw enclosing young animals, possessive grip. Image of Hexagram 61.
  Source of Success: Advantageous Divination lit: Spring Growing Harvesting Trial: **Spring**, YÜAN; **Grow**, HENG; **Harvest**, LI; and **Trial**, CHEN, are the four stages of the Time Cycle, the model for all dynamic processes. They indicate that your question is connected to the cycle as a whole rather than a part of it, and that the origin (Spring) of a favorable result (Harvesting Trial) is an offering to the spirits (Growing).

Repenting extinguished, HUI WANG: previous troubles and consequent remorse will disappear.

● *Outer and Inner Aspects*

⚌ **Open**: vapor rising from the marsh's open surface stimulates and fertilizes; stimulating words cheer and inspire. **Open** begins the yin hemicycle by initiating the formative process.

Connection to the outer: liquifying, casting, skinning off the mold, the Metallic Moment beginning. **Open** stimulates, cheers and reveals innate form.

⚍ **Radiance**: Fire and brightness radiate light and warmth, attached to their support; congregating people see and become aware. **Radiance** ends the yang hemicycle, consuming action in awareness.

Connection to the inner: light, heat, consciousness bring continual change, the Fiery Moment. **Radiance** spreads outward, congregating, becoming aware and changing.

Changing inner awareness **skins** away obsolete outer forms, releasing a stimulating new potential.

● *Hidden Possibility*

Nuclear trigrams **Force**, CH'IEN, and **Ground**, SUN, result in Nuclear Hexagram 44, **Coupling**, KOU. Individual renewal through **skinning couples** you with creative force.

● *Sequence*

The Well tao not permitting not Skinning.
Accepting this lets you use Skinning.

Associated Contexts **Well**, CHING: water well at the center of the fields; rise and flow of water in a well, rise and surge from an inner source; life-water, nucleus of life; found a capital city. The ideogram: two vertical lines crossing two horizontal ones, eight fields with a well at the center. Image of Hexagram 48. **Tao**: way or path; ongoing process of being and the course it traces for each specific person or thing; keyword. The ideogram: go and head, leading and the path it creates. **Not permitting**, PU K'O: not possible; contradicts an inherent principle. The ideogram: mouth and breath, silent consent.

Accepting ... use: activating this hexagram depends on understanding and accepting the previous statement.

- *Contrasted Definitions*

  Skinning: departing anteriority indeed.
  The Vessel: grasping renewal indeed.

  Associated Contexts **Depart**, CH'Ü: leave, quit, remove; repudiate, reject, dismiss. **Anterior/past**, KU: come before as cause; formerly, ancient; reason, purpose, intention; grievance, quarrel, dissatisfaction, sorrow, mourning resulting from previous causes and intentions; situation leading to a divination. **Indeed/is/means**, YEH: intensifier, connective; indicates comment on previous statement.

  Vessel/holding, TING: bronze cauldron with three feet and two ears, sacred vessel used to cook food for sacrifice to gods and ancestors; founding symbol of family or dynasty; melting pot, receptacle; hold, contain, transform; establish, secure; precious, respectable. Image of Hexagram 50. **Grasp**, CH'Ü: lay hold of, take and use, seize, appropriate; grasp the meaning, understand. The ideogram: ear and hand, hear and grasp. **Renew**, HSIN: restore, improve, make or get better; new, fresh; the best, the latest.

- *Symbol Tradition*

  Marsh center possessing fire. Skinning.
  A chün tzu uses regulating the time reckoning to brighten the seasons.

  Associated Contexts **Marsh**, TSE: open surface of a flat body of water and the vapors rising from it; fertilize, enrich; kindness, favor; the Symbol of the trigram Open, TUI. **Center**, CHUNG: inner, central; put in the center; middle, stable point enabling you to face inner and outer changes; middle line of trigram. The ideogram: field divided in two equal parts. Image of Hexagram 61. **Possess**, YU: in possession of, have, own; opposite of lack, WU. **Fire**, HUO: warming and consuming aspect of burning; fire and brightness are the Symbols of the trigram Radiance, LI.

  Chün tzu: ideal of a person who uses divination to order his/her life in accordance with tao rather than wilful intention; keyword. **Use(of)**, YI: make use of, by means of, owing to; employ, make functional. **Regulate**, CHIH: govern well, ensure prosperity; remedy disorder, heal; someone fit to govern land, house and heart. **Time reckoning**, LI: fix times, seasons, calender; reckon the course of heavenly bodies, astronomical events.

Brightness, MING: light-giving aspect of burning, heavenly bodies and consciousness; with fire, the Symbol of the trigram Radiance, LI. **Season,** SHIH: quality of the time; the right time, opportune, in harmony; planning in accord with the time; seasons of the year. The ideogram: sun and temple, time as sacred.

●   *Image Tradition*

> Skinning. Stream, fire, mutually pausing. [I]
> Two women concording in residing.
> Their purposes not mutually acquiring. Spoken thus: Skinning.
>
> Your own day, thereupon a connection to the spirits. [II]
> Skin it and trust it.
>
> Pattern brightening uses stimulating. [III]
> Great Growing uses correcting.
> Skinning is appropriate.
> One's repenting thereupon extinguished.
>
> Heaven and Earth Skinning
> and the four seasons accomplishing. [IV]
> Majestically martial, Skinning fate.
> Yielding reaches to heaven and corresponding reaches the people.
> Actually Skinning's season great in fact.

Associated Contexts **[I] Stream,** SHUI: flowing water; fluid, dissolving; river, tide, flood; the Symbol of the trigram Gorge, K'AN. The ideogram: rippling water. **Mutual,** HSIANG: reciprocal assistance, encourage, help; bring together, blend with; examine, inspect; by turns. **Pause,** HSI: stop and rest, repose; breathe, a breathing-spell; suspended.

Two, ERH: pair, even numbers, binary, duplicate. **Woman(hood),** NÜ: a woman; what is inherently female. **Concord,** T'UNG: harmonize, unite, equalize, assemble; agree, share in; together, at once, same time and place. The ideogram: cover and mouth, silent understanding and perfect fit. Image of Hexagram 13. **Reside(in),** CHÜ: dwell, live in, stay; sit down, fill an office; settled parts of a country. The ideogram: body and seat.

Their/they, one's/one, CH'I: third person pronoun; also: it/its, he/his, she/hers. **Purpose,** CHIH: focus of mind and heart; will, inclination, resolve. The ideogram: heart and scholar, high inner resolve, or heart and go, inner determination. **Acquire,** TE: obtain the desired object; wish for, desire covetously; gains, possessions. The ideogram: go and obstacle, going through obstacles to the goal. **Spoken thus,** YÜEH: designated, termed, called. The ideogram: open mouth and tongue.

[II] Trust(worthy), HSIN: truthful, faithful, consistent over time; integrity; confide in, follow; credentials; contrasts with conforming, FU, connection in a specific moment. The ideogram: person and word, true speech. **It/them/have(it)/'s,** CHIH: expresses possession, directly or as an object pronoun.

[III] Pattern, WEN: intrinsic or natural design and its beauty; stylish, elegant; noble; contrasts with composition, CHANG, a conscious creation. **Stimulate/loosen,** SHUO: rouse to action and good feeling; free from constraint, stir up, urge on; persuade, cheer, delight; set out in words; the Action of the trigram Open, TUI. The ideogram: words and exchange.

    Great, TA: big, noble, important, very; orient the will toward a self-imposed goal, impose direction; ability to lead or guide your life; contrasts with small, HSIAO, flexible adaptation to what crosses your path; keyword. Image of Hexagrams 14, 26, 28, 34. **Grow,** HENG: success through a sacrifice; pervade, persevere; bring to full growth; enjoy; vigorous, effective; second stage of the Time Cycle. **Correct,** CHENG: rectify deviation or one-sidedness; proper, straight, exact, regular; constant, rule, model. The ideogram: stop and one, hold to one thing.

    Appropriate, TANG: suitable; opportune, convenient; adequate, competent; equal to; whole lines in uneven places and opened lines in even places.

    Repent, HUI: dissatisfaction with past conduct causing a change of heart; proceeds from abashment, LIN, shame and confusion at having lost the right way. **Extinguish,** WANG: ruin, destroy; gone, dead, lost without trace; extinct, forgotten, out of mind. The ideogram: person concealed by a wall, out of sight.

[IV] Heaven and Earth, T'IEN TI: dynamic relation between the primal powers and the world it produces; cosmos, natural or human world; keyword. **Four seasons,** SSU SHIH: the four dynamic qualities of time that make up the year and the Time Cycle; the right time, in accord with the time; time as sacred; all-encompassing. **Accomplish,** CH'ENG: complete, finish, bring about; perfect, full, whole; play your part, do your duty; mature. The ideogram: weapon and man, able to bear arms, thus fully developed.

    Majestic, T'ANG: grand, awesome; extending everywhere; repel injustice, correct grievances; lit.: large river and its periodic floods. **Martial,** WU: military, warlike; strong, stern; power to make war. The ideogram: fight and stop, force deterring aggression. **Fate/mandate,** MING: individual destiny; birth and death as limits of life; issue orders with authority; consult the gods. The ideogram: mouth and order, words with heavenly authority.

Yield(to), SHUN: give way and bear produce; comply, agree, follow, obey; unresisting, docile, flexible; nourish, provide; the Action of the trigram Field, K'UN. The ideogram: head and current, water flowing from the head of a river, yielding to the banks. **Reach(to),** HU: arrive at a goal; reach toward and achieve; connect; contrasts with tend-towards, YU. **Heaven,** T'IEN: highest; sky, firmament, heavens; power above the human as opposed to earth, TI, below; the Symbol of the trigram Force, CH'IEN. The ideogram: great and the one above. **Correspond(to),** YING: be in agreement or harmony; resonate together, invoke and fulfil each other; answer to, suitable; relation between the lines (1:4, 2:5, 3:6) when they form the pair opened and whole, supple and strong. The ideogram: heart and obey. **People, person,** JEN: humans individually and collectively; an individual; humankind. Image of Hexagrams 13 and 37.

Actually ... in fact, YI TSAI: stresses the importance of a statement. The ideogram: a dart and done, strong intention fully expressed. **'s/have(it)/it/them,** CHIH: expresses possession, directly or as an object pronoun.

- *Transforming Lines*

  Initial nine

  a) Thonging avails of a yellow cow's Skin.

  b) Thonging avails of yellow cattle.
  Not permitted to use possessing activating indeed.

Like a shaman in the skin mask, you begin the change of awareness. You can not act yet, but nothing can tear you away from this connection. Be open to the impulse when it comes.

Associated Contexts a) **Thong,** KUNG: bind with thongs, secure; well-guarded, strong, stiffened. **Avail of,** YUNG: take advantage of; benefit from; profit by; use for a specific purpose; apply to advantage. The ideogram: to divine and center, applying divination to central concerns. **Yellow,** HUANG: color of the productive middle; associated with the Earthy Moment between the yang and yin hemicycles; color of soil in central China; emblematic and imperial color of China since the Yellow Emperor (2500 BCE). **Cattle**, NIU: ox, bull, cow, calf; kine; power and strength of work animals.

b) **Activate**, WEI: act or cause to act; do, make, manage; make active; attend to, help; because of.

> **Six at second**
>
> *a)* **Your own day, thereupon Skinning it.**
> **Chastising auspicious, without fault.**
>
> *b)* **Your own day Skinning it.**
> **Moving possessing excellence indeed.**

When your time comes, move into the dance. You can change the world. Put everything into solution. Vigorous action to put things in order opens the way. This is definitely not a mistake.

Associated Contexts a) **Chastise**, CHENG: punish, subjugate, discipline; reduce to order; punishing expedition. The ideogram: step and correct, a rectifying move. **Auspicious**, CHI: leads to the experience of meaning; favorable, propitious, advantageous, appropriate; keyword. The ideogram: scholar and mouth, wise words of a sage. **Without fault**, WU CHIU: no error or harm in the situation.

b) **Move**, HSING: move or move something; motivate, emotionally moving; walk, act, do. The ideogram: stepping left then right. **Excellence**, CHIA: superior quality; fine, delicious, glorious; happy, pleased; rejoice in, praise. The ideogram: increasing goodness, pleasure and happiness.

> **Nine at third**
>
> *a)* **Chastising: pitfall, Trial: adversity.**
> **Skinning words three times draw near:**
> **There is a connection to the spirits.**
>
> *b)* **Skinning words three times drawing near.**
> **Furthermore actually wherefore having them.**

Discipline and expeditions won't work now. Danger. The ghosts of the past have arrived. Let the call to action go around three times, then act decisively. You can renew the time. The spirits will help you.

Associated Contexts a) **Chastise,** CHENG: punish, subjugate, discipline; reduce to order; punishing expedition. The ideogram: step and correct, a rectifying move. **Pitfall,** HSIUNG: leads away from the experience of meaning; stuck and exposed to danger, unable to take in the situation; flow of life and spirit is blocked; unfortunate, baleful; keyword. **Trial,** CHEN: test by ordeal; inquiry by divination and its result; righteous, firm; separating wheat from chaff; the kernel, the proven core; fourth stage of the Time Cycle. The ideogram: pearl and divination. **Adversity,** LI: danger; threatening, malevolent demon. This has two aspects: grind, sharpen, improve, perfect, stimulate; and: poisonous, sinister, cruel, contrary. It indicates a spirit or ghost that seeks revenge by inflicting suffering upon the living. Pacifying or exorcizing such a spirit can have a healing effect. The ideogram: sheltering cliff and stinging insect.

Word, YEN: speech, spoken words, sayings; talk, discuss, address. The ideogram: mouth and rising vapor, words as speech. **Three times,** SAN: serial repetition. **Draw near,** CHIU: approach, encounter, come near; follow; approach completion; composed, finished; able, willing; in a little while.

There is ... spirits, YU FU: inner and outer are in accord; confidence of the spirits has been captured; sincere, truthful; proper to take action.

b) **Furthermore,** YU: in addition to; higher degree of. **Actually,** YI: truly, really, at present. The ideogram: a dart and done, strong intention fully expressed. **Wherefore,** HO: interrogative: why? for what reason? what is? and affirmation: therefore, for that reason. **Have(them)/it/'s,** CHIH: expresses possession, directly or as an object pronoun.

Nine at fourth

a) Repenting extinguished, there is a connection to the spirits.
   Amending fate auspicious.

b) Amending fate's auspiciousness.
   Trustworthy purpose indeed.

The great change. Act and have no doubts. All your sorrows will vanish. The spirits are helping you. You are in a position to transform the imaginative basis of your world.

Associated Contexts. a) **There is ... spirits,** YU FU: inner and outer are in accord; confidence of the spirits has been captured; sincere, truthful; proper to take action.

Amend, KAI: correct, reform, make new, alter, mend. The ideogram:

self and strike, fighting your own errors. **Auspicious,** CHI: leads to the experience of meaning; favorable, propitious, advantageous, appropriate; keyword. The ideogram: scholar and mouth, wise words of a sage.

Nine at fifth

a) **Great People: tiger transforming.**
Not yet an augury, there is a connection to the spirits.

b) **Great People: tiger transforming.**
One's pattern luminous indeed.

When the time comes to change, you must change with it. Take a quantum leap. Let your great creative strength be seen. Pursue what you desire. Even before there is an oracle, people will know you are connected to the spirits. Have no fear. Your inner pattern can brighten events.

Associated Contexts a) **Great People,** TA JEN: important, noble, influential; those who impose a ruling principle on their lives; effect of the great within an individual; keyword. **Tiger,** HU: fierce king of animals; extreme yang; opposed to and protects against demoniacs on North– South axis of Universal Compass. **Transform,** PIEN: abrupt, radical, fundamental mutation from one state of being to another; transformation of lines in hexagrams; contrasts with change, HUA, gradual metamorphosis.

Not yet, WEI: temporal negative; something will but has not yet occurred; contrary of already, CHI. Image of Hexagram 64. **Augury,** CHAN: sign, omen; divine by casting lots, sortilege; look at as a sign or augury. **There is ... spirits,** YU FU: inner and outer are in accord; confidence of the spirits has been captured; sincere, truthful; proper to take action.

b) **Luminous,** PING: bright, fire-like, light-giving; alert, intelligent.

Six above

a) **A chün tzu: leopard transforming.**
Small People: Skinning the visage.
Chastising: pitfall.
Residence Trial auspicious.

b) **A chün tzu: leopard transforming.**
One's pattern beautiful indeed.
Small People: Skinning the visage.
Yielding uses adhering to the chief indeed.

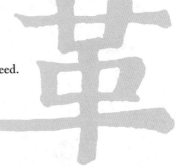

Change your life with grace and elegance. You can ground change in the life around you. Don't simply put on another mask. Stay right where you are for now, and the changes will fall into your hands. Disciplining others or setting out on expeditions close the Way.

Associated Contexts a) **Leopard**, PAO: spotted wild cats, beautiful and independent; mark of high-ranking officers. **Transform**, PIEN: abrupt, radical, fundamental mutation from one state of being to another; transformation of lines in hexagrams; contrasts with change, HUA, gradual metamorphosis.

Small People, HSIAO JEN: lowly, common, humble; those who adjust to circumstances with the flexibility of the small; effect of the small within an individual; keyword. **Visage**, MIEN: face, countenance; honor, character, reputation; front, surface; face to face.

Chastise, CHENG: punish, subjugate, discipline; reduce to order; punishing expedition. The ideogram: step and correct, a rectifying move. **Pitfall**, HSIUNG: leads away from the experience of meaning; stuck and exposed to danger, unable to take in the situation; flow of life and spirit is blocked; unfortunate, baleful; keyword.

Reside(in), CHÜ: dwell, live in, stay; sit down, fill an office; settled parts of a country. The ideogram: body and seat. **Trial**, CHEN: inquiry by divination and its result; righteous, firm; separating wheat from chaff; the kernel, the proven core; fourth stage of the Time Cycle . The ideogram: pearl and divination. **Auspicious**, CHI: leads to the experience of meaning; favorable, propitious, advantageous, appropriate; keyword . The ideogram: scholar and mouth, wise words of a sage.

b) **Beautiful**, WEI: elegant, classic, fine; luxuriant, lush.

Adhere(to), TS'UNG: follow a way, hold to a doctrine, school, or person; hear and comply with, agree to; forced to follow, follower. The ideogram: two men walking, one following the other. **Chief**, CHÜN: effective ruler; preside over, take the lead; influence others; term of respect. The ideogram: mouth and director, giving orders.

50
THE VESSEL ▌ *TING*

Sacred vessel; hold, contain and transform, imagine; meal with spirits, ancestors and noble people; establish, found.

The Vessel describes your situation in terms of imagination and the transformative capacity of a sacred vessel. Its symbol is the cast bronze cauldron, the sacrificial meal and the founding of a noble house. The way to deal with it is to contain and transform your problem through an image. Make an offering and you will succeed. You need to see deeply into what your problem means. Security and a new beginning will come from this awareness. It is a time for reflection, for slowly turning and examining things. This is the origin of great good fortune and meaningful events. It releases transformative energy. It is pleasing to the spirits. Through it they will give you success, effective power and the capacity to bring the situation to maturity.

● *Image of the Situation*

> The Vessel, Spring auspicious.
> Growing.

Associated Contexts **Vessel/holding,** TING: bronze cauldron with three feet and two ears, sacred vessel used to cook food for sacrifice to gods and ancestors; founding symbol of family or dynasty; melting pot, receptacle; hold, contain, transform; establish, secure; precious, respectable. **Spring,** YÜAN: source, origin, head; great, excellent; arise, begin, generating power; first stage of the Time Cycle. **Auspicious,** CHI: leads to the experience of meaning; favorable, propitious, advantageous, appropriate; keyword. The ideogram: scholar and mouth, wise words of a sage.

Grow, HENG: success through a sacrifice; pervade, persevere; bring to full growth; enjoy; vigorous, effective; second stage of the Time Cycle.

● *Outer and Inner Aspects*

☲ **Radiance:** Fire and brightness radiate light and warmth, attached to their support; congregating people see and become aware. **Radiance** ends the yang hemicycle, consuming action in awareness.

Connection to the outer: light, heat, consciousness bring continual change, the Fiery Moment. **Radiance** spreads outward, congregating, becoming aware and changing.

☴ **Ground**: Wind and wood subtly enter from the ground, penetrating and pervading. **Ground** is the center of the yang hemicycle, spreading pervasive action.

Connection to the inner: penetrating and bringing together, the Woody Moment culminating. **Ground** pervades, matches and couples, seeding a new generation.

Inner substance feeds a spreading outer light, cooking and transforming what is **held** in the **vessel**.

- *Hidden Possibility*

Nuclear trigrams **Open**, TUI, and **Force**, CH'IEN, result in Nuclear Hexagram 43, **Deciding**, KUAI. **Holding** and containing things in the **vessel** lets you take **decisive** action and **part** from the past.

- *Sequence*

Skinning beings implies absolutely nothing like a Vessel.
Accepting this lets you use the Vessel.

Associated Contexts **Skin**, KO: take off the covering, skin or hide; change, renew, molt; remove, peel off; revolt, overthrow, degrade from office; leather armor, protection. Image of Hexagram 49. **Being(s)**, WU: creature, thing, any single being; matter, substance, essence; nature of things. **Imply**, CHE: further signify; additional meaning. **Absolutely no(thing)**, MO: complete elimination; not any, by no means. **Like**, JO: same as; just as, similar to.

Accepting ... use: activating this hexagram depends on understanding and accepting the previous statement.

- *Contrasted Definitions*

Skinning: departing from the past indeed.
The Vessel: grasping renewal indeed.

Associated Contexts **Depart**, CH'Ü: leave, quit, remove; repudiate, reject, dismiss. **Past/anterior**, KU: come before as cause; formerly, ancient;

reason, purpose, intention; grievance, quarrel, dissatisfaction, sorrow, mourning resulting from previous causes and intentions; situation leading to a divination. **Indeed/is/means**, YEH: intensifier, connective; indicates comment on previous statement.

Grasp, CH'Ü: lay hold of, take and use, seize, appropriate; grasp the meaning, understand. The ideogram: ear and hand, hear and grasp. **Renew**, HSIN: restore, improve, make or get better; new, fresh; the best, the latest.

- *Symbol Tradition*

> Above wood possessing fire. The Vessel.
> A chün tzu uses correcting the situation to solidify fate.

Associated Contexts **Above**, SHANG: anything above, in all senses; higher, upper, outer; upper trigram; opposite of below, HSIA. **Wood/tree**, MU: all things woody or wooden, alive or constructed from wood; associated with the Woody Moment; wood and wind are the Symbols of the trigram Ground, SUN. The ideogram: a tree with roots and branches. **Possess**, YU: in possession of, have, own; opposite of lack, WU. **Fire**, HUO: warming and consuming aspect of burning; fire and brightness are the Symbols of the trigram Radiance, LI.

Chün tzu: ideal of a person who uses divination to order his/her life in accordance with tao rather than wilful intention; keyword. **Use(of)**, YI: make use of, by means of, owing to; employ, make functional. **Correct**, CHENG: rectify deviation or one-sidedness; proper, straight, exact, regular; constant, rule, model. The ideogram: stop and one, hold to one thing. **Situation**, WEI: place or seat according to rank; post, position, command; right, proper; established, arranged. The ideogram: person and stand, servants in their places. **Solidify**, NING: congeal, freeze, curdle, stiffen; coagulate, make strong or firm. **Fate/mandate**, MING: individual destiny; birth and death as limits of life; issue orders with authority; consult the gods. The ideogram: mouth and order, words with heavenly authority.

- *Image Tradition*

> The Vessel. A symbol indeed. [I]
> Using wood: Ground and fire.
> Growing: cooking indeed.

The all wise person Growing
uses presenting to the Supreme Above. [II]
The great Growing uses nourishing all wise eminences.
Ground and the ear and eye: understanding is brightened.

Supple advances and moves above, [III]
Acquiring the center also corresponding, reaching the strong.
That uses Spring Growing.

Associated Contexts **[I] Symbol,** HSIANG: image invested with intrinsic power to connect visible and invisible; magic spell; figure, form, shape, likeness; pattern, model; create an image, imitate; act, play; writing.

Wood/tree, MU: all things woody or wooden, alive or constructed from wood; associated with the Woody Moment; wood and wind are the Symbols of the trigram Ground, SUN. The ideogram: a tree with roots and branches. **Ground,** SUN: base on which things rest; support, foundation; mild, subtly penetrating; nourishing. The ideogram: stand and things arranged on it, the subtle influence of the ground. Image of Hexagram 57.

Cook, JEN: cook very thoroughly; transform completely. The ideogram: food and full or complete.

[II] All wise, SHENG: intuitive universal wisdom; mythical sages; holy, sacred; mark of highest distinction. The ideogram: ear and inform, one who knows all from a single sound. **People, person,** JEN: humans individually and collectively; an individual; humankind. Image of Hexagrams 13 and 37. **Present(to),** HSIANG: present in sacrifice, offer with thanks, give to the gods or a superior; confer dignity on. **Supreme Above,** SHANG TI: highest power in universe, lord of all.

Great, TA: big, noble, important, very; orient the will toward a self-imposed goal, impose direction; ability to lead or guide your life; contrasts with small, HSIAO, flexible adaptation to what crosses your path; keyword. Image of Hexagrams 14, 26, 28, 34. **Nourish,** YANG: feed, sustain, support; provide, care for; bring up, improve, grow, develop. **Eminent,** HSIEN: moral and intellectual power; worthy, excellent, virtuous; sage second to the all-wise, SHENG.

Ear and eye, ERH MU, organs of perception and awareness; see and understand; observe. **Understand,** TSUNG: perceive quickly, astute, sharp; discriminate intelligently. The ideogram: ear and quick. **Brightness,** MING: light-giving aspect of burning, heavenly bodies and consciousness; with fire, a the Symbol of the trigram Radiance, LI.

[III] Supple, JOU: quality of the opened lines; flexible, pliant, tender, adaptable. **Advance,** CHIN: exert yourself, make progress, climb; be promoted; further the development of, augment; adopt a religion or conviction; offer, introduce. **Move**, HSING: move or move something; motivate, emotionally moving; walk, act, do. The ideogram: stepping left then right.

Acquire, TE: obtain the desired object; wish for, desire covetously; gains, possessions. The ideogram: go and obstacle, going through obstacles to the goal. **Center**, CHUNG: inner, central; put in the center; middle, stable point enabling you to face inner and outer changes; middle line of trigram. The ideogram: field divided in two equal parts. Image of Hexagram 61. **Correspond(to)**, YING: be in agreement or harmony; resonate together, invoke and fulfil each other; answer to, suitable; relation between the lines (1:4, 2:5, 3:6) when they form the pair opened and whole, supple and strong. The ideogram: heart and obey. **Reach(to)**, HU: arrive at a goal; reach toward and achieve; connect; contrasts with tend-towards, YU. **Strong**, KANG: quality of the whole lines; firm, strong, unyielding, persisting.

That uses, SHIH YI: involves and is involved by.

- *Transforming Lines*

  Initial six

  a) The Vessel: toppling the foot.
  Advantageous to issue forth from obstruction. Harvesting.
  Acquiring a concubine, using one's sonhood.
  Without fault.

  b) The Vessel: toppling the foot.
  Not yet rebelling indeed.
  Advantageous to issue forth from obstruction.
  Using adhering to value indeed.

Do something out of the ordinary to establish a connection with the spirit. Turn things on their head. Get rid of the obstruction. This is not a mistake. It will bring you happiness.

Associated Contexts a) **Topple**, TIEN: fall over because top-heavy; overthrow, subvert; top, summit. **Foot**, CHIH: literal foot; foundation, base.

Advantageous/Harvest, LI: advantageous, profitable; acute, insightful; benefit, nourish; third stage of the Time Cycle. **Issue forth(from)**, CH'U: emerge from, come out of, proceed from, spring from; the Action of the trigram Shake, CHEN; contrary of enter, JU. The ideogram: stem with branches and leaves emerging. **Obstruct**, P'I: closed, stopped; bar the way; obstacle; unfortunate, wicked; refuse, disapprove, deny. The ideogram: mouth and not, blocked communication. Image of Hexagram 12.

Concubine, CH'IEH: secondary wife taken without ceremony to ensure a male descendant; handmaid. **One's/one**, CH'I: third person pronoun; also: it/its, he/his, she/hers, they/theirs. **Son(hood)**, TZU: living up to ideal of ancestors as highest human development; act with concern and reverence; male child; offspring, posterity; seed, kernel, egg; sage, teacher; nadir, deepest point, midnight, mid-winter.

Without fault, WU CHIU: no error or harm in the situation.

b) **Not yet**, WEI: temporal negative; something will but has not yet occurred; contrary of already, CHI. Image of Hexagram 64. **Rebel**, PEI: go against nature or usage; insubordinate; perverse, unreasonable.

Adhere(to), TS'UNG: follow a way, hold to a doctrine, school, or person; hear and comply with, agree to; forced to follow, follower. The ideogram: two men walking, one following the other. **Value**, KUEI: regard as valuable, give worth and dignity to; precious, high priced; honorable, exalted, illustrious. The ideogram: cowries (coins) and basket.

Nine at second

a) The Vessel possesses substance.
My companion possesses affliction.
Not able to approach me. Auspicious.

b) The Vessel possesses substance.
Considering places it indeed.
My companion possesses affliction.
Completing without surpassing indeed.

You have something real inside you, a spiritual transformation. Those around you now are afflicted with negative emotions. Stay with the transformation. Don't fear. It is substantial and secure. The way is open. Go your own way.

Associated Contexts a) **Substance**, SHIH: real, strong, full; results, fruits, possessions; essence; honest, sincere. The ideogram: string of coins under a roof, riches in the house.

My/me/I, WO: first person pronoun; indicates an unusually strong emphasis on your own subjective experience. **Companion**, CH'IU: equal, spouse; unite, join in marriage. Also: opponent, rival, enemy; contradict, hate. **Afflict,** CHI: sickness, disorder, defect, calamity; injurious; pressure and consequent anger, hate or dislike. The ideogram: sickness and dart, a sudden affliction.

Able, NENG: enable; ability, power, skill, art; competent, talented; duty, function, capacity. The ideogram: an animal with strong hooves and bones, able to carry and defend. **Approach,** CHI: come near to, advance toward; about to do; soon.

b) **Consider,** SHEN: act carefully, seriously; cautious, attentive, circumspect; still, quiet, sincere. The ideogram: heart and true. **Place,** SO: where something belongs or comes from; residence, dwelling; habitual focus or object. **It/them/have(it)/'s,** CHIH: expresses possession, directly or as an object pronoun.

Complete, CHUNG: end of a cycle that begins the next; last, whole, all; contrasts with exhaust, CH'IUNG, final end. The ideogram: silk cocoons, follow and ice, winter linking one year with the next. **Without,** WU: devoid of; -less as suffix. **Surpass,** YU: exceed; beyond measure, excessive; extraordinary; transgress, blame.

Nine at third

a) **The Vessel: the ears skinned.**
 Its movement clogged.
 Pheasant juice not eaten.
 On all sides rain lessens repenting.
 Completing auspicious.

b) **The Vessel: the ears skinned.**
 Letting go its righteousness indeed.

Everything feels clogged up now. Don't worry about it. This is a transformation of the way you understand things. The cleansing rain will come and wash away your sorrows. Keep going. The way is open.

Associated Contexts. a) **Ear,** ERH: organ of hearing; handle, sides.

Its/it, CH'I: third person pronoun; also: one/one's, he/his, she/hers, they/theirs. **Clog,** SAI: stop up, fill up, close, obstruct, hinder, prevent; unintelligent, dull, hard to understand.

Pheasant, CHIH: clever, beautiful bird associated with the trigram Radiance, LI; rule, arrange, put in order; embrasures on ramparts and forts. **Juice,** KAO: active principle, essence; oil, grease, ointment; fertilizing, rich; genius. **Take in/eat,** SHIH: ingest, swallow, devour; incorporate.

Sides (on all sides), FANG: limits, boundaries; square, surface of the earth extending to the four cardinal points; everywhere. **Rain**, YÜ: all precipitation; sudden showers, fast and furious; associated with the trigram Gorge, K'AN, and the Streaming Moment. **Lessen**, K'UEI: diminish, injure, wane; lack, defect, failure. **Repent**, HUI: dissatisfaction with past conduct causing a change of heart; proceeds from abashment, LIN, shame and confusion at having lost the right way.

Complete, CHUNG: end of a cycle that begins the next; last, whole, all; contrasts with exhaust, CH'IUNG, final end. The ideogram: silk cocoons, follow and ice, winter linking one year with the next.

b) **Let go**, SHIH: lose, omit, miss, fail, let slip; out of control. The ideogram: drop from the hand. **Righteous**, YI: proper and just, meets the standards; things in their proper place; the heart that rules itself; upright, moral rule; contrasts with Harvest, LI, advantage or profit.

Nine at fourth

a) The Vessel: a severed stand.
Overthrowing a princely stew.
Its form soiled. Pitfall.

b) Overthrowing a princely stew.
Wherefore trustworthy thus indeed?

Disaster. Whatever you are contemplating, don't do it. You will betray a trust. The way is closed.

Associated Contexts a) **Sever**, CHE: break off, separate, sunder, cut in two; discriminate, judge the true and false. **Stand**, TSU: base, foot, leg; rest on, support; stance. The ideogram: foot and calf resting.

Overthrow, FU: subvert, upset, defeat, throw down; unstable, move back and forth. **Prince**, KUNG: nobles acting as ministers of state in the capital; governing from the center rather than active in daily life; contrasts with feudatory, HOU, governors of the provinces. **Stew**, SU: cooked or boiled rice and meat; mixed contents of a pot.

Its/it, CH'I: third person pronoun; also: one/one's, he/his, she/hers, they/theirs. **Form**, HSING: shape; body, bodily; material appearance. **Soil**, WU: covered thick; dirty, stain; moisten, enrich. **Pitfall**, HSIUNG: leads away from the experience of meaning; stuck and exposed to danger, unable to take in the situation; flow of life and spirit is blocked; unfortunate, baleful; keyword.

b) **Wherefore**, HO: interrogative: why? for what reason? what is? and affirmation: therefore, for that reason. **Trustworthy**, HSIN: truthful, faithful, consistent over time; integrity; confide in, follow; credentials; contrasts with conforming, FU, connection in a specific moment. The ideogram: person and word, true speech. **Thus**, JU: as, in this way.

Six at fifth

a) The Vessel: yellow ears, metallic rings.
  Advantageous Trial. Harvesting.

b) The Vessel: yellow ears.
  Centering uses activating substance indeed.

A beautiful vision and a loving plan. You have found a way to bring it into the world. This is a great joy. Act on it. It will bring you profit and insight.

Associated Contexts a) **Yellow**, HUANG: color of the productive middle; associated with the Earthy Moment between the yang and yin hemicycles; color of soil in central China; emblematic and imperial color of China since the Yellow Emperor (2500 BCE). **Ear**, ERH: organ of hearing; handle, sides. **Metallic**, CHIN: smelting and casting; all things pertaining to metal, particularly gold; autumn, West, sunset; one of the Five Moments. **Rings**, HSÜAN: handles or ears for carrying a tripod.

  Advantageous Trial, LI CHEN: harvesting; advantageous divination; putting the action in question to the test is beneficial.

b) **Activate**, WEI: act or cause to act; do, make, manage; make active; attend to, help; because of. **Substance**, SHIH: real, strong, full; results, fruits, possessions; essence; honest, sincere. The ideogram: string of coins under a roof, riches in the house.

Nine above

a) The Vessel: jade rings.
  The great auspicious.
  Nothing not advantageous. Harvesting.

b) Jade rings located above.
  Strong and Supple articulated indeed.

This is something truly precious. It can transform your life. The Great Way is open to you now. This can be of benefit to all. It will open a whole new world.

Associated Contexts a) **Jade**, YÜ: all gemstones; precious beauty; delightful, happy; perfect, clear. **Rings**, HSÜAN: handles or ears for carrying a tripod.

Nothing not advantageous, WU PU LI: nothing for which this will not be beneficial; advantageous potential, borderline where the balance is swinging from not Harvesting to actually Harvesting.

b) **Locate(in)**, TSAI: live in, dwell, reside; belong to, involved with, depend on; within. The ideogram: earth and persevere, place on the earth.

Strong and Supple, KANG JOU: field of creative tension between the whole and opened lines and their qualities; field of psychic movement. **Articulate**, CHIEH: separate and distinguish, as well as join, different things; express thought through speech; joint, section, chapter, interval, unit of time; zodiacal sign; moderate, regulate; lit.: nodes on bamboo stalks. Image of Hexagram 60.

51

S H A K E ▮ *C H E N*

Disturbing and fertilizing shock; sexual energy; wake up, stir up; return of life in early spring.

Shake/Rousing describes your situation in terms of a disturbing and inspiring shock. Its symbol is the rituals that open the fields in spring. The way to deal with it is to rouse things to new activity. Make an offering and you will succeed. Re-imagine what you are confronting. Let the shock shake up your old beliefs and begin something new. Don't lose your depth and concentration. What at first seems frightening will soon be a cause to rejoice. This is pleasing to the spirits. Through it they will give you success, effective power and the capacity to bring the situation to maturity. The thunder rolls and everyone is frightened. You can hear them screaming in terror. Then the fright changes to joy and you hear everyone laughing and talking. The sudden shock spreads fear for thirty miles around. Don't lose your concentration. Hold the libation cup calmly so the dark wine arouses and calls the spirits.

● *Image of the Situation*

> **Shake, Growing.**
> **Shake coming: frightening, frightening.**
> **Laughing words, shrieking, shrieking.**
> **Shake scaring a hundred miles.**
> **Not losing the ladle and libation.**

Associated Contexts **Shake,** CHEN: arouse, excite, inspire; thunder rising from below; awe, alarm, trembling; fertilizing intrusion. The ideogram: excite and rain. **Shake** is the **Thunder** trigram doubled and includes that trigram's attributes: *Symbol:* **Thunder,** LEI: rising, arousing power. *Actions:* **Stir up,** TUNG: excite, influence, move, affect; work, take action; come out of the egg or the bud. The ideogram: strength and heavy, able to move weighty things. **Grow,** HENG: success through a sacrifice; pervade, persevere; bring to full growth; enjoy; vigorous, effective; second stage of the Time Cycle.

Come, LAI, and **go,** WANG, describe the stream of time as it flows from future through present to past; come, LAI, indicates what is approaching;

move toward, arrive at; keyword. **Fright**, HSI: frighten or be frightened; alarm, terror; awestruck. The doubled character intensifies this quality.

Laugh, HSIAO: manifest joy or mirth; giggle, laugh at, ridicule; pleased, merry; associated with the Fiery Moment. **Word**, YEN: speech, spoken words, sayings; talk, discuss, address. The ideogram: mouth and rising vapor, words as speech. **Shriek**, YA: shout, yell; warning cry of animals; sounds of someone learning to speak; confused noise, exclamations. The doubled character intensifies this quality.

Scare, CHING: create and spread fear, terrify; apprehensive, alarmed, perturbed. The ideogram: horse and strike, havoc created by a terrified horse. **Hundred**, PO: numerous, many, all; a whole class or type. **Mile**, LI: measure of distance, about 1800 feet; village; street, square.

Lose, SANG: fail to obtain, cease, become obscure; forgotten, destroyed; lament, mourn; funeral. The ideogram: weep and the dead. **Ladle**, PI: ceremonial spoon used to pour libations. **Libation**, CH'ANG: sacrificial liquor, poured out to draw the gods near.

- *Outer and Inner Aspects*

☳ **Shake**: Thunder rises from below, shaking and stirring things up. **Shake** begins the yang hemicycle by germinating new action.

Connection to both inner and outer: sprouting energies thrusting from below, the Woody Moment beginning. **Shake** stirs things up to issue-forth.

- *Hidden Possibility*

Nuclear trigrams **Gorge**, K'AN, and **Bound**, KEN, result in Nuclear Hexagram 39, **Difficulties**, CHIEN. The dynamic thrust of **shake** lets you re-imagine a **difficult** situation.

- *Sequence*

> A lord's implements imply absolutely nothing
> like the long living son.
> Accepting this lets you use Shake.
> Shake implies stirring up indeed.

Associated Contexts **Lord**, CHU: ruler, master, chief; authority. The ideogram: lamp and flame, giving light. **'s/have(it)/it/them**, CHIH: expresses possession, directly or as an object pronoun. **Implements**, CH'I:

utensils, tools; molded or carved objects; use a person or thing suitably; capacity, talent, intelligence. **Imply**, CHE: further signify; additional meaning. **Absolutely no(thing)**, MO: complete elimination; not any, by no means. **Like**, JO: same as; just as, similar to. **Long living**, CHANG: enduring, constant; senior, superior, greater; increase, prosper; respect, elevate. **Son(hood)**, TZU: living up to ideal of ancestors as highest human development; act with concern and reverence; male child; offspring, posterity; seed, kernel, egg; sage, teacher; nadir, deepest point, midnight, mid-winter.

Accepting ... use: activating this hexagram depends on understanding and accepting the previous statement.

Indeed/is/means, YEH: intensifier, connective; indicates comment on previous statement.

● *Contrasted Definitions*

> **Shake: rising up indeed.**
> **Bound: stopping indeed.**

Associated Contexts **Rise up**, CH'I: stand up, lift; undertake, begin, originate.

Bound, KEN: limit, boundary; encounter an obstacle, stop; still, quiet, motionless; confine, enclose, mark off; turn around to look behind; hard, adamant, obstinate; perverse. The ideogram: eye and person turning round to compare and group what is behind. Image of Hexagram 52. **Stop**, CHIH: bring or come to a standstill; the Action of the trigram **Bound**, KEN. The ideogram: a foot stops walking.

● *Symbol Tradition*

> **Reiterated thunder. Shake.**
> **A chün tzu uses anxious fearing to adjust and inspect.**

Associated Contexts **Reiterate**, CHIEN: repeat, duplicate; successive.

Chün tzu: ideal of a person who uses divination to order his/her life in accordance with tao rather than wilful intention; keyword. **Use(of)**, YI: make use of, by means of, owing to; employ, make functional. **Anxious**, K'UNG: apprehensive, alarmed, agitated; suspicious of. The ideogram: heart and sick, agitated within. **Fear**, CHÜ: afraid, intimidated, apprehensive; stand in awe of. **Adjust**, HSIU: regulate, repair, clean up, renovate. **Inspect**, HSING: examine on all sides, careful inquiry; watchful.

• *Image Tradition*

Shake, Growing. [I]
Shake coming: frightening, frightening.
Anxiety involving blessing indeed.

Laughing words, shrieking, shrieking. [II]
Afterwards possessing by consequence indeed.

Shake scaring a hundred miles. [III]
Scaring the distant and fearing the nearby indeed.

Issuing forth permits using guarding
the ancestral temple, field altar, offertory millet. [IV]
Using activating the offering lord indeed.

Associated Contexts [I] **Involve,** CHIH: include, entangle, implicate; induce, cause. The ideogram: person walking, induced to follow. **Bless,** FU: heavenly gifts; make happy; spiritual power and goodwill. The ideogram: spirit and plenty, heavenly gifts in abundance.

[II] **After(wards)/later,** HOU: come after in time, subsequent; put oneself after; the second; attendants, heirs, successors, posterity. **Possess,** YU: in possession of, have, own; opposite of lack, WU. **By consequence(of),** TSE: very strong connection; reason, cause, result; rule, law, pattern, standard; therefore.

[III] **Distance,** YÜAN: far off, remote; keep at a distance; alienated. The ideogram: go and a long way. **Nearby,** ERH: near, close; close relation.

[IV] **Permit,** K'O: possible because in harmony with an inherent principle. The ideogram: mouth and breath, silent consent. **Guard,** SHOU: keep in custody; protect, ward off harm, attend to, supervise. **Ancestry,** TSUNG: clan, kin, origin; those who bear the same surname; ancestral hall and tablets; honor, revere; a doctrine; contrasts with predecessor, K'AO, individual ancestors. **Temple,** MIAO: building used to honor gods and ancestors. **Field altar,** SHE: altar and sacrifices to spirits of place; village, with a common god and field-altar. **Offertory millet,** CHI: grain presented to the god of agriculture; presence of the god in the grain.

Activate, WEI: act or cause to act; do, make, manage; make active; attend to, help; because of. **Offer,** CHI: gifts to gods and spirits. The ideogram: hand, meat and worship.

● *Transforming Lines*

Initial nine

a) Shake coming: frightening, frightening.
After laughing words, shrieking, shrieking.
Auspicious.

b) Shake coming: frightening, frightening.
Anxiety involving blessing indeed.
Laughing words, shrieking, shrieking.
Afterwards possessing by consequence indeed.

A profound shock. Everything is turned upside down. But the anxiety soon turns to joy and a burst of creative energy. Let it move you. The way is open.

Associated Contexts a) **Auspicious**, CHI: leads to the experience of meaning; favorable, propitious, advantageous, appropriate; keyword. The ideogram: scholar and mouth, wise words of a sage.

Six at second

a) Shake coming: adversity.
A hundred thousand lost coins.
Climb up the ninth mound.
No pursuit.
The seventh day: acquiring.

b) Shake coming: adversity.
Riding the strong indeed.

You think you have lost something precious. Don't grieve. Climb the mountain of transformation. Everything you lost will soon return of itself. This shock rouses your dormant creative energy. Everything is renewed and inspired. Move with it. You will not be making a mistake.

Associated Contexts a) **Adversity**, LI: danger; threatening, malevolent demon. This has two aspects: grind, sharpen, improve, perfect, stimulate; and: poisonous, sinister, cruel, contrary. It indicates a spirit or ghost that seeks revenge by inflicting suffering upon the living. Pacifying or exorcizing such a spirit can have a healing effect. The ideogram: sheltering cliff and stinging insect.

Hundred thousand, YI: ten myriads (groups of ten thousand); huge quantity, number beyond imagination. **Coins**, PEI: cowrie shells used for money; adorned with shell; money, riches; precious, valuable.

    Climb, CHI: ascend, scale; climb steep cliffs; rise as clouds. **Nine**, CHIU: number of a transforming whole line; superlative: best, perfect; ninth. **Mound**, LING: grave-mound, barrow; small hill.

    Pursue, CHU: chase, follow closely, press hard; expel, drive out. The ideogram: pig (wealth) and go, chasing fortune.

    Seven, CH'I: number seven, seventh; seven planets; seventh day when moon changes from crescent to waxing; the Tangram game makes pictures of all phenomena from seven basic shapes. **Day/sun**, JIH: actual sun and the time of a sun-cycle, a day. **Acquire**, TE: obtain the desired object; wish for, desire covetously; gains, possessions. The ideogram: go and obstacle, going through obstacles to the goal.

b) **Ride**, CH'ENG: ride an animal or a chariot; have the upper hand, seize the right time; control strong power; overcome the nature of the other; supple opened line above a strong whole line. **Strong**, KANG: quality of the whole lines; firm, strong, unyielding, persisting.

    Six at third

    a) Shake: reviving, reviving.
      Shake moving without blunder.

    b) Shake: reviving, reviving.
      Situation not appropriate indeed.

This shock rouses your dormant creative energy. Everything is renewed and inspired. Move with it. You will not be making a mistake.

Associated Contexts a) **Revive**, SU: regain vital energy, courage or strength; bring to life, cheer up; relief; lit.: herb whose smell revives weary spirits. The doubled character intensifies this quality.

    Move, HSING: move or move something; motivate, emotionally moving; walk, act, do. The ideogram: stepping left then right. **Without**, WU: devoid of; -less as suffix. **Blunder**, SHENG: mistake due to ignorance or fault; contrasts with calamity, TSAI, disaster from without. The ideogram: eye and grow, a film clouding sight.

b) **Situation**, WEI: place or seat according to rank; post, position, command; right, proper; established, arranged. The ideogram: person and stand, servants in their places. **Appropriate**, TANG: suitable; opportune, convenient; adequate, competent; equal to; whole lines in uneven places and opened lines in even places.

Nine at fourth

a) Shake: released from the bog.

b) Shake: released from the bog.
  Not yet shining indeed.

Release fertile energy from the cloud of confusion. Everything is bogged down. What happened? Try to understand where the new impulse comes from.

Associated Contexts a) **Release**, SUI: loose, let go, free; unhindered, in accord; follow, spread out, progress; penetrate, invade. The ideogram: go and follow your wishes, unimpeded movement. **Bog**, NI: wet spongy soil; mire, slush, quicksand; unable to move.

b) **Not yet**, WEI: temporal negative; something will but has not yet occurred; contrary of already, CHI. Image of Hexagram 64. **Shine**, KUANG: illuminate; give off brilliant, bright light; honor, glory, éclat; result of action, contrasts with brightness, MING, light of heavenly bodies. The ideogram: fire above person, lifting the light.

Six at fifth

a) Shake going, coming adversity.
  Intention without losing possesses affairs.

b) Shake going, coming adversity.
  Exposed moving indeed.
  One's affairs located in the center.
  The great without loss indeed.

The creative energy comes and goes. It brings up old memories and quarrels and you must deal with them together. Keep your mind on what you want to do and all will be well. You will have plenty to keep you busy.

Associated Contexts a) **Come**, LAI, and **go**, WANG, describe the stream of time as it flows from future through present to past. Come, LAI, indicates what is approaching; move toward, arrive at; go, WANG, indicates what is departing; proceed, move on; keywords. **Adversity**, LI: danger;

threatening, malevolent demon. This has two aspects: grind, sharpen, improve, perfect, stimulate; and: poisonous, sinister, cruel, contrary. It indicates a spirit or ghost that seeks revenge by inflicting suffering upon the living. Pacifying or exorcizing such a spirit can have a healing effect. The ideogram: sheltering cliff and stinging insect.

Intention, YI: thought, meaning, idea, will, motive; what gives words their significance. The ideogram: heart and sound, heartfelt expression. **Without**, WU: devoid of; -less as suffix. **Affairs**, SHIH: all kinds of personal activity; matters at hand; business, occupation; manage a business, case in court.

b) **Expose**, WEI: exposed to danger, precipitous, unsteady; too high, not upright; uneasy. The ideogram: overhanging rock, person and limit, exposure in an extreme position. **Move**, HSING: move or move something; motivate, emotionally moving; walk, act, do. The ideogram: stepping left then right.

One's, one, CH'I: third person pronoun; also: he/his, she/hers, they/theirs, it/its. **Locate(in)**, TSAI: live in, dwell, reside; belong to, involved with, depend on; within. The ideogram: earth and persevere, place on the earth. **Center**, CHUNG: inner, central; put in the center; middle, stable point enabling you to face inner and outer changes; middle line of trigram. The ideogram: field divided in two equal parts. Image of Hexagram 61.

Great, TA: big, noble, important, very; orient the will toward a self-imposed goal, impose direction; ability to lead or guide your life; contrasts with small, HSIAO, flexible adaptation to what crosses your path; keyword. Image of Hexagrams 14, 26, 28, 34.

Six above

a) Shake: twisting, twisting.
  Observing: terrorizing, terrorizing.
  Chastising: pitfall.
  Shake is not in one's body,
  but in one's neighbor.
  Without fault.
  Matrimonial allying possesses words.

b) Shake: twining, twining.
  Center not yet acquired indeed.
  Although a pitfall, without fault.
  Dreading the neighbor, a warning indeed.

Creative energy twists and turns, driving people around you into a frenzy. Don't try to put this all in order. Stay aloof. Don't get caught in the trap. This is not the right time to do anything. Be cautious about beginning a relationship now.

Associated Contexts a) **Twisting,** SO: string or rope of many strands twisted together; tie up, bind together; reins; ruling ideas, obligations; demand, search for, inquire; scatter, loosen, destroy authority. The doubled character intensifies this quality.

Observe, SHIH: see and inspect carefully; gain knowledge of; compare and imitate. The ideogram: see and omen, taking account of what you see. **Terrorize,** CH'IO: look around in great alarm; frightened and trying to escape. The ideogram: eyes of bird trapped by a hand. The doubled character intensifies this quality.

Chastise, CHENG: punish, subjugate, discipline; reduce to order; punishing expedition. The ideogram: step and correct, a rectifying move. **Pitfall,** HSIUNG: leads away from the experience of meaning; stuck and exposed to danger, unable to take in the situation; flow of life and spirit is blocked; unfortunate, baleful; keyword.

One's/one, CH'I: third person pronoun; also: it/its, he/his, she/hers, they/theirs. **Body,** KUNG: physical being, power and self expression; contrasts with individuality, SHEN, the total personality. **Neighbor,** LIN: person living nearby; extended family; assist, support.

Without fault, WU CHIU: no error or harm in the situation.

Matrimonial allying, HUN KOU: legal institution of marriage; make alliances through marriage rather than force.

b) **Center,** CHUNG: inner, central; put in the center; middle, stable point enabling you to face inner and outer changes; middle line of trigram. The ideogram: field divided in two equal parts. Image of Hexagram 61. **Not yet,** WEI: temporal negative; something will but has not yet occurred; contrary of already, CHI. Image of Hexagram 64. **Acquire,** TE: obtain the desired object; wish for, desire covetously; gains, possessions. The ideogram: go and obstacle, going through obstacles to the goal.

Although, SUI: even though, supposing that, if, even if.

Dread, WEI: stand in awe of, respect, venerate; a just fear. **Warn,** CHIEH: alert, alarm, put on guard; caution, inform; guard against, refrain from (as in a diet). The ideogram: spear held in both hands, warning enemies and alerting friends.

BOUND ▮ KEN

Calm, still, stabilize; bind, come to the limit or boundary; articulating your experiences; becoming individual.

Bound/Stilling describes your situation in terms of recognizing a limit, or coming to the end of a cycle. It is the symbol of meditation and inner realization. The way to deal with it is to calm and stabilize your desire to act in order to understand what has been accomplished. Calm yourself. Don't try to advance. See through your desire. By doing this you stabilize yourself in the world of the spirits and allow them to emerge. Quiet your body. Calm and stabilize your back. This stills your personality so it is not caught up in compulsive actions. Move through your life as if the people were not there. This is not a mistake. It allows you to stabilize and articulate yourself.

● *Image of the Situation*

> **Bound: one's back.**
> **Not catching one's individuality.**
> **Moving through one's chambers**
> **Not seeing one's people.**
> **Without fault.**

Associated Contexts **Bound**, KEN: limit, boundary; encounter an obstacle, stop; still, quiet, motionless; confine, enclose, mark off; turn around to look behind; hard, adamant, obstinate; perverse. The ideogram: eye and person turning round to compare and group what is behind. **Bound** is the **Mountain** trigram doubled and includes that trigram's attributes: *Symbol:* **Mountain**, SHAN: limit, boundary. The ideogram: three peaks, a mountain range. *Action:* **Stop**, CHIH: bring or come to a standstill. The ideogram: a foot stops walking. **One's/one**, CH'I: third person pronoun; also: it/its, he/his, she/hers, they/theirs. **Back**, PEI: spine; opposite of front; behind, rear, hidden; turn the back on; north side; oppose, disobey, transgress. The ideogram: body and north, where the face is south.

  Catch, HUO: take in hunt; catch a thief; obtain, seize; hit the mark, opportune moment; prisoner, spoils, prey; slave, servant. **Individuality**, SHEN: total person: psyche, body and lifespan; character, virtue, duty; contrasts with **body**, KUNG, physical being.

Move, HSING: move or move something; motivate, emotionally moving; walk, act, do. The ideogram: stepping left then right. **Chambers**, T'ING: family room, courtyard, hall; domestic. The ideogram: shelter and hall, a secure place.

See, CHIEN: seeing in all its aspects: vision, being visible, forming mental images; visit, call on, consult. The ideogram: eye above person, active and receptive sight. **People, person**, JEN: humans individually and collectively; an individual; humankind. Image of Hexagrams 13 and 37.

Without fault, WU CHIU: no error or harm in the situation.

- *Outer and Inner Aspects*

☶ **Bound**: Mountains bound, limit and set a place off, stopping forward movement. **Bound** completes a full yin-yang cycle.

Connection to both inner and outer: accomplishing words, which express things fully. **Bound** articulates what is complete and suggests what is beginning.

- *Hidden Possibility*

Nuclear trigrams **Shake**, CHEN, and **Gorge**, K'AN, result in Nuclear Hexagram 40, **Loosening**, HSIEH. Stopping and accepting a limit or **bound** let you **loosen** and liberate bound energy.

- *Sequence*

> Beings not permitted to use completing stirring up.
> Stopping it.
> Accepting this lets you use Bound.
> Bounding implies stopping indeed.

Associated Contexts **Beings not permitted to use ...** : no one is allowed to make use of; nothing can exist by means of. **Complete**, CHUNG: end of a cycle that begins the next; last, whole, all; contrasts with exhaust, CH'IUNG, final end. The ideogram: silk cocoons, follow and ice, winter linking one year with the next. **Stir up**, TUNG: excite, influence, move, affect; work, take

action; come out of the egg or the bud; the Action of the trigram Shake, CHEN. The ideogram: strength and heavy, move weighty things.

It/them/have(it)/'s, CHIH: expresses possession, directly or as an object pronoun.

Accepting ... use: activating this hexagram depends on understanding and accepting the previous statement.

Imply, CHE: further signify; additional meaning. **Indeed/is/means,** YEH: intensifier, connective; indicates comment on previous statement.

- ## Contrasted Definitions

> **Shake: rising up indeed.**
> **Bound: stopping indeed.**

Associated Contexts **Shake,** CHEN: arouse, excite, inspire; thunder rising from below; awe, alarm, trembling; fertilizing intrusion. The ideogram: excite and rain. Image of Hexagram 51. **Rise up,** CH'I: stand up, lift; undertake, begin, originate.

- ## Symbol Tradition

> **Joined mountains. Bound.**
> **A chün tzu uses pondering not to issue forth from his situation.**

Associated Contexts **Join,** CHIEN: add or bring together; unite, absorb; attend to many things. The ideogram: hand grasps two grain stalks, two things at once.

Chün tzu: ideal of a person who uses divination to order his/her life in accordance with tao rather than wilful intention; keyword. **Use(of),** YI: make use of, by means of, owing to; employ, make functional. **Ponder,** SSU: reflect, consider, remember; deep thought; desire, wish. The ideogram: heart and field, the heart's concerns. **Issue forth(from),** CH'U: emerge from, come out of, proceed from, spring from; the Action of the trigram Shake, CHEN; contrary of enter, JU. The ideogram: stem with branches and leaves emerging. **One's/one,** CH'I: third person pronoun; also: it/its, she/hers, he/his, they/theirs. **Situation,** WEI: place or seat according to rank; post, position, command; right, proper; established, arranged. The ideogram: person and stand, servants in their places.

- *Image Tradition*

> Bound: stopping indeed. [I]
> The season stopping, by consequence you stop.
> The season moving, by consequence you move.
> Stirring up and stilling, not letting go their season.
> One's tao: shining brightness.
> Bound: one's stopping.
> Stopping: one's place indeed.
>
> Above and Below, an antagonistic correspondence. [II]
> Not mutually associating indeed.
> That uses not catching one's individuality.
> Moving through one's chambers,
> Not seeing one's people.
> Without fault indeed.

Associated Contexts [I] **Season**, SHIH: quality of the time; the right time, opportune, in harmony; planning in accord with the time; seasons of the year. The ideogram: sun and temple, time as sacred. **By consequence(of)**, TSE: very strong connection; reason, cause, result; rule, law, pattern, standard; therefore.

Still, CHING: quiet, at rest; imperturbable. **Let go**, SHIH: lose, omit, miss, fail, let slip; out of control. The ideogram: drop from the hand.

Tao: way or path; ongoing process of being and the course it traces for each specific person or thing; keyword. The ideogram: go and head, leading and the path it creates. **Shine**, KUANG: illuminate; give off brilliant, bright light; honor, glory, éclat; result of action, contrasts with brightness, MING, light of heavenly bodies. The ideogram: fire above person, lifting the light. **Brightness**, MING: light-giving aspect of burning, heavenly bodies and consciousness; with fire, the Symbol of the trigram Radiance, LI.

Place, SO: where something belongs or comes from; residence, dwelling; habitual focus or object.

[II] **Above and Below**, SHANG HSIA: realm of dynamic interaction between the upper and the lower; the vertical dimension. **Antagonistic**, TI: opposed and equal; competitor, enemy; a contest between equals. **Correspond(to)**, YING: be in agreement or harmony; resonate together, invoke and fulfil each other; answer to, suitable; relation between the lines (1:4, 2:5, 3:6) when they form the pair opened and whole, supple and strong. The ideogram: heart and obey.

Mutual, HSIANG: reciprocal assistance, encourage, help; bring together,

blend with; examine, inspect; by turns. **Associate(with)**, YÜ: consort with, combine; companions; group, band, company; agree with, comply, help. The ideogram: pair of hands reaching downward meets a pair of hands reaching upward, helpful association.

That uses, SHIH YI: involves and is involved by.

● *Transforming Lines*

Initial six

a) Bound: one's feet.
　Without fault.
　Perpetually advantageous Trial. Harvesting.

b) Bound: one's feet.
　Not yet letting go correcting indeed.

When an impulse to action comes, try to hold back before it leads you into compulsive entanglements. This is not a mistake. It can change your whole life for the better.

Associated Contexts a) **Foot**, CHIH: literal foot; foundation, base.
　Advantageous/Harvest, LI: advantageous, profitable; acute, insightful; benefit, nourish; third stage of the Time Cycle. **Perpetual**, YUNG: continuing; everlasting, ever-flowing. The ideogram: flowing water. **Trial**, CHEN: inquiry by divination and its result; righteous, firm; separating wheat from chaff; the kernel, the proven core; fourth stage of the Time Cycle. The ideogram: pearl and divination.

b) **Not yet**, WEI: temporal negative; something will but has not yet occurred; contrary of already, CHI. Image of Hexagram 64. **Correct**, CHENG: rectify deviation or one-sidedness; proper, straight, exact, regular; constant, rule, model. The ideogram: stop and one, hold to one thing.

Six at second

a) Bound: one's calves.
　Not rescuing one's following.
　One's heart not keen.

b) Not rescuing one's following.
　Not yet withdrawing from hearkening indeed.

Though you can stop running after impossible desires, you cannot help others who are on the same course. Though this makes your heart ache, do not fail to listen to the call.

Associated Contexts a) **Calf**, FEI: muscle of lower leg; rely on; prop, rest.

Rescue, CHENG: aid, deliver from trouble; pull out, raise up, lift. The ideogram: hand and aid, a helping hand. **Follow**, SUI: come or go after; pursue, impelled to move; come after in inevitable sequence; move in the same direction, comply with what is ahead; follow a way or religion; according to, next, subsequent. The ideogram: go and fall, unavoidable movement. Image of Hexagram 17.

Heart, HSIN: heart as center of being; seat of mind's images and affections; moral nature; source of desires, intentions, will. **Keen**, K'UAI: sharp, eager, prompt, cheerful; spirited.

b) **Not yet**, WEI: temporal negative; something will but has not yet occurred; contrary of already, CHI. Image of Hexagram 64. **Withdraw(from)**, T'UI: draw back, retreat, recede; decline, refuse. **Hearken**, T'ING: listen to, obey, accept, acknowledge; examine, judge, decide. The ideogram: ear and actualizing-tao, hear and obey.

Nine at third

a) **Bound: one's limit.**
   Assigned to one's loins:
   Adversity smothers the heart.

b) **Bound: one's limit.**
   Exposure smothers the heart indeed.

You are cutting yourself in two, separating yourself from real and legitimate desires. The acrid smoke from this repression smothers your heart. You don't have to suffer like this. It won't help anyone.

Associated Contexts a) **Limit**, HSIEN: boundary, frontier, threshold; restriction, impediment; set a limit. distinguish, separate.

Assign to, LIEH: place according to rank; arrange in order; distinguish, separate. **Loins**, YIN: hips, pelvis, lumbar region; kidneys; respect, honor; work toward a distant aim; money belt.

Adversity, LI: danger; threatening, malevolent demon. This has two aspects: grind, sharpen, improve, perfect, stimulate; and: poisonous, sinister, cruel, contrary. It indicates a spirit or ghost that seeks revenge by

inflicting suffering upon the living. Pacifying or exorcizing such a spirit can have a healing effect. The ideogram: sheltering cliff and stinging insect. **Smother**, HSÜN: suffocate, smoke out; fog, steam, miasma, vapor; broil, parch; offend; evening mists. **Heart**, HSIN: heart as center of being; seat of mind's images and affections; moral nature; source of desires, intentions, will.

b) **Expose**, WEI: exposed to danger, precipitous, unsteady; too high, not upright; uneasy. The ideogram: overhanging rock, person and limit, exposure in an extreme position.

Six at fourth

a) Bound: one's individuality.
  Without fault.

b) Bound: one's individuality.
  Stopping connoting the body indeed.

Still your compulsive actions, emotions and desires. This frees you from mistakes and lets you see where your real motivations lie. It calms and stabilizes the heart.

Associated Contexts b) **Connote**, CHU: imply the meaning; signify. The ideogram: words and imply. **Body**, KUNG: physical being, power and self expression; contrasts with individuality, SHEN, the total personality.

Six at fifth

a) Bound: one's jawbones.
  The words possesses a sequence.
  Repenting extinguished.

b) Bound: one's jawbones.
  Using centering correcting indeed.

If you reflect and restrain your speech, what you say will have order and elegance. When you can communicate like this, your sorrows will vanish.

Associated Contexts a) **Jawbones/brace**, FU: support, consolidate, reinforce, strengthen, stiffen, prop up, fix; rigid, steady, firm; help, rescue; support the mouth that speaks. The ideogram: cart and great.
  Word, YEN: speech, spoken words, sayings; talk, discuss, address. The ideogram: mouth and rising vapor, words as speech. **Possess**, YU: in

possession of, have, own; opposite of lack, WU. **Sequence,** HSÜ: order, precedence, series; follow in order.

Repenting extinguished, HUI WANG: previous troubles and consequent remorse will disappear.

b) **Centering correcting,** CHUNG CHENG: central and correct; make rectifying one-sidedness and error your central concern; reaching a stable center in yourself can correct the situation.

Nine above

a) **Magnanimous Bounding, auspicious.**

b) **Magnanimous Bounding's auspicious.**
   Using munificence to complete it indeed.

Meet people with generosity, honesty and care and you will receive it in return. This is the end of your isolation. You have learned what you need to face your new life. The way is open.

Associated Contexts a) **Magnanimous,** TUN: generous; honest, substantial, important, wealthy; honor, increase; firm, strong. The ideogram: strike and accept, warrior magnanimous in attack and defense. **Auspicious,** CHI: leads to the experience of meaning; favorable, propitious, advantageous, appropriate; keyword. The ideogram: scholar and mouth, wise words of a sage.

b) **Munificence,** HOU: liberal, kind, generous; create abundance; thick, large. The ideogram: gift of a superior to an inferior.

GRADUAL ADVANCE ▮ *CHIEN*

Smooth, adaptable progress; infiltrate, penetrate like water; ceremonies leading to a formal marriage; find a place in the world of symbols.

Gradual Advance describes your situation in terms of gradually achieving a goal. Its symbol is the flight of the wild geese proceeding to a marriage and the soul's journey into the world of symbolic realities. The way to deal with it is to advance slowly and steadily through subtle penetration. Move through the woman and the yin. Through infiltrating, you find the place where you belong. Proceed step by step, and don't try to dominate the situation. This generates meaning and good fortune by releasing transformative energy. You will ultimately achieve mastery and find a new field of activity. Put your ideas to the trial. This brings profit and insight.

- *Image of the Situation*

> **Gradual Advance, the woman converting is auspicious.**
> **Advantageous Trial. Harvesting.**

Associated Contexts **Gradual Advance**, CHIEN: advance by degrees; penetrate slowly and surely, as water; stealthily; permeate throughout; influence, affect. The ideogram: water and cut. **Woman(hood)**, NÜ: a woman; what is inherently female. **Convert**, KUEI: change to another form, persuade; return to yourself or the place where you belong; restore, revert, become loyal; turn into; give a young girl in marriage. The ideogram: arrive and wife, become mistress of a household. Image of Hexagram 54. **Auspicious**, CHI: leads to the experience of meaning; favorable, propitious, advantageous, appropriate; keyword. The ideogram: scholar and mouth, wise words of a sage.

> **Advantageous Trial/Harvesting**, LI CHEN: advantageous divination; putting the action in question to the test is beneficial.

- *Outer and Inner Aspects*

> ☴ **Ground**: Wind and wood subtly enter from the ground, penetrating and pervading. **Ground** is the center of the yang hemicycle, spreading pervasive action.

Connection to the outer: penetrating and bringing together, the Woody Moment culminating. **Ground** pervades, matches and couples, seeding a new generation.

☷ **Bound**: Mountains bound, limit and set a place off, stopping forward movement. **Bound** completes a full yin-yang cycle.

Connection to the inner: accomplishing words, which express things. **Bound** articulates what is complete to suggest what is beginning.

An inner limit provides the basis for gradually advancing on the outer ground.

• *Hidden Possibility*

Nuclear trigrams **Radiance**, LI, and **Gorge**, K'AN, result in Nuclear Hexagram 64, **Not yet Fording**, WEI CHI. Smooth and constant **gradual** advance lets you gather the energy to **ford** the stream of events.

• *Sequence*

Beings not permitted to use completing stopping.
Accepting this lets you use Infiltrating.
Infiltrating implies advancing indeed.

Associated Contexts **Beings not permitted to use ...** : no one is allowed to make use of; nothing can exist by means of. **Complete**, CHUNG: end of a cycle that begins the next; last, whole, all; contrasts with exhaust, CH'IUNG, final end. The ideogram: silk cocoons, follow and ice, winter linking one year with the next. **Stop**, CHIH: bring or come to a standstill; the Action of the trigram Bound, KEN. The ideogram: a foot stops walking.

Accepting ... use: activating this hexagram depends on understanding and accepting the previous statement.

Imply, CHE: further signify; additional meaning. **Advance**, CHIN: exert yourself, make progress, climb; be promoted; further the development of, augment; adopt a religion or conviction; offer, introduce. **Indeed/is/means**, YEH: intensifier, connective; indicates comment on previous statement.

• *Contrasted Definitions*

Gradual Advance: a woman converting awaits a man's move indeed.
Converting Maidenhood: a woman's completion indeed.

Associated Contexts **Await**, TAI: expect, wait for, welcome (friendly or hostile), provide against. **Man(hood)**, NAN: a man; what is inherently male. The ideogram: fields and strength, hard labor in the fields. **Move**, HSING: move or move something; motivate, emotionally moving; walk, act, do. The ideogram: stepping left then right.

   Maiden(hood), MEI: girl not yet nubile, virgin; younger sister; daughter of a secondary wife. The ideogram: woman and not-yet. **Converting Maidenhood** is the Image of Hexagram 54. **'s/have(it)/ it/them**, CHIH: expresses possession, directly or as an object pronoun.

- *Symbol Tradition*

> **Above mountain possessing wood. Gradual Advance.**
> **A chün tzu uses residing in eminent actualizing tao**
> **to improve the vulgar.**

Associated Contexts **Above**, SHANG: anything above, in all senses; higher, upper, outer; upper trigram; opposite of below, HSIA. **Mountain**, SHAN: limit, boundary; the Symbol of the trigram Bound, KEN. The ideogram: three peaks, a mountain range. **Possess**, YU: in possession of, have, own; opposite of lack, WU. **Wood/tree**, MU: all things woody or wooden, alive or constructed from wood; associated with the Woody Moment; wood and wind are the Symbols of the trigram Ground, SUN. The ideogram: a tree with roots and branches.

   Chün tzu: ideal of a person who uses divination to order his/her life in accordance with tao rather than willful intention; keyword. **Use(of)**, YI: make use of, by means of, owing to; employ, make functional. **Reside(in)**, CHÜ: dwell, live in, stay; sit down, fill an office; settled parts of a country. The ideogram: body and seat. **Eminent**, HSIEN: moral and intellectual power; worthy, excellent, virtuous; sage second to the all-wise, SHENG. **Actualize tao**, TE: realize tao in action; power, virtue; ability to follow the course traced by the ongoing process of the cosmos; keyword. The ideogram: to go, straight, and heart. Linked with acquire, TE: acquiring that which makes a being become what it is meant to be. **Improve**, SHAN: make better, reform, perfect, repair; virtuous, wise; mild, docile; clever, skilful, handy. The ideogram: mouth and sheep, gentle speech. **Vulgar**, SU: common people and their desires; inelegant, low; grovelling; the pressure of everyday life.

● *Image Tradition*

Gradually advancing it indeed. [I]
Womanhood converting auspicious.
Advancing and acquiring the situation,
Going possesses achievement indeed.

Advancing uses correcting. [II]
It permits using correcting the fiefdoms indeed.
One's situation: strong acquiring the center indeed.

Stopping and The Ground. [III]
Stirring up not exhausted indeed.

Associated Contexts [I] **Acquire**, TE: obtain the desired object; wish for, desire covetously; gains, possessions. The ideogram: go and obstacle, going through obstacles to the goal. **Situation**, WEI: place or seat according to rank; post, position, command; right, proper; established, arranged. The ideogram: person and stand, servants in their places.

Go, WANG, and **come**, LAI, describe the stream of time as it flows from future through present to past; go, WANG, indicates what is departing from present to past; proceed, move on; keyword. **Achieve**, KUNG: work done, results; real accomplishment, praise, worth, merit. The ideogram: workman's square and forearm, combining craft and strength.

[II] **Correct**, CHENG: rectify deviation or one-sidedness; proper, straight, exact, regular; constant, rule, model. The ideogram: stop and one, hold to one thing.

Permit, K'O: possible because in harmony with an inherent principle. The ideogram: mouth and breath, silent consent. **Fiefdom**, PANG: region governed by a feudatory, an order of nobility.

One's/one, CH'I: third person pronoun; also: it/its, he/his, she/hers, they/theirs. **Strong**, KANG: quality of the whole lines; firm, strong, unyielding, persisting. **Center**, CHUNG: inner, central; put in the center; middle, stable point enabling you to face inner and outer changes; middle line of trigram. The ideogram: field divided in two equal parts. Image of Hexagram 61.

[III] **Ground**, SUN: base on which things rest; support, foundation; mild, subtly penetrating; nourishing. The ideogram: stand and things arranged on it, the subtle influence of the ground. Image of Hexagram 57.

Stir up, TUNG: excite, influence, move, affect; work, take action; come out of the egg or the bud; the Action of the trigram Shake, CHEN. The ideogram: strength and heavy, move weighty things. **Exhaust**, CH'IUNG: bring to an end;

limit, extremity; destitute; investigate exhaustively; end without a new beginning. The ideogram: cave and naked person, bent with disease or old age.

- *Transforming Lines*

   Initial six

   a) The wild geese gradually advance to the barrier.
   The small son's adversity possessing words.
   Lacking fault.

   b) The small son's adversity.
   Righteous, without fault indeed.

First steps. You encounter danger from the past, but the creative energy is still there. This is not a mistake. Have no fear. Speak out.

Associated Contexts a) **Wild geese,** HUNG: large white water bird, symbol of the soul and its spiritual aspirations; wild swan and wild goose as emblems of the messenger and of conjugal fidelity; vast, profound, far-reaching, great; valued, learned. **Barrier,** KAN: boundary, limit; fend off, protect; stream, parapet, river bank; shield, defensive armor; the Ten Heavenly Barriers are part of the calendar system.

   Small, HSIAO: little, common, unimportant; adapting to what crosses your path; ability to move in harmony with the vicissitudes of life; contrasts with great, TA, self-imposed theme or goal; keyword. Image of Hexagrams 9 and 62. **Son(hood),** TZU: living up to ideal of ancestors as highest human development; act with concern and reverence; male child; offspring; posterity; seed, kernel, egg; sage, teacher; nadir, deepest point, midnight, mid-winter. **Adversity,** LI: danger; threatening, malevolent demon. This has two aspects: grind, sharpen, improve, perfect, stimulate; and: poisonous, sinister, cruel, contrary. It indicates a spirit or ghost that seeks revenge by inflicting suffering upon the living. Pacifying or exorcizing such a spirit can have a healing effect. The ideogram: sheltering cliff and stinging insect. **Word,** YEN: speech, spoken words, sayings; talk, discuss, address. The ideogram: mouth and rising vapor, words as speech.

   Lacking, WU: strong negative; does not possess. **Fault,** CHIU: unworthy conduct that leads to harm, illness, misfortune. The ideogram: person and differ, differ from what you should be.

b) **Righteous,** YI: proper and just, meets the standards; things in their proper place; the heart that rules itself; upright, moral rule; contrasts with Harvest, LI, advantage or profit.

   Without fault, WU CHIU: no error or harm in the situation.

Six at second

   a) The wild geese gradually advance to the stone.
   Drinking and eating: feasting, feasting.
   Auspicious.

   b) Drinking and eating: feasting, feasting.
   Not sheer satiation indeed.

A secure place and a warm connection. Enjoy yourself now. The way is open. The journey will resume.

Associated Contexts a) **Wild geese,** HUNG: large white water bird, symbol of the soul and its spiritual aspirations; wild swan and wild goose as emblems of the messenger and of conjugal fidelity; vast, profound, far-reaching, great; valued, learned. **Stone,** P'AN: large conspicuous rock, foundation stone; stable, immovable.

   Drinking and eating, YIN SHIH: comprehensive term for eating, drinking and breathing; a meal, eating together. **Feast,** K'AN: take part in or give a feast; rejoice, give pleasure; pleased, contented. The doubled character intensifies this quality.

b) **Sheer,** SU: plain, unadorned; original color or state; clean, pure. The ideogram: white silk, symbol of mourning. **Satiation,** PAO: full, replete, satisfied; swollen, sated; gratified, flattered.

Nine at third

   a) The wild geese gradually advance to the highlands.
   The husband chastised, not returning.
   The wife pregnant, not nurturing.
   Pitfall.
   Advantageous to resist outlawry. Harvesting.

   b) The husband chastised, not returning.
   A radiant flock of demons indeed.
   The wife pregnant, not nurturing.
   Letting go her tao indeed.
   Advantageous to resist outlawry.
   Yielding mutualizes protection indeed.

Separation. You have taken a wrong turn. Things are falling apart in mutual recrimination. The way is closing and creative energy dispersed. Firmly resist the temptation to become violent or withholding. Find what you can do to help each other.

Associated Contexts a) **Wild geese,** HUNG: large white water bird, symbol of the soul and its spiritual aspirations; wild swan and wild goose as emblems of the messenger and of conjugal fidelity; vast, profound, far-reaching, great; valued, learned. **Highlands,** LU: high, dry land as distinct from swamps; plateau.

Husband, FU: household manager; administer with thrift and prudence; responsible for; sustain with your earnings; old enough to assume responsibility; married man. **Chastise,** CHENG: punish, subjugate, discipline; reduce to order; punishing expedition. The ideogram: step and correct, a rectifying move. **Return,** FU: go back, turn back to the starting point; recur, reappear, come again; restore, recover, retrace; an earlier time or place. The ideogram: step and retrace a path. Image of Hexagram 24.

Wife, FU: responsible position of married woman within the household; contrasts with consort, CH'I, her legal position and concubine, CH'IEH, secondary wives. The ideogram: woman, hand and broom, household duties. **Pregnant,** JEN: carrying a child. **Nurture,** YÜ: bring up, support, rear, raise; increase.

Pitfall, HSIUNG: leads away from the experience of meaning; stuck and exposed to danger, unable to take in the situation; flow of life and spirit is blocked; unfortunate, baleful; keyword.

Advantageous/Harvest, LI: advantageous, profitable; acute, insightful; benefit, nourish; third stage of the Time Cycle. **Resist,** YÜ: withstand, oppose; bring to an end; prevent. The ideogram: rule and worship, imposing ethical or religious limits. **Outlawry,** K'OU: break the laws; violent people, outcasts, bandits.

b) **Radiance,** LI: glowing light, spreading in all directions; light-giving, discriminating, articulating; divide and arrange in order; the power of consciousness. The ideogram: bird and weird, the magical fire-bird with brilliant plumage. Image of Hexagram 30. **Flock,** CH'UN: herd, group; people of same kind, friends, equals; all, entire; move in unison, flock together. The ideogram: chief and sheep, flock around a leader. **Demon(iac),** CH'OU: possessed by a malignant genius; ugly, physically or morally deformed; vile, disgraceful, shameful; drunken. The ideogram: fermenting liquor and soul. Demoniac and tiger are opposed on the Universal Compass North–South axis; the tiger (Extreme Yang) scares away and protects against demoniacs (Extreme Yin).

Let go, SHIH: lose, omit, miss, fail, let slip; out of control. The ideogram: drop from the hand. **Her/she**, CH'I: third person pronoun; also: one/one's, it/its, he/his, they/their. **Tao**: way or path; ongoing process of being and the course it traces for each specific person or thing; keyword. The ideogram: go and head, leading and the path it creates.

Avail of, YUNG: take advantage of; benefit from, profit by; use for a specific purpose; apply to advantage. The ideogram: to divine and center, applying divination to central concerns.

Yield(to), SHUN: give way and bear produce; comply, agree, follow, obey; unresisting, docile, flexible; nourish, provide; the Action of the trigram Field, K'UN. The ideogram: head and current, water flowing from the head of a river, yielding to the banks. **Mutual**, HSIANG: reciprocal assistance, encourage, help; bring together, blend with; examine, inspect; by turns. **Protect**, PAO: guard, defend, keep safe; secure.

Six at fourth

a) The wild geese gradually advance to the trees.
  "Someone" acquiring his rafter.
  Without fault.

b) "Someone" acquiring his rafter.
  Yielding using Ground indeed.

This is a resting-place after a great transition. It will give you shelter for a while. Have no fear, this is not a mistake. The spirit is at work.

Associated Contexts a) **Wild geese**, HUNG: large white water bird, symbol of the soul and its spiritual aspirations; wild swan and wild goose as emblems of the messenger and of conjugal fidelity; vast, profound, far-reaching, great; valued, learned.

Maybe/"someone", HUO: possible, perhaps; term indicates spirit is active. **Rafter**, CHÜEH: roof beams; flat branches.

Without fault, WU CHIU: no error or harm in the situation.

b) **Yield(to)**, SHUN: give way and bear produce; comply, agree, follow, obey; unresisting, docile, flexible; nourish, provide; the Action of the trigram Field, K'UN. The ideogram: head and current, water flowing from the head of a river, yielding to the banks.

Nine at fifth

a) The wild geese gradually advance to the mound.
The wife, three year's time not pregnant.
At completion: absolutely nothing can master them.
Auspicious.

b) Completion: absolutely nothing can master them, auspicious.
Acquiring the place desired indeed.

This is the penultimate step, where your creative energy makes contact with the ancestors and the guardian spirits. This takes time, but when it is finished nothing will stop you. Have no fears. The way is open.

Associated Contexts a) **Wild geese**, HUNG: large white water bird, symbol of the soul and its spiritual aspirations; wild swan and wild goose as emblems of the messenger and of conjugal fidelity; vast, profound, far-reaching, great; valued, learned. **Mound**, LING: grave-mound, barrow; small hill.

Wife, FU: responsible position of married woman within the household; contrasts with consort, CH'I, her legal position and concubine, CH'IEH, secondary wives. The ideogram: woman, hand and broom, household duties. **Three**, SAN: number three, third time or place; active phases of a cycle; superlative; beginning of repetition. **Year's time**, SUI: actual length of time in a year; contrasts with years-revolved, NIEN, number of years elapsed. **Pregnant**, JEN: carrying a child.

Absolutely no(thing), MO: complete elimination; not any, by no means. **Master**, SHENG: have the upper hand, conquer; worthy of, able to; control, check, command.

b) **Place**, SO: where something belongs or comes from; residence, dwelling; habitual focus or object. **Desire**, YÜAN: wish, hope or long for; covet; desired object.

Nine above

a) The wild geese gradually advance to the highlands.
Their feathers permit availing of activating the fundamentals.
Auspicious.

b) Their feathers permit availing of
activating the fundamentals, auspicious.
Not permitting disarray indeed.

The journey ends together in the world of the spirit. It becomes a symbol that can activate fundamental energies in the world we live in. Because you understand what symbols can do, the way will always be open to you.

Associated Contexts a) **Wild geese,** HUNG: large white water bird, symbol of the soul and its spiritual aspirations; wild swan and wild goose as emblems of the messenger and of conjugal fidelity; vast, profound, far-reaching, great; valued, learned. **Highlands,** LU: high, dry land as distinct from swamps; plateau.

Its/it, CH'I: third person pronoun; also: one/one's, he/his, she/hers, they/theirs. **Feathers,** YU: wings, plumes; feathered; quick, flying. **Avail of,** YUNG: take advantage of; benefit from, profit by; use for a specific purpose; apply to advantage. The ideogram: to divine and center, applying divination to central concerns. **Activate,** WEI: act or cause to act; do, make, manage; make active; attend to, help; because of. **Fundamentals,** YI: primary natural powers; the great rituals and dances; origins, essentials; good and do good; correct, proper, just; rule, rite, decorum; paired, matched. The ideogram: person and righteous.

b) **Not permitting,** PU K'O: not possible; contradicts an inherent principle. The ideogram: mouth and breath, silent consent. **Disarray,** LUAN: throw into disorder, mislay, confuse; out of place; discord, insurrection, anarchy.

MARRYING THE MAIDEN ▮
KUEI MEI

Marriage of the younger daughter; a passionate, irregular relationship; change over which you have no control; realize your hidden potential; desire, compulsion.

Marrying the Maiden describes your situation in terms of a change you must go through which is beyond your control. Its symbol is the young woman who is led to a major and unforeseen transformation by forces beyond her control. You are not the one who has chosen. The force involved is larger than you are. The way to deal with it is to accept it and let yourself be led. You cannot escape the situation. It reflects a deep and unacknowledged need. It is moving you towards a new field of activity, the place where you belong. Don't try to discipline people or take control of the situation. That will cut you off from the spirits and leave you open to danger. Don't impose your will, have a plan or a place to go. Being free of such plans will bring you profit and insight. This is a very special situation that, in the long run, can lead to great success.

● *Image of the Situation*

> **Marrying the Maiden, chastising: pitfall.**
> **Not advantageous to have a direction to go.**

Associated Contexts **Marry/convert**, KUEI: change to another form, persuade; return to yourself or the place where you belong; restore, revert, become loyal; turn into; give a young girl in marriage. The ideogram: arrive and wife, become mistress of a household. **Maiden(hood)**, MEI: girl not yet nubile; younger sister, daughter of a secondary wife. The ideogram: woman and not-yet. **Chastise**, CHENG: punish, subjugate, discipline; reduce to order; punishing expedition. The ideogram: step and correct, a rectifying move. **Pitfall**, HSIUNG: leads away from the experience of meaning; stuck and exposed to danger, unable to take in the situation; flow of life and spirit is blocked; unfortunate, baleful; keyword.

Not advantageous to have a direction, WU YU LI: no plan or direction is advantageous; in order to take advantage of the situation, do not impose a direction on events.

- *Outer and Inner Aspects*

⚎ **Shake**: Thunder rises from below, shaking and stirring things up. **Shake** begins the yang hemicycle by germinating new action.

Connection to the outer: sprouting energies thrusting from below, the Woody Moment beginning. **Shake** stirs things up to issue-forth.

⚌ **Open**: vapor rising from the marsh's open surface stimulates and fertilizes; stimulating words cheer and inspire. **Open** begins the yin hemicycle by initiating the formative process.

Connection to the inner: liquifying, casting, skinning off the mold, the Metallic Moment beginning. **Open** stimulates, cheers and reveals innate form.

Rousing energy from without **converts** the **maiden's** potential to stimulate, inspire and give form. These trigrams emphasize the Pivoting Phase, initiating new action.

- *Hidden Possibility*

Nuclear trigrams **Gorge**, K'AN, and **Radiance**, LI, result in Nuclear Hexagram 63, **Already Fording**, CHI CHI. The maiden who stands on the threshold of **marriage** is part of a transition that is **already** underway.

- *Sequence*

> Advancing necessarily possessing a place to Convert.
> Accepting this lets you use Marrying the Maiden.

Associated Contexts **Advance**, CHIN: exert yourself, make progress, climb; be promoted; further the development of, augment; adopt a religion or conviction; offer, introduce. **Necessarily**, PI: unavoidably, indispensably, certainly. **Possess**, YU: in possession of, have, own; opposite of lack, WU. **Place**, SO: where something belongs or comes from; residence, dwelling; habitual focus or object.

Accepting ... use: activating this hexagram depends on understanding and accepting the previous statement.

- *Contrasted Definitions*

> Gradual Advance: the woman converting
> awaits the man's move indeed.
> Marrying the Maiden: womanhood's completion indeed.

Associated Contexts **Gradual Advance**, CHIEN: advance by degrees; penetrate slowly and surely, as water; stealthily; permeate throughout; influence, affect. The ideogram: water and cut. Image of Hexagram 53. **Woman(hood)**, NÜ: a woman; what is inherently female. **Await**, TAI: expect, wait for, welcome (friendly or hostile), provide against. **Man(hood)**, NAN: a man; what is inherently male. The ideogram: fields and strength, hard labor in the fields. **Move**, HSING: move or move something; motivate, emotionally moving; walk, act, do. The ideogram: stepping left then right. **Indeed**, YEH: intensifier, connective; indicates comment on previous statement.

's/have(it)/it/them, CHIH: expresses possession, directly or as an object pronoun. **Complete**, CHUNG: end of a cycle that begins the next; last, whole, all; contrasts with exhaust, CH'IUNG, final end. The ideogram: silk cocoons, follow and ice, winter linking one year with the next.

- *Symbol Tradition*

> Above marsh possessing thunder. Marrying the Maiden.
> A chün tzu uses perpetually completing to know the cracked.

Associated Contexts **Above**, SHANG: anything above, in all senses; higher, upper, outer; upper trigram; opposite of below, HSIA. **Marsh**, TSE: open surface of a flat body of water and the vapors rising from it; fertilize, enrich; kindness, favor; the Symbol of the trigram Open, TUI. **Thunder**, LEI: rising, arousing power; the Symbol of the trigram Shake, CHEN.

Chün tzu: ideal of a person who uses divination to order his/her life in accordance with tao rather than wilful intention; keyword. **Use(of)**, YI: make use of, by means of, owing to; employ, make functional. **Perpetual**, YUNG: continuing; everlasting, ever-flowing. The ideogram: flowing water. **Know**, CHIH: understand, perceive, remember; informed, aware, wise. The ideogram: arrow and mouth, words focused and swift. **Cracked**, PI: broken, ruined, tattered; unfit, unworthy. The ideogram: strike and break.

- *Image Tradition*

> Marrying the Maiden. [I]
> Heaven and Earth's great righteousness indeed.
> Heaven and Earth not mingling and the myriad beings not rising.
> Marrying the Maiden.

A person's completion beginning indeed. [II]
Stimulating uses stirring up.
A place to Marry the Maiden indeed.
Chastising: pitfall.
Situation not appropriate indeed.

Not advantageous to have a direction to go. [III]
Supple riding a strong indeed.

Associated Contexts [I] **Heaven and Earth,** T'IEN TI: dynamic relation between the primal powers and the world it produces; cosmos, natural or human world; keyword. **Great,** TA: big, noble, important, very; orient the will toward a self-imposed goal, impose direction; ability to lead or guide your life; contrasts with small, HSIAO, flexible adaptation to what crosses your path; keyword. Image of Hexagrams 14, 26, 28, 34. **Righteous,** YI: proper and just, meets the standards; things in their proper place; the heart that rules itself; upright, moral rule; contrasts with Harvest, LI, advantage or profit.

Mingle, CHIAO: blend with, communicate, join, exchange; trade, business; copulation; friendship. **Myriad,** WAN: countless; many, everyone; lit.: ten thousand. The ideogram: swarm of insects. **Being(s),** WU: creature, thing, any single being; matter, substance, essence; nature of things. **Rise,** HSING: get up, grow, lift; begin, give rise to, construct; be promoted; flourishing, fashionable. The ideogram: lift, two hands and unite, lift with both hands.

[II] **People, person,** JEN: humans individually and collectively; an individual; humankind. Image of Hexagrams 13 and 37. **Begin,** SHIH: commence, start, open; earliest, first; beginning of a time-span, ended by completion, CHUNG. The ideogram: woman and eminent, beginning new life.

Stimulate/loosen, SHUO: rouse to action and good feeling; free from constraint, stir up, urge on; persuade, cheer, delight; set out in words; the Action of the trigram Open, TUI. The ideogram: words and exchange. **Stir up,** TUNG: excite, influence, move, affect; work, take action; come out of the egg or the bud; the Action of the trigram Shake, CHEN. The ideogram: strength and heavy, move weighty things.

Situation, WEI: place or seat according to rank; post, position, command; right, proper; established, arranged. The ideogram: person and stand, servants in their places. **Appropriate,** TANG: suitable; opportune, convenient; adequate, competent; equal to; whole lines in uneven places and opened lines in even places.

[III] Supple, JOU: quality of the opened lines; flexible, pliant, tender, adaptable. **Ride**, CH'ENG: ride an animal or a chariot; have the upper hand, seize the right time; control strong power; overcome the nature of the other; supple opened line above a strong whole line. **Strong**, KANG: quality of the whole lines; firm, strong, unyielding, persisting.

● *Transforming Lines*

    Initial nine

    a) Marrying the Maiden using the junior sister.
      Halting enables treading.
      Chastising auspicious.

    b) Marrying the Maiden using the junior sister.
      Using persevering indeed.
      Halting enables treading, auspicious.
      Mutualizing and receiving indeed.

You are not in a position of power, but that does not mean you can't influence things and achieve your desire. Put yourself in order and do what you have to do. This lets you partake of mutual benefits.

Associated Contexts a) **Junior sister**, TI: younger woman in family or clan; younger sister, under authority of the first wife.

    Halt, P'O: limp; lame, crippled; indecorous. **Able**, NENG: enable; ability, power, skill, art; competent, talented; duty, function, capacity. The ideogram: an animal with strong hooves and bones, able to carry and defend. **Tread**, LÜ: step, path, track; footsteps; walk a path or way; course of the stars; act, practice; conduct; salary, means of subsistence. The ideogram: body and repeating steps, following a trail. Image of Hexagram 10.

    Auspicious, CHI: leads to the experience of meaning; favorable, propitious, advantageous, appropriate; keyword. The ideogram: scholar and mouth, wise words of a sage.

b) **Persevere**, HENG: continue in the same way or spirit; constant, perpetual, regular; self-renewing; extend everywhere. Image of Hexagram 32.

    Mutual, HSIANG: reciprocal assistance, encourage, help; bring together, blend with; examine, inspect; by turns. **Receive**, CH'ENG: receive gifts or commands from superiors or customers; take in hand; catch falling water. The ideogram: accepting a seal of office.

Nine at second

a) Squinting enables observing.
  Shade people's advantageous Trial. Harvesting.

b) Shade people's advantageous Trial.
  Not yet transforming the rules indeed.

Stay out of sight for now. Don't get involved in struggles for power. Look
at things from an independent perspective. You will learn a lot this way, and
be able to unfold your plans.

Associated Contexts a) **Squint,** MIAO: look at with one eye, glance at;
obstructed vision. **Able,** NENG: enable; ability, power, skill, art; competent,
talented; duty, function, capacity. The ideogram: an animal with strong
hooves and bones, able to carry and defend. **Observe,** SHIH: see and inspect
carefully; gain knowledge of; compare and imitate. The ideogram: see and
omen, taking account of what you see.

  Advantageous/Harvest, LI: advantageous, profitable; acute, insightful;
benefit, nourish; third stage of the Time Cycle. **Shade,** YU: hidden from
view; retired, solitary, secret; dark, obscure, occult, mysterious; ignorant.
The ideogram: small within hill, a cave or grotto. **Trial,** CHEN: inquiry by
divination and its result; righteous, firm; separating wheat from chaff; the
kernel, the proven core; fourth stage of the Time Cycle. The ideogram:
pearl and divination.

b) **Not yet,** WEI: temporal negative; something will but has not yet occurred;
contrary of already, CHI. Image of Hexagram 64. **Transform,** PIEN: abrupt,
radical, fundamental mutation from one state of being to another;
transformation of lines in hexagrams; contrasts with change, HUA, gradual
metamorphosis. **Rules,** CH'ANG: unchanging principles; regular, constant,
habitual; maintain laws and customs.

Six at third

a) Marrying the Maiden using patience.
  Reversing the Marriage: using the junior sister.

b) Marrying the Maiden using patience.
  Not yet appropriate indeed.

You feel in a secondary position. Have patience, ease and courage. In the
end you will reverse things and gain a strategic position. Be ready. You will

sabotage everything if you act publicly as an inferior.

Associated Contexts a) **Patience,** HSÜ: patience symbolized as waiting for hair to grow; hold back, wait for; slow; necessary.

Reverse, FAN: turn and move in the opposite direction; turn around or upside down (180 degrees); change to the opposite position; contrary. **Junior sister,** TI: younger woman in family or clan; younger sister, under authority of the first wife.

b) **Not yet,** WEI: temporal negative; something will but has not yet occurred; contrary of already, CHI. Image of Hexagram 64.

Nine at fourth

a) **Marrying the Maiden by overrunning the term.**
   Procrastinating in Marriage possesses the season.

b) **Overrunning the term's purpose.**
   Possessing awaiting and moving indeed.

Let things go. Forget about deadlines. This will increase your worth. You will know when it is the right time to act.

Associated Contexts a) **Overrun,** CH'IEN: pass the limit; mistake, transgression, disease. **Term,** CH'I: set time, fixed period, agreed date; seasons; person a hundred years old.

Procrastinate, CH'IH: delay, act at leisure, retard; slow, late. **Season,** SHIH: quality of the time; the right time, opportune, in harmony; planning in accord with the time; seasons of the year. The ideogram: sun and temple, time as sacred.

b) **Purpose,** CHIH: focus of mind and heart; will, inclination, resolve. The ideogram: heart and scholar, high inner resolve, or heart and go, inner determination.

Six at fifth

a) **The supreme burgeoning Marries the Maidens.**
   One's chief wife's sleeves:
   Not thus fine as one's junior sister's sleeves.
   The moon almost facing, auspicious.

b) The supreme burgeoning Marries Maidens.
  Not thus fine as one's junior sister's sleeves.
  One's situation located in the center.
  Using valuing movement indeed.

An omen of great future happiness, fertility and power. Be like the moon that is almost full. The time is changing. Accept the secondary position willingly for now. It carries great power. Your success is assured.

Associated Contexts a) **Supreme**, TI: highest, above all on earth; sovereign lord, source of power; emperor. **Burgeon**, YI: beginning of growth after seedburst, CHIA, early spring; associated with the Woody Moment. **Supreme Burgeoning**, TI YI, refers to the great Shang emperor (1191–1151 BCE) who took a wife from the family of King Wen's father in order to assure an heir. This ennobled the line from which the Chou Dynasty came. It is an omen of great happiness and good fortune in the future.

　　One's/one, CH'I: third person pronoun; also: it/its, he/his, she/hers, they/theirs. **Chief**, CHÜN: effective ruler; preside over, take the lead; influence others; term of respect. The ideogram: mouth and director, giving orders. **Sleeve**, MEI: displays signs showing quality and rank of the wearer; symbol of self; womb symbol.

　　Junior sister, TI: younger woman in family or clan; younger sister, under authority of the first wife. **Thus**, JU: as, in this way. **Fine**, LIANG: excellent, refined, valuable; gentle, considerate, kind; natural.

　　Moon, YÜEH: actual moon and moon-month; yin, the sun being yang. **Almost**, CHI: nearly, about to; subtle, almost imperceptible; the first sign. **Face**, WANG: full moon; moon directly facing the sun; 15th day of the moon-month; look at hopefully. **Auspicious**, CHI: leads to the experience of meaning; favorable, propitious, advantageous, appropriate; keyword. The ideogram: scholar and mouth, wise words of a sage.

b) **Locate(in)**, TSAI: live in, dwell, reside; belong to, involved with, depend on; within. The ideogram: earth and persevere, place on the earth. **Center**, CHUNG: inner, central; put in the center; middle, stable point enabling you to face inner and outer changes; middle line of trigram. The ideogram: field divided in two equal parts. Image of Hexagram 61.

　　Value, KUEI: regard as valuable, give worth and dignity to; precious, high priced; honorable, exalted, illustrious. The ideogram: cowries (coins) and basket.

Six above

a) A woman receiving a basket without substance.
A notable disembowelling a goat without blood.
No advantageous direction.

b) Six above, without substance.
Receiving an empty basket indeed.

This is the empty show: no substance, no blood, and no passion. Nothing you can do will help. The time has passed it by. Don't make any more plans. Just leave.

Associated Contexts a) **Receive**, CH'ENG: receive gifts or commands from superiors or customers; take in hand; catch falling water. The ideogram: accepting a seal of office. **Basket**, K'UANG: open basket; put in baskets; bottom of a bed. **Without**, WU: devoid of; -less as suffix. **Substance**, SHIH: real, solid, full; results, fruits, possessions; essence; honest, sincere. The ideogram: string of coins under a roof, riches in the house.

   Notable, SHIH: learned, upright, important man; scholar, gentleman. **Disembowel**, K'UEI: cut open and clean; prepare for sacrifice; stab. **Goat**, YANG: sheep and goats; direct thought and action. **Blood**, HSÜEH: yin fluid that maintains life; money, property.

b) **Empty**, HSÜ: no images or concepts; vacant, unsubstantial; empty yet fertile space.

55

ABOUNDING ▌ *FENG*

Plenty, copious, rich, generous; culminating point, overflowing; activate inner creative energy; sign of great change.

Abounding describes your situation in terms of abundance and fertile profusion. Its symbol is the change in the mandate of heaven given to King Wu that bought a renewal of the time. The way to deal with it is to be exuberant and expansive. Overflow with good feeling, support and generosity. Give with both hands. This is pleasing to the spirits. Through it they will give you success, effective power and the capacity to bring the situation to maturity. Imagine yourself as the king whose power bestows wealth and happiness on all. Rid yourself of sorrow, melancholy and care. Be like the sun at midday. Shed light on all and eliminate the shadows.

● *Image of the Situation*

> **Abounding, Growing.**
> **The king imagines it.**
> **No grief. Properly the sun at the center.**

Associated Contexts **Abound,** FENG: abundant, plentiful, copious; grow wealthy; at the point of overflowing; exuberant, fertile, prolific; rich in talents, property, friends; fullness, culmination; ripe, sumptuous, fat. **Grow,** HENG: success through a sacrifice; pervade, persevere; bring to full growth; enjoy; vigorous, effective; second stage of the Time Cycle.

King(hood), WANG: effective ruler, by authority of the Emperor, from whom others derive their power. **Imagine,** CHIA: create in the mind; fantasize, suppose, pretend, imitate; fiction; illusory, unreal; costume. The ideogram: person and borrow. **It/them/have(it)/'s,** CHIH: expresses possession, directly or as an object pronoun.

Grieve(over), YU: sorrow, melancholy; mourn; anxious, careworn; hidden sorrow. The ideogram: heart, head, and limp, heart-sick and anxious. **Proper,** YI: reasonable of itself; fit and right, harmonious; ought, should. **Sun/day,** JIH: actual sun and the time of a sun-cycle, a day. **Center,** CHUNG: inner, central; put in the center; middle, stable point enabling you

to face inner and outer changes; middle line of trigram. The ideogram: field divided in two equal parts. Image of Hexagram 61.

- *Outer and Inner Aspects*

☳ **Shake**: Thunder rises from below, shaking and stirring things up. **Shake** begins the yang hemicycle by germinating new action.

Connection to the outer: sprouting energies thrusting from below, the Woody Moment beginning. **Shake** stirs things up to issue-forth.

☲ **Radiance**: Fire and brightness radiate light and warmth, attached to their support; congregating people see and become aware. **Radiance** ends the yang hemicycle, consuming action in awareness.

Connection to the inner: light, heat, consciousness bring continual change, the Fiery Moment. **Radiance** spreads outward, congregating, becoming aware and changing.

Inner brightness and warmth permeate the outer world, stirring up **abounding**. These trigrams begin and end the yang hemicycle, emphasizing the fruits of action.

- *Hidden Possibility*

Nuclear trigrams **Open**, TUI, and **Ground**, SUN, result in Nuclear Hexagram 28, **Great Traverses**, TA KUO. **Abounding** generosity for all lets you make the **great** transition.

- *Sequence*

> Acquiring one's place to Marry necessarily implies the great.
> Accepting this lets you use Abounding.
> Abounding implies the great indeed.

Associated Contexts **Acquire**, TE: obtain the desired object; wish for, desire covetously; gains, possessions. The ideogram: go and obstacle, going through obstacles to the goal. **One's/one**, CH'I: third person pronoun; also: it/its, he/his, she/hers, they/theirs. **Place**, SO: where something belongs or comes from; residence, dwelling; habitual focus or object. **Marry/convert**, KUEI: change to another form, persuade; return to yourself or the place where you belong; restore, revert, become loyal; turn into; give a young girl in marriage. The ideogram: arrive and wife, become mistress of a household. Image of Hexagram 54. **Imply**, CHE: further signify; additional meaning.

Necessarily, PI: unavoidably, indispensably, certainly. **Great,** TA: big, noble, important, very; orient the will toward a self-imposed goal, impose direction; ability to lead or guide your life; contrasts with small, HSIAO, flexible adaptation to what crosses your path; keyword. Image of Hexagrams 14, 26, 28, 34.

Accepting ... use: activating this hexagram depends on understanding and accepting the previous statement.

Indeed, YEH: intensifier, connective; indicates comment on previous statement.

● *Contrasted Definitions*

> **Abounding: a numerous past indeed.**
> **Connecting the few: Sojourning indeed.**

Associated Contexts **Numerous,** TO: great number, many; often. **Past/anterior,** KU: come before as cause; formerly, ancient; reason, purpose, intention; grievance, quarrel, dissatisfaction, sorrow, mourning resulting from previous causes and intentions; situation leading to a divination.

Connect, CH'IN: attach to, approach, come near; cherish, help, favor; intimate; relatives, kin. **Few,** KUA: small number; seldom, rarely; unusual, solitary. **Sojourn,** LÜ: travel, stay in places other than your home; itinerant troops, temporary residents; visitor, guest, lodger. The ideogram: banner and people around it, loyal to a symbol rather than their temporary residence. Image of Hexagram 56.

● *Symbol Tradition*

> **Thunder, lightning, altogether the culmination. Abounding.**
> **A chün tzu uses severing litigating to involve punishing.**

Associated Contexts **Thunder,** LEI: rising, arousing power; the Symbol of the trigram Shake, CHEN. **Lightning,** TIEN: lightning flash, electric discharge; sudden clarity; look attentively. **Altogether,** CHIEH: all, the whole; the same sort, all alike; entirely. **Culminate,** CHIH: bring to the highest degree; arrive at the end or summit; superlative.

Chün tzu: ideal of a person who uses divination to order his/her life in accordance with tao rather than wilful intention; keyword. **Use(of),** YI: make use of, by means of, owing to; employ, make functional. **Sever,**CHE: break off, separate, sunder, cut in two; discriminate, judge the true and false. **Litigate,** YÜ: legal proceedings; take a case to court. The ideogram: two dogs and words, barking arguments at each other. **Involve,** CHIH: include, entangle, implicate; induce, cause. The ideogram: person walking, induced to follow. **Punish**, HSING: legal punishment; physical penalties for severe criminal offenses; whip, torture, behead.

- *Image Tradition*

Abounding, the great indeed. [I]
Brightness using stirring up. Anterior Abounding.

The king imagines it. [II]
Honoring the great indeed.
No grief, properly the sun at center.
Properly illuminating Below Heaven indeed.

Sun centering, by consequence going down. [III]
Moon overfilling, by consequence taking in.
Heaven and Earth overfilling emptiness.
Associating with the season, a dissolving pause.
And even more with respect to the people reached.
Even more with respect to the Souls and Spirits reached.

Associated Contexts [I] **Brightness**, MING: light-giving aspect of burning, heavenly bodies and consciousness; with fire, the Symbol of the trigram Radiance, LI. **Stir up**, TUNG: excite, influence, move, affect; work, take action; come out of the egg or the bud; the Action of the trigram Shake, CHEN. The ideogram: strength and heavy, move weighty things.

[II] **Honor**, SHANG: esteem, give high rank to; eminent; put one thing on top of another.
 Illuminate, CHAO: shine light on; enlighten, reflect: care for, supervise. The ideogram: fire and brightness. **Below Heaven**, T'IEN HSIA: the human world, between heaven and earth.

[III] **By consequence(of)**, TSE: very strong connection; reason, cause, result; rule, law, pattern, standard; therefore. **Go down**, TSE: sun setting, afternoon; waning moon; decline.
 Moon, YÜEH actual moon and moon-month; yin, the sun being yang. **Overfill**, YING: at the point of overflowing; more than wanted, stretch beyond; replenished, full; arrogant. The ideogram: vessel and too much. **Take in/eat**, SHIH: eat, ingest, swallow, devour; incorporate.
 Heaven and Earth, T'IEN TI: dynamic relation between the primal powers and the world it produces; cosmos, natural or human world;

keyword. **Empty**, HSÜ: no images or concepts; vacant, unsubstantial; empty yet fertile space.

Associate(with), YÜ: consort with, combine; companions; group, band, company; agree with, comply, help. The ideogram: pair of hands reaching downward meets a pair of hands reaching upward, helpful association. **Season**, SHIH: quality of the time; the right time, opportune, in harmony; planning in accord with the time; seasons of the year. The ideogram: sun and temple, time as sacred. **Dissolving pause**, HSIAO HSI: yin or structure dissolves so that yang or action may emerge; transitional phase of Universal Compass.

Even more, K'UANG: even more so, all the more. **With respect to**, YÜ: relates to, refers to; hold a position in. **People, person**, JEN: humans individually and collectively; an individual; humankind. Image of Hexagrams 13 and 37. **Reach(to)**, HU: arrive at a goal; reach toward and achieve; connect; contrasts with tend-towards, YU.

Souls and Spirits, KUEI SHEN: the whole range of imaginary beings both inside and outside the individual; spiritual powers, gods, demons, ghosts, powers, faculties.

● *Transforming Lines*

Initial nine

a) **Meeting one's equal lord.**
Although a decade, without fault.
Going possesses honor.

b) **Although a decade, without fault.**
Exceeding a decade, calamity indeed.

You meet someone or something that will change the course of your life. It is a deep mutual recognition. Stay with this for a complete cycle of time, a decade. Go through all the stages. It is not a mistake. If you hold onto the connection, it will bring you honor and reward.

Associated Contexts a) **Meet**, YÜ: come on unexpectedly, encounter; occur, happen; pleasant meeting, lucky coincidence; agree. **Equal**, P'EI: on the same level; pair, husband or wife; together. **Lord**, CHU: ruler, master, chief; authority. The ideogram: lamp and flame, giving light.

Although, SUI: even though, supposing that, if, even if. **Decade**, HSÜN: ten days or years; complete time period. **Without fault**, WU: CHIU: no error or harm in the situation.

Go, WANG, and **come**, LAI, describe the stream of time as it flows from future through present to past; go, WANG, indicates what is departing from present to past; proceed, move on; keyword. **Possess**, YU: in possession of, have, own; opposite of lack, WU.

b) **Exceed/traverse**, KU: go beyond, pass by, pass over; excessive, transgress; error, fault. Image of Hexagrams 28 and 62. **Calamity**, TSAI: disaster from outside; flood, plague, drought, blight, ruin; contrasts with blunder, SHENG, indicating personal fault. The ideogram: water and fire, elemental powers.

Six at second

a) Abounding: one's screen.
Sun at center: seeing the Bin.
"Does going acquire doubt and affliction?"
There is a connection to the spirits, like shooting forth.
Auspicious.

b) Possessing conformity, like shooting forth.
Trustworthiness using shooting forth purpose indeed.

The time is full, the moment to act is coming. You can see things that other people can't see. Although you feel isolated and unsure, you have a profound connection to the spirits that is working at a great distance to create connections. Fear not. The way is opening.

Associated Contexts a) **Screen**, P'U: curtain, veil, awning, hanging mat; hide, protect; lit.: luxuriant plant growth.

See, CHIEN: seeing in all its aspects: vision, being visible, forming mental images; visit, call on, consult. The ideogram: eye above person, active and receptive sight. **Bin**, TOU: star constellation that dispenses the fates' Big Dipper; measure and container for grain; gauge, hold, contain.

Go, WANG, and **come**, LAI, describe the stream of time as it flows from future through present to past; go, WANG, indicates what is departing from present to past; proceed, move on; keyword. **Doubt**, YI: suspect, distrust; dubious; surmise, conjecture. **Afflict**, CHI: sickness, disorder, defect, calamity; injurious; pressure and consequent anger, hate or dislike. The ideogram: sickness and dart, a sudden affliction.

There is ... spirits, YU FU: inner and outer are in accord; confidence of the spirits has been captured; sincere, truthful; proper to take action. **Like**, JO: same as; just as, similar to. **Shoot forth**, FA: expand, send out; shoot an arrow; ferment, rise; be displayed. The ideogram: stance, bow and arrow, shooting from a strong base.

Auspicious, CHI: leads to the experience of meaning; favorable, propitious, advantageous, appropriate; keyword. The ideogram: scholar and mouth, wise words of a sage.

b) **Trustworthy,** HSIN: truthful, faithful, consistent over time; integrity; confide in, follow; credentials; contrasts with conforming, FU, connection in a specific moment. The ideogram: person and word, true speech. **Purpose,** CHIH: focus of mind and heart; will, inclination, resolve. The ideogram: heart and scholar, high inner resolve, or heart and go, inner determination.

Nine at third

a) Abounding: one's profusion.
Sun at center: seeing the froth of stars.
Severing one's right arm.
Without fault.

b) Abounding: one's profusion.
Not permitting Great Affairs indeed.
Severing one's right arm.
Completing, not permitting availing of indeed.

You are unable to move at the moment. Do not worry, the time is coming. Look at the omens rising in the sky. You see such extraordinary sights that you lose the capacity to respond. Don't worry. This is not a mistake. A new spirit is being born.

Associated Contexts a) **Profusion,** P'EI: spread and flow in many directions, like rain or rivers; enlarge; irrigate; luxuriant water plants.

See, CHIEN: seeing in all its aspects: vision, being visible, forming mental images; visit, call on, consult. The ideogram: eye above person, active and receptive sight. **Froth,** MO: the minor stars; spume, foam, bubbles; perspire, drool.

Sever, CHE: break off, separate, sunder, cut in two; discriminate, judge the true and false. **Right,** YU: right side, right hand; noble, honorable; make things right. **Arm,** KUNG: the arms as the body's instruments; staunch supporter; officer, minister of state.

Without fault, WU CHIU: no error or harm in the situation.

b) **Not permitting,** PU K'O: not possible; contradicts an inherent principle. The ideogram: mouth and breath, silent consent.

Complete, CHUNG: end of a cycle that begins the next; last, whole, all; contrasts with exhaust, CH'IUNG, final end. The ideogram: silk cocoons, follow and ice, winter linking one year with the next. **Avail of,** YUNG: take advantage of; benefit from, profit by; use for a specific purpose; apply to advantage. The ideogram: to divine and center, applying divination to central concerns.

Nine at fourth

a) Abounding: one's screen.
The sun center: seeing in the Bin.
Meeting one's hidden lord.
Auspicious.

b) Abounding: one's screen.
Situation not appropriate indeed.
Sun centering: seeing the bin.
Shade, not brightening indeed.
Meeting one's hiding lord.
Auspicious movement indeed.

You see the hidden spirit that is moving events and will be able to move with it. These are extraordinary things that most people can't understand. In this solitude and obscurity, you meet something that makes it all clear. The recognition is immediate. Hold onto the connection.

Associated Contexts a) **Screen**, P'U: curtain, veil, awning, hanging mat; hide, protect; lit.: luxuriant plant growth.

See, CHIEN: seeing in all its aspects: vision, being visible, forming mental images; visit, call on, consult. The ideogram: eye above person, active and receptive sight. **Bin**, TOU: star constellation that dispenses the fates; Big Dipper; measure and container for grain; gauge, hold, contain.

Meet, YÜ: come on unexpectedly, encounter; occur, happen; pleasant meeting, lucky coincidence; agree. **Hide**, YI: keep out of sight; remote, distant from the center; equalize by lowering; squat, level, make ordinary; pacified, colorless; cut, wound, destroy, exterminate. Image of Hexagram 36. **Lord**, CHU: ruler, master, chief; authority. The ideogram: lamp and flame, giving light.

Auspicious, CHI: leads to the experience of meaning; favorable, propitious, advantageous, appropriate; keyword. The ideogram: scholar and mouth, wise words of a sage.

b) **Situation**, WEI: place or seat according to rank; post, position, command;

right, proper; established, arranged. The ideogram: person and stand, servants in their places. **Appropriate**, TANG: suitable; opportune, convenient; adequate, competent; equal to; whole lines in uneven places and opened lines in even places.

Shade, YU: hidden from view; retired, solitary, secret; dark, obscure, occult, mysterious; ignorant. The ideogram: small within hill, a cave or grotto.

Move, HSING: move or move something; motivate, emotionally moving; walk, act, do. The ideogram: stepping left then right.

Six at fifth

a) The coming compositionpossesses reward and praise.
  Auspicious.

b) Six at fifth's auspiciousness.
  Possessing reward indeed.

A mandate from heaven. The next chapter in the book of your life is full of beauty, joy and love. Rewards and praise will be showered on you. The way is opening.

Associated Contexts a) **Come**, LAI, and **go**, WANG, describe the stream of time as it flows from future through present to past. Come, LAI, indicates what is approaching; move toward, arrive at; Go, WANG, indicates what is departing; proceed, move on; keywords. **Composition**, CHANG: a well-composed whole and its structure; beautiful creations; elegant, clear, brilliant; contrasts with pattern, WEN, beauty of intrinsic design.

Possess, YU: in possession of, have, own; opposite of lack, WU. **Reward**, CH'ING: gift given from gratitude or benevolence; favour from heaven; congratulate with gifts. The ideogram: heart, follow and deer (wealth), the heart expressed through gifts. **Praise**, YÜ: admire and approve; magnify, eulogize; flatter. The ideogram: words and give, offering words. **Auspicious**, CHI: leads to the experience of meaning; favorable, propitious, advantageous, appropriate; keyword. The ideogram: scholar and mouth, wise words of a sage.

Six above

a) Abounding: one's roof.
  Screening one's dwelling,
  Peeping through one's door.
  Living alone, one without people.
  Three year's time not encountering.
  Pitfall.

b) Abounding: one's roof.
The heavenly border, hovering indeed.
Peeping through one's door.
Living alone, one without people.
Originating from concealing indeed.

You may have been hurt, but now your melancholy and pain are in danger of isolating you. Break out of this trap! Don't shut yourself in. Grasp the changing time and act. If you don't, the way will close.

Associated Contexts a) **Roof**, WU: cover, shelter; house, room, cabin, tent; stop or remain at.

Screen, P'U: curtain, veil, awning, hanging mat; hide, protect; lit.: luxuriant plant growth. **Dwell**, CHI: home, house, household, family; domestic, within doors; live in. The ideogram: roof and pig or dog, the most valued domestic animals. Image of Hexagram 37.

Peep through, K'UEI: observe from hiding; stealthily, furtive. **Door**, HU: inner door, chamber door; a household; contrasts with gate, MEN, the outer door.

Live alone, CH'Ü: lonely, solitary; quiet, still; deserted. **Without**, WU: devoid of; -less as suffix.

Three, SAN: number three, third time or place; active phases of a cycle; superlative; beginning of repetition. **Year's time**, SUI: actual length of time in a year; contrasts with years-revolved, NIEN, number of years elapsed. **Encounter**, TI: see face to face; admitted to an audience; visit, interview.

Pitfall, HSIUNG: leads away from the experience of meaning; stuck and exposed to danger, unable to take in the situation; flow of life and spirit is blocked; unfortunate, baleful; keyword.

b) **Heaven**, T'IEN: highest; sky, firmament, heavens; power above the human as opposed to earth, TI, below; the Symbol of the trigram Force, CH'IEN. The ideogram: great and the one above. **Border**, CHI: limit, frontier; line which joins and divides. The ideogram: place and sacrifice, border between human and spirit. **Hover**, HSIANG: glide; rise, soar, roam.

Origin, TZU: source, beginning, ground; cause, reason, motive; line of descent; path to the origin; yourself, intrinsic. **Conceal**, TS'ANG: hide from view; store up, put aside, accumulate; stores, property; internal organs.

56

SOJOURNING/QUEST ▮ *LÜ*

Journeys, voyages, outside the social network; wander, exile; soldiers on a mission; quest, searcher, wandering sage.

Sojourning/Quest describes your situation in terms of wandering, journeys and living apart. Its symbol is the wandering sage, the king inspecting the borders or the solitary on a quest. The way to deal with it is to mingle with others as a stranger whose identity and mission come from a distant center. You are outside the normal network, on a quest of your own. Make an offering and you will succeed. Be small and flexible. Adapt to whatever crosses your path. This is pleasing to the spirits. Through it they will give you success, effective power and the capacity to bring the situation to maturity. Be willing to travel and search alone. Put your ideas to the trial. This generates meaning and good fortune by releasing transformative energy.

● *Image of the Situation*

> **Sojourning, the small: Growing.**
> **Sojourning, Trial: auspicious.**

Associated Contexts **Sojourn,** LÜ: travel; stay in places other than your home; itinerant troops, temporary residents; visitor, guest, lodger. The ideogram: banner and people around it, loyal to a symbol rather than their temporary residence. **Small,** HSIAO: little, common, unimportant; adapting to what crosses your path; ability to move in harmony with the vicissitudes of life; contrasts with great, TA, self-imposed theme or goal; keyword. Image of Hexagrams 9 and 62. **Grow,** HENG: success through a sacrifice; pervade, persevere; bring to full growth; enjoy; vigorous, effective; second stage of the Time Cycle.

    Trial, CHEN: inquiry by divination and its result; righteous, firm; separating wheat from chaff; the kernel, the proven core; fourth stage of the Time Cycle. The ideogram: pearl and divination. **Auspicious,** CHI: leads to the experience of meaning; favorable, propitious, advantageous, appropriate; keyword. The ideogram: scholar and mouth, wise words of a sage.

- *Outer and Inner Aspects*

☲ **Radiance:** Fire and brightness radiate light and warmth, attached to their support; congregating people see and become aware. **Radiance** ends the yang hemicycle, consuming action in awareness.

Connection to the outer: the Fiery Moment; light, heat and consciousness bring continual change. **Radiance** spreads outward, congregating, generating insight and changing.

☶ **Bound:** Mountains bound, limit and set a place off, stopping forward movement. **Bound** completes a full yin-yang cycle. Connection to the inner: accomplishing words express limits. **Bound** articulates what is complete to suggest what is beginning.

Articulating inner limits provides a stable base for **sojourning's** continually changing awareness,

- *Hidden Possibility*

Nuclear trigrams **Open**, TUI, and **Ground**, SUN, result in Nuclear Hexagram 28, **Great Traverses**. **Sojourning's** cautious observance of the immediate lets you make the **great** transition.

- *Sequence*

Exhausting the great implies necessarily letting go one's residing.
Accepting this lets you use Sojourning.

Associated Contexts **Exhaust**, CH'IUNG: bring to an end; limit, extremity; destitute; investigate exhaustively; end without a new beginning. The ideogram: cave and naked person, bent with disease or old age. **Great**, TA: big, noble, important, very; orient the will toward a self-imposed goal, impose direction; ability to lead or guide your life; contrasts with **small**, HSIAO, flexible adaptation to what crosses your path; keyword. Image of Hexagrams 14, 26, 28, 34. **Imply**, CHE: further signify; additional meaning. **Necessarily**, PI: unavoidably, indispensably, certainly. **Let go**, SHIH: lose, omit, miss, fail, let slip; out of control. The ideogram: drop from the hand. **One's/one**, CH'I: third person pronoun; also: it/its, he/his, she/hers, they/theirs. **Reside(in)**, CHÜ: dwell, live in, stay; sit down, fill an office; settled parts of a country. The ideogram: body and seat.

Accepting ... use: activating this hexagram depends on understanding and accepting the previous statement.

- *Contrasted Definitions*

> **Abounding: numerous anteriority indeed.**
> **Connecting the few: Sojourning indeed.**

Associated Contexts **Abound**, FENG: abundant, plentiful, copious; grow wealthy; at the point of overflowing; exuberant, fertile, prolific; rich in talents, property, friends; fullness, culmination; ripe, sumptuous, fat. Image of Hexagram 55. **Numerous**, TO: great number, many; often. **Anterior/past**, KU: come before as cause; formerly, ancient; reason, purpose, intention; grievance, quarrel, dissatisfaction, sorrow, mourning resulting from previous causes and intentions; situation leading to a divination. **Indeed/is/means**, YEH: intensifier, connective; indicates comment on previous statement.

Connect, CH'IN: attach to, approach, come near; cherish, help, favor; intimate; relatives, kin. **Few**, KUA: small number; seldom, rarely; unusual, solitary.

- *Symbol Tradition*

> **Above mountain possessing fire. Sojourning.**
> **A chün tzu uses brightening consideration**
> **to avail of punishing and is not detained by litigating.**

Associated Contexts **Above**, SHANG: anything above, in all senses; higher, upper, outer; upper trigram; opposite of below, HSIA. **Mountain**, SHAN: limit, boundary; the Symbol of the trigram Bound, KEN. The ideogram: three peaks, a mountain range. **Possess**, YU: in possession of, have, own; opposite of lack, WU. **Fire**, HUO: warming and consuming aspect of burning; fire and brightness are the Symbols of the trigram Radiance, LI.

Chün tzu: ideal of a person who uses divination to order his/her life in accordance with tao rather than wilful intention; keyword. **Use(of)**, YI: make use of, by means of, owing to; employ, make functional. **Brightness**, MING: light-giving aspect of burning, heavenly bodies and consciousness; with fire, the Symbol of the trigram Radiance, LI. **Consider**, SHEN: act carefully, seriously; cautious, attentive, circumspect; still, quiet, sincere. The ideogram: heart and true. **Avail of**, YUNG: take advantage of; benefit from, profit by; use for a specific purpose; apply to advantage. The ideogram: to divine and center, applying divination to central concerns. **Punish**, HSING: legal punishment; physical penalties for severe criminal offenses; whip,

torture, behead. **Detain**, LIU: hold back or on to; delay, remain; slow. **Litigate**, YÜ: legal proceedings; take a case to court. The ideogram: two dogs and words, barking arguments at each other.

● *Image Tradition*

> Sojourning. [I]
> The small Growing.
> Supple acquires the center reaching to the outside
> and yielding reaches to the strong.
>
> Stopping and congregating reaching to brightness. [II]
> That uses the small Growing.
> Sojourning, Trial: auspicious indeed.
> Actually Sojourning's season righteously great in fact.

Associated Contexts **[I] Supple**, JOU: quality of the opened lines; flexible, pliant, tender, adaptable. **Acquire**, TE: obtain the desired object; wish for, desire covetously; gains, possessions. The ideogram: go and obstacle, going through obstacles to the goal. **Center**, CHUNG: inner, central; put in the center; middle, stable point enabling you to face inner and outer changes; middle line of trigram. The ideogram: field divided in two equal parts. Image of Hexagram 61. **Reach(to)**, HU: arrive at a goal; reach towards and achieve; connect; contrasts with tend-towards, YU. **Outside**, WAI: outer, exterior, external; people working in places other than their home; unfamiliar, foreign; the upper trigram, as opposed to inside, NEI, the lower. **Yield(to)**, SHUN: give way and bear produce; comply, agree, follow, obey; unresisting, docile, flexible; nourish, provide; the Action of the trigram Field, K'UN. The ideogram: head and current, water flowing from the head of a river, yielding to the banks. **Strong**, KANG: quality of the whole lines; firm, strong, unyielding, persisting.

[II] Stop, CHIH: bring or come to a standstill; the Action of the trigram Bound, KEN. The ideogram: a foot stops walking. **Congregate**, LI: cling together; depend on, attached to, rely on; couple, pair, herd; the Action of the trigram Radiance, LI. The ideogram: deer flocking together.

That uses, SHIH YI: involves and is involved by.

Actually ... in fact, YI TSAI: stresses the importance of a statement. The ideogram: a dart and done, strong intention fully expressed **'s/have(it)/it/them**, CHIH: expresses possession, directly or as an object pronoun. **Season**, SHIH: quality of the time; the right time, opportune, in harmony; planning in accord with the time; seasons of the year. The ideogram: sun and temple, time as sacred. **Righteous**, YI: proper and just, meets the standards; things in their proper place; the heart that rules itself; upright, moral rule; contrasts with Harvest, LI, advantage or profit.

● *Transforming Lines*

Initial six

a) Sojourning: fragmenting, fragmenting.
Splitting off one's place, grasping calamity.

b) Sojourning: fragmenting, fragmenting.
Purpose exhausted, calamity indeed.

The journey is falling apart before it has begun. You grasp at fragments. People can't understand you. You are in imminent danger. Stop! Do you really want to act like this?

Associated Contexts a) **Fragment**, SO: break into small pieces, broken parts; minute, fine; petty, trivial; annoying; lit.: splinters of precious stones. The ideogram: small and cowrie shells, the tinkling of small coins. The doubled character intensifies this quality.

Split off, SSU: lop off, split with an ax, rive; white (color eliminated). The ideogram: ax and possessive, splitting what belongs together. **Place**, SO: where something belongs or comes from; residence, dwelling; habitual focus or object. **Grasp**, CH'Ü: lay hold of, take and use, seize, appropriate; grasp the meaning, understand. The ideogram: ear and hand, hear and grasp. **Calamity**, TSAI: disaster from outside; flood, plague, drought, blight, ruin; contrasts with blunder, SHENG, indicating personal fault. The ideogram: water and fire, elemental powers.

b) **Purpose**, CHIH: focus of mind and heart; will, inclination, resolve. The ideogram: heart and scholar, high inner resolve, or heart and go, inner determination.

Six at second

a) Sojourning, approaching a resting place.
Cherishing one's own.
Acquiring a youthful vassal: Trial.

b) Acquiring a youthful vassal: Trial.
Completing without surpassing indeed.

You have found a way to come together with others, though you must still take care. You have also made a friend who is willing to help you.

Associated Contexts a) **Approach,** CHI: come near to, advance toward; about to do; soon. **Rest(ing place),** TZ'U: camp, inn, shed; halting-place, breathing-spell; put in consecutive order. The ideogram: two and breath, pausing to breathe.

Cherish, HUAI: dwell on, think of; carry in the heart or womb; cling to. The ideogram: heart and hide, cherish in the heart. **Own,** TZU: possession and the things possessed; avail of, depend on; property, riches.

Youthful, T'UNG: young person between eight and fifteen; young animals and plants. **Vassal,** P'U: servant, menial, retainer; helper in heavy work; palace officers, chamberlains; follow, serve, belong to.

b) **Complete,** CHUNG: end of a cycle that begins the next; last, whole, all; contrasts with exhaust, CH'IUNG, final end. The ideogram: silk cocoons, follow and ice, winter linking one year with the next. **Without,** WU: devoid of; -less as suffix. **Surpass,** YU: exceed; beyond measure, excessive; extraordinary; transgress, blame.

Nine at third

a) Sojourning, burning one's resting place.
Losing one's youthful vassal.
Trial: adversity.

b) Sojourning, burning one's resting place.
Actually truly using injuring.
Using Sojourning to associate with the below.
One's righteousness lost indeed.

You destroy what you have done through violent passions and you frighten your friends away. Try to understand where this comes from. You are confronting danger that has its roots in the past. It you can see it, this disaster could mark a profound change to a new state of being.

Associated Contexts a) **Burn,** FEN: set fire to, destroy completely. **Rest(ing place),** TZ'U: camp, inn, shed; halting-place, breathing- spell; put in consecutive order. The ideogram: two and breath, pausing to breathe.

Lose, SANG: fail to obtain, cease, become obscure; forgotten, destroyed;

lament, mourn; funeral. The ideogram: weep and the dead. **Youthful,** T'UNG: young person between eight and fifteen; young animals and plants. **Vassal,** P'U: servant, menial, retainer; helper in heavy work; palace officers, chamberlains; follow, serve, belong to.

Adversity, LI: danger; threatening, malevolent demon. This has two aspects: grind, sharpen, improve, perfect, stimulate; and: poisonous, sinister, cruel, contrary. It indicates a spirit or ghost that seeks revenge by inflicting suffering upon the living. Pacifying or exorcizing such a spirit can have a healing effect. The ideogram: sheltering cliff and stinging insect.

b) **Actually,** YI: truly, really, at present. The ideogram: a dart and done, strong intention fully expressed. **Truly,** YI: statement is true and precise. **Injure,** SHANG: hurt, wound, grieve, distress; mourn, sad at heart, humiliated.

Associate(with), YÜ: consort with, combine; companions; group, band, company; agree with, comply, help. The ideogram: pair of hands reaching downward meets a pair of hands reaching upward, helpful association. **Below,** HSIA: anything below, in all senses; lower, inner; lower trigram; opposite of above, SHANG.

Nine at fourth

a) Sojourning and abiding.
  Acquiring one's own emblem ax.
  "My heart is not keen."

b) Sojourning and abiding.
  Not yet acquiring the situation indeed.
  Acquiring one's own emblem ax.
  The heart not yet keen indeed.

You have found a place, with responsibility and power to go with it. But these things bring sorrow, not happiness, for deep in your heart you know that you have forsaken what you really feel.

Associated Contents a) **Abide,** CH'U: rest in, dwell; stop yourself; arrive at a place or condition; distinguish, decide; do what is proper. The ideogram: tiger, stop and seat, powerful movement coming to rest.

Own, TZU: possession and the things possessed; avail of, depend on; property, riches. **Emblem ax,** FU: moon-shaped ax, symbol of power to govern.

My/me/I, WO: first person pronoun; indicates an unusually strong

emphasis on your own subjective experience. **Heart,** HSIN: heart as center of being; seat of mind's images and affections; moral nature; source of desires, intentions, will. **Keen,** K'UAI: sharp, eager, prompt, cheerful; spirited.

b) **Not yet,** WEI: temporal negative; something will but has not yet occurred; contrary of already, CHI. Image of Hexagram 64. **Situation,**WEI: place or seat according to rank; post, position, command; right, proper; established, arranged. The ideogram: person and stand, servants in their places.

Six at fifth

a) **Shooting a pheasant.**
   The one arrow extinguishes it.
   Completing uses praising fate.

b) **Completing uses praising fate.**
   Overtaking the above indeed.

You can complete your connection with one try. Your friends will support you. You will receive a mandate from above. This will bring you praise and much increased responsibility.

Associated Contexts a) **Shoot,** SHE: shoot with a bow, point at and hit; project from, spurt, issue forth; glance at; scheme for. The ideogram: arrow and body. **Pheasant,** CHIH: clever, beautiful bird associated with Radiance, LI; rule, arrange, put in order; embrasures on ramparts and forts.

One, the one, YI: single unit; number one; undivided, simple, whole; any one of; first, the first. **Arrow,** SHIH: arrow, javelin, dart; swift, direct as an arrow; marshal together. **Extinguish,** WANG: ruin, destroy; gone, dead, lost without trace; extinct, forgotten, out of mind. The ideogram: person concealed by a wall, out of sight.

Complete, CHUNG: end of a cycle that begins the next; last, whole, all; contrasts with exhaust, CH'IUNG, final end. The ideogram: silk cocoons, follow and ice, winter linking one year with the next. **Praise,** YÜ: admire and approve; magnify, eulogize; flatter. The ideogram: words and give, offering words. **Fate/mandate,** MING: individual destiny; birth and death as limits of life; issue orders with authority; consult the gods. The ideogram: mouth and order, words with heavenly authority.

b) **Overtake,** TI: come up to, reach; arrest, seize; until; also: harmonious, peaceful. The ideogram: go, hand and reach, reaching to seize satisfaction.

Nine above

a) A bird burning its nest.
Sojourning people beforehand laughing,
afterwards crying out and sobbing.
Losing the cattle through change.
Pitfall.

b) Using Sojourning to locate in the above.
One's righteousness burning indeed.
Losing the cattle through change.
Complete absolutely nothing having heard it indeed.

You are being careless and perhaps arrogant. You think you can take this lightly, but you may soon have cause to lament. Everything you care have will vanish. You will soon be crying, not laughing. Consider your attitudes and change your heart or the way will close to you.

Associated Contexts a) **Bird**, NIAO: all feathered animals; associated with the Fiery Moment. **Burn**, FEN: set fire to, destroy completely. **Its/it**, CH'I: third person pronoun; also: one/one's, he/his, she/hers, they/theirs. **Nest**, CH'AO: nest in a tree; haunt, retreat; make a nest.

People, person, JEN: humans individually and collectively; an individual; humankind. Image of Hexagrams 13 and 37. **Before(hand)/earlier**, HSIEN: come before in time; first, at first; formerly, past, previous; begin, go ahead of. **Laugh**, HSIAO: manifest joy or mirth; giggle, laugh at, ridicule; pleased, merry; associated with the Fiery Moment. **After(wards)/later**, HOU: come after in time, subsequent; put oneself after; the second; attendants, heirs, successors, posterity. **Cry out/outcry**, HAO: call out, proclaim; signal, order, command; mark, label, sign. **Sob**, T'AO: cry, weep aloud; wailing children. The ideogram: mouth and omen, ominous sounds.

Lose, SANG: fail to obtain, cease, become obscure; forgotten, destroyed; lament, mourn; funeral. The ideogram: weep and the dead. **Cattle**, NIU: ox, bull, cow, calf; kine; power and strength of work animals. **Change/versatility**, I: a frontier region; sudden and unpredictable change; mental mobility and openness; easy and light, not difficult and heavy; occurs in name of the I CHING.

Pitfall, HSIUNG: leads away from the experience of meaning; stuck and exposed to danger, unable to take in the situation; flow of life and spirit is blocked; unfortunate, baleful; keyword.

b) **Locate(in)**, TSAI: live in, dwell, reside; belong to, involved with, depend on; within. The ideogram: earth and persevere, place on the earth.

Complete, CHUNG: end of a cycle that begins the next; last, whole, all; contrasts with exhaust, CH'IUNG, final end. The ideogram: silk cocoons, follow and ice, winter linking one year with the next. **Absolutely no(thing)**, MO: complete elimination; not any, by no means. **Hear**, WEN: perceive sound; learn by report; news, fame. The ideogram: ear and door.

57

GROUND ▌ SUN

Gently penetrate to the heart; supple, flexible, subtle, determined; enter from below; support, nourish, the base or ground.

Ground describes your situation in terms of the pervasive influence of the ground from which it grows. Its symbol is the healer and shaman who lays out the offerings and unfolds the fates. The way to deal with it is to penetrate to the core of the problem by being supple and adaptable. Make an offering and you will succeed. Enter from below. Let the situation shape you. Be humble and compliant; adapt to whatever crosses your path. Take the pervasive action of the wind, or growing plants extending their roots and branches as your model. This is pleasing to the spirits. Through it they will give you success, effective power and the capacity to bring the situation to maturity. Hold on to your purpose. Have a place to go. Impose a direction on things. See great people. Seek out those who can help and advise you. Think about the great in yourself and how you organize your thoughts. All these things bring profit and insight.

● *Image of the Situation*

> Ground, the small Growing.
> Advantageous to have a direction to go. Harvesting.
> Advantageous to see the Great People.

Associated Contexts **Small**, HSIAO: little, common, unimportant; adapting to what crosses your path; ability to move in harmony with the vicissitudes of life; contrasts with great, TA, self-imposed theme or goal; keyword. Image of Hexagrams 9 and 62. **Ground** is the **Wood** and **Wind** trigram doubled and includes that trigram's attributes: **Ground,** SUN: base on which things rest; support, foundation; mild, subtly penetrating; nourishing. The ideogram: stand and things arranged on it, the subtle influence of the ground. *Symbols:* **Wood/tree,** MU: all things woody or wooden, alive or constructed from wood; associated with the Woody Moment. The ideogram: a tree with roots and branches. **Wind,** FENG: moving air, breeze, gust; weather and its influence on mood and humor; fashion, usage. *Action:* **Enter,** JU: penetrate, go into, enter on, progress; put

into, encroach on; contrary of issue-forth, CH'U. **Grow,** HENG: success through a sacrifice; pervade, persevere; bring to full growth; enjoy; vigorous, effective; second stage of the Time Cycle.

Advantageous/Harvest, LI: advantageous, profitable; acute, insightful; benefit, nourish; third stage of the Time Cycle. **Have a direction to go,** YU WANG: imposing a direction on the flow of time from present to past; have a specific goal or purpose.

See, CHIEN: seeing in all its aspects: vision, being visible, forming mental images; visit, call on, consult. The ideogram: eye above person, active and receptive sight. **Great People,** TA JEN: important, noble, influential; those who impose a ruling principle on their lives; effect of the great within an individual; keyword.

- *Outer and Inner Aspects*

☴ **Ground:** Wind and wood subtly enter from the ground, penetrating and pervading. **Ground** is the center of the yang hemicycle, spreading pervasive action.

Connection to both inner and outer: penetrating and bringing together, the Woody Moment culminating. **Ground** pervades, matches and couples, seeding a new generation.

- *Hidden Possibility*

Nuclear trigrams **Radiance,** LI, and **Open,** TUI, result in Nuclear Hexagram 38, **Diverging,** KUEI. The gentle union of inner and outer in **ground** leads to resolving **diverging** opinions.

- *Sequence*

Sojourning and lacking a place to tolerate.
Accepting this lets you use Ground.
Ground implies entering indeed.

Associated Contexts **Sojourn,** LU: travel, stay in places other than your home; itinerant troops, temporary residents; visitor, guest, lodger. The ideogram: banner and people around it, loyal to a symbol rather than their temporary residence. Image of Hexagram 56. **Lacking,** WU: strong negative; does not possess. **Place,** SO: where something belongs or comes from; residence, dwelling; habitual focus or object. **Tolerate,** JUNG: allow, contain, endure,bear with; accept graciously. The ideogram: full stream bed, tolerating and containing.

Accepting ... use: activating this hexagram depends on understanding and accepting the previous statement.

Imply, CHE: further signify; additional meaning. **Indeed/is/means**, YEH: intensifier, connective; indicates comment on previous statement.

● *Contrasted Definitions*

> Open: seeing and
> Ground: hiding away indeed.

Associated Contexts **Open**, TUI: an open surface, promoting interaction and interpenetration; responsive, free, unhindered, pleasing; opening, passage; the mouth; exchange, barter; straight, direct; meet, gather; place where water accumulates. The ideogram: person, mouth and vapor, speaking with others. Image of Hexagram 58.

Hide away, FU: conceal, place in ambush; secretly, silently; prostrate, fall on your face; humble. The ideogram: man and dog, man crouching.

● *Attached Evidences*

> Ground: actualizing tao's paring indeed.
> Ground: evaluating and occulting.
> Ground: using moving the counterpoise.

Associated Contexts **Actualize tao**, TE: realize tao in action; power, virtue; ability to follow the course traced by the ongoing process of the cosmos; keyword . The ideogram: to go, straight, and heart. Linked with acquire, TE: acquiring that which makes a being become what it is meant to be. **'s/have(it)/it/them**, CHIH: expresses possession, directly or as an object pronoun. **Pare**, CHIH: cut away; form, tailor, carve; invent; limit, prevent. The ideogram: knife and incomplete.

Evaluate, CH'ENG: assess, appraise; weigh, estimate, reckon; designate, name. The ideogram: weigh and grain, attributing value. **Occult**, YIN: screen, obscure, keep from view, keep back; private; retired, not in office.

Use(of), YI: make use of, by means of, owing to; employ, make functional. **Move**, HSING: move or move something; motivate, emotionally moving; walk, act, do. The ideogram: stepping left then right. **Counterpoise**, CH'ÜAN: balance, equalize, plan; act as the position demands, expedient; influential; lit.: balance on a sliding scale.

- *Symbol Tradition*

Following winds. Ground.
A chün tzu uses distributing the mandate to move affairs.

Associated Contexts **Follow**, SUI: come or go after; pursue, impelled to move; come after in inevitable sequence; move in the same direction, comply with what is ahead; follow a way or religion; according to, next, subsequent. The ideogram: go and fall, unavoidable movement. Image of Hexagram 17.

Chün tzu: ideal of a person who uses divination to order his/her life in accordance with tao rather than wilful intention; keyword. **Distribute**,SHEN: give out, spread, scatter, allot, diffuse. **Mandate/fate**, MING: individual destiny; birth and death as limits of life; issue orders with authority; consult the gods. The ideogram: mouth and order, words with heavenly authority. **Affairs**, SHIH: all kinds of personal activity; matters at hand; business, occupation; manage a business, case in court.

- *Image Tradition*

Redoubling Ground uses distributing the mandate.
Strong Ground reaches centering and correcting
and the purpose is moving.
Supple altogether yielding reaches the strong.
That uses the small Growing.
Advantageous to have a direction to go.
Advantageous to see Great People.

Associated Contexts **Redouble**, CH'UNG: repeat, reiterate, add to; build up by layers.

Strong, KANG: quality of the whole lines; firm, strong, unyielding, persisting. **Reach(to)**, HU: arrive at a goal; reach toward and achieve; connect; contrasts with tend-towards, YU. **Centering correcting**, CHUNG CHENG: central and correct; make rectifying one-sidedness and error your central concern; reaching a stable center in yourself can correct the situation. **Purpose**, CHIH: focus of mind and heart; will, inclination, resolve. The ideogram: heart and scholar, high inner resolve, or heart and go, inner determination.

Supple, JOU: quality of the opened lines; flexible, pliant, tender, adaptable. **Altogether**, CHIEH: all, the whole; the same sort, all alike; entirely. **Yield(to)**, SHUN: give way and bear produce; comply, agree, follow, obey; unresisting, docile, flexible; nourish, provide; the Action of the trigram Field, K'UN. The ideogram: head and current, water flowing from the head of a river, yielding to the banks.

That uses, SHIH YI: involves and is involved by.

● *Transforming Lines*

Initial six

a) Advancing, withdrawing.
    Martial People's Advantageous Trial. Harvesting.

b) Advancing, withdrawing.
    Purpose doubted indeed.
    Martial people's Advantageous Trial:
    Purpose regulated indeed.

Make decisions firmly and aggressively. Change directions as many times as you need to. Be decisive. If you hesitate you will undermine your real purpose. This is not a time to be timid.

Associated Contexts a) **Advance,** CHIN: exert yourself, make progress, climb; be promoted; further the development of, augment; adopt a religion or conviction; offer, introduce. **Withdraw(from),** T'UI: draw back, retreat, recede; decline, refuse.

  Martial, WU: military, warlike; strong, stern; power to make war. The ideogram: fight and stop, force deterring aggression. **People, person,** JEN: humans individually and collectively; an individual; humankind. Image of Hexagrams 13 and 37. **Advantageous Trial,** LI CHEN: advantageous divination; fruit of an action is a test or trial; harvesting.

b) **Doubt,** YI: suspect, distrust; dubious; surmise, conjecture.

  Regulate, CHIH: govern well, ensure prosperity; remedy disorder, heal; someone fit to govern land, house and heart.

Nine at second

a) Ground located below the bed.
    Avail of chroniclers and shamans,
    Variegated and similar. Auspicious.
    Without fault.

b) The variegated and similar has auspiciousness.
Acquiring the center indeed.

You must penetrate to the core of this old story, full of sexual intrigue and dark ancestors. Use mediums, who can see and call the spirits, and historians, who know the past. Get to the bottom of it, and free yourself from its grasp. This is not a mistake.

Associated Contexts a) **Locate(in)**, TSAI: live in, dwell, reside; belong to, involved with, depend on; within. The ideogram: earth and persevere, place on the earth. **Below**, HSIA: anything below, in all senses; lower, inner; lower trigram; opposite of above, SHANG. **Bed**, CH'UANG: sleeping place; couch, sofa, lounge; bench around a well.

Avail of, YUNG: take advantage of; benefit from, profit by; use for a specific purpose; apply to advantage. The ideogram: to divine and center, applying divination to central concerns. **Chronicles**, SHIH: histories, records, annals; authoritative record; narrator of events, annalist. **Shaman**, WU: medium of the gods; sorcerer, enchantress; perform magic; wizard, witch.

Variegated, FEN: variegated, spotted; mixed, assorted, confused; cloudy, perplexed. **Similar/like**, JO: same as; just as, similar to. **Auspicious**, CHI: leads to the experience of meaning; favorable, propitious, advantageous, appropriate; keyword. The ideogram: scholar and mouth, wise words of a sage.

Without fault, WU CHIU: no error or harm in the situation.

b) **Have(it)/it/them/'s**, CHIH: expresses possession, directly or as an object pronoun. **Acquire**, TE: obtain the desired object; wish for, desire covetously; gains, possessions. The ideogram: go and obstacle, going through obstacles to the goal. **Center**, CHUNG: inner, central; put in the center; middle, stable point enabling you to face inner and outer changes; middle line of trigram. The ideogram: field divided in two equal parts. Image of Hexagram 61.

Nine at third

a) Pressing Ground, distress.

b) Pressing Ground's distress.
Purpose exhausted indeed.

You are pushing too hard. This only produces confusion. You won't accomplish your desires like this.

Associated Contexts a) **Pressing**, P'IN: on the brink of; imminent, urgent. **Distress**, LIN: shame, regret, humiliation; aware of having lost the right track; leads to repenting, HUI, correcting the direction of mind and life.

b) **Exhaust**, CH'IUNG: bring to an end; limit, extremity; destitute; investigate exhaustively; end without a new beginning. The ideogram: cave and naked person, bent with disease or old age.

Six at fourth

a) Repenting extinguished.
   The fields, catching three kinds.

b) The fields, catching three kinds.
   Possessing achievement indeed.

You are finally in a position to act. You can catch the information, the recognition and the power you need. Act through subtle penetration and you will achieve everything you desire.

Associated Contexts a) **Repenting extinguished**, HUI WANG: previous troubles and consequent remorse will disappear.
   Fields, T'IEN: cultivated land, plantation; also: hunting, game in the fields cannot escape the hunt. The ideogram: square divided into four sections, delineating fields. **Catch**, HUO: take in hunt; catch a thief; obtain, seize; hit the mark, opportune moment; prisoner, spoils, prey; slave, servant. **Three**, SAN: number three, third time or place; active phases of a cycle; superlative; beginning of repetition. **Kinds**, P'IN: species and their essential qualities; sorts, classes; classify, select.

b) **Possess**, YU: in possession of, have, own; opposite of lack, WU. **Achieve**, KUNG: work done, results; real accomplishment, praise, worth, merit. The ideogram: workman's square and forearm, combining craft and strength.

Nine at fifth

a) Trial: auspicious, repenting extinguished.
   Nothing not advantageous.
   Without initiating, possessing completion.
   Before husking, three days.
   After husking, three days.
   Auspicious.

b) **Nine at fifth's auspiciousness.**
Situation correctly centered indeed.

Act now. Everything will benefit. Don't start something new, but go
through with what you have been planning. Act through subtle penetration.
Watch it carefully before it is unveiled, and after it has begun. This is a very
favorable time.

Associated Contexts a) **Trial**, CHEN: inquiry by divination and its
result; righteous, firm; separating wheat from chaff; the kernel, the proven
core; fourth stage of the Time Cycle. The ideogram: pearl and divination.
Auspicious, CHI: leads to the experience of meaning; favorable, propitious,
advantageous, appropriate; keyword. The ideogram: scholar and mouth,
wise words of a sage. **Repenting extinguished**, HUI WANG: previous
troubles and consequent remorse will disappear.

Nothing not advantageous, WU PU LI: nothing for which this will not
be beneficial; advantageous potential, borderline where the balance is
swinging from not Harvesting to actually Harvesting.

Without, WU: devoid of; –less as suffix. **Initial**, CH'U: first step or part;
beginning, incipient; bottom line of hexagram. The ideogram: knife and
garment, cutting out the pattern. **Possess**, YU: in possession of, have, own;
opposite of lack, WU. **Complete**, CHUNG: end of a cycle that begins the
next; last, whole, all; contrasts with exhaust, CH'IUNG, final end. The
ideogram: silk cocoons, follow and ice, winter linking one year with the
next.

Before(hand)/earlier, HSIEN: come before in time; first, at first;
formerly, past, previous; begin, go ahead of. **Husking**, KENG: fruit and grain
husks bursting in autumn; seventh of the Ten Heavenly Barriers in calender
system; bestow, reward; blade or sword; associated with the Metallic
Moment . The ideogram: receiving things in the hand. **Three**, SAN: number
three, third time or place; active phases of a cycle; superlative; beginning of
repetition. **Day/sun**, JIH: actual sun and the time of a sun-cycle, a day.

After(wards)/later, HOU: come after in time, subsequent; put oneself
after; the second; attendants, heirs, successors, posterity.

b) **Situation**, WEI: place or seat according to rank; post, position, command;
right, proper; established, arranged. The ideogram: person and stand,
servants in their places. **Correct**, CHENG: rectify deviation or one-
sidedness; proper, straight, exact, regular; constant, rule, model. The
ideogram: stop and one, hold to one thing. **Center**, CHUNG: inner, central;
put in the center; middle, stable point enabling you to face inner and outer

changes; middle line of trigram. The ideogram: field divided in two equal parts. Image of Hexagram 61.

Nine above

a) Ground located below the bed.
Losing one's own emblem ax.
Trial: pitfall.

b) Ground located below the bed.
Above exhausted indeed.
Losing one's own emblem ax.
Correcting reaches a pitfall indeed.

This is not the time to penetrate the past. You will lose your possessions and your position. Leave it alone and be happy with what you have. If you start digging all over again, the way will close.

Associated Contexts a) **Locate(in)**, TSAI: live in, dwell, reside; belong to, involved with, depend on; within. The ideogram: earth and persevere, place on the earth. **Below**, HSIA: anything below, in all senses; lower, inner; lower trigram; opposite of above, SHANG. **Bed**, CH'UANG: sleeping place; couch, sofa, lounge; bench around a well.

Lose, SANG: fail to obtain, cease, become obscure; forgotten, destroyed; lament, mourn; funeral. The ideogram: weep and the dead. **One's/one**, CH'I: third person pronoun; also: it/its, he/his, she/hers, they/theirs. **Own**, TZU: possession and the things possessed; avail of, depend on; property, riches. **Emblem ax**, FU: moon-shaped ax, symbol of power to govern.

Trial, CHEN: inquiry by divination and its result; righteous, firm; separating wheat from chaff; the kernel, the proven core; fourth stage of the Time Cycle. The ideogram: pearl and divination. **Pitfall**, HSIUNG: leads away from the experience of meaning; stuck and exposed to danger, unable to take in the situation; flow of life and spirit is blocked; unfortunate, baleful; keyword.

b) **Above**, SHANG: anything above, in all senses; higher, upper, outer; upper trigram; opposite of below, HSIA. **Exhaust**, CH'IUNG: bring to an end; limit, extremity; destitute; investigate exhaustively; end without a new beginning. The ideogram: cave and naked person, bent with disease or old age.

Correct, CHENG: rectify deviation or one-sidedness; proper, straight, exact, regular; constant, rule, model. The ideogram: stop and one, hold to one thing.

58

OPEN ▮ *TUI*

Communication, self-expression; opportunity; pleasure, joy, excitement; persuade, exchange; the marketplace.

Open/Expression describes your situation in terms of communication, pleasure and exchange. Its symbol is the dancer and medium who gives voice to the spirits. The way to deal with it is express yourself openly and interact with others. Make an offering and you will succeed. Cheer people up and urge them on. Talk, bargain, barter, exchange information. Enjoy yourself and free others from constraint. This is pleasing to the spirits. Through it they will give you success, effective power and the capacity to bring the situation to maturity.

● *Image of the Situation*

> **Open, Growing,**
> **Advantageous Trial. Harvesting.**

Associated Contexts **Open,** TUI: an open surface, promoting interaction and interpenetration; responsive, free, unhindered, pleasing; opening, passage; the mouth; exchange, barter; straight, direct; meet, gather; place where water accumulates. The ideogram: person, mouth and vapor, speaking with others. **Open** is the **Marsh** trigram doubled and includes that trigram's attributes: *Symbol:* **Marsh/Mists,** TSE: open surface of a flat body of water and the vapors rising from it; fertilize, enrich; kindness, favor. *Action:* **Stimulate,** SHUO: rouse to action and good feeling; stir up, urge on; persuade; set out in words; free from constraint, cheer, delight. The ideogram: words and exchange. **Grow,** HENG: success through a sacrifice; pervade, persevere; bring to full growth; enjoy; vigorous, effective; second stage of the Time Cycle.

> **Advantageous Trial,** LI CHEN: Harvesting advantageous divination; putting the action in question to the test is beneficial.

● *Outer and Inner Aspects*

☱ **Open:** vapor rising from the marsh's open surface stimulates and fertilizes; stimulating words cheer and inspire. **Open** begins the yin hemicycle by initiating the formative process.

Connection to the outer: liquifying, casting, skinning off the mold, the Metallic Moment beginning. **Open** stimulates, cheers and reveals innate form.

- *Hidden Possibility*

Nuclear trigrams **Ground**, SUN, and **Radiance**, LI, result in Nuclear Hexagram 37, **Dwelling People**, CHIA JEN. **Open** exchange and contact with others leads to the security of **people** in their **dwelling**.

- *Sequence*

> Entering and afterwards stimulating it.
> Accepting this lets you use Open.
> Open implies stimulating indeed.

Associated Contexts **Enter,** JU: penetrate, go into, enter on, progress; put into, encroach on; the Action of the trigram Ground, SUN, contrary of issue-forth, CH'U. **After(wards)/later,** HOU: come after in time, subsequent; put oneself after; the second; attendants, heirs, successors, posterity. **It/them/have(it)/'s,** CHIH: expresses possession, directly or as an object pronoun.

Accepting ... use: activating this hexagram depends on understanding and accepting the previous statement.

Imply, CHE: further signify; additional meaning. **Indeed/is/means,** YEH: intensifier, connective; indicates comment on previous statement.

- *Contrasted Definitions*

> Open: seeing and
> Ground: hiding away indeed.

Associated Contexts **See,** CHIEN: seeing in all its aspects: vision, being visible, forming mental images; visit, call on, consult. The ideogram: eye above person, active and receptive sight. **Ground,** SUN: base on which things rest; support, foundation; mild, subtly penetrating; nourishing. The ideogram: stand and things arranged on it, the subtle influence of the ground. Image of Hexagram 57. **Hide away,** FU: conceal, place in ambush; secretly, silently; prostrate, fall on your face; humble. The ideogram: man and dog, man crouching.

● Symbol Tradition

Congregating marshes. Open.
A chün tzu uses partnering friends to explicate repeating.

Associated Contexts **Congregate**, LI: cling together; depend on, attached to, rely on; couple, pair, herd; the Action of the trigram Radiance, LI. The ideogram: deer flocking together.

Chün tzu: ideal of a person who uses divination to order his/her life in accordance with tao rather than wilful intention; keyword. **Use(of)**, YI: make use of, by means of, owing to; employ, make functional. **Partner**, P'ENG: associate for mutual benefit; two equal or similar things; companions, friends, peers; join in; commercial ventures. The ideogram: linked strings of cowries or coins. **Friend**, YU: companion, associate; of the same mind; attached, in pairs. The ideogram: two hands joined. **Explicate**, CHIANG: explain, unfold, narrate; converse, speak; investigate, plan, discuss. The ideogram: speech and crossing beams, speech blending harmoniously. **Repeat**, HSI: series of similar acts; practice, rehearse; familiar with, skilled. The ideogram: two wings and a cap, thought carried by repeated movements.

● Image Tradition

Open stimulating indeed. [I]
Strong centering and supple outside.
Stimulating uses Advantageous Trial.
That uses yielding reaching to heaven and
corresponding reaching to the people.

Stimulating beforehand using the commoners: [II]
The commoners forget their toiling.
Stimulating using opposing heaviness:
The commoners forget their dying.
Stimulating's great:
Actually the commoners encouraged in fact.

Associated Contexts **Strong**, KANG: quality of the whole lines; firm, strong, unyielding, persisting. **Center**, CHUNG: inner, central; put in the center; middle, stable point enabling you to face inner and outer changes; middle line of trigram. The ideogram: field divided in two equal parts. Image of Hexagram 61. **Supple**, JOU: quality of the opened lines; flexible, pliant, tender, adaptable. **Outside**, WAI: outer, exterior, external; people working in places other than their home; unfamiliar, foreign; the upper trigram, as opposed to inside, NEI, the lower.

That uses, SHIH YI: involves and is involved by. Yield(to), SHUN: give way and bear produce; comply, agree, follow, obey; unresisting, docile, flexible; nourish, provide; the Action of the trigram Field, K'UN. The ideogram: head and current, water flowing from the head of a river, yielding to the banks. Reach(to), HU: arrive at a goal; reach toward and achieve; connect; contrasts with tend-towards, YU. Heaven, T'IEN: highest; sky, firmament, heavens; power above the human as opposed to earth, TI, below; the Symbol of the trigram Force, CH'IEN. The ideogram: great and the one above. Correspond(to), YING: be in agreement or harmony; resonate together, invoke and fulfil each other; answer to, suitable; relation between the lines (1:4, 2:5, 3:6) when they form the pair opened and whole, supple and strong. The ideogram: heart and obey. People, person, JEN: humans individually and collectively; an individual; humankind. Image of Hexagrams 13 and 37.

[II] Before(hand)/earlier, HSIEN: come before in time; first, at first; formerly, past, previous; begin, go ahead of. Commoners, MIN: class of workers the state draws on to sustain the social hierarchy; undeveloped potential outside the organized personality.

Forget, WANG: escape the mind; leave undone, disregard, neglect. The ideogram: heart and lost. Their/they, CH'I: third person pronoun; also: one/one's, it/its, he/his, she/hers. Toil, LAO: labor, take pains, exert yourself; burdened, careworn; worthy actions. The ideogram: strength and fire, producing heat.

Oppose, FAN: resist; violate, offend, attack; possessed by an evil spirit; criminal. The ideogram: violate and dog, brutal offense. Heavy, NAN: arduous, grievous, difficult; hardship, distress; harass; contrasts with versatile, I, deal lightly with. The ideogram: domestic bird with clipped tail and drying sticky earth.

Die, SSU: sudden or untimely death; run out of energy; immobile, fixed.

Great, TA: big, noble, important, very; orient the will toward a self-imposed goal, impose direction; ability to lead or guide your life; contrasts with small, HSIAO: flexible adaptation to what crosses your path; keyword. Image of Hexagrams 14, 26, 28, 34.

Actually ... in fact, YI TSAI: stresses the importance of a statement. The ideogram: a dart and done, strong intention fully expressed. Encourage, CH'ÜAN: exhort, stimulate, influence; admonish.

● *Transforming Lines*

Initial nine

a) Harmonious Opening, auspicious.

b) Harmonious Opening's auspiciousness.
Movement not yet doubted indeed.

A beautiful contact. Expect real harmony to develop. The way is open.
Don't hold back.

Associated Contexts a) **Harmony,** HO: concord, union; conciliate; at
peace, mild; fit, tune, adjust. **Auspicious,** CHI: leads to the experience of
meaning; favorable, propitious, advantageous, appropriate; keyword. The
ideogram: scholar and mouth, wise words of a sage.

b) **Move,** HSING: move or move something; motivate, emotionally moving;
walk, act, do. The ideogram: stepping left then right. **Not yet,** WEI:
temporal negative; something will but has not yet occurred; contrary of
already, CHI. Image of Hexagram 64. **Doubt,** YI: suspect, distrust; dubious;
surmise, conjecture.

Nine at second

a) A connection to the spirits through Opening, auspicious.
Repenting extinguished.

b) A connection to the spirits Opening it, auspicious.
Trustworthy purpose indeed.

This contact will open a whole new world. Reach out. The way is open. Old
sorrows and frustrations will simply vanish.

Associated Contexts a) **Connection to the spirits,** FU: accord between
inner and outer in a particular moment; sincere, truthful, verified, reliable,
in accord with the spirits; capture; prisoners, spoils; contrasts with
trustworthy, HSIN, consistent over time. The ideogram: bird's claw
enclosing young animals, possessive grip. Image of Hexagram 61.
Auspicious, CHI: leads to the experience of meaning; favorable, propitious,
advantageous, appropriate; keyword. The ideogram: scholar and mouth,
wise words of a sage.

Repenting extinguished, HUI WANG: previous troubles and consequent
remorse will disappear.

b) **Trustworthy**, HSIN: truthful, faithful, consistent over time; integrity; confide in, follow; credentials; contrasts with conforming, FU, connection in a specific moment. The ideogram: person and word, true speech. **Purpose**, CHIH: focus of mind and heart; will, inclination, resolve. The ideogram: heart and scholar, high inner resolve, or heart and go, inner determination.

Six at third

a) Coming Opening, pitfall.

b) Coming Opening's pitfall.
   Situation not appropriate indeed.

This may look like an interesting opportunity, but there is nothing in it. Turn away or be trapped. The way is closing.

Associated Contexts a) **Come**, LAI, and **go**, WANG, describe the stream of time as it flows from future through present to past; come, LAI, indicates what is approaching; move toward, arrive at; keyword. **Pitfall**, HSIUNG: leads away from the experience of meaning; stuck and exposed to danger, unable to take in the situation; flow of life and spirit is blocked; unfortunate, baleful; keyword.

b) **Situation**, WEI: place or seat according to rank; post, position, command; right, proper; established, arranged. The ideogram: person and stand, servants in their places. **Appropriate**, TANG: suitable; opportune, convenient; adequate, competent; equal to; whole lines in uneven places and opened lines in even places.

Nine at fourth

a) Bargaining Opening, not yet soothing.
   Limiting the affliction possesses rejoicing.

b) Nine at fourth's rejoicing.
   Possessing reward indeed.

You are discussing this opening and everyone's temperature is rising. Put a clear limit on negative emotions. If you actively bargain to seek harmony, the situation will soon be filled with joy.

Associated Contexts a) **Bargain**, SHANG: argue over prices; consult, deliberate, do business; dealers, traveling merchants; hour before sunrise

and sunset. The ideogram: stutter and sentences, repetitive speaking. **Not yet,** WEI: temporal negative; something will but has not yet occurred; contrary of already, CHI. Image of Hexagram 64. **Soothe,** NING: calm, pacify; create peace of mind; tranquil, quiet. The ideogram: shelter above heart, dish and breath, physical and spiritual comfort.

Limit/chain mail, CHIEH: chain-armor; tortoise or crab shell; protective covering; border, limit; protection, support. **Afflict,** CHI: sickness, disorder, defect, calamity; injurious; pressure and consequent anger, hate or dislike. The ideogram: sickness and dart, a sudden affliction. **Possess,** YU: in possession of, have, own; opposite of lack, WU. **Rejoice(in),** HSI: feel and give joy; delight, exult; cheerful, merry. The ideogram: joy (music) and mouth, expressing joy.

b) **Reward,** CH'ING: gift given from gratitude or benevolence; favor from heaven; congratulate with gifts. The ideogram: heart, follow and deer (wealth), the heart expressed through gifts.

Nine at fifth

a) A connection to the spirits through stripping.
   Possessing adversity.

b) A connection to the spirits through stripping.
   Situation correcting appropriate indeed.

This opportunity for connection may be dangerous. Though it is filled with spirit, you are forced to confront past memories and negative experiences. Strip away your old ideas and face up to the challenge. It is time to put the situation straight.

Associated Contexts a) **Connection to the spirits,** FU: accord between inner and outer in a particular moment; sincere, truthful, verified, reliable, in accord with the spirits; capture; prisoners, spoils; contrasts with trustworthy, HSIN, consistent over time. The ideogram: bird's claw enclosing young animals, possessive grip. Image of Hexagram 61. **Strip,** PO: flay, peel, skin; remove, uncover, degrade; split, slice; reduce to essentials; slaughter an animal. The ideogram: knife and carve, trenchant action. Image of Hexagram 23.

Possess, YU: in possession of, have, own; opposite of lack, WU. **Adversity,** LI: danger; threatening, malevolent demon. This has two aspects: grind, sharpen, improve, perfect, stimulate; and: poisonous, sinister, cruel, contrary. It indicates a spirit or ghost that seeks revenge by inflicting suffering upon the living. Pacifying or exorcizing such a spirit can have a healing effect. The ideogram: sheltering cliff and stinging insect.

b) **Situation,** WEI: place or seat according to rank; post, position, command; right, proper; established, arranged. The ideogram: person and stand, servants in their places. **Correct,** CHENG: rectify deviation or one-sidedness; proper, straight, exact, regular; constant, rule, model. The ideogram: stop and one, hold to one thing. **Appropriate,** TANG: suitable; opportune, convenient; adequate, competent; equal to; whole lines in uneven places and opened lines in even places.

Six above

a) **Protracted Opening.**

b) **Six above, protracted Opening.**
   Not yet shining indeed.

Don't let go of this opportunity for connection. Draw it out as far as possible. Express yourself. Keep the possibilities open. You will be very sorry if you simply let go. This could be a lasting source of joy and pleasure.

Associated Contexts a) **Protract,** YIN: draw out, prolong; carried on; lead on, to bring forward; lit.: drawing a bow.

b) **Not yet,** WEI: temporal negative; something will but has not yet occurred; contrary of already, CHI. Image of Hexagram 64. **Shine,** KUANG: illuminate; give off brilliant, bright light; honor, glory, éclat; result of action, contrasts with brightness, MING: light of heavenly bodies. The ideogram: fire above person, lifting the light.

59

DISPERSING ▮ *HUAN*

Dissolve, clear up, scatter; dispel illusions, break up obstacles, eliminate resistance; melt the rigid.

Dispersing describes your situation in terms of the possibility of eliminating misunderstandings, illusions and obstacles. Its symbol is the blood flowing from a sacrifice that disperses the obstacle between the human and the spirit world. The way to deal with it is to clear away what is blocking clarity and understanding. Make an offering and you will succeed. Scatter the clouds, melt the ice, dispel fear and illusions, clear up misunderstandings, and eliminate suspicions. Let the fog lift and the sun shine through. This is pleasing to the spirits. Through it they will give you success, effective power and the capacity to bring the situation to maturity. Be like the king who imagines a temple full of images that unite people and connect them with greater forces. This is the right time to embark on a significant enterprise or to enter the stream of life with a purpose. Put your ideas to the trial. That brings profit and insight.

● *Image of the Situation*

> **Dispersing, Growing.**
> **The king imagines possessing a temple.**
> **Advantageous to step into the Great River. Harvesting.**
> **Advantageous Trial.**

Associated Contexts **Disperse,** HUAN: scatter clouds or crowds; break up obstacles; dispel illusions, fears and suspicions; clear up misunderstandings; dissolve, evaporate, disintegrate, fade, vanish; fog lifting or clearing away. **Grow,** HENG: success through a sacrifice; pervade, persevere; bring to full growth; enjoy; vigorous, effective; second stage of the Time Cycle.

King(hood), WANG: effective ruler, by authority of the Emperor, from whom others derive their power. **Imagine,** CHIA: create in the mind; fantasize, suppose, pretend, imitate; fiction; illusory, unreal; costume. The ideogram: person and borrow. **Possess,** YU: in possession of, have, own; opposite of lack, WU. **Temple,** MIAO: building used to honor gods and ancestors.

Advantageous/Harvest, LI: advantageous, profitable; acute, insightful; benefit, nourish; third stage of the Time Cycle. **Step into the Great River**, SHE TA CH'UAN: consciously moving into the flow of time; enter the stream of life with a goal or purpose; embark on a significant enterprise.

Advantageous Trial, LI CHEN: advantageous divination; putting the action in question to the test is beneficial.

• *Outer and Inner Aspects*

☴ **Ground**: Wind and wood subtly enter from the ground, penetrating and pervading. **Ground** is the center of the yang hemicycle, spreading pervasive action.

Connection to the outer: penetrating and bringing together, the Woody Moment culminating. **Ground** pervades, matches and couples, seeding a new generation.

☵ **Gorge**: Stream ventures and falls into the gorge, flowing on through toil and danger. **Gorge** ends the yin hemicycle by leveling and dissolving forms.

Connection to the inner: flooding and leveling dissolve direction and shape, the Streaming Moment. **Gorge** ventures, falls, toils and flows on.

The inner stream subtly penetrates the outer world, dissolving forms and **dispersing** obstacles.

• *Hidden Possibility*

Nuclear trigrams **Bound**, KEN, and **Shake**, CHEN, result in Nuclear Hexagram 27, **Jaws/Swallowing**, YI. The outward movement of **dispersing** and clearing away obstacles leads to providing nourishment through the **jaws**.

• *Sequence*

Stimulating and afterwards scattering it.
Accepting this lets you use Dispersing.
Dispersing implies Radiance indeed.

Associated Contexts **Stimulate**, SHUO: rouse to action and good feeling; free from constraint, stir up, urge on; persuade, cheer, delight; set out in words; the Action of the trigram Open, TUI. The ideogram: words and exchange. **After(wards)/later**, HOU: come after in time, subsequent;

put oneself after; the second; attendants, heirs, successors, posterity. **Scatter,** SAN: disperse in small pieces; separate, divide, distribute. The ideogram: strike and crumble. **It/them/have(it)/it/them/'s,** CHIH: expresses possession, directly or as an object pronoun.

Accepting ... use: activating this hexagram depends on understanding and accepting the previous statement.

Imply, CHE: further signify; additional meaning. **Radiance,** LI: glowing light, spreading in all directions; light-giving, discriminating, articulating; divide and arrange in order; the power of consciousness. The ideogram: bird and weird, the magical fire-bird with brilliant plumage. Image of Hexagram 30. **Indeed/is/means,** YEH: intensifier, connective; indicates comment on previous statement.

- *Contrasted Definitions*

  Dispersing: Radiance indeed.
  Articulating: stopping indeed.

Associated Contexts **Articulate,** CHIEH: separate and distinguish, as well as join, different things; express thought through speech; joint, section, chapter, interval, unit of time; zodiacal sign; moderate, regulate; lit.: nodes on bamboo stalks. Image of Hexagram 60. **Stop,** CHIH: bring or come to a standstill; the Action of the trigram Bound, KEN. The ideogram: a foot stops walking.

- *Symbol Tradition*

  Wind moves above stream. Dispersing.
  The Earlier Kings used presenting to the supreme
  to establish the temples.

Associated Contexts **Wind,** FENG: moving air, breeze, gust; weather and its influence on mood and humor; fashion, usage; wind and wood are the Symbols of the trigram Ground, SUN. **Move,** HSING: move or move something; motivate, emotionally moving; walk, act, do. The ideogram: stepping left then right. **Above,** SHANG: anything above, in all senses; higher, upper, outer; upper trigram; opposite of below, HSIA. **Stream,** SHUI: flowing water; fluid, dissolving; river, tide, flood; the Symbol of the trigram Gorge, K'AN. The ideogram: rippling water.

Earlier Kings,, HSIEN WANG: ideal rulers of old; the golden age, primal time, power in harmony with nature; model for the chün tzu. **Use(of),** YI:

make use of, by means of, owing to; employ, make functional. **Present(to)**, HSIANG: present in sacrifice, offer with thanks, give to the gods or a superior; confer dignity on. **Supreme**, TI: highest, above all on earth; sovereign lord, source of power; emperor. **Establish**, LI: set up, institute, order, arrange; stand erect; settled principles.

• *Image Tradition*

> **Dispersing, Growing. [I]**
> **Strong coming and not exhausted.**
> **Supple acquiring the situation reaching to the outside**
> **and concording above.**
>
> **The king imagines possessing a temple. [II]**
> **Kinghood thereupon located in the center indeed.**
>
> **Advantageous to step into the Great River. [III]**
> **Riding wood possesses achievement indeed.**

Associated Contexts **[I] Strong**, KANG: quality of the whole lines; firm, strong, unyielding, persisting. **Come**, LAI, and **go**, WANG, describe the stream of time as it flows from future through present to past; come, LAI, indicates what is approaching; move toward, arrive at; keyword. **Exhaust**, CH'IUNG: bring to an end; limit, extremity; destitute; investigate exhaustively; end without a new beginning. The ideogram: cave and naked person, bent with disease or old age.

Supple, JOU: quality of the opened lines; flexible, pliant, tender, adaptable. **Acquire**, TE: obtain the desired object; wish for, desire covetously; gains, possessions. The ideogram: go and obstacle, going through obstacles to the goal. **Situation**, WEI: place or seat according to rank; post, position, command; right, proper; established, arranged. The ideogram: person and stand, servants in their places. **Reach(to)**, HU: arrive at a goal; reach toward and achieve; connect; contrasts with tend-towards, YU. **Outside**, WAI: outer, exterior, external; people working in places other than their home; unfamiliar, foreign; the upper trigram, as opposed to inside, NEI, the lower. **Concord**, T'UNG: harmonize, unite, equalize, assemble; agree, share in; together, at once, same time and place. The ideogram: cover and mouth, silent understanding and perfect fit. Image of Hexagram 13.

[II] Thereupon, NAI: on that ground, because of. **Locate(in)**, TSAI: live in, dwell, reside; belong to, involved with, depend on; within. The ideogram:

earth and persevere, place on the earth. **Center**, CHUNG: inner, central; put in the center; middle, stable point enabling you to face inner and outer changes; middle line of trigram. The ideogram: field divided in two equal parts. Image of Hexagram 61.

[III] **Ride**, CH'ENG: ride an animal or a chariot; have the upper hand, seize the right time; control strong power; overcome the nature of the other; supple opened line above a strong whole line. **Wood/tree**, MU: all things woody or wooden, alive or constructed from wood; associated with the Woody Moment; wood and wind are the Symbols of the trigram Ground, SUN. The ideogram: a tree with roots and branches. **Achieve**, KUNG: work done, results; real accomplishment, praise, worth, merit. The ideogram: workman's square and forearm, combining craft and strength.

- *Transforming Lines*

  Initial six

  a) **Avail of a rescuing horse, invigorating auspicious.**

  b) **Initial six's auspiciousness.**
  Yielding indeed.

This affair is in trouble, and you must come to the rescue. Give it all you've got. If you really rouse yourself, you can open the way for the spirit to flow.

Associated Contexts a) **Avail of**, YUNG: take advantage of; benefit from, profit by; use for a specific purpose; apply to advantage. The ideogram: to divine and center, applying divination to central concerns. **Rescue**, CHENG: aid, deliver from trouble; pull out, raise up, lift. The ideogram: hand and aid, a helping hand. **Horse**, MA: symbol of spirited strength in the natural world, counterpart of dragon, LUNG; associated with the trigram Force, CH'IEN, heaven, T'IEN, and high noon. **Invigorate**, CHUANG: inspirit, animate; strong, robust; full grown, flourishing, abundant; attain manhood (at 30); damage through unrestrained strength. The ideogram: strength and scholar, intellectual impact. Image of Hexagram 34. **Auspicious**, CHI: leads to the experience of meaning; favorable, propitious, advantageous, appropriate; keyword. The ideogram: scholar and mouth, wise words of a sage.

b) **Yield(to)**, SHUN: give way and bear produce; comply, agree, follow, obey; unresisting, docile, flexible; nourish, provide; the Action of the trigram

Field, K'UN. The ideogram: head and current, water flowing from the head of a river, yielding to the banks.

Nine at second

a) Dispersing: fleeing one's bench.
  Repenting extinguished.

b) Dispersing: fleeing one's bench.
  Acquiring the desired indeed.

Let go of what you habitually depend on. Open yourself to the new. This will bring clarity and disperse the obstacles you are confronting. Your frustration will disappear and you will get what you desire.

Associated Contexts a) **Flee**, PEN: run away quickly; urgent, hurry; bustle, confusion; marry without rites. The ideogram: three oxen and fright, a stampede. **One's/one**, CH'I: third person pronoun; also: it/its, he/his, she/hers, they/theirs. **Bench**, CHI: low table used to lean on; side-table; stool or support.

  Repenting extinguished, HUI WANG: previous troubles and consequent remorse will disappear.

b) **Desire**, YÜAN: wish, hope or long for; covet; desired object.

Six at third

a) Dispersing one's body.
  Without repenting.

b) Dispersing one's body.
  Purpose located outside indeed.

Don't identify with your need to express yourself or your craving for personal power. Focus entirely on the needs of your work, outside of personal concerns. That way there will be no cause for sorrow. The blessing can flow.

Associated Contexts a) **One's/one**, CH'I: third person pronoun; also: it/its, he/his, she/hers, they/theirs. **Body/person**, KUNG: physical being, power and self expression; contrasts with individuality, SHEN, the total personality.

  Without repenting, WU HUI: devoid of the sort of trouble that leads to sorrow, regret and the necessity to change your attitude.

b) **Purpose,** CHIH: focus of mind and heart; will, inclination, resolve. The ideogram: heart and scholar, high inner resolve, or heart and go, inner determination.

Six at fourth

a) Dispersing one's flock, Spring auspicious.
Dispersing possessing the hill top.
In no way hiding, a place to ponder.

b) Dispersing one's flock, Spring auspicious.
Shining great indeed.

Let go of the flock that usually surrounds you. You have a great opportunity now, and you need to see it clearly. Go where you can talk to the spirits. This is not simply going into hiding. You need a place to ponder things deeply. The moment you do this, the new will come shining through.

Associated Contexts a) **One's/one,** CH'I: third person pronoun; also: it/its, he/his, she/hers, they/theirs. **Flock,** CH'ÜN: herd, group; people of same kind, friends, equals; all, entire; move in unison, flock together. The ideogram: chief and sheep, flock around a leader. **Spring,** YÜAN: source, origin, head; great, excellent; arise, begin, generating power; first stage of the Time Cycle. **Auspicious,** CHI: leads to the experience of meaning; favorable, propitious, advantageous, appropriate; keyword. The ideogram: scholar and mouth, wise words of a sage.

    Hilltop, CH'IU: hill with hollow top used for worship and as grave-site; knoll, hillock.

    In no way, FEI: strong negative; not so. The ideogram: a box filled with opposition. **Hide,** YI: keep out of sight; remote, distant from the center; equalize by lowering; squat, level, make ordinary; pacified, colorless; cut, wound, destroy, exterminate. Image of Hexagram 36. **Place,** SO: where something belongs or comes from; residence, dwelling; habitual focus or object. **Ponder,** SSU: reflect, consider, remember; deep thought; desire, wish. The ideogram: heart and field, the heart's concerns.

b) **Shine,** KUANG: illuminate; give off brilliant, bright light; honor, glory, éclat; result of action, contrasts with brightness, MING, light of heavenly bodies. The ideogram: fire above person, lifting the light. **Great,** TA: big, noble, important, very; orient the will toward a self-imposed goal, impose direction; ability to lead or guide your life; contrasts with small, HSIAO, flexible adaptation to what crosses your path; keyword. Image of Hexagrams 14, 26, 28, 34.

Nine at fifth

a) Dispersing sweat, one's great crying out.
Dispersing the king's residence.
Without fault.

b) The king's residence, without fault.
Correcting the situation indeed.

You are involved in a great project. Don't think about anything else now. This is not a mistake. In the end this will correct your entire situation. The center is changing. Be part of it.

Associated Contexts a) **Sweat**, HAN: perspiration; labor, trouble. **Dispersing sweat**, HUAN HAN, denotes an imperial edict. **One's/one**, CH'I: third person pronoun; also: it/its, he/his, she/hers, they/theirs. **Great**, TA: big, noble, important, very; orient the will toward a self-imposed goal, impose direction; ability to lead or guide your life; contrasts with small, HSIAO, flexible adaptation to what crosses your path; keyword. Image of Hexagrams 14, 26, 28, 34. **Cry out/outcry**, HAO: call out, proclaim; signal, order, command; mark, label, sign.

Reside(in), CHÜ: dwell, live in, stay; sit down, fill an office; settled parts of a country. The ideogram: body and seat. **Without fault**, WU CHIU: no error or harm in the situation.

b) **Correct**, CHENG: rectify deviation or one-sidedness; proper, straight, exact, regular; constant, rule, model. The ideogram: stop and one, hold to one thing.

Nine above

a) Dispersing one's blood.
Departing far away, issuing forth.
Without fault.

b) Dispersing one's blood.
Distancing harm indeed.

Remove the cause for conflict. Exorcize it. Get rid of it. Send it far away. Then you can emerge into the light and have the place you want. You will make no mistake in doing this.

Associated Contexts a) **One's/one**, CH'I: third person pronoun; also: it/its, he/his, she/hers, they/theirs. **Blood**, HSÜEH: yin fluid that maintains life; money, property.

Depart, CH'Ü: leave, quit, remove; repudiate, reject, dismiss. **Far away,** TI: far, remote; send away, exile. **Issue forth (from),** CH'U: emerge from, come out of, proceed from, spring from; the Action of the trigram Shake, CHEN; contrary of enter, JU. The ideogram: stem with branches and leaves emerging.

Without fault, WU CHIU: no error or harm in the situation.

b) **Distance,** YÜAN: far off, remote; keep at a distance; alienated. The ideogram: go and a long way. **Harm,** HAI: damage, injure, offend; suffer; hurtful, hindrance; fearful, anxious.

60

ARTICULATING ▋ *CHIEH*

Sense the right time and its quality; measure, limit; articulate speech and thought; chapters, intervals, music and ceremonies; loyal and true.

Articulating describes your situation in terms of the relations between things. Its symbol is the joints or openings in the flow of time. The way to deal with it is to articulate and make the connections clear. Make an offering and you will succeed. Express your thoughts. Separate and distinguish things. Make chapters, sections, and units of time. Create a whole in which each thing has its place. This is pleasing to the spirits. Through it they will give you success, effective power and the capacity to bring the situation to maturity. But don't harm yourself or others. Rules that are bitter and harsh will prevent you from putting your ideas to the trial.

● *Image of the Situation*

> **Articulating, Growing.**
> **Bitter Articulating does not permit a Trial.**

Associated Contexts **Articulate**, CHIEH: separate and distinguish, as well as join different things; express thought through speech; joint, section, chapter, interval, unit of time; regulations, limits; zodiacal sign; lit.: nodes on bamboo stalks. **Grow**, HENG: success through a sacrifice; pervade, persevere; bring to full growth; enjoy; vigorous, effective; second stage of the Time Cycle.

Bitter, K'U: taste corresponding to the Fiery Moment; unpleasant, troublesome, painful affliction; take pains; urgent, pressing; dislike, grieve, mortify. **Not permitting**, PU K'O: not possible; contradicts an inherent principle. The ideogram: mouth and breath, silent consent. **Trial**, CHEN: inquiry by divination and its result; righteous, firm; separating wheat from chaff; the kernel, the proven core; fourth stage of the Time Cycle. The ideogram: pearl and divination.

633

- ## Outer and Inner Aspects

☵ **Gorge:** Stream ventures and falls into the gorge, flowing on through toil and danger. **Gorge** ends the yin hemicycle by leveling and dissolving forms.

Connection to the outer: flooding and leveling dissolve direction and shape, the Streaming Moment. **Gorge** ventures, falls, toils and flows on.

☱ **Open:** vapor rising from the marsh's open surface stimulates and fertilizes; stimulating words cheer and inspire. **Open** begins the yin hemicycle by initiating the formative process.

Connection to the inner: liquifying, casting, skinning off the mold, the Metallic Moment beginning. **Open** stimulates, cheers and reveals innate form.

Stimulating words from within **articulate** and transform the undifferentiated stream of events.

- ## Hidden Possibility

Nuclear trigrams **Bound**, KEN, and **Shake**, CHEN, result in Nuclear Hexagram 27, **Jaws/Swallowing**, YI. Discriminating and **articulating** leads to providing nourishment through **jaws**.

- ## Sequence

> Beings not permitted to use completing Radiance.
> Accepting this lets you use Articulating.

Associated Contexts **Beings not permitted to use ...** : no one is allowed to make use of; nothing can exist by means of. **Complete,** CHUNG: end of a cycle that begins the next; last, whole, all; contrasts with exhaust, CH'IUNG, final end. The ideogram: silk cocoons, follow and ice, winter linking one year with the next. **Radiance,** LI: glowing light, spreading in all directions; light-giving, discriminating, articulating; divide and arrange in order; the power of consciousness. The ideogram: bird and weird, the magical fire-bird with brilliant plumage. Image of Hexagram 30.

Accepting ... use: activating this hexagram depends on understanding and accepting the previous statement.

- ## Contrasted Definitions

> Dispersing: Radiance indeed.
> Articulating: stopping indeed.

Associated Contexts **Disperse,** HUAN: scatter clouds or crowds; break up obstacles; dispel illusions, fears and suspicions; clear up misunderstandings; dissolve, evaporate, disintegrate, fade, vanish; fog lifting or clearing away. Image of Hexagram 59. **Indeed/is/means,** YEH: intensifier, connective; indicates comment on previous statement.

Stop, CHIH: bring or come to a standstill; the Action of the trigram Bound, KEN. The ideogram: a foot stops walking.

• *Symbol Tradition*

> **Above marsh possessing stream. Articulating.**
> **A chün tzu uses paring away to reckon the measures.**
> **[A chün tzu uses] deliberating actualizing tao to move.**

Associated Contexts **Above,** SHANG: anything above, in all senses; higher, upper, outer; upper trigram; opposite of below, HSIA. **Marsh,** TSE: open surface of a flat body of water and the vapors rising from it; fertilize, enrich; kindness, favor; the Symbol of the trigram Open, TUI. **Possess,** YU: in possession of, have, own; opposite of lack, WU. **Stream,** SHUI: flowing water; fluid, dissolving; river, tide, flood; the Symbol of the trigram Gorge, K'AN. The ideogram: rippling water.

Chün tzu: ideal of a person who uses divination to order his/her life in accordance with tao rather than wilful intention; keyword. **Use(-of),** YI: make use of, by means of, owing to; employ, make functional. **Pare,** CHIH: cut away; form, tailor, carve; invent; limit, prevent. The ideogram: knife and incomplete. **Reckon,** SHU: count, find the number; give out; sum up, discriminate; also: account, bill, list; fate, destiny; many cares, dilemma. **Measures,** TU: rule, regulation, limit, test; interval in music; capacity, endurance.

Deliberate, YI: consult, discuss, criticize; weigh the options and find the best course; arrange, select; laws, rules. The ideogram: words and right. **Actualize-tao,** TE: realize tao in action; power, virtue; ability to follow the course traced by the ongoing process of the cosmos; keyword. The ideogram: to go, straight, and heart. Linked with acquire, TE, acquiring that which makes a being become what it is meant to be. **Move,** HSING: move or move something; motivate, emotionally moving; walk, act, do. The ideogram: stepping left then right.

● *Image Tradition*

Articulating, Growing. [I]
Strong and Supple apportioning and strong acquiring
the center.
Bitter Articulating does not permit a Trial.
One's tao exhausted indeed.

Stimulating uses moving and venturing. [II]
Appropriate situating uses Articulating.
Centering correcting uses interpenetrating.
Heaven and Earth Articulating and
the four seasons accomplishing.

Articulating used to pare the measures: [III]
Not injuring property,
Not harming the commoners.

Associated Contexts [I] **Solid and Supple**, KANG JOU: field of creative tension between the whole and opened lines and their qualities; field of psychic movement. **Apportion**, FEN: divide for distribution; sort out; allot to. **Strong**, KANG: quality of the whole lines; firm, strong, unyielding, persisting. **Acquire**, TE: obtain the desired object; wish for, desire covetously; gains, possessions. The ideogram: go and obstacle, going through obstacles to the goal. **Center**, CHUNG: inner, central; put in the center; middle, stable point enabling you to face inner and outer changes; middle line of trigram. The ideogram: field divided in two equal parts. Image of Hexagram 61.

One's/one, CH'I: third person pronoun; also: it/its, he/his, she/hers, they/theirs. **Tao**: way or path; ongoing process of being and the course it traces for each specific person or thing; keyword. The ideogram: go and head, leading and the path it creates. **Exhaust**, CH'IUNG: bring to an end; limit, extremity; destitute; investigate exhaustively; end without a new beginning. The ideogram: cave and naked person, bent with disease or old age.

[II] **Stimulate/loosen**, SHUO: rouse to action and good feeling; free from constraint, stir up, urge on; persuade, cheer, delight; set out in words; the Action of the trigram Open, TUI. The ideogram: words and exchange. **Venture**, HSIEN: risk without reserve; key point, point of danger; difficulty, obstruction that must be confronted; water falling and filling the holes on its way; the Action of the trigram Gorge, K'AN: The ideogram: mound and all or whole, everything engaged at one point.

Appropriate, TANG: suitable; opportune, convenient; adequate, competent; equal to; whole lines in uneven places and opened lines in even places. **Situation**, WEI: place or seat according to rank; post, position, command; right, proper; established, arranged. The ideogram: person and stand, servants in their places.

Centering correcting, CHUNG CHENG: central and correct; make rectifying one-sidedness and error your central concern; reaching a stable center in yourself can correct the situation. **Interpenetrate**, T'UNG: mutually penetrate; permeate, flow through, reach everywhere; see clearly, communicate with.

Heaven, T'IEN: highest; sky, firmament, heavens; power above the human as opposed to earth, TI, below; the Symbol of the trigram Force, CH'IEN. The ideogram: great and the one above. **Earth**, TI: ground on which the human world rests; basis of all things, nourishes all things; the Symbol of the trigram Field, K'UN. **Four seasons**, SSU SHIH: the four dynamic qualities of time that make up the year and the Time Cycle; the right time, in accord with the time; time as sacred; all-encompassing. **Accomplish**, CH'ENG: complete, finish, bring about; perfect, full, whole; play your part, do your duty; mature. The ideogram: weapon and man, able to bear arms, thus fully developed.

[III] **Injure**, SHANG: hurt, wound, grieve, distress; mourn, sad at heart, humiliated. **Property**, TS'AI: possessions, goods, substance, wealth. The ideogram: pearl and value.

Harm, HAI: damage, injure, offend; suffer; hurtful, hindrance; fearful, anxious. **Commoners**, MIN: class of workers the state draws on to sustain the social hierarchy; undeveloped potential outside the organized personality.

● *Transforming Lines*

Initial nine

a) **Not issuing forth from the door chambers.**
   Without fault.
b) **Not issuing forth from the door chambers.**
   Knowing interpenetrating is clogged indeed.

This is not a time to act. Stay in your place within. Contemplate what is important to you. This is not a mistake. The way to connect with others is blocked now.

Associated Contexts a) **Issue forth (from)**, CH'U: emerge from, come out of, proceed from, spring from; the Action of the trigram Shake, CHEN; contrary of enter, JU. The ideogram: stem with branches and leaves emerging. **Door**, HU: inner door, chamber door; a household; contrasts with gate, MEN, the outer door. **Chambers**, T'ING: family room, courtyard, hall; domestic. The ideogram: shelter and hall, a secure place.

Without fault, WU CHIU: no error or harm in the situation.

b) **Know**, CHIH: understand, perceive, remember; informed, aware, wise. The ideogram: arrow and mouth, words focused and swift. **Clog**, SAI: stop up, fill up, close, obstruct, hinder, prevent; unintelligent, dull, hard to understand.

Nine at second

a) Not issuing forth from the gate chambers.
   Pitfall.

b) Not issuing forth from the gate chambers, pitfall.
   Letting go the season end indeed.

This is a time to act. Leave your habitual ways of thought. Enter the new. If you don't, you will surely regret it. The way will close and you will be on the outside looking in.

Associated Contexts a) **Issue forth (from)**, CH'U: emerge from, come out of, proceed from, spring from; the Action of the trigram Shake, CHEN; contrary of enter, JU. The ideogram: stem with branches and leaves emerging. **Gate**, MEN: outer door, between courtyard and street; a text or master as gate to a school of thought. **Chambers**, T'ING: family room, courtyard, hall; domestic. The ideogram: shelter and hall, a secure place.

Pitfall, HSIUNG: leads away from the experience of meaning; stuck and exposed to danger, unable to take in the situation; flow of life and spirit is blocked; unfortunate, baleful; keyword.

b) **Let go**, SHIH: lose, omit, miss, fail, let slip; out of control. The ideogram: drop from the hand. **End**, CHI: last or highest point; final, extreme; on the verge; ridgepole of a house.

Six at third

a) Not the Articulating like, by consequence the lamenting like.
   Without fault.

b) Not Articulating's lamenting.
   Furthermore whose fault indeed?

This is the time. You must set limits and create order. If you don't, you will always end up being sorry. Everything will dissolve a flood of tears. If you articulate things now, you will make no mistake.

Associated Contexts a) **Like,** JO: same as; just as, similar to. **By consequence (of),** TSE: very strong connection; reason, cause, result; rule, law, pattern, standard; therefore. **Lament,** CHÜEH: express intense regret or sorrow; mourn over; painful recollections.
   Without fault, WU CHIU: no error or harm in the situation.

b) **'s/have(it)/it/them,** CHIH: expresses possession, directly or as an object pronoun.
   Furthermore, YU: in addition to; higher degree of. **Whose,** SHUI: relative and interrogative pronoun; also: whose? **Fault,** CHIU: unworthy conduct that leads to harm, illness, misfortune. The ideogram: person and differ, differ from what you should be.

Six at fourth

a) **Quiet Articulating, Growing.**

b) **Quiet Articulating's Growing.**
   Receiving tao above indeed.

Articulate your ideas and feelings quietly and peacefully and you meet a warm response. This creates success and inspires friends to join you. Make an offering and you will succeed.

Associated Contexts a) **Quiet/secure,** AN: peaceful, still, settled; calm, tranquilize. The ideogram: woman under a roof, a tranquil home.

*b)***'s/have(it)/it/them,** CHIH: expresses possession, directly or as an object pronoun.
   Receive, CH'ENG: receive gifts or commands from superiors or customers; take in hand; catch falling water. The ideogram: accepting a seal of office.

Nine at fifth

a) **Sweet Articulating auspicious.**
   Going possesses honor.

b) Sweet Articulating's auspiciousness.
  Residing in the situation: centering indeed.

Express yourself with sweetness, grace and delight. The way is open. You meet with honor and esteem. This is a significant time for you both.

Associated Contexts a) **Sweet**, KAN: taste corresponding to the Earthy Moment; agreeable, happy, delightful, refreshing; grateful. **Auspicious**, CHI: leads to the experience of meaning; favorable, propitious, advantageous, appropriate; keyword. The ideogram: scholar and mouth, wise words of a sage.

  Go, WANG, and **come**, LAI, describe the stream of time as it flows from future through present to past; go, WANG, indicates what is departing from present to past; proceed, move on; keyword. **Honor**, SHANG: esteem, give high rank to; eminent; put one thing on top of another.

b) **'s/have(it)/it/them**, CHIH: expresses possession, directly or as an object pronoun.

  Reside(in), CHÜ: dwell, live in, stay; sit down, fill an office; settled parts of a country. The ideogram: body and seat.

  Six above

  a) Bitter Articulating, Trial: pitfall.
    Repenting extinguished.

  b) Bitter Articulating, Trial: pitfall.
    One's tao exhausted indeed.

You are angry and frustrated. You want to impose harsh measures through bitter speech. Don't do it. You will do nothing but harm. If you will only give up your bitterness, the cause for sorrow will disappear.

Associated Contexts a) **Pitfall**, HSIUNG: leads away from the experience of meaning; stuck and exposed to danger, unable to take in the situation; flow of life and spirit is blocked; unfortunate, baleful; keyword .

  Repenting extinguished, HUI WANG: previous troubles and consequent remorse will disappear.

61

CENTERING CONNECTING ▮
CHUNG FU

Sincere, truthful; connect your inner and outer lives; power of a heart at peace; connection to the spirit; a capture, spoils.

Centering and Connecting to the Spirits describes your situation in terms of the need to bring your life into accord with the spirits. Its symbol is the emptied heart open to the spirits. The way to deal with it is to make connecting the inner and the outer parts of your life your central concern. Be sincere, truthful, and reliable. Make your inner vision and your outer circumstances coincide. Empty your heart so you can hear the inner voices. Act through these voices with sincerity and honesty in connecting with others. This will link you to the spirits and they will carry you through. Swim in the stream of the way and gather the pigs and fishes. This generates meaning and good fortune by releasing transformative energy. This is the right time to enter the stream of life with a purpose, or to embark on a significant enterprise. Put your ideas to the trial. That brings profit and insight.

● *Image of the Situation*

> **Centering and connecting to the spirits, hog fish auspicious.**
> **Advantageous to step into the Great River. Harvesting.**
> **Advantageous Trial.**

Associated Contexts **Center**, CHUNG: inner, central; calm, stable; put in the center; stable point which enables you to face inner and outer changes; middle line of trigram. The ideogram: field divided in two equal parts. **Connection to the spirits**, FU: accord between inner and outer in a particular moment; sincere, truthful, verified, reliable, in accord with the spirits; capture; prisoners, spoils; contrasts with trustworthy, HSIN, consistent over time. The ideogram: bird's claw enclosing young animals, possessive grip. **Hog fish**, T'UN YÜ: aquatic mammals; porpoise, dolphin; intelligent aquatic animals whose development parallels the human; sign of abundance and good luck. **Auspicious**, CHI: leads to the experience of meaning; favorable, propitious, advantageous, appropriate; keyword. The ideogram: scholar and mouth, wise words of a sage.

Advantageous/Harvest, LI: advantageous, profitable; acute, insightful; benefit, nourish; third stage of the Time Cycle. **Step into the Great River**, SHE TA CH'UAN: consciously moving into the flow of time; enter the stream of life with a goal or purpose; embark on a significant enterprise.

Advantageous Trial, LI CHEN: advantageous divination; putting the action in question to the test is beneficial.

- *Outer and Inner Aspects*

☴ **Ground**: Wind and wood subtly enter from the ground, penetrating and pervading. **Ground** is the center of the yang hemicycle, spreading pervasive action.

Connection to the outer: penetrating and bringing together, the Woody Moment culminating. **Ground** pervades, matches and couples, seeding a new generation.

☱ **Open**: vapor rising from the marsh's open surface stimulates and fertilizes; stimulating words cheer and inspire. **Open** begins the yin hemicycle by initiating the formative process.

Connection to the inner: liquifying, casting, skinning off the mold, the Metallic Moment beginning. **Open** stimulates, cheers and reveals innate form.

The open **center** stimulates **conforming** by penetrating and coupling the outer and the inner.

- *Hidden Possibility*

Nuclear trigrams **Bound**, KEN, and **Shake**, CHEN, result in Nuclear Hexagram 27, **Jaws/Swallowing**, YI. Creating a **connection** between the **center** and the spirit leads to providing nourishment though the **jaws**.

- *Sequence*

Articulating and trusting it.
Accepting this lets you use Centering Conforming.

Associated Contexts **Articulate**, CHIEH: separate and distinguish, as well as join, different things; express thought through speech; joint, section, chapter, interval, unit of time; zodiacal sign; moderate, regulate; lit.: nodes on bamboo stalks. Image of Hexagram 60. **Trust(worthy)**, HSIN: truthful, faithful, consistent over time; integrity; confide in, follow; credentials;

contrasts with conforming, FU, connection in a specific moment. The ideogram: person and word, true speech. **It/them/have(it)/'s**, CHIH: expresses possession, directly or as an object pronoun.

Accepting ... use: activating this hexagram depends on understanding and accepting the previous statement.

- ## Contrasted Definitions

> Small Traverses: Excess indeed.
> Centering Connecting: trustworthiness indeed.

Associated Contexts **Small**, HSIAO: little, common, unimportant; adapting to what crosses your path; ability to move in harmony with the vicissitudes of life; contrasts with great, TA, self-imposed theme or goal; keyword. **Exceed/traverse**, KU: go beyond, pass by, pass over; excessive, transgress; error, fault. **Small Traverses** is the Image of Hexagram 62. **Indeed**, YEH: intensifier, connective; indicates comment on previous statement.

- ## Symbol Tradition

> Above marsh possessing wind. Centering Connecting.
> A chün tzu uses deliberating litigation to delay death.

Associated Contexts **Above**, SHANG: anything above, in all senses; higher, upper, outer; upper trigram; opposite of below, HSIA. **Marsh**, TSE: open surface of a flat body of water and the vapors rising from it; fertilize, enrich; kindness, favor; the Symbol of the trigram Open, TUI. **Possess**, YU: in possession of, have, own; opposite of lack, WU. **Wind**, FENG: moving air, breeze, gust; weather and its influence on mood and humor; fashion, usage; wind and wood are the Symbols of the trigram Ground, SUN.

Chün tzu: ideal of a person who uses divination to order his/her life in accordance with tao rather than wilful intention; keyword. **Use(of)**, YI: make use of, by means of, owing to; employ, make functional. **Deliberate**, YI: consult, discuss, criticize; weigh the options and find the best course; arrange, select; laws, rules. The ideogram: words and right. **Litigate**, YÜ: legal proceedings; take a case to court. The ideogram: two dogs and words, barking arguments at each other. **Delay**, HUAN: retard, put off; let things take their course, tie loosely; gradually, leisurely; lax, tardy, negligent. **Die**, SSU: sudden or untimely death; run out of energy; immobile, fixed; death penalty.

Image Tradition

Centering Connecting. [I]
Supple located inside and strong acquiring the center.
Stimulating and Ground: Connecting to the spirits.
Thereupon changing the fiefdoms indeed.

Hog fish auspicious. [II]
Trustworthiness extending to hog fish indeed.
Advantageous to step into the Great River.
Riding a wooden dugout, emptiness indeed.

Centering Connecting uses Advantageous Trial. [III]
Thereupon corresponding reaching to heaven indeed.

Associated Contexts [I] **Supple**, JOU: quality of the opened lines; flexible, pliant, tender, adaptable. **Locate(in)**, TSAI: live in, dwell, reside; belong to, involved with, depend on; within. The ideogram: earth and persevere, place on the earth. **Inside**, NEI: within, inner, interior; inside of the house and those who work there, particularly women; the lower trigram, as opposed to outside, WAI, the upper. The ideogram: border and enter, cross a border. **Strong**, KANG: quality of the whole lines; firm, strong, unyielding, persisting. **Acquire**, TE: obtain the desired object; wish for, desire covetously; gains, possessions. The ideogram: go and obstacle, going through obstacles to the goal.

Stimulate/loosen, SHUO: rouse to action and good feeling; free from constraint, stir up, urge on; persuade, cheer, delight; set out in words; the Action of the trigram Open, TUI. The ideogram: words and exchange. **Ground**, SUN: base on which things rest; support, foundation; mild, subtly penetrating; nourishing. The ideogram: stand and things arranged on it, the subtle influence of the ground. Image of Hexagram 57.

Thereupon, NAI: on that ground, because of. **Change**, HUA: gradual, continuous metamorphosis; influence someone; contrasts with transform, PIEN, sudden mutation. The ideogram: person alive and dead, the life-process. **Fiefdom**, PANG: region governed by a feudatory, an order of nobility.

[II] **Extend(to)**, CHI: reach to, draw out, prolong; continuous, enduring.
Ride, CH'ENG: ride an animal or a chariot; have the upper hand, seize the right time; control strong power; overcome the nature of the other; supple opened line above a strong whole line. **Wood/tree**, MU: all things woody or wooden, alive or constructed from wood; associated with Woody

Moment; wood and wind are the Symbols of the trigram Ground, SUN. The ideogram: a tree with roots and branches. **Dugout**, CHOU: hollowed log, canoe; boat, ride or transport by boat. **Empty**, HSÜ: no images or concepts; vacant, unsubstantial; empty yet fertile space.

[III] Correspond(to), YING: be in agreement or harmony; resonate together, invoke and fulfil each other; answer to, suitable; relation between the lines (1:4, 2:5, 3:6) when they form the pair opened and whole, supple and strong. The ideogram: heart and obey. **Reach(to)**, HU: arrive at a goal; reach toward and achieve; connect. **Heaven**, T'IEN: highest; sky, firmament, heavens; power above the human as opposed to earth, TI, below; the Symbol of the trigram Force, CH'IEN. The ideogram: great and the one above.

● *Tranforming Lines*

Initial nine

a) **Precaution auspicious.**
Possessing this, not a swallow.

b) **The initial nine, precaution auspicious.**
Purpose not yet transformed indeed.

Stay alone and quiet and think about what you want to do. That will open the way. If you are always worrying about other people, you will have no peace. Don't take on their problems now.

Associated Contexts a) **Precaution**, YÜ: provide against, preventive measures; anxious, vigilant, ready; preoccupied with, think about, expect; mishap, accident.
    This, T'A: specifically this thing. The ideogram: person and indeed. **Swallow**, YEN: house swallow, martin, swift; retired from official life; easy, peaceful, private; give a feast; relation between elder and younger brother.

b) **Purpose**, CHIH: focus of mind and heart; will, inclination, resolve. The ideogram: heart and scholar, high inner resolve, or heart and go, inner determination. **Not yet**, WEI: temporal negative; something will but has not yet occurred; contrary of already, CHI. Image of Hexagram 64. **Transform**, PIEN: abrupt, radical, fundamental mutation from one state of being to another; transformation of lines in hexagrams; contrasts with change, HUA, gradual metamorphosis.

Nine at second

a) Calling crane located in the yin.
One's sonhood harmonizes with it.
"I possess a loved wine cup.
Myself associating, we will simply spill it out."

b) One's sonhood harmonizing it.
Centering the heart desiring indeed.

This is the profound call of one soul to another. Respond to it. It can change your life. Don't hesitate to answer.

Associated Contexts a) **Call**, MING: bird and animal cries, through which they recognize each other; distinctive sound, song, statement. The ideogram: bird and mouth, a distinguishing call. **Crane**, HAO: large wading birds; sign of long life, wisdom and bliss; messenger to the immortals; relation between father and son. **Yin:** Struction; consolidating, shadowy aspect of phenomena: conserves, substantializes, creates structures; spacial extension; limited, bound, given specific being; build, make something concrete.

One's/one, CH'I: third person pronoun; also: it/its, he/his, she/hers, they/theirs. **Son(hood)**, TZU: living up to ideal of ancestors as highest human development; act with concern and reverence; male child; offspring, posterity; seed, kernel, egg; sage, teacher; nadir, deepest point, midnight, mid-winter. **Harmony**, HO: concord, union; conciliate; at peace, mild; fit, tune, adjust.

I/me/my, WO: first person pronoun; indicates an unusually strong emphasis on your own subjective experience. **Love**, HAO: affection; fond of, take pleasure in; fine, graceful. **Wine cup**, CHIO: libation cup originally in the form of a bird; all small birds; rank of nobility, confer rank on someone.

Myself, WU: first person intensifier; the particular person I am. **Associate(with)**, YÜ: consort with, combine; companions; group, band, company; agree with, comply, help. The ideogram: pair of hands reaching downward meets a pair of hands reaching upward, helpful association. **Simply**, ERH: just so, only. **Spill**, MI: pour out; disperse, spread; waste, overturn; fleeing soldiers; showy, extravagant.

b) **Heart**, HSIN: heart as center of being; seat of mind's images and affections; moral nature; source of desires, intentions, will. **Desire**, YÜAN: wish, hope or long for; covet; desired object.

Six at third

a) Acquiring the antagonist.
   Maybe drumbeating, maybe desisting.
   Maybe weeping, maybe singing.

b) Maybe drumbeating, maybe desisting.
   Situation not appropriate indeed.

This is the profound call of one soul to another. Respond to it. It can change your life. Don't hesitate to answer.

Associated Contexts a) **Antagonist**, TI: opposed and equal; competitor, enemy; a contest between equals.

   Maybe/"someone", HUO: possible but not certain, perhaps. **Drumbeating**, KU: skin or earthenware drums; play a drum; excite, arouse, encourage; joyous, happy. **Desist**, PA: cease, leave off, discontinue, finish; enough.

   Weep, CH'I: lament wordlessly; grieved, heart-broken. **Sing**, KO: chant, sing elegies, sad or mournful songs; associated with the Earthy Moment, turning from yang to yin.

b) **Situation**, WEI: place or seat according to rank; post, position, command; right, proper; established, arranged. The ideogram: person and stand, servants in their places. **Appropriate**, TANG: suitable; opportune, convenient; adequate, competent; equal to; whole lines in uneven places and opened lines in even places.

Six at fourth

a) The moon almost facing.
   The horse team extinguished.
   Without fault.

b) The horse team extinguished.
   Cutting off the above, sorting indeed.

In victory you find an equal and a rival. Back and forth, again and again, you have something to love and fight with that you cannot defeat. In the end you will probably have to change it or leave it.

Associated Contexts a) **Moon**, YÜEH: actual moon and moon-month; yin, the sun being yang. **Almost**, CHI: nearly, about to; subtle, almost imperceptible; the first sign. **Face**, WANG: full moon; moon directly facing the sun; 15th day of the moon-month; look at hopefully.

Horse, MA: symbol of spirited strength in the natural world, counterpart of dragon, LUNG; associated with the trigram Force, CH'IEN, heaven, T'IEN, and high noon. **Team**, P'I: pair, matched horses; fellow, mate; united. **Extinguish**, WANG: ruin, destroy; gone, dead, lost without trace; extinct, forgotten, out of mind. The ideogram: person concealed by a wall, out of sight.

Without fault, WU CHIU: no error or harm in the situation.

b) **Cut off**, CHÜEH: cut short, interrupt, disconnect, break off, sever; destroy, renounce; alienated. The ideogram: silk, knife and knot, cutting through. **Sort**, LEI: group according to kind, class with; like nature or purpose; species, class, genus.

Nine at fifth

a) There is a connection to the spirits, binding thus.
Without fault.

b) There is a connection to the spirits, binding thus.
Situation correcting appropriate indeed.

This relationship connects you on a deep spiritual level. This can truly help people. Put things right. Act energetically. This is not a mistake.

Associated Contexts a) **There is ... spirits**, YU FU: inner and outer are in accord; confidence of the spirits has been captured; sincere, truthful; proper to take action. **Bind**, LÜAN: tie, connect, take hold of; bent, contracted. The ideogram: hand and connect, binding things. **Thus**, JU: as, in this way.

Without fault, WU CHIU: no error or harm in the situation.

b) **Situation**, WEI: place or seat according to rank; post, position, command; right, proper; established, arranged. The ideogram: person and stand, servants in their places. **Correct**, CHENG: rectify deviation or one-sidedness; proper, straight, exact, regular; constant, rule, model. The ideogram: stop and one, hold to one thing. **Appropriate**, TANG: suitable; opportune, convenient; adequate, competent; equal to; whole lines in uneven places and opened lines in even places.

Nine above

a) A soaring sound mounting to heaven.
Trial: pitfall.

b) **A soaring sound mounting to heaven.**
Wherefore permitting long living indeed?

This is enthusiasm that flies above itself and carries you away. There is no real substance here. Ask yourself why you are doing this. Danger. The way is closing. You will fall into the hunter's net.

Associated Contexts a) **Soar**, HAN: fly high; rising sun, the firebird with red plumage; trunk or stem of a plant; vertical support. The ideogram: feathers and dawn. **Sound**, YIN: any sound, particularly music; pronunciation of words. The ideogram: words and hold in the mouth, vocal sound. **Mount**, TENG: ascend, step up; ripen, complete.

   Trial, CHEN: inquiry by divination and its result; righteous, firm; separating wheat from chaff; the kernel, the proven core; fourth stage of the Time Cycle. The ideogram: pearl and divination. **Pitfall**, HSIUNG: leads away from the experience of meaning; stuck and exposed to danger, unable to take in the situation; flow of life and spirit is blocked; unfortunate, baleful; keyword.

b) **Wherefore**, HO: interrogative: why? for what reason? what is? and affirmation: therefore, for that reason. **Permit**, K'O: possible because in harmony with an inherent principle. The ideogram: mouth and breath, silent consent. **Long living**, CHANG: enduring, constant; senior, superior, greater; increase, prosper; respect, elevate.

62

SMALL TRAVERSES ▮
HSIAO KUO

A transition; adapt to each thing; be very careful, very small; yin energy.

Small Traverses describes your situation in terms of a transition through a seemingly overwhelming variety of details. Its symbol is the little bird flying low to escape the nets of the hunter. The way to deal with it is carefully to adapt to each thing in turn. Make an offering and you will succeed. Be very careful and meticulous. Adapt conscientiously to whatever comes. This is pleasing to the spirits. Through it they will give you success, effective power and the capacity to bring the situation to maturity. Put your ideas to the trial. That brings profit and insight. The time allows you to do small things. It does not allow you to do great things. The flying bird leaves this message behind: the above is not suitable, the below is suitable. Don't go up, go down. This generates great good fortune and meaningful events by releasing transformative energy. Keep your sense of purpose. Don't look to others to solve your problems.

● *Image of the Situation*

> Small Traverses, Growing.
> Advantageous Trial. Harvesting.
> Permitting Small Affairs. Not permitting Great Affairs.
> Flying bird: abandoning's sound.
> Above not proper, below proper.
> The great auspicious.

Associated Contexts **Small,** HSIAO: little, common, unimportant; adapting to what crosses your path; ability to move in harmonious relation to the vicissitudes of life; contrasts with great, TA, self-imposed theme or goal; keyword. **Traverse/Exceed,** KU: pass by, pass over; excessive, transgress; error, fault. **Grow,** HENG: success through a sacrifice; pervade, persevere; bring to full growth; enjoy; vigorous, effective; second stage of the Time Cycle.

Advantageous Trial, LI CHEN: advantageous divination; putting the action in question to the test is beneficial harvesting.

Permit, K'O: possible because in harmony with an inherent principle.

The ideogram: mouth and breath, silent consent. **Affairs**, SHIH: all kinds of personal activity; matters at hand; business, occupation; manage a business, case in court. **Not permitting**, PU K'O: not possible; contradicts an inherent principle. **Great**, TA: big, noble, important, very; orient the will toward a self-imposed goal, impose direction; ability to lead or guide your life; contrasts with small, HSIAO, flexible adaptation to what crosses your path; keyword. Image of Hexagrams 14, 26, 28, 34.

Fly, FEI: spread your wings, fly away; let free; swift. **Bird**, NIAO: all feathered animals; associated with the Fiery Moment. **Abandon**, YI: leave behind, forget; die; lose through unawareness. The ideogram: go and value, value is gone. **'s/have(it)/it/them**, CHIH: expresses possession, directly or as an object pronoun. **Sound**, YIN: any sound, particularly music; pronunciation of words. The ideogram: words and hold in the mouth, vocal sound.

Above, SHANG: anything above, in all senses; higher, upper, outer; upper trigram; opposite of below, HSIA. **Proper**, YI: reasonable of itself; fit and right, harmonious; ought, should. **Below**, HSIA: anything below, in all senses; lower, inner; lower trigram; opposite of above, SHANG.

Auspicious, CHI: leads to the experience of meaning; favorable, propitious, advantageous, appropriate; keyword. The ideogram: scholar and mouth, wise words of a sage.

- *Outer and Inner Aspects*

☳ **Shake**: Thunder rises from below, shaking and stirring things up. **Shake** begins the yang hemicycle by germinating new action.

Connection to the outer: sprouting energies thrusting from below, the Woody Moment beginning. **Shake** stirs things up to issue-forth.

☶ **Bound**: Mountains bound, limit and set a place off, stopping forward movement. **Bound** completes a full yin-yang cycle.

Connection to the inner: accomplishing words, which express things. **Bound** articulates what is complete to suggest what is beginning.

Previous accomplishment limits outer stirring-up through an **exceeding** concern with the **small**.

- *Hidden Possibility*

Nuclear trigrams **Open**, TUI, and **Ground**, SUN, result in Nuclear Hexagram 28, **Great Traverses**, TA KUO. An **excessive** concern with adapting through the **small** leads to making the **great** transition.

Sequence

Possessing one's trustworthiness implies necessarily moving it.
Accepting this lets you use Small Exceeding.

Associated Contexts **Possess,** YU: in possession of, have, own; opposite of lack, WU. **One's/one,** CH'I: third person pronoun; also: it/its, he/his, she/hers, they/theirs. **Trustworthy,** HSIN: truthful, faithful, consistent over time; integrity; confide in, follow; credentials; contrasts with conforming, FU, connection in a specific moment. The ideogram: person and word, true speech. **Imply,** CHE: further signify; additional meaning. **Necessarily,** PI: unavoidably, indispensably, certainly. **Move,** HSING: move or move something; motivate, emotionally moving; walk, act, do. The ideogram: stepping left then right.

Accepting ... use: activating this hexagram depends on understanding and accepting the previous statement.

• *Contrasted Definitions*

Small Traverses: Excess indeed.
Centering Connecting: trustworthiness indeed.

Associated Contexts **Indeed/is/means,** YEH: intensifier, connective; indicates comment on previous statement.

Center, CHUNG: inner, central; put in the center; middle, stable point enabling you to face inner and outer changes; middle line of trigram. The ideogram: field divided in two equal parts. **Connection,** FU: accord between inner and outer in a particular moment; sincere, truthful, verified, reliable, in accord with the spirits; capture; prisoners, spoils; contrasts with trustworthy, HSIN, consistent over time. The ideogram: bird's claw enclosing young animals, possessive grip. **Centering Connecting** is the Image of Hexagram 61.

• *Symbol Tradition*

Above mountain possessing thunder. Small Traverses.
A chün tzu uses moving excess to reach to courtesy.
[A chün tzu uses] losing excess to reach to mourning.
[A chün tzu uses] availing of excess to reach to parsimony.

Associated Contexts **Mountain,** SHAN: limit, boundary; the Symbol of the trigram Bound, KEN. The ideogram: three peaks, a mountain range.

Thunder, LEI: rising, arousing power; the Symbol of the trigram Shake, CHEN.

Chün tzu: ideal of a person who uses divination to order his/her life in accordance with tao rather than wilful intention; keyword. **Use(of),** YI: make use of, by means of, owing to; employ, make functional. **Reach(to),** HU: arrive at a goal; reach towards and achieve; connect; contrasts with tend-towards, YU. **Courtesy,** KUNG: display respect, treat courteously, show reverence; affable, decorous, modest, polite; obsequious.

Lose, SANG: fail to obtain, cease, become obscure; forgotten, destroyed; lament, mourn; funeral. The ideogram: weep and the dead. **Mourn,** AI: grieve, lament over something gone; distress, sorrow; compassion. The ideogram: mouth and clothes, display of feelings.

Avail of, YUNG: take advantage of; benefit from, profit by; use for a specific purpose; apply to advantage. The ideogram: to divine and center, applying divination to central concerns. **Parsimonious,** CHIEN: thrifty; moderate, temperate; stingy, scanty.

- *Image Tradition*

> **Small Traverses. [I]**
> **Small implies Traversing and Growing indeed.**
> **Traversing uses Advantageous Trial.**
> **Associating with the season moving indeed.**
>
> **Supple acquiring the center. [II]**
> **That uses Small Affairs, auspicious indeed.**
> **Strong letting go the situation and not centering.**
> **That uses not permitting Great Affairs indeed.**
>
> **Possessing the flying bird's symbol in truth. [III]**
> **Flying bird: abandoning's sound.**
> **Above not proper, below proper.**
> **The great auspicious.**
> **Countering above and yielding below indeed.**

Associated Contexts **[I] Associate(with),** YÜ: consort with, combine; companions; group, band, company; agree with, comply, help. The ideogram: pair of hands reaching downward meets a pair of hands reaching upward, helpful association. **Season,** SHIH: quality of the time; the right time, opportune, in harmony; planning in accord with the time; seasons of the year. The ideogram: sun and temple, time as sacred.

[II] Supple, JOU: quality of the opened lines; flexible, pliant, tender, adaptable. **Acquire,** TE: obtain the desired object; wish for, desire covetously; gains, possessions. The ideogram: go and obstacle, going through obstacles to the goal.

That uses, SHIH YI: involves and is involved by.

Strong, KANG: quality of the whole lines; firm, strong, unyielding, persisting. **Let go,** SHIH: lose, omit, miss, fail, let slip; out of control. The ideogram: drop from the hand. **Situation,** WEI: place or seat according to rank; post, position, command; right, proper; established, arranged. The ideogram: person and stand, servants in their places.

[III] Symbol, HSIANG: image invested with intrinsic power to connect visible and invisible; magic spell; figure, form, shape, likeness; pattern, model; create an image, imitate; act, play; writing. **In truth,** YEN: statement is complete and correct.

Counter, NI: oppose, resist, seek out; contrary, rebellious, refractory. The ideogram: go and rise against, active revolt. **Yield(to),** SHUN: give way and bear produce; comply, agree, follow, obey; unresisting, docile, flexible; nourish, provide; the Action of the trigram **Field,** K'UN. The ideogram: head and current, water flowing from the head of a river, yielding to the banks.

• *Transforming Lines*

Initial six

a) Flying bird: using a pitfall.

b) Flying bird: using a pitfall.
Why this is not thus permitted!

Stay low, stay humble and stay grounded. Don't try to impress people. Don't try to be the best. Don't fly away. If you do you will surely regret it.

Associated Contexts a) **Pitfall,** HSIUNG: leads away from the experience of meaning; stuck and exposed to danger, unable to take in the situation; flow of life and spirit is blocked; unfortunate, baleful; keyword.

b) **Why,** HO: interrogative: why? for what reason? what is? and affirmation: therefore, for that reason. **Thus,** JU: as, in this way.

Six at second

a) Traversing past one's grandfather.
Meeting one's grandmother.
Not extending to one's chief.
Meeting one's servant.
Without fault.

b) Not extending to one's chief.
A servant not permitted to Traverse indeed.

Identify with people in secondary roles. Don't push yourself forward. Gladly accept the supporting position. Don't try to dominate. You will see all your wishes fulfiled. The connections will have deep, enduring value.

Associated Contexts a) **Grandfather**, TSU: second ancestor generation; deceased grandfather, honored more than actual father. **Meet**, YÜ: come on unexpectedly, encounter; occur, happen; pleasant meeting, lucky coincidence; agree.

Grandmother, PI: second ancestor generation; deceased grandmother, venerated as source of her many descendants.

Extend(to), CHI: reach to, draw out, prolong; continuous, enduring. **Chief**, CHÜN: effective ruler; preside over, take the lead; influence others; term of respect. The ideogram: mouth and director, giving orders.

Servant, CH'EN: attendant, minister, vassal; courtier who can speak to the sovereign; wait on, serve in office. The ideogram: person bowing low.

Without fault, WU CHIU: no error or harm in the situation.

Nine at third

a) Traversing. Nowhere exceeding defending against it.
Adhering, maybe killing it.
Pitfall.

b) Adhering, maybe killing it.
Wherefore a pitfall thus indeed.

You overextend yourself. You are in an impossible situation. If you are lucky, you can fend off harm. You are real danger. You must stop acting like this.

Associated Contexts a) **Nothing/nowhere**, FU: strong negative; not a single thing/place. **Defend against**, FANG: keep off, protect from, guard

against; erect a protective barrier. The ideogram: open space and earthen ramparts.

Adhere(to), TS'UNG: follow a way, hold to a doctrine, school, or person; hear and comply with, agree to; forced to follow, follower. The ideogram: two men walking, one following the other. **Maybe/ "someone"**, HUO: possible, perhaps; term indicates spirit is active. **Kill**, CH'IANG: put to death; violent assault; maltreat, misuse; kill an important person.

Pitfall, HSIUNG: leads away from the experience of meaning; stuck and exposed to danger, unable to take in the situation; flow of life and spirit is blocked; unfortunate, baleful; keyword.

b) **Wherefore**, HO: interrogative: why? for what reason? what is? and affirmation: therefore, for that reason. **Thus**, JU: as, in this way.

Nine at fourth

a) Without fault. Traversing.
   Nowhere exceeding meeting it.
   Going adversity necessarily warning.
   No availing of perpetual Trial.

b) Nowhere exceeding meeting it.
   Situation not appropriate indeed.
   Going adversity necessarily warning.
   Completing not permitting long living indeed.

The crisis is over and you have made the connection. This is not a mistake. Take a look at the dangers you have just passed through, the memories and ghosts. Let them be a warning. Don't go back!

Associated Contexts a) **Without fault**, WU CHIU: no error or harm in the situation.

Nothing/nowhere, FU: strong negative; not a single thing/place. **Meet**, YÜ: come on unexpectedly, encounter; occur, happen; pleasant meeting, lucky coincidence; agree.

Go, WANG, and **come**, LAI, describe the stream of time as it flows from future through present to past; go, WANG, indicates what is departing from present to past; proceed, move on; keyword. **Adversity**, LI: danger; threatening, malevolent demon. This has two aspects: grind, sharpen, improve, perfect, stimulate; and: poisonous, sinister, cruel, contrary. It indicates a spirit or ghost that seeks revenge by inflicting suffering upon the living. Pacifying or exorcizing such a spirit can have a healing effect. The ideogram: sheltering cliff and stinging insect. **Warn**, CHIEH: alert, alarm, put on guard; caution, inform; guard against, refrain from (as in a diet). The ideogram: spear held in both hands, warning enemies and alerting friends.

Perpetual, YUNG: continuing; everlasting, ever-flowing. The ideogram: flowing water. **Trial**, CHEN: inquiry by divination and its result; righteous, firm; separating wheat from chaff; the kernel, the proven core; fourth stage of the Time Cycle. The ideogram: pearl and divination.

b) **Appropriate**, TANG: suitable; opportune, convenient; adequate, competent; equal to; whole lines in uneven places and opened lines in even places.

Complete, CHUNG: end of a cycle that begins the next; last, whole, all; contrasts with exhaust, CH'IUNG: final end. The ideogram: silk cocoons, follow and ice, winter linking one year with the next. **Long living**, CHANG: enduring, constant; senior, superior, greater; increase, prosper; respect, elevate.

Six at fifth

a) **Shrouding clouds, not raining.**
Originating from my Western suburbs.
A prince and a string arrow, grasps another located in a cave.

b) **Shrouding clouds, not raining.**
Above climaxing indeed.

The culmination is coming, the autumn rains and the harvest. You make an enduring connection with someone who is in retreat. This will open up a whole new life.

Associated Contexts a) **Shroud**, MI: dense, close together, thick, tight; hidden, secret; retired, intimate. **Clouds**, YÜN: fog, mist, water vapor; connects to the Streaming Moment and Stream, the Symbol of the trigram Gorge, K'AN. **Rain**, YÜ: all precipitation; sudden showers, fast and furious; associated with the trigram Gorge, K'AN, and the Streaming Moment.

Origin, TZU: source, beginning, ground; cause, reason, motive; line of descent; path to the origin; yourself, intrinsic. **My/me/I**, WO: first person pronoun; indicates an unusually strong emphasis on your own subjective experience. **West**, HSI: corresponds to autumn, Harvest and the Streaming Moment; begins the yin hemicycle of Universal Compass. **Suburbs**, CHIAO: area adjoining a city where human constructions and nature interpenetrate; second of the territorial zones: city, suburbs, countryside, forests.

Prince, KUNG: nobles acting as ministers of state in the capital; governing from the center rather than active in daily life; contrasts with feudatory, HOU, governors of the provinces. **String arrow**, YI: arrow with string attached used to retrieve what is shot; seize, appropriate; arrest a criminal. **Grasp**, CH'Ü: lay hold of, take and use, seize, appropriate; grasp the meaning, understand. The ideogram: ear and hand, hear and grasp. **Another**, PEI: yet one more; the other party; exclude, leave out. **Locate(in)**, TSAI: live in, dwell, reside; belong to, involved with, depend on; within. The ideogram: earth and persevere, place on the earth. **Cave**, HSÜEH: hole used for dwelling; cavern, den, pit; open grave.

b) **Climax**, YI: come to a high point and stop, bring to an end; use up, lay aside; decline, reject.

   Six above

   a) Traversing. Nowhere meeting, exceeding it.
   Flying bird radiating it.
   Pitfall.
   That designates Calamity and Blunder.

   b) Nowhere meeting, exceeding it.
   Climaxing overbearing indeed.

Danger and arrogance. You overreach yourself, flying higher and higher. This won't accomplish anything. A disaster from within and without. Change now!

Associated Contexts a) **Nothing/nowhere**, FU: strong negative; not a single thing/place. **Meet**, YÜ: come on unexpectedly, encounter; occur, happen; pleasant meeting, lucky coincidence; agree.

   Radiance, LI: glowing light, spreading in all directions; light-giving, discriminating, articulating; divide and arrange in order; the power of consciousness. The ideogram: bird and weird, the magical fire-bird with brilliant plumage. Image of Hexagram 30.

   Pitfall, HSIUNG: leads away from the experience of meaning; stuck and exposed to danger, unable to take in the situation; flow of life and spirit is blocked; unfortunate, baleful; keyword.

   That, SHIH: preceding statement. **Designate**, WEI: represent in words, assign a name or meaning; report on, talk about. The ideogram: words and belly, describing the essential. **Calamity and Blunder**, TSAI SHENG: disaster from without and within; natural disaster combined with misfortune due to ignorance or fault; ruin, defeat, rout, collapse.

b) **Climax,** YI: come to a high point and stop, bring to an end; use up, lay aside; decline, reject. **Overbearing,** K'ANG: excessive, overpowering authority; disparage; rigid, unbending; excessive display of force.

63

ALREADY FORDING ∎
CHI CHI

Begun, already underway, in progress; everything in place; proceed actively.

Already Fording describes your situation in terms of an action that is already underway. Its symbol is the crossing of a river, the river of life. The way to deal with it is to go on actively with what you are doing. Make an offering and you will succeed. You are in the middle of fording the stream of events. Things are already in their proper places. Adapt to whatever crosses your path. Give aid and encouragement. This is pleasing to the spirits. Through it they will give you success, effective power and the capacity to bring the situation to maturity. Put your ideas to the trial. That brings profit and insight. Stay with the process. That generates meaning and good fortune by releasing transformative energy. Trying to bring things to completion creates disorder. Remain underway.

● *Image of the Situation*

> Already Fording. Growing: the small.
> Advantageous Trial. Harvesting.
> Initiating auspicious.
> Completing: disarraying.

Associated Contexts **Already,** CHI: completed, done, has occurred; past tense, contrary of not-yet, WEI. **Ford,** CHI: cross a river at a ford or shallow place; overcome an obstacle, embark on a course of action; help, relieve; cease. The ideogram: water and level, running smooth over a flat bottom. **Grow,** HENG: success through a sacrifice; pervade, persevere; bring to full growth; enjoy; vigorous, effective; second stage of the Time Cycle. **Small,** HSIAO: little, common, unimportant; adapting to what crosses your path; ability to move in harmony with the vicissitudes of life; contrasts with great, TA, self-imposed theme or goal; keyword. Image of Hexagrams 9 and 62.

    Advantageous Trial, LI CHEN: advantageous divination; putting the action in question to the test is beneficial; harvesting.

    Initial, CH'U: first step or part; beginning, incipient; bottom line of hexagram. The ideogram: knife and garment, cutting out the pattern. **Auspicious**, CHI: leads to the experience of meaning; favorable, propitious, advantageous, appropriate; keyword. The ideogram: scholar and mouth, wise words of a sage.

Complete, CHUNG: end of a cycle that begins the next; last, whole, all; contrasts with exhaust, CH'IUNG, final end. The ideogram: silk cocoons, follow and ice, winter linking one year with the next. **Disarray**, LUAN: throw into disorder, mislay, confuse; out of place; discord, insurrection, anarchy.

● *Outer and Inner Aspects*

☵ **Gorge**: Stream ventures and falls into the gorge, flowing on through toil and danger. **Gorge** ends the yin hemicycle by leveling and dissolving forms.

Connection to the outer: flooding and leveling dissolve direction and shape, the Streaming Moment. **Gorge** ventures, falls, toils and flows on.

☲ **Radiance**: Fire and brightness radiate light and warmth, attached to their support; congregating people see and become aware. **Radiance** ends the yang hemicycle, consuming action in awareness.

Connection to the inner: light, heat, consciousness bring continual change, the Fiery Moment. **Radiance** spreads outward, congregating, becoming aware and changing.

Inner brightness has joined with outer venturing, **already fording** the stream of events.

● *Hidden Possibility*

Nuclear trigrams **Radiance**, LI, and **Gorge**, K'AN, result in Nuclear Hexagram 64, **Not yet Fording**, WEI CHI. The necessity to expend energy in **already fording** is contrasted with building up potential by **not yet fording** the stream of events.

● *Sequence*

> Possessing Traversing, the being necessarily implies Fording.
> Accepting this lets you use Already Fording.

Associated Contexts **Possess**, YU: in possession of, have, own; opposite of lack, WU. **Traverse/Exceed**, KU: go beyond, pass by, pass over;

excessive, transgress; error, fault. Image of Hexagrams 28 and 62. **Being(s)**, WU: creature, thing, any single being; matter, substance, essence; nature of things. **Imply**, CHE: further signify; additional meaning. **Necessarily**, PI: unavoidably, indispensably, certainly.

Accepting ... use: activating this hexagram depends on understanding and accepting the previous statement.

- *Contrasted Definitions*

> Already Fording: setting it right indeed.
> Not yet Fording: manhood exhausted indeed.

Associated Contexts **Set right**, TING: settle, fix, put in place; at rest, repose. **Indeed/is/means**, YEH: intensifier, connective; indicates comment on previous statement.

Not yet, WEI: temporal negative; something will but has not yet occurred; contrary of already, CHI. **Not yet Fording** is the Image of Hexagram 64. **Man(hood)**, NAN: a man; what is inherently male. The ideogram: fields and strength, hard labor in the fields. **Exhaust**, CH'IUNG: bring to an end; limit, extremity; destitute; investigate exhaustively; end without a new beginning. The ideogram: cave and naked person, bent with disease or old age.

- *Symbol Tradition*

> Stream located above fire. Already Fording.
> A chün tzu uses pondering tribulation and
> provides for defending against it.

Associated Contexts **Stream**, SHUI: flowing water; fluid, dissolving; river, tide, flood; the Symbol of the trigram Gorge, K'AN. The ideogram: rippling water. **Locate(in)**, TSAI: live in, dwell, reside; belong to, involved with, depend on; within. The ideogram: earth and persevere, place on the earth. **Above**, SHANG: anything above, in all senses; higher, upper, outer; upper trigram; opposite of below, HSIA. **Fire**, HUO: warming and consuming aspect of burning; fire and brightness are the Symbols of the trigram Radiance, LI.

Chün tzu: ideal of a person who uses divination to order his/her life in accordance with tao rather than wilful intention; keyword. **Use(of)**, YI: make use of, by means of, owing to; employ, make functional. **Ponder**, SSU: reflect, consider, remember; deep thought; desire, wish. The ideogram:

heart and field, the heart's concerns. **Tribulation**, HUAN: distress, grief, affliction. The ideogram: heart and clamor, the heart distressed. **Provide for/provision**, YÜ: ready, prepared for; pre-arrange, take precaution, think beforehand; satisfied, contented, at ease. The ideogram: sonhood and elephant, careful, reverent and very strong. Image of Hexagram 16. **Defend against**, FANG: keep off, protect from, guard against; erect a protective barrier. The ideogram: open space and earthen ramparts. **It/them/have(it)/'s** CHIH: expresses possession, directly or as an object pronoun.

● *Image Tradition*

> **Already Fording, Growing. [I]**
> **The small implies Growing indeed.**
> **Advantageous Trial. Harvesting.**
> **Strong and Supple correcting and the situation**
> **appropriate indeed.**
>
> **Initiating auspicious. [II]**
> **Supple acquiring the center indeed.**
> **Completing and stopping, by consequence disarraying.**
> **One's tao exhausted indeed.**

Associated Contexts **[I] Strong and Supple**, KANG JOU: field of creative tension between the whole and opened lines and their qualities; field of psychic movement. **Correct**, CHENG: rectify deviation or one-sidedness; proper, straight, exact, regular; constant, rule, model. The ideogram: stop and one, hold to one thing. **Situation**, WEI: place or seat according to rank; post, position, command; right, proper; established, arranged. The ideogram: person and stand, servants in their places. **Appropriate**, TANG: suitable; opportune, convenient; adequate, competent; equal to; whole lines in uneven places and opened lines in even places.

[II] Supple, JOU: quality of the opened lines; flexible, pliant, tender, adaptable. **Acquire**, TE: obtain the desired object; wish for, desire covetously; gains, possessions. The ideogram: go and obstacle, going through obstacles to the goal. **Center**, CHUNG: inner, central; put in the center; middle, stable point enabling you to face inner and outer changes; middle line of trigram. The ideogram: field divided in two equal parts. Image of Hexagram 61.

Stop, CHIH: bring or come to a standstill; the Action of the trigram

Bound, KEN. The ideogram: a foot stops walking. **By consequence(of),** TSE: very strong connection; reason, cause, result; rule, law, pattern, standard; therefore.

One's/one, CH'I: third person pronoun; also: it/its, he/his, she/hers, they/theirs. **Tao:** way or path; ongoing process of being and the course it traces for each specific person or thing; keyword. The ideogram: go and head, leading and the path it creates.

- *Transforming Lines*

   Initial nine

   a) **Pulling back one's wheels.**
   Soaking one's tail.
   Without fault.

   b) **Pulling back one's wheels.**
   Righteous, without fault indeed.

You have a great connection, but you are starting too quickly. Hold back. Start slowly. Let yourself be lured on. This is not a mistake.

Associated Contexts a) **Pull back,** YI: pull or drag something toward you; drag behind, take by the hand; leave traces. **Wheel,** LUN: disk, circle, round; revolution, circuit; rotate, roll, by turns.

   Soak, JU: immerse, steep; damp, wet; stain, pollute, blemish; urinate on. **Tail,** WEI: animal's tail; last, extreme; remnants, unimportant.

   Without fault, WU CHIU: no error or harm in the situation.

b) **Righteous,** YI: proper and just, meets the standards; things in their proper place; the heart that rules itself; upright, moral rule; contrasts with Harvest, LI, advantage or profit.

   Six at second

   a) **A wife losing her veil.**
   No pursuit.
   The seventh day: acquiring.

   b) **The seventh day: acquiring.**
   Using centering tao indeed.

It seems like what you hope and care for is lost. Don't worry. Don't chase it. When the time comes, it will find you without trying. Have no cares. You will soon have what you desire.

Associated Contexts a) **Wife**, FU: responsible position of married woman within the household; contrasts with consort, CH'I, her legal position and concubine, CH'IEH, secondary wives. The ideogram: woman, hand and broom, household duties. **Lose**, SANG: fail to obtain, cease, become obscure; forgotten, destroyed; lament, mourn; funeral. The ideogram: weep and the dead. **Her/she**, CH'I: third person pronoun; also: one/one's, it/its, he/his, they/their. **Veil**, FU: screen on person or carriage; hair ornaments; lit.: luxuriant, tangled vegetation that conceals the path.

Pursue, CHU: chase, follow closely, press hard; expel, drive out. The ideogram: pig (wealth) and go, chasing fortune.

Seven, CH'I: number seven, seventh; seven planets; seventh day when moon changes from crescent to waxing; the Tangram game makes pictures of all phenomena from seven basic shapes. **Day/sun**, JIH: actual sun and the time of a sun-cycle, a day.

Nine at third

a) The High Ancestor subjugating souls on all sides.
Three years revolved and he controls it.
Small People, no availing of.

b) Three years revolved controlling it.
Weariness indeed.

You are embarked on a great enterprise. It will take time to complete. Keep a firm purpose. Don't listen to what others try to tell you. Your hearts will win in the end.

Associated Contexts a) **High(ness)**, KAO: high, elevated, lofty, eminent; excellent, advanced. **Ancestry**, TSUNG: clan, kin, origin; those who bear the same surname; ancestral hall and tablets; honor, revere; a doctrine; contrasts with predecessor, K'AO: individual ancestors. **High Ancestor**, KAO TSUNG, is the ceremonial title of a great Shang emperor (1364–1324 BCE) seen as a model of the just warrior and glorious ruler. His spirit is felt to protect his descendants. **Subjugate**, FA: chastise rebels, make dependent; cut down, subject to rule. The ideogram: man and lance, armed soldiers. **Soul**, KUEI: power that creates individual existence; union of volatile-soul, HUN, spiritual and intellectual power, and dense-soul, P'O:

bodily strength and movement. The HUN rises after death, the P'O remains with the body and may communicate with the living. **Sides (on all sides),** FANG: limits, boundaries; square, surface of the earth extending to the four cardinal points; everywhere.

Three, SAN: number three, third time or place; active phases of a cycle; superlative; beginning of repetition. **Years revolved,** NIEN: number of years elapsed; a person's age; contrasts with **year's time,** SUI, length of time in a year. **Control,** K'O: command; check, impede, prevail, obstruct, repress; adequate, able. The ideogram: roof beams support a house, controlling the structure.

Small People, HSIAO JEN: lowly, common, humble; those who adjust to circumstances with the flexibility of the small; effect of the small within an individual; keyword. **Avail of,** YUNG: take advantage of; benefit from, profit by; use for a specific purpose; apply to advantage. The ideogram: to divine and center, applying divination to central concerns.

b) **Weariness,** PAI: fatigue; debilitated, exhausted, distressed; weak.

Six at fourth

a) A token: possessing clothes in tatters.
Completing the day, a warning.

b) Completing the day, a warning.
Possessing a place to doubt indeed.

You are in the middle of a difficult passage. Things could change in a minute. Don't relax yet. Be vigilant and all will come out well.

Associated Contexts a) **Token,** HSÜ: halves of a torn piece of silk which identify the bearers when joined. **Clothes,** YI: upper body garments; dress; cover, husk. **In tatters,** JU: worn-out garments, used for padding or stopping leaks.

Day/sun, JIH: actual sun and the time of a sun-cycle, a day. **Warn,** CHIEH: alert, alarm, put on guard; caution, inform; guard against, refrain from (as in a diet). The ideogram: spear held in both hands, warning enemies and alerting friends.

b) **Place,** SO: where something belongs or comes from; residence, dwelling; habitual focus or object. **Doubt,** YI: suspect, distrust; dubious; surmise, conjecture.

Nine at fifth

a) The Eastern neighbor slaughters cattle.
Not thus the Western neighbor's dedicated offering.
The substance: accepting one's blessing.

b) The Eastern neighbor slaughters cattle.
Not thus the Western neighbor's season indeed.
The substance: accepting one's blessing.
Auspicious, the great coming indeed.

Looking back you can see how real hidden worth is blessed and recognized. Don't try to impress people. The sincerity of your feeling and your dedication to it are what count most. Be yourself. Accept your blessings. Heaven holds out its mandate.

Associated Contexts a) **East,** TUNG: corresponds to Spring, YÜAN, and the Woody Moment, stirs-up and germinates new life-cycle; place of honor and the person in it. **Neighbor,** LIN: person living nearby; extended family; assist, support. **Slaughter,** SHA: kill, murder, execute; hunt game; mow grass. **Cattle,** NIU: ox, bull, cow, calf; kine; power and strength of work animals.

Thus, JU: as, in this way. **West,** HSI: corresponds to autumn, Harvest and the Streaming Moment; begins the yin hemicycle of the Universal Compass. **Dedicate,** YO: offering at the spring equinox, when stores were low; offer a sacrifice with limited resources. The ideogram: spring and thin. **Offer,** CHI: gifts to gods and spirits. The ideogram: hand, meat and worship.

Substance, SHIH: real, strong, full; results, fruits, possessions; essence; honest, sincere. The ideogram: string of coins under a roof, riches in the house. **Accept,** SHOU: accept, make peace with, agree to; at rest, satisfied; patient. **Bless,** FU: heavenly gifts; make happy; spiritual power and goodwill. The ideogram: spirit and plenty, heavenly gifts in abundance.

b) **Season,** SHIH: quality of the time; the right time, opportune, in harmony; planning in accord with the time; seasons of the year. The ideogram: sun and temple, time as sacred.

Great, TA: big, noble, important, very; orient the will toward a self-imposed goal, impose direction; ability to lead or guide your life; contrasts with small, HSIAO, flexible adaptation to what crosses your path; keyword. Image of Hexagrams 14, 26, 28, 34. **Come,** LAI, and **go,** WANG, describe the stream of time as it flows from future through present to past; come, LAI, indicates what is approaching; move toward, arrive at; keyword.

Six above

a) **Soaking one's head.**
Adversity.

b) **Soaking one's head, adversity.**
Wherefore permitting lasting indeed?

You have gotten yourself in too deep. You are faced with dangers you don't have the means to confront. Why go on like this?

Associated Contexts a) **Soak,** JU: damp, wet; immerse, steep; stain, pollute, blemish; urinate on. **Head,** SHOU: literal head; leader, foremost; subject headings; beginning, model; superior, upper, front.

Adversity, LI: danger; threatening, malevolent demon. This has two aspects: grind, sharpen, improve, perfect, stimulate; and: poisonous, sinister, cruel, contrary. It indicates a spirit or ghost that seeks revenge by inflicting suffering upon the living. Pacifying or exorcizing such a spirit can have a healing effect. The ideogram: sheltering cliff and stinging insect.

b) **Wherefore,** HO: interrogative: why? for what reason? what is? and affirmation: therefore, for that reason. **Permit,** K'O: possible because in harmony with an inherent principle. The ideogram: mouth and breath, silent consent. **Last,** CHIU: long, protracted; enduring.

NOT YET FORDING ▮ *WEI CHI*

On the edge of a change; gather your energy, everything is possible; wait for the right moment.

Not Yet Crossing describes your situation in terms of being on the verge of an important change. Its symbol is standing on the edge of a river, getting ready to begin an important passage. The way to deal with it is to gather your energy to make this decisive new move. Make an offering and you will succeed. You are about to launch a plan, cross the river or overcome an obstacle. The possibilities are great. Be sure your plans are in order and that you have accumulated enough energy to make the crossing without getting stuck. This is pleasing to the spirits. Through it they will give you success, effective power and the capacity to bring the situation to maturity. Don't be like the small fox that gets almost across the river and then soaks her tail in the mud of the opposite shore. That would leave you with nowhere to go and nothing to do that would help you.

● *Image of the Situation*

> **Not yet Fording, Growing.**
> **The small fox, a muddy Ford.**
> **Soaking one's tail:**
> **No advantageous direction.**

Associated Contexts **Not yet,** WEI: temporal negative; incomplete, has not yet occurred; contrary of already, CHI. **Ford,** CHI: cross a river at a ford or shallow place; overcome an obstacle, embark on a course of action; help, relieve; cease. The ideogram: water and level, running smooth over a flat bottom. **Grow,** HENG: success through a sacrifice; pervade, persevere; bring to full growth; enjoy; vigorous, effective; second stage of the Time Cycle.

Small, HSIAO: little, common, unimportant; adapting to what crosses your path; ability to move in harmony with the vicissitudes of life; contrasts with great, TA, self-imposed theme or goal; keyword. Image of Hexagrams 9 and 62. **Fox,** HU: crafty, shape-changing animal; used by spirits, often female; ambivalent night-spirit that can create havoc and bestow abundance. **Mud,** HSI: ground left wet by water, muddy shores; danger;

shed tears; nearly. **Soak** , JU: immerse, steep; damp, wet; stain, pollute, blemish; urinate on. **One's/one**, CH'I: third person pronoun; also: it/its, he/his, she/hers, they/theirs. **Tail**, WEI: animal's tail; last, extreme; remnants, unimportant.

No advantageous direction, WU YU LI: no plan or direction is advantageous; in order to take advantage of the situation, do not impose a direction on events.

● *Outer and Inner Aspects*

☲ **Radiance**: Fire and brightness radiate light and warmth, attached to their support; congregating people see and become aware. **Radiance** ends the yang hemicycle, consuming action in awareness.

Connection to the outer: light, heat, consciousness bring continual change, the Fiery Moment. **Radiance** spreads outward, congregating, becoming aware and changing.

☵ **Gorge**: Stream ventures and falls into the gorge, flowing on through toil and danger. **Gorge** ends the yin hemicycle by leveling and dissolving forms.

Connection to the inner: flooding and leveling dissolve direction and shape, the Streaming Moment. **Gorge** ventures, falls, toils and flows on.

Inner venturing blocks outer congregating, **not yet** accumulating the energy necessary to **ford** the stream of events.

● *Hidden Possibility*

Nuclear trigrams **Gorge**, K'AN, and **Radiance**, LI, result in Nuclear Hexagram 63, **Already Fording**, CHI CHI. Accumulating energy for an important move by **not yet fording** is contrasted with being **already** engaged in **fording** the stream of events.

● *Sequence*

Beings not permitted exhaustion indeed.
Accepting this lets you use Not yet Fording completed in truth.

Associated Contexts **Being(s)**, WU: creature, thing, any single being; matter, substance, essence; nature of things. **Not permitting**, PU K'O: not possible; contradicts an inherent principle. The ideogram: mouth and breath, silent consent. **Exhaust**, CH'IUNG: bring to an end; limit, extremity;

destitute; investigate exhaustively; end without a new beginning. The ideogram: cave and naked person, bent with disease or old age. **Indeed,** YEH: intensifier, connective; indicates comment on previous statement.

Accepting ... use: activating this hexagram depends on understanding and accepting the previous statement. **Complete,** CHUNG: end of a cycle that begins the next; last, whole, all; contrasts with exhaust, CH'IUNG: final end. The ideogram: silk cocoons, follow and ice, winter linking one year with the next. **In truth,** YEN: statement is complete and correct.

- *Contrasted Definitions*

> Already Fording: setting right indeed.
> Not yet Fording: manhood exhausted indeed.

Associated Contexts **Already,** CHI: completed, done, has occurred; past tense, contrary of not-yet, WEI. **Already Fording** is the Image of Hexagram 63. **Set right,** TING: settle, fix, put in place; at rest, repose.

Man(hood), NAN: a man; what is inherently male. The ideogram: fields and strength, hard labor in the fields.

- *Symbol Tradition*

> Fire located above stream. Not yet Fording.
> A chün tzu uses considering to mark off the beings residing on all sides.

Associated Contexts **Fire,** HUO: warming and consuming aspect of burning; fire and brightness are the Symbols of the trigram Radiance, LI. **Locate(in),** TSAI: live in, dwell, reside; belong to, involved with, depend on; within. The ideogram: earth and persevere, place on the earth. **Above,** SHANG: anything above, in all senses; higher, upper, outer; upper trigram; opposite of below, HSIA. **Stream,** SHUI: flowing water; fluid, dissolving; river, tide, flood; the Symbol of the trigram Gorge, K'AN. The ideogram: rippling water.

Chün tzu: ideal of a person who uses divination to order his/her life in accordance with tao rather than wilful intention; keyword. **Use(of),** YI: make use of, by means of, owing to; employ, make functional. **Consider,** SHEN: act carefully, seriously; cautious, attentive, circumspect; still, quiet, sincere. The ideogram: heart and true. **Mark off,** PIEN: distinguish by dividing; mark off a plot of land; frame which divides a bed from its stand; discuss and dispute. The ideogram: knife and acrid, biting division. **Reside(in),** CHÜ: dwell, live in, stay; sit down, fill an office; settled parts of

a country. The ideogram: body and seat. **Sides (on all sides)**, FANG: limits, boundaries; square, surface of the earth extending to the four cardinal points; everywhere.

● *Image Tradition*

> **Not yet Fording, Growing. [I]**
> **Supple acquiring the center indeed.**
>
> **The small fox, a muddy Ford. [II]**
> **Not yet issuing forth from the center indeed.**
> **Soaking one's tail:**
> **No advantageous direction.**
> **Not continuing, completing indeed.**
>
> **Although not an appropriate situation. [III]**
> **Strong and Supple corresponding indeed.**

Associated Contexts **[I] Supple**, JOU: quality of the opened lines; flexible, pliant, tender, adaptable. **Acquire**, TE: obtain the desired object; wish for, desire covetously; gains, possessions. The ideogram: go and obstacle, going through obstacles to the goal. **Center**, CHUNG: inner, central; put in the center; middle, stable point enabling you to face inner and outer changes; middle line of trigram. The ideogram: field divided in two equal parts. Image of Hexagram 61.

[II] Issue forth(from), CH'U: emerge from, come out of, proceed from, spring from; the Action of the trigram Shake, CHEN, contrary of enter, JU. The ideogram: stem with branches and leaves emerging.

  Continue, HSÜ: carry on what another began; succeed to, join on, attach to; keep up, follow.

[III] Although, SUI: even though, supposing that, if, even if. **Appropriate**, TANG: suitable; opportune, convenient; adequate, competent; equal to; whole lines in uneven places and opened lines in even places. **Situation**, WEI: place or seat according to rank; post, position, command; right, proper; established, arranged. The ideogram: person and stand, servants in their places.

  Strong and Supple, KANG JOU: field of creative tension between the whole and opened lines and their qualities; field of psychic movement. **Correspond(to)**, YING: be in agreement or harmony; resonate together, invoke and fulfil each other; answer to, suitable; relation between the lines

(1:4, 2:5, 3:6) when they form the pair opened and whole, supple and strong. The ideogram: heart and obey.

● *Transforming Lines*

Initial six

a) **Soaking one's tail.**
   Distress.

b) **Soaking one's tail.**
   Truly not knowing the end indeed.

You start too soon and fall into the water. You don't understand yet, so hold back.

Associated Contexts a) **Distress,** LIN: distress, shame, regret, humiliation; aware of having lost the right track; leads to repenting, HUI, correcting the direction of mind and life.

b) **Truly,** YI: statement is true and precise. **Know,** CHIH: understand, perceive, remember; informed, aware, wise. The ideogram: arrow and mouth, words focused and swift. **End,** CHI: last or highest point; final, extreme; on the verge; ridgepole of a house.

Nine at second

a) **Pulling back one's wheels.**
   Trial: auspicious.

b) **Nine at second, Trial: auspicious.**
   Centering using moving and correcting indeed.

Everything is loaded, but don't start yet. By restraining your eager desires, you can truly open the way. Think about what you want in this matter. You are not quite ready yet. Let yourself be lured into action.

Associated Contexts a) **Pull back,** YI: pull or drag something towards you; drag behind, take by the hand; leave traces. **Wheel,** LUN: disk, circle, round; revolution, circuit; rotate, roll, by turns.
   Trial, CHEN: inquiry by divination and its result; righteous, firm; separating wheat from chaff; the kernel, the proven core; fourth stage of the Time Cycle. The ideogram: pearl and divination. **Auspicious,** CHI: leads to the experience of meaning; favorable, propitious, advantageous,

appropriate; keyword. The ideogram: scholar and mouth, wise words of a sage.

b) **Move,** HSING: move or move something; motivate, emotionally moving; walk, act, do. The ideogram: stepping left then right. **Correct,** CHENG: rectify deviation or one-sidedness; proper, straight, exact, regular; constant, rule, model. The ideogram: stop and one, hold to one thing.

Six at third

a) Not yet Fording, chastising: pitfall.
Advantageous to step into the Great River. Harvesting.

b) Not yet Fording, chastising: pitfall.
Situation not appropriate indeed.

On the edge of the great move. Don't try to discipline people or set everything in order. Step into the river with a clear will and purpose. What you are beginning now will bring all you want.

Associated Contexts a) **Chastise,** CHENG: punish, subjugate, discipline; reduce to order; punishing expedition. The ideogram: step and correct, a rectifying move. **Pitfall,** HSIUNG: leads away from the experience of meaning; stuck and exposed to danger, unable to take in the situation; flow of life and spirit is blocked; unfortunate, baleful; keyword.

Advantageous/Harvest, LI: advantageous, profitable; acute, insightful; benefit, nourish; third stage of the Time Cycle. **Step into the Great River,** SHE TA CH'UAN: consciously moving into the flow of time; enter the stream of life with a goal or purpose; embark on a significant enterprise.

Nine at fourth

a) Trial: auspicious, repenting extinguished.
Shake avails of subjugating souls on all sides.
Three years revolved, possessing gifts in
the great city.

b) Trial: auspicious, repenting extinguished.
Purpose moving indeed.

This is the time to act. The way is open. Your misgivings will simply disappear. Arouse your energy. Get rid of the past. This may take a while, but in the end there will be great achievements. Your entire world will be transformed.

Associated Contexts a) **Trial**, CHEN: inquiry by divination and its result; righteous, firm; separating wheat from chaff; the kernel, the proven core; fourth stage of the Time Cycle. The ideogram: pearl and divination. **Auspicious**, CHI: leads to the experience of meaning; favorable, propitious, advantageous, appropriate; keyword. The ideogram: scholar and mouth, wise words of a sage. **Repenting extinguished**, HUI WANG: previous troubles and consequent remorse will disappear.

Shake, CHEN: arouse, excite, inspire; thunder rising from below; awe, alarm, trembling; fertilizing intrusion. The ideogram: excite and rain. Image of Hexagram 51. **Avail of**, YUNG: take advantage of; benefit from, profit by; use for a specific purpose; apply to advantage. The ideogram: to divine and center, applying divination to central concerns. **Subjugate**, FA: chastise rebels, make dependent; cut down, subject to rule. The ideogram: man and lance, armed soldiers. **Soul**, KUEI: power that creates individual existence; union of volatile-soul, HUN, spiritual and intellectual power, and dense-soul, P'O, bodily strength and movement. The HUN rises after death, the P'O remains with the body and may communicate with the living.

Three, SAN: number three, third time or place; active phases of a cycle; superlative; beginning of repetition. **Years revolved**, NIEN: number of years elapsed; a person's age; contrasts with year's-time, SUI, length of time in a year. **Possess**, YU: in possession of, have, own; opposite of lack, WU. **Gifts**, SHANG: bestow, confer, grant; rewards, gifts; celebrate, take pleasure in. **Great**, TA: big, noble, important, very; orient the will toward a self-imposed goal, impose direction; ability to lead or guide your life; contrasts with small, HSIAO, flexible adaptation to what crosses your path; keyword. Image of Hexagrams 14, 26, 28, 34. **City**, KUO: area of only human constructions; political unit, polis. First of the territorial zones: city, suburbs, countryside, forests.

b) **Purpose**, CHIH: focus of mind and heart; will, inclination, resolve. The ideogram: heart and scholar, high inner resolve, or heart and go, inner determination. **Move**, HSING: move or move something; motivate, emotionally moving; walk, act, do. The ideogram: stepping left then right.

Six at fifth

a) **Trial: auspicious, without repenting.**
A chün tzu's shining.
There is a connection to the spirits. Auspicious.

b) **A chün tzu's shining.**
One's brilliance auspicious indeed.

Act on your plans. The way is open, no sorrow in sight. Your sincere spirit will shine through. Sense what is important. The spirits will help you. The way is open.

Associated Contexts a) **Trial**, CHEN: inquiry by divination and its result; righteous, firm; separating wheat from chaff; the kernel, the proven core; fourth stage of the Time Cycle. The ideogram: pearl and divination. **Auspicious**, CHI: leads to the experience of meaning; favorable, propitious, advantageous, appropriate; keyword. The ideogram: scholar and mouth, wise words of a sage. **Without repenting**, WU HUI: devoid of the sort of trouble that leads to sorrow, regret and the necessity to change your attitude.

's/have(it)/it/them, CHIH: expresses possession, directly or as an object pronoun. **Shine**, KUANG: illuminate; give off brilliant, bright light; honor, glory, éclat; result of action, contrasts with brightness, MING, light of heavenly bodies. The ideogram: fire above person, lifting the light.

There is ... spirits, YU FU: inner and outer are in accord; confidence of the spirits has been captured; sincere, truthful; proper to take action.

b) **One's/one**, CH'I: third person pronoun; also: it/its, he/his, she/hers, they/theirs. **Brilliance**, HUI: sunlight, sunshine, sunbeam; bright, splendid.

Nine above

a) There is a connection to the spirit in drinking liquor.
  Without fault.
  Soaking one's head.
  There is a connection to the spirit in letting go what is passed.

b) Drinking liquor, soaking the head.
  Truly not knowing: articulating indeed.

Associated Contexts a) **Connection to the spirit**, YU FU: inner and outer are in accord; confidence of the spirits has been captured; sincere, truthful; proper to take action. **Drink**, YIN: take in liquid or air; quench thirst, give liquid to; inhale, suck in. **Liquor**, CHIU: alcoholic beverages, distilled spirits; spirit which perfects the good and evil in human nature. The ideogram: liquid above fermenting must, separating the spirits.

Without fault, WU CHIU: no error or harm in the situation. **Head**, SHOU: literal head; leader, foremost; subject headings; beginning, model; superior, upper, front.

Let go, SHIH: lose, omit, miss, fail, let slip; out of control. The ideogram: drop from the hand. **That/what is passed** SHIH: preceding statement, past events.

b) **Truly,** YI: statement is true and precise. **Know,** CHIH: understand, perceive, remember; informed, aware, wise. The ideogram: arrow and mouth, words focused and swift. **Articulate,** CHIEH: separate and distinguish, as well as join, different things; express thought through speech; joint, section, chapter, interval, unit of time; zodiacal sign; moderate, regulate; lit.: nodes on bamboo stalks. Image of Hexagram 60.

PART THREE

周易

CONCORDANCE

CONCORDANCE

A concordance is a tool which has been used to deepen the understanding of some of the world's most important books. The present translation of the *I Ching* makes a Concordance possible for the first time in a Western language. It is an invaluable tool to understand more fully the divinatory context of words and phrases. It also enables you to locate a passage or a hexagram from the memory of a specific word.

Entries in the Concordance are alphabetical, according to the English core words marked in bold in the hexagrams, which translate the Chinese terms. Each sentence in which the term appears is reprinted, along with its hexagram number and location. If, for instance, you remember only a word from an answer given to you by the Oracle and want to find the relevant hexagram again, you can consult the list of phrases in which the word appears. By looking further at other uses of your word, you will acquire a deeper sense of its significance and its relation to the *I Ching* as a whole.

CONCORDANCE TO THE DIVINATORY TEXTS

ABBREVIATIONS

Im	*Image of the Situation*
S	*Sequence*
CD	*Contrasted Definitions*
AE	*Attached Evidences*
ST	*Symbol Tradition*
ImT	*Image Tradition*
1 - 6a/b	*Transforming Lines*

● **Abandon,** YI: leave behind, forget; die; lose through unawareness. The ideogram: go and value, value is gone.

11.2a Not putting off abandoning.
62.Im/ImT Flying bird: abandoning's sound.

● **Abide,** CH'U: rest in, dwell; stop yourself; arrive at a place or condition; distinguish, decide; do what is proper. The ideogram: tiger, stop and seat, powerful movement coming to rest.

9.10 Treading: not abiding indeed.
9.6a/b Already rain, already abiding.
31.3b Truly not abiding indeed.
56.4a/b Sojourning, into abiding.

● **Able,** NENG: enable; ability, power, skill, art; competent, talented; duty, function, capacity. The ideogram: an animal with strong hooves and bones, able to carry and defend.

7.ImT Able to use the crowds correcting:
9.3b Not able correcting the home indeed.
10.3a/b Squinting enabling observing.
10.3a/b Halting enabling Treading.
13.ImT Verily a chün tzu activating enables interpenetrating Below Heaven's purpose.
16.S Possessing the Great and enabling Humbling necessarily Provides for.
26.ImT Ability stopping persisting.
32.ImT Sun[and]Moon acquiring heaven and enabling lasting illumination.
32.ImT The four seasons transforming changes and enabling lasting accomplishment.
32.2b Ability lasting, centering indeed.
34.6a/b Not enabling withdrawing, not enabling releasing.
36.ImT Inside heaviness and enabling correcting one's purpose.

39.ImT Seeing venturing and also enabling stopping.
50.2a Not me able to approach. Auspicious.
54.1a/b Halting enabling treading.
54.2a Squinting enabling observing.

Abound, FENG: abundant, plentiful, copious; ● grow wealthy; at the point of overflowing; exuberant, fertile, prolific; rich in talents, property, friends; fullness, culmination; ripe, sumptuous, fat.
Image of Hexagram 55 and occurs throughout its texts.
55/56.CD Abounding: numerous anteriority indeed.

Above, SHANG: anything above, in all senses; ● higher, upper, outer; upper trigram; opposite of below, HSIA. See also: **Above and Below** and **Supreme Above**
This term occurs in the Symbol Tradition and the Image Tradition of most hexagrams describing the upper trigram and lines. It also occurs at:
6.2b Below origin, above Arguing
6.3b Adhering to the above auspicious indeed.
8.4b Using adhering to the above indeed.
8.5b Commissioning centering above indeed.
9.4b Uniting purposes above indeed.
10.6b Spring auspicious located above.
14.6b Great Possessing the above: auspicious.
16.ST Exalting worship's Supreme Above.
16.6b Dim Providing for located above.
17.6b Exhausting the above indeed.
22.2b Associating with the above, rising indeed.
22.6b Acquiring purpose above indeed.
24.S Above Stripping exhausted, below reversing.
26.3b Uniting purposes above indeed.
27.4b Spreading out shining above indeed.
27.5b Yielding uses adhering to the above indeed.
29/30.CD Above Radiance and below Gorge indeed.
29.6b Six above, letting go tao.
32.6b Rousing Persevering located in the above.
35.3b Moving above indeed.
40.6a A prince avails of shooting a hawk, into the high rampart's above.

41.5b Originating from shielding above indeed.

44.6b Exhausting distress above indeed.

45.3b Ground above indeed.

45.6b The above not yet quiet indeed.

46.S Assembling and the above implies designating's Ascending.

46.1b Uniting purposes above indeed.

46.6b Dim Ascending located in the above.

48.S Confining reaching to the above implies necessarily reversing the below.

48.6b Spring auspicious located in the above.

50.6b Jade rings located above.

54.6b Six above, without substance.

56.5b Overtaking the above indeed.

56.6b Using Sojourning to locate in the above.

57.6b Above exhaustion indeed.

58.6b Six above, protracting Opening.

60.4b Receiving tao above indeed.

61.4b Cutting off the above, sorting indeed.

62.Im Above not proper, below proper.

62.5b Above climaxing indeed.

● **Above and Below,** SHANG HSIA: realm of dynamic interaction between the upper and the lower; the vertical dimension.

4.6b Above and Below yielding indeed.

8.ImT Above and Below corresponding indeed.

9.ImT Supple acquiring the situation and Above and Below corresponding to it.

10.ST A chün tzu uses differentiating Above and Below.

11.ImT Above and Below mingling and one's purpose concording indeed.

12.ImT Above and Below not mingling and Below Heaven without fiefdoms indeed.

14.ImT and Above and Below corresponding to it.

23.3b Letting go Above and Below indeed.

31.S Therefore afterwards possessing Above and Below.

31.S Possessing Above and Below:

52.ImT Above and Below, antagonistic correspondence.

● **Absolutely no(thing),** MO: complete elimination; not any, by no means.

22.3b Completing absolutely nothing: having a mound indeed.

33.2a Absolutely nothing has mastering stimulating.

42.6a/b Absolutely no Augmenting it.

43.2a Absolutely no night time, possessing arms.

50.S Skinning beings implies absolutely nothing like a Vessel.

51.S A lord's implementing implies absolutely nothing like the long living son.

53.5a/b Completing: absolutely nothing has mastering.

56.6b Completing absolutely nothing: having hearing indeed.

Abyss, YÜAN: deep hole or gulf, where backwaters ● eddy and accumulate; whirlpool; deep water.

1.4a/b Maybe capering located in the abyss.

6.ImT Entering into the abyss indeed.

Accept, SHOU: acquiesce, make peace with, agree to; at rest, satisfied; patient.

3-64.S Accepting this lets you use

6.6b Using Arguing accepts submitting.

31.ST A chün tzu uses emptiness to accept people.

35.1b Not yet accepting fate indeed.

35.2a/b Accepting closely woven chain mail: blessing.

47.5b Accepting blessing indeed.

48.3a Together with accepting one's blessing.

48.3b Accepting blessing indeed.

63.5a/b The substance: accepting one's blessing.

Accepting … use: activating this hexagram depends ● on understanding and accepting the previous statement.

This phrase occurs in the Sequence of Hexagrams **3-64.**

Accompany, HSIEH: take or go along with; jointly, ● all at once.

41/42.ImT Associating with the season, accompanying the movement.

Accomplish, CH'ENG: complete, finish, bring ● about; perfect, full, whole; play your part, do your duty; mature. The ideogram: weapon and man, able to bear arms, thus fully developed.

1.ImT The six situations: the season accomplishing.

2.3a Without accomplishing possessing completion.

6.ImT Arguing not permitting accomplishment indeed.

6.3a Without accomplishment.

11.ST The crown prince uses property to accomplish Heaven and Earth's tao.

16.6a Accomplishment: possessing denial.

22.ImT Using changes accomplishing Below Heaven.

30.ImT Thereupon changes accomplishing Below Heaven.

32.ImT The four seasons transforming changes and enabling lasting accomplishment.

32.ImT The all wise person lasting with respect to his tao and Below Heaven the changes accomplishing.

48.6b The great accomplishing indeed.

49.ImT Heaven and Earth Skinning and the four seasons accomplishing.

60.ImT Heaven, Earth: Articulating and the four seasons accomplishing.

Accumulate, CH'U: retain, hoard, gather, herd together; control, restrain; domesticate, tame, train; raise, feed, sustain, bring up. The ideogram: field and black, fertile black soil good for pastures, accumulated through retaining silt.

Image of Hexagrams 9 and 26 and occurs throughout their texts.

7.ST A chün tzu uses tolerating commoners to accumulate crowds.

10.S Beings Accumulating, therefore afterwards possessing

10.CD Small Accumulating: few indeed.

25.CD Great Accumulating: the season indeed.

27.S Beings accumulating therefore afterwards permitting nourishing.

30.Im Growing. Accumulating female cattle. Auspicious.

30.ImT That uses accumulating female cattle, auspicious indeed.

33.3a/b Accumulating servants, concubines, auspicious.

Ache, TS'E: acute pain or grief; pity, sympathy, sorrow, grief.

48.3a Activating my heart aching.

48.3b Moving: aching indeed.

Achieve, KUNG: work done, results; real accomplishment, praise, worth, merit. The ideogram: workman's square and forearm, combining craft and strength.

4.ImT The all wise achieving indeed.

5.ImT Going possesses achievement indeed.

7.3b The great without achievement indeed.

7.6b Using correcting achieving indeed.

17.1a/b Issuing forth from the gate, mingling possesses achievement.

17.4b Brightening achieving indeed.

29.ImT Going possesses achievement indeed.

29.3b Completing without achieving indeed.

32.6b The great without achievement indeed.

39/40.ImT Going possesses achievement indeed.

48.ImT Not yet possessing achievement indeed.

53.ImT Going possessing achievement indeed.

57.4b Possessing achievement indeed.

59.ImT Riding wood possesses achievement indeed.

Acquire, TE: obtain the desired object; wish for, desire covetously; gains, possessions. The ideogram: go and obstacle, going through obstacles to the goal.

2.Im Beforehand delusion, afterwards acquiring.

2.Im/ImT Western South: acquiring partnering.

2.ImT Afterwards yielding acquiring rules.

3.1b The great acquiring the commoners indeed.

6.ImT Solid coming and acquiring the center indeed.

9.ImT Supple acquiring the situation and Above and Below corresponding to it.

11.2a Acquiring honor, into centering moving.

11.2b Enwrapping wasteland, acquiring honor,

12.2b Centering the heart acquiring indeed.

13.ImT Supple acquiring the situation.

13.ImT Acquiring centering and corresponding reaching to Force.

13.6b Purpose not yet acquired indeed.

14.ImT Supple acquiring the dignifying situation, the great centering.

15.6b Purpose not yet acquired indeed.

16.4a The great possesses acquiring.

16.4b Antecedent Provision, the great possesses acquiring.

17.3a Following possessing seeking, acquiring.

18.2b Acquiring centering tao indeed.

18.4b Going, not yet acquiring indeed.

21.ImT Supple acquiring the center and moving above.

21.4a Acquiring a metallic arrow.

21.5a Gnawing parched meat. Acquiring yellow metal.

21.5b Acquiring the appropriate indeed.

22.6b Acquiring purpose above indeed.

23.6a/b A chün tzu acquiring a cart.

25.1b Acquiring purpose indeed.

25.3a Moving people's acquiring:

25.3b Moving people acquiring cattle.

28.2a A venerable husband acquiring his woman consort.

28.5a A venerable wife acquiring her notable

husband.

29.2a/b Seeking, the small acquiring.

29.6a Three year's time, not acquiring. Pitfall.

30.2b Acquiring centering tao indeed.

32.ImT Sun and Moon acquiring heaven and enabling lasting illumination.

32.4b Quietly acquiring the wildfowl indeed.

35.5a/b Letting go, acquiring, no cares.

36.3a Acquiring its great, the head.

36.3b Thereupon acquiring the great indeed.

38.ImT Acquiring the center and corresponding reaching the solid.

39.ImT Going acquires the center indeed.

40.ImT Going acquiring crowds indeed.

40.ImT Thereupon acquiring the center indeed.

40.2a Acquiring a yellow arrow.

40.2b Acquiring centering tao indeed.

41.3a By consequence acquiring his friend.

41.6a Acquiring a servant, without dwelling.

41.6b The great acquiring purpose indeed.

42.5b The great acquiring purpose indeed.

43.2b Acquiring centering tao indeed.

46.5b The great acquiring the purpose indeed.

47.5b Purpose not yet acquired indeed.

48.Im Without losing, without acquiring.

49.ImT Their purposes not mutually acquired.

50.ImT Acquiring the center and corresponding reaching the solid.

50.1a Acquiring a concubine, using one's sonhood.

51.2a The seventh day: acquiring.

51.6b Center not yet acquired indeed.

53.ImT Advancing acquiring the situation.

53.ImT One's situation: solid acquiring the center indeed.

53.4a/b Maybe acquiring one's rafter.

53.5b Acquiring the place desired indeed.

55.S Acquiring one's place to Convert implies necessarily the great.

55.2a Going acquiring doubt, affliction.

56.ImT Supple acquiring the center reaching to the outside and yielding reaching to the solid.

56.2a/b Acquiring a youthful vassal: Trial.

56.4a Acquiring one's own emblem ax.

56.4b Not yet acquiring the situation indeed.

56.4b Acquiring one's own emblem ax.

57.2b Acquiring the center indeed.

59.ImT Supple acquiring the situation reaching to the outside and concording above.

59.2b Acquiring desire indeed.

60.ImT Solid[and]Supple apportioning and solid acquiring the center.

61.ImT Supple located inside and solid acquiring the center.

61.3a Acquiring antagonism.

62.ImT Supple acquiring the center.

63.ImT Supple acquiring the center indeed.

63.2a/b The seventh day: acquiring.

64.ImT Supple acquiring the center indeed.

Activate, WEI: act or cause to act; do, make, manage; make active; attend to, help; because of. ●

1.7b Heavenly actualizing tao not permitting activating the head indeed.

4.6a Not Advantageous: activating outlawry.

10.3a/b Martial people activating: into a Great Chief.

13.ImT Verily a chün tzu activating enables interpenetrating Below Heaven's purpose.

25.ImT Solid originating from the outside coming and activating a lord with respect to the inside.

41.2b Centering using activating purposes indeed.

42.1a Advantageous: availing of activating the great, arousing.

42.4a Harvesting: availing of activating depending on shifting the city.

43.1a Going not mastering, activating faulty.

45.1a Like an outcry, the one handful activates laughing.

48.3a Activating my heart aching.

49.1b Not permitted to use possessing activating indeed.

50.5b Centering uses activating substance indeed.

51.ImT Using activating the offering lord indeed.

53.6a Its feathers permit availing of activating fundamentals.

53.6b Its feathers permit availing of activating.

Actualize tao, TE: realize tao in action; power, ●
virtue; ability to follow the course traced by the ongoing process of the cosmos; keyword. The ideogram: to go, straight, and heart. Linked with acquire, TE: acquiring that which makes a being become what it is meant to be.

1.2b Actualizing tao spreading out throughout indeed.

1.7b Heavenly actualizing tao not permitting activating the head indeed.

2.ST A chün tzu uses munificent actualizing tao

to carry the beings.

2.ImT Actualizing tao uniting without delimiting.

4.ST A chün tzu uses fruiting movement to nurture actualizing tao.

6.3a/b Taking in ancient actualizing tao.

9.ST A chün tzu uses highlighting the pattern to actualize tao.

9.6a Honoring actualizing tao carrying.

9.6b Actualizing tao amassing carrying indeed.

10.AE Treading: actualizing tao's foundation indeed.

12.ST A chün tzu uses parsimonious actualizing tao to cast out heaviness.

14.ImT One's actualizing tao: solid persisting and pattern brightening.

15.AE Humbling: actualizing tao's handle indeed.

16.ST The Earlier Kings used arousing delight to extol actualizing tao.

18.ST A chün tzu uses rousing the commoners to nurture actualizing tao.

18.5b Receiving uses actualizing tao indeed.

24.AE Returning: actualizing tao's root indeed.

26.ST [A chün tzu] uses accumulating one's actualizing tao.

26.ImT A day renewing one's actualizing tao.

29.ST A chün tzu uses rules actualizing tao to move.

32.AE Persevering: actualizing tao's firmness indeed.

32.AE Persevering: using the one actualizing tao.

32.3a/b Not Persevering one's actualizing tao.

32.5a Persevering one's actualizing tao: Trial.

35.ST A chün tzu uses originating enlightening to brighten actualizing tao.

39.ST A chün tzu uses reversing individuality to renovate actualizing tao.

41.AE Diminishing: actualizing tao's adjustment indeed.

42.AE Augmenting: actualizing tao's enriching indeed.

42.5a There is a connection to the spirit, benevolence: my actualizing tao.

42.5b Benevolence: my actualizing tao.

43.ST [A chün tzu uses] residing in actualizing tao, by consequence keeping aloof.

46.ST A chün tzu uses yielding to actualize tao.

47.AE Confining: actualizing tao's marking off indeed.

48.AE The Well: actualizing tao's earth indeed.

53.ST A chün tzu uses residing in eminent actualizing tao to improve the vulgar.

57.AE Ground: actualizing tao's paring indeed.

60.ST [A chün tzu uses] deliberating actualizing tao to move.

Actually, YI: truly, really, at present. The ideogram: ●
a dart and done, strong intention fully expressed.

5.ImT Actually one's righteousness, not confining exhaustion.

7.ImT Actually permitting using kinghood.

7.ImT Actually auspicious, furthermore wherefore faulty?

20.ImT and actually Below Heaven submitting.

23.S Actually involving embellishing, therefore afterwards Growing by consequence used up.

25.S Actually Returning, by consequence not Embroiling.

25.ImT Actually wherefore having it?

31/32.ImT and actually Heaven and Earth, the myriad beings's motives permitting seeing.

34.ImT Actually the correcting Great and Heaven and Earth's motives permitting seeing.

37.ImT Actually correcting Dwelling and Below Heaven set right.

42.5b Actually no questioning it.

45.ImT Actually viewing one's place to assemble.

45.ImT and actually Heaven and Earth, the myriad beings's motives, permitting seeing.

49.3b Furthermore actually wherefore having them.

56.3b Actually truly using injuring.

Actually ... in fact, YI TSAI: stresses the importance ●
of a statement. The ideogram: a dart and done, strong intention fully expressed.

16.ImT Actually Provision's season righteously great in fact.

17.ImT Actually Following the season's righteous great in fact.

25.ImT Actually moving in fact.

27.ImT Actually Jaws's season great in fact.

28.ImT Actually Great Exceeding's season great in fact.

29.ImT Actually venturing's season availing of the great in fact.

33.ImT Actually Retiring's season righteously great in

fact.

38.ImT Actually Polarizing's season availing of the great in fact.

39.ImT Actually knowing in fact.

39.ImT Actually Difficulty's season availing of the great in fact.

40.ImT Actually Loosening's season great in fact.

44.ImT Actually Coupling's season righteously great in fact.

49.ImT Actually Skinning's season great in fact.

56.ImT Actually Sojourning's season righteously great in fact.

58.ImT Actually the commoners encouraged in fact.

● **Add, ERH**: join to something previous; reiterate, repeat; second, double; assistant.

29.4a/b A cup, liquor, a platter added.

● **Adhere(to), TS'UNG**: follow a way, hold to a doctrine, school, or person; hear and comply with, agree to; forced to follow, follower. The ideogram: two men walking, one following the other.

2.3a/b Maybe adhering to kingly affairs:

3.3b Using adhering to wildfowl indeed.

6.3a Maybe adhering to kingly affairs:

6.3b Adhering to the above auspicious indeed.

7.ImT Using the latter poisons Below Heaven and the commoners adhering to it.

8.ImT Yielding adhering to the below indeed.

8.4b Using adhering to the above indeed.

17.1b Adhering to correcting auspicious indeed.

17.6a Thereupon adhering holding fast to it.

24.4b Using adhering to tao indeed.

27.5b Yielding uses adhering to the above indeed.

31.4a Partnering adheres to simply pondering.

32.5b Adhering to the one and completing indeed.

32.5b Adhering to the wife: pitfall indeed.

39.6b Using adhering to valuing indeed.

42.4a/b Notifying the prince, adhering.

49.6b Yielding uses adhering to the chief indeed.

50.1b Using adhering to valuing indeed.

62.3a/b Adhering, maybe killing it.

● **Adjoin, FU**: next to, lean on; join; near, approaching.

23.ST Mountain adjoining with respect to earth. Stripping.

Adjust, HSIU: regulate, repair, clean up, renovate. ●

24.1b Using adjusting individuality indeed.

41.AE Diminishing: actualizing tao's adjustment indeed.

48.4b Adjusting the Well indeed.

51.ST A chün tzu uses anxious fearing to adjust inspecting.

Admonish, CHIEH: make someone obey; rule of ●
conduct, precept, warning. The ideogram: words and warning.

8.5a/b Capital people not admonished.

Adorn, PI: embellish, ornament, deck out, beautify; ●
variegated (flowers); elegant, brilliant; also: energetic, passionate, eager, intrepid; capable of great effort; brave. The ideogram: cowrie shells (money) and flowers, linking ornaments and value.

Image of Hexagram 22 and occurs throughout its texts.

Advance, CHIN: exert yourself, make progress, ●
climb; be promoted; further the development of, augment; adopt a religion or conviction; offer, introduce.

1.4b Advancing, without fault indeed.

5/6.CD Attending: not advancing indeed.

20.3a/b Viewing my birth, advancing, withdrawing.

35.S Prospering implies advancing indeed.

35.ImT Prospering. Advancing indeed.

35.ImT Supple advancing and moving above.

36.S Advancing necessarily possessing a place: injuring.

38.ImT Supple advancing and moving above.

42.ImT Sun advancing without delimiting.

50.ImT Supple advancing and moving above.

53.S Infiltrating implies advancing indeed.

53.ImT Infiltrating's advancing indeed.

53.ImT Advancing acquiring the situation.

53.ImT Advancing uses correcting.

54.S Advancing necessarily possessing a place to Convert.

57.1a/b Advancing, withdrawing.

Advantageous/Harvesting, LI: advantageous, ●
profitable; acute, insightful; benefit, nourish; third stage of the Time Cycle.

Advantageous Trial, LI CHEN: advantageous ●
divination; putting the action in question to the test is beneficial, harvesting.

These terms occur throughout the hexagram text.

Adversity, LI: danger; threatening, malevolent demon. This has two aspects: grind, sharpen, improve, perfect, stimulate; and: poisonous, sinister, cruel, contrary. It indicates a spirit or ghost that seeks revenge by inflicting suffering upon the living. Pacifying or exorcizing such a spirit can have a healing effect. The ideogram: sheltering cliff and stinging insect.

1.3a Nightfall, alarm, like adversity.
6.3a Adversity, completing auspicious.
9.6a The wife, Trial: adversity.
10.5a/b Deciding Treading. Trial: adversity.
18.1a Adversity, completing auspicious.
21.5a Trial: adversity.
21.5b Trial: adversity, without fault.
24.3a/b Pressing Returning. Adversity.
26.1a Possessing adversity.
27.6a/b Antecedent Jaws. Adversity auspicious.
33.1a Retiring tail, adversity.
33.1b Retiring tail's adversity.
33.3a Tied Retiring. Possessing afflicting adversity.
33.3b Tied Retiring's adversity.
34.3a Trial: adversity.
35.4a Trial: adversity.
35.4b Bushy tailed rodents, Trial: adversity.
35.6a Adversity auspicious, without fault.
37.3a Repenting, adversity auspicious.
38.4a Adversity, without fault.
43.Im/ImT Connection, crying out, possessing adversity.
44.3a Adversity.
49.3a Chastising: pitfall, Trial: adversity.
51.2a/b Shake coming: adversity.
51.5a/b Shake going, coming adversity.
52.3a Adversity smothers the heart.
53.1a The small son, adversity possessing words.
53.1b The small son's adversity.
56.3a Trial: adversity.
58.5a Possessing adversity.
62.4a/b Going adversity necessarily warning.
63.6a Adversity.
63.6b Soaking one's head, adversity.

Affairs, SHIH: all kinds of personal activity; matters at hand; business, occupation; manage a business, case in court.

2.3a/b Maybe adhering to kingly affairs:
6.ST A chün tzu uses arousing affairs to plan beginning.
6.1a/b Not a perpetual place, affairs.

6.3a Maybe adhering to kingly affairs:
18.S Using rejoicing Following people implies necessarily possessing affairs.
18.S Corrupting implies affairs indeed.
18.ImT Going possesses affairs indeed.
18.6a/b Not affairs, kingly feudatories.
18.6a Honoring highness: one's affair.
19.S Possessing affairs and afterwards permitting the great.
29.ST [A chün tzu uses] repeating to teach affairs.
33.3b Not permitting Great Affairs indeed.
38.Im Polarizing, Small Affairs auspicious.
38.ImT That uses Small Affairs auspicious.
38.ImT Heaven, Earth, Polarizing and one's affairs concording indeed.
38.ImT The myriad beings Polarizing and their affairs sorted indeed.
41.1a/b Climaxing affairs, swiftly going.
42.1b The below, not munificent affairs indeed.
42.3a/b Augmenting's availing of pitfall affairs.
46.4b Yielding affairs indeed.
51.5a Intention without losing possesses affairs.
51.5b One's affairs located in the center.
55.3b Not permitting Great Affairs indeed.
57.ST A chün tzu uses distributing fate to move affairs.
62.Im Permitting Small Affairs. Not permitting Great Affairs.
62.ImT That uses Small Affairs, auspicious indeed.
62.ImT That uses not permitting Great Affairs indeed.

Affection, AI: love, show affection; benevolent feelings; kindness, regard.

37.5b Mingling mutual affection indeed.

Afflict, CHI: sickness, disorder, defect, calamity; injurious; pressure and consequent anger, hate or dislike. The ideogram: sickness and dart, a sudden affliction.

16.5a Trial: affliction.
16.5b Six at fifth, Trial: affliction.
24.Im Issuing forth, entering, without affliction.
24.ImT That uses issuing forth, entering, without affliction.
25.5a Disentangling's affliction.
33.3a Tied Retiring. Possessing afflicting adversity.
33.3b Possessing afflicting weariness indeed.

36.3a Not permitting affliction: Trial.

41.4a/b Diminishing one's affliction.

50.2a/b My companion possesses affliction.

55.2a Going acquiring doubt, affliction.

58.4a Chain mail afflicting: possessing rejoicing.

Affluence, FU: rich, abundant; wealth; enrich, provide for; flow toward, accrue.

9.5a Affluence: using one's neighbor.

9.5b Not solitary affluence indeed.

11.4a Not affluence: using one's neighbor.

11.4b Fluttering, fluttering: not affluence.

15.5a Not affluence: using one's neighbor.

25.2b Not yet affluence indeed.

37.4a/b Affluence Dwelling, the great auspicious.

46.6b Dissolving, not affluence indeed.

Afoot, T'U: travel on foot; footman, foot soldier; follower, disciple; ruffian, bond servant.

22.1a/b Stowing away the chariot and afoot.

After(wards)/later, HOU: come after in time, subsequent; put oneself after; the second; attendants, heirs, successors, posterity. See also: **Therefore ... afterwards**

This term occurs throughout the hexagram texts.

Age (the), SHIH: an age, an epoch, a generation; the world, mankind; the time, as "in the time of."

28.ST [A chün tzu uses] retiring from the age without melancholy.

Agencies, CH'I: fluid energy, configurative power, vital force; interacts with essence, CHING, to produce things and beings. The ideogram: vapor and rice, heat and moisture producing substance.

31.ImT The two agencies influencing correspondence use mutual associating.

Ail, CHIU: chronic disease; disheartened, distressed by.

10.ImT Treading the supreme situation and not ailing.

All, see: **Sides, on all sides**

All wise, SHENG: intuitive universal wisdom; mythical sages; holy, sacred; mark of highest distinction. The ideogram: ear and inform, one who knows all from a single sound.

4.ImT The all wise achieving indeed.

16.ImT The all wise person uses yielding stirring up.

20.ImT The all wise person uses spirit tao to set up teaching.

27.ImT The all wise person nourishes eminence used to extend to the myriad commoners.

31.ImT The all wise person influencing the people at heart and Below Heaven harmony evening.

32.ImT The all wise person lasting with respect to his tao and Below Heaven the changes accomplishing.

50.ImT The all wise person Growing uses presenting to the Supreme Above.

50.ImT and great Growing uses nourishing all wise eminences.

Ally, see: **Matrimonial allying**

Almost, CHI: nearly, about to; subtle, almost imperceptible; the first sign.

3.3a A chün tzu almost not thus stowing away.

9.6a The moon almost facing.

54.5a The moon almost facing, auspicious.

61.4a The moon almost facing.

Alone, KU: solitary; without a protector; fatherless, orphan like; as a title: the only, unequalled. See also: **Living alone**

38.4a/6a Polarizing alone.

Already, CHI: completed, done, has occurred; past tense, contrary of not yet, WEI.

Image of Hexagram 63 and occurs throughout its texts.

9.6a/b Already rain, already abiding.

19.3a/b Already grieving over it:

29.5a Merely already evened.

Although, SUI: even though, supposing that, if, even if.

3.1b Although a stone pillar, purpose moving correctly indeed.

5.2b Although the small possesses words, using completing auspicious indeed.

5.6b Although not an appropriate situation, not yet the great let go indeed.

6.1b Although the small possesses words, one's differentiation brightening indeed.

21.ImT Although not an appropriate situation, Advantageous:

31.2b Although a pitfall, residing auspicious.

47.4b Although not an appropriate situation, possessing associating indeed.

51.6b Although a pitfall, without fault.

55.1a/b Although a decade, without fault.

64.ImT Although not an appropriate situation.

Altogether, CHIEH: all, the whole; the same sort, all alike; entirely.

11.4b Altogether letting go substance indeed.

32.ImT Strong and Supple altogether corresponding. Persevering.

40.ImT Thunder and Rain arousing and the hundred fruits, grasses, trees, altogether seedburst boundary.

55.ST Thunder, lightning, altogether culminating.

57.ImT Supple altogether yielding reaching the solid.

● **Amass,** CHI: hoard, accumulate, pile up, store up, add up, increase.

9.6b Actualizing tao amassing carrying indeed.

14.2b Amassing centering, not destroying indeed.

46.ST [A chün tzu uses] amassing the small to use the high great.

● **Amble,** HSÜ: walk quietly and carefully; leisurely, tardy, slow; composed, dignified.

47.4a/b Coming, ambling, ambling.

47.5a/b Thereupon ambling possesses stimulating.

● **Amend,** KAI: correct, reform, make new, alter, mend. The ideogram: self and strike, fighting your own errors.

42.ST [A chün tzu uses] possessing excess, by consequence amending.

48.Im/ImT Amending the capital, not amending the Well.

49.4a/b Amending fate auspicious.

● **Ancestry,** TSUNG: clan, kin, origin; those who bear the same surname; ancestral hall and tablets; honor, revere; a doctrine; contrasts with predecessor, K'AO, individual ancestors.

13.2a/b Concording People into ancestry.

38.5a/b Your ancestor gnawing flesh.

51.ImT Issuing forth permits using guarding the ancestral temple, field altar, offertory millet.

63.3a The high ancestor subjugating souls on all sides.

● **Ancient,** CHIU: of old, long before; worn out, spoiled; defunct.

6.3a Taking in ancient actualizing tao. Trial.

6.3b Taking in ancient actualizing tao.

48.1a/b The ancient Well without wildfowl.

● **Anger,** FEN: resentment; cross, wrathful; irritated at, indignant. The ideogram: heart and divide, the heart dividing people.

41.ST A chün tzu uses curbing anger to block the appetites.

Another, PEI: yet one more; the other party; exclude, leave out. ●

62.5a A prince, a string arrow grasping another located in a cave.

Antagonistic, TI: opposed and equal; competitor, ● enemy; a contest between equals.

13.3b Antagonistic solid indeed.

52.ImT Above and Below, antagonistic correspondence.

61.3a Acquiring antagonism.

Antecedent, YU: come before as origin and cause; ● through, by, from; depend on; permit, enter by way of.

16.4a Antecedent Provision.

16.4b Antecedent Provision, the great possesses acquiring.

27.6a/b Antecedent Jaws. Adversity auspicious.

Anterior/past, KU: come before as cause; formerly, ● ancient; reason, purpose, intention; grievance, quarrel, dissatisfaction, sorrow, mourning resulting from previous causes and intentions; situation leading to a divination.

16.ImT Anterior Heaven and Earth thus having it.

16.ImT Anterior Sun and Moon not exceeding.

17/18.CD Following: without anteriority indeed.

22.ImT Anterior Growth.

22.ImT The anterior small, Advantageous: having a direction to go.

30.ImT Anterior Growing.

34.ImT Solid uses stirring up. Anterior Invigorating.

39.2a In no way body's anteriority.

45.ImT Anterior assembling indeed.

49/50.CD Skinning: departing anteriority indeed.

55/56.CD Abounding: numerous anteriority indeed.

55.ImT Brightness using stirring up. Anterior Abounding.

Anxious, K'UNG: apprehensive, alarmed, agitated; ● suspicious of. The ideogram: heart and sick, agitated within.

51.ST A chün tzu uses anxious fearing to adjust inspecting.

51.ImT/1b Anxiety involving blessing indeed.

Appetites, YÜ: drives, instinctive craving; wishes, passions, desires, aspirations; long for, seek ardently; covet.

27.4a His appetites: pursuing, pursuing.

41.ST A chün tzu uses curbing anger to block the appetites.

Apportion, FEN: divide for distribution; sort out; allot to.

21.ImT Strong and Supple apportioning.

22.ImT Above apportioning solid and patterning supple.

60.ImT Strong and Supple apportioning and solid acquiring the center.

Apprehensive, CH'OU: anticipating adversity, afraid of what approaches; chagrined, grieved. The ideogram: heart and autumn, dreading the coming winter.

35.2a Prospering thus, apprehensive thus.

Approach, CHI: come near to, advance toward; about to do; soon.

3.3a/b Approaching stag, lacking precaution.

6.4a/b Returning, approaching fate.

43.Im/ImT Not Advantageous: approaching arms.

50.2a Not me able to approach. Auspicious.

56.2a Sojourning, approaching a resting place.

Appropriate, TANG: suitable; opportune, convenient; adequate, competent; equal to; whole lines in uneven places and opened lines in even places.

This term occurs in the Image Tradition and in the Transforming Lines b) of most hexagrams.

Apron, SHANG: ceremonial garment; skirt, clothes; curtains of a carriage. The ideogram: garment and manifest, clothing as display.

2.5a/b A yellow apron. Spring auspicious.

Argue, SUNG: dispute, plead in court, contend before a ruler, demand justice; wrangles, quarrels, litigation. The ideogram: words and public, public disputation.

Image of Hexagram 6 and occurs throughout its texts.

Arm, KUNG: the arms as the body's instruments; staunch supporter; officer, minister of state.

55.3a/b Severing one's right arm.

Arms, JUNG: weapons; armed people, soldiers; military, violent. The ideogram: spear and armor, offensive and defensive weapons.

13.3a/b Hiding away arms, into the thickets.

40.3b Originating from my involving arms.

43.Im/ImT Not Advantageous: approaching arms.

43.2a Absolutely no night time, possessing arms.

43.2b Possessing arms, no cares.

45.ST A chün tzu uses eliminating arms to implement.

Arouse, TSO: stir up, stimulate, rouse from inactivity; generate; appear, arise. The ideogram: person and beginning. See also: **Rouse**

6.ST A chün tzu uses arousing affairs to plan beginning.

16.ST The Earlier Kings used arousing delight to extol actualizing tao.

30.ST Brightness doubled arousing Radiance.

40.ST Thunder, Rain, arousing. Loosening.

40.ImT Heaven and Earth Loosening and Thunder and Rain arousing.

40.ImT Thunder and Rain arousing and the hundred fruits, grasses, trees, altogether seedburst boundary.

42.1a Advantageous: availing of activating the great, arousing.

Array, PAN: classify and display; arrange according to rank; assign to a group, as soldiers to their units. The ideogram: knife between two gems, separating values.

3.2a/4a/6a Riding a horse, arraying thus.

Arrest, TS'UI: stop, drive back, repress; force obedience, overpower, impel; scorn; destroy; break.

35.1a/b Prospering thus, arresting thus.

Arrow, SHIH: arrow, javelin, dart; swift, direct as an arrow; marshal together. See also: **String arrow**

21.4a Acquiring a metallic arrow.

40.2a Acquiring a yellow arrow.

56.5a The one arrow extinguishing.

Articulate, CHIEH: separate and distinguish, as well as join, different things; express thought through speech; joint, section, chapter, interval, unit of time; zodiacal sign; moderate, regulate; lit.: nodes on bamboo stalks.

Image of Hexagram 60 and occurs throughout its texts.

4.2b Strong and Supple articulating indeed.

27.ST [A chün tzu uses] articulating to drink[and]take in.

37.3b Letting go Dwelling articulating indeed.

39.5b Using centering articulating indeed.

50.6b Strong and Supple articulating indeed.

59.CD Articulating: stopping indeed.

61.S Articulating and trusting it.

64.6b Truly not knowing articulating indeed.

Ascend, SHENG: go up; climb step by step; rise in office; advance through effort; accumulate; bring out and fulfil; lit.: a measure for fermented liquor, ascension as distillation.

Image of Hexagram 46 and occurs throughout its texts.

13.3a Ascending one's high mound.

29.ImT Heaven venturing, not permitting ascending indeed.

45.CD Ascending: not coming indeed.

47.S Ascending and not climaxing necessarily Confines.

Ask why, HO: interjection: why? how? why not?; interrupt with questions; intimidate, heckle. The ideogram: speak and beg, demanding an answer.

41.Im/ImT Asking why having availing of.

Assail, T'U: rush against; abrupt attack; suddenly stricken; insolent, offensive.

30.4a/b Assailing thus, its coming thus.

Assemble, CHÜ: gather, bring together, collect; call to assembly; dwell together, converge; meeting, reunion, collection; meeting place, dwelling place. The ideogram: three (= many) people.

45.S Beings mutually meeting and afterwards assembling.

45.S Clustering implies assembling indeed.

45/46.CD Clustering: assembling and Ascending: not coming indeed.

45.ImT Clustering, assembling indeed.

45.ImT Anterior assembling indeed.

45.ImT Assembling uses correcting indeed.

45.ImT Actually viewing one's place to assemble.

46.S Assembling and the above implies designating's Ascending.

Assign to, LIEH: place according to rank; arrange in order; distinguish, separate.

52.3a Assigned to one's loins:

Associate(with), YÜ: consort with, combine; companions; group, band, company; agree with, comply, help. The ideogram: pair of hands reaching downward meets a pair of hands reaching upward, helpful association.

2.ImT Thereupon associating sorting movement.

6.ST Heaven associating with stream, contradicting movements.

10.3b Not the stand to use associating with moving indeed.

13.ST Heaven associating with fire.

14.S Associating with People Concording implies beings necessarily converting in truth.

17.2b Nowhere joining associating indeed.

19/20.CD Maybe associating with, maybe seeking.

22.2b Associating with the above, rising indeed.

23.2b Not yet possessing associating indeed.

25.ST Below heaven thunder moving. Beings associating

28.2b Exceeding uses mutual associating indeed.

31.ImT The two agencies influencing correspondence use mutual associating.

32.ImT Thunder, wind, mutually associating.

33.ImT Associating with the season moving indeed.

41/42.ImT Associating with the season, accompanying the movement.

44.ImT Not permitting associating with long living indeed.

47.4b Although not an appropriate situation, possessing associating indeed.

48.2b Without associating indeed.

52.ImT Not mutually associating indeed.

55.ImT Associating with the season: dissolving pause.

56.3b Using Sojourning to associate with the below.

61.2a Myself associating, simply spilling it.

62.ImT Associating with the season moving indeed.

Attach, HSI: fasten to, bind, tie; retain, continue; keep in mind, emotionally attached.

12.5a Attaching into bushy mulberry trees.

25.3a Maybe attaching's cattle.

44.1a/b Attaching into a metallic chock.

Attack, KUNG: fight with; aggression; go to work, apply to; rouse by criticizing, put in order; stimulate vital power; urgent desire. The ideogram: toil and strike.

13.4a Nothing controlling attacking.

Attend, HSÜ: take care of, look out for, care or service of; turn your mind to; needs; obstinate, fixed on; wait, await, wait on; hesitate, doubt. The ideogram: rain and stopped, compelled to wait, or rain and origin, providing what is needed.

Image of Hexagram 5 and occurs throughout its texts.

6.CD Attending: not advancing indeed.

Audience, CHIEH: be received by higher powers, receive and pass on; follow in office; inherit, as father and son; associate with. The ideogram: hand and concubine, passed on through natural, not legal, ways.

35.Im Day time sun three times an audience.

35.ImT Day time sun three times an audience indeed.

Augment, YI: increase, advance, promote, benefit, strengthen; pour in more; full, superabundant; restorative. The ideogram: water and vessel, pouring in more.

Image of Hexagram 42 and occurs throughout its texts.

15.ST A chün tzu uses reducing the numerous to augment the few.

15.ImT Heavenly tao lessening overfilling and augmenting Humbling.

41.CD Diminishing, Augmenting.

41.ImT Below Diminishing, above augmenting.

41.ImT Diminishing solid, augmenting supple, possessing the season.

41.ImT Diminishing augmenting, overfilling emptiness.

41.2a Nowhere Diminishing, augmenting it.

41.5a Maybe augmenting's ten: partnering's tortoise.

41.6a/b Nowhere Diminishing, augmenting it.

43.S Augmenting and not climaxing necessarily breaks up.

Augury, CHAN: sign, omen; divine by casting lots, sortilege; look at as a sign or augury.

49.5a Not yet an augury, there is a connection to the spirit.

Auspicious, CHI: leads to the experience of meaning; favorable, propitious, advantageous, appropriate; keyword. The ideogram: scholar and mouth, wise words of a sage. This term occurs throughout the hexagram texts.

Auspicious, HSIANG: omen of good luck and prosperity; sign, auspices.

10.6a Observing Treading, predecessors auspicious.

47.3b Not auspicious indeed.

Avail of, YUNG: take advantage of; benefit from, profit by; use for a specific purpose; apply to advantage. The ideogram: to divine and center, applying divination to central concerns. This term occurs throughout the hexagram texts.

Await, TAI: expect, wait for, welcome (friendly or hostile), provide against.

16.AE Used to await violent visitors.

39.1b Proper to await indeed.

53/54.CD Infiltrating: womanhood converting awaits manhood moving indeed.

54.4b Possessing awaiting and moving indeed.

Alarm, T'I: alarmed and cautious; respect, regard, fear; stand in alarm of. The ideogram: heart and versatile, the heart aware of sudden change.

1.3a Nightfall, alarm, like adversity.

6.Im Arguing, there is a connection to the spirit. Blocking alarm.

6.ImT Blocking alarm, centering auspicious.

9.4a Blood departing, alarm issuing forth.

9.4b There is a connection to the spirit, alarm issuing forth.

43.2a Alarm, an outcry.

Ax, see: **Emblem ax**

Axle strap, FU: fastens the body of a cart to axle and wheels.

26.2a/b Carting, stimulating the axle strap.

34.4a Invigorating into the Great: a cart's axle straps.

Back, PEI: spine; opposite of front; behind, rear, hidden; turn the back on; north side; oppose, disobey, transgress. The ideogram: body and north, where the face is south.

52.Im Bound: one's back.

Bag, NANG: sack, purse; put in a bag; property, salary.

2.4a/b Bundled in the bag.

Bar, PI: close a door, stop up a hole; obstruct, exclude, screen. The ideogram: door and hand, closing the door.

24.ST The Earlier Kings used culminating sun to bar the passages.

Bargain, SHANG: argue over prices; consult, deliberate, do business; dealers, travelling merchants; hour before sunrise and sunset. The ideogram: stutter and sentences, repetitive speaking.

24.ST Bargaining sojourners [used culminating sun] not to move.

58.4a Bargaining Opening, not yet soothing.

Barrier, KAN: boundary, limit; fend off, protect; stream, parapet, river bank; shield, defensive armor; the Ten Heavenly Barriers are part of the calendar system.

53.1a The wild geese Infiltrating into the
   barrier.

● **Basket,** K'UANG: open basket; put in baskets;
bottom of a bed.

54.6a A woman receiving a basket without
   substance.

54.6b Receiving an empty basket indeed.

● **Bass,** FU: freshwater fish, said to go in pairs and be
faithful.

48.2a/b The Well: a gully, shooting bass.

● **Bear,** FU: carry on your back; take on a
responsibility; rely on, depend on; loaded down;
burden, duty; math term for minus.

38.6a Seeing pigs bearing mire.

40.3a/b Bearing, moreover riding.

● **Beater,** CH'Ü: servants who drive animals toward
hunters; order people to their places; drive on, whip
up, animate, exhort.

8.5a The king avails of three beaters.

● **Beautiful,** WEI: elegant, classic, fine; luxuriant, lush.

49.6b One's pattern beautiful indeed.

● **Bed,** CH'UANG: sleeping place; couch, sofa, lounge;
bench around a well.

23.1a/b Stripping the bed, using the stand.

23.2a/b Stripping the bed, using marking off.

23.4a/b Stripping the bed, using flesh.

57.2a,6a/b Ground located below the bed.

● **Before(hand)/earlier,** HSIEN: come before in time;
first, at first; formerly, past, previous; begin, go
ahead of.

This term occurs throughout the hexagram texts.

● **Before zenith sun,** SSU JIH: double hour from 9 to
11 a.m., month of June, both symbolized by the
serpent; about to, on the point of the right time,
moment of transformation.

49.Im/ImT Your own day, thereupon
   connection.

49.2a Your own day, thereupon Skinning it.

49.2b Your own day Skinning it.

● **Begin,** SHIH: commence, start, open; earliest, first;
beginning of a time span, ended by completion,
CHUNG. The ideogram: woman and eminent,
beginning new life.

1.ImT The myriad beings's own beginning.

1.ImT Great brightening completing beginning.

2.1b Yin begins solidifying indeed.

3.S Sprouting implies beings's beginning giving
   birth indeed.

3.ImT Strong and Supple beginning mingling
   and heaviness giving birth indeed.

6.ST A chün tzu uses arousing affairs to plan
   beginning.

18.ImT Completing, by consequence possessing
   the beginning.

32.ImT Completing by consequence possessing
   the beginning indeed.

32.1b Beginning seeking depth indeed.

41/42.CD Increasing, decreasing's beginning
   indeed.

54.ImT A person's completion beginning
   indeed.

● **Being(s),** WU: creature, thing, any single being;
matter, substance, essence; nature of things. See
also: **Beings not permitted to use**

1.ImT The myriad beings's own beginning.

1.ImT The kinds: being diffusing forms.

1.ImT Heads issuing forth from the
   multitudinous beings.

2.ST A chün tzu uses munificent actualizing tao
   to carry the beings.

2.ImT The myriad beings's own birth.

2.ImT Field: munificence carrying the beings.

2.ImT The kinds: being conjoining Growing.

3.S Therefore afterwards the myriad beings
   giving birth in truth.

3.S Overfilling Heaven and Earth's interspace
   implies verily the myriad beings.

3.S Sprouting implies beings's beginning giving
   birth indeed.

4.S Beings giving birth necessarily Enveloping.

4.S Being's immaturity indeed.

5.S Being immature not permitting not
   nourishing indeed.

10.S Beings Accumulating, therefore afterwards
   possessing codes.

11.ImT By consequence of that Heaven and
   Earth mingling and the myriad beings
   interpenetrating indeed.

12.ImT By consequence of that Heaven and
   Earth not mingling and the myriad beings
   not interpenetrating indeed.

13.ST A chün tzu uses sorting the clans to mark
   off the beings.

14.S Associating with People Concording
   implies beings necessarily converting in
   truth.

15.ST [A chün tzu uses] evaluating beings to
   even spreading out.

20.S Being great therefore afterwards
   permitting Viewing.

21.ImT Jaws center possesses being.

24.AE Returning: the small and marking off with respect to beings.

25.ST Below heaven thunder moving. Beings associating Disentangling.

25.ST The Earlier Kings used luxuriance suiting the season to nurture the myriad beings.

27.S Beings accumulating therefore afterwards permitting nourishing.

27.ImT Heaven and Earth nourishes the myriad beings.

31.S Therefore afterwards possessing the myriad beings.

31.S Possessing the myriad beings:

31.ImT Heaven and Earth influencing and the myriad beings changing give birth.

31/32.ImT and actually Heaven and Earth, the myriad beings's motives permitting seeing.

37.ST A chün tzu uses words to possess beings and movement to possess perseverance.

37.5a Beings: care auspicious.

38.ImT The myriad beings Polarizing and their affairs sorted indeed.

44.ImT The kinds: beings conjoining composition indeed.

45.S Beings mutually meeting and afterwards assembling.

45.ImT and actually Heaven and Earth, the myriad beings's motives, permitting seeing.

50.S Skinning beings implies absolutely nothing like a Vessel.

54.ImT Heaven and Earth not mingling and the myriad beings not rising.

63.S Possessing Exceeding being implies necessarily Fording.

64.S Beings not permitted exhaustion indeed.

64.ST A chün tzu uses considering to mark off the beings residing on all sides.

- **Beings not permitted to use**: no one is allowed to make use of; nothing can exist by means of.

  This phrase occurs in the Sequence of Hexagrams 12, 13, 22, 24, 29, 33, 34, 35, 40, 52, 53, 60.

- **Belly**, See: **Left belly**

- **Below**, HSIA: anything below, in all senses; lower, inner; lower trigram; opposite of above, SHANG. See also: **Above and Below**, and **Below Heaven**

  This term occurs in the Symbol Tradition and the Image Tradition of most hexagrams describing the lower trigram and lines. It also occurs at:

1.1b Yang located below indeed.

3.1b Using valuing the mean below.

6.2b Below origin, above Arguing.

15.ImT Heavenly tao fording below and shining brightness.

17.3b Below, purpose stowed away indeed.

23.1b Below using submerging indeed.

24.S Above Stripping exhausted, below reversing.

24.2b Using humanity below indeed.

28.1b Supple located below indeed.

28.4b Not sagging, reaching to the below indeed.

29/30.CD Above Radiance and below Gorge indeed.

31.3b A place to hold on to the below indeed.

42.1b The below, not munificent affairs indeed.

47.4b Purpose located below indeed.

48.S Confining reaching to the above implies necessarily reversing the below.

48.1b The below indeed.

56.3b Using Sojourning to associate with the below.

57.2a,6a/b Ground located below the bed.

62.Im Above not proper, below proper.

Below Heaven, T'IEN HSIA: the human world, between heaven and earth. ●

7.ImT Using the latter poisons Below Heaven and the commoners adhering to it.

12.ImT Above and Below not mingling and Below Heaven without fiefdoms indeed.

13.ImT Verily a chün tzu activating enables interpenetrating Below Heaven's purpose.

17.ImT and Below Heaven Following the season.

18.ImT and Below Heaven regulated indeed.

20.ImT Centering correcting uses Viewing Below Heaven.

20.ImT and actually Below Heaven submitting.

22.ImT Using changes accomplishing Below Heaven.

30.ImT Thereupon changes accomplishing Below Heaven.

31.ImT The all wise person influencing the people at heart and Below Heaven harmony evening.

32.ImT The all wise person lasting with respect to his tao and Below Heaven the changes accomplishing.

37.ImT Actually correcting Dwelling and Below Heaven set right.

44.ImT Below Heaven, the great moving indeed.

55.ImT Properly illuminating Below Heaven indeed.

- **Belt**, see: **Pouched belt**
- **Bench**, CHI: low table used to lean on; side table; stool or support.

  59.2a/b Dispersing: fleeing one's bench.

- **Benefits**, LU: pay, salary, income; have the use of; goods received, revenues; official recognition.

  12.ST [A chün tzu uses] not permitting splendor to use benefits.

  43.ST A chün tzu uses spreading out benefits to extend to the below.

- **Benevolence**, HUI: regard for others, humanity; fulfil social duties; unselfish, kind, merciful.

  42.5a/b There is a connection to the spirit, a benevolent heart.

  42.5a There is a connection to the spirit, benevolence: my actualizing tao.

  42.5b Benevolence: my actualizing tao.

- **Bestow**, HSI: grant, confer upon; reward, gift. The ideogram: metal used in coins and insignia.

  6.6a Maybe bestowing's pouched belt.

  7.2a/b The king three times bestowing fate.

  35.Im/ImT The calm feudatory avails of bestowing horses to multiply the multitudes.

- **Big toe**, see: **Thumb**
- **Bin**, TOU: star constellation that dispenses the fates; Big Dipper; measure and container for grain;gauge, hold, contain.

  55.2a,4a/b Sun centering: seeing the Bin.

- **Bind**, LÜAN: tie, connect, take hold of; bent, contracted. The ideogram: hand and connect, binding things.

  9.5a/b There is a connection to the spirit, binding thus.

  61.5a/b There is a connection to the spirit, binding thus.

- **Bird**, NIAO: all feathered animals; associated with the Fiery Moment.

  56.6a A bird burning its nest.

  62.Im Flying bird: abandoning's sound.

  62.ImT Possessing the flying bird's symbol in truth.

  62.ImT Flying bird: abandoning's sound.

  62.1a/b Flying bird: using a pitfall.

  62.6a Flying bird radiating it.

Birth/give birth to, SHENG: produce, beget, grow, bear, arise; life, vitality. The ideogram: earth and sprout.

  2.ImT The myriad beings's own birth.

  3.S Therefore afterwards the myriad beings giving birth in truth.

  3.S Sprouting implies beings' beginning giving birth indeed.

  3.ImT Strong and Supple beginning mingling and heaviness giving birth indeed.

  4.S Beings giving birth necessarily Enveloping.

  20.3a/b Viewing my birth, advancing, withdrawing.

  20.5a/b Viewing my birth.

  20.6a/b Viewing one's birth.

  28.2a A withered willow giving birth to a sprig.

  28.5a/b A withered willow giving birth to flowers.

  31.ImT Heaven and Earth influencing and the myriad beings changing give birth.

  42.ImT Heaven spreading out, earth giving birth.

  46.ST Earth center giving birth to wood.

Bite, HO: close the jaws, bite through, crush between the teeth. The ideogram: mouth and cover, jaws fit together as a lid fits a vessel.

  Image of Hexagram 21 and occurs throughout its texts.

Bitter, K'U: taste corresponding to the Fiery Moment; unpleasant, troublesome, painful affliction; take pains; urgent, pressing; dislike, grieve, mortify.

  60.Im/ImT Bitter Articulating not permitting Trial.

  60.6a/b Bitter Articulating, Trial: pitfall.

Bless, FU: heavenly gifts; make happy; spiritual power and goodwill. The ideogram: spirit and plenty, heavenly gifts in abundance.

  11.3a Into taking in possesses blessing.

  15.ImT Souls[and]Spirits harming overfilling and blessing Humbling.

  35.2a/b Accepting closely woven chain mail: blessing.

  47.5b Accepting blessing indeed.

  48.3a Together with accepting one's blessing.

  48.3b Accepting blessing indeed.

  51.ImT,1b Anxiety involving blessing indeed.

  63.5a/b The substance: accepting one's blessing.

Block, CHIH: obstruct, stop up, close, restrain, fill up.

 6.Im Arguing, there is a connection to the spirit. Blocking alarm.

 6.ImT Blocking alarm, centering auspicious.

 41.ST A chün tzu uses curbing anger to block the appetites.

Blood, HSÜEH: yin fluid that maintains life; money, property.

 2.6a Their blood: indigo, yellow.

 3.6a/b Weeping blood, coursing thus.

 5.4a/b Attending into blood.

 9.4a Blood departing, alarm issuing forth.

 54.6a A notable disembowelling a goat without blood.

 59.6a/b Dispersing one's blood.

Blunder, SHENG: mistake due to ignorance or fault; contrasts with calamity, TSAI, disaster from without. The ideogram: eye and grow, a film clouding sight. See also: **Calamity[and]Blunder**

 6.2a Without blunder.

 25.Im/ImT One in no way correcting: possessing blunder.

 25.6a Disentangling. Moving possessing blunder.

 51.3a Shake moving without blunder.

Body/person KUNG: physical being, power and self expression; contrasts with individuality, SHEN, the total personality.

 4.3a Not possessing the body.

 39.2a In no way body's anteriority.

 51.6a Shake: not into one's body, into one's neighbor.

 52.4b Stopping connoting the body indeed.

 59.3a/b Dispersing one's body.

Bog, NI: wet spongy soil; mire, slush, quicksand; unable to move.

 5.3a/b Attending into bogs.

 48.1a/b The Well: a bog, not taking in.

 51.4a/b Shake: releasing the bog.

Bonds, YO: cords, ropes; contracts, treaties, legal and moral obligations; moderate, restrain, restrict.

 29.4a Letting in bonds originating from the window.

Border, CHI: limit, frontier, line which joins and divides. The ideogram: place and sacrifice, border between human and spirit.

 11.3b Heaven and Earth, the border indeed.

 29.4b Strong and Supple, the border indeed.

 40.1b Strong and Supple's border.

 55.6b The heavenly border, hovering indeed.

Bound, KEN: limit, boundary; encounter an obstacle, stop; still, quiet, motionless; confine, enclose, mark off; turn around to look behind; hard, adamant, obstinate; perverse. The ideogram: eye and person turning round to compare and group what is behind.

 Image of Hexagram 52 and occurs throughout its texts.

Boundary, CHI: border, limit, frontier; confine.

 40.ImT Thunder and Rain arousing and the hundred fruits, grasses, trees, altogether seedburst boundary.

Bow, HU: wooden bow; curved flag pole; curved, arched.

 38.6a Beforehand stretching's bow.

 38.6a Afterwards stimulating's bow.

Brace/jawbones, FU: support, consolidate, reinforce, strengthen, stiffen, prop up, fix; steady, firm, rigid; help, rescue; support the speaking mouth. The ideogram: cart and great.

 8.ImT Grouping bracing indeed.

 11.ST [The crown prince uses] bracing to mutualize Heaven and Earth's propriety.

 28.3b Not permitted to use possessing bracing indeed.

 31.6a/b Conjoining one's jawbones, cheeks, tongue.

 52.5a/b Bound: one's jawbones.

Break up, CHÜEH: streams diverging; break through an obstacle and scatter; separate, break into parts; cut or bite through; decide, pass sentence. The ideogram: water and deciding.

 34.4a/b The hedge broken up, not ruined.

 43.S Augmenting and not climaxing necessarily breaks up.

 43.S Deciding implies breaking up indeed.

 43/44.CD Deciding: breaking up indeed.

 43/44.CD Solid breaking up supple indeed.

 43.ImT Deciding. Breaking up indeed.

 43.ImT Solid breaking up supple indeed.

 43.ImT Breaking up and harmonizing.

 44.S Breaking up necessarily possesses meeting.

Brightness, MING: light giving aspect of burning, heavenly bodies and consciousness; with fire, a Symbol of the trigram Radiance, LI.

 Image of Hexagram 36 and occurs throughout its texts.

 1.ImT Great brightening completing beginning.

3.4b Brightness indeed.

6.1b Although the small possesses words, one's differentiation brightening indeed.

10.ImT Shining brightness indeed.

10.3b Not the stand to use possessing brightness indeed.

13.ImT Pattern brightening uses persisting.

14.ImT One's actualizing tao: solid persisting and pattern brightening.

14.4b Brightness differentiating clearly indeed.

15.ImT Heavenly tao fording below and shining brightness.

17.4a There is a connection to the spirit, locating in tao uses brightening.

17.4b Brightening achieving indeed.

21.ST The Earlier Kings used brightening flogging to enforce the laws.

21.ImT Stirring up and brightening.

21.6b Understanding not brightened indeed.

22.ST A chün tzu uses brightening the multitudinous standards without daring to sever litigating.

22.ImT Pattern brightening, stopping:

30.ST Brightness doubled arousing Radiance.

30.ST Great People use consecutive brightening to illuminate into the four sides.

30.ImT Redoubling brightness uses congregating to reach to correcting.

35.CD Brightness Hiding: proscribed indeed.

35.ST Brightness issuing forth above earth.

35.ST A chün tzu uses originating enlightening to brighten actualizing tao.

35.ImT Brightness issuing forth above earth.

35.ImT Yielding and congregating reaching to great brightening.

38.ImT Stimulating and congregating reaching to brightness.

43.4b Understanding not brightened indeed.

47.1b Shady, not bright indeed.

48.3a Kingly brightness.

48.3b Seeking kingly brightness:

49.ST A chün tzu uses regulating time reckoning to brighten the seasons.

49.ImT Pattern brightening uses stimulating.

50.ImT Ground and the ear[and]eye: understanding brightened.

52.ImT One's tao: shining brightness.

55.ImT Brightness using stirring up.

55.4b Shade, not brightening indeed.

56.ST A chün tzu uses brightening consideration to avail of punishing and not to detain litigating.

56.ImT Stopping and congregating reaching to brightness.

Brilliance, HUI: sunlight, sunshine, sunbeam; bright, splendid.

64.5b One's brilliance auspicious indeed.

Buckle, JAO: distort, wrench out of shape, collapse, break; weak; flexible, lithe.

28.3a/b The ridgepole buckling. Pitfall.

Bulwark, CH'ENG: city wall, citadel, place walled for defense.

11.6a/b The bulwark returned into the moat.

Bundle in, KUA: enclose, envelop, tie up; embrace, include.

2.4a Bundled in the bag.

2.4b Bundled in the bag, without fault.

Burgeon, YI: beginning of growth after seedburst, CHIA; early spring; associated with the Woody Moment.

11.5a The supreme burgeoning, converting maidenhood.

54.5a/b The supreme burgeoning Converting Maidenhood.

Burn, FEN: set fire to, destroy completely.

30.4a Burning thus. Dying thus. Thrown out thus.

56.3a/b Sojourning, burning one's resting place.

56.6a A bird burning its nest.

56.6b One's righteousness burning indeed.

Bushy, PAO: luxuriant growth, dense thicket; conceal, screen; sleeping mats; wrap as a gift. The ideogram: wrap and bushes.

12.5a Attaching into bushy mulberry trees.

Bushy tailed rodent, SHIH SHU: animals who destroy stored grain; mean, thieving people; timid, skulking, mournful, brooding.

35.4a Prospering, thus bushy tailed rodents.

35.4b Bushy tailed rodents, Trial: adversity.

Butt, CHU: push or strike with the horns; attack, oppose, offend; stirred up, excited; obnoxious; associated with Woody Moment.

34.3a,6a The he goat butts a hedge.

By consequence(of), TSE: very strong connection; reason, cause, result; rule, law, pattern, standard; therefore.

This term occurs throughout the hexagram texts.

Calamity, TSAI: disaster from outside; flood, plague, drought, blight, ruin; contrasts with blunder, SHENG, indicating personal fault. The ideogram: water and fire, elemental powers.

5.3b Calamity located outside indeed.
23.4b Slicing close to calamity indeed.
25/26.CD Disentangling: calamity indeed.
25.3a Disentangling's calamity.
25.3a Capital people's calamity.
25.3b Capital people, calamity indeed.
25.6b Exhaustion's calamity indeed.
26.1b Not opposing calamity indeed.
33.1b Not going, wherefore calamity indeed.
55.1b Exceeding a decade, calamity indeed.
56.1a Splitting off one's place, grasping calamity.
56.1b Purpose exhausted, calamity indeed.

Calamity and Blunder, TSAI SHENG: disaster from without and within; natural disaster combined with misfortune due to ignorance or fault; ruin, defeat, rout, collapse.

24.6a Possessing Calamity and Blunder.
62.6a That designates Calamity and Blunder.

Calf, FEI: muscle of lower leg; rely on; prop, rest.

31.2a Conjoining one's calves.
52.2a Bound: one's calves.

Call, MING: bird and animal cries, through which they recognize each other; distinctive sound, song, statement. The ideogram: bird and mouth, a distinguishing call.

15.2a/b,6a/b Calling Humbling.
16.1a Calling Provision.
16.1b Initial six, calling Provision.
61.2a Calling crane located in yin.

Calm, K'ANG: confident strength and poise; stability, peace, ease; joy, delight.

35.Im/ImT The calm feudatory avails of bestowing horses to multiply the multitudes.

Canons, CHING: standards, laws; regular, regulate; the Five Classics. The ideogram: warp threads in a loom.

3.ST A chün tzu uses the canons to coordinate.
27.2a Rejecting the canons, into the hill top.
27.5a Rejecting the canons.

Caper, YO: play, frolic, dance and leap for joy, frisk, gambol. The ideogram: foot and feather, light footed.

1.4a/b Maybe capering located in the abyss.

Capital, YI: populous fortified city, center and symbol of the domain it rules. The ideogram: enclosure and official seal.

6.2a Converting and escaping one's capital.
8.5a/b Capital people not admonished.
11.6a Originating from the capital, notifying fate.
15.6a Chastising the capital city.
15.6b Chastising the capital city indeed.
25.3a Capital people's calamity.
25.3b Capital people, calamity indeed.
35.6a/b Holding fast avails of subjugating the capital.
43.Im/ImT Notifying originates from the capital.
46.3a/b Ascending: an empty capital.
48.Im/ImT Amending the capital, not amending the Well.

Care, HSÜ: fear, doubt, concern; heartfelt attachment; relieve, soothe, aid; sympathy, compassion, consolation. The ideogram: heart and blood, the heart's blood affected.

11.3a No cares: one's connection.
35.5a/b Letting go, acquiring, no cares.
37.5a Beings: care auspicious.
43.2a No cares.
43.2b Possessing arms, no cares.
45.1a No cares.
46.Im/ImT No cares.

Carry, TSAI: bear, carry with you; contain, sustain; load a ship or cart, cargo; fill in, complete.

2.ST A chün tzu uses munificent actualizing tao to carry the beings.
2.ImT Field: munificence carrying the beings.
9.6a Honoring actualizing tao carrying.
9.6b Actualizing tao amassing carrying indeed.
14.2a/b The great chariot used to carry.
23.6b Commoners: the place to carry indeed.
38.6a Carrying souls, the one chariot.

Cart, YÜ: carrying capacity of a vehicle; contain, hold, sustain.

7.3a/b Legions maybe carting corpses.
7.5a/b The junior son carting corpses.
9.3a Carting stimulating the spokes.
23.6a/b A chün tzu acquiring a cart.
26.2a/b Carting, stimulating the axle strap.
26.3a An enclosed cart, escorting.
34.4a Invigorating into the Great: a cart's axle straps.
38.3a/b Seeing the cart pulled back.

● **Cast out**, PʼI: expel, repress, exclude, punish; exclusionary laws and their enforcement. The ideogram: punish, authority and mouth, give orders to expel.

> 12.ST A chün tzu uses parsimonious actualizing tao to cast out heaviness.
>
> 30.1b Using casting out fault indeed.
>
> 38.1b Using casting out fault indeed.

● **Catch**, HUO: take in hunt; catch a thief; obtain, seize; hit the mark, opportune moment; prisoner, spoils, prey; slave, servant.

> 17.4a/b Following possessing catching.
>
> 30.6a Severing the head. Catching in no way its demons.
>
> 36.4a Catching Brightness Hiding's heart.
>
> 36.4b Catching the heart, intention indeed.
>
> 40.2a The fields, catching three foxes.
>
> 40.6a Without not Advantageous: catching it.
>
> 52.Im/ImT Not catching one's individuality.
>
> 57.4a/b The fields, catching three kinds.

● **Cattle**, NIU: ox, bull, cow, calf; kine; power and strength of work animals.

> 25.3a Maybe attaching's cattle.
>
> 25.3b Moving people acquiring cattle.
>
> 26.4a Youthful cattle's stable.
>
> 30.Im/ImT Accumulating female cattle. Auspicious.
>
> 33.2a Holding on to it: availing of yellow cattle's skin.
>
> 33.2b Holding on avails of yellow cattle.
>
> 38.3a One's cattle hampered.
>
> 49.1a Thonging avails of yellow cattle's Skin.
>
> 49.1b Thonging avails of yellow cattle.
>
> 56.6a/b Losing the cattle, into versatility.
>
> 63.5a/b The Eastern neighbor slaughters cattle.

● **Cave**, HSÜEH: hole used for dwelling; cavern, den, pit; open grave.

> 5.4a Issuing forth originates from the cave.
>
> 5.6a Entering into the cave.
>
> 62.5a A prince, a string arrow grasping another located in a cave.

● **Center**, CHUNG: inner, central; put in the center; middle, stable point enabling you to face inner and outer changes; middle line of trigram. The ideogram: field divided in two equal parts. See also:

Centering correcting

> This term occurs in many hexagrams at the second and/or fifth Transforming Line. It also occurs at: Image of Hexagram 61 and occurs throughout its texts.

3.ImT Stirring up reaching to venturing center.

3.3a Namely, entering into the forest center.

4.ImT Season centering indeed.

4.ImT Using solid centering indeed.

5.ImT Using correcting centering indeed.

6.Im Centering auspicious.

6.ImT Blocking alarm, centering auspicious.

6.ImT Solid coming and acquiring the center indeed.

7.ST Earth center possessing stream.

7.ImT Solid centering and corresponding.

8.ImT Using solid centering indeed.

9.ImT Solid centering and purpose moving.

11.4b Centering the heart desiring indeed.

13.ImT Acquiring centering and corresponding reaching to Force.

14.ImT Supple acquiring the dignifying situation, the great centering.

15.ST Earth center possessing mountain.

17.ST Marsh center possessing thunder.

19.ImT Solid centering and corresponding.

21.ImT Jaws center possesses being.

21.ImT Supple acquiring the center and moving above.

24.ST Thunder located in earth center. Returning.

24.4a/b Centering movement, solitary Returning.

25.ImT Solid centering and corresponding.

26.ST Heaven located in mountain center.

28.ImT Solid Exceeding and centering.

29.ImT Holding fast the heart's Growing, thereupon using solid centering indeed.

36.ST/ImT Brightness entering earth center.

38.ImT Acquiring the center and corresponding reaching to the solid.

39.ImT Going acquires the center indeed.

40.ImT Thereupon acquiring the center indeed.

42.3a There is a connection to the spirit, center moving.

42.4a Center moving.

45.ImT Solid centering and corresponding.

46.ST Earth center giving birth to wood. Ascending.

46.ImT Solid centering and corresponding.

47.ImT Using solid centering indeed.

48.ImT Thereupon using solid centering indeed.

49.ST Marsh center possessing fire. Skinning.

50.ImT Acquiring the center and corresponding reaching to the solid.

51.6b Center not yet acquired indeed.

53.ImT One's situation: solid acquiring the center indeed.

55.Im/ImT No grief. Properly sun centering.

55.ImT Sun centering, by consequence going down.

55.3a Sun centering: seeing froth.

55.4a/b Sun centering: seeing the Bin.

56.ImT Supple acquiring the center reaching to the outside and yielding reaching to the solid.

58.ImT Solid centering and supple outside.

59.ImT Kinghood thereupon located in the center indeed.

60.ImT Strong and Supple apportioning and solid acquiring the center.

62.CD Centering Connection: trustworthiness indeed.

62.ImT Supple acquiring the center.

62.ImT Solid letting go the situation and not centering.

63.ImT Supple acquiring the center indeed.

64.ImT Supple acquiring the center indeed.

64.ImT Not yet issuing forth from the center indeed.

Centering correcting, CHUNG CHENG: central and correct; make rectifying one sidedness and error your central concern; reaching a stable center in yourself can correct the situation.

5.5b Using centering correcting indeed.

6.ImT Honoring centering correcting indeed.

6.5b Using centering correcting indeed.

10.ImT Solid centering correctly.

13.ImT Centering correcting and corresponding.

16.2b Using centering correcting indeed.

20.ImT Centering correcting uses Viewing Below Heaven.

30.ImT Supple congregating reaches to centering correcting.

35.2b Using centering correcting indeed.

42.ImT Centering correcting possessing reward.

44.ImT Solid meeting centering correctness.

44.5b Centering correctness indeed.

48.5b Centering correcting indeed.

52.5b Using centering correcting indeed.

57.ImT Solid Ground reaching to centering correcting and purpose moving.

60.ImT Centering correcting uses interpenetrating.

Chain mail/limits, CHIEH: chain armor; tortoise or crab shell; protective covering; border, limit; protection, support.

16.2a Chain mail into petrification:

35.2a/b Accepting closely woven chain mail: blessing.

58.4a Chain mail afflicting: possessing rejoicing.

Chambers, T'ING: family room, courtyard, hall; domestic. The ideogram: shelter and hall, a secure place.

36.4a Into issuing forth from the gate chambers.

43.Im/ImT Displaying into kingly chambers.

52.Im/ImT Moving one's chambers.

60.1a/b Not issuing forth from the door chambers.

60.2a Not issuing forth from the gate chambers.

60.2b Not issuing forth from the gate chambers, pitfall.

Change, HUA: gradual, continuous metamorphosis; influence someone; contrasts with transform, PIEN, sudden mutation. The ideogram: person alive and dead, the life-process.

1.ImT Force: tao transforming changes.

20.ImT Viewing below and changing indeed.

22.ImT Using changes accomplishing Below Heaven.

30.ImT Thereupon changes accomplishing Below Heaven.

31.ImT Heaven and Earth influencing and the myriad beings changing give birth.

32.ImT The four seasons transforming changes and enabling lasting accomplishment.

32.ImT The all wise person lasting with respect to his tao and Below Heaven the changes accomplishing.

61.ImT Thereupon changing the fiefdoms indeed.

Channel, HO: bed of river or stream; running water.

11.2a Availing of crossing the channel.

Chariot, CH'E: wheeled travelling vehicle; contrasts with cart, YÜ, which carries.

14.2a/b The great chariot used to carry.

22.1a/b Stowing away the chariot and afoot.

38.6a Carrying souls, the one chariot.

47.4a Confined, into a metallic chariot.

Chastise, CHENG: punish, subjugate, discipline; reduce to order; punishing expedition. The ideogram: step and correct, a rectifying move.

9.6a/b A chün tzu chastising: pitfall.

11.1a Chastising auspicious.

11.1b Eradicating thatch grass, chastising auspicious.

15.5b Chastising, not submitting indeed.

15.6a Chastising the capital city.

15.6b Chastising the capital city indeed.

24.6a Culminating into ten years revolved not controlling chastisement.

27.2a Jaws chastising: pitfall.

27.2b Six at second, chastising: pitfall.

30.6a/b Kinghood availing of issuing forth chastising.

34.1a Chastising: pitfall, there is a connection to the spirit.

41.2a Chastising: pitfall.

46.Im/ImT The South, chastising auspicious.

47.2a Chastising: pitfall, without fault.

47.6a Chastising auspicious.

49.2a Chastising auspicious, without fault.

49.3a Chastising: pitfall, Trial: adversity.

49.6a Chastising: pitfall.

51.6a Chastising: pitfall.

53.3a/b The husband chastised, not returning.

54.Im/ImT Chastising: pitfall.

54.1a Chastising auspicious.

64.3a/b Not yet Fording, chastising: pitfall.

Cheek bones, CH'UAN: facial feature denoting character; high cheek bones indicate cruelty.

43.3a Invigorating into the cheek bones:

Cheeks, CHIA: sides of the face; speak, articulate.

31.6a/b Conjoining one's jawbones, cheeks, tongue.

Cherish, HUAI: dwell on, think of; carry in the heart or womb; cling to. The ideogram: heart and hide, cherish in the heart.

7.2a Cherishing the myriad fiefdoms indeed.

56.2a Cherishing one's own.

Chief, CHÜN: effective ruler; preside over, take the lead; influence others; term of respect. The ideogram: mouth and director, giving orders. See also: **Chief and Servant**

7.6a/b The Great Chief possesses fate.

10.3a/b Martial people activating: into a Great Chief.

12.1b Purpose located in a chief indeed.

19.5a/b A Great Chief's propriety.

24.6a Using one's city chief: pitfall.

24.6b Reversing the chief: tao indeed.

37.ImT Dwelling People possess an intimidating chief in truth.

49.6b Yielding uses adhering to the chief indeed.

54.5a One's chief's sleeves:

62.2a/b Not extending to one's chief.

Chief and Servant, CHÜN CH'EN: cooperative relation between those who give orders and those who carry them out. See also: **Servant**

31.S Therefore afterwards possessing Chief and Servant.

31.S Possessing Chief and Servant:

Chock, NI: block used to stop a cart wheel; inquire, investigate.

44.1a/b Attaching into a metallic chock.

Chroniclers, SHIH: histories, records, annals; authoritative record; narrator of events, annalist.

57.2a Availing of chroniclers, shamans.

Chün tzu: ideal of a person who uses divination to order his/her life in accordance with tao rather than wilful intention; keyword.

This term occurs in the Symbol Tradition of all hexagrams except **8, 11, 16, 20, 21, 23, 24, 30, 44, 59**. It also occurs at:

1.3a A chün tzu completing the day: Force, Force.

2.Im A chün tzu possesses directed going.

2.ImT A chün tzu directing moving.

3.3a A chün tzu almost not thus stowing away.

3.3b A chün tzu stowing it:

9.6a/b A chün tzu chastising: pitfall.

11.ImT Inside chün tzu and outside Small People.

11.ImT A chün tzu: tao long living.

12.Im/ImT Not Advantageous: chün tzu, Trial.

12.ImT Inside Small People and outside chün tzu.

12.ImT A chün tzu: tao dissolving indeed.

13.Im Advantageous: chün tzu, Trial.

13.ImT A chün tzu, correcting indeed.

13.ImT Verily a chün tzu activating enables interpenetrating Below Heaven's purpose.

15.Im A chün tzu possesses completing.

15.ImT A chün tzu's completing indeed.

15.1a/b Humbling, Humbling: chün tzu.

15.3a/b Toiling Humbling: chün tzu.

20.1a Chün tzu: distress

20.5a/6a A chün tzu: without fault.

23.ImT A chün tzu honors the dissolving pause to overfill emptiness.

23.6a/b A chün tzu acquiring a cart.

33.4a A chün tzu auspicious.

33.4b A chün tzu lovingly Retiring.

34.3a A chün tzu avails of net.

34.3b A chün tzu: net indeed.

36.1a/b A chün tzu into moving:

40.5a A chün tzu holding fast possesses Loosening.

40.5b A chün tzu possessing Loosening.

43.3a/b A chün tzu: Deciding.

47.ImT Reaching to one's very chün tzu.

49.6a/b A chün tzu: leopard transforming.

64.5a/b A chün tzu's shining.

City, KUO: area of only human constructions; political unit, polis. First of the territorial zones: city, suburbs, countryside, forests.

1.ImT Myriad cities, conjoining, soothing.

7.6a Disclosing the city, receiving a dwelling.

8.ST The Earlier Kings used installing myriad cities to connect the connoted feudatories.

15.6a Chastising the capital city.

15.6b Chastising the capital city indeed.

20.4a/b Viewing the city's shining.

24.6a Using one's city chief: pitfall.

29.ImT The kingly prince sets up venturing used to guard his city.

36.6b Illuminating the four cities indeed.

42.4a Advantageous: availing of activating depending on shifting the city.

64.4a Three years revolved, possessing donating into the great city.

Clan, TSU: extended family with same ancestor and surname; kin, relatives; tribe, class, kind. The ideogram: flag and spear, a rallying point.

13.ST A chün tzu uses sorting the clans to mark off the beings.

Clapper, T'O: board used by watchmen to strike the hours.

16.AE Redoubling gates, smiting clappers.

Classification, HUI: class, collection, series; same kind; put or group together.

11.1a Using one's classification.

12.1a Using one's classification.

Clear, TZU: cultivate wild or overgrown land; reclaim.

25.2a Not clearing the plow land.

Clearly, CHE: make clear, illuminate; shine, emit light; starlight.

14.4b Brightness differentiating clearly indeed.

Climax, YI: come to a high point and stop, bring to an end; use up, lay aside; decline, reject.

22.S Beings not permitted to use unconsidered uniting and climaxing.

26.1a Advantageous: climaxing.

26.1b Possessing adversity, Advantageous: climaxing.

32.ImT Persevering lasting and not climaxing indeed.

41.1a/b Climaxing affairs, swiftly going.

42.S Diminishing and not climaxing necessarily Augments.

43.S Augmenting and not climaxing necessarily breaks up.

47.S Ascending and not climaxing necessarily Confines.

62.5b Above climaxing indeed.

62.6b Climaxing overbearing indeed.

Climb, CHI: ascend, scale; climb steep cliffs; rise as clouds.

51.2a Climbing into the ninth mound.

Clog, SAI: stop up, fill up, close, obstruct, hinder, prevent; unintelligent, dull, hard to understand.

50.3a Its movement clogged.

60.1b Knowing interpenetrating clogging indeed.

Close to, CHIN: near in time or place, next to; approach; recently, lately; familiar.

23.4b Slicing close to calamity indeed.

Closely woven, TZU: compact, close textured, dense, solid, impenetrable. The ideogram: herbs and silk, dense fabric or foliage.

35.2a/b Accepting closely woven chain mail: blessing.

Clothes, YI: upper body garments; dress; cover, husk.

63.4a A token: possessing clothes in tatters.

Clouds, YÜN: fog, mist, water vapor; connects to the Streaming Moment and Stream, the Symbol of the trigram Gorge, K'AN.

1.ImT Clouds moving, rain spreading out.

3.ST Clouds, Thunder, Sprouting.

5.ST Above clouds with respect to heaven.

9.Im/ImT Shrouding clouds, not raining.

62.5a/b Shrouding clouds, not raining.

Cluster, TS'UI: call or pack together; tight groups of people, animals, things; collect, gather, assemble, concentrate; bunch, crowd, collection; lit.: dense, tussocky grass.

Image of Hexagram 45 and occurs throughout its texts.

● **Codes,** LI: rites, rules, ritual; usage, manners; worship, ceremony, observance. The ideogram: worship and sacrificial vase, handling a sacred vessel.

10.S Beings Accumulating, therefore afterwards possessing codes.

15.AE Humbling: using paring the codes.

31.S Therefore afterwards the codes righteously possessing a place to polish.

34.ST A chün tzu uses no codes whatever, nowhere treading.

● **Coins,** PEI: cowrie shells used for money; adorned with shell; money, riches; precious, valuable.

51.2a A hundred thousand lost coins.

● **Cold,** HAN: chilled, wintry; destitute, poor; shiver; fear; associated with the Streaming Moment. The ideogram: person huddled in straw under a roof.

48.5a The Well: limpid, cold springwater taken in.

48.5b Cold springwater's taking in.

● **Collect,** SHOU: gather, harvest; receive what is due; involve, snare, bind, restrain.

48.6a The Well: collecting, no cover.

● **Come,** LAI, and go, WANG, describe the stream of time as it flows from future through present to past; come, LAI, indicates what is approaching; move toward, arrive at; keyword.

5.6a Three people coming.

5.6b Not urging's visitors coming.

6.ImT Solid coming and acquiring the center indeed.

8.Im/ImT Not soothing, on all sides coming.

8.1a Completing coming possesses more auspiciousness.

11.Im The small going, the great coming.

11.ImT The small going, the great coming: auspiciousness Growing.

12.Im/ImT The great going, the small coming.

17.ImT Solid coming and supple below.

22.ImT Supple coming and patterning solid.

24.Im/ImT Partnering coming, without fault.

24.Im/ImT The seventh day coming: Returning.

25.ImT Solid originating from the outside coming and activating a lord with respect to the inside.

29.3a/b Coming's Gorge, the Gorge.

30.4a/b Assailing thus, its coming thus.

31.4a/b Wavering, wavering: going, coming.

39.1a/b Going Difficulties, coming praise.

39.3a/b Going Difficulties, coming reversing.

39.4a/b Going Difficulties, coming continuity.

39.5a/b The great Difficulties, partnering coming.

39.6a/b Going Difficulties, coming ripening.

40.Im/ImT One's coming return auspicious.

42.2b/6b Originating from outside, coming indeed.

45/46.CD Ascending: not coming indeed.

47.2a Scarlet sashes on all sides coming.

47.4a/b Coming, ambling, ambling.

48.Im Going, coming: Welling, Welling.

51.Im/ImT Shake coming: frightening, frightening.

51.1a/b Shake coming: frightening, frightening.

51.2a/b Shake coming: adversity.

51.5a/b Shake going, coming adversity.

55.5a Coming composition.

58.3a/b Coming Opening, pitfall.

59.ImT Solid coming and not exhausted.

63.5b Auspicious, the great coming indeed.

● **Command,** KAO: give orders; insist on, express wishes; official seal. The ideogram: words and announce, verbal commands.

44.ST The crown prince uses spreading out fate to command the four sides.

● **Commission,** SHIH: employ for a task; command, order; messenger, agent. The ideogram: person and office.

7.5b Commissioning not appropriate indeed.

8.5b Commissioning centering above indeed.

41.4a Commissioning swiftly possesses rejoicing.

● **Commoners,** MIN: class of workers the state draws on to sustain the social hierarchy; undeveloped potential outside the organized personality.

3.1b The great acquiring the commoners indeed.

7.ST A chün tzu uses tolerating commoners to accumulate crowds.

7.ImT Using the latter poisons Below Heaven and the commoners adhering to it.

10.ST [A chün tzu uses] setting right the commoners, the purpose.

11.ST [The crown prince] uses the left to right the commoners.

15.3b The myriad commoners submitting indeed.

16.ImT By consequence punishing flogging purifies and the commoners submit.

18.ST A chün tzu uses rousing the commoners to nurture actualizing tao.

19.ST [A chün tzu uses] tolerating to protect the commoners without delimiting.

20.ST The earlier kings used inspecting on all sides, Viewing the commoners to set up teaching.

20.5b Viewing the commoners indeed.

23.6b Commoners: the place to carry indeed.

27.ImT The all wise person nourishes eminence used to extend to the myriad commoners.

42.ImT The commoners stimulated without delimiting.

44.4b Distancing the commoners indeed.

48.ST A chün tzu uses toiling commoners to encourage mutualizing.

58.ImT Stimulating using beforehand the commoners:

58.ImT The commoners forget their toiling.

58.ImT The commoners forget their dying.

58.ImT Actually the commoners encouraged in fact.

60.ImT Not harming the commoners.

● **Companion,** CH'IU: equal, spouse; unite, join in marriage. Also: opponent, rival, enemy; contradict, hate.

50.2a/b My companion possesses affliction.

● **Complete,** CHUNG: end of a cycle that begins the next; last, whole, all; contrasts with exhaust, CH'IUNG, final end. The ideogram: silk cocoons, follow and ice, winter linking one year with the next.

1.ImT Great brightening completing beginning.

1.3a A chün tzu completing the day: Force, Force.

1.3b Completing the day: Force, Force.

2.ImT Thereupon completing possesses reward.

2.3a Without accomplishing possessing completion.

2.7b Using the great to complete indeed.

5.2a Completing auspicious.

5.2b Although the small possesses words, using completing auspicious indeed.

5.6a/b Respecting them: completing auspicious.

6.Im/ImT Completing: pitfall.

6.1a The small possesses words, completing auspicious.

6.3a Adversity, completing auspicious.

6.6a Completing dawn three times depriving it.

8.1a Completing coming possesses more auspiciousness.

8.6b Without a place to complete indeed.

10.4a/b Pleading, pleading: completing auspicious.

12.S Beings not permitted to use completing interpenetrating.

12.6b Obstruction completed, by consequence subverting.

13.S Beings not permitted to use completing Obstructing.

15.Im A chün tzu possesses completing.

15.ImT A chün tzu's completing indeed.

15.3a Possessing completing auspicious.

16.2a Not completing the day.

16.2b Not completing the day, Trial: auspicious.

18.ImT Completing, by consequence possessing the beginning.

18.1a Adversity, completing auspicious.

18.3b Completing without fault indeed.

22.3b Completing absolutely nothing: having a mound indeed.

22.4b Completing without surpassing indeed.

22.5a Distress. Completing auspicious.

23.5b Completing without surpassing indeed.

23.6b Completing, not permitting availing of indeed.

24.S Beings not permitted to use completing using up.

24.6a Completing possesses great destroying.

29.S Beings not permitted to use completing Exceeding.

29.3b Completing without achieving indeed.

29.4a Completing, without fault.

32.ImT Completing by consequence possessing the beginning indeed.

32.5b Adhering to the one and completing indeed.

34.S Beings not permitted to use completing Retiring.

35.S Beings not permitted to use completing Invigorating.

37.3a Completing distress.

37.6a Completing auspicious.

38.3a/b Without initially possessing completion.

39.2b Completing without surpassing indeed.

40.S Beings not permitted to use completing heaviness.

43.ImT Solid long living, thereupon completing indeed.

43.3b Completing without fault indeed.

43.6a Completing: possessing a pitfall.

43.6b Completing not permitting long living indeed.

45.1a There is a connection to the spirit, not completing.

47.4a Possessing completion.

50.2b Completing without surpassing indeed.

50.3a Completing auspicious.

52.S Beings not permitted to use completing stirring up.

52.6b Using munificence to complete indeed.

53.S Beings not permitted to use completing stopping.

53/54.CD Converting Maidenhood: womanhood's completion indeed.

53.5a Completing: absolutely nothing has mastering.

53.5b Completing: absolutely nothing has mastering, auspicious.

54.ST A chün tzu uses perpetually completing to know the cracked.

54.ImT A person's completion beginning indeed.

55.3b Completing, not permitting availing of indeed.

56.2b Completing without surpassing indeed.

56.5a/b Completing uses praising fate.

56.6b Completing absolutely nothing: having hearing indeed.

57.5a Without initially possessing completion.

60.S Beings not permitted to use completing Radiance.

62.4b Completing not permitting long living indeed.

63.Im Completing: disarraying.

63.ImT Completing, stopping by consequence disarraying.

63.4a/b Completing the day, a warning.

64.S Accepting this lets you use Not yet Fording completed in truth.

64.ImT Not continuing, completing indeed.

Complexion, SE: appearance, expression; color, hue; air, manner, deportment; beautiful.

21/22.CD Adorning: without complexion indeed.

Composition, CHANG: a well composed whole and its structure; beautiful creations; elegant, clear, brilliant; contrasts with pattern, WEN, beauty of intrinsic design.

2.3a/b Containing composition permitting Trial.

21.ImT Thunder, lightning, uniting and composing.

44.ImT The kinds: beings conjoining composition indeed.

44.5a Containing composition.

44.5b Nine at fifth, containing composition.

55.5a Coming composition.

Conceal, TS'ANG: hide from view; store up, put aside, accumulate; stores, property; internal organs.

55.6b Originating from concealing indeed.

Concord, T'UNG: harmonize, unite, equalize, assemble; agree, share in; together, at once, same time and place. The ideogram: cover and mouth, silent understanding and perfect fit.

Image of Hexagram 13 and occurs throughout its texts.

11.ImT Above and Below mingling and one's purpose concording indeed.

14.S Associating with People Concording implies beings necessarily converting in truth.

14.CD Concording People: connecting indeed.

38.ST A chün tzu uses concording and dividing.

38.ImT Two women concording: residing.

38.ImT Their purposes not concording: moving.

38.ImT Heaven, Earth, Polarizing and one's affairs concording indeed.

49.ImT Two women concording, residing.

59.ImT Supple acquiring the situation reaching to the outside and concording above.

Concubine, CH'IEH: secondary wife taken without ceremony to ensure a male descendant; handmaid.

33.3a/b Accumulating servants, concubines, auspicious.

50.1a Acquiring a concubine, using one's sonhood.

Conduct, SHUAI: lead; leader, chief, commander; follow, follower.

7.5a/b The long living son conducting Legions.

Confine, K'UN: enclose, restrict, limit; oppressed; impoverish, distress; afflicted, exhausted, disheartened, weary. The ideogram: an enclosed tree.

Image of Hexagram 47 and occurs throughout its texts.

4.4a/b Confining Enveloping. Distress.

5.ImT Actually one's righteousness, not confining exhaustion.

13.4b By consequence confining and reversing by consequence indeed.

48.S Confining reaching to the above implies necessarily reversing the below.

48.CD Confining: mutual meeting indeed.

Congregate, LI: cling together; depend on, attached to, rely on; couple, pair, herd; the Action of the trigram Radiance, LI. The ideogram: deer flocking together.

30.S Falling necessarily possesses a place to congregate.

30.S Radiance implies congregating indeed.

30.ImT Radiance. Congregating indeed.

30.ImT Sun and Moon congregating reach to heaven.

30.ImT The hundred grains, grasses, trees congregating reach to earth.

30.ImT Redoubling brightness uses congregating to reach to correcting.

30.ImT Supple congregating reach to centering correcting.

35.ImT Yielding and congregating reaching to great brightening.

38.ImT Stimulating and congregating reaching to brightness.

56.ImT Stopping and congregating reaching to brightness.

58.ST Congregating marshes.

Conjoin, HSIEN: come into contact with, influence; reach, join together; put together as parts of a previously separated whole; come into conjunction, as the celestial bodies; totally, completely; lit.: broken piece of pottery, the halves of which join to identify partners.

Image of Hexagram 31 and occurs throughout its texts.

1.ImT Myriad cities, conjoining, soothing.

2.ImT The kinds: being conjoining Growing.

19.1a/b Conjunction Nearing, Trial: auspicious.

19.2a/b Conjunction Nearing: auspicious.

32.CD Conjoining: urging indeed.

44.ImT The kinds: beings conjoining composition indeed.

Connect, CH'IN: attach to, approach, come near; cherish, help, favor; intimate; relatives, kin.

5/6.CD Arguing: not connecting indeed.

8.ST The Earlier Kings used installing myriad cities to connect the connoted feudatories.

13/14.CD Concording People: connecting indeed.

55/56.CD Connecting the few: Sojourning indeed.

Connection (to the spirit), FU: accord between inner and outer in a particular moment; sincere, truthful, verified, reliable, in accord with the spirits; capture; prisoners, spoils; contrasts with trustworthy, HSIN, consistent in time. The ideogram: bird's claw enclosing young animals, possessive grip. See also: **There is … spirit.**

Image of Hexagram 61 and occurs throughout its texts.

11.3a No cares: one's connection.

11.4a/b Not warning: using connection.

14.5a Your connection: mingling thus, impressing thus.

14.5b Your connection, mingling thus.

17.5a/b Conformity into excellence. Auspicious.

34.1b One's connection exhausted indeed.

35.1a Net: connection.

38.4a Mingling connection.

38.4b Mingling connection, without fault.

40.4a Partnering culminating, splitting off connection.

43.Im/ImT Connection, crying out, possessing adversity.

44.1a Ruining the pig, connection: hoof dragging.

45.2a Connection, thereupon Advantageous availing of dedicating.

45.5a Without fault: in no way connection.

46.2a Connection, thereupon Advantageous availing of dedicating.

46.2b Nine at second's connection.

49.Im Skinning: your own day, thereupon connection.

49.ImT Your own day, thereupon connection.

58.2a/b Connection Opening, auspicious.

58.5a/b Connection into stripping.

62.CD Centering Connection: trustworthiness indeed.

Connote, CHU: imply the meaning; signify. The ideogram: words and imply.

8.ST The Earlier Kings used installing myriad cities to connect the connoted feudatories.

16.AE Surely, grasping connotes Providing for.

52.4b Stopping connoting the body indeed.

Consecutive, CHI: follow after, continue; take another's place; line of succession, adopt an heir. The ideogram: silk thread and continuous.

30.ST Great People use consecutive brightening to illuminate tending towards the four sides.

Consider, SHEN: act carefully, seriously; cautious, attentive, circumspect; still, quiet, sincere. The ideogram: heart and true.

2.4b Consideration not harmful indeed.

5.3b Respectful consideration, not destroying indeed.

27.ST A chün tzu uses considering words to inform.

50.2b Considering places it indeed.

56.ST A chün tzu uses brightening consideration to avail of punishing and not to detain litigating.

64.ST A chün tzu uses considering to mark off the beings residing on all sides.

Consort, CH'I: single official partner; legal status of married woman (first wife); contrasts with function of wife, FU, head of household, and concubine, CH'IEH, secondary wives.

9.3a/b Husband, consort, reversing eyes.

28.2a A venerable husband acquiring his woman consort.

28.2b A venerable husband, a woman consort.

47.3a/b Entering into one's house. Not seeing one's consort.

Conspicuous, CHU: manifest, obvious, clear.

3/4.CD Enveloping: variegated and conspicuous.

Contain, HAN: retain, embody, cherish; withold, tolerate; lit.: contain in the mouth, put a coin in a corpse's mouth.

2.ImT Containing generosity, the shining great.

2.3a/b Containing composition permitting Trial.

44.5a Containing composition.

44.5b Nine at fifth, containing composition.

Continue, HSÜ: carry on what another began; succeed to, join on, attach to; keep up, follow.

64.ImT Not continuing, completing indeed.

Continuity, LIEN: connected, continuous, attached, annexed, consistent; follow, reach, stick to, join; series.

39.4a/b Going Difficulties, coming continuity.

Contradict, WEI: oppose, disregard, disobey; seditious, perverse.

6.ST Heaven associating with stream, contradicting movements.

15.4b Not contradicting by consequence indeed.

41.5a Nowhere a controlling contradiction.

42.2a Nowhere a controlling contradiction.

Control, K'O: command; check, impede, prevail, obstruct, repress; adequate, able. The ideogram: roof beams support a house, controlling the structure.

4.2a/b The son controlling the dwelling.

6.2a/b,4a Not controlling Arguing.

13.4a Nothing controlling attacking.

13.4b Righteously nothing controlling indeed.

13.5a/b Great legions controlling mutual meeting.

13.5b Words mutualize controlling indeed.

14.3a Small People nowhere controlling.

24.6a Culminating into ten years revolved not controlling chastisement.

41.5a Nowhere a controlling contradiction.

42.2a Nowhere a controlling contradiction.

63.3a/b Three years revolved controlling it.

Convert, KUEI: change to another form, persuade; return to yourself or the place where you belong; restore, revert, become loyal; turn into; give a young girl in marriage. The ideogram: arrive and wife, become mistress of a household.

Image of Hexagram 54 and occurs throughout its texts.

6.2a Converting and escaping one's capital.

6.2b Converting escaping, skulking indeed.

11.5a The supreme burgeoning, converting maidenhood.

14.S Associating with People Concording implies beings necessarily converting in truth.

53.Im Infiltrating, womanhood converting auspicious.

53.CD Infiltrating: womanhood converting awaits manhood moving indeed.

53.CD Converting Maidenhood: womanhood's completion indeed.

53.ImT Womanhood converting auspicious.

55.S Acquiring one's place to Convert implies necessarily the great.

Cook, JEN: cook very thoroughly; transform completely. The ideogram: food and full or complete.

50.ImT Growing: cooking indeed.

Coordinate, LUN: classify, bind, adjust; weave together; lit.: unravel and twist silk together into threads.

   3.ST A chün tzu uses the canons to coordinate.

Corpse, SHIH: dead human body; effigy, statue; inefficient, useless; impersonate.

   7.3a/b Legions maybe carting corpses.
   7.5a/b The junior son carting corpses.

Correct, CHENG: rectify deviation or one sidedness; proper, straight, exact, regular; constant, rule, model. The ideogram: stop and one, hold to one thing. See also: **Centering correcting**

   1.ImT Each one correcting innate fate.
   3.1b Although a stone pillar, purpose moving correctly indeed.
   4.ImT Enveloping used to nourish correcting:
   4.1b Using correcting laws indeed.
   5.ImT Using correcting centering indeed.
   7.ImT Trial: correcting indeed.
   7.ImT Able to use the crowds correcting:
   7.6b Using correcting accomplishing indeed.
   8.5b Situation correctly centered indeed.
   9.3b Not able correcting the home indeed.
   10.5b Situation correcting appropriate indeed.
   12.5b Situation correcting appropriate indeed.
   13.ImT A chün tzu, correcting indeed.
   17.1b Adhering to correcting auspicious indeed.
   17.5b Situation correctly centering indeed.
   19.ImT Great Growing uses correcting.
   19.1b Purpose moving, correcting indeed.
   25.Im One in no way correcting: possessing blunder.
   25.ImT Great Growing using correcting.
   25.ImT One in no way correcting: possessing blunder.
   26.ImT The great correcting indeed.
   27/28.CD Jaws: nourishing correcting indeed.
   27.ImT Nourishing correcting, by consequence auspicious indeed.
   30.ImT Redoubling brightness uses congregating to reach to correcting.
   30.6b Using correcting the fiefdoms indeed.
   33.5b Using correcting the purpose indeed.
   34.ImT The Great implies correcting indeed.
   34.ImT Actually the correcting Great and Heaven and Earth's motives permitting seeing.
   35.1b Solitary moving correcting indeed.
   36.ImT Inside heaviness and enabling correcting one's purpose.

   37.ImT The woman correcting the situation reaching to the inside.
   37.ImT The man correcting the situation reaching to the outside.
   37.ImT Man[and]Woman correcting.
   37.ImT and Dwelling tao correcting.
   37.ImT Actually correcting Dwelling and Below Heaven set right.
   39.ImT Using correcting the fiefdoms indeed.
   45.ImT Assembling uses correcting indeed.
   49.ImT Great Growing uses correcting.
   50.ST A chün tzu uses correcting the situation to solidify fate.
   52.1b Not yet letting go correcting indeed.
   53.ImT Advancing uses correcting.
   53.ImT Permitting using correcting the fiefdoms indeed.
   57.5b Situation correctly centered indeed.
   57.6b Correcting: reaching a pitfall indeed.
   58.5b Situation correcting appropriate indeed.
   59.5b Correcting the situation indeed.
   61.5b Situation correcting appropriate indeed.
   63.ImT Strong and Supple correcting and the situation appropriate indeed.
   64.2b Centering using moving correcting indeed.

Correspond(to), YING: be in agreement or harmony; resonate together, invoke and fulfil each other; answer to, suitable; relation between the lines (1:4, 2:5, 3:6) when they form the pair opened and whole, supple and solid. The ideogram: heart and obey.

   This term occurs in the Image Tradition of most hexagrams.

Corrupt, KU: rotting, poisonous; intestinal worms, venomous insects; evil magic; disorder, error; pervert by seduction, flattery; unquiet ghost. The ideogram: dish and worms, putrefaction and poisonous decay.

   Image of Hexagram 18 and occurs throughout its texts.

Counter, NI: oppose, resist, seek out; contrary, rebellious, refractory. The ideogram: go and rise against, active revolt.

   8.5b Stowing away countering, grasping yielding.
   62.ImT Countering above and yielding below indeed.

Counterpoise, CH'ÜAN: balance, equalize, plan; act as the position demands, expedient; influential; lit.: balance on a sliding scale.

57.AE Ground: using moving the counterpoise.

Countryside, YEH: cultivated fields and grassland, where nature and human construction interact; third of the territorial zones: city, suburbs, countryside, forests.

    2.6a/b Dragons struggling into the countryside.

    13.Im/ImT Concording People, into the countryside.

Couple, KOU: driven encounter, at once transitory and enduring, that is the reflection of primal yin and yang; meet, encounter, copulate; mating animals; magnetism, gravity; to be gripped by impersonal forces.

    Image of Hexagram 44 and occurs throughout its texts.

Course, LIEN: move, flow like ripples spreading on water; unceasing.

    3.6a/b Weeping blood, coursing thus.

Courtesy, KUNG: display respect, treat courteously, show reverence; affable, decorous, modest, polite; obsequious.

    62.ST A chün tzu uses moving Exceeding to reach to courtesy.

Cover, MU: canvas covering; tent, booth, screen, tarpaulin.

    48.6a The Well: collecting, no cover.

Cracked, PI: broken, ruined, tattered; unfit, unworthy. The ideogram: strike and break.

    48.2a The jug cracked, leaking.

    54.ST A chün tzu uses perpetually completing to know the cracked.

Crane, HAO: large stepping into birds; sign of long life, wisdom and bliss; messenger to the immortals; relation between father and son.

    61.2a Calling crane located in yin.

Create, TSAO: make, construct, build, form, establish.

    1.5b Great People creating indeed.

    3.ImT Heaven creating grass, duskiness.

Creeper, see: **Trailing creeper**

Crimson, CH'IH: color associated with the Fiery Moment, South and Actualized Yang; fire, burning; dark complexion; color of new born child; drunk, angry; polished metal; strip, naked, barren; also: sign of official rank. See also: **Scarlet**

    47.5a Confined, into a crimson sash.

Crop, HUO: grain gathered in autumn; reap, harvest.

    25.2a/b Not tilling the crop.

Cross, P'ING: cross a river without a boat; cross a dry or frozen river. The ideogram: horse and ice.

    11.2a Availing of crossing the channel.

Crowds, CHUNG: many people, large group; majority; in common.

    7.S Arguing necessarily possesses crowds rising up.

    7.S Legions imply crowds indeed.

    7.ST A chün tzu uses tolerating commoners to accumulate crowds.

    7.ImT Legions: crowds indeed.

    7.ImT Able to use the crowds correcting:

    8.S Crowds necessarily possess a place to Group.

    13/14.CD Great Possessing: crowds indeed.

    35.3a Crowds, sincerity, repenting extinguished.

    35.3b Crowds: sincerity's purpose.

    36.ST A chün tzu uses supervising the crowds to avail of darkening and Brightening.

    40.ImT Going acquiring crowds indeed.

Crown, LUNG: place above all others; peak; high, surpassing.

    28.4a/b The ridgepole crowning.

Crown prince, HOU: successor to the sovereign. The ideogram: one, mouth and shelter, one with the sovereign's orders.

    11.ST The crown prince uses property to accomplish Heaven and Earth's tao.

    11.ST [The crown prince uses] bracing to mutualize Heaven and Earth's propriety.

    11.ST [The crown prince] uses the left to right the commoners.

    24.ST The crown prince [used culminating sun] not to inspect on all sides.

    44.ST The crown prince uses spreading out fate to command the four sides.

Cry out/outcry, HAO: call out, proclaim; signal, order, command; mark, label, sign.

    13.5a Concording People beforehand crying out sobbing and afterwards laughing.

    43.Im/ImT Connection, crying out, possessing adversity.

    43.2a Alarm, an outcry.

    43.6a Without crying out.

    43.6b Without crying out's pitfall.

    45.1a Like an outcry, the one handful activates laughing.

    56.6a Sojourning people beforehand laughing, afterwards crying out sobbing.

    59.5a Dispersing sweat, one's great crying out.

Culminate, CHIH: bring to the highest degree; arrive at the end or summit; superlative. See also: **Culminating sun**

2.ImT Culminating Field, Spring in fact.
2.1a Treading frost, hardening ice culminating.
2.1b Culminating hardening the ice indeed.
5.3a Involving outlawry culminating.
6.2b Distress culminating, reaping indeed.
10.AE Treading: harmonizing and culminating.
19.Im/ImT Culminating into the eighth moon: possessing a pitfall.
19.4a Culminating Nearing.
19.4b Culminating Nearing, without fault.
24.6a Culminating into ten years revolved not controlling chastisement.
29.ST Streams reiterating culminating.
40.3a Involving outlawry culminating.
40.4a Partnering culminating, splitting off connection.
48.Im/ImT Muddy culmination: Truly not yet the well rope Well.
55.ST Thunder, lightning, altogether culminating.

Culminating sun, CHIH JIH acme of any time period; midday, summer solstice; midpoint of life.

24.ST The Earlier Kings used culminating sun to bar the passages.
24.ST Bargaining sojourners [used culminating sun] not to move.
24.ST The crown prince [used culminating sun] not to inspect on all sides.

Cultivate, CHOU: till fields or gardens; continue successively, like annual plowing. The ideogram: fields and long life.

12.4a Cultivating radiant satisfaction.

Cup, TSUN: quantity a libation vessel contains; glass, decanter, bottle. See also: **Wine cup**

29.4a/b A cup, liquor, a platter added.

Curb, CH'ENG: reprimand, reprove, repress; warn, caution; corrective punishment. The ideogram: heart and action, the heart acting on itself.

41.ST A chün tzu uses curbing anger to block the appetites.

Cut off, CHÜEH: cut short, interrupt, disconnect, break off, sever; destroy, renounce; alienated. The ideogram: silk, knife and knot, cutting through. See also: **Foot cutting** and **Nose cutting**

61.4b Cutting off the above, sorting indeed.

Dare, KAN: have the courage to, try, permit yourself; bold, intrepid; rash, offensive.

22.ST A chün tzu uses brightening the multitudinous standards without daring to sever litigating.

Darken, HUI: make or become dark; last day of the moon; obscure, night, mist.

17.ST A chün tzu uses turning to darkening to enter a reposing pause.
36.ST A chün tzu uses supervising the crowds to avail of darkening and Brightening.
36.ImT Darkening one's Brightness indeed.
36.6a Not Brightening, darkening.

Dawn, CHAO: early morning, before daybreak; opposite of nightfall, HSI.

6.6a Completing dawn three times depriving it.

Day/sun, JIH: actual sun and the time of a sun cycle, a day. See also: **Sun and Moon**

1.3a A chün tzu completing the day: Force, Force.
1.3b Completing the day: Force, Force.
16.2a Not completing the day.
16.2b Not completing the day, Trial: auspicious.
18.Im/ImT Before seedburst three days, after seedburst three days.
24.Im/ImT The seventh day coming: Returning.
26.ImT A day renewing one's actualizing tao.
36.1a Three days, not taking in.
51.2a The seventh day: acquiring.
57.5a Before husking, three days.
57.5a After husking, three days.
63.2a/b The seventh day: acquiring.
63.4a/b Completing the day, a warning.

Daybreak, SU: first light, after dawn; early morning; early, careful attention.

40.Im Daybreak auspicious.
40.ImT Having a direction to go, daybreak auspicious.

Day time, CHOU: daylight half of 24-hour cycle.

35.Im Day time sun three times an audience.
35/36.CD Prospering: day time indeed.
35.ImT Day time sun three times an audience indeed.

Decade, HSÜN: ten days or years; complete time period.

55.1a/b Although a decade, without fault.
55.1b Exceeding a decade, calamity indeed.

Decrease, SHUAI: grow or make smaller; fade, decline, decay, diminish, cut off; grow old; adversity, misfortune.

41/42.CD Increasing, decreasing's beginning indeed.

Dedicate, YO: offering at the spring equinox, when stores are low; offer a sacrifice with limited resources. The ideogram: spring and thin.

45.2a Connection, thereupon Advantageous availing of dedicating.

46.2a Connection, thereupon Advantageous availing of dedicating.

63.5a Not thus the Western neighbor's dedicated offering.

Defend against, FANG: keep off, protect from, guard against; erect a protective barrier. The ideogram: open space and earthen ramparts.

62.3a Nowhere Exceeding defending against it.

63.ST A chün tzu uses pondering distress and providing for defending against it.

Delay, HUAN: retard, put off; let things take their course, tie loosely; gradually, leisurely; lax, tardy, negligent.

39/40.CD Loosening: delay indeed.

40.S Loosening implies delay indeed.

41.S Delaying necessarily possesses a place to let go.

61.ST A chün tzu uses deliberating litigating to delay dying.

Deliberate, YI: consult, discuss, criticize; weigh the options and find the best course; arrange, select; laws, rules. The ideogram: words and right.

60.ST [A chün tzu uses] deliberating actualizing tao to move.

61.ST A chün tzu uses deliberating litigating to delay dying.

Delight, LO: take joy or pleasure in; pleasant, relaxed; also: music as harmony, elegance and pleasure.

5.ST A chün tzu uses drinking and eating to repose delighting.

7/8.CD Grouping: delighting.

16.ST The Earlier Kings used arousing delight to extol actualizing tao.

Delimit, CHIANG: define frontiers, draw limits; boundary, border. See also: **Limit**

2.ImT Actualizing tao uniting without delimiting.

2.ImT Moving, the earth without delimiting.

2.ImT Corresponding earth without delimiting.

19.ST [A chün tzu uses] tolerating to protect the commoners without delimiting.

42.ImT The commoners stimulated without delimiting.

42.ImT Sun advancing without delimiting.

Delude, MI: confused, stupefied, infatuated; blinded by vice; bewitch, fascinate, deceive.

2.Im Beforehand delusion, afterwards acquiring.

2.ImT Beforehand delusion letting go tao.

24.6a/b Deluding Returning. Pitfall.

Demon(iac), CH'OU: possessed by a malignant genius; ugly, physically or morally deformed; vile, disgraceful, shameful; drunken. The ideogram: fermenting liquor and soul. Demoniac and tiger are opposed on the Universal Compass North–South axis; the tiger (Extreme Yang) scares away and protects against demoniacs (Extreme Yin).

20.2b Truly permitting the demoniac indeed.

28.5b Truly permitting the demoniac indeed.

30.6a Severing the head. Catching in no way its demons.

40.3b Truly permitting the demoniac indeed.

53.3b Radiance flocking demons indeed.

Demonstrate, HUI: show, signal, point out. The ideogram: hand and act, giving signals.

15.4a/b Without not Advantageous, demonstrating Humbling.

Dense, TS'UNG: close set, bushy, crowded; a grove.

29.6a Dismissing into dense jujube trees.

Deny, YÜ: retract, repudiate; deterioration, regress.

6.4a/b Denying, quiet Trial.

16.6a Accomplishment: possessing denial.

17.1a/b An office: possessing denial.

Depart, CH'Ü: leave, quit, remove; repudiate, reject, dismiss.

9.4a Blood departing, alarm issuing forth.

49/50.CD Skinning: departing anteriority indeed.

59.6a Departing far away, issuing forth.

Depend on, YI: rely on, trust; conform to; image, illustration.

42.4a Advantageous: availing of activating depending on shifting the city.

Deprive, CH'IH: strip (of rank), take away; undress; put an end to.

6.6a Completing dawn three times depriving it.

Depth, SHEN: deep water; profound, abstruse; ardent, strong, intense, inner; sound the depths.

32.1b Beginning seeking depth indeed.

Designate, WEI: represent in words, assign a name or meaning; report on, talk about. The ideogram: words and belly, describing the essential.

19.5b Moving the center's designating indeed.

37.ImT Father[and]Mother's designating indeed.

37.6b Reversing individuality's designating indeed.

46.S Assembling and the above implies designating's Ascending.

62.6a That designates Calamity and Blunder.

Desire, YÜAN: wish, hope or long for; covet; desired object.

10.1b Solitarily moving desire indeed.

11.4b Centering the heart desiring indeed.

11.5b Center uses moving desire indeed.

53.5b Acquiring the place desired indeed.

59.2b Acquiring desire indeed.

61.2b Centering the heart desiring indeed.

Desist, PA: cease, leave off, discontinue, finish; enough.

61.3a/b Maybe drumbeating, maybe desisting.

Destroy, PAI: ruin, defeat, violate, subvert, break.

5.3b Respectful consideration, not destroying indeed.

14.2b Amassing centering, not destroying indeed.

24.6a Completing possesses great destroying.

Detain, LIU: hold back or on to; delay, remain; slow.

56.ST A chün tzu uses brightening consideration to avail of punishing and not to detain litigating.

Die, SSU: sudden or untimely death; run out of energy; immobile, fixed.

16.5a/b Persevering, not dying.

30.4a Burning thus. Dying thus. Thrown out thus.

58.ImT The commoners forget their dying.

61.ST A chün tzu uses deliberating litigating to delay dying.

Differentiate, PIEN: argue, dispute, criticize; sophisticated, artful. The ideogram: words and sharp or pungent.

6.1b Although the small possesses words, one's differentiation brightening indeed.

10.ST A chün tzu uses differentiating Above and Below.

14.4b Brightness differentiating clearly indeed.

48.AE The Well: using differentiating righteousness.

Diffuse, LIU: flow out, spread, permeate.

1.ImT The kinds: being diffusing forms.

15.ImT Earthly tao transforming overfilling and diffusing Humbling.

29.ImT Stream diffusing and not overfilling.

Dignify, TSUN: honor, make eminent; noble, respected. The ideogram: presenting wine to a guest.

14.ImT Supple acquiring the dignifying situation, the great centering.

15.AE/ImT Humbling: dignifying and shining.

Dim, MING: dark, obscure; misinformed, immature, cavern, the underworld. The ideogram: 16th day of moon month, when the moon begins to dim.

16.6a Dim Providing for.

16.6b Dim Providing for located above.

46.6a Dim Ascending.

46.6b Dim Ascending located above.

Diminish, SUN: lessen, make smaller; take away from; lose, damage, spoil, wound; bad luck; blame, criticize; offer up, give away. The ideogram: hand and ceremonial vessel, offering sacrifice.

Image of Hexagram 41 and occurs throughout its texts.

42.S Diminishing and not climaxing necessarily Augments.

42.CD Diminishing, Augmenting.

42.ImT Above diminishing, below Augmenting.

Direct, YU: move toward a specific place or goal; have a focus. The ideogram: person moving through or over water, direction without visible landmarks. See also: **Having a direction to go** and **Without direction: Advantageous**

2.ImT A chün tzu directing moving.

37.2a Without direction, releasing.

Disarray, LUAN: throw into disorder, mislay, confuse; out of place; discord, insurrection, anarchy.

7.6b Necessarily disarraying the fiefdoms indeed.

10.2b Centering, not originating from disarray indeed.

11.6b One's fate disarrayed indeed.

12.2b Not disarraying the flock indeed.

45.1a/b Thereupon disarraying, thereupon Clustering.

45.1b One's purpose disarrayed indeed.

53.6b Not permitting disarray indeed.

63.Im Completing: disarraying.

63.ImT Completing, stopping by consequence disarraying.

Discard, MIEH: disregard, ignore; petty, worthless, insignificant; trash.

23.1a,2a Discarding the Trial: pitfall.

Disclose, K'AI: open, reveal, unfold, display; enact rites, clear land; final phase of both hemicycles in the Universal Compass. The ideogram: house doors bursting open.

7.6a Disclosing the city, receiving a dwelling.

Discuss, CHO: deliberate; hear opinions; reach and act on a decision. The ideogram: wine and ladle, pouring out wine to open discussion.

41.1a Discussing Diminishing it.

Disembowel, K'UEI: cut open and clean; prepare for sacrifice; stab.

54.6a A notable disembowelling a goat without blood.

Disentangle, WU WANG: free yourself from: disorder, incoherence; foolish, wild, reckless; false, brutish behaviour; vain, idle, futile.

Image of Hexagram 25 and occurs throughout its texts.

26.S Possessing Disentangling therefore afterwards permitting Accumulating.

Dismiss, CHIH: put aside; judge and find wanting.

29.6a Dismissing into dense jujube trees.

Disperse, HUAN: scatter clouds or crowds; break up obstacles; dispel illusions, fears and suspicions; clear up misunderstandings; dissolve, evaporate, disintegrate, fade, vanish; fog lifting or clearing away.

Image of Hexagram 59 and occurs throughout its texts.

Display, YANG: spread, extend, scatter, divulge; publish abroad, make famous. The ideogram: hand and expand, spreading a message.

14.ST A chün tzu uses terminating hate to display improvement.

43.Im Deciding, displaying into kingly chambers.

43.ImT Displaying into kingly chambers.

Dissolve, HSIAO: liquify, melt, thaw; diminish, disperse; eliminate, exhaust. The ideogram: water dissolving differences.

11.ImT Small People: tao dissolving indeed.

12.ImT A chün tzu: tao dissolving indeed.

19.ImT Dissolving, not lasting indeed.

46.6b Dissolving, not affluence indeed.

Dissolving pause, HSIAO HSI: yin or structure dissolves so that yang or action may emerge; transitional phase of the Universal Compass.

23.ImT A chün tzu honors the dissolving pause to overfill emptiness.

55.ImT Associating with the season: dissolving pause.

Distance, YÜAN: far off, remote; keep at a distance; alienated. The ideogram: go and a long way.

4.4b Solitariness distancing substance indeed.

24.1a/b Not distancing Returning.

33.ST A chün tzu uses distancing Small People.

41.AE Diminishing: using distancing harm.

44.4b Distancing the commoners indeed.

51.ImT Scaring the distant and fearing the nearby indeed.

59.6b Distancing harm indeed.

Distress, HUAN: tribulation, grief, affliction. The ideogram: heart and clamor, the heart distressed.

6.2b Distress culminating, reaping indeed.

63.ST A chün tzu uses pondering distress and providing for defending against it.

Distribute, SHEN: give out, spread, scatter, allot, diffuse.

57.ST A chün tzu uses distributing fate to move affairs.

57.ImT Redoubling Ground uses distributing fate.

Distress, LIN: shame, regret, humiliation; aware of having lost the right track; leads to repenting, HUI, correcting the direction of mind and life.

3.3a Going distress.

3.3b Going distress exhausted indeed.

4.1a Using going distress.

4.4a/b Confining Enveloping. Distress.

11.6a Trial: distress.

13.2a Distress.

13.2b Distress: tao indeed.

18.4a Going: seeing distress.

20.1a Chün tzu: distress.

21.3a The small distress.

22.5a Distress. Completing auspicious.

28.4a Possessing more: distress.

31.3a Going distress.

32.3a Trial: distress.

35.6a Trial: distress.

37.3a Completing distress.

40.3a Trial: distress.

44.6a Distress.

44.6b Exhausting distress above indeed.

45.3a The small distress.

47.4a Distress.

57.3a/b Pressing Ground, distress.

64.1a Distress.

Deepen, CHÜN: jump into deep water; deepen; serious, abstruse.

32.1a Deepening Persevering, Trial: pitfall.

32.1b Deepening Persevering's pitfall.

Divide, YI: separate, break apart, sever; oppose; different, foreign, strange, unusual, rare.

38.ST A chün tzu uses concording and dividing.

Docile, HSÜN: amiable, mild, yielding; tame; gradually attained.

2.1b Docilely involving one's tao:

Donate, SHANG: bestow, confer, grant; rewards, gifts; celebrate, take pleasure in.

64.4a Three years revolved, possessing donating into the great city.

Door, HU: inner door, chamber door; a household; contrasts with gate, MEN, the outer door.

6.2a People, three hundred doors.

55.6a/b Peeping through one's door.

60.1a/b Not issuing forth from the door chambers.

Doubled, LIANG: twice, both, again, dual, a pair.

30.ST Brightness doubled arousing Radiance.

Doubt, YI: suspect, distrust; dubious; surmise, conjecture.

9.6b Possessing a place to doubt indeed.

16.4a No doubting.

22.4b Six at fourth. Appropriate situation to doubt indeed.

33.6b Without a place to doubt indeed.

38.6b The flock, doubt extinguished indeed.

41.3b Three by consequence doubting indeed.

46.3b Without a place to doubt indeed.

55.2a Going acquiring doubt, affliction.

57.1b Purpose doubted indeed.

58.1b Movement not yet doubted indeed.

63.4b Possessing a place to doubt indeed.

Drag, CHU: pull along a hurt or malfunctioning foot; difficulties, lame. The ideogram: foot and worm, an infected foot.

44.1a Ruining the pig, connection: hoof dragging.

Dragon, LUNG: powerful spirit energy emerging from waters below; mythical shape changer with supreme power; connected with heaven, T'IEN, and the trigram Force, CH'IEN.

1.ImT The season riding six dragons used going to meet heaven.

1.1a/b Immersed dragon, no availing of.

1.2a/b Seeing dragon located in the fields.

1.5a/b Flying dragon located in heaven.

1.6a/b Overbearing dragon possesses repenting.

1.7a Seeing flocking dragons without a head.

2.6a/b Dragons struggling into the countryside.

Draw near, CHIU: approach, encounter, come near; follow; approach completion; composed, finished; able, willing; in a little while.

49.3a/b Skinning words three times drawing near:

Draw water, CHI: draw water from a well; draw forth, lead; take in a doctrine or example. The ideogram: water and reach to.

48.3a Permitting availing of drawing water:

Dread, WEI: stand in alarm of, respect, venerate; a just fear.

51.6b Dreading the neighbor, a warning indeed.

Drench, CH'IN: soak, penetrate, immerse, steep in; imbued with.

19.ImT Solid drenched and long living.

33.ImT Drenched and long living indeed.

Drink, YIN: take in liquid or air; quench thirst, give liquid to; inhale, suck in.

64.6a There is a connection to the spirit: into drinking liquor.

64.6b Drinking liquor, soaking the head.

Drink and eat, YIN SHIH: comprehensive term for eating, drinking and breathing; a meal, eating together.

5.S Attending implies drinking and eating's tao indeed.

5.ST A chün tzu uses drinking and eating to repose delighting.

6.S Drinking and eating necessarily possesses Arguing.

27.ST [A chün tzu uses] articulating to Drink and take in.

53.2a/b Drinking and eating: feasting, feasting.

Droop, CH'UI: hang down, let fall; bow; condescend to inferiors; almost, near; suspended; hand down from past to future.

36.1a Drooping one's wings.

Drudgery, CHIEN: difficult, hard, repetitive work; hard to cultivate; distressing, sorrowful. The ideogram: sticky earth and a person looking around, hard work in comparison to others.

11.3a Drudgery, Trial: without fault.

14.1a Drudgery by consequence without fault.

21.4a Advantageous: drudgery, Trial.

21.4b Advantageous: drudgery, Trial auspicious.

26.3a Advantageous: drudgery, Trial.

34.6a/b Drudgery by consequence auspicious.

36.Im/ImT Advantageous: drudgery, Trial.

- **Drumbeating,** KU: skin or earthenware drums; play a drum; excite, arouse, encourage; joyous, happy.

30.3a Not drumbeating a jar and singing.

61.3a/b Maybe drumbeating, maybe desisting.

- **Dug out,** CHOU: hollowed log, canoe; boat, ride or transport by boat.

61.ImT Riding a wooden dug out, emptiness indeed.

- **Duskiness,** MAI: obscure, indistinct; insufficient light; times of day when it is not fully light. The ideogram: day and not yet.

3.ImT Heaven creating grass, duskiness.

- **Dwell,** CHI: home, house, household, family; domestic, within doors; live in. The ideogram: roof and pig or dog, the most valued domestic animals.

Image of Hexagram 37 and occurs throughout its texts.

4.2a/b The son controlling the dwelling.

7.6a Disclosing the city, receiving a dwelling.

26.Im/ImT Not dwelling, taking in. Auspicious.

38.S Dwelling tao exhausted, necessarily returning.

38.CD Dwelling People: inside indeed.

41.6a Acquiring a servant, without dwelling.

55.6a Screening one's dwelling.

- **Each one,** KO: every, all, wherever; each separate thing.

1.ImT Each one correcting innate fate.

- **Ear,** ERH: organ of hearing; handle, sides.

21.6a/b Wherefore locking up submerging the ears?

50.ImT Ground and the ear and eye: understanding brightened.

50.3a/b The Vessel: the ears skinned.

50.5a The Vessel: yellow ears, metallic rings.

50.5b The Vessel: yellow ears.

- **Earlier Kings,** HSIEN WANG: ideal rulers of old; the golden age, primal time, power in harmony with nature; model for the chün tzu.

This term occurs in the Symbol Tradition of Hexagrams 8, 16, 20, 21, 24, 25, 59.

- **Earth,** TI: ground on which the human world rests; basis of all things, nourishes all things; the Symbol of the trigram Field, K'UN. See also: **Heaven and Earth**

2.ST Earth potency: Field.

2.ImT The female horse: earth sorting.

2.ImT Moving, the earth without delimiting.

2.ImT Corresponding earth without delimiting.

2.2b Earthly tao shining indeed.

7.ST Earth center possessing stream.

8.ST Above earth possessing stream.

12.ST Heaven, earth, not mingling.

15.ST Earth center possessing mountain.

15.ImT Earth tao lowly and moving above.

15.ImT Earthly tao transforming overfilling and diffusing Humbling.

16.ST Thunder issuing forth from earth impetuously.

19.ST Above marsh possessing earth.

20.ST Wind moving above earth.

23.ST Mountain adjoining with respect to earth.

24.ST Thunder located in earth center.

29.ImT Earth venturing, mountains, rivers, hill tops, mounds indeed.

30.ImT The hundred grains, grasses, trees congregating reaching to earth.

35.ST/ImT Brightness issuing forth above earth.

36.ST/ImT Brightness entering earth center.

36.6a/b Afterwards entering into earth.

38.ImT Heaven, Earth, Polarizing and one's affairs concording indeed.

42.ImT Heaven spreading out, earth giving birth.

44.ImT Heaven, Earth: mutually meeting.

45.ST Above marsh with respect to earth.

46.ST Earth center giving birth to wood.

48.AE The Well: actualizing tao's earth indeed.

60.ImT Heaven, Earth: Articulating and the four seasons accomplishing.

East, TUNG: corresponds to Spring, YÜAN, and the Woody Moment, stirs up and germinates new life-cycle; place of honor and the person in it.

63.5a/b The Eastern neighbor slaughters cattle.

Eastern North: border, limit, completion; boundary between cycles: Mountain; accomplishing words, summing up before new germination; dark, cold, lonely winter night.

2.Im/ImT Eastern North: losing partnering.

39.Im/ImT Not Advantageous: Eastern North.

Eat, see **Take in**

Eight, PA: number of highly valued essentials: eight trigrams, eight immortals, eight compass points; eighth.

19.Im/ImT Culminating into the eighth moon: possessing a pitfall.

Eliminate, CH'U: root out, remove, do away with, take off, keep out; vacate, exchange.

45.ST A chün tzu uses eliminating arms to implement.

Embarrassed, HSIU: conscious of guilt or fault; unworthy; ashamed, confused; shy, blushing. The ideogram: sheep, sheepish feeling.

12.3a/b Enwrapping embarrassing.

32.3a Maybe receiving's embarrassing.

Embellish, SHIH: ornament, paint, brighten, patch up the appearance; apply cosmetics; pretend, make believe.

22.S Adorning implies embellishing indeed.

23.S Actually involving embellishing, therefore afterwards Growing by consequence used up.

Emblem ax, FU: moon shaped ax, symbol of power to govern.

56.4a/b Acquiring one's own emblem ax.

57.6a/b Losing one's own emblem ax.

Eminent, HSIEN: moral and intellectual power; worthy, excellent, virtuous; sage second to the all wise, SHENG.

8.4b Outside Grouping with respect to eminence.

26.ImT Above solid and honoring eminence.

26.ImT Nourishing eminence indeed.

27.ImT The all wise person nourishes eminence used to extend to the myriad commoners.

50.ImT and great Growing uses nourishing all wise eminences.

53.ST A chün tzu uses residing in eminent actualizing tao to improve the vulgar.

Empty, HSÜ: no images or concepts; vacant, unsubstantial; empty yet fertile space.

23.ImT A chün tzu honors the dissolving pause to overfill emptiness.

31.ST A chün tzu uses emptiness to accept people.

41.ImT Diminishing augmenting, overfilling emptiness.

46.3a/b Ascending: an empty capital.

54.6b Receiving an empty basket indeed.

55.ImT Heaven and Earth overfilling emptiness.

61.ImT Riding a wooden dug out, emptiness indeed.

Enable, see: **Able**

Enclose, HSIEN: put inside a fence or barrier; restrain, obstruct, forbid; pen, corral.

26.3a Spoken thus: an enclosed cart, escorting.

37.1a/b Enclosing: possessing Dwelling.

Encounter, TI: see face to face; admitted to an audience; visit, interview.

47.1a Three year's time not encountering.

55.6a Three year's time not encountering.

Encourage, CH'ÜAN: exhort, stimulate, influence; admonish.

48.ST A chün tzu uses toiling commoners to encourage mutualizing.

58.ImT Actually the commoners encouraged in fact.

Encroach, CH'IN: invade, usurp, appropriate; advance stealthily, enter secretly; possessed by a spirit.

15.5a/b Advantageous: availing of encroaching subjugating.

End, CHI: last or highest point; final, extreme; on the verge; ridgepole of a house.

60.2b Letting go the season end indeed.

64.1b Truly not knowing the end indeed.

Enforce, LAI: compel obedience; have charge of; imposed by highest authority; arrest, deliver for punishment.

21.ST The Earlier Kings used brightening flogging to enforce the laws.

Enlighten, CHAO: cast light on, display, show; instruct, give knowledge; manifest, bright, splendid. The ideogram: sun and call, bring into the light.

35.ST A chün tzu uses originating enlightening to brighten actualizing tao.

Enrich, YÜ: make richer (excluding land); material, mental or spiritual wealth; bequeath; generous, abundant. The ideogram: garments, portable riches.

18.4a/b Enriching the father's Corrupting.

35.1a/b Enriching, without fault.

42.AE Augmenting: actualizing tao's enriching indeed.

42.AE Augmenting: long living enriching and not setting up.

Enshroud, YEN: screen, shade from view, hide, cover. The ideogram: hand and cover. See also: **Shroud**

47.ImT Solid enshrouded indeed.

Enter, JU: penetrate, go into, enter on, progress; put into, encroach on; the Action of the trigram Ground, SUN, contrary of issue forth, CH'U.

3.3a Namely, entering into the forest center.

5.6a Entering into the cave.

6.ImT Entering into the abyss indeed.

17.ST A chün tzu uses turning to darkening to enter a reposing pause.

24.Im Issuing forth, entering, without affliction.

24.ImT That uses issuing forth, entering, without affliction.

29.1a Entering into the Gorge, the recess.

29.1b Repeating Gorge, entering Gorge.

29.3a Entering into the Gorge, the recess.

36.ST/ImT Brightness entering earth center.

36.4a/b Entering into the left belly.

36.6a/b Afterwards entering into earth.

47.1a/b Entering into a shady gully.

47.3a/b Entering into one's house.

57.S Ground implies entering indeed.

58.S Entering and afterwards stimulating it.

Envelop, MENG: cover, pull over, hide, conceal; lid or cover; clouded awareness, dull; ignorance, immaturity; unseen beginnings. The ideogram: plant and covered, hidden growth.

Image of Hexagram 4 and occurs throughout its texts.

3.CD Enveloping: variegated and conspicuous.

36.ImT Using the enveloped great: heaviness.

Enwrap, PAO: envelop, hold, contain; patient; take on responsibility, engaged. The ideogram: enfold and self, a fetus in the womb.

4.2a Enwrapping Enveloping.

11.2a Enwrapping wasteland.

11.2b Enwrapping wasteland, acquiring honor, into centering moving.

12.2a Enwrapping receiving.

12.3a/b Enwrapping embarrassing.

44.2a/b Enwrapping possessing fish.

44.4a Enwrapping without fish.

44.5a Using osier, enwrapping melons.

Equal, P'EI: on the same level; pair, husband or wife; together.

16.ST Using equaling the grandfather predecessors.

55.1a Meeting one's equal lord.

Eradicate, PA: pull up, root out, extirpate; extricate from difficulties; elevate, promote.

11.1a Eradicating thatch grass intertwisted.

11.1b Eradicating thatch grass, chastising auspicious.

12.1a Eradicating thatch grass intertwisted.

12.1b Eradicating thatch grass, Trial: auspicious.

Escape, P'U: flee, run away, turn tail; deserter, fugitive. The ideogram: go and first, precipitous flight.

6.2a Converting and escaping one's capital.

6.2b Converting escaping, skulking indeed.

Escort, WEI: accompany, protect, guard, defend, honor; restrain; military outpost.

26.3a Spoken thus: an enclosed cart, escorting.

Establish, LI: set up, institute, order, arrange; stand erect; settled principles.

28.ST A chün tzu uses solitary establishing not to fear.

32.ST A chün tzu uses establishing, not versatility on all sides.

42.6a Establishing the heart, no persevering.

59.ST The earlier kings used presenting into the supreme to establish the temples.

Evade, MIEN: avoid, escape from, get away; be free of, dispense with; remove from office. The ideogram: a hare, known for its evasive skill.

40.ImT Stirring up and evading reaching to venturing.

Evaluate, CH'ENG: assess, appraise; weigh, estimate, reckon; designate, name. The ideogram: weigh and grain, attributing value.

15.ST [A chün tzu uses] evaluating beings to even spreading out.

57.AE Ground: evaluating and occulting.

Even, P'ING: level, make even or equal; uniform, peaceful, tranquil; restore quiet, harmonize.

11.3a Without evening, not unevening.

15.ST [A chün tzu uses] evaluating beings to even spreading out.

20.6b Purpose not yet evened indeed.

29.5a Merely already evened.

31.ImT The all wise person influencing the people at heart and Below Heaven harmony evening.

Even more, K'UANG: even more so, all the more.

16.ImT and even more installing feudatories to move legions reached.

55.ImT and even more with respect to the people reached.

55.ImT Even more with respect to the Souls[and]Spirits reached.

Evidence, TZ'U: verbal proof; instructions, orders, arguments; apology.

42.6b One sided evidence indeed.

Exalting worship, YIN CHIEN: superlative of worship; glorify; intensify feelings of praise and alarm.

16.ST Exalting worship's Supreme Above.

Exceed/Traverse, KU: go beyond, pass over; make the passage; excessive, transgress; error, fault. Image of Hexagrams 28 and 62 and occurs throughout their texts.

16.ImT Anterior Sun and Moon not exceeding.

27.CD Great Exceeding: toppling indeed.

29.S Beings not permitted to use completing Exceeding.

40.ST A chün tzu uses forgiving excess to pardon offenses.

42.ST [A chün tzu uses] possessing excess, by consequence amending.

55.1b Exceeding a decade, calamity indeed.

61.CD Small Exceeding: Excess indeed.

63.S Possessing Exceeding being implies necessarily Fording.

Excellence, CHIA: superior quality; fine, delicious, glorious; happy, pleased; rejoice in, praise. The ideogram: increasing goodness, pleasure and happiness.

17.5a Conformity into excellence. Auspicious.

17.5b Conformity into excellence auspicious.

30.6a Possessing excellence.

33.5a/b Excellence Retiring, Trial: auspicious.

49.2b Moving possessing excellence indeed.

Exhaust, CH'IUNG: bring to an end; limit, extremity; destitute; investigate exhaustively; end without a new beginning. Contrasts with complete, CHUNG, end of a cycle.The ideogram: cave and naked person, bent with disease or old age.

2.6b Their tao exhausted indeed.

3.3b Going distress exhausted indeed.

5.ImT Actually one's righteousness, not confining exhaustion.

8.ImT One's tao exhausted indeed.

16.1b Purpose exhausted, pitfall indeed.

17.6b Exhausting the above indeed.

19.ST A chün tzu uses teaching to ponder without exhausting.

24.S Above Stripping exhausted, below reversing.

25.6b Exhaustion's calamity indeed.

34.1b One's connection exhausted indeed.

38.S Dwelling tao exhausted, necessarily returning.

39.ImT One's tao exhausted indeed.

43.ImT The place to honor thereupon exhausted indeed.

44.6b Exhausting distress above indeed.

47.AE Confining: exhausting and interpenetrating.

47.ImT Honoring the mouth thereupon exhausted indeed.

48.ImT The Well nourishing and not exhausted indeed.

53.ImT Stirring up not exhausted indeed.

56.S Exhausting the great implies necessarily letting go one's residing.

56.1b Purpose exhausted, calamity indeed.

57.3b Purpose exhausted indeed.

57.6b Above exhaustion indeed.

59.ImT Solid coming and not exhausted.

60.ImT,6b One's tao exhausted indeed.

63/64.CD Not yet Fording: manhood exhausted indeed.

63.ImT One's tao exhausted indeed.

64.S Beings not permitted exhaustion indeed.

Experienced, see **Respectable**

Explicate, CHIANG: explain, unfold, narrate; converse, speak; investigate, plan, discuss. The ideogram: speech and crossing beams, speech blending harmoniously.

58.ST A chün tzu uses partnering friends to explicate repeating.

Expose, WEI: exposed to danger, precipitous, unsteady; too high, not upright; uneasy. The ideogram: overhanging rock, person and limit, exposure in an extreme position.

43.ImT One's exposure thereupon shining indeed.

51.5b Exposed moving indeed.

52.3b Exposure smothers the heart indeed.

Extend(to), CHI: reach to, draw out, prolong; continuous, enduring.

27.ImT The all wise person nourishes eminence used to extend to the myriad commoners.

43.ST A chün tzu uses spreading out benefits to extend to the below.

44.2b Righteously not extending to guesting indeed.

61.ImT Trustworthiness extending to hog fish indeed.

62.2a/b Not extending to one's chief.

Extinguish, WANG: ruin, destroy; gone, dead, lost without trace; extinct, forgotten, out of mind. The ideogram: person concealed by a wall, out of sight. See also: **Repenting extinguished**

11.2a Partnering extinguished.

12.5a Its extinction, its extinction.

16.5b Center not yet extinguished indeed.

38.6b The flock, doubt extinguished indeed.

56.5a The one arrow extinguishing.

61.4a/b The horse team extinguished.

• **Extol**, CH'UNG: praise, honor, magnify, revere; eminent, lofty; worthy of worship.

16.ST The Earlier Kings used arousing delight to extol actualizing tao.

• **Eye**, MU: eye and its functions: look, see, glance, observe.

9.3a/b Husband, consort, reversing eyes.

50.ImT Ground and the ear[and]eye: understanding brightened.

• **Face**, WANG: full moon; moon directly facing the sun; 15th day of the moon month; look at hopefully.

9.6a The moon almost facing.

54.5a The moon almost facing, auspicious.

61.4a The moon almost facing.

• **Fade**, JO: lose strength or freshness, wither, wane; fragile, feeble, weak; decayed, ruined; infirm purpose.

28.ImT Roots, tips, fading indeed.

• **Fall**, HSIEN: fall down or into, sink, drop, descend; falling water; the Action of the trigram Gorge, K'AN.

5.ImT Solid persisting and not falling.

29.S Gorge implies falling indeed.

30.S Falling necessarily possesses a place to congregate.

• **Far away**, TI: far, remote; send away, exile.

59.6a Departing far away, issuing forth.

• **Fate/Mandate**, MING: individual destiny; birth and death as limits of life; issue orders with authority; consult the gods. The ideogram: mouth and order, words with heavenly authority.

1.ImT Each one correcting innate fate.

6.4a/b Returning, approaching fate.

7.2a/b The king three times bestowing fate.

7.6a/b The Great Chief possesses fate.

11.6a Originating from the capital, notifying fate.

11.6b One's fate disarrayed indeed.

12.4a/b Possessing fate, without fault.

14.ST [A chün tzu uses] yielding to heaven to relinquish fate.

19.2b Not yet yielding to fate indeed.

25.ImT Heaven's fate indeed.

25.ImT Heavenly fate not shielding.

35.1b Not yet accepting fate indeed.

44.ST The crown prince uses spreading out fate to command the four sides.

44.5b Purpose, not stowing away fate indeed.

45.ImT Yielding to heavenly fate indeed.

47.ST A chün tzu uses involving fate to release purpose.

49.ImT Majestically martial, Skinning fate.

49.4a/b Amending fate auspicious.

50.ST A chün tzu uses correcting the situation to solidify fate.

56.5a/b Completing uses praising fate.

57.ST A chün tzu uses distributing fate to move affairs.

57.ImT Redoubling Ground uses distributing fate.

• **Father(hood)**, FU: ruler of the family; act as a father, paternal, patriarchal; authoritative rule. The ideogram: hand and rod, the chastising father. See also: **Father and Mother** and **Father and Son**

18.1a/b,3a/b Managing the father's Corrupting.

18.4a/b Enriching the father's Corrupting.

18.5a Managing the father's Corrupting.

18.5b Managing the father availing of praise.

37.ImT The father, a father.

• **Father and Mother**, FU MU: cooperative relation between man and woman in ruling and caring for a family.

37.ImT Father and Mother's designating indeed.

• **Father and Son**, fu tzu: proper relation between generations serving and living up to the ideal of the ancestors, carrying on a tradition.

31.S Therefore afterwards possessing Father and Son.

31.S Possessing Father and Son:

• **Fault**, CHIU: unworthy conduct that leads to harm, illness, misfortune. The ideogram: person and differ, differ from what you should be. See also: **Without fault**

7.ImT Actually auspicious, furthermore wherefore faulty?

9.1a Wherefore one's fault? Auspicious.

13.1b Furthermore whose fault indeed?

14.1a In no way faulty.

17.4a Wherefore faulty?

18.3a Without the great: fault.

19.3b Fault not long living indeed.

28.6b Not permitting fault indeed.

30.1b Using casting out fault indeed.

34.6b Fault not long living indeed.

38.1b Using casting out fault indeed.

38.5a Going wherefore faulty?

40.3b Furthermore whose fault indeed.

43.1a Going not mastering, activating faulty.

43.1b Fault indeed.

44.3a Without the great: fault.

53.1a Lacking fault.

60.3b Furthermore whose fault indeed?

Favor, CH'UNG: receive or confer gifts, obtain grace, win favor; dote on a woman; gifted for.

7.2b Receiving heavenly favor indeed.

23.5a/b Using housing people, favor.

Fear, CHÜ: afraid, intimidated, apprehensive; stand in alarm of.

28.ST A chün tzu uses solitary establishing not to fear.

51.ST A chün tzu uses anxious fearing to adjust inspecting.

51.ImT Scaring the distant and fearing the nearby indeed.

Feast, K'AN: take part in or give a feast; rejoice, give pleasure; pleased, contented.

53.2a/b Drinking and eating: feasting, feasting.

Feathers, YU: wings, plumes; feathered; quick, flying.

53.6a Its feathers permit availing of activating fundamentals.

53.6b Its feathers permit availing of activating fundamentals, auspicious.

Feed, K'UEI: prepare and present food; provisions.

37.2a Locating the center, feeding.

Female, P'IN: female sexual organs, particularly of farm animals; concave, hollow. The ideogram: cattle and ladle, a hollow, reproductive organ.

2.Im Field: Spring Growing Advantageous, female horse's Trial.

2.ImT The female horse: earth sorting.

30.Im Growing. Accumulating female cattle.

30.ImT That uses accumulating female cattle, auspicious indeed.

Fetter, CHIH: tie, manacle; restrain and hinder movement, clog wheels; impede.

4.1a Availing of stimulating fettering shackles.

Feudatory, HOU: nobles entrusted with governing the provinces; active in daily life rather than governing from the center; contrasts with prince, KUNG, executives at the court.

3.Im Advantageous: installing feudatories.

3.ImT Proper to install feudatories and not to soothe.

3.1a Advantageous: installing feudatories.

8.ST The Earlier Kings used installing myriad cities to connect the connoted feudatories.

16.Im Providing for, Advantageous: installing feudatories to move legions.

16.ImT and even more installing feudatories to move legions reached.

18.6a/b Not affairs, kingly feudatories.

35.Im Prospering, the calm feudatory avails of bestowing horses to multiply the multitudes.

35.ImT That uses the calm feudatory availing of bestowing horses to multiply the multitudes.

Few, KUA: small number; seldom, rarely; unusual, solitary.

9/10.CD Small Accumulating: few indeed.

15.ST A chün tzu uses reducing the numerous to augment the few.

47.AE Confining: using few grudges.

55/56.CD Connecting the few: Sojourning indeed.

Fiefdom, PANG: region governed by a feudatory, an order of nobility.

7.2b Cherishing the myriad fiefdoms indeed.

7.6b Necessarily disarraying the fiefdoms indeed.

12.ImT Above and Below not mingling and Below Heaven without fiefdoms indeed.

30.6b Using correcting the fiefdoms indeed.

39.ImT Using correcting the fiefdoms indeed.

53.ImT Permitting using correcting the fiefdoms indeed.

61.ImT Thereupon changing the fiefdoms indeed.

Field, K'UN: surface of the world; concrete extension; basis of all existence, where Force or heaven exerts its power; all involving service; earth; moon, wife, mother; courtiers, servants. The ideogram: terrestrial globe and stretch out, stability and extension.

Image of Hexagram 2 and occurs throughout its texts.

1.CD Field: supple.

Field altar, SHE: altar and sacrifices to spirits of place; village, with a common god and field altar.

51.ImT Issuing forth permits using guarding the ancestral temple, field altar, offertory millet.

Fields, T'IEN: cultivated land, plantation; also: hunting, game in the fields cannot escape the hunt. The ideogram: square divided into four sections, delineating fields.

1.2a/b Seeing dragon located in the fields.
7.5a The fields possess wild fowl.
32.4a The fields without wildfowl.
40.2a The fields, catching three foxes.
57.4a/b The fields, catching three kinds.

Fine, LIANG: excellent, refined, valuable; gentle, considerate, kind; natural.

26.3a A fine horse, pursuing.
54.5a/b One's junior sister's sleeves not thus fine.

Fire, HUO: warming and consuming aspect of burning; fire and brightness are the Symbols of the trigram Radiance, LI.

13.ST Heaven associating with fire.
14.ST Fire located above heaven.
22.ST Below mountain possessing fire.
37.ST Wind originating from fire issuing forth.
38.ST Fire above, marsh below.
38.ImT Fire stirring up and above.
49.ST Marsh center possessing fire.
49.ImT Skinning. Stream, fire, mutually pausing.
50.ST Above wood possessing fire.
50.ImT Using wood: Ground, fire.
56.ST Above mountain possessing fire.
63.ST Stream located above fire.
64.ST Fire located above stream.

Firm, FU: constant, fixed, steady; chronic, recurrent. The ideogram: old and enclosure, long preserved.

25.4b Firmly possessing it indeed.
32.AE Persevering: actualizing tao's firmness indeed.
33.2b Firm purpose indeed.
42.3b Firmly possessing it indeed.

Fish, YÜ: scaly, aquatic beings hidden in the water; symbol of abundance; connected with the Streaming Moment. See also: **Hog Fish**

23.5a Threading fish.
44.2a/b Enwrapping possessing fish.
44.4a Enwrapping without fish.
44.4b Without fish's pitfall.

Five, WU: number for active groups: Five Moments, Directions, colors, smells, tastes, tones, feelings; fifth.

This term occurs at the fifth Transforming Line of each hexagram. It also occurs at:

43.ImT Supple riding five solids indeed.

Flee, PEN: run away quickly; urgent, hurry; bustle, confusion; marry without rites. The ideogram: three oxen and fright, a stampede.

59.2a/b Dispersing: fleeing one's bench.

Flesh, FU: muscles, organs, skin, in contrast to bones.

21.2a/b Gnawing flesh, submerging the nose.
23.4a/b Stripping the bed, using flesh.
38.5a/b Your ancestor gnawing flesh.
43.4a The sacrum without flesh.
44.3a The sacrum without flesh.

Flock, CH'ÜN: herd, group; people of same kind, friends, equals; all, entire; move in unison, flock together. The ideogram: chief and sheep, flock around a leader.

1.7a Seeing flocking dragons without a head.
12.2b Not disarraying the flock indeed.
38.6b The flock, doubt extinguished indeed.
53.3b Radiance flocking demons indeed.
59.4a/b Dispersing one's flock, Spring auspicious.

Flog, FA: punish with blows, beat, whip; used to find out the truth.

16.ImT By consequence punishing flogging purifies and the commoners submit.
21.ST The Earlier Kings used brightening flogging to enforce the laws.

Flower, HUA: beauty, abundance; variegated, elegant, blooming, garden like; symbol of culture and literature.

28.5a/b A withered willow giving birth to flowers.

Flutter, P'IEN: fly or run about; bustle, fussy. The ideogram: young bird leaving the nest.

11.4a Fluttering, fluttering.
11.4b Fluttering, fluttering: not affluence.

Fly, FEI: spread your wings, fly away; let free; swift.

1.5a Flying dragon located in heaven.
36.1a Brightness Hiding into flying.
62.Im Flying bird: abandoning's sound.
62.ImT Possessing the flying bird's symbol in truth.
62.ImT Flying bird: abandoning's sound.
62.1a/b Flying bird: using a pitfall.
62.6a Flying bird radiating it.

Follow, SUI: come or go after; pursue, impelled to move; come after in inevitable sequence; move in the same direction, comply with what is ahead; follow a way or religion; according to, next, subsequent. The ideogram: go and fall, unavoidable movement.

Image of Hexagram 17 and occurs throughout its texts.

18.S Using rejoicing Following people implies necessarily possessing affairs.

18.CD Following: without anteriority indeed.

31.3a Holding on to one's following.

31.3b Purpose located in following people.

52.2a/b Not rescuing one's following.

57.ST Following winds. Ground.

Foot, CHIH: literal foot; foundation, base.

21.1a/b Shoes locked up, submerging the feet.

22.1a Adorning one's feet.

34.1a/b Invigorating into the feet.

43.1a Invigorating into the preceding foot.

50.1a/b The Vessel: toppling the foot.

52.1a/b Bound: one's feet.

Foot cutting, YÜEH: crippling punishment for serious crimes.

47.5a/b Nose cutting, foot cutting.

Force, CH'IEN: spirit power, creative and destructive; unceasing forward motion; dynamic, enduring, untiring; firm, stable; heaven, sovereign, father; also: dry up, parched, exhausted, cleared away. The ideogram: sprouts or vapors rising from the ground and sunlight, both fecundating moisture and scorching drought. See also: **Parch**

Image of Hexagram 1 and occurs throughout its texts.

2.CD Force: solid.

10. ImT Stimulating and corresponding reaching to Force.

13. ImT Acquiring centering and corresponding reaching to Force.

13. ImT Force moving indeed.

Ford, CHI: cross a river at a ford or shallow place; overcome an obstacle, embark on a course of action; help, relieve; cease. The ideogram: water and level, running smooth over a flat bottom.

Image of Hexagrams 63 and 64 and occurs throughout their texts.

15. ImT Heavenly tao fording below and shining brightness.

Forest, LIN: area with no mark of human construction; woods, wild luxuriance; wilderness; last of the territorial zones: city, suburbs, countryside, forests.

3.3a Namely, entering into the forest center.

Forget, WANG: escape the mind; leave undone, disregard, neglect. The ideogram: heart and lost.

58. ImT The commoners forget their toiling.

58. ImT The commoners forget their dying.

Forgive, SHE: excuse, pass over, set aside, reprieve.

40.ST A chün tzu uses forgiving excess to pardon offenses.

Form, HSING: shape; body, bodily; material appearance.

1.ImT The kinds: being diffusing forms.

50.4a Its form soiled. Pitfall.

Foundation, CHI: base of wall or building; basis, starting point; found, establish.

10.AE Treading: actualizing tao's foundation indeed.

Four, SSU: number four, fourth; everywhere, all around; the earth with four sides, FANG. See also: **Four seasons** and **Four sides**

This term occurs at the fourth Transforming Line of each hexagram. It occurs also at:

36.6b Illuminating the four cities indeed.

Four seasons, SSU SHIH: the four dynamic qualities of time that make up the year and the Time Cycle; the right time, in accord with the time; time as sacred; all encompassing.

16. ImT and the four seasons not straying.

20. ImT and the four seasons not straying.

32. ImT The four seasons transforming changes and enabling lasting accomplishment.

49. ImT Heaven and Earth Skinning and the four seasons accomplishing.

60. ImT Heaven, Earth: Articulating and the four seasons accomplishing.

Four sides, SSU FANG: the cardinal points; the limits or boundaries of the earth; everywhere, all around. See also: **Sides**

30.ST Great People use consecutive brightening to illuminate into the four sides.

44.ST The crown prince uses spreading out fate to command the four sides.

Fox, HU: crafty, shape changing animal; used by spirits, often female; ambivalent night spirit that can create havoc and bestow abundance.

40.2a The fields, catching three foxes.

64. Im/ImT The small fox, a muddy Ford.

Fragment, SO: break into small pieces, broken parts; minute, fine; petty, trivial; annoying; lit.: splinters of precious stones. The ideogram: small and cowrie shells, the tinkling of small coins.

56.1a/b Sojourning: fragmenting, fragmenting.

Friend, YU: companion, associate; of the same mind; attached, in pairs. The ideogram: two hands joined.

41.3a By consequence acquiring one's friend.

58.ST A chün tzu uses partnering friends to explicate repeating.

Fright, HSI: frighten or be frightened; alarm, terror; alarmstruck.

51.Im/ImT,1a/b Shake coming: frightening, frightening.

Frost, SHUANG: frozen dew, hoar frost, rime; crystallized; severe, frigid.

2.1a Treading frost, hardening ice culminating.

2.1b Treading frost hardening the ice:

Froth, MO: froth of small stars; spume, foam, bubbles; perspire, drool.

55.3a Sun centering: seeing froth.

Fruit, KUO: plants' annual produce; tree fruits; come to fruition, fruits of actions; produce, results, effects; reliable; conclude, surpass. The ideogram: tree topped by a round fruit.

4.ST A chün tzu uses fruiting movement to nurture actualizing tao.

23.6a The ripe fruit not taken in.

40.ImT Thunder and Rain arousing and the hundred fruits, grasses, trees, altogether seedburst boundary.

Full, MAN: as much as possible; replete, bulging, stuffed, abounding; complete; proud.

3.ImT Thunder and Rain's stirring up, fullness overfilling.

Fundamentals, YI: primary natural powers; origins, essentials; good and do good; correct, proper, just; rule, rite, decorum; paired, matched. The ideogram: person and righteous.

53.6a Its feathers permit availing of activating fundamentals.

53.6b Its feathers permit availing of activating fundamentals, auspicious.

Furthermore, YU: in addition to; higher degree of.

7.ImT Actually auspicious, furthermore wherefore faulty?

13.1b Furthermore whose fault indeed?

40.3b Furthermore whose fault indeed?

49.3b Furthermore actually wherefore having them.

60.3b Furthermore whose fault indeed?

Garden, YÜAN: enclosed garden; park, yard; imperial tombs.

22.5a Adorning into a hill top garden.

Gate, MEN: outer door, between court yard and street; a text or master as gate to a school of thought.

13.1a Concording People into the gate.

13.1b Issuing forth from the gate Concording People.

16.AE Redoubling gates, smiting clappers.

17.1a/b Issuing forth from the gate, mingling possesses achievement.

36.4a Into issuing forth from the gate chambers.

60.2a Not issuing forth from the gate chambers.

60.2b Not issuing forth from the gate chambers, pitfall.

Geld, FEN: castrate a pig; deprive, take out.

26.5a A gelded pig's tusks.

Generous, HUNG: liberal, large; vast, expanded; give or share willingly; munificent; develop fully.

2.ImT Containing generosity, the shining great.

Giggle, HSI: laugh or titter uncontrollably; merriment, delight, surprise; foolish.

37.3a/b The wife, the son, giggling, giggling:

Give birth to, see: **Birth**

Glare, TAN: stare intensely; obstruct, prevent. The ideogram: look and hesitate, staring without acting.

27.4a Tiger observing: glaring, glaring.

Gnaw, SHIH: bite away, chew; bite persistently and remove; snap at, nibble; reach the essential by removing the unnecessary. The ideogram: mouth and divination, revealing the essential.

Image of Hexagram 21 and occurs throughout its texts.

38.5a/b Your ancestor gnawing flesh.

Go, WANG, and come, LAI, describe the stream of time as it flows from future through present to past; go, WANG, indicates what is departing from present to past; proceed, move on; keyword. See also: **Go to meet; Let go; Having a direction to go**

3.3a Going distress.

3.3b Going distress exhausted indeed.

3.4a Going auspicious.

3.4b Seeking and going.

4.1a Using going distress.

5.ImT Going possesses achievement indeed.

9.ImT Honoring going indeed.

10.1a/b Sheer Treading going.

11.Im/ImT The small going, the great coming.

11.3a/b Without going, not returning.

12.Im/ImT The great going, the small coming.

18.ImT Going possesses affairs indeed.

18.4a Going: seeing distress.

18.4b Going, not yet acquiring indeed.

25.ImT Disentangling's going.

25.1a Disentangling. Going auspicious.

25.1b Disentangling's going.

26.ST A chün tzu uses the numerous recorded preceding words going to move.

29.ImT Movement possesses honor. Going possesses achievement indeed.

31.3a Going distress.

31.4a/b Wavering, wavering: going, coming.

33.1b Not going, wherefore calamity indeed.

34.4b Honoring going indeed.

35.5a Going auspicious, without not Advantageous.

35.5b Going possessing reward indeed.

38.5a Going wherefore faulty?

38.5b Going possessing reward indeed.

38.6a Going meeting rain, by consequence auspicious.

39.ImT Going acquires the center indeed.

39.ImT Going possesses achievement indeed.

39.1a/b Going Difficulties, coming praise.

39.3a/b Going Difficulties, coming reversing.

39.4a/b Going Difficulties, coming continuity.

39.6a/b Going Difficulties, coming ripening.

40.Im Without a place to go:

40.ImT Going acquiring crowds indeed.

40.ImT Going possesses achievement indeed.

41.1a/b Climaxing affairs, swiftly going.

43.1a Going not mastering, activating faulty.

43.1b Not mastering and going.

43.3a Solitary going, meeting rain.

45.1a,3a/b Going without fault.

48.Im Going, coming: Welling, Welling.

51.5a/b Shake going, coming adversity.

53.ImT Going possessing achievement indeed.

55.1a Going possesses honor.

55.2a Going acquiring doubt, affliction.

60.5a Going possesses honor.

62.4a/b Going adversity necessarily warning.

● **Goat**, YANG: sheep and goats; direct thought and action.

34.3a The he goat butts a hedge.

34.5a/b Losing the goat, into versatility.

34.6a The he goat butts a hedge.

43.4a Hauling along the goat, repenting extinguished.

54.6a A notable disembowelling a goat without blood.

● **Go down**, TSE: sun setting, afternoon; waning moon; decline.

30.3a/b Sun going down's Radiance.

55.ImT Sun centering, by consequence going down.

● **Go to meet**, YA: advance to encounter and receive; invoke; anticipate, face, provide for; govern; drive or tame a horse; extending everywhere, as the imperial power.

1.ImT The season riding six dragons used going to meet heaven.

● **Gorge**, K'AN: dangerous place; hole, cavity, hollow; pit, snare, trap, grave, precipice; critical time, test; risky. The ideogram: earth and pit.

Image of Hexagram 29 and occurs throughout its texts.

● **Gradual Advance**, CHIEN: advance by degrees; penetrate slowly and surely, as water; stealthily; permeate throughout; influence, affect. The ideogram: water and cut.

Image of Hexagram 53 and occurs throughout its texts.

● **Grains**, KU: cereal crops, corn; substantial, well off; income; bless with plenty.

30.ImT The hundred grains, grasses, trees congregating reaching to earth.

● **Grandfather**, TSU: second ancestor generation; deceased grandfather, honored more than actual father.

16.ST Using equaling the grandfather predecessors.

62.2a Exceeding one's grandfather.

● **Grandmother**, PI: second ancestor generation; deceased grandmother, venerated as source of her many descendants.

62.2a Meeting one's grandmother.

● **Grapple**, CHÜ: grasp and detain; restrain, attach to, hook.

17.6a/b Grappling, tying to it.

● **Grasp**, CH'Ü: lay hold of, take and use, seize, appropriate; grasp the meaning, understand. The ideogram: ear and hand, hear and grasp.

4.3a/b No availing of grasping womanhood.

8.5b Stowing away countering, grasping yielding.

16.AE Surely, grasping connotes Providing for.

31.Im/ImT Grasping womanhood auspicious.

44.Im/ImT No availing of grasping womanhood.

49/50.CD The Vessel: grasping renewal indeed.

56.1a Splitting off one's place, grasping calamity.

62.5a A prince, a string arrow grasping another located in a cave.

● **Grass,** TS'AO: all grassy plants and herbs; young, tender plants; rough draft; hastily. See also: **Thatch grass**

3.ImT Heaven creating grass, duskiness.

30.ImT The hundred grains, grasses, trees congregating reaching to earth.

40.ImT Thunder and Rain arousing and the hundred fruits, grasses, trees, altogether seedburst boundary.

● **Great,** TA: big, noble, important, very; orient the will toward a self imposed goal, impose direction; ability to lead or guide your life; contrasts with small, HSIAO, flexible adaptation to what crosses your path; keyword. See also: **Great People, Stepping into the Great River**

Image of Hexagrams **14, 26, 28, 34** and occurs throughout their texts.

1.ImT The great Force, Spring in fact.

1.ImT Great brightening completing beginning.

1.ImT Protection uniting the great harmony.

2.ImT Containing generosity, the shining great.

2.2a Straightening on all sides, great.

2.3b Knowing the shining great indeed.

2.7b Using the great to complete indeed.

3.ImT Great Growing: Trial.

3.1b The great acquiring the commoners indeed.

3.5a The great, Trial: pitfall.

5.6b Although not an appropriate situation, not yet the great let go indeed.

7.3b The great without achievement indeed.

7.6a/b The Great Chief possesses fate.

10.3a/b Martial people activating: into a Great Chief.

10.6b The great possesses reward indeed.

11.Im/ImT The small going, the great coming.

11.2b Using the shining great indeed.

12.Im/ImT The great going, the small coming.

13.CD Great Possessing: crowds indeed.

13.5a/b Great legions controlling mutual meeting.

16.S Possessing the Great and enabling Humbling necessarily Provides for.

16.ImT Actually Provision's season righteously great in fact.

16.4a The great possesses acquiring.

16.4b Antecedent Provision, the great possesses acquiring.

16.4b Purpose: the great moving indeed.

17.ImT Great Growing, Trial: without fault.

17.ImT Actually Following the season's righteous great in fact.

18.3a Without the great: fault.

19.S Possessing affairs and afterwards permitting the great.

19.S Nearing implies the great indeed.

19.ImT Great Growing uses correcting.

19.5a/b A Great Chief's propriety.

20.S Being great therefore afterwards permitting Viewing.

20.ImT The great: Viewing located above.

24.6a Completing possesses great destroying.

25.CD Great Accumulating: the season indeed.

25.ImT Great Growing using correcting.

27.CD Great Exceeding: toppling indeed.

27.ImT Actually Jaws's season great in fact.

27.3b Tao, the great rebelling indeed.

27.6b The great possessing reward indeed.

29.ImT Actually venturing's season availing of the great in fact.

29.5b Centering, not yet great indeed.

30.3a By consequence great old age's lamenting. Pitfall.

31.4b Not yet the shining great indeed.

32.6b The great without accomplishment indeed.

33.CD Great Invigorating: by consequence stopping.

33.ImT Actually Retiring's season righteously great in fact.

33.3b Not permitting Great Affairs indeed.

35.ImT Yielding and congregating reaching to great brightening.

36.ImT Using the enveloped great: heaviness.

36.3a Acquiring its great, the head.

36.3b Thereupon acquiring the great indeed.

37.ImT Heaven and Earth's great righteousness indeed.

37.4a/b Affluence Dwelling, the great auspicious.

38.ImT Actually Polarizing's season availing of the great in fact.

39.ImT Actually Difficulty's season availing of the great in fact.

39.5a/b The great Difficulties, partnering coming.

40.ImT Actually Loosening's season great in fact.

41.6b The great acquiring purpose indeed.
42.ImT One's tao, the great shining.
42.1a Advantageous: availing of activating the great, arousing.
42.5b The great acquiring purpose indeed.
44.ImT Below Heaven, the great moving indeed.
44.ImT Actually Coupling's season righteously great in fact.
44.3a Without the great: fault.
45.Im/ImT Availing of the great: sacrificial victims auspicious.
45.4a/b The great auspicious, without fault.
46.ST [A chün tzu uses] amassing the small to use the high great.
46.ImT That uses great Growing to avail of seeing Great People.
46.1a/b Sincere Ascending, the great auspicious.
46.5b The great acquiring the purpose indeed.
48.6b The great accomplishing indeed.
49.ImT Great Growing uses correcting.
49.ImT Actually Skinning's season great in fact.
50.ImT and great Growing uses nourishing all wise eminences.
50.6a The great auspicious.
51.5b The great without losing indeed.
54.ImT Heaven and Earth's great righteousness indeed.
55.S Acquiring one's place to Convert implies necessarily the great.
55.S Abounding implies the great indeed.
55.ImT Abounding, the great indeed.
55.ImT Honoring the great indeed.
55.3b Not permitting Great Affairs indeed.
56.S Exhausting the great implies necessarily letting go one's residing.
56.ImT Actually Sojourning's season righteously great in fact.
58.ImT Stimulating's great.
59.4b Shining great indeed.
59.5a Dispersing sweat, one's great crying out.
62.Im Permitting Small Affairs. Not permitting Great Affairs.
62.Im The great auspicious.
62.ImT That uses not permitting Great Affairs indeed.
62.ImT The great auspicious.
63.5b Auspicious, the great coming indeed.
64.4a Three years revolved, possessing donating into the great city.

Great People, TA JEN: important, noble, influential; ● those who impose a ruling principle on their lives; effect of the great within an individual; keyword.
1.2a,5a Advantageous: seeing Great People.
1.5b Great People creating indeed.
6.Im/ImT Advantageous: seeing Great People.
12.2a/b Great People Obstructed. Growing.
12.5a/b Great People auspicious.
30.ST Great People use consecutive brightening to illuminate into the four sides.
39.Im/ImT,6a/b Advantageous: seeing Great People.
45.Im/ImT Advantageous: seeing Great People. Growing.
46.Im Availing of seeing Great People.
46.ImT That uses great Growing to avail of seeing Great People.
47.Im/ImT Trial: Great People auspicious.
49.5a/b Great People: tiger transforming.
57.Im/ImT Advantageous: seeing Great People.

Grieve(over), YU: sorrow, melancholy; mourn; ● anxious, careworn; hidden sorrow. The ideogram: heart, head, and limp, heart sick and anxious.
7/8.CD Legions: grieving.
19.3a/b Already grieving over it:
55.Im/ImT No grief. Properly sun centering.

Ground, SUN: base on which things rest; support, ● foundation; mild, subtly penetrating; nourishing. The ideogram: stand and things arranged on it, the subtle influence of the ground.
Image of Hexagram 57 and occurs throughout its texts.
4.5b Yielding uses Ground indeed.
9.ImT Persisting and Ground.
18.ImT Ground and stopping. Corrupting.
20.ImT Yielding and Ground.
28.ImT Ground and stimulating movement.
32.ImT Ground and stirring up.
37.2b Yielding uses Ground indeed.
42.ImT Augmenting stirring up and Ground.
45.3b Ground above indeed.
46.ImT Ground and yielding.
48.ImT Ground reaching to stream and stream above.
50.ImT Using wood: Ground, fire.
50.ImT Ground and the ear[and]eye: understanding brightened.
53.ImT Stopping and Ground.
53.4b Yielding using Ground indeed.
58.CD Ground: hiding away indeed.

61.ImT Stimulating and Ground: Connection.

• **Group**, PI: compare and select, order things and put them in classes; find what you belong with; sort, examine correspondences; choose and harmonize; unite. The ideogram: person who stops walking, looking around to examine and compare.

Image of Hexagram 8 and occurs throughout its texts.

7.CD Grouping: delighting.

9.S Grouping necessarily possesses a place to Accumulate.

• **Grow**, HENG: success through a sacrifice; pervade, persevere; bring to full growth; enjoy; vigorous, effective; second stage of the Time Cycle.

2.ImT The kinds: being conjoining Growing.

3.ImT Great Growing: Trial.

4.Im/ImT Enveloping, Growing.

4.ImT Using Growing movement.

5.Im/ImT Shining Growing, Trial: auspicious.

9.Im Small Accumulating, Growing.

9.ImT Thereupon Growing.

10.Im/ImT Not mauling people. Growing.

11.Im Auspiciousness Growing.

11.ImT The small going, the great coming: auspiciousness Growing.

12.1a Trial: auspicious. Growing.

12.2a/b Great People Obstructed. Growing.

13.Im/ImT Concording People, into the countryside. Growing.

14.Im Great Possessing, Spring Growing.

14.ImT That uses Spring Growing.

14.3a/b A prince availing of Growing, into heavenly sonhood.

15.Im/ImT Humbling, Growing.

17.ImT Great Growing, Trial: without fault.

17.6a The king availing of Growing into the Western mountain.

18.Im/ImT Corrupting, Spring Growing.

19.ImT Great Growing uses correcting.

21.Im Gnawing Bite, Growing.

21.ImT Gnawing Bite and Growing.

22.Im/ImT Adorning, Growing.

22.ImT Anterior Growth.

23.S Actually involving embellishing, therefore afterwards Growing by consequence used up.

24.Im/ImT Returning, Growing.

25.ImT Great Growing using correcting.

26.6a Growing.

28.Im Growing.

28.ImT Thereupon Growing.

29.Im Holding fast the heart Growing.

29.ImT Holding fast the heart's Growing, thereupon using solid centering indeed.

30.Im Growing. Accumulating female cattle. Auspicious.

30.ImT Anterior Growing.

31.Im Conjoining, Growing.

31.ImT That uses Growth Advantageous Trial, grasping womanhood auspicious.

32.Im Persevering, Growing.

32.ImT Persevering Growing, without fault.

33.Im/ImT Retiring, Growing.

33.ImT Retiring and Growing indeed.

45.Im Clustering, Growing.

45.Im/ImT Advantageous: seeing Great People. Growing.

46.Im Ascending, Spring Growing.

46.ImT That uses great Growing to avail of seeing Great People.

46.4a/b Kinghood availing of Growing, into the twin peaked mountain.

47.Im Confining, Growing.

47.ImT Confining and not letting go one's place: Growing.

49.ImT Great Growing uses correcting.

50.Im Growing.

50.ImT Growing, cooking indeed.

50.ImT The all wise person Growing uses presenting to the Supreme Above.

50.ImT and great Growing uses nourishing all wise eminences.

50.ImT That uses Spring Growing.

51.Im/ImT Shake, Growing.

55.Im Abounding, Growing.

56.Im Sojourning, the small: Growing.

56.ImT The small Growing.

56.ImT That uses the small Growing.

57.Im Ground, the small: Growing.

57.ImT That uses the small Growing.

58.Im Open, Growing,

59.Im/ImT Dispersing, Growing.

60.Im/ImT Articulating, Growing.

60.4a/b Quiet Articulating Growing.

62.Im Small Exceeding, Growing.

62.ImT Small implies Exceeding and Growing indeed.

63.Im Already Fording. Growing: the small.

63.ImT Already Fording, Growing.

63.ImT The small implies Growing indeed.

64.Im/ImT Not yet Fording, Growing.

Grudges, YÜAN: bitter feelings, ill will; hate, abhor; murmur against. The ideogram: heart and overturn, upset emotion.

47.AE Confining: using few grudges.

Guard, SHOU: keep in custody; protect, ward off harm, attend to, supervise.

29.ImT The kingly prince sets up venturing used to guard his city.

51.ImT Issuing forth permits using guarding the ancestral temple, field altar, offertory millet.

Guest, PIN: entertain a guest; visit someone, enjoy hospitality; receive a stranger.

20.4a Advantageous: availing of guesting into kinghood.

20.4b Honoring guesting indeed.

44.2a Not Advantageous: guesting.

44.2b Righteously not extending to guesting indeed.

Gully, KU: valley, ravine, river bed, gap. The ideogram: divide and river, a river bed separating hills.

47.1a/b Entering into a shady gully.

48.2a/b The Well: a gully, shooting bass.

Gush, T'O: water surging in streams; falling tears; heavy rain.

30.5a Issuing forth tears like gushing. Sadness like lamenting.

Halt, P'O: limp; lame, crippled; indecorous.

10.3a/b Halting enabling Treading.

54.1a Halting enabling treading.

54.1b Halting enabling treading, auspicious.

Hamper, CH'E: hinder, obstruct, hold or pull back; embarrass; select. The ideogram: hand and limit, grasp and control.

38.3a One's cattle hampered.

Handful, WU: as much as the hand can hold; a little; grasp, hold.

45.1a Like an outcry, the one handful activates laughing.

Handle, PING: haft; control of, power to.

15.AE Humbling: actualizing tao's handle indeed.

Hand washing, KUAN: wash the hands before a sacramental act; ablutions, a basin.

20.Im/ImT Viewing: hand washing and not worshipping.

Harden, CHIEN: make or become hard; establish, strengthen; durable, resolute.

2.1a Treading frost, hardening ice culminating.

2.1b Treading frost hardening the ice:

2.1b Culminating hardening the ice indeed.

Harm, HAI: damage, injure, offend; suffer; hurtful, hindrance; fearful, anxious.

2.4b Consideration not harmful indeed.

14.1a Without mingling harm.

14.1b Without mingling harm indeed.

14.3b Small People harmful indeed.

15.ImT Souls[and]Spirits harming overfilling and blessing Humbling.

31.2b Yielding, not harming indeed.

31.4b Not yet influencing harming indeed.

41.AE Diminishing: using distancing harm.

59.6b Distancing harm indeed.

60.ImT Not harming the commoners.

Harmony, HO: concord, union; conciliate; at peace, mild; fit, tune, adjust.

1.ImT Protection uniting the great harmony.

10.AE Treading: harmonizing and culminating.

10.AE Treading: using harmonizing movement.

31.ImT The all wise person influencing the people at heart and Below Heaven harmony evening.

43.ImT Breaking up and harmonizing.

58.1a/b Harmonious Opening: auspicious.

61.2a/b One's sonhood harmonizing it.

Hate, WU: dislike, dread; averse to, ashamed of; repulsive, vicious, vile, ugly, wicked. The ideogram: twisted bowels and heart, heart entangled in emotion.

14.ST A chün tzu uses terminating hate to display improvement.

15.ImT People tao hating overfilling and loving Humbling.

33.ST [A chün tzu uses] not hating and intimidating.

38.1a/b Seeing hateful people.

Have a direction to go, YU YU WANG: imposing a direction on the flow of time from present to past; have a specific goal or purpose. This phrase occurs 25 times throughout the hexagram texts.

Haul along, CH'IEN: haul or pull, drag behind; pull an animal on a rope; pull toward. The ideogram: ox and halter.

9.2a Hauling along, returning. Auspicious.

9.2b Hauling along, returning, locating in the center.

43.4a Hauling along the goat, repenting extinguished.

44.1b Supple tao hauling along indeed.

44.3b Moving, not yet hauling along indeed.

Have (it)/'s/it/them, chih: expresses possession, directly or as an object pronoun.

This term occurs throughout the hexagram texts.

Hawk, SHUN: bird of prey used in hunting; falcon, kestrel.

40.6a A prince avails of shooting a hawk, into the high rampart's above.

40.6b A prince avails of shooting a hawk.

Head, SHOU: literal head; leader, foremost; subject headings; beginning, model; superior, upper, front.

1.ImT Heads issuing forth from the multitudinous beings.

1.7a Seeing flocking dragons without a head.

1.7b Heavenly actualizing tao not permitting activating the head indeed.

8.6a/b Without a head, Grouping it.

30.6a Severing the head.

36.3a Acquiring its great, the head.

63.6a Soaking one's head.

63.6b Soaking one's head, adversity.

64.6a Soaking one's head.

64.6b Drinking liquor, soaking the head.

Hear, WEN: perceive sound; learn by report; news, fame. The ideogram: ear and door.

43.4a/b Hearing words, not trustworthy.

56.6b Completing absolutely nothing: having hearing indeed.

Hearken, T'ING: listen to, obey, accept, acknowledge; examine, judge, decide. The ideogram: ear and actualizing tao, hear and obey.

5.4b Yielding uses hearkening indeed.

52.2b Not yet withdrawing from hearkening indeed.

Heart, HSIN: heart as center of being; seat of mind's images and affections; moral nature; source of desires, intentions, will.

11.4b Centering the heart desiring indeed.

15.2b Centering the heart acquiring indeed.

24.ImT Reaching to Returning one's seeing Heaven and Earth's heart.

29.Im Holding fast the heart Growing.

29.ImT Holding fast the heart's Growing, thereupon using solid centering indeed.

31.ImT The all wise person influencing the people at heart and Below Heaven harmony evening.

36.4a Catching Brightness Hiding's heart.

36.4b Catching the heart, intention indeed.

42.5a/b There is a connection to the spirit, a benevolent heart.

42.6a Establishing the heart, no persevering.

48.3a Activating my heart aching.

52.2a One's heart not keen.

52.3a Adversity smothers the heart.

52.3b Exposure smothers the heart indeed.

56.4a My heart not keen.

56.4b The heart not yet keen indeed.

61.2b Centering the heart desiring indeed.

Heaven, T'IEN: highest; sky, firmament, heavens; power above the human as opposed to earth, TI, below; the Symbol of the trigram Force, CH'IEN. The ideogram: great and the one above. See also: **Below Heaven** and **Heaven and Earth**

1.ST Heaven moves persistingly.

1.ImT Thereupon primary heaven.

1.ImT The season riding six dragons used going to meet heaven.

1.5a/b Flying dragon located in heaven.

1.7b Heavenly actualizing tao not permitting activating the head indeed.

2.ImT Thereupon yielding receiving heaven.

3.ImT Heaven creating grass, duskiness.

5.ST Above clouds with respect to heaven.

5.ImT Situation reaching to the heavenly situation.

6.ST Heaven associating with stream, contradicting movements.

7.2b Receiving heavenly favor indeed.

9.ST Wind moving above heaven.

10.ST Heaven above, marsh below.

12.ST Heaven, earth, not mingling.

13.ST Heaven associating with fire.

14.ST Fire located above heaven.

14.ST [A chün tzu uses] yielding to heaven to relinquish fate.

14.ImT Corresponding reaching to heaven and the season moving.

14.3a/b A prince availing of Growing, into heavenly sonhood.

14.6a Originating from heaven shielding it.

14.6b Originating from heaven shielding indeed.

15.ImT Heavenly tao lessening overfilling and augmenting Humbling.

18.ImT Heaven moving indeed.

19.ImT Heavenly tao indeed.

20.ImT Viewing heaven's spirit tao.

22.ImT Heavenly pattern indeed.

22.ImT Viewing reaching to the heavenly pattern.

23.ImT Heaven moving indeed.

24.ImT Heaven moving indeed.

25.ImT Heaven's fate indeed.

25.ImT Heavenly fate not shielding.

26.ST Heaven located in mountain center.

26.ImT Corresponding reaching to heaven indeed.

26.6a/b Wherefore heaven's highway?

29.ImT Heaven venturing, not permitting ascending indeed.

30.ImT Sun and Moon congregating reaching to heaven.

32.ImT Sun and Moon acquiring heaven and enabling lasting illumination.

33.ST Below heaven possessing mountain.

34.ST Thunder located above heaven.

36.6a/b Initially mounting into heaven.

38.ImT Heaven, Earth, Polarizing and one's affairs concording indeed.

42.ImT Heaven spreading out, earth giving birth.

43.ST Above marsh with respect to heaven.

44.ST Below heaven possessing wind.

44.ImT Heaven, Earth: mutually meeting.

44.5a/b Possessing tumbling, originating from heaven.

45.ImT Yielding to heaven: fate indeed.

49.ImT Yielding reaching to heaven and corresponding reaching to the people.

55.6b Heaven bordering, hovering indeed.

58.ImT That uses yielding reaching to heaven and corresponding reaching to the people.

60.ImT Heaven, Earth: Articulating and the four seasons accomplishing.

61.ImT Thereupon corresponding reaching to heaven indeed.

61.6a/b A soaring sound mounting, into heaven.

● **Heaven and Earth**, T'IEN TI: dynamic relation between the primal powers and the world it produces; cosmos, natural or human world; keyword.

3.S Possessing Heaven and Earth.

3.S Overfilling Heaven and Earth's interspace implies verily the myriad beings.

11.ST Heaven and Earth mingling.

11.ST The crown prince uses property to accomplish Heaven and Earth's tao.

11.ST [The crown prince uses] bracing to mutualize Heaven and Earth's propriety.

11.ImT By consequence of that Heaven and Earth mingling and the myriad beings interpenetrating indeed.

11.3b Heaven and Earth, the border indeed.

12.ImT By consequence of that Heaven and Earth not mingling and the myriad beings not interpenetrating indeed.

16.ImT Anterior Heaven and Earth thus having it.

16.ImT Heaven and Earth uses yielding stirring up.

24.ImT Reaching to Returning one's seeing Heaven and Earth's heart.

27.ImT Heaven and Earth nourishes the myriad beings.

31.S Possessing Heaven and Earth:

31.ImT Heaven and Earth influencing and the myriad beings changing give birth.

31.ImT and actually Heaven and Earth, the myriad beings's motives permitting seeing.

32.ImT Heaven and Earth's tao.

32.ImT and actually Heaven and Earth, the myriad beings's motives permitting seeing.

34.ImT Actually the correcting Great and Heaven and Earth's motives permitting seeing.

37.ImT Heaven and Earth's great righteousness indeed.

40.ImT Heaven and Earth Loosening and Thunder and Rain arousing.

45.ImT and actually Heaven and Earth, the myriad beings's motives, permitting seeing.

49.ImT Heaven and Earth Skinning and the four seasons accomplishing.

54.ImT Heaven and Earth's great righteousness indeed.

54.ImT Heaven and Earth not mingling and the myriad beings not rising.

55.ImT Heaven and Earth overfilling emptiness.

Heavy, NAN: arduous, grievous, difficult; hardship, distress; harass; contrasts with versatile, I, deal lightly with. The ideogram: domestic bird with clipped tail and drying sticky earth. ●

3.ImT Strong and Supple beginning mingling and heaviness giving birth indeed.

3.2b Six at second's heaviness.

5.1b Not opposing heavy moving indeed.

12.ST A chün tzu uses parsimonious actualizing tao to cast out heaviness.

36.ImT Using the enveloped great: heaviness.

36.ImT Inside heaviness and enabling correcting one's purpose.

39.S Turning away necessarily possesses heaviness.

39.S Difficulties implies heaviness indeed.

39/40.CD Difficulties: heaviness indeed.

39.ImT Difficulties. Heaviness indeed.

40.S Beings not permitted to use completing heaviness.

41.AE Diminishing: beforehand heaviness and afterwards versatility.

58.ImT Stimulating using opposing heaviness:

Hedge, FAN: row of bushes, fence, boundary; protect, fend off, enclose.

34.3a,6a The he goat butts a hedge.

34.4a/b The hedge broken up, not ruined.

He goat, TI YANG: ram or buck; three-year-old male at peak of strength. See also: **Goat**

34.3a,6a The he goat butts a hedge.

Her/she, CH'I: third person pronoun; also: one/one's, it/its, he/his, they/their.

This term occurs throughout the hexagram texts.

Herd, MU: tend cattle; watch over, superintend; ruler, teacher.

15.1b Lowliness uses originating from herding indeed.

Hide, YI: keep out of sight; remote, distant from the center; equalize by lowering; squat, level, make ordinary; pacified, colorless; cut, wound, destroy, exterminate.

Image of Hexagram 36 and occurs throughout its texts.

35.CD Brightness Hiding: proscribed indeed.

55.4a/b Meeting one's hiding lord.

59.4a In no way hiding, a place to ponder.

Hide away, FU: conceal, place in ambush; secretly, silently; prostrate, fall on your face; humble. The ideogram: man and dog, man crouching.

13.3a/b Hiding away arms, into the thickets.

57/58.CD Ground: hiding away indeed.

High(ness), KAO: high, elevated, lofty, eminent; excellent, advanced.

13.3a Ascending one's high mound.

18.6a Honoring highness: one's affair.

40.6a A prince avails of shooting a hawk, into the high rampart's above.

46.ST [A chün tzu uses] amassing the small to use the high great.

63.3a The high ancestor subjugating souls on all sides.

Highlands, LU: high, dry land as distinct from swamps; plateau.

43.5a Reeds, highlands: Deciding, Deciding.

53.3a,6a The wild geese Infiltrating into the highlands.

Highlight, YI: emphasize what is inherently good; concentrate, focus on; virtuous, worthy; an accomplished, graceful woman.

9.ST A chün tzu uses highlighting the pattern to actualize tao.

Highway, CH'Ü: main road, thoroughfare; where many ways meet.

26.6a/b Wherefore heaven's highway?

Hill top, CH'IU: hill with hollow top used for worship and as grave site; knoll, hillock.

22.5a Adorning into a hill top garden.

27.2a Rejecting the canons, into the hill top.

29.ImT Earth venturing, mountains, rivers, hill tops, mounds indeed.

59.4a Dispersing possessing the hill top.

His/he, CH'I: third person pronoun; also: one/one's, it/its, she/hers, they/theirs.

This term occurs throughout the hexagram texts.

Hoary, PO: silvery grey hair; old and venerable, aging.

22.4a Adorning thus, hoary thus.

Hog fish, T'UN YÜ: aquatic mammals; porpoise, dolphin; intelligent aquatic animals whose development parallels the human; sign of abundance and good luck.

61.Im Centering Connection, hog fish auspicious.

61.ImT Hog fish auspicious.

61.ImT Trustworthiness extending to hog fish indeed.

Hold fast (to), WEI: hold together; tie to, connect; reins, net.

17.6a Thereupon adhering holding fast to it.

29.Im/ImT Holding fast the heart Growing.

35.6a/b Holding fast avails of subjugating the capital.

40.5a A chün tzu holding fast possesses Loosening.

Hold on(to), CHIH: lay hold of, seize, take in hand; keep, maintain, look after. The ideogram: criminal and seize.

7.5a Advantageous: holding on to words.

31.3a Holding on to one's following.

31.3b A place to hold on to the below indeed.

33.2a Holding on to it: availing of yellow cattle's skin.

33.2b Holding on avails of yellow cattle.

● **Home,** SHIH: place of rest, dwelling, family; the grave.

9.3b Not able correcting the home indeed.

● **Honor,** SHANG: esteem, give high rank to; eminent; put one thing on top of another.

6.ImT Honoring centering correcting indeed.

9.ImT Honoring going indeed.

9.6a Honoring actualizing tao carrying.

11.2a Acquiring honor, into centering moving.

11.2b Enwrapping wasteland, acquiring honor, into centering moving.

18.6a Honoring highness: one's affair.

20.4b Honoring guesting indeed.

23.ImT A chün tzu honors the dissolving pause to overfill emptiness.

26.ImT Above solid and honoring eminence.

29.Im Movement possesses honor.

29.ImT Movement possesses honor.

34.4b Honoring going indeed.

41.1b Honoring uniting purposes indeed.

43.ImT The place to honor thereupon exhausted indeed.

47.ImT Honoring the mouth thereupon exhausted indeed.

55.ImT Honoring the great indeed.

55.1a Going possesses honor.

60.5a Going possesses honor.

Hoof, TI: pig's trotters and horse's hooves.

44.1a Ruining the pig, connection: hoof dragging.

● **Horns,** CHIO: strength and power; gore; dispute; test your strength; headland.

34.3a Ruining his horns.

35.6a Prospering: one's horns.

44.6a/b Coupling: one's horns.

● **Horse,** MA: symbol of spirited strength in the natural world, counterpart of dragon, LUNG; associated with the trigram Force, CH'IEN, heaven, T'IEN, and high noon.

2.Im Field: Spring Growing Advantageous, female horse's Trial.

2.ImT The female horse: earth sorting.

3.2a,4a,6a Riding a horse, arraying thus.

22.4a A white horse, soaring thus.

26.3a A fine horse, pursuing.

35.Im Prospering, the calm feudatory avails of bestowing horses to multiply the multitudes.

35.ImT That uses the calm feudatory availing of bestowing horses to multiply the multitudes.

36.2a Availing of a rescuing horse, invigorating auspicious.

38.1a Losing the horse, no pursuit, originating from returning.

59.1a Availing of a rescuing horse, invigorating auspicious.

61.4a/b The horse team extinguished.

Hunt, SHOU: hunt with dogs; annual winter hunt; ● military campaign; pursue closely, press hard; burn dry fields to drive game; inspect the frontiers.

36.3a Brightness Hiding into the South, hunting.

36.3b The South: hunting's purpose.

House, KUNG: residence, mansion; surround; fence, ● walls, roof.

23.5a/b Using housing people, favor.

47.3a/b Entering into one's house.

Hover, HSIANG: glide; rise, soar, roam. ●

55.6b Heaven bordering, hovering indeed.

Humanity, JEN: fellow feeling, regard for others; ● benevolence, fulfil social duties; unselfish, kind, merciful.

24.2b Using humanity below indeed.

Humble, CH'IEN: think and speak of yourself in a ● modest way; respectful, unassuming, retiring, unobtrusive; yielding, compliant, reverent, lowly. The ideogram: words and unite, keeping words close to underlying facts.

Image of Hexagram 15 and occurs throughout its texts.

16.S Possessing the Great and enabling Humbling necessarily Provides for.

16.CD Humbling: levity indeed.

Hundred, PO: numerous, many, all; a whole class or ● type.

6.2a People, three hundred doors.

30.ImT The hundred grains, grasses, trees congregating reaching to earth.

40.ImT Thunder and Rain arousing and the hundred fruits, grasses, trees, altogether seedburst boundary.

51.Im/ImT Shake scaring a hundred miles.

Hundred thousand, YI: ten myriads (groups of ten thousand); huge quantity, number beyond imagination.

51.2a A hundred thousand lost coins.

Husband, FU: household manager; administer with thrift and prudence; responsible for; sustain with one's earnings; old enough to assume responsibility; married man.

4.3a Seeing a metallic husband.

8.Im/ImT Afterwards, husbanding: pitfall.

9.3a/b Husband, consort, reversing eyes.

17.2a Letting go the respectable husband.

17.3a/b Tied to the respectable husband.

28.2a A venerable husband acquiring his woman consort.

28.2b A venerable husband, a woman consort.

28.5a A venerable wife acquiring her notable husband.

28.5b A venerable wife, a notable husband.

32.5a The husband, the son: pitfall.

32.5b The husband, the son: paring righteously.

37.ImT The husband, a husband. The wife, a wife.

38.4a Meeting Spring, husbanding.

53.3a/b The husband chastised, not returning.

Husband and Wife, FU FU: the cooperative effort of man and woman in establishing and maintaining a home.

31.S Therefore afterwards possessing Husband and Wife.

31.S Possessing Husband and Wife:

32.S Husband and Wife's tao.

Husking, KENG: fruit and grain husks bursting in autumn; seventh of the Ten Heavenly Barriers in calender system; bestow, reward; blade or sword; associated with the Metallic Moment. The ideogram: receiving things in the hand.

57.5a Before husking, three days.

57.5a After husking, three days.

Hut, LU: thatched hut, cottage, roadside lodge, hovel; house as personal shelter.

23.6a/b Small People Stripping the hut.

I/me/my, WO: first person pronoun; indicates an unusually strong emphasis on your own subjective experience.

4.Im/ImT In no way me seeking youthful Enveloping.

4.ImT Youthful Enveloping seeking me.

5.3b Originating from my involving outlawry.

9.Im/ImT Originating from my Western suburbs.

20.3a/b Viewing my birth, advancing, withdrawing.

20.5a/b Viewing my birth.

27.1a/b Viewing my pendent Jaws.

40.3b Originating from my involving arms.

42.5a There is a connection to the spirit, benevolence: my actualizing tao.

42.5b Benevolence: my actualizing tao.

48.3a Activating my heart aching.

50.2a Not me able to approach. Auspicious.

50.2a/b My companion possesses affliction.

56.4a My heart not keen.

61.2a I possess a loved wine cup.

62.5a Originating from my Western suburbs.

Ice, PING: frozen water; icy, freezing; clear, pure.

2.1a Treading frost, hardening ice culminating.

2.1b Treading frost hardening the ice:

2.1b Culminating hardening the ice indeed.

Illuminate, CHAO: shine light on; enlighten, reflect: care for, supervise. The ideogram: fire and brightness.

30.ST Great People use consecutive brightening to illuminate into the four sides.

32.ImT Sun and Moon acquiring heaven and enabling lasting illumination.

36.6b Illuminating the four cities indeed.

55.ImT Properly illuminating Below Heaven indeed.

Imagine, CHIA: create in the mind; fantasize, suppose, pretend, imitate; fiction; illusory, unreal; costume. The ideogram: person and borrow.

37.5a/b The king imagines possessing a Dwelling.

45.Im/ImT The king imagines possessing a temple.

55.Im/ImT The king imagining it.

59.Im/ImT The king imagines possessing a temple.

Immature, CHIH: small, tender, young, delicate; undeveloped; conceited, haughty; late grain.

4.S Being's immaturity indeed.

5.S Being immature not permitting not nourishing indeed.

Immerse, CH'IEN: submerge, hide in water; make away with; secret, reserved; carefully.

1.1a/b Immersed dragon, no availing of.

Impetuous, FEN: sudden energy; lively, spirited, impulsive; excite, arouse; press on.

16.ST Thunder issuing forth from earth impetuously.

Implements, CH'I: utensils, tools; molded or carved objects; use a person or thing suitably; capacity, talent, intelligence.

45.ST A chün tzu uses eliminating arms to implement.

51.S A lord's implementing implies absolutely nothing like the long living son.

Imply, CHE: further signify; additional meaning. This term occurs in the Sequence of most hexagrams. It also occurs at:

28. ImT Great implies Exceeding indeed.

34. ImT Great Invigorating. The Great implies Invigorating indeed.

34. ImT The Great implies correcting indeed.

62. ImT Small implies Exceeding and Growing indeed.

63. ImT The small implies Growing indeed.

Impress, WEI: impose on, intimidate; august, solemn; pomp, majesty.

14.5a Your connection: mingling thus, impressing thus.

14.5b Impressing thus, having auspiciousness.

37.6a There is a connection to the spirit, impressing thus.

37.6b Impressing thus, having auspiciousness.

Improve, SHAN: make better, reform, perfect, repair; virtuous, wise; mild, docile; clever, skillful, handy. The ideogram: mouth and sheep, gentle speech.

14.ST A chün tzu uses terminating hate to display improvement.

42.ST A chün tzu uses seeing improvement, by consequence shifting.

53.ST A chün tzu uses residing in eminent actualizing tao to improve the vulgar.

Increase, SHENG: grow or make larger; flourishing, exuberant, full, abundant; heaped up; excellent, fine.

41/42.CD Increasing, decreasing's beginning indeed.

Indeed/is/means, YEH: intensifier connective; indicates comment on previous statement.

This term occurs throughout the hexagram texts. It characterizes the Image Tradition and the Transforming Lines b).

Indignation, WEN: irritated, wrathful; feeling of injustice, rage; hateful.

43.3a Like soaking, possessing indignation.

Indigo, HSÜAN: color associated with the Metallic Moment; deep blue black, color of the sky's depths; profound, subtle, deep; veneration of the gods and spirits.

2.6a Their blood: indigo, yellow.

Individuality, SHEN: total person: psyche, body and lifespan; character, virtue, duty; contrasts with body, KUNG, physical being.

24.1b Using adjusting individuality indeed.

37.6b Reversing individuality's designating indeed.

39.ST A chün tzu uses reversing individuality to renovate actualizing tao.

52. Im Not catching one's individuality.

52. ImT That uses not catching one's individuality.

52.4a/b Bound: one's individuality.

Indolence, TAI: idle, inattentive, careless; self indulgent; disdainful, contemptuous.

15/16.CD Provision: indolence indeed.

In fact, TSAI: in actual fact, currently. See also: **Actually ... in fact**

1.ImT The great Force, Spring in fact.

2.ImT Culminating Field, Spring in fact.

Influence, KAN: excite, act on, touch; affect someone's feelings, move the heart. The ideogram: heart and all, pervasive influence.

31. ImT Conjoining. Influencing indeed.

31. ImT The two agencies influencing correspondence use mutual associating.

31. ImT Heaven and Earth influencing and the myriad beings changing give birth.

31. ImT The all wise person influencing the people at heart and Below Heaven harmony evening.

31. ImT Viewing one's place to influence.

31.4b Not yet influencing harming indeed.

Inform, YÜ: tell, warn; talk with, converse, exchange ideas.

27.ST A chün tzu uses considering words to inform.

Initial, initiate, CH'U: first step or part; beginning, incipient; bottom line of hexagram. The ideogram: knife and garment, cutting out the pattern.

This term frequently occurs in the first Transforming Line b).

4.Im/ImT The initial oracle consulting notifying.

36.6a/b Initially mounting into heaven.

38.3a/b Without initially possessing

completion.

57.5a Without initially possessing completion.

63.Im/ImT Initially auspicious.

● **Injure,** SHANG: hurt, wound, grieve, distress; mourn, sad at heart, humiliated.

8.3b Reaching to not truly injuring.

36.S Advancing necessarily possessing a place: injuring.

36.S Hiding implies injury.

37.S Injury with respect to the outside implies necessarily reversing with respect to Dwelling.

56.3b Actually truly using injuring.

60.ImT Not injuring property.

● **Innate,** HSING: inborn character; spirit, quality, ability; naturally, without constraint. The ideogram: heart and produce, spontaneous feeling.

1.ImT Each one correcting innate fate.

● **In no way,** FEI: strong negative; not so. The ideogram: a box filled with opposition.

3.2a In no way outlawry, matrimonial allying.

4.Im/ImT In no way me seeking youthful Enveloping.

8.3a/b Grouping's in no way people.

12.Im/ImT Obstructing it, in no way people.

14.1a In no way faulty.

14.4a In no way one's preponderance.

14.4b In no way one's preponderance. Without fault.

22.4a/b In no way outlawry, matrimonial allying.

25.Im/ImT One in no way correcting: possessing blunder.

30.6a Severing the head. Catching in no way its demons.

38.6a In no way outlawry, matrimonial allying.

39.2a In no way body's anteriority.

45.5a Without fault: in no way connection.

59.4a In no way hiding, a place to ponder.

● **In no way people,** FEI FEN: there are no people, no people are involved; also: worthless people; barbarians, rebels, foreign slaves, captives.

8.3a/b Grouping's in no way people.

12.Im/ImT Obstructing it, in no way people.

● **Inside,** NEI: within, inner, interior; inside of the house and those who work there, particularly women; the lower trigram, as opposed to outside, WAI, the upper. The ideogram: border and enter, cross a border.

8.2a/b Grouping's origin inside.

11.ImT Inside yang and outside yin.

11.ImT Inside persisting and outside yielding.

11.ImT Inside chün tzu and outside Small People.

12.ImT Inside yin and outside yang.

12.ImT Inside supple and outside solid.

12.ImT Inside Small People and outside chün tzu.

19.6b Purpose located inside indeed.

25.ImT Solid originating from the outside coming and activating a lord with respect to the inside.

36.ImT Inside pattern Brightening and outside supple yielding.

36.ImT Inside heaviness and enabling correcting one's purpose.

37/38.CD Dwelling People: inside indeed.

37.ImT The woman correcting the situation reaching to the inside.

39.3b Inside rejoicing in it indeed.

39.6b Purpose located inside indeed.

61.ImT Supple located inside and solid acquiring the center.

● **Inspect,** HSING: examine on all sides, careful inquiry; watchful.

20.ST The Earlier Kings used inspecting on all sides, Viewing the commoners to set up teaching.

24.ST The crown prince [used culminating sun] not to inspect on all sides.

51.ST A chün tzu uses anxious fearing to adjust inspecting.

● **Install,** CHIEN: set up, establish; confirm a position or law.

3.Im/ImT,1a Advantageous: installing feudatories.

8.ST The Earlier Kings used installing myriad cities to connect the connoted feudatories.

16.Im Providing for, Advantageous: installing feudatories to move legions.

16.ImT and even more installing feudatories to move legions reached.

● **In tatters,** JU: worn out garments, used for padding or stopping leaks.

63.4a A token: possessing clothes in tatters.

● **Intention,** YI: thought, meaning, idea, will, motive; what gives words their auspiciousness. The ideogram: heart and sound, heartfelt expression.

18.1b Intention receiving the predecessors indeed.

36.4b Catching the heart, intention indeed.

51.5a Intention without losing possesses affairs.

Interpenetrate, T'UNG: mutually penetrate; permeate, flow through, reach everywhere; see clearly, communicate with.

11.S Pervading implies interpenetrating indeed.

11.ImT By consequence of that Heaven and Earth mingling and the myriad beings interpenetrating indeed.

12.S Beings not permitted to use completing interpenetrating.

12.ImT By consequence of that Heaven and Earth not mingling and the myriad beings not interpenetrating indeed.

13.ImT Verily a chün tzu activating enables interpenetrating Below Heaven's purpose.

38.ImT Man, Woman, Polarizing and their purposes interpenetrating indeed.

47/48.CD The Well: interpenetrating and Confining: mutual meeting indeed.

47.AE Confining: exhausting and interpenetrating.

60.ImT Centering correcting uses interpenetrating.

60.1b Knowing interpenetrating clogging indeed.

Interspace, HSIEN: space between, interval, crevice; vacant, empty.

3.S Overfilling Heaven and Earth's interspace implies verily the myriad beings.

Intertwist, JU: interlaced; entangled roots.

11.1a Eradicating thatch grass intertwisted.

12.1a Eradicating thatch grass intertwisted.

Intimidate, YEN: inspire with fear or alarm; severe, rigid, strict, austere, demanding; a severe father; tight, a closed door.

33.ST [A chün tzu uses] not hating and intimidating.

37.ImT Dwelling People possess an intimidating chief in truth.

In truth, YEN: statement is complete and correct.

3.S Therefore afterwards the myriad beings giving birth in truth.

14.S Associating with People Concording implies beings necessarily converting in truth.

37.ImT Dwelling People possess an intimidating chief in truth.

62.ImT Possessing the flying bird's symbol in truth.

64.S Accepting this lets you use Not yet

Fording completed in truth.

Invigorate, CHUANG: inspirit, animate; strong, robust; full grown, flourishing, abundant; attain manhood (at 30); damage through unrestrained strength. The ideogram: strength and scholar, intellectual impact.

Image of Hexagram 34 and occurs throughout its texts.

33.CD Great Invigorating: by consequence stopping.

35.S Beings not permitted to use completing Invigorating.

36.2a Availing of a rescuing horse, invigorating auspicious.

43.1a Invigorating into the preceding foot.

43.3a Invigorating into the cheek bones:

44.Im Coupling, womanhood invigorating.

59.1a Availing of a rescuing horse, invigorating auspicious.

Involve, CHIH: include, entangle, implicate; induce, cause. The ideogram: person walking, induced to follow.

2.1b Docilely involving one's tao:

5.3a Involving outlawry culminating.

5.3b Originating from my involving outlawry.

23.S Actually involving embellishing, therefore afterwards Growing by consequence used up.

40.3a Involving outlawry culminating.

40.3b Originating from my involving arms.

45.ImT Involving reverence presenting indeed.

47.ST A chün tzu uses involving fate to release purpose.

51.ImT,1b Anxiety involving blessing indeed.

55.ST A chün tzu uses severing litigating to involve punishing.

Issue forth (from), CH'U: emerge from, come out of, proceed from, spring from; the Action of the trigram Shake, CHEN; contrary of enter, JU. The ideogram: stem with branches and leaves emerging.

1.ImT Heads issuing forth from the multitudinous beings.

4.ST Below the mountain issuing forth springwater.

5.4a Issuing forth originates from the cave.

7.1a/b Legions issuing forth using ordinance.

9.4a Blood departing, alarm issuing forth.

9.4b There is a connection to the spirit, alarm issuing forth.

13.1b Issuing forth from the gate Concording People.

16.ST Thunder issuing forth from earth impetuously.

17.1a/b Issuing forth from the gate, mingling possesses achievement.

24.Im Issuing forth, entering, without affliction.

24.ImT That uses issuing forth, entering, without affliction.

29.2b Not yet issuing forth from the center indeed.

30.5a Issuing forth tears like gushing.

30.6a/b Kinghood availing of issuing forth chastising.

35.ST,ImT Brightness issuing forth above earth.

36.4a Into issuing forth from the gate chambers.

37.ST Wind originating from fire issuing forth.

50.1a/b Advantageous: issuing forth from obstruction.

51.ImT Issuing forth permits using guarding the ancestral temple, field altar, offertory millet.

52.ST A chün tzu uses pondering not to issue forth from his situation.

59.6a Departing far away, issuing forth.

60.1a/b Not issuing forth from the door chambers.

60.2a Not issuing forth from the gate chambers.

60.2b Not issuing forth from the gate chambers, pitfall.

64.ImT Not yet issuing forth from the center indeed.

Its/it, CH'I: third person pronoun; also: one/one's, he/his, she/hers, they/theirs.

This term occurs throughout the hexagram texts.

It, see: **Have (it)**

Jade, YÜ: all gemstones; precious beauty; delightful, happy; perfect, clear.

50.6a The Vessel: jade rings.

50.6b Jade rings located above.

Jar, FOU: earthenware vessels; wine jars and drums. The ideogram: jar containing liquor.

8.1a There is a connection to the spirit, overfilling the jar.

29.4a Availing of a jar.

30.3a Not drumbeating a jar and singing.

Jawbones, see: **Brace**

Jaws/swallow, YI: mouth, jaws, cheeks, chin; take in, ingest; feed, nourish, sustain, rear; furnish what is necessary. The ideogram: open jaws.

Image of Hexagram 27 and occurs throughout its texts.

21.ImT Jaws center possesses being. Spoken thus: Gnawing Bite.

Join, CHIEN: add or bring together; unite, absorb; attend to many things. The ideogram: hand grasps two grain stalks, two things at once. See also: **Conjoin**

17.2b Nowhere joining associating indeed.

52.ST Joined mountains. Bound.

Join together, HO: unite for a purpose; assemble friends for a specific aim.

16.4a Partners join together suddenly.

Jug, WENG: earthen jar; jug used to draw water.

48.2a The jug cracked, leaking.

Juice, KAO: active principle, essence; oil, grease, ointment; fertilizing, rich; genius.

3.5a/b Sprouting: one's juice.

50.3a Pheasant juice not taken in.

Jujube tree, CHI: thorny bush or tree; sign of a court of justice or site of official literary examinations.

29.6a Dismissing into dense jujube trees.

Junior, TI: younger relatives who owe respect to their elders.

7.5a/b The junior son carting corpses.

37.ImT The senior, a senior. The junior, a junior.

Junior sister, TI: younger woman in family or clan; younger sister, under authority of the first wife.

54.1a/b Converting Maidenhood using the junior sister.

54.3a Reversing Converting using the junior sister.

54.5a/b One's junior sister's sleeves not thus fine.

Keen, K'UAI: sharp, eager, prompt, cheerful; spirited.

52.2a One's heart not keen.

56.4a My heart not keen.

56.4b The heart not yet keen indeed.

Keep aloof, CHI: keep at a distance; avoid, fear, shun; antipathy. The ideogram: heart and self, keeping to yourself.

43.ST [A chün tzu uses] residing in actualizing tao, by consequence keeping aloof.

Kill, CH'IANG: put to death; violent assault; maltreat

misuse; kill an important person.
62.3a/b Adhering, maybe killing it.

Kinds, P'IN: species and their essential qualities; sorts, classes; classify, select.
1.ImT The kinds: being diffusing forms.
2.ImT The kinds: being conjoining Growing.
44.ImT The kinds: beings conjoining composition indeed.
57.4a/b The fields, catching three kinds.

King(hood), WANG: effective ruler, by authority of the Emperor, from whom others derive their power.
See also: **Earlier Kings**
2.3a/b Maybe adhering to kingly affairs:
6.3a Maybe adhering to kingly affairs:
7.ImT Actually permitting using kinghood.
7.2a/b The king three times bestowing fate.
8.5a The king avails of three beaters.
17.6a The king availing of Growing into the Western mountain.
18.6a/b Not affairs, kingly feudatories.
20.4a Advantageous: availing of guesting into kinghood.
29.ImT The kingly prince sets up venturing used to guard his city.
30.5b Radiance: the kingly prince indeed.
30.6a/b Kinghood availing of issuing forth chastising.
35.2a Into one's kingly mother.
36.ImT The pattern king uses it.
37.5a/b The king imagines possessing a Dwelling.
39.2a/b A king, a servant: Difficulties, Difficulties.
42.2a Kinghood availing of presenting into the supreme, auspicious.
43.Im Deciding, displaying into kingly chambers.
43.ImT Displaying into kingly chambers.
45.Im/ImT The king imagines possessing a temple.
46.4a/b Kinghood availing of Growing, into the twin peaked mountain.
48.3a Kingly brightness.
48.3b Seeking kingly brightness:
55.Im/ImT The king imagining it.
59.Im/ImT The king imagines possessing a temple.
59.ImT Kinghood thereupon located in the center indeed.
59.5a/b Kinghood residing, without fault.

Know, CHIH: understand, perceive, remember; informed, aware, wise. The ideogram: arrow and mouth, words focused and swift.
2.3b Knowing the shining great indeed.
19.5a Knowledge Nearing.
24.AE Returning: using originating knowledge.
39.ImT Actually knowing in fact.
54.ST A chün tzu uses perpetually completing to know the cracked.
60.1b Knowing interpenetrating clogging indeed.
64.1b Truly not knowing the end indeed.
64.6b Truly not knowing articulating indeed.

Lacking, WU: strong negative; does not possess.
3.3a Approaching stag, lacking precaution.
53.1a Lacking fault.
57.S Sojourning and lacking a place to tolerate.

Ladle, PI: ceremonial spoon used to pour libations.
51.Im Not losing the ladle, the libation.

Lament, CHÜEH: express intense regret or sorrow; mourn over; painful recollections.
30.3a By consequence great old age's lamenting.
30.5a Issuing forth tears like gushing. Sadness like lamenting.
45.3a Clustering thus, lamenting thus.
60.3a Not the Articulating like, by consequence the lamenting like.
60.3b Not Articulating's lamenting.

Last, CHIU: long, protracted; enduring.
1.6b Overfilling, not permitting lasting indeed.
19.ImT Dissolving, not lasting indeed.
28.5b Wherefore permitting lasting indeed?
30.3b Wherefore permitting lasting indeed?
31/32.CD Persevering: lasting indeed.
32.S Not permitting using not lasting indeed.
32.S Persevering implies lasting indeed.
32.ImT Persevering. Lasting indeed.
32.ImT Lasting with respect to one's tao indeed.
32.ImT Persevering lasting and not climaxing indeed.
32.ImT Sun and Moon acquiring heaven and enabling lasting illumination.
32.ImT The four seasons transforming changes and enabling lasting accomplishment.
32.ImT The all wise person lasting with respect to his tao and Below Heaven the changes accomplishing.
32.2b Ability lasting, centering indeed.

32.4b No lasting whatever: one's situation.

33.S Beings not permitted to use lasting residing in their place.

63.6b Wherefore permitting lasting indeed?

● **Latter,** TZ'U: what was last spoken of.

7.ImT Using the latter poisons Below Heaven and the commoners adhering to it.

● **Laugh,** HSIAO: manifest joy or mirth; giggle, laugh at, ridicule; pleased, merry; associated with the Fiery Moment.

13.5a Concording People beforehand crying out sobbing and afterwards laughing.

45.1a Like an outcry, the one handful activates laughing.

51.Im/ImT Laughing words, shrieking, shrieking.

51.1a After laughing words, shrieking, shrieking.

51.1b Laughing words, shrieking, shrieking.

56.6a Sojourning people beforehand laughing, afterwards crying out sobbing.

● **Laws,** FA: rules, statutes, model, method.

4.1b Using correcting laws indeed.

21.ST The Earlier Kings used brightening flogging to enforce the laws.

● **Leak,** LOU: seep, drip, ooze out; reveal; forget, let slip.

48.2a The jug cracked, leaking.

● **Left,** TSO: left side, left hand; secondary; deputy, assistant; inferior.

7.4a Legions: the left resting.

7.4b The left resting, without fault.

11.ST [The crown prince] uses the left to right the commoners.

36.2a Brightness Hiding. Hiding into the left thigh.

● **Left belly,** TSO FU: body cavity holding heart and spleen, considered the seat of emotion.

36.4a/b Entering into the left belly.

● **Legions/leading,** SHIH: troops; an organized unit, a metropolis; leader, general, model, master; organize, make functional; take as a model, imitate. The ideogram: heap and whole, organize confusion into functional units.

Image of Hexagram 7 and occurs throughout its texts.

8.CD Legions: grieving.

11.6a No availing of legions.

13.5a/b Great legions controlling mutual meeting.

15.6a Advantageous: availing of moving legions.

15.6b Permitting availing of moving legions.

16.Im Providing for, Advantageous: installing feudatories to move legions.

16.ImT and even more installing feudatories to move legions reached.

24.6a Availing of moving legions:

● **Leopard,** PAO: spotted wild cats, beautiful and independent; mark of high ranking officers.

49.6a/b A chün tzu: leopard transforming.

● **Lessen,** K'UEI: diminish, injure, wane; lack, defect, failure.

15.ImT Heavenly tao lessening overfilling and augmenting Humbling.

50.3a On all sides rain lessens repenting.

● **Let go,** SHIH: lose, omit, miss, fail, let slip; out of control. The ideogram: drop from the hand.

2.ImT Beforehand delusion letting go tao.

3/4.CD Sprouting: seeing and not letting go one's residing.

5.1b Not yet letting go rules indeed.

5.6b Although not an appropriate situation, not yet the great let go indeed.

6.4b Not letting go indeed.

7.1b Letting go ordinance: pitfall indeed.

7.4b Not yet letting go the rules indeed.

8.2b Not originating letting go indeed.

8.5a Letting go the preceding wildfowl.

8.5b Letting go the preceding wildfowl indeed.

9.2b Truly not originating from letting go indeed.

11.4b Altogether letting go substance indeed.

17.1b Not letting go indeed.

17.2a Letting go the respectable husband.

17.3a Letting go the small son.

20.3b Not yet letting go tao indeed.

23.3b Letting go Above and Below indeed.

27.2b Movement letting go sorting indeed.

29.ImT Movement venturing and not letting go one's trustworthiness.

29.1b Letting go tao: pitfall indeed.

29.6b Six above, letting go tao.

35.5a/b Letting go, acquiring, no cares.

36.6b Letting go by consequence indeed.

37.3b Not yet letting go indeed.

37.3b Letting go Dwelling articulating indeed.

38.2b Not yet letting go tao indeed.

41.S Delaying necessarily possesses a place to let go.

47.ImT Confining and not letting go one's place:

Growing.

50.3b Letting go its righteousness indeed.

52.ImT Stirring up, stilling, not letting go one's season.

52.1b Not yet letting go correcting indeed.

53.3b Letting go her tao indeed.

56.S Exhausting the great implies necessarily letting go one's residing.

60.2b Letting go the season ending indeed.

62.ImT Solid letting go the situation and not centering.

64.6a There is a connection to the spirit: letting go that.

Let in, NA: allow to enter; take in, grow smaller; insert; collect. The ideogram: silk and enter, shrinking silk threads.

4.2a Letting in the wife. Auspicious.

29.4a Letting in bonds originating from the window.

Levity, CH'ING: frivolous, think lightly of, unimportant; alert, agile; gentle. The ideogram: cart and stream, empty cart floating downstream.

15.CD Humbling: levity indeed.

Libation, CH'ANG: sacrificial liquor, poured out to draw the gods near.

51.Im Not losing the ladle, the libation.

Lightning, TIEN: lighting flash, electric discharge; sudden clarity; look attentively.

21.ST Thunder, lightning. Gnawing Bite.

21.ImT Thunder, lightning, uniting and composing.

55.ST Thunder, lightning, altogether culminating.

Like/similar, JO: same as; just as, similar to.

1.3a Nightfall, alarm, like adversity.

20.Im/ImT There is a connection to the spirit, like a presence.

30.5a Issuing forth tears like gushing. Sadness like lamenting.

43.3a Like soaking, possessing indignation.

45.1a Like an outcry, the one handful activates laughing.

50.S Skinning beings implies absolutely nothing like a Vessel.

51.S A lord's implementing implies absolutely nothing like the long living son.

55.2a/b There is a connection to the spirit, like shooting forth.

57.2a The variegated like auspicious.

57.2b The variegated like has

auspiciousness

60.3a Not the Articulating like, by consequence the lamenting like.

Limit, HSIEN: boundary, frontier, threshold; restriction, impediment; set a limit, distinguish, separate. See also: **Delimit**

52.3a/b Bound: one's limit.

Limits, see **Chain mail**

Limp, CHIEN: walk lamely, proceed haltingly; weak legged, afflicted, crooked; feeble, weak; unfortunate, difficult. The ideogram: foot and cold, impeded circulation in the feet.

Image of Hexagram 39 and occurs throughout its texts.

Limpid, LIEH: pure, clear, clean liquid; wash clean.

48.5a The Well: limpid, cold springwater taken in.

Lining, TS'OU: line or repair a well.

48.4a/b The Well: lining, without fault.

Liquor, CHIU: alcoholic beverages, distilled spirits; spirit which perfects the good and evil in human nature. The ideogram: liquid above fermenting must, separating the spirits.

5.5a Attending into liquor taken in.

5.5b Liquor taken in, Trial: auspicious.

29.4a/b A cup, liquor, a platter added.

47.2a/b Confined, into liquor taken in.

64.6a There is a connection to the spirit: into drinking liquor.

64.6b Drinking liquor, soaking the head.

Litigate, YÜ: legal proceedings; take a case to court. The ideogram: two dogs and words, barking arguments at each other.

21.Im Advantageous: availing of litigating.

21.ImT Although not an appropriate situation, Advantageous: availing of litigating indeed.

22.ST A chün tzu uses brightening the multitudinous standards without daring to sever litigating.

55.ST A chün tzu uses severing litigating to involve punishing.

56.ST A chün tzu uses brightening consideration to avail of punishing and not to detain litigating.

61.ST A chün tzu uses deliberating litigating to delay dying.

Little, CHIEN: small, narrow, insignificant, petty; diminish, contract.

22.5a Rolled plain silk: little, little.

Live alone, CH'Ü: lonely, solitary; quiet, still; deserted.

55.6a/b Living alone, one without people.

Locate(in), TSAI: live in, dwell, reside; belong to, involved with, depend on; within. The ideogram: earth and persevere, place on the earth.

1.1b Yang located below indeed.

1.2a/b Seeing dragon located in the fields.

1.4a/b Maybe capering located in the abyss.

1.5a/b Flying dragon located in heaven.

2.5b Pattern located in the center indeed.

5.ImT Venturing located in precedence indeed.

5.2b Overflowing located in the center indeed.

5.3b Calamity located outside indeed.

7.2a Locating Legions, centering auspicious.

7.2b Locating Legions, centering auspicious.

9.2b Hauling along, returning, locating in the center.

10.6b Spring auspicious located above.

11.1b Purpose located outside indeed.

12.1b Purpose located in a chief indeed.

14.ST Fire located above heaven.

16.6b Dim Providing for located above.

17.4a There is a connection to the spirit, locating in tao uses brightening.

17.4b There is a connection to the spirit located in tao.

19.6b Purpose located inside indeed.

20.ImT The great: Viewing located above.

24.ST Thunder located in earth center.

26.ST Heaven located in mountain center.

28.1b Supple located below indeed.

31.1b Purpose located outside indeed.

31.3b Purpose located in following people.

32.6b Rousing Persevering located in the above.

34.ST Thunder located above heaven.

37.2a Locating the center, feeding.

37.4b Yielding located in the situation indeed.

39.ImT Venturing located in precedence indeed.

39.6b Purpose located inside indeed.

46.6b Dim Ascending located above.

47.4b Purpose located below indeed.

48.6b Spring auspicious located in the above.

50.6b Jade rings located above.

51.5b One's affairs located in the center.

54.5b One's situation located in the center.

56.6b Using Sojourning to locate in the above.

57.2a,6a/b Ground located below the bed.

59.ImT Kinghood thereupon located in the center indeed.

59.3b Purpose located outside indeed.

61.ImT Supple located inside and solid acquiring the center.

61.2a Calling crane located in yin.

62.5a A prince, a string arrow grasping another located in a cave.

63.ST Stream located above fire.

64.ST Fire located above stream.

Lock up, CHIAO: imprison, lock up the feet; prison, pen.

21.1a/b Shoes locked up, submerging the feet.

21.6a/b Wherefore locking up submerging the ears?

Loins, YIN: hips, pelvis, lumbar region; kidneys; respect, honor; work toward a distant aim; money belt.

52.3a Assigned to one's loins.

Long living, CHANG: enduring, constant; senior, superior, greater; increase, prosper; respect, elevate.

3.6b Wherefore permitting long living indeed?

6.1b Arguing not permitting long living indeed.

7.5a/b The long living son conducting Legions.

11.ImT A chün tzu: tao long living.

12.ImT Small People: tao long living.

12.6b Wherefore permitting long living indeed?

16.6b Wherefore permitting long living indeed?

19.ImT Solid drenched and long living.

19.3b Fault not long living indeed.

23.ImT Small People long living indeed.

24.ImT Solid long living indeed.

33.ImT Drenched and long living indeed.

34.6b Fault not long living indeed.

42.AE Augmenting: long living enriching and not setting up.

43.ImT Solid long living, thereupon completing indeed.

43.6b Completing not permitting long living indeed.

44.ImT Not permitting associating with long living indeed.

51.S A lord's implementing implies absolutely nothing like the long living son.

61.6b Wherefore permitting long living indeed?

62.4b Completing not permitting long living indeed.

Loosen, see **Stimulate**

Loosening/Deliverance, HSIEH: loosen, disjoin, untie, sever, scatter; analyse, explain, understand; release, dispel sorrow; eliminate effects, solve problems; resolution, deliverance. The ideogram: horns and knife, cutting into forward thrust.

> Image of Hexagram 40 and occurs throughout its texts.
> 39.CD Loosening: delay indeed.

Lord, CHU: ruler, master, chief; authority. The ideogram: lamp and flame, giving light.

> 2.Im A lord Advantageous.
> 25.ImT Solid originating from the outside coming and activating a lord with respect to the inside.
> 36.1a A lord: the people possessing words.
> 38.2a/b Meeting a lord, into the street.
> 51.S A lord's implementing implies absolutely nothing like the long living son.
> 51.ImT Using activating the offering lord indeed.
> 55.1a Meeting one's equal lord.
> 55.4a/b Meeting one's hiding lord.

Lose, SANG: fail to obtain, cease, become obscure; forgotten, destroyed; lament, mourn; funeral. The ideogram: weep and the dead.

> 2.Im/ImT Eastern North: losing partnering.
> 34.5a/b Losing the goat, into versatility.
> 38.1a Losing the horse, no pursuit, originating from returning.
> 48.Im Without losing, without acquiring.
> 51.Im Not losing the ladle, the libation.
> 51.2a A hundred thousand lost coins.
> 51.5a Intention without losing possesses affairs.
> 51.5b The great without losing indeed.
> 56.3a Losing one's youthful vassal.
> 56.3b One's righteousness lost indeed.
> 56.6a/b Losing the cattle, into versatility.
> 57.6a/b Losing one's own emblem ax.
> 62.ST [A chün tzu uses] losing Exceeding to reach to mourning.
> 63.2a A wife losing her veil.

Love, HAO: affection; fond of, take pleasure in; fine, graceful.

> 15.ImT People tao hating overfilling and loving Humbling.
> 33.4a Loving Retiring.
> 33.4b A chün tzu lovingly Retiring.
> 61.2a I possess a loved wine cup.

Lowly, PEI: speak and think of yourself humbly; modest, yielding; base, mean, contemptible.

> 15.ImT Earth tao lowly and moving above.
> 15.ImT Lowliness and not permitting passing beyond.
> 15.1b Lowliness uses originating from herding indeed.

Luminous, PING: bright, fire like, light giving; alert, intelligent.

> 49.5b One's pattern luminous indeed.

Luxuriance, MAO: thriving, flourishing, vigorous; highly developed, elegant. The ideogram: plants and flourish.

> 25.ST The Earlier Kings used luxuriance suiting the season to nurture the myriad beings.

Magnanimous, TUN: generous; honest, substantial, important, wealthy; honor, increase; firm, solid. The ideogram: strike and accept, warrior magnanimous in attack and defense.

> 19.6a Magnanimity Nearing.
> 19.6b Magnanimity Nearing's auspiciousness.
> 24.5a Magnanimous Returning.
> 24.5b Magnanimous Returning, without repenting.
> 52.6a/b Magnanimous Bounding auspicious.

Maiden(hood), MEI: girl not yet nubile, virgin; younger sister; daughter of a secondary wife. The ideogram: woman and not yet.

> Image of Hexagram 54 and occurs throughout its texts.
> 11.5a The supreme burgeoning, converting maidenhood.
> 53.CD Converting Maidenhood: womanhood's completion indeed.

Majestic, T'ANG: grand, alarmsome; extending everywhere; repel injustice, correct grievances; lit.: large river and its periodic floods.

Mandate, see **Fate**

> 49.ImT Majestically martial, Skinning fate.

Manage, KAN: cope with, deal with, able; undertake, attend to business; trunk, stem, spine, skeleton.

> 18.1a/b Managing the father's Corrupting.
> 18.2a/b Managing the mother's Corrupting.
> 18.3a/b Managing the father's Corrupting.
> 18.5a Managing the father's Corrupting.
> 18.5b Managing the father availing of praise.

Man(hood), NAN: a man; what is inherently male. The ideogram: fields and strength, hard labor in the fields.

> 31.ImT Below manhood, womanhood.

37.ImT The man correcting the situation reaching to the outside.

38.ImT Man, Woman, Polarizing and their purposes interpenetrating indeed.

53/54.CD Infiltrating: womanhood converting awaits manhood moving indeed.

63/64.CD Not yet Fording: manhood exhausted indeed.

Man and Woman, NAN NÜ: creative relation between what is inherently male and what is inherently female.

31.S Therefore afterwards possessing Man and Woman.

31.S Possessing Man and Woman:

37.ImT Man and Woman correcting.

Manifest, HSIEN: apparent, conspicuous; illustrious; make clear.

8.5a Manifest Grouping.

8.5b Manifest Grouping's auspiciousness.

Mark off, PEIN: distinguish by dividing; mark off a plot of land; frame which divides a bed from its stand; discuss and dispute. The ideogram: knife and acrid, biting division.

13.ST A chün tzu uses sorting the clans to mark off the beings.

23.2a/b Stripping the bed, using marking off.

24.AE Returning: the small and marking off with respect to beings.

47.AE Confining: actualizing tao's marking off indeed.

64.ST A chün tzu uses considering to mark off the beings residing on all sides.

Marsh, TSE: open surface of a flat body of water and the vapors rising from it; fertilize, enrich;kindness, favor; the Symbol of the trigram Open, TUI.

10.ST Heaven above, marsh below.

17.ST Marsh center possessing thunder.

19.ST Above marsh possessing earth.

28.ST Marsh submerging wood.

31.ST Above mountain possessing marsh.

38.ST Fire above, marsh below.

38.ImT Marsh stirring up and below.

41.ST Below mountain possessing marsh.

43.ST Above marsh with respect to heaven.

45.ST Above marsh with respect to earth.

47.ST Marsh without stream.

49.ST Marsh center possessing fire.

54.ST Above marsh possessing thunder.

58.ST Congregating marshes.

60.ST Above marsh possessing stream.

61.ST Above marsh possessing wind.

Martial, WU: military, warlike; strong, stern; power to make war. The ideogram: fight and stop, force deterring aggression.

10.3a Martial people activating: into a Great Chief.

10.3b Martial people activating: into a Great Chief.

49.ImT Majestically martial, Skinning fate.

57.1a/b Martial people's Advantageous Trial.

Master, SHENG: have the upper hand, conquer; worthy of, able to; control, check, command.

33.2a Absolutely nothing has mastering stimulating.

43.1a Going not mastering, activating faulty.

43.1b Not mastering and going.

53.5a Completing: absolutely nothing has mastering.

53.5b Completing: absolutely nothing has mastering, auspicious.

Matrimonial allying, HUN KOU: legal institution of marriage; make alliances through marriage rather than force.

3.2a In no way outlawry, matrimonial allying.

3.4a Seeking matrimonial allying.

22.4a/b In no way outlawry, matrimonial allying.

38.6a In no way outlawry, matrimonial allying.

51.6a Matrimonial allying possesses words.

Maul, TIEH: bite, seize with the teeth; sneering laughter, rebuke. The ideogram: mouth and reach.

10.Im/ImT Not mauling people. Growing.

10.3a/b Mauling people: pitfall.

Maybe/"someone," HUO: possible, perhaps; term indicates spirit is active.

1.4a/b "Someone" capering located in the abyss.

2.3a/b Maybe adhering to kingly affairs:

6.3a Maybe adhering to kingly affairs:

6.6a Maybe bestowing's pouched belt.

7.3a/b Legions maybe carting corpses.

19/20.CD "Someone" associating with it, "someone" is seeking.

25.3a Maybe attaching's cattle.

32.3a Maybe receiving's embarrassing.

41.5a "Someone" augmenting it: ten partnering's tortoise.

42.2a "Someone" Augmenting it: ten partnering's tortoise.

42.2b "Someone" Augmenting it.

42.6a/b Maybe smiting it.

53.4a/b "Someone" acquiring his rafter.
61.3a Maybe drumbeating, maybe desisting.
61.3a Maybe weeping, maybe singing.
61.3b Maybe drumbeating, maybe desisting.
62.3a/b Adhering, maybe killing it.

- **Me,** see: **I/me/my**
- **Mean,** CHIEN: low, poor, cheap; depreciate, undervalue; opposite of value, KUEI.
  3.1b Using valuing the mean below.
- **Measures,** TU: rule, regulation, limit, test; interval in music; capacity, endurance.
  60.ST A chün tzu uses paring to reckon the measures.
  60.ImT Articulating used to pare the measures.
- **Meat,** JU: flesh of animals, pulp of fruit.
  21.3a Gnawing seasoned meat. Meeting poison.
  21.5a Gnawing parched meat. Acquiring yellow metal.
- **Meat bones,** TZU: meat with bones; bones left after a meal.
  21.4a Gnawing parched meat bones.
- **Medicinal herbs,** YAO: plants used as remedies; medical as opposed to other ways of healing.
  25.5a No medicinal herbs, possessing rejoicing.
  25.5b Disentangling's medicinal herbs.
- **Meet,** YÜ: come on unexpectedly, encounter; occur, happen; pleasant meeting, lucky coincidence; agree.
  See also: **Going to meet**
  13.5a/b Great legions controlling mutual meeting.
  21.3a Gnawing seasoned meat. Meeting poison.
  21.3b Meeting poison.
  38.2a/b Meeting a lord, into the street.
  38.3b Meeting a solid indeed.
  38.4a Meeting Spring, husbanding.
  38.6a Going meeting rain, by consequence auspicious.
  38.6b Meeting rain's auspiciousness.
  43/44.CD Coupling: meeting indeed.
  43/44.CD Supple meeting solid indeed.
  43.3a Solitary going, meeting rain.
  44.S Breaking up necessarily possesses meeting.
  44.S Coupling implies meeting indeed.
  44.ImT Coupling. Meeting indeed.
  44.ImT Supple meeting solid indeed.
  44.ImT Heaven, Earth: mutually meeting.
  44.ImT Solid meeting centering correctness.
  45.S Beings mutually meeting and afterwards assembling.
  47/48.CD Confining: mutual meeting indeed.

55.1a Meeting one's equal lord.
55.4a/b Meeting one's hiding lord.
62.2a Meeting one's grandmother.
62.2a Meeting one's servant.
62.4a/b Nowhere Exceeding meeting it.
62.6a/b Nowhere meeting Exceeding it.

- **Melancholy,** MEN: sad, unhappy, chagrined, heavy hearted. The ideogram: gate and heart, the heart confined.
  28.ST [A chün tzu uses] retiring from the age without melancholy.
- **Melon,** KUA: general term for melon, gourd, squash, cucumber; symbol of Heaven and Earth, the cosmos.
  44.5a Using osier, enwrapping melons.
- **Merely,** CHIH: nothing more than.
  24.1a Without merely repenting.
  29.5a Merely already evened.
- **Metallic,** CHIN: smelting and casting; all things pertaining to metal, particularly gold; autumn, West, sunset; one of the Five Moments.
  4.3a Seeing a metallic husband.
  21.4a Acquiring a metallic arrow.
  21.5a Gnawing parched meat. Acquiring yellow metal.
  44.1a/b Attaching into a metallic chock.
  47.4a Confined, into a metallic chariot.
  50.5a The Vessel: yellow ears, metallic rings.
- **Mile,** LI: measure of distance, about 1800 feet; village; street, square.
  51.Im/ImT Shake scaring a hundred miles.
- **Mingle,** CHIAO: blend with, communicate, join, exchange; trade, business; copulation; friendship.
  3.ImT Strong and Supple beginning mingling and heaviness giving birth indeed.
  11.ST Heaven and Earth mingling.
  11.ImT By consequence of that Heaven and Earth mingling and the myriad beings interpenetrating indeed.
  11.ImT Above and Below mingling and one's purpose concording indeed.
  12.ST Heaven, earth, not mingling.
  12.ImT By consequence of that Heaven and Earth not mingling and the myriad beings not interpenetrating indeed.
  12.ImT Above and Below not mingling and Below Heaven without fiefdoms indeed.
  14.1a Without mingling harm.
  14.1b Without mingling harm indeed.
  14.5a Your connection: mingling thus, impressing thus. Auspicious.

14.5b Your connection, mingling thus.

17.1a/b Issuing forth from the gate, mingling possesses achievement.

37.5b Mingling mutual affection indeed.

38.4a Mingling conformity.

38.4b Mingling connection, without fault.

54.ImT Heaven and Earth not mingling and the myriad beings not rising.

● **Mire**, T'U: mud, dirt, filth; besmear, blot out; stupid, pig headed. The ideogram: earth and water.

38.6a Seeing pigs bearing mire.

● **Moat**, HUANG: ditch around city or fort.

11.6a/b The bulwark returned into the moat.

● **Moon**, YÜEH: actual moon and moon month; yin, the sun being yang. See also: **Sun and Moon**

9.6a The moon almost facing.

19.Im/ImT Culminating into the eighth moon: possessing a pitfall.

54.5a The moon almost facing, auspicious.

55.ImT Moon overfilling, by consequence taking in.

61.4a The moon almost facing.

● **More**, T'O: another; add to. See also: **Even more, Furthermore**

8.1a Completing coming possesses more auspiciousness.

8.1b Possessing more auspiciousness indeed.

28.4a Possessing more: distress.

● **Moreover**, CH'IEH: further, and also.

29.3a Venturing moreover reclining.

38.3a One's person stricken, moreover nose cut.

40.3a/b Bearing, moreover riding.

43.4a/b One moves the resting place moreover.

44.3a/b One moves the resting place moreover.

● **Mother(hood)**, MU: child bearing and nourishing. The ideogram: two breasts. See also: **Father and Mother** and **Grandmother**

18.2a/b Managing the mother's Corrupting.

35.2a Into one's kingly mother.

● **Motive**, CH'ING: true nature; feelings, desires, passions. The ideogram: heart and green, germinated in the heart.

31.ImT and actually Heaven and Earth, the myriad beings's motives permitting seeing.

32.ImT and actually Heaven and Earth, the myriad beings's motives permitting seeing.

34.ImT Actually the correcting Great and Heaven and Earth's motives permitting seeing.

45.ImT and actually Heaven and Earth, the myriad beings's motives, permitting seeing.

● **Mound**, LING: grave mound, barrow; small hill.

13.3a Ascending one's high mound.

22.3b Completing absolutely nothing: having a mound indeed.

29.ImT Earth venturing, mountains, rivers, hill tops, mounds indeed.

51.2a Climbing into the ninth mound.

53.5a The wild geese Infiltrating into the mound.

● **Mount**, TENG: ascend, step up; ripen, complete.

36.6a/b Initially mounting into heaven.

61.6a/b A soaring sound mounting, into heaven.

● **Mountain**, SHAN: limit, boundary; the Symbol of the trigram Bound, KEN. The ideogram: three peaks, a mountain range.

4.ST Below the mountain issuing forth springwater.

4.ImT Enveloping. Below mountain possessing venturing.

15.ST Earth center possessing mountain.

17.6a The king availing of Growing into the Western mountain.

18.ST Below mountain possessing wind.

22.ST Below mountain possessing fire.

23.ST Mountain adjoining with respect to earth.

26.ST Heaven located in mountain center.

27.ST Below mountain possessing thunder.

29.ImT Earth venturing, mountains, rivers, hill tops, mounds indeed.

31.ST Above mountain possessing marsh.

33.ST Below heaven possessing mountain.

39.ST Above mountain possessing stream.

41.ST Below mountain possessing marsh.

46.4a/b Kinghood availing of Growing, into the twin peaked mountain.

52.ST Joined mountains.

53.ST Above mountain possessing wood.

56.ST Above mountain possessing fire.

62.ST Above mountain possessing thunder.

● **Mourn**, AI: grieve, lament over something gone; distress, sorrow; compassion. The ideogram: mouth and clothes, display of feelings.

62.ST [A chün tzu uses] losing Exceeding to reach to mourning.

● **Mouth**, K'OU: literal mouth, words going out and food coming in; entrance, hole.

27.Im/ImT Originating from seeking mouth substance.

31.6b The spouting mouth stimulating indeed.

47.ImT Honoring the mouth thereupon exhausted indeed.

● **Move,** HSING: move or move something; motivate, emotionally moving; walk, act, do. The ideogram: stepping left then right. This term occurs throughout the hexagram texts.

● **Mud,** HSI: ground left wet by water, muddy shores; danger; shed tears; nearly.

48.Im/ImT Muddy culmination: Truly not yet the well rope Well.

64.Im/ImT The small fox, a muddy Ford.

● **Mulberry tree,** SANG: literal tree and silk production; tranquility; retired, rural place.

12.5a Attaching into bushy mulberry trees.

● **Multiply,** FAN: augment, enhance, increase; thriving, plentiful.

35.Im Prospering, the calm feudatory avails of bestowing horses to multiply the multitudes.

35.ImT That uses the calm feudatory availing of bestowing horses to multiply the multitudes.

● **Multitude,** SHU: the people; mass, herd; all, the whole.

1.ImT Heads issuing forth from the multitudinous beings.

22.ST A chün tzu uses brightening the multitudinous standards without daring to sever litigating.

35.Im Prospering, the calm feudatory avails of bestowing horses to multiply the multitudes.

35.ImT That uses the calm feudatory availing of bestowing horses to multiply the multitudes.

● **Munificence,** HOU: liberal, kind, generous; create abundance; thick, large. The ideogram: gift of a superior to an inferior.

2.ST A chün tzu uses munificent actualizing tao to carry the beings.

2.ImT Field: munificence carrying the beings.

23.ST Using munificence above to quiet the position below.

42.1b The below, not munificent affairs indeed.

52.6b Using munificence, completing indeed.

● **Mutual,** HSIANG: reciprocal assistance, encourage, help; bring together, blend with; examine, inspect; by turns.

11.ST [The crown prince uses] bracing to mutualize Heaven and Earth's propriety.

13.5a/b Great legions controlling mutual meeting.

13.5b Words mutualize controlling indeed.

28.2b Exceeding uses mutual associating indeed.

31.ImT The two agencies influencing correspondence use mutual associating.

32.ImT Thunder, wind, mutually associating.

37.5b Mingling mutual affection indeed.

44.ImT Heaven, Earth: mutually meeting.

45.S Beings mutually meeting and afterwards assembling.

47/48.CD Confining: mutual meeting indeed.

48.ST A chün tzu uses toiling commoners to encourage mutualizing.

49.ImT Skinning. Stream, fire, mutually pausing.

49.ImT Their purposes not mutually acquired.

52.ImT Not mutually associating indeed.

53.3b Yielding mutualizes protection indeed.

54.1b Mutualizing receiving indeed.

My, see: **I/me/my.** See also: **Myself**

Myriad, WAN: countless; many, everyone; lit.: ten thousand. The ideogram: swarm of insects.

1.ImT The myriad beings's own beginning.

1.ImT Myriad cities, conjoining, soothing.

2.ImT The myriad beings's own birth.

3.S Therefore afterwards the myriad beings giving birth in truth.

3.S Overfilling Heaven and Earth's interspace implies verily the myriad beings.

7.2b Cherishing the myriad fiefdoms indeed.

8.ST The Earlier Kings used installing myriad cities to connect the connoted feudatories.

11.ImT By consequence of that Heaven and Earth mingling and the myriad beings interpenetrating indeed.

12.ImT By consequence of that Heaven and Earth not mingling and the myriad beings not interpenetrating indeed.

15.3b The myriad commoners submitting indeed.

25.ST The Earlier Kings used luxuriance suiting the season to nurture the myriad beings.

27.ImT Heaven and Earth nourishes the myriad beings.

27.ImT The all wise person nourishes eminence used to extend to the myriad commoners.

31.S Therefore afterwards possessing the myriad beings.

31.S Possessing the myriad beings:

31.ImT Heaven and Earth influencing and the myriad beings's changing give birth.

31.ImT and actually Heaven and Earth, the myriad beings's motives permitting seeing.

32.ImT and actually Heaven and Earth, the myriad beings's motives permitting seeing.

38.ImT The myriad beings Polarizing and their affairs sorted indeed.

45.ImT and actually Heaven and Earth, the myriad beings's motives, permitting seeing.

54.ImT Heaven and Earth not mingling and the myriad beings not rising.

- **Myself**, WU: first person intensifier; the particular person I am.

   61.2a Myself associating, simply spilling it.

- **Namely**, WEI: precisely, only that.

   3.3a Namely, entering into the forest center.

- **Near**, LIN: approach or be approached: behold with care, look on sympathetically; condescend; bless or curse by coming nearer; a superior visits an inferior. Image of Hexagram 19 and occurs throughout its texts.

- **Nearby**, ERH: near, close; close relation.

   51.ImT Scaring the distant and fearing the nearby indeed.

- **Necessarily**, PI: unavoidably, indispensably, certainly.

   4.S Beings giving birth necessarily Enveloping.

   6.S Drinking and eating necessarily possesses Arguing.

   7.S Arguing necessarily possesses crowds rising up.

   7.6b Necessarily disarraying the fiefdoms indeed.

   8.S Crowds necessarily possess a place to Group.

   9.S Grouping necessarily possesses a place to Accumulate.

   14.S Associating with People Concording implies beings necessarily converting in truth.

   16.S Possessing the Great and enabling Humbling necessarily Provides for.

   17.S Providing for necessarily possesses Following.

   18.S Using rejoicing Following people implies necessarily possessing affairs.

   30.S Falling necessarily possesses a place to congregate.

36.S Advancing necessarily possessing a place: injuring.

37.S Injury with respect to the outside implies necessarily reversing with respect to Dwelling.

38.S Dwelling tao exhausted, necessarily returning.

39.S Turning away necessarily possesses heaviness.

41.S Delaying necessarily possesses a place to let go.

42.S Diminishing and not climaxing necessarily Augments.

43.S Augmenting and not climaxing necessarily breaks up.

44.S Breaking up necessarily possesses meeting.

47.S Ascending and not climaxing necessarily Confines.

48.S Confining reaching to the above implies necessarily reversing the below.

54.S Advancing necessarily possessing a place to Convert.

55.S Acquiring one's place to Convert implies necessarily the great.

56.S Exhausting the great implies necessarily letting go one's residing.

62.S Possessing one's trustworthiness implies necessarily moving it.

62.4a/b Going adversity necessarily warning.

63.S Possessing Exceeding being implies necessarily Fording.

Neck, MEI: muscular base of neck, shoulders and arms; source of strength in arms and shoulders; persist.

   31.5a/b Conjoining one's neck.

Neighbor, LIN: person living nearby; extended family; assist, support.

   9.5a Affluence: using one's neighbor.

   11.4a Not affluence: using one's neighbor.

   15.5a Not affluence: using one's neighbor.

   51.6a Shake: not into one's body, into one's neighbor.

   51.6b Dreading the neighbor, a warning indeed.

   63.5a/b The Eastern neighbor slaughters cattle.

   63.5a Not thus the Western neighbor's dedicated offering.

   63.5b Not thus the Western neighbor's season indeed.

Nest, CH'AO: nest in a tree; haunt, retreat; make a nest.

56.6a A bird burning its nest.

Net, WANG: emptiness, vacancy; lit.: a net, open spaces between threads; used as a negative. The ideogram: net and lost, empty spaces divide what is kept from what is lost.

34.3a A chün tzu avails of net.

34.3b A chün tzu: net indeed.

35.1a Net: connection.

Nightfall, HSI: day's end, dusk; late; last day of month or year.

1.3a Nightfall, alarm, like adversity.

Night time, YEH: dark half of 24 hour cycle.

43.2a Absolutely no night time, possessing arms.

Nine, CHIU: number of a transforming whole line; superlative: best, perfect; ninth.

1.7b Availing of nines.

14.1b Great Possessing, the initial nine.

32.2b Nine at second, repenting extinguished.

34.2b Nine at second, Trial: auspicious.

40.2b Nine at second, Trial: auspicious.

41.2b Nine at second, Advantageous Trial.

44.5b Nine at fifth, containing composition.

46.2b Nine at second's connection.

51.2a Climbing into the ninth mound.

57.5b Nine at fifth's auspiciousness.

58.4b Nine at fourth's rejoicing.

61.1b The initial nine, precaution auspicious.

64.2b Nine at second, Trial: auspicious.

No advantageous direction, WU YU LI: no plan or direction is advantageous; in order to take advantage of the situation, do not impose a direction on events.

4.3a Without direction: Advantageous.

19.3a Without direction: Advantageous.

25.6a Without direction: Advantageous.

27.3a Without direction: Advantageous.

32.1a Without direction: Advantageous.

34.6a Without direction: Advantageous.

45.3a Without direction: Advantageous.

54.Im/ImT,6a Without direction: Advantageous.

64.Im/ImT Without direction: Advantageous.

North, see: **Eastern North**

Nose, PI: literal nose; the first, original.

21.2a/b Gnawing flesh, submerging the nose.

Nose cutting, YI: punish through loss of public face or honor; contrasts with foot cutting, YEH, crippling punishment for serious crime.

38.3a One's person stricken, moreover nose cut.

47.5a/b Nose cutting, foot cutting.

Not permitting, PU K'O: not possible; contradicts an inherent principle. The ideogram: mouth and breath, silent consent. See also: **Permit**

1.6b Overfilling, not permitting lasting indeed.

1.7b Heavenly actualizing tao not permitting activating the head indeed.

5.S Being immature not permitting not nourishing indeed.

6.ImT Arguing not permitting accomplishment indeed.

6.1b Arguing not permitting long living indeed.

12.ST [A chün tzu uses] not permitting splendor to use benefits.

15.S Possessing the Great implies not permitting using overfilling.

15.ImT Lowliness and not permitting passing beyond.

18.2a Not permitting Trial.

23.6b Completing, not permitting availing of indeed.

25.5b Not permitting testing indeed.

27.5a Not permitting stepping into the Great River.

28.S Not nourishing, by consequence not permitting stirring up.

28.3b Not permitted to use possessing bracing indeed.

28.6b Not permitting fault indeed.

29.ImT Heaven venturing, not permitting ascending indeed.

32.S Not permitting using not lasting indeed.

33.3b Not permitting Great Affairs indeed.

36.3a Not permitting affliction: Trial.

36.5b Brightness not permitted to pause indeed.

43.6b Completing not permitting long living indeed.

44.ImT Not permitting associating with long living indeed.

49.S The Well tao not permitting not Skinning.

49.1b Not permitted to use possessing activating indeed.

53.6b Not permitting disarray indeed.

55.3b Not permitting Great Affairs indeed.

55.3b Completing, not permitting availing of indeed.

60.Im/ImT Bitter Articulating not permitting Trial.

62.Im Permitting Small Affairs. Not permitting Great Affairs.

62.ImT That uses not permitting Great Affairs indeed.

62.1b Wherefore not permitted thus indeed.

62.2b A servant not permitted Exceeding indeed.

62.4b Completing not permitting long living indeed.

64.S Beings not permitted exhaustion indeed.

Notable, SHIH: learned, upright, important man; scholar, gentleman.

28.5a A venerable wife acquiring her notable husband.

28.5b A venerable wife, a notable husband.

54.6a A notable disembowelling a goat without blood.

Nothing not advantageous, WU PU LI: nothing for which this will not be beneficial; advantageous potential, borderline where the balance is swinging from not Advantageous to actually Advantageous.

2.2a/b Not repeating: nothing not Advantageous.

3.4a Nothing not advantageous.

14.6a Auspicious, Nothing not advantageous.

15.4a/b Nothing not advantageous, demonstrating Humbling.

15.5a Nothing not advantageous.

19.2a/b Nothing not advantageous.

23.5a Nothing not advantageous.

28.2a Nothing not advantageous.

33.6a/b Rich Retiring, nothing not advantageous.

35.5a Going auspicious, nothing not advantageous.

40.6a Nothing not advantageous: catching it.

50.6a Nothing not advantageous.

57.5a Nothing not advantageous.

Nothing/nowhere, FU: strong negative; not a single thing/place. See also: **Absolutely nothing**

13.4a Nothing controlling attacking.

13.4b Righteously nothing controlling indeed.

14.3a Small People nowhere controlling.

17.2b Nowhere joining associating indeed.

22.1b Righteously nothing to ride indeed.

34.ST A chün tzu uses no codes whatever, nowhere treading.

41.2a Nowhere Diminishing, augmenting it.

41.5a Nowhere a controlling contradiction.

41.6a/b Nowhere Diminishing, augmenting it.

42.2a Nowhere a controlling contradiction.

62.3a Nowhere Exceeding defending against it.

62.4a/b Nowhere Exceeding meeting it.

62.6a/b Nowhere meeting Exceeding it.

Notify, KAO: proclaim, order, decree; advise, inform, tell. The ideogram: mouth and ox head, imposing speech.

4.Im/ImT The initial oracle consulting notifying.

4.Im/ImT Obscuring, by consequence not notifying.

11.6a Originating from the capital, notifying fate.

42.3a Notifying the prince, availing of the scepter.

42.4a/b Notifying the prince, adhering.

43.Im/ImT Notifying originates from the capital.

Not yet, WEI: temporal negative; something will but has not yet occurred; contrary of already, CHI. Image of Hexagram 64 and occurs throughout its texts.

3.5b Spreading out not yet shining indeed.

5.1b Not yet letting go rules indeed.

5.6b Although not an appropriate situation, not yet the great let go indeed.

7.4b Not yet letting go the rules indeed.

9.ImT Spreading out, not yet moving indeed.

13.6b Purpose not yet acquired indeed.

15.6b Purpose not yet acquired indeed.

16.5b Center not yet extinguished indeed.

18.4b Going, not yet acquiring indeed.

19.2b Not yet yielding to fate indeed.

20.3b Not yet letting go tao indeed.

20.6b Purpose not yet evened indeed.

21.4b Not yet shining indeed.

23.2b Not yet possessing associating indeed.

25.2b Not yet affluence indeed.

29.2b Not yet issuing forth from the center indeed.

29.5b Centering, not yet great indeed.

31.4b Not yet influencing harming indeed.

31.4b Not yet the shining great indeed.

35.1b Not yet accepting fate indeed.

35.6b Tao not yet shining indeed.

37.1b Purpose not yet transformed indeed.

37.3b Not yet letting go indeed.

38.2b Not yet letting go tao indeed.

40.4b Not yet an appropriate situation indeed.

43.5b Center not yet shining indeed.

44.3b Moving, not yet hauling along indeed.

45.2b Centering, not yet transforming indeed.

45.5b Purpose not yet shining indeed.
45.6b The above not yet quiet indeed.
47.5b Purpose not yet acquired indeed.
47.6b Not yet appropriate indeed.
48.Im/ImT Muddy culmination: Truly not yet the well rope Well.
48.ImT Not yet possessing achievement indeed.
49.5a Not yet an augury, there is a connection to the spirit.
50.1b Not yet rebelling indeed.
51.4b Not yet shining indeed.
51.6b Center not yet acquired indeed.
52.1b Not yet letting go correcting indeed.
52.2b Not yet withdrawing from hearkening indeed.
54.2b Not yet transforming the rules indeed.
54.3b Not yet appropriate indeed.
56.4b Not yet acquiring the situation indeed.
56.4b The heart not yet keen indeed.
58.1b Movement not yet doubted indeed.
58.4a Bargaining Opening, not yet soothing.
58.6b Not yet shining indeed.
61.1b Purpose not yet transformed indeed.
63.CD Not yet Fording: manhood exhausted indeed.

- **Nourish**, YANG: feed, sustain, support; provide, care for; bring up, improve, grow, develop.
    4.ImT Enveloping used to nourish correcting:
    5.S Being immature not permitting not nourishing indeed.
    26.ImT Nourishing eminence indeed.
    27.S Beings accumulating therefore afterwards permitting nourishing.
    27.S Jaws imply nourishing indeed.
    27.CD Jaws: nourishing correcting indeed.
    27.ImT Nourishing correcting, by consequence auspicious indeed.
    27.ImT Viewing one's place to nourish indeed.
    27.ImT Viewing one's origin: nourishing indeed.
    27.ImT Heaven and Earth nourishes the myriad beings.
    27.ImT The all wise person nourishes eminence used to extend to the myriad commoners.
    28.S Not nourishing, by consequence not permitting stirring up.
    28.CD Jaws: nourishing correcting indeed.
    48.ImT The Well nourishing and not exhausted indeed.

50.ImT and great Growing uses nourishing all wise eminences.
No ... whatever, FEI: strongest negative; not at all!
    32.4b No lasting whatever: one's situation.
    34.ST A chün tzu uses no codes whatever, nowhere treading.
Nowhere, see: **Nothing**
Numerous, TO: great number, many; often.
    15.ST A chün tzu uses reducing the numerous to augment the few.
    26.ST A chün tzu uses the numerous recorded preceding words going to move.
    55/56.CD Abounding: numerous anteriority indeed.
Nurse, TZU: love, care for and shelter; act as a mother. The ideogram: child and shelter.
    3.2a Woman[and]Son, Trial: not nursing.
    3.2a/b Ten years revolved, thereupon nursing.
Nurture, YÜ: bring up, support, rear, raise; increase.
    4.ST A chün tzu uses fruiting movement to nurture actualizing tao.
    18.ST A chün tzu uses rousing the commoners to nurture actualizing tao.
    25.ST The Earlier Kings used luxuriance suiting the season to nurture the myriad beings.
    53.3a/b The wife pregnant, not nurturing.

Oblations, SSU: sacrifices offered to the gods and the dead.
    47.2a Advantageous: availing of presenting oblations.
    47.5a/b Advantageous: availing of offering oblations.
Obscure, TU: confuse, muddy, agitate; muddled, cloudy, turbid; agitated water; annoy through repetition.
    4.Im/ImT Twice, three times: obscuring.
    4.Im/ImT Obscuring, by consequence not notifying.
    4.ImT Obscuring Enveloping indeed.
Observe, SHIH: see and inspect carefully; gain knowledge of; compare and imitate. The ideogram: see and omen, taking account of what you see.
    10.3a/b Squinting enabling observing.
    10.6a Observing Treading, predecessors auspicious.
    27.4a Tiger observing: glaring, glaring.
    51.6a Observing: terrorizing, terrorizing.
    54.2a Squinting enabling observing.

Obstruct, P'I: closed, stopped; bar the way; obstacle; unfortunate, wicked; refuse, disapprove, deny. The ideogram: mouth and not, blocked communication.
Image of Hexagram 12 and occurs throughout its texts.
7.1a Obstructing virtue: pitfall.
11.CD Obstructing, Pervading: reversing one's sorting indeed.
13.S Beings not permitted to use completing Obstructing.
33.4a Small People obstructing.
33.4b Small People obstructing indeed.
50.1a/b Advantageous: issuing forth from obstruction.

Occult, YIN: screen, obscure, keep from view, keep back; private; retired, not in office.
57.AE Ground: evaluating and occulting.

Offense, TSUI: crime, sin, fault; violate laws or rules; incur blame, incriminated. The ideogram: net and wrong, entangled in guilt.
40.ST A chün tzu uses forgiving excess to pardon offenses.

Offer, CHI: present gifts to gods and spirits. The ideogram: hand, meat and worship.
47.5a/b Advantageous: availing of offering oblations.
51.ImT Using activating the offering lord indeed.
63.5a Not thus the Western neighbor's dedicated offering.

Offertory millet, CHI: grain presented to the god of agriculture; presence of the god in the grain.
51.ImT Issuing forth permits using guarding the ancestral temple, field altar, offertory millet.

Office, KUAN: government officials, magistrates, dignitaries.
17.1a An office: possessing denial. Trial: auspicious.
17.1b An office: possessing denial.

Old age, TIEH: seventy or older; aged, no longer active.
30.3a By consequence great old age's lamenting. Pitfall.

On all sides, see: **Sides**

One's/one, CH'I: third person pronoun; also: it/its, he/his, she/hers, they/theirs.
This term occurs throughout the hexagram texts.

One, the one, YI: single unit; number one; undivided, simple, whole; any one of; first, the first.

32.AE Persevering: using the one actualizing tao.
32.5b Adhering to the one and completing indeed.
38.6a Carrying souls, the one chariot.
41.3a By consequence Diminishing the one person.
41.3a/b The one person moving.
45.1a Like an outcry, the one handful activates laughing.
56.5a The one arrow extinguishing.

One sided, P'IEN: excessive, partial, selfish; long for, bent on; lit.: inclined to one side.
42.6b One sided evidence indeed.

Ooze, TIEH: exude moisture; mud; slime; turbid, tainted.
48.3a/b The Well: oozing, not taking in.

Open, TUI: an open surface, promoting interaction and interpenetration; responsive, free, unhindered, pleasing; opening, passage; the mouth; exchange, barter; straight, direct; meet, gather; place where water accumulates. The ideogram: person, mouth and vapor, speaking with others.
Image of Hexagram 58 and occurs throughout its texts.

Oppose, FAN: resist; violate, offend, attack; possessed by an evil spirit; criminal. The ideogram: violate and dog, brutal offense.
5.1b Not opposing heavy moving indeed.
26.1b Not opposing calamity indeed.
58.ImT Stimulating using opposing heaviness:

Oracle consulting, SHIH: yarrow stalk divination; find your allotted destiny.
4.Im/ImT The initial oracle consulting notifying.
8.Im/ImT Retracing the oracle consulting: Spring, perpetual Trial.

Ordinance, LÜ: law, fixed regulation; regulate by law, divide into right and wrong. The ideogram: writing and move, codes that govern action.
7.1a/b Legions issuing forth using ordinance.
7.1b Letting go ordinance: pitfall indeed.

Origin, TZU: source, beginning, ground; cause, reason, motive; line of descent; path to the origin; yourself, intrinsic.
1.ST A chün tzu uses originating strength not to pause.
5.3b Originating from my involving outlawry.
5.4a Issuing forth originates from the cave.
6.2b Below origin, above Arguing.

8.2a/b Grouping's origin inside.

8.2b Not originating letting go indeed.

9.Im/ImT Originating from my Western suburbs.

9.1a/b Returning originating from tao.

9.2b Truly not originating from letting go indeed.

10.2b Centering, not originating from disarray indeed.

11.6a Originating from the capital, notifying fate.

14.6a Originating from heaven shielding it.

14.6b Originating from heaven shielding indeed.

15.1b Lowliness uses originating from herding indeed.

24.AE Returning: using originating knowledge.

24.5b Centering originating from the predecessor indeed.

25.ImT Solid originating from the outside coming and activating a lord with respect to the inside.

27.Im/ImT Originating from seeking mouth substance.

27.ImT Viewing one's origin: nourishing indeed.

29.4a Letting in bonds originating from the window.

35.ST A chün tzu uses originating enlightening to brighten actualizing tao.

37.ST Wind originating from fire issuing forth.

38.1a Losing the horse, no pursuit, originating from returning.

40.3b Originating from my involving arms.

41.5b Originating from shielding above indeed.

42.ImT Above origin, below the below.

42.2b,6b Originating from outside, coming indeed.

43.Im/ImT Notifying originates from the capital.

44.5a/b Possessing tumbling, originating from heaven.

55.6b Originating from concealing indeed.

62.5a Originating from my Western suburbs.

- **Osier**, CH'I: willow branches used to make baskets.

44.5a Using osier, enwrapping melons.

- **Outcry**, see: Cry out

- **Outlawry**, K'OU: break the laws; violent people, outcasts, bandits.

3.2a In no way outlawry, matrimonial allying.

4.6a Not Advantageous: activating outlawry.

4.6a Advantageous: resisting outlawry.

4.6b Advantageous: availing of resisting outlawry.

5.3a Involving outlawry culminating.

5.3b Originating from my involving outlawry.

22.4a/b In no way outlawry, matrimonial allying.

38.6a In no way outlawry, matrimonial allying.

40.3a Involving outlawry culminating.

53.3a Advantageous: resisting outlawry.

53.3b Advantageous: availing of resisting outlawry.

Outside, WAI: outer, exterior, external; people working in places other than their home; unfamiliar, foreign; the upper trigram, as opposed to inside, NEI, the lower.

5.3b Calamity located outside indeed.

8.4a Outside Grouping it.

8.4b Outside Grouping with respect to eminence.

11.ImT Inside yang and outside yin.

11.ImT Inside persisting and outside yielding.

11.ImT Inside chün tzu and outside Small People.

11.1b Purpose located outside indeed.

12.ImT Inside yin and outside yang.

12.ImT Inside supple and outside solid.

12.ImT Inside Small People and outside chün tzu.

25.ImT Solid originating from the outside coming and activating a lord with respect to the inside.

31.1b Purpose located outside indeed.

36.ImT Inside pattern Brightening and outside supple yielding.

37.S Injury with respect to the outside implies necessarily reversing with respect to Dwelling.

37/38.CD Polarizing: outside indeed.

37.ImT The man correcting the situation reaching to the outside.

42.2b,6b Originating from outside, coming indeed.

56.ImT Supple acquiring the center reaching to the outside and yielding reaching to the solid.

58.ImT Solid centering and supple outside.

59.ImT Supple acquiring the situation reaching to the outside and concording above.

59.3b Purpose located outside indeed.

Overbearing, K'ANG: excessive, overpowering authority; disparage; rigid, unbending; excessive display of force.

    1.6a/b Overbearing dragon possesses repenting.

    62.6b Climaxing overbearing indeed.

Overfill, YING: at the point of overflowing; more than wanted, stretch beyond; replenished, full; arrogant. The ideogram: vessel and too much.

    1.6b Overfilling, not permitting lasting indeed.

    3.S Overfilling Heaven and Earth's interspace implies verily the myriad beings.

    3.S Sprouting implies overfilling indeed.

    3.ImT Thunder and Rain's stirring up, fullness overfilling.

    8.1a There is a connection to the spirit, overfilling the jar.

    15.S Possessing the Great implies not permitting using overfilling.

    15.ImT Earthly tao transforming overfilling and diffusing Humbling.

    15.ImT Heavenly tao lessening overfilling and augmenting Humbling.

    15.ImT Souls[and]Spirits harming overfilling and blessing Humbling.

    15.ImT People tao hating overfilling and loving Humbling.

    23.ImT A chün tzu honors the dissolving pause to overfill emptiness.

    29.ImT Stream diffusing and not overfilling.

    29.5a/b Gorge not overfilled.

    41.ImT Diminishing augmenting, overfilling emptiness.

    55.ImT Moon overfilling, by consequence taking in.

    55.ImT Heaven and Earth overfilling emptiness.

Overflow, YEN: flow over the top; inundate, spread out; abundant, rich.

    5.2b Overflowing located in the center indeed.

Overrun, CH'IEN: pass the limit; mistake, transgression, disease.

    54.4a Converting Maidenhood overrunning the term

    54.4b Overrunning the term's purpose.

Overtake, TI: come up to, reach; arrest, seize; until; also: harmonious, peaceful. The ideogram: go, hand and reach, reaching to seize satisfaction.

    56.5b Overtaking the above indeed.

Overthrow, FU: subvert, upset, defeat, throw down; unstable, move back and forth.

    50.4a/b Overthrowing a princely stew.

Own, TZU: possession and the things possessed; avail of, depend on; property, riches.

    1.ImT The myriad beings's own beginning.

    2.ImT The myriad beings's own birth.

    56.2a Cherishing one's own.

    56.4a/b Acquiring one's own emblem ax.

    57.6a/b Losing one's own emblem ax.

Parch, KAN: dry up; dried, exhausted, desiccated; cleaned away, gone. See also: **Force**

    21.4a Gnawing parched meat bones.

    21.5a Gnawing parched meat. Acquiring yellow metal.

Pardon, YU: forgive, indulge, relax; lenient.

    40.ST A chün tzu uses forgiving excess to pardon offenses.

Pare, CHIH: cut away; form, tailor, carve; invent; limit, prevent. The ideogram: knife and incomplete.

    15.AE Humbling: using paring the codes.

    32.5b The husband, the son: paring righteously.

    57.AE Ground: actualizing tao's paring indeed.

    60.ST A chün tzu uses paring to reckon the measures.

    60.ImT Articulating used to pare the measures.

Parsimonious, CHIEN: thrifty; moderate, temperate; stingy, scanty.

    12.ST A chün tzu uses parsimonious actualizing tao to cast out heaviness.

    62.ST [A chün tzu uses] availing of Exceeding to reach to parsimony.

Part, KUAI: separate, fork, cut off, decide; pull or flow in different directions; certain, settled; prompt, decisive, stern.

    Image of Hexagram 43 and occurs throughout its texts.

    10.5a/b Deciding Treading. Trial: adversity.

    44.CD Deciding: breaking up indeed.

Partner, P'ENG: associate for mutual benefit; two equal or similar things; companions, friends, peers; join in; commercial ventures. The ideogram: linked strings of cowries or coins.

    2.Im/ImT Western South: acquiring partnering.

    2.Im/ImT Eastern North: losing partnering.

    11.2a Partnering extinguished.

    16.4a Partners join together suddenly.

    24.Im/ImT Partnering coming, without fault.

31.4a Partnering adheres to simply pondering.

39.5a/b The great Difficulties, partnering coming.

40.4a Partnering culminating, splitting off connection.

41.5a Maybe augmenting's ten: partnering's tortoise.

42.2a Maybe Augmenting's ten: partnering's tortoise.

58.ST A chün tzu uses partnering friends to explicate repeating.

Passage, KUAN: market gate, customs house, frontier post; limit, crisis, important point.

24.ST The Earlier Kings used culminating sun to bar the passages.

Pass beyond, YÜ: go beyond set time or limits; get over a wall or obstacle; pass to the other side.

15.ImT Lowliness and not permitting passing beyond.

Past, see **Anterior**

Pattern, WEN: intrinsic or natural design and its beauty; stylish, elegant; noble; contrasts with composition, CHANG, a conscious creation.

2.5b Pattern located in the center indeed.

9.ST A chün tzu uses highlighting the pattern to actualize tao.

13.ImT Pattern brightening uses persisting.

14.ImT One's actualizing tao: solid persisting and pattern brightening.

22.ImT Supple coming and patterning solid.

22.ImT Above apportioning solid and patterning supple.

22.ImT Heavenly pattern indeed.

22.ImT Pattern brightening, stopping:

22.ImT People pattern indeed.

22.ImT Viewing reaching to the heavenly pattern.

22.ImT Viewing reaching to the people pattern.

36.ImT Inside pattern Brightening and outside supple yielding.

36.ImT The pattern king uses it.

49.ImT Pattern brightening uses stimulating.

49.5b One's pattern luminous indeed.

49.6b One's pattern beautiful indeed.

Patience, HSÜ: patience symbolized as waiting for hair to grow; hold back, wait for; slow; necessary.

5.ImT Attending: patience indeed.

22.2a/b Adorning: one's patience.

54.3a/b Converting Maidenhood using patience.

Pause, HSI: stop and rest, repose; breathe, a breathing spell; suspended. See also: **Dissolving Pause**

1.ST A chün tzu uses originating strength not to pause.

17.ST A chün tzu uses turning to darkening to enter a reposing pause.

36.5b Brightness not permitted to pause indeed.

46.6a Advantageous: into not pausing's Trial.

49.ImT Skinning. Stream, fire, mutually pausing.

Pay tribute, CHI: compulsory payments; present property to a superior.

45.6a/b Paying tribute: sighs, tears, snot.

Peak, TING: top, summit, crown; carry on the head; superior. See also: **Twin peaked**

28.6a Exceeding stepping into submerges the peak. Pitfall.

Peep through, K'UEI: observe from hiding; stealthily, furtive.

20.2a Peeping through Viewing.

20.2b Peeping through Viewing: woman Trial.

55.6a/b Peeping through one's door.

Pendent, TO: hanging; flowering branch, date or grape clusters.

27.1a/b Viewing my pendent Jaws.

People, person, JEN: humans individually and collectively; an individual; humankind. See also: **Great People** and **Small People**

Image of Hexagrams 13 and 37 and occurs throughout their texts.

4.1a/b Advantageous: availing of punishing people.

5.6a Three people coming.

6.2a People, three hundred doors.

7.Im Respectable people auspicious.

8.3a/b Grouping's in no way people.

8.5a Capital people not admonished. Auspicious.

8.5b Capital people not admonished.

10.Im/ImT Not mauling people. Growing.

10.2a/b Shade people, Trial: auspicious.

10.3a/b Mauling people: pitfall.

10.3a/b Martial people activating: into a Great Chief.

12.Im/ImT Obstructing it, in no way people.

14.S Associating with People Concording implies beings necessarily converting in truth.

14.CD Concording People: connecting indeed.

15.ImT People tao hating overfilling and loving Humbling.

16.ImT The all wise person uses yielding stirring up.

18.S Using rejoicing Following people implies necessarily possessing affairs.

20.ImT The all wise person uses spirit tao to set up teaching.

22.ImT People pattern indeed.

22.ImT Viewing reaching to the people pattern.

23.5a/b Using housing people, favor.

25.3a Moving people's acquiring:

25.3a Capital people's calamity.

25.3b Moving people acquiring cattle.

25.3b Capital people, calamity indeed.

27.ImT The all wise person nourishes eminence used to extend to the myriad commoners.

31.ST A chün tzu uses emptiness to accept people.

31.ImT The all wise person influencing the people at heart and Below Heaven harmony evening.

31.3b Purpose located in following people.

32.ImT The all wise person lasting with respect to his tao and Below Heaven the changes accomplishing.

32.5a Wife people: auspicious.

32.5b Wife people, Trial: auspicious.

36.1a A lord: the people possessing words.

38.CD Dwelling People: inside indeed.

38.1a/b Seeing hateful people.

38.3a One's person stricken, moreover nose cut.

41.3a Three people moving.

41.3a By consequence Diminishing the one person.

41.3a/b The one person moving.

49.ImT Yielding reaching to heaven and corresponding reaching to the people.

50.ImT The all wise person Growing uses presenting to the Supreme Above.

52.Im/ImT Not seeing one's people.

54.ImT A person's completion beginning indeed.

54.2a/b Advantageous: shade people's Trial.

55.ImT and even more with respect to the people reached.

55.6a/b Living alone, one without people.

56.6a Sojourning people beforehand laughing, afterwards crying out sobbing.

57.1a/b Martial people's Advantageous Trial.

58.ImT That uses yielding reaching to heaven and corresponding reaching to the people.

Permit, K'O: possible because in harmony with an • inherent principle. The ideogram: mouth and breath, silent consent. See also: **Beings not permitted to use**

2.3a/b Containing composition permitting Trial.

3.6b Wherefore permitting long living indeed?

7.ImT Actually permitting using kinghood.

12.6b Wherefore permitting long living indeed?

15.6b Permitting availing of moving legions.

16.6b Wherefore permitting long living indeed?

18.6b Purpose permitted by consequence indeed.

19.S Possessing affairs and afterwards permitting the great.

20.S Being great therefore afterwards permitting Viewing.

20.2b Truly permitting the demoniac indeed.

21.S Permitting Viewing and afterwards possessing a place to unite.

25.4a Permitting Trial.

25.4b Permitting Trial, without fault.

26.S Possessing Disentangling therefore afterwards permitting Accumulating.

27.S Beings accumulating therefore afterwards permitting nourishing.

28.5b Wherefore permitting lasting indeed?

28.5b Truly permitting the demoniac indeed.

30.3b Wherefore permitting lasting indeed?

31.ImT and actually Heaven and Earth, the myriad beings's motives permitting seeing.

32.ImT and actually Heaven and Earth, the myriad beings's motives permitting seeing.

34.ImT Actually the correcting Great and Heaven and Earth's motives permitting seeing.

40.3b Truly permitting the demoniac indeed.

41.Im/ImT Without fault, permitting Trial.

41.Im/ImT Two platters permit availing of presenting.

41.4b Truly permitting rejoicing indeed.

45.ImT and actually Heaven and Earth, the myriad beings's motives, permitting seeing.

48.3a Permitting availing of drawing water.

51.ImT Issuing forth permits using guarding the ancestral temple, field altar, offertory millet.

53.ImT Permitting using correcting the fiefdoms indeed.

53.6a Its feathers permit availing of activating fundamentals.

53.6b Its feathers permit availing of activating fundamentals, auspicious.

61.6b Wherefore permitting long living indeed?

62.Im Permitting Small Affairs. Not permitting Great Affairs.

63.6b Wherefore permitting lasting indeed?

Perpetual, YUNG: continuing; everlasting, ever flowing. The ideogram: flowing water.

2.7a Advantageous: perpetual Trial.

2.7b Availing of the sixes, perpetual Trial.

6.1a/b Not a perpetual place, affairs.

8.Im/ImT Retracing the oracle consulting: Spring, perpetual Trial.

22.3a Perpetual Trial auspicious.

22.3b Perpetual Trial's auspiciousness.

42.2a Perpetual Trial auspicious.

45.5a Spring, perpetual Trial.

52.1a Advantageous: perpetual Trial.

54.ST A chün tzu uses perpetually completing to know the cracked.

62.4a No availing of perpetual Trial.

Persevere, HENG: continue in the same way or spirit; constant, perpetual, regular; self renewing; extend everywhere.

Image of Hexagram 32 and occurs throughout its texts.

5.1a Advantageous: availing of persevering.

5.1b Advantageous: availing of persevering, without fault.

16.5a/b Persevering, not dying.

31.CD Persevering: lasting indeed.

37.ST A chün tzu uses words to possess beings and movement to possess perseverance.

42.6a Establishing the heart, no persevering.

54.1b Using persevering indeed.

Persist, CHIEN: strong, robust, dynamic, tenacious; continuous; unwearied heavenly bodies in their orbits; the Action of the trigram Force, CH'IEN.

1.ST Heaven moves persistingly.

5.ImT Solid persisting and not falling.

6.ImT Venturing and persisting.

9.ImT Persisting and Ground.

11.ImT Inside persisting and outside yielding.

13.ImT Pattern brightening uses persisting.

14.ImT One's actualizing tao: solid persisting and pattern brightening.

25.ImT Stirring up and persisting.

26.ImT Solid persisting: staunch substance, resplendent shining.

26.ImT Ability stopping persisting.

43.ImT Persisting and stimulating.

Person, see **Body**

Pervade, T'AI: spread and reach everywhere, permeate, diffuse; communicate; extensive, abundant, prosperous; smooth, slippery; extreme, extravagant, prodigal. The ideogram: person in water, connected to the universal medium.

Image of Hexagram 11 and occurs throughout its texts.

Petrify, SHIH: become stone or stony; rocks, stony land; objects made of stone; firm, decided; a barren womb.

16.2a Chain mail into petrification:

47.3a Confined, into petrification.

Pheasant, CHIH: clever, beautiful bird associated with the trigram Radiance, LI; also: embrasures on ramparts and forts; arrange, put in order.

50.3a Pheasant juice not taken in.

56.5a Shooting a pheasant.

Pig, SHIH: all swine; sign of wealth and good fortune; associated with the Streaming Moment.

26.5a A gelded pig's tusks.

38.6a Seeing pigs bearing mire.

44.1a Ruining the pig, connection: hoof dragging.

Pillar, HUAN: post or tablet marking a grave.

3.1a Stone pillar.

3.1b Although a stone pillar, purpose moving correctly indeed.

Pitcher, P'ING: clay jug or vase.

48.Im/ImT Ruining one's pitcher.

Pitfall, HSIUNG: leads away from the experience of meaning; stuck and exposed to danger, unable to take in the situation; flow of life and spirit is blocked; unfortunate, baleful; keyword. This term occurs 76 times throughout the hexagram texts.

Place, SO: where something belongs or comes from; residence, dwelling; habitual focus or object. See also: **Resting place**

6.1a/b Not a perpetual place, affairs.

8.S Crowds necessarily possess a place to Group.

8.6b Without a place to complete indeed.

9.S Grouping necessarily possesses a place to Accumulate.

9.6b Possessing a place to doubt indeed.

21.S Permitting Viewing and afterwards possessing a place to unite.

23.6b Commoners: the place to carry indeed.

27.ImT Viewing one's place to nourish indeed.

30.S Falling necessarily possesses a place to congregate.

30.4b Without a place to tolerate indeed.

31.S Therefore afterwards the codes righteously possessing a place to polish.

31.ImT Viewing one's place to influence.

31.3b A place to hold on to the below indeed.

32.ImT Viewing one's place to Persevere.

32.3b Without a place to tolerate indeed.

33.S Beings not permitted to use lasting residing in their place.

33.6b Without a place to doubt indeed.

36.S Advancing necessarily possessing a place: injuring.

40.Im Without a place to go:

41.S Delaying necessarily possesses a place to let go.

43.ImT The place to honor thereupon exhausted indeed.

45.ImT Actually viewing one's place to assemble.

46.3b Without a place to doubt indeed.

47.ImT Confining and not letting go one's place: Growing.

48.AE The Well: residing in one's place and shifting.

50.2b Considering places it indeed.

52.ImT Stopping: one's place indeed.

53.5b Acquiring the place desired indeed.

54.S Advancing necessarily possessing a place to Convert.

54.ImT A place to Convert Maidenhood indeed.

55.S Acquiring one's place to Convert implies necessarily the great.

56.1a Splitting off one's place, grasping calamity.

57.S Sojourning and lacking a place to tolerate.

59.4a In no way hiding, a place to ponder.

63.4b Possessing a place to doubt indeed.

Plain silk, PAI: unbleached, undyed silk.

22.5a Rolled plain silk: little, little.

Plan, MOU: plot, ponder, deliberate; project, device, stratagem.

6.ST A chün tzu uses arousing affairs to plan beginning.

Platter, KUEI: wood or bamboo plate; sacrificial utensil.

29.4a/b A cup, liquor, a platter added.

41.Im/ImT Two platters permit availing of presenting.

41.ImT Two platters corresponding possess the season.

Plead, SU: defend or prosecute a case in court; enter a plea; statement of grievance.

10.4a/b Pleading, pleading: completing auspicious.

Plow land, YÜ: newly opened fields, after two or three years plowing.

25.2a Not tilling the crop. Not clearing the plow land.

Poison, TU: noxious, malignant, hurtful, destructive; despise.

7.ImT Using the latter poisons Below Heaven and the commoners adhering to it.

21.3a Gnawing seasoned meat. Meeting poison.

21.3b Meeting poison.

Polarize, K'UEI: separate, oppose; contrary, mutually exclusive; distant from, absent, remote; animosity, anger; astronomical or polar opposition: the ends of an axis, 180 degrees apart.

Image of Hexagram 38 and occurs throughout its texts.

37.CD Polarizing: outside indeed.

Polish, TS'O: file away imperfections; wash or plate with gold; confused, in disorder, mixed. The ideogram: metal and old, clearing away accumulated disorder.

30.1a Treading, polishing therefore.

30.1b Treading, polishing it respectfully.

31.S Therefore afterwards the codes righteously possessing a place to polish.

Ponder, SSU: reflect, consider, remember; deep thought; desire, wish. The ideogram: heart and field, the heart's concerns.

19.ST A chün tzu uses teaching to ponder without exhausting.

31.4a Partnering adheres to simply pondering.

52.ST A chün tzu uses pondering not to issue forth from his situation.

59.4a In no way hiding, a place to ponder.

63.ST A chün tzu uses pondering distress and providing for defending against it.

Position, CHAI: dwelling site, good situation in life; consolidate, reside, fill an office.

23.ST Using munificence above to quiet the position below.

Possess, YU: in possession of, have, own; opposite of lack, wu. This term occurs throughout the hexagram texts and in the Image of Hexagram 14.

Potency, SHIH: power, influence, strength; authority, dignity; virility. The ideogram: strength and skill.

2.ST Earth potency: Field.

Pouched belt, P'AN TAI: sash that serves as a purse; money belt.

6.6a Maybe bestowing's pouched belt.

Praise, YÜ: admire and approve; magnify, eulogize; flatter. The ideogram: words and give, offering words.

2.4a Without fault, without praise.

18.5a Availing of praise.

18.5b Managing the father availing of praise.

28.5a Without fault, without praise.

39.1a/b Going Difficulties, coming praise.

55.5a Possessing reward, praise auspicious.

56.5a/b Completing uses praising fate.

Precaution, YÜ: provide against, preventive measures; anxious, vigilant, ready; preoccupied with, think about, expect; mishap, accident.

3.3a Approaching stag, lacking precaution.

3.3b Approaching stag, without precaution.

45.ST [A chün tzu uses] warning, not precautions.

61.1a Precaution auspicious.

61.1b The initial nine, precaution auspicious.

Precede, CH'IEN: come before in time and thus in value; anterior, former, ancient; lead forward.

5.ImT Venturing located in precedence indeed.

8.5a Letting go the preceding wildfowl.

8.5b Letting go the preceding wildfowl indeed.

26.ST A chün tzu uses the numerous recorded preceding words going to move.

39.ImT Venturing located in precedence indeed.

43.1a Invigorating into the preceding foot.

Predecessor, K'AO: deceased ancestor, especially the grandfather; the ancients; aged, long lived; consult, verify. The ideogram: old and ingenious, the old wise man.

10.6a Observing Treading, predecessors auspicious.

16.ST Using equaling the grandfather predecessors.

18.1a Predecessors without fault.

18.1b Intention receiving the predecessors indeed.

24.5b Centering originating from the predecessor indeed.

Pregnant, JEN: carrying a child.

53.3a/b The wife pregnant, not nurturing.

53.5a The wife, three year's time not pregnant.

Prepare, PEI: make ready, provide for; sufficient.

14.5b Versatility and without preparing indeed.

Preponderance, P'ENG: forceful, dominant; over bearing, encroaching. The ideogram: drum beats, dominating sound.

14.4a In no way one's preponderance.

14.4b In no way one's preponderance. Without fault.

Presence, YUNG: noble bearing; prestige, dignity; imposing; haughty, conceited; lit.: a large head.

20.Im/ImT There is a connection to the spirit, like a presence.

Present (to), HSIANG: present in sacrifice, offer with thanks, give to the gods or a superior; confer dignity on.

41.Im/ImT Two platters permit availing of presenting.

42.2a Kinghood availing of presenting into the supreme, auspicious.

45.ImT Involving reverence presenting indeed.

47.2a Advantageous: availing of presenting oblations.

50.ImT The all wise person Growing uses presenting to the Supreme Above.

59.ST The Earlier Kings used presenting into the supreme to establish the temples.

Pressing, P'IN: on the brink of; pressing, urgent.

24.3a Pressing Returning.

24.3b Pressing Returning's adversity.

57.3a/b Pressing Ground, distress.

Primary, T'UNG: origin, beginning; first of a class; clue, hint; whole, general.

1.ImT Thereupon primary heaven.

Prince, KUNG: nobles acting as ministers of state in the capital; governing from the center rather than active in daily life; contrasts with feudatory, HOU, governors of the provinces. See also: **Crown prince**

14.3a/b A prince availing of Growing, into heavenly sonhood.

29.ImT The kingly prince sets up venturing used to guard his city.

30.5b Radiance: the kingly prince indeed.

40.6a A prince avails of shooting a hawk, into the high rampart's above.

40.6b A prince avails of shooting a hawk.

42.3a Notifying the prince, availing of the scepter.

42.4a/b Notifying the prince, adhering.

50.4a/b Overthrowing a princely stew.

62.5a A prince, a string arrow grasping another located in

Procrastinate, CH'IH: delay, act at leisure, retard; slow, late.

16.3a Procrastinating possesses repenting.

54.4a Procrastinating Converting possesses the season.

Profusion, P'EI: spread and flow in many directions, like rain or rivers; enlarge; irrigate; luxuriant water plants.

55.3a/b Abounding: one's profusion.

Proper, YI: reasonable of itself; fit and right, harmonious; ought, should.

3.ImT Proper to install feudatories and not to soothe.

11.ST [The crown prince uses] bracing to mutualize Heaven and Earth's propriety.

19.5a/b A Great Chief's propriety.

39.1b Proper to await indeed.

55.Im/ImT No grief. Properly sun centering.

55.ImT Properly illuminating Below Heaven indeed.

62.Im/ImT Above not proper, below proper.

Property, TS'AI: possessions, goods, substance, wealth. The ideogram: pearl and value.

11.ST The crown prince uses property to accomplish Heaven and Earth's tao.

60.ImT Not injuring property.

Propriety, see: **Proper**

Proscribe, CHU: exclude, reject by proclamation; denounce, forbid; reprove, seek as a criminal; condemn to death; clear away.

35/36.CD Brightness Hiding: proscribed indeed.

Prospering, CHIN: grow and flourish as young plants in the sun; increase, progress, permeate, impregnate; attached to. The ideogram: sun and reaching, the daylight world.

Image of Hexagram 35 and occurs throughout its texts.

Protect, PAO: guard, defend, keep safe; secure.

1.ImT Protection uniting the great harmony.

19.ST [A chün tzu uses] tolerating to protect the commoners without delimiting.

53.3b Yielding mutualizes protection indeed.

Protract, YIN: draw out, prolong; carried on; lead on, to bring forward; lit.: drawing a bow.

45.2a/b Protracting auspicious, without fault.

58.6a Protracting Opening.

58.6b Six above, protracting Opening.

Provide for, YÜ: ready, prepared for; pre-arrange, take precaution, think beforehand; satisfied, contented, at ease. The ideogram: sonhood and elephant, careful, reverent and very strong.

Image of Hexagram 16 and occurs throughout its texts.

15.CD Provision: indolence indeed.

17.S Providing for necessarily possesses Following.

63.ST A chün tzu uses pondering distress and providing for defending against it.

Psyche, LING: life force, vital energy; spirit of a being; magical action or influence.

27.1a Stowing away simply the psyche tortoise.

Pull back, YI: pull or drag something towards you; drag behind, take by the hand; leave traces.

38.3a/b Seeing the cart pulled back.

63.1a/b Pulling back one's wheels.

64.2a Pulling back one's wheels.

Punish, HSING: legal punishment; physical penalties for severe criminal offenses; whip, torture, behead.

4.1a/b Advantageous: availing of punishing people.

16.ImT By consequence punishing flogging purifies and the commoners submit.

55.ST A chün tzu uses severing litigating to involve punishing.

56.ST A chün tzu uses brightening consideration to avail of punishing and not to detain litigating.

Purify, CH'ING: clean a water course; limpid, unsullied; right principles.

16.ImT By consequence punishing flogging purifies and the commoners submit.

Purpose, CHIH: focus of mind and heart; will, inclination, resolve. The ideogram: heart and scholar, high inner resolve, or heart and go, inner determination.

3.1b Although a stone pillar, purpose moving correctly indeed.

4.ImT Purpose corresponding indeed.

9.ImT Solid centering and purpose moving.

9.4b Uniting purposes above indeed.

10.ST [A chün tzu uses] setting right the commoners, the purpose.

10.3b Purpose solid indeed.

10.4b Purpose moving indeed.

11.ImT Above and Below mingling and one's purpose concording indeed.

11.1b Purpose located outside indeed.

12.1b Purpose located in a chief indeed.

12.4b Purpose moving indeed.

13.ImT Verily a chün tzu activating enables interpenetrating Below Heaven's purpose.

13.6b Purpose not yet acquired indeed.

14.5b Trustworthiness uses shooting forth purpose indeed.

15.6b Purpose not yet acquired indeed.

16.ImT Providing for. Solid corresponding and purpose moving.

16.1b Purpose exhausted, pitfall indeed.

16.4b Purpose: the great moving indeed.

17.3b Below, purpose stowed away indeed.

18.6b Purpose permitted by consequence indeed.

19.1b Purpose moving, correcting indeed.

19.6b Purpose located inside indeed.

20.6b Purpose not yet evened indeed.

22.6b Acquiring purpose above indeed.

25.1b Acquiring purpose indeed.

26.3b Uniting purposes above indeed.

31.1b Purpose located outside indeed.

31.3b Purpose located in following people.

31.5b Purpose, the tips indeed.

33.2b Firm purpose indeed.

33.5b Using correcting the purpose indeed.

35.3b Crowds: sincerity's purpose.

36.ImT Inside heaviness and enabling correcting one's purpose.

36.3b The South: hunting's purpose.

37.1b Purpose not yet transformed indeed.

38.ImT Their purposes not concording: moving.

38.ImT Man, Woman, Polarizing and their purposes interpenetrating indeed.

38.4b Purpose moving indeed.

39.6b Purpose located inside indeed.

41.1b Honoring uniting purposes indeed.

41.2b Centering using activating purposes indeed.

41.6b The great acquiring purpose indeed.

42.4b Using Augmenting purpose indeed.

42.5b The great acquiring purpose indeed.

44.5b Purpose, not stowing away fate indeed.

45.1b One's purpose disarrayed indeed.

45.5b Purpose not yet shining indeed.

46.ImT Purpose moving indeed.

46.1b Uniting purposes above indeed.

46.5b The great acquiring the purpose indeed.

47.ST A chün tzu uses involving fate to release purpose.

47.4b Purpose located below indeed.

47.5b Purpose not yet acquired indeed.

49.ImT Their purposes not mutually acquired.

49.4b Trustworthy purpose indeed.

54.4b Overrunning the term's purpose.

55.2b Trustworthiness using shooting forth purpose indeed.

56.1b Purpose exhausted, calamity indeed.

57.ImT Solid Ground reaching to centering correcting and purpose moving.

57.1b Purpose doubted indeed.

57.1b Purpose regulated indeed.

57.3b Purpose exhausted indeed.

58.2b Trustworthy purpose indeed.

59.3b Purpose located outside indeed.

61.1b Purpose not yet transformed indeed.

64.4b Purpose moving indeed.

Pursue, CHU: chase, follow closely, press hard; expel, drive out. The ideogram: pig (wealth) and go, chasing fortune.

26.3a A fine horse, pursuing.

27.4a His appetites: pursuing, pursuing.

38.1a Losing the horse, no pursuit, originating from returning.

51.2a No pursuit.

63.2a No pursuit.

Put off, HSIA: delay; put at a distance; far away, remote in time.

11.2a Not putting off abandoning.

Question, WEN: ask, inquire about, examine; clear up doubts; convict and sentence.

42.5a No question, Spring auspicious.

42.5b Actually no questioning it.

Quiet/security, AN: peaceful, still, settled; calm, tranquilize. The ideogram: woman under a roof, a tranquil home.

2.Im/ImT security Trial auspicious.

6.4a Denying, security Trial. Auspicious.

6.4b Denying, security Trial.

11.S Therefore afterwards quieting.

13.3b Quieting movement indeed.

23.ST Using munificence above to quiet the position below.

32.4b Quietly acquiring the wildfowl indeed.

45.6b The above not yet quiet indeed.

60.4a/b Quiet Articulating Growing.

● **Quit,** CHAN: stop, change because unsuccessful; unable to advance.

3.2a Sprouting thus, quitting thus.

● **Radiance,** LI: glowing light, spreading in all directions; light giving, discriminating, articulating; divide and arrange in order; the power of consciousness. The ideogram: bird and weird, the magical fire bird with brilliant plumage.

Image of Hexagram 30 and occurs throughout its texts.

12.4a Cultivating radiant satisfaction.

29.CD Above Radiance and below Gorge indeed.

53.3b Radiance flocking demons indeed.

59.S Dispersing implies Radiance indeed.

59/60.CD Dispersing: radiance indeed.

60.S Beings not permitted to use completing Radiance.

62.6a Flying bird radiating it.

● **Rafter,** CHÜEH: roof beams; flat branches.

53.4a/b Maybe acquiring one's rafter.

● **Rain,** YÜ: all precipitation; sudden showers, fast and furious; associated with the trigram Gorge, K'AN, and the Streaming Moment. See also: **Thunder and Rain**

1.ImT Clouds moving, rain spreading out.

9.Im/ImT Shrouding clouds, not raining.

9.6a/b Already rain, already abiding.

38.6a Going meeting rain, by consequence auspicious.

38.6b Meeting rain's auspiciousness.

40.ST Thunder, Rain, arousing.

43.3a Solitary going, meeting rain.

50.3a On all sides rain lessens repenting.

62.5a/b Shrouding clouds, not raining.

● **Rampart,** YUNG: defensive wall; bulwark, redoubt.

13.4a/b Riding one's rampart.

40.6a A prince avails of shooting a hawk, into the high rampart's above.

● **Reach(to),** HU: arrive at a goal; reach toward and achieve; connect; contrasts with tend towards, YU.

This term occurs throughout the hexagram texts.

● **Reap,** TO: harvest, collect, gather up, pick; arrange. The ideogram: hand and join, taking in both hands.

6.2b Distress culminating, reaping indeed.

● **Rebel,** PEI: go against nature or usage; insubordinate; perverse, unreasonable.

27.3b Tao, the great rebelling indeed.

40.6b Using Loosening rebelling indeed.

50.1b Not yet rebelling indeed.

● **Receive,** CH'ENG: receive gifts or commands from superiors or customers; take in hand; catch falling water. The ideogram: accepting a seal of office.

2.ImT Thereupon yielding receiving heaven.

7.2b Receiving heavenly favor indeed.

7.6a Disclosing the city, receiving a dwelling.

12.2a Enwrapping receiving.

18.1b Intention receiving the predecessors indeed.

18.5b Receiving uses actualizing tao indeed.

32.3a Maybe receiving's embarrassing.

54.1b Mutualizing receiving indeed.

54.6a A woman receiving a basket without substance.

54.6b Receiving an empty basket indeed.

60.4b Receiving tao above indeed.

● **Recess,** TAN: pit within a large cave, entered from the side.

29.1a,3a Entering into the Gorge, the recess.

● **Reckon,** SHU: count, find the number; give out; sum up, discriminate; also: account, bill, list; fate, destiny; many cares, dilemma. See also: **Time reckoning**

60.ST A chün tzu uses paring to reckon the measures.

● **Recline,** CHEN: lean back or on; soften, relax; head rest, back support; stake to tie cattle.

29.3a Venturing moreover reclining.

● **Record,** SHIH: write down, inscribe; memorize, learn; recognize; annals, monuments.

26.ST A chün tzu uses the numerous recorded preceding words going to move.

● **Recur,** HSÜAN: return to the same point; orbit, revolve; spiral.

10.6a One's recurring Spring auspicious.

● **Redouble,** CH'UNG: repeat, reiterate, add to; build up by layers.

16.AE Redoubling gates, smiting clappers.

29.ImT Redoubling venturing indeed.

30.ImT Redoubling brightness uses congregating to reach to correcting.

57.ImT Redoubling Ground uses distributing fate.

● **Reduce,** P'OU: diminish in number; collect in fewer, larger groups.

15.ST A chün tzu uses reducing the numerous to augment the few.

Reeds, KUAN: marsh and swamp plants, rushes.

    43.5a Reeds, highlands: Deciding, Deciding.

Regulate, CHIH: govern well, ensure prosperity; remedy disorder, heal; someone fit to govern land, house and heart.

    18.ImT and Below Heaven regulated indeed.

    49.ST A chün tzu uses regulating time reckoning to brighten the seasons.

    57.1b Purpose regulated indeed.

Reiterate, CHIEN: repeat, duplicate; successive.

    29.ST Streams reiterating culminating. Repeating Gorge.

    51.ST Reiterated thunder.

Reject, FU: push away, expel, brush off; oppose, contradict; perverse, proud. The ideogram: hand and do not, pushing something away.

    27.2a Rejecting the canons, into the hill top.

    27.3a Rejecting Jaws. Trial: pitfall.

    27.5a Rejecting the canons.

Rejoice(in), HSI: feel and give joy; delight, exult; cheerful, merry. The ideogram: joy (music) and mouth, expressing joy.

    12.6a Beforehand Obstruction, afterwards rejoicing.

    18.S Using rejoicing Following people implies necessarily possessing affairs.

    22.5b Possessing rejoicing indeed.

    25.5a No medicinal herbs, possessing rejoicing.

    26.4b Possessing rejoicing indeed.

    39.3b Inside rejoicing in it indeed.

    41.4a Commissioning swiftly possesses rejoicing.

    41.4b Truly permitting rejoicing indeed.

    46.2b Possessing rejoicing indeed.

    58.4a Chain mail afflicting: possessing rejoicing.

    58.4b Nine at fourth's rejoicing.

Release, SUI: loose, let go, free; unhindered, in accord; follow, spread out, progress; penetrate, invade. The ideogram: go and follow your wishes, unimpeded movement.

    34.6a/b Not enabling withdrawing, not enabling releasing.

    37.2a Without direction, releasing.

    47.ST A chün tzu uses involving fate to release purpose.

    51.4a/b Shake: releasing the bog.

Relinquish, HSIU: let go of, stop temporarily, rest; resign, release; act gently, enjoy; relaxed. The ideogram: person leaning on a tree.

    12.5a Relinquishing Obstruction.

    14.ST [A chün tzu uses] yielding to heaven to relinquish fate.

    24.2a Relinquishing Returning.

    24.2b Relinquishing Returning's auspiciousness.

Renew, HSIN: restore, improve, make or get better; new, fresh; the best, the latest.

    26.ImT A day renewing one's actualizing tao.

    49/50.CD The Vessel: grasping renewal indeed.

Renovate, HSIU: repair, mend, clean, adorn; adjust, regulate; cultivate, practice, acquire skills.

    39.ST A chün tzu uses reversing individuality to renovate actualizing tao.

Repeat, HSI: series of similar acts; practice, rehearse; familiar with, skilled. The ideogram: two wings and a cap, thought carried by repeated movements.

    2.2a/b Not repeating: without not Advantageous.

    29.Im Repeating Gorge.

    29.ST Streams reiterating culminating. Repeating Gorge.

    29.ST [A chün tzu uses] repeating to teach affairs.

    29.ImT,1a Repeating Gorge.

    29.1b Repeating Gorge, entering Gorge.

    58.ST A chün tzu uses partnering friends to explicate repeating.

Repent, HUI: dissatisfaction with past conduct causing a change of heart; proceeds from distress, LIN, shame and confusion at having lost the right way. See also: **Repenting extinguished** and **Without repenting**

    1.6a/b Overbearing dragon possesses repenting.

    16.3a Skeptical Providing for, repenting.

    16.3a Procrastinating possesses repenting.

    16.3b Skeptical Providing for possesses repenting.

    18.3a The small possesses repenting.

    37.3a Repenting, adversity auspicious.

    47.6a/b Stirring up repenting possesses repenting.

    50.3a On all sides rain lessens repenting.

Repenting extinguished, HUI WANG: previous troubles and consequent remorse will disappear.

    31.4a/b Trial: auspicious, repenting extinguished.

    32.2a Repenting extinguished.

    32.2b Nine at second, repenting extinguished.

    34.4a Repenting extinguished.

    35.3a Crowds, sincerity, repenting extinguished.

35.5a Repenting extinguished.

37.1a Repenting extinguished.

38.1a,5a Repenting extinguished.

43.4a Hauling along the goat, repenting extinguished.

45.5a Repenting extinguished.

49.Im Repenting extinguished.

49.ImT One's repenting thereupon extinguished.

49.4a Repenting extinguished, there is a connection to the spirit.

52.5a Repenting extinguished.

57.4a Repenting extinguished.

57.5a Trial: auspicious, repenting extinguished.

58.2a Repenting extinguished.

59.2a Repenting extinguished.

60.6a Repenting extinguished.

64.4a/b Trial: auspicious, repenting extinguished.

Repose, YEN: rest, leisure, peace of mind; banquet, feast. The ideogram: shelter and rest, a wayside inn.

5.ST A chün tzu uses drinking and eating to repose delighting.

17.ST A chün tzu uses turning to darkening to enter a reposing pause.

Rescue, CHENG: aid, deliver from trouble; pull out, raise up, lift. The ideogram: hand and aid, a helping hand.

36.2a Availing of a rescuing horse, invigorating auspicious.

52.2a/b Not rescuing one's following.

59.1a Availing of a rescuing horse, invigorating auspicious.

Reside(in), CHÜ: dwell, live in, stay; sit down, fill an office; settled parts of a country. The ideogram: body and seat.

3/4.CD Sprouting: seeing and not letting go one's residing.

3.1a Advantageous: residing in Trial.

17.3a Advantageous: residing in Trial.

27.5a/b Residing in Trial auspicious.

31.2a Pitfall. Residing auspicious.

31.2b Although a pitfall, residing auspicious.

33.S Beings not permitted to use lasting residing in their place.

38.ImT Two women concording: residing.

43.ST [A chün tzu uses] residing in actualizing tao, by consequence keeping aloof.

48.AE The Well: residing in one's place and shifting.

49.ImT Two women concording, residing.

49.6a Residing in Trial auspicious.

53.ST A chün tzu uses residing in eminent actualizing tao to improve the vulgar.

56.S Exhausting the great implies necessarily letting go one's residing.

59.5a/b Kinghood residing, without fault.

60.5b Residing in the situation: centering indeed.

64.ST A chün tzu uses considering to mark off the beings residing on all sides.

Resist, YÜ: withstand, oppose; bring to an end; prevent. The ideogram: rule and worship, imposing ethical or religious limits.

4.6a Advantageous: resisting outlawry.

4.6b Advantageous: availing of resisting outlawry.

53.3a Advantageous: resisting outlawry.

53.3b Advantageous: availing of resisting outlawry.

Respect(ful), CHING: reverent, attentive; stand in alarm of, honor; inner respect; contrasts with courtesy, KUNG, good manners. The ideogram: teacher's rod taming speech and attitude. See also: **With respect to**

5.3b Respectful consideration, not destroying indeed.

5.6a/b Respecting them, completing auspicious.

6.6b Truly not standing respectfully indeed.

30.1a Respecting it.

30.1b Treading, polishing it respectfully.

Respectable/experienced, CHANG: worthy of respect; standard by which others are measured.

7.Im Experienced people auspicious.

17.2a Letting go the respectable husband.

17.3a/b Tied to the respectable husband.

Resplendent, HUI: glorious, sun like, refulgent; brighten.

26.ImT Solid persisting: staunch substance, resplendent shining.

Rest(ing place), TZ'U: camp, inn, shed; halting place, breathing spell; put in consecutive order. The ideogram: two and breath, pausing to breathe.

7.4a Legions: the left resting.

7.4b The left resting, without fault.

43.4a/b One moves the resting place moreover.

44.3a/b One moves the resting place moreover.

56.2a Sojourning: approaching a resting place.

56.3a/b Sojourning: burning one's resting place.

Restrict, YEN: keep in order, maintain discipline; subjugate, repress; narrow, obedient.

32.AE Persevering: variegated and not restricting.

Retire(from), TUN: withdraw; run away, flee; conceal yourself, become obscure, invisible; secluded, non-social. The ideogram: walk and swine (wealth and luck), satisfaction through walking away.

Image of Hexagram 33 and occurs throughout its texts.

28.ST [A chün tzu uses] retiring from the age without melancholy.

34.S Beings not permitted to use completing Retiring.

Retrace, YÜAN: repeat, another; trace to the source. The ideogram: pure water at its source.

8.Im/ImT Retracing the oracle consulting: Spring, perpetual Trial.

Return, FU: go back, turn back to the starting point; recur, reappear, come again; restore, recover, retrace; an earlier time or place. The ideogram: step and retrace a path.

Image of Hexagram 24 and occurs throughout its texts.

1.3b Reversing returning tao indeed.

6.4a/b Returning, approaching fate.

9.1a/b Returning originating from tao.

9.2a Hauling along, returning. Auspicious.

9.2b Hauling along, returning, locating in the center.

11.3a/b Without going, not returning.

11.6a/b The bulwark returned into the moat.

23.CD Returning: reversing indeed.

25.S Actually Returning, by consequence not Embroiling.

38.S Dwelling tao exhausted, necessarily returning.

38.1a Losing the horse, no pursuit, originating from returning.

40.Im/ImT One's coming return auspicious.

53.3a/b The husband chastised, not returning.

Reverence, HSIAO: filial duty, respect and obedience owed to elders; loyalty, dignity, confidence, self respect; brave in battle; period of mourning for deceased parents.

45.ImT Involving reverence presenting indeed.

Reverse, FAN: turn and move in the opposite direction; turn around or upside down (180 degrees); change to the opposite position; contrary.

1.3b Reversing returning tao indeed.

3.2b Reversing rules indeed.

9.3a/b Husband, consort, reversing eyes.

11/12.CD Obstructing, Pervading: reversing one's sorting indeed.

13.4b By consequence confining and reversing by consequence indeed.

23/24.CD Returning: reversing indeed.

24.Im Reversing Returning one's tao.

24.S Above Stripping exhausted, below reversing.

24.ImT Returning, Growing. Solid reversing.

24.ImT Reversing Returning one's tao.

24.6b Reversing the chief: tao indeed.

37.S Injury with respect to the outside implies necessarily reversing with respect to Dwelling.

37.6b Reversing individuality's designating indeed.

39.ST A chün tzu uses reversing individuality to renovate actualizing tao.

39.3a/b Going Difficulties, coming reversing.

48.S Confining reaching to the above implies necessarily reversing the below.

54.3a Reversing Converting using the junior sister.

Revive, SU: regain vital energy, courage or strength; bring to life, cheer up; relief; lit.: herb whose smell revives weary spirits.

51.3a/b Shake: reviving, reviving.

Reward, CH'ING: gift given from gratitude or benevolence; favor from heaven; congratulate with gifts. The ideogram: heart, follow and deer (wealth), the heart expressed through gifts.

2.ImT Thereupon completing possesses reward.

10.6b The great possesses reward indeed.

26.5b Possessing reward indeed.

27.6b The great possessing reward indeed.

35.5b Going possessing reward indeed.

38.5b Going possessing reward indeed.

42.ImT Centering correcting possessing reward.

46.ImT Possessing reward indeed.

47.2b Center possessing reward indeed.

55.5a Possessing reward, praise auspicious.

55.5b Possessing reward indeed.

58.4b Possessing reward indeed.

Rich, FEI: fertile, abundant, fat; manure, fertilizer. See also: **Enrich**

33.6a/b Rich Retiring, nothing not advantageous.

Ride, CH'ENG: ride an animal or a chariot; have the upper hand, seize the right time; control strong power; overcome the nature of the other; supple opened line above a solid whole line.

1.ImT The season riding six dragons used going to meet heaven.

3.2a,4a,6a Riding a horse, arraying thus.

3.2b Riding a solid indeed.

13.4a/b Riding one's rampart.

16.5b Riding a solid indeed.

21.2b Riding a solid indeed.

22.1b Righteously nothing to ride indeed.

40.3a/b Bearing, moreover riding.

43.ImT Supple riding five solids indeed.

47.3b Riding a solid indeed.

51.2b Riding a solid indeed.

54.ImT Supple riding solid indeed.

59.ImT Riding wood possesses achievement indeed.

61.ImT Riding a wooden dug out, emptiness indeed.

- **Ridgepole**, TUNG: highest and key beam in a house; summit, crest.

  28.Im Great Exceeding, the ridgepole sagging.

  28.ImT The ridgepole sagging.

  28.3a/b The ridgepole buckling. Pitfall.

  28.4a/b The ridgepole crowning. Auspicious.

- **Right**, YU: right side, right hand; noble, honorable; make things right. See also: **Set right**

  11.ST [The crown prince] uses the left to right the commoners.

  55.3a/b Severing one's right arm.

- **Righteous**, YI: proper and just, meets the standards; things in their proper place; the heart that rules itself; upright, moral rule; contrasts with Harvest, LI, advantage or profit.

  5.ImT Actually one's righteousness, not confining exhaustion.

  9.1b One's righteousness auspicious indeed.

  13.4b Righteously nothing controlling indeed.

  16.ImT Actually Provision's season righteously great in fact.

  17.ImT Actually Following the season's righteous great in fact.

  17.4b One's righteousness: pitfall indeed.

  19/20.CD Nearing Viewing's righteousness.

  22.1b Righteously nothing to ride indeed.

  24.3b Righteous, without fault indeed.

  31.S Therefore afterwards the codes righteously possessing a place to polish.

  32.5b The husband, the son: paring righteously.

  33.ImT Actually Retiring's season righteously great in fact.

  36.1b Righteously not taking in indeed.

37.ImT Heaven and Earth's great righteousness indeed.

40.1b Righteous, without fault indeed.

44.ImT Actually Coupling's season righteously great in fact.

44.2b Righteously not extending to guesting indeed.

48.AE The Well: using differentiating righteousness.

50.3b Letting go its righteousness indeed.

53.1b Righteous, without fault indeed.

54.ImT Heaven and Earth's great righteousness indeed.

56.ImT Actually Sojourning's season righteously great in fact.

56.3b One's righteousness lost indeed.

56.6b One's righteousness burning indeed.

63.1b Righteous, without fault indeed.

- **Rings**, HSÜAN: handles or ears for carrying a tripod.

  50.5a The Vessel: yellow ears, metallic rings.

  50.6a The Vessel: jade rings.

  50.6b Jade rings located above.

- **Ripe**, SHIH: mature, full grown; great, eminent.

  23.6a The ripe fruit not taken in.

  39.6a/b Going Difficulties, coming ripening.

- **Rise**, HSING: get up, grow, lift; begin, give rise to, construct; be promoted; flourishing, fashionable. The ideogram: lift, two hands and unite, lift with both hands.

  13.3a/b Three year's time not rising.

  22.2b Associating with the above, rising indeed.

  42.AE Augmenting: using the rising Harvest.

  54.ImT Heaven and Earth not mingling and the myriad beings not rising.

- **Rise up**, CH'I: stand up, lift; undertake, begin, originate.

  7.S Arguing necessarily possesses crowds rising up.

  44.4a Rising up: pitfall.

  51/52.CD Shake: rising up indeed.

- **River**, CH'UAN: water flowing between banks; current, channel; associated with the Streaming Moment and the trigram Gorge, K'AN. See also: **Step into the Great River**

  29.ImT Earth venturing, mountains, rivers, hill tops, mounds indeed.

- **Rodent**, see: **Bushy tailed rodent**

- **Roll**, SHU: gather into a bundle, bind together; restrain.

  22.5a Rolled plain silk: little, little.

Roof, WU: cover, shelter; house, room, cabin, tent; stop or remain at.
    55.6a/b Abounding: one's roof.

Root, PEN: origin, cause, source of nourishment; essential. The ideogram: tree with roots in earth.
    24.AE Returning: actualizing tao's root indeed.
    28.ImT Roots, tips, fading indeed.

Rope, see: **Stranded ropes** and **Well rope**

Rotten, LAN: corrupt, putrid, antiquated, worn out, dirty; a running sore; boil over.
    23/24.CD Stripping: rotten indeed.

Rouse, CHEN: stir up, excite, stimulate; issue forth; put in order. The ideogram: hand and shake, shaking things up. See also: **Arouse**
    18.ST A chün tzu uses rousing the commoners to nurture actualizing tao.
    32.6a Rousing Persevering: pitfall.
    32.6b Rousing Persevering located in the above.

Ruin, LEI: destroy, break, overturn; debilitated, meager, emaciated; entangled.
    34.3a Ruining his horns.
    34.4a/b The hedge broken up, not ruined.
    44.1a Ruining the pig, connection: hoof dragging.
    48.Im/ImT Ruining one's pitcher:

Rules, CH'ANG: unchanging principles; regular, constant, habitual; maintain laws and customs.
    2.ImT Afterwards yielding acquiring rules.
    3.2b Reversing rules indeed.
    5.1b Not yet letting go rules indeed.
    7.4b Not yet letting go the rules indeed.
    29.ST A chün tzu uses rules actualizing tao to move.
    54.2b Not yet transforming the rules indeed.

Ruminate, HSIANG: ponder and discuss; examine minutely, learn fully, watch over, pay attention to. The ideogram: word and sheep, ruminating on words.
    34.6b Not ruminating indeed.

Sacrifice, CHIEH: make offerings to gods and the dead; depend on, call on, borrow; lit.: straw mat used to hold offerings.
    28.1a/b A sacrifice availing of white thatch grass.

Sacrificial victims, SHENG: the six sacrificial animals: horse, ox, lamb, cock, dog and pig.
    45.Im/ImT Availing of the great: sacrificial victims auspicious.

Sacrum, T'UN: lower back where it joins legs; buttocks, seat, lower spine.

    43.4a The sacrum without flesh.
    44.3a The sacrum without flesh.
    47.1a The sacrum Confined, into stump wood.

Sad, CH'I: unhappy, low in spirits, distressed; mourn, sorrow over; commiserate with.
    30.5a Issuing forth tears like gushing. Sadness like lamenting.

Sag, NAO: yield, bend, distort, twist; disturbed, confused.
    28.Im Great Exceeding, the ridgepole sagging.
    28.ImT The ridgepole sagging.
    28.4b Not sagging, reaching to the below indeed.

Sands, SHA: beach, sandbanks, shingle; gravel, pebbles; granulated. The ideogram: water and few, areas laid bare by receding water.
    5.2a/b Attending into sands.

Sash, FU: ceremonial belt of official which holds seal of office.
    47.2a Scarlet sashes on all sides coming.
    47.5a Confined, into a crimson sash.

Satiation, PAO: full, replete, satisfied; swollen, sated; gratified, flattered.
    53.2b Not sheer satiation indeed.

Satisfaction, CHIH: fulfilment, gratification, happy in realizing your aim; take pleasure in, fulfil a need.
    11.5a/b Using satisfaction, Spring auspicious.
    12.4a Cultivating radiant satisfaction.

Scare, CHING: create and spread fear, terrify; apprehensive, alarmed, perturbed. The ideogram: horse and strike, havoc created by a terrified horse.
    51.Im/ImT Shake scaring a hundred miles.
    51.ImT Scaring the distant and fearing the nearby indeed.

Scarlet, CHU: vivid red signifying honor, luck, marriage, riches, literary accomplishment; culmination of the Woody Moment.
    47.2a Scarlet sashes on all sides coming.

Scatter, SAN: disperse in small pieces; separate, divide, distribute. The ideogram: strike and crumble.
    59.S Stimulating and afterwards scattering it.

Scepter, KUEI: sign of rank that gives you freedom to report to the prince.
    42.3a Notifying the prince, availing of the scepter.

Scold, HO: rebuke, blame, demand and enforce obedience; severe, stern.
    37.3a/b Dwelling People, scolding, scolding:

Screen, P'U: curtain, veil, awning, hanging mat; hide, protect; lit.: luxuriant plant growth.

55.2a,4a/b Abounding: one's screen.

55.6a Screening one's dwelling.

- **Scrutinize,** CH'A: investigate, observe carefully, learn the particulars, get at the truth. The ideogram: sacrifice as central to understanding.

    22.ImT Using scrutinizing the seasons transforming.

- **Season,** SHIH: quality of the time; the right time, opportune, in harmony; planning in accord with the time; seasons of the year. The ideogram: sun and temple, time as sacred.

    1.ImT The six situations: the season accomplishing.

    1.ImT The season riding six dragons used going to meet heaven.

    4.ImT Season centering indeed.

    14.ImT Corresponding reaching to heaven and the season moving.

    16.ImT and the four seasons not straying.

    16.ImT Actually Provision's season righteously great in fact.

    17.ImT and Below Heaven Following the season.

    17.ImT Actually Following the season's righteous great in fact.

    20.ImT and the four seasons not straying.

    22.ImT Using scrutinizing the seasons transforming.

    25/26.CD Great Accumulating: the season indeed.

    25.ST The Earlier Kings used luxuriance suiting the season to nurture the myriad beings.

    27.ImT Actually Jaws's season great in fact.

    28.ImT Actually Great Exceeding's season great in fact.

    29.ImT Actually venturing's season availing of the great in fact.

    32.ImT The four seasons transforming changes and enabling lasting accomplishment.

    33.ImT Associating with the season moving indeed.

    33.ImT Actually Retiring's season righteously great in fact.

    38.ImT Actually Polarizing's season availing of the great in fact.

    39.ImT Actually Difficulty's season availing of the great in fact.

    40.ImT Actually Loosening's season great in fact.

    41.ImT Two platters corresponding possess the season.

41.ImT Diminishing solid, augmenting supple, possessing the season.

41.ImT Associating with the season, accompanying the movement.

42.ImT Associating with the season, accompanying the movement.

44.ImT Actually Coupling's season righteously great in fact.

46.ImT Supple using the season, Ascending.

48.1b The season stowed away indeed.

49.ST A chün tzu uses regulating time reckoning to brighten the seasons.

49.ImT Heaven and Earth Skinning and the four seasons accomplishing.

49.ImT Actually Skinning's season great in fact.

52.ImT The season stopping, by consequence stopping.

52.ImT The season moving, by-consequence moving.

52.ImT Stirring up, stilling, not letting go one's season.

54.4a Procrastinating Converting possesses the season.

55.ImT Associating with the season: dissolving pause.

56.ImT Actually Sojourning's season righteously great in fact.

60.ImT Heaven, Earth: Articulating and the four seasons accomplishing.

60.2b Letting go the season ending indeed.

62.ImT Associating with the season moving indeed.

63.5b Not thus the Western neighbor's season indeed.

Seasoned, HSI: dried meat, prepared for a journey. ●

    21.3a Gnawing seasoned meat. Meeting poison.

Second, see: **Twice** and **Two** ●

See, CHIEN: seeing in all its aspects: vision, being ● visible, forming mental images; visit, call on, consult. The ideogram: eye above person, active and receptive sight.

    1.2a,5a Advantageous: seeing Great People.

    1.2a/b Seeing dragon located in the fields.

    1.7a Seeing flocking dragons without a head.

    3/4.CD Sprouting: seeing and not letting go one's residing.

    4.3a Seeing a metallic husband.

    6.Im/ImT Advantageous: seeing Great People.

    18.4a Going: seeing distress.

24.ImT Reaching to Returning one's seeing Heaven and Earth's heart.

31.ImT and actually Heaven and Earth, the myriad beings's motives permitting seeing.

32.ImT and actually Heaven and Earth, the myriad beings's motives permitting seeing.

34.ImT Actually the correcting Great and Heaven and Earth's motives permitting seeing.

38.1a/b Seeing hateful people.

38.3a/b Seeing the cart pulled back.

38.6a Seeing pigs bearing mire.

39.Im/ImT,6a/b Advantageous: seeing Great People.

39.ImT Seeing venturing and enabling stopping.

42.ST A chün tzu uses seeing improvement, by consequence shifting.

45.Im/ImT Advantageous: seeing Great People. Growing.

45.ImT and actually Heaven and Earth, the myriad beings's motives, permitting seeing.

46.Im Availing of seeing Great People.

46.ImT That uses great Growing to avail of seeing Great People.

47.3a/b Entering into one's house. Not seeing one's consort.

52.Im/ImT Not seeing one's people.

55.2a,4a/b Sun centering: seeing the Bin.

55.3a Sun centering: seeing froth.

57.Im/ImT Advantageous: seeing Great People.

57/58.CD Open: seeing

- **Seedburst,** CHIA: seeds bursting forth in spring; first of the Ten Heavenly Barriers in calendar system; begin, first, number one; associated with the Woody Moment.

  18.Im/ImT Before seedburst three days, after seedburst three days.

  40.ImT Thunder and Rain arousing and the hundred fruits, grasses, trees, altogether seedburst boundary.

- **Seek,** CH'IU: search for, aim at, wish for, desire; implore, supplicate; covetous.

  3.4a Seeking matrimonial allying.

  3.4b Seeking and going.

  4.Im/ImT In no way me seeking youthful Enveloping.

  4.Im/ImT Youthful Enveloping seeking me.

  17.3a Following possessing seeking, acquiring.

  19/20.CD Maybe associating with, maybe seeking.

27.Im/ImT Originating from seeking mouth substance.

29.2a/b Seeking, the small acquiring.

32.1b Beginning seeking depth indeed.

48.3b Seeking kingly brightness:

- **Seize,** CHÜ: grasp, lay hands on; lean on, rely on; maintain, become concrete; testimony, evidence.

  47.3a/b Seizing into star thistles.

- **Senior,** HSIUNG: elder; recognized as one to whom respect is due.

  37.ImT The senior, a senior. The junior, a junior.

- **Sequence,** HSÜ: order, precedence, series; follow in order. The name of a section of each hexagram. It also occurs at:

  52.5a Words possessing sequence.

- **Servant,** CH'EN: attendant, minister, vassal; courtier who can speak to the sovereign; wait on, serve in office. The ideogram: person bowing low. See also: **Chief and Servant**

  33.3a/b Accumulating servants, concubines, auspicious.

  39.2a/b A king, a servant: Difficulties, Difficulties.

  41.6a Acquiring a servant, without dwelling.

  62.2a Meeting one's servant.

  62.2b A servant not permitted Exceeding indeed.

- **Set right,** TING: settle, fix, put in place; at rest, repose.

  10.ST [A chün tzu uses] setting right the commoners, the purpose.

  37.ImT Actually correcting Dwelling and Below Heaven set right.

  63/64.CD Already Fording: setting right indeed.

- **Set up,** SHE: establish, institute; arrange, set in order; spread a net. The ideogram: words and impel, establish with words.

  20.ST The Earlier Kings used inspecting on all sides, Viewing the commoners to set up teaching.

  20.ImT The all wise person uses spirit tao to set up teaching.

  29.ImT The kingly prince sets up venturing used to guard his city.

  42.AE Augmenting: long living enriching and not setting up.

- **Seven,** CH'I: number seven, seventh; seven planets; seventh day when moon changes from crescent to waxing; the Tangram game makes pictures of all phenomena from seven basic shapes.

24.Im/ImT The seventh day coming:
Returning.

51.2a The seventh day: acquiring.

63.2a/b The seventh day: acquiring.

Sever, CHE: break off, separate, sunder, cut in two; discriminate, judge the true and false.

22.ST A chün tzu uses brightening the multitudinous standards without daring to sever litigating.

30.6a Severing the head. Catching in no way its demons.

50.4a The Vessel: a severed stand.

55.ST A chün tzu uses severing litigating to involve punishing.

55.3a/b Severing one's right arm.

• **Shackles**, KU: chains used to secure prisoners; restrain freedom of action; self restraint, good principles.

4.1a Availing of stimulating fettering shackles.

• **Shade**, YU: hidden from view; retired, solitary, secret; dark, obscure, occult, mysterious; ignorant. The ideogram: small within hill, a cave or grotto.

10.2a/b Shade people, Trial: auspicious.

47.1a/b Entering into a shady gully.

47.1b Shady, not bright indeed.

54.2a/b Advantageous: shade people's Trial.

55.4b Shade, not brightening indeed.

• **Shake**, CHEN: arouse, excite, inspire; thunder rising from below; alarm, trembling; fertilizing intrusion. The ideogram: excite and rain.

Image of Hexagram 51 and occurs throughout its texts.

52.CD Shake: rising up indeed.

64.4a Shake avails of subjugating souls on all sides.

• **Shaman**, WU: medium of the gods; sorcerer, enchantress; perform magic; wizard, witch.

57.2a Availing of chroniclers, shamans.

• **Sheer**, SU: plain, unadorned; original color or state; clean, pure. The ideogram: white silk, symbol of mourning.

10.1a/b Sheer Treading going.

53.2b Not sheer satiation indeed.

• **Shield**, YU: protect; defended by spirits; heavenly kindness and protection. The ideogram: numinous and right hand, spirit power.

14.6a Originating from heaven shielding it.

14.6b Originating from heaven shielding indeed.

25.ImT Heavenly fate not shielding.

41.5b Originating from shielding above indeed.

• **Shift**, CH'IEN: move, change, transpose; improve, ascend, be promoted; deport, dismiss, remove.

42.ST A chün tzu uses seeing improvement, by consequence shifting.

42.4a Advantageous: availing of activating depending on shifting the city.

48.AE The Well: residing in one's place and shifting.

• **Shine**, KUANG: illuminate; give off brilliant, bright light; honor, glory, éclat; result of action, contrasts with brightness, MING, light of heavenly bodies. The ideogram: fire above person, lifting the light.

2.ImT Containing generosity, the shining great.

2.2b Earthly tao shining indeed.

2.3b Knowing the shining great indeed.

3.5b Spreading out not yet shining indeed.

5.Im/ImT Shining Growing, Trial: auspicious.

10.ImT Shining brightness indeed.

11.2b Using the shining great indeed.

15.AE Humbling: dignifying and shining.

15.ImT Heavenly tao fording below and shining brightness.

15.ImT Humbling dignifying and shining.

20.4a/b Viewing the city's shining.

21.4b Not yet shining indeed.

26.ImT Solid persisting: staunch substance, resplendent shining.

27.4b Spreading out shining above indeed.

31.4b Not yet the shining great indeed.

35.6b Tao not yet shining indeed.

42.ImT One's tao, the great shining.

43.ImT One's exposure thereupon shining indeed.

43.5b Center not yet shining indeed.

45.5b Purpose not yet shining indeed.

51.4b Not yet shining indeed.

52.ImT One's tao: shining brightness.

58.6b Not yet shining indeed.

59.4b Shining great indeed.

64.5a/b A chün tzu's shining.

• **Shoes**, CHÜ: footwear, sandals.

21.1a/b Shoes locked up, submerging the feet.

• **Shoot**, SHE: shoot with a bow, point at and hit; project from, spurt, issue forth; glance at; scheme for. The ideogram: arrow and body.

40.6a A prince avails of shooting a hawk, into the high rampart's above.

40.6b A prince avails of shooting a hawk.

48.2a/b The Well: a gully, shooting bass.

56.5a Shooting a pheasant.

● **Shoot forth**, FA: expand, send out; shoot an arrow; ferment, rise; be displayed. The ideogram: stance, bow and arrow, shooting from a solid base.

4.1a Shooting forth Enveloping.

14.5b Trustworthiness uses shooting forth purpose indeed.

55.2a/b There is a connection to the spirit, like shooting forth.

55.2b Trustworthiness using shooting forth purpose indeed.

● **Shriek**, YA: shout, yell; warning cry of animals; sounds of someone learning to speak; confused noise, exclamations.

51.Im/ImT,1b Laughing words, shrieking, shrieking.

51.1a After laughing words, shrieking, shrieking.

● **Shroud**, MI: dense, close together, thick, tight; hidden, secret; retired, intimate. See also: **Enshroud**

9.Im/ImT Shrouding clouds, not raining.

62.5a/b Shrouding clouds, not raining.

● **Sides (on all sides)**, FANG: limits, boundaries; square, surface of the earth extending to the four cardinal points; everywhere. See also: **Four sides**

2.2a Straightening on all sides, great.

2.2b Straightening used on all sides indeed.

8.Im/ImT Not soothing, on all sides coming.

20.ST The Earlier Kings used inspecting on all sides, Viewing the commoners to set up teaching.

24.ST The crown prince [used culminating sun] not to inspect on all sides.

32.ST A chün tzu uses establishing, not versatility on all sides.

42.ImT One's Augmenting without sides.

47.2a Scarlet sashes on all sides coming.

50.3a On all sides rain lessens repenting.

63.3a The high ancestor subjugating souls on all sides.

64.ST A chün tzu uses considering to mark off the beings residing on all sides.

64.4a Shake avails of subjugating souls on all sides.

● **Sigh**, TZU: lament, express grief, sorrow or yearning.

45.6a/b Paying tribute: sighs, tears, snot.

● **Similar**, see **Like**

● **Simply**, ERH: just so, only.

27.1a Stowing away simply the psyche tortoise.

31.4a Partnering adheres to simply pondering.

61.2a Myself associating, simply spilling it.

● **Sincere**, YÜN: true, honest, loyal; according to the facts; have confidence in, permit, assent. The ideogram: vapor rising, words directed upward.

35.3a Crowds, sincerity, repenting extinguished.

35.3b Crowds: sincerity's purpose.

46.1a/b Sincere Ascending, the great auspicious.

● **Sing**, KO: chant, sing elegies, sad or mournful songs; associated with the Earthy Moment, turning from yang to yin.

30.3a Not drumbeating a jar and singing.

61.3a Maybe weeping, maybe singing.

● **Situation**, WEI: place or seat according to rank; post, position, command; right, proper; established, arranged. The ideogram: person and stand, servants in their places.

1.ImT The six situations: the season accomplishing.

5.ImT Situation reaching to the heavenly situation.

5.6b Although not an appropriate situation, not yet the great let go indeed.

8.5b Situation correctly centered indeed.

9.ImT Supple acquiring the situation and Above and Below corresponding to it.

10.ImT Treading the supreme situation and not ailing.

10.3b Situation not appropriate indeed.

10.5b Situation correcting appropriate indeed.

12.3b Situation not appropriate indeed.

12.5b Situation correcting appropriate indeed.

13.ImT Supple acquiring the situation.

14.ImT Supple acquiring the dignifying situation, the great centering.

16.3b Situation not appropriate indeed.

17.5b Situation correctly centering indeed.

19.3b Situation not appropriate indeed.

19.4b Situation appropriate indeed.

21.ImT Although not an appropriate situation, Advantageous: availing of litigating indeed.

21.3b Situation not appropriate indeed.

22.4b Six at fourth. Appropriate situation to doubt indeed.

32.4b No lasting whatever: one's situation.

33.ImT Solid: appropriate situation and corresponding.

34.5b Situation not appropriate indeed.

35.4b Situation not appropriate indeed.

37.ImT The woman correcting the situation reaching to the inside.

37.ImT The man correcting the situation reaching to the outside.

37.4b Yielding located in the situation indeed.

38.3b Situation not appropriate indeed.

39.ImT Appropriate situation, Trial: auspicious.

39.4b Appropriate situation, substance indeed.

40.4b Not yet an appropriate situation indeed.

43.4b Situation not appropriate indeed.

45.4b Situation not appropriate indeed.

45.5a/b Clustering: possessing the situation.

47.4b Although not an appropriate situation, possessing associating indeed.

50.ST A chün tzu uses correcting the situation to solidify fate.

51.3b Situation not appropriate indeed.

52.ST A chün tzu uses pondering not to issue forth from his situation.

53.ImT Advancing acquiring the situation.

53.ImT One's situation: solid acquiring the center indeed.

54.ImT Situation not appropriate indeed.

54.5b One's situation located in the center.

55.4b Situation not appropriate indeed.

56.4b Not yet acquiring the situation indeed.

57.5b Situation correctly centered indeed.

58.3b Situation not appropriate indeed.

58.5b Situation correcting appropriate indeed.

59.ImT Supple acquiring the situation reaching to the outside and concording above.

59.5b Correcting the situation indeed.

60.ImT Appropriate situating uses Articulating.

60.5b Residing in the situation: centering indeed.

61.3b Situation not appropriate indeed.

61.5b Situation correcting appropriate indeed.

62.ImT Solid letting go the situation and not centering.

62.4b Situation not appropriate indeed.

63.ImT Strong and Supple correcting and the situation appropriate indeed.

64.ImT Although not an appropriate situation.

64.3b Situation not appropriate indeed.

● **Six**, LU: transforming opened line; six lines or places of a hexagram; sixth.

1.ImT The six situations: the season accomplishing.

1.ImT The season riding six dragons used going to meet

2.7b Availing of the sixes, perpetual Trial.

Skeptical, YÜ: doubtful, cynical; wonder at, wide ●
eyed surprise.

16.3a Skeptical Providing for, repenting.

16.3b Skeptical Providing for possesses repenting.

Skin, KO: take off the covering, skin or hide; change, ●
renew, molt; remove, peel off; revolt, overthrow, degrade from office; leather armor, protection.

Image of Hexagram 49 and occurs throughout its texts.

33.2a Holding on to it: availing of yellow cattle's skin.

50.S Skinning beings implies absolutely nothing like a Vessel.

50.CD Skinning: departing anteriority indeed.

50.3a/b The Vessel: the ears skinned.

Skulk, TS'UAN: sneak away and hide; furtive, ●
stealthy; seduce into evil. The ideogram: cave and rat, rat lurking in its hole.

6.2b Converting escaping, skulking indeed.

Slaughter, SHA: kill, murder, execute; hunt game; ●
mow grass.

63.5a/b The Eastern neighbor slaughters cattle.

Sleeve, MEI: displays signs showing quality and rank ●
of the wearer; symbol of self; womb symbol.

54.5a One's chief's sleeves:

54.5a One's junior sister's sleeves not thus fine.

Slice, CH'IEH: cut, carve, mince; urge, press; a ●
resumé.

23.4b Slicing close to calamity indeed.

Small, HSIAO: little, common, unimportant; ●
adapting to what crosses your path; ability to move in harmony with the vicissitudes of life; contrasts with great, TA, self imposed theme or goal; keyword. See also: **Small People**

Image of Hexagrams 9 and 62 and occurs throughout their texts.

3.5a The small, Trial: auspicious.

5.2a The small possesses words.

5.2b Although the small possesses words, using completing auspicious indeed.

6.1a The small possesses words, completing auspicious.

6.1b Although the small possesses words, one's differentiation brightening indeed.

10.CD Small Accumulating: few indeed.

11.Im The small going, the great coming.

11.ImT The small going, the great coming: auspiciousness Growing.

12.Im/ImT The great going, the small coming.
17.2a/b Tied to the small son.
17.3a Letting go the small son.
18.3a The small possesses repenting.
21.3a The small distress.
22.Im The small, Advantageous: having a direction to go.
22.ImT The anterior small, Advantageous: having a direction to go.
24.AE Returning: the small and marking off with respect to beings.
29.2a/b Seeking, the small acquiring.
33.Im/ImT The small: Advantageous Trial.
38.Im Polarizing, Small Affairs auspicious.
38.ImT That uses Small Affairs concording indeed.
45.3a The small distress.
46.ST [A chün tzu uses] amassing the small to use the high great.
53.1a The small son, adversity possessing words.
53.1b The small son's adversity.
56.Im Sojourning, the small: Growing.
56.ImT The small Growing.
56.ImT That uses the small Growing.
57.Im Ground, the small: Growing.
57.ImT That uses the small Growing.
61.CD Small Exceeding: Excess indeed.
63.Im Already Fording. Growing: the small.
63.ImT The small implies Growing indeed.
64.Im/ImT The small fox, a muddy Ford.

Small People, HSIAO JEN: lowly, common, humble; those who adjust to circumstances with the flexibility of the small; effect of the small within an individual; keyword.
7.6a/b Small People, no availing of.
11.ImT Inside chün tzu and outside Small People.
11.ImT Small People: tao dissolving indeed.
12.ImT Inside Small People and outside chün tzu.
12.ImT Small People: tao long living.
12.2a Small People auspicious.
14.3a Small People nowhere controlling.
14.3b Small People harmful indeed.
20.1a Small People: without fault.
20.1b Small People: tao indeed.
23.ImT Small People long living indeed.
23.6a/b Small People Stripping the hut.
33.ST A chün tzu uses distancing Small People.
33.4a Small People obstructing.

33.4b Small People obstructing indeed.
34.3a/b Small People avail of Invigorating.
40.5a There is a connection to the spirit, into Small People.
40.5b Small People withdrawing indeed.
49.6a/b Small People: Skinning the visage.
63.3a Small People, no availing of.

Smite, CHI: hit, beat, attack; hurl against, rush a position; rouse to action. The ideogram: hand and hit, fist punching.
4.6a Smiting Enveloping.
16.AE Redoubling gates, smiting clappers.
42.6a/b Maybe smiting it.

Smooth, T'AN: plain, leveled; even, make smooth; tranquil, composed, at ease.
10.2a Treading tao, smoothing, smoothing.

Smother, HSÜN: suffocate, smoke out; fog, steam, miasma, vapor; broil, parch; offend; evening mists.
52.3a Adversity smothers the heart.
52.3b Exposure smothers the heart indeed.

Snot, YI: mucus from the nose; snivel, whine.
45.6a/b Paying tribute: sighs, tears, snot.

Soak, JU: immerse, steep; damp, wet; stain, pollute, blemish; urinate on.
22.3a Adorning thus, soaking thus.
43.3a Like soaking, possessing indignation.
63.1a Soaking one's tail.
63.6a Soaking one's head.
63.6b Soaking one's head, adversity.
64.Im/ImT,1a/b Soaking one's tail:
64.6a Soaking one's head.
64.6b Drinking liquor, soaking the head.

Soar, HAN: fly high; rising sun, the firebird with red plumage; trunk or stem of a plant; vertical support. The ideogram: feathers and dawn.
22.4a A white horse, soaring thus.
61.6a/b A soaring sound mounting, into heaven.

Sob, T'AO: cry, weep aloud; wailing children. The ideogram: mouth and omen, ominous sounds.
13.5a Concording People beforehand crying out sobbing and afterwards laughing.
56.6a Sojourning people beforehand laughing, afterwards crying out sobbing.

Soil, WU: covered thick; dirty, stain; moisten, enrich.
50.4a Its form soiled. Pitfall.

Sojourn, LU: travel, stay in places other than your home; itinerant troops, temporary residents; visitor, guest, lodger. The ideogram: banner and people around it, loyal to a symbol rather than their temporary residence.

Image of Hexagram 56 and occurs throughout its texts.

24.ST Bargaining sojourners [used culminating sun] not to move.

55.CD Connecting the few: Sojourning indeed.

57.S Sojourning and lacking a place to tolerate.

● **Solidify**, NING: congeal, freeze, curdle, stiffen; coagulate, make solid or firm.

2.1b Yin begins solidifying indeed.

50.ST A chün tzu uses correcting the situation to solidify fate.

● **Solitary**, TI: alone, single; isolated, abandoned.

4.4b Solitariness distancing substance indeed.

9.5b Not solitary affluence indeed.

10.1b Solitarily moving desire indeed.

24.4a/b Centering movement, solitary Returning.

28.ST A chün tzu uses solitary establishing not to fear.

35.1b Solitary moving correcting indeed.

43.3a Solitary going, meeting rain.

● **"Someone,"** see **Maybe**

● **Son(hood)**, TZU: living up to ideal of ancestors as highest human development; act with concern and reverence; male child; offspring, posterity; seed, kernel, egg; sage, teacher; nadir, deepest point, midnight, mid winter. See also: **Father and Son** and **Woman[and]Son**

4.2a/b The son controlling the dwelling.

7.5a/b The long living son conducting Legions.

7.5a/b The junior son carting corpses.

14.3a/b A prince availing of Growing, into heavenly sonhood.

17.2a/b Tied to the small son.

17.3a Letting go the small son.

18.1a Possessing sonhood.

32.5a The husband, the son: pitfall.

32.5b The husband, the son: paring righteously.

36.ImT The winnowing son uses it.

36.5a The winnowing son's Brightness Hiding.

36.5b The winnowing son's Trial.

37.ImT The father, a father. The son, a son.

37.3a/b The wife, the son, giggling, giggling:

50.1a Acquiring a concubine, using one's sonhood.

51.S A lord's implementing implies absolutely nothing like the long living son.

53.1a The small son, adversity possessing words.

53.1b The small son's adversity.

61.2a/b One's sonhood harmonizing it.

● **Soothe**, NING: calm, pacify; create peace of mind; tranquil, quiet. The ideogram: shelter above heart, dish and breath, physical and spiritual comfort.

1.ImT Myriad cities, conjoining, soothing.

3.ImT Proper to install feudatories and not to soothe.

8.Im/ImT Not soothing, on all sides coming.

58.4a Bargaining Opening, not yet soothing.

● **Sort**, LEI: group according to kind, class with; like nature or purpose; species, class, genus.

2.ImT The female horse: earth sorting.

2.ImT Thereupon associating sorting movement.

11/12.CD Obstructing, Pervading: reversing one's sorting indeed.

13.ST A chün tzu uses sorting the clans to mark off the beings.

27.2b Movement letting go sorting indeed.

38.ImT The myriad beings Polarizing and their affairs sorted indeed.

61.4b Cutting off the above, sorting indeed.

● **Soul**, KUEI: power that creates individual existence; union of volatile soul, HUN, spiritual and intellectual power, and dense soul, P'O, bodily strength and movement. The HUN rises after death, the P'O remains with the body and may communicate with the living.

38.6a Carrying souls, the one chariot.

63.3a The high ancestor subjugating souls on all sides.

64.4a Shake avails of subjugating souls on all sides.

● **Souls and Spirits**, KUEI SHEN: the whole range of imaginal beings both inside and outside the individual; spiritual powers, gods, demons, ghosts, powers, faculties.

15.ImT Souls and Spirits harming overfilling and blessing Humbling.

55.ImT Even more with respect to the Souls and Spirits reached.

● **Source of Success: Advantageous Divination**, see **Spring Growing Harvest Trial**

● **Sound**, YIN: any sound, particularly music; pronunciation of words. The ideogram: words and hold in the mouth, vocal sound.

61.6a/b A soaring sound mounting, into heaven.

62.Im/ImT Flying bird: abandoning's sound.

South, NAN: corresponds to summer, Growing, and the Fiery Moment; end of the yang hemicycle; reference point of compass; rulers face South, thus true principles and correct decisions. See also: **Western South**

36.3a Brightness Hiding into the South, hunting.

36.3b The South: hunting's purpose.

46.Im/ImT The South, chastising auspicious.

- **Spill**, MI: pour out; disperse, spread; waste, overturn; fleeing soldiers; showy, extravagant.

  61.2a Myself associating, simply spilling it.

- **Spirit(s)**, SHEN: independent spiritual powers that confer intensity on heart and mind by acting on the soul, KUEI; gods, daimones. See also: **Souls and Spirits**

  20.ImT Viewing heaven's spirit tao.

  20.ImT The all wise person uses spirit tao to set up teaching.

- **Splendor**, JUNG: glory, elegance, honor, beauty; flowering; elaborate carved corners of a temple roof.

  12.ST [A chün tzu uses] not permitting splendor to use benefits.

- **Split off**, SSU: lop off, split with an ax, rive; white (color eliminated). The ideogram: ax and possessive, splitting what belongs together.

  40.4a Partnering culminating, splitting off connection.

  56.1a Splitting off one's place, grasping calamity.

- **Spoken thus**, YÜEH: designated, termed, called. The ideogram: open mouth and tongue.

  9.ImT Spoken thus: Small Accumulating.

  13.ImT Spoken thus: Concording People.

  13.ImT Concording People: spoken thus.

  14.ImT Spoken thus: Great Possessing.

  21.ImT Jaws center possesses being. Spoken thus: Gnawing Bite.

  26.3a Spoken thus: an enclosed cart, escorting.

  47.6a Spoken thus: stirring up repenting possesses repenting.

  49.ImT Their purposes not mutually acquired. Spoken thus: Skinning.

- **Spokes**, FU: braces that connect hub and rim of wheel; tributaries.

  9.3a Carting stimulating the spokes.

- **Spout**, T'ENG: spurt, burst forth; open mouth, loud talk.

  31.6b The spouting mouth stimulating indeed.

- **Spread out**, SHIH: expand, diffuse, distribute, arrange, exhibit; add to, aid. The ideogram: flag and indeed, claiming new country.

  1.ImT Clouds moving, rain spreading out.

  1.2b Actualizing tao spreading out throughout indeed.

3.5b Spreading out not yet shining indeed.

9.ImT Spreading out, not yet moving indeed.

15.ST [A chün tzu uses] evaluating beings to even spreading out.

27.4b Spreading out shining above indeed.

42.ImT Heaven spreading out, earth giving birth.

43.ST A chün tzu uses spreading out benefits to extend to the below.

44.ST The crown prince uses spreading out fate to command the four sides.

Sprig, T'I: tender new shoot of a tree, twig, new branch.

28.2a A withered willow giving birth to a sprig.

Spring, YÜAN: source, origin, head; great, excellent; arise, begin, generating power; first stage of the Time Cycle.

1.ImT The great Force, Spring in fact.

2.ImT Culminating Field, Spring in fact.

2.5a/b A yellow apron. Spring auspicious.

6.5a/b Arguing. Spring auspicious.

8.Im/ImT Retracing the oracle consulting: Spring, perpetual Trial.

10.6a One's recurring Spring auspicious.

10.6b Spring auspicious located above.

11.5a/b Using satisfaction, Spring auspicious.

14.Im Great Possessing, Spring Growing.

14.ImT That uses Spring Growing.

18.Im/ImT Corrupting, Spring Growing.

24.1a Spring auspicious.

26.4a Spring auspicious.

26.4b Six at fourth, Spring auspicious.

30.2a/b Yellow Radiance. Spring auspicious.

38.4a Meeting Spring, husbanding.

41.Im/ImT,5a Spring auspicious.

41.5b Six at fifth, Spring auspicious.

42.1a/b Spring auspicious, without fault.

42.5a No question, Spring auspicious.

45.5a Spring, perpetual Trial.

46.Im Ascending, Spring Growing.

48.6a There is a connection to the spirit, Spring auspicious.

48.6b Spring auspicious located in the above.

50.Im The Vessel, Spring auspicious.

50.ImT That uses Spring Growing.

59.4a/b Dispersing one's flock, Spring auspicious.

Spring Growing Harvesting Trial: Spring, YÜAN; **Grow,** HENG; **Harvest,** LI; and **Trial,** CHEN, are the four stages of the Time Cycle, the model for all dynamic processes. They indicate that your question is connected to the cycle as a whole rather than a part of it, and that the origin (Spring) of a favorable result (Advantageous Trial) is an offering to the spirits (Growing).
> 1.Im Force: Spring Growing Harvesting Trial.
> 2.Im Field: Spring Growing Harvesting, female horse's Trial.
> 3.Im Spring Growing Harvesting Trial.
> 17.Im Spring Growing Harvesting Trial.
> 19.Im Nearing, Spring Growing Harvesting Trial.
> 25.Im Spring Growing Harvesting Trial.
> 49.Im Spring Growing Harvesting Trial.

Springwater, CH'ÜAN: headwaters of a river; pure water. The ideogram: water and white, pure water at the source.
> 4.ST Below the mountain issuing forth springwater.
> 48.5a The Well: limpid, cold springwater taken in.
> 48.5b Cold springwater's taking-in.

Sprout, CHUN: begin or cause to grow; assemble, accumulate, bring under control; hoard possessions; gather soldiers in a military camp; difficult, arduous. The ideogram: sprout piercing hard soil.
> Image of Hexagram 3 and occurs throughout its texts.

Squint, MIAO: look at with one eye, glance at; obstructed vision.
> 10.3a/b Squinting enabling observing.
> 54.2a Squinting enabling observing.

Stability, CH'IH: firm, prepared for; careful, respectful.
> 17/18.CD Corrupting: by consequence stability indeed.

Stable, KU: shed or pen for cattle and horses.
> 26.4a Youthful cattle's stable.

Stag, LU: mature male deer with horns.
> 3.3a/b Approaching stag, lacking precaution.

Stand, TSU: base, foot, leg; rest on, support; stance. The ideogram: foot and calf resting.
> 6.6b Truly not standing respectfully indeed.
> 10.3b Not the stand to use possessing brightness indeed.
> 10.3b Not the stand to use associating with moving indeed.

> 23.1a/b Stripping the bed, using the stand.
> 27.1b Truly not the stand to value indeed.
> 50.4a The Vessel: a severed stand.

Standard, CHENG: measure, test, limit, rule; musical interval; subjugate, regulate; capacity, endurance.
> 22.ST A chün tzu uses brightening the multitudinous standards without daring to sever litigating.

Star thistles, CHI LI: spiny weeds that entangle the feet; caltrops, metal snares.
> 47.3a/b Seizing into star thistles.

Staunch, TU: firm, solid, reliable; pure; consolidate, establish; sincere, honest.
> 26.ImT Solid persisting: staunch substance, resplendent shining.

Step into, SHE: walk in or through the water; spend time on something; contrasts with ford, CHI, to cross. The ideogram: step and water.
> 28.6a Exceeding stepping into submerges the peak. Pitfall.
> 28.6b Exceeding stepping into's pitfall.

Step into the Great River, SHE TA CH'UAN consciously moving into the flow of time; enter the stream of life with a goal or purpose; embark on a auspicious enterprise.
> 5.Im/ImT Advantageous: stepping into the Great River.
> 6.Im/ImT Not Advantageous: stepping into the Great River.
> 13.Im/ImT Advantageous: stepping into the Great River.
> 15.1a Availing of stepping into the Great River. Auspicious.
> 18.Im/ImT Advantageous: stepping into the Great River.
> 26.Im/ImT Advantageous: stepping into the Great River.
> 27.5a Not permitting stepping into the Great River.
> 27.6a Advantageous: stepping into the Great River.
> 42.Im/ImT Advantageous: stepping into the Great River.
> 59.Im/ImT Advantageous: stepping into the Great River.
> 61.Im/ImT Advantageous: stepping into the Great River.
> 64.3a Advantageous: stepping into the Great River.

Steps, CHIEH: stairs leading to a gate or hall; grade, degree, rank; emulate, rise.

   46.5a/b Trial: auspicious, Ascending steps.

Stew, SU: cooked or boiled rice and meat; mixed contents of a pot.

   50.4a/b Overthrowing a princely stew.

Still, CHING: quiet, at rest; imperturbable.

   52.ImT Stirring up, stilling, not letting go one's season.

Stimulate/loosen, SHUO: rouse to action and good feeling; free from constraint, stir up, urge on; persuade, cheer, delight; set out in words; the Action of the trigram Open, TUI. The ideogram: words and exchange.

   4.1a Availing of stimulating fettering shackles.

   9.3a Carting stimulating the spokes.

   10.ImT Stimulating and corresponding reaching to Force.

   17.ImT Stirring up and stimulating.

   19.ImT Stimulating and yielding.

   26.2a/b Carting, stimulating the axle strap.

   28.ImT Ground and stimulating movement.

   31.ImT Stopping and stimulating.

   31.6b The spouting mouth stimulating indeed.

   33.2a Absolutely nothing has mastering stimulating.

   38.ImT Stimulating and congregating reaching to brightness.

   38.6a Afterwards stimulating's bow.

   42.ImT The commoners stimulated without delimiting.

   43.ImT Persisting and stimulating.

   45.ImT Yielding uses stimulating.

   47.ImT Venturing uses stimulating.

   47.5a/b Thereupon ambling possesses stimulating.

   49.ImT Pattern brightening uses stimulating.

   54.ImT Stimulating uses stirring up.

   58.S Entering and afterwards stimulating it.

   58.S Open implies stimulating indeed.

   58.ImT Open stimulating indeed.

   58.ImT Stimulating uses Advantageous Trial.

   58.ImT Stimulating using beforehand the commoners:

   58.ImT Stimulating using opposing heaviness:

   58.ImT Stimulating's great.

   59.S Stimulating and afterwards scattering it.

   60.ImT Stimulating uses movement venturing.

   61.ImT Stimulating and Ground: Connection.

Stir up, TUNG: excite, influence, move, affect; work, take action; come out of the egg or the bud; the Action of the trigram Shake, CHEN. The ideogram: strength and heavy, move weighty things.

   2.2b Six at second's stirring up.

   3.ImT Stirring up reaching to venturing center.

   3.ImT Thunder and Rain's stirring up, fullness overfilling.

   16.ImT Yielding uses stirring up. Provision.

   16.ImT Providing for: yielding uses stirring up.

   16.ImT Heaven and Earth uses yielding stirring up.

   16.ImT The all wise person uses yielding stirring up.

   17.ImT Stirring up and stimulating. Following.

   21.ImT Stirring up and brightening.

   24.ImT Stirring up and using yielding movement.

   25.ImT Stirring up and persisting.

   28.S Not nourishing, by consequence not permitting stirring up.

   32.ImT Ground and stirring up.

   34.ImT Solid uses stirring up. Anterior Invigorating.

   38.ImT Fire stirring up and above.

   38.ImT Marsh stirring up and below.

   40.ImT Loosening. Venturing uses stirring up.

   40.ImT Stirring up and evading reaching to venturing. Loosening.

   42.ImT Augmenting stirring up and Ground.

   47.6a/b Stirring up repenting possesses repenting.

   51.S Shake implies stirring up indeed.

   52.S Beings not permitted to use completing stirring up.

   52.ImT Stirring up, stilling, not letting go one's season.

   53.ImT Stirring up not exhausted indeed.

   54.ImT Stimulating uses stirring up.

   55.ImT Brightness using stirring up. Anterior Abounding.

Stone, P'AN: large conspicuous rock, foundation stone; stable, immovable.

   3.1a Stone pillar.

   3.1b Although a stone pillar, purpose moving correctly indeed.

   53.2a The wild geese Infiltrating into the stone.

Stop, CHIH: bring or come to a standstill; the Action of the trigram Bound, KEN. The ideogram: a foot stops walking.

4.ImT Venturing and stopping. Enveloping.

18.ImT Ground and stopping. Corrupting.

22.ImT Pattern brightening, stopping:

23.ImT Yielding and stopping it.

26.ImT Ability stopping persisting.

31.ImT Stopping and stimulating.

33/34.CD Great Invigorating: by consequence stopping.

39.ImT Seeing venturing and enabling stopping.

51/52.CD Bound: stopping indeed.

52.S Stopping it.

52.S Bounding implies stopping indeed.

52.ImT Bound: stopping indeed.

52.ImT The season stopping, by consequence stopping.

52.ImT Bound: one's stopping.

52.ImT Stopping: one's place indeed.

52.4b Stopping connoting the body indeed.

53.S Beings not permitted to use completing stopping.

53.ImT Stopping and Ground.

56.ImT Stopping and congregating reaching to brightness.

59/60.CD Articulating: stopping indeed.

63.ImT Completing, stopping by consequence disarraying.

● **Strong**, KANG: quality of the whole lines; firm, strong, unyielding, persisting.

This term occurs throughout the hexagram texts in the Image Tradition and in the Transforming Lines b). It also occurs at:

1/2.CD Force: solid.

43/44.CD Supple meeting solid indeed.

43/44.CD Solid breaking up supple indeed.

● **Strong and Supple**, KANG JOU: field of creative tension between the whole and opened lines and their qualities; field of psychic movement.

3.ImT Strong and Supple beginning mingling and heaviness giving birth indeed.

4.2b Strong and Supple articulating indeed.

21.ImT Strong and Supple apportioning.

29.4b Strong and Supple, the border indeed.

32.ImT Strong and Supple altogether corresponding. Persevering.

40.1b Strong and Supple's border.

50.6b Strong and Supple articulating indeed.

60.ImT Strong and Supple apportioning and solid acquiring the center.

63.ImT Strong and Supple correcting and the situation appropriate indeed.

64.ImT Strong and Supple corresponding indeed.

● **Stow(away)**, SHE: set aside, put away, store; halt, rest in; temporary lodgings, breathing spell.

3.3a A chün tzu almost not thus stowing away.

3.3b A chün tzu stowing it:

8.5b Stowing away countering, grasping yielding.

17.3b Below, purpose stowed away indeed.

22.1a/b Stowing away the chariot and afoot.

27.1a Stowing away simply the psyche tortoise.

44.5b Purpose, not stowing away fate indeed.

48.1b The season stowed away indeed.

● **Straighten**, CHIH: correct the crooked, reform, repay injustice; proceed directly; sincere, upright, just; blunt, outspoken.

2.2a Straightening on all sides, great.

2.2b Straightening used on all sides indeed.

13.5b Using centering straightening indeed.

47.5b Using centering straightening indeed.

● **Stranded ropes**, HUI MO: three stranded ropes; royal garments; beautiful, honorable.

29.6a Tying availing of stranded ropes.

● **Stray**, T'E: wander blindly; deviate, err, alter, doubt; excess.

16.ImT and the four seasons not straying.

20.ImT and the four seasons not straying.

● **Stream**, SHUI: flowing water; fluid, dissolving; river, tide, flood; the Symbol of the trigram Gorge, K'AN. The ideogram: rippling water.

6.ST Heaven associating with stream, contradicting movements.

7.ST Earth center possessing stream.

8.ST Above earth possessing stream.

29.ST Streams reiterating culminating. Repeating Gorge.

29.ImT Stream diffusing and not overfilling.

39.ST Above mountain possessing stream.

47.ST Marsh without stream.

48.ST Above wood possessing stream.

48.ImT Ground reaching to stream and stream above. The Well.

49.ImT Skinning. Stream, fire, mutually pausing.

59.ST Wind moves above stream.

60.ST Above marsh possessing stream.

63.ST Stream located above fire.

64.ST Fire located above stream.

● **Street**, HSIANG: public space between dwellings, public square; side street, alley, lane. The ideogram: place and public.

38.2a/b Meeting a lord, into the street.

Strengthen, CH'IANG: invigorate, test; compel, rely on force; determined, sturdy; overcome a desire.

1.ST A chün tzu uses originating strength not to pause.

Stretch, CHANG: draw a bow taut; open, extend, spread, display; make much of.

38.6a Beforehand stretching's bow.

Stricken, YAO: afflicted by fate; untimely, premature death; tender, delicate, young; pleasing. The ideogram: great with a broken point, interrupted growth.

38.3a One's person stricken, moreover nose cut.

String arrow, YI: arrow with string attached used to retrieve what is shot; seize, appropriate; arrest a criminal.

62.5a A prince, a string arrow grasping another located in a cave.

Strip, PO: flay, peel, skin; remove, uncover, degrade; split, slice; reduce to essentials; slaughter an animal. The ideogram: knife and carve, trenchant action.

Image of Hexagram 23 and occurs throughout its texts.

24.S Above Stripping exhausted, below reversing.

24.CD Stripping: rotten indeed.

58.5a/b Connection into stripping.

Struggle, CHAN: fight with, combat; make war, join battle; hostilities; alarmed, terrified.

2.6a/b Dragons struggling into the countryside.

Stump, CHU: trunk, bole, stalk; wooden post; keep down, degrade.

47.1a The sacrum Confined, into stump wood.

Subjugate, FA: chastise rebels, make dependent; cut down, subject to rule. The ideogram: man and lance, armed soldiers.

15.5a/b Advantageous: availing of encroaching subjugating.

35.6a/b Holding fast avails of subjugating the capital.

63.3a The high ancestor subjugating souls on all sides.

64.4a Shake avails of subjugating souls on all sides.

Submerge, MIEH: plunge under water, put out afire; exterminate, finish, cut off. The ideogram: water and destroy.

21.1a/b Shoes locked up, submerging the feet.

21.2a/b Gnawing flesh, submerging the nose.

21.6a/b Wherefore locking up submerging the ears?

23.1b Below using submerging indeed.

28.ST Marsh submerging wood.

28.6a Exceeding stepping into submerges the peak. Pitfall.

Submit, FU: yield to, serve; undergo.

6.6b Using Arguing accepts submitting.

15.3b The myriad commoners submitting indeed.

15.5b Chastising, not submitting indeed.

16.ImT By consequence punishing flogging purifies and the commoners submit.

20.ImT and actually Below Heaven submitting.

Substance, SHIH: real, solid, full; results, fruits, possessions; essence; honest, sincere. The ideogram: string of coins under a roof, riches in the house.

4.4b Solitariness distancing substance indeed.

11.4b Altogether letting go substance indeed.

26.ImT Solid persisting: staunch substance, resplendent shining.

27.Im/ImT Originating from seeking mouth substance.

39.4b Appropriate situation, substance indeed.

50.2a/b The Vessel possesses substance.

50.5b Centering uses activating substance indeed.

54.6a A woman receiving a basket without substance.

54.6b Six above, without substance.

63.5a/b The substance: accepting one's blessing.

Suburbs, CHIAO: area adjoining a city where human constructions and nature interpenetrate; second of the territorial zones: city, suburbs, countryside, forests.

5.1a/b Attending into the suburbs.

9.Im/ImT Originating from my Western suburbs.

13.6a/b Concording People into the suburbs. Without repenting.

62.5a Originating from my Western suburbs.

Subvert, CHING: undermine, overturn, overthrow; falling; pour out, empty; waste, squander. The ideogram: man, head and ladle, emptying out old ideas.

12.6a Subverting Obstruction.

12.6b Obstruction completed, by consequence subverting.

Suddenly, TSAN: quick, prompt, abrupt action; collect together. The ideogram: clasp used to gather the hair.

16.4a Partners join together suddenly.

Suiting, TUI: correspond to, agree with, consistent; pair; parallel sentences in poetic language.

25.ST The Earlier Kings used luxuriance suiting the season to nurture the myriad beings.

Sun/day, JIH: actual sun and the time of a sun cycle, a day.

24.ST The earlier kings used culminating sun to bar the passages.

24.ST Bargaining sojourners [used culminating sun] not to move.

24.ST The crown prince [used culminating sun] not to inspect on all sides.

30.3a/b Sun going down's Radiance.

35.Im Day time sun three times an audience.

35.ImT Day time sun three times an audience indeed.

42.Im/ImT Sun advancing without delimiting.

55.Im/ImT No grief. Properly sun centering.

55.ImT Sun centering, by consequence going down.

55.2a,4a/b Sun centering: seeing the Bin.

55.3a Sun centering: seeing froth.

Sun and Moon, JIH YÜEH: the two dimensions of calendar time that define any specific moment; time as interlocking cycles.

16.ImT Anterior Sun and Moon not exceeding.

30.ImT Sun and Moon congregating reaching to heaven.

32.ImT Sun and Moon acquiring heaven and enabling lasting illumination.

Supervise, LI: oversee, inspect, administer; visit subordinates; headquarters.

36.ST A chün tzu uses supervising the crowds to avail of darkening and Brightening.

Supple, JOU: quality of the opened lines; flexible, pliant, tender, adaptable. See also: **Strong and Supple**

This term occurs throughout the hexagram texts in the Image Tradition and in the Transforming Lines b).

Supreme, TI: highest, above all on earth; sovereign lord, source of power; emperor.

10.ImT Treading the supreme situation and not ailing.

11.5a The supreme burgeoning, converting maidenhood.

42.2a Kinghood availing of presenting into the supreme, auspicious.

54.5a/b The supreme burgeoning Converting Maidenhood.

59.ST The Earlier Kings used presenting into the supreme to establish the temples.

Supreme Above, SHANG TI: highest power in universe, lord of all.

16.ST Exalting worship's Supreme Above.

50.ImT The all wise person Growing uses presenting to the Supreme Above.

Surely, KAI: preceding statement is undoubtedly true.

16.AE Surely, grasping connotes Providing for.

Surpass, YU: exceed; beyond measure, excessive; extraordinary; transgress, blame.

22.4b Completing without surpassing indeed.

23.5b Completing without surpassing indeed.

26.2b Centering without surpassing indeed.

39.2b Completing without surpassing indeed.

50.2b Completing without surpassing indeed.

56.2b Completing without surpassing indeed.

Swallow, YEN: house swallow, martin, swift; retired from official life; easy, peaceful, private; give a feast; relation between elder and younger brother.

61.1a Possessing this, not a swallow.

Swallowing, see: **Jaws**

Sweat, HAN: perspiration; labor, trouble. Dispersing sweat, HUAN HAN, denotes an imperial edict.

59.5a Dispersing sweat, one's great crying out.

Sweet, KAN: taste corresponding to the Earthy Moment; agreeable, happy, delightful, refreshing; grateful.

19.3a/b Sweetness Nearing.

60.5a/b Sweet Articulating auspicious.

Swiftly, CH'UAN: quickly; hurry, hasten.

41.1a/b Climaxing affairs, swiftly going.

41.4a Commissioning swiftly possesses rejoicing.

Symbol, HSIANG: image invested with intrinsic power to connect visible and invisible; magic spell; figure, form, shape, likeness; pattern, model; create an image, imitate; act, play; writing.

23.ImT Viewing symbols indeed.

50.ImT The Vessel. A symbol indeed.

62.ImT Possessing the flying bird's symbol in truth.

Tail, WEI: animal's tail; last, extreme; remnants, unimportant. See also: **Bushy tailed rodent**

10.Im,3a,4a Treading a tiger tail.

10.ImT That uses Treading a tiger tail.

33.1a/b Retiring tail, adversity.

63.1a Soaking one's tail.

64.Im/ImT,1a/b Soaking one's tail:

- **Take in/eat**, SHIH: eat, ingest, swallow, devour; incorporate.

5.5a Attending into liquor taken in.

5.5b Liquor taken in, Trial: auspicious.

6.3a Taking in ancient actualizing tao. Trial.

6.3b Taking in ancient actualizing tao.

11.3a Into taking in possesses blessing.

21/22.CD Gnawing Bite: taking in indeed.

23.6a The ripe fruit not taken in.

26.Im/ImT Not dwelling, taking in. Auspicious.

36.1a Three days, not taking in.

36.1b Righteously not taking in indeed.

47.2a/b Confined, into liquor taken in.

48.1a/b The Well: a bog, not taking in.

48.3a/b The Well: oozing, not taking in.

48.5a The Well: limpid, cold springwater taken in.

48.5b Cold springwater's taking in.

50.3a Pheasant juice not taken in.

55.ImT Moon overfilling, by consequence taking in.

- **Tao**: way or path; ongoing process of being and the course it traces for each specific person or thing; keyword. The ideogram: go and head, leading and the path it creates. See also: **Actualize tao**

1.ImT Force: tao transforming changes.

1.3b Reversing returning tao indeed.

2.ImT Beforehand delusion letting go tao.

2.1b Docilely involving one's tao:

2.2b Earthly tao shining indeed.

2.6b One's tao exhausted indeed.

5.S Attending implies drinking and eating's tao indeed.

8.ImT One's tao exhausted indeed.

9.1a/b Returning originating from tao.

10.2a Treading tao, smoothing, smoothing.

11.ST The crown prince uses property to accomplish Heaven and Earth's tao.

11.ImT A chün tzu: tao long living.

11.ImT Small People: tao dissolving indeed.

12.ImT Small People: tao long living.

12.ImT A chün tzu: tao dissolving indeed.

13.2b Distress: tao indeed.

15.ImT Heavenly tao fording below and shining brightness.

15.ImT Earth tao lowly and moving above.

15.ImT Heavenly tao lessening overfilling and increasing Humbling.

15.ImT Earthly tao transforming overfilling and diffusing Humbling.

15.ImT People tao hating overfilling and loving Humbling.

17.4a There is a connection to the spirit, locating in tao uses brightening.

17.4b There is a connection to the spirit located in tao.

18.2b Acquiring centering tao indeed.

19.ImT Heavenly tao indeed.

20.ImT Viewing heaven's spirit tao.

20.ImT The all wise person uses spirit tao to set up teaching.

20.1b Small People: tao indeed.

20.3b Not yet letting go tao indeed.

24.Im/ImT Reversing Returning one's tao.

24.4b Using adhering to tao indeed.

24.6b Reversing the chief: tao indeed.

26.6b Tao: the great moving indeed.

27.3b Tao, the great rebelling indeed.

29.1b Letting go tao: pitfall indeed.

29.6b Six above, letting go tao.

30.2b Acquiring centering tao indeed.

32.S Husband and Wife's tao.

32.ImT Lasting with respect to one's tao indeed.

32.ImT Heaven and Earth's tao.

32.ImT The all wise person lasting with respect to his tao and Below Heaven the changes accomplishing.

35.6b Tao not yet shining indeed.

37.ImT and Dwelling tao correcting.

38.S Dwelling tao exhausted, necessarily returning.

38.2b Not yet letting go tao indeed.

39.ImT One's tao exhausted indeed.

40.2b Acquiring centering tao indeed.

41.ImT One's tao moving above.

42.ImT One's tao, the great shining.

42.ImT Woody tao, thereupon moving.

42.ImT Total Augmenting's tao.

43.2b Acquiring centering tao indeed.

44.1b Supple tao hauling along indeed.

49.S The Well tao not permitting not Skinning.

52.ImT One's tao: shining brightness.

53.3b Letting go her tao indeed.

60.ImT,6b One's tao exhausted indeed.

60.4b Receiving tao above indeed.

63.ImT One's tao exhausted indeed.

63.2b Using centering tao indeed.

Tatters, see: **In tatters**

Teach, CHIAO: instruct, show; precept, doctrine.

19.ST A chün tzu uses teaching to ponder without exhausting.

20.ST The Earlier Kings used inspecting on all sides, Viewing the commoners to set up teaching.

20.ImT The all wise person uses spirit tao to set up teaching.

29.ST [A chün tzu uses] repeating to teach affairs.

Team, P'I: pair, matched horses; fellow, mate; united.

61.4a/b The horse team extinguished.

Tears, T'I: weep, cry; water from the eyes.

30.5a Issuing forth tears like gushing. Sadness like lamenting.

45.6a/b Paying tribute: sighs, tears, snot.

Temple, MIAO: building used to honor gods and ancestors.

45.Im/ImT The king imagines possessing a temple.

51.ImT Issuing forth permits using guarding the ancestral temple, field altar, offertory millet.

59.Im/ImT The king imagines possessing a temple.

59.ST The Earlier Kings used presenting into the supreme to establish the temples.

Ten, SHIH: goal and end of reckoning; whole, complete, all; entire, perfected, the full amount; reach everywhere, receive everything. The ideogram: East–West line crosses North–South line, a grid that contains all.

3.2a/b Ten years revolved, thereupon nursing.

24.6a Culminating into ten years revolved not controlling chastisement.

27.3a/b Ten years revolved, no availing of.

41.5a Maybe augmenting's ten: partnering's tortoise.

42.2a Maybe Augmenting's ten: partnering's tortoise.

Term, CH'I: set time, fixed period, agreed date; seasons; person a hundred years old.

54.4a Converting Maidenhood overrunning the term.

54.4b Overrunning the term's purpose.

Terminate, O: cut off, check, extinguish, bring to a standstill. The ideogram: go and why, no reason to move.

14.ST A chün tzu uses terminating hate to display improvement.

Terrorize, CH'IO: look around in great alarm; frightened and trying to escape. The ideogram: eyes of bird trapped by a hand.

51.6a Observing: terrorizing, terrorizing.

Test, SHIH: compare, try, experiment; tempt.

25.5b Not permitting testing indeed.

That, what is passed, SHIH: preceding statement, past events.

11.ImT By consequence of that Heaven and Earth mingling and the myriad beings interpenetrating indeed.

12.ImT By consequence of that Heaven and Earth not mingling and the myriad beings not interpenetrating indeed.

62.6a That designates Calamity and Blunder.

64.6a There is a connection to the spirit: letting go what is passed.

That uses, SHIH YI: involves and is involved by.

10.ImT That uses Treading a tiger tail.

14.ImT That uses Spring Growing.

24.ImT That uses issuing forth, entering, without affliction.

30.ImT That uses accumulating female cattle, auspicious indeed.

31.ImT That uses Growth Advantageous Trial, grasping womanhood auspicious.

35.ImT That uses the calm feudatory availing of bestowing horses to multiply the multitudes.

38.ImT That uses Small Affairs, concording indeed.

46.ImT That uses great Growing to avail of seeing Great People.

48.ImT That uses a pitfall indeed.

50.ImT That uses Spring Growing.

52.ImT That uses not catching one's individuality.

56.ImT That uses the small Growing.

57.ImT That uses the small Growing.

58.ImT That uses yielding reaching to heaven and corresponding reaching to the people.

62.ImT That uses Small Affairs, auspicious indeed.

62.ImT That uses not permitting Great Affairs indeed.

Thatch grass, MAO: thick grass used for the roofs of humble houses.

11.1a Eradicating thatch grass intertwisted.

11.1b Eradicating thatch grass, chastising auspicious.

12.1a Eradicating thatch grass intertwisted.

12.1b Eradicating thatch grass, Trial: auspicious.

28.1a/b A sacrifice availing of white thatch grass.

- **There is a connection to the spirit,** YU FU: inner and outer are in accord; confidence of the spirits has been captured; sincere, truthful; proper to take action. This phrase occurs 29 times throughout the hexagram texts.

- **Their/they,** CH'I: third person pronoun; also: one/one's, it/its, he/his, she/hers.

  This term occurs throughout the hexagram texts.

- **Them,** see: **have(it)**

- **Therefore,** JAN: follows logically, thus.

  30.1a Treading, polishing therefore.

- **Therefore afterwards,** JAN HOU: logical consequence of, necessarily follows in time.

  3.S Therefore afterwards the myriad beings giving birth in truth.

  10.S Beings Accumulating, therefore afterwards possessing codes.

  11.S Therefore afterwards quieting.

  20.S Being great therefore afterwards permitting Viewing.

  23.S Actually involving embellishing, therefore afterwards Growing by consequence used up.

  26.S Possessing Disentangling therefore afterwards permitting Accumulating.

  27.S Beings accumulating therefore afterwards permitting nourishing.

  31.S Therefore afterwards possessing the myriad beings.

  31.S Therefore afterwards possessing Man and Woman.

  31.S Therefore afterwards possessing Husband and Wife.

  31.S Therefore afterwards possessing Father and Son.

  31.S Therefore afterwards possessing Chief and Servant.

  31.S Therefore afterwards possessing Above and Below.

  31.S Therefore afterwards the codes righteously possessing a place to polish.

- **Thereupon,** NAI: on that ground, because of.

  1.ImT Thereupon primary heaven.

1.ImT Thereupon Advantageous Trial.

2.ImT Thereupon yielding receiving heaven.

2.ImT Thereupon associating sorting movement.

2.ImT Thereupon completing possesses reward.

3.2a/b Ten years revolved, thereupon nursing.

9.ImT Thereupon Growing.

17.6a Thereupon adhering holding fast to it.

28.ImT Thereupon Growing.

29.ImT Holding fast the heart's Growing, thereupon using solid centering indeed.

30.ImT Thereupon changes accomplishing Below Heaven.

36.3b Thereupon acquiring the great indeed.

40.ImT Thereupon acquiring the center indeed.

42.ImT Woody tao, thereupon moving.

43.ImT One's exposure thereupon shining indeed.

43.ImT The place to honor thereupon exhausted indeed.

43.ImT Solid long living, thereupon completing indeed.

45.1a/b Thereupon disarraying, thereupon Clustering.

45.2a Connection, thereupon Advantageous availing of dedicating.

46.2a Connection, thereupon Advantageous availing of dedicating.

47.ImT Honoring the mouth thereupon exhausted indeed.

47.5a/b Thereupon ambling possesses stimulating.

48.ImT Thereupon using solid centering indeed.

49.Im/ImT Your own day, thereupon connection.

49.ImT One's repenting thereupon extinguished.

49.2a Your own day, thereupon Skinning it.

59.ImT Kinghood thereupon located in the center indeed.

61.ImT Thereupon changing the fiefdoms indeed.

61.ImT Thereupon corresponding reaching to heaven indeed.

Thicket, MANG: underbrush, tangled vegetation, thick grass, jungle; rustic, rude, socially inept.

  13.3a/b Hiding away arms, into the thickets.

Thigh, KU: upper leg that provides power for walking; strands of a rope.

31.3a/b Conjoining one's thighs.

36.2a Brightness Hiding. Hiding into the left thigh.

● **This,** T'A: specifically this thing. The ideogram: person and indeed.

61.1a Possessing this, not a swallow.

● **Thistle,** see: **Star thistle**

● **Thong,** KUNG: bind with thongs, secure; well guarded, strong, stiffened.

49.1a Thonging avails of yellow cattle's Skin.

49.1b Thonging avails of yellow cattle.

● **Thread,** KUAN: string together; string of a thousand coins.

23.5a Threading fish.

● **Three,** SAN: number three, third time or place; active phases of a cycle; superlative; beginning of repetition. See also: **Twice, three times**

5.6a Three people coming.

6.2a People, three hundred doors.

6.6a Completing dawn three times depriving it.

7.2a/b The king three times bestowing fate.

8.5a The king avails of three beaters.

13.3a/b Three year's time not rising.

18.Im/ImT Before seedburst three days, after seedburst three days.

29.6a Three year's time, not acquiring. Pitfall.

29.6b Pitfall: three year's time indeed.

35.Im Day time sun three times an audience.

35.ImT Day time sun three times an audience indeed.

36.1a Three days, not taking in.

40.2a The fields, catching three foxes.

41.3a Three people moving.

41.3b Three by consequence doubting indeed.

47.1a Three year's time not encountering.

49.3a/b Skinning words three times drawing near:

53.5a The wife, three year's time not pregnant.

55.6a Three year's time not encountering.

57.4a/b The fields, catching three kinds.

57.5a Before husking, three days.

57.5a After husking, three days.

63.3a/b Three years revolved controlling it.

64.4a Three years revolved, possessing donating into the great city.

● **Throughout,** P'U: universal, all; great, pervading light. The ideogram: sun and equal, equal to the sun.

1.2b Actualizing tao spreading out throughout indeed.

● **Throw out,** CH'I: reject, discard, abandon, push aside, break off: renounce, forget.

30.4a Burning thus. Dying thus. Thrown out thus.

● **Thumb/big toe,** MU: in lower trigram: big toe; in upper trigram: thumb; the big toe enables the foot to walk, as the thumb enables the hand to grasp.

31.1a/b Conjoining one's big toes.

40.4a/b Loosening and the thumbs.

● **Thunder,** LEI: rising, arousing power; the Symbol of the trigram Shake, CHEN.

3.ST Clouds, Thunder, Sprouting.

16.ST Thunder issuing forth from earth impetuously.

17.ST Marsh center possessing thunder.

21.ST Thunder, lightning.

21.ImT Thunder, lightning, uniting and composing.

24.ST Thunder located in earth center.

25.ST Below heaven thunder moving.

27.ST Below mountain possessing thunder.

32.ST Thunder, wind, Persevering.

32.ImT Thunder, wind, mutually associating.

34.ST Thunder located above heaven.

40.ST Thunder, Rain, arousing.

42.ST Wind, thunder.

51.ST Reiterated thunder.

54.ST Above marsh possessing thunder.

55.ST Thunder, lightning, altogether culminating.

62.ST Above mountain possessing thunder.

● **Thunder and Rain,** LEI YÜ: fertilizing shock of storms; associated with the trigrams Shake, CHEN, and Gorge, K'AN.

3.ImT Thunder and Rain's stirring up, fullness overfilling.

40.ImT Heaven and Earth Loosening and Thunder and Rain arousing.

40.ImT Thunder and Rain arousing and the hundred fruits, grasses, trees, altogether seedburst boundary.

● **Thus,** JU: as, in this way. See also: **Spoken thus** and **Thus ... thus**

3.2a,4a,6a Riding a horse, arraying thus.

3.3a A chün tzu almost not thus stowing away.

3.6a/b Weeping blood, coursing thus.

9.5a/b There is a connection to the spirit, binding thus.

14.5b Your connection, mingling thus.

14.5b Impressing thus, having auspiciousness.

16.ImT Anterior Heaven and Earth thus having it.

22.4a A white horse, soaring thus.

35.4a Prospering, thus bushy tailed rodents.

37.6a There is a connection to the spirit, impressing thus.

37.6b Impressing thus, having auspiciousness.

50.4b Wherefore trustworthy thus indeed?

54.5a/b One's junior sister's sleeves not thus fine.

61.5a/b There is a connection to the spirit, binding thus.

62.1b Wherefore not permitted thus indeed.

62.3b Wherefore a pitfall thus indeed.

63.5a Not thus the Western neighbor's dedicated offering.

63.5b Not thus the Western neighbor's season indeed.

Thus ... thus, JU ... JU: when there is one thing, then there must be the second thing.

3.2a Sprouting thus, quitting thus.

14.5a Your connection: mingling thus, impressing thus. Auspicious.

22.3a Adorning thus, soaking thus.

22.4a Adorning thus, hoary thus.

30.4a Assailing thus, its coming thus.

30.4a Burning thus. Dying thus. Thrown out thus.

30.4b Assailing thus, its coming thus.

35.1a/b Prospering thus, arresting thus.

35.2a Prospering thus, apprehensive thus.

45.3a Clustering thus, lamenting thus.

Tie(to), HSI: connect, attach to, bind; devoted to; relatives. The ideogram: person and connect, ties between humans.

17.2a/b Tied to the small son.

17.3a/b Tied to the respectable husband.

17.6a/b Grappling, tying to it.

29.6a Tying availing of stranded ropes.

33.3a Tied Retiring. Possessing afflicting adversity.

33.3b Tied Retiring's adversity.

Tiger, HU: fierce king of animals; extreme yang; opposed to and protects against demoniacs on North–South axis of Universal Compass.

10.Im,3a,4a Treading a tiger tail.

10.ImT That uses Treading a tiger tail.

27.4a Tiger observing: glaring, glaring.

49.5a/b Great People: tiger transforming.

Till, KENG: plow; labor at, cultivate.

25.2a/b Not tilling the crop.

Time reckoning, LI: fix times, seasons, calendar; reckon the course of heavenly bodies, astronomical events.

49.ST A chün tzu uses regulating time reckoning to brighten the seasons.

Tips, MO: growing ends, outermost twigs; last, most distant.

28.ImT Roots, tips, fading indeed.

31.5b Purpose, the tips indeed.

Together with, PING: also, both, at the same time. The ideogram: two people standing together.

48.3a Together with accepting one's blessing.

Toil, LAO: labor, take pains, exert yourself; burdened, careworn; worthy actions. The ideogram: strength and fire, producing heat.

15.3a/b Toiling Humbling: chün tzu.

48.ST A chün tzu uses toiling commoners to encourage mutualizing.

58.ImT The commoners forget their toiling.

Token, HSÜ: halves of a torn piece of silk which identify the bearers when joined.

63.4a A token: possessing clothes in tatters.

Tolerate, JUNG: allow, contain, endure, bear with; accept graciously. The ideogram: full stream bed, tolerating and containing.

7.ST A chün tzu uses tolerating commoners to accumulate crowds.

19.ST [A chün tzu uses] tolerating to protect the commoners without delimiting.

30.4b Without a place to tolerate indeed.

32.3b Without a place to tolerate indeed.

57.S Sojourning and lacking a place to tolerate.

Tongue, SHE: tongue in the mouth; clapper in a bell, valve in a pump, hook of a clasp; talkative, wordy.

31.6a/b Conjoining one's jawbones, cheeks, tongue.

Topple, TIEN: fall over because top heavy; over throw, subvert; top, summit.

27.CD Great Exceeding: toppling indeed.

27.2a Toppling Jaws.

27.4a/b Toppling Jaws. Auspicious.

28.CD Great Exceeding: toppling indeed.

50.1a/b The Vessel: toppling the foot.

Tortoise, KUEI: turtles; armored animals, shells and shields; long living; oracle consulting by tortoise shell; image of the macrocosm: heaven and earth, between them the soft flesh of humans.

27.1a Stowing away simply the psyche tortoise.

41.5a Maybe augmenting's ten: partnering's
tortoise.

42.2a Maybe Augmenting's ten: partnering's
tortoise.

- **Total**, FAN: all, everything; world, humankind.

42.ImT Total Augmenting's tao.

- **Trailing creeper**, KO LEI: lush, fast growing hanging
plants; spread rapidly and widely; numerous
progeny.

47.6a/b Confined, into trailing creepers.

- **Transform**, PIEN: abrupt, radical, fundamental
mutation from one state of being to another;
transformation of lines in hexagrams; contrasts with
change, HUA, gradual metamorphosis.

1.ImT Force: tao transforming changes.

15.ImT Earthly tao transforming overfilling and
diffusing Humbling.

22.ImT Using scrutinizing the seasons
transforming.

23.ImT Supple transforming solid indeed.

32.ImT The four seasons transforming changes
and enabling lasting accomplishment.

37.1b Purpose not yet transformed indeed.

45.2b Centering, not yet transforming indeed.

49.5a/b Great People: tiger transforming.

49.6a/b A chün tzu: leopard transforming.

54.2b Not yet transforming the rules indeed.

61.1b Purpose not yet transformed indeed.

- **Traverse**, see **Exceed**
- **Tread**, LÜ: step, path, track; footsteps; walk a path
or way; course of the stars; act, practice; conduct;
salary, means of subsistence. The ideogram: body
and repeating steps, following a trail.

Image of Hexagram 10 and occurs throughout its
texts.

2.1a Treading frost, hardening ice culminating.

2.1b Treading frost hardening the ice:

9.CD Treading: not abiding indeed.

11.S Treading and Pervading.

30.1a Treading, polishing therefore.

30.1b Treading, polishing it respectfully.

34.ST A chün tzu uses no codes whatever,
nowhere treading.

54.1a Halting enabling treading.

54.1b Halting enabling treading, auspicious.

- **Tree**, see: **Wood**
- **Trial**, CHEN: inquiry by divination and its result;
righteous, firm; separating wheat from chaff; the
kernel, the proven core; fourth stage of the Time
Cycle. The ideogram: pearl and divination.

2.Im/ImT Quiet Trial auspicious.

2.3a/b Containing composition permitting
Trial.

2.7b Availing of the sixes, perpetual Trial.

3.ImT Great Growing: Trial.

3.2a Woman[and]Son, Trial: not nursing.

3.5a The small, Trial: auspicious.

3.5a The great, Trial: pitfall.

5.Im/ImT Shining Growing, Trial: auspicious.

5.5a Trial: auspicious.

5.5b Liquor taken in, Trial: auspicious.

6.3a Taking in ancient actualizing tao. Trial.

6.4a Denying quiet Trial. Auspicious.

6.4b Denying quiet Trial.

7.Im Legions: Trial.

7.ImT Trial: correcting indeed.

7.5a Trial: pitfall.

8.Im/ImT Retracing the oracle consulting:
Spring, perpetual Trial.

8.2a,4a Trial: auspicious.

9.6a The wife, Trial: adversity.

10.2a/b Shade people, Trial: auspicious.

10.5a/b Deciding Treading. Trial: adversity.

11.3a Drudgery, Trial: without fault.

11.6a Trial: distress.

12.1a Trial: auspicious. Growing.

12.1b Eradicating thatch grass, Trial:
auspicious.

15.2a/b Calling Humbling. Trial: auspicious.

16.2a Trial: auspicious.

16.2b Not completing the day, Trial: auspicious.

16.5a Trial: affliction.

16.5b Six at fifth, Trial: affliction.

17.ImT Great Growing, Trial: without fault.

17.1a An office: possessing denial. Trial:
auspicious.

17.4a Following possessing catching. Trial:
pitfall.

18.2a Not permitting Trial.

19.1a/b Conjunction Nearing, Trial: auspicious.

20.2b Peeping through Viewing: woman Trial.

21.5a Trial: adversity.

21.5b Trial: adversity, without fault.

22.3a/b Perpetual Trial auspicious.

23.1a,2a Discarding the Trial: pitfall.

25.4a Permitting Trial.

25.4b Permitting Trial, without fault.

27.Im/ImT Jaws, Trial: auspicious.

27.3a Rejecting Jaws. Trial: pitfall.

27.5a/b Residing in Trial auspicious.

31.4a/b Trial: auspicious, repenting extinguished.
32.1a Deepening Persevering, Trial: pitfall.
32.3a Trial: distress.
32.5a Persevering one's actualizing tao: Trial.
32.5b Wife people, Trial: auspicious.
33.5a/b Excellence Retiring, Trial: auspicious.
34.2a Trial: auspicious.
34.2b Nine at second, Trial: auspicious.
34.3a Trial: adversity.
34.4a Trial: auspicious.
35.1a,2a Trial: auspicious.
35.4a Trial: adversity.
35.4b Bushy tailed rodents, Trial: adversity.
35.6a Trial: distress.
36.3a Not permitting affliction: Trial.
36.5b The winnowing son's Trial.
37.2a Trial: auspicious.
39.Im Trial: auspicious.
39.ImT Appropriate situation, Trial: auspicious.
40.2a Trial: auspicious.
40.2b Nine at second, Trial: auspicious.
40.3a Trial: distress.
41.Im/ImT Without fault, permitting Trial.
41.6a Trial: auspicious.
42.2a Perpetual Trial auspicious.
44.1a Trial: auspicious.
45.5a Spring, perpetual Trial.
46.5a/b Trial: auspicious, Ascending steps.
46.6a Advantageous: into not pausing's Trial.
47.Im/ImT Trial: Great People auspicious.
49.3a Chastising: pitfall, Trial: adversity.
49.6a Residing in Trial auspicious.
56.Im Sojourning, Trial: auspicious.
56.ImT Sojourning, Trial: auspicious indeed.
56.2a/b Acquiring a youthful vassal: Trial.
56.3a Trial: adversity.
57.5a Trial: auspicious, repenting extinguished.
57.6a Trial: pitfall.
60.Im/ImT Bitter Articulating not permitting Trial.
60.6a/b Bitter Articulating, Trial: pitfall.
61.6a Trial: pitfall.
62.4a No availing of perpetual Trial.
64.2a Trial: auspicious.
64.2b Nine at second, Trial: auspicious.
64.4a/b Trial: auspicious, repenting extinguished.
64.5a Trial: auspicious, without repenting.

Truly, YI: statement is true and precise.

6.6b Truly not standing respectfully indeed.
8.3b Reaching to not truly injuring.
9.2b Truly not originating from letting go indeed.
20.2b Truly permitting the demoniac indeed.
27.1b Truly not the stand to value indeed.
28.5b Truly permitting the demoniac indeed.
31.3b Truly not abiding indeed.
40.3b Truly permitting the demoniac indeed.
41.4b Truly permitting rejoicing indeed.
48.Im/ImT Muddy culmination: Truly not yet the well rope Well.
56.3b Actually truly using injuring.
64.1b Truly not knowing the end indeed.
64.6b Truly not knowing articulating indeed.

Trustworthy, HSIN: truthful, faithful, consistent over time; integrity; confide in, follow; credentials; contrasts with connection, FU, connection in a specific moment. The ideogram: person and word, true speech.
14.5b Trustworthiness uses shooting forth purpose indeed.
29.ImT Movement venturing and not letting go one's trustworthiness.
43.4a/b Hearing words, not trustworthy.
47.Im/ImT Possessing words not trustworthy.
49.ImT Skinning and trusting it.
49.4b Trustworthy purpose indeed.
50.4b Wherefore trustworthy thus indeed?
55.2b Trustworthiness using shooting forth purpose indeed.
58.2b Trustworthy purpose indeed.
61.S Articulating and trusting it.
61/62.CD Centering Connection: trustworthiness indeed.
61.ImT Trustworthiness extending to hog fish indeed.
62.S Possessing one's trustworthiness implies necessarily moving it.

Tumble, YÜN: fall with a crash, fall from the sky; roll down.
44.5a/b Possessing tumbling, originating from heaven.

Turn away, KUAI: turn your back on something and focus on its opposite; contradict, cross purposes; cunning, crafty; perverse; contrasts with return, FU, going back to the start.
38.S Dwelling tao exhausted, necessarily turning away.
38.S Polarizing implies turning away indeed.

39.S Turning away necessarily possesses heaviness.

Turn to, HSIANG: direct your mind towards, seek.

17.ST A chün tzu uses turning to darkening to enter a reposing pause.

Tusk, YA: teeth of animals; toothlike, jagged, gnaw; ivory; a tax collector.

26.5a A gelded pig's tusks.

Twice, three times, TSAI SAN: serial repetition.

4.Im/ImT Twice, three times: obscuring.

Twine, SO: string or rope of many strands twisted together; tie up, bind together; reins; ruling ideas, obligations; demand, search for, inquire; scatter, loosen, destroy authority.

51.6a/b Shake: twining, twining.

Twin peaked, CH'I: mountain with two peaks; forked road; diverge, ambiguous. The ideogram: mountain and branched. Twin peaked Mountain, CH'I SHAN, is the ancestral shrine of the Chou Dynasty.

46.4a/b Kinghood availing of Growing, into the twin peaked mountain.

Two, ERH: pair, even numbers, binary, duplicate. See also: **Twice, three times**

31.ImT The two agencies influencing correspondence use mutual associating.

38.ImT Two women concording: residing.

41.Im/ImT Two platters permit availing of presenting.

41.ImT Two platters corresponding possess the season.

49.ImT Two women concording, residing.

Unconsidered, KOU: offhand, impromptu, improvised; careless, improper; illicit.

22.S Beings not permitted to use unconsidered uniting and climaxing.

Understand, TS'UNG: perceive quickly, astute, sharp; discriminate intelligently. The ideogram: ear and quick.

21.6b Understanding not brightened indeed.

43.4b Understanding not brightened indeed.

50.ImT Ground and the ear[and]eye: understanding brightened.

Uneven, PEI: any difference in level; inclined, falling down, tipped over, dilapidated; also: rising; bank, shore, dam, dikes.

11.3a Without evening, not unevening.

Unite, HO: join, match, correspond, agree, collect, reply; unison, harmony; also: close, shut the mouth. The ideogram: mouth and assemble.

1.ImT Protection uniting the great harmony.

2.ImT Actualizing tao uniting without delimiting.

9.4b Uniting purposes above indeed.

21.S Permitting Viewing and afterwards possessing a place to unite.

21.S Gnawing Bite implies uniting indeed.

21.ImT Thunder, lightning, uniting and composing.

22.S Beings not permitted to use unconsidered uniting and climaxing.

26.3b Uniting purposes above indeed.

41.1b Honoring uniting purposes indeed.

46.1b Uniting purposes above indeed.

Unsteady and unsettled, NIEH WU: badly based; unquiet, hazardous; uneasy, anxious; dizzy, giddy as on a high place.

47.6a Into the unsteady and unsettled.

Urge, SU: strong specific desire; quick, hurried; call, invite.

5.6a Possessing not urging's visitors.

5.6b Not urging's visitors coming.

31/32.CD Conjoining: urging indeed.

Use(of), YI: make use of, by means of, owing to; employ, make functional.

This term occurs throughout the hexagram texts.

Use up, CHIN: exhaust, use all; ended, an empty vessel.

23.S Actually involving embellishing, therefore afterwards Growing by consequence used up.

24.S Beings not permitted to use completing using up.

Value, KUEI: regard as valuable, give worth and dignity to; precious, high priced; honorable, exalted, illustrious. The ideogram: cowries (coins) and basket.

3.1b Using valuing the mean below.

27.1b Truly not the stand to value indeed.

39.6b Using adhering to valuing indeed.

50.1b Using adhering to valuing indeed.

54.5b Using valuing movement indeed.

Variegated, TSA: mingled, variegated, mixed; disorder.

3/4.CD Enveloping: variegated and conspicuous.

32.AE Persevering: variegated and not restricting.

Variegated, FEN: variegated, spotted, mixed, assorted, confused; cloudy, perplexed.

57.2a The variegated like auspicious.

57.2b The variegated like has auspiciousness.

● **Vassal**, P'U: servant, menial, retainer; helper in heavy work; palace officers, chamberlains; follow, serve, belong to.

56.2a/b Acquiring a youthful vassal: Trial.

56.3a Losing one's youthful vassal.

● **Veil**, FU: screen on person or carriage; hair ornaments; lit.: luxuriant, tangled vegetation that conceals the path.

63.2a A wife losing her veil.

● **Venerable**, LAO: term of respect due to old age.

28.2a A venerable husband acquiring his woman consort.

28.2b A venerable husband, a woman consort.

28.5a A venerable wife acquiring her notable husband.

28.5b A venerable wife, a notable husband.

● **Venture/danger**, HSIEN: risk without reserve; key point, point of danger; difficulty, obstruction that must be confronted; water falling and filling the holes on its way; the Action of the trigram Gorge, K'AN. The ideogram: mound and all or whole, everything engaged at one point.

3.ImT Stirring up reaching to venturing center.

4.ImT Enveloping. Below mountain possessing venturing.

4.ImT Venturing and stopping.

5.ImT Venturing located in precedence indeed.

6.ImT Arguing. Solid above, venture below.

6.ImT Venturing and persisting.

7.ImT Movement venturing and yielding.

29.ImT Redoubling venturing indeed.

29.ImT Movement venturing and not letting go one's trustworthiness.

29.ImT Heaven venturing, not permitting ascending indeed.

29.ImT Earth venturing, mountains, rivers, hill tops, mounds indeed.

29.ImT The kingly prince sets up venturing used to guard his city.

29.ImT Actually venturing's season availing of the great in fact.

29.2a Gorge possessing venturing.

29.3a Venturing moreover reclining.

39.ImT Venturing located in precedence indeed.

39.ImT Seeing venturing and enabling stopping.

40.ImT Loosening. Venturing uses stirring up.

40.ImT Stirring up and evading reaching to venturing.

47.ImT Venturing uses stimulating.

60.ImT Stimulating uses movement venturing.

● **Verily**, WEI: the epitome of; in truth, the only; very important.

3.S Overfilling Heaven and Earth's interspace implies verily the myriad beings.

13.ImT Verily a chün tzu activating enables interpenetrating Below Heaven's purpose.

47.ImT Reaching to one's very chün tzu.

● **Versatility/change**, I: sudden and unpredictable change; mental mobility and openness; easy and light, not difficult and heavy; occurs in name of the I CHING.

14.5b Versatility and without preparing indeed.

32.ST A chün tzu uses establishing, not versatility on all sides.

34.5a/b Losing the goat, into versatility.

41.AE Diminishing: beforehand heaviness and afterwards versatility.

56.6a/b Losing the cattle, into versatility.

● **Vessel**, TING: bronze cauldron with three feet and two ears, sacred vessel used to cook food for sacrifice to gods and ancestors; founding symbol of family or dynasty; melting pot, receptacle; hold, contain, transform; establish, secure; precious, respectable.

Image of Hexagram 50 and occurs throughout its texts.

● **View**, KUAN: contemplate, observe from a distance; look at carefully, gaze at; also: a monastery, an observatory; scry, divine through liquid in a cup. The ideogram: see and waterbird, observe through air or water.

Image of Hexagram 20 and occurs throughout its texts.

19/20.CD Nearing Viewing's righteousness.

21.S Permitting Viewing and afterwards possessing a place to unite.

22.ImT Viewing reaching to the heavenly pattern.

22.ImT Viewing reaching to the people pattern.

23.ImT Viewing symbols indeed.

27.Im/ImT Viewing Jaws.

27.ImT Viewing one's place to nourish indeed.

27.ImT Viewing one's origin: nourishing indeed.

27.1a/b Viewing my pendent Jaws.

31.ImT Viewing one's place to influence.

32.ImT Viewing one's place to Persevere.

45.ImT Actually viewing one's place to

assemble.

Violent, PAO: fierce, oppressive, cruel; strike hard.

16.AE Used to await violent visitors.

Virtue, TSANG: essential force or quality; generous, good, dexterous.

7.1a Obstructing virtue: pitfall.

Visage, MIEN: face, countenance; honor, character, reputation; front, surface; face to face.

49.6a/b Small People: Skinning the visage.

Visitor, K'O: guest; stranger, foreign, from afar; squatter.

5.6a Possessing not urging's visitors.

5.6b Not urging's visitors coming.

16.AE Used to await violent visitors.

Vulgar, SU: common people and their desires; inelegant, low; grovelling; the pressure of everyday life.

53.ST A chün tzu uses residing in eminent actualizing tao to improve the vulgar.

Warn, CHIEH: alert, alarm, put on guard; caution, inform; guard against, refrain from (as in a diet). The ideogram: spear held in both hands, warning enemies and alerting friends.

11.4a/b Not warning: using connection.

45.ST [A chün tzu uses] warning, not precautions.

51.6b Dreading the neighbor, a warning indeed.

62.4a/b Going adversity necessarily warning.

63.4a/b Completing the day, a warning.

Wasteland, HUANG: wild, barren, deserted, unproductive; jungle, moor, heath; reckless, neglectful.

11.2a Enwrapping wasteland.

11.2b Enwrapping wasteland, acquiring honor, into centering moving.

Waver, CH'UNG: irresolute, hesitating; unsettled, disturbed; fluctuate, sway to and fro.

31.4a/b Wavering, wavering: going, coming.

Weariness, PAI: fatigue; debilitated, exhausted, distressed; weak.

33.3b Possessing afflicting weariness indeed.

63.3b Weariness indeed.

Weep, CH'I: lament wordlessly; grieved, heart broken.

3.6a/b Weeping blood, coursing thus.

61.3a Maybe weeping, maybe singing.

Well, CHING: water well at the center of the fields; rise and flow of water in a well, rise and surge from an inner source; life water, nucleus of life; found a capital city. The ideogram: two vertical lines crossing two horizontal ones, eight fields with a well at the center.

Image of Hexagram 48 and occurs throughout its texts.

47.CD The Well: interpenetrating

49.S The Well tao not permitting not Skinning.

Well rope, YÜ: rope used to draw water.

48.Im/ImT Muddy culmination: Truly not yet the well rope Well.

West, HSI: corresponds to autumn, Harvest and Streaming Moment; begins the yin hemicycle of the Universal Compass. See also: **Western South**

9.Im/ImT Originating from my Western suburbs.

17.6a The king availing of Growing into the Western mountain.

62.5a Originating from my Western suburbs.

63.5a Not thus the Western neighbor's dedicated offering.

63.5b Not thus the Western neighbor's season indeed.

Western South: neutral Earthy Moment between the yang and yin hemicycles; bring forth concrete results, ripe fruits of late summer.

2.Im/ImT Western South: acquiring partnering.

39.Im/ImT Difficulties, Advantageous: Western South.

40.Im/ImT Loosening. Advantageous: Western South.

Wheel, LUN: disk, circle, round; revolution, circuit; rotate, roll, by turns.

63.1a/b Pulling back one's wheels.

64.2a Pulling back one's wheels.

Wherefore, HO: interrogative: why? for what reason? what is? and affirmation: therefore, for that reason.

3.6b Wherefore permitting long living indeed?

7.ImT Actually auspicious, furthermore wherefore faulty?

9.1a Wherefore one's fault? Auspicious.

12.6b Wherefore permitting long living indeed?

16.6b Wherefore permitting long living indeed?

17.4a Wherefore faulty?

21.6a/b Wherefore locking up submerging the ears?

25.ImT Actually wherefore having it?

26.6a/b Wherefore heaven's highway?

28.5b Wherefore permitting lasting indeed?

30.3b Wherefore permitting lasting indeed?

33.1b Not going, wherefore calamity indeed.

38.5a Going wherefore faulty?

49.3b Furthermore actually wherefore having them.

50.4b Wherefore trustworthy thus indeed?

61.6b Wherefore permitting long living indeed?

62.1b Wherefore not permitted thus indeed.

62.3b Wherefore a pitfall thus indeed.

63.6b Wherefore permitting lasting indeed?

White, PO: associated with autumn, Harvest and the Metallic Moment; clear, immaculate; plain, pure, essential; explicit; color of death and mourning.

22.4a A white horse, soaring thus.

22.6a White Adorning.

22.6b White Adorning, without fault.

28.1a/b A sacrifice availing of white thatch grass.

Whose, SHUI: relative and interrogative pronoun; also: whose?

13.1b Furthermore whose fault indeed?

40.3b Furthermore whose fault indeed.

60.3b Furthermore whose fault indeed?

Wife, FU: responsible position of married woman within the household; contrasts with consort, CH'I, her legal position and concubine, CH'IEH, secondary wives. The ideogram: woman, hand and broom, household duties. See also: **Husband and Wife**

4.2a Letting in the wife. Auspicious.

9.6a The wife, Trial: adversity.

28.5a A venerable wife acquiring her notable husband.

28.5b A venerable wife, a notable husband.

32.5a Wife people: auspicious.

32.5b Wife people, Trial: auspicious.

32.5b Adhering to the wife: pitfall indeed.

37.ImT The husband, a husband. The wife, a wife.

37.3a/b The wife, the son, giggling, giggling:

53.3a/b The wife pregnant, not nurturing.

53.5a The wife, three year's time not pregnant.

63.2a A wife losing her veil.

Wildfowl, CH'IN: all wild and game birds; untamed.

3.3b Using adhering to wildfowl indeed.

8.5a Letting go the preceding wildfowl.

8.5b Letting go the preceding wildfowl indeed.

32.4a The fields without wildfowl.

32.4b Quietly acquiring the wildfowl indeed.

48.1a/b The ancient Well without wildfowl.

Wild goose, HUNG: large white water bird, symbol of the soul and its spiritual aspirations; wild swan and wild goose as emblems of the messenger and of conjugal fidelity; vast, profound, far reaching, great; valued, learned.

53.1a The wild geese Infiltrating into the barrier.

53.2a The wild geese Infiltrating into the stone.

53.3a,6a The wild geese Infiltrating into the highlands.

53.4a The wild geese Infiltrating into the trees.

53.5a The wild geese Infiltrating into the mound.

Willow, YANG: all thriving, fast growing trees; willow, poplar, tamarisk, aspen. The ideogram: tree and expand.

28.2a A withered willow giving birth to a sprig.

28.5a/b A withered willow giving birth to flowers.

Wind, FENG: moving air, breeze, gust; weather and its influence on mood and humor; fashion, usage; wind and wood are the Symbols of the trigram Ground, SUN.

9.ST Wind moving above heaven.

18.ST Below mountain possessing wind.

20.ST Wind moving above earth.

32.ST Thunder, wind, Persevering.

32.ImT Thunder, wind, mutually associating.

37.ST Wind originating from fire issuing forth.

42.ST Wind, thunder. Augmenting.

44.ST Below heaven possessing wind.

50.ST Above wind possessing fire.

57.ST Following winds.

59.ST Wind moves above stream.

61.ST Above marsh possessing wind.

Window, YU: opening in wall or roof to let in light; open, instruct, enlighten.

29.4a Letting in bonds originating from the window.

Wine cup, CHIO: libation cup originally in the form of a bird; all small birds; rank of nobility, confer rank on someone.

61.2a I possess a loved wine cup.

Wings, YI: birds' wings; sails, flanks, side rooms; brood over, shelter and defend.

36.1a Drooping one's wings.

Winnow, CHI: separate grain from chaff by tossing it in the wind; separate the valuable from the worthless, good from bad; sieve, winnowing basket; fan out.

36.ImT The winnowing son uses it.
36.5a The winnowing son's Brightness Hiding.
36.5b The winnowing son's Trial.

Withdraw(from), T'UI: draw back, retreat, recede; decline, refuse.

20.3a/b Viewing my birth, advancing, withdrawing.
33.S Retiring implies withdrawing indeed.
33/34.CD Retiring: by consequence withdrawing indeed.
34.6a/b Not enabling withdrawing, not enabling releasing.
40.5b Small People withdrawing indeed.
52.2b Not yet withdrawing from hearkening indeed.
57.1a/b Advancing, withdrawing.

Withered, K'U: dry up; dry wood, dried up bogs; decayed, rotten. The ideogram: tree and old.

28.2a A withered willow giving birth to a sprig.
28.5a/b A withered willow giving birth to flowers.

Without, WU: devoid of; less as suffix. This term occurs throughout the hexagram texts.

Without fault, WU CHIU: no error or harm in the situation. This term occurs throughout the hexagram texts.

Without repenting, WU HUI: devoid of the sort of trouble that leads to sorrow, regret and the necessity to change your attitude.

13.6a/b Concording People into the suburbs. Without repenting.
24.1a Without merely repenting.
24.5a Without repenting.
24.5b Magnanimous Returning, without repenting.
31.5a Without repenting.
34.5a Without repenting.
59.3a Without repenting.
64.5a Trial: auspicious, without repenting.

With respect to, YÜ: relates to, refers to; hold a position in.

5.ST Above clouds with respect to heaven.
8.4b Outside Grouping with respect to eminence.
23.ST Mountain adjoining with respect to earth.

24.AE Returning: the small and marking off with respect to beings.
25.ImT Solid originating from the outside coming and activating a lord with respect to the inside.
32.ImT Lasting with respect to one's tao indeed.
32.ImT The all wise person lasting with respect to his tao and Below Heaven the changes accomplishing.
37.S Injury with respect to the outside implies necessarily reversing with respect to Dwelling.
43.ST Above marsh with respect to heaven.
45.ST Above marsh with respect to earth.
55.ImT and even more with respect to the people reached.
55.ImT Even more with respect to the Souls and Spirits reached.

Woman(hood), NÜ: a woman; what is inherently female. See also: **Man and Woman** and **Woman and Son**

4.3a/b No availing of grasping womanhood.
20.2a Advantageous: woman Trial.
20.2b Peeping through Viewing: woman Trial.
28.2a A venerable husband acquiring his woman consort.
28.2b A venerable husband, a woman consort.
31.Im Grasping womanhood auspicious.
31.ImT Below manhood, womanhood.
31.ImT That uses Growth Advantageous Trial, grasping womanhood auspicious.
37.Im Dwelling People, Advantageous: woman Trial.
37.ImT The woman correcting the situation reaching to the inside.
38.ImT Man, Woman, Polarizing and their purposes interpenetrating indeed.
44.Im Coupling, womanhood invigorating.
44.Im/ImT No availing of grasping womanhood.
53.Im Infiltrating, womanhood converting auspicious.
53/54.CD Infiltrating: womanhood converting awaits manhood moving indeed.
53/54.CD Converting Maidenhood: womanhood's completion indeed.
53.ImT Womanhood converting auspicious.
54.6a A woman receiving a basket without substance.

- **Woman[and]Son**, NÜ TZU: particular relation between a woman and her child.

  3.2a Woman[and]Son, Trial: not nursing.

- **Wood/tree**, MU: all things woody or wooden, alive or constructed from wood; associated with the Woody Moment; wood and wind are the Symbols of the trigram Ground, SUN. The ideogram: a tree with roots and branches.

  28.ST Marsh submerging wood.

  30.ImT The hundred grains, grasses, trees congregating reaching to earth.

  40.ImT Thunder and Rain arousing and the hundred fruits, grasses, trees, altogether seedburst boundary.

  42.ImT Woody tao, thereupon moving.

  46.ST Earth center giving birth to wood.

  47.1a The sacrum Confined, into stump wood.

  48.ST Above wood possessing stream.

  50.ImT Using wood: Ground, fire.

  53.ST Above mountain possessing wood.

  53.4a The wild geese Infiltrating into the trees.

  59.ImT Riding wood possesses achievement indeed.

  61.ImT Riding a wooden dug out, emptiness indeed.

- **Word**, YEN: speech, spoken words, sayings; talk, discuss, address. The ideogram: mouth and rising vapor, words as speech.

  5.2a The small possesses words.

  5.2b Although the small possesses words, using completing auspicious indeed.

  6.1a The small possesses words, completing auspicious.

  6.1b Although the small possesses words, one's differentiation brightening indeed.

  7.5a Advantageous: holding on to words.

  13.5b Words mutualize controlling indeed.

  26.ST A chün tzu uses the numerous recorded preceding words going to move.

  27.ST A chün tzu uses considering words to inform.

  36.1a A lord: the people possessing words.

  37.ST A chün tzu uses words to possess beings and movement to possess perseverance.

  43.4a/b Hearing words, not trustworthy.

  47.Im/ImT Possessing words not trustworthy.

  49.3a/b Skinning words three times drawing near:

  51.Im/ImT Laughing words, shrieking, shrieking.

  51.1a After laughing words, shrieking, shrieking.

  51.1b Laughing words, shrieking, shrieking.

  51.6a Matrimonial allying possesses words.

  52.5a Words possessing sequence.

  53.1a The small son, adversity possessing words.

- **Worship**, CHIEN: honor the gods and ancestors; make sacrifice; recommend or introduce yourself. The ideogram: leading animals to green pastures.

  16.ST Exalting worship's Supreme Above.

  20.Im/ImT Viewing: hand washing and not worshipping.

- **Yang**: Action; dynamic and light aspect of phenomena: arouses, transforms, dissolves existing structures; linear thrust; stimulus, drive, focus; direct or orient something.

  1.1b Yang located below indeed.

  11.ImT Inside yang and outside yin.

  12.ImT Inside yin and outside yang.

- **Years revolved**, NIEN: number of years elapsed; a person's age; contrasts with year's time, SUI, length of time in a year.

  3.2a/b Ten years revolved, thereupon nursing.

  24.6a Culminating into ten years revolved not controlling chastisement.

  27.3a/b Ten years revolved, no availing of.

  63.3a/b Three years revolved controlling it.

  64.4a Three years revolved, possessing donating into the great city.

- **Year's time**, SUI: actual length of time in a year; contrasts with years revolved, NIEN, number of years elapsed.

  13.3a/b Three year's time not rising.

  29.6a Three year's time, not acquiring. Pitfall.

  29.6b Pitfall: three year's time indeed.

  47.1a Three year's time not encountering.

  53.5a The wife, three year's time not pregnant.

  55.6a Three year's time not encountering.

- **Yellow**, HUANG: color of the productive middle; associated with the Earthy Moment between the yang and yin hemicycles; color of soil in central China; emblematic and imperial color of China since the Yellow Emperor (2500 BCE).

  2.5a/b A yellow apron. Spring auspicious.

  2.6a Their blood: indigo, yellow.

  21.5a Gnawing parched meat. Acquiring yellow metal.

  30.2a/b Yellow Radiance. Spring auspicious.

  33.2a Holding on to it: availing of yellow cattle's skin.

33.2b Holding on avails of yellow cattle.

40.2a Acquiring a yellow arrow.

49.1a Thonging avails of yellow cattle's Skin.

49.1b Thonging avails of yellow cattle.

50.5a The Vessel: yellow ears, metallic rings.

50.5b The Vessel: yellow ears.

Yield(to), SHUN: give way and bear produce; comply, agree, follow, obey; unresisting, docile, flexible; nourish, provide; the Action of the trigram Field, K'UN. The ideogram: head and current, water flowing from the head of a river, yielding to the banks.

2.ImT Thereupon yielding receiving heaven.

2.ImT Supple yielding, Advantageous Trial.

2.ImT Afterwards yielding acquiring rules.

4.3b Movement not yielding indeed.

4.5b Yielding uses Ground indeed.

4.6b Above and Below yielding indeed.

5.4b Yielding uses hearkening indeed.

7.ImT Movement venturing and yielding.

8.ImT Yielding adhering to the below indeed.

8.5b Stowing away countering, grasping yielding.

11.ImT Inside persisting and outside yielding.

14.ST [A chün tzu uses] yielding to heaven to relinquish fate.

16.ImT Yielding uses stirring up. Provision.

16.ImT Providing for: yielding uses stirring up.

16.ImT Heaven and Earth uses yielding stirring up.

16.ImT The all wise person uses yielding stirring up.

19.ImT Stimulating and yielding.

19.2b Not yet yielding to fate indeed.

20.ImT Yielding and Ground.

23.ImT Yielding and stopping it.

24.ImT Stirring up and using yielding movement.

27.5b Yielding uses adhering to the above indeed.

31.2b Yielding, not harming indeed.

35.ImT Yielding and congregating reaching to great brightening.

36.ImT Inside pattern Brightening and outside supple yielding.

36.2b Yielding used by consequence indeed.

37.2b Yielding uses Ground indeed.

37.4b Yielding located in the situation indeed.

45.ImT Yielding uses stimulating.

45.ImT Yielding to heaven: fate indeed.

46.ST A chün tzu uses yielding to actualize tao.

46.ImT Ground and yielding.

46.4b Yielding affairs indeed.

49.ImT Yielding reaching to heaven and corresponding reaching to the people.

49.6b Yielding uses adhering to the chief indeed.

53.3b Yielding mutualizes protection indeed.

53.4b Yielding using Ground indeed.

56.ImT Supple acquiring the center reaching to the outside and yielding reaching to the solid.

56.ImT Supple acquiring the center reaching to the outside and yielding reaching to the solid.

57.ImT Supple altogether yielding reaching the solid.

58.ImT That uses yielding reaching to heaven and corresponding reaching to the people.

59.1b Yielding indeed.

62.ImT Countering above and yielding below indeed.

Yin: Struction; consolidating, shadowy aspect of phenomena: conserves, substantializes, creates structures; spacial extension; limited, bound, given specific being; build, make something concrete.

2.1b Yin begins solidifying indeed.

11.ImT Inside yang and outside yin.

12.ImT Inside yin and outside yang.

61.2a Calling crane located in yin.

Your, CHÜEH: intensifying personal pronoun, specifically you! your!; intensify, concentrate, tense, contract; lit.: muscle spasms.

14.5a Your connection: mingling thus, impressing thus. Auspicious.

14.5b Your connection, mingling thus.

38.5a/b Your ancestor gnawing flesh.

Youthful, T'UNG: young person between eight and fifteen; young animals and plants.

4.Im/ImT In no way me seeking youthful Enveloping.

4.Im/ImT Youthful Enveloping seeking me.

4.5a/b Youthful Enveloping. Auspicious.

20.1a Youthful Viewing.

20.1b Initial six, youthful Viewing.

26.4a Youthful cattle's stable.

56.2a/b Acquiring a youthful vassal: Trial.

56.3a Losing one's youthful vassal.

FURTHER READING

For a portable, concise version of the I Ching, based on the work in this volume, see:

STEPHEN KARCHER, *How to Use the I Ching: Working with the Oracle of Change*, (HarperCollins, 2001).

● *Basic Commentary*

The work of Hellmut Wilhelm, son of the translator Richard Wilhelm, is a fundamental source of insight into the philosophy and use of the *I Ching*.

HELLMUT WILHELM, *Change: Eight Lectures on the I Ching*, trans. Cary F. Baynes, (Princeton: Princeton University Press, Bollingen Series lxii, 1960).

HELLMUT WILHELM, *Heaven, Earth and Man in the Book of Changes*, Seven Eranos Lectures, (Seattle and London: University of Washington Press, 1977).

HELLMUT WILHELM, "On Sacrifice in the I Ching," (Spring *1972*, 74-89.)

In the last 50 years, a school of thought has developed that sees the *I Ching* primarily as a sociological and historical document. Though it ignores the imaginative and spiritual significance of the book, it provides interesting information on the book's various levels and layers, the culture surrounding its origins, and old meanings for many of the divinatory terms. This critical approach employs Western analytical methods. It originated in China largely in reaction to the moralistic imperial stance taken by official philosophers. A primary source, with an interesting Foreword by an exponent of a different school of thought, is:

JULIAN K. SCHUTSKII, *Researches on the I Ching*, (Princeton: Princeton University Press, 1979).

Perhaps the best current example of such scholarship in English is a translation and commentary on the oldest known manuscript of the *I Ching* (from the tombs at *Mawangdui,* dated to c. 168 BCE). It is very technical and includes an extensive multi-lingual bibliography.

- RICHARD ALAN KUNST, The Original Yijing: A Text, Phonetic Transcription and Indexes with Sample Glosses, (Ann Arbor: University Microfilms, 1985).

  Richard Rutt's Yijing summarizes and collates most modern scholarship in usable fashion:

- RICHARD RUTT, ZHOUYI: The Book of Changes, (Richmond, Surrey: Curzon Press, 1996).

  A bibliography of works in English on *Yijing*.

- EDWARD A. HACKER, STEVE MOORE, LORRAINE PATSCO: *An Annotated Bibliography of the I Ching*, (New York and London: Routledge, 2002).

- *The Great Treatise or Commentary on the Attached Evidences*

  The *Hzi t'zu chuan* or *Ta chuan*, the "Great Treatise" attached to the *I Ching*, was "for 2,000 years one of the most influential statements in Chinese tradition on knowing how the cosmos worked and how humans might relate to it" (Peterson). An excellent description and analysis, which relates divination with the *I* to various magical traditions, is:

- WILLARD PETERSON, "Making Connections: 'Commentary on the Attached Verbalizations' of the Book of Changes," (Harvard Journal of Asiatic Studies, 42/1, June 1982, 67–112.)

  A good modern translation is:

- STEPHEN KARCHER, Ta chuan: The Great Treatise, NY: St Martins Press, 2000.

  For Chinese ideas on how the *I Ching* works, see:

- WILLARD PETERSON, "Some Connective Concepts in China," Eranos 57/1988.

- *Divination*

  An overview:

- STEPHEN KARCHER, *The Illustrated Encyclopedia of Divination*, (HarperCollins, 2001).

- GEORGE KERLIN PARK, "Divination," *Encyclopedia Britannica*, 15th ed., Macropedia, v. 5, 916–20.

- MICHAEL LOEWE AND CARMEN BLACKER, eds, *Oracles and Divination*, (Boulder CO: Shambala, 1981).

  The best examination of divination in classical Mediterranean culture has never been translated into English:

- A. BOUCHÉ-LECLERQ, *L'histoire de la divination dans l'antiquité*, 4 vol., (Paris, 1879, rpt. Aalen: Scientia Verlag, 1978).

  See also:

- H. W. PARKE, *Greek Oracles*, (London, 1967).

  A very interesting look at the shift in divinatory methods which produced the *I Ching*, also not translated, is:

- H. W. PARKE, "De la tortue a l'achillée," in *Divination et Rationalité*, ed. Jean-Paul Vernant, (Paris: Editions du Seuil, 1974).

- LEON VANDERMEERSCH, "The Origin of Milfoil Divination and the Primitive I Ching," unpublished paper presented at the Workshop on Divination and Portent Interpretation, University of California, Berkeley, June 20–July 1, 1983; published in French in *Hexagrammes* 4/1989, (Paris).

  See also:

- NGO VAN XUYET, *Divination, magie et politique dans la Chine ancienne*, (Paris: Presses Universitaires de France, 1976).

  The closest living analogy to the divinatory process of the *I Ching* is African Ifa divination, probably developed from the Arabic geomantic system that shadowed European high culture for centuries. See:

- PHILLIP PEEK, ed., *African Divination Systems: Ways of Knowing*, (Bloomington: Indiana University Press, 1991).

- WILLIAM BASCOM, *Ifa Divination*, (Bloomington: Indiana University Press, 1969).

- JUDITH GLEASON, with Awotunde Aworinde and John Olaniyi Ogundipe, *A Recitation of Ifa, Oracle of the Yoruba*, (New York: Grossman, 1973).

- JEAN SERVIER, "Une ouverture sur le monde: magie et religion en Afrique du Nord. Une technique divinatoire: la geomancie," *Eranos 46/1977*, English translation, *Eranos 62/1993*.

Works from a classical Jungian perspective are:

- C. G. JUNG, *Synchronicity: An Acausal Connecting Principle*, trans. R. F. C. Hull, (Princeton: Princeton University Press, Bollingen Series xx, 1960).

  C. G. JUNG, Foreword to *The I Ching or Book of Changes. The Richard Wilhelm Translation rendered into English by Cary F. Baynes*, 3rd ed., (Princeton: Princeton University Press, Bollingen Series xix, 1967), reproduced in *CW 11*.

- MARIE-LOUISE VON FRANZ, *On Divination and Sychronicity: the Psychology of Meaningful Chance*, (Toronto: Inner City Books, 1980).

An examination of how the "magic spells" used in divination became the "magic of philosophy" is:

- PEDRO LAIN ENTRALGO, *The Therapy of the Word in Classical Antiquity*, eds and trans L. J. Rather and John M. Sharp, (New Haven: Yale University Press, 1970).

- STEPHEN KARCHER, "Oracle's Contexts: Gods, Dreams, Shadow, Language," *Spring 53/1992*.

- STEPHEN KARCHER, "Making Spirits Bright: Divination and the Demonic Image," *Eranos 61/1992*.

- STEPHEN KARCHER, "Which Way I Fly is Hell: Divination and the Shadow of the West," *Spring 55/1994*.

- STEPHEN KARCHER, "Jung the Tao and the Classic of Change," *Harvest/1999*.

- ## *Correlative Systems and the Universal Compass*

The most extensive and detailed examination of the fundamental ideas and categories involved in the "correlative systems" of traditional Chinese science is:

● JOSEPH NEEDHAM, *Science and Civilization in China*, Volume 2, (Cambridge: Cambridge University Press, 1956).

The source for most of these systems, the report of the discussions held under Imperial auspices in 79 CE, is translated and examined in:

● TJAN TJOE SOM, PO HU TUNG: *The Comprehensive Discussions in the White Tiger Hall*, 2 vol., (Leiden: E.J. Brill, 1952).

A rare but extremely valuable discussion of divinatory and cosmological systems and their social and ideological function is:

● STEPHAN D. R. FEUCHTWANG, *An Anthropological Analysis of Chinese Geomancy*, (Vientiane, Laos: Editions Vithagna, 1974).

A technical, difficult but remarkable analysis of the systems in Chinese medicine is:

● MANFRED PORKERT, *The Theoretical Foundations of Chinese Medicine: Systems of Correspondence*, (Cambridge MA: MIT Press, 1974).

On the origin, development and decline of traditional Chinese cosmology, see:

● SARAH ALLEN, *The Shape of the Turtle: Myth, Art and Cosmos in Early China*, (New York: State University of New York Press, 1991).

● JOHN B. HENDERSON, *The Development and Decline of Chinese Cosmology*, (New York: Columbia University Press, 1984).

A simple, concise encyclopedia of motifs in the "hidden symbolic language" of Chinese myth is:

● WOLFRAM EBERHARD, *A Dictionary of Chinese Symbols*, trans. G. L. Campbell, (London and New York: Routledge/Methuen, 1986).

● *Chinese History, Traditional Culture and the Warring States Period*

Interesting accounts of ancient China:

● PATRICIA BUCKLEY (ed.), *The Cambridge Illustrated History of China*, (Cambridge: Cambridge University Press, 1996).

● MARCEL GRANET, *Chinese Civilization*, (London: Routledge and Kegan Paul, 1930), translation of *La civilisation chinoise*, (Paris, 1929).

What is possibly the best single volume on Chinese thought written in this century remains untranslated:

- MARCEL GRANET, *La pensée chinoise*, (Paris, 1934).

An excellent source on ancient China is:

- HENRI MASPERO, *China in Antiquity*, trans. Frank A. Kierman of La Chine antique (Paris, 1965), (University of Massachusetts Press, 1978).

See also:

- HERRLEE G. CREEL, *The Birth of China*, (New York: Ungar Press, 1937).

- A. C. GRAHAM, *Disputers of the Tao: Philosophical Argument in Ancient China*, (LaSalle, IL: Open Court, 1985).

- DAVID KEIGHTLY, *Sources of Shang History*, (Berkeley: University of California Press, 1978).

- DAVID ROY AND TSUEN-HSUIN TSIEN, eds, *Ancient China: Studies in Early Civilization*, (Hong Kong: Chinese University Press, 1978).

- BENJAMIN SCHWARTZ, *The World of Thought in Ancient China*, (Cambridge MA and London: Harvard University Press, 1985).

A stunning look at early Chinese art and archeological artifacts:

- JESSICA RAWSON (ed.), *Mysteries of Ancient China*, (London: British Museum Press, 1996).

- XIAONENG YANG (ed.), *The Golden Age of Chinese Archeology*, (National Gallery of Art, Washington, New Haven: Yale University Press, 1999).

- *Philosophy, Religion, Literature*

Three sources on philosophy:

- SARA ALLEN, *The Way of Water*, (Buffalo, NY: SUNY Press, 2000).

- FUNG YULAN, *A History of Chinese Philosophy*, trans. Derk Bodde, 2 vols., (Princeton: Princeton University Press, 1952–3).

- ARTHUR WALEY (trans.), *The Book of Songs*, (London: Allen and Unwin, 1937/1969).

Excerpts from the "Taoist oriented *summa* of Chinese philosophy of the early Han" (c. 145 BCE), with a consideration of the key ideas of resonance and interconnection, is:

- CHARLES LE BLANC, *Huai Nan Tzu: Philosophical Synthesis in Early Han Thought*, (Hong Kong: Hong Kong University Press, 1985).

Classic studies of the Way in literature and meditation:

- HAROLD W. ROTH, *Original Tao: The Inward Training*, (New York: Columbia University Press, 1999).

- ARTHUR WALEY, *The Way and its Power: A Study of the Tao Tê Ching and its Place in Chinese Thought*, (1934, rpt. New York: Grove Press, 1958).

An interesting and insightful description of the Five Classics, the central works of later culture, is found in:

- BURTON WATSON, *Early Chinese Literature*, (New York: Columbia University Press, 1962).

Diverse perspectives on the "way" and its many permutations in religious practices come from:

- HOLMES WELCH AND ANNA SEIDEL, eds, *Facets of Taoism: Essays in Chinese Religion*, (New Haven: Yale University Press, 1979).

Discussions and documents from the Confucian and neo-Confucian school are found in:

- WM. THEODORE DU BARY, *Neo-Confucian Orthodoxy and the Learning of the Mind-Heart*, (New York: Columbia University Press, 1981).

- WING-TSIT CHAN (trans.), *Reflections on Things at Hand: The Neo-Confucian Anthology Compiled by Chu Hsi and Lü Tzu-Ch'ien*, (New York: Columbia University Press, 1967).

● I Ching: History and Key Commentators

An excellent overview of various historical views on divination, preparatory to an equally interesting consideration of a key Sung Dynasty figure, is:

- J. A. ADLER, *Divination and Philosophy: Chu Hsi's Understanding of the I Ching*, (Ann Arbor: University Microfilms, 1984),

For "historicist" speculations on the first assembling of the book in the late

Chou period and the sort of diviners who used it, see:

● EDWARD LOUIS SHAUGHNESSY, *The Composition of the Zhouyi*, (Ann Arbor: University Microfilms, 1983).

On the two fundamental schools of interpretation, *hsiang-shu* or "image-number," first associated with the *fang shih* or traveling magicians and diviners, and *i-li* or "moral-principle," first associated with the scholar-philosopher *Wang Pi* (226–273 CE), see:

● KENNETH J. DE WOSKIN, ed. and trans., *Doctors, Diviners and Magicians of Ancient China: Biographies of Fang Shih*, (New York: Columbia University Press, 1983).

● T'ANG YUNG-T'UNG, "Wang Pi's New Interpretation of the I-Ching and Lun-yü", trans. Walter Liebenthal, Harvard Journal of Asiatic Studies, 10/2 (1947).

● HOWARD GOODMAN, *Exegetes and Exegeses of the Book of Changes in the 3rd Century AD: Historical and Scholastic Contexts for Wang Pi*, (Ann Arbor: University Microfilms, 1985).

● RICHARD JOHN LYNN, *The Classic of Changes* (as interpreted by Wang Bi), (New York: Columbia University Press, 1994).

On the pivotal Sung Dynasty re-interpretation of the *I Ching* (c.1100 CE), which altered the course of Chinese culture, see Adler, cited above, and:

● KIDDER SMITH JR, PETER K. BOL, JOSEPH A. ADLER AND DON WYATT, *Sung Dynasty Uses of the I Ching*, (Princeton: Princeton University Press, 1990).

An extremely interesting look at a later interpreter whose perspective adds much to the modern psychological sense of the *I Ching* is:

● LARRY SCHULTZ, *Lai Chih-te (1525–1604) and the Phenomenology of the Classic of Change*, (Ann Arbor: University Microfilms, 1982).

An extensive examination of the mathematical aspects of *I Ching* divination is:

● LEO REISINGER, *Das I Ging: Eine formalwissenschaftliche Untersuchung des chinesichen Orakels*, (Acta Ethnologica et Linguistica 25/1972, Vienna).

A reconstruction of ancient practices involved in oracle consultation can be found in:

- SHIH-CHUAN CHEN, "How to Form a Hexagram and Consult the I Ching," (Journal of the American Oriental Society 92, April-June 1972).

The most significant accomplishment of twentieth-century sinology has just been published, the Ricci Dictionary, fruit of over forty years of research. This elegant and comprehensive tool is a must for anyone interested in Chinese thought and culture.

- *Dictionaire Ricci de caractères chinois*, (Insituts Ricci, Paris-Taipei, Descleè de Brouwer, 1999).

UPPER TRIGRAMS

LOWER TRIGRAMS

	FORCE	FIELD	SHAKE	GORGE
FORCE	1	11	34	5
FIELD	12	2	16	8
SHAKE	25	24	51	3
GORGE	6	7	40	29
BOUND	33	15	62	39
GROUND	44	46	32	48
RADIANCE	13	36	55	63
OPEN	10	19	54	60

• A Key to the Hexagrams

To find the hexa-
gram that the
Oracle has given
you as an answer to
your question, locate
the lower trigram
on the left and the
upper trigram on
the top of the chart
above. Then turn to
the hexagram text
that the number
indicates.

UPPER TRIGRAMS

LOWER TRIGRAMS

BOUND	GROUND	RADIANCE	OPEN	
26	9	14	43	FORCE
23	20	35	45	FIELD
27	42	21	17	SHAKE
4	59	64	47	GORGE
52	53	56	31	BOUND
18	57	50	28	GROUND
22	37	30	49	RADIANCE
41	61	38	58	OPEN